Praise for Volker Ullrich's

Hitler

A *New York Times* Bestseller

"Striking. . . . Highly detailed and always interesting. . . . Full, intelligent, and lucidly written." —*London Review of Books*

"A superb biography of the Führer's pre-war years. . . . Readable and compelling. . . . Absorbing." —*Daily Telegraph* (London)

"Excellent. . . . A thorough and thoroughly readable work of synthesis, which succeeds in combining the personal and the political into a coherent whole." —*Financial Times*

"It succeeds brilliantly. . . . [Deserves] to be read as widely as possible." —*The Times* (Book of the Week)

"Insightful. . . . Acutely argued. . . . Volker Ullrich compellingly tells us once again that no one could have been under any illusion about Hitler's general intentions." —*The New Statesman* (London)

"This is a major achievement." —*Literary Review*

"Timely, given the increase in right-wing intransigence throughout the world, and one of the best works on Hitler and the origins of the Third Reich to appear in recent years." —*Kirkus Reviews*

Volker Ullrich

Hitler

Volker Ullrich is a historian and journalist whose previous books in German include biographies of Bismarck and Napoleon, as well as a major study of Imperial Germany, *Die nervöse Grossmacht 1871–1918* (The Nervous Superpower). From 1990 to 2009, Ullrich was the editor of the political book review section of the influential weekly newspaper *Die Zeit*.

Hitler

Hitler

Ascent 1889–1939

VOLKER ULLRICH

TRANSLATED FROM THE GERMAN BY

Jefferson Chase

VINTAGE BOOKS

A Division of Penguin Random House LLC

New York

FIRST VINTAGE BOOKS EDITION, OCTOBER 2017

Copyright © 2016 by Volker Ullrich
Translation copyright © 2016 by Jefferson Chase

All rights reserved. Published in the United States by Vintage Books, a division of Penguin Random House LLC, New York, and distributed in Canada by Random House of Canada, a division of Penguin Random House Canada Limited, Toronto. Originally published in Germany by S. Fischer Verlag. Copyright © 2013 by S. Fischer Verlag GmbH, Frankfurt am Main. This translation originally published in hardcover in the United States by Alfred A. Knopf, a division of Penguin Random House LLC, New York, in 2016.

Vintage and colophon are registered trademarks of Penguin Random House LLC.

The Library of Congress has catalogued the Knopf edition as follows:
Names: Ullrich, Volker.
Title: Hitler : ascent, 1889–1939 / Volker Ullrich ; translated from the German by Jefferson Chase.
Other titles: Adolf Hitler. English
Description: First American edition. | New York : Alfred A. Knopf, 2016.
Identifiers: LCCN 2015047202
Subjects: LCSH: Hitler, Adolf, 1889–1945. | Hitler, Adolf, 1889-1945—Political and social views. | Hitler, Adolf, 1889–1945—Psychology. | Personality—Case studies. | Heads of state—Germany—Biography. | Dictators—Germany—Biography. | Germany—History—1933–1945. | Germany—Politics and government—1933–1945. | National socialism.
Classification: LCC DD247.H5 U4513 2016 | DDC 943.086092—dc23
LC record available at http://lccn.loc.gov/2015047202

Vintage Books Trade Paperback ISBN: 978-1-101-87205-5
eBook ISBN: 978-0-385-35439-4

Author photograph © Roswitha Hecke

www.vintagebooks.com

Printed in the United States of America
10 9 8 7 6 5 4 3 2 1

Contents

Illustrations

Hitler's father Alois Hitler, *c*.1880 (*akg-images*).

Hitler's mother Klara Hitler, *c*.1885 (*akg-images*).

Hitler as a small child, 1891 (*akg-images*).

Class photo with the 10-year-old Adolf Hitler, Leonding, 1899 (*Bildarchiv Preussischer Kulturbesitz*).

Hitler as a boy (*Bildarchiv Preussischer Kulturbesitz*).

Hitler at a patriotic event on Munich's Odeonsplatz, 2 August 1914 (*Bildarchiv Preussischer Kulturbesitz/Heinrich Hoffmann*).

Hitler with his comrades in Bavarian RIR 16, 1915 (*Bundesarchiv Koblenz, 146-1974-082-44, Scherl/Presse Hoffmann*).

Flyer announcing Hitler's appearance in Zirkus Krone on 11 January 1922 (*Bundesarchiv Berlin-Lichterfelde, NS 26/1242*).

One of the first portraits of Hitler by Heinrich Hoffmann, September 1923 (*Bildarchiv Preussischer Kulturbesitz/BSB/Heinrich Hoffmann*).

Hitler speaking in Munich's Zirkus Krone in 1923 (*Bildarchiv Preussischer Kulturbesitz/BSB/Heinrich Hoffmann*).

Group photo of the defendants at Hitler's trial, 1 April 1924 (*Bildarchiv Preussischer Kulturbesitz/BSB/Heinrich Hoffmann*).

Publicity pamphlet advertising one of Hitler's flying tours, 1932.

Hitler and Hermann Göring at a meeting of the Düsseldorf Industrial Club, 26 January 1933 (*Bildarchiv Preussischer Kulturbesitz/BSB/Heinrich Hoffmann*).

The "Cabinet of National Concentration" on 30 January 1933 (*Bildarchiv Preussischer Kulturbesitz/BSB/Heinrich Hoffmann*).

"The Day of Potsdam": Hitler bows before Hindenburg, 21 March 1933 (*Bundesarchiv Koblenz, 183-S38324*).

Three typical Hitler poses during his 10 February 1933 speech in Berlin's Sportpalast (*AKiP Freie Universität Berlin*).

Hitler digging the first turf for the construction of the autobahn, 23 September 1933 (*ullstein bild/Süddeutsche Zeitung/Photo Scherl*).

Hitler's first meeting with Mussolini, Venice, 14 June 1934 (*ullstein bild/Roger-Viollet*).

Hitler supporters making the pilgrimage to the Berghof (*Bildarchiv Preussischer Kulturbesitz/BSB/Heinrich Hoffmann*).

Albert Speer unveiling his "dome of light" on the Zeppelin Field at the Nuremberg rally of 1936 (*Bundesarchiv Koblenz, 183-1982-1130-502, Scherl*).

Leni Riefenstahl during the filming of *Triumph of the Will*, September 1934 (*Bildarchiv Preussischer Kulturbesitz/Friedrich Rohrmann*).

"Pillory parade" in Gelsenkirchen in August 1935 (*Stadtarchiv Nürnberg Sig. E39 Nr. 1747/17-20*).

Hitler enters Berlin's Olympic Stadium, 1 August 1936 (*Bundesarchiv Koblenz, 146-1976-033-17*).

Hitler looking at blueprints and models for the Nuremberg rally site (*Bundesarchiv Koblenz, 146-1971-016-31*).

The planned North–South Axis in Berlin (*Bundesarchiv Koblenz, 146III-373*).

Hitler's office in the New Reich Chancellery, 1939 (*Bildarchiv Preussischer Kulturbesitz/BSB/Heinrich Hoffmann*).

The concealable window in the Great Hall at the Berghof.

Hitler and Eva Braun on the Obersalzberg, autumn of 1938 (*Bildarchiv Preussischer Kulturbesitz/BSB/Heinrich Hoffmann*).

Group photo from the Berghof New Year's Eve party in 1938 (*ullstein bild/Roger-Viollet*).

Defaced windows of Jewish-owned businesses in Berlin, June 1938 (*Stiftung Neue Synagoge Berlin – Centrum Judaicum*).

Onlookers watch as the Old Synagogue in Essen burns, 9 November 1938 (*Stadtbildstelle Essen*).

Mussolini in Berlin during his state visit, 27 September 1937.

Hitler speaks from the balcony of Vienna's Hofburg Palace, 15 March 1938 (*Bundesarchiv Koblenz, 183-1987-0922-500*).

Hitler at the German Gymnastics and Sports Festival in Breslau, 31 July 1938 (*Bildarchiv Preussischer Kulturbesitz/Hans Hubmann*).

Czech president Emil Hácha with Hitler in his office at the Chancellery, 15 March 1939 (*Bildarchiv Preussischer Kulturbesitz*).

Hermann Göring congratulates Hitler on his fiftieth birthday, 20 April 1939 (*Bundesarchiv Koblenz, 183-1988-0202-503, Scherl*).

A military parade on Berlin's new East–West Axis in honour of Hitler's fiftieth birthday (*Bildarchiv Preussischer Kulturbesitz/BSB/Archiv Heinrich Hoffmann*).

Every effort has been made to trace and contact copyright holders. The publishers will be pleased to correct any mistakes or omissions in future editions.

Introduction

"The fellow is a catastrophe, but that's no reason not to find him interesting as a personality and destiny," wrote Thomas Mann in his essay "Brother Hitler," adding that no one should feel "above dealing with this murky figure."[1]

As the Third Reich recedes ever further into the past, one might think that interest in the most malevolent person in twentieth-century history would diminish. The exact opposite has been the case. Both in Germany and without, the public's fascination with Hitler comes in recurrent waves, and the obsession with the Führer seems only to have increased in the new millennium. "There's never been so much Hitler," wrote the historian Norbert Frei in 2005, sixty years after the end of the Second World War and the demise of the Third Reich.[2] Indeed, on the occasion of that anniversary, unprecedented media attention was paid to the Führer and his cohorts. Hitler was everywhere—in the cinema and on television, on the covers of magazines and in the pages of popular history books. There is no reason to believe the situation will be any different at any future anniversary.

The global entertainment industry has long since appropriated and transformed Hitler into a sensationalist, pop-cultural icon of horror, guaranteed to send the maximum shivers down audiences' spines. The leader of the National Socialist German Workers' Party, or NSDAP, and the man who so dominated the course of world events from 1933 to 1945 remains—to cite journalist Jens Jessen—the "hardest of all drugs for generating attention."[3] Hitler stirs up more emotions than any other historical figure, including Stalin. That is, of course, due to the scale of the crimes that Germans committed under his leadership.

Parallel to but largely independent of the entertainment market, academic historians around the world have pressed forward with investigations concerning nearly every aspect of Hitler and National Socialism. No historical topic has been more thoroughly researched in all its nooks and crannies—today the literature on the subject fills whole libraries. And yet academic interest in this "murky figure" never wanes. The riddles surrounding Hitler—the questions of how and why he could come to power and hang on to it for more than a decade—demand ever-new explanations. There has been no shortage of biographical approaches to these questions, but only four have stood the test of time: Konrad Heiden's two-volume *Hitler: A Biography*, written in the mid-1930s from Swiss exile; Alan Bullock's canonical *Hitler: A Study in Tyranny* from the early 1950s; Joachim Fest's sweeping portrait *Hitler: A Biography*, first published in 1973; and Ian Kershaw's standard-setting *Hitler 1889–1936: Hubris* and *Hitler 1936–1945: Nemesis* from 1998 and 2000.[4]

Heiden's biography represents an attempt to "identify the historical significance of the phenomenon of Hitler at the height of his power."[5] As the Munich correspondent for the liberal *Frankfurter Zeitung* newspaper between 1923 and 1930, Heiden witnessed Hitler's rise to national prominence first-hand. The book is based both on the author's own observations and on information from sources close to Hitler in his days as a political agitator, and Heiden resisted the twin temptations of mythologising or ridiculing its subject. "The 'hero' of this book," Heiden wrote in his preface, dated 1935, "is neither a superman nor a puppet. He is a very interesting contemporary and, viewed quantitatively, a man who has stirred up the masses more than anyone else in human history."[6] Later research has corrected a number of biographical details Heiden got wrong. Nonetheless, his work is full of convincing conclusions and clever analyses, for instance concerning Hitler's skill as an orator and his uncanny "dual nature."[7]

This first Hitler biography was enthusiastically received by German exiles. "Constantly with Konrad Heiden's scorching Hitler biography," noted Thea Sternheim, the ex-wife of playwright Carl Sternheim, in late October 1935. "A spotlight upon Germany. Suddenly, you thank God for the existence of this sort of human conscience. Might not this book be the first decisive breach in the infernal crime that is taking place right now in Germany?"[8] The art patron and diplomat Harry Kessler, who like Sternheim lived in French exile, was also full of praise. "A clever and convincing book," he wrote in his journal. "'A failed

man and a failed people have joined forces.' How accurate."[9] The
Gestapo and the Security Service tried to track down Heiden, who
had moved to France, but when the Wehrmacht invaded that country
in 1940, he was able to flee via Lisbon to the United States.[10]

Alan Bullock's thrilling 1952 debut, *Hitler: A Study in Tyranny,* has
been the starting point for all subsequent academic study of the "Hitler
phenomenon." The British historian had advance access to confiscated
German documents which had been used as evidence at the Nuremberg
Trials and which were about to be made public.[11] Bullock depicted the
German dictator as a completely unprincipled opportunist driven solely
by lust for power at its most raw and pure.[12] In his conclusion, Bullock
cited the former Danzig (Gdansk) Senate President Hermann
Rauschning, a German exile whose 1938 book *The Revolution of Nihilism*
had greatly influenced views of Hitler at the time. In it, Rauschning
asserted that National Socialism was "the very essence of a movement,
pure dynamism, a revolution with various slogans that it was always
willing to change." One thing, according to Rauschning, that National
Socialism was *not* was "a world view and a doctrine."[13]

The thesis that Hitler was basically a power-hungry political opportunist came in for some heavy historical revision in the following
decades. Above all, historian Eberhard Jäckel convincingly demonstrated in the late 1960s that Hitler did indeed maintain a consistent
world view, no matter how extreme and insane, and that this perspective guided his actions. Jäckel argued that the two most important
elements of Hitler's world view were the "removal of the Jews" and
the conquest of "living space in the east." Ever since the 1920s, Jäckel
showed, Hitler held true to these two axiomatic, fixed ideas with
rigorous consistency.[14] Both Fest and Kershaw adopted this insight,
and the present book will reaffirm it as well.

Joachim Fest's Hitler biography, coming more than twenty years
after Bullock's, is impressive for its style—Jäckel gushed that "No one
since Thomas Mann has written about Hitler in such good German
prose"[15]—while historian Karl-Dietrich Bracher praised "the author's
talent for dense and sweeping interpretation."[16] Somewhat sheepishly,
many academic historians asked why the journalist Fest, and not one
of their own, had been able to achieve this.[17]

Fest not only came up with an unprecedented psychological portrait
of Hitler's personality, he also located the Führer firmly in the context

of his epoch. Fest identified the most important phenomenon in Hitler's rise as the convergence of individual and general factors, "the difficult-to-decipher correspondence between the man and the times and the times and the man."[18] To illustrate what he meant, Fest interspersed his chronological narrative with "intermediary reflections" that brought together individual biographical details and collective historical developments. The result was the paradoxical conclusion that Hitler, who despised revolution, was "the German form of revolution," idiosyncratically combining both modern and reactionary elements.[19]

Fest's interpretation, based on already-published sources rather than original archive research, has attracted criticism. Some scholars have rightly pointed out that Fest dramatically downplays the role of the conservative elites who ushered Hitler through the doors of power.[20] And it is impossible to overlook the educated, bourgeois contempt for the half-ignorant *arriviste* that Fest displays on several occasions, for instance, in his snide critique of Hitler's poor writing in *Mein Kampf.*[21] Fest's assessment of Hitler is also heavily influenced by the Führer's favourite architect and Nazi armaments minister, Albert Speer. As a journalist, Fest had helped Speer write his 1969 memoirs; in return Speer provided information for Fest's Hitler biography. As a result, Fest's account guilelessly passes on a number of legends, for instance the idea that Speer was an apolitical specialist who fell under the helpless sway of the dictator.[22]

Yet despite all these objections, Fest landed a real coup. In one review, historian Klaus Hildebrand predicted that Fest's pioneering work would represent "the definitive book on Adolf Hitler for quite some time."[23] That held true for twenty-five years until another British historian, Ian Kershaw, took up the challenge of a major Hitler biography. Kershaw had access to sources not available to Fest, most significantly the diaries of Joseph Goebbels from his years as Gauleiter of Berlin and then propaganda minister.[24]

In his introduction, Kershaw confessed that, to an extent, he approached Hitler from the "wrong" direction—from the structures of Nazi rule, which had been the subject of his earlier research. In contrast to Fest, Kershaw was less interested in the "strange" character of the man than in the social conditions and forces that had made Hitler possible. "The task of the biographer . . . ," Kershaw wrote, is "to focus not upon the personality of Hitler, but squarely and directly

upon *the character of his power—the power of the Führer.*" To explain
the sinister force of this power, Kershaw argued, it was necessary to
focus more on the expectations and motivations of German society
than on Hitler himself.[25] He was aiming for nothing less than a biography that embedded Hitler in a social and political context.[26]

Kershaw tried to show that in many situations Hitler didn't need
to do very much at all since German society—everyone from the
underlings surrounding him to ordinary people on the street—were
increasingly inclined to anticipate and fulfil the Führer's every wish,
"working towards him."[27] Critics accused Kershaw of supporting an
image of Hitler that made the dictator look "interchangeable, superfluous or at most weak."[28] In fact, Kershaw did not minimise the
historical role played by Hitler and his insane, ideological fixations,
but he did illustrate that without the readiness of many people to
work for the man in charge, there would have been no way he could
have achieved his murderous aims. Kershaw's main thesis was that
the dynamism of the Nazi regime arose from the interplay of Hitler's
intentions with activism emanating from subordinate individuals and
institutions. The results were ever more radical "solutions." With this
explanation, Kershaw ended the long-standing, fruitless debate between
"intentionalist" and "structuralist" schools of German historiography.[29]

"Our libraries contain 120,000 studies of Hitler—Kershaw's is their
Central Massif," concluded Frank Schirrmacher, publisher of the
Frankfurter Allgemeine Zeitung, in his rave review of Kershaw's work.[30]
So after such a monumental Hitler biography, is there really a need
for another one? More than fifteen years have passed since Kershaw's
first volume appeared in 1998. Since then the wheels of historical
research have continued to turn—at an ever-faster pace. Recent works
on Hitler himself encompass everything from the Führer's relationship
to Munich and Berlin and an analysis of his physiognomy to wild
speculations about his alleged homosexuality. There has also been a
tremendous amount published on surrounding figures, from Goebbels
and Eva Braun all the way to Nazi sculptor Arno Breker and Hitler's
personal physician Karl Brandt. In addition, a host of scholars have
written monographs on topics ranging from the economy and the
German Foreign Ministry under Nazism to consumerism and corruption in the Third Reich. Last but not least, recent years have seen the

editing and publication of Hitler's complete notes and speeches up until 1933, the official Reich Chancellery documents under Hitler's reign, and Goebbels's complete diaries. All of this material first appeared after Kershaw had finished his work.[31]

Bringing it all together and synthesising it would be justification enough for a new Hitler biography, but that is not all I intend to do. On the contrary, my aim is to refocus attention on Hitler, who necessarily had to remain a bit anaemic in Kershaw's account, without neglecting the social factors that propelled his meteoric rise. Along the way, I hope to put to the test several assumptions that recur throughout the literature on Hitler. One of them is that the Führer was basically an ordinary person with limited intellectual horizons and severely restricted social skills. As Karl-Dietrich Bracher once formulated it, the basic problem with approaching Hitler is to explain "how such a narrow-minded, unpleasant fellow could found and carry a movement of such immense dimensions and consequences."[32] Kershaw rephrased the question as: "How do we explain how someone with so few intellectual gifts and social attributes . . . could nevertheless have such an immense historical impact, could make the entire world hold its breath?"[33]

But what if those premises are wrong? What if Hitler's horizons and intellectual abilities were not so crassly underdeveloped? Kershaw, like most of the Hitler biographers before him, sees the Führer's sole talent as his ability to excite the base instincts of the masses.[34] Hitler was undoubtedly an extraordinarily gifted speaker, and that capability was of inestimable importance to his rise to power during the 1920s and '30s. But the chairman of the NSDAP was not just an excellent demagogue. He was also a fairly gifted actor who had mastered the art of appearing in a variety of masks and roles. Perhaps no one realised this better than Charlie Chaplin in his 1940 film *The Great Dictator*. When Albert Speer saw it in 1972, he praised the comedian for "having penetrated Hitler's character a lot further than any other contemporary person."[35]

Joachim Fest wrote of Hitler leading "a strange existence characterised by roles"—this will be one leitmotif for my depiction of the Führer.[36] The artistry with which Hitler was able to conceal his real intentions from both friends and foes was another main key to his success as a politician. Seventeen years after the fall of the Third Reich, in his memoirs the former Finance Minister Lutz Schwerin von Krosigk identified "bottomless mendacity" as Hitler's primary personal characteristic. "He wasn't even honest towards his most intimate confidants," Krosigk recalled. "In my opinion, he was so thoroughly untruthful that he could no longer recognise the difference between lies and truth."[37] Krosigk's moral condemnation reveals that Hitler—the consummate role player who had repeatedly got the better of his conservative allies—continued to fool them even after his death.

Hitler liked to present himself as a frustrated artist who had been driven involuntarily into politics, and the myth of the "artist-politician" has influenced many biographies. This obscures the fact that Hitler was a well-below-average painter and architect, however: his great gift was for politics alone. In his ability to instantaneously analyse and exploit situations, he was far superior not only to his rivals within the NSDAP but also to the politicians from Germany's mainstream parties. There is no other way to explain why he emerged victorious in all of the crises within the Nazi Party leading up to 1933. Or how he was able, within a few months after his appointment as chancellor, to subjugate his conservative coalition partners in the "cabinet of national concentration," although they were convinced that they had co-opted him for their ends. This astonishing process will be discussed in detail in the chapter entitled "Totalitarian Revolution." Furthermore, I will try to show that Hitler's unusually improvisational and personal style of leadership, which created constant responsibility conflicts and an anarchic tangle of offices and portfolios, was anything but an expression of political incompetence. On the contrary, it served to make Hitler's own supremacy essentially unassailable.

Another cliché holds that Hitler's personal life outside politics was completely irrelevant—indeed, that the Führer didn't have a genuine private life. Even his first biographer Heiden wrote that Hitler was a demagogue who could only connect with people en masse and lacked the "courage" to have a private life.[38] Bullock characterised him as an uprooted individual without a home or a family, while Fest described "a human void around [Hitler]," simply dismissing the idea of his having personal relationships.[39] Kershaw expanded on this thesis, arguing that Hitler was entirely consumed by his role as Führer. "Hitler's private life was his life as a political creature. If you take away the political, little to nothing remains," the historian told the *Frankfurter Allgemeine Zeitung* when the first volume of his biography appeared. "In a sense, he was an empty shell."[40] Not surprisingly the leading exponent of structuralist German history, Hans Mommsen, also favoured this interpretation, writing that there was actually no private sphere whatsoever behind Hitler's public appearances—a striking example of how the mythology surrounding the Führer has influenced the writing of history.[41]

This book will attempt to correct that picture and show that the putative void in Hitler's non-political existence is a myth. In a sense, previous biographers have fallen for the role Hitler played best, the one that concealed his private life and cast him as someone who had renounced all personal relations to devote himself to "*Volk* and Reich." The chapters concerning Hitler's relationships with women and the circles he entertained at his country house in Bavaria will show how little the cliché of the impersonal Führer corresponds to reality. Hitler's private life was in fact far more varied than many of his contemporaries and later historians imagined. It is untrue that he was fundamentally incapable of having personal relationships. Characteristically, however, he made no clear distinction between political and private spheres: for him the two were unusually intertwined. This realisation sheds new light on Hitler's specific style of rule.

"Are we permitted to depict Hitler as a human being?" the German media asked in 2004 with the release of Bernd Eichinger's film *Downfall*, which depicted the Führer, played by veteran actor Bruno Ganz, during his final days in the bunker in Berlin.[42] The only answer is: not only are we permitted, we are *obliged* to. It is a huge mistake to assume that a criminal on the millennial scale of Hitler must have been a monster. Naturally it would be simpler to reduce him to a psychopath who used political action to realise his homicidal impulses. For a long time this tendency to demonise Hitler dominated historical research and prevented us from having a clear view of the actual man. In February 1947, from the isolation of his cell in Spandau prison, Albert Speer remarked on the growing tendency in post-Nazi German society "to depict Hitler as a carpet-chewing hotheaded dictator who blew his stack on the slightest of occasions." Speer thought that was both wrong and dangerous, noting: "If there are no human characteristics in the picture of Hitler, if one ignores his power of persuasion, his winning qualities and the Austrian charm he was capable of displaying, one will never do justice to him as a phenomenon."[43] In the mid-1970s, after reading his memoirs, the film-maker Leni Riefenstahl wrote to Speer that, for her, the question remained:

> What was it about Hitler that allowed him to impress and indeed bewitch not just the German people, but many foreigners as well? . . . I can never forget or forgive the terrible things that happened in Hitler's name, nor do I want to. But I also don't want to forget what a massive effect he had on people. That would be to make things too easy for us. These two seeming contradictions within his personality—this schizophrenia—were likely what produced the enormous energy within his person.[44]

Such references to Hitler's unique dual nature, the conjunction of winning characteristics and criminal energy, should not be dismissed as mere attempts by Speer or Riefenstahl to distract attention from their own culpability. On the contrary, we must take such statements seriously if we want to understand the seductive force Hitler possessed not just for his own entourage, but for large segments of the German population. In the chapter with the somewhat unsettling title "Hitler as Human Being," I have tried to use just this approach to go beyond what Fest called examining an "un-person" and gain insights into Hitler's habits and characteristics.[45]

Hitler was without doubt the focal point of the Nazi regime, and the Third Reich lived and died with him. For that reason, anyone who wants to understand both the monstrous and attractive sides of National Socialism must also examine both Hitler as a motivating force and the forces that motivated him. That will be the subject of the chapter entitled "Cult and Community," which will seek to illuminate the reciprocal relationship between the dictator and German society and the reasons for Hitler's enormous popularity.

To depict Hitler in human terms is not to elicit sympathy for him or to downplay his crimes. This biography seeks to show the sort of person he was since the 1920s: a fanatic Jew-hater, who could tactically conceal his anti-Semitism but who never lost sight of his aim of "removing" Jews from German society. For that reason, I will pay special attention to the question of how Hitler, once in power, tried to realise this goal and what sort of support he received.

Sections devoted to German foreign policy after 1933 will illustrate how doggedly Hitler pursued the goal, which he had also maintained since the mid-1920s, of conquering "living space in the east." This remained true even when he appeared publicly in the guise of a man of peace who was only striving for a revision of the Treaty of Versailles. The subsequent chapter, entitled "The Way to War," will then describe how the dictator gradually turned from the politics of revision to the politics of expansion, which aimed to give the Third Reich not only undisputed hegemony on the Continent but world domination.

The present volume is concerned with the "years of ascent," but by no means do I want to give the impression that Hitler enjoyed an uninterrupted success story. On the contrary, I will show that his career was permanently threatening to come undone—most significantly after his failed putsch in 1923 and the Nazis' disastrous electoral defeat in November 1932. Hitler's path to power was anything but inevitable: in January 1933, it would have been eminently possible to prevent his nomination as Reich chancellor. The chairman of the NSDAP profited from a unique constellation of crises that he was able to exploit cleverly and unscrupulously. He also benefited from his domestic adversaries' tendency, from the very inception of his political career, to underestimate his abilities. A similar lack of appreciation for Hitler's gifts later convinced foreign statesmen that they could control his aggression. That was an illusion, from which the world first awoke when Hitler crassly violated the Munich Agreement in March 1939. With that, the dictator had crossed the line. Nemesis was at hand—although none of Hitler's contemporaries, and certainly not the man himself, realised how close it was.

This book does not pretend to offer a fully new interpretation of history. In light of the achievements of my predecessors from Heiden to Kershaw, that would be utterly arrogant. But I do hope that the first volume of this biography succeeds in bettering our understanding of the man Stefan Zweig described as "bringing greater disaster upon the world than anyone in our times."[46] In particular, I hope that Hitler's personality emerges more clearly in all its astonishing contradictions and contrasts so that our picture of the man is more complex and nuanced. Hitler was not a "man without qualities."[47] He was a figure with a great many qualities and masks. If we look behind the public persona which Hitler created for himself and which was bolstered by his loyal followers, we can see a human being with winning and revolting characteristics, undeniable talents and obviously deep-seated psychological complexes, huge destructive energy and a homicidal bent. My aim is to deconstruct the myth of Hitler, the "fascination with monstrosity" that has so greatly influenced historical literature and public discussion of the Führer after 1945.[48] In a sense, Hitler will be "normalised"—although this will not make him seem more "normal." If anything, he will emerge as even more horrific.

Writing about the pivotal figure in German and European history is without doubt the most difficult task for a historian and demands the greatest responsibility. There will always be aspects of Hitler we cannot explain. German publisher Rudolf Augstein was probably right in his review of Fest's work when he questioned whether there could ever be *the* definitive biography of Hitler.[49] People will never stop pondering this mysterious, calamitous figure. Every generation must come to terms with Hitler. "We Germans were liberated from Hitler, but we'll never shake him off," Eberhard Jäckel concluded in a lecture in 1979, adding: "Hitler will always be with us, with those who survived, those who came afterwards and even those yet to be born. He is present—not as a living figure, but as an eternal cautionary monument to what human beings are capable of."[50]

I

The Young Hitler

"I have no idea when it comes to my family history," Hitler remarked in August 1942 in one of his countless monologues at his Wolfsschanze headquarters. "I'm the most limited person in the world in this area. I am a fully non-familial being, someone who by his very nature isn't focused on relationships. It's not in me. I belong to my ethnic community."[1] The German dictator had good reason to declare his lack of interest in family history. Several obscure bits of his family story had already begun to occasion rumours and speculation when Hitler began his political career in the early 1920s. They have made historians rack their brains ever since, and even today not all of the questions surrounding Hitler's origins have been cleared up.

Hitler's family biography takes us to Waldviertel, an agricultural region of northern Austria that borders on Bohemia in what is now the Czech Republic. On 17 June 1837, in a village called Strones, an unmarried daughter of a small farmer, named Marie Anna Schicklgruber, gave birth to a son she named Alois. Children born out of wedlock were nothing unusual—that sort of thing happened all the time in the countryside. But at the age of almost 42, the mother was extraordinarily old for the times. Nonetheless, five years later she married the 50-year-old miller's assistant, Johann Georg Hiedler, from the village of Spital. The couple apparently lived in poverty, and as far as we know, even before Marie Anna's death in 1847 the child was entrusted to Johann Georg's younger brother Johann Nepomuk, who was one of the wealthier farmers in Spital. The younger Hiedler brother—who spelled his last name Hüttler—raised his foster son as his own. Alois grew up in a sheltered environment with Hiedler's three daughters. He went to a vocational *Volksschule* and then learned the cobbler trade in Vienna.

For a young man of such humble origins and limited education, Alois Schicklgruber had a remarkable professional career. In 1855, at the age of 19, he decided to give up his trade and get a job in the financial administration of the Austrian monarchy. A shining example of both ambition and devotion to duty, he climbed the social ladder, rung by rung. By 1875 he had become a customs official in the town of Braunau, a rank in the Austrian civil service normally reserved for people who had attended a university-track academy or *Gymnasium*.[2] But then, one year later, something strange happened. In early 1876, Johann Nepomuk and three witnesses turned up at the office of notary Josef Penker in the town of Weitra, not far from Spital, and declared that Alois Schicklgruber was actually the biological son of his brother Johann Georg Hiedler, who had died nineteen years previously. In the protocol drawn up by the notary and signed by the three witnesses, the name was recorded as "Hitler"—in those days the spelling of names seems to have been considered relatively unimportant. One day later, the pastor in the township of Döllersheim, where Strones is located, amended the parish register, adding "Georg Hitler" as Alois's father, striking the name "Schicklgruber" and replacing "illegitimate" with "legitimate."[3]

Historians have always been puzzled why the legal identity of Alois's father was determined, and his name changed, so late.[4] If Johann Georg Hiedler was truly Alois's father, as became the orthodoxy in the Third Reich, why had he not acknowledged his son when he married Marie Anna in 1842? And why had he let his brother raise the boy? Was Johann Nepomuk, as some have speculated, perhaps the true father?[5] The fact that Johann Nepomuk, and not Alois himself, initiated the name change would seem to speak for that scenario. But why then did Johann Nepomuk not admit that he was Alois's natural father, preferring instead to hide behind his long-deceased brother? Was he trying to head off a family scandal? Or did he just want to free his foster son, whose social rise had greatly impressed him, from the stigma of his illegitimate birth? The late date of Johann Nepomuk's trip to the notary would argue against this: the circumstances of Alois Schicklgruber's birth do not seem to have harmed his career prospects all those years. There is considerable evidence that the farmer, who was as sly as he was wealthy, wanted to shield his inheritance from the Austrian tax authorities. Alois was Johann Nepomuk's main heir, and as an officially acknowledged blood relation, he had to pay less tax on what he inherited.

Whatever the truth may be, the identity of Adolf Hitler's paternal grandfather remains uncertain. It is hard to overlook the irony that the man who would later demand that all Germans prove their "Aryan origins" was himself incapable of demonstrating his own— no matter how much the Führer's official genealogy tried to convey the contrary impression. On 12 March 1932, one day before the election that pitted Hitler against Hindenburg for the office of Reich president, the *Bayerischer Kurier* newspaper remarked how strange it was that "the talkative Adolf Hitler is so silent about his ancestors and about how far back his family name goes." A short while before, the Viennese newspaper the *Wiener Sonn- und Montagszeitung* had sensationally revealed that Hitler's father had actually been called "Schücklgruber" (*sic*) and that the name had been changed for inheritance purposes.[6]

Rumours that there were Jews in Hitler's family have no proven foundation. They sprang up in the early 1920s, and after the Second World War they seemed to be supported by a reliable source. In his memoirs, written before the notorious general governor of occupied Poland was executed in Nuremberg in 1946, Hans Frank wrote that Hitler's paternal grandfather had been a Jewish merchant in Graz named Frankenberger, in whose household Marie Anna Schicklgruber had worked.[7] But subsequent research revealed that no Jewish family by that name lived at the time in either Graz or indeed the entire Steiermark region.[8] There is no evidence that Hitler ever took speculations about his supposed Jewish grandfather seriously—to say nothing of feeling threatened by them.

We could dismiss the 1876 name change as a rather bizarre tangential episode, if it had not had such momentous historical importance. "Nothing that the 'old man' did pleased Hitler more than that," the Führer's childhood friend August Kubizek later recalled. "He thought 'Schicklgruber' was too coarse, too rural, too complicated and impractical. 'Hiedler' was too boring and soft for him. But 'Hitler' had a nice ring to it and was memorable."[9] In fact, there is every reason to doubt that someone named Schicklgruber would have ever been able to play the role of political messiah. "Heil Schicklgruber!" would likely have elicited only laughter.

In public, Alois Hitler wanted to be seen as an upstanding civil servant. A former colleague in Braunau described him as an unlikeable pedant who insisted on procedure above all else and lived a withdrawn life, with little social contact.[10] Photographs show him trying to look dignified in his official uniform, with its buttons spit-polished and a flashing sabre at his side. But Alois Hitler's private life was less orderly and controlled. An internal restlessness led him to change addresses frequently, and in his love life the seeming paragon of respectability was also remarkably fickle. Indeed, for the times and the moral conventions of his social circles, he was positively debauched. He married three times. His first marriage came in 1873, at the age of 36, when he wedded Anna Glasl, a civil servant's daughter from Braunau who was fourteen years his senior; they were divorced seven years later. The customs official had begun a fling with a 19-year-old barmaid named Franziska ("Fanni") Matzelsberger, which could hardly fail to attract attention in a town of 3,000 inhabitants. In May 1883, one month after the death of his first wife, Alois married his lover, who had borne him an illegitimate son, also named Alois, two years previously. Two weeks after their wedding ceremony, Fanni gave birth to their second child, a daughter named Angela.

But the family's fortunes took a downturn. That year, Fanni caught tuberculosis, a common disease at the time. While she was wasting away, Alois began a relationship with Klara Pölzl, a former housekeeper whom he hired to look after his two children. Born in 1860 in Spital, Klara was twenty-three years his junior. She was the daughter of a small farmer named Johann Baptist Pölzl and his wife Johanna, who was herself the daughter of Johann Nepomuk Hüttler.[11] That means, if the notarised declaration of 1876 was correct, that Alois and Klara were second cousins; and if Johann Nepomuk was actually Alois's true father, Alois would have been Klara's half-uncle. In August 1884, Fanni died at the age of 23, and as Klara was already carrying his child, Alois decided to forgo the customary year of mourning and to marry her immediately. That was easier said than done, however: the local pastor refused to marry the two because they were so closely related. Alois Hitler thus had to petition the bishop's seat in Linz for special dispensation and, after some back and forth, it was granted.[12] On 7 January 1885, Alois and Klara were finally allowed to get married.

Klara Hitler gave birth to three children in quick succession—Gustav in 1885, Ida in 1886 and Otto in 1887—but all died young. This was not uncommon at a time of high child mortality. At around 6:30 p.m. on 20 April 1889, she brought her fourth child into the world on the second floor of an inn in Braunau where the Hitlers were living. The child was baptised Adolf on Easter Monday.[13] His mother was 28; his father 51 years old.

There are few reliable eyewitness accounts of Adolf Hitler's earliest years. What Hitler himself wrote about his childhood in *Mein Kampf* is a calculated mixture of half-truths and legends which the leader of the 1923 putsch, imprisoned in Landsberg Castle, hoped would put him in a good light and help him become the Führer of a new greater German empire. After 1933, Hitler arranged for the confiscation of all private documents that might have revealed information about his childhood and youth. In April 1945, a few days before his suicide in his Berlin bunker, Hitler had his adjutant Julius Schaub destroy these records.[14] Most of the information we do have, therefore, is second-hand titbits and contemporaries' later sketches, which must be taken with a grain of salt since they were informed by knowledge of Hitler's subsequent life.[15]

"Today I consider it a lucky twist of fate that Providence deemed I would be born in Braunau am Inn," Hitler wrote in the first lines of *Mein Kampf*. "For this small town is located on the border between those two German states whose reunification must be, at least for those of us who are young, a lifelong goal to be achieved with any and all means."[16] But Braunau did not actually play much of a role in Hitler's childhood. In 1892 his father, who had been promoted to senior customs official, was transferred to Passau on the German side of the border. It was here that Hitler acquired the Bavarian accent which he would retain throughout his life and which would help make him such an effective rabble-rouser in the Munich beer halls of the early 1920s.[17]

In later years, Hitler liked to imply that he had grown up in humble circumstances, but this was far from the case.[18] As a senior customs official Alois Hitler earned an annual salary of 2,600 crowns—roughly the same as what a school principal would have made. Even when he retired in 1895 at the age of 59, he received a pension of 2,200 crowns and would not have had to make many cutbacks.[19] The Hitlers were comfortably middle class. The household consisted of Alois, Klara and Alois's two children from his second marriage, Alois Jr. and Angela; and of Adolf, his brother Edmund (who was born in 1894 but died in 1900 of rubella) and his sister Paula, who was born in 1896. Also residing in the Hitlers' apartment was Klara's younger, unmarried sister Johanna Pölzl, who helped out with the family. Aunt "Hanni" had a hunchback and, apparently, mild learning difficulties.[20]

Alois Hitler was a strict, short-tempered patriarch who demanded unquestioning respect and obedience from his children and used the switch whenever his expectations were not met. His oldest son Alois Jr. suffered particularly from his temper and left home at the age of 14. Adolf, who was seven years younger, also came in for the odd beating, but his sister Paula was probably exaggerating when she claimed during an interrogation in 1946 that he had received "a good thrashing" every day.[21] The senior customs official was not all that concerned about his children. He devoted most of his free time to his hobby, beekeeping, and enjoyed going to taverns to drink a few glasses of beer and discuss the state of the world with acquaintances.[22] We should also be sceptical about Hitler's later claims that his father's alcohol consumption was excessive and that he had once had to carry him home, drunk, from the tavern.[23] Hitler tended to depict his father negatively to cast his mother in a more favourable light. After a conversation with the Führer in August 1932, Goebbels noted in his diary: "Hitler endured almost an identical childhood to mine. His father a domestic tyrant, his mother a source of goodness and love."[24]

Klara Hitler was a quiet, modest, obedient woman who patiently bore her husband's self-important airs and protected her children as best she could from his outbreaks of rage. The early death of her first three children was an enormous loss, and she was all the more determined to shower her fourth child Adolf with maternal care. He was the coddled favourite, while Klara's stepchildren, Alois and Angela, often felt neglected. "He was spoiled from early morning to late at night," opined William Patrick Hitler, Alois Jr.'s son, in New York in 1943. "The stepchildren were forced to listen to endless stories about how wonderful Adolf was."[25] For the young Hitler, maternal affection compensated for excessive paternal strictness. "Without exception he always spoke of his mother with profound love," August Kubizek recalled.[26] Even late in life, Hitler carried a small photo of Klara in his breast pocket, and an oil portrait of his mother was one of the few personal possessions that he kept in his bedroom right up until his death.

Most psychologists assume that the first years of an individual's life determine how his personality develops, and few historians (and even fewer psychological historians) have been able to withstand the temptation to find traces of the monster in the young Hitler. The violence he suffered at his father's hand has often been cited as a source of the murderous policies he pursued as a dictator.[27] But biographers should be careful about drawing far-reaching conclusions from Hitler's early childhood. Physical punishment was an accepted method of child-rearing in those days, and it was hardly uncommon for turn-of-the-century middle-class families to feature an authoritarian, punitive father on the one hand and a loving mother on the other. From all we know, Hitler seems to have had a fairly normal childhood. In any case there are no obvious indications of an abnormal personality development to which Hitler's later crimes can be attributed. If Hitler had a problem, it was an overabundance rather than a paucity of motherly love. That may have contributed to his exaggerated self-confidence, his tendency towards being a know-it-all and his disinclination to exert himself in areas he found unpleasant. These characteristics were already evident during Hitler's schooldays.

In 1895, the year he retired, Alois Hitler acquired a farm in Hafeld, an area of the town of Fischlham. There that May, the 6-year-old Hitler started attending the one-room schoolhouse. "When I was in the first grade, I listened in on the pupils from the second and later the third and the fourth," Hitler later said.[28] In 1897, Alois sold the farm and rented an apartment in the nearby market town of Lambach, where Hitler continued his schooling and was briefly a member of the boys' choir at the local Benedictine monastery. In the autumn of 1898, the family moved yet again, this time to the village of Leonding near Linz, where Alois Hitler had purchased a house right next to the town cemetery. It would later become a site for Nazi pilgrimages after the *Anschluss* between Germany and Austria in 1938. "Very small and primitive," Goebbels remarked after visiting Hitler's boyhood home in March 1938. "I was led into the room that was his empire . . . This was where a genius was made. I was overcome by a feeling of solemn significance."[29]

Adolf Hitler was a lively pupil who easily mastered the challenges of the village school and got excellent marks. "The laughably easy task of learning at school left me so much free time that I saw more of the sun than of my room," Hitler wrote in *Mein Kampf*.[30] He played soldiers with the other village youngsters and enjoyed taking command. "The Boer War was going on," recalled one of Hitler's classmates. "The kids from Leonding under Hitler's leadership were the Boers while the kids from [nearby] Untergamberg were the English. Things often got pretty heated afterwards at the Hitlers' house as well, because our commander Adolf left his father waiting for so long for the tobacco he was supposed to buy."[31]

In the evening, like many boys his age, he devoured the Westerns of novelist Karl May. He read them "by candlelight and, with the help of a magnifying glass, by moonlight," Hitler recalled in a February 1942 monologue at the Wolfsschanze.[32] During the Second World War, especially at difficult times, Hitler would frequently take out a book by May and praise the Native American character Winnetou as "the embodiment of a company leader."[33] Hitler saw himself as "the leader of a little gang" of his Leonding schoolmates and a class photo supports that idea.[34] The 10-year-old occupies the middle of the top row with his arms crossed and his face slightly overexposed "in a pose of demonstrative superiority."[35] The young boy was obviously not plagued by self-doubt.

But in September 1900 the transition from a village primary to an urban secondary school in Linz brought an abrupt end to Hitler's sunny childhood. Hitler, now 11, had to walk an hour to and from school, and he was no longer the indisputable leader of the class. He was just one of many pupils and he also carried the stigma, in the eyes of his well-heeled Linz classmates, of being a country yokel. Hitler had a hard time submitting to a more regimented school routine, and he no longer effortlessly got good grades as he had before. Already in his first year he failed maths and natural science and had to repeat a grade. In the years that followed, he barely progressed. In 1924, his former teacher Eduard Huemer remembered him as a "gaunt, pale youth" who was "definitely talented" but "not diligent." Considering his "undeniable gifts," Huemer said, Hitler "should have done far better." With his teachers, Hitler was "rebellious, independent, dogmatic and hot-tempered," often reacting to their corrections and admonitions with "scarcely concealed distaste."[36] As he entered puberty, the lively, curious young boy became an introverted, moody adolescent who positioned himself as an outsider.

In *Mein Kampf*, Hitler characterised his poor school performance as an act of rebellion not so much against his teachers as against his father. His father, he claimed, had wanted to force him down the path towards a career as a civil servant, which ran completely contrary to his nature. "I never wanted to become a civil servant, no, no, no," Hitler wrote. "The thought of being trapped in an office, of no longer being the master of my own time but rather being compelled to devote my entire life to filling out forms, made me yawningly nauseous."[37] There are good reasons to doubt Hitler's depiction, however. If his father had truly intended for him to enter the civil service, he would have sent him to a classical *Gymnasium* and not to a *Realschule*, which steered pupils towards technical and mercantile jobs.[38] Hitler's talent for drawing was recognised at an early age, and this seems to have been the reason for Alois's decision. But contrary to what he wrote in *Mein Kampf*, this does not mean that Hitler decided at the age of 12 to devote himself to art rather than become a civil servant. His father's embittered rejection of Hitler's artistic ambitions— "Artistic painter, never, over my dead body!"—is most likely the stuff of legend.[39]

We can safely assume, though, that the tension between father and son was increasing at this time. Alois Hitler must have sensed that his adolescent son was becoming more independent and rebellious. But what likely angered him most was not some disagreement about his son's future career, but rather Adolf's demonstrative unwillingness to put in the work needed to get into a better school. Born out of wedlock in the rural provinces, Alois had laboured hard to climb the social ladder, and he expected his son, who had enjoyed a far better start in life, to be diligent and determined about securing his status in society. In the best of all worlds, his son would have climbed a few rungs in the social hierarchy to a level that Alois's humble origins and lack of education had put beyond his reach. Instead, the adolescent Adolf was surprisingly lazy and intractable. This no doubt enraged his ambitious father.

But on 3 January 1903, before the conflict could truly come to the boil, Alois Hitler suddenly died at the age of 65 while having a morning drink in the Wiesinger Inn in Leonding. This unexpected event "plunged us all into the deepest sorrow," Hitler wrote in *Mein Kampf*.[40] In truth, the sudden passing of the patriarchal tyrant probably came as a relief to Alois's wife and even more so to his children. The family was provided for: Klara Hitler received a widow's pension sufficient to maintain a comfortable existence.[41] Usually she spent her summers with Adolf and Paula at her sister's home in Weitra. His cousins would later recall that Hitler had played with them occasionally but preferred to go off on his own and paint, draw or read one of the books he had brought along.[42]

Hitler's grades did not improve. In 1903–4 he was only promoted after taking a supplementary test and agreeing to transfer to a different school. His mother enrolled him in another *Realschule* in Steyr, eighty kilometres away from Linz, where he lived with foster parents. For the first time Adolf was separated from his mother, and he was apparently quite homesick. Even as Reich chancellor, he still complained about "how he had been filled with yearning and resentment when his mother sent him to Steyr."[43] One of his teachers there recalled a "medium-sized, somewhat pale pupil" who "acted somewhat shy and cowed, probably because it was the first time he had been away from home."[44] But Hitler did not stay in Steyr very long. In the autumn of 1905, with his grades remaining poor, he faked an illness and convinced his mother to take him out of school. He would retain a deep hatred of schools and teachers for the rest of his life. "Teachers—I can't stand them," he once remarked. "The ones who are any good are the exceptions to the rule."[45] Among the few good ones in Hitler's eyes was his history teacher in Linz, Leopold Poetsch, whom he singled out for praise in *Mein Kampf*. Poetsch, Hitler wrote, had known how "not just to captivate but to motivate when he spoke."[46]

By the time the drop-out Hitler returned to his family, Klara had already sold their house in Leonding. In June 1905 she rented an apartment in Humboldtstrasse 31 in Linz. Her stepdaughter Angela had just moved in with her new husband, a civil servant named Leo Raubal, so only four people lived in the apartment: Klara, Adolf, Paula and Hanni. For a while a boarder, a pupil named Wilhelm Hagmüller, also ate lunch with the Hitlers.

Linz, the provincial capital of Upper Austria, had some 60,000 inhabitants around 1900, many of whom like the Hitlers originally came from the countryside. Thanks to its location on the right bank of the Danube, the city had become an important railway crossing, and its main attraction was its central train station, which was a stopping point for the express trains that connected Munich and Vienna. For a provincial capital, Linz had a lot of culture on offer. During Hitler's time there, the director of the Linz Conservatory, August Göllerich, developed an impressive repertoire of operas and established a reputation as a leading interpreter of Liszt, Wagner and Bruckner.[47]

In retrospect, Hitler described the two years he spent in Linz before moving to Vienna as "almost a beautiful dream."[48] His life was one of comfortable idleness. Hitler had no intention of starting an apprenticeship. At the age of 16, he spent most of his days in his room drawing, painting and reading. He also took long walks along Linz's main boulevard, which led from the train station to the bridge over the Danube; he was always neatly attired, affecting the airs of a dandified university student, swinging a black walking stick with a delicate ivory handle.[49] In the evenings, he attended the operas in Linz's *Landestheater*. It is presumably here that he met his friend August Kubizek, the son of a decorator and upholsterer, in 1905.[50]

In the autumn of 1953, three years before his death, Kubizek published his recollections of the "friend from his youth." They are significant in so far as they are the only substantial account of Hitler's Linz years, but they must be read critically since they are based on an earlier shorter manuscript that Kubizek had written for the Nazi Party archives in 1943 at the behest of Hitler's secretary Martin Bormann. Not surprisingly, Kubizek's recollections are full of admiration for the later Führer. Nonetheless, although he embellished the odd incident post-war and his memory occasionally failed him, Kubizek's memoirs remain a credible source.[51]

Kubizek is the author of the only description of Hitler as a young man, and it is worth quoting extensively:

Hitler was of medium build and thin. Even then he was a bit taller than his mother. He didn't seem all that strong. On the contrary, he was somewhat gangly and slight ... His nose was straight and well proportioned, nothing unusual. He had a high forehead that sloped back slightly, and I found it unfortunate that he was already in the habit of brushing his hair as deeply as possible over it . . . In my entire life, I have never met a person . . . whose eyes dominated his face as much as my friend's. He had his mother's light-coloured eyes and a greatly intensified version of her penetrating stare . . . It was uncanny how his eyes changed their expression, especially when Adolf spoke. Adolf literally spoke with his eyes . . . When he visited me at home for the first time and I introduced him to my mother, she said to me that night before going to bed: "Your friend has such remarkable eyes!" I remember that all too well. There was more fear than admiration in her voice.[52]

Hitler's eyes would always be described as his most extraordinary feature. Many people thought they were the secret of his attractiveness to women.[53]

The two young friends could hardly have differed more in personality. "While I was a quiet, somewhat dreamy boy, sensitive, adaptable and conciliatory," Kubizek wrote, "Hitler was very wild and temperamental. Harmless things, like a couple of hasty words, could make him explode with anger."[54] Although he was a year younger than Kubizek, Hitler dominated their relationship, doing most of the talking. "He felt compelled to speak and needed someone to listen," Kubizek recalled.[55] It was in early life then that the egomaniacal Hitler developed the habit of holding monologues that was to make life so hard for his entourage later on.

The bond between two such unequal young men was their joint passion for music, especially Richard Wagner. "My youthful enthusiasm for the master of Bayreuth knew no limits," Hitler wrote in *Mein Kampf*.[56] Such enthusiasm was common among many adults in both the Habsburg monarchy and the German Reich. Thomas Mann, for instance, wrote in 1907 that people had to experience Wagner's art "to understand anything about our age."[57] Hitler read everything he could find on Wagner. Sometimes, when out on an extended walk in Linz with his friend, he would suddenly stop and recite a passage from Wagner's correspondence or his diaries.[58] *Lohengrin* always remained Hitler's favourite opera. The Hitlers' boarder Hagmüller recalled the young Adolf pacing his room in Humboldtstrasse singing "Du Schwan zieh hin."[59]

Kubizek described Hitler as being completely enraptured at a performance of the early Wagner opera *Rienzi*, which tells the story of the medieval Italian populist Cola di Rienzi, who freed Rome from tyranny but was ultimately betrayed by his people and died in the rubble of the burning Italian capital. For a long time, Kubizek recalled, Hitler was silent. Then he led his friend up to the top of the Freinberg hill, clasped his hands and the words began to spill out. "In grand, captivating images, he told me about his future and the future of his people," Kubizek wrote. "He spoke of a special mission that would one day be his. I . . . could hardly follow him. It took me many years to understand what these hours of otherworldly rapture had meant to my friend." While visiting the Wagner Festival in Bayreuth in August 1939, Hitler recalled that evening on Freinberg and turned to Winifred Wagner with the remark, "That was the hour everything started."[60] Obviously, this account was driven by the desire to transform the *Rienzi* episode into a moment of profound political awakening: Kubizek's projection and Hitler's need for exaggerated self-importance dovetailed perfectly. But if we filter out the mythologising, we can see the role the young Hitler's passion for Wagner played in his unstable psyche. It gave him the intoxicating feeling of being much more important than he was. It helped him escape into a dream world, where his own future was not dark but bright and clear.

More than once Hitler announced that he felt an artistic calling and loathed any sort of middle-of-the-road "breadwinning" job. His friend Kubizek, who himself aspired to a career in music, admired Hitler for the apparent seriousness with which he pursued his ambitions. Hitler was constantly drawing and sketching, and he developed fantastical plans for remaking Linz that included a new gigantic Danube bridge and a new concert hall. "I felt as though I had entered an architect's office," Kubizek wrote, recalling the first time he visited Hitler's room.[61] But the bold urban developer never seems to have asked himself whether the sketches he put on paper could ever be realised. He cocooned himself in a bizarre, alternative world somewhere between dream and reality.

The same is true for the 17-year-old Hitler's "first love." In Kubizek's more-than-ample account, the two friends encountered a beautiful blonde girl named Stefanie Isac in the spring of 1906 while out for an evening stroll through the centre of town. Hitler immediately developed a huge crush on her and could think of nothing else, although he never dared to introduce himself. For her part, Stefanie never noticed that she had a secret admirer. Kubizek explained his friend's unusual reticence with the idea that actually meeting the girl would have destroyed Hitler's ideal picture of her as the embodiment of everything feminine. No matter whether Kubizek's tale of young romance was true, it reflects Hitler's characteristic disinclination to let cold, hard reality get in the way of wishful thinking.[62]

For two weeks in early May 1906, Hitler travelled to Vienna for the first time and was overwhelmed by the many sights the metropolis had to offer—the museums, the State Opera, the Austrian parliament, the town hall, the Ringstrasse—which reminded him of the "magic of *A Thousand and One Nights*."[63] On two evenings, Hitler attended the opera to see productions of *Tristan* and *The Flying Dutchman* by Gustav Mahler and with sets designed by Alfred Roller. He sent four postcards back to Kubizek and these are the earliest surviving examples of Hitler's handwriting. His hand was full of verve and astonishingly adult, although the 17-year-old was no master of spelling, grammar and punctuation. The occasional grandiloquent, melodramatic tone presaged his later speeches and writings. Describing the State Opera on his second postcard, Hitler wrote:

> The interior of the palace is not uplifting. Whereas the outside is full of powerful majesty that gives the structure the gravity of a monument to art, the interior triggers admiration rather than makes one appreciate the dignity. Only when the powerful waves of sound flood the space and the rushing of the wind yields to those aural waves, does one feel sublimity and forget the gold and velvet with which the interior is burdened.[64]

Even this brief postcard excerpt contained five spelling and grammatical errors.

The visit convinced Hitler that he had to move to the Austrian capital. "In his mind, he was no longer in Linz, but lived at the centre of Vienna," Kubizek recalled.[65] But then his mother suddenly fell seriously ill, disrupting his plans. In January 1907, Klara's Jewish family doctor, Eduard Bloch, diagnosed breast cancer. Thirty-four years later in American exile, Bloch described how the young Hitler had taken the terrible news: "His long, pale face twisted. Tears flowed from his eyes. Did his mother have no chance, he asked."[66] On 18 January, Klara

Hitler was operated on in the Barmherzige Schwestern hospital in Linz.[67] She was discharged on 5 February and seemed to be on the mend. Because she could not manage the flights of stairs up to the Hitlers' third-floor apartment in Humboldtstrasse, the family moved to the borough of Urfahr on the other side of the Danube in mid-May 1907, where they occupied a small but bright apartment in the first floor of a new building on Blütenstrasse 3.

In early September 1907, with his mother's condition apparently stable, Hitler travelled again to Vienna to take the entrance test for the Academy of Fine Arts. One hundred and twelve candidates applied. Hitler made it past the first round, in which thirty-three candidates were weeded out, but he failed to clear the second one, in which only twenty-eight applicants got through. "Too few heads. Sample drawing unsatisfactory" was the admissions committee's verdict.[68] Hitler had gone to Vienna convinced that he would pass the exam with flying colours, so the rejection hit him all the harder—like "an abrupt blow from nowhere," as he would write in *Mein Kampf*.[69] When he asked for an explanation, the academy director told him that his talent lay in architecture, not art. But he could not study architecture because he had not completed the *Gymnasium*. "Downtrodden, I left Theophil Hansen's marvellous building," Hitler later wrote.[70] People have perennially speculated about how history might have turned out had Hitler passed that admissions test. Most likely not only his life story, but Germany's and the world's would have taken a different course.

When Hitler returned to Linz in October, his mother's health had deteriorated and he tended to her with great devotion. "Adolf read her every wish from her eyes and showed her the tenderest sort of care," Kubizek recalled. "I had never seen him be so solicitous and gentle."[71] That account tallies with the observations of Dr. Bloch, who made daily house calls to ease his patient's pain. In the night of 20–21 December 1907, Klara Hitler died at the young age of 47. The doctor found her son the next morning at her death bed. "In almost forty years of practice, I have never seen a young man so utterly filled with pain and grief as the young Adolf Hitler," Bloch recalled in November 1938.[72]

After his rejection by the Academy of Fine Arts, which he concealed from his family and friends, it was doubly difficult for Hitler to get over his mother's death. In her he likely lost the only person he ever loved.[73] Yet there is no evidence that her doctor's Jewishness was at the root of his pathological hatred for Jews.[74] On 23 December, the day of Klara Hitler's funeral, the 18-year-old Hitler appeared in Bloch's office and declared, "I will be forever grateful to you, Doctor."[75] And he did not forget his gratitude in his later years. In 1938, when he celebrated Austria's incorporation into the German Reich with a triumphant march into his "home city" of Linz, he is said to have asked: "Tell me, is good old Dr. Bloch still alive?"[76] Alone among Linz's Jews, Bloch was put under the special protection of the Gestapo. In late 1940, he and his wife were able to flee to the United States via Portugal.

After New Year's Day 1908, Hitler visited his parents' graves in Leonding. "Adolf was very composed," wrote Kubizek. "I knew how deeply his mother's death had shaken him . . . I was astonished how calmly and clearly he spoke about it."[77] There was nothing keeping Hitler in Linz now, and he immediately started preparing his move to Vienna. Together with his sister Paula, he applied to the Linz authorities for orphans' pensions. They were each entitled to 25 crowns a month. The inheritance from their father of 625 crowns each was deposited in a closed account they could not access until they had reached the age of 24, but the two siblings could make use of an inheritance of 2,000 crowns from their mother. Hitler was by no means wealthy, as some have claimed, but the money was enough to live on in Vienna for a year without having to work regularly.[78]

On 4 February, the owner of the house on Blütenstrasse, Magdalena Hanisch, asked her Viennese friend Johanna Motloch to try to convince the set designer Alfred Roller, who was also a professor at the Academy of Applied Arts, to intervene on Hitler's behalf. "He's a serious, ambitious young man, very mature for his age of 19, from a completely respectable family," Hanisch wrote. Roller promptly answered: "Young Hitler should come see me and bring samples of his work so that I can see what they're like." Several days later, Hanisch described Hitler's reaction to her friend: "He read the letter silently, word for word, with reverence and a happy smile on his face, as though he wanted to memorise it." Could it be, after his disappointment the preceding October, that a door was opening to the sort of artistic life he coveted? In a letter to Johanna Motloch, Hitler expressed his "deepest gratitude" for giving him "access to the great master of stage design."[79] It is strange, therefore, that in Vienna he never took Roller up on his offer. If we believe Hitler's later explanations, the reason was shyness. In one of his table talks he claimed that he had been too nervous during his early days in Vienna to approach a person like Roller. That, he said, was as impossible for him "as speaking before five people."[80]

On 12 February 1908, Hitler left for Vienna. His bags contained his books and a few important family documents such as letters from his mother, which he ordered to be burned in 1945.[81] He had convinced Kubizek, who brought him to the train station, to move to Vienna as well to get musical training at the conservatory. His sister Paula and aunt Hanni initially remained in the apartment in Urfahr, but Hanni soon moved back to Waldviertel to be near her relatives. Twelve-year-old Paula then went to live with her half-sister Angela Raubal.[82] As he had done on his last visit in October, Hitler moved in with the unmarried seamstress Maria Zakrey in the courtyard of Stumpergasse 29 of the Viennese district of Mariahilf, an area for "little people." On 18 February, he sent a postcard to Kubizek that read: "I eagerly await news of your arrival . . . All of Vienna is waiting. So come soon."[83]

2

The Vienna Years

"Vienna was and is the most difficult, if also the most thorough, school I went through," Hitler wrote in *Mein Kampf*. "I came to the city half a boy and left it as a quiet, serious adult."[1] The five years from 1908 to 1913 that Hitler spent in the capital of the Austro-Hungarian Empire were deeply significant. In many respects the impressions his new environment made upon him and the experiences he had there greatly influenced his character and his political views. It was no accident that he would always come back to these years in the monologues he later held in his headquarters.

Fin-de-siècle Vienna was a major European metropolis—with around two million inhabitants, it was the continent's fourth most populous city after London, Paris and Berlin. The seat of the Habsburg monarchy was not only famous for its glorious past. With its industry, large commercial firms, banks and modern means of transport, it was also a vibrant economic centre, and its theatres, concert halls, artists' studios, publishing houses and newspapers made it a hive of culture as well. "Hardly any other city in Europe had such cultural urgency as Vienna," wrote Viennese author Stefan Zweig, looking back on the years before the First World War.[2] Modernists in various branches of culture—the painters Gustav Klimt, Egon Schiele and Oskar Kokoschka, the architects Otto Wagner and Adolf Loos, the writers Arthur Schnitzler and Hugo von Hofmannsthal, the composer Arnold Schönberg and many others—were creating a furore.[3] Emperor Franz Josef I, nearly 80 years old, still resided in the Hofburg Palace. When Hitler moved to Vienna in 1908, the aged monarch—a guarantee, so it seemed, of absolute stability and a symbol of lasting leadership—celebrated the sixtieth anniversary of his rule with a series of gala dinners and a parade full of pomp.[4]

But the glamorous façade concealed deep social cracks. The splendid architecture of Ringstrasse and the broad boulevards that expressed the self-confidence of the aristocracy and the bourgeoisie, as well as their need to show off, stood in stark contrast to the shabby tenement buildings in the outer districts where working-class families lived in cramped quarters. "From a social perspective, Vienna around the turn of the century was one of the most difficult cities," Hitler remarked in *Mein Kampf.* "Gleaming wealth alternated abruptly with repellent poverty."[5] But Vienna was more than just a city of stark social contrasts. It also attracted and magnified the problems of the multinational Austro-Hungarian state. Other than Berlin, no European city had such a high rate of immigration. Between 1880 and 1910 the city's population doubled. The largest group of immigrants were the Czechs—by 1910 every fifth person in Vienna had Czech roots.[6] Vienna's Jewish population was also proportionally larger than in most other European cities. In 1910, over 175,000 Jews lived there—that was 8.7 per cent of the total population. The poorer segment of this group, chiefly immigrants from the eastern parts of the empire—Hungary, Galicia and Bukovina—lived in the Leopoldstadt district, nicknamed "Matzo Island" in the local slang.[7]

Among Vienna's ethnic Germans and in the German-speaking parts of the Austro-Hungarian Empire, this massive immigration gave rise to fears of "foreignisation," of losing the cultural and political hegemony that German Austrians considered their birthright. In reaction, numerous radical nationalist associations, political parties and popular movements had formed since the end of the nineteenth century.[8] That, of course, provoked counter-reactions from other ethnic and cultural groups. One of the main arenas for nationalist conflict was the Reichsrat or Imperial Council, the parliament of the western half of the Austro-Hungarian Empire. In 1907, with the introduction of universal suffrage for men over the age of 24, Germans were no longer the strongest faction there, and the verbal duels fought between the spokesmen for various nationalities, right out in the public eye, were so bitter that many people believed the Habsburg monarchy was in crisis and the multinational state would soon be dissolved. Nowhere was the oft-cited *fin-de-siècle* mood—the intimation of coming seismic shifts and catastrophes—more palpable than in Vienna. "Everyone is stopped and waiting, maître d's, hansom cab drivers and governments,"

wrote the Viennese satirist Karl Kraus in 1899. "Everyone's waiting for
the end. Let's hope the apocalypse is pleasant, Your Highness."[9]

Immediately upon arriving in Vienna, Hitler told readers of *Mein Kampf*,
he was cast into "a world of misery and poverty."[10] This was intentionally misleading. The financial cushion of his maternal inheritance, his
orphan's pension and occasional gifts from Aunt Hanni meant that
the new arrival could continue his idle existence. In late February 1908,
after Kubizek had joined him, the two friends moved into the larger
room in Maria Zakrey's apartment on Stumpergasse. Their rent was
20 crowns a month. Kubizek passed the entrance examination to the
conservatory on the first go, so while his friend pursued his studies,
Hitler whiled away his days with no goal or plan. He tended to get up
late, a habit he retained even as Nazi Party leader and Reich chancellor,
and when Kubizek returned from the conservatory, he usually found
Hitler making sketches or brooding over his books.

Hitler would often read until the early hours of the morning.
"Books, always books," recalled Kubizek. "I can't picture Adolf
without books. Books were his whole world."[11] Hitler's favourite
reading material was Germanic myths and heroic sagas, closely
followed by art and architectural histories. But he also read contemporary works such as the plays of Ibsen and Frank Wedekind's *Spring
Awakening*.[12] He quickly memorised everything he found important
and useful and forgot the rest. In *Mein Kampf*, he would devote a
long section to the "Art of Proper Reading," which he claimed to
have mastered from an early age. This consisted of "separating what's
valuable from what's worthless so as to retain the former in your
head for ever while not even seeing the latter, if possible, and definitely not carrying around senseless ballast."[13]

Whenever they could, the two friends attended the Vienna State
Opera. "Before the world war, the opera was something wonderful!"
Hitler still rhapsodised in 1942. "The culture there—unparalleled!"[14]
Often he and Kubizek had to stand in line for hours to get one of the
coveted standing-room tickets. As they had in Linz, they found Wagner
particularly intoxicating. "For Adolf everything else receded in importance before this unique mystical world the great master conjured up
for us," Kubizek recalled.[15] Gustav Mahler had got fed up with being
attacked by anti-Semites, and given up the directorship of the opera

in 1907, but both young Wagnerians took the side of the Jewish conductor and composer in the controversy surrounding his interpretations of the operas.[16]

Otherwise, Hitler's taste in art remained utterly uninfluenced by Viennese modernism. He had no time for the works of Klimt and the Secession. Hitler preferred traditional art: the late romanticism of Arnold Böcklin, the neo-baroque monumental paintings of Hans Makart and above all the idyllic genre works of the Munich painter Eduard Grützner.[17] "As a young man in Vienna I once saw a Grützner in the window of an art dealership," he later told his "court photographer" Heinrich Hoffmann. "I was so thrilled I couldn't take my eyes off it."[18] By contrast, Hitler regarded all abstract painting as "nothing more than crippled spattering."[19] He had equally little sympathy for the pioneers of a new functionalism in architecture like Adolf Loos. Hitler's architectural heroes were the neoclassicists Karl Friedrich Schinkel and Gottfried Semper, and he spent hours staring up at the majestic buildings on Ringstrasse.[20] "He forgot not just the time, but everything around him," Kubizek wrote. "At home he would make me sketches of floor plans and longitudinal cuts, trying to recreate every interesting detail . . . For him Ringstrasse became a living object of study that allowed him to test his architectural knowledge and argue for his ideas."[21]

As time passed, Kubizek began to notice a change in his friend's behaviour. Hitler would explode in rage at the slightest provocation, cursing a world that allegedly conspired against him. He was also prone to bouts of depression, in which he tortured himself with self-critical reproaches. Phases of frantic activity alternated with stretches of lethargy in which he succumbed to total idleness.[22] One day, Hitler stunned Kubizek by announcing that he was going to write an opera called "Wieland the Blacksmith," although he had only had a few months of piano lessons—from early October 1906 to late January 1907—and no idea at all how to compose music. Kubizek was forced to assist him in this adventurous project, until one day after several sleepless nights in which Hitler had worked himself into a frenzy, he gave up on the idea.[23] The same thing happened with other projects. When an idea took hold of him, Hitler would immediately set to work in a blaze of activity only to suddenly lose interest and devote his attention to something else.

In his 1938 essay "Brother Hitler," Thomas Mann recognised "a manifestation of an artist's nature" in the young man's daydreaming. "Although it makes me feel ashamed," Mann wrote,

> everything is there: the tendency to be "difficult," the laziness and pathetic amorphousness of adolescence, the refusal to be accommodated, the what-do-you-really-want, the semi-idiotic vegetation of a social and spiritual bohemian, the arrogant, self-inflated refusal of all reasonable and honourable activity—and on what basis? For the sake of an obscure intimation that one is destined for something indefinable, which would make people burst into laughter if it were ever possible to name.[24]

In their room on Stumpergasse, the two friends began to get on each other's nerves. Not only did Hitler feel disturbed in his auto-didactic studies whenever Kubizek practised the piano, he was also jealous that his room-mate proudly went to the conservatory every morning and enjoyed one success after another, while he, who felt himself called to be an artist, had had the doors of the Academy of Fine Arts slammed in his face. The excitable 19-year-old had still not told Kubizek about his rejection, but one night after they had fought yet again, it burst out of him. "They rejected me," Hitler confessed. "I was thrown out, excluded." His confession was accompanied by a wave of insults. As Kubizek recalled:

> "This academy!" Hitler yelled. "Nothing but a pack of cramped, old, outmoded servants of the state, clueless bureaucrats, stupid creations of the civil service! The whole academy should be dynamited!" His face was pale, his lips were pressed so tightly together that they went white. His eyes were glowing. How uncanny his eyes were! As if all the hatred of which he was capable were burning in those eyes.[25]

It was one of the rare moments when the otherwise secretive Hitler opened up to another person. The arrogant pose, with which Hitler sought to demonstrate his superiority over his friend, actually concealed his own massive uncertainty as to his future as an artist.

Perhaps that was one of the reasons why the young Hitler, in Kubizek's account, began to get interested in politics. On numerous occasions, he visited the Imperial Council and listened in the gallery to the debates, which were conducted in ten different languages. In retrospect, he claimed to have been outraged by what he called a "pathetic spectacle—a gesticulating, wildly motioning mass shrieking in every key at once and over them all a harmless old uncle, who worked himself into a sweat, ringing a bell and trying to restore the dignity of the house with words of conciliation, then warning."[26] Such scenes, Hitler would have his readers believe in *Mein Kampf*, had produced his deeply ingrained contempt for parliamentarianism and the entire concept of democratic majority rule. Kubizek, who once tagged along with Hitler and soon decided to leave, disgusted by the tumult, observed his friend reacting quite differently: "He stood up, his fists clenched and his face burning with excitement. I decided to remain seated quietly, although I had no idea what the debate was about."[27]

There can be no doubt that the incendiary political climate in Vienna greatly influenced the young man from the provinces, who was susceptible to radical slogans. As a pupil back in Linz, he had got involved in the German School Association, whose mission was to set up German-language schools and kindergartens in multilingual areas.[28] Hitler was convinced of the cultural superiority of everything German before he arrived in the Austrian capital. "When I came to Vienna, my sympathies were already fully and exclusively with the pan-Germanic movement," he wrote—this time plausibly—in *Mein Kampf*.[29] Georg Ritter von Schönerer, the founder of the movement in Austria, was one of the politicians the new arrival in Vienna most admired. Schönerer's desire to unite the German part of Austria with Imperial Germany, which entailed the dissolution of the multinational Habsburg state, must have exercised a considerable fascination on the young Hitler. He would later praise the fervent nationalist and Bismarck admirer Schönerer for "recognising more clearly than anyone else the inevitable end of the Austrian state."[30] It is uncertain whether the 19-year-old Hitler had much time for the cult of personality that grew up around Schönerer within the pan-Germanic movement. But he did take over some elements of that cult, for example the "Heil" greeting and the title Führer, into the NSDAP.[31]

By the turn of the century Schönerer was past the height of his power—1907 was the last time he had a seat in the council. His fight against the Catholic Church, pursued under the slogan "Let's get free of Rome," had offended a lot of his Catholic sympathisers. In *Mein Kampf*, Hitler criticised the "free of Rome" campaign as a major mistake, saying that Schönerer had possessed "insufficient understanding of the psyche of the broad masses."[32] But what Schönerer lacked, Hitler found in another politician: Karl Lueger, the Vienna mayor and founder of the Christian Social Party, who was at the height of his popularity at the beginning of the twentieth century. Lueger's political activity, Hitler wrote in *Mein Kampf*, was focused on the middle classes, which were threatened with extinction and who gave him an "unshakeable base that was willing to make sacrifices and fight tenaciously."[33]

As a disciple of Schönerer, Hitler maintained in one of his later monologues, he had initially opposed the Christian Social Party, but with time he had developed a "great personal respect" for Lueger. "I heard him speak for the first time in the Volkshalle in the city hall," Hitler recalled. "I was of two minds. I wanted to hate him, but I couldn't help admiring him. He had a great talent for speaking."[34] Lueger's oratorical skills were not the only quality Hitler admired. He also appreciated Lueger's rigorous Germanophile policies, advanced with the slogan "Vienna is German and must remain German."[35] Moreover, Hitler was impressed with the remarkable modernisation of the city's infrastructure for which the mayor had been responsible since taking office in 1897. Lueger had not only municipalised Vienna's gas and electricity suppliers and its public transport system, he also oversaw improvements to healthcare and social benefits, and established parks and other green areas. "Lueger was the greatest example of a local politician and the most brilliant mayor we've ever had," Hitler later said as Reich chancellor.[36] When Lueger died in March 1910, his young admirer Hitler was among the hundreds of thousands of people who lined the streets to watch the funeral procession.[37]

Next to Lueger's Christian Social Party, the Social Democrats were the strongest political force in pre-war Vienna. Hitler's relationship with them was strangely ambiguous. On the one hand, he was moved by the social misery that he encountered everywhere in the city. He spent weeks drawing up plans for social housing blocks so that the working population would have cheaper and better accommodation.[38] On the other hand, he was scared of sinking down into the proletariat himself. "Perhaps," Kubizek mused, "the unbelievable energy he poured into his autodidactic studies masked the instinctive attempt to protect himself from the misery of the masses by acquiring the broadest and most thorough education he could."[39] Hitler attended a number of workers' demonstrations in Vienna, but he found them more threatening than inspiring. "For almost two hours," he wrote in *Mein Kampf* of one such incident, "I stood there and watched with bated breath the unsettling human dragon-worm that slowly crawled by. Anxious and downcast, I finally left the square and wandered home."[40]

As a pan-Germanic sympathiser and a radical nationalist, Hitler loathed the Austrian Social Democrats' internationalist policy of mutual understanding with Slavic peoples. He suspected the Social Democratic leadership of exploiting the hardship of the working populace for their own gain. "Who are the leaders of these people living in misery?" Kubizek recalled Hitler asking after a demonstration. "They're not men who have experienced the hardships of the little guy themselves, but rather ambitious, power-hungry politicians, some of whom have no idea of reality and who are getting rich off the misery of the masses."[41] Hitler concluded his bitter indictment with a tirade against political profiteering. Opposition to the Social Democratic outlook, which he considered "un-German" and corrupt, would remain a constant in Hitler's political world view. It was part of the poisonous legacy of his Vienna years.

In early June 1908, at the end of his second semester, Kubizek travelled back to Linz to spend the holidays with his parents. When Hitler brought him to the train station Kubizek did not suspect that it would be thirty years before he would see his friend again. Left behind in Vienna, Hitler sent Kubizek several postcards and two longish letters in which he described his "hermit's existence" with forced good cheer. He reported that he had killed a "monster bedbug" in their room and got over a "bronchial flu." Hitler also stressed that he had been anything but lazy in his friend's absence: "I'm writing a lot right now, usually in the afternoons and evenings."[42] In the latter half of August, Hitler sent one last postcard from Waldviertel, where he was visiting relatives. Then he broke off all contact. When Kubizek returned to Vienna in November 1908, Zakrey informed him that Hitler had moved out without leaving a forwarding address.[43]

In September 1908, Hitler had applied for a second time to the Academy of Fine Arts. This time he was not even invited to take the entrance exam.[44] This may well be the reason he abandoned his friend so suddenly and with no explanation. Hitler's self-confidence was badly shaken. His dream of a great artistic career seemed to be over. Hitler's recurrent tirades even as Reich chancellor against the Academy "schoolmasters" who had "rejected him as untalented" showed how deeply he had been insulted.[45] The young Hitler no doubt felt that he and his mission were being utterly neglected and he decided to withdraw completely in the autumn of 1908. He broke off contact not only with Kubizek but with his family as well. On 18 November, he rented a new apartment on Felberstrasse 22, near the western train station and not far from Stumpergasse. He lived there until 20 August 1909.[46]

We have no reliable information about Hitler's time on Felberstrasse. For three quarters of a year, it is as though he had disappeared from view. But we can assume that his financial situation was getting worse and worse every month. He must have just about used up his maternal inheritance by that point, and his orphan's pension alone was not enough to live on. For the first time, Hitler had to make the sort of hard sacrifices he later boasted about. "For months I didn't have a hot meal," he claimed in one of his monologues. "I lived off milk and dried bread."[47]

An episode Hitler described at length in *Mein Kampf* may have happened at this time. "In order not to starve," Hitler claimed, he had worked on a building site. Here the conversations of the unionised construction workers had "enraged him to the extreme." Everything was dragged through the dirt—the nation, the fatherland, the authority of law, religion and morality. When he dared contradict them, the construction workers threatened to throw him from the scaffolding. He quit the job, one experience richer.[48] It seems unlikely, however, that this story was true. Hitler probably invented it as an illustration of how heroically he had combated the "false teachings" of Marxism even as a 20-year-old.[49]

On 22 August 1909, Hitler moved to cheaper quarters on Sechshauser Strasse 58. Previously, when registering his address, he had described himself on the forms as an "artist" or a "student." Now he called himself a "writer," although he had yet to publish a line.[50] On 16 September, he had to vacate his room, probably because he could not pay the rent. Under the heading "new address," his deregistration card read "unknown." It seems that Hitler had no fixed address during the following months. Looking back on the autumn of 1909 in January 1914, he wrote that it had been an "endlessly bitter time." Even five years later, he still carried "mementoes in the form of frost boils on my fingers, hands and feet."[51] This may be one of Hitler's typical exaggerations, but there is no doubt that he had hit rock bottom.[52] The young man, who according to Kubizek had always dressed properly and was extremely conscious of hygiene, was now one of the army of homeless people who slept on Vienna's park benches or gathered in the city's soup kitchens for a hot meal and to warm up when the weather was cold.[53]

In the late autumn of 1909, Hitler went to the Meidling homeless shelter, which offered some 1,000 people a bed and soup and bread every night. There he made the acquaintance of the man in the neighbouring cot, a convicted vagrant named Reinhold Hanisch. As Hanisch recalled in May 1933: "On the metal cot to my left was a spindly young man with bloody feet. I still had some bread from the farmers, and I shared it with him. Back then, I spoke in a thick Berlin dialect. He was crazy about Germany. I had wandered through his home town Braunau am Inn so it was easy to follow his stories."[54] Every morning the men using the shelter had to pack their things. They were not allowed to return until the evening. In the meantime, Hanisch and Hitler tried to earn some money as day labourers, but Hitler did not hold out long shovelling snow. "He had no winter coat and was frozen blue," Hanisch recalled.[55]

When the 20-year-old Hitler, who was too weak for physical labour, boasted to his new friend that he had gone to the Academy of Fine Arts, Hanisch hit upon the idea of exploiting Hitler's artistic talent. He suggested that Hitler paint postcards, which Hanisch would then sell in taverns. They would split the profits. Pressed by his new partner, Hitler asked his aunt Hanni for 50 crowns to buy paint and brushes. Business was better than expected: on 9 February 1910, the two men were able to quit the homeless shelter for a men's home on Meldemannstrasse 27.[56] Hitler would spend his next three years there.

The men's home in the working-class district of Brigittenau on the periphery of Vienna was a modern facility for its time, offering its more than 500 residents comfortable accommodation compared with the homeless shelter. Residents did not have to sleep in large halls; instead, every man got a small sleeping chamber with a bed, a table, a bureau and, as a special attraction, electric light. There were also a number of common rooms including a large reading room with a library, where nine newspapers were laid out, and a small "writing room."[57] Hitler sat there during the day, drawing and painting. Mostly he depicted Viennese landmarks such as the Karlskirche, the Stephansdom and the town hall on his postcards which Hanisch sold to tourists and frame-sellers. At 8 p.m. each night, Hitler withdrew to his chamber to devote himself to his autodidactic studies. "I painted to earn money and learned for the joy of it," he wrote in *Mein Kampf*. "I think the people around me then thought I was an oddball."[58]

And indeed the 21-year-old would-be artist was an outsider in the colourful society of the men's home, in which unmarried workers and small-time clerks lived side by side with dissipated university graduates. Hitler avoided other people's company. He did not drink or smoke and had little to say when the conversation turned to women. Female visitors were strictly forbidden on Meldemannstrasse as they were in all men's homes, but Hitler does not seem to have tried to find female companionship anyway. He would have had ample opportunities to do so during his time with Kubizek, who reported that female eyes were always on Hitler whenever the two friends went to the opera. Kubizek had asked himself what the attraction was. Was it Hitler's "extraordinarily light eyes" or the "strangely strict expression on his ascetic face"? Perhaps, Kubizek concluded, it was Hitler's "manifest uninterest in the members of the opposite sex" that had made women "want to test this male source of resistance."[59] Whatever the reasons may have been, the young Hitler was an ascetic within the erotically charged atmosphere of pre-war Vienna, in which Arthur Schnitzler's sex-themed play *La Ronde* and Klimt's explicit paintings caused such scandals. But there is no plausible reason to conclude that Hitler was attracted to men and was unable to acknowledge his true inclinations.[60] He had no shortage of potential contacts of this sort in his time in the men's home, but there is not the slightest indication of any homosexual orientation.

Paying prostitutes to initiate him into the ways of love, as was common among men of his age from middle-class backgrounds, was out of the question for Hitler: according to Kubizek, he was terrified of contracting syphilis.[61] Perhaps Hitler was following his role model Schönerer, who recommended that male members of the pan-Germanic

movement remain celibate until they were 25. "Nothing is more beneficial to young people than extended celibacy," Schönerer argued. "It
trains every muscle, makes the eyes gleam, quickens the wits, refreshes
the memory, inspires the imagination and fortifies the will. With this
feeling of strength, one sees the world, as it were, through a colourful
prism."[62] If Hitler stuck to such a vow of celibacy, which seems likely,
he would have still been a virgin when he left Vienna at the age of 24.[63]

We can only speculate about the consequences of Hitler's dormant
sex life. Perhaps it was connected to his aversion, recognisable from
a young age, to physical contact with others and his idealised views
of women such as we encountered in his silent love for Stefanie in
Linz. Possibly it was one cause of the short-temperedness from which
Kubizek had suffered so much during their time together. But many
men and women at the turn of the century suffered from
nervousness—or as doctors fashionably called it, "neurasthenia." This
had less to do with repressed sexuality than with the enormous accel-
eration of every aspect of daily life thanks to modern means of
transport and communication.[64]

The business partners Hanisch and Hitler soon quarrelled. To keep
both their heads above water, Hitler had to paint a postcard a day.
But sometimes he preferred to read the newspaper or take part in
political discussions in the reading room. He needed to be in the
"proper mood for artistic creation," Hitler said whenever Hanisch
nagged him to get on with his painting.[65] Hanisch also resented the
fact that Hitler increasingly befriended another resident of the men's
home, a 31-year-old copper-polisher from a Jewish family named Josef
Neumann, who peddled wares of various sorts. Neumann also sold
Hitler's paintings, putting him in direct competition with Hanisch. In
June 1910, Hitler disappeared with Neumann from the men's home,
only to return five days later.[66] Quite possibly the two men had tried
to establish an economic existence elsewhere. If so, the plan had
quickly failed and, in July, Neumann informed the authorities that he
was leaving Vienna. Hitler was forced to depend on Hanisch.

Nonetheless, the two fell out for good a few weeks later. Hitler
accused Hanisch of cheating him out of the price of two paintings,
and an acquaintance of his from the men's home officially filed
charges against Hanisch. On 5 August 1910, Hitler testified at the
Brigittenau police station that "For roughly two weeks, Hanisch has

not returned to the men's home, taking with him a painting by me entitled 'Parliament,' which was worth 50 crowns, and a water-colour worth 9 crowns."[67] Hanisch was given seven days in jail, in part because he had registered in another men's home in mid-July under a false name. From that point on, Hitler sold his paintings himself, primarily doing business with two Jewish owners of picture-framing and art shops, Jakob Altenberg and Samuel Morgenstern. They paid so well that Hitler was finally able to stand on his own two feet.[68]

In late March 1911, Hitler's aunt Johanna died, and the family learned that he had received large sums of money from her. Angela Raubal, whose husband had died the previous year and who was now forced to support not only her own three children but also Hitler's sister on a widow's pension, took the chance to claim the entirety of the orphans' benefit, which had previously been split between Adolf and Paula. In early May, Hitler was summoned at the behest of the district court in Linz to appear before the Leopoldstadt district court in Vienna. There he declared that he was able to support himself and agreed that the entire orphans' pension should be given to his sister.[69] This statement is one of the few documents we have concerning Hitler in 1911 and 1912. He then reappears in 1913, in an account by a man named Karl Honisch who lived in the men's home for a few months and wrote extensively about his time there for the NSDAP main archive in 1939.[70]

In this account, Hitler seemed strangely frozen in time. Honisch described him sitting at his familiar working spot in the window arch of the writing room: "Slight of build, with drawn cheeks and a dark shock of hair that kept falling down his forehead, dressed in a worn-out dark suit, he worked diligently from early in the morning until late afternoon."[71] No one even thought of occupying Hitler's customary spot. He had become something of a fixture in the men's home, respected and even admired by the others for his painting skills. "We were proud to have an artist among our ranks," recalled Honisch, who in 1939 was of course at pains to present Hitler in a positive light.[72] Hitler was a "friendly and likeable fellow" who "showed an interest in the travails of all the others" while taking care "not to get too close to anyone." For that reason, the others were careful not to take "liberties."[73]

Hitler, as Honisch presented it, rarely revealed much of himself. When he did, it was because the discussion turned to politics, and he felt compelled to take a stand within the small circle of "intelligentsia" in the men's home. "On such occasions he would stand up, toss his brush or pencil across the table and state his views with a fiery temperament, not shying away from strong expressions," Honisch recalled. "His eyes flashed, and he would jerk his head back to keep the shock of hair out of his forehead." At the end of such outbursts, Hitler would suddenly fall silent and sit back down at his easel with a resigned gesture, "as if to say, 'What a shame that I wasted my words on you since you don't understand them.'"[74] Hitler was particularly prone to anger when the talk was of "the Reds and the Jesuits"—Social Democrats and Catholics. Honisch did not recall Hitler making any anti-Semitic statements, however. So what was his attitude towards Jews at this point?

Hitler was no anti-Semite when he arrived in Vienna. The recollections of Dr. Bloch are more plausible on this score than those of Kubizek, who claimed that Hitler had held anti-Semitic opinions even back in Linz.[75] In *Mein Kampf*, Hitler himself wrote that he was first converted to Jew-hatred in Vienna: "At that time, I underwent the greatest internal upheaval I have ever experienced. I went from cosmopolitan weakling to fanatic anti-Semite."[76] Most of Hitler's biographers have taken this statement at face value, for it seems plausible that Hitler's obsession with Jews was a compensatory mechanism for his failure as an artist. Joachim Fest, for instance, writes that "his previously vagabond hatred . . . had finally found an object."[77] But the historian Brigitte Hamann has shown that Hitler's account was just one of the many legends with which the demagogue, writing in the early 1920s, tried to suggest that his world view had developed in a straight line. Hitler did not experience an anti-Semitic epiphany in Vienna. The reality is far murkier than historians have traditionally assumed.[78]

One thing is certain: Hitler would not have been able to avoid contact with anti-Jewish movements during his Vienna years. The Austrian capital in the early twentieth century was a major stomping ground for anti-Semites. In particular, the immigration of Jews from eastern Europe had given rise to fears that Vienna was being "Jewified," and the successes enjoyed by some of these immigrants, who knew the value of education and worked hard to climb the social ladder, elicited envy and resentment among many native Viennese.[79] Numerous politicians played on anti-Semitic sentiments. Hitler's idol Schönerer combined his fight on behalf of "Germanity" with a racial anti-Semitism previously unknown in Austria. Lueger, too, was not above employing slogans like "Greater Vienna must not become Greater Jerusalem" or pillorying the "Jewish press."[80] It would have been unusual if such sentiments had no influence whatsoever on the young Hitler.

Fin-de-siècle Vienna was fertile ground for crass racist theories. Pan-Germanic newspapers and pamphlets discussed the obscure teachings of Guido von List, who divided humanity into Aryan "masters" and the non-Aryan "herd," as well as the fantasies about racist breeding put forward by List's disciple Joseph Adolf (Jörg) Lanz von Liebenfels. In 1906, Lanz founded Ostara, "the first and only journal devoted to the researching and cultivation of the master race and its dominance."[81] Hitler read the Alldeutsches Tageblatt (Pan-German Daily), whose offices were located not far from Stumpergasse, and it is likely that he was also acquainted with Ostara. But although Lanz later claimed to have "given Hitler his ideas," we do not know what sort of influence the journal may have had on the future dictator.[82] Without doubt, part of the poisoned legacy of Hitler's Vienna years was that, in the course of his autodidactic studies, he was introduced to the broad repertoire of anti-Semitic clichés and prejudices popular among local nationalists and racists. But this doesn't mean that he already identified with them.

On the contrary, Hitler had no problems in his day-to-day interactions with the Jewish residents of the men's home, and he even maintained something approaching a friendship with Neumann. "Neumann was a good-hearted fellow who liked Hitler a lot and whom Hitler greatly respected," recalled Hanisch.[83] Among Hitler's Jewish acquaintances in the men's home were the locksmith's assistant Simon Robinson, who occasionally gave Hitler small sums of money, and the salesman Siegfried Löffner, who helped Hitler peddle his postcards. The fact that Hitler sold his pictures to Jewish merchants also argues against the notion that he already felt a strong antipathy towards Jews. Hanisch was probably being truthful when he asserted: "Hitler was by no means a Jew-hater in those days—that came later."[84] This statement is backed up by the recollection of an anonymous man from Brünn who resided at the home in early 1912: "Hitler got along well with Jews. Once he said that they were a clever people who stuck together better than the Germans."[85]

At the same time, Hitler's statements about Jews, as quoted by Hanisch, were very contradictory. On the one hand, he praised Jews for being the first civilised nation because they had done away with polytheism in favour of belief in a single god. He also praised charitable Jewish organisations in Vienna, from which he as a pauper had personally benefited, dismissed anti-Semitic claims that Jews carried out ritual murder, and defended the cultural achievements of Jews like the poet Heinrich Heine and the composer Gustav Mahler. On the other hand, he once supposedly answered the question of why Jews always remained foreigners in whatever nation they lived by saying that they were "a race unto themselves." He also occasionally remarked that Jews "smelled different."[86] Thus Hitler seems to have shared some of the anti-Semitic prejudices and clichés that abounded in German nationalist circles, but he was a long way away from the paranoid Jew-hatred that would become the centrepiece of his political activity. By no means did he have a "closed world view" or strict anti-Semitic convictions, so contrary to what his first biographer Konrad Heiden concluded, Hitler—or at least the public persona of "Hitler"—was anything but a finished product by the end of his Vienna years.[87] He would have to have further dramatic, life-changing experiences before he became an obsessive anti-Semitic demagogue lecturing in Munich's beer halls.

Hitler did not attract any attention with radical views in the coffee house he began to frequent in his final weeks in Vienna. On the contrary, the owner, Maria Wohlrab, later described him as a serious, introverted young man who read a lot and did not say much. Occasionally a woman came with him, and on his last visit, she was quoted as saying, "Dolfi, go to Germany."[88] It is doubtful that, thirty years after the fact, Wohlrab was able to remember her reticent customer quite as well as she made out, but Hitler had talked in the men's home about his desire to emigrate to Germany. He found Munich, the Bavarian capital, particularly alluring. There, he thought, he would be able to develop his artistic talent better than in Vienna, and he was attracted by the city's galleries with their impressive art collections. But first he had to wait for his twenty-fourth birthday on 20 April 1913 so he could claim his paternal inheritance. The original sum of 652 crowns in 1903 had grown into 819 crowns, 98 hellers—a sizeable amount of money indeed. The district court in Linz paid it out to Hitler on 16 May.[89]

Hitler spent the days that followed busily preparing for his move. He bought new clothes and told the authorities in Vienna that he was leaving the city. On 25 May he was on a train to Munich. Travelling with him was a 20-year-old apprentice pharmacist named Rudolf Häusler, who had moved into the men's home in February 1913. The two probably became close because Häusler's biography recalled Hitler's own. Häusler came from a well-situated Viennese family, but had got thrown out of school for playing a youthful prank, whereupon his strict father had banned him from the family home. Hitler, who was four years older, had taken him under his wing, introduced him to the world of Wagner's operas and persuaded him to come along to Munich. As he had previously done for Kubizek, Hitler had convinced Häusler's mother Ida, who remained devoted to her son, to let him go.[90] Upon arriving in Munich, Hitler and Häusler rented a small room in the fourth-floor apartment of the tailor Joseph Popp on Schleissheimerstrasse 34, on the edge of the bohemian Schwabing district. When he registered himself with the residence authorities on 29 May 1913, Hitler listed his occupation as "artistic painter." Under the rubric "expected length of stay," he wrote "2 years."[91] The new arrival thus intended to remain in Munich for the foreseeable future.

Looking back in 1924 on his time before the First World War, Hitler positively gushed about Munich.[92] Many aspects of the Bavarian capital could hardly fail to appeal to the young man. By the start of the twentieth century, Munich had become known as the "Athens on the Isar River," a major cultural metropolis that attracted growing numbers of painters, sculptors and writers.[93] Hitler was not interested at all in the avant-garde of the *Blaue Reiter* school around Vassily Kandinsky, but he was drawn to the Alte Pinothek with its collection of old masters, the Neue Pinothek, which contained the private collection of Ludwig I of Bavaria, and the Count Adolf Friedrich von Schack collection, which included works by Hitler's favourite Böcklin, Anselm Feuerbach, Carl Spitzweg and the late Romantic Moritz von Schwind.[94] He was also impressed by Munich's imposing architecture and its grand boulevards. In *Mein Kampf* he rhapsodised about the "magic" of the royal Munich Residenz, "that wonderful marriage of primeval strength and fine artistic sentiment."[95]

Hitler apparently also felt quite at home in the bohemian milieu of Schwabing with its vivid mixture of determined artists and eccentric do-gooders. The anarchist writer Erich Mühsam once described Schwabing's population as "painters, sculptors, poets, models, slackers, philosophers, founders of new religions, revolutionaries, reformers, sexual ethicists, psychoanalysts, musicians, architects, people who do arts and crafts, runaway daughters from respectable families, eternal students, the diligent and the lazy, those hungry for and tired of life, people with bushy locks and dapperly parted hair."[96] Among this cast of eccentrics the introverted, peculiar young Hitler did not stand out, and he could give in to his disinclination towards regular working hours and his fondness for daydreaming. Like many of the regulars at Café Stefanie, nicknamed Café Megalomania, Hitler believed he had a higher calling without knowing precisely what it was or how it could be achieved.

In one of his later monologues, Hitler talked about what he called his "decision to keep working as an autodidact": "I went to Munich with joy in my heart. I intended to keep learning for three more years and then, when I turned 28, to become a draughtsman at Heilmann and Littmann [a major construction company]. I would have taken part in the first competition, and I told myself that, then, people would see that this fellow had talent."[97] In reality, Hitler did nothing concrete in Munich to prepare himself for a career as an architectural draughtsman. Instead, he continued to pursue his chosen lifestyle. Every two or three days he would paint a picture. As had been the case in Vienna, these were mostly copies of postcards featuring famous city landmarks—the Hofbräuhaus, the Feldherrnhalle, the Frauenkirche, the Alte Hof or the Theathinerkirche. He would then try to sell his works in shops and beer gardens.

The Munich doctor Hans Schirmer recalled that one evening in the Hofbräuhaus garden, a "modest-looking young man who seemed to have been through a lot" approached his table and tried to sell him an oil painting. Schirmer did not have enough money on him, so he asked Hitler to come to his apartment the next day, where he ordered two further works, which Hitler promptly delivered. "I concluded that this man had to work very hard in order to earn money for the basic necessities," Schirmer remembered.[98] Gradually, Hitler built up a set of loyal customers, from whom he could earn a reasonable living.

But on 18 January 1914, Hitler was abruptly ripped from his cosy, bohemian existence. An officer from the Munich criminal police appeared at the Schleissheimerstrasse apartment and handed Hitler a letter from the magistrate's office in Linz ordering him to appear in two days' time for military examination.[99] As someone born in 1889, Hitler should have registered for the draft in the late autumn of 1909 and submitted to an examination in the spring of 1910, but he had done neither. One likely reason why Hitler left Vienna was to avoid these duties. "Illegally absent because whereabouts unknown," read his file in Linz. Since August 1913, police there had been trying to track Hitler down, and in mid-January 1914 they succeeded. On 19 January, he was taken to the Austro-Hungarian general consulate in Munich. Only now did Hitler realise that he was in serious trouble: refusing to appear for the draft carried a penalty of four weeks to one year of imprisonment and a fine of 2,000 crowns.

Hitler must have got a nasty shock. On 21 January, he wrote a letter justifying his behaviour. It was three and a half pages, quite long by Hitler's standards, and represents the most extensive surviving sample of his early handwriting.[100] In it, he admitted to not registering in Linz in 1909, but claimed that he had done so in Vienna in February 1910 but had never heard anything further from the authorities. That laid the blame on bureaucratic negligence: it had "never occurred to him" to attempt to evade military service. He also tried to win over the magistrate in Linz with an extensive and sometimes exaggerated description of his years of privation in Vienna:

> Despite great desperation, amidst often more than dubious company, I kept my name respectable and remained entirely guiltless in the eyes of the law and untroubled by my own conscience except for my failure to register for military service, which I was not even aware of. That is all I feel responsible for. I would ask to be allowed to pay a small sum of money to atone for this and declare myself willing to do so.

Hitler also asked to be examined in Salzburg, which was closer to Munich, rather than Linz. The general consulate passed on Hitler's letter to the Linz magistrate, noting that it was "well worth taking into consideration," and Hitler got what he wanted. On 5 February 1914, he was given a military examination in Salzburg and was deemed "unsuitable for combat and support duty, too weak, incapable of firing weapons."[101] Hitler was then allowed to return to Munich.

Häusler had moved out of their shared room when Hitler was away. In all likelihood, he could no longer bear living in such close confines with a room-mate who read until the early hours and liked to hold forth. But Hitler seems to have had little difficulty paying the entire rent on his own. He continued to frequent the cafés of Schwabing, although he did not make any close friends. Nor did he establish contact with any of the local chapters of ultranationalist organisations like the Pan-Germanic League, which was the largest of its kind in Wilhelmine Germany and had an influential spokesman in the publisher Julius F. Lehmann. His landlady characterised Hitler as a reticent young man who had secluded himself in his room "like a hermit" and refused all invitations to eat dinner together, saying that he had to work.[102]

Hitler's lack of social contact was the external symptom of a deep inner uncertainty. Having spent a year in Munich, he had to admit that he had made no progress and that his precarious existence as "artistic painter" did not offer many prospects for the future. But out of nowhere the beginning of the First World War in early August 1914 would release him from his frustrating lack of prospects.

3

The Experience of War

"As probably was the case for every German, the most unforgettable and exciting time in my life had begun," Hitler wrote rather melodramatically in *Mein Kampf*. "Everything previous paled into nothingness compared to the events of this giant struggle."[1] The First World War was Hitler's defining experience and marks a caesura in his life. Having failed to achieve his lofty artistic ambitions, after seven years of privations, disappointments and rejections, the 25-year-old loner finally thought he had found a way out of his disoriented, useless existence. Hitler would never have developed as he did had he not fought in the First World War, and it was the war that made his political career possible in the first place.[2]

On 28 June 1914, when Hitler heard the news that the Austro-Hungarian heir to the throne, Archduke Franz Ferdinand, and his wife had been assassinated in Sarajevo, he was sitting, as was his wont, over his books in his room on Schleissheimerstrasse. Given the tense situation in Europe, and in particular the drastically deteriorating relationship between Austria–Hungary and Serbia over the previous years, Hitler had no doubt that "a stone had begun to roll and there was no stopping it."[3] He was hardly alone in thinking that a major European conflict was inevitable. People all the way up to the highest echelons of political and military power in Wilhelmine Germany shared that view. In point of fact, however, war could have been averted in July 1914, had the Reich leadership in Berlin, urged on by military commanders, not decided to use the assassination as a pretext for a test of strength with the Triple Entente of France, Britain and Russia. The aim was to drive apart the powers "encircling" Germany and alter the European balance of power in the Reich's favour. On 5 and 6 July, not only did Germany assure its ally Austria–Hungary of its complete support in the event of military action against Serbia; Berlin also encouraged Vienna to respond quickly and with determination. Chancellor Theobald von Bethmann Hollweg was all too aware that Germany was incurring a tremendous risk in issuing Austria–Hungary such a blank cheque. "Military action against Serbia could lead to a world war," he admitted on the evening of 6 July to an intimate, Foreign Ministry Legation Secretary Kurt Riezler.[4]

The public had little idea of what was going on in the governing cabinets in Berlin and Vienna as the crisis continued to escalate. Hitler, too, followed the general assumption that "ruling circles in Vienna" were the ones pushing for war and that Germany had no other option than stay unswervingly loyal to its ally.[5] Hardly anyone realised how slyly Bethmann Hollweg manoeuvred Imperial Russia into the role of the aggressor in the final stage of the crisis so that the tsar could be blamed for the war. "Ruthlessly and under all circumstances, Russia must be made into the source of injustice," the chancellor told Kaiser Wilhelm II on 26 July.[6] Bethmann Hollweg's plan worked. The German public believed that their country was defending itself from enemy attack and put aside all domestic quarrels and class enmity to come together as a nation.

By late July 1914 in Munich, as in most big German cities, public demonstrations of patriotism were sometimes ending in wild excesses. When the band leader at a café refused to play the patriotic song "Die Wacht am Rhein" (The Watch on the Rhine), for example, the premises were ransacked.[7] In early August, as war became more and more certain, there were outpourings of enthusiasm. On 2 August, a crowd of many thousands assembled on Odeonsplatz in front of the Feldherrnhalle. "All the melodies, military tunes and enthusiastic words that resonated up to the heavens sounded like a song of songs about German might and German self-confidence," reported one eyewitness.[8] Among the jubilant masses was the "artistic painter" Adolf Hitler, and a picture taken by his later "court photographer" Heinrich Hoffmann shows him getting carried away by the euphoric atmosphere.[9] In Mein Kampf, Hitler described his feelings with his characteristic bent towards exalted language: "Even today, I am not ashamed to say that I, overcome by tempestuous enthusiasm, sank to my knees and thanked heaven with an overflowing heart that I was fortunate enough to live in these times."[10]

Many people felt the way Hitler did. Suddenly everything that confined and divided Germans seemed to have disappeared, leaving an intoxicating sensation of togetherness. "To be honest, I must acknowledge that there was something grand, captivating and even seductive about this eruption of the masses, which was difficult to resist," recalled Stefan Zweig many years later.[11] Even the anarchist and pacifist Erich Mühsam found himself "somehow captivated by the general uproar unleashed by angry passion." In his diary, Mühsam wrote: "The confidence of the Germans, their pious and intense enthusiasm, is harrowing, but also grand. There's a spiritual unity there that I hope to see some day employed for great cultural works."[12]

But not everyone joined in the chorus of glee. There was little enthusiasm for war in the German countryside. "Deep concern is making the rounds among the many, often large farming families whose fathers will be going away, whose sons, horses and wagons will be commissioned by the military, and whose harvests still have to be brought in," reported the *Münchener Neueste Nachrichten* on 4 August 1914.[13] In the big cities, too, enthusiasm for the war was largely confined to the middle classes. Blue-collar workers, particularly those who were members of the SPD and the trade unions, were in a serious, almost despondent mood. "What do we care if the heir to the throne of Austria was murdered?" one worker in Hamburg was overheard remarking in a bar. "I'm glad I'm too old to go [to war]," said another. "I have no desire to get shot and killed for anyone else."[14] The attitudes in Munich's working-class districts in late July 1914 would hardly have been much different.

Intellectuals, writers and artists were most likely to get caught up in the intoxication of the "August experience." The reasons varied from dissatisfaction with the ossified structures of Wilhelmine society, to weariness with bourgeois complacency and the comfort of a long stretch of peace, to the longing for adventure, challenges and feelings of community. "How could the artist, the soldier in the artist, not have thanked God for the breakdown of a peaceful world of which he was so very sick?" asked Thomas Mann, who was living in Munich at the time. "War! What we experienced was cleansing, liberation and an enormous sense of hope."[15]

The "artist" Adolf Hitler felt something very similar. In *Mein Kampf* he recalled that the war seemed like "liberation from the annoying sensibilities of youth" and a way out of the idle cycles of his oddball existence.[16] The prospect of belonging to a community and of devoting himself to a seemingly worthy national cause enlivened Hitler. If *Mein Kampf* is to be believed, on 3 August 1914, he wrote a letter beseeching King Ludwig III of Bavaria to allow him to join a Bavarian regiment despite being an Austrian citizen. One day later Hitler received permission by special cabinet order.[17] This account is very implausible, however.[18] It is much more likely that in the chaos of the first days of military mobilisation, as hordes of patriotic enthusiasts were signing up for military service, no one bothered to check Hitler's citizenship. Otherwise he would never have been allowed to serve in the Bavarian army.

Hitler first tried to volunteer on 5 August, but he was sent away, and it was not until 16 August that he was inducted into Recruit Depot VI of the 2nd Bavarian Infantry Regiment. This replacement battalion was quartered in a school that had been hastily converted into barracks. Here Hitler was given field uniform and equipment, and he underwent basic military training.[19] On 1 September, he was transferred to the reconstituted 16th Reserve Infantry Regiment. The "List Regiment," nicknamed after its first commander, Colonel Julius List, was a rather ragtag bunch. Young volunteers served together with older men known as "replacement reserves." Munich students and artists marched side by side with farmers, rural labourers, small entrepreneurs, artisans, workers and professionals. The regiment thus represented a cross section of ages and social classes.[20]

On 10 October 1914, it left Munich for combat training at Lechfeld, an outwash plain near the city of Augsburg. "The first five days at Lechfeld were the hardest of my life," Hitler wrote in a letter to his landlady, Anna Popp. "Every day we have a long march, major exercises and a night-time march of up to forty-two kilometres, followed by major brigade manoeuvres."[21] Hitler's biggest concern during these weeks, if we take him at his word, was that the war would be won by the time he got to the front. "This alone robbed me time and again of my peace of mind," he claimed in *Mein Kampf.*[22] Any worries proved unfounded. The German army may have advanced rapidly through Belgium and northern France, but the retreat of German troops to the Marne in early September 1914 spelled the end of the original plan of destroying the French army by squeezing it in a surprise pincer movement. Realistically, the war was already lost for Germany. The Chief of the General Staff, Helmuth von Moltke—the nephew of the great, victorious Prussian commander—suffered a nervous break-down and was replaced on 14 September by Reich Minister of War Erich von Falkenhayn. But the scale of the military disaster was kept secret from the public. As a result, broad segments of German society, and in particular volunteers eager to get to the front, maintained dangerous illusions about the true situation.

Early in the morning on 21 October, the List Regiment was loaded onto three trains and taken to the Western Front. "I'm immensely looking forward to it," wrote Hitler.[23] In Ulm, the first stop on the journey, Hitler sent a postcard to Joseph Popp with "best regards on my way to Antwerp."[24] The next morning the train reached the River Rhine, which had long been a bone of contention between Germany and France. Hitler still recalled this moment in March 1944: "I saw the Rhine for the first time when my regiment was sent west in 1914. I will never forget the feelings that welled up in me when I first caught sight of this historic river."[25] Via Cologne and Aachen, the train continued to Belgium. There Hitler could see the traces of war. The train station in Liège, he reported, was "badly shot up," and the city of Louvain was a "pile of rubble."[26] Two months before, from 25 to 28 August, German troops had committed a number of war crimes in Louvain, massacring 248 Belgian civilians, destroying parts of the old city centre and setting fire to the city's famous university library.[27]

On 23 October, Hitler and his comrades arrived in Lille, where the din from the battlefields of Flanders could be easily heard. Falkenhayn had stuck with the general staff's offensive tactics. By strengthening the German army's right flank he hoped to surround the French and British armies. This was the beginning of the famous "Race to the Sea," a series of battles leading ever closer to the English Channel. The attacking Germans suffered heavy casualties, particularly among young volunteers who naively ran into enemy machine-gun fire. The 6th Bavarian Reserve Division, of which the List Regiment was part, was deployed in the middle of the First Battle of Ypres. On 27 October, after three days of rest to recover from the journey, the regiment was ordered to march to the front. There, in the early hours of 29 October, as part of an assault on the Flemish village of Gheluvelt, Hitler received his "baptism of fire" in a forest along the road to Becelaere. It was a life-changing experience about which he reported in detail in a letter to the Munich court assessor Ernst Hepp, who before the war had purchased two of his watercolours and occasionally invited him out for a meal.[28]

The letter, which Hitler wrote on 5 February 1915, three months after the events described, is an astonishing document.[29] It showed that Hitler was not only a keen observer, but had a talent for putting his experiences into words—even if he had not quite overcome his poor spelling and punctuation. "Around 6 a.m. we met up with the other companies at an inn," Hitler wrote.

> At 7 our day began. We marched in columns through a forest to our right and emerged with our ranks intact in an elevated field. Four marksmen were dug in ahead of us. We took up positions behind them in large trenches and waited . . . Finally came the command "Forwards." We climbed out of our holes and sprinted across the field . . . towards a small farmstead. Left and right shells were exploding, and in the middle English bullets were humming, but we paid them no mind. For ten minutes we took cover and then again came the command "Forwards' . . . Now the first of our numbers were falling. The English had trained their machine guns on us. We threw ourselves on the ground and slowly crawled forward in a furrow. Sometimes we had to stop because someone had got shot and could no longer move, and we had to lift him out of the furrow.

The decimated attackers sought shelter in a stretch of forest. "Overhead there was whining and rushing, and shredded tree trunks and branches were flying all around us," Hitler continued. "Shells would hit the underbrush and throw clouds of stones, soil and sand in the air. They uprooted the mightiest of trees and covered everything in a horrible, stinking yellow-green mist. We couldn't stay there for ever, and if we were going to fall, it was better to do so out in the open." The soldiers sprinted across the fields of the farmstead and jumped into the first British trench. "By my side were men from Württemberg, and under me were dead and wounded Englishmen," Hitler wrote. "I suddenly realised why my landing had been so soft." They were soon engaged in bitter hand-to-hand combat.

Anyone who didn't surrender got cut down. We cleaned out trench after trench in this fashion. Finally we reached the main road . . . To the left were several farmsteads that were still occupied, and we came under heavy fire. One after another of our number crumpled . . . We charged four times and were beaten back every time. There was only one soldier left from my group besides me, and in the end he fell too. A bullet tore its way through my right sleeve, but miraculously, I remained without a scratch . . . We fought like this for three days until finally the English were taken care of.

The List Regiment was first withdrawn from battle on 1 November and the survivors marched back to the village of Werwick. They had suffered enormous casualties: "In four days, our regiment had shrunk from 3,500 to 600 men. There were only three officers left in the entire regiment."[30] Among the dead was their commander, Colonel List.

Without doubt, Hitler's first encounter with the bloody realities of war was a traumatic experience, which seared the images of battle into his memory. He could still recall them vividly when he wrote *Mein Kampf* during his Landsberg incarceration, and in late July 1924 read the most recently written passages to his fellow inmate Rudolf Hess.[31] In a letter to his future wife Ilse Pröhl, Hess described the scene: "The champion of the people read ever more slowly and hesitantly . . . He took longer and longer pauses. Then he suddenly lowered the manuscript, put his head in his hands—and sobbed."[32]

The terrible price paid by the List Regiment had brought only insignificant territorial gains. After Germany's second attempt to decide matters in the west had failed, the front lines hardened in November 1914. Exhausted soldiers hunkered down in their trenches along an 800-kilometre-long line from Nieuport on the Belgian coast to the Swiss border. "A web of dugouts, trenches with embrasures, saps, wire entanglements and landmines—in short, an almost impregnable position," was how Hitler described the trench-warfare system in a letter from January 1915.[33] Hitler himself, however, did not have to stay at the very front line. A few days after being promoted to private first class on 3 November 1914, he was transferred to the regimental staff, where until the end of the war he served as one of several dispatch runners. These runners were responsible for bringing the regimental commander's orders to the front lines during battle, if other lines of communication to the battalion and company leaders no longer functioned. It was a dangerous job.[34] In early December 1914, Hitler himself wrote that since he had been made a runner, he had "risked his life every day and looked death in the eye."[35]

In mid-November 1914, the new regimental commander, Philipp Engelhardt, recommended Private Hitler for the Iron Cross, Second Class, but soon afterwards a shell hit the tent where Engelhardt was conferring with several company leaders. The commander was seriously wounded, and several members of his staff were killed. Hitler had left the tent five minutes previously—as so often would be the case later in his life, luck was on his side.[36] On 2 December, he received his Iron Cross from the regimental adjutant, Lieutenant Georg Eichelsdörfer. "It was the happiest day of my life," he wrote in a letter to Joseph Popp. "Of course almost all of my comrades, who deserved one too, are dead." Hitler asked Popp to save the newspaper announcement of his award. "If the good Lord keeps me alive, I'd like it as a memento."[37]

Since late November 1914, the regimental staff had been pinned down by heavy fire in the totally destroyed town of Messines, not far from the front. "Day after day for the past two months, the air and ground have shaken with the howling and cracking of shells and the explosions of shrapnel," Hitler wrote in late January 1915.

> The hellish concert starts early at 9 a.m. and ends at 1 p.m., only to reach its crescendo in the afternoon between 3 and 5. At 5 it's over. It's eerie when the cannons begin to thunder in the night. They start in the distance and get closer and closer. Gradually rifle fire is added, and after half an hour things calm again. Only the flares still gleam, and in the distance to the west you can see the searchlights and hear the constant artillery fire of the heavy armoured ships. But we won't leave this place, come hell or high water.[38]

In his letters to Munich, Hitler complained that the constant fighting was making him "dulled" and what he missed most was regular sleep. He felt very nervous, admitting that uninterrupted heavy artillery fire "ruined even the strongest of nerves in time."[39] But on 24 December 1914, something very unusual happened on the battlefields of Flanders. Almost everywhere, the weapons went silent. German and British soldiers crawled from their trenches, first alone and then in groups. They met one another in no man's land, exchanged gifts and agreed a ceasefire for the following day. It seemed like a miracle. The same men who had only the day before tried their best to kill one another stood together, laughing, chatting, smoking and toasting each other's health. "We were as happy as children," an officer from Saxony noted in his diary.[40]

The 16th Reserve Infantry Regiment (RIR 16) was also involved in the fraternisation. In a letter to his parents dated 28 December 1914, one member of the regiment wrote: "It was very moving. Between the trenches, the most hateful and bitter enemies stood around a Christmas tree singing carols. I'll never forget the sight as long as I live."[41] Hitler did not record his reaction to the "Christmas miracle on the front," but according to one of the other runners, he had remarked disapprovingly: "Something like this should be out of the question in wartime."[42]

In his later monologues, Hitler repeatedly returned to his experiences during the First World War. If he were twenty or twenty-five years younger, he remarked in July 1941, a few weeks after Germany had invaded the Soviet Union, he would volunteer for the front. "I was a passionate soldier," he said.[43] But was Hitler really the brave front-line fighter sharing "the misery of millions of Germans who squatted in their trenches for weeks at a time, permanently subject to mortal fear," as he claimed at an NSDAP meeting in Munich in September 1930?[44] In the 1920s and increasingly in the 1930s, doubts arose as to Hitler's depiction of his military past. In the spring of 1932, two veterans of the List Regiment published articles in left-wing newspapers, the *Braunschweiger Volksfreund* and the weekend edition of the *Hamburger Echo*, in which they accused Hitler of spending the war in the safety of the regiment's main headquarters, and not at the front as he claimed.[45] Runners did indeed enjoy easier conditions than the soldiers in the trenches: they had dry quarters and were given better food, and they were not permanently exposed to machine-gun fire and sharpshooters' bullets. "Every soldier in the trenches thought that the regimental staff members were lucky bastards," another former comrade wrote to Hitler in March 1932. "It's true, and no one can deny it, that things were much better in the staff than they were in the company."[46] But that does not mean that the runners' job was without risk. For them the biggest danger came from artillery shells striking behind the front lines.

After 1933, the NSDAP party archive began to collect statements from former comrades at the front who testified that Hitler had shown "constant engagement" and not shied away from any "dangerous route." One of them reported that he had always been surprised that Hitler came back from his deliveries unwounded.[47] These statements must be treated sceptically since they obviously served to support Hitler's own version of his wartime experiences. The reports of Hitler's military superiors are more believable. Lieutenant Colonel Friedrich Petz, who succeeded Engelhardt and commanded the regiment until March 1916, wrote in February 1922:

> Hitler was an extremely hard-working, willing, conscientious and dutiful soldier, who was also completely reliable and obedient towards his superiors . . . Particularly worth stressing are his personal daring and the heedless courage he displayed when confronting dangerous situations and all the dangers of battle. His iron calm and cold-bloodedness never deserted him. When the situation was at its most dangerous, he always volunteered to make deliveries to the front and carried them out successfully.[48]

It is possible that Petz sympathised with the ambitious young right-wing matador in Munich, which may explain why his assessment was so positive. But Fritz Wiedemann, the adjutant in the List Regiment from January 1916 to April 1917, offered a similar, if less upbeat, assessment after 1945. Hitler, he said, had been the "paradigm of the unknown soldier carrying out his duty silently and calmly."[49] This assessment carries all the more weight because Wiedemann had every reason to be critical of the former private. After being named Reich chancellor, Hitler had appointed Wiedemann his personal adjutant, but in early 1939 he had stripped him of that post and banished him as a consul general, first to San Francisco and then to Tianjin, China. Wiedemann subsequently distanced himself from Hitler and after the war voluntarily testified against other Nazi leaders at the Nuremberg trials.[50]

When we weigh up all the sources, we can conclude that Hitler did not stand out as particularly brave but neither did he occupy a "shirker's job" guaranteed to keep him out of harm's way. Attempts to cast Hitler as a coward are misleading.[51] Even an outspoken critic of Hitler like the writer Alexander Moritz Frey, who also served in the List Regiment and was forced to emigrate from Germany after 1933, stated in 1946: "If people say he was cowardly, that's not accurate. He wasn't brave either. He lacked the coolness for that."[52]

Yet if Private Hitler was such a dutiful soldier, why was he never promoted? In 1948, Wiedemann amused everyone in the courtroom in Nuremberg by stating that Hitler "lacked leadership qualities"—the German word he used was *Führerqualitäten*. In his 1964 memoirs, Wiedemann reiterated that in his opinion Hitler did not have what it took to become a superior officer. His posture was "sloppy . . . with his head usually sloping towards his left shoulder" and his answers, when asked questions, were "anything but militarily brief."[53] Max Amann—a sergeant major in RIR 16 and later NSDAP chairman and party publisher—testified after the war that Hitler had not wanted to be put up for promotion. When Amann informed him one day that he was being considered for promotion to junior officer, Hitler supposedly reacted with "horror" saying: "Please don't do that—I have more authority without an officer's bars than with them."[54] We cannot be sure whether this story is true, or whether Hitler feared that he could be transferred to another regiment and given a more dangerous job, if promoted.

Hitler did not deny that he, like many other volunteers, quickly lost the idealism of August 1914 when confronted with the shocking reality of the war: the mass, machine-like killing on the battlefield. "The romance of battle had been replaced by horror," he wrote in *Mein Kampf*. "My enthusiasm cooled, and fear of death strangled my exaggerated jubilations."[55] Hitler also made no secret of the fact that he was afraid of dying, and that his self-preservation instincts worked against his sense of duty. "He admits quite openly, and without any sense of shame, that his nerves were more sensitive than other people's," Rudolf Hess reported in June 1924. "In any case, almost everyone felt that way, more or less strongly. Anyone who denies that either didn't see battle or is a liar."[56] In the end, though, Hitler assured the readers of *Mein Kampf*, his sense of duty won out: "My will finally regained complete control."[57]

The experience of being forced to toughen up while growing ever more indifferent to human suffering was one of the main lessons Hitler would take from the First World War. At the front, he asserted during a night-time round of tea in his headquarters in October 1941, "people were often subjected to demands on their nerves that the military leadership could not imagine . . . The key was to stay hard . . . You can only defeat death with death."[58] He summarised his experience even more vividly in February 1942: "Either the fire at the front sweeps you away because you succumb to cowardice or you overcome your inner weakling and become hard."[59] For Hitler, the war seemed to confirm what he had read in pan-Germanic pamphlets and newspapers in Vienna, namely that in human society, as in nature, only the strong would survive, while the weak would drop dead in their tracks. More than once in his monologues, Hitler confirmed that such social Darwinist beliefs, which he would maintain until the end of his life, originated in his experience of the war. "I went to the battlefield with the purest idealism," Hitler said, "but when you see thousands get injured and killed, you become aware that life is a constant, terrible struggle, which serves to preserve the species—someone has to die so that others may survive."[60]

Hitler was respected by his comrades in the regimental staff, yet, as was the case in the men's home in Vienna, here too a distance remained that could scarcely be bridged. His comrades sensed that Hitler was different—"a little bit eccentric" was how Amann later put it.[61] Hitler still neither drank nor smoked. From early 1915 he no longer received any letters, and he did not seek contact with French women or join the others on their brothel visits. A fellow runner named Balthasar Brandmayer described how Hitler had responded to the suggestion that they reward themselves for a job well done with a visit to a French mademoiselle: "'I'd die of shame if I made love to a French woman' interjected Hitler in his provincial Bavarian dialect. The others laughed their heads off. 'If it isn't the friar,' someone joked. Hitler's expression grew serious. 'Do you not have any German sense of honour in you?' Hitler countered."[62] There is no reliable evidence for the contention that in 1916 and 1917 Hitler had an affair with a French woman named Charlotte Lobjoie and that she gave birth to an illegitimate son in March 1918.[63] Nor is there any trustworthy indication that Hitler had a homosexual relationship with another regimental runner named Ernst Schmidt.[64] Given the riskiness of their job, runners had to depend on one another: they got to know each other's strengths and weaknesses and formed a community aimed at mutual survival. But as far as we know, Hitler's friendship with Schmidt never went beyond camaraderie. And it would be hard to square a homosexual relationship with the fact that even after he was named Reich chancellor and had reason to fear scandals, Hitler kept in contact with Schmidt, even visiting their old battlegrounds with him and Amann after Germany defeated France in 1940.[65]

Hitler felt more comfortable in the exclusively male world of the regiment than in civilian society, and his experience of war would determine his views on military hierarchies and greatly influence the organisational structure of the NSDAP. In the army he did not have to earn his daily bread, and life was governed by discipline and order. He seems not to have had much difficulty integrating into the system of command and obedience. Hitler behaved obediently, even subserviently towards his superiors.[66] He took no part in the crude amusements and coarse jokes of his comrades, and he remained an outsider among them. In the photographs that survive from this period, he appears on the margins, an extremely thin figure with a fixed, almost stony stare. When he does put his arm around one of his comrades, the gesture feels artificial and alien.[67]

One photograph shows a white fox terrier which ran away from the British front lines in January and which Hitler adopted in January 1915. He was very attached to the animal, teaching it a number of tricks. Once, in January 1942, when the situation at the Eastern Front took a dramatic turn for the worse, Hitler spent half the night telling stories about "Foxl." "I was very fond of him," he reminisced. "I shared everything with him, and he slept with me at night . . . I would never have given him up, not for any price." In September 1917, when the regiment was redeployed to Alsace, Foxl suddenly disappeared. It was a major blow for Hitler. "The bastard who took him away doesn't know what he did to me," Hitler complained in 1942.[68] In later life, Hitler's pronounced affection for dogs stood in stark contrast to the coldness with which he treated even those people who belonged to his most intimate circle.

Unlike in the Vienna men's home, Hitler seems to have kept his political views to himself during the war. "I was a soldier and didn't want to make things political," he wrote in *Mein Kampf*.[69] In Nuremberg in 1947, when asked whether Hitler gave political speeches during the war, Amann also answered with a definite "No."[70] The only time Hitler's anger arose against his comrades was when someone doubted that the Central Powers would win the war. "There is no way we can lose the world war," Hitler would protest.[71] In a rare moment of openness, in a letter to Ernst Hepp in early February 1915, he did give a hint as to his political views. Those soldiers who were lucky enough to see their homeland again, Hitler wrote, "will find it purer and cleansed of foreignness." He added his hope "that the daily sacrifices and suffering of hundreds of thousands of us . . . will not only smash Germany's enemies abroad but also destroy our internal internationalism—that would be worth more than any territorial gains."[72]

Thus, while annexationist circles in heavy industry, conservative parties and nationalist associations may have seen the war in terms of territorial conquests, for Hitler it was a struggle in which Germany defended itself abroad against international enemies while restoring its domestic, ethnic homogeneity and shattering the power of the "internationalist" Social Democratic labour movement at home. The fact that the SPD had supported the Imperial German government and approved lines of credit for the war on 4 August 1914 apparently did nothing to alter Hitler's negative view of the party. The prejudices and phobias acquired during his Vienna years were too deeply ingrained to be dislodged.

From March 1915 to September 1916, RIR 16 dug in near the town of Fromelles, where it was responsible for defending a 2.3-kilometre stretch of the front. In the respites between battles, Hitler had time to do a bit of painting and to read books. "I carried five volumes of Schopenhauer around with me throughout the war," he later boasted. "I learned a lot from him."[73] We don't know how intensely Hitler studied Schopenhauer's philosophy, but he was certainly familiar with the basics of *The World as Will and Idea*, including the notion that all geniuses, and especially artistic ones, were destined to be misunderstood. Reading Schopenhauer may also have strengthened Hitler's conviction that strength of will could help him not only lead a life of sexual asceticism, but overcome his fears of dying.

In late September 1916, Hitler's regiment was redeployed to the south, just in time to be sent into the Battle of the Somme, which had been raging since 1 July. One of the bloodiest battles of the First World War, almost 20,000 British troops died on the first day alone, and by the time the fighting was over, 419,000 British and 204,000 French soldiers had been killed or wounded; German casualties totalled some 465,000.[74] "This is not war, but a mutual annihilation using technological strength," wrote Vice-Sergeant Hugo Frick from another regiment to his mother in October 1916. "Beyond the word horrible, there's no describing the hardships and mortal fear we endure here."[75]

Again luck was initially on Hitler's side, but on 5 October a shell hit the entrance to the bunker where the regimental staff runners had sought cover. Hitler took some shrapnel in his left thigh. Adjutant Wiedemann wrote that as he bent down over the wounded man, Hitler said: "It's not so bad, Lieutenant. I want to stay with you in the regiment."[76] In January 1942, Hitler recalled: "Strangely enough, in the moment when you're wounded you hardly feel the pain. You sense a blow, and think, that's nothing. The pain only comes when you're transported away."[77] Hitler's injuries proved not to be as serious as initially feared. He was given medical treatment in a field hospital near the town of Hermies and then sent to a Red Cross hospital in Beelitz, south of Berlin, where he recovered from 9 October to 1 December 1916. "What a difference!" Hitler wrote in *Mein Kampf*. "From the mud of the battlefield to the gleaming white beds of that wonderful building! You hardly dared to lie down in them at first. It took a while to get used to this new world."[78]

In the hospital in Beelitz, Hitler encountered soldiers who were sick of the war and had no qualms about saying so. In *Mein Kampf*, he expressed his outrage at those "miserable scoundrels" who had poked fun at the "beliefs of respectable soldiers with all the means of their poor eloquence." Hitler was especially scandalised by a soldier who had inflicted an injury on himself to get away from the conflict.[79] For Hitler, who apparently continued to believe in the war, such forms of rebellion indicated the demise of military morale. We do not know whether he himself ever doubted that Germany would emerge victorious, as virtually no first-hand documents—letters or anything else—of his opinions from the second half of the war survived.

On 4 November 1916, the convalescent Hitler was granted permission to travel to Berlin. It was his first time in the capital of the Reich whose chancellor he would become seventeen years later. What he saw and heard there hardly lifted his spirits. "Everywhere, people's suffering was great," he recalled in *Mein Kampf*. "This million-strong city was starving. There was great dissatisfaction."[80] Since the winter of 1915/16 it had become increasingly difficult to supply Germany's major cities with necessities, and there were long queues in front of grocery shops. Women and children stood for hours in all kinds of weather to obtain a pound of butter, a couple of eggs or a piece of meat. People's disgruntlement with such intolerable conditions grew the longer they went on, and eventually led to public unrest and spontaneous strikes. Such protests also became increasingly political, directly targeting the prevailing social hierarchy, the privileged and the wealthy. In April 1916, a Berlin police officer reported: "The mood in general is very downbeat. Everyone longs for an end to the war . . . People are dissatisfied with the measures taken by the government, which have failed to combat inflation and profiteering sufficiently. Soldiers leave for the battlefield embittered. The general view is that the war is being fought not for the fatherland, but for capitalism."[81]

Nothing was left of the enthusiasm for war in August 1914. Exhaustion and longing for peace now set the tone among urban populations. Hitler would experience this when he was discharged from the hospital on 2 December 1916 and sent to Munich, where he reported to a replacement battalion of RIR 16. He no longer recognised the city. "Anger, sullenness and complaints wherever you went!" he recalled in *Mein Kampf*.[82] People's disgruntlement was, on the one hand, directed against "the Prussians," who were hated equally by Bavarian soldiers and civilians. In August 1917, a policeman jotted down remarks made by Bavarian soldiers during a rail journey: "The soldiers' main wish was for a speedy end to the war, and they mentioned that Germany was also at fault for prolonging it . . . As long as Bavaria was allied with Prussia, there would be war, for the big-mouthed Prussians had been involved every time there was war."[83]

As social tensions increased, anti-Semitic resentment played a larger and larger role in public dissatisfaction. Jews were accused not just of shamelessly profiting from the misery of the general populace, but of trying to shirk military service by whatever means they could. Since late 1915, the Prussian War Ministry had practically been flooded with complaints about Jewish "shirking." People of the Jewish faith, contended a campaign primarily launched by the influential Pan-Germanic League, were using their wealth and resources to ride out the war in desk jobs at headquarters in the rear. The Jewish industrialist and writer Walther Rathenau was appointed director of the Raw Materials Division of the Prussian War Ministry in August 1914 but was forced to resign in March 1915 after receiving numerous threats. In 1916 he wrote about the growing waves of anti-Semitism: "The more Jews fall in this war, the more their enemies will contend that they all hid far behind the front lines and engaged in profiteering. The hatred will double and triple."[84]

Rathenau's fears were all too justified. On 11 October 1916, only a few weeks after these remarks, Prussian Minister of War Adolf Wild von Hohenborn ordered a review of the types of military service being performed by Jews. The so-called "Jewish census" was an abomination as the government was reacting to completely unfounded anti-Semitic accusations—at the very time when many Jewish Germans were sacrificing their lives for their fatherland. "Two years of absolute sacrifice for our homeland and then this!" wrote Georg Meyer, a captain in a Bavarian artillery regiment, when he heard about the census. "It's like someone boxed my ears."[85]

It is difficult to imagine that Hitler, who had been exposed to Jewish stereotypes in his years in Vienna, would have remained completely unaffected by the increasingly radical anti-Semitic defamations circulating towards the end of the war. If we believe what he wrote later on, it was in his barracks with the replacement battalion in Munich in December 1916 that he first saw the "truth" about alleged Jewish shirking: "The offices were full of Jews. Almost every clerk was a Jew, and almost every Jew a clerk."[86] In *Mein Kampf*, Hitler also reproduced the common stereotype of Jews as wartime profiteers: "Here [in the economy] Jews had in fact become 'indispensable.' The spider slowly began sucking the blood through the pores of the people."[87]

We have no way of knowing for sure whether Private Hitler thought in these terms in late 1916 and early 1917. If his experiences of the home front did in fact make him more susceptible for the Jew-hatred that was going round, he concealed it from his comrades. In any case, there is no record of him making any anti-Semitic statements.[88] Wiedemann was astonished when he encountered Hitler again in the 1920s as a popular anti-Semitic politician. He never discovered the origin of Hitler's fanatical Jew-hatred: his interactions with officers and comrades in RIR 16 did not offer "the slightest indication" of anti-Semitism.[89]

*

Interestingly, Hitler neither visited his former landlords, the Popps, nor any other pre-war acquaintances in Munich. Reminders of his civilian existence seemed to make him uncomfortable. He was bored in the barracks and longed to get back to the front. "At the moment I'm undergoing dental treatment, but I'll report immediately and voluntarily for the front," Hitler wrote to Karl Lanzhammer, the regiment's bicyclist, on 19 December 1916. Two days later he told Brandmayer: "I'm sitting with swollen cheeks in my four walls thinking of you. There was a transport a few days ago to the regiment. Unfortunately I wasn't on it."[90] The regimental staff had become Hitler's adoptive family. In a letter to Wiedemann, in which he declared himself once again "battle ready," he said that he greatly longed "to return to my old regiment and old comrades."[91] Wiedemann fulfilled Hitler's wish. On 5 March 1917, Hitler celebrated his return to the front.

By that time his regiment had been redeployed to La Bassée. In late April 1917, under the leadership of regimental commander Major Anton von Tubeuf, it moved to the area of Arras in northern France. In mid-July it returned to the scene of Hitler's first action in Flanders, where it was thrown into the Third Battle of Ypres. On 31 July, in the course of a major offensive, British forces unveiled a new weapon: tanks. "It was our misfortune that our leadership back then didn't recognise the value of technological weaponry," Hitler opined in August 1941. "If we'd had 400 tanks in the summer of 1918, we would have won the world war."[92] Hitler was partly right. Germany's army commanders had in fact decided too late to build a German tank, and they could no longer make up the lost ground—although that was not what decided the war.[93]

In early August 1917, having suffered heavy casualties, Hitler's regiment was withdrawn from the battle in Flanders and redeployed to a quieter stretch of front in Alsace. Here, on 17 September, Hitler was awarded the Military Merit Cross, Third Class. Later that month, for the first time, he was given an eighteen-day home furlough, which he spent in Berlin visiting the parents of a comrade named Richard Arendt, who lived in the district of Prenzlauer Berg. Unlike his quick visit in November 1916, this time around Hitler got to enjoy all of Berlin's cultural attractions.[94] "The city is grandiose," he wrote to Ernst Schmidt on 6 October. "A true world city. The traffic is also immense. Out and about almost the whole day long. Finally have the chance to study the museums more closely. In short, I have everything I need."[95] Hitler sent three postcards to Amann alone. In one of them, he expressed his regret that his days in Berlin were passing so quickly.[96] On 17 October, he returned to his regiment, which had been redeployed to the province of Champagne.

Amidst the labourers, artisans and lowly office workers who populated Prenzlauer Berg, it could not have escaped Hitler during his second Berlin visit how explosive the situation in the capital had become. In April 1917, Berlin had been hit by the first major strikes by workers in the armaments industries. As was also the case in other big German cities, the effects of the February Revolution in Russia were making themselves felt. "We have to do as they did in Russia, then everything will be different," a police informant overheard a working-class woman in front of a Hamburg grocery shop saying, and such statements surely reflected a widespread feeling.[97] The anti-war protest movement coalesced around the Independent Social Democratic Party of Germany (USPD), which had constituted itself as an alternative to the mainstream SPD in April 1917. Although military and civilian authorities took draconian action against opponents of the war, they failed to impose calm. "The populace no longer has any hopes of a favourable outcome to the war," a Berlin police officer reported in mid-July 1917. "There is a fervent longing for an end to the war at any price."[98] In December of that year, the tension was ratcheted up even further after justified fears that negotiations over the Treaty of Brest-Litovsk with the Bolsheviks, who had come to power in Russia, could fail due to the inflexibility of the German delegation.

In late January 1918, the general dissatisfaction led to a massive strike. Hundreds of thousands of workers demonstrated in Berlin, Hamburg, Munich, Nuremberg and many other cities for a swift end to the carnage. "I can tell you, when I saw the procession of serious-looking workers and women move so silently and united through the streets, I felt jubilation running through me," a Hamburg office worker wrote to her boyfriend at the front.[99] As far as we can tell from soldiers' intercepted letters, the news of the strikes drew a mixed response, with some soldiers expressing their unconditional support, while others were dumbfounded or rejected the protest. The spectrum extended from "All of my comrades rejoiced at the strike" to "Do these lunatics really think the strike will end the war more quickly?"[100] Private Hitler belonged to the latter group. In *Mein Kampf* he dismissed the strike as "the biggest criminal act of the entire war," which served only to strengthen "the enemy peoples' faith in their ultimate victory."[101] Hitler blamed the leadership of the Majority Social Democratic Party (MSPD) for the protests, even though, unlike the USPD, the MSPD had not been involved in declaring the strike and only cooperated with it in Berlin and other places to ensure the popular movement ended as soon as possible. "Once the unrest had broken out," Berlin Police President Heinrich von Oppen noted on 29 January 1918, "the respectable SPD joined the movement against their will so as not to be shunted completely into the background."[102]

In March 1918, after dictating terms of peace to Russia in the Treaty of Brest-Litovsk, the German Army Supreme Command made one last attempt to decide the war in Germany's favour with a massive military offensive in the west. Initial triumphs seemed to justify the wildest of hopes. On 21 March, German forces attacked along a broad line from Cambrai in northern France to St. Quentin in the south, advancing as many as sixty kilometres. But after a few days the advance stalled, and none of the three subsequent offensives in April, May and July 1918 could turn the tide. By late May, the vanguard of the German army had reached the Marne and was once again only a few days' march from Paris, but the strategic position of the German forces had worsened as the bulging front lines were vulnerable to counter-offensives. The Army Supreme Command had pushed things too far and exhausted Germany's offensive capabilities. On 18 July, the French counter-attacked and achieved a major breakthrough of German lines. The Allies had regained the initiative and could count on reinforcements in the form of fresh American troops.

The List Regiment took part in all the offensives—on the Somme, the Aisne and the Marne—resulting in further heavy casualties. Half of the regiment's men were killed or wounded in April 1918 alone.[103] Hitler remained unharmed, and on 4 August 1918, after the regiment was withdrawn from the defensive battle on the Marne and redeployed in a recovery position in La Cateau, he received the Iron Cross, First Class—an accolade not usually given to privates. The Jewish lieutenant Hugo Gutmann, who had replaced Wiedemann as regiment adjutant, may have put Hitler forward for that distinction, although we cannot be sure. If he had been nominated by Gutmann, Hitler never thanked him. Instead, he later remarked: "We had a Jew in our regiment, Gutmann, a coward beyond compare. He was awarded the Iron Cross, First Class. It was an outrage and a disgrace."[104]

On 8 August 1918, four days after Hitler received his decoration, British tanks broke through German lines near Amiens. This "black day" for the German army was the final turning point of the war. Exhaustion and war fatigue were more evident than ever before, and at the front there were reports of breached discipline and disobedience. Things were also boiling over in garrisons on the home front, with increasing numbers of soldiers trying to avoid the transports to the front lines. "The letters contain hardly a trace of patriotism," reported a military censor in early September 1918. "Individual interest in the war has been pushed to the background. Almost to a man, the soldiers take the view: 'I'm going to avoid the front as best I can!'"[105] Nonetheless, it was a good four weeks until the Supreme Command, which since August 1916 had been led by Paul von Hindenburg and Erich Ludendorff, acknowledged their military bankruptcy. On 29 September in the Belgian town of Spa, the two commanders declared to Imperial Germany's entire military leadership that the war was lost and Germany would have to sue for a ceasefire. A parliamentary government under Prince Max von Baden would be formed to this end, and the mainstream Social Democrats, as the largest party in the Reichstag, would be part of the new regime.

Hitler was no longer at the front when these events took place. On 21 August he had gone to Nuremberg to take part in a course for radio and telephone operators, and after that, from 10 to 27 September, he spent his second home furlough in Berlin. With the exception of a brief remark he made in his headquarters in October 1941, we have no accounts of this time. Hitler seems to have spent most of it on Berlin's Museum Island, looking at the various art collections, and we do not know whether he saw the signs of impending revolutionary crisis or ignored them.[106] After he returned to the front, his regiment took up position near Comines, where it had first been stationed in the autumn of 1914, although now it was charged with repulsing British attacks, not going on the offensive. In the night of 13–14 October, Hitler and several of his comrades became the victims of a mustard gas attack. "As morning dawned, the pain was increasing by the quarter of an hour, and around seven, I stumbled back with burning eyes, clutching my last message of the war," Hitler wrote in *Mein Kampf*. "A few hours later, my eyes had turned into burning coals, and everything had grown dark around me."[107] He was given emergency treatment in a Bavarian army field hospital near Oudenaarde and then taken to the reserve military hospital in Pasewalk near Stettin (today the city of Szeczin in Poland). He arrived on 21 October. This is where Hitler experienced the beginning of the German revolution of 1918–19.

Scholars today still disagree on how close Hitler came to going blind and what sort of treatment he received in Pasewalk.[108] His patient file went missing but it seems fairly certain that the poison gas attack had left him with inflammation of the conjunctiva and the eyelids, and that, at least temporarily, he could hardly see. In a letter from 1921, Hitler himself reported that in the Pasewalk hospital his blindness had receded relatively quickly and his vision gradually returned.[109] The supposition that Hitler was never seriously poisoned by mustard gas and that his "blindness" was caused by hysteria is far less likely. And there is no truth whatsoever to the wild theory that one of the doctors who treated him, psychiatrist Edmund Forster, cured his hysterical blindness using hypnosis but forgot to wake Hitler from his trance, thus turning the later dictator into a victim of medical negligence.[110]

No doubt the news of Germany's military collapse and the revolutionary unrest of early November 1918 shook Hitler greatly. He had felt comfortable as a soldier and had grown fond of his regiment, and suddenly everything he identified with was simply wiped out. For Hitler and many others who blindly hoped for a positive outcome to the war, the search for scapegoats had begun—and what could have been easier than to look where the Pan-Germanic League and the far right had already identified them? In the autumn of 1918, as Germany acknowledged military defeat, right-wing propaganda intensified. Defamation of Jewish "shirkers" and "wartime profiteers" was now combined with the stab-in-the-back legend, which held that the German army at the front had been undermined and cheated of victory by traitorous Jews and Social Democrats at home. Military leaders and their supporters used such fairy tales in an attempt to avoid responsibility for the demise of the empire. In late October 1918, the deputy chairman of the Pan-Germanic League, Lord Konstantin von Gebsattel, was already calling for the "situation to be used for fanfares against the Jews who should be made into lightning rods for all the injustice."[III]

In *Mein Kampf*, Hitler tried to represent his shock at German defeat and revolution as a political epiphany. In early November 1918, he claimed, revolutionary sailors had already appeared in Pasewalk. A few days later, Hitler wrote, an "abominable intimation" became reality. On 10 November, the hospital chaplain told the patients that the Hohenzollern dynasty had been deposed and that Germany was now a republic. When the aged clergyman added that the war was lost and Germany was dependent on the "mercy of the victors," Hitler was overcome:

> Everything went black again, and I felt and stumbled my way back to my sickbed and buried my burning head in my blanket and pillow . . . Everything had been in vain . . . Must not now the graves open of all the hundreds of thousands who had once marched out, believing in the fatherland, never to return? . . . Had everything happened only so that a band of criminals could get their hands on our fatherland? . . . In the nights that followed, my hatred grew, my hatred for those responsible for this deed.

Hitler closed this passage with the oft-cited sentence: "I decided to become a politician."[112]

But Hitler did not make any such sudden determination. His decision to put his artistic and architectural ambitions on the back burner and devote himself to politics seems to have gradually coalesced during 1919. The historian Ernst Deuerlein was right when he wrote: "Hitler did not come to politics—politics came to Hitler."[113] As far as his ideological development was concerned, the Pasewalk episode marks the transition between the defining experience of war and the equally defining experience of revolution and counter-revolution in Munich. Hitler's hatred for the "November criminals" combined phobia of the Left with resentment of Jews. But he would have to go through further life-changing experiences before the *bête noire* of "Jewish Bolshevism" would become the focus of his world view.

4

The Leap into Politics

"I became a politician against my will," Hitler claimed in January 1942. "Some people think it will be tough for me when I'm no longer as busy as I am now. On the contrary, the day I leave politics and put all the worries, hardships and irritations behind me will be the happiest of my life."[1] The notion that Hitler only got into politics out of love for his country, and that his actual calling was that of an artist, was part of the dictator's carefully maintained image. In fact, politics was the one arena in which he could use his rhetorical talents and demagogic skills. As hesitant as he was when he initially tested the waters, Hitler would soon trump all his rivals within the chauvinist-nationalist camp and become the Führer of a far-right-wing party of brawlers.

Hitler's political career began in Munich, and the post-war Bavarian capital contained all the conditions that made Hitler's rise possible in the first place. With the declaration of the Bavarian Soviet Republic in the spring of 1919 the radical pendulum swung very far to the left, and the counter-revolution was correspondingly radical on the right. Hitler instinctively knew how to exploit this situation. He also had some influential patrons in military circles helping to pave his way into politics.

On 19 November 1918, Hitler was discharged from the hospital in Pasewalk. The private, who by this time was almost 30 years old, was one of millions of ordinary soldiers who returned to their home garrisons for demobilisation. His mood must have been bleak. He had no job, no family and no real social contacts, and he faced the prospect of being plunged back into his insecure pre-war existence. When he returned to Munich on 21 November, his only plan was to delay getting discharged from the army for as long as possible. He was assigned to the 7th Company of the 1st Replacement Battalion of the 2nd Infantry

Regiment. There he met again several of his former comrades from RIR 16, including Ernst Schmidt.[2]

Things were changing apace in the Bavarian capital. Revolution broke out on 7 November, two days before it did in Berlin. The leader was Kurt Eisner, the chairman of Munich's tiny USPD faction, who had only been released in mid-October from Stadelheim prison, where he had been incarcerated since the January strikes. In the late afternoon of 7 November, after a mass demonstration in Munich's Theresienwiese park, Eisner bravely led a gang of followers and stormed one military garrison after another. They met with no resistance. It was a clear sign of how hollow monarchist authority had become in Bavaria during the war. The next morning, the revolutionaries proclaimed a "Free State of Bavaria" on bright red placards and declared that the Wittelsbach dynasty had been deposed. That afternoon, the USPD and the MSPD formed a joint government. Eisner became both president and foreign minister while the chairman of the MSPD, Erhard Auer, took over the Interior Ministry; from the outset, he was Eisner's main cabinet rival.[3] The fact that the revolution proceeded nonviolently and that the first pronouncements of the new government were quite moderate helped extend support for the president well beyond the working classes. "Isn't it something wonderful? We've achieved a revolution without shedding a drop of blood!" Eisner declared. "It's a historical first!"[4]

The turbulence of the early days of November had calmed down by the time Hitler returned to Munich, but tension quickly developed in the governing cabinet between Eisner and the MSPD ministers. Like their colleagues in the Council of People's Deputies in revolutionary Berlin, the MSPD cabinet members were vigorously opposed to enshrining the workers' and soldiers' councils or soviets—as they were named after the Russian example—which had formed spontaneously at the start of the revolution, in a future democratic constitution. They regarded them as provisional institutions that would only exist until the election of a constitutional convention. Eisner, on the other hand, favoured cooperation between the soviets and parliament, and this put him on a collision course with Auer, who pushed for early Bavarian elections in the hope of making the soviets obsolete and undermining Eisner's position. After a meeting of ministers on 5 December, the election was scheduled for 12 January 1919.

Another point of conflict was Eisner's clear admission of German war guilt. On 23 November, he allowed the *Berliner Tageblatt* newspaper to publish excerpts of reports made by the Bavarian consul in Berlin from July and August 1914, which proved that the Reich leadership had ramped up the conflict between Austria–Hungary and Serbia as a way of bringing about a decisive test of strength with the Entente.[5] Eisner's move not only attracted condemnation from the MSPD ministers but opened him up to accusations of "treason" from nationalists. Eisner now became the target of vitriolic anti-Semitic attacks. The son of a Jewish merchant from Berlin, and a career journalist in the SPD, Eisner was defamed as a "Galician Jew," whose real name was supposedly Salomon Kosmanowsky. "Will we be able to believe in the future that we tolerated such blackguards in Germany for even one single day?" the outraged navy captain Bogislaw von Selchow asked in his diary on 25 November 1918.[6]

According to a statement by Ernst Schmidt, Hitler did not talk much about the revolution upon returning to Munich, but it was clear "how bitter he felt."[7] He had no love lost for the Wittelsbach dynasty. He was more dismayed that soldiers' soviets now had their say in the garrisons, which offended his sense of order and discipline. "I found the whole business so disgusting that I decided to leave as soon as possible," he wrote in *Mein Kampf*.[8] He was probably even more offended by the atmosphere of exuberance that broke out in Munich and other big cities in the first weeks and months after the revolution. All of Germany was hit by a dance craze. It was taking on "terrible dimensions," one member of Eisner's ministerial cabinet complained: "Women are going crazy, and tavern owners are powerless to stop them."[9]

Given the circumstances, Hitler probably welcomed it when he and Schmidt were transferred to the southern Bavarian town of Traunstein im Chiemgau in December 1918. There they were assigned as guards in a camp for prisoners of war and civilian inmates. Hitler spent more than a month in Traunstein, and during that time he again disappears almost completely from view. Before the camp was dissolved in mid-January—and not, as he recalled in *Mein Kampf*, in March—Hitler returned to Munich.[10] In mid-February, the replacement battalion of the 2nd Infantry Regiment was restructured, and Hitler was assigned to the 2nd Demobilisation Company. Next to nothing is known about his activities in this period. He probably spent most of his time in the barracks. Occasionally, resuming his old habits, he appears to have gone to the opera with Schmidt. From 20 February to 8 March he may have been ordered to stand guard at Munich's central train station, but this cannot be verified.[11]

Meanwhile, conflicts were becoming radicalised in a way that would completely change the face of the revolution in Munich and Bavaria. The spark was Eisner's murder on 21 February 1919. That day the president was on his way to the Bavarian parliament, the Landtag, to dissolve his cabinet after his party had suffered a crushing defeat in the election of 12 January. The USPD had received only 2.5 per cent of the vote and 3 parliamentary seats compared with 33 per cent and 61 seats for the MSPD. The strongest party was the Bavarian People's Party (BVP), which received 35 per cent of the vote and 66 seats, even though it had only been founded the previous November. Eisner's assassin, who shot him twice in the back of the head, was a 22-year-old army lieutenant and Munich University law student, Count Anton Arco auf Valley. In a note he wrote before the attack, Arco described his motivations: "Eisner is a Bolshevist and a Jew. He's not German. He doesn't feel German and he undermines all patriotic thoughts and emotions. He is a traitor to his country."[12] Only a few hours after the murder, the barman Alois Lindner, who was a member of the workers' council, fired two shots at Eisner's rival Auer, seriously wounding him. The revolutionary elements within Munich's working classes were convinced that Auer had been complicit in the assassination since he had done everything in his power to damage Eisner's public reputation in the preceding months.

"We are beginning to suspect that the bullet that killed Eisner has ushered in a new epoch of the revolution," the writer Ricarda Huch noted in her diary on 26 February.[13] Her hunch was right. On 22 February, delegates of the workers' and soldiers' soviets from all over Bavaria assembled in Munich to form a "Central Soviet of the Bavarian Republic." The Augsburg schoolteacher Ernst Niekisch, a member of the left wing of the MSPD, was elected chairman. After difficult negotiations with representatives of the soviets and the political parties, the Central Soviet decided to reconvene the Landtag, which had been dissolved. On 17 March, that body elected Johannes Hoffmann, the former minister of culture in the Eisner government, as Bavaria's new state president. But he was unable to calm the turmoil within the working classes. The news that Hungary had become a republic of soviets under the leadership of Béla Kun encouraged all those who dreamed of a similar experiment in Munich, and in the night of 6–7 April, the Central Soviet proclaimed a Bavarian Soviet Republic. The Hoffmann government fled to Bamberg, where it declared itself to be "the sole legitimate power in Bavaria."[14]

"It's the first part of Germany to go Bolshevik," the art patron and diplomat Count Harry Kessler commented. "If the Communists hang on there, it will be a German and European event of the first order."[15] Yet the Communists themselves refused to get involved. The head of the Bavarian branch of the newly formed German Communist Party (KPD), Eugen Leviné, rejected the new government as "a fake soviet republic," since it was headed by men who had previously treated Communists with deep mistrust. The new chairman of the Central Soviet was the writer Ernst Toller, who had gone from military volunteer to pacifist in the course of the war and had joined the USPD. The twelve representatives in the soviet government included respected figures like the independent socialist and writer Gustav Landauer, who took over the Education Ministry, as well as eccentrics like the anarchist Silvio Gesell, whose unorthodox suggestions for reforming the currency created a panic among Bavaria's wealthy.

The Toller experiment only lasted a week. After the Hoffmann government and loyalist troops failed in their attempt on 13 April, Palm Sunday, to overthrow the Soviet Republic in a putsch, the Communists under Leviné decided that their time had come. That very night, a conference of factory and garrison soviets declared the Central Soviet dissolved. A fifteen-member committee was appointed as the new government, with a five-member council serving as its executive and Leviné as its chairman. A nine-day general strike was called to give workers the opportunity to form a "Red Army."

The central government in Berlin had now had enough. On 16 April, Reich Prime Minister Philipp Scheidemann (MSPD) announced to his cabinet that he would approve the Hoffmann government's request for military support. The Prussian lieutenant Ernst von Oven was put in charge of the mission. The troops who intervened included paramilitary Freikorps volunteers under Franz Ritter von Epp and his right-hand man, later SA leader Ernst Röhm, as well as a navy brigade under Captain Hermann Ehrhardt, who would be one of the leaders of the Kapp putsch in March 1920.[16] The hastily assembled units of the "Red Army" under sailor Rudolf Egelhofer had no chance against this force of 30,000 men.

By late April, Munich was completely encircled. Deliveries of food were no longer reaching the Bavarian capital, and the city's monetary system collapsed. Last-minute attempts to avoid bloodshed failed. Reich Defence Minister Gustav Noske (MSPD) wanted to make an example of Munich, and Egelhofer drastically overestimated his followers' determination. Apparently on the latter's orders, the left-wing rebels shot and killed ten hostages, including seven members of the far-right-wing Thule Society, in the Luitpold *Gymnasium* on 30 April. The executions came as revenge for atrocities committed by the Freikorps as they marched on Munich, but the public was outraged by the "hostage murder." The adherents of the Soviet Republic also vigorously denounced it, but the event remained alive in Munich's collective memory as an example of "the Red reign of terror." In terms of cruelty, however, it was dwarfed by the deeds of the Reich troops as they marched on Munich and entered the city in early May.

By 3 May, the resistance of the "Red Army" was broken. No German city had ever experienced the level of White Terror that followed. More than 600 people were killed, many of them innocent civilians. Landauer was arrested on 2 May and brutally murdered by Freikorps paramilitaries when he was delivered to Stadelheim prison. Egelhofer was discovered in his hiding place the same day. After being tortured, he was shot in the head in the royal residence's inner courtyard on 3 May. After a brief trial before a kangaroo court, Leviné was put in front of a firing squad in Stadelheim on 5 May. Toller was able to hide until 4 May. He got off with five years in prison. On 7 May 1919, Erich Mühsam, who had also been involved in the Soviet Republic, noted in his diary from Eberbach prison: "That's the revolution I so longed for. After half a year of bloodletting, I can only shudder in horror."[17]

What did Hitler do and think in those dramatic weeks between Eisner's assassination and the demise of the Soviet Republic? In *Mein Kampf*, he barely mentioned it, and his silence fuelled speculation early on that he was trying to gloss over an unpleasant chapter in his biography—that is, the fact that he had initially sided with the leftists.

Konrad Heiden lent credence to this idea in the mid-1930s when he asserted that Private Hitler and his comrades had defended the Social Democrats against the Communists.[18] What is beyond doubt is the fact that on 3 April 1919 Hitler was elected the liaison of his demobilisation battalion, something that would never have happened had he publicly opposed the revolution. But can we therefore conclude that Hitler must have been close to the Majority Social Democrats?[19]

It would be extremely bizarre for Hitler to support the political party to which he had developed such an aversion in his Vienna days and which he had come to loathe even more during wartime. Thus it must have been tactics, not conviction, that made him seemingly lean towards the Majority Social Democrats in the first months of the revolution. After 9 November 1918, the MSPD represented the last hope of everyone who feared that the revolution would lead to a socialist remaking of society. Indeed, the majority of Germany's conservative middle classes supported the MSPD's call for quick elections on national and local levels. They did so not because they had suddenly been converted into passionate adherents of parliamentary democracy but because they wanted to preserve the traditional social order and private property. In Bavaria, it was Eisner's great rival Auer who had become "the best hope of those fundamentally opposed to the revolution."[20] In his later monologues, Hitler occasionally praised Auer and other MSPD leaders: "In the case of the leaders of 1918, I draw a distinction. Some of them ended up in it like Pilate in the Creed. They never intended to spark a revolution. Noske was one, as were Ebert, Scheidemann, Severing, and Auer in Bavaria."[21]

Joachim Fest argued plausibly that Hitler's behaviour in the spring of 1919 was a mixture of "desperation, passivity and opportunistic adaptation."[22] It is possible (although the photographic evidence is not incontrovertible) that Hitler was part of the funeral procession of 26 February in which Eisner's body was carried through Munich city centre to the Eastern Cemetery.[23] During the two Bavarian soviet republics, Hitler neither volunteered to join the Hoffmann government in Bamberg nor did he attach himself to one of the many Freikorps units. On 13 April, the day of the Palm Sunday putsch, he allegedly urged his comrades to keep out of the fighting: "We're no pack of revolutionary guards for a gang of vagrant Jews!"[24] But this anecdote may be apocryphal. Hitler's second election as liaison on 15 April, two days after the declaration of the second Bavarian Soviet Republic, shows in any case that he was not an open opponent of the revolution.[25] He seems to have already learned the art of disguise, refusing to take a stand, and may have kept a low profile in the reasonable belief that the soviet experiment would be short-lived. But the story he told in Mein Kampf, of having attracted the displeasure of the Communist authorities and of forcibly resisting the threat to arrest him on 27 April 1919, appears to be entirely fictional.[26]

Immediately after the demise of the council government, Hitler dropped his guard and openly aligned himself with the counter-revolutionaries. On 9 May, we suddenly find him as a member of a three-person commission charged with investigating the behaviour of his regiment's soldiers during the two soviet republics. In Mein Kampf he described this as "my first more or less purely political activity."[27] He had no qualms about informing on comrades who, in contrast to himself, had shown genuine sympathy for the revolution. He denounced Georg Dufter, who had been elected along with him to the battalion council of the 1st Demobilisation Company on 15 April, as the "worst and most radical rabble-rouser within the regiment . . . who had constantly spread propaganda for the soviet republic."[28] Hitler was rewarded for these services. When his company was disbanded in early May, he was able to avoid being discharged from the army. From June 1919 onwards, he was a member of the demobilisation office of the 2nd Infantry Regiment.[29] This post was to prove enormously significant in his political career.

The Hoffmann government only returned to Munich in late August 1919. From early May until then, power rested with the military, in particular with Reichswehr Group Commando 4, which was formed on 11 May under General Arnold von Möhl and to which all army units stationed in Bavaria were subordinated. An edict of 20 May defined the army's main priority as being able "to carry out, in conjunction with the police, stricter surveillance of the populace and [to] recognise its moods and potential points of resistance early enough so that the ignition of any new unrest can be discovered and extinguished in its inception."[30] The "intelligence department" of the Group Commando, which was headed as of late May by Captain Karl Mayr, was charged with carrying out this mission. Mayr, an ambitious and scheming officer, was to become the "midwife of Hitler's political career."[31]

Hitler initially attracted Mayr's attention with his work on the investigatory commission. "When I first met him, he was like a tired stray dog looking for a master," wrote the anonymous author of an article that appeared in a U.S. magazine in 1941 and who we can reasonably assume was Mayr.[32] For his part, the army captain was looking for reliable liaisons who could spread "counter-propaganda" among the troops, educating them about the dangers of Bolshevism and reigniting the spirit of nationalism and militarism. A list likely drawn up by the intelligence department in early July featured the name "Hittler [sic], Adolf."[33] But before Private Hitler could get to work, he was sent on a training course. He was not, as had been previously assumed, part of the first such course, which took place from 5 to 12 June at Munich University. He participated in the third one held from 10 to 19 July in the Museum Society's space at the Palais Porcia.[34]

Karl Mayr exploited his connections in lining up the speakers, including his old school chum, the nationalist historian Karl Alexander von Müller, who lectured about post-Reformation German history and the political history of the world war.[35] Also taking part was Müller's brother-in-law, the engineer Gottfried Feder from Murnau, who had created a stir in pan-Germanic, chauvinist circles in Munich with his May 1919 "Manifesto on Breaking the Interest Slavery of Money." The self-appointed economic theorist saw Mammonism— people's fixation on money and the drive to acquire more and more of it—as the main evil of his times. Feder put the blame on the lending practices of the financial markets, which he regarded as being in the hands of Jews. Breaking "interest slavery" meant making it impossible for people to earn a living from their capital without working and taking up the cause of "creative" capital against "money grabbing." On 6 June, Feder gave his first lecture in front of 300–400 people, who kept interrupting him with applause. He returned for the July course.[36] Hitler was impressed, writing in Mein Kampf: "For the first time in my life I fundamentally got to grips with international stock-market and loan capital."[37] Feder's theories, which combined anti-capitalist with anti-Semitic resentments, would become an integral part of the Nazi Party's early ideology.

In his memoirs, Müller recalled that as the hall was emptying after his lecture, a group of people remained behind, transfixed by a man who was speaking to them with growing passion and an unusual guttural voice. "I had the strange feeling that he had got them excited and at the same time that their interest had given him his voice," remembered the historian. "I saw a pale, drawn face underneath a decidedly unmilitary shock of hair, with a trimmed moustache and remarkably large, light blue, fanatically cold, gleaming eyes."[38] For the first time, someone had remarked on what was Hitler's greatest skill: his oratorical ability. "Do you know that one of your trainees is a natural-born public speaker?" Müller asked Mayr, who then invited Hitler to join them. "The man came up to the podium, moving awkwardly, as if both defiant and embarrassed. Our conversation yielded nothing of interest."[39] The future champion of the German people had not yet grown into that role. His public bearing did not match his natural speaking ability. Being in the presence of a famous history professor must also have daunted Hitler and reminded him of his failure at school. On more than one occasion in *Mein Kampf*, Hitler's inferiority complex in this regard led him to excoriate "the so-called 'intelligentsia' who . . . in their never-ending arrogance look down on everyone who hasn't been run through the obligatory schools and been pumped full of the necessary knowledge."[40]

Mayr did not care about Hitler's lack of diplomas: he immediately took to the private. In late July 1919, when an "educational commando" was formed to hold anti-Bolshevik classes at the temporary camp in Lechfeld for soldiers returning from the front, Hitler was named one of twenty-six instructors.[41] During the five-day course from 20 to 25 August, Hitler not only gave lectures with titles such as "Conditions of Peace and Reconstruction" and "Very Social and Economic Political Catchphrases," he also spoke during the discussions following the other lectures.[42] These days at Lechfeld were Hitler's political initiation. For the first time in his life, he received affirmation and recognition from a larger circle of people, and he realised the effect his speaking ability could have on an audience. "I began with enthusiasm and passion," he wrote five years later in *Mein Kampf*. "I suddenly had the opportunity to talk to a larger audience, and what I had always instinctively assumed without knowing was confirmed: I could 'speak well.'"[43] Several people on the course confirmed this impression. "Herr Hittler [*sic*] especially," one attendee remarked, "is a born public speaker, whose commitment and natural demeanour commands the attention of an audience and forces its members to think."[44]

Hitler's first recorded anti-Semitic statement comes from his time in Lechfeld. The director of the camp, First Lieutenant Walther Bendt, reported that during a "nice, clear, impassioned lecture . . . about capitalism" Hitler had touched upon "the Jewish question."[45] Hitler had obviously adopted some of the ideas in Feder's talk, but he also incorporated the radical anti-Semitic sentiments that were spreading like an epidemic, particularly among soldiers, in Munich and elsewhere in Bavaria.[46] Even mainstream conservative circles had attacked Eisner as a tool of "Jewish Bolshevism," and after Munich's "liberation" the hate campaign was directed against other prominent representatives of the soviet governments who had Jewish backgrounds, such as Toller, Leviné, Mühsam and Towia Axelrod. In May 1919, the *Bayrisches Bauernblatt* newspaper, the main organ of the Christian Farmers' Association, which was published by the BVP politician Georg Heim, wrote: "The gallery of famous men from the time of the soviet republics is a picture album full of criminals. Foreign riff-raff, mostly from the district office of Jerusalem, have targeted the innocent Bavarian people as an object of exploitation and have filled their pockets."[47] The soviet republics were frequently described as a "Jewish tyranny" and conflated with the *bête noire* of Bolshevism. In October 1919, in light of the anti-Semitic propaganda spreading throughout society, the intelligence department of the Munich police deemed an anti-Jewish pogrom "entirely possible."[48] On the other hand, police authorities typically dismissed complaints from the leaders of the Jewish community and the Central Association of German Citizens of the Jewish Faith by claiming that "hatred of Jewishness has been greatly encouraged by the fact that most Communist leaders are Jewish."[49]

Like a sponge, Hitler sucked up popular anti-Jewish sentiments and the anti-Semitic slogans of ethnically chauvinist brochures and pamphlets.[50] His turn towards fanatical anti-Semitism, which he would later claim had originated in Vienna, actually took place amidst the revolution and counter-revolution in Munich. From then on, the *bête noire* of "the Jew" as the incarnation of all evil occupied the centre of his racist world view, and he expressed this idea with such unmistakable clarity in Lechfeld that Walther Bendt had to tell him to be more moderate to avoid creating the impression of Jew-baiting. Hitler was ordered to be more "careful in discussing the Jewish question," and to "avoid making overly direct references to this race, which is foreign to the German people."[51]

Karl Mayr was not only aware of Hitler's anti-Semitic views, but seems to have shared them. On 10 September 1919, the captain told Hitler to answer a letter from a former course participant, Adolf Gemlich. Gemlich had asked for advice as to whether Jews represented "a national danger," and if so, what approach the ruling Social Democrats were taking to this threat.[52] Hitler's extensive reply, dated 16 September, can be regarded with utter justification as *the* key document in his early biography. It featured all of the anti-Semitic prejudices he had acquired in the preceding months, including the idea that Jews were "a racial and not a religious community," combined into one neurotic complex. As a race, Hitler argued, Jews were incapable of assimilating. "After thousands of years of inbreeding," he wrote to Gemlich, "the Jew has generally preserved his race and its innate traits better than most of the people in whose midst he lives." As a disciple of Gottfried Feder, Hitler saw boundless greed, the "dance around the golden calf," as one of those characteristics. "His power is the power of money, which in the form of interest infinitely reproduces itself in his hands without any effort on his part," Hitler instructed Gemlich. "Everything that inspires people to strive for something higher—be it religion, socialism or democracy—is for a Jew just a means serving the end of satisfying monetary greed and the desire to rule. His effect on other peoples is that of racial tuberculosis."[53]

Hitler put on the airs of the coolly rational analyst, arguing that political anti-Semitism should not be based on outbursts of emotion, which would only lead to pogroms. In this regard, Hitler was taking sides in a debate between "cultural" and "pogrom" anti-Semitism unleashed by the Leipzig anti-Semite Heinrich Pudor in August 1919. Pudor had argued against combating Jews solely with laws and regulations, demanding that all means, including pogroms, should be used to break "Jewish tyranny."[54] The anti-Semitic German-Nationalist Protection and Defiance Federation had distanced itself from this "incitement to pogroms" and revived the demand of the Pan-Germanic League for Jews to be legally classified as foreigners.[55] Hitler, too, preferred what he called "the anti-Semitism of reason" to "emotional anti-Semitism." The former, he wrote to Gemlich, would necessarily lead to a "controlled legal fight against and eradication of Jewish advantages." Only a "government of national strength," he added, would be able to achieve this end. In his view, Germany's current government was too dependent on Jews, who had been, after all, "the driving forces of revolution."[56]

Hitler would never lose sight of the central goal of removing Jews from German society, and it was by no means the eccentric idea of a lone individual. There was a large amount of consensus among the reconstituted army, the Reichswehr, and the Freikorps that this was a desirable objective. Mayr agreed with Hitler's "very clear explanations," expressing reservations only about the mention of the "interest problem." Interest, Mayr objected, was not a Jewish invention, but rather a fundamental institution of property and an element of healthy business acumen—one had to combat excesses but not, as Feder did, "throw the baby out with the bathwater." On the other hand, Mayr completely agreed that "what people call the ruling social democracy was completely chained to Jewry." He also reaffirmed that "all harmful elements—including the Jews—should be cast out or quarantined like pathogens."[57]

On 12 September 1919, four days before he composed his letter to Gemlich, Hitler attended his first meeting of the German Workers' Party (Deutsche Arbeiterpartei, DAP). One day, Hitler wrote in *Mein Kampf*, he had received orders from his superiors to investigate this political association.[58] Historians have therefore often assumed that Hitler was essentially acting as an undercover agent at Mayr's behest, but that view has been disproven. Mayr was already quite well informed about the DAP and the culture surrounding it and would have had no need for such information. And Hitler certainly did not spy on the organisation. As the attendance list makes clear, Hitler came not alone, but in the company of several comrades from the Lechfeld commando. Their presence there is more likely to have reflected Reichswehr Group Commando 4's interest in gaining influence over the DAP.[59]

The party was one of many ethnically chauvinist, nationalist groups that evolved after 1918 from the Pan-Germanic League, the most influential right-wing agitation group of the pre-war and war years. The Thule Society in Munich was one of their organisational nuclei, and it was run by its chairman, the dubious figure of Baron Rudolf von Sebottendorff, like a secret lodge. Its members encompassed

Munich bigwigs like the publisher Julius F. Lehmann, one of the founders of the Munich chapter of the Pan-Germanic League, and several lesser-known adherents of right-wing ethnic chauvinism who would later play a role in the development of Nazi ideology. They included Feder, the journalist Dietrich Eckart, and the students Hans Frank, Rudolf Hess and Alfred Rosenberg.[60]

The Thule Society provided a platform for counter-revolutionary activities. It used the swastika as its symbol and had its own newspaper, the *Münchener Beobachter*. It did not just restrict its appeal to middle-class circles, but also reached out to blue-collar workers. One of its founders, the sports journalist Karl Harrer, was charged with establishing contact with the locomotive mechanic Anton Drexler, who had made a name for himself during the war as a follower of the nationalist German Fatherland Party and who had founded the "Free Workers' Committee for a Just Peace" in March 1918.[61] Together Harrer and Drexler established a "political workers' circle," out of which the DAP was born on 5 January 1919. Drexler became the chairman of the Munich chapter, and Harrer took over the office of "Reich chairman"—a pompous title considering that the newly formed party had only thirty members and would remain a fringe group in the months to come.[62]

A grand total of forty-one people attended the DAP meeting at the Sterneckerbräu tavern on 12 September. Feder spoke on the topic "How and by what means can we get rid of capitalism?" Hitler was already familiar with Feder's ideas, so he spent the time observing the audience. "The impression it made on me was neither good nor bad," Hitler would write in *Mein Kampf*. "It was just another one of many newly formed associations." After the lecture, when Hitler was about to leave, one of those in attendance, a Professor Baumann, vigorously argued that Bavaria should break away from Prussia and join the Republic of Austria. Hitler felt he had no choice but to speak out and rebuff the "educated gentleman" in no uncertain terms, whereupon Baumann left the tavern "with his tail between his legs."[63] But Hitler's version of events does not square with reality—the name Baumann only appears on the attendance lists a couple of months later.[64] It seems more likely that Hitler spoke, as he had in the Lechfeld camp, in an attempt to impress those around him. After the meeting, Drexler followed Hitler and gave him a copy of his pamphlet "My Political

Awakening." "That one's got quite a mouth on him! We could use that!" the party chairman was supposed to have remarked.[65]

The next day Hitler read Anton Drexler's pamphlet and recognised a number of details from his own "political awakening." What seems to have impressed him most, though, was the idea of fusing nationalism and socialism, of freeing the working classes from the "false teachings" of Marxism and winning them over for the nationalist cause. To his surprise, Hitler wrote in *Mein Kampf*, a week later he received a postcard informing him that he had been accepted as a member of the DAP and inviting him to take part in the party's next committee meeting. But what he experienced in a shabby tavern in Herrnstrasse exceeded his most pessimistic expectations: "It was clubby small-mindedness ... Notwithstanding a couple of general ideas, they had nothing. No political programme, no pamphlet, nothing at all printed up, not even membership cards or one lousy stamp. All they had was faith and goodwill."[66]

Why did Hitler join a political party that he himself described as a "mixture of a lodge and an early evening drinking club"?[67] The rudimentary nature of the group seems to have been part of the appeal. "Such a ridiculously small entity with a couple of members," Hitler wrote, "had not yet ossified into an 'organisation' but rather remained open to each individual finding something to do."[68] In other words, the DAP offered Hitler the opportunity to get ahead quickly and shape the party according to his own ideas.

With his characteristic fondness for superlatives, in *Mein Kampf* Hitler described his decision to join the DAP as the "most decisive resolution" of his life.[69] Some have pointed out that as a member of Germany's new armed forces, the Reichswehr, Hitler was prohibited from joining a political organisation, but this is incorrect: Hitler was, in fact, still a member of the old German army.[70] Nor was he the seventh member of the DAP, as legend had it, but the seventh member of the committee Drexler had asked him to join as a general recruitment specialist. As of February 1920, the party began to maintain an alphabetical membership list, which began with the number 501 to give the impression that it had more members than it did; Hitler's membership number was 555.[71]

From the very beginning Hitler's goal was to turn what was a sect-like regulars' table at a tavern into an effective political party. In October 1919 a DAP office was set up in a side room at the Sterneckerbräu. It contained a typewriter used to compose flyers for meetings. Hitler told later of distributing the flyers himself, and of the number of listeners gradually rising "from eleven to thirteen, then seventeen, twenty-three and thirty-four."[72] By the middle of the month, the party gambled on attracting a larger audience. When it published an ad in the *Münchener Beobachter* for an event in the city's Hofbräuhaus, more than a hundred people turned up. Hitler was the second speaker of the evening. For the 30-year-old, his first public speech was a watershed, and his memories of it in *Mein Kampf* nearly repeat the passage about the episode in the Lechfeld camp: "I talked for thirty minutes, and what I used to sense internally without really knowing it was now confirmed by reality: I could speak well."[73]

These lines were written five years after the fact, but they still communicate the euphoria Hitler must have felt when he discovered his great gift. The positive response of his audience gave him the validation that made up for the many disappointments of his early years. Max Amann no longer recognised Hitler when he ran into him around this time. "There was an unfamiliar fire burning in him," Amann recalled after the war. "I was at two or three of his meetings . . . He yelled and indulged in histrionics. I'd never seen the like of it. But everyone said, 'This fellow means what he says.' He was drenched in sweat, completely wet. It was unbelievable."[74]

More and more people began attending DAP events, and in no time, Hitler advanced to become the party's star speaker. On 13 November 1919, before an audience of 130 in the Eberlbräu beer cellar, Hitler used his strongest language yet to condemn the Treaty of Versailles, which had been signed at the end of June. "As long as the earth has existed," Hitler thundered, "no people have ever been forced to declare themselves willing to sign such a shameful treaty." The person who wrote up a report of the event for the Munich police noted someone yelling out "The work of Jews!" at this point. Hitler combined his criticism of the treaty with scabrous personal attacks on Reich Finance Minister Matthias Erzberger, who had signed the armistice agreement in the woods of Compiègne on 11 November 1918. Hitler bellowed that he was certain that "the man who had hung such a treaty around our necks would not be in his post for much longer and would not even be a schoolteacher in Buttenhausen (cry from the audience: He'll get it like Eisner)."[75] Indeed, Erzberger would be forced by right-wing nationalists to resign in 1920, and he would be murdered in 1921. The *Münchener Beobachter* reported that "repeated frenetic applause greeted Hitler's graceful speech."[76]

Hitler's rise within the DAP did not escape the notice of the Reichswehr. In late October 1919 a position as an assistant to the educational officer was created for him in the staff of the 41st Rifleman's Regiment at Prinz Arnulf Garrison. Hitler later described himself as an "educational officer," which was impossible since as a private he would never have been allowed to hold an officer's position.[77] While maintaining his connection to Karl Mayr in the intelligence department of the Group Commando, he increasingly shifted his focus to propaganda activities for the DAP. On 10 December, he spoke in the Deutsches Reich restaurant. The title of his talk was "Germany as it faces its worst humiliation." He made no bones about who he considered responsible for military defeat and revolution: "the Jews, who alone are profiting from it and don't shy away from inciting civil war with their rabble-rousing and base agitation." Hitler insisted on the idea of "Germany for Germans!"[78] He was even more outspoken at a meeting on 16 January 1920. "We refuse to tolerate our destiny being ruled by a foreign race," Hitler thundered. "We demand a stop to Jewish immigration."[79] Any intimation that Hitler moderated his anti-Semitism at the beginning of his political career is completely mistaken. From the very start, he appeared as a radical anti-Semite—and this was precisely why he seems to have appealed to his audience. The anti-Semitism boiling over in Munich in the autumn of 1919 ensured that Hitler's speeches would resonate with his listeners.

DAP Reich Chairman Harrer viewed Hitler's aggressive public stance with unease. He would have preferred to continue running the party as a secret sect like the Thule Society. But in December 1919, using a new set of rules that tied down the seven-man party committee to certain principles, Hitler succeeded in stripping Harrer of practically all his power.[80] Harrer resigned from his post on 5 January 1920, and together with Anton Drexler, who succeeded Harrer, Hitler began to work on a party programme to be announced at the next mass meeting in February 1920. The twenty-five points the two men hammered out in Drexler's apartment on Burghausener Strasse 6 contained no original ideas. On the contrary, they were a cross section of ideas in currency among ethnic-chauvinist and anti-Semitic circles at the time.

At the top of the agenda (Point 1) was the demand for all ethnic Germans to be united within a greater Germany. This was followed by demands for the revocation of the Treaty of Versailles (Point 2) and the return of Germany's colonies (Point 3). Point 4 clearly expressed the party's anti-Semitic orientation, reading "Only an ethnic comrade [*Volksgenosse*] can be a citizen. Only someone who is of German blood, irrespective of religion, can be an ethnic comrade. Thus no Jew can be an ethnic comrade." This was followed by the demands that Jews in Germany be treated as foreigners under the law (Point 5) and that all further Jewish immigration be halted (Point 8).

Gottfried Feder's influence made itself felt in demands for "the eradication of work-free, effortless income" (Point 11) and the "confiscation of all wartime profits without exception" (Point 12). Demands for the nationalisation of big business, for profit-sharing and for an expansion of the pension system (Points 13–15) were designed to appeal to the working classes. A promise to communalise large department stores (Point 16) was aimed at the middle classes, and the prospect of land reform (Point 17) at farmers. The programme also contained the slogans "communal welfare comes before selfishness" (Point 24) and "strengthening of central authority" (Point 25), combined with the pledge to fight against "the corrupting parliamentary system" (Point 6). As a whole the programme left no doubt that the aim was to get rid of the democracy of the young Weimar Republic and create an authoritarian government for an ethnic community, which would no longer have any room for Jews.[81]

Drexler and Hitler chose the Hofbräuhaus as the location for announcing this programme, and the DAP advertised the event with garish red posters. Initial fears that not enough people would show up proved to be unfounded. On the evening of 24 February 1920, around 2,000 people squeezed into the Hofbräuhaus's main first-floor hall. Hitler was the second speaker, but he was the one who really got the crowd whipped up with his attacks on the Treaty of Versailles, Erzberger and, above all, the Jews. The police transcript of the event read: "First chuck the guilty ones, the Jews, out and then we'll purify ourselves. (Enthusiastic applause.) Monetary fines are no use against the crimes of fencing and usury. (Beatings! Hangings!) How shall we protect our fellow human beings against this band of bloodsuckers? (Hang them!)"[82]

Hitler then read out the individual points of the party manifesto, whereupon numerous opponents from the political Left, who were also in attendance, raised their voices in protest. The police observer noted: "There was often great tumult and I was convinced that fights were going to break out at any moment."[83] Party legend later romanticised the meeting of 24 February into a heroic, foundational act of the Nazi movement. Hitler himself laid the groundwork for this, ending the first volume of *Mein Kampf* with the words: "A fire was sparked, from whose embers the sword would necessarily come which would restore freedom to the German Siegfried and life to the German nation . . . The hall gradually emptied. The movement was under way."[84] The mainstream Munich press paid little attention to the event: the DAP, which would rename itself the NSDAP on 24 February 1920, was still too insignificant. The thirty-seven-line report on the meeting in the *Münchener Neueste Nachrichten* newspaper failed to mention Hitler by name. Even the *Völkischer Beobachter* (as the *Münchener Beobachter* had been known since late 1919) restricted itself to a brief note.[85]

On 31 March 1920, Hitler was discharged from the military, but he would continue to remain close to the milieu of the Reichswehr, to which he was indebted for crucial help in starting his political career.[86] Over the course of just a few months, the unknown private had made himself irreplaceable as the (NS)DAP's most effective speaker. This was the first step of his meteoric rise. Hitler's task now was to expand the party's base and establish himself at its head. Supported by powerful patrons, the beer-cellar demagogue was about to become a public attraction—in Munich and beyond.

5

The King of Munich

"It was a wonderful time," Hitler recalled in one of his monologues. "In my memory, it was the best time of all."[1] Even long after he had become Reich chancellor, Hitler enjoyed thinking back to the early years of the NSDAP in Munich. He regarded them as the party's heroic period, the "time of struggle," in which he and his followers had come together as an oath-bound community and overcome monsters of all varieties. "Our old National Socialists were something wonderful," Hitler reminisced. "Back then you had little to gain by being in the party and everything to lose."[2] Hitler largely credited himself with turning the NSDAP from a tiny sect into a player in Bavarian politics within four years. As a "complete unknown," he boasted, he had set out to "conquer a nation."[3] Fifteen years later, he would achieve his goal. Nonetheless, the German dictator never forgot that the Bavarian capital had been the springboard for his astonishing career, and he showed his gratitude in August 1935 by granting Munich the title "capital of the movement."[4]

Without Hitler, the rise of National Socialism would have been unthinkable. In his absence, the party would have remained one of many ethnic-chauvinist groups on the right of the political spectrum. Nonetheless, the special conditions of the immediate post-war years in both Bavaria and the German Reich were also crucial: without the explosive mixture of economic misery, social instability and collective trauma, the populist agitator Hitler would never have been able to work his way out of anonymity to become a famous politician. The circumstances at the time played into Hitler's hands, and he was more skilful and unscrupulous about using them than any of his rivals on the nationalist far right.

In March 1920, right-wing opponents of democracy under the leadership of the East Prussian civil servant Wolfgang Kapp and the commander of Reichswehr Group Commando 1 in Berlin, General Baron Walther von Lüttwitz, made the first attempt to topple the Weimar Republic. The putsch collapsed within a few days after workers brought public life to a standstill with a powerful general strike, but in Bavaria counter-revolutionary forces thought the time was ripe to force the government under Johannes Hoffmann to resign. On 16 March, the Landtag elected the government president of Upper Bavaria, Gustav von Kahr, the new Bavarian state president.[5]

Under Kahr, politics lurched dramatically to the right. Kahr was an outspoken monarchist whose express aim was to turn Bavaria into a "cell of order" in the Reich. He immediately issued an edict to stem the immigration of "Eastern Jews" to Bavaria, with which the government bent to the will of the ethnic-chauvinistic right and encouraged anti-Semitic currents within the populace.[6] In the months that followed, Munich became an Eldorado for opponents of the Weimar Republic throughout Germany. Corvette Captain Hermann Ehrhardt, whose naval brigade had formed the military backbone of the Kapp–Lüttwitz putsch and who was wanted by the police, found refuge there, and in his new headquarters in Munich's Franz-Josef-Strasse, he and some like-minded comrades founded a new secret society, "Organisation Consul," whose purpose was to murder leading representatives of the Weimar Republic. On 9 June 1921 the USPD faction leader in the Bavarian Landtag, Karl Gareis, became their first victim. On 26 August 1921, the Centre Party politician and the ex-Reich Finance Minister Matthias Erzberger was also killed, and the murder of Foreign Minister Walther Rathenau followed on 24 June 1922. Bogislaw von Selchow, who saw this racist movement as an "elementary, new force" in Germany, laid part of the blame for Rathenau's murder with the Jewish foreign minister himself. "One should not stir up the embers within the German people in such turbulent times," he wrote, "by having a member of a foreign race represent them abroad."[7] This was not an isolated voice. The general tenor within nationalist circles was no different.

In the summer of 1920, the man who had pulled the strings behind the failed putsch, the retired general Erich Ludendorff, also moved to Munich. His residence, a luxurious villa in the south of the city, now became a focal point for counter-revolutionary activities throughout Bavaria.[8] Tolerated by the authorities, countless paramilitary organisations were permitted to lead their shady existences in the southern German state, including the citizens' militias that had been founded after the demise of the Bavarian Soviet Republic and soon numbered 300,000 men. The presence of this counter-revolutionary private army had enormous influence on everyday life and political culture in Munich in the early 1920s. "They institutionalised Bavaria's rejection of the Versailles settlement and its hatred for the Weimar Republic," writes the historian David Clay Large. "Above all, they despised Berlin as Germany's new mecca of left-wing politics, multiethnic society, and avant-garde culture."[9]

Extremists who wanted to topple the state were encouraged by Munich Police President Ernst Pöhner and the director of Political Division VI, Wilhelm Frick, who looked the other way when confronted with the assassinations carried out by Organisation Consul. Hitler and the NSDAP also enjoyed the protection of these two officials right from the start. They had held a "protective hand" over the National Socialist Party and Hitler, Frick testified at the trial after the Beer Hall Putsch of 1923, because they were seen as the "seed of renewal in Germany."[10] Hitler realised how much he owed these early supporters. In *Mein Kampf*, he praised Pöhner and Frick for being "Germans first and civil servants second."[11] In late March 1942, Hitler would compliment Frick as someone who had "always behaved beyond reproach, helpfully pointed the way and enabled the party to maximise its effect."[12]

Already in the first year of its existence, the NSDAP became the most active of the ethnic-chauvinist groups in Munich. Hardly a week passed without a meeting or a rally. Since the quantum leap of 24 February 1920, party events were now held at the largest beer halls: the Hofbräuhaus, the Bürgerbräukeller, the Kindlkeller and the Hackerbräukeller. Audience sizes ranged from 800 to 2,500—in the second half of 1920, levels of 3,000 were reached. In December 1920, the Bavarian District Defence Commando VII concluded with satisfaction that "the lively activity of the National Socialist German Workers' Party in arranging meetings . . . has a beneficial, patriotic effect."[13] On 3 February 1921, the NSDAP staged their first event in the

Zirkus Krone on Marsstrasse, at the time the largest covered arena in Munich. More than 6,000 people gathered there to hear Hitler speak. "The hall lay in front of me like a gigantic shell," he recalled in *Mein Kampf.* "After the first hour, ever louder eruptions of spontaneous applause were beginning to interrupt me. After two hours they ebbed away again and the consecrated silence fell that I later experienced over and over in this space . . . For the first time, we left the realms of an ordinary, everyday party."[14]

It was Hitler who drew in the crowds week after week. In 1920 alone, he appeared as the main speaker twenty-one times, and he served as a member of panel discussions on numerous other occasions. He also appeared in the Bavarian countryside, as the NSDAP sought to expand its appeal beyond Munich: in the early autumn of 1920, he also made four speeches during the Austrian election campaign. Taken together, it was a gruelling workload.[15] Hitler's main priority at this point was to attract attention to his still relatively small party and secure its place in the public sphere. "Who cares whether they laugh at us or insult us, treating us as fools or criminals?" Hitler wrote in *Mein Kampf.* "The point is that they talk about us and constantly think about us."[16] The better known the party became, the more its membership rolls swelled—from 190 members in January 1920 to 675 in May, and from 2,500 in January 1921 to 3,300 in August. Hitler was optimistic. There was no reason "to doubt the party's rise because of its small size at present," he told the chairman of the recently formed local Nazi chapter in Hanover, Gustav Seifert, in October 1921.[17]

Contrary to what many people still believe, Hitler did not speak extemporaneously: he diligently prepared for all his public appearances. He would fill a dozen pages with catchwords and slogans to keep him focused during his two- to three-hour performances. Right before the start of events, he would pace his room and run through the fundamental points of his speech, repeatedly interrupted by telephone calls from followers reporting on the atmosphere in the venue. Hitler usually arrived half an hour late to ratchet up the excitement. He would then place his notes to his right and occasionally glance down at them to reassure himself.[18]

His speeches followed a set pattern. As a rule, Hitler began calmly, almost hesitantly. As the historian John Toland put it, Hitler spent the first ten minutes or so gauging the mood of his audience with the fine sense of an actor.[19] Only when he was convinced of their approval did he begin to relax. He then started to punctuate his remarks with dramatic gestures—throwing his head back, extending his right arm and underlining particularly vivid sentences with his finger or hammering on the lectern with his fists. At the same time his tone and choice of words became more aggressive. The more clearly an audience signalled with applause and calls of approval that the spark had caught, the more Hitler increased his volume and tempo. His own excitement was infectious. By the end of his speeches, after a furious crescendo, the entire venue would be in a state of intoxicated fervour, and the orator himself, covered in sweat, would accept the congratulations of his entourage.[20]

A variety of factors contributed to Hitler's power as a speaker, starting with his full-bodied and flexible voice—"his best weapon," as it has been called[21]—which he used like an instrument. "If one minute there was a vibrato to lament the undeserved fate of an aggrieved and repeatedly betrayed people, the next there would be the approach of a cleansing thunderstorm, only for Hitler's voice to erupt suddenly in emotional displays that swept his audience irresistibly into mass ecstasy," Hitler's friend Ernst "Putzi" Hanfstaengl wrote.[22] Prior to 1928, Hitler spoke without the help of microphones or loudspeakers: his earliest followers heard the natural power of his baritone voice without any of the distortion of technological amplification.

Hitler was skilled at choosing his words to appeal to an audience. As Hanfstaengl put it, he had mastered the "language of the post-war little guy," peppering his speeches not only with the coarse phrases of a former military man, but also with irony and sarcasm.[23] He was good at responding to hecklers so he mostly kept the laughter on his side. Moreover, Hitler's speeches clearly touched a nerve. Like no one else, he was able to express what his audience thought and felt: he exploited their fears, prejudices and resentments, but also their hopes and desires. "A virtuoso playing the soul of the masses like a keyboard" was how Hanfstaengl put it, adding: "Well beyond the measure of his inspiring rhetoric, this person seemed to have a gift for coupling the gnostic desire of the time for a strong leader with his own sense of personal mission. This conflation made every conceivable hope and expectation seem realistic."[24]

That effect Hitler derived not just from *what* he said, but *how* he said it. He had become the Unknown Soldier from the world war who shared the problems and desires of his audience, and thus radiated an aura of veracity and authenticity. "The first thing you felt was that here was someone who meant what he said, who didn't want to convince you of anything he didn't believe entirely himself," observed Hans Frank, who first heard one of Hitler's speeches in January 1920 at the age of 19. "He spoke from the bottom of his own soul and all of our souls."[25] This was the "unity of the word and the man" that Hitler's first biographer, Konrad Heiden, identified as the secret to the agitator's success. During the high points of his speeches, Heiden wrote, Hitler was "someone seduced by himself," someone who was so inseparable from his words "that a measure of authenticity flowed over the audience even when he was telling obvious lies."[26]

From his very earliest speeches, Hitler liked using religious imagery and motifs. When he referenced the Bible, he sometimes went so far as to compare himself with Jesus Christ: "We may be small, but there was once a man who stood up for himself in Galilee, and today his teachings rule the entire world."[27] Conversely, many people who had been disoriented by the war and were looking for a political messiah attached their hopes and desires to Hitler, the man who propagated his ethnic gospel with such missionary fervour. Hitler seemed like "a second Luther" to the merchant Kurt Lüdecke, who was part of the demagogue's inner circle for a time. "I experienced an exaltation that could be likened only to a religious conversion," he wrote in 1938.[28] Such experiences were typical of many people who attended Hitler's speeches; even those who were initially sceptical about the NSDAP were surprised to find themselves part of a community that got emotionally carried away.

Some of the appeal of Hitler's appearances was the increasing cleverness with which they were staged. They combined, as Joachim Fest put it, "the spectacular elements of the circus and the grand opera with the uplifting ceremony of the church's liturgical ritual."[29] Parades with flags and marching-band music prepared the crowd. Anticipation rose, all the more so the longer the speaker kept his audience waiting. Karl Alexander von Müller described the entrance of the local matador in the following terms: "Suddenly, at the back entrance, there was movement. Commands barked out. The speaker at the

podium fell silent in mid-sentence. Everyone jumped up to shout 'Heil!'
The man everyone had been waiting for strode to the stage with his
entourage, his right arm raised rigidly in the air."[30] Even those who
were not caught up in the feverish atmosphere were entertained by
Nazi events, not least because beer flowed freely.[31]

Hitler possessed an extraordinary sense of political symbolism. The
swastika flag became the party emblem very early on, in 1921,
combining the colours of the German Reich—black, white and red—
with a symbol which had long been in use among ethnic-chauvinist
circles; Ehrhardt's navy brigade, for instance, had worn it on their
steel helmets during the Kapp–Lüttwitz putsch.[32] There were also the
pennant that became the sign of the SA, and the "Heil" greeting,
which was made mandatory within the movement in 1926.[33] The
National Socialists also had no qualms about adopting leftist propaganda techniques. They announced their meetings on garish red
posters, and they distributed flyers from trucks to the general populace.
One goal was to seduce workers away from leftist parties, although
in the beginning it was worried members of the lower middle classes,
uprooted former soldiers and impoverished university graduates who
flocked to Hitler's events.[34]

Hitler adapted the content of his speeches to suit the tastes of
his lower-middle-class, nationalist-conservative, ethnic-chauvinist
and anti-Semitic listeners, even though his repertoire of topics was
quite limited. His speeches typically began with a look back at
"wonderful, flourishing Germany before the war," in which "orderliness, cleanliness and precision" had ruled and civil servants had
gone about their work "honestly and dutifully."[35] Again and again,
Hitler directed his audience's attention to the "great heroic time of
1914,"[36] when the German people, unified as seldom before, had been
dragged into a war forced upon them by the Entente powers. This
idealised vision of the past allowed Hitler to paint the present day
in hues that were all the darker. Everywhere you looked now, there
was only decline and decay. "Why do we stand today amidst the
ruins of the Reich Bismarck created so brilliantly?" Hitler asked in
a speech in January 1921, on the fiftieth anniversary of the founding
of the German Reich.[37] His answer was always the same: the revolution of 1918–19 had been Germany's downfall, casting it into slavery.[38]
Those primarily responsible were Jews and leftists whom he described

as "revolutionary" or "November criminals."[39] They had undermined Germany's armed forces, cheating the country of the victory it had earned and delivering it up helplessly to its enemies. "The 'utterly fearless' army was 'stabbed from behind' by 'Jew-socialists' bribed with Jewish money," was how a USPD pamphlet cited a statement by Hitler at a meeting in the Hofbräuhaus in April 1920.[40] Paul von Hindenburg and Erich Ludendorff, the former heads of the Third Supreme Command, had launched the stab-in-the-back legend during an effectively staged appearance before the investigations committee of the German National Assembly in November 1919. This myth then became a constant component within the propaganda arsenal of right-wing nationalists.[41]

Polemical attacks on the Treaty of Versailles occupied a central position in Hitler's campaigns, playing upon widespread bitterness about what was perceived as a shameful and humiliating peace. The conditions of the treaty, Hitler repeatedly hammered into his listeners' heads, were "unfulfillable," since they stripped Germany down to its "last shirt" and condemned it to "serfdom" for the foreseeable future. A peace had been dictated to the German people, Hitler raged, such as had "never been seen before in 6,000 years of human history." Compared with Versailles, the Treaty of Brest-Litovsk, which Imperial Germany had dictated to revolutionary Russia in March 1918, had been "child's play."[42] That was a crass reversal of actual fact: the terms of the Treaty of Versailles had been relatively mild compared with those that the Soviet government had been forced to accept.

Hitler combined his agitation against the Versailles Treaty with hateful attacks on the Weimar Republic and its leading representatives. By turns he excoriated Germany's new democratic order as a "republic of scoundrels," a "Berlin Jew government" and a "criminal republic."[43] In his eyes all democratic politicians, including Reich President Friedrich Ebert, were incompetent and corrupt. Playing upon Ebert's training as a saddler, a profession that included mattress-making, Hitler said of Germany: "Ripped and torn, full of holes and defective in every sense, with coils sticking out and ruptured knots, it is in extreme need of restoration. But one particular aspect of our Reich mattress stands out above all, Herr Ebert. It's full of lice, completely full of lice."[44] Hitler defamed former Reich Finance Minister Erzberger as "a typical new-fangled German state criminal."[45] In early 1922, he turned his hateful sights on Foreign Minister Rathenau, whom he accused of "betraying and selling out the German people" by making concessions to the victorious Allies.[46] This was very much in the spirit of the nationalist campaign of defamation against "fulfilment politicians"— those leaders who thought Germany should live up to its commitments in the Treaty of Versailles; Hitler's tirades further contributed to the poisonous atmosphere in which both Erzberger and Rathenau were murdered. According to Hitler, Weimar Germany's elected representatives were tools of "international stock-market and interest capital," which held Germany in its clutches and was sucking the lifeblood out of the country.[47] The once-so-successful Reich had thereby been reduced, he claimed, to "a colony of global capital and its henchmen . . . and hopelessly condemned to slavery."[48]

But the political demagogue did not just adopt and magnify the worries and resentments of his audience. In the Nazi Party's twenty-five-point manifesto Hitler also offered hope for the future. "Our most effective criticism is our programme," he noted before a speech in August 1920. "Its brevity. Our will."[49] Even in his earliest speeches, Hitler vowed to annul the Treaty of Versailles: "As soon as we have the power, we'll rip up this scrap of paper."[50] He made no bones of his view that economic recovery depended upon "smashing interest slavery."[51] The goal of "national rebirth" meant, externally, the creation of a "greater Germany" and, internally, the foundation of an "ethnic community" (*Volksgemeinschaft*) that abolished the chasm between the bourgeoisie and the working class.[52] "We must become a people of honest hard workers," Hitler proclaimed.

> And to do that, we can't have any classes any more, no bourgeois and no workers. We need to become a people of brothers, who are prepared to make sacrifices for the national cause . . . There should be no drivel about classes and no preferment of one segment of the people in national questions . . . People who work with their heads and those who work with their hands need to realise that they belong together and that only together can we get our people back on their feet again.[53]

That, Hitler said again and again, was the path "to genuine, German socialism in contrast to the class-warfare socialism preached by Jewish leaders."[54]

Right from the start, Hitler wanted to eradicate Weimar democracy. "Let's do away with the party graft that divides our people," he exclaimed in April 1920. On this topic, too, he called upon widespread anti-democratic and anti-parliamentarian sentiments. He never tired of preaching the merits of "a relentless battle against this entire parliamentary brood, this whole system."[55] Democracy was to be replaced with "a government of power and authority" that would "ruthlessly clean out the pigsty."[56] When he demanded a "dictator who is also a genius . . . a man of iron who is the embodiment today of the Germanic spirit," Hitler was speaking to the hearts of his audience.[57] Germany, he declared in May 1921, "will only be able to live if the pigsty of Jewish corruption, democratic hypocrisy and socialist betrayal is swept clean by an iron broom—and that broom will be made in Bavaria."[58] Hitler made no secret about what he would do with the post-war revolutionaries. "We demand a German national court, before which all the men of 1918 and 1919 can be held responsible," he thundered. The police report of a Hitler speech in September 1922 noted "minutes of frenetic applause" after he demanded "a final reckoning with the November criminals."[59]

Reading through Hitler's speeches from the period 1920–22, it seems amazing that he attracted larger and larger audiences with such repeated mantra-like phrases. But perhaps it was the monotonous repetition of his accusations, vows of revenge and promises for the future that was the key to his success.[60] In the chapter in *Mein Kampf* that focuses on propaganda, Hitler wrote:

> The receptivity of large masses is very limited. Their capacity to understand things is slight whereas their forgetfulness is great. Given this, effective propaganda must restrict itself to a handful of points, which it repeats as slogans as long as it takes for the dumbest member of the audience to get an idea of what they mean.[61]

Hitler's analysis was hardly original. In fact, it recalled a pre-war book by the Frenchman Gustave Le Bon entitled *The Psychology of the Masses*, which by 1919 was in its third edition. Like Hitler, Le Bon described the masses as stupid, egotistical, feminine, fickle, incapable of accepting criticism and ruled by uncontrollable urges.[62] Hitler presumably became acquainted with Le Bon's ideas through a book by the Munich neurologist J. R. Rossbach called *The Soul of the Masses*, which appeared in 1919 and quoted the Frenchman extensively.[63]

Ironically, therefore, the beer-cellar rabble-rouser, who liked to depict himself as a man of the people, in fact despised the masses, which he regarded as nothing more than a tool to be manipulated to achieve his political ambitions. In this respect, too, Hitler was no exception, but rather a mouthpiece of the cultural pessimism represented in particular by the authors associated with the "conservative revolution" in the Weimar Republic.[64] Nonetheless, unlike those theoreticians, Hitler knew how to draw a mass audience, and that in turn attracted the interest of nationalistic conservatives. As the doctor and "racial hygiene" expert Max von Gruber, who like many Munich University professors was an early Nazi sympathiser, recalled: "In upper-middle-class circles, one looked on with delight as Hitler achieved what we could not: winning over the circles of the little people and undermining Social Democracy. We overlooked the dangers his demagoguery presented, were it ever to be successful. The cure was worse than the disease."[65]

A central motif running through almost all of Hitler's speeches was his declaration of war on the Jews. From the very beginning, he treated this topic in the most radical of terms. One vivid example was his speech "Why are we anti-Semites?," given in the Hofbräuhaus on 20 August 1920 in front of 2,000 people. It is the only speech from Hitler's first year as a political propagandist that has been preserved in its entirety.[66] It contains all of the anti-Jewish stereotypes Hitler had picked up in his autodidactic study of works such as Richard Wagner's "Judaism in Music" (1850), Houston Stewart Chamberlain's *Foundations of the Nineteenth Century* (1899), Theodor Fritsch's *Handbook on the Jewish Question* (1907) and Adolf Wahrmund's *The Law of the Nomad and Today's Jewish Domination* (1887).[67] All in all, the speech was a murky mixture of pseudo-scientific and vulgar anti-Semitic clichés.

Hitler began his address with the contention that, unlike the northern European Aryan races, Jews were incapable of any productive work and cultural achievement. Because they had never been able to form a state, they had no alternative but to live as "nomads . . . parasites on the bodies of other peoples . . . as a race within other races and a state within other states." Driven by their two most prominent racial characteristics, "Mammonism and materialism," they had accumulated enormous wealth "without putting in the sweat and effort required of all other mortals." With that, Hitler arrived at his favourite subject, international "interest and stock-market capital," which dominated "practically the entire world . . . with sums of money growing beyond all measure and—what's worst—with the effect of corrupting all honest work." The National Socialists, Hitler claimed, had come forth to combat this destructive force by "awakening, augmenting and inciting the instinctual antipathy of our people for Jewry." As he had previously argued in his letter to Adolf Gemlich in September 1919, Hitler defined his ultimate, unchangeable goal as "the removal of Jews from our people."

The police report noted that Hitler was rewarded with lengthy applause and calls of approval at this juncture. All in all, he was interrupted fifty-six times during his two-hour speech by positive audience outbursts. It seems that he had precisely tapped into the anti-Semitic mood that had spread like a highly contagious fever through the Bavarian capital after the demise of the soviet republic. A reporter sent to the event by the Social Democratic *Münchener Post* newspaper wrote: "You have to grant Hitler one thing: he's the cagiest of the rabble-rousers plying their unholy trade in Munich at the moment."[68]

It was a small step from global "stock-market and interest capital" holding Germany in its vice-like grip to the nightmare of a "worldwide Jewish conspiracy." With the publication in German of the *Protocols of the Elders of Zion* in 1919, conspiracy theory had become a stock element of ethnic-chauvinistic German propaganda. This pamphlet, which soon ran through 100,000 copies, contained fake reports about alleged secret meetings at the first Zionist Congress in Basle, Switzerland, in 1897, which had supposedly yielded strategies for establishing global Jewish dominance. In his notes for a meeting on 12 August 1921, Hitler mentioned the *Protocols* for the first time.[69] A report on a speech Hitler gave on 21 August 1921 in Rosenheim, where the first NSDAP chapter outside Munich had been founded on 18 April 1920, also read: "Hitler shows from the book *The Elders of Zion* . . . that establishing their rule, by whatever means, has always been and will always be the Semites' goal."[70]

By 1920 at the latest, the supposed Jewish drive to rule the world had become a fixed part of Hitler's world view. "The only Jewish goal—global domination," Hitler noted in early December. By

September 1921, he was jotting down: "The question of questions, Jewry's struggle for world domination, it's a new crime." The conclusions Hitler drew from this idea were unambiguous, and he repeatedly and unmistakably shared them with his audiences: "The German people can only be free and healthy if it is liberated from Jewish bandits." The "resolution of the Jewish question" was "the main issue" for National Socialists.[71] Thus even in the early 1920s, no resident of Munich who had attended a Hitler speech or read about one in the newspapers could have been in any doubt about what Hitler intended to do with the Jews. But hardly anyone seems to have disapproved. On the contrary, storms of applause greeted precisely the most anti-Semitic passages of Hitler's speeches, strongly suggesting that they were the source of much of the speaker's appeal. When he demanded that Jews be "removed" from Germany by some unspecified means, therefore, Hitler and his audience were on the same wavelength. Both were carried away by the racist wishful thinking of a fully homogenous ethnic community.

There is a further, previously unknown indication that Hitler's hateful anti-Semitic tirades were not just a populist strategy but reflected the core of his political convictions. In August 1920, Hitler received a visit from a young Munich law student, Heinrich Heim, who would later go on to be a ministerial counsel and an adjutant of Martin Bormann, responsible for taking notes during Hitler's monologues in his headquarters. Hitler had made an "extraordinarily good" impression on him, Heim reported in a letter. He had been "friendly and earnest, a deep, distinguished character blessed with the strongest will." As far as the "Jewish question" was concerned, Heim describes Hitler's views as follows:

One has to root out the bacterium in order to restore the body's natural defences. As long as the Jew remains active it will not be possible to break down the masses into rational individuals . . . and make them immune to his influence. He utterly rules out a Germanification of Jews in a larger or smaller sense. As long as Jews remain with their pernicious effects, Germany cannot convalesce. When it comes to the existence or non-existence of a people, one cannot draw a line at the lives of blinkered ethnic comrades and even less so at the lives of a hostile, dangerous, foreign tribe.[72]

Hitler would cling to his conviction that his battle against Jews was a matter of life or death right up until his suicide in his bunker in Berlin in late April 1945. In Vienna he had got to know anti-Semitic clichés and prejudices without identifying with them. Imperial Germany's military defeat, which nationalist circles explained by scapegoating Jews in particular, no doubt also reinforced Private Hitler's anti-Semitic leanings. But it was the experience of left-wing revolution and right-wing counter-revolution in Munich in 1918 and 1919 which vehemently radicalised anti-Jewish resentment in the Bavarian capital and made Hitler into what he would remain for the rest of his life: a fanatic anti-Semite whose primary political mission was to expunge a "dangerous, foreign tribe."

Even after Hitler was discharged from the military in late March 1920, Captain Mayr kept supporting his protégé wherever he could. In September 1920, Mayr wrote to Wolfgang Kapp, the unsuccessful leader of the putsch who had fled to Sweden, that the NSDAP should "provide the basis for the strong assault troop we envision." The party's programme, he conceded, was "somewhat amateurish and full of holes," but it would get better, and he had assembled a number of "very capable young men," above all Hitler, who was "a motivational force" and a "first-rate popular speaker." Mayr concluded his letter by pointing out that the National Socialists' Munich chapter now had 2,000 members, compared to fewer than a hundred in the summer of 1919.[73]

In late March 1920, Mayr had arranged for Hitler and the right-wing journalist Dietrich Eckart to fly to Berlin to support the provisional government declared by the putsch, but they arrived after the attempted coup d'état had already collapsed. "The way you look and talk—people are going to laugh at you," was the alleged reaction of Captain Waldemar Pabst, one of the men behind the murders of Communist leaders Rosa Luxemburg and Karl Liebknecht in January 1919 and a co-organiser of the 1920 putsch, when he saw Hitler and Eckart.[74] Pabst would not be alone in underestimating Hitler. Indeed, the fact that the conservative elites often failed to appreciate Hitler's ability to influence people and get his way was a major factor in his success.

Dietrich Eckart was more than Hitler's travelling companion: he was one of the most important mentors of his early political career. Eckart was twenty years Hitler's senior, and Ernst Hanfstaengl remembered him as "a perfect example of an old-fashioned Bavarian with the appearance of a walrus."[75] Eckart had unsuccessfully tried to make a career for himself as a playwright in pre-war Berlin but his only success had been a translation of Ibsen's *Peer Gynt*. In 1915, he moved to Munich and joined the city's pan-Germanic and nationalist circles. Beginning in December 1918, with the support of the Thule Society, he began publishing the magazine *Auf gut deutsch* (In Plain-spoken German), which soon became a platform for anti-Semitic authors. In August 1919, he gave a lecture to the members of the DAP, although he never joined either that party or the NSDAP. He met Hitler sometime in the winter of 1919–20 and liked what he saw, although it is no doubt a legend that the first time Eckart encountered Hitler, he proclaimed, "That's Germany's next great man—one day the whole world will talk about him."[76] But he did immediately appreciate Hitler's extraordinary rhetorical gift and his immense appeal to the masses. Testifying to the Munich police after the Beer Hall Putsch in November 1923, Eckart said that he had recognised right from the start that Hitler was "the right man for the whole movement."[77]

The two men developed a close, almost symbiotic relationship. As Joachim Fest noted, Eckart was "the first person from an educated, upper-middle-class background whose presence Hitler could tolerate without his deep-seated complexes breaking out."[78] Eckart helped the 30-year-old, who was eager to learn and still malleable, write his first print articles. "Stylistically I was still an infant," Hitler would later admit.[79] Eckart also encouraged his anti-Semitic convictions and opened the doors to wealthy Munich personages. Last but not least, he supported Hitler and the NSDAP financially. In December 1920, Eckart allowed the party to use his house and property as security for a 60,000-mark Reichswehr fund loan in order to acquire the *Völkischer Beobachter*.[80] Hitler was effusive in his expressions of gratitude: "Without your helpful intervention, this would not have worked. Indeed, I believe that our prospects of acquiring a newspaper would have been postponed for many months. I am so attached to the movement in body and soul that you can hardly imagine how happy I am at achieving a goal we have desired for so long."[81] In October 1921, after he had been made editor-in-chief of the *Völkischer Beobachter*, Eckart reciprocated with a copy of his *Peer Gynt* translation dedicated to his "dear friend" Adolf Hitler.[82]

Their relationship dramatically cooled in the course of 1922, however. The more confident and composed Hitler became, the less need he had for a political mentor. In March 1923, Hitler transferred the editorship of the *Völkischer Beobachter* to Alfred Rosenberg. Nonetheless, Hitler maintained fond memories of his friend, who died of a heart attack in late December 1923. The second volume of *Mein Kampf* concludes with an elegy to the man, "who was one of the best and who devoted his life to awakening his and our people with his writing, his thinking and, finally, his deeds."[83] Years later, Hitler confided to his secretary Christa Schroeder that he had never again found a friend with whom he felt so deeply connected in "a harmony of thinking and feeling." His friendship with Eckart was "one of the best things he had experienced in the 1920s."[84] In his monologues, Hitler deemed Eckart's services "imperishable," honouring him as "a guiding light of the early National Socialist movement."[85]

Dietrich Eckart was the man who introduced Hitler to Alfred Rosenberg. Born in 1893 in Russian Reval (today's Tallinn) as the son of a merchant, Rosenberg completed a degree in architecture in Moscow during the war. In November 1918 he moved to Munich, where he became part of the so-called "Baltic Mafia," alongside Riga-born Max Erwin von Scheubner-Richter and the illustrator of chauvinistic pamphlets Otto von Kursell.[86] In Moscow Rosenberg had experienced the Russian Revolution first-hand and considered it the work of Jews. The first article he wrote for Eckart's *Auf gut deutsch* bore the headline "The Russian-Jewish Revolution." One of his first works, *Russia's Gravediggers*, began with a passage programmatically entitled "Jewish Bolshevism" which clearly defined the enemy with which Rosenberg was obsessed and which he continued to attack in countless publications. His 1922 book *Plague in Russia* explicitly aimed at opening his contemporaries' eyes to the gruesomeness of the "Jewish-Bolshevik experiment."

Rosenberg's nightmare scenarios had a huge impact on Hitler. Beginning in the summer of 1920, Hitler's speeches clearly reveal that he began to see revolutionary Russia through the lens of Rosenberg's writings and with reference to the *idée fixe* of a global Jewish conspiracy. "Russia has been completely abandoned to starvation and misery," Hitler proclaimed in June 1920, "and no one is to blame but the Jews." By the end of that month, Hitler was arguing that Bolshevism actually brought about the opposite of what it promised: "Those who are on top in Russia are not the workers but, without exception, Hebrews." Hitler spoke of a "Jewish dictatorship" and a "Moscow Jew government" sucking the life out of the Russian people and called on the NSDAP to become "a battering ram of German character" against the "dirty flood of Jewish Bolshevism."[87] Hitler's anti-Semitism had initially contained a strain of anti-capitalism. Now it acquired an additional, anti-Bolshevist dimension. With that, the later German dictator's world view was essentially complete.

Along with Eckart and Rosenberg, the university student Rudolf Hess was a party member of the first hour, but he did not provide political advice or ideological slogans: he was one of the still-rare breed of Hitler disciples. Born in 1894 in Alexandria as the son of a wealthy German merchant, Hess had also volunteered for military service in 1914 and experienced the end of the war as a pilot in a fighting squadron on the Western Front. Typically for his generation, Hess had trouble readjusting to civilian life. He joined the Thule Society and helped overthrow the Bavarian Soviet Republic as part of Franz Ritter von Epp's Freikorps. He, too, met Hitler through Eckart, and in early June 1920 he became a member of the NSDAP. While still enrolled at the University of Munich, where he studied with, among others, the professor of geography and originator of geopolitics, Karl Haushofer, he became one of Hitler's most devoted followers. "I spend nearly every day with Hitler," he told his parents in September 1920, and the following April he wrote to his cousin: "Hitler . . . has become a dear friend. A splendid person! . . . He comes from a humble background and has acquired a vast knowledge on his own, which I greatly admire." Hess described what attracted him to Hitler's political programme as follows: "His fundamental idea is to build a bridge between various classes of the people and to establish socialism on a national basis. That of course automatically includes battling against Jewry."[88]

In May 1921, Hess accompanied Hitler as an NSDAP delegation was invited to exchange ideas with President von Kahr—a clear signal that the Bavarian government was beginning to take the National Socialists seriously as a political force. Hitler declared that his only mission was "to convert radical workers to a nationalist frame of mind" and asked that he be allowed to continue his work "undisturbed." Kahr was

impressed. "These warmly made and upstanding, truthful declarations," the president wrote in his unpublished memoirs, made an
"excellent impression."[89] After that meeting, without Hitler's knowledge, Hess wrote a long letter to Kahr in which he praised the NSDAP's
propagandist as someone who combined "a rare sensitivity for the
public mood, keen political instincts and enormous strength of will."
That, Hess explained, was why Hitler had so quickly become "an
equally feared and respected personality in political battles and a man
whose power extended much further than the public suspects." Hess
concluded his letter with the words: "He is a rare, scrupulously honourable and pure character, full of deeply felt goodness: he is religious
and a good Catholic. He has only one goal: the welfare of the country."[90]

Not all of the leading members of the NSDAP shared Hess's worshipful
enthusiasm. For many, Hitler's industriousness was a thorn in their
sides. Some were jealous, while others feared that his activism and the
blunt nature of his propaganda were leading the party down a political
dead end. In the spring of 1921, tension increased within the leadership. The main issue was the NSDAP's efforts to merge with like-
minded ethnic-chauvinist parties and groups. One of the first targets
was the German Socialist Party (Deutsche Sozialistische Partei, or
DSP) which had been founded, also under the patronage of the Thule
Society, by the mechanical engineer Alfred Brunner. Its programme
scarcely differed from that of the NSDAP. The DSP also advocated the
idea of a nationalist socialism to combat "Jewish" capitalism, although
their anti-Semitism was less aggressive and their activity extended to
northern Germany instead of being virtually restricted to Munich and
Bavaria. By mid-1920 the DSP had 35 local chapters with 2,000 members.
Like the NSDAP, it was little more than a fringe party on the far right;
it seemed only logical for the two to join forces.[91]

Previously, the NSDAP had insisted on maintaining its independence
and had rebuffed all attempts by the DSP to make contact. Nonetheless,
in early August 1920, at a conference of national socialists from
Germany, Austria and Czechoslovakia in Salzburg, an agreement
seemed to be in the offing. A coordination committee was established
to pave the way for the merger. Hitler, who spoke at Salzburg, had
apparently succumbed to the enthusiasm for unity. In any case, he
carried with him a card signed by party chairman Drexler, which

proudly announced "the unification of all national socialists in the German-language realm."[92] But the NSDAP's propagandist quickly distanced himself from the Salzburg agreements. In January 1921, he summarised his reasons for opposing the fusion of the NSDAP with the DSP. By founding so many local chapters, Hitler argued, the DSP had "so splintered its strength that it's everywhere and nowhere at once." He also criticised it "for losing itself in the democratic principle," because the party had been willing to participate in parliamentary elections. By contrast Hitler demanded that the NSDAP rely on radical, anti-parliamentarian mass propaganda.[93]

Not all of the NSDAP's leaders agreed. Indeed, the majority felt that the prospects for the merger with the DSP had not been exhausted and shared the DSP's frustration with "the fanatic upstart" who was trying to put the brakes on the fusion of the two parties.[94] In late March 1921, Drexler made a surprise appearance at the DSP party conference in the town of Zeitz and provisionally agreed to sanction a merger. The leadership of the unified party would move to Berlin. Hitler, who had not been consulted, was outraged, threatening to resign from the party if the plan was carried out. He succeeded in postponing the decision, but the issue remained up in the air. Indeed, in the spring of 1921, Hitler was neither able nor willing to take the drastic steps needed to resolve it. His behaviour during this period bears all the hallmarks of uncertainty and indecisiveness. He interpreted the unfamiliar resistance from the party leadership, including Drexler, as a personal attack and was correspondingly thin-skinned. "As a man who still mistrusted himself and his prospects, he was full of inferiority complexes towards all those who had already become something or were about to surpass him," former Freikorps leader Gerhard Rossbach recalled. "He was subservient and uncertain, often crude when he felt he was being curtailed."[95]

Hitler opposed all attempts to fuse ethnic-nationalist parties because he was afraid of losing the starring role his rhetorical skills had earned him in the NSDAP. Soon he also felt threatened from another quarter, the German Works Association, which was founded in March 1921 by the Augsburg University lecturer Otto Dickel. Dickel had created a stir in far-right circles with his book *The Resurrection of the West*, a reply to Oswald Spengler's *The Decline of the West*.[96] In June 1921, while Hitler was in Berlin with Eckart trying to raise funds for the chronically underfunded NSDAP, the party invited Dickel to hold a lecture in the Hofbräuhaus, the site of Hitler's greatest triumphs. Here Dickel met with an enthusiastic response, and a subsequent party newsletter welcomed the arrival of another "popular and powerful speaker."[97]

A party meeting was arranged in Augsburg for 10 July to discuss merging with both the Nuremberg chapter of the DSP and Dickel's German Works Association. Hitler got wind of the discussion while still in Berlin and arrived in Augsburg in advance of the NSDAP delegation and threatened to prevent "any form of unification." During the three hours of discussions, Hitler repeatedly exploded in anger, ultimately storming out of the hall in a rage, much to the embarrassment of his party comrades. He resigned from the NSDAP the following day.[98]

Hitler's emotional reaction is understandable: he saw his political existence threatened. The fact that a lecturer with a doctorate seemed about to steal his thunder must have summoned up all of the hatred for teachers and professors he had accumulated in Linz and Vienna. In a letter of 5 January 1922 to the tiny NSDAP chapter in Hanover, Hitler would express his "profound satisfaction" that the group had eventually rebuffed Dickel and his organisation: "Your negative opinion of our so-called educated people, who take every idiot down this precarious path, is unfortunately all too justified . . . A Dr. Dickel who is simultaneously a Works Association mouthpiece and a scion of the West is of no importance to us. On the other hand, a Dickel who claims to be a National Socialist, if only in his mind, is an enemy and needs to be combated."[99]

Hitler's reaction to his perceived competition presaged how he would later behave in crisis situations.[100] He was risking everything. After humming and hawing for months about fundamental decisions, he suddenly issued an "all or nothing" ultimatum—in the hope that he would be able to blackmail the party leadership. It is possible that Hitler's political career could have ended abruptly in June 1921, had Eckart not intervened. Anton Drexler, who was torn between his distaste for Hitler's prima donna posturing and his fear of losing his biggest public draw, eventually relented and asked Hitler under what circumstances he would return to the party.

That gave Hitler the chance to turn the situation to his advantage in one fell swoop, and he seized the opportunity. On 14 July, he told the party committee that he would only rejoin the organisation if six conditions were "strictly fulfilled." Hitler demanded that an extraordinary party conference be called within a week, at which he would put himself forward as "chairman with dictatorial powers of responsibility," in order to carry out, with the help of a newly formed action committee, "a ruthless cleansing of the party of all those elements that have intruded upon it." He also demanded that Munich be irrevocably declared the "seat of the movement," that no changes in the name of the party and its programme be permitted for the span of six years, and that all efforts to merge with other parties cease immediately. Those who wanted to cooperate with the NSDAP would have to join it, negotiations would require Hitler's personal approval, and he alone would choose the negotiators. Never again did Hitler want to be overruled and isolated by the majority of the party leadership. His sixth and final demand was that the NSDAP boycott a meeting planned for August in Linz that was intended as a follow-up to the conference in Salzburg the year before.[101] Hitler claimed that he was not making his demands because he was thirsty for power, but because without "iron leadership" the NSDAP would soon cease to be a party fighting for national socialism. In reality of course, Hitler was clearly demonstrating that side of his personality which had already emerged when he booted Karl Harrer out of the DAP in January 1920. Hitler's goal was unlimited power and that meant, first of all, achieving an unrestricted leadership role within his own party.

The majority of the committee members acceded to Hitler's demands because they thought the party could not do without him. In recognition of his "enormous knowledge, his sacrifices for and contributions to the growth of the movement and his rare rhetorical gift," the committee was willing to grant him dictatorial powers. It was "utterly delighted" that Hitler wanted to take over the position of chairman, which Drexler had repeatedly offered him.[102] On 26 July, Hitler rejoined the NSDAP as member number 3,680.

Hitler's adversaries did not give up without a fight, however. On the morning of 29 July, the day of the extraordinary party conference, they circulated a pamphlet entitled "Adolf Hitler—Traitor?" It argued that Hitler's lust for power and personal ambition had seduced him into sowing "dissent and fragmentation" within the party, playing into the hands of "Jewry and its helpers." It accused Hitler of trying to use the party as a springboard for corrupt purposes and "of trying to grab sole power for himself so that he could push the party in a completely different direction when the moment was right." Hitler was a "demagogue," whose only talent was his speaking ability. He also fought in "true Jewish fashion" by twisting the facts. The pamphlet urged party members to resist "this interloping megalomaniac and bigmouth."[103] A poster made by the anti-Hitler faction but prohibited by the Munich police contained the words: "The tyrant must be deposed. And we will not rest until we've seen the last of 'His Majesty Adolf I,' the current 'King of Munich.'"[104] The *Münchener Post* gleefully reprinted the pamphlet.

Hitler's adversaries played right into his hands. When he took to the stage of the Hofbräuhaus that night to excoriate the anonymous authors of the pamphlet, Hitler was applauded "almost without end." He said he had filed legal charges against his opponents and denied—falsely—that he had ever sought to become party chairman, claiming that he had only given in to a request by Drexler.[105] The 554 party members in attendance unanimously voted Hitler into that position. Drexler was shunted off into the office of honorary chairman. They also approved Hitler's amendments to the party charter, which gave the chairman "directorial responsibility," thereby cementing Hitler's claim to absolute leadership.[106]

The "Führer party" was born, as was the stylised image of Hitler as the leader of the movement. "No one could have served a cause . . . more selflessly, sacrificially, passionately and honestly," Dietrich Eckart wrote in the *Völkischer Beobachter* on 4 August. Hitler's "iron fist," he gushed, had put an end to the "spectre" haunting the party. "What else is needed to show that he deserves our trust and to what extent?" Eckart asked.[107] Hess also took Hitler's critics to task: "Can you really be so blind as not to see that this man alone has the leadership personality enabling him to wage the battle? Do you really think that the masses would pack Zirkus Krone without him?"[108]

A few days after grabbing party power, Hitler founded his own paramilitary organisation: the SA. The beginnings of the National Socialist storm troopers lie in 1920, when the DAP/NSDAP began to organise security for their meetings to prevent them from being disrupted by "Marxist hecklers." Later that year the security forces became the NSDAP's "gymnastics and sports division." The growth of the organisation was accelerated by the dissolution of the Bavarian citizens' militias, to which President von Kahr had been forced to agree by the Allies and the Reich government. Most of the militiamen joined "patriotic" associations like the League of Bavaria and the Reich, which considered themselves home-front defence organisations, but some also went into the Nazi Party's Security Service. Now, in early August 1921, Hitler ordered that the "gymnastics and sports division" be transformed into the party's battle-ready army. Its mission was to "put its strength as a battering ram at the disposal of the movement" and to "embody the idea of a free people defending itself."[109]

A key figure in this development was Reichswehr Captain Ernst Röhm. Born in 1887 as the son of a railway official, Röhm was a typical front-line officer who had trouble adjusting to civilian life after 1918. He had been wounded three times during the war: a bit of shrapnel had taken off half his nose, and his cheek bore the scars of a grazing shot. His dismay at Germany's defeat and the left-wing revolution led him to align himself with the counter-revolutionary forces; like Hess he was one of the activists of the Epp Freikorps. In late 1919, he became member number 623 of the DAP and he soon came into close contact with Hitler: he was one of the few party comrades allowed to address Hitler informally after he became Führer.

Röhm replaced Mayr as Hitler's most important connection to the Reichswehr. As a staff officer in the Epp Brigade, as the Freikorps was known after it had been absorbed into the regular military, he supplied the citizens' militias with weapons, ammunition and military hardware, and after the militias were disbanded, he ensured that these were not turned over to the Allies. Röhm thus had a secret arsenal at his disposal, which could be distributed as needed to paramilitary organisations.[110] He now played a central role in transforming the *Sturmabteilung* (SA), as it became known in September 1921, into precisely such an organisation. "You too shall be trained as a storm troop," Hitler told his SA men in October 1921. "We must be strong not only in words, but in deeds against our enemy, the Jew."[111] Starting in the autumn of 1921, the SA not only protected NSDAP events but began disrupting those of the Nazis' political enemies and beating up Jews on the streets.[112] Even years later, Hitler still felt compelled to defend the SA's use of violence. Politics back then was "made on the street," he proclaimed in one of his monologues as Führer, saying that he had explicitly sought out people with no scruples about behaving brutally.[113]

The SA spread fear and terror throughout Munich. In mid-September 1921, they broke up a meeting of the Bavaria League in the Löwenbräukeller, battering the organisation's leader, engineer Otto Ballerstedt, and throwing him off the stage so that his head started bleeding.[114] That had legal consequences. In January 1922, Hitler was sentenced to three months in Stadelheim prison for inciting public violence, although he only ended up serving a little more than a month, from 24 June to 27 July. "At least he has a cell to himself," Hess reported. "He can work, make his own food, receive visitors twice a week . . . and read newspapers. The peace and quiet is good for his nerves and his voice."[115]

In September 1921 Gustav von Kahr resigned as president after deputies in the Bavarian Landtag, including those from his own party, the BVP, withdrew their support for him. Police President Pöhner, one of Hitler's most determined supporters, also left office. Under Kahr's successor, Count Hugo Lerchenfeld-Köfering, relations between Berlin and Munich improved somewhat, and the Munich police began to pay more attention to the activities of the NSDAP and the SA. In late October, Hitler was summoned and told that he could face deportation from Bavaria if he did not keep his men under control. He pledged "to do everything in his power to head off unrest."[116] That was an empty promise. On 4 November, a pitched battle took place in the Hofbräuhaus, with the SA brutally throwing protestors, largely left-wing workers, out of the beer hall. "My heart almost cries out with joy when I recall the old battle experiences," Hitler wrote in *Mein Kampf*.[117] Nazi propaganda later transformed "the Battle of the Hofbräuhaus" into a trial by fire for the SA. In any case, the violence paid off. The NSDAP's political enemies were intimidated, and SA gangs unabashedly roamed Munich's streets. "We'll beat our way to the top" was one of their slogans.[118] Even Reich President Friedrich Ebert got a taste of the Nazis' domination of Munich's public spaces when he paid an official visit to the Bavarian capital on 12 and 13 June 1922. No sooner had he arrived at the train station than he was yelled and spat at. The British consul general reported that Ebert was booed wherever he went and that there was no state guard or raising of flags in his honour.[119]

In the wake of Walther Rathenau's murder on 24 June 1922, relations between Berlin and Munich deteriorated again. One day after it had been passed by the Reichstag, the Bavarian government lifted Ebert's Law on the Protection of the Republic, which allowed the state to ban organisations that called for political assassinations or tried to overthrow democracy. In its stead, a new ordinance was proclaimed, whose most important provision was that Bavarian criminals should not be brought up in front of the new Republic Criminal Court in Leipzig. Still Bavaria's far-right-wing associations thought that Munich had made too many concessions to Berlin, and on 16 August they staged a major demonstration on Munich's Königsplatz. The NSDAP marched to it in closed-rank formation, led by the SA. Hitler, the event's second speaker, pilloried the attempt to "subject Bavaria to Berlin's course" and demanded an "extraordinary law . . . against international exploitation and usury."[120] By then it was abundantly clear that the beer-cellar rabble-rouser and his movement could no longer be ignored as a major player on the political Right.

The growing Nazi influence was even more apparent at a "Germany Day" event staged by the Union of Fatherland Associations in the northern Bavarian city of Coburg on 14 and 15 October 1922. Hitler had been invited to speak, and he arrived in a specially chartered train with 800 SA men. City leaders asked him to help avoid confrontations with left-wing groups by not entering the city in closed formation accompanied by marching music, but Hitler refused. The inevitable followed. The SA's martial posturing provoked pitched street battles in which the storm troopers showed that they deserved their reputation as brutal thugs. In the end, Hitler crowed in *Mein Kampf,* "there wasn't a trace of anything red left on the streets."[121] Coburg would become a Nazi hotspot, and Germany's later Reich chancellor ordered a special medal to be made up for those who had participated in the orgy of violence.

Such undeniable propaganda successes helped the NSDAP expand. Local Nazi chapters were founded in a number of cities and towns beyond Munich.[122] In October 1922 Julius Streicher, who like Hitler was a rabid anti-Semite, subordinated his Nuremberg chapter of the German Works Community to the NSDAP. With that, the DSP's resistance to being swallowed by Hitler's party dissolved. Hitler's insistence that others join *him* had proved a success. By the end of 1922, the NSDAP had around 20,000 members, and its radius of action now went beyond Bavaria's borders.[123] The party's new headquarters at Corneliusstrasse 12, which had replaced the old Sterneckerbräu ones in November 1921, were an increasingly busy hive of various types of activity.

Most of the new party members came from the lower middle classes. The largest group were artisans (20 per cent) followed by small businessmen and shopkeepers (13.6), white-collar workers (11.1) and farmers (10.4). Unskilled labourers represented only 9.5 per cent, and specialised workers 8.5.[124] The NSDAP was thus essentially a middle-class movement, and the proportion of university graduates, students and professors in Munich was striking.[125] Conversely, despite the fact that their propaganda was explicitly directed at blue-collar workers, the Nazis did not do well with that demographic group. In a letter to Reichswehr Major Konstantin Hierl in July 1920, Hitler admitted that it was "difficult to win over workers who have belonged to the same [socialist] organisations for decades." Nonetheless, Hitler reiterated that the NSDAP's goal was to become "a popular movement not a class organisation."[126] But in 1922, the party was far from achieving that aim, no matter how Hess may have tried to give the contrary impression in a description of a Hitler appearance in Zirkus Krone. Hess did, however, provide a clear vision of the Nazi ideal: "The blue-collar worker sits next to the factory owner, and the judge next to the hansom cab driver. Nowhere do you see a scene like this nowadays." There was no way of holding back Nazism, Hess predicted, because it is "born itself of the working classes."[127]

The sarcastic nickname coined by his enemies, the "King of Munich," was becoming an ever more accurate description of Hitler's status. But his private life remained carefully concealed from inquisitive eyes. Since May 1920, Hitler had lived in a room on Thierschstrasse 41, which had been allocated to him by the Munich housing authority. For the woman who sub-let him the room, he was an ideal tenant. He always paid his rent and telephone bills on time, seldom had female visitors and did not draw much attention to himself.[128] The gaunt young man also seemed not to attach much importance to his appearance. Mostly he wore a threadbare blue suit, a beige trench coat and an old grey felt hat. His only unusual fashion accessory was a sjambok—a type of riding crop—with a silver handle and loop that he always carried with him.[129]

One of the few people who were allowed to visit Hitler at home was Ernst Hanfstaengl. Born in 1887 into an established Munich publishing family, Hanfstaengl had studied at Harvard and directed the New York branch of his father's art publishing house, before returning to Munich in 1921 with his wife Helene, the daughter of a German-American businessman. In November 1922 he attended a Hitler speech in the Kindlkeller and was immediately fascinated by Hitler's "phenomenal personality as a speaker." He was keen to make Hitler's acquaintance, and before long the privileged son of an upper-class family was part of the rabble-rouser's entourage.[130]

In his memoirs, Hanfstaengl recorded his impressions of Hitler's spartan domicile: "The room . . . was clean and pleasant, if somewhat narrow and not exactly luxuriously furnished. The floor was covered by cheap, scuffed linoleum and a few small, worn-out rugs. On the wall across from his bed . . . were a chair, a table and a crudely built shelf holding Hitler's treasured books."[131] They included Hermann Stegemann's *History of the First World War*, Erich Ludendorff's *Politics and the Waging of War*, Heinrich von Treitschke's *German History of the Nineteenth Century*, Carl von Clausewitz's *On War*, Franz Kugler's biography of Friedrich the Great, Houston Stewart Chamberlain's Wagner biography, Gustav Schwab's *Most Beautiful Sagas of Classical Antiquity* and Sven Hedin's wartime memoirs as well as a number of popular novels, detective stories and—slightly concealed according to Hanfstaengl—*The Illustrated History of Morals* and *The History of Erotic Art* by the Jewish author Eduard Fuchs.[132]

Hanfstaengl shared Hitler's interest in history, art and music. He was a fine pianist himself and soon discovered how to put the often irritable Wagner enthusiast Hitler in a good mood. Whenever Hanfstaengl played the first bars of the overture to Wagner's *Meistersänger* on the piano in the landlady's parlour, it was as if Hitler were transformed. "He would immediately stand up and pace up and down in the room, swinging his arms like a conductor and whistling along with every note in a strangely penetrating, but absolutely on-key vibrato," Hanfstaengl recalled. "He knew the entire prelude by heart, and since he had an excellent ear for the spirit of the music, I gradually began to have fun with our duets."[133]

What did Hitler live off? The authors of the anonymous anti-Hitler pamphlet in July 1921 had asked this question, and it continues to occupy historians. Hitler's early sources of income remain unclear. He himself testified in front of a court in January 1921 that he had never received "a penny" for his work for the NSDAP, but that he did get paid for speeches he gave outside the party, for instance to the German-Nationalist Protection and Defiance Federation.[134] It's highly doubtful whether Hitler could live from those lecture fees alone. There is clear evidence that he was supported by sympathisers.[135] Moreover, even early on in his career, Hitler charmed well-heeled elderly ladies. Most prominent among them was Hermine Hoffmann, the widow of a school principal, who mothered Hitler in her house in Solln on the periphery of Munich. "You simply must come to lunch on Sunday," she wrote to her "respected and dear friend" Hitler on one presumably typical occasion in February 1923. Hitler was also invited to stay the night: "Recent times have brought so much commotion that you owe it to our holy cause to rest and recover for a couple of hours out here in the peace and quiet."[136]

Hitler also got the occasional meal from Dora Lauböck, the wife of Government Counsel Theodor Lauböck, who founded the Nazi chapter in the town of Rosenheim. Whenever Hitler travelled, he always made sure to send the Lauböcks a postcard, and when Theodor was transferred to Munich, their relationship became even closer. Hitler spent Christmas with the couple in 1922, and the Lauböcks' son Fritz served as Hitler's private secretary in 1923.[137]

Even if the ascetic Hitler did not require much personally, the party coffers were perennially empty because membership fees and revenues from events were not enough to cover the running costs; the *Völkischer Beobachter* also had to be heavily subsidised.[138] Thus Hitler had no choice but to scrounge around for people to help finance the NSDAP's endeavours. One of the earliest patrons was the Augsburg manufacturer Gottfried Grandel, who also supported Eckart's publication *Auf gut deutsch*.[139] Another supporter was the chemist Emil Gansser, who worked for Siemens in Berlin and was friends with Eckart. As Karl Burhenne, the director of Siemens's social-political department, wrote in March 1922, Gansser had followed the development of "the Hitlerian movement" for two years and was convinced that "generous, if discreet support for this healthy initiative, which arose from the people, would relatively quickly influence the political circumstances in Germany . . . in the most favourable sense possible."[140] On 29 May 1922, after

Gansser's encouragement, Hitler held a talk at the "National Club of 1919," whose membership included not only officers and civil servants, but entrepreneurs. Hitler knew how to adapt to his audiences so that his lectures were usually received well.[141] After that speech, the NSDAP appears to have received donations from Berlin industrialists such as Ernst von Borsig and the coffee manufacturer Richard Franck.[142] After mediation by Gansser and Hess, who was studying at Zurich Polytechnic in the winter term of 1922–3, Hitler also established contact with Germanophile circles in Switzerland in order to solicit funds. In late August 1923, he and Gansser visited Swiss army general Ulrich Wille and his family in their Zurich villa. As a family member noted in her diary: "Hittler [sic] very likeable. The man positively vibrates when he speaks. He speaks wonderfully."[143]

When Hitler did not have to appear at party events and travel around in search of money, he reverted to the haphazard daily routines of his pre-war existence. "You never quite knew where he was," Hanfstaengl recalled. "Essentially he was a bohemian who had no roots anywhere."[144] Gottfried Feder even wrote to Hitler to express his worries "about our great work, the German liberation movement of national socialism, and you whom we acknowledge without envy to be its passionate leader." Hitler was difficult to reach and devoted too little time to important party matters, Feder complained; he seemed to enjoy "relaxing in artistic circles and in the company of beautiful women."[145] Hitler was notorious for always being late and for having no sense of planning his working day. He preferred to spend his free time in Munich's cafés and watering holes: in Café Neumayr, a beer bar on the edge of the Viktualienmarkt; in Café Heck in the Hofgarten; and in Osteria Bavaria, an artists' tavern on Schellingstrasse. Hitler would spend hours there drinking coffee and eating cake with his intimates, his "sweet tooth" apparent in the fact that he could not get enough of gateau heaped with whipped cream.[146]

Hitler's circle of acquaintances was a motley crew. It included hooligans like Christian Weber, a former horse trader who also carried around a whip, Hitler's bodyguard Ulrich Graf, and his chauffeur Emil Maurice, another feared brawler. With these three thugs at his side, the National Socialist leader could move through Munich with the cockiness of a minor mafioso.[147] Also part of the clique were Hitler's former sergeant Max Amann, whom Hitler made party secretary in

July 1921 and also head of the party's publishing house, the Eher Verlag; the young journalist Hermann Esser, who had served as Karl Mayr's press spokesman and who was considered the second-best speaker in the party after Hitler; and Johann Klintzsch, a former member of the Ehrhardt Brigade, who had been put in charge of building up the SA in August 1921. But Hitler's circle also contained more genteel, intellectual members like Eckart, Hess, the "party philosopher" Rosenberg and Hanfstaengl. Hitler felt at home in what historian Martin Broszat has called a "bizarre mix of bohemians and condottieri."[148] In their company he was able to relax and hold his monologues while his true followers hung on his every word.

Hermann Göring once mocked Hitler's entourage as a "club of provincial skittle enthusiasts with extremely limited horizons"[149]—although this did not prevent Göring from joining it. Born in 1893 as the son of a high-ranking colonial administrator, he had made a name for himself as a fighter ace in the First World War. He was the final commander of the famous Richthofen Squadron and was awarded Germany's highest military medal, the *Pour le Mérite*, in June 1918. After the war, he had made his way doing various jobs in Sweden and Denmark. In early February 1922, he married Carin von Kantzow, born the Swedish Baroness von Fock, and moved with her to Munich. Göring met Hitler in October or November 1922 at a Nazi event and soon joined the party. Less than half a year later, Hitler put him in charge of the SA. "A famous combat pilot and a bearer of the *Pour le Mérite*—what a propaganda coup!" Hitler is said to have gushed. "What's more, he has money and doesn't cost me a penny. That's very important."[150]

Hanfstaengl and Göring were not the only ones who lent the provincial NSDAP a bit of cosmopolitan flair. Thanks to the help he received from influential patrons, Hitler gained entry into elevated social circles early on. In June 1921, Eckart introduced him to the salon of Helene Bechstein, the wife of a wealthy Berlin piano-maker. The elegant lady of the house developed a maternal affection for the ambitious politician thirteen years her junior and did everything she could to help him fit in with polite society. She bought him new outfits, taught him etiquette and repeatedly gave him money. Hitler was also a regular guest at the dinners the Bechsteins hosted at the Four Seasons Hotel in Munich.[151]

Hitler was frequently invited to Hanfstaengl's apartment on Gentzstrasse on the fringe of the Schwabing district. It was here that the historian Karl Alexander von Müller met him again and insightfully described Hitler's appearance:

> Through the open door, you could see him greeting the hostess, almost subserviently, in the narrow hallway. He put away his riding crop and took off his velour hat and trench coat, then took off a belt with a revolver and hung that up as well on a coat hook. That was strange, like something out of [the Westerns of] Karl May . . . The man who entered was no longer the clumsy, sheepish instructor in a badly fitting uniform whom I had met in 1919. You could see the confidence he'd gained from his public appearances in his eyes. Nonetheless, there was still something gauche about him, and you had the unpleasant feeling that he could sense you had noticed it and held that against you.[152]

Hitler's insecurity revealed the fear of the parvenu that he would never be taken entirely seriously in the upper-class circles to which he was now granted access.

The Hanfstaengls introduced Hitler to Elsa Bruckmann, the wife of the publisher Hugo Bruckmann, whose authors included Houston Stewart Chamberlain. Their salon, which prior to 1914 had offered a wide circle of renowned artists and men of letters the chance to exchange ideas, was increasingly becoming a meeting place for chauvinist and anti-Semitic authors and politicians.[153] Elsa Bruckmann heard Hitler speak for the first time in Zirkus Krone in February 1921, and as she later recalled, she felt "reawakened" by his voice. Yet she first seems to have sought contact with him during his imprisonment at Landsberg, and it was not until December 1924 that Hitler participated for the first time in the Bruckmanns' salon in their villa on Karolinenplatz 5.[154] When Hugo Bruckmann died in September 1941, Hitler praised his "services to the early NSDAP." At the Bruckmanns' house, Hitler recalled, he had met all the important men in the nationalist scene in Munich.[155]

Munich social elites were probably less captivated by the aggressive anti-Semitism with which Hitler regularly enraptured his beer-hall audiences than by his bizarre appearance and eccentric behaviour. "He had the aura of a magician, a whiff of the circus and of tragic embitterment, and the harsh shine of the 'famous beast,'" was how Joachim Fest put it.[156] Members of good society simply had to see the man all of Munich was talking about, and even those who found his political radicalism repellent regarded him a fascinating object of study, whose mere presence guaranteed an evening's entertainment. Thus he was passed from one salon to another, where he elicited a mixture of spine-tingling excitement and half-concealed amusement.[157]

In the autumn of 1923, Hitler gained access via the Bechsteins to the Wagner family in Bayreuth. "Full of reverence," wrote Winifred Wagner, the composer's daughter-in-law, after Hitler visited the family's Villa Wahnfried for the first time on 1 October. "Deeply moved, he examined everything that was directly connected with R[ichard] W[agner]—the downstairs rooms with his desk, the grand piano, his pictures and books, etc."[158] Hitler talked about his days as a young man in Linz and the huge impression Wagner's operas had made on him. By the time he left, he had won over not just Winifred but Wagner's son Siegfried as well. "Thank God that there are still German men!" Siegfried exclaimed. "Hitler is a splendid fellow, a true slice of the German soul."[159] On 28 September 1923, Hitler held his first public speech in Bayreuth, after which he paid a visit to the ageing and frail Houston Stewart Chamberlain. In a letter to Hitler on 7 October, Chamberlain also praised him as "an awakener of souls from sleep and idleness." In Chamberlain's opinion, Hitler was not at all the fanatic he had been depicted as: "The fanatic heats up people's heads, but you warm their hearts. The fanatic wants to drown people out, while you seek only to convince them, which is why you succeed." Hitler's visit, Chamberlain added, had renewed his faith: "The fact that Germany has given birth to a Hitler in the hour of its greatest need shows that it is still alive and well."[160]

Just as Hitler absorbed chauvinist and anti-Semitic ideas like a sponge during the early years of his phenomenal rise from obscurity to political prominence, he now learned how to move in various social circles and play changing roles. The tone Hitler used in his public speeches might not be to everyone's taste, Hess wrote in June 1921, but he could also speak in different modes.[161] The ability to adapt his behaviour and speech to almost any given audience demonstrated his second greatest talent after his rhetorical skills: his acting ability. Ernst Hanfstaengl had immediately noted the startling accuracy with which Hitler could imitate people's voices and personality quirks. His parodies were "masterly, good enough for cabaret."[162] Hitler was also able to use this skill as a mimic to conform to the image people had of him. "He had become a versatile actor on the political stage, calculating and with many different faces," writes historian Lothar Machtan.[163] A cunning mastery of the art of disguise was one of Hitler's most prominent traits as a politician.

By 1923 Hitler was known well beyond Bavaria's borders, but there is not a single photograph of him from this time. For four years he succeeded in preventing any picture of himself from being published, the dictator bragged years later, in April 1942, in a lunchtime monologue at the Wolfsschanze.[164] Hitler's refusal to allow himself to be photographed was apparently part of his public image: it only increased people's interest in him. "What does Hitler look like?" asked illustrator Thomas Theodor Heine in the May 1923 edition of *Simplicissimus* magazine, only to conclude after twelve satiric attempts: "These questions must remain unanswered. Hitler is not an individual at all. He's a condition."[165] Yet Hitler's shyness in front of the camera also caused conflicts. In April 1923, on a visit to Berlin with Hanfstaengl, Hitler was recognised in an amusement park by press photographer Georg Pahl, who took his picture. Hitler immediately attacked Pahl, hitting at the camera with his walking stick. Only after a lengthy back and forth did Pahl agree to hand over the negative.[166] Hitler's drastic reaction may have been caused by the fact that the NSDAP was officially banned in Prussia under the Law on Protecting the Republic. The party leader, who was wanted by the Prussian authorities, would have wanted to remain incognito.

In early September 1923, a press photographer finally succeeded in getting a shot of Hitler at the "Germany Day" in Nuremberg. After that, Hitler stopped hiding from the camera and commissioned Heinrich Hoffmann to take his portrait. The *Berliner Illustrierte Zeitung* newspaper of 16 September 1923 published the first-ever Hitler portrait with the caption: "Adolf Hitler, the leader of the Bavarian National Socialists, who thus far refused to let himself be photographed has now been unfaithful to that principle."[167]

Hoffmann would soon become Hitler's court photographer. In 1909, at the age of 24, Hoffmann had established his own studio on Schellingstrasse and made a name for himself within the art scene for his pictures of artworks and artists. In 1918 and 1919 he was the most important chronicler of the revolution in Munich, although he did not sympathise with the Left. After the demise of the soviets, he supported counter-revolutionary propaganda, joined a militia and became a member of the NSDAP in April 1920. We do not know when he first met Hitler, but after Hitler's first sitting for him, Hoffmann became part of the party leader's entourage—not just as photographer, but as a witty entertainer who, like Hanfstaengl, knew how to keep everyone in a good mood.[168]

"The Fascists have grabbed power in Italy with a coup d'état. If they can hold on to it, this will be a historic event with unpredictable consequences not just for Italy, but for all of Europe," Count Harry Kessler presciently commented on 29 October 1922 after Mussolini's "March on Rome."[169] The Italian Fascists' seizure of power was wind in the National Socialist sails. "Mussolini has shown what a minority can accomplish, if the holy national will lives inside it," Hitler declared at a public event in November 1922, demanding "the formation of a national government along Fascist lines in Germany."[170] Impressed by the events in Italy, a small group of Hitler followers began to propagate an image of the Führer that drew heavily from Il Duce. In early November in the Hofbräuhaus, Hermann Esser explicitly proposed that "Germany's Mussolini is named Adolf Hitler."[171]

There was no cultish worship of the Führer in the early days of the NSDAP. Indeed, the term "Führer" first occurred in the *Völkischer Beobachter* in December 1921, and for a time it remained an exception. On posters or newspaper advertisements for events, the party chairman was usually referred to as "Herr Adolf Hitler" or "party comrade Hitler." That practice changed after Mussolini's "March on Rome." Hitler was now styled into a charismatic Führer and the future saviour of the nation.[172] In the autumn of 1922, the University of Munich held a contest for the best essay on the topic "What qualities will the man have who leads Germany back to the top?" Rudolf Hess won first prize for his encomium to the coming political messiah. In one passage, Hess wrote:

Deep knowledge in all areas of the life of the state and its history, the ability to learn lessons from them, belief in the purity of his own cause and in ultimate victory, and an untamable strength of will give him

the power of captivating oration that make the masses celebrate him . . .
Thus we have a picture of the dictator: sharp in intellect, clear and
honest, passionate yet under control, cool and bold, daring, decisive
and goal-oriented, without qualms about the immediate execution of
his plans, unforgiving towards himself and others, mercilessly hard yet
tender in his love for his people, tireless in his work, with an iron fist
clothed in a velvet glove, capable of triumphing over himself. We still
don't know when he will intervene to save us all, this "man." But he
is coming. Millions sense that.

In a February 1923 letter to Karl Alexander von Müller, from whom
he was taking classes, Hess confirmed that he had Hitler in mind.
Hess sent Müller the manuscript of his essay with the words: "Some
of what is contained in the enclosed document is wishful thinking.
But in many respects it is indeed the picture I have after being around
Hitler, often on a daily basis, for two and a half years."[173]

Dietrich Eckart and Alfred Rosenberg, too, continually projected
messianic expectations onto Hitler, praising him as the strong hand
that would liberate Germany from its humiliation and shame and lead
it into a new golden age. The first high point of the new Führer cult
came on Hitler's thirty-fourth birthday on 20 April 1923. The *Völkischer
Beobachter* ran a banner headline reading "Germany's Führer," and the
lead article was a poem by Eckart that ended with the couplet: "Open
your hearts! Who wants to see, will see! / The strength is there, before
which the night must flee!" In the same issue, Rosenberg also celebrated Hitler's influence, which was "growing from month to month"
and becoming "more captivating." Throngs of desperate people
longing for a "Führer of the German people," Rosenberg asserted,
were looking "ever more expectantly to *the* man in Munich." This was
a manifestation of "that mysterious reciprocal influence between the
Führer and his followers . . . which has become so characteristic of
the German liberation movement today."[174]

Hitler did indeed receive a number of birthday congratulations
from ordinary people who treated him as the coming "national
messiah." A letter from Breslau (today's Wrocław) read: "The eyes of
all tormented Germans are today looking towards your Führer figure."
One supporter wrote in the name of "all loyal followers in Mannheim":
"We will persist and, if necessary, die in the fight in which you are

our Führer and role model, the fight to free our fatherland from humiliation and shame."[175]

According to the sociologist Max Weber, the power of a charismatic politician depends on his having a community of followers who are convinced that he possesses extraordinary abilities and has been called by destiny.[176] For Hitler, this group had crystallised in 1922, and they went on a publicity offensive in November that year with the aim of building a cult of the charismatic Führer. Historian Ludolf Herbst is correct when he writes of the "invention of a German messiah."[177] Conversely, the attempt to inflate the chairman of the NSDAP into a long-awaited national saviour would not have been successful if Hitler had not possessed several extraordinary political skills, above all his talent as an orator and an actor. The charisma ascribed to him and the charisma he projected fed off one another, and this symbiotic relationship alone can explain why the idea of Hitler as the "Führer of a Germany to come" could have such mass appeal.[178]

Did Hitler already see himself in the role in which his admirers saw him? As late as May 1921, he had still admitted to the editor-in-chief of the pan-Germanic *Deutsche Zeitung* newspaper, Max Maurenbrecher, that there were limits to his abilities. "He was not the Führer and statesman who could save the fatherland from sinking into chaos," Maurenbrecher reported Hitler saying, "but the agitator who could gather the masses . . . He needed someone bigger behind him, whose commands he could orient himself around." Likewise in June 1922, he told the advocate of the "conservative revolution," Arthur Moeller van den Bruck: "I'm just a drummer and a gatherer."[179] But his self-image seems to have changed in the autumn of 1922 as a result of being deified by those around him. "We need a strong man, and the National Socialists will produce him," Hitler declared in December 1922, leaving little doubt that he meant himself.[180] The idea was reinforced by the first portrait Hoffmann took of Hitler. It showed Hitler in what would become his familiar Führer pose: his posture stiff and manly, his arms folded or his left hand pressed firmly against his hip, his brows knitted and his lips pressed thin under his neatly trimmed moustache. Hitler's body language and facial expression were intended to communicate will-power, decisiveness and strength.[181]

Along with his increasing self-styling, Hitler also started concealing himself. As early as July 1921, his internal party critics had noted that he flew into a rage every time he was asked about his previous occu-pation.[182] Hanfstaengl remarked that Hitler immediately closed up "like an oyster" whenever the conversation turned to his past—he was like Lohengrin whom Elsa von Brabandt was not allowed to ask the forbidden question.[183] Hitler's inflated self-image was difficult to square with his considerably less than impressive career before 1914, which is why, even before sitting down to write *Mein Kampf*, he started revising his past to make it conform with his sense of being on a national mission. In an initial biographical sketch he composed in late November 1921 for a certain "Herr Doktor" within the NSDAP, most likely Emil Gansser, he already depicted himself as an autodidact from a humble background who had become an anti-Semite after going through the school of hard knocks in Vienna, before finding a suitable political "movement" in 1919 in the "seven-member German Workers' Party."[184]

In early November 1922, the Munich correspondent for the Cologne newspaper *Kölner Anzeiger* wrote: "It is today a given that none of the biggest halls in Munich, not even Zirkus Krone, is large enough to accommodate the storm of people when Hitler speaks. Thousands have to go home after failing to be admitted." The correspondent for the conservative but democratic paper went on to describe how he himself had been captivated by the speaker's "overwhelming strength of conviction."[185] In late January 1923, Karl Alexander von Müller attended a talk by Hitler and was dumbfounded by how much he had changed since the time he had been in Müller's audience:

> He passed me closely by, and I could see he was a different person than the fellow I encountered here and there in private homes. His gaunt, pale features seemed to have been pinched together by an obsessive rage, and cold flames darted from his eyes, which seemed to glance right and left for enemies to be put down. Was it the masses that gave him this mysterious power? Or did it flow from him to them?[186]

A woman from Munich who attended a hopelessly overfilled event a few days later in the Löwenbräukeller offered one answer to Müller's questions. He had so warmed to and spoken so passionately about his subject that his speech couldn't leave anyone unaffected, she wrote to Hitler the very next day: "For us . . . those hours were a wonderful experience and constantly reminded me of the days when our troops marched out of Berlin in August 1914. Hopefully we will experience such hours once again."[187]

Hitler's increasing significance was not lost on foreign observers. Britain's consul general in Munich, William Seeds, who had dismissed Hitler as a bit player in April 1922, reported in December: "During the last few months . . . Herr Hitler has developed into something much more than a scurrilous and rather comic agitator." An observer from the British embassy in Berlin, John Addison, advised that it was unwise "to treat him as if he were a mere clown." The British Foreign Office instructed Seeds to keep Hitler under close observation in future.[188]

In the space of only four years, Hitler had gone from an unknown soldier in the First World War to a popular public speaker who was a main attraction in Munich and who had begun to capture the imagination of people beyond Bavaria. He owed his phenomenal rise to the particular social and political crises of the post-war period, which provided an unusually advantageous situation for a right-wing populist of his ilk. On the other hand, his success was also down to his highly developed sensitivity to the unique chance that had opened up to him in the extremely anti-Semitic political climate in Munich. Initially uncertain and clumsy in his personal behaviour, he grew step by step into the role of the party leader who dispatched all his competitors for power and collected a horde of blindly loyal followers. Hitler refined his rhetorical and acting repertoire until he was comfortable that his posturing would produce the desired effect. The more intoxicating his triumphs in the large arenas of the Bavarian capital became, the more confident he grew in the role ascribed to him by his disciples. He was no longer the "drummer," but rather the "saviour," called to rescue Germany from its "humiliation and misery," and lead it to new heights, much as the national saviour Rienzi had done for Rome.

As stubbornly as he clung to his obsessive anti-Semitism, he was all the more capable of adapting when it came to fitting in with the social conventions of upper-class salons. He realised how important it was to be connected to influential patrons like the Bechsteins, Bruckmanns and Wagners, and he knew how to use them for his own ends. In this phase of intensive political apprenticeship, Hitler already possessed all the characteristics that would later typify him as a politician: the ability to overwhelm audiences rhetorically, the capacity to trick others and to disguise himself, as well as extreme tactical cleverness.

Wartime comrades encountering him again scarcely believed that this was the same quiet, nondescript man they had known as a private at the front. "My dear Hitler, anyone who has had the opportunity to follow you from the founding of the movement until now can hardly fail to express admiration," a former member of the List Regiment wrote on the occasion of Hitler's birthday in 1923. "You have achieved something that probably no other man in Germany could have, and we, your former comrades, are at the disposal of your will. Thousands and thousands of men think this way."[189]

6

Putsch and Prosecution

"When I fell flat on my face in 1923, the only thing I thought about was getting back up again," Hitler once tersely remarked about the failed Beer Hall Putsch of 8 and 9 November 1923.[1] It was no surprise that Hitler did not enjoy talking about this event, which after his rejection by the Vienna Academy of Fine Arts represented his second-biggest failure. After four years of what seemed like an unstoppable rise to populist political prominence, Hitler suddenly plummeted back into irrelevance. His own fate and that of his movement seemed to have been sealed. The *New York Times* concluded that the putsch represented the certain end of Hitler and his National Socialist supporters.[2]

If the Bavarian judicial system had enforced the letter of the law, Hitler would have spent many years in prison for his attempted coup d'état, making a political comeback almost inconceivable. Thus the leader of the NSDAP had every reason to be grateful to his judge for giving him the minimum sentence. Moreover, he was also allowed to use his trial as a stage for self-aggrandisement, during which he styled his dilettantish attempt at armed rebellion into a heroic defeat. The failed putsch was to become a central element in Nazi Party legend. The party comrades who died in it were glorified as "blood witnesses" to the movement's struggle, and Hitler would dedicate the first volume of *Mein Kampf* to them. After 1933, 8 and 9 November 1923 would become the high point of the Nazi calendar. Every year, Hitler would commemorate those events with a speech to the "old fighters" in the Bürgerbräukeller, a ceremony which ended with a ritual re-creation of the Nazis' march from the beer hall to the Feldherrnhalle, where four policemen and fourteen Nazis had been killed.[3]

The year 1923 had started with a bang. On 11 January, French and Belgian troops entered the industrial Ruhr Valley region to punish Germany for falling behind in its reparations payments for the First World War. A wave of animosity arose throughout the country, and the simmering German nationalism reminded some observers of the mood in August 1914. The politically independent Reich Chancellor Wilhelm Cuno, who had led a minority government formed by the parties of the political centre since November 1922, called upon Germans to engage in "passive resistance." Economic life along the Rhineland and Ruhr Valley pretty much came to a standstill. The French and Belgian occupiers responded by imposing harsh sanctions, arresting striking workers and taking railways and mines into their own hands. This only increased German outrage. "1923 looks as though it will be a year of destiny for Germany," prophesied Georg Escherich, the founder of the anti-Communist Bavarian home guards. "It's a matter of existence or non-existence."[4]

Much to the surprise of his supporters, Hitler did not join the "unified front" against the French and Belgians. He was more concerned with redirecting the general hostility at Germany's purported enemies within. On the evening of 11 January, Hitler gave a speech in Zirkus Krone in which he excoriated the "November criminals." By "stabbing the army in the back," Hitler raged, political leaders at the end of the First World War had left Germany defenceless and exposed to "total enslavement." A Germany reborn vis-à-vis the rest of the world would only be possible "when the criminals are held accountable and condemned to their just fates." The "babble about a unified front," Hitler proclaimed, only served to distract the German people from their main task.[5] Hitler thus refused to take part in a demonstration by the Fatherland Associations against Germany's arch-enemy France in Munich on 14 January. It was a sign of how self-confident he had become in his ability to stake out political positions on his own.

The economic consequences of "passive resistance" were disastrous. The only way the Reich could cover the costs for wages in the dormant factories, mines and companies was to print massive amounts of money. The devaluation of the reichsmark, which had already begun at the end of the war, reached a dizzying pace. Overnight, the middle and working classes saw their savings disappear, while financial adventurers and speculators exploited the chance to amass huge fortunes.

The demise of the currency was accompanied by the decay of fundamental social values. Cynicism was the mood of the day. In his book
Defying Hitler, Sebastian Haffner described the dramatic events his
generation went through: "We had just put the great game of war
and the shock at how it ended behind us, as well as a very disillusioning
political lesson in revolution, and now we were treated to the daily
spectacle of all rules of life breaking down, and age and experience
being revealed as bankrupt."[6]

One side effect of the almost apocalyptic despair produced by
spiralling currency devaluation was the appearance of travelling
preachers known in popular parlance as "inflation saints." They
included Friedrich Muck-Lamberty, nicknamed the "messiah of
Thuringia," who intoxicated audiences with his troupes of dancers
and performers, and the former sparkling-wine manufacturer Ludwig
Christian Häusser, who employed modern advertising methods to
attract masses of people to his sermons.[7]

In Bavaria, Hitler was the one attracting the desire for religious
awakening and salvation of those who had fallen down the social
ladder or who feared they might be about to. The National Socialists
were one of the main profiteers from Germany's economic catastrophe. "While other political events are poorly attended due to the
enormous entry fees and beer prices, the halls are always full when
the National Socialists put on one of their mass meetings," Munich
police reported.[8] Crowds of people felt drawn to the NSDAP and
Hitler's tirades against capitalist and Jewish criminals and usurers: the
sudden impoverishment of broad segments of the German populace
made Hitler's words seem much more plausible. In Munich the
National Socialists were stronger than all the other parties on the right
and in many other towns and cities the movement was flourishing
too, Rudolf Hess reported in early 1923. Between February and
November 1923, the party picked up 35,000 new members. By the time
of the putsch, total enrollment was 55,000. Maria Endres, who worked
at the party headquarters in Corneliusstrasse, recalled that so many
people wanted to sign up that she could hardly process all the membership applications.[9]

Rumours that the National Socialists were planning a putsch had
been circulating since the autumn of 1922. In early November, Count
Harry Kessler reported that the diplomat and author Victor Naumann

had told him that Hitler and his de facto deputy Hermann Esser had complete control over the streets. They had a "large, well-organised and armed group of followers," capable of striking any day "against the Jews and against Berlin." The Reichswehr, Naumann warned, would be "unable to resist."[10] On the other hand, the president of Bavaria, Eugen von Knilling (BVP), who had just succeeded Lerchenfeld-Köfering, told the American consul in Munich, Robert Murphy, in November 1922 that Hitler did not have it in him to become anything more than a populist speaker and would fail to achieve the successes of either Benito Mussolini or Kurt Eisner. "He has not the mental ability," Knilling scoffed, "and furthermore the government is now on its guard, as was not the case in 1918."[11] Knilling was yet another person who gravely underestimated Hitler's abilities and the danger he represented. But not all members of the Bavarian government shared the president's estimation. In an official note from mid-December 1922, the ministerial councillor in the Bavarian Interior Ministry, Josef Zetlmeier, described the Nazi movement as "undoubtedly a threat to the state." If the Nazis were able to realise even some of their "grim ideas" concerning Jews, Social Democrats and banking capital, Zetlmeier warned, there would be "considerable unrest and bloodshed." Hitler had heeded none of the official admonitions to be more moderate, which was not surprising given the energy of a movement "that was aiming for dictatorship." Zetlmeier called upon the Bavarian government to change its practice of tacit tolerance towards the NSDAP.[12]

And in fact the Bavarian government, alarmed by persistent rumours of a putsch, did impose some restrictions on the annual Nazi Party conference scheduled for late January 1923 in Munich. The large rally planned for the Königsplatz was forbidden, and only small gatherings and marches were permitted outdoors. In a heated discussion with Pöhner's successor as police president, Eduard Nortz, on 25 January, Hitler threatened to use violence to get his way. "He would lead the columns of his supporters, and the government could get out their guns and shoot him, if they wished," Hitler was quoted as braying. The first shot would precipitate a bloodbath, and the government would be finished. "We'll meet again at Philippi," Hitler said, quoting Shakespeare, and stormed out of the room.[13] The Bavarian government took him at his word and declared a state of emergency throughout

Bavaria on 26 January. Hitler might have suffered an embarrassing defeat if his influential patrons had not intervened on his behalf. Thanks to mediation by Röhm and Ritter von Epp, Hitler was granted an audience with the commander of the Reichswehr in Bavaria, Lieutenant General Otto von Lossow, to whom he swore that there would be no attempted putsch. Hitler repeated his solemn promise to Gustav von Kahr, who was once again the head of government in Upper Bavaria. Lossow and Kahr then had a word with Knilling. Another meeting was scheduled with Nortz for the evening of 26 January. Hitler suddenly behaved quite tamely, pledging "on all his honour that the party conference would not give rise to a single objection." The event was allowed to proceed with only minor restrictions.[14]

Hitler, however, was unwilling to observe any limits. On the evening of 27 January, the NSDAP staged twelve gatherings—not the six that had been approved. "Celebrated by the masses like a saint," Hitler spoke at every one of them, and he scarcely missed an opportunity to heap scorn on the Knilling government. "So, Herr Minister, where do you get your information that the National Socialists are planning a putsch?" Hitler asked sarcastically. "Of course, the milkwoman must have told him! A tram conductor said something to that effect, and an operator overheard something of that sort in a telephone conversation. And the *Münchener Post* newspaper wrote that." National Socialists, Hitler boasted, had no need for putsches since they were not a "soon-to-be-extinct" political party but rather a youthful movement that was growing in strength and numbers from week to week. They could wait for their day to come, and when it did, it would not require a putsch to clear away the old government: a small breeze would suffice.[15]

During the three-day party conference, Munich was more or less in Nazi hands. Columns of marching SA men were everywhere on the streets, and the party's disregard for official rules resulted in a severe loss of face for the Bavarian state president. Carl Moser von Filseck, the envoy of the state of Württemberg to Bavaria, noted that people generally felt the government had "completely embarrassed itself" and damaged its reputation.[16] Yet instead of learning that the idea of coexisting with Hitler and his movement was illusory, government officials maintained their accommodating attitude towards the NSDAP. One reason was that they feared they would lose popular support if they moved decisively to block Nazi activities. After all, in nationalist circles the Nazis were considered useful allies in the struggle against the socialist left. The Bavarian military leadership also saw a "healthy core of the Hitler movement" capable of instilling patriotism in the minds of the working classes. "We did not want to suppress the Hitler movement with force, but rather to place it on the solid ground of what was possible and attainable," Lossow later testified during Hitler's trial.[17]

The Reichswehr leadership also considered paramilitary units in general, including the SA, as a secret military reserve they could activate in case of a conflict. In early February 1923, after Ernst Röhm's encouragement, a "Working Association of Patriotic Fighting Organisations" was constituted—at its core were the SA and paramilitary Freikorps organisations like Bund Oberland and Reichsflagge. Its military leader was the retired first lieutenant Hermann Kriebel, formerly chief of staff for the citizens' militias. The Reichswehr itself trained the association's members. Its involvement in this changed the character of the SA, which went from being a party militia to a fighting force reorganised along military lines under its new boss Göring. The storm troopers were organised into companies, battalions and regiments. The self-defined task of the Working Association, as spelled out in a memorandum by Hitler in mid-April 1923, was: "1. To take over political power. 2. To brutally cleanse the fatherland of its internal enemies. 3. To train the nation, both in terms of its will and practical skills, for the day when the fatherland will be liberated, the period of November betrayal will come to an end and we will be able to hand over a German empire to our sons and grandsons."[18] These paramilitary organisations were quick to demonstrate their determination to act outside the law. On 15 April they staged large-scale military exercises in the moorland north of Munich and violated the non-military zone around the Bavarian Landtag when they marched back into the city. Hitler also inspected a Nazi parade directly in front of the home of the Prussian envoy on Munich's Prinzregentenstrasse—a clear provocation. "Hitler is becoming a megalomaniac," remarked the director of the press office at the Bavarian Foreign Ministry in reaction to the lack of police curtailment of the Nazi leader.[19]

At the same time, young SA men were increasingly throwing their weight around in the streets. When they forced the owner of a bookshop in Brienner Strasse to remove works they found objectionable from his main window display, he complained in an angry letter to Hitler about "thugs posing as dictators." At the end of one of Hitler's appearances, a woman who had been taking notes of his speech was subjected to a humiliating body search by the SA security men in the venue. Her companion, a female doctor, was outraged: "What we encountered there was sheer terror, worse than anything in the Eisner era." Jews were accosted and even physically attacked on the streets; Jewish shopkeepers were accused of stirring up animosity towards Hitler's cause "in the most unheard-of fashion."[20]

In late April, Hitler decided that it was again time to test the Bavarian government. The bone of contention was 1 May, which was both the German Labour Day celebrated by leftists and the anniversary of Munich's conservative "liberation" from the rule of the soviets in 1919. Hitler demanded the government ban the SPD's and the unions' celebrations on Munich's Theresienwiese; and when it refused, he called upon the Working Association to prevent the "Reds" from holding their parade by "aggressive intervention including the use of weapons."[21] In the early morning hours of 1 May, some 2,000 paramilitaries assembled on the Oberwiesenfeld in the north of the city. They were armed with rifles and machine guns from the Reichwehr's arms depot, in direct defiance of Lossow's orders. While they were still forming their ranks—with Hitler, decked out in a steel helmet and wearing his Iron Cross, First Class, at their centre—they were encircled by units of the Bavarian police. In addition, Reichswehr troops were put on alert in their barracks. This time, the Bavarian government and the military leadership were willing to confront the challenge head-on and show Hitler that there were limits to his power. "The decisive and unambiguous stance of the police forces manning the cordon was to thank for the fact that any inclination towards action on the part of those assembled on the Oberwiesenfeld was quickly banished," the final report by the Munich Police Directorship would conclude.[22]

Around noon, a Reichswehr commando appeared and demanded that the stolen weapons be returned. Hermann Kriebel and other hotheads wanted to resist this order, but Hitler shied away from an armed battle with the Reichswehr and the police, which, as he knew all too well, could quickly put an end to his political ambitions. The paramilitaries handed over the weapons and dispersed. By that time the leftist festivities on Theresienwiese had ended without disturbance. Munich breathed a sigh of relief. The confrontation that so many people feared had been averted.

For Hitler, the ignominious end to his 1 May agitation was an early political blow. Years later in his monologues, he still spoke of it as the "greatest humiliation" of his life.[23] He tried to buoy the spirits of his disappointed SA men by telling them that their day would come, but that could not paper over his own loss of prestige in the wake of the fiasco.[24] Hitler had "no clear goals and is pushed by backstage figures who increasingly called for a 'deed' of salvation," noted Georg Escherich, who had only known Hitler since that February and who had an unfavourable impression of him, describing him as "a small-time demagogue who can only sling slogans." Escherich publicly accused Hitler of being unable to constrain the "desperadoes" in his own ranks.[25] Many observers at the time thought Hitler had passed his zenith. U.S. Consul Murphy reported to Washington that the National Socialists were "on the wane."[26] That impression, however, was mistaken. The defeat of 1 May only temporarily slowed the Hitler movement's momentum.

Nonetheless, Hitler faced the unpleasant reality that the Bavarian state prosecutor's office, after prodding by the Bavarian interior minister, had begun investigating him for "forming an armed mob." That was a criminal offence subject to punishment by several months' imprisonment. Hitler threatened to reveal details about the secret collaboration between the SA and the militias with the Reichswehr, should it come to a trial. After that Bavarian Minister of Justice Franz Gürtner, who had only been in office since August 1922, postponed the investigation—for reasons of state—until a "calmer time." No progress was ever made towards indicting Hitler.[27] It was another instance of how the accommodating Bavarian government was utterly unable to restrain the demagogue.

After all the excitement of the previous months, Hitler apparently needed a rest and temporarily withdrew from the limelight. He travelled to the remote mountain village on the Obersalzberg near Berchtesgaden, where his friend Dietrich Eckart, who had fled the threat of arrest, had been hiding out for some time. Using the alias "Wolf," he checked into the Pension Moritz, a guest house run by a couple who were well disposed towards the Nazi leader. It was then, he later recalled, that he "fell in love with the landscape . . . For me the Obersalzberg had become a magnificent place."[28] It was only with difficulty that he was coaxed back to Munich on 10 June to take part in the Fatherland Associations' memorial for Leo Schlageter, an insurgent in the Ruhr region who had carried out a number of bombings, for which he was sentenced to death by French occupiers and executed on 26 May 1923. Hitler returned to his mountain idyll immediately after his speech. Rudolf Hess, who visited in July, found him in excellent health: "Thankfully, Hitler is now getting some rest and relaxation in the mountains. It's an unusual sight to see him in lederhosen with his knees exposed and his shirtsleeves rolled up. He looks better than he did before."[29]

Joachim Fest believes that Hitler lapsed into his old habits of lethargy and idleness on the Obersalzberg.[30] Hess, however, painted a different picture: "His life is still strenuous, morning till night. One meeting follows another, and sometimes he doesn't even take time to get a bite to eat in between."[31] Hitler was now being chauffeured comfortably from one event to another in the new Mercedes-Benz he had just acquired.

Starting in the summer of 1923, the economic and political crisis in Germany came to the boil, which did not allow the head of the NSDAP to absent himself from Munich for very long. Hyperinflation was reaching its high point. "In August, [the exchange rate with] the dollar reached one million," Sebastian Haffner recalled.

> We read the news with bated breath, as though the reports were of some astonishing new record. Fourteen days later we could only laugh about it. It was as if the dollar had gained a tenfold of energy from surpassing the million mark. Its value began to increase by increments of hundreds of millions and even billions. By September, the million-mark note was practically worthless. The billion became the new standard unit, and by the end of October it was the trillion.[32]

The bottomless plunge in the value of the reichsmark meant hardship and despair for broad segments of the German populace. An eyewitness in south-western Germany reported in late August that the mood was unusually depressed: "There's unemployment and hunger on many

people's doorsteps, and no one knows how to ward off these dangers."
In October the Senior state official of Upper Bavaria compared the
mood to that of November 1918: "Statements to the effect that it makes
no difference whether everything is smashed to bits . . . are no rarity."[33]

A wave of demonstrations, strikes and food riots shook the entire
country. In August, Wilhelm Cuno stepped down as chancellor, to be
replaced by the chairman of the German People's Party (Deutsche
Volkspartei, or DVP), Gustav Stresemann, who had gone from being
a national expansionist and supporter of Erich Ludendorff in the First
World War to a converted democrat who believed the parliamentary
system was the least of all evils. He formed a grand coalition with
the German Democratic Party (Deutsche Demokratische Partei, or
DDP), the Centre Party and the SPD. The new government faced the
daunting task of stopping hyperinflation, since without a stable
currency, economic recovery would be impossible. But that demanded
an end to the financially ruinous struggle in the Ruhr. On 26 September
1923, the government announced it was ceasing the policy of passive
resistance. The political Right immediately launched an emotionally
charged campaign accusing Stresemann and his grand coalition of
capitulating to foreign interests.[34]

Resentments towards "Red Berlin" were greater in Bavaria than in
other parts of Germany, and resistance towards this governmental
change of course formed immediately. On 1 and 2 September, the
Fatherland Associations convened for a "Germany Day" in Nuremberg.
"The streets were a sea of black-red-and-white and white-and-blue
flags," reported the Nuremberg-Fürth police department, referring to
the colours of Imperial Germany and Bavaria.

> Masses of people surrounding the guests of honour and the parade
> called out "Heil" in greeting . . . It was a joyous expression of relief
> of hundreds of thousands of despondent, cowed, mistreated, desperate
> people who thought they glimpsed a sliver of hope of liberation from
> enslavement and destitution. Many men and women stood there crying,
> overcome with emotion.[35]

In Nuremberg there was a public display of solidarity between Hitler
and Ludendorff. Hess had introduced the two men in 1921, and at his
trial in February 1924, Hitler said that he had been very happy to make

the acquaintance of the general, whom he had once "idolised." For his part, Ludendorff testified that after their first meeting he had foreseen Hitler's rise. "Here was someone the people could understand, someone morally elevated who could offer salvation," Ludendorff stated. "That was how Herr Hitler and I found our way to one another."[36] As a wartime hero, Ludendorff was particularly valuable to Hitler. With Ludendorff backing him, the leader of the NSDAP could realistically hope that the Reichswehr would support his plans for a coup d'état. The events of 1 May had taught Hitler that without military support, all his plans were condemned to failure from the very start.

Another major result of Nuremberg was the founding of a Patriotic Fighting Association, which united the activist cores of militia organisations like the SA, the Bund Oberland and the Reichsflagge. Here, too, Hermann Kriebel functioned as military leader, while the diplomat Max Erwin von Scheubner-Richter ran the day-to-day operations. On 25 September, Hitler was made the association's "political leader." Its "action plan" was utterly unambiguous: the goal of "putting down Marxism," that document read, required the association "to seize the instruments of state power in Bavaria." Furthermore, "The national revolution must not be allowed to precede the takeover of political power in Bavaria. On the contrary, the takeover of the political instruments of power of the state is the precondition for a national revolution."[37]

The constant invocation of an imminent national revolution fuelled right-wing hopes that a coup d'état would soon be at hand. Rumours of a putsch again made the rounds and ratcheted up the feverish mood. Hitler and his movement felt increased pressure to act. Wilhelm Brückner, the leader of the SA's Munich regiment, warned that the day was fast approaching when he would be unable to restrain his men: "If nothing happens now, the men will simply start devouring things."[38]

Mountains of letters from all parts of Germany arrived at the NSDAP's headquarters in September and October, urging Hitler to take action. As one correspondent put it, all hope rested on the "rescuer from Bavaria" who would clean out the Aegean stables with his "iron broom." With a "truly energetic act," comparable to Mussolini's take-over in Italy, Hitler could do Germany an "extraordinary service." Ordinary people were waiting for the signal to "storm forward" and

prayed that "Our Lord might lead our Hitler to complete victory."
One of the letter-writers was a resident of the affluent Munich district
of Bogenhausen, who had attended every speech Hitler gave in Zirkus
Krone for the previous two years and queued for hours to secure a
good spot, so that she could "take in every word, every subtlety of
tone, and call out 'Heil' to our honoured Führer from close proximity."
She wrote in early November: "Now may the Almighty make your
arm as strong as your words are beautiful so that the day of liberation
will be upon us."[39] Such overwhelming declarations of loyalty must
have strengthened the Nazi leadership's belief that they had to hurry
up and take action.

Hitler further whipped up enthusiasm with a rabble-rousing speech in
Zirkus Krone on 5 September. The German people, he said, were in
the grip of a "great emotion": "There are only two possibilities—either
Berlin goes on the march and ends up in Munich, or Munich goes on
the march and ends up in Berlin."[40] In mid-September, Hess described
Hitler being welcomed as a messiah at a "Germany Day" in Hof:

> In no time at all, six halls were filled beyond capacity, and masses of
> people lined up outside, hoping in vain for admittance . . . In one venue
> he was once again suddenly seized by something indescribable. It
> grabbed me so fiercely that I had to clench my teeth . . . There were
> many good, critical minds in the hall—and by the end, they all were
> beside themselves with enthusiasm.[41]

When would the big day come? That was the question on everyone's
minds. Hitler himself still did not know in mid-September, although
Hess had "rarely" seen him "so serious." Hitler, Hess recorded, was
conscious of his "responsibility . . . concerning the start, his decision
to toss the fire onto the powder keg."[42] For 27 September alone, the
NSDAP chairman had fourteen mass events planned in Munich. In a
sense, the date was a prelude that would bring judgement day closer.

But something Hitler had failed to anticipate intervened. On
26 September, the Knilling cabinet declared a state of emergency,
appointing Kahr "general state commissar" and giving him near-
dictatorial powers. On the one hand, the move was directed against
the national government in Berlin, which had just proclaimed the end
of Germany's passive resistance in the Ruhr. But it was also aimed at

the Hitler movement, whose increasing readiness to stage a putsch had not remained concealed from the Bavarian authorities. As one of the first measures taken under the new order, Kahr prohibited the Nazi events scheduled for 27 September. Hitler registered his "most vigorous" protest but failed to get the ban lifted.[43] Thereafter the relationship between Kahr and Hitler was chilly, with the latter seeking to marginalise the new state commissar. Kahr, Hitler fumed, was "a milquetoast civil servant who lacked political instincts and a firm will" and was as such "not the right man to lead a decisive battle." Hitler's message was unmistakable: he and he alone was the man destined to become "the pioneer of the great German liberation movement."[44]

The atmosphere in Munich throughout October was one of feverish tension, as Kahr and Hitler circled one another like mistrustful tomcats. Cordial overtures alternated with obvious threats. Even those well initiated into local politics found it difficult to orient themselves amidst all the political manoeuvring and game-playing, and the situation was made even more opaque by the continuing rivalry between Bavaria and the Reich. On 26 September, in reaction to Kahr's appointment, Reich President Friedrich Ebert had also declared a state of emergency and charged Reich Defence Minister Otto Gessler with asserting the nation state's monopoly on the legitimate use of violence. A day later, Gessler banned the *Völkischer Beobachter* for publishing a slanderous article about Reich Chancellor Stresemann and the Head of Army Command Hans von Seeckt. However, Lossow defied the order as given against Kahr's will, whereupon Ebert dismissed him from his post as Bavaria's highest military commander. That went too far for Kahr, who reconfirmed Lossow's command over Reichswehr troops in Bavaria. The break between Munich and Berlin was complete. Bavaria was now essentially ruled by a triumvirate of Kahr, Lossow and Colonel Hans von Seisser, the head of the Bavarian police.[45]

At times, the conflict between Bavaria and the Reich obscured the stand-off between the triumvirate and the restless far-right circles around Hitler and the Fighting Association. But the tug of war was continuing behind the scenes. Everyone on the right agreed that the goal was to get rid of Weimar democracy and establish a national dictatorship. But leaders did not see eye to eye on how to achieve this end, who should become the nation's new leader and when action should be taken. In Kahr, Lossow and Seisser's opinion, the national revolution would have to begin in Berlin. They knew that there were plans in the Reich capital to form a "directory," which would assume power after the expected fall of the Stresemann government. Along with General von Seeckt, it was to encompass the former director of the Stinnes conglomerate, Friedrich Minoux, and Germany's ambassador to the United States, Otto Wiedfeldt.[46] The triumvirate wanted to join forces with these men. For that reason it was important, Kahr testified at Hitler's trial, "to gather nationalist forces in Bavaria and to create a strong Bavaria capable of lining up beside and supporting the directory."[47] In other words, Kahr and consorts hoped that they themselves would not have to take the initiative, but rather leave that up to Reichswehr leaders in Berlin and their contacts in northern Germany. Hitler and the Fighting Association would be required to subordinate themselves to the goal of "concentrating nationalist forces in order to create a firm and vigorous state authority" in Bavaria. In a press conference on 1 October, Kahr declared that the Association was welcome to participate but would have to integrate itself into the whole. Demands for special treatment would not be tolerated.[48]

In the minds of Hitler and the Association, in contrast, the "national dictatorship" would be proclaimed in Bavaria, followed by a "march upon Berlin." In a speech to SA leaders on 23 October, Hitler described his vision: "To unfurl the German flag in the final hour in Bavaria and to call into being a German army of liberation under a German government in Munich." In a speech at Zirkus Krone on 30 October, Hitler was even more explicit: "Bavaria has a great mission . . . We have to break through our limitations and do battle with the Marxist brood in Berlin . . . We have to take the fight to them and stab them through the heart." And Hitler left no doubt as to who would lead the planned coup d'état: "For me the German question will first be solved when the black-red-and-white swastika flag flies from Berlin's Imperial City Palace."[49] Hitler planned to put the military leadership of the putsch in Ludendorff's hands. The First World War general's reputation, Hitler hoped, would encourage the Reichswehr to fall in line. But Hitler reserved the political leadership of the coup d'état for himself—a sure sign that he no longer saw himself as a mere drummer, but as the coming Führer. At his later trial he said: "The man who feels called to lead a people doesn't have the right to say:

'If people want me or come and get me, then I'll do it.' He has a duty to do it."[50]

While the triumvirate played for time, Hitler pressed for action. He considered his hand forced not just by the expectations of his supporters throughout Germany and the Fighting Association men in Munich, but by the shift in political conditions. When the Reichswehr moved against socialist–communist "united front" governments in Saxony and Thuringia in late October and early November, it removed one of the pretexts right-wing conspirators in Munich cited for the need to push Bavarian troops to the borders with those central German states. Moreover, the establishment of a new central bank, the Rentenbank, which issued a revalued reichsmark in mid-October, made it clear that the Stresemann government was tackling the currency crisis. Hitler and the other leaders of the Association were under pressure. Hitler may have promised Seisser on 1 November not to move against the Reichswehr or the Bavarian police or attempt a putsch,[51] but he also demanded that the triumvirate take action: "It's high time. Economic misery is so pushing our people that we have to act or risk our supporters going over to the Communists."[52]

In early November Seisser travelled to Berlin on behalf of the triumvirate to confer about the situation. In a conversation with the head of the Reichswehr, he mentioned the "severe pressure" being exerted by all radical nationalist groups on Kahr to get him to "intervene against Berlin" with the goal of creating a "national dictatorship." Seeckt declared that this was his objective as well, but made it crystal clear that "the legal path would have to be followed." A "march on Berlin" of the sort supported by Hitler and his followers was out of the question.[53] On 6 November, Kahr summoned the leaders of the Fatherland Associations, including Hermann Kriebel from the Fighting Association, and warned them not to act on their own. "I alone and nobody else will give the sign to march," he declared. Lossow said he agreed and reminded those present of the failed Kapp–Lüttwitz putsch of 1920. "I am prepared to support a right-wing dictatorship, if it has a chance to succeed," Lossow declared. "But if we're just going to be rushed into a putsch, which will come to a pathetic end in five or six days, then count me out."[54]

The meeting of 6 November made it absolutely clear that the triumvirate was unwilling to seize the initiative. The three leaders wanted to wait and see what course developments in northern Germany took and then perhaps join forces with the "directory." After his grandiloquent pronouncements of the previous weeks, however, Hitler could not afford to remain idle for much longer. "We couldn't keep preparing our people for the cause and reeling them back in," he admitted at his trial. "We couldn't keep them constantly agitated. We had to make a clear decision."[55] Before the night of 6 November was even over, Hitler decided to attack, a decision that was confirmed the next day by the leaders of the Fighting Association. The date was set for 11 November, the anniversary of the armistice in the First World War. Kriebel suggested taking the fighting units out to the Fröttmaninger heath on Munich's northern border for night-time exercises on 10 November and then marching them into the city the following day. But this plan was abandoned when it emerged that Kahr had called a meeting in the Bürgerbräukeller for the evening of 8 November. Everyone who was anyone in Munich politics was set to attend.

The last-minute scheduling of Kahr's meeting convinced Hitler that Kahr was trying to head him off at the pass. He even suspected that the general state commissar might try to reinstate the Wittelsbach dynasty—rumours to that effect had been circulating in Munich since the beginning of November. Hitler was dead set against the restoration of the monarchy. "Never," he had dictated to his secretary Fritz Lauböck in late September, "will the National Socialist German Workers' Party accept any attempt to move the utterly degenerate Houses of Hohenzollern and Wittelsbach and their repulsive courts to again take over the government of our German people."[56]

So Hitler decided to move the putsch forward to 8 November. If his supporters succeeded in seizing the Bürgerbräukeller, they would have the unique opportunity to bring the entire political class of Munich under their control. The plan was to leave the triumvirate with no other option by presenting them with a fait accompli. "We have to force them to get involved and then they won't be able to turn back," Hitler told Ernst Hanfstaengl.[57] At his trial, he declared that he had wanted to give the three hesitant leaders "a push from behind . . . so that they would finally jump into the water they always found too cold."[58]

Over the course of 8 November, the leaders of the Fighting Association received their orders, in part by motorcycle courier. The circle of those in the know was kept small in an attempt to preserve the element of surprise.[59] Early that morning, Hitler secured the support of Ernst Pöhner, his former patron in the police force, whom he promised the office of Bavarian president in the post-putsch government. Pöhner was surprised by Hitler's plan, but he welcomed the fact that someone was taking action. "When Hitler asked me, I answered without hesitation: 'Yes, I'm with you,'" Pöhner testified at Hitler's trial.[60] At 9 a.m., Hitler summoned Hess by telephone and tasked him with arresting all the members of the Bavarian government present in the Bürgerbräukeller. "I assured him with a handshake of my complete discretion, and we parted ways until the evening," Hess wrote afterwards.[61]

Around noon, Hitler marched into the offices of the *Völkischer Beobachter*, "with his riding crop in hand—the very picture of grim determination," and told the astonished Rosenberg and Hanfstaengl: "The time to act has come . . . But don't reveal a word of this to any living soul." Hitler told them to come to the Bürgerbräukeller that evening and to make sure to bring their pistols.[62] In this fashion, the inner circles of the conspiracy were gradually informed about the putsch. Having been pushed forward, the entire undertaking was hasty and improvised. There was no time for intensive preparations, which would be one main reason why the putsch failed.

Even before the official start time of 8 p.m. the Bürgerbräukeller was filled beyond capacity. Outside the doors crowded hundreds of people who had failed to get in. Shortly after Kahr had begun his speech, Hitler rode up in his Mercedes with Alfred Rosenberg, his bodyguard Ulrich Graf and Anton Drexler, who was only told then what was in store. "Best of luck," the honorary NSDAP chairman is supposed to have remarked drily.[63] Seeing the unexpectedly large crowds before the Bürgerbräukeller, Hitler began to fret that his storm troopers would not be able to follow him without inciting a panic that could have doomed the whole endeavour. Spontaneously, Hitler went up to the policemen on duty in front of the venue and ordered them to clear the street. Thus it was that, in the words of Konrad Heiden, "the police cleared the way, on Hitler's command, for Hitler's putsch."[64]

Soon the first trucks full of armed SA men arrived, and the "Stosstrupp Hitler," a special troop about one hundred men strong, secured the entrance to the beer hall and surrounded the building.

Hitler, dressed in a dark suit for the occasion, entered the foyer, where he paced nervously.[65] Finally, at around 8:45 p.m., he smashed a beer glass Hanfstaengl had handed him on the floor, drew his pistol and stormed into the beer hall proper, while at the entrance SA men under the command of Göring took up positions with machine guns. "Obviously you couldn't just go in with a palm frond," Hitler said during his trial in an attempt to justify his martial posturing.[66] "Pale, a dark lock of hair hanging down his forehead, and with a pistol-wielding storm trooper on either side," Hitler began to negotiate the clogged way to the stage.[67] When he was ten steps away from Kahr, he got up on a chair and fired a shot into the ceiling to quiet the tumult. Then he took the stage and proclaimed excitably: "National revolution is under way. The hall is under the control of 600 heavily armed men. No one is allowed to leave. If things don't immediately quieten down, I will have a machine gun posted on the gallery. The Bavarian government has been deposed. The Reich government has been deposed. A provisional government has been formed."[68]

Hitler then asked Kahr, Lossow and Seisser to accompany him into an adjoining room, guaranteeing their safety. In his unpublished memoirs, Kahr described feeling "anger and disgust," but he hoped that the police would soon put an end to the entire spectacle. Kahr was playing for time. As they left the main hall, Lossow had whispered "Play along," and the three men had exchanged glances, agreeing to do precisely that.[69] At least that was their official version afterwards. In fact, it is doubtful that the triumvirate spontaneously agreed to play along with Hitler in order to turn on him later. Much to his surprise and despite being as persuasive as he could, Hitler met with resistance in the adjoining room. Sweating, foaming at the mouth and waving his pistol about in excitement, Hitler declared: "No one gets out of this room alive without my permission." Then he calmed down and apologised for having taken this drastic step, saying he had no choice. "What's done is done," Hitler said. "There's no turning back." He explained briefly the future make-up of the Bavarian and Reich governments: "Pöhner becomes president with dictatorial powers. You [indicating Kahr] will be Bavarian administrator. Reich government: Hitler. National army: Ludendorff. Seisser: minister of police." Hitler said he knew how difficult it was for the three men to agree to this plan, but he wanted to make it easier for them to "take the plunge."

He followed that up with a threat: he had four bullets in his gun, three for them and one for himself. Kahr, who was outraged at being treated in such fashion, responded coolly: "You can arrest me, have me shot or shoot me yourself. I don't care whether I live or die."[70] Ten minutes passed without Hitler making any progress whatsoever.

Outrage was also spreading throughout the beer hall. Many of the respectable Munich citizens in attendance were shocked by what they were experiencing and called out "theatre," "South America" and "Mexico" to express their dissatisfaction.[71] In an attempt to calm things down, Göring took to the stage and told the crowd with his booming military drone that the action was not directed against Kahr. On the contrary, they hoped Kahr would join them. And in any case, Göring added, the people had their beer so they had every reason to be satisfied.[72] That snotty remark only enraged the crowd all the more.

Hitler returned to the hall, and what happened next still dumbfounded one of the eyewitnesses, the historian Karl Alexander von Müller, more than forty years later when he wrote his memoirs. Hitler, who had seemed insane to most of the audience only a few minutes before, suddenly mastered the situation. In a short speech—"an oratorical masterpiece that would have done any actor proud," as Müller described it—Hitler completely turned the mood in the beer hall. "It was like someone turning a glove inside out," the historian wrote. "It was almost like a bit of hocus-pocus, like a magic trick." When he was certain he had people on his side, Hitler asked the crowd: "The Herren Kahr, Lossow and Seisser are outside. They're wrestling with their decision. Can I tell them that you stand behind them?" "Yes! Yes!" Müller reported the crowd echoing from all sides. With a triumphal voice, Hitler got in one last, theatrical line: "Tomorrow will see a German nationalist government, or it will see us dead."[73]

At that moment, Erich Ludendorff—accompanied by cries of "Heil!"—appeared on the scene. Max Erwin von Scheubner-Richter had been instructed to bring him by car to the Bürgerbräukeller, although it is unlikely that the general would not have been informed in advance about the attempted putsch. A few hours previously, at 4 p.m., he had turned up unannounced at Kahr's office and declared in the presence of Lossow and Seisser that "everything demanded a decision." Kahr invoked the well-known plan to establish a directory and had once again dismissed the idea of a right-wing dictatorship proceeding from Bavaria. Ludendorff took his leave with the thinly veiled threat that "the people may take matters into their own hands in the end."[74] By contrast, that evening he acted as though he had been surprised by Hitler's action. "Gentlemen, I'm just as astonished as you are," he said. "But the step has been taken, and the fatherland and our great national cause are at stake, so I can only advise you: come with us and do as we do." Ludendorff's appearance immediately altered the atmosphere in the adjoining room. The pistols were put away, and both sides seemed to want to discuss the matter "like civilised people." Lossow was the first to give in after Ludendorff appealed to him as a fellow military man, and Seisser followed. Only Kahr held out. But in the end, he relented in the face of united insistence, telling the others: "I am prepared to take over directing Bavaria's fate as the placeholder of the monarchy." Hitler had no intention whatsoever of restoring the monarchy, but he needed Kahr's support, so he replied: "There's nothing standing in the way of that." He himself, Hitler said, would inform Crown Prince Rupprecht that the uprising was not directed against the House of Wittelsbach, but aimed to redress the injustice that had been done to it in November 1918. With simulated subservience, Hitler promised: "Your Excellency, I assure you that from now on I will stand behind you as loyally as a dog."[75]

Hitler now demanded that the others return with him to the hall to publicly seal their agreement. Again Kahr resisted, objecting that he could not re-enter a space from which he had been led in such humiliating fashion. Hitler reassured him: "You'll be received with great applause—they'll kneel before you." In the end they all retook the stage to thunderous acclaim from the audience. His face an iron mask, Kahr spoke first, telling the crowd that he saw himself as a "placeholder of the monarchy" and had only decided with a heavy heart, and for the good of Bavaria and Germany, to support the uprising. Hitler shook his hand for a long time with an expression of "gleaming, completely open, almost childlike joy," as Müller recalled. After the tension of the initial hour of the putsch, Hitler found himself in a state approaching euphoria. With quasi-religious fervour, he once again addressed the crowd:

> In the coming weeks and months, I intend to fulfil the promise I made myself five years ago to the day as a blind cripple in an army hospital:

never to rest or relax until the criminals of November 1918 are brought to the ground! Until a Germany of power and greatness, of freedom and majesty, has been resurrected on the ruins of Germany in its pathetic present-day state! Amen.

Afterwards Ludendorff, "sallow with suppressed internal excitement," declared that he was placing himself "at the disposal of the German national government." Lossow and Seisser also stated their support after being bidden by Hitler to the lectern.[76] Hitler triumphantly shook their hands as well. He—and not Ludendorff—was the star of the evening. The "drummer" had discarded his mask and impressively underscored his ambition to lead the "national revolution."

Hardly anyone in the beer hall would have suspected that this fraternal-looking ceremony was a calculated put-on. "We were all more deeply moved than rarely before," Hitler himself later said, describing the atmosphere.[77] Most of the people in attendance shared the sentiment that they were witnessing a historic moment. Many were unable to join in the German national anthem, which was sung at the end, because they were so overcome with emotion. Before the crowd dispersed, as arranged, an SA commando under Hess arrested all the members of the Knilling cabinet in the audience. They were taken to the villa of the pan-Germanic publisher Julius F. Lehmann.

It was at that point, just as he seemed to have succeeded in his surprise offensive, that Hitler made his decisive mistake. Having received news that the seizure of the military barracks housing pioneer units had run into difficulties, he decided to go there with Friedrich Weber, the head of the Bund Oberland paramilitary group. That left Kahr, Lossow and Seisser under Ludendorff's supervision. When Hitler returned, he discovered to his horror that the general had allowed the triumvirate to leave the beer hall with only a promise that they would stick to the agreement they had made. When Hitler expressed his scepticism, Ludendorff responded sharply that he would tolerate no doubts being cast upon a German officer's word of honour.[78]

Hitler's misgivings soon proved justified. Hardly had Kahr, Lossow and Seisser left the beer hall when they used their freedom to betray Hitler and Ludendorff and order action taken against them. The putsch was thus condemned to failure since everything depended on getting the triumvirate behind the uprising. The rebels had made no further plans about occupying key institutions like army and police barracks, transport and communication centres and newspaper offices. Now their dilettantish preparations and improvised activism would come back to haunt them—and the one responsible for the fiasco was clearly Hitler, who had moved forward the putsch. The only success the rebels achieved was Ernst Röhm taking over Lossow's local defence commando. Among Röhm's followers was a 23-year-old man with metal-rimmed spectacles, an unemployed agriculture expert named Heinrich Himmler, for whom the putsch marked the start of a political career that would make him the second most powerful man in the Third Reich.[79]

Meanwhile, the triumvirate had hardly been idle. Since his office was occupied by SA men, Lossow drove from the Bürgerbräukeller to the city military headquarters. The generals present welcomed him with the question, "Surely, Your Excellency, this was all a bluff?" Bavaria's military leader may have vacillated in the preceding hours, but now he assured his subordinates that the declaration he had made in the beer hall was "just a show he had been forced to perform under the threat of violence."[80] Shortly after 11 p.m. the officers went to the barracks of the 19th Infantry Regiment in order to coordinate their counter-measures. At around 1 a.m. on 9 November, Kahr and Seisser joined them. The triumvirate agreed on the text for a radio message to be broadcast at 2:50 a.m. on all Munich stations: "General State Commissar von Kahr, General von Lossow and Colonel Seisser reject the Hitler putsch. Statements they were forced to make at gunpoint at the meeting in the Bürgerbräukeller are invalid. People should beware of the misuse being made of their names."[81] Local authorities and border police were instructed to arrest the leaders of the coup d'état should they try to flee.

The insurgents failed to realise that things had turned against them. After midnight, they were still putting up a "proclamation to the German people" on advertising columns and building walls. It announced that "the government of the November criminals" had been deposed and replaced by a "provisional national German government."[82] In reality, the momentum had long since shifted to the triumvirate, who spent the night issuing orders to bolster troop numbers in Munich and put down the uprising.[83] An emissary sent by Hitler and Kriebel to the barracks early in the morning to determine Lossow's position was immediately arrested. The general took him into custody with the words: "There's no negotiating with rebels." And Kahr chimed in: "The assurances forced from us with a pistol are null and void."[84]

As dilettantish as the putsch and as burlesque as the scenes in the Bürgerbräukeller may have been, what happened in the night of 9 November was all the more serious since in many respects it foreshadowed what would take place ten years later, after Hitler had been named Reich chancellor.[85] For several hours, storm troopers thought they had seized political power and began to carry out terror campaigns against their political adversaries and Jewish citizens in Munich. Immediately after the conclusion of the Bürgerbräu gathering, members of the Stosstrupp Hitler marched to the headquarters of the left-wing *Münchener Post* newspaper and caused considerable damage. Shortly after midnight they forced their way into the apartment of editor-in-chief and SPD politician Erhard Auer and tried to arrest him. Only Auer's wife and son-in-law were at home, so the SA men took them along in Auer's stead and kept them locked in a room in the Bürgerbräukeller. The chairman of the Central Association of Jewish Citizens in Munich, Ludwig Wassermann, was already detained there after the insurgents had identified him leaving the beer hall. Over the course of the night, SA men swarmed out taking Jewish hostages wherever they could get them, but several prominent Jewish families had quickly fled the city or gone into hiding. On the morning of 9 November, members of the Bund Oberland moved into the Bogenhausen district, considered a neighbourhood full of wealthy Jews, and began carrying out arrests on the flimsy basis of address books and nameplates on doors. Those detained were locked up in the Bürgerbräukeller, where they joined eight city councillors from left-wing parties whom the Stosstrupp Hitler had apprehended that morning at the city Rathaus.[86]

The British consul general in Munich, Robert Clive, reported on 11 November: "As instances of the sort of thing we should have had to expect if Hitler was in power, I may mention that orders were immediately given the same night to round up the Jews."[87] Indeed, only the rapid collapse of the putsch prevented much worse abuses. The pocket of a Nazi lawyer who worked for the Bavarian Supreme Court, Baron Theodor von der Pfordten, and who was shot dead in front of the Feldherrnhalle around noon on 9 November, contained a draft constitution that was to take effect after the successful putsch. It decreed that "all risks to security and useless consumers of food" be brought to "collection camps." Those who tried to resist being transported were to be sentenced to death, together with "members of the Jewish people," who had profited from the war and resisted the confiscation of their assets.[88] In early summer 1923, Ernst Hanfstaengl recalled, Hitler had mentioned with "great and quasi-intoxicated admiration" the Roman dictator Sulla's policies of proscription, expropriation and execution as a "model for the indispensable cleansing of post-war Germany from the pustulent Bolshevik hordes." Even during his subsequent trial Hitler made little secret of his aims. The putsch was intended to bring about the "most overwhelming transformation of Germany in . . . historical memory since the founding of the state of New Brandenburg-Prussia."[89]

By the early hours of the morning, the conspirators finally realised that they could not count on the triumvirate, and every new report from the outside world confirmed that the Reichswehr and police were preparing to respond to the coup. In the Bürgerbräukeller, the previous night's euphoria was replaced by sobriety. Hitler vacillated between hope and despair. On the one hand, during the night, he charged Gottfried Feder with drawing up a proclamation nationalising the banks. On the other hand, he seemed to accept the inevitable. He was quoted as saying: "If it comes off, everything's fine. If it doesn't, we'll hang ourselves."[90] The leaders of the uprising conferred for hours about what to do next. Kriebel suggested an orderly retreat to Rosenheim, the epicentre of the movement, but Ludendorff refused, stating that he did not want the "ethnic-popular movement to end in the dirt of the streets."[91] Instead he proposed to stage a protest march to the centre of town. With Hitler having run out of ideas, the general finally seemed to grow in stature and halted any further discussion with a command to march. But there was little hope of winning over popular sentiment for their cause by it and somehow reversing their fortune.[92]

The march formed at around noon. At the front, Hitler, Ludendorff, Scheubner-Richter, Weber, Graf and Göring led around 2,000 paramilitaries and cadets from Munich's Infantry School, who had joined the rebels under the leadership of the former Freikorps commander Gerhard Rossbach. After overrunning a police cordon at Ludwigs Bridge, the march continued on to the Isar Gate and Marienplatz, Munich's central square. Thousands of onlookers had gathered and cheered the demonstrators on. "The enthusiasm was unprecedented," Hitler later said, "and I couldn't help but remark to myself during the march that the people were behind us."[93] But the demonstrators could hardly fail to notice that many of the posters proclaiming their new government had been torn down or were covered over with Kahr's renunciation of the rebellion.[94] The marchers continued on to Residenzstrasse singing the old military song "O Deutschland hoch in Ehren" (O Germany, high in honour). Shortly before the march reached the Odeonsplatz near the Feldherrnhalle, a mêlée broke out between the demonstrators and police. Then came a gunshot—no one has ever determined who fired it—and the two sides exchanged heavy fire for thirty seconds.[95] In the end, fourteen members of the putsch and four policemen lay dead on the cobblestones.

Max Erwin von Scheubner-Richter was one of the first casualties. He had locked arms with Hitler, who fell with him, dislocating his left shoulder. Göring was seriously wounded by a bullet to the hip. While the rest of the vanguard of the demonstration instinctively dropped to the ground and then fled backwards chaotically, Ludendorff marched straight and stiff as a candle through the police lines and allowed himself to be arrested without resistance on Odeonsplatz.

Amidst the tumult, Hitler had got up and made his way down a side street, where Dr. Walter Schultze, head of the SA medical service, found him and pulled him into a car. It headed south at high speed. Seventy kilometres outside Munich, just before the village of Uffing am Staffelsee, the motor gave out. Together with the doctor and an orderly, Hitler proceeded on foot to Hanfstaengl's holiday home. "Just after 7 p.m., the servant girl came and said that somebody had knocked quietly on the door," Helene Hanfstaengl recalled.

> I went downstairs and to my astonishment I heard Hitler's unmistakable, if weakened, voice. I quickly opened the door. There he stood, pale as a ghost, without a hat, his face and his clothing covered in dirt and his left arm hanging from his shoulder at a strange angle. Two men, a young doctor and an orderly, were supporting him.[96]

The fugitive, who had not slept for many hours, was still in shock. He lamented the deaths of Ludendorff and Graf, who had thrown himself in front of his boss to protect him. In fact, the former had emerged from the gunfight unscathed, while the latter had been seriously wounded. Hitler was in great pain from his dislocated shoulder. It was not until the following day that the doctor succeeded in resetting the joint. A sling prevented Hitler from donning his jacket so Helene Hanfstaengl gave him a blue bathrobe that belonged to her husband, recalling: "The patient smiled and said he felt like a Roman emperor."

Over the course of the afternoon of 11 November, Hitler grew ever more restless. He had sent the orderly to the Bechsteins in Munich to ask if they would loan Hitler their car so he could flee across the Austrian border, but the car did not arrive, and Hitler knew that his hideaway would not remain undiscovered for long. At 5 p.m. the phone rang. It was Hanfstaengl's mother, who lived nearby and reported that police were searching her home. "Now all is lost," Helene Hanfstaengl recalled Hitler saying. He reached for his revolver, which he had placed atop a cupboard, but she managed to take it off him and hid it in a flour container. "Then, I got some paper and a fountain pen and asked him to write down instructions for his closest comrades, while there was still time—one page per person," Helene Hanfstaengl reported. Hitler obediently did as he was told.[97]

A short time later, cars pulled up and police surrounded the house. The young police lieutenant Rudolf Belleville, an acquaintance of Hess, introduced himself and politely requested to search the premises. Helene Hanfstaengl led him upstairs and opened a door. "In the room stood Hitler in white pyjamas with his arm in a sling," read the official police report. "Hitler was staring absent-mindedly and when informed that he was being taken into custody, he extended his hand to the arresting officer and said that he was at his disposal."[98] Hitler was brought that same day to Landsberg prison and put in cell number 7. To make room for him, its previous occupant—Eisner's murderer, Count Anton Arco auf Valley—had been moved elsewhere.[99]

The seriously wounded Göring had been treated at a private clinic in Munich and was apprehended trying to cross the border with Austria, but thanks to police bungling, he succeeded in getting away to Innsbruck. He was joined there by a host of others who had taken part in the putsch, including Hermann Esser and Ernst Hanfstaengl. Hess hid out in the apartment of his paternal professor Karl Haushofer.

He then also fled to Austria before turning himself in to the Bavarian authorities in April 1924 after Hitler's conviction. Gottfried Feder, who had also escaped injury, found refuge with friends in Czechoslovakia from late November 1923 to mid-January 1924. Ernst Pöhner and Wilhelm Frick, who had conspired with the uprising, had already been arrested during the night of 8–9 November. Ernst Röhm had been apprehended in the afternoon of 9 November after the home defence commando he had taken over surrendered. Erich Ludendorff, who had essentially turned himself in, was released on his word of honour.[100]

After the coup was put down, Munich was like a pressure cooker, with "members of the so-called better classes" openly hostile to the Reichswehr and the police. "When we marched through Maximilienstrasse," a police captain reported, "we were greeted with insults like 'Jew-protectors!—Traitors to the fatherland!—Bloodhounds—Heil Hitler—Down with Kahr'—and the like. When we crossed Odeonsplatz, pedestrians yelled, whistled, jeered and shook their fists at us."[101] In the days following the attempted putsch, there were demonstrations against the "clique of traitors"—Kahr, Lossow and Seisser—in Munich and other Bavarian cities. "It was clear that the feeling of the crowd was all for Hitler," reported British Consul General Clive to London.[102] Students in particular tended to sympathise with Hitler and his co-conspirators. At a mass event at the University of Munich on 12 November, speakers were repeatedly interrupted by cries of "Up with Hitler, down with Kahr." As the university dean called upon those present to sing the German national anthem, the audience sang the Freikorps song "Swastika on a Steel Helmet" instead. Together with the professor of medicine, Ferdinand Sauerbruch, the historian Karl Alexander von Müller tried "to bring the students to reason," as he put it.[103] It took a while for the situation to calm down, and when it did, developments in the Reich were partially responsible. By mid-November 1923, the worst of Germany's crisis was over. Currency reform had throttled hyperinflation, and the economy had begun to recover. Weimar democracy had survived. A period of stabilisation commenced, signalling the end of the immediate post-war era.[104]

During his first days of imprisonment at Landsberg, Hitler was completely demoralised and toyed with the idea of suicide. He went on hunger strike, probably in an attempt to end his life, but that just landed him in the infirmary. "He sat there before me in his chair like a lump of misery, badly shaven, exhausted, and listened to my simple words with a tired smile and complete indifference," prison guard Franz Hemmrich recalled.[105] Hitler revealed to prison psychologist Alois Maria Ott that "I've had enough. I'm done. If I had a revolver, I'd use it." Ott succeeded in calming his patient down, and with the help of Hitler's lawyer, they convinced him to end his hunger strike.[106] Visitors, however, remained shocked by Hitler's condition. He was pale, haggard and, as Hess learned by letter, "emotionally very down."[107] Nonetheless, little by little, he recovered. When his half-sister Angela Raubal spoke with him for half an hour in mid-December, he was back in good mental and psychological form. "Physically he is quite well," she told her brother Alois. "His arm still gives him trouble, but they think it is almost healed. How moving is the loyalty he is accorded these days."[108]

Among those who still had complete faith in Hitler were the Wagners. They had happened to be in Munich on 9 November for the scheduled premiere of Siegfried Wagner's symphonic poem *Happiness*. The concert was cancelled after the putsch was put down, and the Wagners returned to Bayreuth embittered. "There has never been such a scandalous betrayal!" the outraged Siegfried proclaimed. "Even people as pure as Hitler and Ludendorff aren't immune from such dirty tricks being played on them . . . How much easier the Jews and the clerics have it." His wife Winifred tried to bolster the spirits of disappointed NSDAP followers in Bayreuth: "Believe me, despite everything, Adolf Hitler is the man of the future. He'll draw the sword from the German oak." In early December 1923, Winifred wrote a letter to her "dear esteemed friend Hitler," in which she sent him the libretto for Siegfried's *The Blacksmith of Marienburg*. "Perhaps this little book will help you pass a long hour or two," she wrote. She told Hitler that she and Siegfried would be visiting their mutual friends the Bechsteins and assured him he would be there in spirit. On 6 December, Winifred told a friend that she had sent her idol in Landsberg "a care package with a woollen blanket, jacket, socks, warm linings and books." In the run-up to Christmas she turned Villa Wahnfried into a veritable collection point for packages of affection ultimately bound for Landsberg. Siegfried was delighted: "My wife is fighting like a lioness for Hitler! Wonderful!"[109]

On 13 December 1923, the deputy state prosecutor Hans Ehard travelled to Landsberg to interrogate Hitler. He initially refused to make any statement at all. "He wasn't a criminal, and he refused to be interrogated like a criminal," the protocol recorded Hitler saying. When Ehard pointed out that such recalcitrance only meant that he would spend longer in investigative custody, Hitler responded that he was solely interested in justifying his actions and his mission before history and that he rejected any authority the court might claim to pass judgement upon him. He would only play "his best trumps . . . in the courtroom." Then one would see whether "certain gentlemen" would dare to "raise their hand in perjury"—a reference to Kahr, Lossow and Seisser.

Realising that he was getting nowhere with the stubborn inmate, Ehard sent his stenographer out of the room and talked with Hitler off the record for five hours. Hitler was initially mistrustful, but he thawed out and was soon drowning the state prosecutor in wave after wave of words. It became immediately clear what Hitler's defence strategy would be. He would dispute the accusation of high treason by claiming that not only had the representatives of legal state power in Bavaria participated in the coup but that they had planned everything that had been decided in the Bürgerbräukeller together months in advance. "In their hearts they stood by the cause and only changed their minds later," Ehard reported Hitler saying.[110]

One open question was where the trial should take place. Despite his opposition to the 1922 Law on the Defence of the Republic, Hitler preferred the State Court in Leipzig because he hoped judges there would be less favourably disposed towards the triumvirate than those in Munich. "In Leipzig, various gentlemen might well enter the court as witnesses and leave it as prisoners," he told Ehard. "That of course wouldn't be the case in Munich. Here that wouldn't be allowed."[111] In fact, the powers that be in Bavaria had no interest in revealing to the public how entwined Kahr and Lossow, who both resigned before the start of the trial, had been in the plans for the coup d'état. It was decided to hold the main trial in Munich's First District Court; the venue was the former war academy on Blutenburgstrasse 3. On 26 February 1924, under the scrutiny of the German and international press, proceedings were opened against Hitler, Ludendorff, Röhm, Pöhner, Frick, Kriebel, Weber and the SA leaders Wilhelm Brückner,

Robert Wagner and Heinz Pernet. The building was protected with barbed wire and guards, and anyone entering was thoroughly frisked. The courtroom was full to the very last seat.[112]

Hitler, who was transferred to the court's holding cells on 22 February, seemed confident about the outcome of the trial. "What can they do to me?" he bragged to Hanfstaengl, who had hastened back to Munich after a warrant had been issued for his arrest. "I only need to say a few things, especially about Lossow, and there will be a big scandal."[113] Shortly before 9 a.m. on 26 February, the defendants and their counsel entered the courtroom. Ludendorff took the lead in a simple blue suit, followed by Pöhner and then Hitler in a dark jacket bearing his Iron Cross, First Class. "He looks good," a court reporter remarked. "Imprisonment has not left any marks on him." While the other defendants immediately took their seats, Hitler remained standing for a minute and surveyed the courtroom audience.[114]

The prosecutor named Hitler "the soul of the whole undertaking,"[115] and right from the initial days of the trial there was no question who was the focus of attention. In his four-hour self-defence, Hitler took the entire responsibility for the putsch: "Ultimately, I was the one who wanted it. In the end, the other gentlemen only took action with me." On the other hand, he disputed the state's charges, claiming that there was no such thing as "high treason against the national traitors of 1918." Moreover, if this were a case of high treason, he was surprised that "the gentlemen who wanted the same things we did and held talks to prepare them" were not sitting beside him on the defendants' bench. He was talking about Kahr, Lossow and Seisser, and Hitler promised to make revelations about them in the closed segment of the trial.[116]

The leading judge was Georg Neidhardt, who had already revealed his political colours at Count Anton Arco's trial when he had attributed "the most fervent love of his people and his fatherland" to Eisner's murderer.[117] At Hitler's trial, too, Neidhardt did not conceal his sympathies and allowed Hitler to use the tribunal as a pulpit. Occasionally, when Hitler launched attacks against government representatives or raised his voice to volumes he was accustomed to use at party meetings, the judge did order him to be more moderate. Otherwise, Neidhardt gave Hitler every licence, even the opportunity to cross-examine witnesses, including the members of the triumvirate. Swapping the role of the defendant for that of the prosecutor, Hitler used all of the rhetorical skills at his disposal to direct blame at those he felt had abandoned him on 9 November.

Lossow was the only one to put up any effective resistance, showing how transparent Hitler's pretence of selflessness really was. The Führer of the National Socialists, Lossow countered, considered himself "the German Mussolini," and his followers celebrated him as "the German messiah." Lossow denied ever supporting a national dictatorship under Hitler and Ludendorff. "I wasn't some unemployed Chetnik who thought that the only way of gaining honour and dignity was to launch another putsch," Lossow huffed.[118] The barb stung, and Hitler showered Lossow with crass insults. Neidhardt deemed him to be out of order, but there were no consequences. The general decided to leave the courtroom and never returned.[119]

The journalist Hans von Hülsen wrote of an "unworthy piece of theatre," adding: "What was unfolding there was Munich's version of political carnival."[120] To the very end of the trial, Hitler was allowed to play the master of ceremonies. In his concluding speech, a paradigm of calculating rhetoric, he invoked the hour "when the masses who wander the streets today with our cross [i.e. the swastika] will unite with those who lined up against them on 8 November." Turning directly to the judges, he announced:

> Not you will render the final verdict, but the goddess of the Last Judgement who will rise from our graves as "history" . . . And while you may find us "guilty," this eternal goddess of the eternal court will tear up the prosecutor's petition and the court's verdict with a smile, for *she* will acquit us.

When asked by Neidhardt if he had anything to add, Röhm replied, "After the statements of my friend and Führer Adolf Hitler, I eschew any further words." The other defendants followed suit.[121]

The verdicts were announced on 1 April. The court was unusually jam-packed, and many in the gallery had brought flowers for the defendants. Given the course of the trial, it was no great surprise that Ludendorff, who appeared in full general's regalia with all his medals, was acquitted. Much to the court's dismay, Ludendorff remarked that the ruling was "a shame this uniform and these medals do not deserve." The court stenographer noted: "Feverish cries of 'Heil!'"[122] Hitler, Weber, Kriebel and Pöhner were found guilty of the "crime of high treason" with a minimum sentence of five years' imprisonment, although their sentences could be suspended for good behaviour after only six months. The court also ruled that Hitler, who "is so German in his thinking and feeling," was exempt from possible deportation to Austria under the Law for the Defence of the Republic. That drew "bravos" from the gallery. Brückner, Röhm, Pernet, Wagner and Frick were given suspended sentences of one year and three months.[123] The sentences were scandalously mild, and the press rushed out of the courtroom to pass them along via telephone. The *Münchener Neueste Nachrichten* reported: "Shortly after 11:15 a.m., Ludendorff drove off in a car to vigorous cries of 'Heil . . .' Hitler, Kriebel and the other convicted defendants appeared in the window of the court building and were also greeted by the masses . . . with boisterous cries of 'Hooray' and 'Heil.'"[124]

"Munich is chuckling over the verdict, which is regarded as an excellent joke for All Fools Day," commented *The Times* in London,[125] but the court's ruling came in for sharp criticism among adherents of the Weimar Republic. "Judicial murder has been carried out against the republic in Munich," wrote the left-wing journal *Die Weltbühne*.[126] In fact, the court's verdict praised the defendants as "having acted in a purely patriotic spirit, led by the most noble, selfless will."[127] It was the moral equivalent of an acquittal. The court failed to mention that the putsch had cost four policemen their lives, and that SA commandos had terrorised the Munich populace during the night of the attempted coup and that the draft constitution found on the dead rebel Pfordten had contained an outline for a system of concentration camps. The verdict was a travesty of justice, and as such it foreshadowed what would happen to Germany's judicial system in the Third Reich. Hitler knew he had reason to be grateful to Neidhardt. In September 1933, he named the judge president of the Bavarian Supreme Court in Munich.[128]

The putsch and subsequent trial established Hitler's notoriety well beyond Bavaria. For months, the media were fascinated by the man who had been able to turn a fiasco into a propaganda triumph. Most observers were convinced that Hitler would return to prominence once his time in Landsberg was served. For Hitler, a five-year apprenticeship was over. He had gone from being the "drummer" for a movement to becoming the "Führer" of an anticipated "national revolution."[129] The most important lesson he learned from the failed enterprise of 8 and 9 November was that he was going to have to take another path if he wanted to come to power. Instead of a putsch, he needed to ensure at least the pretence of legality in cooperation with the Reichswehr. It was while imprisoned in Landsberg, Hitler recollected in February 1942, that he "became convinced that violence would not work since the state is too established and has all the weapons in its possession."[130]

Several of Hitler's main characteristics and behavioural patterns came to the fore even more clearly during the critical days of November 1923. Among them were the extreme vacillations between euphoria, apathy and depression. Hitler had repeatedly announced that he would kill himself if the putsch failed, and this latent tendency towards self-annihilation would accompany him throughout his political career. In his 1940 book *Germany: Jekyll & Hyde*, Sebastian Haffner rightly called Hitler "a potential suicide par excellence."[131]

Another constant was the all-or-nothing attitude of the political gambler. Consciously or not, he seemed to be imitating the Prussian king Friedrich the Great, whom he much admired and whose biography he knew from Franz Kugler's 1840 *History of Friedrich the Great*. In 1740, Friedrich had bet everything on a single card by launching a surprise attack against Silesia, and he had repeatedly demonstrated a near-suicidal proclivity for risk-taking during the Seven Years War from 1756 to 1763.[132] Forced to act, Hitler had similarly gone all out when he detained and blackmailed the triumvirate.[133] Once he had decided to strike what he hoped would be a decisive blow, Hitler had no more time for counter-arguments. "Herr Hitler does not engage with objections," Lossow said at the trial by way of explaining Hitler's missionary convictions and immunity to criticism. "He is the Chosen One and everyone else has to accept whatever he says."[134]

As far as we know, however, none of Hitler's entourage ever made any attempts to restrain him. Although they were only initiated at a late stage into the plans for the putsch, they followed his call without hesitation.[135] That is another indication of how unquestioned his authority as Führer had become within the party. The failed putsch would do nothing to undermine this status. On the contrary, it reinforced Hitler's image as a man who not only talked, but acted in critical situations—and who was willing to take great personal risks. He would continue to feed off this aura even after he became Germany's chancellor.

7

Landsberg Prison and Mein Kampf

"Landsberg was my state-paid university," Hitler once remarked to his legal adviser Hans Frank.[1] After years of frenetic political activity and weeks of a trial that had demanded his entire attention, incarceration in Landsberg prison offered Hitler a not necessarily unwelcome break. "Among the many lucky aspects of Hitler's political career, these nine months of non-interruption were one of the most valuable gifts," his biographer Konrad Heiden concluded.[2] As an inmate, Hitler had time to reflect on the debacle of 8–9 November and learn his lessons. He also used his involuntary stay behind bars to continue his autodidactic studies. He once again had the chance "to read and to learn," he wrote to Siegfried Wagner in early May 1924, whereas previously he had barely had time to acquaint himself with the "newly published works on the ethnic-nationalist book market."[3] All his reading now was going to serve the book he had decided to write. Without Landsberg, there would have been no *Mein Kampf*, Hitler recalled in 1942, since it was only there that he had achieved conceptual clarity about things "he had largely intuited" before.[4] It had been stupid of the government, he claimed, to imprison him: "They would have been better off letting me speak and speak again and never find my peace of mind."[5]

Imprisonment only encouraged Hitler's belief in himself and his historic mission. In Landsberg, he recalled, "he had gained the level of confidence, optimism and faith that could no longer be shaken by anything."[6] His sense of being the Chosen One, which he had vaguely felt already in his youth, was now set in stone. And his fellow inmates, first and foremost Hess, did everything they could to strengthen his conviction that he was meant to play the role of the tribune as in Wagner's *Rienzi*. In mid-June 1924 Hess wrote to his later wife Ilse Pröhl: "Hitler is the 'man of the future' in Germany, the 'dictator' whose flag will fly sooner or later over public buildings in Berlin. He himself has faith enough to move mountains."[7] Nowhere does that peculiar symbiotic relationship between the messianic hopes and expectations projected by Hitler's disciples and Hitler's own self-image as national saviour emerge more clearly than in Hess's letters from Landsberg.

"Hitler's punishment is the sort handed out for a gentleman's indiscretion—a holiday disguised by some legalese," the journalist Carl von Ossietzky protested in late April 1924.[8] And indeed, the conditions at Landsberg were more like a spa than a prison, and Hitler enjoyed a wide variety of privileges. His "cell" was a large, airy, comfortably furnished room with an expansive view. In addition to the hearty food cooked by the prison kitchen, Hitler constantly received care packages; his quarters reminded some visitors of a "delicatessen."[9] For his thirty-fifth birthday on 20 April, Hitler was showered with gifts, letters and telegrams. "His quarters and the common room looked like a forest of flowers," commented one of the prison guards. "It smelled like a greenhouse."[10] In Munich, supporters of the NSDAP, which had been banned, and former front-line soldiers held an event to honour the man who, in their words, "sparked the current flame behind the idea of liberty and the ethnic consciousness of the German people."[11]

Hitler's admirers and his political followers kept up a continuous pilgrimage to Landsberg. In April and May, Hitler was receiving upwards of five visitors per day from all over Germany. "Every social class and age was represented," recalled one of the guards.

> There were bearded guys in lederhosen and crudely nailed shoes, cosmopolitan gentlemen from industry and high society, clergymen of both Christian confessions, rural lower-middle-class folks, lawyers, former military officers, professors, farmers, artists, day labourers, aristocrats, booksellers, publishers and newspaper editors. All of them came—sometimes for the strangest of reasons.[12]

Among the flood of visitors were older ladies who enjoyed mothering Hitler. Hermine Hoffmann spoiled him with sweets and whipped cream, Helene Bechstein brought a gramophone, and Elsa Bruckmann waited two hours to speak to him. In her essay "My First Trip to the

Führer," written in 1933, Bruckmann described her first encounter with Hitler as though she had met a saint:

> Finally, someone came and got me. I was led through a number of long corridors and approached Hitler, who was dressed in Bavarian lederhosen and a yellow linen jacket. He looked simple and chivalrous, and his eyes were bright. The moment of our encounter was so important for me because I perceived the same simple greatness, the same mature and genuine nature and the same life flowing from the roots, in the *person* who stood across from me as I had previously experienced at a distance in the great Führer and orator within the total spectacle of mass events . . . I brought him best regards from a great man who was still alive then and who had foreseen the Führer's destiny: Houston Stewart Chamberlain, who was also our friend.[13]

Bruckmann's account of their meeting is extremely stylised. Nonetheless, it does reveal Hitler's talent for slipping into the roles he assumed would most impress the people he met. In the presence of this upper-class salon lady, Hitler presented himself as a humble man of the people in traditional Bavarian dress. Hitler also wore lederhosen with suspenders and a white linen shirt with a tie when he took his daily walk through the prison yard, often accompanied by one of his disciples.[14] Well fed and enjoying the fresh air, he quickly recovered from the physical demands of the preceding years. "The Tribune looks splendid," Hess wrote to Ilse Pröhl on 18 May. "His face is no longer so drawn. The involuntary break is good for him."[15]

Hess first arrived at Landsberg in mid-May. Initially, he was housed on the first floor, in the so-called "commanders' wing," which also contained Hitler, Kriebel, Weber and Hitler's chauffeur Emil Maurice. Maurice, who was brought to Landsberg in April, served as the group's connection to the "lansquenet" contingent in the prison: some forty members of the Stosstrupp Hitler, who had been sentenced to imprisonment at a subsequent trial.[16] Hitler also assumed the role of Führer vis-à-vis other prisoners. Each new arrival had to report to him for inspection. "I hardly had time to look around in my cell," recalled inmate Hans Kallenbach, "when Emil Maurice appeared and ordered me to report to the Führer immediately. The old Nazi drive was present even here!"[17]

Despite the physical proximity to his underlings, Hitler was careful to maintain a sense of distance from them, refusing, for instance, to participate in sporting activities. When Ernst Hanfstaengl advised the 35-year-old, who was putting on weight, to join in, Hitler shot back: "No, no. That's out of the question. It would be bad for discipline. A Führer can't afford to be beaten by his followers, even at gymnastics or games."[18]

Communal lunch in the prison's large common room always followed a set ritual. Hitler's fellow inmates would wait, standing silently behind their chairs, for the cry "Attention!" The Führer would then walk, accompanied by his inner circle, through the rows of his faithful followers and sit down at the top end of the table.[19] A similar ceremony was maintained at the social evenings every Saturday. "When the Führer arrived, the house band would strike up a welcome march and then segue into a lansquenet or military song everyone could sing along to," Hans Kallenbach wrote. As a rule Hitler would give a short speech that concluded with his followers crying "Never say die! Sieg heil!" "On those evenings," Kallenbach recalled, "the leader and those he led kept alive the true spirit of front-line soldiers."[20]

Not only did the guards do nothing to disrupt these activities: many of them sympathised with the aims of National Socialism, treating Hitler with great respect and greeting him under their breath with "Heil!"[21] Rudolf Belleville, the officer who arrested Hitler and who served as a guard for several weeks in the summer of 1924, greeted Hess with the words: "Hello, I know you. I'm a National Socialist too." Belleville, Hess recorded, told him that it still brought "tears to his eyes" when he remembered taking Hitler into custody.[22] Whenever Hitler gave his speeches, the guards would gather in the hallway and listen in.[23] Inmates were also allowed to publish a prison newspaper, "The Landsberg Honorary Citizen," to which Hitler occasionally contributed articles and caricatures.[24] Thus life in this unusual jail was varied and entertaining, and the all-male inmates pleasantly whiled away their time there. None of them felt that they had done anything wrong—let alone harboured moral qualms.

Hitler instructed his fellow inmates, he later claimed, to behave in a way that "no one in the facility could fail to become a committed National Socialist by the time he was released."[25] But no huge amount of persuasion was necessary. Hitler scrupulously avoided any conflict with the prison authorities, preferring to achieve "peacefully and amicably what was possible." He said he had no desire to play the role of the "wild man" and strictly forbade his followers from disobeying the prison rules.[26] His true concern was no doubt his parole. By being openly cooperative, Hitler wanted to ensure he would be released after six months, on 1 October 1924.

Yet while a tight-knit fellowship was forming behind prison walls, in the outside world, the ethnic-chauvinistic movement was quickly disintegrating into a host of rival groups. Gustav von Kahr had immediately banned the NSDAP and the various organisations of the Fighting Association on 9 November 1923. The *Völkischer Beobachter* was forced to cease publication, and party property was confiscated.[27] Directly before he went to prison, Hitler had dictated to Helene Hanfstaengl a message for Alfred Rosenberg, asking him to lead the movement in his absence.[28] It is unclear why Hitler chose Rosenberg, who was hardly the most practically oriented mind. Perhaps it was Rosenberg's obvious lack of leadership qualities that appealed to Hitler, who did not want a competitor appearing on the scene while he was away.[29] In his first newsletter, dated 3 December 1923 and signed by "Rolf Eidhalt" (an anagram of Adolf Hitler), Rosenberg announced that despite everything the leadership of the party was "once again in good hands." Nonetheless, the ban meant that "the party from now on must be run as a secret organisation," and everyone concerned would have to pitch in to "prevent the dissipation of our movement."[30]

Yet that was precisely what happened. Hitler was the lynchpin who integrated and maintained a balance between divergent forces and interests, and the party sorely missed him. "The ups and downs in the movement after Hitler's arrest were the best indication of his exceptional leadership personality," commented one of his followers after the Führer's release from Landsberg.[31] Rosenberg lacked the necessary authority to hold the party together, and as Hanfstaengl observed, "everywhere busybodies and opportunists from the second or third ranks are trying to push their way forward."[32] The movement was riven with people who felt they needed to make their mark and were jealous of everyone else. Moreover, because of its weak organisational structure beyond Munich, it quickly emerged that the NSDAP was ill-equipped to deal with life as an illegal body. For that reason, in January Rosenberg and his deputy Hans Jacob founded another party, the Greater German Popular Community (Grossdeutsche Volksgemeinschaft, or GVG), which they had no trouble officially registering, even though it was a transparent surrogate for the NSDAP.[33] But if they hoped it would serve as a reservoir for all of Hitler's adherents, they were disappointed. A bitter rivalry soon broke out between Rosenberg, on the one hand, and Hermann Esser, who returned from Austrian exile in May, and Julius Streicher on the other. In early June, Rosenberg was forced out, and Esser and Streicher formed a new leadership duo. In a newsletter, they immediately demanded that "the emphasis of the old Hitler movement must continue to be extra-parliamentary."[34]

This declaration was primarily directed against the Ethnic Block (Völkischer Block, or VB), another umbrella organisation of ethnic-chauvinist and National Socialist Bavarian groups, which had also formed in January 1924 and which had announced its intention to participate in the electoral process. In the Bavarian Landtag elections of 6 April, the VB recorded a remarkable triumph, immediately winning 17.1 per cent of the votes and 23 parliamentary seats, which made it the third-strongest political force in Bavaria behind the BVP (32.8 per cent of the vote) and the SPD (17.2 per cent). In Munich, the VB attracted 25.7 per cent of the vote—more than any other party.[35] For the national elections the following month, the VB had concluded an alliance with the Ethnic German Liberation Party (Deutschvölkische Freiheitspartei, or DVFP), which had been founded by three rebel members of the German National People's Party (Deutschnationale Volkspartei, or DNVP), Albrecht von Graefe, Reinhard Wulle and Wilhelm Hennig, and which had its power base in northern Germany. The DVFP sensed a chance to occupy the vacuum left behind by the ban on the NSDAP and become the leading force within the ethnic-nationalist movement. Their ambitions were bolstered by Erich Ludendorff, who called for all rival ethnic-chauvinist and National Socialist groups to unite under the umbrella of one organisation.[36]

In the Reichstag elections on 4 May 1924, the unified list of ethnic-chauvinist parties got 6.5 per cent of the vote and 32 parliamentary seats. Twenty-two of them went to representatives of the DVFP, compared with only 10 for the National Socialists, whose deputies included Röhm, Feder, Frick and Gregor Strasser, a pharmacist from Landshut who would soon play a leading role in the NSDAP.[37] The most famous member of the faction was Ludendorff, who twice visited Hitler in Landsberg and tried to win him over to the idea of an association of all ethnic-chauvinist groups. Hitler behaved in conciliatory fashion, while expressing reservations.[38] But he could not prevent the Reichstag deputies from uniting under the banner of the "National Socialist Liberation Party," when they met as a faction on 24 May. A short time later, the following declaration was published in the press: "It is the will of ethnic-popular leaders General Ludendorff, Hitler and Graefe that their followers should in future form one political organisation throughout the Reich."[39] Ludendorff underscored the validity of the declaration, by claiming that Hitler had come out "clearly and unambiguously for the necessity of the merger of the DVFP and the National Socialist Workers' Party into one party outside the Reichstag as well."[40]

Many of Hitler's followers were opposed to the transition to parliamentary participation and the idea of a fusion with the DVFP. National Socialists in northern Germany were particularly alarmed.[41] In late May they sent a four-man delegation led by Ludolf Haase, a party comrade from Göttingen, to Landsberg to discuss their concerns with Hitler, but the Führer was as evasive as he had been with Ludendorff. As far as the elections were concerned, Hitler had already written to Siegfried Wagner at the beginning of the month, telling him that he would have found it "more correct to avoid participating at least this time around."[42] But apparently he was no longer opposed to the parliamentary strategy in principle. Hitler, at least in Hess's summary, took the view that "after others had gone to parliament against his will, activity in parliament would have to be seen . . . as one of many means to combat the present system." That did not mean constructive participation in the parliamentary process, but rather opposition and obstruction. The idea was "to extend parliament or, better said, parliamentarianism, *ad absurdum*."[43]

In fact, Hitler never budged an inch in his rejection of a merger of the NSDAP and the DVFP, even though to the disappointment of the northern German contingent he refused to give them a statement to that effect. His priority was to keep out of the internal party squabbles and unsavoury personal intrigues, which he correctly recognised could only damage his aura as Führer. As he told Ludolf Haase on 16 June, he could hardly be expected "to intervene in any way or assume any responsibility" from the confines of Landsberg. He had decided "to withdraw from public politics until such a time as his restored liberty made it possible for him to genuinely lead."[44] A short time later Hermann Fobke, a law student and former member of the Stosstrupp Hitler who also served time at Landsberg, told friends in northern Germany Hitler thought "that the wagon has gone so far off the road as to require a complete start from scratch when he goes free." Nonetheless, Hitler was confident that within a few days of his release he would have "all the reins firmly in his grasp."[45]

On 7 July, Hitler publicly announced his decision. In a press release, he stated that he had "stepped down from the leadership of the National Socialist movement" and would refrain from "all political activities for the duration of his imprisonment." An additional reason was given for his decision: "Herr Hitler is writing a substantial book and wants to preserve the free time necessary for it." He therefore requested his supporters not to pay any more visits to Landsberg.[46] The pilgrimages did not abate, however, so Hitler was forced to repeat his request on 29 July. In the future, Hitler would only receive visitors who stated their purpose in advance and who were approved. "In all other cases, as much as I regret it, I'm compelled to turn visitors away," Hitler wrote.[47]

Hitler's withdrawal encouraged the ethnic-chauvinist movement to spin further out of control. A conference on 20 July in Weimar that was intended to bring unity ended in tumult, with various sides trading insults. Such scenes made him sick, declared Ludendorff, adding that if that was the German ethnic movement, then he would take his leave and express his regret that he had mistakenly spent time in its midst.[48] A follow-up conference, also in Weimar, in mid-August may have achieved the merger of the NSDAP and DVFP into a "National Socialist Liberation Movement," but that was merely a declaration on paper. Despite individual appeals for unity and solidarity, the disintegration of the NSDAP and the ethnic-chauvinist movement continued apace.[49]

Though constantly pressured by his followers to put his foot down, Hitler stuck rigidly to his policy of not taking sides and keeping silent about what he thought. He had to "behave with complete neutrality," he told the northern German delegation, in order to be able to carry out the reorganisation of the party impartially as soon as he was released. "Whoever doesn't obey then, will be out—regardless of who they are," he threatened.[50] This approach helped Hitler avoid getting drawn into fights between various groups and sub-groups. "His person remains elevated above small quarrels," Hess noted in mid-August 1924. "When he's back on the outside, his authority will ensure that everything will quickly be under control again." Hess speculated that the constant feuding in the party and the movement were not altogether unwelcome for Hitler: "He thereby shows our people outside that they can't get anything done without him and that it's not as easy as they thought to do the work he does."[51] Some of Hitler's followers even suspected that he deliberately encouraged the disputes "in order to secure his position at the very top."[52] Indeed, Hitler's behaviour while in Landsberg seems to have been an example of a technique of rule that he would develop to perfection as Reich chancellor. Divide and conquer was the best way to cement his own claim to leadership.[53]

The declarations of July 1924 were the first indications the public got that Hitler was writing a book. In fact, he had been at it since the first weeks of his imprisonment. Even at his trial, when he was cross-examined by Hans Ehard on 13 December 1923, Hitler mentioned his plan to write a testimonial that would "tear the mask" from his detractors' faces.[54] The prison director granted him permission to procure a typewriter, and prison guard Franz Hemmrich provided him with a table and paper.[55] Hitler's testimonial has not been preserved, but its contents can be reconstructed from his speeches in front of the court.[56] After he was sentenced on 1 April, Hitler continued writing. One of the first products of his work was an essay entitled "Germany's Awakening" that appeared in a pan-Germanic monthly—many passages are repeated word for word in *Mein Kampf*.[57] Hitler's motivation for putting pen to paper remained constant. As he told Siegfried Wagner on 5 May, he was writing "to comprehensively settle accounts with those gentlemen who enthusiastically cried 'Hurrah' on 9 Nov. only to try to prove the 'ill-considered nature of the insane undertaking' on the 10th."[58]

In early June, Eher Verlag—the Nazi publishing house—had announced the appearance of Hitler's book, then entitled "4½ Years of Struggle Against Lies, Stupidity and Cowardice," for publication in July. The hastily sketched contents indicated that this was to be a one-volume work, but Hitler's decision to withdraw from politics changed that.[59] What was originally a settling of accounts was expanded to include autobiographical sections.[60] Hitler began working intensively on the manuscript in the second half of June. By the end of the month, he read Hess the section on his experience on the Western Front in 1914 (*Mein Kampf*, Chapter 5) and discussed the design of the cover with him.[61] On 23 July he returned to Hess's cell asking whether he could read him the chapter about Munich which he had just completed (*Mein Kampf*, Chapter 4). "I'm still overwhelmed by my impressions," Hess told his girlfriend. When Hess praised what Hitler had written, the latter had beamed. "What a mixture of the sober, mature superiority of the man with boundless boyish joy," Hess wrote.[62]

It is a myth that Hitler often dictated passages until the small hours of the morning to Hess, who, serving as his secretary, typed them up. Many of Hitler's biographers have simply passed on this legend from the memoirs of prison guard Otto Lurker.[63] In reality, Hitler typed the manuscript himself, using the "hunt-and-peck" system, after he had outlined his thoughts by hand on sheets of paper.[64] In a letter from late July, Hess described his role in the composition of *Mein Kampf*. "Hitler regularly reads to me from his book," Hess wrote. "Whenever a chapter is done, he takes it to me. He explains it to me and we discuss the odd point."[65] By early August, Hitler hoped he would be finished writing in a few days and he solemnly invited Hess to proofread the final draft with him.[66] But that never seems to have happened. Hitler kept postponing finishing the manuscript. In late August, he was still working on it constantly and did not wish to be disturbed.[67] In September, prison director Otto Leybold witnessed him working on the draft "for several hours each day."[68] By the time he was released from Landsberg on 20 December 1924, large sections of the manuscript were finished. Emil Maurice claimed that he hid them in the wooden body of his gramophone and smuggled them out.[69]

The appearance of the book was delayed for months. That was partly due to the financial difficulties in which Eher Verlag found itself. "Debts, debts, debts everywhere," publisher Max Amann complained to Hanfstaengl.[70] But politics also played an important role: Hitler did not want the publication of the book to damage his efforts to get the ban on the NSDAP lifted and to found the party anew.[71] This was the context in which not only the title was changed—it was advertised as of February 1925 as *Mein Kampf* (My Struggle)—but the overall structure as well. What had been conceived as one volume was now to appear in two. The first volume ended with the announcement of the Nazi Party manifesto on 24 February 1920, while several programmatic chapters were reserved for volume two.[72] In April 1925, Hitler made the final changes to volume one on the Obersalzberg. Josef Stolzing-Cerny, the *Völkischer Beobachter*'s music critic, and Hess's fiancée Ilse Pröhl helped with the editing.[73]

The first volume of *Mein Kampf* appeared on 18 July 1925, but it would be a while before the second volume was published. It was not until the autumn of 1926 that Hitler once again withdrew to the Obersalzberg to dictate the final parts to one of his secretaries.[74] Hess, who had in the meantime become Hitler's private secretary, did the final editing.[75] On 11 December of that year, the second volume appeared in the bookshops. Hess had prophesied that it would unleash a "wave of astonishment, anger and admiration . . . throughout the German lands," but sales were initially sluggish, which may have been because of the relatively expensive price tag of 12 marks per volume.[76] By the end of 1925, the 10,000-strong first edition of the first volume was sold out, but demand for the second volume was nowhere near as great.[77] It was not until the Nazis' electoral triumphs in 1930 that sales picked up again—in particular the cheaper popular one-volume edition proved to be a big hit. Almost 228,000 copies had been sold by the end of 1932, and after Hitler came to power in 1933, that figure naturally shot up. About 4,000 copies were being sold every day, Hitler told Hess in April 1933: "Good old Amann can't fund enough printing works to keep up with the demand." Public libraries and schools were required to buy copies, and starting in 1936, state employees performing civil marriage ceremonies were instructed to give newly-weds a copy of *Mein Kampf*. During the Second World War, there was a lightweight-paper edition for soldiers. By 1944, almost twelve and a half million copies had been printed.[78]

If he had suspected he would one day become Reich chancellor, he would never have written *Mein Kampf*, Hitler once remarked to Hans Frank.[79] That was sheer sophistry. Hitler was visibly proud of his book and often gave away signed copies of it as gifts.[80] Not only did *Mein Kampf* make him a rich man, it also played a significant role in his political career. The book served two purposes. On the one hand, by connecting his biography and his political programme, Hitler could portray his life up until his entry into politics as a prelude to his historic mission. His early years of deprivation and disappointment emerged as an essential stage of his development, as the incubation period of a political genius who had been hardened by real life. On the other hand, the book underscored his claim to party leadership in an intellectual sense. It was proof that Hitler was both a politician and a theorist, a combination that, as he crowed in *Mein Kampf*, tended to occur only very rarely in human history.[81] That was one reason for the book's utterly pretentious style. Hitler was keen to show that, despite his incomplete formal education, he was just as well read and knowledgeable as any university professor.[82]

Prison guards Lurker and Hemmrich recalled that Hitler built up an extensive library in Landsberg, which took up "a large part of his room with its nice-looking pictures and flowers."[83] But it is hard to determine what he read and what might have served as sources for *Mein Kampf*. He hardly ever discussed his reading habits and was loath to acknowledge who he took ideas from by name. Otto Strasser, the brother of Gregor, thought he could identify the anti-Semitic notions of Houston Stewart Chamberlain and Paul de Lagarde.[84] Other sources that left their mark on *Mein Kampf* were Arthur de Gobineau's teachings on the inequality of human races; Hans F. K. Günther's *Racial Ethnology of the German People*, which was in its third edition by 1923 and which publisher J. F. Lehmann had given Hitler with a personal dedication; and the racist pamphlet by American carmaker Henry Ford, "The International Jew: The World's Foremost Problem," which had appeared in German translation in 1922 and became a huge hit. "I regard Ford as my inspiration," Hitler allegedly told an American reporter.[85] For the second volume, Hitler apparently used American eugenicist Madison Grant's *The Passing of the Great Race*, which had been published in German in 1925, also by Lehmann, and which argued that racial mixing was the cause of the demise of peoples and cultures.[86] This book did not give Hitler any new ideas, but it did reinforce his already strong convictions. That seems to have been typical of Hitler's reading habits in Landsberg: he did not read in order to test but rather in order to confirm his opinions. Hitler was constantly in search of mosaic stones that could be added to his already existing world view.[87]

As a result, *Mein Kampf* contained little that was original. On the contrary, the two-volume work essentially summarised the things

Hitler had said in countless speeches before November 1923, although it did maintain the pretence of systematising the highlights of Hitler's reading and presenting them as a consistent, coherent world view.[88] At the core of Hitler's interpretation of history were the categories "people and race"—the title of Chapter 11 of the first volume of *Mein Kampf*. Hitler saw the "racial question" as the "key not only to world history but to human culture itself."[89] That distinguished his understanding of history from Marxist thought: for Hitler, races and not classes were the motors of events. Consequently, racial and not class warfare determined the course of historical development. Hitler saw his racial theory as being based on the laws of nature and particularly a supposed natural tendency towards racial purity. "The fox is always a fox, the goose a goose and the tiger a tiger," Hitler argued. For him, any mixing of races was a violation of the "iron logic of nature" that would automatically lead to decadence and decay. "The reason all the great cultures of the past collapsed," Hitler proposed, "was that the original creative race died of blood poisoning."[90]

Hitler combined his biological racial theory with the social Darwinist ideas he had internalised as a soldier. Nature's only wish was "the victory of the strong and the destruction or unconditional subordination of the weak." There was no room for humanitarian considerations in the pitiless "fight for survival" between peoples: "Whoever wants to live must fight, and whoever does not want to fight in this world of eternal tests of strength does not deserve to live." Within this profoundly inhumane logic, the ultimate goal was the "breeding towards perfection" of the races until the point, somewhere in the distant future, when "the best form of humanity is in charge, having taken possession of the earth."[91] Aryans, who were deemed the sole "creative race," were the ones to carry out this task. On that score, Hitler was absolutely clear: "Everything we see today of human culture and artistic, scientific and technological achievements is almost exclusively the creative work of the Aryan."[92]

In Hitler's Manichaean world view, the "Jewish race" was the negative mirror image of the Aryan one. Many passages in *Mein Kampf* are word-for-word repetitions of anti-Semitic tirades like his "Why we are anti-Semites" speech from August 1920. "The Jew" was scapegoated into the incarnation of everything evil, and the fight against him was correspondingly the most important part of Hitler's political mission.

Compared to his earlier statements, however, *Mein Kampf* did radicalise the measures to be taken to combat this threat. In late July, when asked by one of his visitors at Landsberg whether his attitude towards Jews had changed, Hitler replied: "Yes indeed . . . I've realised that I was far too mild! In the course of working on my book, I've come to see that in future we will have to employ the most severe means if we are to triumph. I'm convinced that this is a question of survival not just for our people, but for all peoples. The Jew is a global plague."[93]

Hitler was convinced he was acting in the interests not just of the German people but of all the world's peoples in striving for the "elimination of the Jews." His obsession was so all-consuming that the anti-Jewish struggle took on apocalyptic dimensions. "If the Jew triumphs over the peoples of the world with his Marxist faith," Hitler warned, "the crowning moment will be humanity's *danse macabre*, for the planet will fly through the ether unpopulated as it did millions of years ago." That doomsday scenario yielded the following conclusion: "Thus I believe that I am acting according to the will of the Almighty Creator. By defending myself against the Jew, I am fighting for the work of Our Lord."[94] Saul Friedländer has characterised this sort of vulgar, extreme, quasi-religious hostility towards Jews as "redemptive anti-Semitism" and traces its origins back to the Wagner circle and, in particular, the influence of Chamberlain.[95]

Hitler no longer spoke of deporting or driving out Jews: he now used words like "destruction" and "eradication." He also availed himself on numerous occasions in *Mein Kampf* of the language of parasitology, by describing Jews as vermin that needed to be exterminated.[96] His anti-Semitic paranoia now included murderous fantasies, as revealed by a passage near the end of the second volume of *Mein Kampf*: "If at the beginning and over the course of the [First World] war we had subjected twelve to fifteen thousand of these Hebraic corrupters of the people to the same poison gas that hundreds of thousands of our best productive Germans had to endure in the field, then the sacrifice of millions of lives at the front would not have been in vain."[97]

Hitler's foreign-policy views were also radicalised in *Mein Kampf*. Originally Hitler had entered politics demanding an abrogation of the Treaty of Versailles, a settling of accounts with Germany's "archenemy" France, the restitution of German colonies and the restoration of Germany's 1914 borders. These were the sorts of revisionist views prevalent throughout pan-Germanic, ethnic-chauvinist and nationalist circles. In *Mein Kampf*, Hitler now shifted his emphasis to the idea that a nation with an expanding population like Germany needed territory large enough to feed its people and continue to increase its political power. The notion that Germany needed "living space" can be traced back to the geopolitical ideas of Professor Karl Haushofer. These had considerable influence on the foreign policy of Hitler, who likely learned about them from Haushofer's student Hess.[98] In Landsberg, Hitler also read the 1897 book *Political Geography* by the geopolitical scientist and co-founder of the Pan-Germanic League Friedrich Ratzel, which Haushofer had brought for Hess.[99]

How was "living space" to be conquered? In Chapter 4 of *Mein Kampf*'s first volume, which criticised pre-1914 German foreign policy, Hitler wrote: "If one wants territory in Europe, it can more or less only happen to the detriment of Russia. The new Reich would have to march in the footsteps of the Teutonic Knights and conquer with the German sword the soil that the German plough would till in order to provide our people with their daily bread."[100] Hitler's turn of phrase left no doubt that he believed any eastward expansion would require military action. Hitler was even more explicit in Chapter 14 of *Mein Kampf*'s second volume, entitled "Eastern Orientation or Eastern Policy," in which he proclaimed the German people's right "to an appropriate territory on this earth" as one of his central foreign-policy goals. "We will stop the eternal movement of the Germanic tribes to the south and west of Europe," Hitler wrote, "and train our sights on land to the east. We will finally wind down the colonial and trade policies of the pre-war period and go over to a land policy for the future."[101]

Hitler envisioned such a war for living space as a relatively risk-free endeavour. He saw the Soviet Union as being in the hands of "Jewish Bolsheviks," which in his logic meant that Russia's racial foundation had been decisively weakened. "The gigantic empire to the east is ripe for collapse," Hitler wrote. "And the end of Jewish domination in Russia will spell the end of Russia as a state. We have been chosen by destiny to bear witness to a catastrophe that will provide the most powerful confirmation of the accuracy of ethnic-popular racial theory."[102] This passage sets out and combines Hitler's two most important goals: the destruction of "Jewish Bolshevism" and the conquest of "living space in the east." Despite all the tactical flexibility and political manoeuvrability he was to show later in his career, Hitler always insisted on these two goals with dogmatic rigidity.

"It will always remain one of the great mysteries of the Third Reich," wrote Victor Klemperer in *LTI*, his 1946 analysis of Nazi language, "how this book could have been disseminated throughout the public sphere, and how nonetheless Hitler achieved his twelve-year rule. The bible of National Socialism was in circulation years before his rise to power."[103] Indeed, in *Mein Kampf*, Hitler had spelled out with exemplary clarity everything he intended to do if he was ever given power. Did the people who voted for him and who cheered him on not read it? Historians have long assumed they did not.[104] Many of them cite the anecdote which Otto Strasser told in his 1940 book *Hitler and I*. When at the party conference in Nuremberg in 1927 Strasser had admitted to a circle of party functionaries that he had not read all of *Mein Kampf*, but merely memorised some of the more striking sentences, he claimed that others, including his brother Gregor and Joseph Goebbels, acknowledged not having read it either.[105] If that was the case among Hitler's most immediate subordinates, must it not also be true for his millions of followers— not to mention the many people who were not involved in the NSDAP?

Historian Othmar Plöckinger, however, has dismissed the idea of *Mein Kampf* being an "unread bestseller" as a myth that in the early years after the Second World War helped Germans to justify and excuse their behaviour.[106] When it appeared in 1925, the first volume of *Mein Kampf* attracted a broad, mostly negative reaction in the mainstream press. In the Berlin magazine *Das Tagebuch*, liberal-left pundit Stefan Grossmann published an extensive review in which he questioned "the sanity of the author of these memoirs." The liberal *Frankfurter Zeitung* newspaper opined that Hitler was "over and done with" after publishing his confession. On the other hand, the *Augsburger Neueste Nachrichten* called Hitler a "highly gifted man," writing: "[He is] a true fighter for the convictions he has won in a life of struggle. Anyone who wants to get more closely acquainted with Hitler's unique personality and to understand his actions should get hold of this book. Whether he sees it positively or critically, it is useful reading."[107] After the Nazis' electoral successes in 1929 and 1930, many people apparently followed this advice. Not only did *Mein Kampf*'s sales figures explode, but daily newspapers began mentioning the book more and more frequently. And by no means were the majority of the opinions as critical as the one published by Hellmut von Gerlach in the June 1932 issue of *Die Weltbühne*. "Whoever has read Hitler's autobiography *Mein Kampf*," Gerlach wrote, "will ask himself in horror how a sadistic master of confusion could become the preferred leader of a good third of the German people."[108]

By the early 1930s at the latest, *Mein Kampf* had established itself as the party bible. Of course, not everyone who received the book after 1936 as a wedding gift studied it in detail, but it must be assumed that convinced National Socialists read at least major parts of it. The fact that the book was borrowed relatively frequently from libraries in the first years of the Third Reich also speaks for a genuine popular interest in it.[109]

In late August 1924, Hitler was still convinced that he would be released once the first six months of his sentence were up on 1 October.[110] By mid-September, he was comparing prices for a car he intended to buy when he got out of prison. "The difficulty for me is that in case of my release on 1 October, I cannot expect any major revenue from my work before mid-December so that I see myself compelled to ask for some sort of advance or a loan," the automotive enthusiast Hitler wrote to Jakob Werlin, the head of the Munich office of Benz & Cie (later Daimler-Benz), who had visited him in Landsberg.[111]

If the prison authorities had got their way, Hitler would indeed have been released at the first possible opportunity. Otto Leybold was a great fan of his famous inmate. "I can't find any fault with him," the prison director told Franz Hemmrich. "He's an idealist . . . When I hear him, I could almost become a National Socialist myself."[112] In a report he wrote on 15 September, Leybold praised Hitler as a "man of order and discipline." He was "content, humble and eager to please," someone who "did not make any demands" and was "at pains to accept the restrictions accompanying his incarceration." Hitler had always behaved "politely and never in insulting form" towards prison employees. In Leybold's opinion, Hitler had become "more mature and calmer" during his detention so that there was no reason to expect him to pose any further danger.[113]

Munich Deputy Police President Friedrich Tenner was of a different opinion. After his release, Tenner protested, Hitler—who was "more than ever the soul of the movement"—would "resume his ruthless battle with the government and not shy away from breaking the law."[114] The head prosecutor of Munich's First District Court, Ludwig Stenglein, also came out against granting Hitler early release. Considering their behaviour during the trial and their incarceration, Stenglein objected, there was no sign that the convicts had given up their "state-threatening" views or would abide by the law in future. On 29 September, after Munich's Third Criminal Division had nonetheless granted Hitler's appeal for early release, state prosecutors filed an appeal to the Bavarian Supreme Court.[115] That ruled out Hitler being set free on 1 October, which turned the mood bleak among his supporters in Landsberg.[116]

Hitler, however, did not seem particularly concerned. What bothered him more were considerations within the Bavarian government about whether he should be deported to Austria. In October 1924, the government sent a representative to Vienna to negotiate "Austria potentially taking over Hitler." But the border control in Passau had already received instructions to deny Hitler entry to the country. The Austrian government stuck to its view that by "emigrating" to Bavaria and serving in the Bavarian army Hitler had forfeited his Austrian citizenship.[117] On 16 October, after being erroneously informed that he had been stripped of his Austrian citizenship, Hitler declared that he did not perceive this as a loss because he had never "felt like an Austrian citizen but rather always like a German."[118] In early April 1925 he officially applied to be released from Austrian citizenship. The government in Vienna granted his request by the end of the month.[119] Hitler was henceforth stateless: he would not become a German citizen until 1932.

The Bavarian Supreme Court rejected the Munich prosecutors' appeal on 6 October 1924. The latter made one final attempt to get permission for Hitler's early release revoked, but when Leybold once again put in a good word for his model prisoner, the court ruled that Hitler should be let go on 20 December.[120] The results of national elections on 7 December may have influenced that decision. The National Socialist Liberation Movement only polled 3 per cent of the vote, less than half of what it had got in May.[121] Ethnic right-wing radicalism seemed to have passed its zenith, and many people no longer saw it posing much of a threat. In this context, a well-to-do

Munich woman petitioned Bavarian President Heinrich Held "to make peace with that most German of Germans, Adolf Hitler." With the vote having gone against his party, the woman argued, there was no need to keep him behind "dungeon walls." She added: "If the German people had twenty Hitlers, we'd be in a lot better shape today."[122]

When he left Landsberg, Hitler asserted in February 1942, everyone from the director to the guards wept. "We won them all over," he bragged.[123] Gregor Strasser and Anton Drexler had come with a car, intending to chauffeur Hitler immediately to a meeting with Ludendorff. "The competition for him has started even earlier than I expected," wrote Hess. "[Hitler] had no intention of going with them. He was outraged, saying that for the meantime he wanted to rest and nothing else."[124] Hitler's relationship with Ludendorff had cooled noticeably during his incarceration. The party leader had not forgotten how the general had let Kahr, Lossow and Seisser "escape" on 8 November.[125] He also resented Ludendorff not only for getting himself elected to the Reichstag but for taking the lead in efforts to merge the DVFP and the NSDAP. "Ludendorff had another think coming," when Hitler was released, Hess wrote on 11 December. "He doesn't know the Tribune at all!"[126]

Instead of going to meet Ludendorff, Hitler had himself picked up by Adolf Müller, the owner of the printing press used by Eher Verlag, and his photographer Heinrich Hoffmann. Hoffmann took a shot of Hitler posing before the Landsberg city gate, which ran in numerous newspapers with the caption "Hitler leaves Landsberg."[127] Arriving back in Munich, he found his apartment in Thierschstrasse full of flowers and laurel wreaths. "My dog almost knocked me back down the stairs from sheer joy," Hitler recalled.[128] Three days later, Hitler paid his respects at the Bruckmanns' salon on Karolinenplatz. "How nice it is here," he was said to have remarked on seeing the splendour of the place, before writing in the Bruckmanns' guestbook: "Whoever is broken by sorrow deserves no joy."[129] He spent Christmas with the Hanfstaengls, who had swapped their apartment in Gentzstrasse for a villa in Pienzenauerstrasse near the Herzogpark. "Please, Hanfstaengl, play me the *Liebestod*," Hitler requested when he arrived at the house. The sound of Wagner's music, Hanfstaengl recalled, dissolved Hitler's tension: "He seemed relaxed, almost giddy, as he greeted my wife . . . He apologised again for what had happened in Uffing, hummed a funny melody for our daughter Hertha and couldn't stop praising our new home."[130]

A newsletter circulating among the local groups of the VB at the end of December 1924 greeted Hitler with the words: "The man of strong action and unwavering political goals has come back to us."[131] But during the first few weeks after Christmas, Hitler refrained from involving himself in politics. He visited the inmates who remained behind in Landsberg and devoted himself to readying *Mein Kampf* for publication. "He had to run around a lot because of those left behind in Landsberg and because of his book," a former fellow inmate from Munich recalled.[132] Hitler was carefully checking out the terrain to avoid any missteps when he returned to the arena of politics. "Hitler is maintaining his icy silence," the *Bayerischer Anzeiger* newspaper reported on 21 January 1925, "as well as the aloofness his supporters find so unnerving."[133]

8

Führer on Standby

"I'm no longer unknown, and that's the most important springboard for us as we give it another try," Hitler told Ernst Hanfstaengl after his release from Landsberg. He also reassured Hanfstaengl's wife Helene: "I promise you one thing . . . The next time I'm not just going to topple off my perch."[1] Hitler had already decided in prison to reconstitute the NSDAP, and since he refused to take sides among the warring factions, his aura had remained undamaged. Thus he was in an excellent position to unite most of the rival individuals and groups behind him. It was his intention from the very start to transform the NSDAP into an unquestioning instrument for his own will. To further this aim, his power base in Munich had to remain the seat of the party. Hitler attached sacral importance to the birthplace of Nazism: "Rome, Mecca, Moscow—every one of these places embodies a world view!" he proclaimed. "We shall remain in the city that saw the first party comrades shed their blood for our movement. It must become the Moscow of our movement!"[2] He added: "The holiest site is the one in which there has been the most suffering."[3]

But conditions in Munich had changed since the rise of the NSDAP in the early 1920s. After the post-war political crises and hyperinflation, the Weimar Republic consolidated itself between 1924 and 1928. Once the reichsmark had been stabilised, the German economy recovered surprisingly quickly. In 1927, industrial production again reached pre-war levels. Real wages also grew at a healthy rate, while unemployment, which had stood at 20 per cent in the winter of 1923–4, was receding. The worst was seemingly over, and a cautious optimism was spreading through society.

Germany could also celebrate some progress in foreign policy. With the adoption in 1924 of the Dawes Plan, which tied reparations payments to the state of the economy, Germany received assurances that the military occupation of the Ruhr region would end within a year. Under Gustav Stresemann, who served as Germany's foreign minister through a succession of governments from 1924 to 1929, relations continually improved with the Entente countries, in particular with France. In the 1925 Treaty of Locarno, Germany recognised its western border laid out in the Treaty of Versailles and guaranteed that the Rhineland would be kept demilitarised. In return, France and Belgium waived demands for further territorial concessions. In 1926, after these agreements had come into force, Germany was ceremoniously inducted into the League of Nations. The event marked the country's return to the international community.[4]

When Germans today talk about the "Golden Twenties," however, they don't primarily mean economic recovery and political successes, but rather "Weimar culture," an unusually rich flourishing of creativity and experimentalism.[5] Around 1923–4, the ecstatic pathos and social utopianism of expressionism gave way to New Objectivity, a cooler and socially more realistic outlook that set the tone in painting, literature and architecture. The most concrete expression of this attitude was Walter Gropius's Bauhaus movement in Weimar and later Dessau. Bauhaus was an experimental laboratory for new functional architecture, furniture and home appliances. New media such as vinyl records, radio and sound film facilitated the rise of modern mass culture, whose offerings could be enjoyed by people beyond the privileged upper classes. Sports like football, athletics, boxing and bicycle- and car-racing became increasingly popular. In his autobiography the journalist Sebastian Haffner identified a veritable "sports mania" that took hold of him and many other young people in the mid-1920s.[6] The capital of the Golden Twenties was undeniably Berlin, full of cinemas and dance halls where American imports like the Shimmy and the Charleston were all the rage. Women's fashion was more practical and casual, and the page-boy haircut became a symbol of female emancipation. Attitudes towards sex were unprecedentedly liberal. All these experiences, impulses and distractions worked against the previous trend towards political radicalism—but only as long as Germany's fragile economic recovery continued.

The times were no longer favourable for Hitler. "Today, inflation no longer nourishes the desperation politics of a putsch," the *Bayerischer*

Anzeiger newspaper reasoned. "The conditions have changed, and Hitler will have to adjust his policies."[7] Nonetheless, as Hitler's newly appointed personal secretary Hess noted, the "Tribune" was "in good spirits" and "full of his old energy" as he set about reconstituting the Nazi Party. "The superfluous fat gained at L[andsberg] is gone," Hess wrote. "Once again he hardly has any free time. The hunt is back on!"[8] Hitler had carefully prepared his return to the political stage. The first step was to get the Bavarian government to lift the ban on the NSDAP. In early January 1925, therefore, Hitler paid a visit to the Bavarian state president and chairman of the BVP, Heinrich Held. He expressed regrets for the attempted putsch, requested that his co-conspirators still detained in Landsberg be released, and promised to stay within the bounds of the law in future. At the same time, he distanced himself from attacks made by Ludendorff and other representatives of the far right upon the Catholic Church. Held's reaction was cool. The Bavarian government, he said, would under no circumstances tolerate conditions like those in the run-up to 9 November 1923 and would use "every means of state authority" to prevent a repeat of the past. But he did ultimately agree to lift the ban on the NSDAP and the *Völkischer Beobachter*. "The beast is tamed," Held is said to have remarked. "Now we can loosen the shackles."[9] Hitler was only able to launch his second political career because his adversaries criminally underestimated him.

On 26 February, ten days after the ban was lifted, the *Völkischer Beobachter* resumed publication. In the first edition's lead article, "How to Make our Movement Strong Again," and another piece entitled "Appeal to the Former Members of the National Socialist German Workers' Party," Hitler called for an end to the quarrels of the past: "Let us stand as before shoulder to shoulder, loyally as brothers in a great fighting community."[10] In the appended guidelines for a "new founding" of the party, all members had to reapply. However, Hitler made it clear that the most basic goal of the party had not changed in the slightest: "The entire strength of the movement is to be directed at the German people's most terrible enemy: Jewry, Marxism and the parties that are allied with them or support them—the Centrists and the democrats."[11]

A day later Hitler made a public appearance in the Bürgerbräukeller, the place where he had launched the attempted putsch a year and a half earlier. The venue was crammed beyond capacity hours before the start of the event, and when Hitler finally appeared, he was greeted with frenetic applause. Several prominent figures—Ludendorff, Rosenberg, Röhm and Gregor Strasser—were not in attendance, and the party's original founder Anton Drexler, who had just failed in his attempt to push out Hermann Esser and Julius Streicher, stayed away as well. Publisher Max Amann moderated the event in his stead. By no means did Hitler show any signs of reform. On the contrary, he took up exactly where he had left off in November 1923. The largest part of his two-hour speech consisted of hateful anti-Jewish tirades that whipped the audience into a frenzy. "The Jew," he proclaimed, was a "tool of the devil" that had plunged Germany into misery, and the battle against this "global plague" could only be won "when the swastika flag flies atop every workshop and factory." The entire strength of the movement, Hitler demanded, must be focused on achieving this goal.

Only towards the end of his speech did Hitler get around to addressing what was actually the topic of the event—the reconstitution of the party. He repeated his appeal to "all those who have remained National Socialists" to bury the hatchet and unite around him. At no point was there the slightest doubt about Hitler's claim to leadership: "For nine months I haven't said a word. Now I lead the movement, and no one has the right to place me under any conditions." Hitler was assuming complete responsibility for the past, and now, more than a year after the attempted coup, party members could decide his fate: "If I've done well, then you should stop condemning me. If I've done badly, then I will put my office back in your hands. (Cries of 'Never!')"[12] This theatrical ending was followed by a prearranged scene of reconciliation between the rival leaders of the NSDAP's successor organisations. Julius Streicher, Arthur Dinter and Hermann Esser of the Pan-Germanic Ethnic Community publicly shook hands on the podium with Rudolf Buttmann, Gottfried Feder and Wilhelm Frick of the VB. "The reuniting of the two feuding brothers" was a success, Hess noted. That evening, Hitler had himself chauffeured in his new Mercedes to Bayreuth by Winifred Wagner, whom he had invited to the Bürgerbräukeller.[13]

Yet despite the public pretence of unity, the quarrels continued. The Pan-Germanic Ethnic Community was dissolved in March 1925, and the majority of its members joined the NSDAP, but the membership of the VB had reservations. Of the twenty-three VB deputies in the Bavarian Landtag, only six went over to the new Nazi faction, which had been formed under Buttmann's leadership. Ludendorff and Gregor Strasser had already stepped down from the Reich leadership of the National Socialist Liberation Movement on 12 February. But many of the people who sympathised with its aims saw Ludendorff, and not Hitler, as the true leader of the ethnic-chauvinist camp. Moreover, in early May, Anton Drexler, who was completely disillusioned with Hitler, founded an organisation of his own, the National-Social People's League (Nationalsozialer Volksbund, or NSVB), from the remnants of the VB in Munich, although it never seriously rivalled the NSDAP.[14]

Hitler's first post-prison appearance had unpleasant consequences. On 7 March, the Bavarian government banned him from speaking in public. The authorities were particularly disconcerted by his statement that "Either the enemy will march over our dead bodies, or we will march over his"—a threat that completely negated Hitler's promises to stay within the bounds of the law.[15] Most of Germany's other federal states, including Prussia, followed suit and prohibited Hitler from speaking as well. That robbed the party leader of his most effective weapon, his ability to stir audiences with his words. On the other hand, he was still allowed to take the podium at closed party meetings and events, and the Bruckmanns' salon served as a kind of substitute public forum. There Hitler spoke a number of times in front of specially invited audiences of between forty and sixty guests, most of them influential representatives of business, science and culture. Here Hitler had to make a very different impression than he did in the feverish, intoxicated atmosphere of a mass event. Even in his external appearance, as the historian Karl Alexander von Müller noted, Hitler adapted to the social circumstances by donning a dark-blue jacket or even a tuxedo. This was "an entirely new school of propaganda, dissimulation and seduction," wrote Müller. The historian was also struck by Hitler's physiognomic changes: "His thin, pale, sickly, oft empty-seeming face had become pinched, which caused his facial bones, from his forehead to his chin, to emerge more starkly. His enthusiasm had yielded to an unmistakable streak of severity. Essentially he had already become how people would later remember him."[16]

If Hitler wanted to realise his ambition of absolute leadership of the NSDAP, he had to get rid of his political rivals, in particular

Ludendorff, from whom he had already distanced himself while in Landsberg. It was no accident that Hitler failed to mention Ludendorff once in his speech on 27 February. Only after the staged reconciliation of the rival factions did he pay tribute to the general "who will always be the German people's military leader." Conversely, Ludendorff felt disappointed by Hitler. The party chairman suffered from "a psychotic fortress mentality," Ludendorff complained privately. The general had already announced in early February that he would withdraw from politics if Hitler reconstituted the NSDAP, although Ludendorff retained his Reichstag mandate.[17]

Hitler was soon gifted an unforeseen chance to deal a blow to Ludendorff's reputation. On 28 February 1925, worn out by the constant attacks of his enemies, Reich President Friedrich Ebert died at the age of 54. Hitler persuaded Ludendorff to stand as a candidate for the far right in the resulting elections. The other candidates were the Duisburg mayor Karl Jarres for the moderately right-wing DNVP and DVP, the Social Democrat Otto Braun, the Centre Party leader Wilhelm Marx and the Communist Ernst Thälmann. Hitler knew that Ludendorff stood no chance, but on the surface he did everything to suggest that the reconstituted NSDAP was completely behind the general's candidacy. The *Völkischer Beobachter* published constant appeals to its readers to vote for Ludendorff with the slogan "He who wants freedom must choose the man with the iron fist."[18]

The first round of voting on 24 March was a debacle for Ludendorff, who only received 286,000 votes, or 1.1 per cent of the ballots cast, by far the fewest of any of the candidates. "Bismarck too was not made chancellor of the German people by the result of an election," Hitler wrote in a disingenuously encouraging article in the *Völkischer Beobachter.*[19] In truth, Hitler was delighted. "Very good so—now we've taken care of him," Hitler allegedly remarked after Ludendorff's complete defeat became clear.[20] Because none of the candidates achieved an absolute majority, however, a run-off election was called for 26 April. Former Field Marshal Paul von Hindenburg, representing all the parties on the right, won a narrow victory over Marx, who stood for the SPD, the DDP and the Centre Party. Hindenburg's election might have been prevented had not Thälmann insisted on running for the KPD. The Communists thus played a role in installing a dyed-in-the-wool monarchist in Germany's highest political office. "Who would have imagined two years ago that Paul von Hindenburg could become German president?" exulted the right-wing paramilitary leader Georg Escherich. "Now we have an unimpeachable, reasonable man at the head of the Reich."[21] In fact, Hindenburg had a fractured relationship with the democratic institutions of the Weimar Republic, and the fatal consequences would become apparent when German democracy came under attack in the 1930s.

Hitler, who had called upon the members of his party to vote for Hindenburg, was satisfied with the election outcome, which saw "the top hat give way to the steel helmet." Under Hindenburg, Hitler reasoned, "a better future would be coming for Germany."[22] Ludendorff, however, was no longer a suitable figurehead for the far-right, ethnic-chauvinist movement, and he immediately sank into political irrelevance. In September 1925, he founded a group called the Tannenberg League, but under the influence of his second wife, the physician Mathilde von Kemnitz, it was transformed into a sect that spread abstruse conspiracy theories about Freemasons, Jews and Jesuits and preached neopagan religious beliefs.[23]

The other rival whom Hitler manoeuvred onto the margins was Ernst Röhm. While Hitler was confined in Landsberg, the former army captain had organised members of the disbanded SA and the Fighting Association into a new paramilitary group, the Frontbann. Röhm intended it to be a militia independent from the party, which collided with Hitler's aim of subjugating the SA to the NSDAP. "The purpose of the new SA," read Hitler's guidelines of 26 February 1925, "remains the same as the original one of before February 1923: to steel the bodies of our youth, to teach them discipline and commitment to our great, common ideal and to train them to become a security and propaganda service for the party."[24] Their differences caused Hitler and Röhm to fall out. In late April 1925, Röhm resigned as the head of the SA and the Frontbann and withdrew from the movement; in 1928, he became a military adviser in Bolivia. Hitler named Franz Pfeffer von Salomon as his successor in November 1926.

Before November 1923, the NSDAP had essentially been a home-grown Bavarian product, only weakly represented in northern Germany. Hitler now wanted to change that. Even before the party was officially reconstituted on 27 February 1925, he had charged Gregor Strasser with building up the party in north-western Germany. Strasser, whose storm battalion had taken part in the Beer Hall Putsch, had become one of the far right's best-known politicians during Hitler's imprisonment. In April 1924, he was elected a VB deputy to the Bavarian Landtag and had quickly become the chairman of his parliamentary faction. Together with Ludendorff and Albrecht von Graefe, he had been part of the Reich leadership triumvirate of the National Socialist Liberation Movement, and he won a mandate to represent that group in the Reichstag in December 1924. Strasser was not only a good public speaker, but an organisational talent. He valued Hitler as an irreplaceable unifying figure for the movement, and later told an intimate that he had found Hitler's "tempestuous and winning personality" impossible to resist.[25] But unlike most people in the Führer's entourage, Strasser did not blindly worship him. As Strasser himself once remarked, he was not "one of those proverbial satellites who always revolves around the sun to draw light from it."[26] Hitler's bohemian habits infuriated Strasser, and although he was a committed anti-Semite himself, he did not share Hitler's rabid Jew-hatred.

Like that of many war veterans, Strasser's notion of "national socialism" reflected his experience in the trenches. But Strasser was more a socialist than a nationalist, and he took the anti-capitalist planks in the party programme quite seriously. In a reflection on the new year in the *Völkischer Beobachter* in early 1926, Strasser wrote: "We National Socialists fight passionately not only for national liberation but with great conviction for social justice, for the nationalisation of the economy."[27] The immunity Strasser enjoyed as a member of the Reichstag and the privilege of free rail travel given to deputies granted him great mobility, which he used tirelessly to promote the NSDAP in northern and western Germany. By the end of 1925, there were already 262 local Nazi chapters in those regions—almost four times as many as there had been at the time of the Beer Hall Putsch.[28]

Strasser's most important associate was a young intellectual named Paul Joseph Goebbels. Born in 1897 as the son of a business manager in the western German industrial city of Rheydt (today's Mönchengladbach), Goebbels suffered from a clubbed right foot—the deformity was the source of a deep-seated inferiority complex for which Goebbels tried to compensate with intellectual achievements. After graduating from high school in 1917, Goebbels studied German literature in Bonn, and he received his doctorate in Heidelberg in 1921 with a dissertation about the Romantic dramatist Wilhelm Schütz. But that did not satisfy Goebbels's ambitions. He longed to make a name for himself as a writer or a journalist and applied for a job at the liberal *Berliner Tageblatt* in January 1924. The application was summarily rejected, which was likely one of the roots of Goebbels's hatred of Jews and the "Jewish press." For a short time he worked at a branch of Dresdner Bank in Cologne, and his experiences of rampant hyperinflation encouraged his critical attitudes towards capitalism. The frustrated young man first became aware of Hitler in connection with the latter's trial in Munich in early 1924. The Führer "spoke straight from my soul," Goebbels would tell Hitler two years later. "God granted you the ability to articulate our suffering. You put our pain into words of deliverance and transformed confidence in the coming miracle into sentences."[29]

After visiting the unity conference of right-wing parties in Weimar in August 1924, where he met Gregor Strasser for the first time, Goebbels and a friend from school formed the local Rheydt chapter of the National Socialist Liberation Movement (NSFB). It was at the organisation's meetings that the physically slight intellectual with the pronounced limp discovered his rhetorical abilities. For several months he took over as the editor of *Völkische Freiheit*, the weekly "fighting newsletter" of the NSFB in Elberfeld, in Germany's industrial heartland. When the NSDAP was reconstituted in February 1925, Goebbels immediately joined. On the recommendation of Karl Kaufmann, a Strasser intimate, he was made the secretary of the North Rhineland party district or Gau, whereupon he moved to Elberfeld. Goebbels quickly became known as one of the party's most effective speakers, and his public appearances constantly provoked fights with Communists in the industrial Ruhr Valley.

Goebbels and Strasser both emotionally rejected capitalism and rapturously embraced socialism: "National and socialist!" Goebbels wrote in his diary. "What has priority and what comes second? There's no doubt about the answer among us here in the west. First socialist redemption, and then national liberation will arrive like a powerful storm wind."[30] Goebbels also shared Strasser's antipathy for the "dirty, whorish dealings" within the Nazi Party's Munich headquarters.[31] They particularly despised Hermann Esser, who they thought exerted a bad influence on Hitler; and they considered it their main goal to free the party chairman from the putative clutches of the Munich clique and tie him to the "socialist" line of the Strasser wing of the NSDAP. As a means of creating an opposite pole to the "decadent Munich direction," a "Working Association North-west" was founded at a meeting in Hagen on 10 September 1925.[32] The organisation, based in Elberfeld, was a loose association of the Gaue in northern and western Germany, with Strasser as its director and Goebbels as its secretary. Goebbels also edited the fortnightly newsletter, the *Nationalsozialistische Briefe*. The working association was not directed against Hitler: on the contrary, it explicitly recognised his right to lead the party. In its statutes, adopted on 9 October, all the regional party leaders, the Gauleiter, pledged "to put aside all selfish aims and serve in the spirit of camaraderie the National Socialist idea under the Führer Adolf Hitler."[33]

At this point, Goebbels still had his doubts whether Hitler, whom he met for the first time in person at a Gauleiter convention in Weimar in July 1925, would in fact be able to fulfil the role of the much-longed-for political messiah. When Goebbels finished reading the first volume of *Mein Kampf* in mid-October, he asked himself: "Who is this man? Half plebian, half deity! Is he in fact Christ or only John the Baptist?"[34] But by the time Goebbels encountered Hitler for a second time, at a Gau conference in Braunschweig on 6 November, his doubts were resolved. Hitler had greeted him "like an old friend," Goebbels rejoiced in his diary. "Those large, blue eyes. Like stars ... This man has everything he needs to become king. He is a born popular Tribune. The coming dictator."[35]

At the first meeting of the working association on 22 November in Hanover, Strasser unveiled the draft of a "comprehensive manifesto of national socialism." It was intended to make the NSDAP party programme more specific on a number of points, not replace it. The general thrust was most clear in Strasser's demand that key industries be nationalised, by "transferring ownership of most of the means of production to the general public." On the foreign-policy front, Strasser envisioned all Germans being united in a "greater German empire" that would be the basis for a Central European customs union and a "United States of Europe."[36] The new Reich should try to conclude an alliance with Bolshevik Russia, Strasser argued in an article in the *Völkischer Beobachter*, and the deal should be concluded in the spirit of mutual German and Russian opposition to the capitalist West and to the order imposed by the Treaty of Versailles.[37]

On 24 January 1926, the north-western Gauleiter came together for a second time to discuss the revised party programme. In attendance also was Gottfried Feder from Munich, who had vigorously protested in the name of the NSDAP against any changes to the earlier twenty-five-point manifesto. Feder took copious notes during the debates—much to the dismay of many conference participants, who feared that Hitler would be informed about any critical remarks they made. The decision about whether to write a new programme was postponed, while Strasser's draft and all other suggestions were passed along to a committee. The conference did, however, vote to support a popular referendum, sponsored by the SPD and the Communists, calling for the expropriation of German princes without compensation.[38]

Initially, Hitler had not paid much attention to the doings of the Working Association North-west. As was his wont with internal party conflicts, he let things take their course. In July 1925 he attended the Wagner Festival in Bayreuth for the first time. Accompanied by his Munich patroness, Elsa Bruckmann, he resided with the Bechsteins and enjoyed the luxury. It was not until the seventh day of the festival that Hitler met Winifred Wagner. The two called one another "Winnie" and "Wolf," and Wagner was soon one of the few people allowed to address Hitler with the informal second-person pronoun "du." "Those were sunny days," Hitler recalled in February 1942. "I was 36 years old and had not a care in the world. The sky was hung with violins. I was popular enough that everyone treated me well without wanting anything from me. People left me in peace. During the day I walked around in my lederhosen, to the festival I wore a tuxedo or tails."[39]

After the festival, Hitler retreated for several weeks to a guest house in Berchtesgaden to resume work with Max Amann on the second volume of *Mein Kampf*.[40] He only returned to Munich at the end of September. With the party leader nearly invisible for two months, Gregor Strasser was ambitiously making a name for himself in north-western Germany. Hitler did not yet see Strasser as a rival. On the contrary, at the NSDAP leadership conference in Landshut in October 1925, Hitler praised Strasser "for opening up large sections of Germany to National Socialism."[41]

Hitler only began to see the activities of the working association as a threat to his own leadership in January 1926, when, probably at Feder's behest, he was given Strasser's draft party programme.[42] "Hitler is furious about the manifesto," Goebbels noted.[43] Only then did Hitler feel compelled to intervene, and as he had in previous crisis situations, he now could not engineer the decisive test of strength quickly enough. At short notice, he called a leadership conference for 14 February in Bamberg. Goebbels was confident that the spokesmen for the working association would be successful in advocating their suggestions for the party programme. "In Bamberg we'll play the role of the standoffish beauty and win Hitler over to our side," Goebbels predicted. "In every city, I see with great joy that our spirit, i.e. the socialist one, is on the march. No one puts their faith any more in Munich. Elberfeld shall become the mecca of German socialism."[44]

The conference, however, did not go at all as Goebbels anticipated. The representatives from northern and western Germany were in a clear minority among the approximately sixty participants, and from the very start, Hitler was intent on confronting them. In a speech that went on for hours, he dismissed the ideas of the working association point by point. When it came to foreign policy, Hitler advocated alliances with Britain and Italy, both of which made for potential partners owing to shared differences with Germany's "mortal enemy" France. Hitler categorically rejected any agreement with Russia, which, he said, would lead to the "immediate political Bolshevisation" of Germany. As he had outlined in *Mein Kampf*, he made the acquisition of "territory and soil" the centrepiece of his foreign policy, demanding that Germany "reorient itself towards the east and colonise the area as it had in the Middle Ages." He also ruled about the expropriation of the German princes, declaring that aristocrats were, in the first instance, Germans. "We will not tolerate that what belongs to them is being taken from them," Hitler thundered. "We believe in the law and will not give a Jewish system of exploitation any legal justification for completely plundering our people." Finally, Hitler forbade any discussions about the party programme. It was "the movement's article of faith" and thus "sacrosanct."[45]

Goebbels felt as though he had been slapped in the face. "Was this the real Hitler?" he asked. "A reactionary? . . . The Russian question: completely off the mark. Italy and England: Germany's natural allies.

How horrible! Our main task is to smash Bolshevism. Bolshevism is a Jewish instrument! We must inherit Russia!" Goebbels was also shocked by Hitler's attitude towards the expropriation issue. "The law must remain the law for aristocrats as well," he noted in horror. "No questioning of private property! How terrible!"[46] Yet despite his profound disappointment, the otherwise so loquacious secretary of the Elberfeld faction did not dare oppose Hitler openly. While Goebbels stubbornly remained silent, it was left to Gregor Strasser to defend their positions, and he was apparently so shocked by Hitler's fury that he failed miserably. "Hesitant, tremulous and clumsy" was how Goebbels described Strasser's reply. Feder characterised Strasser as "a beaten dog."[47] The triumph of the Munich faction was absolute. In the wake of the Bamberg conference, the Working Association North-west was finished politically, even if it did not immediately disband. In early March 1926, Strasser wrote to the Gauleiter asking them to send back all the copies of his draft manifesto, saying that he had "promised Herr Hitler to bring about the total recall of the programme."[48] It was the last time there would be any debate about the party's main political orientation.

Hitler was clever enough not to revel in his victory. Instead of humiliating his rivals he sought to win them over with conciliatory gestures. When Gregor Strasser was injured in a car accident in Landshut, Hitler made a point of visiting him in his sickbed.[49] The following September, Strasser was called to join the party leadership in Munich as propaganda director; he succeeded Hermann Esser, the very object of the initial attacks by the working association.[50] Hitler was particularly eager to court Goebbels, whose political talent he had recognised early on and whose need for praise and acknowledgement were equally obvious. The way he massaged the bruised ego of the "little doctor" demonstrated his instinctive understanding of people. "Once he's here, I'll win him over to our side," Hitler told his intimates in Munich. "I'll take care of him myself. The rest of you keep your hands off."[51] In late March, Hitler invited Goebbels to come to Munich and give a speech at the prestigious Bürgerbräukeller. The man from the Rhineland was courted as soon as he arrived in Munich on the evening of 7 April. Hitler sent his personal Mercedes to pick him up. "What a reception!" Goebbels crowed.[52] During the drive to his hotel, he saw giant posters advertising his speech the following evening.

"My heart was beating so hard it almost burst," Goebbels noted about his two-and-a-half-hour address. "I was giving everything I had. There were cheers and commotion. At the end, Hitler embraced me, tears in his eyes. I'm so overjoyed." The next day, Hitler gave Goebbels a personal tour of the party headquarters. The two men met several times, and Hitler employed his full power of persuasion to quell Goebbels's doubts. In the end, Goebbels was converted: "I am relieved on all counts. He is a man who only sees the big picture. Such an effervescent mind can be my leader. I bow before my superior, the political genius!"

On 19 April, Goebbels spoke alongside Hitler in Stuttgart, and the two celebrated Hitler's thirty-seventh birthday when the clock struck midnight. "Adolf Hitler, I love you, because you are simultaneously great and simple," Goebbels gushed in his diary.[53] In mid-June Hitler spoke in Essen. "A wonderful triad of gestures, facial expressions and words," Goebbels noted. "A born motivator! One could conquer the world with this man."[54] In July, Goebbels was permitted to spend a few days with Hitler on the Obersalzberg, and he requited that honour with a pledge of absolute loyalty: "Yes, this is a man I can serve. This is what the creator of the Third Reich looks like . . . I am knocked sideways. This is how he is: as sweet-natured, good-hearted and mild as a child; as sly, clever and adroit as a cat; as roaringly great and gigantic as a lion. A capital fellow, a true man."[55] Goebbels's conversion was complete. In late October 1926, Hitler named him Gauleiter of Greater Berlin, one of the most significant posts in the party's struggle for political power.

Hitler's triumph over the Strasser faction consolidated his position within the party, and at the party conference in Munich on 22 May 1926, he had his leadership confirmed by the rank and file. His re-election as party chairman was a foregone conclusion: the delegates burst out laughing when Max Amann asked if "someone other than Adolf Hitler should lead the party in the future." The newly ratified constitution of the NSDAP declared the party programme of 24 February 1920 as "immutable" and decreed that the party chairman be given "the most generous leeway . . . and independence from majority decisions of committees." In his state-of-the-party address, Hitler stressed that the organisation was in a "better than previous" position one year after its reconstitution. The NSDAP, Hitler said, had gained a foothold

throughout Germany and recruited a number of "first-rate speakers."
He specifically mentioned "our friend from Elberfeld, Goebbels," which
the latter noted with great satisfaction in his diary.[56]

At the first post-ban NSDAP rally, on 3 and 4 July 1926 in Weimar, the
once-fractious party was the picture of harmony. Weimar was chosen
because Thuringia was one of the few German states where Hitler
was still allowed to speak publicly. All petitions that could have been
the source of conflict were sent in advance to "special commissions"
so that the impression of internal unity would not be disrupted. In
his speech at the German National Theatre on the afternoon of 4 July,
Hitler summoned party members' faith and readiness for sacrifice.
"Deep and mystical—almost like a Gospel," Goebbels noted. "I thank
destiny for giving us this man!"[57] After his speech, Hitler, dressed in
an overcoat and puttees and with raised right arm, stood in an open-
top car and inspected a parade of several thousand SA men. The
Weimar rally was a milestone in the NSDAP's transition to a "Führer
party." There had been no objections to Hitler's claim of absolute
leadership, and the reconciliation of rival factions seemed to have
succeeded. Summing up the proceedings in the *Völkischer Beobachter*,
Rosenberg wrote: "Longing became strength. That is one of the major
results from Weimar. And it has its flag. And its Führer."[58]

In truth, the Nazi Party's development in 1926 and 1927 was far
less impressive than party propaganda made it out to be. Growth in
membership was slow. In late 1925, the party had little more than
27,000 members, and in late 1926 that figure was still only 50,000. It
was not until March 1927 that enrolment reached 57,477—the number
of members the NSDAP had had in November 1923. By the end of
1927, the number had reached 72,590 people.[59] Even in Munich, where
the party had its headquarters, the signs of stagnation were unmistakable. Little remained of the party's dynamism, its near-constant
presence on the streets from the early 1920s. Between 1926 and the
spring of 1928, the Munich chapter never counted more than 2,500
members and thus failed to match its strength of 1923.[60] Local meetings were, as a rule, poorly attended, and only a small percentage
of members were actively involved in party life. The declining willingness of members to pay their dues also indicated that interest
was waning.[61]

Moreover, the rivalries of 1924 persisted even after the carefully staged reconciliation. The everyday life of the party was full of feuding and resentment. In Munich, Goebbels's rise in Hitler's favour was viewed with envy. In February 1927 an essay by the Berlin Gauleiter in the *Nationalsozialistische Blätter* (National Socialist Newsletter) caused a furore. "This ever more intolerable youth has been insolent enough . . . to rebuke Frick so that even this level-headed man is upset," Rudolf Buttmann wrote to his wife. "H[itler] will no doubt put the upstart scribbler back in his place in writing."[62] In fact, Hitler merely had Gottfried Feder give Goebbels a mild scolding. Just as he had in Landsberg, the Führer declined to involve himself or take sides in quarrels between his underlings.

As reflected in their election results, in the first few years after the party was reconstituted, the NSDAP played only a marginal role in German politics. The party got a scant 4,607 votes (1.7 per cent) in the Landtag election in Mecklenburg-Schwerin on 6 June 1926 and only 37,725 (1.6 per cent) in a state poll in Saxony on 31 October 1926. The NSDAP did slightly better in Thuringia on 30 January 1927, taking 27,946 votes (3.5 per cent).[63] Hitler may have been convinced, as Hess reported in early 1927, that the party was headed for an imminent "upturn" but that was not the case.[64] In March 1927, the Reich commissioner for public order, who was charged with monitoring the NSDAP, deemed that overall the party had made no progress: "It has not been able to bring its membership anywhere near the level it had in 1923."[65] By the summer of 1927, the liberal Reichstag deputy and lecturer at the German Academy of Politics in Berlin, Theodor Heuss, opined that the NSDAP was merely "a reminder of the period of inflation."[66] Foreign observers felt likewise. In a memorandum in late 1927, the British Foreign Office's Germany expert John Perowne suggested that Hitler's star was declining: "His figure and that of Ludendorff fade into insignificance."[67]

With the NSDAP's popularity fading, Bavarian Interior Minister Karl Stützel saw no reason to extend the ban on Hitler appearing publicly. On 5 March 1927, after considerable dithering, the prohibition was lifted, and Hitler was free to speak again. The following day, he took to the stage in the town of Vilsbiburg, and on 9 March he celebrated a triumphant comeback in Zirkus Krone. Some 7,000 people packed the venue, among them "members of the better classes, ladies in fur coats and representatives of the intelligentsia." "Lust for the sensational lay in the hot, sickly-sweet air," noted a Munich police observer. At around 9 p.m., Hitler finally appeared with his entourage. "The people acted happy and excited, waving, constantly crying 'Heil,' standing on the benches and stamping their feet. Then a fanfare as in the theatre. Immediate silence." The dramaturgy of Hitler's appearances had not changed since 1923. Hitler marched into the auditorium, followed by two rows of drummers and some 200 SA men in rank and file. "The people greeted him in the Fascist way with outstretched arms . . ." the police observer wrote. "Music blared. Flags were paraded, and spit-polished standards with wreathed swastikas and eagles copied from Ancient Roman insignia."

The observer seems to have been less than impressed by Hitler's rhetorical skills. Hitler began slowly, but then the words came tumbling out, barely comprehensible: "He gesticulated with his hands and arms, jumped about this way and that and sought to keep his audience captivated. Whenever he was interrupted by applause, he theatrically extended his arms." Nor was the police observer, obviously no Nazi sympathiser, captivated by what Hitler had to say:

> In his speech, Hitler used vulgar comparisons, tailor-made to the intellectual capacities of his listeners, and he did not shy away from even the cheapest allusions . . . His words and opinions were simply hurled out with dictatorial certainty as if they were unquestionable principles and facts. All this manifests itself in his language as well, which is like something merely expulsed.[68]

At Hitler's second appearance in Zirkus Krone in late March, however, the hall was only two-thirds full. In early April, around 3,000 people showed up, and on 6 April Hitler was only drawing half that number. "Hitler back in front of empty seats," the Social Democratic *Münchener Post* newspaper gleefully reported.[69] After his involuntary two-year hiatus, Hitler no longer possessed the appeal as a speaker he once had. That had less to do with fatigue, even among his Munich followers, than with his refusal to take account of all the recent changes in his speeches, which still relied upon the crisis rhetoric of 1923. Hitler stodgily ignored all signs of economic recovery. "The German collapse continues," he asserted in December 1925, declaring a few months later: "Today we are a pitiable people, plagued by misery and poverty . . . Seven years on from 1918, we can say that we have sunk lower and lower."[70] Hitler liked to use comparisons with Italy under Mussolini to portray conditions in Germany in the worst possible light. "There they have a flourishing economy, while here we have a decrepit industrial sector with twelve million unemployed," he declared at a rally in Stuttgart in April 1926.[71] In reality, an average of only two million Germans were unemployed that year.

Hitler paired his extreme exaggeration of Germany's economic plight with extremist polemics against Gustav Stresemann's policy of international reconciliation. For Hitler, the 1924 Dawes Plan was nothing but a grandiose way of sapping the German people's energy. The 1925 Treaty of Locarno represented "boundless subordination and the deepest dishonour."[72] As he had previously with Walther Rathenau, Hitler did not shy away from *ad hominem* attacks on Stresemann, accusing him of being a traitor. For Hitler, reaching any agreements with Germany's "irreconcilable enemy" France was like "trying to form a coalition between the goose and the fox." The German foreign minister owed his office to "the grace of France," Hitler sneered, and thus was more concerned about the interests of his French colleague Aristide Briand than those of the German people.[73]

Hitler took the same view that conservatives in general did of "Weimar culture," seeing it only as a symptom of decadence and decline. In Hitler's mind, German literature and art had been "made obscene and dirty." Even in the birthplace of German classicism itself, Weimar, Hitler raged in one of his speeches, "the poisoners of the German soul are leading their filthy existence and defiling the sites of the most elevated art with nigger and jazz music." One task of National Socialism was to "clean out this manure."[74] Hitler blamed the "degeneration" of German culture on the "corrosive" influence of Jews. Not only did Jews control the economy via the banks and the stock exchanges, Hitler thundered in August 1925, they also dominated German journalism, literature, art, theatre and cinema: "Today, they are in almost complete control culturally just as they are in total control economically over the entire world."[75] Incarceration had done nothing to dampen Hitler's fanatic anti-Semitism, which he put on display not only at closed party meetings, but in public mass events. No other speaker in the NSDAP—not even Goebbels or Julius

Streicher—raged more furiously against the "Galician riff-raff and criminal gangs ... the international Jewish stranglers of blood ... [and] the drones of international high finance."⁷⁶ The people of the world, he promised in June 1927, would "breathe easier" once they were liberated from the Jews. On 24 February 1928, the eighth anniversary of the announcement of the party programme, Hitler may have proclaimed: "If [the Jew] behaves, he can stay—if not, out with him!" But in the same breath he insisted that *We* are the masters of our house" and issued an unmistakably murderous threat: "One cannot compete with parasites, one can only remove them."⁷⁷

Hitler could, of course, moderate his anti-Semitism when he was speaking before smaller, select audiences. One example is the speech he gave on 28 February 1926 in front of an exclusive conservative-nationalist club in Hamburg, in the great hall of the luxury Atlantic Hotel. Here Hitler's talk avoided any mention of the "Jewish question," focusing instead on the "danger of the Marxist movement." His understanding of the term "Marxist" was very broad, however, and included both the Social Democrats and the Communists. But because the moderate Hamburg SPD, which cooperated with bourgeois liberals, was not a suitable target for attack, Hitler concentrated his bile on the KPD, whose leader, Ernst Thälmann, came from the northern German port city. Hitler deliberately called upon the fears of his audience, which included leading Hamburg merchants, of the Communists coming to power. "If Communism were to triumph today, two million people would be making their way to the gallows," he prophesied. But there was a way of "smashing and eradicating the Marxist world view," which was the aim of his own movement. The NSDAP, Hitler proclaimed, knew "that toxins could only be combated with anti-toxins," and the party would not rest "until the last Marxist has either been converted or eliminated." The initially reserved audience greeted these words with frenetic applause, and at the end of the speech, when Hitler proclaimed his vision of a "Germany of freedom and power," he was showered with ovations and shouts of "Heil."⁷⁸

For Hitler the categories "Jewish" and "Marxist" were interchangeable. Depending on the situation, his warnings for the future could oscillate between "the international Jewish world enemy" and "the international Marxist poisoning of peoples." On occasion he would combine the two objects of hatred. "The Jew is and remains the world's enemy, and his greatest weapon, Marxism, is and remains a plague for humanity," he wrote in February 1927 in the *Völkischer Beobachter*.[79] By destroying Marxism, Hitler believed that he could eradicate class conflict and create a "genuine ethnic-popular community." He was also constantly coming up with new phrases to describe the marriage of nationalism and socialism, the unification of "workers of the mind and workers of the fist." National Socialism knew neither bourgeois nor proletarian, only "the German working for his people."[80] Sometimes Hitler recalled his experiences at the Western Front as a harbinger of the sort of national community he envisioned. "There once was a place in Germany without class divisions," he declared in a speech. "That was among the companies of soldiers at the front. There were no recognisable bourgeois and proletarian characteristics there. There was the company and only the company."[81]

One of the few new topics Hitler adopted after 1924 was the necessity, first advanced in December 1925, of acquiring "living space" to secure adequate food supplies for the German people. His speech at the Weimar rally in 1926 made a special point of emphasising the demand that population size and available territory be calibrated—by force if necessary. "We have to solve this question with a rough hand and a sharp sword," Hitler proclaimed.[82] After finishing the second volume of *Mein Kampf* in the autumn of 1926, he had repeatedly included the "space question" in his speeches. Hitler made no bones of the fact that he intended to resolve this issue with violence as soon as Germany's military position was strong enough. In his first public speech after the Bavarian ban was lifted, in Vilsbiburg, he had cited the example of eastern colonisation in the Middle Ages. Back then, Hitler claimed, "the territory east of the Elbe River had been conquered with the sword and handed over to the fist of the German farmer." In early April 1927 in Zirkus Krone, he addressed an imaginary enemy: "And should you not give us space in the world, then we will take that space ourselves."[83] Later in 1927, Hitler took to citing the title of a popular novel of the previous year: Hans Grimm's *Volk ohne Raum*—"A People without Space." Then, in early February 1928, he first publicly used the term *Lebensraum*—"living space."[84] Hitler rarely made it explicitly clear that the territory in question would come at the expense of the Soviet Union, but his audience could hardly have been under any illusions about the direction in which his expansionism was aimed.

Hitler's full-throated proclamations must have appeared rather delu-
sional at a time when the NSDAP was still only a marginal player
within German politics. To dispel doubts among his followers, Hitler
seized every occasion to stress how crucial "blind, fanatical belief"
was to the ultimate triumph of the movement. If one had "the holiest
of faiths," he reassured them, "even what is most impossible becomes
possible."[85] That prompted Hess to write to their former fellow
Landsberg inmate Walter Hewel in late March 1937:

> This is where the great popular leader coincides with the great founder
> of a religion. An apodictic belief has to be installed in listeners. Only
> then can the mass of followers be led where they are supposed to be
> led. They will follow their leader even in the face of setbacks, but only
> if they have been instilled with absolute faith in the absolute rectitude
> of their own will, of the Führer's mission and the mission of their people.[86]

National Socialism depicted itself as a political religion. "What does
Christianity mean for us today?" Goebbels scoffed. "National Socialism
is a religion."[87] This view corresponded to the party's inflation of itself
to a "community of faith" and its programme to an "ideological
creed." Like the biblical apostles, the task of the Führer's disciples was
to spread Nazi principles "like a gospel among our people."[88] This was
one reason why Hitler staunchly refused to consider any amendment
of the original twenty-five-point NSDAP manifesto. "Absolutely not,"
he told Hanfstaengl. "It's staying as it is. The New Testament, too, is
full of contradictions, but that did nothing to hinder the spread of
Christianity."[89] At the Nazi Party's 1925 Christmas celebrations, Hitler
drew a revealing parallel between early Christianity and the "movement." Christ had also been initially mocked, and yet the Christian
faith had become a massive global movement. "We want to achieve
the same thing in the arena of politics," Hitler stated. A year later he
was explicitly casting himself as Jesus's successor, who would complete
his work. "National Socialism," Hitler proclaimed, "is nothing other
than compliance with Christ's teachings."[90]

In his public speeches, especially in their final crescendos, Hitler
often utilised religious vocabulary. He would conclude with a final
"Amen!" or invoke his "faith in a new Holy German Empire" or call
upon "Our Lord to give me the strength to continue my work in the

face of all the demons."[91] He constantly warned his followers that there would be no shortage of sacrifices along the way. Here, too, he drew parallels with early Christianity: "We have a path of thorns to go down and are proud of it." The "blood witnesses" who had lost their lives for the Nazi movement, Hitler promised, would enjoy the sort of reverence once reserved for the Christian martyrs.[92] To reinforce this idea, the annual party rally rituals included the reverent handing over of the "bloody banner" carried during the putsch of 1923, combined with a personal oath of loyalty to the Führer.

Yet although the Nazis had no scruples about appropriating religious sentiments and customs for political purposes, they also maintained strict neutrality towards the Christian confessions. In his lead article concerning the reconstitution of the party in February 1925, Hitler had opposed any attempt to "drag religious quarrels into the movement," insisting that the "members of both confessions must be able to peacefully coexist" in the NSDAP.[93] Hitler was thus enraged when the Gauleiter of Thuringia and author of the anti-Semitic bestseller *Sin against Blood*, Arthur Dinter, began promoting the "pure gospel of the saviour" and advocated dismantling the Protestant and Catholic Churches. In late September 1927, Hitler removed Dinter from office,[94] informing him the following July: "As the leader of the National Socialist movement and as a person who has a blind faith in belonging one day to the ranks of those who make history, I see your activity as damaging the National Socialist movement by connecting the party with your reformist goals." Dinter was subsequently kicked out of the NSDAP.[95]

The party made little headway from the mid-1920s, as the period of relative stability for the Weimar Republic continued. Nonetheless, those years were crucial to its internal development. It was then that the foundations were laid for the movement's later dramatic rise. "It may not be visible from the outside and it may be more in silent preparation for future triumphs," Hess wrote to Walter Hewel in late November 1927, "but gradually the predictions for the year 1927, and our cause, are coming to pass."[96] Between 1925 and 1928, the NSDAP was irrevocably transformed into a "Führer party," focused around a single leader at its head. "There can be no doubt who the leader and commander is," Hess wrote. In that letter to Hewel, Hess expanded upon the importance for the movement of the so-called "Führer principle," based on "absolute authority directed downwards and absolute duty directed upwards." As Hess explained, Hitler "issues commands to the Gauleiter, the Gauleiter issue commands to the Ortsgruppenführer [local leaders] and the Ortsgruppenführer issue commands to the broad masses of supporters directly under them. Duty . . . follows the reverse path." This, for Hess, represented "Germanic democracy."[97]

The system relied on party members' sense of personal connection to their Führer and their unquestioning subordination. Anyone who violated this principle was sure to be sanctioned. When a local Nazi leader from the Munich district of Schwabing, Ernst Woltereck, complained about Hitler's unsatisfactory public image and threatened to resign, Hitler called a meeting of the Schwabing chapter in June 1926, at which he made clear that the party was built on authority and subordination. He as Führer would not tolerate a minor chapter leader criticising his superiors. "Were this to be tolerated," Hitler asserted, "the party would be dead and buried."[98] In May 1927, frustrated by the lack of progress the party was making, the Munich SA under Edmund Heines rebelled. Once again Hitler took a hard line, ordering that "those who refuse to subordinate themselves have no place in the party and especially not in the SA."[99] By the end of the month, Heines had been expelled from both the party and the SA. When internal disagreements did not call his leadership into question, however, Hitler refused to get involved. Indeed, his leadership style encouraged rivalries between his subordinates. In his crudely Darwinist world view, such feuds were part of a process of natural selection that would favour the strongest and most capable of his followers. "He keeps considerable distance from minor everyday questions," Hess wrote approvingly. That contributed to his aura as a "coolly superior . . . born politician of stature—a statesman."[100]

Before the Beer Hall Putsch, individual party members worshipped their leader to varying degrees, but between 1926 and 1928 devotion was institutionalised. The "Heil Hitler" greeting was made mandatory for all NSDAP members "in recognition of Hitler's position of unlimited leadership and as a kind of canonisation during his lifetime," as Hanfstaengl described it.[101] Nazi propaganda became obsessed with popularising the Führer cult and ensuring that it spread to the smallest party chapter. Among the most effective pieces of propaganda were

Heinrich Hoffmann's first photographic brochures, "Germany's Awakening in Word and Image," from 1924 and 1926. They reinforced Hitler's quasi-religious aura as a man who had emerged from the people and who was preaching the gospel of love for the fatherland.[102] Goebbels, who after his "conversion" had become a fervent admirer of the party chairman, emerged as one of the active propagators of Hitler's larger-than-life status. Only those in the know, wrote Goebbels in July 1926 in the *Völkischer Beobachter*, could judge "what Adolf Hitler's personality had meant for the solidarity of the movement in the past few years of struggle." In Goebbels's view, Hitler alone had prevented the movement from being "scattered in a thousand winds."[103]

Here, too, we can see how Hitler's sense of mission and the expectations of those who saw him as the coming messiah, the saviour of Germans, reinforced each other. As Hess wrote in November 1927: "For me, being constantly in his presence, it is astonishing to see how he grows day by day, continually acquiring new fundamental wisdom, developing new ways of dealing with problems, gushing with ideas and constantly excelling himself in his speeches."[104] The Nazi Party rally in August 1927, the first one to take place in Nuremberg, became an extended celebration of the Führer. Hitler himself was deeply involved in the preparations, calling upon his "German ethnic comrades to join the coalescing army of a young Germany in which the faith in the Führer and not the weakness of the majority is decisive."[105] Between 15,000 and 20,000 of his supporters showed up in Nuremberg. On 21 August, after the "consecration of standards" in Luitpoldshain Park, Hitler—dressed in a brown SA shirt—inspected the columns of his subordinates on the main market square. There, as one report had it, he was "enthusiastically greeted and given flowers."[106] The young Berliner Horst Wessel, who took part, later recalled: "Flags, enthusiasm, Hitler, all of Nuremberg a brown army camp. It made an enormous impression."[107]

As the cult of the Führer was established, the party also became more organised. In March 1925, Philipp Bouhler took over the post of the secretary of the Munich party, with Franz Xaver Schwarz as treasurer. Other key figures included Hess, who acted as an intermediate between Hitler and the Reich leadership, and Max Amann, the head of the party's publishing house. In September 1926, Gregor Strasser succeeded Hermann Esser as Reich director of propaganda. In January 1928, the retired major Walter Buch became chairman of an investigatory and mediating committee which had been set up in December 1925 to settle internal party conflicts. It was an "essential institution"[108] and Buch understood that the main purpose of the body was to keep disagreements under wraps. One of his major aides was Hans Frank, later Governor General of occupied Poland.[109] In June 1925, the party headquarters had relocated from its provisional home at the offices of Eher Verlag in Thierschstrasse 15, to Schellingstrasse 50, where Hitler's photographer Hoffmann had provided the use of several rooms. "We are establishing our new offices," Hess reported. "At the moment it is still provisional. The Tribune hopes to build our own headquarters soon, with all the modern furnishings."[110] Here the pride of the party was a handwritten central card catalogue of all members. On 2 January 1928, Hitler appointed Gregor Strasser as Reich organisational director, with the party chairman himself now assuming responsibility for the propaganda division.[111] Strasser unified party organisation throughout the Reich. Among other things, the Gaue were redrawn to reflect Germany's electoral districts. The result was an efficient bureaucratic apparatus that provided the framework for later mass mobilisation.

In addition, a network of special bodies and associations was formed to attract various groups and professions. In February 1926, the National Socialist German Students' League came into being, and a German literature student from a highly respected Weimar family, Baldur von Schirach, took over the organisation in July 1928. In August 1927, Alfred Rosenberg initiated the founding of the Fighting League for German Culture, whose aim was to oppose the "corrosive" influence of artistic modernism; its supporters included the Bruckmanns, Hitler's influential Munich patrons. In January 1928 the German Women's Order was subsumed as the "Red Swastika" by the NSDAP: it would become the National Socialist Women's League in 1931. In September 1928, Hans Frank founded the League of National Socialist Lawyers, and 1929 would see the establishment of the National Socialist League of German Teachers, the National Socialist League of School Pupils and the National Socialist League of Doctors. As of 1926, the Hitler Youth was appealing to 14- to 18-year-old boys; in 1929 it was joined by the League of German Girls.[112]

In the spring of 1925, Hitler had told his old associate and occasional bodyguard Julius Schreck to form a "Staff Guard" along the lines of the Stosstrupp Hitler. It was soon renamed the Schutzstaffel, or SS.

Its membership initially consisted of a few hundred men responsible for the personal safety of the Führer. They considered themselves an elite body that united the best and most active forces within the party. Their leader received the somewhat pompous title of Reichsführer-SS, but as of 1926 the SS was subordinated to the reconstituted SA under Pfeffer von Salomon. Heinrich Himmler became deputy Reichsführer-SS in September 1927, eventually taking over the organisation in January 1929.

Born in 1900 as the son of a *Gymnasium* teacher in Munich, Himmler grew up in a sheltered, well-educated Catholic environment and, like his two brothers, enjoyed an excellent humanist education. He was a typical representative of what Germans called the "war youth generation": he was too young to have served at the front but old enough for the First World War to be one of the defining experiences of his life. Even after defeat and revolution had put an end to his dream of becoming a military officer, the physically frail Himmler still worshipped the ideal of the soldier. Noticeably self-conscious in his dealings with others, he learned to conceal his insecurities behind a shield of coldness, severity and sobriety.[113] He studied agricultural sciences at Munich University in the early 1920s, when he became involved in paramilitary associations. After the Beer Hall Putsch, the unemployed university graduate put his future in the hands of Hitler's party, earning his spurs as a rural agitator for the NSDAP in northern Bavaria. In 1926, Gregor Strasser named him deputy propaganda director at Munich party headquarters. In contrast to other Nazi leaders, Himmler does not seem to have undergone an epiphany that drew him into Hitler's charismatic orbit. Hitler himself maintained his distance from the externally nondescript, pedantic Himmler, but valued him as a skilled organiser. Upon becoming Reichsführer-SS, Himmler devoted all his attention to liberating the organisation from subordination to the SA leadership and to establishing its reputation as a disciplined, elite formation utterly loyal to Hitler. He encouraged solidarity within his "order" with a number of cult rituals, and instituted a strict code of behaviour to which SS men were expected to conform.[114]

With the party's progress beginning to stagnate again, Hitler increased his efforts to elicit support from the business community. In June 1926 he spoke for the first time to fifty or sixty representatives of Ruhr

Valley industry. As he had talked to the nationalist club in Hamburg, Hitler did not engage in any of his customary tirades against Jews, focusing instead on "dealing with Marxism." He also tried to assuage industrialists' fears about his economic and political aims, assuring them that he would stand up for the inviolability of private property. "The free market will be protected as the most sensible or only possible economic order," the *Rheinisch-Westfälische Zeitung* newspaper, a mouthpiece of heavy industry, wrote in summing up Hitler's speech. The paper's publisher, Theodor Reismann-Grone, had supported the NSDAP since the early 1920s.[115]

In late April in Essen, Hitler spoke again to a large circle of invited guests from the realms of business and politics. This time he sought support for his idea of symbiotically merging nationalism and socialism and reinstituting "the authority of personality." Hess, who accompanied him, described the effect of Hitler's speech: "I seldom heard him like that. Irritated by the icy silence [of the audience] during the first hour, he increased his intensity so much that by the end the audience of around 400 broke out in hurricanes of applause in ever-decreasing intervals!" According to Hess, Emil Kirdorf—the 80-year-old patriarch of Rhineland and Westphalian industry and long-time director of the Gelsenkirchner Bergwerk mining company—"stood up, visibly moved, at the end and shook the Tribune's hand."[116]

On 4 July 1927, Elsa Bruckmann arranged a meeting between Kirdorf and Hitler at her home in Munich. The leader of the NSDAP and the industrialist talked for four hours, after which the latter was so impressed that he asked Hitler to put his thoughts down in a pamphlet that Kirdorf would distribute to the most important business figures in the Ruhr Valley. Hugo Bruckmann had it printed up as a brochure entitled "The Road to Resurgence." Hitler sent it to Kirdorf in August with the request that "the honourable Privy Councillor" help spread the thoughts therein among his circles. In this brochure, Hitler again made it clear that he did not intend to attack private industry. On the contrary, he wrote, "only a strong nationalist state can provide industry with the protection and the freedom to continue to exist and develop." Hitler also played down his anti-Semitism, although in one passage he mentioned "the international Jew" disparagingly as the "most active propagator of the theory of pacifism, reconciliation between peoples and eternal world peace."[117]

The pamphlet does not seem to have created much of a stir. Leading industrialists in the Ruhr Valley kept their distance from the NSDAP, which at the time was regarded as barely more than a marginal party. "Hitler won't bring much joy either to us or the region," magnate Paul Reusch wrote to Albert Vögler, the chairman of the United Steelworks, in December 1927.[118] Hess's report that month, that "excellent progress" was being made in the Ruhr Valley—"the important people simply follow the Tribune"—was clearly wishful thinking.[119] Even Kirdorf, who joined the NSDAP on 1 August 1927 and attended the party rally in Nuremberg as an honorary guest, turned his back on the party a year later, dismayed at its constant anti-capitalist agitation in the Ruhr Valley. He did, however, remain a supporter of Hitler personally. After the 1929 Nuremberg rally, the industrialist wrote to the party chairman: "Anyone who had the privilege of taking part in the rally . . . even though he may be sceptical or opposed to specific points in the party programme, has to acknowledge the significance of your movement for the recovery of our German fatherland and hope that it is a success."[120] Hitler's courting of Ruhr industrialists may not have yielded many concrete results, and it certainly did not land him massive donations, as was speculated in the contemporary press; nonetheless, it was not a total failure since it established Hitler as an economic moderate. This reputation would serve him very well after 1930, when the NSDAP's electoral breakthrough had made the party far more interesting to businessmen and entrepreneurs.

As 1927 came to an end, Hitler was confident. "I know again that Providence will lead me where I had hoped to arrive four years ago," he wrote to Winifred Wagner on 30 December 1927. "A time will come when pride in your friend will be your reward for many things for which at present I cannot repay you."[121] Hitler pinned his hopes on the Reichstag election scheduled for 20 May 1928. In January of that year, Hitler reckoned the party could win fifteen seats, although he also said, "If we get twenty-five, we'll enter into a government coalition, only to leave it with aplomb, the first time circumstances permit."[122] The NSDAP began campaigning intensively. On the evening of 14 May, Hitler appeared alongside the leading candidate, General Franz von Epp, at twelve large-scale Munich events. "We feel like soldiers," Hitler proclaimed on one occasion, "soldiers of a coming

German army, of a new Reich and of the ideas that shall forge this Reich."[123] Goebbels noted that Hitler had never looked forward to an election as much as this one, hoping that "the results will be commensurate to the willingness for sacrifice we have shown thus far."[124]

The outcome was a major setback for the NSDAP. The clear winners of the election were the left-wing parties. The SPD's share of the vote rose from 26 to 29.8 per cent, and the KPD's from 9 to 10.6 per cent. The Social Democrat Hermann Müller formed a grand coalition consisting of the SPD, the Centre Party, the BVP, the DDP and the DVP. The big loser was the conservative German National People's Party (DNVP), which saw its share of the vote decline from 20.5 to 14.2 per cent. The NSDAP only polled 2.6 per cent, slightly down from their last election results in December 1924.[125] Instead of fourteen, the party now had only twelve Reichstag deputies. They included Epp, Goebbels, Frick, Gregor Strasser, Feder and Göring, who had returned from Sweden to Germany in the autumn of 1927 under a general amnesty declared by Reich President von Hindenburg. Hitler put a positive spin on the election, which also saw the VB take a catastrophic 0.9 per cent. That caused Hitler to crow that in future there would be "only one ethnic-popular movement"—the NSDAP.[126] But his followers were bitterly disappointed. Gregor Strasser complained that 20 May had given National Socialists "no cause for satisfaction," while Goebbels merely noted, "Depression in me."[127]

The NSDAP had not performed poorly everywhere, but its weakness in urban industrial centres was marked. The party had polled only 1.6 per cent in Berlin, despite Gauleiter Goebbels using every trick in the book after the temporary ban on the NSDAP in the Prussian capital was lifted.[128] By contrast, the party had made notable gains in rural parts of Schleswig-Holstein and Lower Saxony, taking 5.2 per cent in the Weser-Ems electoral district of north-western Germany. Still, the best results were limited to the traditional Nazi strongholds of Franconia (8.1 per cent), Upper Bavaria/Swabia (6.23 per cent) and the Palatinate (5.7 per cent). In Munich, they took almost 8 per cent of the vote and remained the third most popular party behind the SPD (24 per cent) and the BVP (17 per cent). Fearing that the NSDAP might once more be banned, Hitler swore that he would sacrifice everything to prevent a grand coalition of conservatives and Social Democrats. "Munich is the headquarters of the party and must be

protected," he declared. To that end, he refused to rule out participating in a Bavarian government, but insisted that in any coalition the
party must control the Justice Ministry so as to ensure there were no
future prohibitions of the movement.[129]

For the party leadership, one lesson of the election was to shift
their propaganda focus to rural Germany. "There better results can
be achieved with lower costs in terms of time, energy and money
than in the big cities," the *Völkischer Beobachter* wrote in late May.[130]
By the autumn of 1927, the party had already stepped up its efforts to
appeal to the rural population of northern Germany. On 10 December,
Hitler spoke for the first time to several thousand farmers from
Schleswig-Holstein, assuring them that the NSDAP was particularly
keen to represent their interests.[131] In April 1928, to head off potential
criticism, he amended Point 17 of the party programme, which called
for a "law on the confiscation of property without compensation for
public purposes." The amendment stipulated that this demand only
concerned "illicitly acquired property" and was aimed "primarily at
Jewish firms that speculated in property."[132]

After the election, Hitler retreated for a few weeks to Berchtesgaden.
In October 1928, he rented Haus Wachenfeld for 100 marks. It was a
simple holiday home in the Alpine style, owned by Margarete Winter,
the widow of a northern German businessman. Hitler was accompanied by his half-sister Angela Raubal. "I immediately called my sister
in Vienna," Hitler recalled in 1942. "I told her, I've rented a house. 'Do
you want to come run the household?' She came, and we moved in
without delay. It was wonderful. My first Christmas up there was
marvellous!" In 1933 he would convince the widow to sell him the
house, which he later expanded into his "Berghof."[133]

In June and July 1928, Hitler used a trip to the Obersalzberg to
tackle a new book project, having given up his original idea of writing
his war memoirs for Bruckmann Verlag publishers. Apparently he had
hit upon the latter idea after receiving a copy of Ernst Jünger's 1926
book *Fire and Blood*, which the author had inscribed with the dedication "For the national leader Adolf Hitler." After *Storm and Steel*, *Battle
as Internal Experience* and *Copse 125*, it was Jünger's fourth book about
his time as a soldier. Hitler, who made copious pencil notes in his
copy of *Fire and Blood*, sent a thank-you letter to Jünger. "I've read all
your works," he wrote. "I've learned to appreciate you as one of the

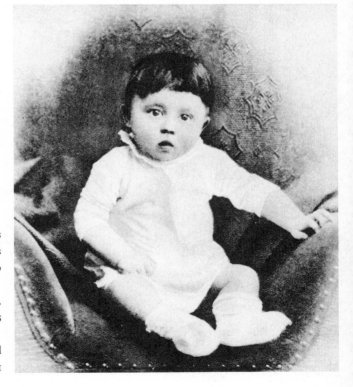

Above left: Hitler's father, Alois
Hitler, in his custom official's
uniform, *c.* 1880

Above right: Hitler's mother,
Klara Hitler, *c.* 1885

Right: Hitler as a small
child, 1891

Above: Class photo with the ten-year-old Adolf Hitler (*top, middle*), Leonding, 1899

Left: Hitler as a boy

Opposite top: Hitler at a patriotic event in Munich's Odeonplatz, 2 August 1914

Opposite bottom: Hitler (*right*) with his comrades in Bavarian RIR 16, and his fox terrier "Foxl," in 1915

Above: NSDAP flyer announcing
Hitler's appearance in Zirkus
Krone on 11 January 1922

Left: One of the first portraits of
Hitler by Heinrich Hoffmann,
September 1923

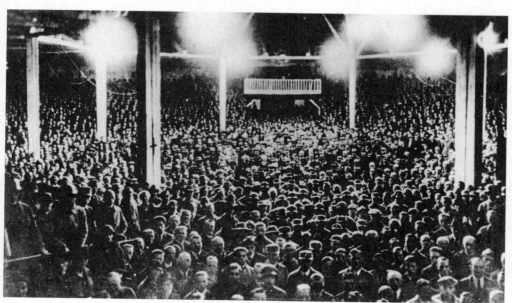

Hitler speaking in Munich's Zirkus Krone in 1923, before the putsch

Group photo of the defendants at Hitler's trial, 1 April 1924: (*from left to right*) Heinz Pernet, Friedrich Weber, Wilhelm Frick, Hermann Kriebel, Erich Ludendorff, Hitler, Wilhelm Brückner, Ernst Röhm and Robert Wagner

Hitler with fellow Landsberg inmates: (*from left to right*) Hitler, Emil Maurice, Hermann Kriebel, Rudolf Hess and Friedrich Weber

Left: Advertising brochure for Hitler's book, early June 1924

Below: Hitler outside the Landsberg city gate after his release from prison, 20 December 1924

Right: Hitler wearing lederhosen and brown shirt in an unpublished photograph by Heinrich Hoffmann, spring 1927

Below: Hitler at a party rally in Weimar, 3–4 July 1926

The Berlin Sportpalast during a National Socialist campaign event in September 1930

Hitler is celebrated by supporters after his testimony at the Reich Court in Leipzig,
25 September 1930

few powerful shapers of his experiences at the front. So my joy at receiving a copy of *Fire and Blood* from you personally, with your friendly dedication, was all the greater."[134] In September 1926, Elsa Bruckmann had told her husband that Hitler "is considering composing a war book and believes that everything is growing more vivid and is ripening within him; images are crystallising around the core which he had conceived, and are now crying out for completion."[135] In fact, Hitler never seems to have committed a word to paper; at least, no manuscript fragments have ever been discovered.

What did survive were 234 typed manuscript pages from the summer of 1928, which the American historian Gerhard L. Weinberg published as *Hitler's Second Book* in 1961.[136] Apparently Hitler dictated this text to his secretary over the course of a few weeks. In late June 1928, Hess described the content of the book in a letter to his parents: "Saturday–Sunday we're going to Berchtesgaden, where I have an appointment . . . with the Tribune who is writing a new and apparently quite fine book about foreign policy."[137] Hitler had indeed formed a plan to present his foreign-policy views in a larger context. His interest had been sparked by the problematic status of southern Tyrol, which he had already discussed in a brochure in February 1926, a preview from the second volume of *Mein Kampf*.[138] There he had announced his willingness to renounce German claims on southern Tyrol in favour of pursuing an alliance with Italy, which made him the target of nationalist attacks in the 1928 elections.[139]

But southern Tyrol was not the focus of the Second Book. In fact, the draft work recorded the basic principles that he had been promoting in his speeches since 1926. One was that "the battle for survival of a people" resided in bringing about a balance between population and territory, so that foreign policy was "the art of securing a people its necessary living space." He also made it clear that eastern Europe was the only part of the continent where Germany could pursue its "territorial policies"—a view that ruled out any alliances with Russia and meant that Germany would have to court Italy and Britain as allies. In the afterword, Hitler stressed that the book was not an "essay on the Jewish question," but he could not resist putting his paranoid anti-Semitic world view on display yet again: "Because they have no productive capabilities of their own, the Jewish people is not able to build a territorially manifested state. It relies on the labour and crea-

tive activity of other people as the basis for its own existence. The
Jew thus leads a parasitic existence among the lives of other people.
The ultimate goal of the Jewish struggle for survival is the enslave-
ment of all productively active peoples."[140]

On 13 July 1928, Hitler gave a speech to 5,000 people in Berlin about
"German foreign policy," in which he summarised the core points of
the Second Book.[141] After the event, he took off with Goebbels for a
week's holiday on the North Sea island of Norderney. He did not
continue working on his book manuscript, and over the course of
1929, he seems to have decided against publishing it.[142] We can only
speculate about the reasons behind his decision. Possibly Max Amann
was concerned that the book would be a commercial failure. The sales
figures for *Mein Kampf* had declined dramatically in 1927 and 1928, and
the demand for another Hitler book may have appeared slight.
Probably more significant, however, was the chance that opened up
in early 1929 for the Nazi Party to work together with right-wing
nationalists who were demanding a popular referendum on the Young
Plan. Hitler's wild attacks on mainstream politicians in the Second
Book would have hardly served to further that cause.[143] Scruples about
how the book would be received outside Germany probably did not
play a role, even if Hitler later used that argument to explain why he
had not published it. In the mid-1930s he told Albert Speer that he
was glad he had suppressed the Second Book: "What political difficulties would it cause me now!"[144]

With his movement in the doldrums, Hitler cancelled the 1928 party
rally and instead called a "Führer conference" in Munich in late August
to run parallel to a general party conference. In his role as party
chairman, Hitler was at pains to elevate the mood of his supporters,
which was visibly depressed. Those who make history are always in
the minority, Hitler told his followers. The fact alone that both the
other parties and the general public now opposed the NSDAP was
"almost mathematical reason for the eventual, certain triumph of our
movement."[145] But he was unable to completely dispel party members'
scepticism. Even Goebbels found Hitler's comments "Somewhat
tired—Munich level—I'm sick of that."[146] Discontent was not limited
to the grass roots but was also beginning to be felt in the NSDAP
headquarters. In response to a complaint from a Franconian Landtag

deputy that some people had erected a protective wall around Hitler, denying others access to him, Walter Buch shot back that department heads in the party headquarters also had "to wait for days for contact with Herr Hitler."[147] However, the chairman of the investigatory and mediation committee himself became increasingly concerned about the Führer's unreliability as well as his contemptuous treatment of his fellow party officials. In October 1928, he drafted a letter raising an issue that had been "weighing on my soul" for many weeks, namely that "you, Herr Hitler, are gradually developing a contempt for people that fills me with frightful concern."[148]

Hitler could belittle loyal followers in the most hurtful fashion. The Gauleiter of Lower Bavaria, Otto Erbersdobler, witnessed one typical scene in March 1929. Hitler had ordered local SA men to drive in trucks to a Nazi event in Upper Bavaria, but in order to save money, Pfeffer von Salomon had them take the train. The following day, at the party's Munich headquarters, Hitler gave Salomon "a real going-over . . . screaming at him for a good ten minutes and punctuating his already unequivocal remarks by lashing the table with his riding crop." Hitler forbade anyone in future from "deviating from his original orders even in the slightest." The party chairman concluded his sermon with the words: "Do we understand one another, party comrade von Pfeffer [sic]?" Salomon maintained his bearing, and Hitler shook his hand in the end.[149]

Hitler's behaviour towards his subordinates was governed by how useful he thought them to be.[150] "I never heard any praise or positive off-the-cuff remarks about party comrades," recalled Albert Krebs, who was the leader of the party's Hamburg chapter from 1926 to 1928 and briefly the city's Gauleiter. With the "sharp sense of scent of an animal," Hitler was able to distinguish between people "who invested him with boundless trust and quasi-religious faith" and those "who saw and judged him with critical distance and according to rational criteria." Hitler did not much care for the latter category, although he only showed it to those concerned when he felt they could no longer be of any use to him.[151]

Creating dissatisfaction was Hitler's habit at public events by immediately withdrawing and ignoring local party members after bathing in mass adulation. Hitler kept his distance, ever concerned with maintaining his aura of inapproachability. In the spring of 1928, when Krebs gave him a tour of the newly refurbished headquarters of the Hamburg

NSDAP, Hitler barely acknowledged the party comrades working there, although they were buoyant and clearly eager to get close to their hero. Hitler allowed Krebs to introduce them only with "visible reluctance" and later made a "number of sarcastic remarks" that Hamburg was to blame for his "inability to fulfil his hopes more quickly."[152]

The NSDAP's prospects palpably improved in the spring of 1929, however, and the critical voices faded. In the winter of 1928–9, the German economy went again into decline. In February, the number of people registered as unemployed once more broke the three-million mark.[153] Prices for agricultural produce were falling, meaning that many farmers could no longer keep up with their interest payments. Many went bankrupt, and their property was auctioned off. In the northern German state of Schleswig-Holstein, a rural movement formed in opposition to the central government. Farmers took to the streets for demonstrations under black flags. A radical group led by a farmer named Claus Heim even carried out bomb attacks against local tax and government offices.[154] The relatively stable period of the Weimar Republic was over.

Hitler felt his prognoses were being confirmed. "Everything is happening exactly as we predicted," he crowed in late March 1929. "The German economy is on its deathbed."[155] Once again, the NSDAP was the party to profit most from the incipient crisis. Between October 1928 and October 1929, the number of party members increased from around 100,000 to 150,000.[156] The Nazis also achieved spectacular results in the elections to Germany's student parliaments in 1928 and 1929.[157] In November 1928, Hitler spoke to an audience of 2,500 Munich University students in the Löwenbräukeller and was greeted with rapturous applause.[158]

The popularity of the NSDAP also grew by leaps and bounds among the rural population. "Happily, progress is being made everywhere," Hess reported in October 1928 about a tour by Hitler of northern Germany. "The best . . . was the farmers of Dithmarschen to whom the Tribune spoke in Heide in Schleswig-Holstein: fine specimens of men, giant in stature, gnarled . . . They sat there like blocks of ice for the first hour, but gradually they were drawn in, and the applause at the end was so furious it shocked all those who thought they knew this taciturn coast-dwelling folk."[159] In the district of Dithmarschen support for the NSDAP grew after the so-called "Blood Night" in the small village of Wöhrden on 7 March 1929. Here a brawl broke out between SA men and adherents of the KPD, which left two SA men dead and a number of people injured. That provided the NSDAP with an excuse to stage a political rally, and Hitler attended the funeral for the deceased. A police observer noted that Hitler's appearance "made a huge impression on the populace." Afterwards farmers' wives wore swastikas on their aprons, and some villagers began greeting one another with "Heil." Many farmers were "extraordinarily bitter and prepared to commit all sorts of violent acts," the police observer noted, adding that some saw the National Socialists as their "rescuers."[160]

The NSDAP registered significant increases in votes in the local state and district elections in the spring and summer of 1929. In elections in Saxony on 12 May, for instance, their share of the vote rose from 1.6 to 5 per cent. It was, Goebbels wrote, "a triumph that exceeded all our expectations."[161] The following month, in the northern German state of Mecklenburg-Schwerin, Hitler's party polled twice as well as it had in the previous election, drawing 4.1 per cent of the vote. And in the elections for the city council in Coburg in southern Germany in late June, the NSDAP achieved the first district majority in its history.[162]

At its rally in Nuremberg in early August 1929, the party abundantly displayed their new self-confidence. Its political leadership touted the event as "not just the largest rally of the movement, but the largest rally of politically active, nationalist Germany itself."[163] Somewhere between 40,000 (so the police estimated) and 100,000 Nazi supporters arrived by train from all over Germany and transformed the Bavarian city once again into "a brown army camp." Hitler kept a "Nuremberg diary" for the *Illustrierter Beobachter*, a party newspaper that had been founded in 1926, in which he described the concluding event on Nuremberg's central market square: "Showered again and again with flowers, the brown warriors of the Third Reich march by with quick steps for three and a half hours."[164] Hitler neglected to mention that SA troops had committed numerous acts of violence. The ancient capital of the Holy Roman Empire of the German Nation was forced to endure a four-day state of emergency.[165]

The places of honour in the grandstand were occupied by Hitler's admirers Winifred Wagner and Emil Kirdorf as well as the vice-chairman of the paramilitary veterans' organisation, the Stahlhelm, Theodor Duesterberg, and one of the sons of former German emperor

Wilhelm II, Prince August Wilhelm, who would apply to join the NSDAP in December.[166] Goebbels was none too pleased: "I'm getting to know Prince August Wilhelm. Fairly senile. All these Stahlhelm reactionaries who are propped up on the grandstand are not at all what I'd like to see."[167] Hitler, however, had decided to make common cause with conservative nationalists to shoot down the Young Plan. It stipulated that France evacuate the Rhineland in 1930 and, in contrast to the heavy monetary burdens under the Dawes Plan, brought Germany financial relief but expanded the duration of German reparations payments for the First World War to 1988. For the entire German right wing, agreeing to it was tantamount to accepting the Treaty of Versailles with its "war guilt" clause.[168]

The hostility towards the plan was led by the media mogul Alfred Hugenberg, who had been elected chairman of the DNVP in October 1928 and was steering the party on a course of uncompromising opposition to what he called "the Weimar system." Hugenberg's empire included the Scherl publishing house in Berlin, the news agency Telegraphen-Union, the advertising company Allgemeine Anzeigen and the film studio Universum Film AG (Ufa). Hugenberg also provided provincial newspapers with syndicated articles and thus had enormous influence even over periodicals that he did not own. On his initiative, a "Reich Committee for the German Referendum" was formed. Its members included the leaders of the DNVP, the Stahlhelm, the Pan-Germanic League, the Reichslandbund and the Vaterland Leagues. Hitler also signed on, after it was agreed that the campaign would be directed not just against the Young Plan but the "lie" of Germany's culpability for the First World War.[169] But Hitler's decision to participate did not meet with the universal approval of his underlings. "Some of the signatories of this call [for a referendum]!" Goebbels carped to his diary. "Dear God! With regard to Hitler I can only say: 'I'm sorry to see you in company like this!'"[170] Ultimately Hitler succeeded in reassuring the Berlin Gauleiter that he had no intention of being manipulated by conservative nationalists. On the contrary, he was using the referendum to advance his own aims. The National Socialists, Hitler promised, "would force their way to the forefront and unmask the DNVP."[171]

The referendum, which aimed to institute a Law against the Enslavement of the German People, was a failure. While its backers did succeed, just barely, in getting enough signatures to force a vote, only 13.8 per cent of the electorate turned out for the plebiscite on 22 December 1929—far below the 50 per cent participation needed to pass the referendum. Nonetheless, the NSDAP's involvement in the initiative paid dividends. Hitler was now an accepted figure in traditional conservative and nationalist circles, and with the help of Hugenberg's press empire, he had been in the public eye for months. At the conclusion of the campaign, Hitler and Hugenberg made a joint appearance in the packed Zirkus Krone, at which it was clear that the press mogul was no match for the Nazi chairman as a public speaker.[172] The NSDAP in general looked like a dynamic young movement, far superior to its conservative allies in terms of organisation and will-power. The Landtag elections in the autumn of 1929 also suggested that Hitler's party benefited from their opposition to the Young Plan. On 27 October in Baden, the NSDAP polled 7 per cent, and in Thuringia on 8 December, it took 11.3 per cent of the vote. The party also did well in district elections that November.[173]

On the morning of 3 October 1929, Reich Foreign Minister Gustav Stresemann died after suffering two strokes. One of the most important advocates of Weimar democracy was gone. "It is an irreparable loss whose consequences cannot be foreseen," wrote Count Harry Kessler, who was in Paris at the time. "Everyone here is talking about it—the hairdressers, the waiters, the chauffeurs and the newspaper sellers ... All of Paris is treating his death almost like a national tragedy." A similar mood prevailed among the pro-democracy camp in Germany. In Berlin 200,000 people turned out to accompany Stresemann to his final resting place on 6 October. "It was a popular funeral, not a state function," Kessler wrote.[174]

Three weeks later, on 24 October 1929, Black Friday plunged the global economy into turmoil. The crisis Hitler had waited for was now at hand. It was no coincidence that at precisely that moment Hitler exchanged his humble lodgings in Thierschstrasse for a nine-room apartment on the second floor of Prinzregentenstrasse 16 in the upper-class district of Bogenhausen.[175] The breakthrough to power seemed to be in reach, and Hitler needed a new domicile that would reflect his new status within German politics.

9

Dark Star Rising

"In the past I have been a prophet in many things . . . at least concerning the big picture," Hitler declared in a private missive in early February 1930. Previously, he had refused to set a timetable for Nazi success. Now he claimed he could predict with "near oracular certainty" that "Germany will have overcome the lowest point of its humiliation in two and a half to three years." He went on: "I believe that our triumph will come about in this period. With that our phase of decay will be over, and the resurgence of our people will begin."[1] In the spring of 1930 such predictions looked like the fantasies of a provincial politician convinced that he was on a divine mission. But only a few months later, after the Reichstag election of 14 September, the NSDAP could celebrate a sudden, massive upsurge in support. The Führer, previously a curiosity on the outer fringe of the political right wing, found himself catapulted into the centre of German politics. All at once what had been vague promises to his followers seemed on the verge of becoming reality. Hitler's party was very close to assuming power.

This development was hardly a total surprise. The Landtag and district elections in 1929 had shown that the NSDAP was on the rise, as the party noticeably increased its share of the vote wherever it chose to stand. Moreover, the campaign against the Young Plan had allowed it to position itself as *the* protest party on the far right. But the Nazis' definitive breakthrough towards becoming a mass party only happened with the onset of the Great Depression. The economic crisis hit Germany particularly hard.[2] The upturn during the Golden Twenties had been financed with short-term foreign credit, particularly from the United States, and after Black Friday, American banks had to call in their loans. That hastened the collapse of the German economy, which had already begun to decline in 1928 and 1929. The number of unemployed leapt from 1.3 million in September 1929 to 3.4 million in February 1930. One year later 5 million people were out of work, and at the height of the crisis in 1932, Germany had 6 million jobless. In fact, the number of people who were out of work was far higher, since the official statistics did not include those who, for whatever reasons, did not register at unemployment offices. In the words of the historian Hans-Ulrich Wehler, the Weimar Republic was "cast down into the abyss of an unprecedented economic depression."[3]

The psychological consequences were overwhelming. The trying experiences of the post-war period of turmoil and hyperinflation had left many Germans without the emotional strength to deal with an economic crisis that exceeded everything that had come before. An apocalyptic mood of hopelessness began to take hold, even among those segments of the populace that were not primarily affected by the Depression. Faith in democratic institutions and democratic political parties dissolved, and anti-parliamentary sentiment, already rife in the Weimar Republic, was given a huge boost. Those in power appeared to have no solutions to the crisis, and the more helpless they seemed to be, the greater the demand became for a "strong man," a political messiah who would lead Germany out of economic misery and point the way towards renewed national greatness. More than any other German politician, Hitler presented himself as the answer to these hopes for salvation.[4] The hour was at hand for the man who already enjoyed the quasi-religious worship of his supporters and who had long identified with the role of the charismatic Führer.

By early 1930, it was clear that the Weimar Republic was built on sand. On 27 March, the grand coalition of Social Democratic Chancellor Hermann Müller collapsed after the SPD and the DVP became embroiled in a petty quarrel about whether to raise unemployment insurance contributions from 3.5 to 4 per cent. Underlying the squabbling was a fundamental disagreement about who should bear the brunt of the costs of combating the economic crisis. After Stresemann's death, under the leadership of its new chairman, Ernst Scholz, the big-business-friendly DVP had become more conservative, and influential forces within the party, supported by the Reich Association of German Industry (RDI), were calling for it to end its cooperation with the Social Democrats.[5] Conversely, the SPD felt that it could no longer demand any further political compromises of its constituency. The supply of common ground, as Müller put it when he announced the end of the grand coalition, was exhausted. The liberal *Frankfurter Zeitung* newspaper called 27 March 1930 a "black day," and indeed the date marked a watershed in the history of the Weimar Republic. Henceforth, no government would enjoy a parliamentary majority. The dissolution of German democracy was under way.[6]

Reich President Paul von Hindenburg and his closest advisers were by no means dismayed that government and parliament were shooting themselves in the foot. Hindenburg had long been pondering how to remove the SPD from power and subordinate Germany's political parties to an authoritarian rule by the presidency.[7] That was the brief handed to Heinrich Brüning, the chairman of the Centre Party, who was appointed Germany's new chancellor. He governed without a parliamentary majority in the interest of Hindenburg and his camarilla, relying on the president's support and on Article 48 of the Reich constitution, which accorded the president extensive powers in states of emergency. As a result Brüning was able to form a cabinet of "experts" that excluded the SPD. This was equivalent to a tacit abrogation of the constitution. From the very beginning of his tenure, Brüning made no secret of the fact that he was willing to dissolve the Reichstag and rule by emergency decree if parliament refused to follow his lead.[8]

The NSDAP played no part in their plans as Hindenburg and Brüning installed this presidential regime. The Nazi faction in parliament was too small to merit attention. Nonetheless, the government's turn away from parliamentarianism and the undermining of democracy played into Hitler's hands. When the Brüning cabinet was formed on 30 March 1930, Goebbels noted: "Perhaps this cabinet will be immediately brought down. Then the Reichstag will be dissolved. Bravo! These are marvellous times!"[9] The NSDAP could count on increasing its share of the vote if fresh elections were called. Thus the party actively worked towards a dissolution of parliament, for instance by supporting a vote of no confidence brought against Brüning on 4 April. The new chancellor survived that motion, however, after the DNVP withheld support. "The DNVP as a whole caved in . . ." Goebbels noted. "The boss is furious."[10] That very day, Hitler announced he was quitting the committee advocating the popular referendum against the Young Plan.[11] On 12 April, when the budget came up for a decisive vote, the DNVP again sided with the government, sparing Brüning's cabinet an early parliamentary defeat.

Right from the start, Hitler was set on unscrupulously exploiting the political and economic crisis, and the way that the state government of Thuringia was formed in early 1930 amply illustrated Hitler's strategy. In Landtag elections in December 1929, the NSDAP had polled 11.3 per cent in Thuringia, giving them six parliamentary seats. If the conservative and liberal parties wanted to govern without the SPD, they needed the support of the National Socialists. Hitler decided that the party would join a governing coalition, but only if it were given two key ministries, those of the interior and of culture and popular education. "He who possesses these two ministries and uses his power within them unscrupulously and with determination can achieve the extraordinary," Hitler wrote in a confidential missive on 2 February. The Interior Ministry gave the NSDAP oversight of the state police force; the Culture Ministry put the party in charge of the entire Thuringian school and educational system. Hitler was not interested in participating in government per se: he was aiming to take over the executive branch from the inside. As his candidate for both ministerial posts, Hitler put forward Wilhelm Frick, his comrade from the Beer Hall Putsch. The DVP initially rejected the appointment. "So I travelled to Weimar and informed these gentlemen, succinctly and in no uncertain terms, that either Dr. Frick would be our minister or there would be fresh elections," Hitler related. The potential coalition was set a deadline of three days to accept Frick. New elections were anathema to the centre-right parties since they would certainly have strengthened the NSDAP's position. Thus the DVP gave in to Hitler's ultimatum, and on 23 January 1930, Wilhelm Frick was named Thuringia's new interior and education minister.[12]

During his fourteen-month term in office, Wilhelm Frick gave Thuringians a preview of what would be visited upon Germany as a whole when the Nazis came to national power on 30 January 1933. Veteran, highly skilled civil servants suspected of sympathising with the SPD were fired and replaced with Nazi stooges. Prayers were made mandatory in schools in order, as Frick told the Landtag, to "prevent the people being swindled by Marxism and the Jews." The University of Jena was given a chair in racial sciences, which was filled by the notorious anti-Semite Hans F.K. Günther. The new director of the Weimar

Academy of Art and Architecture, the National Socialist true believer Paul Schultze-Naumburg, removed modernist works of art from the city's Royal Museum. There was little resistance to such iconoclasm. The former home of Goethe and Schiller had become a Nazi strong-hold: in the 1929 elections, the Nazis had polled 23.8 per cent of the vote in the city of Weimar.[13]

It took quite some time before the Thuringian DVP realised what sort of partners it had taken on board. Eventually, on 1 April 1931, the party supported a vote of no confidence brought by the SPD, which led to Frick's downfall. But in September 1932, the NSDAP would return to power on the back of an election in which the party took 42 per cent of the vote. Frick, for his part, earned Hitler's gratitude for putting Thuringia "at the centre of the national, political and economic renovation of Germany" and was made Reich interior minister when Hitler became chancellor the following year.[14]

By the spring of 1930, it was also clear that the NSDAP would do well in the Landtag election in Saxony the following June. Unfortunately for Hitler, the long-simmering conflict between Goebbels and the Strasser brothers was about to break out in public. On the surface, the rivalry revolved around who would be responsible for Nazi publicity in Berlin and be given commensurate authority. With their Kampf Verlag publishing house, the Strassers directly competed with Goebbels's periodical *Der Angriff*. But the competition was also about ideological issues. Unlike Goebbels and his brother Gregor, Otto Strasser had never backed away from the "socialist" line of the Working Association North-west. Since Gregor was busy as Reich organisational director, Otto was primarily responsible for Kampf Verlag's publica-tions, which promoted a mélange of nationalist and anti-capitalist ideas with a pronounced anti-Western and pro-Soviet slant.[15]

The power struggle between Goebbels and Otto Strasser escalated in late January 1930, when Kampf Verlag announced it would begin publishing a daily newspaper in Berlin in March. "This is a true stab in the back," Goebbels fumed, lobbying Hitler to block the new peri-odical and to make *Der Angriff* into a daily paper.[16] Hitler promised to rein in Otto Strasser but did nothing, and when the first issue of *Der Nationale Sozialist* appeared on schedule on 1 March, Goebbels's patience was at an end. He threatened to resign from the party and confided to his diary: "Hitler . . . has broken his word to me five times.

That's a bitter realisation and I'm drawing my conclusions from it. Hitler has gone into hiding. He's not making any decisions. He's not leading. He's just going with the flow."[17] Goebbels's annoyance about Hitler's lack of intervention was increased by his disappointment that the party chairman declined to attend Horst Wessel's funeral on 1 March. The former university student and SA Sturmführer had been shot by a Communist in late January and died of his wounds on 23 February. Goebbels had decided to mould him into "a new martyr for the Third Reich" and make him the focus of ritual celebrations. "Die Fahne hoch"—"Hold High the Flag"—the song which Wessel had written, became the official party anthem and was played after the German national anthem at official state functions as of 1933.[18]

The fact that Hitler shied away from getting involved in the Goebbels–Strasser conflict had less to do with indecisiveness than his desire to avoid making public the fact that the party was internally divided on the verge of its political breakthrough. But in late April, at an internal NSDAP leadership conference in Munich, Hitler dropped his guard. "A complete excoriation of Strasser, Kampf Verlag and the salon Bolshevists," a relieved Goebbels crowed. "Hitler is leading once again. Thank God. Everyone enthusiastically behind him. Strasser and his crowd have been smashed."[19] At the end of the conference, Hitler named Goebbels Reich propaganda director. For the latter that was the icing on the cake: he now took over the office that Gregor Strasser had given up, in Hitler's favour, in 1927.

Hitler, however, was not ready to break once and for all with Otto Strasser and his supporters. In late May he made one last attempt at an amicable reconciliation, summoning the dissident to his Berlin residence, the Hotel Sanssouci on Linkstrasse. For two days Hitler employed all of his rhetorical talents in an attempt to win over Strasser, but the latter proved surprisingly unimpressed by the characteristically long-winded mix of enticements and threats. Strasser categorically refused to consider Hitler's offer of naming him Reich press secretary if he would sell Kampf Verlag to Max Amann. The core of the two men's disagreement, however, was their varying interpretation of what was meant by the term "socialism" in the party programme. Strasser accused Hitler of "choking off revolutionary socialism in the interest of keeping the party legal and . . . cooperating with the mainstream right-wing parties (Hugenberg, Stahlhelm, etc.)." An agitated

Hitler responded: "I am a socialist . . . But what you mean by socialism is nothing but crass Marxism. The masses of workers only want *panem et circenses*. They have no comprehension of any sort of ideals." Hitler also reaffirmed his axiomatic belief that race and not class warfare was the motor of history. "There can only be one revolution, the revolution of race," he proclaimed. "There is no economic, political or social revolution. The fundamental struggle is always the same: the struggle of a racially inferior lower class against a dominant high race. The day the higher race forgets this iron law, it has lost the battle."

Strasser wanted certainty, so he posed the cardinal question of what Hitler intended to do after coming to power. Would he, for instance, preserve the assets of large privately owned companies like Krupp? "Of course!" Hitler replied. "Do you think I'm crazy enough to destroy German heavy industry?" Strasser shot back: "If you want to retain the capitalist regime . . . you have no right to talk about socialism."[20] With that, all bridges were burned. After their discussion, Hitler described Strasser as "an intellectual white Jew" and "the purest sort of Marxist."[21] He waited to take action until after the Saxony election on 22 June, in which the NSDAP almost tripled their share of the vote to 14.4 per cent and emerged as the second-strongest party behind the SPD (33.4 per cent) and ahead of the KPD (13.6 per cent).[22] Eight days later, Hitler ordered Goebbels in an open letter to purge the Berlin party chapter of all "salon Bolshevists," telling him to "act ruthlessly and severely."[23] Goebbels read Hitler's message out loud at a general party meeting in Berlin on 30 June, where it was greeted with cries of "String them up!" With satisfaction, Goebbels noted in his diary: "The whole thing ended with an oath of loyalty to the movement, to Hitler and to me!"[24]

Otto Strasser and his followers avoided being expelled from the party by voluntarily resigning their membership. "The socialists are leaving the NSDAP," read the headline in Strasser's mouthpiece, *Der Nationale Sozialist*. But he had overestimated his status within the party. Few NSDAP supporters followed his call. Strasser founded the Fighting Society of Revolutionary National Socialists, later known as the Black Front, but these organisations never attracted more than a few thousand members. Gregor Strasser had already broken with his brother. Otto's tendency to act on his own, Gregor claimed, had "fully destroyed their relationship."[25] In any case, the crisis within the party was resolved without attracting much notice in the wider public.

Hitler's rise in the spring and summer of 1930 was significantly aided by mistakes made by the Brüning government. Immediately after taking office, the new chancellor sought to combat the effects of the Depression with a rigid austerity programme. State expenditures were slashed, taxes and levies increased, and civil servants and salaried employees were forced to make emergency financial contributions. What followed was inevitable. On 16 July, the Reichstag refused to approve the government's draft proposal for covering its obligations. Brüning declared that he was unwilling to engage in any more negotiations with parliament and pushed through the proposal by emergency presidential decree. The SPD faction then sponsored a successful motion to lift the state of emergency, whereupon Brüning announced that he was dissolving the Reichstag. It was a short-sighted decision. After the election results in Saxony, it was clear to all political observers that the NSDAP would emerge as the big winner from fresh elections, which were called for 14 September 1930.[26]

"Hurrah" was how Goebbels greeted the dissolution of parliament. The propaganda director immediately started organising the Nazi campaign—it was his chance to demonstrate his abilities in the new post. Germany had never quite seen a campaign like it. "In the run-up to 14 September, there must not be a single city, village or hamlet where we National Socialists have not staged a large-scale gathering," Goebbels demanded in an "extraordinary memo" on 23 July. The party's central election goal was to soften up the "Marxist November state" to the point where it could be taken over. Some 1,500 NSDAP representatives gave speeches, and in the last four weeks of campaigning alone, the party held 34,000 events.[27] Hitler was the main attraction. People turned out en masse wherever he made an appearance. Four days before the election, 16,000 people came to hear him speak in Berlin's Sportpalast auditorium—Goebbels claimed that 100,000 Berliners had tried to get tickets. When Hitler arrived at the venue, the propaganda director noted, he was greeted with a "tempest of jubilation" similar to a "hurricane."[28]

Hitler's campaign speeches followed the same pattern. He began with a polemic against the Weimar "system" which he blamed for Germany's decline and decay, comparing Western parliamentarianism to a "worn-out tailcoat." Democracy, Hitler claimed, was fundamentally unable to solve Germany's problems because it privileged the rule of the majority over "the authority of personality." Hitler then went after the other political parties, which, he claimed, represented only special interests and never the people as a whole. "Twelve years of unlimited rule by the old parliamentary parties have turned Germany into an object for exploitation and made it the laughing stock of the entire world," Hitler thundered. The NSDAP, he told his audience, represented a "new popular German movement" that overcame class conflicts and the selfish interests of specific social castes: "There is only one movement that recognises the German people as a whole, rather than individual groups, and that movement is ours." In this respect, the NSDAP was a model for what Hitler had in store for all of Germany: the creation of a *Volksgemeinschaft*, a racially defined ethnic-popular community. This Hitler defined as a form of social "organisation that no longer knows proletarians, bourgeois, farmers, artisans, etc. but rather is constituted by people from all parts of Germany and all groups of [its] population." The idea of the *Volksgemeinschaft* seems to have particularly fascinated Hitler's audience. He could count on storms of applause every time he invoked it. The concept was inseparably linked with the promise of national revival, similar to that of the Prussian "uprising" against Napoleon in 1813. "What we're promising is not an improvement in material conditions for an individual class of people, but rather the multiplication of the strength of the nation since only this will put us on the path to power and to the liberation of the entire people," Hitler told his listeners in the Sportpalast. He often ended his speeches by appealing to his audience's religious need for salvation with a vision of "a powerful German empire of honour and liberty, strength and power and majesty" instead of "the current state of decline."[29]

Some historians have advanced the thesis that Hitler consciously played down the Jewish question in the 1930 election to avoid putting off potential voters.[30] But that is far from the truth. When Hitler opened the campaign in Munich on 18 July, he complained that "the Jew in Germany can get away with anything . . . and is pretty much above the law." He promised that he would unmask "the lies of the Marxist party," which had been fashioned "with true Jewish dexterity." One week after his Munich speech, Hitler told a crowd in Nuremberg that Marxism was nothing but "a cover for the Jew" whose only aim was "to grab all the money he can for himself." Hitler then added that the time was already at hand when "the Jew" would be treated as he had been "hundreds of years ago." A police observer summarised the content of Hitler's speech in Würzburg on 5 August as follows: "He tried to depict the Jews as a race of foreign blood and described them as parasites on the body of the people." Five days after that in Kiel, Hitler accused Jews of trying to "completely emasculate" Germany. "But they're on the wrong track," he bellowed. "There is still blood in our people, the blood of millennia." A police report noted that this passage of Hitler's speech was met with applause and cries of "Out with the Jews in Germany." Hitler repeatedly referred to Jews as a contaminant that could have no place in the *Volksgemeinschaft* he envisioned. In early September in Augsburg, he declared: "The so-called Communist International only exists to promote the interests of a certain race that is not part of us and only aims at the destruction of everything national so that it can rule internationally."[31]

Hitler was convinced that Jews dominated both the press and the financial markets. Thus everyone in his audience knew who he was referring to when he spoke of "international finance spiders" that were growing fat on the misery of the nation, or when he asserted that "Today international high finance is Germany's lord and master." The fact that Hitler omitted the adjective "Jewish" from such statements may indicate that he was trying to moderate his tone without altering his basic message. In any case, the hundreds of thousands of people who drank in Hitler's words were well aware that Jews in Germany would be in for rough times if the Nazis came to power. Nor could there have been much confusion about Hitler's foreign-policy aims when he claimed that overcoming "a lack of [living] space" was "the perennial task of every healthy people." On 18 August, he told an audience in Cologne that "We have 20 million people too many, and our territory is limited"; three days later, in Koblenz, he emphasised, "We want the German people to fight for its living space."[32] The destruction of "Jewish Marxism" and the conquest of "living space" remained Hitler's two main aims, and he made no secret of either during the 1930 election campaign.

"On 14 September let's give a sound thrashing to all those who have an interest in deceiving the people," the NSDAP encouraged voters four days ahead of the poll.[33] Hitler repeatedly depicted the election as a day of reckoning that would become a turning point in German history. The leitmotif he chose for his speech in Nuremberg on 7 September was "The people are arising, the storm is breaking loose"—lines cribbed from a poem by Theodor Körner about Germany's "wars of national liberation" against Napoleon.[34] The signs were auspicious, and Hitler expected that the NSDAP would significantly improve its margin of the vote. The "ever-cautious Tribune," wrote Hess on the eve of the election, anticipated winning 60 to 70 seats.[35] In fact the result exceeded even the most wildly optimistic expectations. The NSDAP went from 2.6 to 18.3 per cent of the vote, earning 107 seats in parliament compared to their previous 12. There had never been such a landslide improvement for a party in a German election. "A great victory has been fought for and won," Hitler declared in the packed Zirkus Krone on 16 September. "The National Socialist movement can say that it has put its most difficult times behind it."[36]

While the SPD remained the strongest party with 24.5 per cent, its share of the vote had declined by 5.3 per cent from 1928, while the KPD had gone from 10.6 to 13.1 per cent. All in all, the left-wing parties basically trod water. The Catholic camp also remained stable, with the Centre Party and the BVP taking 11.8 and 3 per cent of the vote respectively, compared with 12.1 and 3.1 in 1928. The election's big losers were parties of the political centre and the mainstream conservatives. The DNVP only received 7 per cent of the vote, half of its total from the already disastrous 1928 election. The DVP declined from 8.7 to 4.5 per cent, while the DDP, which had changed its name to the German State Party (DSP) in July, went from 4.9 to 3.8 per cent.[37] The National Socialists were the main beneficiaries from these parties' electoral losses, taking increased numbers of votes in all parts of Germany where moderates and traditional conservatives declined. The NSDAP also profited from the high turnout since they received a greater percentage of ballots than the other parties from previous non-voters. The historian Jürgen Falter has shown that a third of all regular DNVP voters, a quarter of all DVP and DDP voters, a seventh of all non-voters and a tenth of all SPD voters cast their ballots with the NSDAP. The conservative and liberal middle classes were thus more susceptible to the Nazi lure than those coming from the Social Democratic milieu. The National Socialists also made their biggest gains in overwhelmingly Protestant northern and eastern Germany, while voters in Catholic areas proved more resistant.

In his contemporary analysis of the election results, the sociologist Theodor Geiger wrote of "a middle-class panic," but that was only half the story. The NSDAP may have attracted a high number of middle-class voters, but the party also appealed to workers—less to an industrial workforce than to agricultural labourers, artisans and those employed in medium-sized businesses. By contrast, unemployed industrial workers usually preferred the KPD under Ernst Thälmann to Hitler's party. On the whole, however, the NSDAP was more of a party for the entire German people than any of its competitors, collecting the social protest vote from all sections of society. During the campaign it had presented itself as a dynamic, young movement ready to inherit the future; and indeed, on average, Nazi Party members were much younger than the adherents of other parties, although young voters were not the decisive factor in the NSDAP's electoral success. Young SA men on the streets may have been an integral part of the National Socialists' image, but the party received ballots in equal measure from young and old alike.[38]

"Fantastic . . . ." Goebbels described the reaction in the Sportpalast on the evening of 14 September. "Celebration upon celebration. An entrancing mood of battle. The bourgeois parties of the middle have been crushed." The following day he wrote: "Joy for us and despair for our enemies. In one fell swoop, 107 seats, Hitler is beside himself with glee."[39] The supporters of Weimar democracy felt crushed by the election results. "A black day for Germany," Count Harry Kessler commented. "[The country] now faces a crisis of state that can only be overcome if all forces supporting or at least willing to tolerate the republic join together and strictly adhere to the common cause." Otherwise, Kessler wrote, there was the threat of "a civil war and, in the longer term, a new Great War."[40] In Dresden, the university lecturer Victor Klemperer had the same fears. "107 National Socialists," he wrote in his diary the morning after the election. "What a humiliation! How near we are to a civil war!"[41] The writer Thea Sternheim noted in Berlin: "A move to the right was to be expected, but not such a decisive one. Most people from a Jewish background are fully disoriented" and fear for the worst.[42] Bella Fromm, the society columnist writing for the liberal *Vossische Zeitung*, detected panic after the election. "Should we leave Germany and wait it out abroad?" she asked. Fromm, like many assimilated Jews, could not yet bring herself to think of emigrating but, as she recorded in her diary, "It's astonishing how many people now think that it might be clever to do this."[43]

The *Frankfurter Zeitung* wrote of an "election of embitterment," in which the majority of voters had articulated their dissatisfaction with "the methods of governing or rather non-governing, the indecisive parliamentary palaver of the past few years." The journalist also believed that economic hardship had pushed many desperate Germans into Hitler's waiting arms.[44] A "hazardous adventure" was how Carl von Ossietzky described the NSDAP's electoral triumph in *Die Weltbühne*: "This was a Waterloo not just for the bourgeois parties, but for the whole idea of government by the people ... Germany's bourgeoisie has opted for Hitler's fascism. It has chosen to be stripped of its rights and humiliated."[45] Another *Die Weltbühne* writer tried to explain Hitler's success as the result of a "deep depression" that had gripped "the apolitical segments of society" in particular: "The petty bourgeoisie followed in droves the pied piper of Munich and his Berlin disciple Goebbels."[46] Count Harry Kessler, on the other hand, saw the political breakthrough of National Socialism as "the fever outbreak suffered by the mortally ill German lower-middle classes." These were beyond salvation, Kessler thought, although they could "bring unspeakable misery upon Europe as they resisted their demise."[47] But interpretations of Nazism that viewed the phenomenon as a sociological by-product of the decline of this or that class ignored what was new about the movement: its diffuse character as a populist party enabled it to integrate heterogeneous interests and subordinate them to the charismatic figure of the Führer.

Nazi electoral success also occasioned worries abroad. The British ambassador to France, Ronald Hugh Campbell, wrote from Paris that the Nazi triumph was seen as an "unpleasant surprise" and a turning point that could have significant consequences for international relations.[48] French Foreign Minister Aristide Briand felt "personally hurt" and informed his German counterpart Julius Curtius that Paris would be forced to act with "the greatest possible reserve" in its future dealings with Germany.[49] In Britain, too, the election results were seen to make normal relations with Germany much more difficult. In his initial analysis on 18 September, the British ambassador in Berlin, Horace

Rumbold, attributed Nazi success to the widespread mood of protest against economic misery, which Hitler and his movement in their youthful élan had been able to harness and turn into votes. The Foreign Office feared that Hitler's radical agitation against the Treaty of Versailles would harden French attitudes towards Germany as well as lead Brüning to adopt a more uncompromising foreign policy. A Foreign Office memo read: "There will be . . . a stiffening of the German foreign policy for Brüning will surely try to exploit the Nazi bogey."[50]

The British press also emphasised that the election had been dominated by protest. The *Manchester Guardian* wrote that the NSDAP had been able to mobilise a million disgruntled non-voters, while *The Times* had an alternative explanation for Nazi success: "They have succeeded, momentarily at any rate, in winning a large section of Young Germany." Controversially, in the *Daily Mail* on 24 September, the newspaper magnate Viscount Rothermere praised the Nazi triumph as an important milestone in the rebirth of the German nation that would usher in a new epoch in British–German relations; the article was reprinted the following day in the *Völkischer Beobachter*. For Rothermere, the NSDAP represented a new generation of Germans who would extend a hand of reconciliation towards Britain. A strong Germany was in Britain's interest as a bulwark against Bolshevism, he argued. "Western civilisation" could only profit if a government inspired by "healthy principles" came to power in Berlin, as it had done eight years ago with Mussolini in Italy.[51] Such remarks were a harbinger of efforts made by some in the British Establishment to curry favour with Hitler's Germany after 1933.

The spectacular results of September opened up the prospect that Hitler could come to power legally. "The constitution only stipulates the means, not the end," the Führer declared on election night. "And no power in the world can force us from the path of legality."[52] Yet Hitler was unable to reap any immediate benefits of his election triumph. The shock at the NSDAP's unexpected success led the moderate parties to close ranks. In early October 1930, the SPD faction in the Reichstag decided to tolerate the Brüning government. The Social Democrats would no longer support any vote of no confidence or block the unpopular austerity measures Brüning had instituted via emergency fiat. It was a difficult decision since it opened the SPD up to attacks by their left-wing competitors, the KPD. But there was no alternative if the Social Democrats wanted to maintain their last bastion of power, the government of Prussia under State President Otto Braun, who led a coalition with the Centre Party and the DSP. The policy of tolerance made the SPD a "silent partner" in the Brüning government. But this had not been Hindenburg's original plan of tactic presidential governance and was the source of potential friction between the president and the chancellor.[53]

On 5 October 1930, in the course of coalition negotiations with the Reichstag parties, Heinrich Brüning met Hitler for the first time, accompanied by Wilhelm Frick and Gregor Strasser, in the apartment of the minister for the occupied territories, Gottfried Treviranus. The chancellor informed Hitler that the rigorous domestic austerity programme was an attempt to get the Allies to reduce and eventually cancel Germany's reparations payments, and he appealed to the "former front-line soldier" to support the project with constructive opposition, thereby holding out the "prospect of working together in the future." Hitler answered with a monologue that went on for an hour. "He began so shyly and hesitantly that Treviranus and I felt sorry for him and began to encourage him with brief interjections," Brüning later recalled. "After a quarter of an hour we realised that this was the wrong approach. His voice was getting louder and louder." Hitler slipped into his public-speaking mode. As Brüning remembered:

> Ever more frequently he used the word "annihilating," first directed against the SPD, then against the "reactionaries" and finally against France as our arch-enemy and Russia as the hotbed of Bolshevism. When he was part of the government, he said, he would insist that Germany put down all of these enemies with the help of England, Italy and America.

When Brüning asked Hitler how he intended to keep Germany solvent, given that the mere news of the NSDAP's electoral triumph had led to a flight of foreign capital from the country, Hitler simply kept on talking. "One thought flashed through my mind: Mussolini," Brüning recalled. Although Brüning and Hitler parted amicably, it was clear that involving the NSDAP in the government was out of the question, although Brüning refused to categorically rule out a right-wing coalition in the future.[54]

"Late at night the boss and Frick return from Brüning," Goebbels confided to his diary. "We're staying in opposition. Thank God . . . Hitler seems to have made quite an impression with Br[üning]. He was very happy."[55] But in truth, Hitler had come away wounded from the meeting. The chancellor had made it clear that he did not take Hitler seriously as a politician, thus prodding Hitler's weak spot, his inferiority complex.[56] For the next year, Hitler avoided any further encounter with Brüning, and he set his party on a course of vehement opposition to the government cabinet.

Compensating for the affront was the attention Hitler now received as the rising star of German politics. Electoral triumph had catapulted the Führer into the centre of public interest. "You have no idea how the situation of the movement and H[itler] has literally changed overnight, since the night of the election," Hess told his parents. "We've suddenly become 'acceptable' in polite society. People who would previously have given H a wide berth now suddenly have to talk with him. The domestic and foreign press is beating down our doors."[57]

Several days after the election, Hitler offered Ernst Hanfstaengl the post of NSDAP foreign press officer. Because of Hanfstaengl's connections to the Anglo-Saxon world in particular, Hitler told him, he could "provide the party with a valuable service."[58] Hanfstaengl accepted the offer and began building up contacts to representatives of the foreign press. In the latter half of September and the first half of October, Hitler gave a series of interviews to the *Daily Mail*, *The Times* and papers belonging to William Randolph Hearst's U.S. news empire. In them, he sought to dissipate the fears that his party's electoral success had raised among Germany's former enemies. Hitler presented himself as a patriotic politician who knew the value of rational argument and whose only goal was to find a peaceful way of relieving Germany of the burdens placed upon it by the Treaty of Versailles and the Young Plan. The alternative to the necessity of revising these agreements, Hitler argued, was the Bolshevisation of Germany, which could not be in the interest of the Western powers. Much like Rothermere, Hitler claimed that his movement represented a "Young Germany" that wanted only to coexist peacefully with other nations. This younger generation, Hitler added, could not be held responsible for the First World War and therefore rejected any further "payment of tributes." *Daily Mail* correspondent Rothay Reynolds subsequently wrote of the NSDAP chairman's great modesty and seriousness, explaining to readers that Hitler's charisma came not from his eloquence or his ability to hold an audience, as was often proposed, but rather from the depth of his convictions.[59]

But not everyone was taken in by Hitler's act. In Germany, too, there were warning voices. To many people's surprise, on 17 October, Nobel Prize-winning author Thomas Mann issued an impassioned "Appeal to Reason" in Berlin's Beethoven-Saal auditorium. The call was combined with a complex analysis of the intellectual and social preconditions for National Socialism. The Hitler movement would never have reached such a level of "mass emotional conviction," Mann asserted, if it had not been preceded by "the sense of the beginning of a new epoch and . . . a new spiritual situation for humanity." People had turned away from the fundamental principles of a civil society— "liberty, equality, education, optimism and belief in progress"—and faith in reason to embrace "the forces of the unconscious, of unthinking dynamism and of pernicious creativity," which rejected everything intellectual. Fed by those tendencies and carried by a "gigantic wave of eccentric barbarism and primitive, populist fair-ground barking," National Socialism pursued "a politics of the grotesque . . . replete with Salvation Army allures, reflexive mass paroxysms, amusement-park chiming, cries of hallelujah and mantra-like repetition of monotonous slogans until everyone foamed at the mouth." Mann did not just excoriate the NSDAP. He also drew political conclusions. Only the Social Democrats, he said, seemed to be capable of stopping the forward march of the National Socialists. For that reason, he believed, the "political home" of respectable, middle-class German citizens had to be the SPD. Mann's speech was repeatedly interrupted by hostile interjections, orchestrated by Arnolt Bronnen, a former exponent of literary expressionism and friend of Bertolt Brecht who had converted to Nazism. "Our people spit on the head of Thomas Mann, who shamelessly insulted us in his lecture 'Appeal to Reason,'" noted Goebbels.[60]

Mann's speech largely fell on deaf ears. The majority of middle-class Germans treated the National Socialists along the lines described by the historian Friedrich Meinecke in December 1930: "People laugh at their economic demands, and the upper ten thousand dutifully berate their rowdyism on the street, as the conventions of polite society demand; yet these very circles continue, quietly yet unabatedly, to murmur about how useful National Socialism might become."[61] Sebastian Haffner, who came from the educated upper-middle class and was finely attuned to changes in attitude, spoke in 1939 about people's "fascination with the monster," that "strange haze and intoxication of should-be opponents who cannot come to terms with the phenomenon" and instead "turn themselves over, increasingly defencelessly, to the magic of the horrible and the thrill of evil."[62] The erosion of the political centre, reflected in the dramatic decline in support for the DDP/DSP and the DVP, was primarily the result of the radicalisation of voters from the middle classes, whose fears of dropping down the social ladder and anti-parliamentarian longings pushed them in droves into the hands of the National Socialists. The comprehensive criticism of the Weimar Republic by intellectual spokesmen of the anti-democratic "conservative revolution"—Oswald Spengler, Arthur Moeller van den Bruck, Ernst Jünger, Edgar Julius Jung and Carl Schmitt—had paved the way for a movement that wanted to do away with German democracy as soon as possible.[63]

Not all liberal and left-wing intellectuals were as prescient as Thomas Mann. Even an otherwise acute observer of his times like Theodor Wolff, the editor-in-chief of the *Berliner Tageblatt*, fooled himself about the character of the Nazi movement and its leader. On 14 September 1930, before the first election results were released, Wolff wrote an editorial warning people not to "overestimate the fairground party." Even if the NSDAP sent a few more deputies to parliament, they remained a "society of incompetents." Wolff added: "Most probably this will be the National Socialists' day in the sun, and their fall from grace will follow soon. The crown worn by the kings of the rabble-rousers will slip, and Herr Hitler will fade into the sunset."[64] Carl von Ossietzky, editor-in-chief of the influential cultural magazine *Die Weltbühne*, was even further off the mark. Shortly before the election, he had reassured his readers: "The National Socialist movement has a noisy present, but no future at all. The rather bizarre notion that Adolf Hitler had been called to save the nation is pure mysticism." And mysticism, Ossietzky predicted, could intoxicate people, but never satisfy them in the long run.[65] When the outcome of the election had proved him wrong, Ossietzky called for the Brüning government to be dismissed. "Brüning has made fascism something big," Ossietzky wrote. "It's better to have an openly right-wing government than a prolongation of Brüning's. This pointy-nosed man with a face like parchment, this caricature of piety with his Iron Cross First Class dangling from his rosary, must simply disappear."[66] Ossietzky was equally insulting towards Hitler, calling him a "half-insane rascal," a "pathetic dunderhead," a "nowhere fool" and a "big mouth."[67] But attempts to depict the NSDAP leader as ridiculous could not combat the phenomenon of Adolf Hitler. Nor did they undermine the tendency of his supporters to see him as the national saviour.

It was common in left-wing circles to think that, if the Nazis ever got a share of power, they would soon be undone by their own incompetence. A remarkable exception was the dramatist Ernst Toller, who had served five years in prison for participation in the Munich Soviet Republic. "Reich Chancellor Hitler is waiting just outside the gates of Berlin," Toller wrote in *Die Weltbühne* on 7 October 1930, warning against the dangerous illusion that the Nazis would bankrupt themselves if allowed to rule for a brief period. One should not underestimate Hitler's "will to power and determination to keep it," Toller cautioned. The dramatist was in no doubt that as chancellor Hitler would eradicate all democratic progress with a stroke of his pen: "Overnight, all republican civil servants, judges and police officers will be fired in favour of a reliable, fascist cadre . . . Hundreds of thousands of Hitlerites are waiting for jobs!" Toller also predicted that a Hitler regime would brutally terrorise socialists, communists, pacifists and the few surviving democrats, and that once he felt strong enough, the Nazi leader would even go after the trade unions. "For once there is truth to the phrase: it's one minute to midnight," Toller wrote.[68]

A few days after the election, Hitler was given the opportunity to spell out in public how he planned to come to power and what he would do after he did. On 23 September, a Reich court in Leipzig began hearing a case concerning three young Reichswehr officers from the southern German city of Ulm who had violated an order from the Defence Ministry by establishing contact with and promoting the NSDAP. On the third day of the trial, the National Socialist lawyer for the defence called Hitler as a witness. Many people had collected outside the court building, and a number of foreign reporters had also come to see the man who had suddenly become the great hope of millions of people. "The atmosphere positively crackled with excitement," Hanfstaengl observed, when Hitler appeared before the court and the judge began to question him.[69] The judge warned him not to give an "hour-long propaganda speech"—a reference to the 1924 trial at which the Munich judge had allowed Hitler to use the courtroom as a pulpit. After calmly beginning his testimony, however, Hitler began to get excited, earning himself a reprimand. "You're not here to make political speeches," the judge told him again. "Calm down and keep your statements objective."

When asked about the NSDAP's attitude towards state monopoly on legitimate force, Hitler answered that the Reichswehr was "the most important instrument in the restoration of the German state and the German people." Any attempt to corrode it, he added, was insanity. If his party came to power, he told the judge, he would ensure the military, which the Treaty of Versailles had restricted to 100,000 men, would once again become a "great German people's army." Hitler also reiterated his promise from countless campaign speeches that he would "under no circumstances use illegal means" to achieve his ends. Whenever, as in the case of Otto Strasser, one of his subordinates had violated his instructions, he had "immediately intervened." The NSDAP did not need to resort to violence, Hitler boasted, because after the next election, it would be Germany's strongest party. "In this constitutional way," Hitler said, "we will try to achieve decisive majorities in all legislative bodies so that, if we're successful, we can remould the state in a form that corresponds to our ideas . . . If our movement is victorious in its entirely legal battle, there will be a German national court, there will be retribution for November 1918, and heads will roll."[70]

Hitler could hardly have stated any more clearly that he was only prepared to renounce violence until he came to power. His adherence to the Weimar constitution was a tactical ploy to gain the NSDAP political room for manoeuvre and legal protection, which it used to undermine stability and ultimately to bring down German democracy. Goebbels belied the NSDAP's seeming support for law and order when he remarked to one of the officers on trial in Leipzig, Richard Scheringer, that Hitler's testimony had been a "clever move." "What do the authorities think they can do to us now?" Goebbels asked. "They were waiting to make their move. But now we're strictly legal. Legal no matter what."[71]

In the summer of 1930, at the request of the Prussian interior minister, Carl Severing of the SPD, the political division of the Berlin police put together a memorandum on the character of the Hitler movement. It considered a wealth of material, concluding that "the NSDAP was an organisation hostile to the state that strives to undermine the constitutionally enshrined republican form of state." Statements seemingly to the contrary by Hitler only served "to cloak [the movement] in legality so as to avoid problems with the authorities."[72] Nonetheless, in a cabinet meeting on 19 December 1930, the Reich ministers unanimously agreed that there was nothing they could do about the NSDAP. Heinrich Brüning himself warned against using "the same mistaken methods that were applied before the war against the Social Democrats."[73] The Prussian memorandum disappeared in a filing cabinet in the Reich Chancellery.

The military leadership, which had played a decisive role in the transition to rule by presidential decree in March 1930 and which was a key element in the new political constellation, began to revise its stance towards the NSDAP. Impressed by Hitler's vow in Leipzig to keep things legal, Reich Defence Minister Wilhelm Groener and his closest political adviser, General Kurt von Schleicher, argued that Hitler's party should no longer be considered a revolutionary movement bent on overthrowing the state but a serious political force that would have to be involved in Germany's future. The military hoped to co-opt the Nazis' enthusiasm for the armed forces for their own ends and recruit party members for the national defence. Military leaders also thought that involving the NSDAP would exert a moderating, domesticating influence on the movement.[74] For his part Hitler had not forgotten the lesson he had learned from the Beer Hall Putsch: that the path to power depended upon the support or at least the neutrality of the military. The way he presented himself in Leipzig was calculated to bring about a rapprochement with military leaders. In mid-January 1931, he met with the chief of the general staff, General Kurt von Hammerstein. The purpose of the meeting is clear from a short entry in Goebbels's diary: "We have to get the army on our side."[75]

But when the new Reichstag first met on 13 October 1930, it was immediately apparent how hollow Hitler's promise of legality was. Despite a prohibition on uniforms at parliamentary sessions in Prussia, the 107 NSDAP deputies appeared in their brown shirts and swastika armbands. Nazis also staged a provocative demonstration in Berlin's city centre. Horrified, Count Kessler wrote: "All afternoon and evening, there were large masses of Nazis who demonstrated and smashed the windows of the [Jewish-owned] department stores Wertheim, Grünfeld, etc., in Leipziger Strasse. In the evening on Potsdamer Platz, crowds chanted 'Germany awake,' 'Death to Judah' and 'Heil, heil.'" They had to be dispersed by police on horseback and in trucks.[76] The fact that this "attack on shop windows" was directed almost exclusively against Jewish businesses suggests that it was a coordinated act, not a spontaneous outburst of public sentiment.[77] In interviews with the foreign press, Hitler distanced himself from the unrest, calling it the work of "rowdies, shoplifters, plunderers and Communist provocateurs" and claiming that his movement had nothing to do with it.[78] Hitler's denials were transparent lies. In his response to a speech in the Reichstag by Gregor Strasser, the Bavarian SPD deputy Wilhelm Hoegner said the events of 13 October had belied the Nazis' promises to stay within the bounds of legality: "We do not believe that yesterday's wolves have transformed themselves overnight into pious lambs watched over by peaceful shepherds."[79]

Although as the second most powerful faction the NSDAP was represented in the Reichstag presidium and on all parliamentary committees, their attitude from the very beginning of the legislative period was one of obstructionism. The party's only aim was to bring the Reichstag to a standstill by subverting negotiations, filing frivolous motions and submitting nonsensical queries.[80] At the same time Goebbels pressed ahead with extra-parliamentary actions. In early December, he organised the disruption of the world premiere of the film *All Quiet on the Western Front*, based on Erich Maria Remarque's 1929 anti-war novel, in the Mozartsaal cinema on Berlin's Nollendorfplatz. "After 10 minutes, the cinema already resembled a madhouse," Goebbels noted in his diary. "The police were powerless, and the embittered crowd turned on the Jews . . . 'Jews out!' they cried. 'Hitler is at the gates.' The police sympathised with us . . . The screening was cancelled, as was a second one. We've won." On 12 December, after further protests against the film, authorities banned it from being shown. It was the first act of capitulation in the face of Nazi terror. "The National Socialist street is dictating behaviour to the government," Goebbels crowed.[81]

The Reichstag changed its procedural rules in an attempt to break the National Socialists' policy of obstruction, so on 10 February 1931 the NSDAP faction, along with forty-one delegates from the DNVP and four from the rural protest party, the Landvolk, began boycotting parliamentary sessions. NSDAP faction leader and Reichstag vice-president Franz Stöhr declared that his party would only rejoin the "Young [Plan] Parliament" if it saw a possibility "to flout a particularly pernicious measure by the majority Reichstag, which is hostile to the people."[82] On 26 March, the Reichstag went into recess; it would not reconvene until October.

By early 1931, the growing radicalism of political conflicts created conditions that were akin to a civil war.[83] In most cases, it was the SA who started the violence. Packs of SA men tried to create an atmosphere of intimidation and convince their political enemies of their omnipresence by marching through working-class districts or suddenly appearing en masse in smaller "red" towns. Such acts of provocation, which often precipitated brawls, were like invasions of hostile territory. As a rule, public action taken by the German communists and socialists were aimed at defending themselves against the SA's increasingly aggressive behaviour in working-class areas, which the police frequently refused to prevent and thus tacitly supported.[84] Hitler's oft-repeated contentions that the street fights were "without exception the work of Communists and Social Democratic activists" and that the SA was "mostly outnumbered and only defending itself" were a crass reversal of the facts.[85]

Nonetheless, SA violence was a double-edged sword for the party leadership. Rowdyism constantly threatened to get out of hand and give the lie to Hitler's assurances that the party was acting within the bounds of the law. In the midst of the 1930 campaign, this conflict had broken out openly, reflecting an unresolved yet fundamental structural problem running through the entire history of the SA. It was unclear whether the SA was an ancillary apparatus that only existed to help the NSDAP come to power, or whether it was, in parallel to the party, a "self-defence organisation" of equal status which would be given a key military role in the new "Third Reich." Dissatisfied by a chronic lack of funding and the fact that the organisation had not been consulted about the list of candidates for the Reichstag election, the Berlin chapter of the SA, under its commander, Walter Stennes, refused to provide security for party events. The conflict escalated to the point that in late August 1930, while Goebbels was away campaigning in Breslau, SA men stormed the Gau directorship's headquarters and caused significant damage.[86] Hitler hurried to Berlin to nip the rebellion in the bud. In a Nazi clubhouse in Chausseestrasse, he tried to regain the trust of some 2,000 SA men. The police report noted that his "hoarse voice became an almost hysterical scream." Hitler's speech ended with a melodramatic oath of solidarity: "We will use this hour to swear that nothing will drive us apart, if God grants us His assistance against all the devils! May Almighty God bless our struggle."[87]

"Stennes seems to want to keep calm," Goebbels noted on 3 September.[88] Yet although the revolt was over for the time being, the underlying conflict continued to percolate. Hitler had relieved the SA leader, Pfeffer von Salomon, of his duties and nominally taken over command himself. Otto Wagener, previously Pfeffer's chief of staff, was in charge of the day-to-day running of the organisation. Wagener had previously been the managing director of a small industrial company and had only joined the party at the Nuremberg rally in 1929. Then, at the end of November 1930, at a meeting of SA leaders in Munich, Hitler astonished everyone by announcing that Ernst Röhm, who had just returned from Bolivia, would be taking over as SA leader. Röhm, of course, had been rudely pushed aside in 1925 due to disagreements with Hitler about the role of the SA, so this was most likely a concession by Hitler to the still-dissatisfied SA leaders, most of them former military officers and Freikorps fighters, who saw Röhm as one of their own. In early January 1931, Röhm assumed the post of SA chief of staff.

Just as the NSDAP was achieving its great political breakthrough, the SA developed into a mass organisation. In January 1931, it had 77,000 members. One year later that figure had risen to 290,000, and by August 1932, the SA numbered 445,000 men. It recruited from diverse segments of society, although the percentage of working-class members was higher than in the Nazi Party as a whole. The SA particularly appealed to young unemployed men from middle-class backgrounds who worried about falling to the bottom of the social ladder. The organisation offered them not only a social safety net, for instance free food in SA soup kitchens or a place to stay in SA men's homes, but also a forum for releasing their aggression. The SA "storm

pubs," with their atmosphere of incipient violence, were like outposts
for a coming German civil war and greatly shaped the fearsome public
image of Hitler's brown-shirted battalions.[89]

The SA's thirst for action, however, threatened to scupper the
strategy of legality that the party leadership had chosen to pursue.
On 18 February 1931 Hitler had to deny in the *Völkischer Beobachter* the
rumour that the NSDAP was preparing "a coup d'état by means of
force." He also warned SA men be on guard against "spies and provocateurs" trying to tempt them into breaking the law: "Our legality will
smash and deflect all measures taken by those currently in possession
of state power."[90] Hitler's appeal was not universally popular. Goebbels
noted in his diary: "Great disgruntlement among the SA with Munich."[91]
At a meeting of the Munich SA brigade in early March 1931, Hitler
had to defend himself against the charge that he was "too cowardly"
to fight with illegal means. Hitler told those present that he did not
want to send them out to be cut down by machine guns, because he
needed them for more important tasks, namely constructing the Third
Reich.[92] Hitler had even more reason to fear that the SA, and perhaps
the party as a whole, could be banned when Hindenburg issued an
emergency decree on 28 March giving the Brüning government
additional powers to combat political extremism. The NSDAP chairman
saw himself forced to intervene again to end the simmering conflict
within the Berlin SA. On 30 March, he ordered all party members to
strictly observe the emergency decree. Anyone violating that command
would be immediately kicked out of the party. At a leadership conference in Weimar on 1 April, he announced that Stennes had been fired.
"This has been the greatest but perhaps final crisis of the party—we
have to get through it," Goebbels noted. The Berlin Gauleiter travelled
with a "broken-looking" Hitler on the night train back to Munich. "A
sad trip," he recorded. "I feel sorry for Hitler. He's thin and pale."[93]

Stennes and his supporters did not take his dismissal lying down.
That very day, 1 April, they occupied the Berlin Gau directorate and
the offices of *Der Angriff*; and the following day, they issued a statement condemning Hitler's "un-Germanic and uninhibited despotism
within the party and [his] irresponsible demagoguery."[94] But the
attempt to extend the rebellion beyond Berlin to north-western
Germany failed. In Munich Hitler and Goebbels immediately took
counter-measures. On 2 April, Hitler entrusted Goebbels as Berlin

Gauleiter with unlimited authority to "take the renewed cleansing of the party into his own hands and carry it out."[95] The 4 April edition of the *Völkischer Beobachter* contained a long article by Hitler, in which he justified the demotion and exclusion of Stennes from the party. For months, Hitler wrote, the "retired policeman . . . who had never really been a National Socialist . . . had tried to infuse the poison of disloyalty into the minds of courageous SA men" by depicting the party as "settled, timid and bourgeois." That conspiracy, Hitler claimed, had been uprooted: "I know that eight million unemployed will breathe more easily now that we have put a stop to the dirty work of those who would destroy Germany's final hope for the future."[96] Faced with the choice of following the "founder and Führer" Adolf Hitler or a "pack of mutineers," SA units all over Germany hastened to declare their loyalty to the party leadership. The revolt quickly collapsed. Only a few hundred men supported Stennes. By 16 April, at an event in the Sportpalast, Stennes's successor could present a Berlin SA that took orders only from Hitler. "Many wept," Goebbels recorded. "It was a great hour. The game is up for Stennes. The SA Berlin is solidly in the fold."[97] But the events of the spring of 1931 had long-term political consequences as they led to the rise of the SS, which at the time was still subordinate to the SA. During the crisis, the SS had proved absolutely loyal to the party leadership, and the resulting political capital left that group able to rival the SA.

After the September elections, people at the Nazi Party headquarters in Munich had to work through the night to process all the new membership applications. At the end of 1930, the NSDAP had 389,000 members; by the end of 1931, that number had risen to 806,294.[98] Space at Schellingstrasse 50 had long been insufficient to meet the demands of the organisation, and the building was not grand enough for a party that aspired to take over power. Hitler therefore decided to purchase the Palais Barlow on elegant Brienner Strasse. Built in 1828, it had been on the market since 1928; the contract of sale was finalised in late May 1930. The price for this prime piece of Munich property was more than 800,000 marks, some of which was raised by Hitler calling upon members to pay special one-off dues.[99] The building had to be significantly renovated, and Hitler hired the architect Paul Ludwig Troost, whom he had met in late September 1930 at the Bruckmanns' salon. Troost was primarily known as an interior designer who specialised in luxury ocean liners like the MS *Europa*. He had come to Hitler's attention in the late 1920s, and the NSDAP chairman had furnished his private apartment partly with Troost's designs. The architect was bowled over by the favour shown to him by the man who had become one of Germany's leading political lights. "Personally, Hitler is a capital fellow, very educated and modest—it's moving," Troost's wife Gerdy wrote to an acquaintance in November 1930. "So much feeling for and understanding of architecture. My Paulus says he's never met anyone like him."[100] Troost quickly became Hitler's preferred architect and received commissions for new party buildings on Arcisstrasse and the "House of Art," which was completed in 1937.

Hitler closely followed the construction work. Starting in the autumn of 1930, he had regular meetings with Troost, and every time Goebbels was in Munich, he took him to the building site. "A tour of the new party home," Goebbels noted in July 1930. "Pompous and grand. Hitler is in his element." Four months later Goebbels recorded: "The boss was at the site. He showed me the latest progress. My room was fabulous. The whole place is a jewel." At the same time, Goebbels was worried that Hitler's enthusiasm for architecture might lead him to neglect more pressing political tasks. On 26 February 1931, as the conflict with the Berlin SA was coming to a head, Goebbels noted: "All the boss's thoughts on the party home. At a time like this. I don't like that."[101]

The new party headquarters opened in March 1931. In the *Völkischer Beobachter*, Hitler looked back upon the party's humble origins and praised its new home as "the perfect marriage of functionality and beauty."[102] The former vestibule on the ground floor had become the "Hall of Banners" while the forecourt on the first floor was christened the "Hall of Standards." It led to an opulent room for gatherings known as the "Hall of Senators." In the basement there was a canteen. The card catalogue containing the names of party members was housed in an extension to the northern side of the Palais. The first two floors as well as the previously unused top floor were filled with offices. Bursting with pride, Hess wrote to his parents: "The showcase rooms, including the Führer's office, are so wonderfully beautiful that they could be used to receive any representatives of foreign states . . . My office is directly next to the Führer's, and next to his are the people who work for me, my office manager and two typists."[103]

Hitler's office was in a large room in the corner of the first floor. In addition to a bust of Mussolini and a portrait of Friedrich the Great, it contained a painting depicting an attack by the List Regiment in Flanders. But anyone who hoped that the clean lines of his office would inject discipline into Hitler's working habits was disappointed. Hitler quickly lapsed into his chaotic unpredictability, much to the dismay of those who worked with him. He loathed bureaucracy and did not think much of appointments. The Nazi lawyer Hans Frank remembered Hitler seldom being at the "Brown House," as the Nazi headquarters became known, and if his underlings brought important documents to their party leader, he might suddenly go to the telephone or have himself driven away, leaving his visitor in limbo. Sometimes Hitler would keep an appointment and quickly dispatch whatever bureaucratic business it concerned, only to subject his unfortunate interlocutor to an hour-long monologue about whatever topic he found particularly fascinating at the moment.[104] Hitler preferred to meet up with his old chums in his favourite café, Heck am Hofgarten. Goebbels was horrified by this "bunch of petty bourgeois." "How can a person like Hitler stand these people for even five minutes?" he repeatedly asked himself as he tried to protect his boss from the corrupting influence of others. "He has to get out of this Munich scene."[105] What Goebbels failed to recognise was that Hitler's Munich clique helped him wind down. With them he could relax and hold court away from the demands that his rise to a much-loved and much-hated political star had placed upon him.

The Palais Barlow had ample room for the expanding party apparatus. The existing departments of organisation and propaganda were joined by new ones like the economic department under Otto Wagener, the agrarian division under Richard Walter Darré, the legal department under Hans Frank and, in August 1931, the Reich press office run by the business journalist Otto Dietrich, the son-in-law of publisher Theodor Reismann-Grone.[106] But the Brown House was much more than an administrative headquarters. For the masses of true believers it was a "temple devoted to the cult of the Führer" and "a site of almost sacred significance."[107] For disgruntled SA men, on the other hand, the luxury villa was the headquarters of the Munich "bigwigs," and for the Nazis' political adversaries, it became an object of scorn since the building's splendour sharply contrasted with the lip service the party paid to socialism. With an eye towards Hitler's luxury apartment on Prinzregentenstrasse and the party headquarters, the Munich anarchist Erich Mühsam composed a poem:

> In Munich the Nazis
> Have two fine palazzis
> One serves as Hitler's home
> In the other he learns to rule alone
> For the Third Reich and its dons
> With swastikas made of bronze
> Granite and building blocks so brown
> Like prison towers over the town
> Loom the palaces all around.
> The Nazi star gleams shiny
> But what's the source of the money
> That's something kept underground.[108]

In fact, we do know where the NSDAP got the money to pay for the Palais Barlow: the industrialist Fritz Thyssen personally guaranteed a 300,000-mark bank loan for the party.[109] Thyssen, the eldest son of the legendary steel tycoon August Thyssen, was the supervisory board chairman and largest shareholder of the Vereinigte Stahlwerke, the biggest steelworks in Europe. He first heard Hitler speak shortly before the Beer Hall Putsch and then met Hitler and Ludendorff in Max Erwin von Scheubner-Richter's apartment. The NSDAP leader made a "very good impression," Thyssen testified in 1948. Initially, Thyssen supported the traditional nationalists and the policy of fundamental opposition which the DNVP began pursuing under Alfred Hugenberg from October 1928. In July 1929, he joined Hugenberg and Hitler in promoting the referendum on the Young Plan. After the September 1930 election, Thyssen advocated a right-wing coalition that included the National Socialists and started supporting the NSDAP financially. Most of his monetary favours went to Göring, Hitler's personal representative in Berlin whose task it was to establish useful contacts among the wealthy and well-born and make the party suitable for high society. Göring used two donations of at least 50,000 marks apiece for personal purposes, refurbishing his large Berlin apartment to reflect his growing status and financing his extravagant lifestyle. Nonetheless, Thyssen considered the donations money well spent, as Göring was a leader of the NSDAP's "moderate" wing in contrast to its anti-capitalist faction.[110]

Thyssen was not the only prominent economic figure who wanted to see the National Socialists claim a share of power. Another was Hjalmar Schacht, who resigned as Reichsbank president in March 1930 when he argued that the conditions of the Young Plan, which he himself had helped negotiate, were being altered to Germany's detriment.[111] Schacht had originally co-founded the left-liberal DDP, but by February 1930 there was no mistaking where his new political sympathies lay. At a social occasion at the home of a banker, Schacht's wife openly wore a necklace with a swastika pendant. When questioned about this by the society reporter of the *Vossische Zeitung*, Schacht replied: "Why not give the National Socialists a chance? They seem pretty gutsy to me."[112] After the September election, Schacht made his admiration of the NSDAP known publicly, saying that one "could not govern in the long term against the will of 20 per cent of the electorate."[113] In December, Schacht's old friend, Deutsche Bank chairman Emil Georg von Stauss, invited him to his villa in Berlin's exclusive Wannsee district to have dinner with Hermann Göring. Stauss was a deputy in what was left of the DVP faction in the Reichstag, and he had extended his feelers to test the possibility of collaborating with the NSDAP. The dinner seems to have gone swimmingly. Schacht recalled Göring as an "urbane and pleasant man of society," and on 5 January 1931, Schacht was invited to Göring's apartment. Thyssen, the NSDAP's new patron, was also in attendance.[114]

Goebbels, who was present as well, wrote: "Schacht strikes me as something of an *arriviste*, whereas Thyssen is one of the old guard. Excellent. He may be a capitalist, but it's hard to have anything against captains of industry like this."[115] After dinner, Hitler joined the group. "His manner was neither pretentious nor laboured; on the contrary, he acted naturally and modestly," Schacht recalled in his memoirs. "There was nothing to betray the fact that he was the leader of the second-strongest party in the Reichstag. After all the rumours we had heard and all the public criticisms we had read, we were pleasantly surprised by the whole atmosphere."[116] As was his wont, Hitler held a long monologue, during which the other guests barely got a word in edgeways. Schacht was nevertheless impressed. After that initial meeting, he already recognised "that Hitler's propagandistic force has excellent prospects among the German populace, as long as the economic crisis is not solved and the masses are not thereby diverted away from radicalism." Soon afterwards, Schacht claimed, he had encouraged Brüning to invite the National Socialists to join the governing coalition as a way of "directing the movement into orderly channels."[117]

Contact with Schacht was also very important for Hitler. Not only was Schacht held in high regard by industrialists and bankers, Hitler also valued his financial expertise, of which he himself possessed none. The former Reichsbank president was "no doubt the leading mind we have in Germany in the money sector and the financial economy," Hitler told Wagener.[118] Schacht would prove eminently useful when the NSDAP came to power.

"The economic sector is increasingly coming our way," Goebbels rejoiced, while Hess claimed that "extremely prominent representatives of business" were secretly asking for meetings with the party.[119] But in fact, the chummy behaviour of a Thyssen, Schacht or Stauss was not typical of Germany's economic elites. There is little justification for left-wing claims that the National Socialists owed their electoral triumph to financial support from big business or that Hitler was a lap dog of major industrialists.[120] The NSDAP financed their election campaigns largely from the party coffers—from membership dues, entry fees and small private donations. Thus the Nazi breakthrough to becoming a mass movement cannot be attributed to support from big business.[121] Nonetheless, with their often unbridled polemics against the Weimar system, trade unions and the social welfare state, large-scale business entrepreneurs contributed indirectly to the success of the radical right. It was no coincidence that industrialist circles welcomed the disempowerment of the German parliament and the establishment of rule by Brüning's cabinet supported by the president.[122]

After 14 September, the captains of industry could no longer ignore the National Socialists, but the majority still treated the radical right-wing party with caution. The business classes were justifiably skittish since no one was sure what economic course the party would pursue, and fears that the anti-capitalist strains within Nazi propaganda were not just rhetoric were bolstered by a number of parliamentary motions the NSDAP sponsored in October 1930. They included proposals to nationalise large banks, to ban the trading of securities and to restrict interest rates to 5 per cent. Business circles were particularly concerned that the NSDAP nominated Gottfried Feder as its spokesman in the debates about the 1931 budget. Feder's constant calls for Germany to "break the yoke of interest slavery" had earned him a reputation as an anti-capitalist eccentric.[123] At the end of 1930, the *Deutsche Allgemeine Zeitung* newspaper published an editorial that voiced the concerns of big business about the nebulous policies of the NSDAP. It predicted that the conflict between the anti-capitalist and more moderate wings of the party would become more intense and that the outcome was "fully uncertain."[124]

Hitler was at pains to dispel such fears, knowing that resistance from Germany's major business figures would make it more difficult for him to achieve his political goals. "You underestimate these men's political influence . . . and that of the economy in general," Hitler reprimanded Otto Wagener. "I have the feeling that we won't be able to conquer [the chancellor's office in] Wilhelmstrasse over their heads."[125] In September 1930, Hitler met the chairman of the Hamburg–America ocean line HAPAG, the former chancellor Wilhelm Cuno, to assure him that the NSDAP would support entrepreneurial initiative and private capital, and only intervene in cases of illicitly acquired wealth.[126] He made similar remarks the following month in Munich to Theodor Reismann-Grone. The publisher noted down his impressions of Hitler in his diary: "An Austrian officer type . . . I spoke first, but he quickly interrupted and dominated the conversation. The power of his words lies in his temperament, not in his intellect. He shakes things up. That's what the German people need. You can only beat speed with more speed. He described the destruction of Marxism as his life's goal."[127] In early December, Hitler spoke for a second time to Hamburg's National Club of 1919 in the Hotel Atlantik, but he avoided addressing any current issues, instead offering vague promises that once the "tributes" had been eradicated and Germany had regained its political power, the economy would flourish. "I have pledged myself to a new doctrine," he said at the end of his speech. "Everything that serves the best interest of my people is good and proper."[128] The well-heeled Hamburg audience, who once again showered Hitler with applause, remained pretty much in the dark as to where the NSDAP stood on economic questions and what it intended to do if it came to power.

Hitler refused to commit himself to an economic programme for the future because he wanted to keep his options regarding German industry open and because he did not want to alienate the "socialist" wing of his own party. In the spring of 1931, Hans Reupke—a lawyer working for the Confederation of German Industry who had secretly joined the NSDAP in May 1930—published a pamphlet entitled "National Socialism and the Economy" in which he assured his readership that the party had refined its anti-capitalist slogans into anti-materialist ones. Goebbels was outraged, writing: "This is a crass betrayal of socialism." He complained to Hitler and later noted with satisfaction: "Reupke dressed down by the boss."[129] But in truth what bothered the NSDAP chairman was less the content of Reupke's pamphlet than the idea of a fight being carried out in public. Wagener also bore the brunt of Hitler's vacillations. In 1932, the director of the NSDAP's economic-political division wanted to publish a collection of essays under the title "The Economic Programme of the NSDAP," but Hitler killed the idea of Eher Verlag bringing out the volume. The collection was internally circulated and stamped with the words "For official use only."[130]

The industrialists who did donate money to the NSDAP after 14 September regarded it as a kind of political insurance in case the party's rise continued and it gained a share of power. But as a rule, the donations were made not to the party as a whole, but to individuals thought to exercise "moderating" influence. Along with Göring, the prime recipient was Gregor Strasser, who was considered the second most powerful Nazi after Hitler. Also receiving money was the former business editor of the *Börsen-Zeitung* in Berlin, Walther Funk, who had given up that post to devote himself to improving relations between the NSDAP and captains of industry. Funk, who officially joined the party in June 1931, quickly advanced to become Hitler's most important economic adviser, putting himself in direct competition with Wagener.[131]

As far as we know, Hitler himself did not receive any donations from businessmen, nor did he solicit any. He had no need for them. Since 1930, royalties from *Mein Kampf* increased dramatically, and he seems to have paid taxes on only a fraction.[132] At public events, Hitler liked to brag that he did not receive a salary from the party, but he claimed expenses for his numerous appearances as well as fees for his articles in the *Völkischer Beobachter* and the *Illustrierter Beobachter*—significant sources of side income. He also demanded substantial payments for interviews he granted to the foreign press as well as the occasional articles he wrote for the Hearst newspaper empire.[133] The party covered the costs for Hitler's personal staff: his private secretary, chauffeur and bodyguard. Hitler had enough money at his disposal to keep up his large apartment on Prinzregentenstrasse and his holiday home on the Obersalzberg, pursue his passion for expensive Mercedes and, as of February 1931, reside in the elegant Hotel Kaiserhof on Mohrenstrasse, diagonally across from the Reich Chancellery, whenever he was in Berlin.[134]

The Nazis benefited more from the policies of the Brüning government than from the big-business donations. Despite the fact that the number of unemployed was rising from month to month, the chancellor continued his deflationary economic policies. Brüning was willing to accept mass unemployment and impoverishment in favour of his primary goal of eradicating German reparations payments. "Since the spring of 1931," the historian Heinrich August Winkler has written, "the thread running through Brüning's policies was not how to overcome but how to politically exploit the Depression."[135] As hard currency poured out of the country, the government was approaching insolvency. On 20 June 1931, U.S. President Herbert Hoover suggested imposing a one-year moratorium on German reparations payments. Brüning welcomed Hoover's initiative as an intermediary step towards getting rid of reparations once and for all. After protracted negotiations, France also agreed to the moratorium, but that move failed to have the expected calming influence on the financial markets. On 13 July, one week after the moratorium's imposition, one of Germany's largest commercial banks, Danatbank, collapsed. There was a widespread run on banks and savings institutions, forcing the government to suspend all banking operations for two days. "Ominous days for Germany . . ." the diarist Thea Sternheim wrote. "Panic everywhere."[136]

The worsening of the financial crisis in the spring and summer of 1931 was wind in the sails of the NSDAP. In Landtag elections in Oldenburg on 17 May, the Nazis polled 37.2 per cent. For the first time ever they were the largest faction in a regional parliament. They also took 26.2 per cent of the vote in the city parliament election in Hamburg, becoming the second-strongest party in the city after the SPD. In Landtag elections in Hesse on 15 November, the NSDAP captured 37.1 per cent of the vote, which put the party well ahead of the rest of the pack.[137] But despite this series of electoral successes, Hitler was no closer to his goal of taking power. As early as January, Goebbels had expressed his fear that "everything is taking too long and the party's momentum could freeze up." After the Nazis' triumph in Oldenburg, Goebbels noted: "Hitler is always a source of strength and optimism. You have to be an optimist to lead our cause to victory."[138]

In July 1931, Hitler again enlisted the support of Alfred Hugenberg and Stahlhelm leader Franz Seldte. In a joint telegram to Brüning in the name of "the entire national opposition," the three men insisted that Germany could no longer bear "the burdens imposed upon it" and therefore should consider any new reparations obligations towards France as non-binding.[139] Hitler also decided to support a public referendum put forth by the Stahlhelm to get rid of the ruling coalition in Prussia and replace it with a government "that reflects the popular will unequivocally expressed in the election of 14 September 1930." On 9 August 1931, the eve of the referendum, Hitler issued a plea to his supporters: "As long as the Social Democrats and the Centre Party are not overcome, Germany will not be able to rise anew. And the position from which the Social Democrats today rule Germany is Prussia."[140] But the referendum was a failure: only 37.1 per cent of voters supported the premature dissolution of the Prussian Landtag. For Goebbels, this was a "grim defeat" into which the Stahlhelm had pulled the NSDAP. "We must get away from the bourgeois mush," he demanded of Hitler. "We must be more imperious and rigorous. We must be National Socialists. That's the source of salvation."[141]

What Berlin National Socialists considered a "more rigorous" approach was made abundantly clear on the evening of 12 September 1931, the start of the Jewish New Year. Some 500 SA men ran wild on the major shopping boulevard Kurfürstendamm, chanting "Germany awaken—Judah must die," harassing passers-by and brutally assaulting people they thought were Jewish. During the unrest, the newly appointed head of the Berlin SA, Count Wolf-Heinrich von Helldorf, drove up and down the boulevard in an open-top car with his assistant Karl Ernst issuing instructions. The Central Association of German

Citizens of the Jewish Faith later spoke of "pogrom-like rioting," while the Social Democratic newspaper *Vorwärts* described what had happened as a "shameful excess" and "an insult to culture." In subsequent trials, thirty-three of the rioters who had been arrested were given jail sentences of up to a year and nine months. Helldorf and Ernst, however, each got off lightly with six months in jail and a 100-mark fine. They appealed, and in February 1932, they were cleared of charges of disturbing the peace. The sentences of most of the others who had been convicted were also significantly reduced. "What is certain," wrote the *Berliner Tageblatt*, "is that with this verdict one of the most serious acts of terror has gone unatoned for, in particular by those who bore the most responsibility for it."[142] Once again, the goddess of German justice had shown that she was blind in her right eye. The SA took the affair as encouragement in their strategy of occupying public spaces and subjecting everyone present to their visible domination.

On 15 September in Munich, Hitler again cautioned his SA Gruppenführer to be "extraordinarily cautious" and "not to get drawn out," adding that "the legal path is the only secure one at the moment." But he also suggested that he sympathised with actions like the one taken on Kurfürstendamm. In large cities, Hitler said, the SA faced the necessity "of undertaking something to satisfy the revolutionary mood of the people." The party would have to publicly distance itself from the SA leaders who had been involved, but Hitler assured his henchmen: "You can be certain that the party will not forget their services and will restore them to their posts as soon as the time is ripe."[143] It was the clearest signal yet that Hitler's insistence on legality was a purely tactical manoeuvre. Once he had gained political power, he planned to overthrow the democratic state.

Yet although Hitler's adherence to legal means was transparently hollow, the leaders of the German military and the Reich government redoubled their efforts in the autumn of 1931 to co-opt the NSDAP into the governing coalition. On 9 September, Hess reported that various parties had tried to convince Brüning "to involve Hitler at least partly in the government." Hess said that as a condition, Hitler had insisted on fresh elections, "which would result in another huge triumph for the movement."[144] The Reich president himself was at the forefront of the move to involve the NSDAP in the government, in the form of a "concentration of national forces" that would span the entire German right wing from Brüning to Hitler. The head of the ministerial office in the Reichswehr Ministry, General Kurt von Schleicher, told Brüning's secretary Erwin Planck on 20 September that Hindenburg had insisted on a "reconstitution of the cabinet to enable cooperation with the far right."[145] Schleicher had been in contact with the NSDAP via Ernst Röhm since the spring, and on 3 October, he met Hitler. At that meeting, the latter reiterated his willingness to join the Brüning cabinet, but only after fresh elections. "First we will be willing to forgo Prussia, once we've achieved a significant position of power in the Reich," was how Goebbels summarised Hitler after the meeting. "In Prussia, a state commissioner will suffice to force Marxism to its knees."[146] Schleicher, who had a follow-up meeting with Hitler a few days later, came away with a positive impression: "An interesting man with an extraordinary speaking talent. In his plans he tends to get above himself, however. One has to tug him back down to reality by his coat-tails."[147] The general-turned-politician Schleicher believed he would be capable of influencing Hitler's political ambitions, thereby "taming" him. For Schleicher, that mistake would ultimately prove fatal.

On the morning of 10 October, Brüning met Hitler. The chancellor would later recall that the leader of the NSDAP possessed "a far greater aura of self-confidence." Again, Hitler did not reject the idea of joining the government, but he did refuse to endorse Hindenburg, who was standing for re-election in early 1932. "On the face of it, it was an extremely cordial conversation," Brüning wrote in his memoirs.[148] At the chancellor's request, Hindenburg met with Hitler and Göring for two hours that very evening. The Reich president was none too pleased that during his appearances in East Prussia young National Socialists had greeted him with cries of "Germany awaken!" But Hitler was able to defuse the situation by slipping into the role of the First World War private full of reverence for the former field marshal.[149] Hindenburg made it clear to the two Nazi leaders that he would vigorously oppose any attempt to gain power without his consent. Their meeting ended without yielding any concrete results. Hitler talked a good game, Hindenburg was quoted as saying, but was best suited for the office of postmaster "so that he can lick me from behind—on my stamps."[150] But other sources suggest that Hitler made a more positive impression on Hindenburg than has often been assumed. "Hitler was very appealing," the Reich president told one of his old comrades, General Karl von Einem. In a letter to his daughter of 14 October, Hindenburg wrote that the "national opposition" had failed to use its first chance. But he did not rule out a second one: "If the right wing had not issued repeated refusals, everything would have been all right."[151] Hitler, too, was satisfied. "The result: we're fit for good society," Goebbels noted. "The old man has met us face to face. The boss called him worthy of respect."[152]

In the autumn of 1931, Hindenburg approved the reconstitution of the governing cabinet. Brüning agreed to dismiss several ministers, including Interior Minister Joseph Wirth from the left wing of the Centre Party, whom Hindenburg considered insufficiently conservative. Wirth was replaced on an interim basis by Reichswehr Minister Wilhelm Groener, who thereby became the second most powerful man in the cabinet. Chancellor Brüning took over the Foreign Ministry himself. The new cabinet was less tightly connected to political parties than the old one since the DVP was no longer represented. That fact was a sign that the business circles were distancing themselves from Brüning.[153] On 16 October, the new Brüning cabinet barely survived a vote of no confidence—thanks only to votes from the SPD faction. A short time before, in a long open letter to the chancellor, Hitler tried to justify why the NSDAP continued to strictly oppose the government. Hitler thought the idea of reviving Germany economically before entering into negotiations with the Western powers to revise the Treaty of Versailles was putting the cart before the horse. Without an end to reparations, he argued, there could be no economic recovery. Brüning's deflationary economic policies, Hitler scoffed, were like declaring the operation a success after the patient had died. The criticism was not without justification. Hitler failed to mention, however, that the National Socialists were the main beneficiaries of these policies, which had only worsened Germany's economic crisis.[154]

On the evening of 10 October, directly after their meeting with Hindenburg, Hitler and Göring, with Goebbels in tow, drove to the central German town of Bad Harzburg, where the "national opposition" was set to stage a joint event the following day. The man behind it was Alfred Hugenberg, and Bad Harzburg had been selected because it was located within Braunschweig, which the National

Socialists had governed with the DNVP since October 1930. The entire anti-republican German right wing had gathered there. Along with the leaders of the NSDAP, the DNVP, the Stahlhelm, the Reichslandbund and the Pan-Germanic League, there was Hohenzollern Prince Eitel Friedrich, former chief of the army command and now DVP deputy General von Seeckt, and Hjalmar Schacht, who went public with his political change of heart with a scathing speech about Brüning's economic policies.[155] Large-scale industry was barely represented. Aside from Thyssen and United Steelworks director Ernst Brandi, the representatives of big business were mostly second-rate figures like Ernst Middendorf, the director general of the petroleum company Deutsche Erdöl AG, or the Hamburg shipyard owner Rudolf Blohm. "It was a shame that industry failed to turn up in Harzburg," Schacht complained in a letter a few days later.[156]

Hitler had only reluctantly agreed to participate in the event, appearing hours late to a preparatory meeting on 10 October. "Hitler is enraged that people are trying to push us against a wall," Goebbels noted. "I had to talk to him for another hour. More distance to the right."[157] The NSDAP chairman had not come to Bad Harzburg to show solidarity but to underline his predominance within the German far right and show his potential allies that he was not merely a "drummer boy" they could exploit for their own purposes. The only thing Hitler did on the morning of 11 October was to inspect a parade of SA and SS units; he left as soon as Stahlhelm formations appeared. He also skipped the communal lunch, disingenuously claiming that he could not dine at a table while his SA men's stomachs were growling.[158] After a lengthy and heated quarrel with Hugenberg, he appeared late to the afternoon rally at the local entertainment hall, and his speech and the manifesto he read out left no doubt as to who would have the say in the future. The National Socialists, Hitler proclaimed, "were prepared to take any and all responsibility for forming national governments at both the Reich and Land levels," and in this spirit they were ready to "extend their hands in loyal cooperation to the other associations of the nationalist opposition."[159]

The "Harzburg Front," as the alliance came to be known, was a fragile construct, characterised by mistrust between the putative partners. Everyone suspected everyone else of pursuing a hidden personal agenda. "Hitler and Hugenberg are in a clinch like two boxers trying to prevent the opponent from drawing back and landing a dangerous blow—that was clear well before the Harzburg conference," wrote the *Vossische Zeitung* newspaper.[160] The only things the principals truly agreed on were their rejection of the Weimar "system" and their desire to bring down the Brüning government. There was no joint programme for how to overcome Germany's economic and political crises. Hugenberg, who frequently had himself praised in his newspapers as the leader (Führer) of the right-wing and conservative camp, was forced to acknowledge that Hitler would by no means be content with the role of junior partner. Yet conversely, no matter how brusquely he behaved in Bad Harzburg, Hitler did not want to cause a major rift on the right. He still needed the support of mainstream figures of respectability to pose a credible threat to the Brüning government.[161] Nonetheless, he made no secret of his claim to a leading role for himself and his movement. One week after the Harzburg conference, he summoned 100,000 members of the SA, the SS and the Hitler Youth to Braunschweig, urging them to "hold their nerve in the final minute."[162] For Goebbels, this demonstration was "our answer to Harzburg and Brüning."[163]

Then, on 25 November 1931, ten days after the Nazis' electoral triumph in Hesse, a bombshell went off that threatened to destroy all of Hitler's plans. A Nazi deputy in the Hessian state parliament who had been forced to step down for using a fake doctoral title turned over sensitive documents to the police in Frankfurt. They were the minutes of a meeting held by Gauleiter in early August at the Boxheim vineyard near the town of Lampertsheim. The "Boxheim documents," as they became known, included a series of proclamations and ordinances to be issued in the event that the National Socialists seized power in the wake of an alleged Communist uprising. In order to restore public security, the Gauleiter had decided, it would be necessary "to take drastic and ruthless measures using armed force." Every order of the SA and local militias was to be obeyed, and any resistance would be punished by death. Anyone caught possessing a firearm would be "shot on the spot." Civil servants, employees and workers who refused to go to work were also threatened with execution.[164] The author of the documents was the court assessor Werner Best, the head of the Gau legal department and the chairman designate of the Landtag faction in Hesse—an ambitious young lawyer who apparently wanted to show his party comrades how semi-legal tricks could be used to disguise a seizure of power as an act of self-defence.

There was a considerable stir when these plans became public: they seemed to confirm every fear about the National Socialists' violent intentions. "A Brutal Fascist Regime of Violence—Hesse to be German Fascism's Experiment," read the headline of the SPD-affiliated *Hessische Volkszeitung*.[165] The Social Democratic and liberal press called for legal consequences, but the public prosecutor Karl August Werner tried to play down the incident. He was acting on orders from Brüning, who did not want the controversy to affect ongoing negotiations between the Centre Party and the NSDAP about forming a coalition government in Hesse. (Those negotiations would break down in December.) On 30 November, legal proceedings against Best began but the investigation was purposely drawn out, and in October 1932 the fourth senate of the Reich court declared that, owing to lack of evidence, Best could no longer be legally pursued.

The conciliatory attitude of legal authorities towards the National Socialists stood in stark contrast to the rigour with which they went after the political Left. In late November 1931, the left-wing journalist Carl von Ossietzky was sentenced to a year and a half in prison for "betraying military secrets." After a demonstration by the League for Human Rights, at which journalist Leopold Schwarzschild and author Arnold Zweig spoke, among others, Thea Sternheim noted: "The most horrible thing . . . is the fact that all the speakers assume that we are on the threshold of the Third Reich, that the grim fantasies of purveyors of violence laid out in the Hessian document will become reality."[166]

For Hitler the revelations were extremely embarrassing because they cast a shadow on his pledges to keep the party within the bounds of legality. He immediately dispatched Göring to assure Hindenburg that the party had nothing "in the slightest" to do with the Boxheim documents and was standing by its "standpoint of the strictest legality, which has been expressed often enough in the past."[167] In early December, Ernst Hanfstaengl succeeded in convincing Hitler to hold an international press conference in the Hotel Kaiserhof and reassure the general public about his plans for the future. In front of the foreign correspondents in attendance, the NSDAP chairman dismissed as nonsense the idea that the party would jettison its commitment to legality at the last minute when poised to assume power. On the other hand, Hitler said, he could not forbid fellow party members from playing through the scenario of a Communist uprising. Once again, Hitler over-dramatised the threat posed by the Communists to divert attention away from the danger represented by the National Socialists. The decisive battle against Bolshevism would be fought in Germany, Hitler thundered, and the Nazis saw it as their mission to win this struggle.[168] Hanfstaengl was very taken by Hitler's debut in front of the foreign press. He had spoken "rationally, persuasively and in measured tones," Hanfstaengl found, and had stuck to "cool irony" in his polemic asides "without seeming crude or overbearing."[169]

Hitler's pose as a moderate politician who kept his emotions strictly in check convinced the sceptics at the press conference, but in interviews with the journalists and diplomats, he made mixed impressions. Hubert R. Knickerbocker, who talked to Hitler in the Brown House in late 1931, was impressed by his winning smile and the fact that Hitler himself had adjusted Knickerbocker's chair for him. Still, the American journalist was subjected to a monologue in which Hitler seemed to forget the presence of his interlocutor. Knickerbocker described Hitler's voice getting faster and louder, and his gaze was directed at some indeterminate point in the distance, as if he were speaking to an auditorium.[170] To the U.S. ambassador to Germany, Frederick M. Sackett, too, who spoke with Hitler in December 1931, the Nazi chairman seemed "as if he were addressing a large audience." "While he talked vigorously, he never looked me in the eye," Sackett noted. When briefing U.S. Secretary of State Henry Stimson, the ambassador predicted that if Hitler came to power he would be unable to hold on to it for very long. "He is certainly not the type from which statesmen evolve," Sackett sniffed.[171]

American journalist Dorothy Thompson, the wife of Nobel Prize-winning author Sinclair Lewis, was even harsher in her opinion. Thompson was granted an interview by Hitler in his suite in the Hotel Kaiserhof in November 1931, and she published her account of that conversation in a short book entitled *I Saw Hitler* in 1932. "I was convinced I was meeting the future dictator of Germany," Thompson wrote.

In something less than fifty seconds I was quite sure that I was not. It took just about that time to measure the startling insignificance of this man who has set the world agog. He is formless, almost faceless, a man whose countenance is a caricature, a man whose framework seems cartilaginous, without bones. He is inconsequent and voluble, ill-poised, insecure. He is the very prototype of the Little Man. A lock of lank hair falls over an insignificant and slightly retreating forehead. The back head is shallow. The face is broad in the cheek bones. The nose is large but badly shaped and without character. His movements are awkward, almost undignified and most un-martial.

Nonetheless, even Thompson found things to like about the Nazi leader: "And yet, he is not without a certain charm . . . the soft, almost feminine charm of the Austrian! . . . The eyes alone are notable. Dark grey and hyperthyroid—they have the peculiar shine which often distinguishes geniuses, alcoholics and hysterics." Thompson, too, was subjected to a monologue:

> The interview was difficult, because one cannot carry on a conversation with Adolf Hitler. He speaks always, as though he was addressing a mass meeting. In personal intercourse he is shy, almost embarrassed. In every question he seeks for a theme that will set him off. Then his eyes focus in [sic] some far corner of the room; a hysterical note creeps into his voice which rises sometimes almost to a scream. He gives the impression of a man in a trance.[172]

In many respects Thompson's observations mirror those of the writer Klaus Mann, who witnessed several months later how Hitler ate one strawberry tart after another "with half-infantile, half-predatory greed" in Munich's Carlton tearoom. Thomas Mann's eldest son had numerous opportunities to study Hitler, whom he called "an evil philistine with a hysterically opaque gaze in his pale, swollen visage." In his autobiography, *The Turning Point*, Klaus Mann wrote:

> It was certainly not very pleasant to sit that close to such a creature; but still I could not keep my eyes off this vile mug. I had never found him particularly attractive, neither in pictures nor in person on the illuminated grandstand; but the ugliness I encountered now exceeded all my expectations. The vulgarity of his features was soothing and made me feel better. I looked at him and thought: "You will never win, Schicklhuber, even if you scream your head off. You want to rule Germany? You want to become its dictator—with a nose like that? You must be joking . . . You will never win power!"[173]

Mann's account is an excellent example of how a purely aesthetic reaction to Hitler—in this case, revulsion at his physical appearance—could lead observers to underestimate the man and his political tenacity.

These impressionist observations were not the only efforts to come to terms with Hitler. Various attempts were made in 1931 and 1932 to analyse the phenomenon of Hitler and National Socialism. One of the most impressive was Theodor Heuss's *Hitler's Way*, which the author finished in December 1931 and which quickly ran through eight editions. The future president of the post-war Federal Republic of Germany captured the dual nature of the Nazi movement. On the one hand, Heuss found, it inhabited a world of strong emotions and passions. These were evident in the Führer cult, the pseudo-religious faith followers invested in one man and his world view, and the mass psychosis triggered by his public appearances. On the other hand, though, there was the bureaucratic apparatus, the strongly organised, highly efficient party machinery aimed solely at acquiring political power. "Rationalistic power calculations coexist side by side with unbridled emotions," wrote Heuss, who identified the same contradiction in Hitler himself. Hitler was, on the one hand, a "master of emotional ecstasy combining the techniques of the trained mass psychologist and someone inspired by the primeval passion that comes from the exuberance of mass emotion." On the other hand, Heuss regarded Hitler simply as "a politician who wants power." Heuss saw Hitler's pledges to respect the law for what they were—tactical manoeuvres to achieve that goal:

> Today legality means being formed or confirmed by the will of the majority. The man who mocks democracy subjects himself, vowing legality, to its methods and its very idea. In so doing, he suggests to his followers that this is not the result of a change of heart, but the manifestation of a period of adjustment, an attempt to win time that requires patience. The goal is to gain the majority of votes tomorrow or the day after tomorrow—and the majority means power.

Heuss noted Hitler's new moderate tone in his speeches: "He curses far less. He does not rip the Jews to shreds any more. He can talk for hours without even using the word Jew." But Heuss was under no illusions that Hitler had truly reined in his anti-Semitism. On the contrary, moderation was simply a response "to the tactical need not to appear monomaniacal." Heuss also presciently recognised that "the taking of territory in the European east is the core principle of Hitler's foreign policy." The achievement of this end would require war, no matter what Hitler occasionally said to the contrary: "He rejects the notion that he is promoting a new war, but he assumes that there has to be a new war and consequently that the point of German foreign policy is to ensure that the new war ends in victory for Germany."[174] Those who read Heuss's analysis were well informed not just about the road Hitler had travelled to get to where he was by 1931, but what lay in store should he ever come to power.

Unfortunately, most of Heuss's contemporaries were a long way from seeing the situation that clearly. Victor Klemperer described the predominant mood at the end of 1931 as one of desperation: "People simply want to keep on living without comprehending how and why. They're completely numb." And Count Harry Kessler noted laconically: "It's a sad New Year, the end of a catastrophic year and the beginning of what looks to be an even more catastrophic one."[175]

Hitler and Women

"The days are sad right now," wrote Hitler, pouring out his sorrows in a letter to Winifred Wagner on 30 December 1931. "I can't seem to get over this great loneliness." He had passed through Bayreuth on Christmas Eve, but had not had the heart to visit her. "How can a person take pleasure in anything if he is sad inside?" he added.[1] Hitler's unhappiness had a concrete personal cause. On the morning of 19 September 1931, his niece Geli Raubal had been found dead in his apartment on Munich's Prinzregentenstrasse. Next to her lay the pistol that Hitler kept in his desk drawer for protection.

It is not surprising that this incident attracted widespread attention, since at the time the rising new star of German politics was being courted from many sides as a potential coalition partner. For a brief period, Hitler's private life came into public focus, only to quickly disappear once more. For historians, Raubal's death provides an occasion to pose one of the central biographical questions: what sort of relationship did Hitler have with the female sex?

The question is difficult to address and will probably never be answered definitively. Hitler's first biographer, Konrad Heiden, wrote of his "opaque erotic life," and little evidence has emerged since the 1930s to alter that verdict.[2] Hitler always played a game of hide-and-seek with his private life—even towards those closest to him. Authentic personal documents are a rarity: most of the material that existed was probably destroyed by Julius Schaub at the end of the war. It is hardly surprising, then, that no chapter of Hitler's biography contains more rumours and legends than his relations with women. The most bizarre among them is the perpetual canard about his abnormal genitalia. This myth is based on a former classmate's story that a goat bit off half his penis as a young man and the assertion made by a Soviet army doctor who performed a post-mortem on Hitler in 1945 that he was missing his left testicle. According to everything we know from his personal doctor Theodor Morell, Hitler's sexual organs were perfectly normal. Speculation that he was physically unable to have sex is completely unfounded.[3]

Attempts to discover something pathological in Hitler's sex life also lead us astray. The only real ammunition for this argument comes from Hanfstaengl's 1970 memoirs, which include an anecdote designed to appeal to readers' prurience. One evening when he had left the room to order a taxi, Hanfstaengl wrote, Hitler used the opportunity to "kneel down" in front of Helene Hanfstaengl, declare himself as "her slave" and "lament his pitiful destiny, which had condemned him to the bittersweet experience of making her acquaintance too late." Helene only just succeeded in getting the grovelling Hitler back on his feet before her husband returned to the room to witness this ambiguous situation.[4] It is all too easy to conclude that a man who would later order monstrous crimes to be committed must have been sexually perverse, which is why historians have been so eager to credit this idea.[5]

Likewise, the claim especially popular among German exiles in the 1930s that Hitler was homosexual has been disproved. Historian Lothar Machtan made this idea the centre of a study that was marketed with great hullabaloo in 2001. Machtan claimed to have shown "that Hitler loved men . . . and that realising this is essential for understanding both his person and his career," even though he had to "domesticate his same-sex passion" since homosexuality would have been "a fatal handicap for a political career."[6] For Machtan, Hitler's "virile posturing and need to impress others was basically just a desperate attempt to cover up his feminine nature."[7] Machtan tried to cite hard evidence to make his interpretation more plausible, but was unable to produce even a single genuine piece of proof that the idea of Hitler's homosexuality was anything but speculation.

A further curious variation within the broad spectrum of conjectures about Hitler's physical urges holds that he was completely asexual. The main evidence for this hypothesis is a remark passed on by his long-standing secretary Christa Schroeder that her boss "needed eroticism but not sex." According to Schroeder, Hitler gained satisfaction from the "ecstasy of the masses," while his relations with women had been purely "platonic."[8] Joachim Fest picked up such statements, interpreting Hitler's rhetorical flights as "compensation mechanisms for his dead-end sexuality."[9] This characterisation informs the popular idea that as an egomaniac who believed he was on a historic mission, Hitler was incapable of developing emotional bonds with women. The popular historian Guido Knopp put it succinctly: "In the end, Hitler only loved himself."[10] That is no doubt true in a sense, but is hardly sufficient to explain the complex story of Hitler's relationships with women.

There is no doubt that Hitler was susceptible to feminine charms. "What beautiful women there are," he exclaimed in late January 1942 in the Wolfsschanze.

> We were sitting in the Bremen Ratskeller and a woman came in, and you would have thought Olympus had opened up! Simply incandescent! The diners all put down their forks and knives and feasted their eyes on this woman! Then, later in Braunschweig, I could have kicked myself afterwards! All the men there felt the same way. A blonde thing jumped up at my car to give me a bouquet of flowers. Everyone could remember her. But no one thought of asking the girl for her address so that I could write her a thank-you note. She was big and blonde and wonderful![11]

Hitler also remembered his youthful crush from Linz, Stefanie, as "big and blonde and wonderful." The 17-year-old had not dared approach her, remaining an admirer from afar. "In my youth in Vienna, I also encountered many beautiful women," he concluded his monologue in 1942. But as far as we know, he never succeeded in getting to know any of them. Christa Schroeder recalled Hitler describing a woman named Emilie from his Vienna days as his "first love."[12] As the historian Brigitte Hamann has determined, the woman in question was the 17-year-old sister of Hitler's friend Rudolf Häusler—a shy, sheltered girl to whom Hitler had once given a drawing but with whom he definitely had not had an affair.[13] Moreover, there is no indication that Hitler had any contact with women during his time in Munich before the First World War, when he basically lived like a hermit.

Was it shyness or self-imposed asceticism that inclined Hitler to avoid getting to know members of the opposite sex? We do not know, and we can only speculate whether Hitler masturbated, as young men in his situation are wont to do. Onanism, which generations of priests, doctors and teachers had condemned as a serious sin, engendered feelings of guilt in adolescents of all social classes. In his study of neurasthenic conditions around the turn of the century, the historian Joachim Radkau characterised masturbation as the great illicit thrill of the time.[14] Perhaps this was one cause of Hitler's reticence around women. On the other hand, we should remember that after leaving school and failing to get accepted to the Vienna Academy of Fine Arts, the young Hitler felt like a failure—hardly the best position from which to conquer young ladies' hearts.

By the time he went off to war in 1914, at the age of 25, Hitler apparently had had no sexual experiences with women whatsoever, and that fact seems not to have changed in his four years on the Western Front. His comrades in the field, whose preferred topic of conversation was sex, often made fun of him for his lack of interest—whether it was play-acted or genuine—but they ultimately accepted him as what he seemed to be: a somewhat bizarre saint who was strangely abstinent when it came to sensual pleasures.[15] After 1918, the soldiers who had survived the carnage and the women who had done without their men for so long were eager to make up for lost time. The general relaxation of morals, manifested, for example, in the "dance mania," was a response to such desires. It has been speculated that Hitler overcame his skittishness around women and plunged into the whirlpool of physical pleasures in the first, wild, post-war years, which also marked the beginning of his political career.[16] In fact, his rivals within the Nazi Party in the summer of 1921 accused him of "excessive contact with women."[17] But all we have are second-hand rumours. In 1923, he was alleged to have had an affair with Jenny Haug, the sister of his chauffeur at the time. That at least was the story told by Konrad Heiden, who claimed to have it on good authority.[18]

Nonetheless, even then Hitler preferred to keep the company of maternal patrons like Hermine Hoffmann, Helene Bechstein and Elsa Bruckmann, who took the ambitious but uncouth and somewhat lost young politician under their wings.[19] There was certainly a measure of rivalry between Hitler's "surrogate mothers." In March 1942 he recalled that a Munich society lady was excluded from the Bruckmanns' salon after the hostess had noticed her making eyes at him. "She was very beautiful and would have found me interesting—nothing more," Hitler remarked.[20] Helene Bechstein was so taken by Hitler that she would have liked to see him marry her only daughter, Lotte. "He couldn't kiss," the then 15-year-old publishing heiress later said when asked why she had not had a liaison with Hitler.[21]

Winifred Wagner also conformed to the image of a "surrogate mother," even though she was eight years younger than Hitler. In November 1926, after reading a biography of Mussolini, she tried to understand her relationship with the friend she so greatly admired. Men who were "called to such exalted positions," she wrote to an acquaintance, had to be "fully isolated inside" since their mission demanded that they be "above and outside others." Relations with a female represented "the only bridge and contact with the rest of humanity" and were thus of "inestimable significance" to such men, whose character was almost completely formed by their mothers. Unconsciously, both Mussolini's and Hitler's relationships with women, Wagner wrote, were influenced by "the desire for their deceased mothers."[22] Wagner knew what a major role Klara Hitler had played in her son's life and how much Hitler had suffered because of her early death. Thus she tried to be a surrogate mother to him, even though her own feelings for the man she nicknamed "Wolf" were more than just maternal.

During Hitler's time in Landsberg, prison director Otto Leybold noticed that as a bachelor he seemed better able to adjust to incarceration than his fellow prisoners who were married. "He isn't drawn to women," Leybold remarked, "and he treats those he encounters during visits here with the utmost politeness without getting involved in serious political discussions with them."[23] In fact, Hitler was always quite solicitous around women. Like an old-school cavalier, he greeted them by kissing their hands and gave his voice a soft, insinuatingly warm tone. Those who only knew him as a bellowing, wildly gesticulating rabble-rouser were usually astonished at how charming Hitler could be in private. Leybold, however, was correct in his observation that Hitler did not want women getting involved in his political affairs. History had proved beyond the shadow of a doubt, he proclaimed years later over lunch in the Wolfsschanze, that "women, no matter how clever, are unable to separate reason from emotion in politics."[24]

Hitler maintained a traditional view of women. Politics and work were the domain of men, while women were responsible for keeping house, taking care of their husbands and raising children. "The man's world is large compared to the woman's," Hitler pontificated in one of his monologues. "Man belongs to duty, and only now and again do his thoughts turn to women. The woman's world is her husband. Only now and again does she think of anything else. That is the big difference." Women depended on men for protection, Hitler repeatedly stressed. Without it they were lost: "That's why a woman loves a hero. He gives her a sense of safety. She wants a heroic man."[25] Hitler could not conceive of a relationship in which men and women were equal partners.

Hitler decided early on in life to forgo marriage and traditional family life. In June 1924, when his fellow inmate in Landsberg, Rudolf Hess, suggested moving his sister Paula from Vienna to Munich, Hitler dismissed the idea "with every sign of horror," protesting that it would only be "a burden and an inhibition." Hitler was afraid his sister might try to influence his decisions. "For the same reason," wrote Hess, "he refused to get married and avoided, as he himself hinted, strong feelings of attachment to women. He had to be ready at any time to face all perils and if necessary die without the slightest personal, human thought."[26] Hitler would stay true to the principle of never binding himself to a woman in marriage—so as to prevent personal concerns from limiting his political latitude—until shortly before his suicide in his Berlin bunker.

After Hitler was released from Landsberg, there was talk in Nazi circles in Munich of him having a relationship with Ernst Hanfstaengl's sister Erna. The rumours persisted, so that in early March 1925 Hitler felt compelled to publicly deny them, declaring, "I am so married to politics that I cannot even consider another 'engagement.'"[27] Yet that attitude did not rule out relationships with women. After Hitler's stretch in prison, his new chauffeur, the good-looking Emil Maurice, was tasked with "chatting up girls" when driving his boss around. But as Maurice told Christa Schroeder after the war, Hitler and the women had merely socialised and conversed in the evenings after big events. Hitler had given them money, but had not asked for anything in return.[28] It seems that Hitler liked relaxing in the company of beautiful women after strenuous speaking appearances. When he was interrogated in June 1945, Maurice said he was certain that "neither Hitler's short nor his long amorous relationships had resulted in sexual congress."[29]

The same was apparently true for Hitler's relationship with Maria Reiter. Hitler met her in Berchtesgaden in the autumn of 1926 while he was completing the second volume of *Mein Kampf*, but the public first learned of the existence of Hitler's "unknown lover" in 1959, when Reiter was "sensationally discovered" by the West German news weekly *Stern*.[30] Not all of the information supplied by Reiter, who was living then in obscurity in a Munich suburb, was credible. Nonetheless, in a number of respects, the magazine report does shed light on Hitler's complex relationship with women.

Maria Reiter was born on 23 December 1909 in Berchtesgaden. Her father was a tailor and one of the founders of the local chapter of the Social Democratic Party. Her mother ran a women's fashion shop on the ground floor of the Deutsches Haus, the hotel Hitler stayed at in the autumn of 1926.[31] A few weeks before Reiter met Hitler, her mother had died. Her older sister took over the shop, while Maria helped out as a salesgirl. Hitler had observed the blonde, blue-eyed Reiter for quite some time before introducing himself. Their first conversation revolved around the dogs they took for walks in a nearby park. "German shepherds are truly loyal and friendly," Hitler is supposed to have said. "I can no longer imagine life without this dog. Do you not feel the same way?"

At the time, Reiter was 16, Hitler 37 years old. Like his father, Hitler preferred younger women, and he made no secret of it: "There is nothing better than educating a young thing," he would declare in 1942. "A girl of 18, 19, 20 years is as malleable as wax. A man needs to be able to put his stamp on a girl. Women themselves want nothing different!"[32] That was obviously Hitler's rationalisation for the problem he had with women of his own age, who displayed self-confidence, were well educated and let him know that they saw through his charming but artificial poses. Encounters with such women stirred feelings of inferiority, as he had displayed by his nonplussed behaviour when interviewed by Dorothy Thompson in 1931.[33]

With "Mimi," "Mizzi" or "Mitzerl," as he soon called his new acquaintance, Hitler could play the role of the vastly superior, paternal friend. He courted her, inviting her and her sister to an NSDAP event in the Deutsches Haus and devoting his entire attention to her at the subsequent private reception. In response to the hotel owner's daughter's somewhat indiscreet question as to why he was not married, Hitler declared that he "first had to rescue the German people lying on the ground." Reiter remembered Hitler touching her legs with his knee and stepping firmly on her toes with his foot as he said this. Such rather crude advances continued later in her sister's apartment, when Hitler suddenly placed himself in front of her with a penetrating glare and asked: "Don't you want to give me a kiss goodnight?" When Reiter resisted, protesting that she had never kissed a man, the change in Hitler's manner was instantaneous: "He pursed his lips, and his gaze lost the warmth it had just had," Reiter reported.

There is some evidence that Reiter's story was genuine. Henriette Hoffmann—the young daughter of Hitler's court photographer Heinrich and later wife of Hitler Youth leader Baldur von Schirach—described a similar incident. Hoffmann claimed that one evening in her father's apartment Hitler approached her after the other guests had left: "Herr Hitler wore an English trench coat, holding a grey velour hat in his hand, and said something that wasn't like him at all. He asked very seriously: 'Don't you want to kiss me?'" Henriette Hoffmann, too, rejected this advance: "No please, Herr Hitler, I really can't." In response, "He said absolutely nothing, rapped the palm of his hand with his riding crop and slowly descended the stairs to the front door."[34]

How should we interpret this type of behaviour? Apparently, despite all his charm, Hitler was unable to approach women confidently in any way that went beyond the mere exchange of pleasantries. His lack of experience may have played a role in this, but it may also have been an inability or unwillingness to empathise with the wishes and needs of the women he fancied. Thus Hitler launched sudden advances and then turned his back equally abruptly, if his clumsy forays did not meet with approval. He seemed to have lacked an internal emotional compass.

Despite being rejected, Hitler did not end his relationship with Maria Reiter. He accompanied her to her mother's grave, suggested that they use the informal "du" form of address and asked her to call him "Wolf"—a privilege enjoyed by few women other than Winifred Wagner. They did eventually kiss, although if we believe Reiter's account, it came about under strange circumstances. Maurice had chauffeured the couple to a forest behind the Bischofswiesen area of Berchtesgaden. He remained in the car, while Hitler led the 16-year-old girl into a clearing, placed her in front of a tall fir tree and stared at her "as a painter does at a model." Then, according to Reiter, Hitler pulled her close: "He took a firm hold of my neck and kissed me. He didn't know what he was doing."

Lothar Machtan has interpreted this scene as proof of Hitler's homosexuality, asking, "How could he know what he was doing if desire did not show him the way?"[35] Another interpretation is more plausible: Hitler may have felt desire but was uncertain how far he should take it. Perhaps he feared that his new girlfriend, if things went beyond one kiss, would make demands on him. In January 1942, he recalled the incident: "Miezel was pretty as a picture. I knew a great many women back then, and many of them liked me a lot. But why should I get married and leave behind a wife? . . . Back then, this thought led me to pass up on several chances. I forcibly restrained myself."[36]

Maria Reiter seems to have believed that Hitler's intentions were serious. After he left Berchtesgaden, she wrote him long letters. Most of the time, he responded with brief postcards with basically the same message: "My dear child! Receive my most heartfelt greetings. I think of you all the time. Yours, Wolf."[37] In the few letters he wrote to her, he complained about being overworked and having too little time for his private life while pledging his enduring affection: "Yes, child, you truly don't know what you mean to me and how fond I am of you."[38] When Reiter turned 17 on 23 December 1926, Hitler visited her and stayed for Christmas. She gave him two sofa cushions embroidered with swastikas; he gave her a leather-bound two-volume edition of *Mein Kampf*. In late 1927, she visited him in Munich, but nothing came of it aside from an innocent tête-à-tête in his apartment on Thierschstrasse. Then, in the summer, Hitler abruptly ended their romance after party headquarters received anonymous letters accusing him of rape. In 1930, Reiter married a hotelier and moved to Seefeld in Tyrol. She later said she visited Hitler in Munich in the summer of 1931, claiming to have spent the night in his apartment on Prinzregentenstrasse, but this story should be viewed sceptically. By that point, there was a new woman in Hitler's life: his niece Geli Raubal.

*

None of the women in Hitler's life fired the imaginations of both contemporaries and later historians as much as Raubal. Konrad Heiden called her "Hitler's great lover," and most other commentators shared the view that Hitler's niece was the only woman, other than his mother, for whom he developed deeper feelings.[39] The speculations and rumours surrounding Hitler and Raubal make it difficult to view the subject objectively. What kind of relationship did they have, and was it really so central in Hitler's biography?

Angela (Geli) Raubal was born on 4 June 1908 in Linz, a few months after the 19-year-old Hitler had moved to Vienna.[40] She was the second of three children from the marriage of Hitler's half-sister Angela with the tax official Leo Raubal. Leo died in 1910, leaving the family, which at times included Hitler's sister Paula, in difficult financial straits. The situation only improved when Angela Raubal took up the position of director at a home for female apprentices in Vienna in October 1915. Her ambition was to ensure that her children got a good education. After primary school, Geli became one of the first girls to get a degree from Linz's prestigious, university-track *Akademisches Gymnasium* in June 1927. Three years previously, she and her older brother Leo had visited their now-famous uncle in Landsberg. There, prison guard Franz Hemmrich related, Hitler had greeted her with a hug and given her a "hearty kiss on the lips."[41] After she graduated, Hitler invited her entire class to Munich. Geli stayed at the Bruckmanns' villa, and she and her class were treated to an appearance by the NSDAP chairman at afternoon tea. "We stood in rows before him," recalled Geli's classmate Alfred Maleta, who would go on to become the president of the Austrian National Council after the war. "He greeted every one of us with a firm handshake, an audible click of his heels and a penetrating stare with his watery blue eyes, which was obviously meant to be enthralling."[42]

In August 1927, Geli Raubal took part in the Nuremberg rally, and afterwards Hitler went on tour through Germany with her, her mother Angela and Rudolf Hess. "The Tribune's young niece is a tallish, attractive teenager, always cheerful and as clever with words as her uncle," Hess wrote. "Even he can hardly compete with her quick-witted mouth." Hitler wanted her to attend university in Germany, but was convinced that "she would barely get past the second semester before someone would marry her."[43] Henriette Hoffmann also described Geli as "tall, cheerful and self-confident," adding: "Photos didn't do justice to her charm. None of the pictures my father took captured her."[44] In the autumn of 1927, she moved to Munich, where she began studying medicine.

In no time, the attractive young woman was the much-admired centre of attention among the regulars at Café Heck. Her "tomboyish, easy-going manner" captivated the men, Heinrich Hoffmann recalled. "When Geli was at the table, everything revolved around her," Hoffmann wrote, "and Hitler never tried to dominate the conversation. Geli was a magician. Thanks to her natural ways, entirely free of flirtatiousness, her mere presence put everyone present in the best of spirits. Everyone rhapsodised about her, most of all her uncle, Adolf Hitler."[45]

The same was true of Emil Maurice. The chauffeur always hovered around Geli whenever he drove Hitler's entourage to a picnic on Chiemsee Lake in the big black Mercedes. Maurice would get his mandolin out of the trunk and sing Irish folk songs. Hitler never went swimming. At most, he would remove his shoes and socks and carefully bathe his pale feet in the shallow water. Geli and Henriette Hoffmann, whom she befriended, would seek out a spot concealed behind bushes and go skinny-dipping. "We swam naked and let the sun dry us off," Hoffmann recalled. "We wanted to get a complete tan."[46]

Shortly before Christmas 1927, Maurice told his boss about his feelings for Geli, which she apparently reciprocated, effectively asking Hitler for her hand in marriage. Hitler reacted with a fit of rage. He had never seen his boss so angry, Maurice later recalled: "I seriously think he would have liked to shoot me dead at that moment."[47] Hitler threatened to send Geli back to her mother in Vienna, if a number of conditions were not met. Maurice and Geli, who had secretly got engaged, were to submit to a two-year trial phase. "Remember, Maurice," Geli wrote in her Christmas letter to her fiancé, "we have two full years in which we can only kiss now and then under the watchful eye of U[ncle] A[dolf]." But they submitted to Hitler's will, with Geli writing, "I'm so happy I can stay with you."[48] Hitler, however, had no intention of permitting her any further contact with his chauffeur. In January 1928, Maurice was fired without notice and quickly became a *persona non grata*.[49]

We can only speculate about the reason for Hitler's furious reaction. Maurice believed it was jealousy. Hitler, he thought, had fallen in love with his niece, "but it was a strange, unacknowledged love."[50] By contrast, Hitler's long-time housekeeper Anni Winter thought that Hitler was only trying to live up to his role as Geli's guardian: "He only wanted the best for her. She was a foolish girl."[51] Whatever the case may have been, from the spring of 1928, Geli was an integral part of Hitler's entourage. She accompanied her uncle to the cinema, the theatre and the opera, and even when she went shopping, he trotted behind her "like a patient lamb."[52] In July, the two spent several days on holiday with Goebbels and Angela Raubal, on the island of Heligoland.[53] It went without saying that Geli was in attendance in November 1928, when Hitler made his first appearance in Berlin's Sportpalast. "The boss is here," noted Goebbels. "Energised as ever. With his pretty niece you'd almost want to fall in love with."[54] Geli spent Christmas 1928 with Hitler on the Obersalzberg at Haus Wachenfeld, which her mother now ran. There they also celebrated her twenty-first birthday in June 1929.[55] In early August she was seen again at Hitler's side at the Nuremberg rally. Goebbels was happy: "Geli Raubal. A beautiful child. Had dinner with her, her mother and the boss in his room. We laughed a lot."[56]

Without doubt, Geli Raubal enjoyed being the centre of attention and having the men in Hitler's circle compete for her favour. She would have been flattered that "Uncle Alf," as she called Hitler, was so fond of her and allowed her to participate in his breathtaking rise in 1929–30 and the aura of power and success it brought. Hitler loved appearing in public at her side. As Maurice put it, Hitler was "proud of being seen with such an enchanting person."[57] But as much as Hitler enjoyed the company of this young woman, he avoided any displays of intimacy even in his innermost circle. "Never did Hitler reveal his feelings in society," Heinrich Hoffmann observed. "He always behaved completely correctly towards Geli. It was only his gaze and his warm tone that betrayed his affection."[58]

Nonetheless, Geli Raubal's constant presence at Hitler's side gave rise early on to rumours within the Nazi Party. In October 1928, Goebbels wrote in his diary that soon-to-be Hamburg Gauleiter Karl Kaufmann had told him "crazy things" about Hitler: "He and his niece Geli and Maurice. The tragedy that is woman. It's enough to make you desperate. Why do we all have to suffer so because of this woman? I have complete faith in Hitler. I understand everything. The true and the untrue."[59] But Goebbels himself repeatedly complained that Hitler got distracted from serious business by "too many stories with women."[60] There is no way of settling whether Hitler had intimate relations with his niece. Opinion was divided within his circle. Hanfstaengl was convinced of the "incestuous character" of the relationship, writing that Hitler's "inhibited sex drive found willing fulfilment and completion" in Geli's "directionless libidinousness."[61] By contrast, on the basis of conversations with Anni Winter, Christa Schroeder felt confident that Hitler had loved Geli without ever having had sex with her.[62]

In October 1929, Geli gave up her room in a boarding house and moved into Hitler's Prinzregentenstrasse apartment—a sign of just how close their relationship had become. She was given a cheery corner room which she could decorate as she pleased. Hitler's household personnel—Anni and Georg Winter, his former landlady Maria Reichert and his cleaning woman, Anna Kirmair—were not exactly thrilled about their new flatmate. They thought Geli was exploiting her uncle's generosity, and that he was spoiling her. Geli had quit studying medicine to train, in accordance with her uncle's wishes, as a singer. To that end, Hitler hired the bandleader Adolf Vogl, whom he had known since May 1919, and paid for private lessons at a singing school.[63] In July 1930, Hitler and Geli travelled together with the Bechsteins to the Bayreuth Wagner Festival and then visited the Passion Play in Oberammergau.[64] But Geli does not seem to have taken her singing career very seriously. She preferred to amuse herself in the company of others and read the serialised novels in the newspapers—something Hitler often complained about.[65]

As far as we can tell, Geli Raubal increasingly came to view life on Prinzregentenstrasse as a burden. Here she was entirely subjected to her uncle's control. His solicitousness shaded over into rules and coercion. Hitler continued to buy her fashionable clothing and shoes without complaint,[66] but when the amateur photographer wanted to buy herself an expensive Leica camera to replace her Rolleiflex, Hitler refused. "Geli sulked and they finished the walk without her saying a word," reported Julius Schaub, who had served as Hitler's "constant companion" since 1925 and who would be promoted to his personal assistant in 1933.[67] Hitler jealously watched over his niece's every step and increasingly sought to restrict her freedom. She enjoyed going out, but when she wanted to attend a carnival ball in 1931, Hitler only gave in after Heinrich Hoffmann and Max Amann agreed to serve as chaperones. When Hoffmann reproached him, Hitler answered: "What Geli sees as coercion is simply caution. I want to prevent her from falling into the hands of someone unworthy."[68] That was no doubt an excuse: Hitler did not want to share Geli with anyone else.

Thus, as Henriette Hoffmann observed, the carefree young thing gradually became melancholic and introverted,[69] and quarrels erupted with increasing frequency on Prinzregentenstrasse. In mid-September 1931, Hitler forbade his niece from making a trip to Vienna, which she probably intended as a way of escaping her uncle's watchful eye for a time. On the evening of 17 September, Julius Schaub's wife, who went with her to a theatre production, described her as "absent, disconsolate, almost tear-stained."[70]

The following day, before Hitler left for a campaign trip to northern Germany, the two butted heads again, and after Hitler's departure, Geli locked herself in her room. When she failed to appear for breakfast on 19 September and did not respond to knocks at her door, Anni Winter summoned her husband. Together they broke down the door and were greeted by a terrible sight. Geli lay sprawled on the floor, her nightgown covered in blood. Her head rested on one arm; the other was outstretched towards the sofa, where they found a 6.35-millimetre Walther pistol.[71] The Winters immediately notified Hess, who hurried to the apartment with Nazi Party treasurer Franz Xaver Schwarz. Hess then returned to the Brown House, where he tried to telephone Hitler.

As was his wont, Hitler had spent the previous night at the Deutscher Hof hotel in Nuremberg and continued his journey north that morning. Shortly after he had set off, his car was overtaken by a taxi. A bellboy told Hitler that a Mr. Hess from Munich urgently needed to speak with him. Hitler's entourage turned around, and Hitler rushed to a phone booth. Heinrich Hoffmann, who had followed him, listened in. "Hitler exclaimed hoarsely, 'That's terrible,'" Hoffmann recalled after the war. "He then screamed down the phone line: 'Hess, give me a clear answer yes or no—is she still alive? Hess, on your honour as an officer, don't lie to me. Hess! Hess!' Hitler stumbled out of the telephone booth. His hair hung down, dishevelled, in his face. His gaze was unsteady. I only saw him like that on one other occasion: in the Reich Chancellery bunker in April 1945."[72]

Even if we assume that Hoffmann wanted to make his account as dramatic as possible, the news of Geli Raubal's death no doubt shook Hitler to the core. He raced back to Munich. His car was pulled over by the police in the town of Ebenhausen—the speeding ticket was preserved.[73] Hitler arrived back on Prinzregentenstrasse at 2:30 p.m. and was able to see the body before it was taken to the viewing hall at Munich's Eastern Cemetery. By that time the police investigation had already been concluded.[74]

Only after Hess and Schwarz had left the apartment at around 10:15 a.m. did Georg Winter call the police. Two detective superintendents and a police doctor were sent to investigate. Their report concluded that "death was caused by a gunshot wound to the lung and rigor mortis indicated that it had occurred many hours (17–18) previously." All the evidence, as the officers saw it, pointed to suicide, even though there was no note or anything expressing suicidal intentions in Raubal's room. "There was only a partially completed letter to a female friend in Vienna on the table, which contained no indication of extreme world-weariness," the report noted.[75] When questioned, Hitler's servants could think of no reasons why Raubal might have killed herself, although Maria Reichert did say that she had been "very emotional of late."[76]

That afternoon, after arriving at his apartment, Hitler had already overcome the initial shock, making a composed impression on the police officers who interviewed him. While he admitted quarrelling with his niece about her future, he played down the significance of the fight. Geli, he said, had wanted to continue her education in Vienna since she did not feel up to being a singer. "I agreed on the condition that her mother, who lives in Berchtesgaden, accompanied her," Hitler said. "When she said she didn't want that, I came out against the plan. She must have been very angry about it, but she did not get particularly upset and said goodbye to me quite calmly when I left on Friday afternoon." His niece had been "the only relative he was close to," Hitler told the police, and her death had shaken him badly. The police report then recorded a remark which suggested that he was already thinking about the political fallout of Raubal's death: "And now this had to happen to *him*."[77]

Hitler's political adversaries were not above making use of the scandal. In an article entitled "A Mysterious Affair," the Social

Democratic *Münchener Post* tried to sow doubt that Raubal's death had been a suicide. The newspaper reported that a massive row had broken out in Hitler's apartment because his niece had announced her engagement. The *Post* also claimed that Raubal had been found with a broken nose and other serious injuries.[78] The article prompted the state prosecutor to order the police doctor to re-examine the body. His conclusions were unambiguous: aside from the gunshot wound to Raubal's chest, the body revealed no signs of violence—to the nose or anywhere else. The two women employed by the city to take care of bodies in the morgue confirmed these findings.[79] In a denial written on the evening of 21 September and published by the *Post* the following day, Hitler rejected such speculations as falsehoods. His niece had wanted to travel to Vienna "to have a vocal coach reassess her voice." There had been "no scene" and "no excitement," Hitler attested, when he left the apartment on 18 September.[80]

Still, rumours about the causes of Raubal's death persisted. According to one, Hitler had his niece murdered by the SS because she had got pregnant by a Jewish university student. Another held that Hitler had killed Raubal himself in a fit of rage—an equally absurd idea since he was in Nuremberg at the time.[81] The idea that Raubal's death had been an accident—that she had been playing around with Hitler's pistol and unintentionally pulled the trigger—also enjoyed currency. Winifred Wagner believed in this story, and Hitler himself appears to have found some consolation in it. When she was interviewed by American investigators in Berchtesgaden in May 1945, Angela Raubal told them that an accident was the most likely explanation for her daughter's death because Geli had had no reason to commit suicide.[82] The accident thesis is hardly plausible, however, since we know from Henriette Hoffmann that Geli Raubal was well acquainted with Hitler's pistol. The two women had even done target practice with it near Munich.[83]

If all the signs point towards a suicide, why did Raubal kill herself? Contemporaries and historians have racked their brains over this question. Some have tried to establish a connection between Raubal's death and Hitler's allegedly abnormal sexual proclivities. One key witness for this theory is Otto Strasser, who told representatives of the American Office of Strategic Studies in 1943 that Hitler had compelled Raubal to engage in perverse sexual practices and spiced up his tale with a series of disgusting details.[84] In his memoirs, Hanfstaengl also contended that Raubal had told him: "My uncle is a monster. No one can imagine the things he expects of me." Hanfstaengl illuminated this somewhat cryptic statement with an anecdote. On the way home after an evening the three of them had spent together, Hanfstaengl wrote, Hitler had issued wild threats against his enemies and underscored his words with a resounding crack of his riding crop. Hanfstaengl happened to be watching Raubal's face and was shocked to see an "expression of fear and disgust . . . that distorted her face at this whistling sound."[85] This was Hanfstaengl's none-too-subtle way of insinuating that Geli Raubal was the victim of Hitler's sado-masochistic lust. But Hanfstaengl also invented pornographic drawings by Hitler that allegedly showed Raubal in poses "that every professional model would have refused [to adopt]."[86]

Other observers have speculated that Raubal might have been jealous because Hitler had been courting other women and she feared that she was "beginning to lose her power over 'Uncle Alf.'"[87] But that would only be plausible if we assume that Geli Raubal had developed a deeper, romantic affection for Hitler—of which there is no evidence. It seems that the question of Raubal's motives will never be definitively answered. Most likely, Raubal felt unable to live up to the expectation of becoming a singer and was worn down by Hitler's need to control her, which restricted her freedom and hemmed in her own initiative. She may have felt that Prinzregentenstrasse was her "golden cage."[88] Perhaps, in an increasingly intolerable situation, she saw no other way out than to take her own life. At her mother's request, her body was taken to Vienna and buried on 23 September in the city's central cemetery.

Hitler did not attend the funeral, retreating instead for several days to the house of the *Völkischer Beobachter* publisher, Adolf Müller, on Tegernsee Lake. In his memoirs, his companion Heinrich Hoffmann remembered Hitler as seeming like a "totally broken man." There were even fears that Hitler might harm himself, and his chauffeur Julius Schreck confiscated his pistol. For a time Hitler was said to have even considered giving up his political career.[89]

That, at least, was the story, which also found its way into serious literature on Hitler. Joachim Fest wrote that "for weeks Hitler seemed close to a nervous breakdown and repeatedly decided to withdraw from politics."[90] But that idea does not accord with the fact that by 24 September, Hitler was already meeting with Goebbels and Göring in Berlin. Reportedly he was more withdrawn than usual but seemed fully in control of himself. And that evening he spoke in top form to 10,000 supporters in Hamburg.[91] Two days later, he travelled to Vienna incognito and laid flowers on Geli Raubal's grave.

His niece's death no doubt affected Hitler deeply, and his grief was real, not put on for show. He kept her room in Prinzregentenstrasse unchanged, and his servants were required to keep a fresh bouquet of flowers there at all times. Later, Hitler commissioned Munich sculptor Ferdinand Liebermann to create a bronze bust of Raubal. On the first anniversary of her death, Hitler visited her grave, accompanied by his half-sister and Goebbels. But after that, his period of mourning was over. The whole affair was never again directly mentioned in his entourage.[92]

The private tragedy did not put a damper on Hitler's political plans. On the contrary, he was able to make capital out of it, stylising himself once and for all as a politician who had foresworn personal happiness on behalf of his mission to serve the German people. This trick impressed even his closest friends within the party. In late October 1931, Goebbels noted after a conversation with Hitler: "Then he spoke of Geli. He loved her very much. She was his 'good comrade.' He had tears in his eyes . . . This man, at the pinnacle of success, is without any personal happiness, devoted only to the happiness of his friends."[93] Hitler also told Otto Wagener how much he missed Raubal: "Her cheery laughter was always a real joy, and her harmless chatter was such fun." But Hitler immediately added: "Now I'm completely free, internally and externally. Now I belong only to the German people and my mission."[94] In November 1931, Hess remarked that Geli Raubal had been Hitler's "sunshine" and that he would surely miss the few hours of relaxation with her in his own home. "Because his mission so totally occupies him," Hess went on, "the poor man can't grant himself the benefit of a marriage."[95] Hitler's strategy of cloaking himself in the aura of a man without a private life convinced not only his contemporaries. It also made its mark on history. How else to explain why all the serious Hitler biographers—from Heiden and Bullock to Fest and Kershaw—assumed that there was not much of interest to relate about the private life of this "non-person"?[96]

Nonetheless, as Fest wrote, Raubal's death was "one of the key moments of Hitler's life as an individual" which changed him, since his niece was the only woman besides his mother for whom he had felt deep emotion.[97] Thus Hitler's ability to love, if one could even use the phrase, was further limited, and Hitler himself increasingly isolated. In the words of Henriette Hoffmann, from that point on the "tender element" was missing in his life, and the "seed of inhumanity" planted.[98] But this was a far-fetched interpretation, which ignored the fact that in the Hotel Kaiserhof in the late summer of 1931, Hitler met a woman with whom he began to flirt straight away: Magda Quandt.

Apparently Hitler did not know that Goebbels had already begun an affair with the ex-wife of industrialist Günther Quandt in February of that year. For Magda Quandt's part, the attraction seems to have been mutual. Goebbels, at least, was jealous. "Magda loses herself a bit around the boss," he complained to his diary in late August 1931. "I'm suffering greatly . . . I didn't sleep a wink." A few days later he wrote: "Magda must invite the boss home and tell him about us. Otherwise love and a silly jealousy will come between us."[99] The clarifying talk took place in mid-September, only a few days before Geli Raubal's suicide. Magda Quandt told Hitler she intended to marry Goebbels, who noted happily: "Hitler resigned. He is very lonely. He has no luck with women . . . His angel, he said. He loves Magda. But he doesn't begrudge me my happiness. 'A clever and beautiful woman. She'll challenge you instead of hemming you in.' He embraced my hands, with tears in his eyes."[100]

On 19 December 1931, Magda Quandt and Joseph Goebbels got married. They had come to an understanding with Hitler, who served as best man: he became part of their relationship and could bask as an oft-invited guest in their affection. In Magda Goebbels, he had also found an attractive woman who could stand by his side on public occasions and take the role of a first lady once the Nazis had risen to power.[101] At the same time, Goebbels continued to ponder how he could help Hitler overcome the loss of Geli Raubal. In January 1932, the two men once again discussed "marriage questions." Goebbels noted: "He feels very lonely. Longing for a woman whom he never finds. Touching and moving. He likes Magda a lot. We have to find him a good woman. Someone like Magda."[102]

Hitler, however, reacted sensitively when he thought people were trying to pair him off with someone. "I like having beautiful women around me, but I can't stand it when someone tries to force something on me," he told the actress Leni Riefenstahl, with whom he had a rendezvous on the North Sea beach at Horumersiel in May 1932 and who became Hitler's star film director after he assumed power.[103] And what the Goebbelses did not know was that soon after Raubal's suicide, Hitler had intensified his relationship with a young Munich woman whom he had known for some time. She would play the most important role in Hitler's life of any woman, save his mother.

Eva Braun was born on 6 February 1912 as the middle of three daughters of the schoolteacher Friedrich Braun and his wife Franziska, a seamstress.[104] The household was affluent, and the children were baptised and raised as Catholics. From 1918 to 1922, Eva went to primary school; afterwards she attended the high school for girls on Munich's Tengstrasse. In 1928, she had a year of finishing school in the prestigious "Institute of English Fräuleins" in the town of Simbach on the German–Austrian border. There she not only learned how to run a household, but also typing and accountancy. In September 1929, she responded to a newspaper advertisement and was promptly taken on as an intern at Heinrich Hoffmann's atelier, Photohaus Hoffmann. In his memoirs, Hoffmann described her as "of medium build and very watchful of her waistline . . . Dark blond hair framed her round face. With her blue eyes, you could say that she was attractive, if somewhat doll-like. A standard sort of beauty like you see in popular advertisements."[105]

Probably in October 1929, several weeks after joining Hoffmann, Eva Braun met Hitler. Later, Braun described the meeting to her sister Ilse. One evening, as Eva climbed up a ladder to file away some documents, her boss appeared with a gentleman who stared quite directly at her legs. "I climbed down, and Hoffmann introduced us: 'Herr Wolf— our good little girl Eva.' Then he said: 'Do us a favour, Fräulein Braun, and fetch us some beer and meat loaf from the restaurant on the corner.'" While he ate, the stranger continued to devour her with his eyes, and after he left, Hoffmann asked her: "'Did you not guess who Herr Wolf really is? Don't you ever look at our photos? . . . It's Hitler himself, our Adolf Hitler!' 'That was *him*?' I replied."[106]

It is unclear whether this account is fact or fiction, but there is no doubting that the 40-year-old Hitler felt instantly drawn to Hoffmann's 18-year-old assistant. She may have reminded him of "Mimi" Reiter, and as he had done with her, Hitler turned on the paternal charm, paying Eva Braun compliments, giving her small gifts and taking her out every once in a while.[107] It was not until Geli Raubal's death that their relationship intensified, and opinions differ as to when and if Eva Braun became Hitler's lover. Christa Schroeder, who considered her boss to be an asexual being, always believed that the relationship was just for show. She even claimed that Braun had told her hairdresser that she had never had sex with Hitler, but that strains credibility.[108] Henriette Hoffmann, on the other hand, was convinced that the "love affair" started in the winter of 1931–2, only a few months after Raubal's suicide. Hoffmann also offered up a couple of details about their early days together: "After Geli's death, Frau Winter was in charge of Hitler's apartment, and she was a stickler for morals. Hitler had to do what a high school student does who wants to take a girl to his room in his parents' house. He had to get Frau Winter and her husband tickets to the theatre so he could enjoy a private hour with Eva."[109] But if Hitler tried to keep his affair secret from his housekeeper, he had no success. After the war, Anni Winter repeatedly testified that Braun and Hitler became intimate in the early months of 1932.[110] And if anyone would have known for sure, it was her. Eva Braun's biographer Heike Görtemaker has also uncovered evidence to suggest that a love affair commenced in early 1932.[111] But nothing is absolutely certain.

In contrast to Geli Raubal, Eva Braun was not allowed to accompany Hitler to public events, and from the very beginning Hitler was very discreet about the relationship, even amongst party friends. On the one hand, he felt this was necessary due to the sudden interest in his private life that his niece's suicide had whipped up. Moreover, the visible presence of a lover would have undermined his attempts to portray himself as a Führer who sacrificed his private life on behalf of his ceaseless service to the German nation. "I have another bride: Germany," he proclaimed over and over. "I *am* married: to the German people and its destiny."[112] His role model for this persona was most likely Wagner's operatic hero Rienzi. In Act Five of the opera, the popular tribune reacts to his sister Irene's accusation that he has never loved with the words:

Well I did love, too, oh Irene
Don't you remember my love?
I loved painfully my exalted bride
Because I saw her deeply humiliated
Outrageously mistreated, horribly disfigured
Rejected, dishonoured, abused and scorned! . . .
My life I devoted only to her
Only to her, my youth and strength as a man
For I wanted to see her, my exalted bride
Crowned the queen of the world
Know this: My bride's name is Rome![113]

Part of Hitler's strategy of self-concealment was his private and perhaps honest admission to his inner circle that he had "overcome the need to possess a woman physically."[114] Eva Braun was probably the ideal woman for the female role Hitler envisioned: she seemed to be willing not just to meet his sexual needs but also to play along with the masquerade. For Hitler, this was an easy relationship, initially without much commitment. When asked by his former superior officer and later assistant Fritz Wiedemann whether he did not find the bachelor's life troublesome, Hitler allegedly responded with a smile: "It has its advantages. And as far as love is concerned, I keep a girl in Munich."[115]

The year of decisions—1932—was full with election campaigning anyway. For long stretches of time, Hitler resided in Berlin's Hotel Kaiserhof near the Reich Chancellery, which he was soon to take over. He had little time for his girlfriend in Munich. Eva Braun felt neglected. In the latter half of the year, she allegedly tried to commit suicide with her father's pistol. Her sister Ilse claimed that Eva had been found on her parents' bed but that she had been able to summon a doctor, a brother-in-law of Heinrich Hoffmann, herself. He had her taken to hospital.[116]

Did Eva Braun really try to kill herself? Heinrich Hoffmann reported that Hitler, who had hurried to her sickbed, had asked the doctor the same question, and when the answer came in the affirmative, Hitler vowed to take better care of her in the future: "You heard it, Hoffmann. The girl did this out of love for me."[117] Christa Schroeder saw the incident as "blackmail": Eva Braun wanted to tie Hitler more closely to herself by faking a suicide attempt.[118] If that was Braun's intention, she succeeded. On the verge of gaining power, Hitler could ill afford another scandal casting a dubious light on his private life. He began spending more time with Braun.

On 1 January 1933, Braun and Hitler attended a performance of Wagner's *Meistersinger* in Munich's National Theatre, accompanied by Hess and his wife, Hoffmann and several other members of Hitler's entourage. Afterwards, they all celebrated at the Hanfstaengls. Ernst Hanfstaengl recalled that Hitler was "bright-spirited and entertaining as in the early '20s." In the Hanfstaengls' guest book, Hitler wrote "On the first day of the new year," and he assured his host: "This year belongs to us. I'll give you that in writing."[119]

II

Bids and Bluffs

"The endgame for power has begun," Joseph Goebbels wrote on 7 January 1932. "It may continue for the entire year. A game that will be played to the end with tempo, cleverness and a bit of finesse." These oft-quoted sentences are contained not in Goebbels's diary, but in his book *From the Hotel Kaiserhof to the Reich Chancellery*, published by Eher in 1934.[1] In substantially altering and stylising his original notes, Goebbels—the chief promoter of the Führer myth—tried to suggest that Hitler's inspired political instincts alone manoeuvred the NSDAP to power on 30 January 1933. Hitler's press director took the same line in his essay "With Hitler to Power," published by Eher Verlag in the autumn of 1933. Otto Dietrich praised the Führer as a "one-of-a-kind and unique personality" blessed with "instinctive anticipation." Hitler, Dietrich maintained, planned all his steps, maintained "absolute calm," and "wore down and quashed the opponents facing him with his iron will" until there was no longer anyone denying him his just deserts—the German chancellorship.[2]

This narrative had little to do with reality. Hitler's path to power was hardly an inevitable and triumphal march. It was a contest that could have ended either way. The National Socialists had declared 1932 to be "the year of decisions,"[3] and in five major elections the party had the opportunity to demonstrate its organisational and propagandistic strength. The NSDAP again achieved major successes, becoming by far the largest party in the Reichstag in the elections of late July 1932. The chancellor's office on Wilhelmstrasse did indeed seem ripe for the taking. But by inflexibly insisting on all-or-nothing and refusing to share power with anyone else, Hitler also sent his party down a dead-end street. In the elections of early November, the NSDAP suffered significant losses for the first time. Its aura of invincibility was tarnished, and the party's trust in its leadership shaken. The NSDAP went through its worst crisis since the ban on the party of 1923–4. By the end of 1932, the German economy also showed initial signs of recovery. The depths of the Depression seemed to lie in the past. Thus, there were good reasons to think that the danger posed by the Nazis could have been averted. "The development of this, the German year of 1932, will be an object of most intense study for future historians and politicians," the left-wing journalist Leopold Schwarzschild wrote in his weekly *Das Tage-Buch* on 31 December. Only with the benefit of hindsight, Schwarzschild predicted, would humanity be able to understand "what historic miracle deflected the line [of events] at the last minute."[4]

At the start of the year, Hitler had encouraged optimism. In his New Year's address, he contended that Germany was preparing "to go National Socialist with great rapidity." The party had fifteen million supporters—"a triumph without parallel in the history of our people."[5] In an interview with the Japanese newspaper *Tokyo Asahi Shimbum* on 3 January, he said he was confident that his party "would soon seize power in Germany . . . and found a new, Third Reich."[6] Hitler, knew, however, that he was dependent on support from others, including business circles. In the autumn of 1931, as Hess reported, he had already put a lot of effort, "with great success," into "undermining the remaining pillars of support for the current government in the industrial and banking worlds."[7] In fact, it was Chancellor Brüning's misguided policy of deflation, which worsened the Depression, that had cost him support from big business, but that did not mean that the NSDAP immediately profited. Many entrepreneurs remained deeply sceptical about a movement whose leading representatives spoke with forked tongues where economic policies were concerned. To improve his party's image and recommend himself as a future head of government, therefore, Hitler accepted an invitation on 26 January 1932 to speak to the Industrial Club of Düsseldorf, the meeting point for the economic elite of Rhineland-Westphalia.[8]

Some 700 people packed the large ballroom in Düsseldorf's Park Hotel. Hitler himself had to enter through a side door because Nazi supporters and opponents were clashing violently in front of the building. To fit in, he had swapped his brown uniform for a dark frock coat and striped trousers. Anyone who expected him to talk about what measures a Hitler government would introduce to end the Depression came away sorely disappointed, however. In his two-and-a-half-hour speech, Hitler merely reiterated what he had said on similar occasions, for instance to Hamburg's National Club of 1919: that only a strong state could set the parameters for a flourishing economy, and that whoever believed in the concept of private property had to reject the idea of democracy. "It is nonsense to build upon the concept of achievement, the value of personality and thus personal authority in an economic sense," Hitler told his audience, "while rejecting the authority of personality and replacing it with the law of greater numbers—democracy—in a political sense." Hitler once again summoned the bogeyman of Bolshevism, which, if it continued to be successful, "would subject the world to a transformation as total as Christianity had in its day." The National Socialist movement was the only force that could prevent Germany from sinking into "Bolshevist chaos." Hitler added: "And if people accuse us of being impatient, we proudly embrace that charge. We have made an undying vow to pull out the last roots of Marxism in Germany." Hitler studiously avoided any openly anti-Semitic pronouncements and only hinted at his ambition of conquering "living space" in Russia. On the contrary, he ended his speech by stressing that a revitalised Germany under his leadership would be prepared to live in "friendship and peace" with its neighbours.[9]

A number of legends have sprung up around Hitler's appearance in the Düsseldorf Industrial Club. Most of them originated in Dietrich's essay "With Hitler to Power." Dietrich had been present at the speech, and his supposedly authentic account described Hitler whipping an initially cool audience into a frenzy. "Their faces began to blush, their eyes hung on the Führer's lips and you could feel their hearts warming," Dietrich wrote. "At the beginning they only put their hands together hesitantly, but soon salvos of applause erupted. When Adolf Hitler was finished, he had won a battle." For Dietrich, 26 January 1932 was the "memorable day" on which Hitler achieved his "breakthrough" with the western German captains of industry: "The ice was broken— the National Socialist idea had found fertile soil in important and influential circles within the system."[10]

But the American historian Henry A. Turner and others following in his footsteps have corrected this outmoded narrative about the relationship between National Socialism and major German industry.[11]

By no means had the entire economic elite of the Ruhr Valley attended Hitler's speech. The early Hitler admirer Fritz Thyssen was present of course, as were Ernst Poensgen and Albert Vögler from United Steelworks, Ernst Brandi from the Mining Association and mining magnate Karl Haniel, who was also the Industrial Club's chairman. But a number of leading representatives remained conspicuously absent, including Gustav Krupp von Bohlen und Halbach, the chairman of the Reich Association of German Industry, as well as the steelworks manager Paul Reusch, Carl Duisberg from IG Farben, Fritz Springorum from Hoesch Steelworks and mining entrepreneur Paul Silverberg.[12]

The crowd's reaction to Hitler was also by no means as positive as Dietrich's report had its readers believe. When Thyssen concluded his short word of thanks with the word's "Heil, Herr Hitler," most of those in attendance found the gesture embarrassing.[13] Hitler's speech also did little to increase major industrialists' generosity when it came to party donations. Even Dietrich himself admitted as much in his far more sober memoirs from 1955: "At the ballroom's exit, we asked for donations, but all we got were some well-meant but insignificant sums. Above and beyond that there can be no talk of 'big business' or 'heavy industry' significantly supporting, to say nothing of financing, Hitler's political struggle."[14] On the contrary, in the spring 1932 Reich presidential elections, prominent representatives of industry like Krupp and Duisberg came out in support of Hindenburg and donated several million marks to his campaign.[15]

The main political topic in the early months of 1932 was whether Hindenburg would be re-elected. To spare the 85-year-old the strain of a second election, Chancellor Brüning had hit upon the idea of asking the Reichstag to extend his period of office. That, however, required a change in the constitution and a two-thirds majority, which was only possible if the National Socialists and the radical right-wing nationalists were on board.[16] On the evening of 6 January, Brüning sent Defence and Interior Minister Wilhelm Groener to meet Hitler in order to persuade the NSDAP chairman to support the idea. "A likeable impression, modest, orderly man who wants the best," was Groener's take on Hitler. "External appearance of an ambitious auto-didact. Hitler's intentions and goals are good but he's an enthusiast, glowing and multifaceted."[17] A series of negotiations commenced. Hitler initially seemed willing to compromise but he made his support for Hindenburg's candidacy contingent upon the Reichstag being dissolved and fresh elections called. Brüning was having none of that, since in the event of the expected NSDAP election victory he would no longer have a parliamentary majority tolerating him.

On 12 January, Hitler informed Brüning that despite "his great personal respect for the Reich president," he had no choice but to reject the suggested extension of the term of office. As a reason, he cited constitutional concerns. These were well founded but sounded hollow coming from Hitler's mouth since the NSDAP chairman had never left any doubt that as soon as possible after taking power, the National Socialists intended to do away with the constitution.[18] Hitler's decision, however, confronted him with a dilemma. If Hindenburg did decide to run for a second term despite his advanced age, Hitler would have to throw his hat in the ring, and the risk of losing a direct duel with the "victor of Tannenberg," who was very popular among right-wingers, was great. Hitler's aura as the seemingly invincible Führer rushing from one victory to the next might be damaged. On 19 January, Goebbels discussed the "Reich presidency question" for the first time with Hitler: "I'm pleading for him to run. He alone will take Hindenburg out of the running. We calculate with numbers, but the numbers are deceiving. Hitler has to become Reich president. That's the only way. That's our slogan. He hasn't decided yet. I'll continue to drill away."[19]

Much to Goebbels's dismay, Hitler put off making a decision for weeks and weeks. Apparently he was more sceptical about his chances than his head of propaganda. "Hitler is waiting too long," Goebbels complained on 28 January. Two days later, he noted: "When will Hitler decide? Does he not have the nerve? If so, we need to give it to him."[20] It was not until 3 February, when Goebbels had largely concluded preparations for the election in the Brown House, that Hitler signalled his willingness to run against Hindenburg. The announcement of Hitler's decision was delayed until after Hindenburg had declared his candidacy and the SPD had come out in support of him. The logic behind this was obvious: if the pro-democracy camp supported the man they had so vigorously opposed in 1925, Hitler would be all the better able to claim that only he represented the nationalist right wing. "First Hindenburg has to commit himself, and the SPD has to come out in support," Goebbels noted. "Only then our decision. Machiavelli. But correct."[21]

Similar calculations also led Hindenburg to delay announcing *his* decision for as long as he could. In late January, he told Brüning that he would only accept a nomination to run for president if it "did not meet with the joint resistance of the entire right wing."[22] It was not enough for the Reich president that a petition in early February calling on him to run, which was sponsored by Berlin Lord Mayor Heinrich Sahm, quickly attracted more than three million signatures. It was only on 15 February, when the Kyffhäuser League, the umbrella association of German veterans' groups, pledged their loyalty that Hindenburg announced that he would seek re-election. "A day of fateful significance for Germany," Reich Chancellery State Secretary Hermann Pünder noted in his journal.[23] Hitler waited another week before having Goebbels proclaim his candidacy in a speech in Berlin's Sportpalast on the evening of 22 February. "Ten minutes of enthusiasm, ovations, the people stood up and cheered me," Goebbels wrote in his diary.[24] "The roof almost caved in. It's fantastic. If this keeps up, we'll win."

But one hurdle remained. To run for the office, Hitler had to be a German citizen. In July 1930, Wilhelm Frick—then Thuringian interior minister—had made a misguided attempt to secure Hitler citizenship by nominating him commissioner for gendarmes in the town of Hildburghausen. When this failed bit of foolishness became public knowledge in February 1932, people were baffled. In the meantime, the party leadership believed it had hit on a far more elegant solution. The NSDAP interior minister of Braunschweig, who was part of a coalition government with the DNVP and the DVP, was instructed to have Hitler made a civil servant, which would have been a first step towards German citizenship. The original plan was to appoint him extraordinary professor of "Organic Social Theory and Politics" at Braunschweig's Technical University.[25] But that was too much even for the NSDAP's coalition partners. Instead, Hitler was appointed government counsel for Braunschweig's consulate in Berlin. There, on the afternoon of 26 February, Hitler accepted his appointment certificate and swore to "be loyal to the Reich and Land constitutions, obey the law and faithfully fulfil the duties" of his office.[26] With that his official "duties" were already over. He immediately applied for a leave of absence, which was granted as a matter of course, until after the Reich presidential elections. The appointment was only a means to a political end. "Just got word that he's been named Braunschw[eig] counsel—which makes him citizen Hitler," Goebbels cynically noted in his diary on 26 February. "Congratulations."[27]

Alfred Hugenberg's nationalists were excited by neither Hindenburg nor Hitler and nominated a candidate of their own: Theodor Duesterberg, the vice-chairman of the Stahlhelm veterans' association. With that the fragile Harzburg Front finally fell apart. The KPD once again put forward their chairman, Ernst Thälmann. The SPD and the Centre Party, however, decided to forgo candidates of their own and support Hindenburg. In the party newspaper *Vorwärts* the SPD leadership declared:

Hitler in place of Hindenburg means chaos and panic in Germany and the whole of Europe, an extreme worsening of the economic crisis and of unemployment, and the most acute danger of bloodshed within our own people and abroad. Hitler in place of Hindenburg means the triumph of the reactionary part of the bourgeoisie over the progressive middle classes and the working class, the destruction of all civil liberties, of the press and of political, union and cultural organisations, increased exploitation and wage slavery.

The declaration ended with the slogan: "Defeat Hitler! Vote for Hindenburg!"[28]

The political fronts of 1925 had been reversed. "What a bizarre country," Thea Sternheim noted in February 1932. "Hindenburg as the pet of the pro-democracy camp. Years ago when I heard of his election . . . I threw up out of fear and horror. Today, in the face of the fascist threat, a democrat has to anxiously hope for Hindenburg's re-election."[29] The SPD's support for Hindenburg was exactly what the NSDAP needed to go on the offensive. In the Reichstag session on 23 February, Goebbels caused a scandal when he declared that Hindenburg had "betrayed the interests of his former voters" and clearly aligned himself with Social Democracy. "Tell me who praises you, and I'll tell who you are!" Goebbels sneered, adding that Hindenburg was drawing praise from the "gutter press in Berlin and the party of deserters." In response to this defamation, SPD deputy Kurt Schumacher, who had been badly wounded after volunteering for military service in 1914, spoke up angrily: "If there is one thing we admire about National Socialism it's the fact that it has succeeded, for the first time in German politics, in the complete mobilisation of human stupidity."[30] Goebbels refused to apologise for his outburst and was sent out of the chamber. Hitler did not conceal his delight, gushing, "Now battle has been declared."[31]

Immediately thereafter, the National Socialists kicked off their campaign, making use of the latest technology. Goebbels distributed 50,000 gramophone records of him delivering a campaign speech. A ten-minute sound film, designed to be shown on big-city squares, depicted Hitler as the coming saviour of the German people. Shrill posters reinforced the central message that Nazi propaganda had been advancing since mid-February: "Down with the system! Power to the National Socialists!"[32] In his first campaign speech, on 27 February at the Sportpalast, which the *Völkischer Beobachter* covered in a story headlined "The Signal to Attack," Hitler told 25,000 listeners that the "gigantic battle ahead" was not just about the presidency but about the "system" created on 9 November 1918, which in its thirteen years of existence had led Germany to the brink of the abyss. This was the tenor of all Hitler's subsequent speeches: "For thirteen years we've been plaintiffs. Now the hour is at hand, my ethnic comrades. On 13 March, after thirteen years, we must become judges over that which has been destroyed by one side and over those internal values of our people which the other side has built up again!"[33] Describing the audience's reaction, Goebbels noted: "The people were beside themselves. An hour of euphoria. Hitler is a true man. I love him."[34]

Between 1 and 11 March, Hitler maintained an exhausting schedule, speaking in Hamburg, Stettin (Szczecin), Breslau (Wrocław), Leipzig, Bad Blankenburg, Weimar, Frankfurt am Main, Nuremberg, Stuttgart, Cologne, Dortmund and Hanover. He attracted huge crowds wherever he went. The *Hamburger Tageblatt* newspaper wrote about his reception in the Sagebielsäle hall, which was packed to the rafters: "A crowd of many thousands—a grey, dull, suffering army—seems to want to wipe away all its tears, anxiety and worry in a communal scream, which is both greeting and homage at once."[35] The *Schlesische Zeitung* wrote about Hitler's appearance in Breslau's Jahrhunderthalle, before which Hitler kept the 50,000 audience members waiting for hours:

They came from far and wide, from Hirschberg, Waldenburg, Sulau and Militsch, from all parts of Silesia. Many endured hours of travel in cramped circumstances or on the roof of an omnibus in order to hear their Führer . . . The people waited hour upon hour, the mood festive, not impatient. People brought lunch and dinner with them. Ambulant merchants pushed their way through the crowd selling fruit and refreshments. Orderlies and nurses stood at the ready. It was a vivid, lively scene.[36]

Even more than during the Reichstag elections in September 1930, Hitler's campaign stops in the spring of 1932 were mass spectacles. For many Germans, even those who had not yet become party members, seeing Hitler was a must. They projected their desires onto him as their national saviour, someone who would release the country from misery and lead it to new prosperity. Hitler knew how to exploit these desires, denouncing the thirteen years of the Weimar Republic in ever-darker terms as a time of unmitigated decay and contrasting it with the bright future of a unified German "ethnic community."

The chairman of the NSDAP studiously avoided attacking Hindenburg, however, having assured the Reich president in late February that he would do battle in "chivalric fashion."[37] Hitler was well aware that he could not afford to damage his relationship with Hindenburg beyond repair—for he could never come to power without permission from the president, should he fail to win the election. Thus he rarely passed up an opportunity to express his admiration for the former field marshal. At the same time, he indicated that Hindenburg was a man of the past whereas the future belonged to himself and his movement. "Venerable old man," Hitler rhetorically addressed the president at his appearance in Nuremberg on 7 March, "you no longer bear the weight of Germany's future on your shoulders. We must bear it on *our* shoulders. You can no longer assume responsibility for us; we, the war generation—must take it on ourselves. Venerable old man, you can no longer protect those who we want to destroy. Therefore, step aside and clear the way!"[38]

Hitler's primary target for attack was the SPD, which he claimed was hiding behind the Hindenburg myth in an attempt to avoid taking responsibility. "Believe me," he sneered in every one of his campaign speeches, "if I had done nothing in my life other than to lay this party at the field marshal's feet, it would be a historic achievement. What a lovely transformation this party has undergone! What once was the party of the revolutionary proletariat is now a party of dutiful voters for the 85-year-old field marshal they used to hate so intensely."[39] Hitler was consciously trying to drive a wedge between the Social Democratic leadership and their constituency. He knew that if SPD voters cast their ballots for Hindenburg, his chances of electoral victory were slim.

Nevertheless Nazi propaganda was optimistic. "The current, continually repeated message is: Adolf Hitler is not only our candidate—he is the future president," Goebbels wrote in a memo to Gau functionaries. "The entire party's confidence in victory must be elevated into blind faith."[40] Goebbels himself vacillated between hope and anxiety. "The prognoses for Hitler, especially among p[arty] c[omrades], reach the levels of the fantastic," he noted on 6 March. "I see a danger in this. We shouldn't get ahead of ourselves and underestimate the enemy."[41] But only a few days later, Goebbels was confident of victory: "Spoke late at night with Hitler. He is in Stuttgart. Going from one triumph to the next. Everything is good. This will be a success."[42] Hitler was also convinced he could beat Hindenburg. In an interview with *New York Post* correspondent Hubert Knickerbocker on the eve of the election, 12 March, he predicted that he and Hindenburg would both get around 12 million votes and thus fail to secure an absolute majority. But in the run-off election on 10 April, Hindenburg would not have a chance. It had been irresponsible of Brüning, Hitler said, to have convinced the old man to stand for re-election, when his defeat was so easily foreseeable.[43]

Given such high expectations, the result of the election must have shocked the entire NSDAP: with 18 million votes (49.8 per cent) Hindenburg soundly defeated Hitler, who got just over 11 million (30.1 per cent). Nonetheless, Hindenburg just missed out on an absolute majority so a run-off was required. Thälmann had received 5 million votes (13.2 per cent) and Duesterberg 2.5 million (6.8 per cent).[44] The disappointment among Nazi supporters was so great that in many places swastika flags were flown at half mast.[45] Goebbels wrote in his diary: "We are beaten. Terrible prospects . . . The party comrades are depressed and downcast. A major coup is needed. Phoned Hitler. He's completely disappointed by the result. We set our sights too high."[46] On election night, Hitler was already at work on an announcement to the party that downplayed the disaster. The NSDAP, he pointed out, had doubled their share of the vote compared to September 1930: "Today, we have risen to become the undisputed strongest party in Germany." Hitler called upon NSDAP members to renew "the attack upon the front of Centrists and Marxists in the sharpest form." The party could not afford to lose a single day. Every party member had to give "his all and his utmost" if the Nazi movement was to be victorious.[47]

After 1933, Otto Wagener retroactively described Hitler's reaction to the March 1932 election result as his "finest hour." On that "fateful evening," Wagener opined, "the Führer rose above himself" and restored one's faith with his "uncompromising, volcanic will."[48] Ernst Hanfstaengl, however, experienced a very different Hitler at home on Prinzregentenstrasse on 13 March. Hitler sat brooding in a darkened room like "a disappointed and discouraged gambler who had wagered beyond his means."[49] In a speech at an NSDAP event in Weimar on 15 March, Hitler was forced to admit that he had "miscalculated," having been unable to believe that Social Democrats, "down to a man," would vote for Hindenburg.[50] Indeed, SPD followers had adhered to the instructions of their party leadership with remarkable discipline.

Between the initial election and the run-off, the idea briefly arose of Crown Prince Wilhelm running for president. In a letter to Hitler, Wilhelm II's eldest son asked the Nazi leader for support, and Hitler apparently agreed to stand aside if Hindenburg did likewise. He may have speculated that if he helped the crown prince become president, the crown prince would appoint him German chancellor out of gratitude. This plan was predestined to fail. Hindenburg had no intention of standing aside shortly before he was certain to win re-election, and Wilhelm II vetoed the idea from his Dutch exile in Doorn. Crown Prince Wilhelm then officially endorsed Hitler.[51]

In an interview with the Berlin correspondent of the *Daily Express*, Sefton Delmer, on 21 March, Hitler declared that he would run a campaign the likes of which the world had never seen.[52] Hindenburg had declared an "Easter truce," a moratorium on campaigning lasting from 20 March to 3 April, so by that time there was only a week left of activity before the run-off election. The lack of time, as Goebbels noted in his diary, required "completely new" methods of propaganda. The primary innovation was to charter an aeroplane so that Hitler could appear at a number of mass events every day.[53] On 3 April, Hitler embarked in a Junkers D-1720 from Munich on his first "flying tour of Germany," which would take him to more than twenty major campaign stops from the Saxon Nazi strongholds Dresden, Leipzig, Chemnitz and Plauen to Berlin and Potsdam, then via Pomerania to Lauenberg, Elbing and Königsberg in East Prussia. On 6 April, he flew back to southern Germany, appearing in Würzburg, Nuremberg and Regensburg. The following day supporters could see him in Frankfurt am Main, Darmstadt and Ludwigshafen. The day after that, he appeared in Düsseldorf, Essen and Münster, and on 9 April, the last day of campaigning, he spoke in Böblingen, Schwenningen and Stuttgart. "No one was able to avoid this wave of propaganda," wrote Otto Dietrich, who had helped organise the flying tour. "It awakened sporting interests and spoke to the masses' need for sensation as much as it addressed people's political interests . . . It was a form of political propaganda that left even American methods in its shadow."[54]

Indeed, this new strategy would prove to be extraordinarily successful. Hitler was said to have spoken to 1.5 million people within a few days. Between 150,000 and 200,000 people attended Hitler's speech in Berlin's Lustgarten on 4 April—the event was also captured on sound film.[55] There would be three other flying tours in 1932, and they helped popularise the Führer cult. The slogan "Hitler over Germany," which party newspapers published in screaming headlines, suggested not only that Hitler was omnipresent: it also symbolised his claim to be above classes and parties and anticipated the coming "ethnic community." The fact that the Nazis were the only party to follow the American model and use the aeroplane as a campaign tool also lent them an aura of visionary modernity. And the fact that Hitler never cancelled an event, even when the weather made flying risky, solidified the myth that he was a "national saviour" willing to sacrifice himself and unafraid of any danger. The audience at such events was usually kept waiting for hours, after which—in the words of historian Gerhard Paul—Hitler "would descend from the clouds in his plane like a messiah and announce his message of salvation."[56]

Hitler drove himself to complete exhaustion. "My God, how this man works himself into the ground," remarked Winifred Wagner. "Anyone familiar with his antipathy for flying knows what a sacrifice that was for him!"[57] Indeed, in contrast to the heroic legends spread, above all, by Otto Dietrich,[58] Hitler was very afraid of flying—something

his entourage was at pains to conceal. Delmer, the only foreign journalist to accompany Hitler on one of his flying tours, recalled how the
others on board the Lufthansa plane captained by Hans Baur fawned
over Hitler, trying to distract him. Hitler requited their efforts with
irritated disregard. Delmer described him sitting and staring indifferently out of the window, his chin in his right hand and cotton balls in
his ears, barely moving except to scratch his neck now and then. "It
was an entirely new picture of Hitler for me, and a complete contrast
to the glad-hand extrovert who had said goodbye to Magda Goebbels
and the others at Tempelhof," Delmer wrote. "Since that time I have
travelled with many of the top statesmen of the world. But never again
have I seen such a contrast between the public and the private figure
as in Hitler." As soon as the plane landed, Hitler's demeanour abruptly
changed. He straightened his back and once more assumed his "Führer
posture":

> Here he stood bareheaded, erect and unsmiling, his shoulders squared
> back, his mouth set in martial resolution, his hands raised to the salute.
> Then as the roars of the welcoming crowd swelled to a crescendo he
> went over to phase two of his pose. His eyes widened to show their
> whites and a "light" came into them. A light intended to denote kindly
> understanding of people's needs, fearless confidence, the light in the
> eyes of a Messiah predestined to lead Germany to its place in the sun.[59]

Local dignitaries usually showed up to meet Hitler's plane. Young
girls would give him bouquets of flowers, while SA bands would provide
appropriate music. Frequently, Communist protestors would slow
Hitler's motorcade during the trip from the landing strip to wherever
he was appearing. In the Baltic Sea port of Elbing, for example,
Delmer witnessed Hitler's bodyguards, under the command of Sepp
Dietrich, jumping from their cars to beat demonstrating workers with
plastic truncheons and brass knuckles.[60] The police did nothing to
stop them. It was an indication that the National Socialists already
felt like the masters of Germany, entitled to take the law into their
own hands.

In his speeches, Hitler repeated his never-ending complaints about
thirteen years of alleged financial mismanagement in Germany,
combined with promises to clean up the "party gang" as soon as he

came to power. It was taxing for his entourage to have to listen to the nearly identical tirades, varied only slightly to reflect where he was speaking. In Potsdam, for example, he compared the development of the NSDAP to the rise of the small state of Brandenburg which became the global power Prussia. "When we began, we were small, disdained and ridiculed, and we slowly worked our way up to become a National Socialist movement," Hitler said. "Today we have more than 11 million people behind us. The largest organisation Germany has ever seen marches under our banner."[61]

In early April, Hitler was put in an uncomfortable position when the left-liberal newspaper *Welt am Montag* published a bill from the Hotel Kaiserhof under the headline "This Is How Hitler Lives." According to the bill, Hitler and his entourage had spent 4,008 reichsmarks within ten days in March 1932. The figure was in fact exaggerated. The bills from the hotel for the years 1931 and 1932 have been preserved, and they show that Hitler and the three or four people who usually accompanied him typically spent between 606 and 829 marks for a four-day stay. For the five days between 28 April and 2 May 1932, Hitler paid 837 marks for five people and seven rooms.[62] Nonetheless, the sums were considerable and stood in marked contrast to Hitler's image as a man of the people with simple tastes who had retained his modest lifestyle. In a declaration on 7 April, the NSDAP chairman hastily declared the published bill a fake, and in his speeches, he continued to contrast himself with the "bigwigs" from the other parties as an unworldly politician who did not have any wealth of his own: "I don't need any—I live like a bird in the wild."[63]

The results of the election announced on the evening of 10 April were less disappointing for the National Socialists than those of 13 March. Hindenburg was re-elected as expected with a 53 per cent majority, but Hitler had gained around 2 million additional ballots and increased his share of the vote to 36.8 per cent—he seems to have won over the majority of Duesterberg's support after the latter withdrew his candidacy. Thälmann only got 10.2 per cent, after many KPD supporters boycotted the election.[64] The results of the vote did nothing to calm the nerves of defenders of the Weimar Republic, however. "Yesterday Hindenburg was re-elected in Germany, but despite that success, what horrific growth of the Hitler party," wrote Thea Sternheim from Paris. "The battle is not over yet, not by a long shot."[65]

The NSDAP leadership regained some of their former confidence. "An overwhelming victory for us . . ." Goebbels commented. "Hitler is entirely happy. Now we have a springboard for the Prussian elections."[66]

There were state elections on 24 April not only in Prussia, but in Bavaria, Württemberg and Anhalt as well, and voters in Hamburg were choosing a new mayor. The day after the 10 April result, Goebbels was already gearing up for the next round of polls: "14 days of election propaganda. We want to produce our masterpiece."[67] On 16 April, Hitler set off on his second flying tour, this time including the provinces, where he sparked enormous interest. "The masses stood for seven hours waiting for the Führer," reported the *Völkischer Beobachter* about an event in Donauwörth in southern Bavaria.[68] But Hitler concentrated his efforts on Prussia, the biggest and most important of the German states. The poll, he emphasised, would determine the destiny of Prussia, and he promised to topple the governing SPD-led coalition under Otto Braun and continue the legacy of "Friedrich the Great's Prussia, which had been a unique model of cleanliness, order and discipline for centuries." Prussia, Hitler thundered, had been a "standard-bearer of German freedom" in the 1813 campaign against Napoleon, and it would likewise become "a standard-bearer of the new, great social unification of the German nation."[69]

The Nazis celebrated major electoral gains in the elections of 24 April. In Prussia, they improved their share of the vote from 1.8 per cent in 1928 to 36.3 per cent, taking 162 seats and becoming the largest party in the Landtag. The coalition between the SPD, the Centre and the State Party lost their majority, but formed the acting government because the NSDAP lacked the absolute majority needed to force the election of a new state president. In Bavaria, the BVP got 32.6 per cent and just edged out the NSDAP, whose share of the vote rose from 6.1 to 32.5 per cent. In Württemberg, the Nazis received 26.4 per cent of the vote and became the strongest party, and in the Social Democratic stronghold Hamburg, the NSDAP took 31.2 per cent, surpassing the SPD's 30.2 per cent. The best result came in Anhalt, where the party received 40.9 per cent of ballots cast.[70] Yet despite these impressive results, the Nazis failed to convert their strength into positions in government in Prussia, Bavaria, Württemberg or Hamburg. Anhalt was the only place in which they succeeded in replacing the Social Democratic state president. Amidst all the euphoria over the NSDAP's "phenomenal victory," Goebbels's diary betrays a certain helplessness: "What now? Something has to happen. We have to gain power. Otherwise we will triumph ourselves to death."[71]

As was often the case, unexpected external events rather than any ingenious inspiration from Hitler came to the NSDAP's assistance. Hindenburg and Brüning fell out because the Reich president was angry that he had been re-elected with Social Democratic and Catholic Centrist votes rather than those of right-wing nationalists for whom he felt the greatest affinity. "What an ass I was to stand a second time," Hindenburg is reported to have remarked.[72] On 11 April, when Brüning congratulated Hindenburg in the name of his cabinet, the former field marshal was visibly irritated and signalled that the German chancellor's days were numbered.[73]

The issue of a potential ban on the SA and SS worsened the mood between Hindenburg and Brüning. On 17 March, Prussian Interior Minister Carl Severing ordered the NSDAP's and the SA's offices in Prussia searched. The material confiscated showed that the SA had been put on high alert on the day of the 13 March election. Hitler protested against the search order but also called upon the SA and SS not to let themselves be "provoked into breaking the law."[74] At a conference in Berlin on 5 April, the interior ministers of the German states, and in particular those of Prussia and Bavaria, lobbied Reich interim Interior Minister Groener to do something about the Nazi paramilitary organisations. After much humming and hawing, Groener decided to act. In a memo to Brüning on 10 April, he suggested that Hindenburg's re-election was an auspicious moment to rein in the "Brownshirt columns." It took a considerable amount of persuading, but Brüning finally convinced Hindenburg that a ban was necessary, and on 13 April, the president issued an emergency decree for the "Assurance of State Authority," which dissolved all the paramilitary organisations of the NSDAP.[75]

Count Harry Kessler was surprised "that the issue could be resolved so quickly with the stroke of a pen" and that the SA and SS allowed themselves to be disarmed "as timidly as lambs." Kessler decided that this reflected "Hitler's weak feminine character," which made the Nazi chairman, like Wilhelm II before him, "a big mouth with nothing to back it up when the situation turned serious."[76] Kessler could hardly have been more wrong in his assessment of both the political situation and Hitler. The National Socialists were informed about the imminent ban and had sufficient time to take counter-measures. Overnight the Brownshirts may have disappeared from Germany's streets, but the organisational cohesion of the SA and the SS remained intact, and their members continued to be active under the general umbrella of the party. The emergency decree thus actually did little to dissolve the organisations.[77] In an address on 13 April, Hitler made it clear that he saw the ban as a temporary impediment and that the cards would be reshuffled after the Landtag elections on 24 April. He therefore instructed his followers not to give "those who momentarily hold power any excuses to cancel the elections." Hitler promised: "If you do your duty, our propaganda will redirect this attack by General Groener a thousand-fold back upon himself and his allies."[78]

Hitler knew that Hindenburg had signed the decree against his better judgement and that there was great opposition to the ban within the Reichswehr leadership. On 15 April, Hindenburg had ordered Groener to review whether Social Democratic militias like the Reich Banner Black-Red-Gold should be banned as well. The tone of Hindenburg's order was anything but cordial, and included with it was incriminating material against the Reich Banner, which Hindenburg had been given by Army Commander-in-Chief General Kurt von Hammerstein.[79] What ultimately sealed the fate of Groener—and with him that of the entire Brüning cabinet—was the fact that he lost the support of his political patron, the head of the Ministerial Bureau in the Defence Ministry, General Kurt von Schleicher. Schleicher opposed the ban because he viewed the SA street fighters as a potentially useful tool for rebuilding Germany's military might, and he began to actively undermine Groener. Schleicher also continued to advocate tying the NSDAP to a governing coalition as a means of "taming" the party. In this he was of one mind with Hindenburg, who had long pushed for the cabinet to be expanded to the political right and who blamed Brüning for relying on the SPD to tolerate his government.[80]

On 28 April, Schleicher secretly met with Hitler to discuss the conditions under which the NSDAP chairman would join or at least tolerate a governing coalition. According to Goebbels, the conversation—in which Kurt von Hammerstein also took part—went well, and agreement was reached. In May Goebbels reported that the two generals "were continuing to stir things up . . . Brüning and Groener must go!" At a second secret meeting on 7 May, Hitler, Schleicher, Hindenburg's state secretary, Otto Meissner, and the president's son, Oskar von Hindenburg, scripted the demise of the Brüning government. Goebbels summarised: "Brüning is to fall this week. The old man will revoke his trust. Schleicher is throwing himself behind that . . . Then there will be a presidential cabinet. The Reichstag is dissolved. The emergency laws revoked. We will be free to act and can deliver our *coup de grâce*."[81] Hitler had refused to join the government but he had agreed to tolerate a more right-wing, interim presidential cabinet if fresh elections were scheduled and the ban on the SA and SS lifted. Hitler could be more than satisfied with this arrangement. He had not tied himself down and still held all the trump cards. "The boss is relaxed and good-humoured," Goebbels noted. "We're conferring over the next election campaign. It's going to be a huge hit."[82]

But the conspiracy did not go to plan. Brüning was able to stave off his demise by warning Hindenburg of the negative foreign-policy effects his dismissal would have, and by threatening to make the former field marshal's ingratitude known to the Reichstag.[83] The German parliament convened once again on 9 May. In his role as speaker for the NSDAP faction, Göring directly attacked Groener and demanded that the ban on the SA and SS be lifted. Groener delivered his rebuttal the following day, but weakened by illness and constantly distracted by jeers from Nazi deputies, he did not make a very good impression. "Unfortunately, Groener was catastrophically bad in defending his position in front of parliament," wrote the German State Party deputy and post-war German President Theodor Heuss. "We knew he couldn't speak off the cuff, which is why he mostly read out statements. But he was completely agitated, and his head was covered in bandages because of boils. He looked awful, tried to speak extemporaneously and was unable to finish his sentences because he was constantly interrupted."[84] After this disastrous performance, Groener had to go, and Schleicher and Hammerstein lobbied for his dismissal. "So far so good," Goebbels joked. "If the cloak falls so does the duke."[85] On 12 May, Groener announced that he would step down as Reich defence minister. However, he wanted to stay on as interior minister. Hindenburg had departed that day for his family's estate in East Prussian Neudeck, so the decision was postponed. To all intents and purposes, though, Groener's career was over on 12 May, and with him the Brüning cabinet had lost its most important pillar.[86]

While Hindenburg was in Neudeck, Brüning's enemies continued to "burrow away" at the ground beneath his feet.[87] Goebbels's diaries reveal how systematically they went about their work: "The crisis is going according to script . . . A series of calls with Hitler. He is very satisfied" (14 May). "Everyone is celebrating Pentecost. Except Brüning who's beginning to wobble. Time to give him a push" (18 May). "Mission Schleicher going well. Brüning completely isolated. Desperately looking for new ministers. Schleicher refused Defence. He's going the whole hog" (19 May). "Schleicher continues to undermine. A list of ministers is being discussed . . . Poor Brüning. He's on short rations" (20 May).[88] On 25 May, Werner von Alvensleben, a Schleicher intimate who served as a contact with the National Socialists, reported that Brüning would be "out the door" in three days' time. He also had a finished cabinet list with the name of the new chancellor: Franz von Papen.[89]

In Neudeck, Hindenburg was exposed to the influence of his extremely conservative fellow aristocrats, who encouraged the idea of firing Brüning. On 20 May, Brüning's cabinet had drawn up a draft of an emergency decree empowering the Reich commissioner for eastern assistance, Hans Schlange-Schöningen, to buy bankrupt estates at compulsory auctions and release them for settlement by farmers. The main lobbying organisation for the large landholders, the Reichslandbund, was infuriated by what it saw as "agrarian Bolshevism" and kicked up a storm with Hindenburg. When Otto Meissner presented him with the draft emergency decree on 25 May, Hindenburg refused to sign it.[90] Moreover, he communicated via his state secretary his "urgent wish" to Brüning that "the cabinet should be reformed and moved to the right."[91] This was tantamount to asking for his resignation.

When Hindenburg returned to Berlin on 28 May, the die was already cast. In a decisive conversation on the morning of 29 May, Brüning told Hindenburg that he could no longer put up with the "undermining of himself and the government from unqualified quarters, in particular the Reichswehr." In order to continue his work, Brüning said, he needed "certain guarantees" and above all "a new demonstration of trust by the Reich president."[92] Hindenburg brusquely rejected this and told Brüning he would no longer authorise the government to draft emergency decrees. The break was complete. Around noon on 30 May, Brüning handed in his resignation request. His final meeting with Hindenburg lasted three and a half minutes.[93] That was how coldly Hindenburg dismissed the man who had helped him get re-elected only seven weeks previously. Brüning's intimate Hermann Pünder remarked that, even though Brüning did not let it show, he was "internally and justifiably outraged."[94] He also rejected Hindenburg's request that he serve as Germany's future foreign minister.

"Yesterday the bomb went off," Goebbels crowed. "At 12 o'clock, Brüning handed in the resignation of his entire cabinet to the old man. With that the system has collapsed."[95] By contrast, the democrat Count Kessler reacted to the news of Brüning's dismissal with horror: "Backroom interests have got their way as in the time of [Wilhelm II]," Kessler complained on 30 May. "Today marks the beginning of the end for the parliamentary republic."[96] And indeed the fall of Brüning represented a watershed. His departure, as historian Heinrich August Winkler pointed out, signalled the end of the "moderate phase of presidential rule."[97] At the same time, it is also true that while in office Brüning had helped undermine parliamentary democracy and bolster the power of the Reich president and the Reich military leadership by largely removing the Reichstag from the process of political decision-making. To some extent, the chancellor fell victim to a development he himself had partially initiated.

Late in the afternoon of 30 May, as part of his consultations with the leaders of the various political parties, Hindenburg received Hitler and Göring. The NSDAP chairman declared his willingness to engage in "productive cooperation" with a Reich government under Franz von Papen, but he also reiterated the conditions he had negotiated with Schleicher: a quick dissolution of the Reichstag and the lifting of the ban on the SA.[98] He received assurances on both counts. Goebbels noted with satisfaction: "Discussion with the old man went well . . . SA ban is gone. Uniforms allowed and Reichstag dissolved. That's the most important thing. The man is Papen. That's irrelevant. Elections, elections! Straight to the people! We're all very happy."[99] The Nazi leadership considered it a given that the new government was nothing more than an interim solution. They assumed that they would achieve such an overwhelming result in the next Reichstag elections that Hindenburg would have no choice but to appoint Hitler the leader of the government. Local elections in Oldenburg on 29 May and Mecklenburg-Schwerin on 5 June, in which the NSDAP took 48.4 and 49 per cent of the vote respectively and won a majority of seats in the two Landtage,[100] strengthened the conviction that they would achieve a similar triumph in the next national poll. "We have to divorce ourselves from Papen as soon as possible," Goebbels was already writing in his diary on 6 June.[101]

The new chancellor Franz von Papen, an old-school gentleman from a venerable Westphalian aristocratic family, was a Centre Party backbencher in the Prussian Landtag who had never made much of a political name for himself. He had served as a battalion commander on the Western Front during the First World War, however, which recommended him in Hindenburg's eyes. And Papen's lack of political experience was a major advantage in the view of Schleicher, who pulled Papen's name out of a hat in the hope the new chancellor would be all the more malleable as Schleicher increased his own political power. Lutz Schwerin von Krosigk would later recall: "He [Schleicher] wanted to pull the political strings and needed a 'mouthpiece chancellor,' who was able to speak but did not have a political will of his own."[102] In the new cabinet the political general, who had previously kept his manoeuvring behind the scenes, assumed the role of minister of defence and entered the public spotlight for the first time. Baron Konstantin von Neurath, previously ambassador to Britain, became foreign minister; Baron Wilhelm von Gayl was made interior minister; and the director of the East Prussian Land Society, Baron Magnus von Braun, was promoted to minister of food and agriculture. The Finance Ministry fell to Krosigk, a count who had been ministerial director there since 1929. The Postal Services and Transport Ministry went to Baron Paul von Eltz-Rübenach, previously president of the Reichsbank directorship in Karlsruhe, and the Labour Ministry was taken over by Hugo Schäffer, a former director of the Krupp concern and president of the Reich Insurance Office. Franz Gürtner, who had protected Hitler in his capacity as Bavarian minister of justice, assumed control of the Reich Justice Ministry. The only cabinet member retained from the Brüning government was Economics Minister Hermann Warmbold. All in all, deeply conservative representatives of the landed eastern German aristocracy dominated the body, leading the SPD newspaper *Vorwärts* to speak, with considerable justification, of a "cabinet of barons."[103] The new government had little support across the social and political spectrum. Not only the SPD and the KPD declared their opposition: the Centre Party, who blamed Papen for the betrayal of Brüning, also withheld their support.

Papen met with Hitler for the first time on 31 May. In his 1952 memoirs, Papen recalled that Hitler had struck him more as a bohemian than as a politician. The aristocrat noticed little of the "magnetic force of attraction" often ascribed to the NSDAP chairman. "He behaved politely and modestly," Papen wrote. Brüning and Groener's first impression of Hitler had been markedly similar. Apparently this was a role Hitler played to win over others and lure them into a false sense of security concerning his real intentions. When asked whether he would potentially participate in a later government, Hitler became evasive. "He did not want to tie himself down before the results of the election were out," Papen recalled. "But I could tell that he considered my cabinet an interim solution and that he would continue the fight to make his party the strongest in the land and himself chancellor."[104]

Hindenburg dissolved the Reichstag as promised on 4 June. The 31st of July was set as the date for new elections. On 16 June, the ban on the SA was lifted. Hitler's two conditions for tolerating the Papen cabinet were thereby fulfilled. Bavarian State President Held had protested in vain at a meeting between Papen and representatives of the German states on 11 June that Hindenburg's 13 million voters would not understand these measures. Held called them the equivalent of a "carte blanche for murder, manslaughter and the worst sort of terrorising of everyone who thought differently [than the Nazis]."[105] Many people's worst fears had come true: violence escalated to previously unseen levels as National Socialists now engaged in bloody street battles on a daily basis. "We are getting closer and closer to civil war," Harry Kessler observed. "Day for day, Sunday for Sunday, this is a continuous St. Bartholomew's Day Massacre."[106] One of the worst clashes occurred on 17 July in Altona just outside Hamburg. After conferring with Carl Severing, the SPD police president had granted permission for 7,000 SA men to march provocatively through the left-wing districts of the city. Seventeen people died, and many were seriously wounded in the ensuing violence. "The shock at this new bloody Sunday is widespread and deep," wrote Kessler.[107]

The escalation in violence the Papen government had helped bring about served as an excuse to realise one of its most important aims, namely to chip away at the republican "Prussian bulwark." Despite the electoral debacle of 24 April, the fragile coalition between the SPD, the Centre and the German State parties had remained in office. Nonetheless, by June 1932, the once-so-powerful SPD state president, Otto Braun, had resigned and passed on his duties to his former deputy, Welfare Minister Heinrich Hirtsiefer of the Centre Party. Rumours were already swirling that a Reich commissioner could be appointed for Prussia. In the short term, Papen favoured a different solution. On 6 June, he called upon the president of the Prussian Landtag, the National Socialist Hanns Kerrl, to begin "without delay" trying to form a new coalition between the NSDAP, the Centre Party and the DNVP.[108] Negotiations quickly stalled. "No shared responsibility in Prussia either. Either total power or opposition," Goebbels noted in his diary to summarise Hitler's logic.[109] The Centre Party was willing to accept a conservative nationalist, but not a National Socialist, as state president. In early July, attempts to form a majority government in Prussia were deemed a failure, and the Landtag went into indefinite recess.

With that the focus shifted to the second option of subjecting Prussia to Reich administration. In a Reich ministers' conference on 11 July, Interior Minister von Gayl declared that "the psychological moment had come for a Reich intervention." The Prussian government was concentrating exclusively on combating the Nazi movement while "insufficiently" addressing "the Communist threat." In the protocol, Papen said that the meeting had agreed upon "deploying a Reich commissioner in Prussia."[110] On 14 July, Papen, Gayl and State Secretary Meissner went to Neudeck to get Hindenburg's unconditional authorisation to carry out this planned coup. The date of the "Ordinance on the Restoration of Security and Order in the Territory of Prussia" was left open. The conspirators were waiting for a suitable excuse to have it go into force.[111]

That excuse was the "Bloody Sunday" in Altona, back then an exclave part of Prussia, of 17 July. The next day, Heinrich Hirtsiefer, Carl Severing and Prussian Finance Minister Otto Klepper were ordered to report to the Reich Chancellery on the morning of 20 July.

Without further ado, Papen told them that Hindenburg had appointed him Reich commissioner of Prussia and had relieved the ministers of their duties. Papen added that he would personally take over the duties of Prussian state president and that he had appointed Essen Lord Mayor Franz Bracht as acting Prussian interior minister. Hirtsiefer's and Severing's objections that this procedure was "unheard-of" and "without precedent in history" left Papen entirely unimpressed.[112] Immediately after the meeting, he declared a military state of emergency in Berlin and throughout Brandenburg province. Lieutenant General Gerd von Rundstedt, who would be promoted all the way up to general field marshal in Hitler's Wehrmacht, was put in command. In a letter to Papen, the outgoing Prussian government officials complained and announced that they would challenge the decision in Germany's highest court.[113] That made it clear that resistance to the coup d'état would be restricted to legal means—which was tantamount to capitulation. "In Berlin everything calm," noted Goebbels with glee. "SPD and unions completely tame. They won't do a thing. Reichswehr entering. The swine have lost power."[114]

Would the Prussian authorities have been capable of resisting? This question has been hotly debated. It is clear that if Prussian leaders had mobilised their police forces, the Papen government would have responded with the Reichswehr, and there is no doubt which side would have won that battle. Moreover, the Prussian police, especially the higher-ranking officers, were by no means as loyal to the Weimar Republic as many liked to pretend after 1945.[115] Reich Banner activists were most eager to fight, and they were greatly disappointed by the passivity of the SPD leadership. "I saw Reich Banner people weeping around that time," the Lower Silesian SPD secretary, Otto Buchwitz, later recalled. "Older functionaries threw their membership books on the ground at our feet."[116] But realistically, the Reich Banner would have been no match for the right-wing paramilitary organisations.

The most effective means of protest would probably have been a general strike. That was a possibility feared not only by the "cabinet of barons" but also within Hitler's circles. "Is a general strike coming?" asked Goebbels. "I don't think so, but wait and see. Feverish tension."[117] Goebbels no doubt recalled the fact that a general strike had meant the end of the Kapp–Lüttwitz putsch. But the situation in the summer of 1932 was very different from that in the spring of 1920. Back then,

Germany had enjoyed full employment. In 1932, there were 6 million jobless, and all indications were that a call for strike action would have found little support. Moreover, the Prussian "coup" was not as blatantly unconstitutional as the Kapp putsch. In 1920 right-wing conspirators tried to topple a legitimate government; in 1932, action was taken by the Reich government and Reich president against a state government that had lost its parliamentary majority.

Thus it is hard to fault Social Democrats and trade unions for not wanting to risk civil war. They can, however, be blamed for sitting back and letting things take their course. Abandoning the bastion of Prussia without resistance demoralised the supporters of democracy and encouraged their enemies. Immediately after the "coup," the new masters began to "cleanse" the Prussian civil service of democrats, and the National Socialists would continue this process immediately after taking power. The historian Karl-Dietrich Bracher rightly pointed out that the "Prussia coup" was a prelude to the Nazi assumption of power on 30 January 1933.[118] On 25 October 1932, Germany's highest court delivered its verdict. It could hardly have been more contradictory. On the one hand, the judges upheld the Reich president's right to appoint Reich commissioners. On the other, they declared the complete exclusion of the Prussian government unconstitutional. This verdict did nothing to alter the new power relations. The former Prussian government was rehabilitated, in a formal sense, but it led little more than a shadow existence alongside the Reich commissioner.[119]

Hitler began campaigning in early July 1932. He had already set the basic tenor at a conference of Gauleiter in Munich on 8 June, where he declared that 31 July had to be turned into "a general reckoning by the German people with the policies of the past fourteen years and those responsible for them."[120] The main slogans promoted by the Reich propaganda directorship were "Germany awaken! Give Adolf Hitler power!" and "Down with the system, its parties and its exponents!"[121] In mid-July Hitler made a shellac recording distributed at a price of 5 marks by the Eher Verlag.[122] After that, he went on his third flying tour, which included appearances in fifty cities all over Germany. The scenes were familiar. Tens of thousands of people waited to hear him, often for hours, wherever he went. On 19 July in Stralsund, people remained patient until long after midnight.[123] The following evening in Bremen, Hitler's fully illuminated aeroplane flew a couple of loops over the local football stadium before landing—this was intended to symbolise that the Führer was an enlightened deus ex machina, who was above the squabbles of political fighting.[124] By the time the election marathon was over, a local newspaper in the town of Gladbek would describe Hitler as making "a tired, worn-out impression."[125] Ernst Hanfstaengl, who accompanied Hitler on his travels, would write in his memoirs of a "murderous chase from mass event to mass event, from city to city." The Nazi chairman, Hanfstaengl recalled, was utterly exhausted: "Truth be told, we were nothing more than the corner men of a boxer and had our hands full trying to get Hitler fit again between rounds of speeches."[126]

Hitler seldom said anything new. He began his speeches by sketching the general economic and political decay, which he blamed on the Weimar "system." This was followed by a promise to get rid of "the nepotism of parties." One of his goals, he told a crowd in Eberswalde on 27 July, was "to sweep the thirty different political parties out of Germany."[127] At that point, Hitler invoked the "miracle" of the National Socialist movement, which had grown from a handful of people to a massive organisation that would stay true to its principles instead of agreeing to "putrid compromises." The Nazis, Hitler proclaimed, were interested in "the future of the German people," not in parliamentary seats or ministerial positions. The NSDAP was not a party representing narrow interests or classes of people: it was a "party of the German people" whose greatest service was to have "filled millions of people with renewed hope."[128] Hitler was careful not to be too critical of the new presidential cabinet. In Tilsit Hitler told his audience on 15 July: "When my enemies say, 'You're providing cover for the Papen government,' I have to say, 'Be happy Papen is governing and not I.'"[129]

Hitler entirely left out any shrill anti-Semitism, obviously in an attempt to win some votes from the socially liberal middle classes. In his speech in Kiel on 20 July, for example, when Hitler spoke of a "sub-humanity" which the Nazis wanted to "do away with," he deliberately left it open exactly who was meant.[130] Nonetheless he never lost sight of the central tenets of his world view. He was merely concealing them, for tactical reasons, in public. In the introduction he wrote at the time for the official guidelines for the Nazi Party's Political Organisation, Hitler grandiloquently proclaimed that the Nazi movement had not only recognised but "consciously honoured" for the first time ever "blood and race, personality and its value, struggle as a phenomenon of the ongoing selection of the fittest, soil and living space as determining, compelling and driving forces."[131]

At the end of July 1932, Hitler was celebrating another electoral result. "A great victory has been achieved," he crowed. "The National Socialist German Workers' Party is now clearly the strongest party in the German Reichstag."[132] On the surface, the Nazis' victory was indeed impressive. They took 37.3 per cent of the vote, a growth of 19 per cent, and formed the largest parliamentary faction with 230 seats. The Communists also recorded slight gains, from 13.1 to 14.5 per cent, while the Social Democrats' share declined from 24.5 to 21.6 per cent. The Centre Party and the BVP registered modest rises from 11.8 to 12.5 and 3 to 3.2 per cent respectively. The DNVP saw their share of the vote decline from 7 to 5.9 per cent, while the DVP and the German State Party suffered dramatic losses, going from 4.7 to 1.2 and 3.8 to 1 per cent respectively. "The centre is fully destroyed," noted the DNVP deputy Reinhold Quaatz drily.[133]

On close inspection, however, the results were less impressive for the NSDAP. Compared with the presidential run-off election on 10 April, the party's share of the vote had increased by only 0.6 per cent, suggesting that the party could have reached its limits. Count Kessler concluded with satisfaction: "Not only have the Nazis failed to reach their goal. For the first time there are clear signs of standstill and an ebbing of their flood."[134] Goebbels saw the situation in similar terms. "We won't get an absolute majority like this," he noted in his diary. "We need another way." On the question of what this "other way" might be, Goebbels wrote: "We have to come to power now and eliminate Marxism. By hook or by crook. Something has to give. Our time in opposition is at an end. Deeds are what we need now."[135]

Hitler was uncertain as to what his next steps should be and retreated to Adolf Müller's house on Tegernsee Lake, as he had after Geli Raubal's death. There he met Goebbels on 2 August, who noted in telegraph style immediately thereafter: "Hitler ponders. Difficult decisions ahead. Legal? With Centre? Nauseating!"[136] Indeed, for a short time, Hitler seems to have considered forming a coalition with the Centre Party, with whom the Nazis would have had a parliamentary majority. But he quickly dropped the idea since it would have entailed sharing power—and that with a party he had repeatedly defamed in past elections as one of the pillars, together with the SPD, of the "system" he so loathed. As he always did when faced with tough choices, Hitler procrastinated. On 3 August, to distract himself, he attended a performance of *Tristan and Isolde* with Goebbels in Munich. Afterwards they enjoyed some "music and light conversation" at the Hanfstaengls.[137] Still, no sooner had Hitler returned to Berchtesgaden than he made up his mind. Hitler would go and see Kurt von Schleicher to demand the chancellorship for himself and four further ministries for his party. Frick would be interior, Göring aviation, Strasser labour and Goebbels popular education minister. "That means complete power or nothing," Goebbels noted. "That's the way. The worst thing is to back down. [Hitler] believes the barons will give in. But what about the old man?"[138] That was the great uncertain factor in Hitler's calculations. Would Hindenburg be willing to name him chancellor?

On 5 August, Hitler met Schleicher at a secret location in the town of Fürstenberg near Berlin, and he apparently convinced the defence minister, during the course of an "hours-long walk," that there was no way around him becoming chancellor.[139] In any case, upon returning to the Obersalzberg, Hitler immediately called together his paladins and told them that everything had gone well. "In one week the deal will be done," Goebbels recorded. "The boss will become chancellor and Prussian state president. Strasser Reich and Prussian interior minister. Goebbels Prussian culture and Reich education minister. Darré in charge of both agriculture ministries. Frick permanent secretary in the Reich Chancellery. Göring aviation. Justice remains ours. Warmbold economics. Crosigk [*sic*] finance. Schacht Reichsbank. A cabinet of men." We do not know whether Hitler had in fact negotiated all these positions with Schleicher, or whether Goebbels was being over-optimistic. What is certain is that Schleicher wanted to keep the Defence Ministry, which is probably why he thought that he could control a Chancellor Hitler. By contrast Goebbels and Hitler agreed that, should they get those positions, the National Socialists would have achieved their aims. "We'll never give up power—they'll have to cart out our dead bodies," Goebbels wrote. "This is a total solution. It will cost some blood, but it cleanses and purifies. A job well done. We'll work like berserkers. We talk the whole evening, and I draw up plans deep into the night. I can't believe it. We're at the gates of power."[140]

The Nazi leadership were not the only ones who thought definitive triumph was at hand. The party grass roots and the SA also started preparing for what looked like their certain "seizure of power." SA units around Berlin were assembled to present a threatening backdrop and underscore the Nazis' claim to power. "Make the fine gentlemen nervous," Goebbels noted. "That's the point of the exercise."[141] On 10 August, on returning to his apartment in Berlin, Harry Kessler noted that the cellar rooms of the building's concierge, an ardent Nazi supporter, were brightly illuminated: "Music was playing on the radio, and the door was wide open so that people could simply wander in from the street. A party and a mood of victory! People are already in the 'Third Reich!'"[142] But the celebrations were premature. Although on 10 August the newspapers had treated Hitler's ascension to the chancellorship as a foregone conclusion, Kessler sensed a change in mood the following day: "The opposition of the old man seems to have stiffened."[143] News to that effect had also made its way to the Nazi leadership meeting in the southern Bavarian town of Prien am Chiemsee. "The old man refuses to play along," Goebbels wrote in his diary. "Doesn't want Hitler . . . In any case, we now have to keep our nerve and stay strong."[144] So what had happened?

On the morning of 10 August, after Hindenburg had returned from Neudeck, Papen informed him that circles within the NSDAP and the Centre Party were trying to replace his government with one led by Hitler. While Centre deputies believed that they could achieve a parliamentary majority with the Nazis, Papen explained, Hitler imagined a government installed by presidential decree with him as chancellor. "The chancellor," State Secretary Meissner noted, "left the decision up to the Reich president and declared that he would not try to block the formation of a new government." Hindenburg stated that he wanted to stick with a government of presidential decree under Papen. As much as Hindenburg "wished to bring in the National Socialist movement and get it to cooperate," Meissner recorded, he refused with equal conviction to appoint Hitler Reich chancellor, fearing that Hitler's cabinet would be Nazi Party-centred and partisan. Hindenburg personally held it against Hitler that he had broken his promise to tolerate the Papen cabinet and felt there was no guarantee that Hitler, if named chancellor, would respect "the character of a presidential government."[145] In other words, Hindenburg was concerned with preserving his own sphere of influence. Finally, Hindenburg's rejection of Hitler reflected the antipathy of a representative of the old Wilhelmine elite for an upstart. "I cannot entrust the empire of Kaiser Wilhelm and Bismarck to a private from Bohemia," Hindenburg is alleged to have told one of his assistants.[146] (During Prussia's 1866 war against Austria, Hindenburg had passed through a Bohemian town called Braunau and mistook it for Hitler's birthplace.)

On the afternoon of 10 August, Franz von Papen convened his cabinet and informed the ministers about his meeting with Hindenburg. The priority, he said, was "to involve the right-wing movement in the state" without entrusting Hitler with political leadership. In the wake of Hindenburg's veto, Schleicher also distanced himself from the agreement he had reached with Hitler, speaking only of involving the NSDAP in the government and not of making Hitler chancellor. The majority of ministers agreed with this position. Summarising the results of the cabinet meeting, Papen said that coming negotiations with Hitler would determine "to what extent the National Socialists would have to be involved in the government to dislodge them from the opposition."[147]

On 12 August, Hitler travelled by car to Berlin, spending the night at the Goebbelses' in the nearby town of Caputh. Decisive talks with the government were scheduled for the following day. "Is the fruit of ten years of work now ripe?" Goebbels noted in his diary. "I hope so, but I hardly dare believe it."[148] On the morning of 13 August, Hitler met Schleicher at the Defence Ministry before heading to Papen at the Chancellery. Hundreds of people milled about the government district, expecting to witness a historic occasion.[149] But Hitler was about to learn for himself, as he had already heard from others, that Hindenburg had refused to name him chancellor. Papen offered to make him vice-chancellor, but Hitler brusquely refused. As the leader of the strongest party in the Reichstag, Hitler fumed, there was no way he would "subordinate himself to another chancellor." The conversation went on for two hours and grew quite heated, as Papen tried in vain to convince Hitler that a movement as large as the NSDAP could not remain "permanently in opposition." In the end, Papen had to inform Hindenburg that the negotiations had failed.[150] By 2 a.m., when Hitler arrived at Magda Goebbels's apartment on Reichskanzlerplatz, it appeared that his second chance at power had come and gone.

But then, at 3 p.m. that afternoon, Hermann Pünder's successor at the Reich Chancellery, Erwin Planck (the son of the famous physicist), called with the news that Hindenburg wanted to speak with him. At first Hitler refused: "The decision has been made—what's the point of me going?" But Planck seems to have created the impression that Hindenburg's mind was not completely made up. "Brief vague hope," noted Goebbels. "Everyone kept their fingers crossed."[151] The meeting with Hindenburg took place after 4 p.m. Hitler brought along Wilhelm Frick and Ernst Röhm, while Hindenburg had Papen and Otto Meissner at his side. When the president asked whether Hitler would be willing to participate in a government under Papen, the Nazi Party chairman responded that the idea was out of the question—for the reasons he had enumerated that morning. "Given the significance of the National Socialist movement, he had no choice but to demand full leadership of the government and the party," Meissner noted Hitler as saying. Hindenburg categorically refused Hitler's demand, declaring that "in front of God, his conscience and his country he could not justify giving the entire power of government to a single party and especially not one so hostile towards people who thought differently." Hindenburg urged Hitler to play his role in the political opposition in a gentlemanly fashion and suggested that he would not bear any grudges: "We two are old comrades and want to remain so. The road ahead may bring us together again. So I extend my hand as a comrade."[152] After barely half an hour, the meeting was over.

Hitler had held his temper in front of Hindenburg, but as soon as he was out in the hall of the Reich Chancellery, he vented his rage, accusing Papen and Meissner of deceiving him. The two had allowed Planck to suggest that Hindenburg's mind was open, Hitler fumed, when in fact the decision had already been made.[153] "How do you intend to rule?" he asked Papen. "Does the government believe it can work with this Reichstag?" Papen nonchalantly dismissed these objections. "The Reichstag?" he replied. "I'm surprised that you of all people think the Reichstag is important."[154] On the evening of 13 August, the government issued an official communiqué that chronicled the conversation in a way that publicly embarrassed Hitler. The Nazi leader had demanded the "entire power of state," which Hindenburg had been forced to reject "because his conscience and sense of national duty forbade him from transferring complete authority to the National Socialist movement, which would use it one-sidedly."[155] A few days later Planck told Pünder that the communiqué had been modelled on the Ems Dispatch, which Bismarck had used in 1870 to cast aspersions on France and provoke the Franco-Prussian War.[156] In a statement hastily prepared by Frick and Röhm, Hitler replied that he had demanded the "leadership" of the government, that is the position of chancellor, and not the entire power of state,[157] but that was not sufficient to limit the damage. The nationalist circles sympathetic to the Nazis came to believe, with considerable justification, that Hitler was incapable of compromise and was banging his head against a wall. The impression arose that the Nazi leader was less concerned about the welfare of Germany than with securing unfettered power for himself and his followers.

August the 13th was a major setback for Hitler. The politician whose instincts were regarded as fail-safe had gone after the big jackpot and come up short. Or to borrow a different metaphor from Alan Bullock: Hitler had "knocked on the door of the Chancellery, only to have the door publicly slammed in his face."[158] This sort of rejection painfully reminded the NSDAP chairman of his failed November 1923 putsch, and he repeatedly invoked it over the next weeks. At a Gau conference in Nuremberg he compared the current situation with that of a decade before, declaring: "The party battles and comes close to victory, but at the last moment the same old conspiracy against it always appears. A tiny bunch of reactionaries with no future join together with Jews and try to prevent the party's imminent triumph at the last minute." Unlike in 1923, however, the Nazi Party was not going to be lured into a putsch but would "hold its nerve and not give in."[159] But appeals like this could not compensate for the deep disappointment of Hitler's followers at their renewed failure to take control. Especially within the SA, whose members believed they had entered the antechambers of power, discontent was rife. Ernst Röhm declared that it had never been so difficult to maintain calm among his brown-shirted battalions.[160]

Hitler immediately had himself driven back to Munich on the evening of 13 August. "Well, we'll just have to see how things progress now," his companions heard him remark during the journey.[161] For a few days, he retreated to the Obersalzberg. Karl Weigand, a correspondent for the *New York American* who interviewed Hitler on 18 August in Haus Wachenfeld, found him still fuming at being dismissed by Hindenburg.[162] But in a conversation that same day with Louis P. Lochner from the *Manchester Guardian*, Hitler denied revived rumours that he was planning a "march on Berlin." His storm troopers were sufficiently disciplined, Hitler said, and would not take a single step from the path of legality.[163]

Belying that claim in early August, the SA had engaged in a whole series of politically motivated acts of violence in East Prussia, Upper Silesia and Schleswig-Holstein. They primarily targeted members of the KPD and the Reich Banner and claimed a number of lives. Attacks were also directed at trade union buildings, left-wing newspapers and Jewish locations like the main synagogue in the city of Kiel.[164] These acts of terror, wrote Count Harry Kessler, gave a small taste of what the Nazis would do "in larger fashion and throughout the Reich if they achieved victory."[165] Within the Reich cabinet, which had consulted on 9 August about proposed "measures for restoration of public safety," Papen attributed the new wave of violence to a Nazi attempt to "unsettle the public" and to force through the idea that "Hitler had to take the leadership of the government." To do nothing, Papen argued, would be tantamount to "the government committing suicide." That very day, the cabinet drafted an emergency decree making politically motivated manslaughter a capital crime. Special courts were set up in Berlin and the East Prussian district of Elbing to prosecute the perpetrators more quickly.[166]

A few hours later, in the night of 9–10 August, one of the most grisly murders of the pre-1933 years took place in the Upper Silesian village of Potempa. Nine uniformed SA men forced their way into the apartment of the miner and KPD supporter Konrad Pietrzuch, dragged him out of bed and kicked him to death in front of his mother and his brother.[167] Since this crime was carried out after the emergency decree had come into force, the perpetrators were subject to the new stricter punishment. Less than two weeks later, on 22 August, the special court in the town of Beuthen rendered its verdict: five of the perpetrators were sentenced to death, one was given two years in prison and three were acquitted. The verdict elicited outraged protest from the National Socialists. Hitler sent those convicted a telegram which read: "In light of this monstrously bloodthirsty verdict,

I feel connected to you in boundless loyalty. From this moment on, your freedom is a matter of honour for us, and the fight against a government, under which this judgment was possible, is our duty."[168] On 24 August, in an article headlined "The Jews Are to Blame," Goebbels openly expressed sentiments that Hitler had suppressed, for tactical reasons, in his campaign speeches the previous month: "Never forget it, comrades! Repeat it out loud a hundred times a day until the words follow you into your deepest dreams: The Jews are to blame! And they will not evade the criminal tribunal that they deserve."[169]

By openly declaring his solidarity with the murderers of Potempa, Hitler had let the mask slip, revealing his oft-sworn respect for the law as a means of deceiving the public. By that point, anyone in Germany could have figured out what would await the country if the Nazis ever came to political power. "In the entire country, who can comprehend that the leader of such a large political movement could so callously dare to declare his respect for these drunken murderers?" asked the *Frankfurter Zeitung*.[170] Kessler saw the affair as the clear beginning of a popular disenchantment with the Nazi Party, writing that "13 August and Potempa are poison in its body."[171] But once again Hitler was bailed out by the Papen government upon which he had just declared war. In early September, the sentences of the five main perpetrators were commuted to life in prison. In March 1933, a few weeks after Hitler was named chancellor, they were pardoned.[172]

Nonetheless, the fact that Hitler had unmistakably revealed that a government led by him would do away with the rule of law and legalise political murder did not scare people off as much as Kessler hoped it would. Hjalmar Schacht, for example, who had been part of the cabinet negotiated between Hitler and Schleicher, hastened to assure the NSDAP leader of his "unalterable affection." Although he knew that Hitler did not need words of consolation, Schacht wrote, perhaps a word of "most genuine sympathy" would not be unwelcome:

> Your movement is borne internally of such powerful truth and necessity that victory in one form or another is a matter of course. In times of the movement's rise, you have not let yourself be seduced by false idols. And I am completely convinced that now, at a time when you have been forced onto the defensive, that you will resist that temptation. If you stay true to yourself, your success is guaranteed.

Schacht concluded his letter by promising: "You can count on me as a faithful helper."[173] This was essentially a job application, made by a graduate of Hamburg's prestigious Johanneum *Gymnasium* and a long-time president of the Reichsbank, for a leading position in the Third Reich whose arrival he so deeply wished for.

But how to proceed after 13 August? The situation was tied up in knots. Papen had come no closer to his goal of tying the National Socialists to the government, just as Hitler had made no progress towards achieving the decisive position of power in a cabinet that ruled by presidential decree—his desired launching pad for eradicating the Weimar "system" and erecting a dictatorship. After Hindenburg's categorical rebuff, he seemed to have no chance of reaching this goal in the short term. So the question was whether to negotiate with the Centre Party about a coalition or, as Hitler had already threatened, to steer the NSDAP towards a stricter course of opposition to Papen's cabinet. On 25 August, Hitler discussed the three possibilities with Goebbels in Berchtesgaden. "Either a cabinet by presidential decree. Most agreeable but least likely," noted the latter. "Or the Centre with us. Unpleasant but relatively easy to have at present. Or the most blunt sort of opposition. Very unpleasant, but if necessary, possible."[174] While the two men conferred, Gregor Strasser arrived and reported on conversations he had had with ex-Chancellor Brüning two days earlier in the southern German town of Tübingen. According to Brüning's memoirs, Strasser had hinted that Hitler would forgo the office of chancellor in return for a swift agreement between the Centre and Nazi Parties.[175] Hitler would never have made such a commitment, as Goebbels's diaries make clear: "Strasser very supportive of the Centre solution. Hitler and I, on the other hand, for a continuation of the idea of the cabinet by presidential decree."[176] Brüning and Hitler met once more on 29 August in the house of a manufacturer in the Berlin suburb of Grunewald, but an alliance between the two was impossible. Under no circumstances was Brüning prepared to hand over the offices of Prussian president and interior minister, with their control over the police, or to accept Hitler as chancellor of a conservative–Nazi coalition.[177] Nonetheless the Nazis proceeded with informal coalition talks with the Centre Party because the spectre of a majority coalition in parliament put pressure on Hindenburg and his circles and threatened the nationalist DNVP with complete marginalisation.

"There are many indications that Hitler and Brüning will reach agreement and that both we and the economy are facing a terrible regime," Hugenberg wrote on 19 August to Albert Vögler, the chairman of the United Steelworks.[178]

The Papen government countered Hitler's declaration of hostilities with a two-pronged strategy. It altered economic policy by instituting a series of measures to stimulate the domestic economy, by reducing taxes on businesses that hired new employees and by relaxing labour agreements, as employers had long demanded.[179] At the same time, the cabinet intensified its pursuit of plans first suggested by Interior Minister von Gayl at a ministerial meeting on 10 August: namely to dissolve the Reichstag and delay new elections beyond the sixty-day window prescribed by Article 25 of the Weimar Constitution. "Without doubt we will come into conflict with the constitution, but that's primarily a matter for the Reich president," read the minutes of that meeting.[180] On 30 August, Papen, Schleicher and Gayl went to Neudeck. Arguing that an "emergency of state" justified extraordinary measures, they succeeded in securing Hindenburg's support for indefinitely postponing new elections. The Reich president also issued them a blank cheque to dissolve the Reichstag.[181]

The same day that Hindenburg gave the Papen cabinet permission to violate the constitution, the newly elected Reichstag convened for its inaugural session. Beforehand, Hitler underscored "the movement's claim to power" in a speech to the NSDAP parliamentary faction, saying he had never been "more relaxed or confident."[182] Hermann Göring was elected Reichstag president with votes from the NSDAP, the Centre Party and the BVP. Although the position of first vice-president traditionally went to the second-strongest party—in this case the Social Democrats—their candidate, Paul Löbe, was defeated by a Centre Party deputy put forward by the National Socialists. The result was, in the words of the *Völkischer Beobachter*, "a Marxist-free Reichstag presidium." The NSDAP's strategy was obvious. The Nazis had got wind of the Papen cabinet's emergency plan and wanted to demonstrate, as Göring declared in a speech on 30 August, that "the new Reichstag has a large nationalist majority capable of functioning, so that in no sense is there a state of governmental emergency."[183]

Hitler took things one step further. Late in the evening of 31 August, he assembled his paladins in Göring's apartment for a "secret conference."

Goebbels noted: "Bold plan drawn up. We'll try to topple the old man. Silence and preparation of the essence. The old man doesn't want us. He's completely in the hands of the reactionaries. Thus, he himself must go."[184] The idea was to topple Hindenburg using Article 43 of the Weimar Constitution, which foresaw the removal of the Reich president if a two-thirds majority of the Reichstag backed a popular referendum and the German people were in favour of it. Hindenburg's authority would have suffered just from such a resolution being drawn up. On 8 and 10 September, delegations from the NSDAP and the Centre Party met in Göring's villa to discuss common action against Hindenburg. In Goebbels's estimation, the Centre Party was not completely disinclined, but their representatives asked for more time to think things over.[185] It was not until Brüning threatened to leave the party "if a single member of the faction conducted further negotiations in this direction" that the idea of cooperating with the Nazis was dropped.[186] The former Reich chancellor himself had good reason to revenge himself on Hindenburg for his humiliating dismissal, but Brüning knew that if Hindenburg fell, his successor would in all likelihood be Hitler.

While negotiating with the Centre Party, Hitler stepped up his attacks on the Papen cabinet. In his speech in the Sportpalast on 1 September, he excoriated it as "a political regime that rules by the bayonet." Hitler scoffed at the notion that serial dissolutions of the Reichstag represented a threat to the National Socialists: "For all we care, do it a hundred times. We'll emerge as the victors. I'm not going to lose my nerve. My will is unshakeable, and I can outwait my adversaries."[187] Three days later, at the NSDAP Gau conference in Nuremberg, Hitler attacked the "reactionary clique" of aristocrats in the cabinet: "Do they truly think I can be bought off with a few ministerial seats? I don't want anything to do with them . . . They can't imagine how totally meaningless that all is to me. If God wanted things to be the way they are, we'd have all been born with monocles."[188] A further three days later, in a speech at Zirkus Krone on 7 September, Hitler even depicted himself as a defender of the German constitution: "We have a right to say that we will form the government. The fine gentlemen refuse to grant us this right. I'll pick up the glove tossed on the ground . . . They say that the constitution is obsolete. I say, only now does it make sense."[189]

*

On 12 September, the Reichstag met for its first working session. On the agenda was a governmental declaration by Papen, which was to be followed by several days of general debate. But the session took an unexpected turn. Before business had even been opened, Communist deputy Ernst Torgler seized the floor, demanding an immediate vote on the motions brought by his party, which included rejecting emergency governmental measures and a declaration of no confidence in the Papen government. The KPD initiative could have been blocked had a single deputy objected, but that did not happen. In the general confusion that ensued Wilhelm Frick moved for a half-hour adjournment. While Papen used the break to have messengers fetch Hindenburg's order to dissolve the Reichstag issued on 30 August, Hitler instructed the NSDAP faction to support the Communist motion. Hitler's intent was to demonstrate, for all to see, how little parliamentary support the Papen government had.

After the session was reopened, Göring in his capacity as Reichstag president began to explain the various voting procedures, studiously ignoring the Reich chancellor, who repeatedly requested the floor from the government bench while brandishing a red folder containing Hindenburg's decree. "In that situation," Papen recalled in his memoirs, "I had no choice but to lay the dissolution order on Göring's desk, to roars and yells from the deputies, and to leave the building with my government."[190] Shortly thereafter, Göring announced the results of the vote. Five hundred and twenty-two Reichstag members had voted to withdraw confidence in the Papen government, while only forty-two DNVP and DVP deputies had rejected the motion. "It was the most humiliating defeat imaginable," Goebbels noted.[191] The psychological effects of the vote were massive. The rug was pulled from under Papen's feet, and his protestations that the dissolution decree had been presented before the vote, thereby rendering it moot, did nothing to undo the damage. The fact was, as Kessler concluded, that "more than nine-tenths of the Reichstag and the German people are against this chancellor of 'national concentration.'"[192] In the wake of the overwhelming defeat, the Papen cabinet decided on 14 and 17 September to back off from the emergency plan agreed with Hindenburg and schedule new parliamentary elections on 6 November, the last possible day within the sixty-day deadline.[193] In a conversation with Brüning's former deputy Hermann Pünder in October 1932, Kurt von Schleicher admitted that the Papen cabinet had failed in its main task of "tying the NSDAP to the government" but asserted that the Nazis had been "completely demystified." In the coming weeks, Schleicher predicted, support for both the National Socialists and the Centre Party would erode so that a parliamentary majority would no longer be possible. At that point, he believed, the Reichstag would be willing to tolerate the government in order to avoid yet another vote.[194]

"Election prospects extremely pessimistic," Goebbels noted in late September. "We'll have to work until we burst. Then perhaps we'll succeed again."[195] After four difficult elections, fatigue was beginning to show both among the populace in general and the Nazis' supporters. The SA in particular had little desire to focus all its energy on an election again after the disappointment of 13 August. For the first time, the numbers of Nazi Party members declined: from 455,000 in August to 435,000 in October 1932. From around the country came reports of a "downcast" mood and a "tendency to complain."[196] Moreover, the constant election campaigns had depleted the party coffers, and it was difficult to find additional resources. "Procuring money is difficult," Goebbels complained. "The fat cats are with Papen."[197] The Papen government, whose new economic programme was very much to the liking of entrepreneurs, could indeed count on the support of big business. Their donations went nearly exclusively to parties that favoured Papen and his cabinet, that is the DNVP and the DVP.[198]

In contrast to many of his underlings, Hitler projected optimism. The Papen government would soon collapse "like a house of cards," he told the *Daily Mail* on 24 September.[199] In a speech at the Reich propaganda conference in the Brown House on 6 October, Hitler tried to mobilise party members for the coming election: "We National Socialists will give the nation an unprecedented display of our strength of will . . . I head into this struggle with absolute confidence. Let the battle commence. In four weeks, we'll emerge victorious from it."[200] The main Nazi campaign slogan was "Against Papen and the reactionaries."[201] The diplomat Ulrich von Hassell, who visited Hitler in his Munich apartment on 23 September after being named Germany's ambassador to Italy, found the NSDAP leader still extremely bitter towards Papen and Hindenburg. "Hitler said he would place no limits upon his agitation against this government, which had fought against and 'betrayed' him," wrote Hassell. "He made no bones about his feelings towards the barons."[202] The Nazi propaganda instructions issued by Goebbels ran in the same vein. Papen, Goebbels instructed, should be depicted as an "equally ambitious and incompetent representative of the reactionary old boys' club."[203]

Hitler knew what was at stake. If he did not succeed in bettering or at least maintaining his level of support from the 31 July election, it would threaten the aura of inevitable triumph surrounding National Socialism, and the momentum that had carried the movement from success to success could be reversed. He therefore submitted to an even more gruelling election campaign. The fourth "flying tour of Germany," which he began in his Junkers 52 on 11 October, lasted three and a half weeks and took him to every corner of the country, including such provincial places as East Frisia or the Bergisches Land, which he had previously skipped. Hitler started all his speeches by justifying his decision not to join the Papen cabinet on 13 August. It was a sign of how disappointed he was at his failure to seize the office of chancellor. He had not wanted to be a "minister by Papen's grace," he told the crowds, adding that he was not cut out for such a "decorative role." Using different imagery, he said that he did not want to get on board a train he would have to get off a few months later. Papen and his reactionary clique, Hitler fumed, were not interested in granting him political influence but simply getting him to "shut up."[204] Repeatedly, Hitler stressed that he was interested neither in getting a ministerial post nor in sharing power with anyone else: "The only thing that appeals to me is leadership itself, true power, and we National Socialists have a sacred right to it."[205] His opponents should be under no illusions about his "enormous determination." Hitler had chosen his path, he assured his audiences, and would pursue it to the end: "A man like me may perish. A man like me may be beaten to death. But a man like me cannot yield!" One word that did not exist in the National Socialist vocabulary, Hitler crowed, was "capitulation."[206] But the fact that Hitler felt forced to make such assurances suggests that his confidence in victory was partially play-acted, that he himself may have feared a possible setback. Indeed, while the Nazi press once again boasted about how successful Hitler's propaganda tour was, attendance was in reality declining. Nuremberg's Luitpoldhalle auditorium was only half full for Hitler's appearance on 13 October.[207] A substantial number of voters who had flocked to the putative saviour in July turned their backs on him after 13 August. "They say he's come up short," Konrad Heiden wrote, describing the mood among parts of the German populace. "He's just another misguided fanatic, who overreaches and achieves nothing. A falling comet in the November fog."[208]

As if to bolster the impression that he himself had closed the doors to power with his inflexible fanaticism, Hitler gave free rein to his anti-Semitic hatred in his election campaign. Strangely, none of Hitler's biographers have remarked on this shift, although it is perfectly evident. In all of his speeches, Hitler falsely claimed that Papen's economic programme was the brainchild of the Jewish banker Jakob Goldschmidt, the former director of the Danatbank, and was "welcomed above all by Jews." No speech was complete without a tirade against the "Jewish press of Berlin" or an invocation of the spectre of "Jewish-internationalist Bolshevism," which Hitler characterised as a "plague that has beset almost the entire European continent and threatens to attack us." On 30 October in Essen, Hitler thundered: "Either the German people will escape from the hands of the Jews or it will degenerate into nothing. I want to be its advocate and lead it into a unified German empire."[209] Once again Hitler had made it perfectly plain that there would be no room for Jews in the new ethnically defined state.

But bourgeois voters were less disconcerted by Hitler's naked anti-Semitism than by his polemics against Papen's "reactionary clique" and the anti-capitalist, class-warfare tone of the party's propaganda, which seemed to clash with the slogan of "ethnic community." On 25 September, Goebbels had insisted that "right now the most radical socialism has to be advanced."[210] The Berlin Gauleiter put these words into practice when he saw to it that the NSDAP supported a strike by the city's public transport workers a few days before the election. Together with the Communist-dominated Revolutionary Union Opposition (RGO), the Nazi Factory Cell Organisation (NSBO) formed picket lines and brought traffic in Berlin to a standstill. "All yesterday: strike," Goebbels noted on 5 November. "Our people in the lead. Grave acts of terror. Already 4 dead. Revolutionary mood in Berlin. Press on!"[211] Goebbels maintained constant contact with Hitler during the strike, and Goebbels noted with satisfaction that Hitler supported his position, even though cooperating with the Communists was likely to cost the Nazis votes. "Hitler has gone Marxist for the moment—the

Berlin transport strike," the Hamburg schoolteacher Luise Solmitz wrote in her diary on the day of the election.[212] In July she had voted for the NSDAP, but she switched to the DNVP on 6 November. Solmitz was obviously not alone among conservative-nationalist voters: Hugenberg's party increased its share of the vote from 5.9 to 8.9 per cent.

For the National Socialists, the 6 November election was a catastrophe. The party lost 2 million voters, and their overall share of the vote declined by 4.2 per cent to 33.1 per cent. They only picked up 196 parliamentary seats, a decrease of 34. Along with the DNVP, the big winners of the election were the KPD, who increased their share of the vote from 14.5 to 16.9 per cent and took 100 seats in the Reichstag. The SPD and the two Catholic parties suffered small declines in support: the SPD dropped from 21.6 to 20.4 per cent, the Centre from 12.5 to 11.9 per cent and the BVP from 3.2 to 3.1 per cent. The DVP did slightly better, rising from 1.2 to 1.9 per cent, and the German State Party held steady at 1 per cent. Overall turnout declined by almost 4 per cent compared with July, falling to 80.6 per cent—which probably hurt the NSDAP more than any other party.[213] The major liberal papers in Berlin depicted the election as a sensation. "The National Socialist idea has lost its power to win people over," wrote the *Vossische Zeitung*. "The aura is gone . . . the magic has failed. The faith is flagging . . . Hitler's failure as a politician and a statesman has become apparent."[214] Goebbels, who had hoped a few days before the vote that the result would not be "all that bad," also had to admit: "We suffered a heavy defeat . . . We now face some difficult struggles."[215]

For Hitler personally, 6 November represented a third painful defeat within the year 1932. His charismatic aura, which was based on his magnetic effect on the masses and their belief in him as a political messiah, was coming under fire. Hitler of course did his best to put a positive spin on the results in his post-election speech. The "massive attack on the Nazi Party" had been repelled, he claimed, and the Papen government had suffered a "debilitating defeat" since the DNVP, which supported the status quo, had been unable to break the 10-per-cent mark. The message for National Socialists, Hitler said, was "to continue the fight against this regime until it has been ultimately eradicated."[216] But he was unable to lift the NSDAP out of the deep depression that had set in throughout the party.[217] For the first time, there were considerable doubts about Hitler's political judgement. Did not the Nazi strategy of all-or-nothing condemn the party to eternal opposition, many Hitler followers asked? Would the next election bring an even worse defeat? Hitler seems to have been utterly unmoved by such concerns. After a long meeting with Hitler on 9 November, Goebbels noted: "No reconciliation. Hold steady! Papen must go. There can be no compromises. The reactionaries will be left scratching their heads. We don't do things by halves."[218]

Papen had every reason to be happy with the election result, which meant that the NSDAP and the Centre Party no longer had a parliamentary majority and Hitler could no longer threaten him with a "black and brown" coalition. Papen thus believed he would be greeted more receptively on 13 November when he issued a written invitation for Hitler to join his cabinet along the lines of what he had proposed in August. The 6 November election, Papen wrote, had created "a new situation" and a "new possibility to concentrate all [of Germany's] nationalist forces." The bitterness of the election, Papen suggested, should be forgotten in order to jointly serve "the welfare of the country."[219] The Nazi Party leadership suspected that this was yet another attempt to lure Hitler into a trap. "No repeat of 13 August—that would be a catastrophe," Goebbels noted in his diary, leaving no doubt as to what the main obstacle was. "Hitler must be Reich chancellor! *Conditio sine qua non*."[220]

Hitler took three days before refusing Papen's request to discuss the possibility of National Socialist participation in the government. He was at most prepared to engage in a written exchange of ideas. "Under no circumstances," Hitler wrote in his reply to Papen, "will I tolerate a repeat of the proceedings of 13 August."[221] In a cabinet meeting on 17 November Papen admitted that his efforts to ally Germany's nationalist parties had failed. Papen dissolved the cabinet "in order to clear the way . . . for the Reich president to open negotiations with the leaders of the political parties."[222] Hindenburg accepted Papen's resignation but asked him to continue to temporarily administer the government's business.

Harry Kessler celebrated the news of Papen's resignation: "Finally! This perpetually smiling, foolhardy dilettante has done more damage in six months than any of his predecessors in a comparable period."[223] The socialist newspaper *Vorwärts* reported the news under the headline: "Cabinet of lords deposed!"[224] People in Social Democratic circles remembered all too well that Papen had been the one who had destroyed the last bulwark of the Weimar Republic with his 20 July coup d'état against Prussia. Yet it was entirely unclear who would succeed Papen as chancellor or whether a way out of the political crisis could be found. The only thing that was clear, Kessler noted on 19 November, was the absolute impenetrability and uncertainty of the situation: "Everything more or less depends on chance and the good or bad moods of four or five individuals."[225]

On 18 November, Hindenburg commenced negotiations with party leaders. His goal remained to form a "cabinet of national concentration," ranging from the Centre Party to the National Socialists. The first man he received was Alfred Hugenberg, who came out in favour of continuing rule by presidential decree and against making Hitler chancellor. He had been "unable to discover much respect for agreements in Hitler," Hugenberg said.[226] DVP Chairman Eduard Dingeldey also warned against Hitler, calling him "an unpredictable person easily subject to outside influences." No one, Dingeldey argued, could rule out Hitler "trying to seize power even against the will of the Reich president."[227] The chairman of the Centre Party, Ludwig Kaas, was more moderate in his views, as was the leader of the BVP, Fritz Schäffer. Both argued that the National Socialists should be part of the new government. But both declined to offer suggestions about who should be Reich chancellor, saying that was a matter for Hindenburg alone. Schäffer even contended that the danger resided "less in Hitler himself than in the people surrounding him," since they were obsessed with the idea of a "single-party dictatorship." For that reason, any Hitler-led government would have to include "counterweights and strong personalities" in order to prevent abuses of power.[228]

Hitler was invited by telephone to a personal audience with Hindenburg at 11:30 a.m. on 19 November. The day before that, he flew with Wilhelm Frick and Gregor Strasser to Berlin. Goebbels advised him to treat Hindenburg like a father: "Cajole him in the most primitive fashion and try to gain his trust." The Nazi leaders sat together until late at night. "We ate, laughed, chatted and made some music," Goebbels noted in his diary. "Hitler was very relaxed . . . God willing, may everything turn out well."[229] As they had on 13 August, Nazi supporters congregated on Wilhelmstrasse, cheering Hitler on as he arrived for his appointment with Hindenburg. It was the third time he had met with the Reich president, but the first in which he had insisted on a private discussion. Only during the second half of their meeting, which lasted more than an hour, was State Secretary Meissner allowed to join the two men. Once again, Hindenburg appealed to Hitler as the "leader of a large movement," whose nationalist sentiment he respected, not to rule out the invitation to be part of a nationalist government. "The times are too serious for everyone to follow his own personal interests and go his own way," Hindenburg argued according to Meissner's minutes. "We have to put our differences behind us and come together in an emergency community." Hitler stuck to his guns, telling Hindenburg he would only join a governing cabinet if he received "political leadership," that is the office of chancellor. He did, however, signal willingness to compromise on the further composition of such a cabinet. By no means, he assured Hindenburg, did he want to fill the remaining ministerial posts exclusively with National Socialists. When Hindenburg asked him if he was willing to initiate discussions with other parties about the policies of a potential coalition, Hitler responded that the Reich president first needed to call upon him to form a government. At this point, Hitler suggested an idea to which he presumed Hindenburg would be receptive: "I think I could find a basis upon which I and the new government would receive an enabling law from the Reichstag." The possibility of ruling by virtual decree via an enabling law was a legal option in times of crisis—albeit one that required a two-thirds parliamentary majority. Stresemann had already used such a law during the crisis of October 1923. An enabling law had the advantage of allowing the government to act independently of the institutions of the Reichstag for a time without constantly having to approach the Reich president for emergency decrees. Hindenburg said that he would think over Hitler's suggestion and then speak to him again.[230]

The most important result to come out of 19 November was that after his one-to-one meeting, Hindenburg seemed no longer categorically opposed to Hitler's chancellorship. Nonetheless, Hitler's entourage was uncertain as to whether this was really a "serious attempt to come together" or another attempt by the other side to "screw us," as Goebbels coarsely put it.[231] That issue was resolved on 21 November, when Hindenburg received Hitler a second time and charged him with forming a government—but only under the condition that he create "a stable working majority with a set, unified agenda in the Reichstag." That would only be possible if Hitler secured the support of the Centre Party as well as the DNVP, and for Hitler, Hugenberg's party was clearly a lost cause. Otto Meissner had informed Hitler about Hindenburg's intentions in advance, allowing him to respond with a carefully prepared letter he now presented to the Reich president. In it, Hitler demanded that he be given "the authority that all previous bearers of Your Excellency's presidential power have possessed"—i.e. the comprehensive powers of a chancellor of a presidential cabinet enjoyed by Brüning and Papen. Hindenburg was by no means prepared to accede to this demand. With that, negotiations had broken down to all intents and purposes, even if Hindenburg assured Hitler: "You will always find my door open."[232]

Hitler's meetings with Hindenburg led to a correspondence between Hitler and Meissner that once more laid out the fundamental difference between a presidential cabinet and a parliamentary government based on a majority in the Reichstag.[233] On 23 November, Hitler officially renounced Hindenburg's mandate to negotiate with other parties to form a parliamentary majority as "impossible to fulfil for internal reasons." One day later, in a letter from Meissner, Hindenburg officially refused Hitler's request to be charged with the leadership of a presidential cabinet. Hindenburg's justification essentially repeated the arguments of 13 August. The Reich president felt unable to take responsibility for entrusting his "comprehensive presidential powers to the leader of a party that had always stressed its desire to rule exclusively and that was negatively inclined towards the measures which [Hindenburg] himself personally favoured and judged politically and economically necessary." Under such circumstances, the letter read, there was reason to fear that a Hitler-led presidential government "would inevitably become a single-party dictatorship exacerbating the tensions within the German people in a way incompatible with [Hindenburg's] oath of office and conscience."[234] Having already exchanged opinions with Meissner, Hitler expected his request to be refused and reacted calmly. "The old man doesn't trust him, and the feeling is mutual," Goebbels noted. "The farce is over. Papen will be back no doubt . . . The barons have won again. But for how long?"[235]

Hindenburg did not change his mind even when a small group of industrialists, bankers and agricultural producers submitted a petition on 19 November calling upon the president to give the "leader of the largest nationalist group"—i.e. Hitler—"responsible directorship" of a presidential cabinet.[236] The initiator of this action was Wilhelm Keppler, a middle-class entrepreneur, whom Hitler had made an economic adviser in the spring of 1932. At the behest of Hjalmar Schacht, a department named after Keppler was set up to "harmonise the National Socialist economic policies . . . with the flourishing of the private sector."[237] But the petition had not attracted nearly the amount of support from the business sector as its initiators expected. It contained only nineteen signatures, a little fewer than half of whom came from the so-called "Keppler Circle": Schacht, bankers Kurt von Schröder (the owner of the Stein bank in Cologne) and Friedrich Reinhart (a Commerzbank board member), the industrialist August Rosterg and Ilseder Steelworks supervisory board member Ewald Hecker. Hamburg merchant circles were prominently represented with four signatories: Emil Helfferich, Franz Witthoeft, Carl Vincent Krogmann (later mayor of Hamburg under the Nazis) and Kurt Woermann. Five signatories were large-scale agriculturalists—they were led by the president of the Reichslandbund, Count Eberhard von Kalckreuth. The Ruhrlade—an organisation representing the interests of the Ruhr Valley's twelve leading industrialists—provided only one signatory, Fritz Thyssen, a long-time Hitler admirer.[238] Schacht had already informed Hitler on 12 November that most representatives of heavy industry—in keeping with the ponderousness of that designation—were not going to take part in the petition.[239] The director of the United Steelworks, Albert Vögler, told Schröder on 21 November that he, Gutehoffnungshütte Supervisory Board Chairman Paul Reusch and Hoesch General Director Fritz Springorum agreed with the petition's "solution to the current crisis" but had declined to sign it because they "always avoided taking any sort of political position."[240] This suggests a change of mood in Hitler's favour that was probably influenced by the electoral gains of the KPD in the November election and the renewed fears among business leaders that Germany could be "Bolshevised." Still, the majority of industrialists stuck by Papen as their preferred choice for chancellor. That being the case, the petition was hardly going to sway Hindenburg. The greatest impression was probably made by the fact that it had been signed by Kalckreuth, since the lobbyists for the large landowners east of the Elbe had usually regarded Hindenburg as their advocate. In January 1933, their influence would prove particularly fateful.

After the attempt to form a "cabinet of national concentration" including the Nazis had failed, Hindenburg had no option other than to appoint either Papen or another one of his intimates chancellor. And aside from Papen, the only other option was Schleicher, the *éminence grise* of the presidential government. On 23 November, the general and Reich defence minister had already sounded out Hitler as to whether he would support a cabinet headed by him. Hitler answered in the negative and stressed that he would not allow any of his people to join such a cabinet. Given the circumstances, Schleicher said at a ministerial conference on 25 November, there "was nothing to be gained by a change of chancellor."[241] In fact, however, Schleicher had already decided to jettison Papen since, contrary to expectations, his protégé had proved to be anything but a passive puppet and had long since emancipated himself politically. Papen's greatest capital was the trust he had built up with Hindenburg during the five months of his chancellorship, which Papen now sought to cash in against Schleicher. On 26 November, Hindenburg refused to honour Papen's request not to be charged with forming a new government. "It broke his heart," Hindenburg wrote, that Papen too now wanted to abandon him.[242] Schleicher assumed responsibility for negotiating with the leaders of the political parties to get them to tolerate a Papen cabinet. But the sly general in fact used the meetings to test out the possibilities of becoming chancellor himself.[243]

The NSDAP leadership waited to see how "the Papen–Schleicher wrestling match" would turn out,[244] and Hitler studiously remained absent from Berlin, decamping to Weimar where he had a number of speaking engagements before the upcoming Thuringian local elections. Sefton Delmer visited him in his home away from home, the Hotel Elephant on Weimar's central market square, on 27 November, and Hitler appeared confident that the great day was at hand for the National Socialist movement, and that it would triumph in four months at the latest. After the interview Delmer asked him whether he aimed to restore the Hohenzollern monarchy once he assumed power. Hitler answered that he had no intention of being "a racehorse for an imperial jockey who wants to jump on my back precisely at the moment when

I cross the finishing line."[245] On 30 November, Hitler refused an invitation from Meissner to come to Berlin for another meeting with the Reich president. His tone was cordial, but his message was clear: as long as neither side had changed its position, there was no point in further talks. Hitler could not allow public hopes to be raised, he wrote, "which would inevitably lead to disappointment when they went unfulfilled."[246] The trauma of 13 August was still fresh.

By the time Hindenburg invited Papen and Schleicher to a meeting in the late afternoon of 1 December, it was clear that a decision on the chancellor question would have to be made. Schleicher reported on the lack of progress he had made with his negotiations but advocated "waiting to see how the Nazi camp would develop." He also revealed for the first time how, in his mind, a cabinet led by him might be able to find a way out of the crisis. Schleicher's idea was to get some National Socialists, under the leadership of Gregor Strasser, to join the cabinet, thereby dividing the NSDAP and establishing a "vertical front" from the trade unions through the bourgeois parties to dissident Nazis that would be willing to support measures necessary to stimulate the economy and lower unemployment. Hindenburg found that the prospects of success for this endeavour were too uncertain. He refused to accept further delay and asked Papen to continue heading the government. Papen agreed under the condition that "he would be given all the authority of the presidency in the conflict with the Reichstag that was sure to come." Hindenburg agreed, saying that it was a matter of "preserving Germany from the damage that would result from a violation of the duties of the Reichstag."[247] In other words, Hindenburg had decided upon a "battle cabinet" that would institute the emergency plans drawn up in August and September and dissolve the Reichstag, postpone new elections indefinitely and force through changes to the constitution that would divorce the government from the parliament. Schleicher made no secret of the fact that he could not support this decision because openly violating the constitution would lead to a de facto civil war. "You have a difficult road ahead, little monk," he threatened Papen when the meeting broke up.[248]

On the morning of 2 December, Papen convened his cabinet to inform them of Hindenburg's decision. It was a dramatic meeting. With the lone exception of Postal and Transport Minister

Eltz-Rübenach, the ministers all came out against a new incarnation of the Papen government. When Meissner remarked that this would not move the Reich president to reconsider "a decision he had made after much difficult deliberation," Schleicher played his trump card. In response to Justice Minister Gürtner's question as to "whether the Reichswehr was ready to meet all coming eventualities," Schleicher summoned Lieutenant Colonel Eugen Ott into the cabinet. In the preceding weeks, Schleicher had ordered him to test the Reichswehr's readiness to deal with internal unrest and simultaneously secure Germany's borders. The results of those tests were negative. Ott's report left a "devastating impression" on those at the meeting, as Finance Minister von Krosigk noted in his diary.[249] Papen immediately declared that the situation had changed and that he would have to renounce his mandate to form a government. Hindenburg only reluctantly accepted the resignation of his preferred chancellor. "Then in God's name we will have to let Herr von Schleicher try his luck," Papen recalled Hindenburg's words.[250] Even after he had stepped down as chancellor, Papen was allowed to keep his government apartment in Wilhelmstrasse. Hindenburg wanted him in close proximity as an adviser. This constellation of individuals would prove particularly significant in January 1933.

Hitler and his entourage welcomed Schleicher's nomination. "Very good—it's the old man's final evasive manoeuvre," Goebbels noted. "We'll immediately start complaining and extract whatever there is to be extracted."[251] But there was also resistance within the Nazi leadership to the idea of immediate confrontation. Gregor Strasser in particular demanded a change in the course of all-or-nothing. Many historians have asserted that Schleicher offered him the post of vice-chancellor and Prussian state president at a secret meeting on 4 December, but it is far from certain whether that was indeed the case. The only primary source for the meeting is Goebbels's *From the Hotel Kaiserhof to the Reich Chancellery*, but his diaries contain no mention of it or anything comparable to Goebbels's assertion in the book that "not only did Strasser not refuse but said that he intended to run in the next election with a list of his own." It is quite likely that Goebbels invented the meeting after the fact to make the idea of Strasser's "grave betrayal of the Führer and the party" seem more plausible.[252]

Whatever the real story may have been, no one disputes that Gregor Strasser advocated greater flexibility towards the Schleicher cabinet and did not regard the chancellor's office as a categorical precondition for joining the government. He was strengthened in those views by the results of the Thuringian election on 4 December. Although Hitler had been heavily involved in the campaign, the NSDAP suffered heavy losses. Compared with the Reichstag election of 31 July the party lost 40 per cent of its votes.[253] The headline of the article about the election in the *Berliner Tageblatt* read: "Nimbus Destroyed," and the newspaper wrote: "Since the NSDAP has thus far existed solely on the psychotic belief in certain victory, the reversal of this tendency must hit them all the harder." For the *Frankfurter Zeitung*, the outcome of the Thuringian election was proof that "Less and less, and not more and more, is Herr Hitler justified to appear in public claiming to be the leader of the nation . . . 4 December has put Herr Hitler back among the ranks of all the other political leaders where he belongs."[254] It no longer seemed inconceivable that the NSDAP would suffer dramatic losses in the next Reichstag election and see its movement decline. The mood of depression that had taken hold of the party since 6 November worsened. In December 1932, Munich's political police observed the first signs of disintegration: "Numerous resignations occur every day, dues arrive irregularly and expulsions because of arrears become more and more frequent . . . All sections of the party . . . give the impression of being run down."[255] This backdrop explains why the conflict between Hitler and Gregor Strasser would flare up as it did.

The rivalry had been simmering for quite some time, and Goebbels had done everything in his power to discredit his former mentor and now adversary with Hitler, particularly by suggesting that Strasser was using the task of organising the party to increase his own power. "Strasser has got his hands on the party with organisational changes— very subtle," Goebbels noted in late June 1932. "Hitler is to be gradually pushed aside. Honorary president. Hitler doesn't want to see it. He needs to be stirred up." Goebbels's constant undermining of the "party Mephisto," as he nicknamed Strasser, had its desired effect. In early September, Goebbels noted in his diary: "At noon a long conversation with Hitler. He greatly distrusts Strasser. Wants to knock his power within the party from his hands."[256] But it was no mean feat to strip Strasser of power since the Reich organisational director enjoyed great respect with the party rank and file; he was also considered by western German industrialists as one of the few National Socialists with whom one could do business. In September 1932, for example, August Heinrichsbauer, the editor of an important business journal in the city of Essen, informed Strasser that "several leading gentlemen" of industry were concerned about Hitler's all-or-nothing principle. "Adherence to this principle in practice," Heinrichsbauer argued, was "tantamount to self-destruction." The NSDAP would enter into a "voluntary isolation" from which it would be difficult to escape. Moreover, the party's "out-of-bounds, Marxist-style agitation" risked the trust "that is essential for taking over the highest forms of authority."[257] After the election defeat in November, Strasser thought the time was right to introduce a new strategy and lead the party from opposition into government. He spelled that out to Hitler in no uncertain terms. Hitler interpreted this as a challenge to his authority and reacted with commensurate venom. He was "furious with Strasser" for engaging in "sabotage," Goebbels noted on 9 November.[258]

In late November 1932, things came to an initial head when Hitler, Göring, Strasser, Frick and Goebbels debated the party's future stance towards the Schleicher cabinet in Weimar. "Strasser was for participation; otherwise he sees no hope," Goebbels summarised. "Hitler vehemently against him. Kept his line."[259] The conflict was ratcheted up a notch at a Reich leaders' conference in the Hotel Kaiserhof on 5 December. Beforehand Strasser and Frick had had a meeting with Schleicher at which the chancellor threatened to dissolve the Reichstag again should the National Socialists not tolerate his cabinet. Again, Strasser spoke out for a compromise while Hitler remained adamant.[260] In the afternoon of 5 December, a day before the new Reichstag convened for its first session, Hitler ordered NSDAP deputies to take a hard line, arguing that "Never has a great movement been victorious if it went down the path of compromise." The leader of the Nazis' parliamentary faction, Frick, then pledged his "unshakeable and inviolable loyalty" on behalf of the entire faction to the Führer.[261] During Hitler's speech, Goebbels observed, Strasser's face "turned to stone."[262] Strasser no doubt sensed that his views had isolated him within the faction and that there was no way of getting his way against Hitler in the party.

On the morning of 8 December, Strasser wrote to Hitler announcing his intention to resign from all his party offices and give up his Reichstag mandate. In justifying his decision, Strasser wrote that he thought Hitler's strategy of trying to create political chaos in the hope that the chancellorship would then drop into his lap was "wrong, dangerous and not in the general German interest." At the same time, Strasser assured Hitler that his resignation was not designed to put him at the "centre of an opposition movement within the party." On the contrary, he wished to "return to the party rank and file without any hard feelings." For that reason, Strasser wrote, he would be leaving both Berlin and Germany for an extended period.[263]

Immediately after writing that letter, Strasser summoned the NSDAP state inspectors present in Berlin, who each supervised numerous Gaue after a reform of the party organisation, to his office. In a hoarse voice, Strasser informed them of his decision. Hitler, he said, had not been following a "clear line" since August 1932 other than "wanting to become chancellor at all costs." Since there was no realistic chance of that happening, Hitler was risking the disintegration and decay of the movement. There were two ways to achieve power, Strasser argued. The legal one—in which case Hitler should have accepted the position of vice-chancellor and tried to use it as a polit- ical lever. And the illegal option—which would have entailed trying to seize power violently through the SS and SA. Strasser would have followed his Führer down either path. But he was no longer prepared to wait until some indeterminate point in the future when Hitler was named chancellor. Strasser also made no bones of the fact that his resignation was personally motivated, complaining vigorously that Göring, Goebbels and Röhm all enjoyed more of Hitler's favour than he did. For Strasser this was a demotion which he had not deserved and was no longer willing to tolerate. As one eyewitness to the meeting described it, Strasser's surprise announcement left the state inspectors utterly dismayed. They tried to get him to reconsider, but Strasser refused, announcing that his decision was "final and thus immutable."[264]

Strasser had his letter delivered to the Hotel Kaiserhof that very morning, and it created a massive stir among Hitler and his entourage. Hitler feared that it could be the harbinger of an inner-party rebellion and immediately took counter-measures. At noon, he held an audience with the state inspectors in his hotel suite, mustering all his powers of persuasion and melodrama to secure their loyalty. Hitler began his address on a very sombre note: "If one individual turns disloyal and abandons me in the most difficult hour of the party, I can overcome that. If you all intend to abandon me, my life's work and my struggle for it no longer makes any sense, and the movement will collapse. Without this movement and the life's mission that goes with it, I have nothing . . ."—at this point, Hitler glanced over at the bust of his niece Geli Raubal—". . . tying me to this earth. In that case, I will bear the consequences and would only ask that you decorate my body and my coffin with the banner I once created for the movement and as a symbol of a new Germany."

After this prelude, Hitler demanded that the state inspectors "openly and honestly" reveal the reasons Strasser had named for his resignation. Robert Ley did so, whereupon Hitler commenced a long monologue in which he tried to refute Strasser's arguments one by one. Becoming vice-chancellor, Hitler countered, would have quickly led to fundamental differences with Papen, who would have dismissed any initiative with a cold smile and the statement that he was the chancellor and the head of the cabinet and that Hitler could resign if he did not like his course. With that Papen and his backers would have succeeded in publicly demonstrating that Hitler was incapable of governing. "I refuse to go down this road and still wait until I'm offered the chancellorship," Hitler said. "The day will come, and probably sooner than we think." Even less promising was the illegal path to power, since Hindenburg and Papen would not hesitate to issue orders for the army to shoot. "Gentlemen," Hitler said, "I am not so irresponsible as to hound Germany's youth and the war generation, the best of Germany's manhood, in front of police and Reichswehr machine guns. Gregor Strasser will never see the day when that happens!"

Hitler also rejected all criticism of how he had treated his long-term comrade. He had been aware for quite some time that Strasser had become "reserved, sombre and reticent" towards him. "Is that my fault?" Hitler asked. "Can I help it if Göring and Goebbels show up for uninvited visits more often than Strasser? . . . Are these sufficient reasons for one of my most intimate and oldest colleagues to turn his back on the movement?" At this point, Hitler used his thespian ability and modulated his tone, becoming, as Hinrich Lohse, the state inspector of the northern Gaue, recalled, "ever more calm, human, friendly and solicitous." In the end, none of those in attendance at the two-hour meeting were able to resist Hitler's seductive logic. "He triumphed," Lohse remembered. "In the gravest test the movement had faced he proved to his uncertain yet indispensible foot soldiers, who then collected themselves, that he was the master and Strasser was the vassal."[265]

Nonetheless the mood that evening in the Goebbelses' apartment was subdued, with Hitler looking "very pale." At 3 a.m., Goebbels, Röhm and Himmler were summoned to an emergency meeting in the Hotel Kaiserhof. There they inspected the latest edition of the *Tägliche Rundschau* newspaper, which broke the news of Strasser's resignation and speculated that only if he took over the party leadership would the NSDAP be able to break free of its "hopeless confusion." Hitler saw his fears of a conspiracy confirmed. "If the party falls apart, I'll put an end to everything in three minutes," Goebbels quoted Hitler as saying.[266] As he had after the failed putsch of 1923, Hitler toyed with the idea of suicide; it would not be the last time before 30 April 1945, when he did in fact end his own life in the bunker beneath the Reich Chancellery. Despite the mood of despair, however, Hitler was astonishingly quick to take organisational measures. Strasser's office was to be restructured and the institution of the state inspectors abolished. Hitler himself took over the leadership of political organisation, naming Robert Ley, previously the NSDAP's Reich Inspector II, as his deputy. The Nazi departments for agriculture and education were made autonomous and handed over to Walther Darré and Goebbels respectively.[267]

Strasser's resignation was the top news story of 10 December. All the major newspapers led with it. Wild rumours flew around. But it soon became clear that the departure of this once-so-powerful man would not lead to a schism within the NSDAP. Strasser had accepted he would have to take a lesser role a long time before. He had no desire to engage in a power struggle with Hitler. The day of his resignation, he boarded a train to Munich from where he travelled on to Tyrol. He would not return from this holiday until shortly before Christmas. For two weeks, not even his close friends knew where he was.[268] The only Nazi leader to sympathise with him was Gottfried Feder, who had played an important role in Hitler's rise in the early 1920s but who no longer enjoyed much political influence.[269] On the afternoon of 9 December, Hitler once again spoke to the inspectors and Gauleiter before addressing Nazi Reichstag deputies. Goebbels noted: "Annihilating towards Strasser and even more towards Feder. The people howled in anger and pain. Huge triumph for Hitler. In the end a spontaneous declaration of loyalty. Everyone shook Hitler's hand. Strasser is isolated. A dead man."[270] Two days later, after the party leadership had met in the Brown House in Munich, Goebbels remarked: "Everyone rallying around Hitler. Joy that the Strasser affair was liquidated so quickly."[271]

But the crisis within the party was not quite over yet. Strasser's resignation caused what Goebbels described as "great unrest" among the party rank and file.[272] There were doubts about Hitler's leadership mixed with confusion as to where to go from here. Hitler spent the weeks before Christmas travelling to the Gaue to shore up morale among party functionaries. On 10 December in Breslau, in a sign of how dramatic the situation was, he compared the NSDAP's struggle with that of Friedrich the Great in the Seven Years War. The Prussian king, Hitler said, had also had to deal with repeated setbacks but had triumphed in the end. Anyone hoping for a "collapse of the movement," Hitler thundered, "was fooling himself—it stood as immovable as a cliff in the ocean."[273] The following day in Leipzig, he declared: "I am proud of the knowledge that the entire movement stands behind me more determined than ever. The party has not been seized by crisis. It's already put this crisis behind it."[274] This was little more than whistling in the dark. Hitler's words so obviously contradicted the true situation that he was unlikely to have convinced many of his followers. Goebbels's diary offers a more accurate account, with its mentions of declining attendance at Nazi events and the party's hopeless finances.[275] On Christmas Eve Goebbels concluded: "1932 has been one long run of bad luck. It should be smashed to pieces."[276]

In conversation with Bavarian State President Held on 10 December, the newly appointed Chancellor von Schleicher stated that he considered the National Socialist danger to have been "overcome."[277] The tenor of the opinion pieces in the major liberal newspapers at the end of the year was similar. "The massive National Socialist attack on the democratic state has been repelled," the Berlin correspondent of the *Frankfurter Zeitung*, Rudolf Kircher, declared. Julius Elbau titled his review article in the *Vossische Zeitung* "Year of Decision." Yet Elbau also complained that the republic had not been saved because Germans had defended it. "Its attackers got rid of one another," Elbau wrote. "It was a march through the valley of the devil that makes you shudder when you look back at it."[278] The *Berliner Tageblatt* already consigned the Hitler movement to the realm of history: "All over the world, people talked about . . . what was his first name again, Adalbert Hitler? And later? He disappeared."[279]

In the newspaper *Der deutsche Volkswirt*, the liberal journalist Gustav Stolper assured his readers: "The year 1932 has brought an end to Hitler's luck." The movement had reached its high point on 31 July, Stolper argued, and its decline had begun on 13 August. "Since then Hitlerism has been collapsing to an extent and at a rate that are comparable only with its rise," Stolper wrote. "Hitlerism is perishing according to the same laws by which it lived." The Social Democratic politician and former Reich Finance Minister Rudolf Hilferding agreed. In the SPD theoretical journal *Die Gesellschaft*, he wrote that 13 August had "marked a sudden shift in the drama—what is thus far the decisive turn . . . Herr Hitler descends the steps of the palais—it's the demise of fascism."[280]

"I believe we've turned the corner," Thomas Mann wrote to Hermann Hesse on 22 December. "We seem to be past the peak of the insanity."[281] People abroad, too, breathed a sigh of relief that the wave which had borne National Socialism seemed to be over. In the British Foreign Office, experts attributed Hitler's declining influence to his mule-headed insistence on total political authority: "Hitler's obstinacy in demanding complete power . . . has caused him to miss the bus."[282] Harold Laski, the British political scientist and Labour politician, remarked that Hitler would likely end up as an old man in a Bavarian village, telling his friends in an evening beer garden about how he once almost toppled the German Reich.[283]

Critical observers were not the only ones in late 1932 and early 1933 who were convinced that the National Socialist movement would inevitably fade into insignificance. Some Hitler supporters felt much the same way. On 31 December 1932, Luise Solmitz vented her disappointment in her diary: "This year takes with it a great hope . . . Adolf Hitler. The man who awakened us and led us towards national unity . . . is ultimately only the leader of a party that is sliding into certain desperation. I still can't accept this bitter disappointment."[284]

Of course, there were other voices that warned against drawing conclusions too hastily. In a letter to the industrialist Robert Bosch on 29 December, the journalist, political scientist and liberal politician Theodor Heuss expressed the hope that "all the fuss around Hitler will not survive this current crisis." At the same time, he added: "But it would be dangerous to underestimate the movement as a power factor since thousands of people are fighting for their economic survival within the [party] apparatus."[285] In the New Year's edition of *Die Weltbühne*, Carl von Ossietzsky also expressed his satisfaction that Hitler's party, which had knocked on the doors of power at the start of the year, was now "rocked by a serious crisis." But Ossietzsky, too, warned against overheated expectations: "The economic situation is still perfect for breeding further desperadoes."[286] With almost 5.8 million Germans still out of work in late 1932, unemployment was still very high, and in January that figure once again exceeded 6 million.[287] The reasons for the rise, however, were seasonal, and the figures were better than those of the previous years. The worst of the crisis was over and cautious optimism started to spread. "Land in sight!" read the headline of the business section of the *Frankfurter Zeitung* on 1 January 1933.[288]

12

Month of Destiny: January 1933

"The amazing thing about my life," Heinrich Brüning quoted Hitler as saying in early February 1933, just after being appointed German chancellor, "is that I'm always rescued just when I myself have given up."[1] And indeed, the NSDAP's prospects at the beginning of 1933 looked anything but rosy. Hitler's party was in deep crisis, with many members feeling deflated and resigned. Dissatisfaction with the party leadership was threatening to make the SA explode. In short, the National Socialist movement seemed further away from power than it had been at the start of 1932. In a letter to his friend Winifred Wagner in early 1933, Hitler complained about "all the difficult and onerous work" he had had to take on in the preceding weeks. New worries were constantly being added to old ones, Hitler carped. "I now know," he wrote, "why Wagner and his destiny in particular meant more to me as a young man than many other great Germans. It is no doubt the same misery of an eternal struggle against hatred, envy and incomprehension."[2]

Despite the confidence he projected externally, Hitler's dissatisfaction with his situation was clearly evident in the New Year's message he dictated on the Obersalzberg on 30 December—his droning voice could be heard echoing throughout Haus Wachenfeld.[3] That evening, Hitler read out his message to his paladins. Goebbels raved: "No reconciliation. A battle to the last drop of blood . . . Hitler is grand. Radicalism at its most extreme."[4] Gone were all tactical considerations that Hitler had maintained in order to preserve an aura of middle-of-the-road respectability at his appearances in front of business circles and during his 1932 campaign. The fanatic, anti-Semitic beer-cellar rabble-rouser re-emerged, articulating his obsession in language that was both exceedingly aggressive and pseudo-religiously convoluted:

"In almost all states of the world, the international Jew as an intellectual inspirer conducts the battle of the deficiently gifted inferior race against culture—and therefore against the talent of a higher breed that creates and secures human life, whose capacity to resist has been exhausted by liberalism." In Russia, Hitler added, the "Jewish intellectual leadership of the world revolution" had already done its destructive work, and the plan was "to infect the rest of the world via a network of connections and bases." Only one country, Hitler claimed, was standing up to this threat—Mussolini's Italy, which had found in Fascism "a dominant ideal capable of reshaping its entire life anew": "There we see the only state and the only people who have overcome the bourgeois, class-defined state and thereby achieved the preconditions for overcoming and rooting out Marxism."

Hitler reiterated his refusal to compromise in any form, stating that at this moment he was "utterly decided not to sell the first-born child of our movement for the pittance of being allowed to participate, without power, in a government." He would fight "down to his last breath" against bartering "the proudest and greatest uprising of the German people for a couple of ministerial seats."[5] There seemed to be no doubt that Hitler was sticking to his all-or-nothing strategy, and the party seemed headed for political marginalisation.

Four weeks later, Hitler was German chancellor. This turnabout, which astonished a great many people at the time, was no "triumph of the will" or "seizure of power," as Nazi propaganda would soon claim. It was the result of sinister intrigues behind the scenes in which a handful of figures, most notably former Chancellor von Papen, pulled the strings. "Herr Hitler was a defeated man when he was given victory," the journalist and sociologist Leopold Schwarzschild remarked in an article entitled "Chancellor Hitler" in early February 1933. "He had already lost the contest for governmental authority, when he was offered the opportunity to win it *ex post facto*."[6]

The decisive factor in the political intrigue was access to Hindenburg, or, as Konrad Heiden more casually wrote, "who had the old man's ear."[7] Ultimately the destiny of Germany depended on the Reich president. In his definitive Hindenburg biography, Wolfram Pyta convincingly showed that the ageing German president was not merely a marionette in the hands of his camarilla, as earlier historians had depicted him. On the contrary, Hindenburg remained in control of his decisions at all times.[8] He played the leading part in the drama that preceded Hitler's appointment to the chancellorship. Papen, State Secretary Meissner and Hindenburg's son Oskar—although the Weimar Constitution had not foreseen a role played by the president's son—were the most significant members of the supporting cast.

The beginning of the drama took place on 4 January, when Papen met with Hitler—an event which the historian Karl-Dietrich Bracher has rightly described as the "hour when the Third Reich was born."[9] It was arranged by the banker Kurt von Schröder, a member of the "Keppler Circle" and a signatory of the petition to Hindenburg of 19 November 1932. On 16 December, after a speech by Papen to the Berlin Gentlemen's Club, he had started conversing with the former Reich chancellor. The idea was broached—historians disagree whether by Papen or Schröder—of organising a tête-à-tête with Hitler, and Schröder immediately informed Keppler of Papen's willingness to meet the NSDAP chairman. "In the current situation the wish to arrange a discussion between P[apen] and H[itler] seems to me to be very crucial," Keppler wrote on 19 December, adding that Papen "could surely judge best of all . . . what the old man's mood was like these days and how resistance from that quarter could be best overcome."[10] That very day, Keppler wrote to Hitler offering to mediate. As a location for the meeting he suggested Schröder's house just outside Cologne, and he assured Hitler that he could vouch for the banker's "absolute reliability."[11] On 26 December, Keppler informed Schröder that Hitler would be arriving in Cologne on the morning of 4 January. He hoped that the "skill" of the host would succeed in "removing the final barriers during the conversation." From his estate at Wallerfangen an der Saar in south-western Germany, Papen agreed to the date and place.[12]

The planned meeting opened up interesting prospects for both Papen and Hitler. Papen had not got over being politically outmanoeuvred by his former patron Schleicher and was eager to get revenge, seeing a deal with Hitler as a way of forcing Schleicher from office and once more playing a major role himself. For his part, Hitler recognised that a possible understanding with Papen offered the chance of getting out of the dead end into which he had led his party and reversing his own fortunes. He knew that Papen retained privileged access to Hindenburg and hoped that the aristocrat could help break down the president's resistance to the idea of Hitler becoming chancellor.[13] Both sides insisted that the meeting be kept secret. Hitler, who was scheduled to open the campaign for the Landtag elections in Lippe-Detmold in western Germany on 4 January, did not travel directly to the first event there, but took the night train from Munich to Bonn. At the train station, his chauffeur Schreck was already waiting with a Mercedes limousine and drove Hitler and his travelling companions to the Hotel Dreesen in Bad Godesberg for breakfast. A short time later, a second automobile with curtained windows picked up Hitler, Himmler and Hess for the trip to Schröder's Cologne villa. Keppler, who had come from Berlin, showed up a short time later, while Papen arrived at 11:30 a.m.[14]

Hitler and Papen immediately withdrew for two hours into Schröder's office, with their host accompanying them as a silent witness. Schröder recalled Hitler opening the conversation by attacking Papen for his government's handling of the Potempa case. Papen replied that they should put their past differences behind them and try to arrive at a common basis for a new government that would consist of conservatives and National Socialists. It seems that Papen suggested something along the lines of a "duumvirate," in which he and Hitler would share power. To make this idea more appealing, he dangled the positions of defence and interior ministers before Hitler's nose, whereupon Hitler commenced one of his feared monologues in which he justified his insistence upon the chancellorship. However, he would accept Papen adherents in his cabinet, as long as they supported the changes he wanted to institute after taking office. The first measures Hitler specified were "the removal of all Social Democrats, Communists and Jews from leading positions" and the "re-establishment of order in public life." There was still a considerable gap between the two men's positions, but they did promise to continue their discussions.[15]

On 6 January, Keppler wrote to Schröder that "the meeting had a very positive effect in the desired direction." Hjalmar Schacht, too, thanked the banker for the "courageous initiative in paving the way for an understanding between men whom we both greatly admire and whose cooperation could perhaps bring about a positive solution most quickly." Hopefully, Schacht wrote, "the conversation in your house will be of historical importance."[16] Schacht's hope would come true. The meeting in Cologne was the starting point of a process that concluded on 30 January 1933. Hitler, who had been at his wits' end in the final days of December, saw himself catapulted back into the contest for power. The most important thing to emerge from the Cologne meeting was that Papen and Hitler agreed to put aside their enmity and work together to topple Schleicher. Although the contours of a new government had not been discussed in detail, and the all-important question of the chancellorship remained unanswered, the first step had been taken. Hitler could be sure that Papen would bring his influence with Hindenburg to bear to advance the solution they were going to negotiate. On 9 January, Hitler spoke with Goebbels, who then noted in his diary: "Papen dead set against Schleicher. Wants to topple and eradicate him entirely. Has the old man's ear. Even stays with him. Arrangement with us prepared. Either the chancellorship or the ministries of power: defence and interior. Worth listening to."[17]

The attempt to keep the conspiratorial meeting secret failed. When Papen got out of his car in front of Schröder's house, he was photographed by a waiting reporter. One day later, the pro-Schleicher *Tägliche Rundschau* newspaper ran a story with the headline: "Hitler and Papen against Schleicher."[18] The Catholic newspaper *Germania* compared the revelation with "prodding an anthill" and wrote that it had given rise to a flurry of wild speculation.[19] In a joint declaration on 5 January, Papen and Hitler tried to dispel the idea that their discussions had been directed against the new Reich chancellor. The meeting had merely been about exploring "the possibility of a broad national front of unity," the two men declared, and their talks had "not touched at all" on the current cabinet.[20] This disingenuous declaration did not succeed in putting the issue to rest. For days, the newspapers were filled with "a huge amount of guessing" as to what the purpose of Hitler and Papen's meeting had been.[21]

Initially Schleicher did not appear all that worried. At tea with the French ambassador, André François-Poncet, on 6 January, the chancellor spoke disparagingly about his predecessor. When next they met, Schleicher said, he would tell Papen: "My dear little Franz, you've committed another blunder."[22] On 9 January, Papen personally went to Schleicher and tried to convince him that the Cologne meeting had been about finding a place for Hitler in Schleicher's government—an assertion that Papen would repeat in his memoirs. It is hard to imagine that the former army general believed such an obvious lie, but in a joint communiqué the two men did assert that their discussion "completely belied" the reports of a falling-out between them.[23] That same day, Papen also reported to Hindenburg about his meeting with Hitler. If we believe Otto Meissner's memoirs, Papen said that Hitler "had given up his previous demands for the entire power of government and was now prepared in theory to participate in a coalition government with other right-wing parties." In response, Hindenburg charged Papen with continuing to negotiate with Hitler "on a personal and strictly confidential basis."[24] With that the Reich president consciously and in full knowledge of the consequences became a participant in a conspiracy aimed at creating a new government of "national concentration" behind the current Reich chancellor's back. It was the same sort of government that Hitler's intransigence had blocked in the autumn of 1932.[25]

Schleicher was no longer assured of the Reich president's support. As early as 10 January, Goebbels learned that the chancellor could by no means count on an executive order dissolving parliament if the Reichstag staged a vote of no confidence when it reconvened in late January. Schleicher, Goebbels noted, was on "a downward slope."[26] And indeed, the chancellor's position in early January was precarious. In a government statement he had made via radio on 15 December 1932, Schleicher had presented himself as a "socially responsible general," promising not just to take measures to boost employment, but also to revoke the ordinance of the Papen cabinet from 5 September that allowed employers to pay lower wages than those contained within the official labour agreements. These announcements alienated business leaders, and Schleicher further awakened mistrust with the "sacrilegious" assertion that he supported "neither capitalism nor socialism" and that he was not impressed by concepts like "private or planned economy."[27] On the other hand, Schleicher never succeeded in garnering the support of trade unions. While his policy of state-financed job creation met with approval in union circles, the Social Democrats, who were closely allied with the unions, stuck to their position of "absolute opposition" to the chancellor, whom they rightfully accused of being in part responsible for the coup d'état in Prussia in July 1932.[28]

Any hopes Schleicher had placed in cooperating with Gregor Strasser proved unrealistic. On 6 January, the Reich chancellor introduced the former NSDAP organisational director to Hindenburg, who agreed in principle to appointing Strasser vice-chancellor and labour minister. But Schleicher did not force the issue. Once news had got around about Papen and Hitler's Cologne meeting, there was very little chance that a significant part of the NSDAP would support Schleicher's government.[29]

To make matters worse for Schleicher, his cabinet was coming under attack from the Reichslandbund, the lobbying organisation of Germany's wealthy aristocratic landowners. It accused the government of not doing enough to protect big farmers against cheap food imports and of fore-closing on bankrupt agricultural enterprises. On 11 January, Hindenburg received a delegation from the Reichslandbund, consisting of four committee members, which included the National Socialist Werner Willikens. The organisation's president, Count Eberhard von Kalckreuth, painted the situation in the blackest terms. If immediate measures were not taken to "improve economic conditions in agriculture," disaster was imminent. Hindenburg immediately ordered Schleicher and his ministers for agriculture and economics to listen to the complaints and to take action.[30] Shortly after this meeting, however, a declaration that the Reichslandbund had given to the press before seeing Hindenburg was published. It accused the government of hastening the "impover-ishment of German agriculture" in a fashion "unimaginable even under a purely Marxist regime." Schleicher responded to this attack by refusing to negotiate in future with representatives of the Reichslandbund.[31]

In many respects the anti-Schleicher conspiracy resembled the campaign against Brüning's purported "agrarian Bolshevism" that had led to his dismissal in late May 1932. Hindenburg, who as the owner of a large estate in Neudeck was thoroughly receptive to the concerns of the East Elbian agrarians, was once again easily influenced. Schleicher's position, already weakened by Papen and the failure of the plans for a "cross-party front," was further undermined. "Schleicher has a conflict with the Landbund—the farmers are going wild," Goebbels noted. In a revised version of his diary from 1934, he was even more explicit: "That serves us quite well at the moment."[32] But perhaps even more damaging to Schleicher was the deterioration since late 1932 of his relationship with Oskar von Hindenburg, who served as a military adjutant and close adviser to his father. We do not know what precisely caused the rift between the two men, but the consequences were serious. Schleicher lost his most important advocate in the house of Hindenburg.[33]

As if the situation were not bad enough, the DNVP also distanced itself from the government. On 13 January, Alfred Hugenberg offered to join the Schleicher cabinet as minister of economics and agriculture, but only on the condition that the chancellor implemented a strictly authoritarian regime that ruled independently of parliament. Schleicher, however, had made clear in his radio address of 15 December that he "could hardly sit on the point of a bayonet" and "could not rule for very long without broad popular approval behind him" and therefore refused Hugenberg's offer.[34] Consequently, a week later, on 21 January, the DNVP Reichstag faction attacked the Schleicher government in tones no less harsh than the Landbund. Schleicher's government "tended towards internationalist socialism," the faction declared in a statement. "It runs the risk of Bolshevism in the countryside and is liquidating the authoritarian idea that the Reich president created when he appointed the Papen cabinet."[35]

All of this was grist for the mill of Schleicher's enemies. During the night of 10–11 January, after attending a performance of Verdi's *La Traviata*, Hitler met again with Papen in a villa belonging to the sparkling-wine merchant Joachim von Ribbentrop in the wealthy Berlin district of Dahlem. Ribbentrop, a former military officer who had gone into business after the First World War and got rich by marrying the daughter of winemaker Otto Henkell, had met Hitler in August 1932 and joined the NSDAP soon thereafter. Thanks to the excellent social contacts Ribbentrop enjoyed as a member of the exclusive Gentlemen's Club, he was an ideal mediator between conservative circles and the National Socialists.[36] We do not know precisely what Hitler and Papen discussed at their second meeting, but apparently they did not make much progress since Hitler declined at short notice an invitation to continue the exchange of opinions over lunch in Dahlem on 12 January. "Everything still up in the air," noted Goebbels.[37]

Hitler's attention at this time was focused on the Landtag election in Lippe-Detmold, which he hoped would prove that the NSDAP had recovered from the crisis of the end of the previous year and was back on the path to victory. "Lippe is the first opportunity to go from the defensive back on the offensive," Goebbels announced in his capacity as propaganda director.[38] The small region of 174,000 inhabitants, including 117,000 eligible voters, was flooded by an unprecedented wave of propaganda in the first two weeks of January. The NSDAP sent all their well-known speakers there, including Goebbels, Göring, Frick and Prince August Wilhelm. Hitler himself spoke at sixteen events in ten days. In an article entitled "Hitler Hits the Villages," the *Lippische Landes-Zeitung* concluded: "The NSDAP must be in serious trouble if the great 'Führer' himself is travelling to tiny villages."[39] Because the venues in Lippe were too small, Nazi campaign directors rented three tents, the largest of which could accommodate 4,000 people. In order to fill them, audience members were brought in great numbers from elsewhere: six specially chartered trains arrived on 4 January alone for Hitler's appearance at the opening of the campaign.[40]

Hitler's speeches offered little that was new. Once again, he justified his decision not to join the government in August and November 1932: "If I wanted to sell myself for a plate of lentils, I would have already done so." Whoever conquered the hearts of people, Hitler boasted, would inevitably be given the power of government one day. He had inherited a "thick peasant's skull" from his ancestors, he told audiences, and could wait until "Providence deems the time is at hand." Attentive listeners might have pricked up their ears at Hitler's repeated assertion that he did not want to enter the halls of power "through the back door but rather through the main gate." This—entry into the Chancellery—was precisely what Hitler was busily preparing in his meetings with Papen. Hitler's only reference of local interest was when he utilised the myth of the Germanic warrior Arminius to promote the Nazi ethnic-popular community. On 5 January, he invoked "the first communal, powerful and successful appearance of the German nation under Arminius against Roman tyranny," adding: "Internal fragmentation and squandering of strength has caused great injury to the German people down the years. The National Socialist ethnic-popular community will put an end to this situation."[41] One week later, Hitler and Goebbels visited the monument to Arminius near Detmold, which commemorated the Battle of the Teutoburg Forest at which the Roman general Varus's legions had been annihilated in A.D. 9. "Was covered in fog and made such a grand impression," Goebbels noted. "Defiant towards France. That's always been the thrust of German politics."[42]

Unnoticed by the public, Hitler established his election headquarters in Grevenburg, a waterfront estate belonging to Baron Adolf von Oeynhausen, right on the border with Lippe. From there, he could get to all parts of the small state with ease. "No inquisitive journalist's nose discovered our scent, and no reporter found our tracks," Otto Dietrich reported. "We arrived and then disappeared again without anyone knowing where from or where to."[43] The constant topic of evening conversations around the fireplace was Gregor Strasser, whose intentions were still unclear to Hitler and his consorts. They knew that Strasser had returned to Berlin at the start of January and that Schleicher had proposed making him vice-chancellor in a new cabinet. When it became known in Grevenburg on 12 January that Strasser had been received by Hindenburg, the Nazi leadership's worst fears seemed to have been confirmed. "That's how I imagine a traitor," Goebbels fumed. "I knew it all along. Hitler is very dismayed. Everything depends on Lippe."[44]

By the evening of 15 January, the results were in. The NSDAP had received 39,064 votes (39.5 per cent), 6,000 more than in November but still 3,500 fewer than in the election of June 1932.[45] The *Vossische Zeitung* newspaper commented: "If the concentrated and massive Hitler propaganda is only able to win a minority in this entirely Protestant and primarily rural region—39 per cent against 61 per cent—we can only conclude that the demands for 100 per cent power are a presumption consisting of deception and self-deception."[46] The influential editor in chief of the *Berliner Tageblatt*, Theodor Wolff, was even more pointed: "In truth, Hitler has brought home from his heroic struggle in Lippe only a fly impaled on the tip of his sword."[47] By contrast, Nazi propaganda celebrated the election result as a triumph. "The party is back on the offensive," Goebbels noted with satisfaction. "It was worth it in the end."[48] The *Völkischer Beobachter* also interpreted the election result as a success: "[It is] incontrovertible evidence that the stagnation of the NSDAP has been fully overcome and a new upward development has begun. The National Socialist wave is rising once more."[49] This sort of propaganda had a psychological effect. Hitler's position within the party was reinforced, and that put him in a better bargaining position with Papen.

Hitler also used this new momentum to settle accounts with Gregor Strasser at a Gauleiter conference in Weimar on 16 January. There he spoke for three solid hours, and if anyone present sympathised with the former NSDAP Reich organisational director, he did not speak up. "Hitler has achieved a complete victory," Goebbels recorded. "The Strasser issue has been dealt with . . . Everyone is abandoning him . . . I'm glad this is happening to this fraud. He'll end up as nothing, just as he deserves."[50] Strasser's career was over. To avoid being expelled from the party, he had to pledge to avoid any political activity for two years, and Hitler cancelled a meeting with him planned for 24 January in Munich at short notice.[51] The party leader never forgave the colleague he had formerly valued so much for putting him in a tight spot. Hitler would have Strasser murdered during the Night of the Long Knives on 30 June 1934.

From Weimar, Hitler went directly to Berlin to continue secret talks about the formation of a government under his leadership. The NSDAP chairman was "in the best of moods and obviously quite satisfied with how things were going," Wilhelm Keppler told Kurt von Schröder.[52] On 17 January, Hitler met Hugenberg and the DNVP parliamentary chairman, Otto Schmidt-Hannover, in Göring's apartment. The former partners in the Harzburg Front had bitterly attacked one another in the November election, but now relations were more relaxed. On 28 December 1932, Hugenberg had written to Hitler directly and suggested discussing whether they might not be able to restore unity and end "the political division of parts of the movement for national renewal that actually belong together."[53] A rapprochement with the NSDAP was part and parcel of the DNVP's increasing distance from the Schleicher cabinet. The two men's talks on 17 January yielded no concrete results, but Hitler did assure Hugenberg of a major post in his cabinet if he was made chancellor. Hitler was quite contemptuous of Hindenburg, dismissing him as "not an independent factor," a man who talked "like a gramophone record" and "whose political vocabulary consisted of the same eighty sentences." For his part, Hugenberg seemed to "have found lots of common ground with Hitler, although their mutual understanding was not perfect," DNVP Deputy Chairman Reinhold Quaatz noted after being extensively briefed about the meeting that evening.[54]

At noon on 18 January, Hitler, Röhm and Himmler once again travelled to Ribbentrop's villa in Dahlem to continue talks with Papen. His position strengthened by the Lippe election results, Hitler demanded the chancellorship more forcefully than at the earlier meetings. Papen responded that he did not have enough influence to get Hindenburg to grant this wish, whereupon the negotiations seemed once again to have reached a dead end. To overcome the blockade, Ribbentrop suggested introducing Hitler to Oskar von Hindenburg. Then the discussion broke up without a date for the next meeting being agreed.[55] Papen wrote to the Ruhr Valley industrialist Fritz Springorum that he had tried "in every way to bring about a national concentration but had been greeted by fierce resistance from Hitler who objected, after the Lippe elections, to becoming the junior partner in a governing cabinet."[56] At this point, Papen still hoped to become chancellor himself—an option that would have been welcome to most Ruhr industrialists.

Although Hitler was quite preoccupied by the conspiracy to over-throw Schleicher, he still found plenty of opportunities for entertainment. On the evening of 18 January, he and Goebbels took in the film *The Rebel*, directed by and starring Luis Trenker, about a Tyrolean student who sacrifices his life in the anti-Napoleonic resistance. "A great achievement," Goebbels gushed: "a Tyrolean national uprising. Fantastic crowd scenes . . . It shows you what film can do. And what we will do with film some day." Hitler was so carried away that he watched the film a second time the next evening. Then they sat together and reminisced at Göring's residence until 5 a.m. "Hitler very funny," Goebbels noted. "We laughed ourselves silly."[57]

Despite the tug of war for political power, Hitler retained his daily routine and tried to project calm and confidence. On most afternoons, he could be seen taking tea and cake with his entourage in the Hotel Kaiserhof. Late in the evening, after the political work was done, Hitler usually relaxed in the company of Joseph and Magda Goebbels. It was rare for him to leave before 3 a.m. Goebbels fretted about his health: "The boss doesn't feel well at all. He gets too little sleep and doesn't eat enough."[58] On 20 January, Hitler put on a star performance in front of 10,000 party functionaries in the Sportpalast. "A storm of applause erupted such as cannot be described in words," wrote the Nazi newspaper *Der Angriff* about Hitler's entrance into the auditorium. "You thought the place would collapse. The music was drowned out. The Führer strode to the front of the hall through a forest of arms raised in salute, accompanied by SS men and his constant companions."[59] Once again, Hitler told his followers not to be discouraged by setbacks or be infected by "accursed defeatism"—a jibe at Strasser—but to work with determination towards the "great goal," the establishment of a "new ethnic-popular community." In conclusion he appealed to his audience: "We have to forge our will and make it even harder. We have to consecrate this will with camaraderie and obedience. With it, we will defy every misery of this age. May our will become the will of the German people and overcome the time of great misery!"[60] Hitler's entire speech aimed to prepare the party faithful for an extended struggle for power. No one listening would have been able to imagine that in only ten days' time Hitler would be appointed Reich chancellor.

During the afternoon of 22 January, at the Nicolai cemetery in the Berlin district of Prenzlauer Berg, Hitler unveiled a memorial to Horst Wessel, the SA street fighter who had been elevated to a martyr after his death in February 1930. Hitler praised Wessel as a "blood witness," whose song "Die Fahne hoch"—"Hold High the Flag"—had already become a "battle hymn for millions." By sacrificing his life, Hitler said, Wessel had created a "monument more lasting than stone and bronze."[61] Before the Berlin SA units assembled at the cemetery, they had marched past the Karl-Liebknecht-Haus, the KPD headquarters, on Bülowplatz. Berlin's police president had refused permission for a Communist counter-demonstration and deployed 14,000 police officers to prevent clashes between the two groups. Everything proceeded relatively calmly. The KPD leadership had called upon their followers not to let themselves be provoked by the SA march. Nazi propaganda, however, celebrated the absence of confrontation as a great victory. "The SA marched," Goebbels noted. "Massive loss of prestige for the KPD. Bülowplatz is ours. We've won a battle."[62] The Social Democratic *Vorwärts* commented:

> The fact that on 22 January 1933 in Berlin Hitler's brown hordes were allowed to march outside the windows of the KPD headquarters with the conscious intention of challenging and humiliating their enemies, and that they were able to do so without any possibility of effective resistance, was a very bitter pill for the *entire* labour movement.[63]

That evening, Hitler gave another speech dedicated to Horst Wessel in the Sportpalast and then left at around 10 p.m. to travel with Frick and Göring to Dahlem, where Papen was waiting. Notably, State Secretary Meissner and Oskar von Hindenburg were also present. To keep their participation at the meeting secret, the two men had conspicuously attended the opera on Unter den Linden and discreetly slipped out of the theatre before the final curtain.[64] Shortly after arriving in Ribbentrop's villa, Hitler asked the president's son for a private word. What the two men talked about during their two-hour discussion has been the subject of much speculation. It is hardly probable, as one rumour had it, that Hitler threatened to reveal that the president had improperly transferred the Neudeck estate to his son Oskar in 1928 to avoid paying inheritance tax. It is quite possible, however, that Hitler may have promised to use his influence, if made chancellor, to wipe out the debts on the estate that had resulted from extensive renovations.[65] Hitler was apparently unable to overcome all of Oskar von Hindenburg's reservations, but on the trip back to central Berlin, the president's son did tell Meissner he had been taken with what Hitler had to say.[66] Hitler for his part was less impressed. "Young Oskar is an unusual picture of stupidity," he remarked a few days later to Goebbels.[67]

More significant was the fact that after his private talk with the younger Hindenburg, Hitler had made clear progress in his negotiations with Papen. For the first time, the man who had Hindenburg's ear suggested that he might warm to the idea of Hitler becoming chancellor while contenting himself with the post of vice-chancellor.[68] But when Papen visited President von Hindenburg on the morning of 23 January to argue for that idea, he was rebuffed. Ribbentrop took on the task of breaking the bad news to Hitler.[69] That evening, the latter travelled to Munich, where he met Goebbels at the Brown House. Hitler still seemed confident about how things were developing. "Terrain smoothed," noted Goebbels. "Papen wants to be vice-chancellor. Schleicher's position very precarious. He seems to suspect nothing."[70] In Hitler's absence, Frick and Göring continued negotiations with Papen in Dahlem. They agreed that the best way to overcome Hindenburg's resistance to a Hitler chancellorship was to present him with a cabinet of "national concentration" that would reunite all former members of the Harzburg Front. Ribbentrop succinctly noted: "Decision reached about a national front to support Papen with Hindenburg."[71] On the evening of 21 January, Meissner had told

Hugenberg: "Hindenburg attaches great importance to the participation of the German nationalists." The German president also wanted to retain the right to appoint the Reich defence and foreign ministers himself, arguing that according to Germany's constitution he was head of state and represented the Reich under international law and therefore bore direct responsibility for those positions.[72]

The Reich chancellor's demise was getting closer and closer. "Schleicher's position is very bad," Goebbels noted on 22 January. "When will he fall?"[73] Two days before that, the Reichstag Council of Elders decided that Germany's parliament would indeed be called to session on 31 January. Given that only the tiny DVP faction had declared its support for the government, Schleicher was headed for a devastating vote of no confidence, just like Papen before him. Schleicher had already threatened on 16 January to present parliament with a written dissolution order in case the Reichstag put such a vote on the agenda. In so doing he was resorting to the same plan his predecessor had drawn up towards the end of his tenure: dissolving the Reichstag and postponing fresh elections beyond the sixty-day limit imposed by the German constitution, to the autumn, in the hope that the economy would further recover later in 1933. Surprisingly Foreign Minister von Neurath and Finance Minister Schwerin von Krosigk, who had rejected a violation of the constitution in early 1932, both supported Schleicher's idea.[74] The question, though, was whether Hindenburg could be persuaded—especially since Schleicher had got Papen and his government dismissed by arguing that precisely this sort of violation of the constitution would lead to civil war.

Schleicher received his answer on 23 January at a meeting with Hindenburg, who declared that while "he would consider dissolving the Reichstag, he could not take responsibility for postponing the election beyond the deadline specified by the constitution."[75] This decision was hardly a surprise. By resorting to Papen's old emergency plan, Schleicher was admitting that, just like his predecessor, he had failed to establish a broad parliamentary majority to tolerate his government. Hindenburg found it presumptuous that the chancellor would try to take the same escape route that he had used to drive his predecessor from office. By this point the Reich president seems to have decided to drop Schleicher—a decision made easier since he was being kept informed about the secret negotiations between Papen and Hitler and knew that a potential alternative was emerging. It is possible that Hindenburg was also influenced by the fact that a few days previously in the parliamentary budget committee, talk had turned to the misuse of public funds for the restoration of debt-ridden aristocratic estates. The so-called "Eastern Help scandal" made waves, especially as several of Hindenburg's friends were implicated. They in turn accused Schleicher of not protecting them and stepped up their attacks upon him.[76]

The Social Democrats and the Centre Party were greatly alarmed by rumours about Schleicher's intention to cancel the fresh elections mandated by a dissolution of parliament. On 25 January, the SPD party leadership and the leaders of the Social Democratic parliamentary faction "vehemently protested against the plan to proclaim a so-called emergency legal situation," arguing that it would amount to a coup d'état.[77] The Prussian state president, Otto Braun, even spoke of a "call for high treason."[78] In a letter of 26 January, the chairman of the Centre Party, Prelate Ludwig Kaas, also warned the Reich chancellor that he was headed down a legally unjustifiable path: "Moving back the date of the election would be an undeniable violation of the constitution with all the legal and political consequences that would entail."[79] These protests by Germany's two largest democratic parties further undermined Schleicher's position. What the pro-democracy politicians did not realise was that the biggest danger was not posed by Schleicher's suggested violation of the constitution, but by the installing of a cabinet of "national concentration" under Hitler.

On the morning of 28 January, Schleicher called a cabinet meeting and announced that he would only appear before the Reichstag on 31 January if the Reich president gave him an order to dissolve parliament. He said he did not want to present the public with a "pointless spectacle of certain defeat." If Hindenburg refused as expected to issue such an order, Schleicher would submit the cabinet's resignation. Shortly after noon, once the ministers had approved this plan, the chancellor adjourned the meeting and made his way to see the president. As he had five days previously, Hindenburg coolly rejected Schleicher's request for a dissolution order, saying that Schleicher had failed "to win over a parliamentary majority" and that another solution would have to be found.[80] After only twenty minutes, Schleicher returned to his cabinet with the news that he "might as well have been talking to a wall" and that "the old man seemed not to register arguments, but simply to be reciting words he had memorised." Finance Minister von Krosigk noted in his diary: "We are all deeply shaken. The Schleicher cabinet has been toppled after two months by the Reich president withdrawing his confidence."[81] Shortly after his dismissal of Schleicher, Hindenburg officially called upon Papen to start negotiations to form a new government. "He is now unabashedly playing the role of the president's favourite since he has nothing else behind him and almost the entire German people against him," wrote Harry Kessler, who believed Germany was headed for another Papen-led cabinet. "It sickens me to think that we will once again be ruled by this infamous oaf and reckless gambler . . . The whole thing is a mix of corruption, back-room dealings and nepotism that recalls the worst days of the absolutist monarchy."[82]

On 27 January, the day before Schleicher's resignation, Hitler returned from Munich to Berlin. That afternoon, in Göring's office, Hitler and Frick met with Hugenberg and Otto Schmidt-Hannover. Göring opened the meeting by announcing that Papen now supported Hitler being named chancellor and that Franz Seldte, the leader of the Stahlhelm, had agreed to join a Hitler-led cabinet. But Hugenberg still remained reserved, rejecting Hitler's demand that a Nazi be named the Prussian interior minister, which would have given the NSDAP control over the police force in the largest German state. The DNVP chairman also demanded that Schmidt-Hannover be made state secretary in the Reich Chancellery and that a further DNVP member be appointed Reich press spokesman. Hitler would not hear of this, and the meeting, Ribbentrop noted, "ended in quarrel."[83] Hitler was so outraged at Hugenberg's behaviour that he wanted to depart immediately for Munich, and Göring and Ribbentrop only just managed to persuade him to stay in Berlin. Old fears resurfaced that the conservatives would derail him just before he reached his goals, as they had the preceding August. "Hitler is very sceptical and mistrustful," Goebbels noted. "With justification. These people are one big gang of swindlers."[84] Rumours circulating in Berlin that Papen was about to be called to head a "battle cabinet" only strengthened Hitler's distrust.[85] In any case, he refused to meet that evening with the former chancellor. Negotiations seemed once again to be on the verge of breaking down.

It was Papen who kept them going. On the evening of 27 January, he declared that the importance of the quarrel between Hugenberg and Hitler should not be exaggerated. The main thing was that he, Papen, "had now come out fully in favour of Hitler as chancellor" and was willing to do everything to persuade Hindenburg. For Ribbentrop, this assurance was the "turning point in the whole matter."[86]

Indeed, over the course of 28 January, Papen succeeded in finally overcoming Hindenburg's resistance to the idea of Hitler as chancellor—on the condition that the NSDAP leader formed his government "within the framework of the constitution and with the assent of the Reichstag." Hugenberg, who met with Papen that afternoon, also proved to be far more conciliatory now that Schleicher had resigned, remarking that "We need to enter into a pact with Hitler and try to limit his power as much as possible." Hugenberg wanted to be named the economics minister of both the Reich and Prussia, arguing that uniting the two positions made political sense. Hitler for his part told Papen that Hugenberg could pick and choose which posts he wanted—with the exception of Reich interior minister and Prussian state commissioner, which were to be reserved for Nazis.[87] On the surface this was a remarkable compromise and a striking turnabout from Hitler's previous policy of all-or-nothing. In reality, however, Hitler was gambling that by using those two positions the National Socialists could consolidate power as they had in Thuringia in 1930. Papen contacted Finance Minister von Krosigk, who agreed to join the Hitler cabinet as long as he was "able to work professionally."[88] Konstantin von Neurath and Paul von Eltz-Raubach likewise agreed to continue in their previous posts.

When Papen reported to Hindenburg late in the evening of 28 January about how negotiations were progressing, the president was pleased at what he considered Hitler's "moderation." Hindenburg was also impressed by the fact that most of the conservative ministers whom he favoured and who had served in Papen's and Schleicher's cabinets would be retained. The president decided to replace Schleicher at the Defence Ministry with one of his confidants, Lieutenant General Werner von Blomberg, the commander of the military district in East Prussia, who was at the time a member of the German delegation to a disarmament conference in Geneva.[89] Oskar von Hindenburg was charged with summoning Blomberg back to Berlin by telephone. With that, no obstacles to a Hitler cabinet remained. Still, those closest to

Hitler feared that Hindenburg might still change his mind. "The old man is unpredictable," Goebbels warned. "We should be under no illusions about that!"[90]

On 29 January, the last deals were done. That morning the negotiators agreed on the make-up of the cabinet, with Papen accepting Hitler's proposal to make Frick Reich interior minister. For his part Hitler had to swallow—"with barely concealed resentment"—Hindenburg's appointment of Papen and not himself as Reich commissioner of Prussia. By way of compensation, Göring was named Prussian interior minister and deputy Reich commissioner, which gave him control over the Prussian police—something Hugenberg had wanted to prevent. As a new condition for his participation, Hitler demanded that fresh elections be called and a subsequent enabling law be passed. This was an idea he had already proposed in his negotiations with Hindenburg in November 1932,[91] although it required the assent of both his conservative-nationalist coalition partners and above all the German president.

That afternoon, at a meeting with Hugenberg and Stahlhelm leaders Franz Seldte and Theodor Duesterberg, Papen sought to overcome the final objections to a Hitler cabinet. Hugenberg was promised the Economics Ministry as well as that of agriculture in both Prussia and the Reich. The prospect of being in charge of such a mega-ministry was so appealing that he agreed to support the deal Papen had negotiated with Hitler. Seldte, who was tipped for the Labour Ministry, also agreed to join the cabinet. Only Duesterberg, who had been subject to scathing attacks from National Socialists only months before for having a Jewish grandfather,[92] warned against "the dynamics of Hitler's nature and his fanatic mass movement." Hugenberg brushed aside such concerns, arguing that the dominance of traditional conservatives in the cabinet would neutralise the threat of Nazi abuse of power and "fence Hitler in." Duesterberg prophesied that Hugenberg "would one night have to flee through his ministerial gardens in his underwear to avoid arrest."[93] Few traditional conservatives were that prescient. Most were aware of the risk entailed by a pact with Hitler but believed the Nazi leader could be kept in check. "If we go with Hitler, we have to restrain him," DNVP Deputy Chairman Quaatz wrote in his diary on 29 January.[94] It would not be long before it became apparent how utterly misplaced all ideas of restraining Hitler actually were.

What Papen failed to mention to Hugenberg was that Hitler had insisted on fresh elections—a demand that the DNVP chairman would hardly have accepted since the NSDAP was likely to gain votes at the conservatives' expense, making it all the more difficult to rein in Hitler. When Papen briefed Göring about the outcome of the meeting, he also gave the impression that "everything was a done deal." Göring immediately passed on the message to the Nazi leadership anxiously waiting in the Hotel Kaiserhof. Goebbels remained sceptical: "We don't yet dare believe it. Is Papen being honest? Who knows?"[95] There were persistent rumours in Berlin that Hindenburg ultimately wanted to appoint a Papen–Hugenberg "battle cabinet" without Nazi involvement but that the Reichswehr would not tolerate such a move. Later that afternoon Hitler met with General Kurt von Hammerstein, the head of the army chief of command, at the Bechsteins' villa. There the NSDAP chairman was asked "whether he thought the negotiations with the Reich presidential palace about assuming power were genuine or just for show." If the latter were the case, Hammerstein promised, the military command would try to use its influence in Hitler's favour, although Schleicher would likely retain the post of defence minister. Hitler disingenuously said that nothing had been decided yet and promised to notify Hammerstein as soon as he "saw things clearly."[96]

That evening, Schleicher and Hammerstein sent their go-between Werner von Alvensleben to Goebbels's apartment, where Hitler and Göring were waiting. His task was to gain information about the status of negotiations, but he went well beyond that, taking it upon himself to announce: "If the folks on Wilhelmstrasse are only pretending to negotiate with you, then the Reich defence minister and the army chief of staff would have to alert the garrison in Potsdam and sweep the entire pigsty on Wilhelmstrasse clean."[97] The Nazi leadership interpreted this ill-advised statement as proof that Hindenburg intended to appoint a Papen–Hugenberg cabinet and that the Reichswehr was considering a coup d'état. It was hardly beyond the realm of possibility that Hindenburg would be deposed and his son Oskar arrested. "So it's a coup," Goebbels commented. "A threat. In earnest or a joke? Reported to Göring and Hitler waiting in the room next door. Göring spoke immediately to Meissner and Papen . . . We deliberated at length. Hitler in full motion."[98] The NSDAP chairman took the rumours very seriously and had the leader of the

Berlin SA, Count Wolf-Heinrich von Helldorff, put all Brownshirts in the German capital on high alert. The Nazi leadership also charged the "trustworthy" police major Walter Wecke, later commander of the Hermann Göring Regiment, with "preparing for a lightning strike to occupy Wilhelmstrasse with six police battalions."[99]

Although it soon emerged that the rumours of a coup were entirely unfounded, they served to hasten the pace of developments. Papen saw his conviction that there was no time to lose reinforced, and late in the evening on 29 January, he presented Hindenburg with a final list of cabinet members. As had been agreed, it contained only three National Socialists: Hitler as chancellor, Frick as interior minister and Göring as Reich minister without portfolio, deputy Prussian interior minister and Reich commissioner for aviation. Three of the party-unaffiliated ministers had previously served in the Papen and Schleicher cabinets: Foreign Minister von Neurath, Finance Minister von Krosigk and Postal and Transport Minister Eltz-Rübenach. Reichswehr Minister von Blomberg, Economic and Agriculture Minister Hugenberg and Labour Minister Seldte were new appointments. The post of justice minister was left vacant because Papen wanted Hindenburg to think that negotiations with the Centre Party were under way and one ministry had to be left open in case of agreement; the position was intended to go to Franz Gürtner, who had held it under Papen and Schleicher. Swearing-in ceremonies were scheduled for 11 a.m. the following day.[100]

The Reich president's decision was not announced publicly, so on 30 January 1933 the morning newspapers were still in the dark as to what was going on. Some still thought that the appointment of a Papen–Hugenberg cabinet excluding the National Socialists was the most likely outcome. The *Frankfurter Zeitung* speculated that Hitler would once again make impossible demands to avoid the responsibility of power.[101] Schleicher had thought much the same, having told his cabinet on 16 January that "Hitler didn't really want to come to power."[102] But the leader of the NSDAP was on the verge of his greatest triumph. Hitler and his entourage stayed up until 5 a.m. in the Goebbelses' apartment, ever fearful that some unforeseen events would throw everything back up in the air.[103] When Blomberg arrived at the Anhalter Bahnhof train station early that morning, Oskar von Hindenburg immediately took him to Wilhelmstrasse, where at 9 a.m. he was sworn in as the new Reich defence minister.

Meanwhile Papen summoned Hugenberg, Seldte, Duesterberg and Schmidt-Hannover to his apartment on Wilhelmstrasse to inform them that the new cabinet was about to be made official. When Duesterberg and Schmidt-Hannover protested against the hasty appointment of Hitler as chancellor, a "flustered" Papen interjected: "If a new government has not been formed by 11 a.m. the Reichswehr will be marching, and we will face a military dictatorship under Schleicher and Hammerstein." Soon afterwards Hitler and Göring arrived. Once more, the NSDAP chairman demonstrated what a fine actor he was, immediately going up to Duesterberg, taking his hand and declaring in a solemn voice and with tears in his eyes: "I greatly regret the personal insults to you in my newspapers. I give you my word that I did not order them."[104]

Around 10:45 a.m., a quarter of an hour before the scheduled swearing-in ceremonies, the group proceeded through the ministerial gardens to the Reich Chancellery, where Hindenburg had been residing since the summer of 1932, while the presidential palace was being renovated. Duesterberg later recalled that, as the other ministers designate arrived one by one, with the exception of Eltz-Rübenach, who had fallen ill, Hitler, Papen and Hugenberg negotiated the final unresolved questions in Meissner's office. It was only now that Papen and Hitler revealed to the DNVP chairman that Hitler intended to dissolve the Reichstag and call for new elections. Hugenberg was taken aback and vehemently protested, arguing that the November 1932 election had accurately mirrored the relative strengths of the parties and that a fresh poll was unnecessary. In a grand gesture, Hitler gave his word of honour that the make-up of the cabinet would not change, regardless of the outcome of a new election. But the blindsided Hugenberg refused to give in even after Papen pleaded with him not to endanger the agreement, which had been so hard to reach. The formation of the new government looked as though it would fall through literally at the last minute. The appointed time for the swearing-in ceremony came and went, and Hindenburg was getting impatient. Meissner burst into the room, watch in hand, and complained: "It's 11:15. You can't keep the Reich president waiting any longer." Duesterberg recalled: "At that point, Hugenberg relented. Hitler had got his way. Proud and triumphant, with his underlings in his wake, he marched victoriously up the stairs to the first floor, where the elderly gentleman was awaiting the new cabinet."[105]

Hindenburg greeted the men and expressed his satisfaction that "the nationalist Right has finally been unified," whereupon Papen read out the list of ministers. After being sworn in, Hitler gave a short speech in which he asked the Reich president to have faith in him and the new government.[106] At around noon, the ceremony was concluded. In his diary, Goebbels wrote: "[Hindenburg] was quite moved at the end. That's the way it should be. Now we have to win him over completely."[107] Hitler's followers had been waiting on tenterhooks in the Hotel Kaiserhof, and when the freshly appointed chancellor returned there, to cheers from a crowd of admirers, everyone breathed a sigh of relief. "We all had tears in our eyes," noted Goebbels. "We shook Hitler's hand. He deserved this. Enormous celebrations." Goebbels had not got a cabinet post, but he had received Hitler's promise that he would be put in charge of the Education Ministry after the next election. "Right down to work," he noted. "The Reichstag will be dissolved. New elections in four weeks. Until then I'm free of any office."[108] Later that day, Hitler gave a speech in which he thanked his party comrades for the "loyalty and devotion" that had made his political triumph possible. "The task that lies before us is massive," he added. "We will have to be equal to it and we will be."[109]

That evening, National Socialists celebrated Hitler's appointment as chancellor with a torchlit parade lasting hours. "There's a jubilant mood tonight in Berlin," wrote Harry Kessler, who was as surprised as most people by Hitler's elevation to chancellor. "SA and SS men, together with uniformed Stahlhelm members, are making their way through the streets, and the pavements are crowded with onlookers. In and around the Hotel Kaiserhof, it's a veritable carnival."[110] Hitler, who greeted the marching columns of his supporters from the illuminated window of his new office, was euphoric. "The good doctor is a true wizard," he praised Goebbels, who had hastily organised the celebrations. "Where did he get all the torches?"[111] A few windows further down, Hindenburg stood stiff as a statue and received tributes from SA men. The newly appointed Nazis lost no time in exploiting the possibilities of radio. Speeches by Göring and Goebbels were broadcast on all stations in Germany except Bavaria's Bayerischer Rundfunk. Göring compared the mood to that of August 1914, when "a nation also set out for new territory," thereby establishing the melodramatic tone of Nazi propaganda, which would soon transform 30 January 1933 into a "day of national uprising."[112] Things only calmed down after midnight. While Hitler remained in the Chancellery and held one of his digressive monologues,[113] Goebbels went to Potsdam to visit Prince August Wilhelm. There the celebrations continued for hours. "Everything completely intoxicating," Goebbels noted. "At home at 3 a.m. Fall into bed as though dead. Exhausted."[114]

January the 30th, 1933 saw something happen that hardly anyone would have thought possible at the end of December 1932. At the relatively young age of 43, Hitler had become the chancellor of the most powerful state in central Europe. Even his closest confidants like Goebbels regarded this twist of fate as "something out of a fairy tale."[115] Hess wrote to his wife on 31 January: "Am I dreaming or am I awake? I'm sitting in the chancellor's office on Wilhelmplatz. Ministry employees silently approach on soft carpets bringing files for the Reich chancellor." Even the day before, Hess had been afraid that everything would fall apart, especially as Hitler had confided to him that "a couple of times things were on a knife-edge" because of "intransigence" from Hugenberg, the "old shrew" in the cabinet.[116]

The formation of a "Cabinet of National Concentration" also seemed like a miracle to the NSDAP's supporters. "It's as though we've been blessed and are walking on air in an unbelievable dream," wrote Emerentia Krogmann, the wife of the northern German wholesaler Carl Vincent Krogmann. "Hitler is Reich chancellor! It's true! Farewell Marxism! Farewell Communism! Farewell parliament! Farewell Jews!— Here's to Germany!"[117] Luise Solmitz from Hamburg, who had turned away from Hitler in disappointment at the end of 1932, was equally enthusiastic: "What a cabinet!!! We didn't dare to dream of this last July. Hitler, Hugenberg, Seldte, Papen!!! A large portion of my German hopes are attached to each one of them. National Socialist vigour, German nationalist reason, the apolitical Stahlhelm and the unforgettable Papen . . . This is a memorable 30 January."[118]

Hitler's conservative coalition partners also believed they had achieved their goals. When an acquaintance warned Papen about Hitler's thirst for power, he replied: "You're wrong. We engaged him for our ends."[119] And in response to accusations of betrayal from the Pomeranian estate owner Ewald von Kleist-Schmenzin, the vice-chancellor shot back: "What do you want? I have Hindenburg's confidence. In two months, we'll have pushed Hitler so far into a corner he'll squeak."[120] It was impossible to underestimate more fatally Hitler's will to power and determination to dispose of his conservative cabinet members as soon as possible. Hugenberg was famously quoted as telling the Leipzig mayor, Carl Goerdeler, the day after Hitler's appointment that he had committed "the greatest act of foolishness" in his life by concluding an alliance with the "biggest demagogue in world history," but it is unlikely that Hugenberg said any such thing.[121] The super-minister felt that he was the most powerful figure in Hitler's cabinet and believed, along with the other conservatives, that they could keep the new chancellor in check and direct him for their own purposes. Another bit of fiction is the oft-repeated story of Erich Ludendorff writing to Hindenburg at the end of January and accusing the Reich president of "delivering [Germany] up to one of the biggest demagogues of all time." Ludendorff is supposed to have stated: "I solemnly prophesy that the man will cast our empire into the abyss and bring unimaginable misery to our nation. Coming generations will curse you in your grave for this decision."[122] These would have been prophetic words indeed, had Ludendorff actually written them. The reality, however, was that while Ludendorff was initially sceptical of the Hitler government, the two men would re-establish contact after Hindenburg died in August 1934. In April 1937, Hitler and Ludendorff met in Munich and were officially "reconciled." The "hero of Tannenberg" was a useful spokesman for the Führer's drive to rearm the Wehrmacht. When Ludendorff died that December, the Nazis staged a pompous state funeral for the former general.[123]

Not only Hitler's conservative helpers, but many of his democratic opponents initially assumed that Papen and Hindenburg would hold the true power in the cabinet. On 31 January, Harry Kessler recorded a conversation he had had with the banker and politician Hugo Simon: "He sees Hitler as a prisoner of Hugenberg and Papen. 'The poor fellow,' who's not very clever, has been delivered up, hands and feet bound, to those cagey conspirators." Kessler apparently shared this estimation. A few days later, he predicted that the government would not last long since only the intrigues of the "windbag" Papen were holding it together: "Hitler must have already realised that he has fallen into a trap. His hands and feet are tied in government, and he has no room to manoeuvre either forward or back."[124] The *Vossische Zeitung* initially consoled itself with the idea that Hitler had not succeeded with his policy of "all or nothing": "He moves into Wilhelmstrasse not as a dictator who knows no other law than his own will. This is not a Hitler cabinet. It is a Hitler–Papen–Hugenberg government that is full of contradictions, even if it clearly agrees that a complete break has to be made with what came before it." However, the newspaper called this government "a dangerous experiment that can only be followed with profound concern and deepest distrust."[125]

Jewish circles were also worried, although several prominent figures warned against panic. In an editorial on 2 February, Ludwig Holländer, the director of the Central Association of German Citizens of the Jewish Faith, wrote: "Despite the times, German Jews will not lose the composure granted them by the knowledge of their inalienable connection to everything truly German."[126] Fairly typical of the reaction of conservative and patriotic German Jews to Hitler's appointment as chancellor was the 30 January diary entry of the Breslau teacher and historian Willy Cohn: "I fear that this means civil war! The right wing will be initially victorious, but in the end there'll be communism! And then a left-wing revolution will come, and it won't be nearly this mild. If Hitler abides by the constitution, however, he'll be doomed with his own people too. In any case, times are gloomy, especially for us Jews!" The following day Cohn noted that the National Socialists had behaved like victors on the streets, but he stuck by his prognosis: "They too will be unable to deal with the economic crisis, and then there'll be a massive turn to the left."[127] Cohn's fear of communism still outweighed his worries about National Socialism—an attitude that was to change very soon.

Representatives of Germany's political Left also had the wrong ideas about the new government. "The Harzburg Front has been resurrected in the Hitler–Papen–Hugenberg cabinet," the SPD leadership and the Social Democratic parliamentary faction asserted in a statement to party members on 30 January, warning against "undisciplined behaviour." The battle was to be pursued on "the basis of the constitution" in order not to give the new right-wing government any pretence for doing away with that document.[128] The KPD did call for a general strike to protest "the fascist dictatorship of Hitler, Hugenberg and Papen," but Communist appeals to form a common front fell on deaf ears among Social Democrats, who remembered all too well being defamed by the Communists as "social fascists."[129]

Union leaders also did not put much stock in extraparliamentary protests. "Organisation and not demonstration is the watchword of the hour," General German Trade Union Association chairman, Theodor Leipart, stated on 31 January.[130] For many representatives of the Social Democratic labour movement, Hitler was a hostage of the old reactionary elites, the large agricultural estate owners in the east and the major industrialists in the west. Policy, in their view, would be set not by the new chancellor, but by Vice-Chancellor von Papen and the "economic dictator" Hugenberg, who would soon succeed in demystifying the messiah from Braunau. People on the left failed to recognise both Hitler's determination to seize total power or the dimensions of the danger he presented. Most Social Democratic and trade union leaders had grown up in the Wilhelmine Empire, and some had directly experienced Bismarck's campaign against the SPD. They may have suspected that the new government would pass anti-socialist legislation, but they could not imagine that National Socialism would seriously try to destroy the entire organised labour movement.

In his book *Defying Hitler*, written in British exile in 1939, Sebastian Haffner recalled the "icy fright" that had been his first reaction to the news that Hitler had been named chancellor: "For a moment I almost physically sensed the odour of blood and filth surrounding this man Hitler. It was a bit like being approached by a threatening and disgusting predator—it felt like a dirty paw with sharp claws in my face." But on the evening of 30 January 1933, Haffner—then a young intern at Berlin's Superior Court of Justice—calmly discussed the prospects of the new government with his father, a liberal Prussian educational reformer. The two men agreed that the Hitler-led cabinet would do some damage but would not stay in office for very long. "A conservative-reactionary government on the whole, with Hitler as its mouthpiece," Haffner later recalled their conclusion. "That was the main difference to the last two governments that had followed after Brüning . . . No, all things considered, this government was no great cause for alarm."[131] In line with this statement, many Germans reacted to Hitler's appointment as chancellor with indifference. There had been three changes of government in 1932, and people had almost come to expect such shifts. In the weekly cinema newsreels, the swearing-in of the new cabinet came last—after the major sporting events.[132] Only a handful of particularly keen observers recognised that

Alfred Hugenberg and Hitler, in a contemporary photomontage uniting the unequal partners in the Harzburg Front

Hitler's office in Munich's Brown House, with a bust of Mussolini and a portrait of Friedrich the Great

Top: Eva Braun posing on a desk in Heinrich Hoffmann's atelier in 1930

Above: Maria Reiter at the age of sixteen, when she first met Hitler. The dedication on the back of the photo reads "In eternal memory, your Mizzi Reiter, 26 August 1926."

Left: Hitler's niece Geli Raubal

Above: Hitler posing for the cameras of Richard Wagner's grandsons, Wieland and Wolfgang, 1931

Right: Official photo announcing the continuation of the marriage between Joseph and Magda Goebbels, October 1938

HITLER
über Deutschland

Left: Publicity pamphlet advertising one of Hitler's flying tours, 1932

Below: Hitler and Hermann Göring at a meeting of the Düsseldorf Industrial Club, 26 January 1933, at which Fritz Thyssen read a declaration ending with "Heil, Herr Hitler"

Opposite top: The "Cabinet of National Concentration" on 30 January 1933: (*sitting, left to right*) Hermann Göring, Hitler, Franz von Papen; (*standing, right*) Alfred Hugenberg

Opposite bottom: "The Day of Potsdam": Hitler bows before President Paul von Hindenburg, 21 March 1933

Above and left:
Three typical Hitler poses during his
speech in Berlin's Sportpalast on
10 February 1933

Below: Hitler digging the first turf for the
construction of the autobahn near Darmstadt, 3 September 1933

Top: Hitler's first meeting
with Mussolini, Venice,
14 June 1934

Right: Supporters making
the pilgrimage to the
Berghof, Hitler's residence
on the Obersalzberg

Albert Speer unveiling his '"Dome of Light" on the Zeppelin Field at the Nuremberg rally of 1936

Leni Riefenstahl during the filming of *Triumph of the Will*, September 1934

30 January had been an irreversible turning point. Thea Sternheim, who learned of Hitler's appointment while in Paris, wrote in her diary: "Hitler as chancellor. On top of everything else, now this intellectual humiliation. The last straw. I'm going home. To vomit."[133] Klaus Mann noted: "News that Hitler has become Reich chancellor. Horror. Never thought it possible. (The land of unlimited possibilities . . .)"[134]

For most foreign diplomats, on the other hand, 30 January did not mark a major caesura. Sefton Delmer heard from his contacts in the British embassy that Hitler was a "chancellor in handcuffs," held hostage by Papen and Hugenberg.[135] The British ambassador, Horace Rumbold, advocated taking a wait-and-see approach to the new government. He too saw Hitler as the weaker partner in the coalition and considered the vice-chancellor the true architect of the political alliance: "It may be said that the Hitler movement has been saved for the time being, largely owing to the instrumentality of Herr von Papen." Rumbold predicted that conflicts would soon erupt since Papen and Hugenberg's goal of restoring the monarchy could not be squared with Hitler's plans. The ambassador regarded it as a positive sign that Neurath had remained foreign minister, which he took as an indication that German foreign policy was not going to change.[136]

The formation of the Hitler–Papen–Hugenberg cabinet had been kept secret until the very last minute, the French ambassador, André François-Poncet, reported to Paris on the evening of 30 January. He was most concerned about the possible consequences for Germany's foreign policy. The new government with Hitler at the top represented *"une expérience hasardeuse"* for all of Europe and not just Germany, since Hitler would try to bring about revisions of the Treaty of Versailles. Nonetheless, François-Poncet recommended that his government stay calm and wait to see how things developed. When he met Hitler for the first time on 8 February at a reception hosted by Hindenburg for the diplomatic corps, the ambassador was relieved. The new chancellor struck him as "dull and mediocre," a kind of miniature Mussolini without any initiative or ideas of his own. François-Poncet thought he understood why the Reich president's advisers had argued that it would be easy to use and control Hitler.[137]

The Swiss senior envoy in Berlin, Paul Dinichert, received the news of the new government's formation at lunch with some "elevated German personalities." In his report to Berne on 2 February, Dinichert wrote: "None of them seemed to have had any intimation. Heads were shaken. 'How long can this last?' 'It could have been worse.' The conversation went round in circles." The Swiss diplomat recognised that Hitler's appointment was the result of a "political game of chess and puzzle-solving," in which "the watchful and ever-active Herr von Papen, backed up by Hindenburg's unique trust in him," had pulled the strings. But like so many other observers, Dinichert failed to recognise the true import of the new constellation of power when he wrote: "Hitler, who for years insisted on ruling by himself, has been yoked, hemmed in or constrained (take your pick) with two of his disciples between Papen and Hindenburg."[138]

January the 30th, 1933 was thus not seen at the time as the major date in world history it rightfully appears now. In fact, the date marked the start of a fateful process that saw the new man in the chancellor's office quickly seize complete power and that ultimately ended in the fathomless crimes of the wars of annihilation against Poland and the Soviet Union and the mass murder of European Jews. Historians have perennially tried to answer the question of whether Hitler's rise to power could have been halted. Doubtlessly, there were powerful tendencies, deeply anchored in German history, which promoted the success of National Socialism. They included an anti-Western nationalism that rejected the "ideas of 1789," that felt particularly provoked by Germany's unexpected defeat in the First World War and the perceived humiliation of the Treaty of Versailles, and that took refuge in stab-in-the-back legends and lies about Germany's lack of responsibility for the war, so as to prevent any sort of self-critical examination of who was responsible for the disaster of 1918. Other factors included the anti-Semitism that already permeated all strata of German society except the Social Democratic working classes in the Wilhelmine Empire, and which had been radicalised by the First World War and in particular by the revolutionary months of 1918 and 1919; the influence of pre-democratic elites, above all the military, Eastern Elbian aristocratic landowners, large-scale industrialists and civil servants within the government and the justice system, whose power had basically remained untouched in the democratic Weimar Republic; the structural shortcomings of the Weimar Constitution, making the Reich president into something of an ersatz kaiser and allowing him to rule by emergency decree, which in the hands of a dedicated monarchist like Hindenburg was practically an invitation to abuse political power during the economic crisis of 1929 and 1930; and finally the unwillingness of Germany's political parties to compromise, which was partially to blame for the chronic functional difficulties of parliamentary democracy and which culminated in the collapse of the grand coalition in March 1930, ringing in the phase of rule by presidential decree.[139]

However, despite all of these weaknesses, which were primarily the result of the failure to break decisively enough with the legacy of Wilhelmine authoritarianism when the Weimar Republic was founded in 1918 and 1919, it was by no means inevitable that political power would be handed over to Adolf Hitler. There were repeated opportunities to end Hitler's run of triumphs. The most obvious one was after the failed putsch of November 1923. Had the Munich rabble-rouser been forced to serve his full five-year term of imprisonment in Landsberg, it is extremely unlikely that he would have been able to restart his political career.[140] Hindenburg's unnecessary dismissal of Brüning in late May 1932 was also, in the words of the historian Heinrich August Winkler, a "decisive turning point in the German crisis of state" after 1930. Had Brüning remained in office, Papen would not have been able to destroy the "democratic bulwark" of Prussia, and Reichstag elections would not have been held until September 1934—by which point Germany's economy would have probably recovered somewhat and extremist parties would have lost some of their appeal.[141] Instead the Reichstag election of 31 July made the NSDAP Germany's strongest party and supported Hitler's claims to power.

Yet even in late January 1933, Hitler would have been denied power if Hindenburg had granted Schleicher's request for an order to dissolve parliament and given him what he had once agreed to for Papen: permission to postpone new Reichstag elections for more than sixty days. Hindenburg could have also ignored the parliamentary vote of no confidence and retained Schleicher in office. That option would have been akin to tacitly imposing a military dictatorship, but it would have been an opportunity to play for time, until the economic situation had likely improved.[142] It is very doubtful whether Hitler would have dared to mobilise the SA for an armed battle against the Reichswehr under such circumstances. Crucially, Hindenburg allowed himself to be persuaded by Papen and his advisers that a cabinet of "national concentration," in which Hitler would supposedly be contained and tamed by a majority of traditional conservative ministers, was the least risky way out of the crisis. A significant role in the final act of this drama was played by East Elbian aristocratic landowners, who used their access to Hindenburg to urge him to appoint Hitler chancellor. Like the traditional conservative majority in the cabinet and the clique surrounding Hindenburg, they underestimated Hitler's determination and ability to free himself from all attempts at political control and realise his dreams of total power. All of these groups operated under the illusion that they had "engaged" or co-opted Hitler to give them the mass backing they desired for their authoritarian policies. "The history of Hitler is the history of people underestimating him," wrote the historian Veit Valentin shortly after the end of the Second World War.[143]

Nonetheless, if Hitler's rise to chancellor was by no means the inevitable result of the Weimar Republic's crisis of state, it was also more than just a historical mishap, as some observers, most recently the historian Eberhard Jäckel, have claimed down the years.[144] Without the specific social and political conditions of the post-war and hyperinflationary period, the decommissioned private would have remained an antisocial outsider. The situation in the Bavarian capital proved perfect soil for Hitler's hateful, anti-Semitic tirades and his diatribes against the "November criminals" and the "dictates" of the Treaty of Versailles. Without the consequences of the Great Depression, which hit Germany particularly hard, the NSDAP would never have become a mass movement. And it was the chairman of the NSDAP who best understood how to articulate and exploit people's desires for a saviour who would inject order into chaos, create an ethnic-popular community in place of party squabbling and class warfare, and lead the Reich to new greatness.

Hitler can be accused of a lot of things, but one cannot say that he was not frank about his intentions. With astonishing openness in both *Mein Kampf* and countless speeches, he announced exactly what he would do if he came to power. Hitler's main domestic aims were to destroy the Weimar system, which he had ruthlessly exploited from within, to completely "root out" Marxism, by which he meant both the SPD and KPD, and to remove Jews from Germany by whatever means necessary. In terms of foreign policy, Hitler never left any doubt that he wanted to revise the Treaty of Versailles and, in the longer term, conquer "living space" in eastern Europe, which inevitably entailed war with Poland and the Soviet Union. Those who brought him to power agreed with his aims of preventing a return to parliamentary democracy, getting rid of the shackles of the Treaty of Versailles as quickly as possible, rearming Germany's military and restoring Germany's status as a major world power. As far as Hitler's long-term wishes were concerned, his conservative coalition partners believed either that he was not serious or that they could exert a moderating influence on him. In any case, they were severely mistaken. Right from the beginning, Hitler thought in completely different dimensions. In December 1941, as the planned Blitzkrieg against the Soviet Union stalled before Moscow, Hitler looked back on 1933 and remarked: "When I took power it was a decisive moment for me. Should we keep the old calendar? Or should we take the new world order to be a sign for a new beginning in time? I told myself: the year 1933 is nothing less than the renewal of a millennial condition."[145]

13

Hitler as Human Being

Who was the man who on 30 January 1933, at the relatively young age of 43, moved into the Chancellery, the building where his idol and founder of the German Reich, Otto von Bismarck, had once resided? This is not an easy question to answer: it is hard to penetrate behind Hitler's public persona and get at the private person. Hitler remained a mystery even to some of his closest associates. In his memoirs, Hitler's press spokesman, Otto Dietrich, wrote of his "non-transparent, Sphinx-like personality."[1] Likewise Hitler's early friend Ernst Hanfstaengl, who observed the Nazi leader from close proximity for many years, admitted that he was never able to find the key to unlock the depths of Hitler's being. "What he really thought or felt," Hanfstaengl confessed, "remained a book with seven seals."[2] During his first interrogation at Kransberg Castle in June and July 1945, Albert Speer told his captors that for him Hitler remained "a riddle, full of contrasts and outright contradictions."[3] In 1947, the former French ambassador André François-Poncet concluded: "It seems as though there was something to him that we'll never grasp."[4] And the head of the office of the German president, Otto Meissner, who served Hitler as loyally as he had the Führer's predecessors, wrote in his memoirs: "Judging the essence of this strange person . . . will remain forever controversial . . . Even those who knew him for years and followed his development have difficulty drawing reliable conclusions. He was a loner, full of mistrust, who closed himself off and only occasionally permitted a glance at his inner life."[5]

Previous biographers have tried to make a virtue of necessity by attributing Hitler's seeming opacity to the "emptiness of what was left of an existence outside politics," as Ian Kershaw put it.[6] But these are hasty conclusions. As we saw with regard to Hitler's relationships with women, we cannot strictly distinguish between the private and political spheres. Upon closer examination, we can see that the putative void was part of Hitler's persona, a means of concealing his personal life and presenting himself as a politician who completely identified with his role as leader and who had renounced all private relationships for the sake of his historic mission. Thus, as German chancellor, Hitler repeatedly claimed that he no longer had a private life.[7] If we refuse to accept this self-styled image, we need to look behind the curtain that separated Hitler's public persona and role from the human being with his characteristic habits and behaviour.

The main reason it is so difficult to decipher "the riddle of Hitler" is the fact that his personality contained so many astonishing contrasts and contradictions. As early as 1936, Konrad Heiden described Hitler's "dual nature." Like a medium, Heiden argued, the *human being* Adolf Hitler channelled and created, through a monstrous act of will, the *phenomenon* Adolf Hitler: "In moments of repose, the latter lies curled up and hidden within the former, only to emerge in moments of intensity to conceal the former behind its larger-than-life puppet's mask." For Heiden, this split personality is what made it so difficult to reach reliable conclusions about Hitler.[8]

More than one of Hitler's acquaintances confirmed this impression. Otto Dietrich pointed to Hitler's "uncanny dual nature," arguing that the Führer's internal contradictions were so intense that they became "the dominant characteristic of his entire being." On the one hand, Dietrich asserted, Hitler possessed extraordinary capabilities and gifts. On the other, and particularly in conjunction with his fanatical anti-Semitism, he could be intellectually primitive and boorish. In Hitler's breast, Dietrich wrote, "respectable sensibilities and ice-cold heartlessness, love and horrific cruelty lived side by side."[9] Looking back, Albert Speer was also struck by the many faces Hitler had displayed. In 1965, twenty years after the end of the Third Reich, Speer noted in his Spandau cell:

> I could easily say that he was cruel, unjust, unapproachable, cold, lacking restraint, self-pitying and crude, for he was indeed all those things. But he was also the precise opposite. He could be a caring patriarch, an understanding superior, a likeable, measured, proud man who was enthusiastic about everything great and beautiful.[10]

Hanfstaengl painted a similar picture when he recalled Hitler. "He could be charming and then, a short time later, utter views that intimated terrible abysses," Hanfstaengl wrote.

He could develop grandiose ideas and be primitive to the point of banality. He was able to convince millions that his iron will and strength of character alone would guarantee victory, and yet even as German chancellor he remained a bohemian whose unreliability had those who worked with him pulling out their hair.[11]

There are countless statements of this kind, and they are more than just belated attempts to justify fascination with the figure of Hitler.

As a rule, people who got a close look at the Führer for the first time were rarely impressed. After a meeting with Hitler in December 1931, the industrialist Günther Quandt deemed him the very definition of average.[12] Sefton Delmer described him as an everyday person reminiscent of a travelling salesman or a junior officer.[13] As we saw, the American reporter Dorothy Thompson called Hitler the exact prototype of the little man on the street.[14] William Shirer, the correspondent for America's Universal News Service, also came away disappointed after seeing Hitler in September 1934 at the Nuremberg rally. "His face," Shirer wrote in his diary, "had no particular expression at all—I expected it to be stronger—and for the life of me I could not quite comprehend what hidden springs he undoubtedly unloosened in the hysterical mob which was greeting him so wildly."[15]

Hitler's appearance was hardly winning. Finance Minister von Krosigk, who met Hitler for the first time when the new chancellor was sworn in on 30 January 1933, recalled the Führer's face as being unremarkable. "There was nothing harmonious about his features, nor did they have the irregularity that expresses individual human spirit," Krosigk wrote. "A lock of hair that flopped down over his forehead and the rudiments of a moustache only two fingers wide gave his appearance something comic."[16] Hitler's moustache was the feature that everyone noticed. Early on, Hanfstaengl had urged him to shave it off, arguing that it was fodder for caricaturists. "My moustache will be all the rage one day—you can bet on that," Hitler replied.[17] Around 1925 or 1926 he told Adelheid Klein, a friend in Munich: "Imagine my face without the moustache! . . .

My nose is much too big. I have to soften it with the moustache!"[18] Indeed, Hitler's large, fleshy nose was rather disproportionate to the rest of his face. Klaus Mann called it the "most foul and most characteristic" aspect of Hitler's physiognomy.[19] For his part Albert Speer claimed that he only noticed how ugly and disproportionate Hitler's face was in the final months of the Third Reich, when the Führer's appeal was declining. "How did I not notice that in all the years?" he wondered in his Spandau prison cell in late November 1946. "Curious!"[20]

Almost everyone who came into contact with Hitler was struck by another feature. Upon seeing the young Hitler for the first time in 1919, Karl Alexander von Müller immediately noted his "large, light-blue, fanatically and coldly gleaming eyes."[21] Lieselotte Schmidt, an assistant and nanny to Winifred Wagner, had a different impression. Like her mistress, she admired Hitler and found that his eyes shone with goodness and warmth. "One glance from his lovely violet-blue eyes was enough to sense his gentle temperament and good heart," Schmidt said in 1929.[22] Otto Wagener, the economic adviser who entered Hitler's service that same year and still professed his admiration of the Führer in a British POW camp in 1946, recalled:

> From the first moment, his eyes captivated me. They were clear and large and calm. He stared at me full of self-confidence. But his gaze did not come from his eyeballs. On the contrary, I felt it came from somewhere far deeper, from infinity. You could read nothing in his eyes. But they spoke and wanted to say something.[23]

Christa Schroeder, one of Hitler's secretaries from 1933 onwards, was somewhat more sober: "I found Hitler's eyes very expressive. They looked interested and probing and always became more animated whenever he spoke."[24] The playwright Gerhart Hauptmann also noted Hitler's "strange and lovely eyes" after meeting the Führer at the inauguration of the Reich Culture Chamber in November 1933.[25]

Whether people perceived Hitler's gaze as cold or benevolent, impenetrable or friendly and inquisitive depended both on the given situation and their political views. "What admirers praise as the power of his eyes strikes neutral observers as a greedy stare without that hint of decency that makes a gaze truly compelling," wrote the Hitler detractor Konrad Heiden. "His gaze repels more than it captivates."[26]

But even critical observers sometimes praised his eyes. "Hitler's eyes were startling and unforgettable," wrote Martha Dodd, the daughter of the U.S. ambassador to Germany, William Edward Dodd, after being introduced to Hitler by Hanfstaengl in 1933. "They seemed pale blue in colour, were intense, unwavering, hypnotic."[27]

Alongside his eyes, Hitler's hands attracted the most attention. "So expressive in their movements as to compete with the eyes" was how Houston Stewart Chamberlain put it in a fawning letter to Hitler in 1923.[28] For Krosigk, Hitler's hands were nervous, delicate and "almost feminine."[29] In 1933, when the philosopher Karl Jaspers voiced doubts as to whether someone as uneducated as Hitler could lead Germany, his colleague Martin Heidegger replied: "Education is irrelevant . . . just look at those lovely hands."[30] Many of Heidegger's contemporaries shared his admiration for the Führer's hands. In an article for the December 1936 edition of *New Literature*, the head of German radio characterised Hitler's delicate hands as being the tools of an "artist and great creator."[31] And in October 1942, while imprisoned in a British POW camp, General Ludwig Crüwell opined: "His hands are truly striking—lovely hands . . . He's got the hands of an artist. My eyes were always drawn to his hands."[32]

But more impressive than his eyes and hands was Hitler's talent for speaking. His appearance may have made him seem average and everyday, but as soon as he took to the stage, he was transformed into a demagogue the likes of which Germany had never known. Admirers and detractors were in absolute agreement on this point. In his essay "Brother Hitler," Thomas Mann attributed Hitler's rise to his "eloquence, which although unspeakably base, has huge sway over the masses."[33] Heiden wrote of "an incomparable barometer of mass moods,"[34] while Otto Strasser spoke of an "unusually sensitive seismograph of the soul." Strasser also compared Hitler to a "membrane" broadcasting the most secret longings and emotions of the masses.[35] Krosigk concurred. "He sensed what the masses were longing for and translated it into firebrand slogans," the Reich finance minister wrote. "He appealed to the instincts slumbering in people's unconsciousness and offered something to everyone."[36] The American journalist Hubert R. Knickerbocker, who had encountered Hitler as a seemingly polite, small-time politician in the NSDAP's Munich headquarters in 1931, was astonished by a public appearance that same evening. "He was an evangelist speaking at a tent meeting, the Billy Sunday of German politics," the Pulitzer Prize winner wrote. "Those he had converted followed him, laughed with him, felt with him. Together they mocked the French. Together they hissed off the Republic. Eight thousand people became one instrument on which Hitler played his symphony of national passion."[37] As Knickerbocker realised, the secret to Hitler's success lay in the mutual identification between speaker and audience—in the exchange of individual and collective sensitivities and neuroses.

It was not only the faithful whom Hitler managed to put under his spell. "There won't be anyone like him for quite some time," Rudolf Hess wrote in 1924 while imprisoned in Landsberg, "a man who can sweep away both the most left-wing lathe operator and the right-wing government official in a single mass event."[38] Hess's view was no exaggeration. Numerous contemporaries who rejected Hitler and his party struggled to resist the lure of Hitler's overwhelming rhetoric—indeed, some succumbed to it. In his memoirs, the historian Golo Mann described the impression a Hitler speech made on him as a 19-year-old student in the autumn of 1928. "I had to steel myself against the energy and persuasive force of the speaker," Mann wrote. "A Jewish friend of mine, whom I had brought along, was unable to resist. 'He's right,' he whispered in my ear. How many times had I heard this phrase 'He's right' uttered by listeners from whom I would have least expected it?"[39]

Hitler's talent for persuasive oration gave him a hypnotic sway over crowds. Part of his secret was his unusually powerful and variable voice. "Those who only know Hitler from the events of later years, after he had mutated into an immoderately thundering dictator and demagogue at the microphone, have no idea what a flexible and mellifluous instrument his natural, non-amplified voice was in the early years of his political career," noted Hanfstaengl.[40] It was Hitler's voice, at a speech in Weimar in March 1925, that won over Baldur von Schirach, later the Nazis' Reich youth leader, at the age of 18. "It was a voice unlike any other I had heard from a public speaker," Schirach recalled. "It was deep and rough, resonant as a cello. His accent, which we thought was Austrian but was actually Lower Bavarian, was alien to central Germany and compelled you to listen."[41]

But Hitler was not only a gifted orator. He was also an extraordinarily talented actor. "Once, in a moment when he let his guard down, he called himself the greatest actor in Europe," Krosigk recalled.[42] That statement was one of the excessive flights of fancy to which the dictator became increasingly prone in his later years. Nonetheless, Hitler had an undeniable ability to don different masks to suit various occasions and to inhabit changing roles. "He could be a charming conversation partner who kissed women's hands, a friendly uncle who gave children chocolate, or a man of the people who could shake the callused hands of farmers and artisans," remarked Albert Krebs, the Gauleiter of Hamburg.[43] When invited to the Bechstein and Bruckmann salons or to afternoon tea at the Schirachs' in Weimar, he would play the upstanding, suit-and-tie-wearing bourgeois to fit in with such social settings. At NSDAP party conferences, he dressed in a brown shirt and cast himself as a prototypical street fighter who made no secret of his contempt for polite society.

Hitler adapted his speeches to people's expectations. In front of the Reichstag, he talked like a wise statesman. When he spoke to a circle of industrialists he was a man of moderation. To women he was the good-humoured father who loved children, while in front of large crowds he was a fiery volcano. To his fellow party members he was the truest and bravest soldier who sacrificed himself and was therefore allowed to demand sacrifices of others.[44] André François-Poncet, who witnessed Hitler's various appearances at the Nuremberg rally in 1935, was impressed by the Führer's ability to intuit the mood of each given audience. "He found the words and tone he needed for all of them," the French ambassador remarked. "He ran the gamut from biting to melodramatic to intimate and lordly."[45] The man who succeeded François-Poncet in 1938, Robert Coulondre, was also surprised by the man he met at the Berghof retreat when he presented his letter of credence in November. "I was expecting a thundering Jove in his castle and what I got was a simple, gentle, possibly shy man in his country home," Coulondre reported. "I had heard the rough, screaming, threatening and demanding voice of the Führer on the radio. Now I became acquainted with a Hitler who had a warm, calm, friendly and understanding voice. Which one is the true Hitler? Or are they both true?"[46]

As flexible as Hitler may have been in choosing from his repertoire of roles in response to various situations and demands, he was all the more stubborn as Reich chancellor in adhering to the ideological fixations that had become a coherent world view from the early 1920s.

First and foremost in this outlook were his fanatic anti-Semitism, which saw the removal of Jews from German society as an absolute necessity, and his aggressive expansionism, which went far beyond mere revision of the Treaty of Versailles to include the central imperative of conquering "living space" in eastern Europe.

Still, when Hitler wanted to win someone over, he could turn on the charm. Albert Krebs described a typical scene in which Hitler greeted Count Ernst von Reventlow, a prominent member of a radical anti-Semitic and anti-Communist party, the DVFP, who had come over to the NSDAP in 1927. As Krebs recounted it, Hitler came rushing down the steps of the Nazi headquarters in Munich, gave Reventlow a two-handed handshake and greeted him as "My dear Count" with a slight quaver in his voice. "Everyone in attendance knew that Hitler's real feelings about the count were anything but affectionate and benevolent," a bemused Krebs remarked.[47] Hitler was even able to fake affection for people whom he despised in reality. In 1931, he won over the second wife of deposed German emperor Wilhelm II to such an extent that she spoke of how charming he had been and how his mien and eyes had been "without a trace of falsehood."[48] Likewise in 1933, Hitler addressed Prince August Wilhelm, who helped win over members of the aristocracy to the Nazis, with a subservient "Your Imperial Majesty."[49] As soon as he had assumed power, Hitler quickly abandoned August Wilhelm—as well as any support he may have hinted at for a restoration of the monarchy. Indeed, he repeatedly expressed to Goebbels his utter contempt for the Hohenzollern family.[50]

If necessary Hitler could even cry at will. He did so at the melodramatic ceremony in August 1930 when the Berlin SA pledged its loyalty and on the morning of 30 January 1933 when he apologised to Theodor Duesterberg.[51] Friends and foes alike saw him as a master of deception, which makes it so difficult to comprehend the essence of the man.[52] "He had a form for expressing everything—agitation, moral outrage, sympathy, emotion, fidelity, condolence and respect," wrote Ernst von Weizsäcker, state secretary at the German Foreign Ministry from 1938 to 1942, in his post-war memoirs.[53] "Those who had not observed in other contexts what Hitler really thought about human rights and other higher principles could easily be taken in by his act."[54] Even Speer wrote that in retrospect he was "entirely unsure when and where Hitler was truly himself, independent of play-acted roles, tactical considerations and gleefully told lies."[55]

Among Hitler's skills was his ability to mimic people's gestures and speech. He enjoyed entertaining his entourage by imitating Max Amann, who had lost his left arm and who spoke quickly and repetitively in Bavarian dialect. "You could just picture Amann shrugging his armless shoulder and frantically waving his right hand," Christa Schroeder reported. Hitler's caricature of Mathilde von Kemnitz, Erich Ludendorff's second wife, was also a big hit. "Hitler peeled away the pious, philosophic, rationalist, erotic and other layers of this high-born woman until all that was left was an evil, pungent onion," recalled Krebs.[56] After Hitler visited Goebbels and his family in December 1936, the propaganda minister noted: "The Führer was very funny, ridiculing the pastors and princes. It was very refreshing. He imitated them one after another like a professional actor."[57] Nor was Hitler above parodying foreign leaders. After a visit by Mussolini to Berlin in September 1937, Speer recalled Hitler mocking Il Duce's characteristic posturing: "His chin thrust forward, his legs spread and his right hand jammed on his hip, Hitler bellowed Italian or Italian-sounding words like *giovinezza, patria, victoria, macaroni, belleza, bel canto* and *basta*. Everyone around him made sure to laugh, and it was indeed very funny."[58]

Hitler could imitate sounds as well as voices and typically enlivened his recollections of serving in the First World War with sound effects. "In order to depict the barrage of fire at the Battle of the Somme more vividly, he used a large repertoire of the firing, descent and impact noises made by French, English and German howitzers and mortars," wrote Hanfstaengl, "the general impression of which he would vividly augment by imitating the hammering tack-tack of the machine guns."[59]

In addition to his rhetorical and thespian skills, Hitler possessed a third great gift: a stupendous memory.[60] Fritz Wiedemann, Hitler's former regimental commander who became the Führer's personal assistant in 1934, was astonished at the number of wartime details Hitler could recall that he himself had forgotten.[61] Legendary and much feared by military leaders was Hitler's head for numbers—whether they were the calibre, construction and range of firearms or the size, speed and armour of a warship.[62] He knew the navy calendar, which he kept by his bedside, by heart.[63] Indeed, from all indications he had a nearly photographic memory.[64] He would not only recognise people, but recall when and where they had met, leading Christa Schroeder to wonder how so many facts could fit inside one human brain.[65] The speed with which Hitler read was also an indication of his astonishing memory. "He could scan not just one but three or four lines at a time," reported Otto Wagener. "Sometimes it looked as though he had only glanced at a paragraph or a whole article, and yet afterwards he knew what it contained."[66] Hitler could recite whole passages of Clausewitz or Schopenhauer, sometimes passing them off as thoughts of his own.[67] He could also hum or whistle all the motifs in complex pieces of music like the prelude to Wagner's *Meistersänger*.[68]

Hitler had never completed his basic education, let alone graduated from university, and he tried to catch up by reading the books he had missed out on in his youth. A typical autodidact, he delighted in showing off what he knew to the university-educated members of his entourage. The young Rudolf Hess was just one of the people who admired how much Hitler had taught himself. "No matter whether he speaks about the construction of streets, the future of the auto-mobile as a means of mass transport, like in America, or the arma-ments on warships, you notice how deeply he's studied things," Hess gushed.[69] "Where did he get all of that?" Wagener asked himself after being impressed by Hitler's knowledge of geography and history.[70] "He reads and knows a lot," noted Goebbels. "A universal mind."[71]

Of course, Hitler's knowledge was just as unsystematic and incom-plete as it was varied. He simply ignored whatever did not mesh with his world view. "He had no concept of knowledge for knowledge's sake," Karl Alexander von Müller wrote. "Everything he knew was thoroughly connected with some purpose, and at the heart of every purpose were Hitler himself and his political power."[72] The school drop-out never overcame his need to display his self-taught and carefully memorised selective knowledge. He was forever in search of others' recognition and approval, and getting it made him "happy as a young boy," as Hess observed in Landsberg in 1924 after praising some early passages of *Mein Kampf*. When in April 1927 the *Bochumer Zeitung* called Hitler "Germany's best rhetorician," his private secretary found him to be "all smiles." It was, Hitler said, "the first time this had been acknowl-edged by a newspaper not associated with us."[73] Hitler may have projected exaggerated self-confidence in his public role as charismatic leader, but his feelings of inadequacy from early failures also ran deep. As a result he was very prickly when confronted with people who obviously knew more about a topic than he did.[74] His antipathy towards intellectuals, professors and teachers was particularly pronounced. "The vast majority of people who consider themselves educated," he fumed to Wagener in the early 1930s, "are a superficial demimonde, pretentious and arrogant bunglers, who don't even realise how laughably amateurish they are."[75] Once, over lunch at the Reich Chancellery, he even proclaimed that in the future there would only be *one* book of any real significance, and that he himself would write it "after he retired."[76] Conversely, Hitler was visibly flattered when, in July 1932, a professor of clinical psychology at the University of Bonn announced a lecture entitled "Political Psychology as Practical Psychology in *Mein Kampf.*" Hitler spoke of his "great joy" that for the first time a university professor had used his book as the basis for a lecture.[77]

As is typical for many autodidacts, Hitler believed he knew better than specialists and experts and treated them with an arrogance that was but the reverse of his own limited horizons. Speer called him "a genius of dilettantism."[78] Hitler was very reluctant to admit to any gaps in his education, even when filling them would have been in the interest of his political career. Hanfstaengl tried in vain to get Hitler to learn English after he was released from his imprisonment in Landsberg. Although Hanfstaengl himself offered to tutor Hitler twice a week, the party leader dismissed the idea with the words "My language is German, and that suffices."[79] Attempts to get him to travel abroad and see the world from a different perspective also fell on deaf ears. Sometimes Hitler would claim that he did not have any time to travel; on other occasions he argued that his party rivals would exploit his absence and challenge his supremacy.[80] As a result, the politician who assumed power in Germany in 1933 had seen nothing of the world except for four years of military service in Belgium and France during the First World War.

As a parvenu, Hitler lived in constant fear of not being taken seriously or, even worse, making himself look ridiculous. He frequently stumbled in his attempts in the 1920s to adapt to new social demands. The widow of Max Erwin von Scheubner-Richter, one of the sixteen Nazis who died during the putsch of November 1923, remarked that Hitler always seemed "somewhat gloomy" in society.[81] Hitler had to ask his *salonnière* patroness Elsa Bruckmann to show him how to eat dishes like lobster or artichokes.[82] Helene Bechstein kitted him out with a new suit, starched shirts and patent leather boots, whereupon Hanfstaengl reported: "The result was that for a while Hitler always turned up in patent leather boots, regardless of the time of day, until I took the liberty of suggesting that such footwear was hardly appropriate for daytime—not to mention for a leader of a workers' movement."[83] Hitler's fondness for lederhosen also clashed with the Führer cult his acolytes began to celebrate from 1922. Hess was appalled when Hitler turned up at the Obersalzberg with exposed knees and rolled-up sleeves.[84] In late 1926 and early 1927, he posed in lederhosen and a brown shirt for a series of portraits by his official photographer Heinrich Hoffmann.[85] After that, Hitler gradually gave up traditional southern German forms of dress because they clashed with his self-styled image as the messiah for all Germans. Nonetheless he retained his habit of commissioning a photo by Hoffmann before wearing a new article of clothing in public.[86] He never allowed himself to be seen in a bathing suit. For one thing, Hitler could not swim and refused to learn. For another, he cited the cautionary example of a cover of the *Berliner Illustrierte Zeitung* from August 1919 that had depicted Reich President Friedrich Ebert and Reich Defence Minister Gustav Noske in swimming trunks during a visit to the Baltic Sea. That image gave the right-wing press in Germany a welcome opportunity to ridicule those leaders of the Weimar Republic.[87]

Hitler also refused to take dance lessons, something he found as contemptible as learning foreign languages. "Dancing is an occupation unworthy of a statesman," he proclaimed. Even when Hanfstaengl pointed out that Hitler's role model Friedrich the Great had been no stranger to the dance floor, the Nazi leader remained adamant: "All these balls are a pure waste of time, and what's more the waltz is much too effeminate for a man."[88] At the Reich president's reception for the diplomatic corps on 9 February 1933, many people noticed how uncertain the freshly appointed Chancellor Adolf Hitler was on his new terrain. Bella Fromm, the society reporter for the *Vossische Zeitung* newspaper, noted in her diary:

Everyone's eyes were on Hitler, and the former military private, somewhat grumpy and awkward, seemed to feel ill at ease with his role.

The tails of his tuxedo constrained him, and he repeatedly reached for the area where his uniform belt would be. Every time he felt the absence of this cooling and encouraging handhold, he seemed to get more uncomfortable. He constantly played with his handkerchief and betrayed all the signs of stage fright.[89]

"I believe my life is the greatest novel in world history," Hitler wrote in late September 1934 to Adelheid Klein, a friend who some people suspected was his lover.[90] Hitler was perhaps echoing the statement attributed to Napoleon: "What a novel my life is!" Like the French emperor, the German Führer was never completely able to escape the aura of the *arriviste*. Even after a series of domestic and foreign political triumphs had bolstered his self-confidence, he still appeared quite nervous during official receptions. He was plagued, in the words of Christa Schroeder, "by fear of making a faux pas."[91] When he entertained, he checked every detail, casting a final eye over his table and even inspecting the flower arrangements. He seemed most relaxed when he received artists: among them he seemed at his most natural.[92]

Against this backdrop, it is easier to understand Hitler's pronounced and oft-noted tendency to engage in extended monologues: it was most likely an attempt to conceal his own social inadequacies. In early 1920, Hitler reverently received Heinrich Class, the founder of the Pan-Germanic League, only to leave the older far-right agitator "dizzy" with a monologue that lasted for hours.[93] After interviewing Hitler for the first time in early May 1931, Sefton Delmer described how the oral floodgates were opened: "I asked a question, and his answer swelled into a speech as new thoughts poured into his imaginative and unusually lively mind. Before you could stop him, he was yelling as if he had a huge crowd in front of him and not a single English reporter."[94] The diplomat Ulrich von Hassell described a similar transformation after a meeting with Hitler in Munich in early February 1932, at which the Führer "repeatedly suffered outbreaks of passion and reverted to his public-speaking voice, his lips quivering and his eyes fixed in their peculiarly intense stare."[95] Often a single word was enough to prompt Hitler's manic need to talk. People at the Nazi Party headquarters in Munich dreaded such moments because every item of business that day would have to be postponed.[96] Anyone with the temerity to interrupt Hitler would immediately

attract the ire of the loquacious party leader. "Hitler was an inde-
fatigable talker," Otto Dietrich remarked. "Talking was an element
of his very being."[97] Such verbal diarrhoea was a burden on those
around him. Hitler's interlocutors had to tolerate his endless monologues without contradiction, signalling their encouragement and
interest while interjecting the odd word that would inspire the speaker
to further flights of fancy. As a rule, Hitler was so intoxicated by his
own words that he never noticed whether they were having any real
effect on those who had to listen.

Yet Hitler could behave entirely differently in smaller, more private
circles. In such situations, he was a likeable conversationalist who told
entertaining stories instead of holding lectures. He enjoyed recalling his
wartime experiences, the founding of the Nazi Party and the November
putsch.[98] Here, Hitler assumed the role of good-humoured patriarch
who told jokes and laughed at the harmless jokes of others.[99] It was a
seductive persona. "Hitler is as touching as a father," Goebbels noted
in his diary in June 1929. "I like him very much. He's the most likeable
of men because he's so kindly. He has a big heart." Eighteen months
later, Goebbels wrote: "With Hitler this noon . . . He's very relaxing.
The boss as a family father. He's very interested in my welfare."[100]

The Gauleiter of Berlin and later propaganda minister was doubtlessly the colleague with whom Hitler maintained the most intense
contact and discussed the most personal matters. But Goebbels was
mistaken to believe that Hitler took him into complete confidence
and told him everything that was on his mind.[101] In fact, there was no
one to whom Hitler completely opened up. Even in the early 1920s,
Karl Alexander von Müller was struck by the "deep loneliness that
surrounded and doubly separated him from every environment." Nor
did he reveal himself to Elsa Bruckmann and her husband despite
their seeming intimacy—while they believed he did because he allowed
them a tiny glimpse of himself here and there.[102] In his memoirs,
Speer wrote that he had never met a man who "so rarely showed
his true feelings or concealed them again so quickly when he did."
There had been moments when Speer felt he and Hitler had grown
closer, but they were illusory: "If you cautiously took up his affectionate tone, he would immediately erect an insurmountable, defensive wall."[103] Joachim von Ribbentrop, Hitler's foreign minister, also

concluded that the man worshipped by millions of Germans was essentially a loner. "Just as I never got close to him, I never observed anyone else doing so either," Ribbentrop wrote. "There was something indescribably distancing about his very nature."[104]

Hitler's need to maintain distance from others was probably less the product of inferior social skills than of his conviction that he was a messiah who should be surrounded by an aura of unapproachability. Familiarity and intimacy were anathema to him. Even in his closest circles very few people were allowed to address him informally,[105] and he seems to have never had anything approaching a best friend. Hitler was afraid of "moments of uncontrolled affection and spontaneous intimacy," claimed Otto Strasser. "For him the idea of letting himself go was a sheer horror."[106] Perhaps that helps explain Hitler's difficult relationships with women. The Führer particularly hated the thought that people knew him before 1914 or were aware that he had been a lowly private in the First World War. Typically, when he attended a reunion of his regiment during the 1920s, he was unable to connect with his former comrades and quickly left.[107]

Hitler felt most comfortable with the street thugs from the Nazi Party's "early years of struggle," whom he regularly met up with in Munich's Café Heck. Among them, he could let out his vulgar, petit-bourgeois side without fear of being greeted with wrinkled noses. "It's awful to see him talking nonsense with those philistines," Goebbels complained in March 1931.[108] Yet after coming to power, Hitler largely divorced himself from such circles. The comradely tone his old acquaintances would habitually strike up did not suit his new role as Reich chancellor, so Hitler kept them at a distance, insisting that they too address him as "my Führer."[109] The only exception was the evening of 8 November, when the tradition of beer-cellar meetings was revived for a night. Then and only then did Hitler allow himself to sit down with his oldest party comrades in Café Heck.[110]

Beginning in 1933, the Führer also distanced himself from his earlier social patrons. On 21 April of that year, Helene Bechstein complained that the previous day she wanted to congratulate Hitler personally on his birthday but had been prevented from seeing him by his assistant Wilhelm Brückner, who told her that the Reich chancellor did not have a minute to spare.[111] Hitler did repay his former patron with the occasional acknowledgement, such as having her awarded the Golden

Party Emblem in December 1933, but their relationship was never again what it had been—particularly as Bechstein repeatedly criticised aspects of the Nazi regime.[112] Hitler kept in somewhat closer contact with the Bruckmanns in Munich, giving them not just the Golden Party Emblem but presenting them with a car.[113] Still, Elsa Bruckmann could not help but notice that her former protégé visited her much less frequently than before. In a letter written in March 1934, she griped that the Führer was "now quite hard to get hold of."[114]

So did Hitler truly exist "without any inner connection to other people," as Gregor Strasser claimed and as every one of his biographers from Heiden to Kershaw have suggested?[115] Put in such black-and-white terms, that was certainly not the case. Hitler enjoyed something like substitute families in several private circles, including the Hoffmanns. Even after becoming chancellor, he paid regular visits to his court photographer in the latter's villa in the Bogenhausen district of Munich. "When the weather was nice, the chancellor and Führer often took off his jacket and lay down on the lawn in his shirtsleeves," noted one eyewitness. "He felt at home with the Hoffmanns. Once he had them bring him a volume of [Bavarian satirist] Ludwig Thoma, from which he read aloud."[116]

Hitler also enjoyed the status of unofficial family member with the Wagner clan in Bayreuth. Speer noticed that the Führer appeared more relaxed than usual in their company: "With the Wagner family he felt comfortable and freed from the need to represent political power."[117] He had been on informal terms with the matron of the house, Winifred Wagner, since 1926, and he was also quite relaxed with the four Wagner children, letting them photograph him, taking them for rides in his big Mercedes and telling them bedtime stories. "He was very touching with the children," Winifred Wagner later recalled. Her assistant Lieselotte Schmidt described a private visit by Hitler to Bayreuth in early May 1936 in bathetic terms: "He looks with increasingly misty eyes from the children to their mother and back again and knows that if there is such a thing as home for him on this earth, there is none better than in the Villa Wahnfried among these people."[118]

In Berlin, Hitler's social contacts were by and large restricted to the Goebbels family. He was the best man at Magda and Joseph Goebbels's wedding in December 1931, and before 1933 he often spent his evenings at their Berlin apartment. After taking power, he also paid frequent visits to their summer houses in Kladow and on Schwanenwerder Island in Lake Wannsee. They would go boating together, and often Hitler's visits would stretch well into the night.[119] The dictator took an intense interest in the Goebbelses' family life. He visited Magda in hospital when she gave birth to her children, and the family and Hitler jointly celebrated their birthdays. Hitler enjoyed playing with the Goebbelses' daughters, especially the eldest one, Helga, once even declaring that if Helga were twenty years older, and he twenty years younger, she would have been the woman of his life.[120] On the Goebbelses' fifth wedding anniversary on 19 December 1936, Hitler personally brought congratulatory flowers late in the evening. "We are very moved and honoured," noted the propaganda minister in his diary. "He feels very at home with us."[121] In the autumn of 1938, when Goebbels was pondering a divorce to pursue an affair with the Czech actress Lida Baarova, Hitler vetoed the idea. Part of his motivation was no doubt that he did not want to lose his ersatz family.[122]

When choosing his subordinates, Hitler was guided not by emotions, but by his estimation of people's usefulness. The most important criteria were absolute loyalty, discretion and obedience. Hess, who became Hitler's private secretary in 1925, was an ideal subordinate and enjoyed great favour in the years leading up to 1933. When Hess married his long-time fiancée Ilse Pröhl on 20 December 1927, Hitler as a matter of course assumed his place beside Hess's old friend Karl Haushofer as a best man.[123] "Wolf [Hitler's nickname] is so attached to Hess—he's constantly singing his praises," Winifred Wagner wrote in June 1928.[124] It was also a bonus for those who aspired to join the elite ranks of the future leadership if they were good public speakers capable of whipping up a crowd. That was the reason why Hitler stuck by an obviously corrupt functionary like Hermann Esser—and why Goebbels could launch such a meteoric career in the NSDAP and secure a special place in Hitler's estimation.[125] It is striking that Hitler tended to surround himself with men from humble origins who did not have an overabundance of formal education. He was not terribly bothered if a subordinate had a "flaw in the weave," a dark secret in their past or family history: on the contrary, Hitler knew that such "flaws" made it easier to tie that person to him, or remove him if necessary.[126]

Hitler did not, however, enjoy parting with people to whom he had become accustomed. He felt a pronounced sense of solidarity with the "old street brawlers," and it took a lot for the Führer to formally break with any of them.[127] Astonishingly, he was quite skittish about reprimanding anyone face to face. Instead he tended to vent his displeasure to others over lunch or dinner. That, recalled Nazi Agriculture Minister Richard Walter Darré, "was enough since through various channels the person concerned would get word and immediately beg for forgiveness."[128]

Hitler had a keen eye for others' weaknesses and deficiencies and knew how to exploit them. He could assess someone's personality after only a brief acquaintance, leading his first biographer, Konrad Heiden, to dub him "a good judge and captor of people."[129] In response to the question of why he and so many others had succumbed to Hitler's spell, Speer wrote: "He not only knew how to play the masses like an instrument. He was also a master psychologist vis-à-vis individuals. He could sense the most secret hopes and fears of everyone he met."[130] Hitler instinctively knew who had submitted completely to him and who retained reservations, reacting to the latter with knee-jerk animosity.[131] Anyone attempting to penetrate his carefully guarded private life was sure to earn his ever-watchful mistrust, and those who had seen his moments of weakness or unsettled him would inevitably become targets for revenge.[132] Hitler's prodigious memory ensured no insult would ever be forgotten. The deeply insecure *arriviste* was a man who held a grudge.

Even before 1933, Hitler tended to give the same task to various subordinates, assuming that competition would yield better results. At the same time, he realised that they would neutralise one another and therefore be unable to threaten his own leadership. Divide and conquer was Hitler's strategy, and he would perfect and personify it during his years as Germany's dictator.[133] Speer characterised Hitler style of leadership as "a carefully balanced system of mutual enmity." No matter how significant his area of responsibility, none of Hitler's subordinates could imagine he possessed any stable authority of his own.[134]

Part and parcel of this style of rule was Hitler's tendency to inform as few people as possible about his plans—or to keep them secret altogether. Even Goebbels, who believed that he was on an intimate footing with the "boss," occasionally got upset about Hitler's secrecy. "We're all left feeling around in the dark," the propaganda minister once complained.[135] Christa Schroeder bore witness to Hitler's extraordinary capacity to keep a secret: "He was convinced that people only had to know as much as they needed to fulfil the tasks of their office."[136] Doling out small doses of powerful knowledge was one of Hitler's preferred means of playing his subordinates against one another and encouraging them to compete for his favour.

For all the self-confidence he projected, Hitler's shaky sense of self-worth made him overreact whenever anyone dared to contradict him. Before 1933, he may have been willing to listen to alternative views and change his own in one-to-one conversations. But as Wagener made clear, he would not tolerate anyone correcting him in public: "On those occasions, he would rage like a tiger who suddenly found himself in a cage and was now trying to break through the bars."[137] Nearly all of his subordinates had to endure fits of rage similar to the one Franz Pfeffer von Salomon was treated to in 1930. "He just started screaming, yelling at me," the later head of the Gestapo in Kassel reported. "A thick blue vein swelled on his forehead, and his eyes bugged out. His voice broke. I feared that he was going to hurt himself."[138] The spectacle of an enraged Hitler was neither very pleasant nor all that impressive. "Spittle literally dripped from the corners of his mouth and ran over his chin," Albert Krebs noted, although he also asked himself whether such fits of rage were genuine or play-acted, since Hitler seldom lost control of himself.[139] There was a similar ambiguity to Hitler's speeches. No matter how ecstatic Hitler seemed to get, he rarely let himself get carried away to the point where he made ill-considered statements. "His temperament appeared to get the better of him, releasing itself in cascades of bellowed sentences," remarked Baldur von Schirach, "but in reality he had himself totally under control."[140] Schwerin von Krosigk made a similar observation. Hitler may have let himself get carried away by his emotions, but he always knew how to steer them with cold rationalism. "That was perhaps the most extraordinary gift of this born public speaker," concluded the Reich finance minister, "this mixture of fire and ice."[141]

The paradoxical phrase "fire and ice" is an apt description for the most curious aspect of Hitler's behaviour. The more likeable, warm and considerate he could be in his private life, the colder, more

unfeeling and ruthless he behaved when it came to achieving his
political goals. Possibly, this was the result of the violence to which
Hitler, like many men of his generation, had been exposed in the First
World War. Soldiers had been trained to be hard, inured to human
suffering, and that had left its mark, particularly as it was reinforced
by the violent confrontations, just shy of a civil war, that followed in
post-war Germany. The former Private Hitler may not have taken part
himself in the street battles fought by paramilitary Freikorps, but he
had begun his political career within a Munich milieu of counter-
revolutionary militancy in which right-wing brawlers and neighbourhood vigilantes were the norm. From the very beginning, violence
had been an acceptable means of combating one's political adversaries,
and during the November putsch, Hitler showed that he was not above
risking people's lives. At the same time, his martial speechifying in
the Bürgerbräu beer cellar that day revealed that the role of the firebrand who did not shy away from violence had not come entirely
naturally. Before he could act, he had to whip himself into a psychological frenzy. The same pattern would repeat itself when Hitler purged
the SA leadership on the Night of the Long Knives in June 1934.

In early 1931, to deal with Stennes's revolt, Hitler called together
Berlin Brownshirts and associated groups to a meeting in the
Sportpalast auditorium. There he employed an extraordinary tactic
for assuring himself of their loyalty. For Speer, then a member of the
Nazi Transport Corps, it was his initial first-hand experience of Hitler.
"We stood there in silence for hours," Speer recalled.

> Finally he appeared with a small entourage . . . But instead of taking
> the podium as we expected, Hitler waded into the ranks. Everyone
> was completely still. Then he began to walk past the columns of men,
> one by one. All you could hear in this huge space were his footsteps.
> It took hours. Finally, he came to my column. His eyes were locked
> on the men standing at attention, as though he were trying to bind
> them with his gaze. When he got to me, I had the feeling that a pair
> of staring eyes had taken possession of me for the foreseeable future.[142]

Hitler also used the ritual of fixing people with a stare on lesser occasions when he wanted to test the loyalty of a subordinate. Speer
reported him doing this in a tearoom on the Obersalzberg. "I had to

summon up almost superhuman energy to combat the growing urge to look down," Speer recalled. "Then suddenly Hitler closed his eyes and turned to the woman seated beside him."[143]

The suggestive, binding power Hitler exercised over others reflected the self-delusional power he had over himself. Other people found Hitler so convincing, Krosigk remarked in 1945, because he was carried away himself by the momentum of his own words and thought, and completely believed in the truth of what he said. Even intelligent, strong-willed people found it difficult not to be moved and convinced by Hitler. People sometimes approached the Führer with the intention of contradicting him, Krosigk said, only for Hitler to "turn their heads round completely—in no time and with a minimum of effort."[144] The regional Nazi leaders—the Gauleiter—may have acted like dictators in their respective districts, but in Hitler's presence they became small and obedient. "They couldn't summon the courage to contradict him," wrote Speer. "They seemed to have abandoned themselves to him."[145]

    A portrait of Friedrich the Great hung in Hitler's office at the Nazi Party headquarters in Munich, but the Prussian king's sense of duty and work ethic were in many respects foreign to his Austrian admirer. Hitler did not keep regular office hours, and he placed no value on punctuality. For a brief period after he assumed power, that seemed to change. "The boss seems unusually solid," raved Hess in the first weeks of Hitler's chancellorship. "And the punctuality!!! Always a few minutes early!!! . . . A new era is dawning!"[146] But soon Hitler reverted to his old habits. Before 1933, Hanfstaengl would often have to comb the streets of Munich to find the party leader and drag him to foreign press interviews.[147] Hitler's unpredictability and contempt for rules constantly tried the patience of his subordinates. Schirach would later claim he had never seen Hitler work at a desk, either at his Munich apartment or at the Nazi Party headquarters. "For him, desks were mere pieces of decoration," the Nazi youth leader wrote.[148] Otto Wagener also noted that Hitler's desk at party headquarters was always empty. Sometimes, when others were talking, Hitler would doodle with a pencil or colouring pens, but Wagener never saw his boss write anything down. "He created by speaking," Wagener concluded. "He thought things through while he was talking."[149] It was up to his subordinates to identify the core of Hitler's digressive flights of fancy and translate it into practical instructions. That was not always easy, even for his closest associate Goebbels. In March 1932, the future propaganda minister noted in his diary: "Too erratic. Big plans, but difficult to realise and overcome opposition."[150]

Nonetheless, there is little truth to the idea that Hitler's bohemian pretensions left him incapable of doing concentrated work. When necessary, for instance when he had to prepare major speeches for the Reichstag or the Nuremberg rallies, he could devote himself to his political tasks with great diligence. Sometimes he would disappear for days. "The amount he worked was enormous," Fritz Wiedemann reported. "He worked through half the night."[151] Even as chancellor, Hitler did not use ghost writers: he dictated his speeches himself to his secretaries. Christa Schroeder remembered how Hitler would begin by writing down some main points while standing at his desk. Then he would start dictation, at first calmly but growing ever faster. "One sentence would follow the next without pause, while he paced up and down the room," Schroeder recalled. "Sometimes he would stop and stare silently at Lenbach's portrait of Bismarck, lost in thought and collecting himself before he started to wander around again." Gradually his voice would rise to maximum volume, and Hitler would gesticulate wildly, his face turning red. "Sometimes during dictation, my heart would start violently pounding—that's how infectious Hitler's excitement was," Schroeder remembered. When he was finished dictating, Hitler would correct the manuscript with a fountain pen. It would then be copied, often multiple times. When he had finished with a speech, Schroeder recalled, Hitler always seemed relieved.[152]

As a politician, the Führer oscillated between phases of seeming lethargy—in which he actually, away from the public eye, thought intensely about his plans—and periods of feverish, almost frenetic activity.[153] Hitler had a lifelong habit of postponing difficult decisions for as long as possible, once leading Goebbels to complain that his boss was a "hesitator" and "procrastinator."[154] Such was the stress Hitler felt when faced with such decisions that he started biting his fingernails.[155] But when he had reached a decision, he would erupt with great energy, and no cautionary words or objections from others could deter him from taking enormous risks. Hitler often followed what he called his "intuition." Frequently, he would greet his underlings out of the blue with the announcement: "I thought things over last night and have come to the following conclusion . . ."[156] In his first interrogation by the Allies in the summer of 1945, Speer told them that Hitler would get "intimations," displaying a kind of sixth sense for coming events and developments.[157] Goebbels, too, credited him with "a fabulous nose, instinctual political genius."[158] What his admirers overlooked was the fact that despite his alleged infallible instincts Hitler made numerous blunders on the road to power and ultimately only achieved his goal because others opened the door to the Chancellery for him.

Hitler's idiosyncratic work habits and decision-making reflected his self-image as an artist who had been forced into politics. And his entourage lapped up the idea of the artist-politician. "You know Hitler," Gregor Strasser once remarked to Otto Wagener. "He's an artist. His ideas come to him from somewhere in the beyond. They're intangible even to him. He develops them in front of our very eyes. He murmurs them to himself in our presence."[159] Goebbels concurred. "Hitler is himself an artist," the future propaganda minister noted in early December 1932 after a party attended by Leni Riefenstahl and the actress Gretl Slezak. "That's why all artists like him so much."[160] Speer also thought of Hitler as a frustrated artist who would have much rather been an architect than a politician.[161]

As we know from Hess's letters during their joint incarceration in Landsberg, Hitler was obsessed with architectural plans. Among other things, he made a sketch for a "great national building" in Berlin with a "100-metre covering dome" that would be larger than St. Peter's Basilica in Rome.[162] After his release, Hitler continued to pursue his plans. In December 1928, Hess wrote to his parents: "As an architect he already has plans in his head for expanding Berlin into the metropolis of the new German empire, and he's put some of them on paper in the form of marvellous sketches . . . We've often laughed, though with a serious undertone, when we've walked through Berlin, which he knows like the back of his hand, and he's swept away ugly, old housing blocks with a wave of his hand so that other existing or coming ones will have more room to shine."[163] From the very beginning, the construction projects Hitler envisioned were monumental: he was enamoured of everything gigantic.[164] The autodidact Hitler was keen to keep abreast of the latest publications on architecture, construction and art history. His Munich housekeeper, Anni Winter, said in 1945 that his private library consisted mainly of such works and that he read avidly in them.[165] Hitler bought them at the L. Werner bookshop in Munich, which specialised in architecture, and receipts preserved from 1931 to 1933 attest that he was a very good customer.[166] As he revealed in a private letter, he did not just get involved in architecture as a way of "resting and recuperating" from being Reich chancellor.[167] With the help of his favourite architect Speer, he actually set about making his megalomaniacal ideas reality—something few of his pre-1933 followers would have thought possible.

After architecture, Hitler's great passion was for the fine arts, in particular painting, although his understanding of and taste in art had hardly developed since his Vienna years. The failed artist and architect who considered himself a neglected genius felt deep-seated antipathy for avant-garde modernism, which he saw as a socially corrosive phenomenon advanced by "world Jewry." He never tired of railing against the art of the Weimar "system." "What has been foisted as art on the German people since 1922 is just some deformed spatters," Hitler raged in one of his table talks. "From the rapid demise of art in the 'system period,' you can see how devastating the influence of the Jews has been in this area."[168] By contrast, Hitler regarded the nineteenth century as an artistic heyday in which Germans had brought forth their "greatest artistic achievements."[169] Hitler's favourite artists— Adolph von Menzel, Anselm Feuerbach and Arnold Böcklin—all worked during that epoch, and the main rooms in a sketch Hitler made in 1925 for a new German national museum were dedicated to those three painters.[170] Hitler began collecting paintings in the late 1920s. At first he hung them in his private apartment in Munich. Later he also decorated the walls of his residence in the Reich Chancellery and the Berghof. With Hoffmann at his side, he was always in search of new acquisitions, especially works by Carl Spitzweg and Eduard von Grützner.[171] Even after becoming chancellor, Hitler would occasionally announce, all of a sudden, that he was going to a gallery such as Karl Haberstock's in Berlin's ritzy Kurfürstenstrasse. When he acquired Böcklin's *Battle of the Centaurs* in May 1935, Goebbels wrote that Hitler was "as happy as a child."[172]

Another constant from his early years in Linz and Vienna was Hitler's passion for Richard Wagner. "The Führer told me about Richard Wagner, whom he deeply reveres and knows better than any other," Goebbels noted in June 1937.[173] On 13 February 1933, a scant two weeks after taking power, Hitler was the guest of honour at the celebrations marking the fiftieth anniversary of Wagner's death at Leipzig's Gewandhaus. Until the start of the Second World War, he travelled every year to the Wagner Festival in Bayreuth, declaring it "his only chance to relax."[174] Hitler made sure that the chronically money-losing festival was given sufficient funds. He also declared that it was to be held annually and offered his opinions about which singers and musicians should be cast.[175] Alongside Wagner, Hitler enjoyed operettas—he saw Franz Lehar's *The Merry Widow* and Strauss's *Die Fledermaus* multiple times—and he was also a ballet enthusiast.[176]

In addition, Hitler was an avid cinema-goer. Even in the tense months leading up to the November putsch, he regularly went to the movie theatre on Munich's Sendlinger Torplatz. There, together with Ernst Hanfstaengl, he enjoyed the silent film *Fridericus Rex*. Hanfstaengl recounted that Hitler especially liked the scene in which the young Friedrich the Great is forced to witness the execution of his childhood friend Katte. "Off with the head of anyone who goes against the reasons of state," Hitler exclaimed, "be it even your own son!"[177] In October 1926, he and Hess went to see *Ben Hur*[178] and even in the hectic years before he took power, Hitler kept up with all the new releases, either in Berlin or elsewhere. In early 1932, he and Goebbels took in the erotically charged feature *Girls in Uniform*. "A fabulous, unpretentious, compelling film," Goebbels raved. "Achieves the greatest effects by the simplest means. Charming girls. I'm completely taken in and dumbfounded. Hitler too."[179] A bit later, the two men admired Greta Garbo in *Yvonne*.[180] And as 30 January 1933 approached, Hitler watched the historical film *The Rebel* not once but twice.[181] Hitler remained a film buff after becoming chancellor, but instead of going to the cinema, he had films screened privately in the Chancellery or at his retreat on the Obersalzberg.

Hitler was passionate about cars in general and Mercedes-Benz in particular. "I love automobiles," he admitted in January 1942. "I have to say that I owe the best moments of my life to the automobile."[182] He was intimately acquainted with all models of cars and, according to Schirach, was constantly reading up in magazines about valves, camshafts, suspensions, steering systems, motor specifications and handling.[183] In Landsberg, Hess was struck by Hitler's admiration for the Taylor system that allowed the Ford factory in Detroit to produce

800 cars a day. "Our industry should put in the effort and achieve similar results," Hitler opined.[184] There was no way, however, that Hitler would have bought an American car: all his life he remained true to Mercedes-Benz. The company had helped him at the start of his political career to acquire his first car, and Jakob Werlin, who ran the Mercedes dealership in Munich, was part of Hitler's entourage. In 1931, Hitler got the latest Mercedes, the eight-cylinder 770 with 7.7 litres of cubic capacity, the largest and most expensive passenger car of the time. Racing driver Rudolf Caracciola personally delivered the vehicle to Munich.[185] Hitler would have liked to see all prominent Nazis drive Mercedes, but he was never able to implement this wish.[186] Conversely, in the decisive year of 1932, the southern German carmaker intensified its connections with the NSDAP leadership. "There is no reason to decrease the attention we've paid to Herr Hitler and his friends," Mercedes director Wilhelm Kissel wrote to Werlin. "He will be able to count on us . . . just as he has in the past."[187] The carmaker made good on its word, providing the new Reich chancellor with a further luxury Mercedes for a song in June 1933. In return, Mercedes expected to be given preferential treatment in the blossoming automobile sector.[188]

As Hitler himself could not drive, he had himself chauffeured around by a series of drivers—Emil Maurice, Julius Schreck and Erich Kempka.[189] Hitler always sat in the front seat next to his chauffeur, studying the map. Before 1933, he loved going fast, and the luxury Mercedes models easily did over 100 kilometres an hour. "He couldn't see another car on the road in front without ordering his driver to pass it and leave it in the dust," Otto Dietrich reported.[190] After he became chancellor, Hitler set his drivers a speed limit, and for security reasons he now never went anywhere without a commando of bodyguards. But in the years before he took power, Hitler logged hundreds of thousands of kilometres, and sometimes it was inner restlessness and not business that made him take to the roads. "We lead the lives of gypsies," Goebbels remarked in January 1929.[191] Hitler often travelled the 150 miles between Munich and Berchtesgaden in an open-top car, regularly stopping at the Lambach Inn on the northern shore of Lake Chiemsee. He loved to picnic for hours by the side of the road with his entourage. It was a chance for him to briefly slip out of the role of Führer. "Picnic under the pines," Goebbels jotted down in July 1933.

"Four hours amidst nature. Hitler very happy. A normal person among normal people."[192]

Hanfstaengl reported that when he was in a good mood, Hitler was an unusually entertaining travel companion, who would hum whole passages from Wagner operas.[193] He and his entourage usually stayed up late in hotels, although Hitler often began to brood at some point. "The cheerful conversation would die down, if he no longer took part," Wagener recalled. "One or the other person would say good night, and Hitler would ask others to keep him company. You'd still be sitting there hours later . . . talking about everything under the sun except matters of work and present concerns."[194]

Various sources from his inner circle describe Hitler as leading an extremely simple, almost ascetic existence.[195] But that is only half the story. Hitler's supposedly modest personal needs were part of his carefully cultivated, partly fictional persona as a man of the people. His passion for fast and expensive cars, his choice of the Palais Barlow as Nazi Party headquarters and his huge apartment on Munich's posh Prinzregentenstrasse do not conform to that image. Speer turned up his nose at the interior design:

> Carved oak furniture, books in glass cases, embroidered cushions with delicate inscriptions and resolute party slogans. In one corner was a bust of Richard Wagner. The walls were full of idyllic paintings, framed in gold, by Munich School artists. Nothing betrayed the fact that this man had been the chancellor of Germany for three years. The air smelled of heated oil and sour leftovers.[196]

Schirach on the other hand found Hitler's apartment too bourgeois: "A wealthy factory owner or merchant might have lived like that, or an artistically aware but old-fashioned collector."[197]

"My surroundings have to make a grand impression so that they highlight my own simplicity," Hitler once remarked, and his modesty concerning his wardrobe was similarly calculated.[198] Hitler favoured unfussy uniforms made by the tailor Wilhelm Holters near the Chancellery. His suits were made by Michael Werner in Munich.[199] Hitler did not like to have his tailors take his measurements, and when they were allowed to do so, the procedure could not take more than a few minutes.[200] Hitler personally had little use for medals. He himself wore only the Iron Cross, First Class and the Golden Party Emblem—although he had no objections to those around him filling their chests with medals and badges: that too only increased the effect of his calculated modesty.[201]

Hitler had a relatively relaxed attitude towards money and seems not to have possessed a normal bank account.[202] Nor did he carry a wallet. If he needed money, an assistant would give it to him, or he would carry it loosely in his pocket. His aides Julius Schaub and Wilhelm Brückner paid his bills,[203] and Max Amann managed Hitler's income, which grew rapidly thanks to royalties from the sales of *Mein Kampf*. That income allowed him to initially refuse to accept his salary as Reich chancellor. He announced that decision in February 1933 with great pomp, underscoring his desire to nourish the public legend of the ascetic Führer.[204] In fact, he silently reversed that decision a year later. After Hindenburg's death, Hitler also received the Reich president's salary and an annual expense fund.[205]

Part of the legend of Hitler's asceticism was the fact that he did not eat meat or smoke cigarettes and only rarely drank alcohol. Wagener and Hitler's housekeeper Anni Winter reported that Hitler decided to become a vegetarian after the death of Geli Raubal in 1933.[206] In fact he had already begun to cut down his consumption of meat and alcohol after being released from Landsberg in late 1924. "In my experience, meat and alcohol harm my body," he told Hanfstaengl. "I have decided to summon the will-power necessary to do without both, as much as I enjoy them."[207] He stuck to his resolution, although aside from occasional scornful remarks about "cadaver-eaters," he did not mind if others chose not to follow him down this path. At dinner during the wedding of Schirach and Henriette Hoffmann in late March 1932, Hitler shook his head in dismay at the gigantic roast of beef and sighed: "Oh you Venus flytraps!" He himself only had some spaghetti with tomato sauce and an apple.[208] Sefton Delmer characterised meals with Hitler on the campaign trail in April 1932 as being a bit of trial. An "aura of isolation" surrounded the teetotalling vegetarian, making everyone at the table feel rather uncomfortable.[209]

Contrasting markedly with this sort of asceticism was Hitler's insatiable appetite for cake and sweets. When first introduced to Hitler, Hanfstaengl immediately noticed that he could not seem to get enough of Viennese pastries with whipped cream.[210] Schirach was completely dumbfounded when he first sat down with Hitler in 1928, shortly after he himself was named leader of the Nazi Students' Association:

> At tea time, I couldn't believe my eyes. He put so many lumps of sugar in his cup that there was hardly any room for the tea, which he then slurped down noisily. He also ate three or four pieces of cream pie. Hitler noticed my surprise. He glanced down critically at himself, smiled mischievously and said, "I shouldn't be eating this much. I'm getting fat. But I've got such a sweet tooth." He said this and then ordered another slice of pie.[211]

Years of consuming such huge quantities of sugary food took their toll. Hitler had very bad teeth and was forced to submit to extensive dental work in late 1933.[212]

As Schirach's anecdote illustrates, the Hitler of the late 1920s was indeed able to laugh at himself. He gradually lost this capacity as the Führer cult became increasingly excessive, and Hitler identified more and more with the role in which he was cast by his disciples and by Nazi propaganda. As Speer described the change: "He usually let others tell the jokes, and his laughter was loud and unconstrained. Sometimes, he would be bent over in laughter and have to wipe the tears from his eyes. He liked to laugh, but fundamentally it always came at others' expense."[213] There was nothing liberating about Hitler's laughter. It always contained a hint of ridicule and scorn, and Hitler habitually concealed his face with his hand whenever he laughed.[214]

The Führer was very mindful of his health. Indeed, his fear of illness betrayed unmistakable signs of hypochondria. Hitler was worried that he would die young and be unable to realise his plans. "'When I'm no longer here' has become his mantra," noted Goebbels in February 1927. "What a horrible thought!"[215] The following year, when he suffered a bout of severe stomach cramps, Hitler believed he had contracted cancer and was fated to die young like his mother. Initially he refused to consult a doctor, but eventually Elsa Bruckmann convinced him to see a certain Dr. Schweninger—the son of the Bismarck's personal physician. He diagnosed a chronic irritation of Hitler's stomach lining and put the Nazi leader on a strict diet.[216] Hitler's health improved, but he never lost his fear of dying young.

In February 1932, the morning after a speech by Hitler in Hamburg during the Reich presidential election, Albert Krebs found him hunched at his breakfast table in the Hotel Atlantic, looking tired and morose. Hitler then gave a long lecture about the advantages of vegetarianism, which incongruently revealed his fear of getting cancer. "'I've got no time to wait!' he said, looking at me over the edge of his plate of soup," Krebs recalled. "'If I did, I wouldn't be running for this office . . . But I can't afford to lose another year. I must come to power soon, if I'm to be able to take care of the gigantic tasks ahead in the time I have left. I must! I must!'" Krebs saw this "pathological mix of fear of mortality and messianic conviction" as the key to understanding why Hitler was so impatient about pursuing his political plans. "Someone who plans things beyond all normal dimensions and simultaneously fears that he won't live to see fifty has no option to move slowly and wait for his goal to come into reach and the fruits of his labours to ripen," Krebs concluded.[217] Even after Hitler attained power, he still regularly worried that he would not live long.[218] The irony was, as one of his doctors attested, that Hitler was in robust health. The symptoms of the nervous condition that he began to show over the years are hardly surprising, considering the pressure he was under.[219]

Hitler's fear of assassination was only slightly less pronounced than his anxiety about dying from illness. Thus, when Hitler moved into the Hotel Kaiserhof in Berlin in 1932, he suspected the kitchen staff were trying to poison him, and Magda Goebbels had to deliver him food prepared in her kitchen.[220] The director of household at the Reich Chancellery, Arthur Kannenberg, repeatedly complained about how difficult it was to cook for Hitler. "You would not believe how careful we have to be," he sighed. "When my wife cooks his food, no one's allowed to get within ten metres of the pots." Lieselotte Schmidt also reported that when Hitler stayed in Bayreuth, one of his entourage was posted to make sure no one poisoned his food.[221] One of the reasons Hitler appointed Wilhelm Brückner as his assistant was his hefty stature. Brückner, Hitler said, "offered a certain assurance that no one will dare approach me."[222] Hitler took other precautions as well. He carefully locked not only his hotel rooms, but also his bedroom at the Chancellery, and as of 1933, two commandos of police and SS bodyguards watched over his safety.[223] Both Hitler and his chauffeur carried pistols when they went out for drives.[224] Still the

Nazi Party leader and Reich chancellor knew that there was no such thing as absolute safety. He worried that one day he would be gunned down by a sharpshooter in some auditorium. "There's nothing you can do about it," Hitler said in the summer of 1936. "The best protection will always be enthusiastic masses of people."[225]

Hygiene was very important to the Führer. Hitler often took multiple baths a day, especially when he returned sweaty from public-speaking appearances.[226] Part of his morning routine from his early days on Thierschstrasse was doing expander exercises to strengthen his arms. This allowed him to keep his right arm raised for extended periods of time as columns of SA paraded past him for inspection. "It was a matter of years of training," Speer wrote. "None of his underlings could have matched that feat."[227] Hitler did not play any sports, but he did follow major sporting events with great interest. After car racing, his favourite was boxing. Not long after assuming power, he invited German heavyweight champion Max Schmeling to visit him at the Chancellery, and when Schmeling defeated Joe Louis in June 1936, Hitler insisted upon being given an extensive summary of the fight. Two years later he stayed up late to follow the rematch and was reportedly shocked when Louis knocked out Schmeling in the first round. "A terrible defeat," noted Goebbels. "Our newspapers were too confident of victory. Now our entire people is depressed."[228]

Even after 1933, Hitler tended to go to bed late, frequently after midnight, and get up late as well. He traced his night-owl rhythm back to his "street-fighting years": "After the meetings I had to get together with my comrades, and anyway I was so wound up by speeches that I couldn't sleep until morning."[229] But there was another reason for Hitler's nocturnal habits: he hated being alone. "It was striking how he shied away from it," Dietrich reported. "It often seemed to me that he was afraid of his own inner dialogues."[230] Goebbels offered a similar analysis: "Hitler needs to have people around him. Otherwise, he broods too much."[231] This provides another example of Hitler's peculiar dual personality: a dictator who kept other people at a distance but sought out company to avoid being alone with himself. Hitler may have had a keen eye for others' weak spots, but he was clearly unwilling to acknowledge his own psychological shortcomings.

In 1924, a graphologist who sympathised with the Nazis analysed Hitler's handwriting. The results, which he communicated by letter

to a local Nazi leader in Göttingen, Ludolf Haase, were anything but
positive. The analyst was deeply concerned about Hitler's downward-
sloping handwriting, which "clearly indicates a personality who, despite
whatever energy it possesses, will inevitably fail in the final, decisive
moment."[232] The philosopher Hermann von Keyserling offered an even
more damning appraisal a few months after Hitler was appointed
chancellor. Having studied the Führer intensely, Keyserling wrote to
Harry Kessler, he had come to the following conclusion: "The handwriting and physiognomy are of a decidedly suicidal character. He is
someone longing for death and he therefore embodies a basic characteristic of the German people, who have always been enamoured
by death and whose recurrent experience is the fate of the Nibelungs."
Keyserling was right, Kessler commented.[233] But there were not many
people in Germany who saw things this way. On the contrary, it was
not long after 30 January 1933 that the new man in the Chancellery
would achieve unforeseeable popularity.

14

Totalitarian Revolution

"Now we can really get started," Hitler told NSDAP Youth Leader Baldur von Schirach on the evening of 5 February 1933, five days after moving into the Chancellery. "We have power and we're going to keep it. I'm never leaving here."[1] The new Reich chancellor was by no means omnipotent, but he was determined to seize total power. The constellation of the government of "national concentration" Hindenburg had appointed meant that Hitler had to hold back and take into account his conservative coalition partners, who made up the majority of his cabinet. But as he confided to intimates, he saw the alliance formed on 29 and 30 January as an interim solution, an unavoidable transitional phase on the path towards unlimited authority.

Rarely has a political project been revealed as a chimera so quickly as the idea that conservatives in the government cabinet would "tame" the National Socialists. Those who "believed that Hitler is constrained in his cabinet by the lack of his own personnel," wrote Theodor Heuss on 7 February, were overlooking the fact "that these calculations contained some very dubious assumptions."[2] Papen, Hugenberg and their allies had indeed convinced themselves that they had "boxed in" Hitler so tightly that they could restrain his thirst for power and co-opt him and his movement for their own ends. Soon they would be forced to recognise how utterly mistaken they had been. "We had the wrong idea about the powers of the majority within a presidentially appointed government," Hugenberg admitted in May 1933 in a conversation with Richard Breiting, the editor-in-chief of the *Leipziger Neueste Nachrichten* newspaper.[3] The other members of the cabinet were no match for Hitler's tactical cleverness and his notorious mendacity. Within weeks, he had their backs to the wall and succeeded in securing the sort of favour with Hindenburg that Papen had formerly claimed for himself.

The vice-chancellor found himself in the role of the apprentice magician who could not control the evil spirits he had summoned.

Contemporary observers took note of the drama playing itself out in Berlin. "When the Hitler–Papen cabinet came to power, there were assurances that Hitler would be kept in check . . . by a government of conservative nationalists," reported French Ambassador André François-Poncet in early April 1933. "Six weeks later we find that all the dams that were supposed to hold back the waves of the Hitler movement have been washed away."[4] Nonetheless, there is little truth to the notion of a careful strategic plan behind Hitler's rapid seizure of power. What National Socialist propaganda later celebrated as the targeted action directed by the Führer's intuitive genius was actually a series of improvised decisions with which the Nazi leadership responded to and exploited unforeseeable situations.[5] Administrative measures "from above" and violent activities "from below" reinforced one another and drove developments.

It was astonishing not just how quickly but how easily Hitler turned political Germany on its head. "All counterweights to his power were suddenly swallowed up and disappeared," noted the Romance literature professor Victor Klemperer in his diary as early as March 1933. "This complete collapse of the existing powers, worse still their utter absence . . . has truly shaken me."[6] There was hardly any resistance. Instead, almost all institutions and social groups within Germany bent over backwards to accommodate and support the new regime. The process of *bringing* things and people "into line"—*Gleichschaltung*—would never have gone so smoothly and successfully had it not corresponded with a widespread wish to *be brought* into line.[7] Within only eighteen months, Hitler would rid himself of all rivals for power and establish a "Führer dictatorship."

On the afternoon of 30 January, Hitler held his first cabinet meeting. It was intended to demonstrate that the new government was capable of action and was tackling its duties from the outset. The political situation was clear. As he had demanded in his negotiations with Papen, Hitler wanted new elections to gain a parliamentary majority that would pass an enabling act in the Reichstag. A few hours previously, Hugenberg's resistance to the idea had almost scuppered the new government. Moreover, the night before, Papen had told

Hindenburg that negotiations were under way with the Centre Party to join the government, which was why the position of justice minister had been kept open. These unresolved issues bled over into the cabinet meeting. Hugenberg came out against both fresh elections and involving the Centre Party in the government, arguing that the latter "would endanger the formation of a unified will." Instead, he suggested banning the KPD and redistributing their parliamentary seats, which would yield a parliamentary majority.

Hitler did not think the beginning of his chancellorship was an opportune moment for such a draconian move. Banning the Communist Party would cause domestic unrest and perhaps lead to a general strike, he told the cabinet. He added: "It is nothing short of impossible to ban the 6 million people who stand behind the KPD. But perhaps in the coming election after the dissolution of the Reichstag, we can win a majority for the current government."[8] Hitler, too, was uninterested in expanding the coalition to include the Centre Party. But with an eye towards the promises he had given Hindenburg, he agreed to "sound out" Centre Party representatives. With that, subsequent talks with Centre Party Chairman Ludwig Kaas and Parliamentary Leader Ludwig Perlitius were destined to fail.[9] Hitler demanded parliament be suspended for at least a year, while the Centre leaders would only support a suspension of around two months. They also made their participation contingent upon being given written answers to a series of questions that would provide reliable information about the government's intentions. Hitler used such demands as a pretext for telling his cabinet that very afternoon that "there is no point to further negotiations with the Centre . . . new elections will be unavoidable."

Hitler sought to reassure his conservative coalition partners by promising the outcome of the election would have no influence on the composition of the cabinet. Then it was Papen—and not Hitler—who made a radical suggestion. It should be made clear, the vice-chancellor declared, that the next election would be the last one and that a return to the parliamentary system would be ruled out "for ever." Hitler gladly adopted this proposal, saying that the upcoming Reichstag election would indeed be the final one and that a return to parliamentary democracy was "to be avoided at all costs."[10] Using this argument, and with support from Papen and Meissner, Hitler succeeded in convincing Hindenburg that it was necessary to dissolve the Reichstag. Hindenburg's decree, dated 1 February, justified the decision to hold new elections as giving the German people the opportunity to "have their say on the formation of a new government of national solidarity." The date for the vote was set as 5 March. Hitler had achieved his most immediate goal without any serious resistance from his cabinet.[11]

On the evening of 1 February, Hitler delivered a governmental declaration, approved by his cabinet, over the radio. It was the first time he had addressed the German people over the airwaves, and the veteran speaker, who thrived on direct contact with his audience, displayed all the signs of stage fright. "His whole body was shaking," observed Hjalmar Schacht.[12] In his address, Hitler combined the attacks on the democratic "betrayal" of November 1918 and the Weimar Republic from his 1932 campaign speeches ("fourteen years of Marxism have brought Germany to the brink of ruin") with appeals to conservative, Christian, nationalist values and traditions. The first task of his government, Hitler said, was to overcome class hostilities and restore "the unity of our people in spirit and will." Christianity, Hitler added, was to be "the basis of our morals," the family the "basic cell of our body as a people and a state," and respect for "our great past" the foundation for the education of Germany's young people. The chancellor sounded tones of moderation concerning his foreign policy. A Germany that had recovered its equality with other states, Hitler promised, would stand for "the preservation and solidification of peace, which the world needs now more than ever." Hitler did not neglect to direct some flattering words in the direction of the "honourable Reich president," and he ended his speech with the same appeal he was to utter innumerable times in the future: "Now, German people, give us the span of four years and then you may pass judgement upon us!"[13]

From Hitler's governmental declaration, it was easy to get the impression that he, as head of government, intended to be more moderate and would revise the goals he had formulated prior to 1933. But it was clear on the evening of 3 February, when Hitler paid his introductory visit to the commanders of the German army and navy, that any such impressions were mistaken. The meeting called by new Defence Minister Werner von Blomberg took place in the official apartment of the army chief of staff, Kurt von Hammerstein, and Hitler was initially ill at ease among all the high-ranking officers. "He

made strange humble little bows in every direction and was at a loss,"
one participant remarked.[14] Only after dinner, when he began a speech
that would last two hours, did he shed his nervousness. No trace was
left of the moderation he had displayed only two days earlier in his
radio address. On the contrary, Hitler, with astonishing frankness, laid
out for his military commanders what he intended to do in the years
to come.[15]

Hitler defined his government's first goal as to "reclaim political
power," which would have to be the "purpose of the entire state leadership." Domestically there would have to be a "complete reversal" of
present conditions. Pacifist tendencies would no longer be tolerated.
"Anyone who refuses to convert has to be forced," an officer attending
the meeting quoted Hitler. "Marxism is to be utterly rooted out."[16]
Germany's youth and its entire population, Hitler declared, had to be
aligned along the ideas that "only battle can save us and everything
else must be subordinated to this thought." The "sternest, authoritarian
state leadership" and "the removal of the cancerous damage of democracy" were necessary to strengthen Germany's "will to defend itself."
In the part of his speech that dealt with foreign policy, Hitler said his
first goal would be "to fight against Versailles" by achieving military
equality and rearming the Wehrmacht. "Universal conscription has to
be reintroduced," Hitler demanded. The phase of rearmament, Hitler
said, would be the most "dangerous" one, since France could decide
to launch pre-emptive military strikes. Hitler apparently did not specify
what he intended for Germany once it had regained its status as a
major military power. But he did hint at two options, and left the
officers in no doubt as to which one he favoured: "Perhaps the achievement of new export possibilities; perhaps—and probably better—conquest of new living space in the east and its ruthless Germanification."[17]

With that, Hitler had pulled back the curtains and given military
leaders a backstage look at his plans for territorial expansion, the same
ones he had laid out in principle in *Mein Kampf*. It is unlikely that the
generals in attendance realised that they could be heading for a racist
war of extermination with the Soviet Union. What Hitler told them
largely reflected the military leadership's own ideas. The generals could
easily identify with a battle against Marxism and pacifism, demands
for a revision of the Treaty of Versailles, a rearming of Germany's
military and the restoration of its status as world power. The military

leadership was especially pleased to hear Hitler promise that the Wehrmacht would remain the country's only legitimate military force and that it would not be used to put down domestic opponents. The latter, Hitler declared, was the job of National Socialist organisations, particularly the SA. General Ludwig Beck, who was named chief of the Troop Office in the autumn of 1933, may have later claimed that he soon forgot what Hitler had actually said at the meeting, but this is scarcely credible. Beck was among the officers who had unreservedly greeted the change of power in January 1933 as, in his own words, "one of the first major rays of light since 1918."[18] Admiral Erich Raeder, the navy chief of command, was probably more truthful when he testified after the war that Hitler's keynote speech had been "extraordinarily well received by everyone who heard it."[19]

The partnership concluded by Hitler and the military leadership on 3 February 1933 benefited both sides. The Reich chancellor could now concentrate on crushing the political Left and bringing German society as a whole into line with Nazi ideals without any fears of the military intervening. The military leadership in turn had received a guarantee for its monopoly position and was assured that its concerns would enjoy the highest priority within the new government. "For the next four or five years," Hitler told his cabinet, "our main principle will be: everything for the Wehrmacht." Germany's future, Hitler pontificated, depended "solely and exclusively on the rebuilding of the Wehrmacht."[20]

"Attack on Marxism" was the chief slogan Hitler chose for the approaching election.[21] "This time it's a matter of cut and thrust," noted Goebbels, who went through all aspects of the campaign with Hitler on 3 February.[22] From the very beginning, the vote did not take place under fair circumstances. On 4 February, Hindenburg issued a Decree for the Protection of the German People that allowed the government to curtail the right to free speech and free assembly and subjected the two left-wing parties, the SPD and the KPD, to massive restrictions.[23] Moreover, unlike before 1933, the NSDAP now had direct access to the airwaves. Goebbels and Hitler agreed on a division of labour: "Hitler will speak on all radio stations, and I'll do the accompanying reports."[24]

On 10 February the National Socialists kicked off the campaign with an event in Berlin's Sportpalast. "Entirely alone, serious and measured, cordially greeting people, the Führer, Reich Chancellor

Adolf Hitler, the leader of young Germany, is striding through the masses!" Goebbels announced at the start of his radio report. "One month ago, he spoke here in the Sportpalast as the head of a scorned, defamed and ridiculed opposition party. Now we can say: what a turnabout in Divine Providence."[25] The next day Goebbels noted with satisfaction in his diary that his twenty-minute report had gone swimmingly, and that he had not felt any stage fright at all.[26] As was his wont, Hitler began his speech at a markedly leisurely, almost hesitant pace, only to whip himself into an oratorical frenzy. His words about his government policies were astonishingly general. Hitler repeated his attacks on the "political parties of disintegration," which had brought Germany to its knees in the preceding fourteen years, confirmed his intention to "root out Marxism and related phenomena in Germany," promised to replace "lazy democracy" with "the virtue of personality and the creative power of the individual" and asked for "four years" to bring about the "renewal of the nation." He closed with an echo of the Lord's Prayer: "I unwaveringly maintain the conviction that the hour will come in which the millions who now hate us will stand behind us and greet the German Reich of greatness, majesty and justice that we will jointly create, tenaciously deserve and obtain through great sacrifice. Amen."[27]

Goebbels gushed: "Lots of pathos at the end. 'Amen!' That's really powerful. It works. All of Germany will be beside itself."[28] Not only Hitler's admirers were impressed. Even a critical mind like the Leipzig writer Erich Ebermayer, son of Chief Reich Prosecutor Ludwig Ebermayer, noted after listening to the speech on the radio: "The man is obviously growing into the job. What an instrument radio is for mass propaganda! And how few of Hitler's rivals know how to use it at all! Did radio not exist before 30 January? Incomprehensible!"[29]

The National Socialists did not only use radio. They also sought to co-opt Hindenburg's aura for their own propaganda. One of their campaign posters showed Hitler, the anonymous First World War soldier, and the former field marshal standing shoulder to shoulder. The caption read: "The marshal and the private fight with us for peace and equal treatment." Another poster featuring Hitler's and Hindenburg's heads appealed to voters: "Never will the Reich be destroyed if you stick together and stay true."[30] The DNVP concluded an electoral alliance with the Stahlhelm and other conservative-nationalist groups called the "Battle Front Black, White and Red." At Hugenberg's request, Papen ran as their lead candidate in order to, as he wrote, "serve the common cause and to call, side by side with the National Socialists, for participation from all forces who want to renew our German fatherland under the leadership of Field Marshal von Hindenburg in faith, justice and unity."[31] The "Battle Front" too sought to exploit Hindenburg's mythic status by playing up Papen's connection to the Reich president. "If Hindenburg trusts him, so can Germany," read one campaign poster featuring images of both men. "Vote for his close associate, Vice-Chancellor von Papen."[32]

But Hitler and the NSDAP profited more than their conservative coalition partners from popular regard for the former field marshal, and they raked in election donations. At the beginning of the campaign, Goebbels had complained about empty party coffers. That changed on 20 February, when Göring hosted a reception for twenty-seven leading industrialists, including the president of the Reich Association of German Industry, Gustav Krupp von Bohlen und Halbach, United Steelworks General Director Albert Vögler, IG Farben board member Georg von Schnitzler and Hoesch chairman of the board Fritz Springorum. Hitler, who spoke for an hour and a half, once again reaffirmed his belief in private property, denied rumours that he was planning any wild economic experiments and stressed that "only the NSDAP offers salvation from the Communist danger." Fresh elections had been called, Hitler declared, to "allow the people to be heard once more." And with rare frankness, he revealed the hollowness of his insistence upon remaining within the boundaries of the law. "He was no friend of illegal measures," one of the industrialists recorded Hitler saying. "But he would not allow himself to be forced from power even if he could not reach his goal of an absolute majority." Once Hitler had left, Göring declared without further ado that the "coffers of the party, the SS and the SA were empty" and that the business sector would have to bear the costs of the election, "which would be the last one for the foreseeable future." After Göring, too, had withdrawn from the meeting, Hjalmar Schacht spoke up to present those in attendance with a bill for the campaign: 3 million reichsmarks were to be raised, of which three quarters would go to the NSDAP and one quarter to the "Battle Front Black, White and Red."[33] A satisfied Goebbels noted on 21 February: "Göring just brought the news that the 3 million for the election are there. Great stuff! I alerted the entire propaganda division, and one hour later the machines were rattling away. Our campaign is on."[34]

In his capacity as acting Prussian interior minister, Göring had already begun to "cleanse" the Prussian police and administration of the few remaining democrats who had survived Papen's coup of 20 July 1932. Fourteen police presidents in Prussian cities as well as numerous other senior municipal officers were sent into retirement in February 1933 alone. "Göring is cleaning house," Goebbels declared on 16 February. "We are gradually enmeshing ourselves in governmental administration."[35] The following day, Prussian police departments were instructed to "support the national propaganda with all their might, combat the activities of organisations hostile to the state with the most severe means and, if necessary, to have no qualms about using firearms." To be perfectly clear, Göring added: "Police officers who use their weapons in the performance of their duties will be covered by me regardless of the consequences. Conversely, those who hesitate to do their duty will suffer disciplinary action."[36] This "fire-at-will decree" was in effect a licence to kill, as Count Harry Kessler recognised: "From now on all of us who do not stand on the so-called 'national' ground, i.e. who are not Nazis, can be killed with impunity."[37]

On 22 February, Göring also ordered the creation of an auxiliary police force consisting of members of the "national associations"—the SS, the SA and the Stahlhelm—ostensibly for the purpose of combating "increasing unrest from radical left-wing and especially Communist quarters."[38] With that the Brownshirts were finally given the opportunity they had long coveted to settle the score with their hated left-wing adversaries. The following weeks were marked by attacks on election events, arbitrary detentions, physical abuse and murders. The police did nothing to prevent the SA from terrorising people. Social Democrats were mistreated, but Communists got the worst of it. As of early February, it became practically impossible for them to assemble in public, and almost without exception, Communist newspapers were banned. On 23 February, police carried out a large-scale raid on Karl Liebknecht House, the KPD's headquarters, confiscating, as was extensively reported in the papers and on radio the following day, many tons of "highly seditious material" allegedly calling for the government to be overthrown.[39] Fears of an imminent armed KPD uprising were encouraged. In democratic, left-wing circles, rumours circulated that the Nazis were planning a "bloodbath" by faking an assassination attempt on Hitler as a pretext for taking revenge. "It is said that lists have been drawn up of those to be systematically murdered," Kessler wrote.[40] In the midst of this ominous atmosphere, news broke in the evening of 27 February that the Reichstag was on fire.

The question of who was responsible for the burning of the Reichstag has prompted a decades-long debate that has never been resolved. Because the event was so useful to the National Socialists, suspicions arose immediately that the Nazis themselves had started the fire. Conversely, the Nazi leadership did not waste any time at all in blaming the KPD, although not a shred of evidence was presented. The most likely explanation is the one first advanced by Fritz Tobias in the early 1960s that the Dutch Communist revolutionary Marinus van der Lubbe, who was arrested at the scene, acted on his own, without anyone pulling the strings behind him.[41] But there is no way of being certain, and there probably never will be. In any case, more important than continuing debates about whether van der Lubbe was the sole arsonist is what sort of advantages the National Socialists derived from the Reichstag fire.

The initial reactions of the top NSDAP leaders on the evening of 27 February suggest that they, too, were surprised. Hitler was with the Goebbelses, as was his habit, when Hanfstaengl called around 10 p.m. and told them that the Reichstag was in flames. At first they thought it was a bad joke,[42] but the news was soon confirmed. Hitler and Goebbels hurried to the scene, where they met Göring. He greeted all those who arrived with a tirade about who was to blame, although the origins of the blaze had yet to be investigated. "This is the beginning of the Communist uprising," Göring raged. "Now they will strike. We have not a minute to lose!"[43] Goebbels accepted this version of events without question, noting: "Arson in 30 spots. Committed by the Communists. Göring a whirlwind of action. Hitler is enraged."[44] Indeed, at the scene of the fire, Hitler worked himself up into a state of extreme agitation. After the war, Rudolf Diels, whom Göring named head of the Gestapo, the Secret State Police, in April 1933, recalled:

> He yelled, completely out of control, in a way I had never seen before, as if he was about to burst. "Now there'll be no more mercy. Anyone

who gets in our way will be cut down . . . Every Communist functionary will be shot on the spot. The Communist deputies must be hanged from the gallows this very evening. Everybody connected with the Communists is to be arrested. There's no more taking it easy on the Social Democrats and the Reich Banner either."

Hitler would not hear of it when Diels said he thought the man arrested, Marinus van der Lubbe, was a lunatic. "This is a very clever, carefully planned matter," Hitler raged. "The criminals thought this through very thoroughly. But comrades, they've miscalculated, haven't they?"[45]

Nor did Hitler restrain himself in the company of Franz von Papen, who had hurried to the Reichstag from the Gentlemen's Club, where he had been dining with Hindenburg. "This is a sign from God, Herr Vice-Chancellor!" Hitler told him. "If this fire is, as I believe, the work of Communists, we will have to crush this deadly pestilence with an iron fist!"[46] It is difficult to say whether Hitler and his paladins became victims of their own propaganda and truly believed that the Communists were behind the act of arson. But it is beyond doubt that the Nazis were not at all unhappy about the Reichstag fire. On the contrary, it was a welcome excuse to strike a decisive blow against the KPD. Later that evening, when the Nazi leadership assembled in the Hotel Kaiserhof, the mood was positively relaxed. "Everyone was beaming," Goebbels noted. "This was just what we needed. Now we're completely in the clear."[47] The Nazis' conservative coalition partners reacted in similar fashion. When Finance Minister Schwerin von Krosigk, who was having dinner at the French embassy, received word of the fire, he exclaimed, much to the bewilderment of the other guests, "Thank God!"[48]

By the night of 27–28 February, the KPD's leading functionaries and almost all of the party's Reichstag deputies had been arrested. Party offices were closed, and all Communist newspapers were banned until further notice. The arrests continued in the days that followed. On 3 March, KPD Chairman Ernst Thälmann was located and detained. By mid-March more than 10,000 political opponents of Nazism found themselves in "protective custody" in Prussia alone. Among them were left-wing intellectuals like Carl von Ossietzky, Erich Mühsam and Egon Erwin Kisch.[49]

The meeting of Hitler's cabinet on the morning of 28 February was naturally dominated by the events of the previous evening. Hitler asserted that the "psychologically correct moment" had arrived for "a ruthless reckoning with the KPD." He said: "It would be senseless to wait any longer. The KPD is determined in the extreme. The battle against them cannot be made dependent on legal considerations." Göring reiterated the statement that the Nazi leadership had agreed upon the previous evening: it was "impossible that one person alone could have performed this act of arson." On the contrary, the Communists had "initiated this attack." The material confiscated in the Karl Liebknecht House suggested that the Communists intended to form "terrorist groups," set public buildings on fire, poison the food served in public kitchens and take "the wives and children of ministers and other high-ranking personalities hostage."[50] Although it was easy to see that this nightmare scenario was a crass invention, none of the conservative ministers objected. That very afternoon, the cabinet approved the draft of a Decree for the Protection of the People and the State submitted in the morning by Interior Minister Wilhelm Frick. The first paragraph "suspended until further notice" funda-mental civil rights including personal liberty, freedom of speech and the press, the right to assemble, the privacy of letters and telephone conversations and the inviolability of house and home. The second paragraph enabled the government to "temporarily take over" the responsibilities of the upper administration of Germany's states "in order to restore public security and order."[51] That opened the door not only for the Nazis to persecute anyone who disagreed with them but also to bring Germany's often resistant states into line.

The decree of 28 February was, in the words of one German histor-ian, "the emergency law upon which the National Socialist dictatorship based its rule until it itself collapsed,"[52] and as early as 1941 the polit-ical scientist Ernst Fraenkel characterised it as the "constitutional document" of the Third Reich.[53] Hindenburg had no qualms about signing the emergency decree, which was sold to him as a "special ordinance to fight Communist violence." Unwittingly or not, he helped transfer political authority from the office of the Reich president to the Reich government.[54] In a speech in Frankfurt am Main on 3 March, Göring made it abundantly clear what he intended to do with the new powers he had been granted. The measures he ordered, Göring promised, would not be diluted by any legal considerations: "In this regard, I am not required to establish justice. In this regard, I am required to eradicate and eliminate and nothing more!"[55] This sort of language and the violent measures that accompanied Göring's words must have horrified anyone who maintained any vestige of faith in the rule of law. Papen was not among them. When François-Poncet drew his attention to foreign diplomats' concern at the National Socialists' growing terror campaigns, Papen brushed aside any worries: "It's no big deal. When they've scraped the velvet from their horns, everything will be fine."[56]

Nor did the SA's brutal persecution of Communists draw any condemnation from the middle classes. On the contrary, the *bête noire* of a "Communist threat," reinforced by years of propaganda, led many people to see draconian measures as justified. "Finally, an iron broom over Prussia!" gushed Luise Solmitz.[57] Elisabeth Gebensleben, the wife of the deputy mayor of Braunschweig, did not have any scruples either: "The ruthless intervention of the national government may be somewhat alienating for many people, but there needs to be a thorough cleansing and clearing up. The anti-national forces must be rendered harmless. Otherwise no recovery will be possible."[58] If appearances do not deceive, the suppression of the political Left in Germany, and especially the Communists, did nothing to dampen Hitler's popularity. On the contrary, it increased his approval among the general populace. If Hitler stayed his course, one report from Catholic Upper Bavaria read, he would surely "have the trust of the great proportion of the German people" in the upcoming Reichstag election.[59]

The U.S. ambassador, Frederick Sackett, termed the elections on 5 March a "farce," since the left-wing parties "were completely denied their constitutional right to address their supporters during the final and most important week of the campaign."[60] Discrimination was also all too apparent on election day itself. "In front of the polling station only Nazi and Black, White and Red posters, nothing from the State Party, the SPD or the KPD," wrote Kessler.[61] Bearing that in mind, the result of the vote was all the more astonishing. Despite the extraordinarily high voter turnout of 88.8 per cent, the NSDAP came up clearly short of their stated goal of an absolute majority. The Nazis took 43.9 per cent of the vote—an increase of 10.8 per cent over the November 1932 election. To secure their majority, they needed the support of the Battle Front Black, White and Red, which only received 8 per cent of the vote, less than the DNVP had got the preceding November. The SPD took 18.3 per cent of the vote (down 2.1 per cent), and despite everything, the KPD still polled 12.3 per cent (down 4.6 per cent). Notwithstanding all the obstacles placed in their way, the two left-wing parties still managed to capture almost a third of the vote. The Centre Party (11.2 per cent) and the BVP (2.7 per cent) maintained their support while the State Party (0.9 per cent) and the DVP (1.1 per cent), which had basically become fringe parties, continued their respective declines.[62] "The splendid German people!" the writer Erich Ebermayer commented. "Despite everything, the working classes still solidly stand behind their leadership. The Catholics still solidly stand by their Church. There are still upstanding democrats! 48.2 per cent of the electorate had the courage to vote against Hitler or stay at home. I see this day as a victory and a reassurance."[63]

But there was no reason to be reassured. The NSDAP registered strong gains in those regions—Catholic Bavaria and Württemberg and metropolitan Berlin—where it had previously performed poorly, and the party also seemed to have mobilised the majority of previous non-voters. "A glorious victory," noted Goebbels, who had kept track of the incoming results with Hitler in the Chancellery. "Above all in southern Germany. More than a million [votes] in Berlin. Fantastic numbers. We're all in a state of something like intoxication. One surprise after another. Hitler is very moved. We're swimming in bliss."[64] Ambassador Sackett also reported that Hitler had achieved an "unprecedented triumph": "Democracy in Germany has received a blow from which it may never recover." The Third Reich long heralded by the Nazis, Sackett added, had now become reality.[65]

The turnaround noticeably changed the way Hitler behaved in his cabinet. Previously, he had shown respect for his conservative coalition partners and moderated cabinet meetings rather than trying to impose his will upon them. "He rarely gets his way in the cabinet," Goebbels had noted on 2 March,[66] and the ministers were impressed not only by Hitler's knowledge of the issues, but by his ability to "distil what is essential in every problem" and to "summarise concisely the results of a long discussion."[67] But in the first meeting after the election, on 7 March, Hitler began throwing his weight around. "He considers the results of 5 March to be a revolution," read the minutes of the meeting.

"In the end, there will no longer be Marxism in Germany. An Enabling Law approved by a two-thirds majority is necessary. He, the Reich chancellor, is deeply convinced that the Reichstag will pass such a law. The representatives of the KPD will not appear at the inauguration of the Reichstag because they find themselves in detention." Hitler could also expect to encounter no resistance from his ministers—Papen made that clear when he expressed the gratitude of the cabinet to Hitler for his "admirable performance in the election."[68]

On 11 March, Hitler succeeded in getting cabinet approval for the creation of a Reich Ministry for Popular Enlightenment and Propaganda. With that he kept the promise he had made to Goebbels on 30 January but which violated the express assurances he had given his coalition partners that the make-up of the cabinet would not change after the election. With the exception of Alfred Hugenberg, who objected, the members of the cabinet all accepted this breach of the coalition agreement without protest.[69] On 13 March, Hindenburg signed the certificate making Goebbels Reich propaganda minister. "What a journey," the latter wrote in his diary. "A government minister at the age of 35. Hard to believe. I have Hitler to thank. He is a good person and a brave warrior." The next day, Hindenburg swore in the new minister, prompting Goebbels to comment that he was "like an elderly father." The new minister added: "I thanked him that he had chosen me despite my youth. That moved him. Meissner assisted very well. A complete success."[70] With the new Propaganda Ministry, the Nazi leadership had created an instrument for influencing and manipulating the public, and it was to play an important role in the party's gradual consolidation of power. In his first press conference on 16 March, Goebbels announced his and his ministry's intention "to work on the people until they accept our influence."[71]

No sooner had the Reichstag election been held than Hitler began planning the next step on the path towards monopolising political power: bringing the non-National Socialist German states into line. It was imperative, Hitler announced to his cabinet, to "boldly tackle the Reich states problem."[72] Goebbels seconded that sentiment: "Time to clamp down! We can no longer show any consideration. Germany is in the midst of a revolution. Resistance is futile."[73] Measures had been taken to bring Hamburg into line even before the election. Citing the Reichstag Arson

Ordinance of 28 February, Interior Minister Frick had pressured the city senate, a coalition of the SPD, State Party and DVP, to take more vigorous action against the Communists. Although the Social Democrat senator for police affairs, Adolph Schönfelder, acceded to these demands and had seventy-five KPD functionaries arrested, the local NSDAP repeatedly raised the alarm and called upon Frick to maintain order by appointing a Reich commissioner for law enforcement in Hamburg. On 2 March, Frick demanded that the Social Democrat *Hamburger Echo* newspaper be banned for raising doubts as to whether Communists had truly been behind the Reichstag fire, and the city's SPD senators were forced to resign to preserve the remnants of their dignity. Nonetheless, the SPD did remarkably well in the elections on 5 March, taking 26.9 per cent of the vote—a decline of only 1.7 per cent compared with the previous November. The KPD received 17.6 per cent, a loss of 4.3 per cent. With 44.5 per cent, the two left-wing parties outpolled the NSDAP (38.8 per cent) by nearly 6 percentage points. That, of course, did not stop the Nazis from claiming that they had received a mandate to remake the Hamburg senate along their own lines. Only an hour after polling stations had closed, Frick ordered that responsibility for the Hamburg police be transferred to SA leader Alfred Richter. What was left of the senate caved in. A new senate consisting of six National Socialists, two conservative nationalists, two members of the Stahlhelm and one representative each from the DVP and State Party was formed on 8 March.[74]

Germany's other states were brought into line in the same way, with pressure from the party grass roots combining effectively with pseudo-legal measures ordered by the Reich government. Typically the local Gau leadership would start the process by demanding that a Nazi be appointed police president. The SA would stage marches, government offices would be occupied, and the swastika flag raised before public buildings. Under the pretext of having to re-establish "peace and order," the Reich Interior Ministry would intervene and appoint Reich commissioners. In this fashion, Bremen, Lübeck, Hesse, Baden, Württemberg, Saxony and Schaumburg-Lippe were brought into line between 6 and 8 March.[75]

On 9 March, the final bastion, Bavaria, fell. Bavarian President Held initially resisted when the Gauleiter of Bavaria, Adolf Wagner, with support from Röhm and Himmler, demanded that the former Freikorps commander Franz Ritter von Epp be installed as general state commissioner. But when Frick appointed Epp anyway that evening, the Bavarian State Ministry had no choice but to give in. On the night of 9–10 March, leading BVP representatives were detained and abused. The worst mistreatment was reserved for Bavarian Interior Minister Karl Stützel, who was particularly hated because he had treated the NSDAP less leniently than his predecessors. Full of outrage, the leader of the Bavarian Catholic Farmers' movement, Georg Heim, reported to Hindenburg that Stützel "was dragged out of bed, in his nightshirt and barefooted, by adherents of Epp's party, beaten bloody and taken to the Brown House . . . These are conditions the like of which I've never seen in my Bavarian homeland, not even under the Communist rule of terror."[76] Hindenburg forwarded this message to Hitler without comment; the author never received a response. Reich Commissioner Epp named Gauleiter Wagner acting Bavarian interior minister and Himmler acting Bavarian police director. The former naval officer Reinhard Heydrich, not even 30 years old, took charge of Police Division IV, which was responsible for political crimes. For both Himmler and Heydrich, these positons were springboards from which they eventually came to dominate the Third Reich's entire police and security apparatus.[77]

Three days after this staged volte-face, Hitler flew to Munich and expressed his satisfaction that "Bavaria has joined the broad front of the awakening nation." Following a triumphant drive through the streets of the Bavarian capital, he laid a gigantic wreath in front of the Feldherrnhalle to commemorate the casualties of the putsch of 9 November 1923. Its inscription read: "And in the end you did achieve victory!"[78] On 16 March, the Held cabinet, as the representatives of the last state to be brought into line, officially resigned. That cleared the way for a government consisting almost exclusively of National Socialists. By late March, a Preliminary Law for Bringing the States into Line ordered that seats in all regional parliaments be allocated according to the results of the national election of 5 March. KPD mandates were annulled. One week later, on 7 April, the Reich government issued the Second Law for Bringing the States into Line with the Reich. It installed "Reich governors," eradicating once and for all the sovereignty of the regional German states.[79]

This law gave Hitler the leverage to reorder the power structure in Prussia as well. He himself assumed the authority of Reich governor, rendering Papen's position as Reich commissioner obsolete. On

10 April, Göring was named Prussian state president, and two weeks later Hitler assigned him the authority of the governorship. As the British ambassador, Horace Rumbold, accurately reported to Foreign Secretary John Simon, Papen's loss of influence put Prussia completely under National Socialist control and meant that even friends of Hindenburg had to kowtow to Göring and his lackeys.[80] Within a matter of weeks, the vice-chancellor, who as recently as 30 January had depicted himself as the ringmaster taming the Nazis, had been pushed to the political margins.

If Hitler's coalition partners had hoped that SA terror activities would die down in the wake of the election, these hopes were disappointed. On the contrary, the violence only increased. "What I termed terror prior to 5 March was but a mild prelude," remarked Victor Klemperer on 10 March.[81] In many cities and communities, SA men occupied town halls and exacted revenge on representatives of the Weimar "system." SPD offices and newspapers were also occupied, their furnishings destroyed, and their employees abused and taken to cellars and holding cells, where they, together with already-detained Communists, were mercilessly tortured by Hitler's henchmen. Rudolf Diels bluntly described what such a torture chamber was like in the spring of 1933:

> The victims we found there were close to starvation. They had been confined for days in narrow closets in an attempt to force "confessions" from them. The "interrogations" began and ended with beatings. Around a dozen brutes had taken turns beating the victims with iron bars, plastic batons and whips. Knocked-out teeth and broken bones bore witness to the torture. When we entered the space, whole rows of living skeletons were lying on rotten straw, their wounds festering. To a man, their bodies were covered with blue, yellow and green bruises from inhuman beatings. Many of their eyes were swollen shut, and blood had congealed under their nostrils. There was no groaning or complaint. They simply waited for the end to come or for the next beating to commence . . . Hieronymus Bosch and Pieter Bruegel never imagined anything so horrific.[82]

Rampant SA terror tactics created a climate of fear and intimidation. "We're forced to acknowledge that all parts of the opposition are completely demoralised," noted Harry Kessler on 8 March. "The open departure from the rule of law, and the general feeling that justice no longer exists, has a tyrannical effect."[83] In a letter of 14 March, Theodor Heuss wrote:

> Numerous rumours have it that there are many brutal excesses away from the public eye, that people are being dragged from their homes and beaten in the Brownshirt barracks. As long as the Nazi government doesn't punish some of their members who are out of control and make examples of them, I fear that the situation won't calm down. Thus far, these people have always been able to count on support from above.[84]

In a statement on 10 March, Hitler cautioned his supporters against "compromising the great work of national renewal with individual actions," and two days later in a radio address he called for the "strictest and most blind discipline." The NSDAP's victory, Hitler said, was "so immense that we cannot feel any petty desires for vengeance."[85] But such public lip service notwithstanding, Hitler was by no means willing to restrain the SA. That emerged with utter clarity in a long letter he sent to Papen on 11 March.

The vice-chancellor had provoked Hitler's ire by complaining that SA men had harassed foreign diplomats. He had the feeling, Hitler wrote, that "a planned barrage was going on with the intent of stopping the national uprising and definitely of intimidating the movement that carried it." SA men, Hitler claimed, had shown "unprecedented discipline," and he was fearful that history would conclude that, "at a decisive moment, perhaps infected by the weakness and cowardice of the bourgeois world, we proceeded with velvet gloves instead of an iron fist." No one, Hitler vowed, would keep him from fulfilling his mission: "the destruction and eradication of Marxism." The next few sentences expressed only contempt for the conservative coalition partners who had handed him the levers of power only a few months before, leaving no doubt that Hitler was no longer willing to consider their interests. "If the conservative nationalists and other bourgeois have suddenly lost their nerve and think they have to write open letters to me, they should have done so before the election . . ." Hitler wrote, mockingly. "I most insistently request of you, my dear Herr Vice-

Chancellor, to refrain from addressing such complaints to me in the future."[86]

Still, the more uncontrolled violence "from below" there was, the more it became a problem for the Nazi leadership, since it endangered their claim that they were restoring "law and order" after the civil-war-like conditions before 1933. For that reason, Nazi leaders stepped up their efforts to institutionalise the terror tactics used against their enemies. At a press conference in Munich on 20 March, Heinrich Himmler announced the establishment of a concentration camp in a former munitions factory near the small city of Dachau. Initially, as a state facility, Dachau was guarded by Bavarian police, but on 11 April the SS assumed command. The Dachau camp became the first cell from which a national system of terror germinated. It was a kind of laboratory, under the direction of the SS, where experiments could be carried out with the forms of violence that would soon be used in the other concentration camps within the Reich. The German media reported extensively about Dachau, and the stories that were told about what went on there acted as a powerful deterrent to opposition to the Nazis. "Dear God, strike me numb / Lest to Dachau I do come" was an oft-repeated saying in the Third Reich.[87]

But the mood in the spring of 1933 was not just one of terror and fear. Most Germans were enthusiastic about what they saw as a national renewal. "There were celebrations, relief, spring and intoxication in the air," Luise Solmitz wrote on the day of the election.[88] Many people shared the sense of being present at the dawning of a new era and felt reminded of the euphoria of August 1914. As Sebastian Haffner observed: "I saw old women with shopping bags stop and stare with glittering eyes at the wormlike army of marching and loudly singing Brownshirts. 'You can really *see* it, can't you?' they said. 'How things are looking up everywhere.'"[89] While many supporters of the political Left withdrew, demoralised, into private niches, those sections of the middle classes that had previously kept their distance hastened to embrace the National Socialists, with flags flying. "Now everyone is a Nazi," Goebbels noted on 24 February. "Makes me sick."[90] On 30 January, the NSDAP had had 850,000 members; only three months later they had been joined by 2 million others. On 1 May 1933, the party leadership had to declare a temporary moratorium on new memberships because Nazi administrators could no longer deal with the flood of applications.[91] Erich Ebermayer, one of the few who had retained a measure of critical distance, described the "flip-flop of the middle classes' as "the most shameful aspect of this entire time."[92]

The majority of the new party members were bandwagon jumpers who joined in hopes of improving their career opportunities, not out of political conviction. The desire to be on the winning side was combined with the attempt to gain material advantage from the political changes, be it preferential treatment in the search for employment or actual positions in the public sector or the party administration. A joke quickly made the rounds that NSDAP stood for "Na, suchst du auch'n Pöstchen"—"So you too want a little job."[93] New members were at pains to prove that their "conversions" were genuine, for instance by ostentatiously displaying party emblems. Bella Fromm, the reporter for the *Vossische Zeitung*, observed: "Our colleagues who previously wore their party badge discreetly under their lapels now put them on show for everyone to see."[94] Another way of declaring political allegiance was to use the greeting "Heil Hitler," and Sefton Delmer noted that the people most apt to use the new social address were those who had dismissed Hitler as a "clown" just a few weeks earlier.[95] The Polish journalist Count Anton Sobanski, who visited Berlin in the spring of 1933, found the sight of people spontaneously performing the raised right-arm salute extremely alienating.[96] On 13 July 1933, a decree by Frick made the "German greeting" mandatory for all civil servants.[97]

Others indicated their support for the new regime by flying the swastika flag. On 11 March, Hindenburg ordered that the swastika be flown alongside the black-red-and-white banner of Imperial Germany. "These flags combine the glorious past of the German Empire and the powerful rebirth of the German nation," Hindenburg wrote.[98] With that, the Weimar Republic was symbolically dead and buried, and those who refused to conform and openly rejected the new regime were increasingly ostracised. "It feels like there's an airless layer surrounding the few of us who refuse to convert," Ebermayer complained in his diary. "The best of my young friends are declaring their allegiance to National Socialism . . . You can't talk to them at all. They simply *believe*. And there are no rational arguments against faith."[99] Sebastian Haffner, then a legal clerk, had similar experiences. As of March 1933, the atmosphere in the discussion group he regularly attended became increasingly poisonous. Several of the members joined the NSDAP. Open discussions were no longer possible and, in late May, the group disbanded.[100]

The inauguration of the newly elected Reichstag was scheduled for 21 March in Potsdam's Garrison Church. Goebbels, as Germany's first propaganda minister, had assumed responsibility for organising the ceremony,[101] and both the location and date were symbolic. March the 21st was not only the beginning of spring but also signified "national renewal," since it was the date when Bismarck had called to order the first Reichstag after the founding of the German Empire in 1871. Moreover the church crypt in Potsdam contained the coffins of the "Soldier King" Friedrich Wilhelm I and his son Friedrich the Great, making it the perfect location for a propaganda spectacle intended to symbolise the connection between Prussian tradition and National Socialism.[102] The state celebrations began in the morning with services in the main churches of both major denominations, although Hitler and Goebbels declined to attend. Instead, they laid wreaths at the graves of Horst Wessel and other "martyrs of the movement."[103]

Around noon, Hitler and Hindenburg met in front of the Garrison Church. The president wore his Prussian field marshal's uniform, while Hitler had swapped his party uniform for a formal black jacket, which made him visibly uncomfortable. One observer commented that he seemed like "a nervous *arriviste* being introduced by a powerful patron to an alien social circle."[104] In the imperial box, where the seat belonging to Kaiser Wilhelm II had been left empty, Hindenburg greeted Crown Prince Wilhelm by raising his field marshal's baton. The gesture was intended to express Hindenburg's connection to the Hohenzollern dynasty, conveniently ignoring the fact that relations between the field marshal and the royal family had been irreparably damaged when Hindenburg ostensibly abandoned the Kaiser to his fate in 1918.[105] The president's welcoming address was kept short, in the military tradition. With the election of 5 March, Hindenburg stated, the German people had backed the government he had appointed "with a clear majority" and provided the "constitutional basis for its work." With that, Hindenburg threw his weight behind the fiction that Hitler's consolidation of power was completely legal. SPD deputies did not attend the ceremony, and KPD representatives were either in detention or had gone underground. Hindenburg called on those members of the

Reichstag who were in attendance to look beyond "selfishness and party quarrels" and support the "difficult work" of the government "for the blessing of a free, proud and internally unified Germany."[106]

Speaking after Hindenburg, Hitler was initially inhibited, his voice subdued, but gradually he grew more confident. Theodor Heuss, who attended the ceremony as a State Party deputy, found Hitler's speech "moderate," if also "very general," and remarked that it contained "several good formulations but no concrete specification of goals."[107] Very much in the tenor of his address of 1 February, Hitler began by painting a grim picture of the "internal decay" that the revolution of 1918 had brought upon Germany before all the more vividly heralding the "great work of national revival." The core of Hitler's speech, however, was a tribute to Hindenburg, whom Hitler directly addressed at a number of junctures. Hitler not only praised the president's "generous decision" to entrust "young Germany" with the leadership of the Reich on 30 January 1933. He also underlined Hindenburg's military achievements, declaring: "Your wonderful life is a symbol for all of us of the indestructible vitality of our people."[108] Goebbels noted afterwards: "His best speech. All were moved at the end."[109] Hindenburg himself was also deeply impressed. "The Reich president could hardly conceal how moved he was—there were tears in his eyes," remarked Hamburg's mayor, Carl Vincent Krogmann.[110] After the speech, Hindenburg went up to Hitler, and the two men shook hands. The marriage of the "old" and the "new" Germany—the central message of the day—was thereby sealed.

"The Day of Potsdam" had an extraordinary public resonance. Like millions of others Elisabeth Gebensleben followed the events by radio. "We are all still under the sway of what we experienced yesterday," she wrote to her daughter, in Holland, on 22 March.

> Rarely in history has a nation enjoyed such a day of celebration, of national enthusiasm and of cheering joy. It was a day that released all of what is best and most holy in our people, which had been bound by tight constraints for many years, so that it could flow out in limitless celebrations of the most profound gratitude.[111]

The Potsdam spectacle even swayed social circles previously sceptical towards the "national revival." It seemed as though Hitler were about to transform himself from a narrow-minded party leader into a statesman and a "people's chancellor," who bridged gaps and reconciled contradictions instead of polarising people. "He has grown in stature—it can't be denied," commented Erich Ebermayer. "As surprising as it may be to his opponents, a true statesman seems to be developing from the demagogue and party leader, the fanatic and rabble-rouser." What most impressed Ebermayer was Hitler's carefully staged bow before Hindenburg: "The aged field marshal extends his hand to the private from the First World War. The private bows deeply above the hand of the field marshal . . . No one could avoid feeling deeply moved."[112]

"The Day of Potsdam" represented the "definitive breakthrough" in Hitler and Hindenburg's personal relationship.[113] When he appointed the cabinet of "national concentration" on 30 January, the latter had still had considerable reservations about the former, exemplified among other things by the fact that the new chancellor was only allowed to address Hindenburg in the presence of Papen. In the first weeks of his chancellorship, Hitler therefore concentrated particularly on gaining Hindenburg's trust with expressions of seeming affection. "The main thing is to win over the old man completely," Hitler told Baldur von Schirach on 5 February. "We must not do anything to upset him right now."[114] Hitler, a fine actor, was quickly able to gain Hindenburg's favour and push Papen from his privileged position. "He's now on good footing with the old man," Goebbels reported on 17 February.[115] On a long train journey from his headquarters in East Prussia to Berlin in May 1942, Hitler himself recalled that his relationship with Hindenburg had improved after ten days to the point that Papen no longer had to be present as a monitor when the two men spoke. After three weeks, Hitler said, the "old gentleman" had behaved with "paternal affection."[116]

Hitler was probably exaggerating: Papen recalled that it took until April before he was no longer required to be present for consultations.[117] But it is certain that Hindenburg already began showing Hitler his favour in February, for example by defending him against external criticism. On 17 February, the BVP chairman and Bavarian finance minister, Fritz Schäffer, warned Hindenburg that Hitler would "try to violently seize total power," and complained that "upstanding people" such as Social Democrats were being "labelled Marxists and excluded from the community of the German people." He received the following answer: "After some initial hesitations, he, the Reich president, found Herr Hitler to be a man of the most honest national intentions and was glad that the leader of this major movement is working together with him and other right-wing groups."[118] Hindenburg was quite pleased with the results of the 5 March election, noting with satisfaction that "once and for all we're done with all this going to the polls." The "parliamentary hullabaloo," the president said, had always been "deeply alien and unsavoury" to him.[119]

The ceremony in the Garrison Church, so effectively staged by Goebbels, marked a new high point of Hindenburg's appreciation for Hitler. "The old man very happy about Potsdam," the propaganda minister noted.[120] Three days after the ceremony, Hindenburg told Hamburg's mayor Krogmann that he "had only got to know and value Hitler after appointing him chancellor." While it was well known, Hindenburg said, that he had had reservations about Hitler because of the latter's "demands for sole power," he now recognised the great gifts and abilities of the chancellor.[121] Hitler had succeeded in replacing Papen as Hindenburg's favourite. Now, after exploiting the aura of the "hero of Tannenburg" to improve his own political reputation, he was going to emerge from the shadow of the aged Reich president and put himself "at the forefront as a charismatic leader in his own right."[122]

Anyone who thought that Hitler's bow before Hindenburg meant that he acknowledged the president's pre-eminence and was ready to give up his pursuit of absolute power would learn better only two days later, when the Reichstag met in the Kroll Opera House to decide whether to pass the Enabling Act. Hitler not only wanted to strip parliament of power but also to "liberate himself from the constraints of the Reich president and his right to issue emergency decrees, which had thus far been the basis of his rule."[123] The Law to Remedy the Distress of the People and the Reich, as the Enabling Act was officially known, had first been debated in Hitler's cabinet on 15 March. Interior Minister Frick stressed that the legislation had to be worded broadly enough "so that we can deviate from every provision of the Reich constitution." Once again, the conservative-nationalist ministers expressed no objections. Hugenberg alone queried "whether the laws to be issued by the government on the basis of the Enabling Act would require any active role at all from the Reich president." Otto Meissner, and not Hitler, brushed this implicit criticism aside, stating that it was "not necessary" for the Reich president to participate in issuing laws, nor would he demand the right to do so.[124]

Article 76 of the Reich constitution, however, stipulated that any constitutional amendments had to be approved by a two-thirds parliamentary majority, with at least two thirds of the Reichstag's members present. Frick calculated for the cabinet how this majority could be achieved. If the 81 KPD seats were invalidated from the 647 mandates in total, only 378 deputies would need to vote for the Enabling Act and not 432. Together with the Battle Front Black, White and Red, the NSDAP had won 340 seats on 5 March. The government thus needed the support of the Centre Party. In order to ensure that two thirds of deputies attended the parliamentary session, parliamentary rules were changed so that "Reichstag members absent without excuse" would also be considered in attendance.[125] Hitler was eager to gain the support of the Centre Party because, as he explained at a cabinet meeting on 20 March, in which the wording of the law was approved, "that would strengthen the government's prestige abroad." The Enabling Act was limited to four years (Article 5) and allowed the Reich government to decree national laws "outside the process envisioned by the Reich constitution" (Article 1). It was permissible for such laws "to deviate from the constitution" (Article 2). In place of the Reich president, the Reich chancellor was allowed to formulate and publish laws (Article 3). In addition, the Reich government was granted the right to negotiate contracts with foreign countries without consulting the Reichstag (Article 4).[126]

On the afternoon of 23 March, the Reichstag convened under circumstances unprecedented in German parliamentary history. The National Socialists had arranged for an intimidating backdrop. "The entire square in front of the Kroll Opera House was swarming with fascists," the SPD deputy Wilhelm Hoegner remembered.

We were received with wild chanting: "We want the Enabling Act." Young men with swastikas on their chests look us up and down insolently and blocked our way. They made us run the gauntlet while they shouted out insults like "Centrist swine" and "Marxist sow" . . . When we Social Democrats had taken our seats on the outside left of the

assembly, SA and SS men positioned themselves in a semicircle in front
of the exits and along the walls behind us. The expressions on their
faces told us that nothing good was in store.[127]

A gigantic swastika flag hung at the front end of the grandstand,
where the members of the government were seated, as if this was a
Nazi Party event and not the session of an institution representing
the people. Hitler appeared again in a brown shirt, after presenting
himself in civilian clothing two days before.

After being greeted by the NSDAP faction with a "threefold Heil,"
Hitler launched into a two-and-a-half-hour speech, which started with
repetition of his tirade about the "national decay caused by the mistaken
teachings of Marxism," before moving on to a very general sketch of
the government's plans "to create a genuine ethnic-popular community" and "morally cleanse the body of the people." When it came to
the economy, Hitler promised something for everyone. Agriculture
would once again be made profitable for farmers; the middle
classes would be protected from excessive competition; labourers and
office workers would enjoy increased spending power; the unemployed
would be reintegrated into the production process; and the interests
of the export economy would receive additional attention. As far as
foreign policy was concerned, Hitler struck a conciliatory note.
Germany only wanted "the same rights and freedoms" as other countries and aimed to "live in peace with the world." Only at the very end
of his speech did Hitler discuss the Enabling Act, which he claimed
was needed because the government of "national uprising" could not
do its job if "it had to request and negotiate permission from the
Reichstag in every case." Hitler promised that his government would
only make use of the new law "in so far as it is necessary to take
measures that affect the life and death of the nation." Neither the
existence of the Reichstag nor that of the Reich Council was threatened, the German local states were not to be eradicated, and the rights
of the Churches would not be curtailed. That final promise was directed
at the Catholic Centre Party, whose support for the Enabling Act was
still uncertain. After these promises came an unconcealed threat: "Now,
gentlemen, you may decide whether it's to be war or peace."[128]

When Hitler had finished, Göring declared a two-hour recess, and
the parliamentary factions withdrew for consultations. For the Social

Democrats, there was nothing to discuss. The detention, in violation of his parliamentary immunity, of one of their most prominent members, former Prussian Interior Minister Carl Severing, as he tried to enter the opera house, had shown once again what lay in store for the political Left.[129] By contrast, there were heated debates within the Centre faction, with a majority, led by Party Chairman Ludwig Kaas, voting to accept the legislation. They argued that in the preceding negotiations Hitler had dangled the prospect of written assurances that the Enabling Act would only be used under specific circumstances. This promise was nothing but one of the feints at which Hitler was so uniquely expert—the plan was never to mail the letter in question. Former Chancellor Brüning, who had described the Enabling Act that morning in a faction meeting as "the most horrific thing ever demanded of a parliament," tried to the very end to get his party to withhold support. It was "better to go under with honour," he said, than to reach out to a political movement that "won't allow the Centre any air to breathe." But both he and a like-minded minority within the faction ultimately agreed to vote with the majority.[130]

The parliamentary session reconvened shortly after 6 p.m., with SPD Chairman Otto Wels taking the floor. After the persecution Social Democrats had suffered in recent days, he declared, no one could expect him to support the Enabling Act: "You can take away our liberty and our lives, but not our honour." It was a courageous speech considering the murderous atmosphere in the makeshift parliamentary hall. It was the last time for twelve years that anyone would make a public declaration of support for democratic principles and the rule of law in front of the Reichstag. "No enabling law gives you the power to destroy ideas that are eternal and indestructible," Wels said and went on to pay tribute to those who were being pressured and persecuted. "Your determination and loyalty deserve admiration. Your courage in your convictions and unbroken confidence are signs of a brighter future to come." At this point the parliamentary protocol recorded repeated "laughter from the National Socialists."[131]

Hardly had Wels finished speaking than Hitler hurried to the podium to attack him: "You've shown up late, but you've shown up. The nice theories you've just put forth here, Herr Deputy, have been communicated a bit too late to world history." Hitler's reply seemed to have been extemporaneous, and it has been often cited as evidence of his gift with words. But the truth is that the editor-in-chief of *Vorwärts*, Friedrich Stampfer, had earlier distributed the text of Wels's speech as a press release, which gave Hitler time to prepare his answer to it.[132] "You've never seen anyone cut down like that," Goebbels crowed. "Hitler was on a roll. It was a massive success."[133] In fact, the Reich chancellor's speech revealed his true, brutal, power-hungry face, which he had kept concealed behind the mask of the respectable statesman in Potsdam. "Gentlemen, you are whiny and unfit for the current age, if you already speak of persecution," Hitler snarled at the Social Democrats. He even went so far as to admit that his overtures to secure support for the Enabling Act were a calculated manoeuvre: "Only because we have Germany and its misery and the necessities of national life clearly in view do we appeal at this hour to the German Reichstag to approve what we could have seized for ourselves anyway." In conclusion, Hitler once again directly addressed the Social Democrats: "I think that you will not vote for this law because your innermost mentality is incapable of comprehending the intention that animates us ... I can only say: I do not want you to vote for it! Germany should be free, but not through any action of yours!" The protocol recorded: "Long, frenetic cries of 'Heil' from the National Socialists and the rows of spectators. Applause from the conservative nationalists."[134]

Hitler could not have expressed any more clearly that his emphasis on "legality" had been mere lip service and that his government was going to do away with all norms of separation of powers and the rule of law. Nonetheless, that did not prevent the spokesmen of the Centre Party, the Bavarian People's Party, the German State Party, the German People's Party and Christian People's Service from voting for the Enabling Act on behalf of their factions—"in the expectation of an orderly development," as Reinhold Maier from the State Party put it.[135] In the final roll call 441 deputies voted yes, while 94 representatives of the decimated SPD faction voted no. With that, the "blackest day" in German parliamentary history was over.[136] On 24 March in cabinet, Hugenberg expressed his gratitude for the "excellent success" to Hitler. He particularly praised Hitler's reply to Wels's speech, which had "generally been received as giving the SPD a complete dressing-down."[137] As far as the definitive removal of parliamentary democracy and persecution of its last defenders, the Social Democrats, were concerned, there was complete agreement between National Socialists and conservative nationalists.

The Enabling Act concluded the first phase of the Nazi consolidation of power, and the next step was pre-programmed. In shutting down parliament as a state legislative organ, the political parties sacrificed their *raison d'être*. But Hitler's government had not just made itself independent of the Reichstag, which henceforth would merely rubber-stamp and celebrate the regime's decisions. It had also got rid of the president's authority to issue emergency decrees.[138] This marked the definitive end of the idea of "taming Hitler," which depended on the ability to call upon the powers of the president's office. Hitler was no longer constrained in any way by his conservative coalition partners, even though he kept them in his cabinet for the time being to maintain appearances. "So now we are the masters," declared Goebbels, who sat with Hitler in the Chancellery on the evening of 23 March to listen to a rebroadcast of the Führer's reply to Wels on the radio.[139] Although the Enabling Act, which took effect the following day, was limited to four years, it was extended three times and remained the basis of National Socialist rule until the demise of the regime.

A mere week later, on 1 April, the Hitler government launched its next offensive, calling for the first boycott of Jewish businesses, lawyers and doctors. Since Hitler had taken power on 30 January, anti-Semitic agitation had risen noticeably. Physical attacks on Jews and Jewish businesses had become part of everyday life in many cities and areas. Usually they were organised by local SA and party activists.[140] The day after the 5 March election, gangs of SA thugs went after Jewish pedestrians on Berlin's Kurfürstendamm. "In several parts of Berlin a large number of people, most of whom appeared to be Jews, were openly attacked in the streets and knocked down," the Berlin correspondent of the *Manchester Guardian* wrote. "Some of them were seriously injured. The police could do no more than pick up the injured and take them off to hospital."[141] Reports like this in foreign newspapers caused outrage. On 26 March, some 250,000 people in New York and more than a million across the United States protested against the Hitler regime's anti-Jewish discrimination and persecution.[142]

Both Nazi propaganda and reports by German diplomats described international criticism as a Jewish "atrocity propaganda" against which the Third Reich had to defend itself.[143] The Nazi-organised national boycott of Jewish businesses, doctors and lawyers was intended to punish German Jews for foreign criticism and to channel the "wild" activities of the SA towards a common end. Goebbels and Hitler likely decided to stage the boycott when they had met on the Obersalzberg on 26 March. "I am writing a call for an anti-Jewish boycott," Goebbels noted after the meeting. "That will put an end to the agitation abroad."[144] A "Central Committee for Defence against Jewish Atrocity and Boycott Agitation" planned and organised the initiative. It was chaired by the Nuremberg Gauleiter, Julius Streicher, the publisher of the viciously anti-Semitic newspaper *Der Stürmer*. The NSDAP leadership's appeal was published on 28 March in the *Völkischer Beobachter*. It called on all Nazi Party groups to form immediate action committees so that the boycott could commence "abruptly" on 1 April and be carried out everywhere "down to the smallest village." The boycott slogan was: "No good German still buys from a Jew and lets himself be talked into purchases by a Jew or his backers."[145]

On 29 March, Hitler informed his cabinet about the planned initiative, leaving no doubt that he had ordered the boycott and stood behind it personally. "He was convinced that a boycott of 2–3 days would convince Jews that their atrocious anti-German agitation was hurting themselves the most," read a protocol of the cabinet meeting.[146] Two days later, some of his ministers voiced concerns. Finance Minister von Krosigk feared "massive losses in sales tax revenues," while Transport Minister Eltz-Rübenach was concerned the initiative would hurt the German economy, citing the fact that all foreign passages aboard the ships MS *Europa* and MS *Bremen* had been cancelled. Hitler appeared to be flexible, saying that he would be willing to postpone the boycott until 4 April if the governments of Britain and the United States issued immediate statements condemning foreign criticism of Nazi Germany. Otherwise, Hitler threatened, the boycott would go ahead as planned for Saturday 1 April, although there would be a two-day pause between then and 4 April.[147] In fact, both foreign governments agreed to the statement demanded on the evening of 31 March, but that was deemed too late. The mobilised party grass roots were itching for action, and Hitler would have lost face, even had he wanted to call off the boycott. "I don't know whether my name will be held in honour in Germany in 200 or 300 years,"

Hitler told the Italian ambassador, Vittorio Cerruti, on the eve of the boycott. "But I'm absolutely certain that in 500 or 600 years the name Hitler will be universally glorified as the name of the man who once and for all eradicated the global pestilence that is Jewry."[148]

On the morning of 1 April, SA men took up positions with placards in front of Jewish businesses, doctors' offices and legal firms all over Germany and tried to get people to participate in the boycott. "The Jewish businesses—and there were a lot of them in the streets in the east—were open, and SA men planted themselves, their feet spread wide apart, before their front doors," recalled Sebastian Haffner, who witnessed the boycott in Berlin.[149] Reports differed about how the public reacted. "A murmur of disapproval, suppressed but still audible," went through the country," wrote Haffner in retrospect.[150] The British ambassador also concluded that the boycott had not been popular but that neither had public opinion swung around in Jews' favour.[151] There were plenty of contemporary stories about customers who deliberately visited Jewish businesses, doctors and lawyers on 1 April. But these people were no doubt a courageous minority. The majority seem to have followed the wishes of the regime. They withheld their patronage, stood by and looked on.[152]

Many German Jews were deeply shocked by the first government-organised national anti-Semitic initiative. "I always felt German," Victor Klemperer wrote in his diary. "And I always thought the twentieth century and central Europe were different than the fourteenth century and Romania. A mistake."[153] Klemperer was not alone among patriotic German Jews in feeling that in one fell swoop all guarantees against a return to medieval barbarism had been swept away. The boycott was also greeted with shame and horror by Gentile Germans critical of the regime. Count Kessler, who had resided in Paris since deciding not to return to Germany, remarked on 1 April: "This contemptible boycott of Jews in the Reich. This criminal act of insanity has destroyed all the trust and respect Germany had regained in the past fourteen years."[154]

Although the boycott was not resumed on 4 April, local SA and party groups staged repeated actions against Jewish businesses in the weeks and months that followed,[155] and the Hitler government began using less conspicuous methods of forcing Jews from German society. On 7 April, the regime issued the Law Concerning the Re-establishment of a Professional Civil Service, which not only allowed the government to dismiss state employees considered politically unreliable, but also mandated that civil servants from "non-Aryan backgrounds" be sent into early retirement. Jewish state employees who had fought at the front in the First World War, or whose fathers or sons had fallen, were exempt from the law.[156] In a letter to Hitler, Hindenburg had urged him to adopt these exceptions. "If they were good enough to fight and shed their blood for Germany," Hindenburg wrote, "they should be considered worthy enough to serve their fatherland in their jobs."[157] This did not mean that Hindenburg was generally unhappy about the discriminatory measures. In late April, when Sweden's Prince Carl, the head of the Swedish Red Cross, tried to intervene on behalf of German Jews, the Reich president rejected those attempts by saying that a peaceful and orderly national revolution was taking place—a development all the more remarkable because "the now-victorious National Socialist movement has been the victim of serious injustice from Jewish and Jewish–Marxist quarters."[158] Hindenburg's intervention on behalf of Jewish war veterans was thus not a rejection of the regime's anti-Semitic policies but rather an expression of his loyalty towards those who had fought in the First World War.

It is telling how Hitler reacted to Hindenburg's letter. On the one hand, he justified his policies by arguing that the German people had to defend themselves against "Jews swamping certain professions," and that Jews had remained "an alien element that had never merged with the German people." On the other, he lavished praise upon the Reich president for intervening on behalf of Jewish veterans "in such generous human fashion," and he promised to "be true to this noble sentiment as broadly as possible." The next sentence he wrote epitomised Hitler as a master of dissimulation: "I understand your internal rationale, and by the way, I myself often suffer under the difficult fate of being forced to make decisions that as a human being I would prefer one thousandfold to avoid."[159] Hitler still could not afford to alienate Hindenburg, so he slipped into a role that he knew would please the Reich president: that of the polite, modest, adaptable politician who was selflessly doing his burdensome duty and who was forced to act harshly towards Jews and "Marxists" in the interest of the German people and not because that was what he himself wanted.

The Civil Service Law of 7 April was a watershed, marking the first time that the German government curtailed the legal equality of

German Jews. It was the first step in a gradual process of reversing the legal emancipation of German Jews completed in 1871. Further discriminatory laws—including the Law on the Licensing of Lawyers and the Law to Combat Overcrowding of Universities—were also issued in April.[160] Still, only a small minority of German Jews could imagine at this point that the course being taken, in line with Hitler's lunatic ideological fixations, would end in their complete "removal" from the German "ethnic-popular community." One of the few who did was Georg Solmssen, spokesman for the board of directors of Deutsche Bank. On 9 April, he wrote to the chairman of the bank's supervisory board: "I fear that we stand at the beginning of a development that is consciously directed towards economically and morally eradicating all members of the Jewish race [sic] living in Germany according to careful plans."[161]

If there was a social force capable of halting the National Socialists' takeover of German institutions in the April of 1933, it might have been the free trade unions which together made up the Confederation of German Trade Unions (ADGB). But in fact the unions had been destroyed by the beginning of May without having put up any serious resistance—an unprecedented phenomenon that marked the nadir of the German labour movement.[162] In his first two months in power, Hitler was uncertain about how to deal with the unions. His initial hesitation was a measure of his respect for such organisations, whose four million members had considerable potential for putting up a fight. But the unions' surprising vacillation between passivity and ingratiation soon convinced Hitler that they would offer no opposition.

In late February, the confederation had begun to distance itself from the SPD, with which it had been allied for decades, and to move towards the National Socialists. On 21 March, Confederation Chairman Theodor Leipart directly approached Hitler with a request for a meeting. The letter was sycophantic in tone—Leipart signed off with the phrase "With the deepest respect and subservience"—and amounted to a declaration of principles concerning future union activity by the confederation's leaders. It contained an astonishing concession: "The social tasks of unions must be fulfilled regardless of the nature of the political regime."[163] On 9 April, the confederation's leadership officially offered to place union organisations "at the service of the state" and suggested the appointment of a "Reich commissioner for unions."[164] But Hitler did not deem either this offer or Leipart's letter of 21 March worthy of an answer.

Typically, the Nazi leadership requited the unions' attempts to cosy up to the regime with a carrot-and-stick approach to the working classes. Union buildings were targeted for violent attacks by the SA, and union functionaries in various places were arrested and physically abused. In vain, Leipart turned to Hindenburg as "the shepherd and guarantor of the civil rights anchored in the constitution," asking him to "put an end to the legal uncertainty that threatens the lives and property of German workers in numerous German cities."[165] Leipart's protests were futile. The fundamental constitutional rights he cited had long been abrogated by Hitler and his coalition—with Hindenburg's consent.

At the same time, the Hitler regime stepped up its efforts to prise the working classes away from traditional labour organisations and win them over to the "national uprising." In late March, Goebbels suggested to the cabinet that 1 May, historically a day of activism for the workers' movement in Germany, be declared a "holiday of national labour" along the lines of the recent ceremonies in Potsdam.[166] Whereas the Day of Potsdam had served to celebrate the symbolic unification of Prussia and National Socialism, 1 May was conceived as a way of cementing Nazism's connection to the German working classes. Ideological appropriation and violence against opponents were two sides of the same coin. In early April, an "Action Committee for the Protection of German Labour," chaired by NSDAP Reich Organisational Director Robert Ley, was tasked with drawing up a plan to disempower the trade unions. Hitler gave it the green light from the Obersalzberg on 17 April. Goebbels was once more at the centre of the decision-making process. May the 1st will be celebrated in a "major way," he noted, and then: "The union headquarters will be occupied on 2 May. 'Brought into line.' A couple of days of uproar, and then they will be ours."[167] On 21 April, Ley informed the Gauleiter about these plans: "On Tuesday, 2 May 1933, at 10 a.m., we will start to bring the independent labour unions into line." The goal, Ley announced, was "to give workers the feeling that this action is not directed against them, but against an outmoded system no longer in the interests of the German nation."[168]

The ADGB's executive committee was still under the illusion it could come to some sort of arrangement with the regime. In mid-April it welcomed the decision to declare 1 May a holiday and expressed support for the new significance given to the occasion: "In keeping with his status, the German worker should take to the streets on 1 May and show that he is a full member of the German ethnic-popular community."[169] On 1 May 1933, union members and Nazis marched together under swastika banners. The main event took place on Berlin's Tempelhofer Feld, formerly a parade ground for the Imperial military. Goebbels had taken charge of organising the spectacle, which he hoped would be his second propaganda masterpiece.[170] More than 1 million people took up formation in twelve blocks in front of a gigantic grandstand amidst a sea of flags and banners brightly illuminated by spotlights. In his speech, which was again broadcast on all German radio stations, Hitler appropriated the traditional symbolism of 1 May for the German labour movement, attempting to conflate it with the idea of the "ethnic-popular community." He adroitly drew parallels between the rhetoric of social reconciliation and the ideas of "workers of the mind and the fist"—a phrase that suggested equality and that no doubt impressed many previously sceptical members of the working classes, as did the event as a whole.[171] "Fantastic flush of enthusiasm," noted Goebbels, who was awe-struck by the spectacle he had staged. Even a critical observer like André François-Poncet was unable to resist the lure of mass suggestion. The effect of Hitler's "sometimes hoarse, and then once more cutting and wild" voice, he wrote, was augmented by the "theatrical props," the interplay of light and shadow, the banners and uniforms and insistent rhythms of the music, so that even the French ambassador thought he could sense a "hint of reconciliation and unity."[172]

But those illusions were dispelled the very next day. Storm troopers occupied union headquarters and took labour leaders, including Leipart, into "protective custody." Goebbels was pleased, noting, "Everything is running like clockwork."[173] Leipart's attempt to save his organisation with what bordered on self-annihilating conformity had failed. A few days later, the German Labour Front was founded under Robert Ley. This was a mammoth umbrella organisation of Nazified workers' organisations and proved to be a most effective tool for integrating the working classes into the Nazi state.[174] German labourers no longer had a body independent of the government to represent their interests. On 19 May the Law on the Administrators of Labour replaced negotiated wage and labour agreements with binding state decrees. A major principle of the socially equitable Weimar Constitution thereby disappeared with the stroke of a pen.[175]

In a diary entry on 3 June, Goebbels announced with brutal directness what was to follow the dissolution of the unions: "All parties will have to be destroyed. We alone will remain."[176] The KPD had already been suppressed; the SPD was next in line. The regime took immediate repressive action in response to the Social Democratic parliamentary faction's refusal to support the Enabling Act. Disappointment and resignation spread among SPD members and increasing numbers quit the party. After witnessing the Nazis' move against the unions, the SPD feared that it could be banned, and those worries were fuelled when Göring confiscated the party's assets on 10 May. Earlier that month, several members of the Social Democratic leadership had travelled to the Saarland, which was still under the administration of the League of Nations, to prepare for potential emigration. But they disagreed amongst themselves. Was it better to move the party abroad and organise the fight against the regime in exile or to use the legal means that remained to salvage within Germany what could be salvaged? Adherents of the latter point of view were behind the majority of the SPD Reichstag delegates who opted to endorse Hitler's "peace speech" on 17 May—which we will examine in detail in the next chapter. This not only improved Hitler's political standing abroad, but also overshadowed the party's rejection of the Enabling Act. The result was a schism in the party leadership. On 21 May in Saarbrücken, several top party leaders, including Otto Wels, decided to move to Prague and pursue illegal resistance from outside Germany. Those Social Democrats who stayed behind in Berlin under the leadership of Paul Löbe, however, claimed to speak for the party in its entirety. Their hopes that Hitler would become more conciliatory if they compromised were soon dashed.

On 18 June the first edition of *Neuer Vorwärts*, a relaunch of the Social Democrats' traditional party newspaper, was published in the Czech city of Karlovy Vary, containing a sharply worded declaration of war on the Hitler regime by the leadership of the SPD in exile. That provided Interior Minister Frick with a welcome pretext to prohibit, in a decree to local state governments on 21 June, the SPD from engaging in any political activity as a "party hostile to the state and people."[177] A wave of arrests of SPD functionaries and Reichstag and Landtag deputies followed. During the "Köpenick Blood Week" in late July 1933, a rolling SA commando attacked the largely Social Democratic Berlin district, arresting more than 500 men and torturing them so brutally that 91 of them died. Among those murdered in this fashion was a member of the SPD executive committee and the former state president of Mecklenburg-Schwerin, Johannes Stelling. Exiled Social Democratic circles described his death as follows: "After the worst sort of mistreatment, he was dumped nearly unconscious outside an SA barracks, where he was detained once again by plainclothes SA men. He was thrown in a car, taken into custody and tortured to death. His body, which had been beaten beyond recognition, was later fished out of the Dahme river in a closed, weighted-down sack."[178] This sort of atrocity had already become possible in Germany in the summer of 1933, without anyone from the country's traditional elites or middle classes—to say nothing of the conservative cabinet ministers—raising a word of protest.

"SPD dissolved—Bravo!" crowed Goebbels. "We won't have long to wait for the total state."[179] And indeed, the centrist middle-class parties could no longer hold on. In late June and early July, the German State Party and the German People's Party dissolved. After the election of 5 March, these liberal parties had lost so much support that hardly anyone noticed when they disappeared.[180] The situation was different with the conservative German National People's Party (DNVP), which, after all, still sat at meetings as the NSDAP's coalition partner. In late April, Labour Minister Seldte had announced that he was joining the Nazi Party and passing on the leadership of the Stahlhelm to Hitler. This association of First World War veterans was gradually Nazified, and most of its members assigned to the SA.[181] In early May, the DNVP changed its name to the German National Front as a way of demonstrating that it was just as opposed to parliamentary democracy as the NSDAP. But the name change did nothing to prevent more and more of its members from defecting to the Nazi Party. In addition, party centres were increasingly subject to attacks by the SA and SS. On 17 May 1933, Alfred Hugenberg and the deputy leader of the German National Front, Friedrich von Winterfeld, complained to the president about attempts throughout Germany "to concentrate power entirely in National Socialist hands and push aside all other men of nationalist sentiment." Hindenburg answered that he was convinced the Reich chancellor had only the best intentions at heart and was "working in the interest of the fatherland and justice with a clear conscience." Unfortunately, Hitler's subordinates "pushed things too far," Hindenburg conceded, but that problem would diminish over time. He appealed to both Hugenberg and Winterfeld to "maintain the unity that we concluded and sealed with our hearts' blood on 30 January so that what has since been achieved never falls apart."[182]

DNVP Chairman Hugenberg himself contributed to the inexorable downfall of this formerly so self-confident and power-orientated conservative party. At the International Economic Conference in London in mid-June, without consulting with the other members of the German delegation, Hugenberg presented a memorandum demanding the return of Germany's former colonies in Africa as well as land in eastern Europe for new settlements for his "people without space." The latter in fact reflected Hitler's plans for the future, but no one was supposed to raise the issue in public, least of all at an international conference. Hitler could now cannily portray Hugenberg as an incorrigible representative of the Wilhelmine thirst for world power and himself as a relative moderate. Hugenberg's position within the cabinet became untenable and even his conservative colleagues refused to intervene on his behalf. On 27 June, Hitler informed his ministers that Hugenberg had offered to resign. He personally regretted this step, claimed the Führer, barely able to conceal his delight at marginalising his rival, but "the best thing would be for the German National People's Party to disappear."[183] The party announced its dissolution that very day. A "friendship agreement" with the NSDAP promised to protect former DNVP members against "all forms of humiliation and disadvantage."

With no further ado, the "economic dictator," who had believed that together with Papen he could restrain Hitler, departed the political stage. "They've got their just deserts for their contemptible betrayal of the German people," commented Harry Kessler. "Papen will have his turn too."[184] In September Hugenberg was craven enough to communicate in a letter to his "most esteemed Herr Hitler" his immutable "life's wish" that the work they had jointly begun on 30 January be carried out to its "happy conclusion." When Hitler subsequently declared himself "pleasantly moved" that Hugenberg had maintained his "comradely sentiments" despite his departure from the cabinet, Hugenberg did not neglect to solemnly assure Hitler on the first anniversary of his "seizure of power" that he stuck by "all the ideas and goals that initially brought us together."[185] As Hugenberg's successor at the head of the Economics Ministry, Hindenburg named Kurt Schmitt, the head of the Allianz insurance company and a Nazi Party member. Richard Walter Darré was made minister of food and agriculture. Hitler also succeeded in allowing Rudolf Hess, in his function as "deputy of the Führer," to attend all future cabinet meetings.[186] With that the Nazi Party had a cabinet majority. "The worst is behind us," noted Goebbels. "The revolution is taking its course." Goebbels personally profited from Hugenberg's resignation, inheriting his governmental apartment.[187]

The end of the Catholic parties was hardly any less disgraceful. By June, mass resignations of party members combined with state repression had diminished the Centre Party's will to continue. The party's position became completely impossible when the Vatican, in its negotiations over a concordat with the Nazi regime, agreed that priests would be prohibited in future from engaging in any party-political activity. That was effectively the full capitulation of political Catholicism. The National Socialists rebuffed attempts by the Centre Party to liquidate itself under the same terms as the DNVP,[188] and on 5 July the party decided to dissolve. The previous day, its Bavarian sister, the BVP, had also disbanded after being given promises that its members who had been taken into custody would be released.[189] On 14 July, the Reich government issued the Law Prohibiting the Reconstitution of the Parties. It proclaimed the NSDAP to be the "only political party in Germany" and made the attempt to preserve or found any other party a prosecutable offence.[190] The one-party state became a reality. National Socialist domination of Germany, reported the Swiss chargé d'affaires in Berlin, was "a fact that will have to be reckoned for a considerable time."[191]

Hitler had needed only five months to consolidate power. "Everything that existed in Germany outside the Nazi Party," wrote François-Poncet in early July, "has been destroyed, dispelled, dissolved, co-opted or sucked in." Considering the political situation he found on 1 February and the conditions under which he became German chancellor, the French ambassador concluded, Hitler had "successfully performed a lightning-quick manoeuvre."[192] Indeed, the changes in political conditions proceeded so rapidly that many contemporaries could hardly keep up with them. "It is a turbulent time that brings something new every day," Theodor Heuss wrote in late June.[193] Looking back at the summer of 1933, Sebastian Haffner described the situation of non-Nazi Germans as "one of the most difficult a human being could find himself in . . . a state of being completely and hopelessly overwhelmed as well as suffering from the after effects of the shock of being bowled over." Haffner concluded: "The Nazis had us completely at their mercy. All bastions had fallen, and any form of collective resistance had become impossible."[194] Victor Klemperer saw things much the same. On 9 July 1933, he noted in his diary: "And now this monstrous internal tyranny, the break-up of all the parties, the daily emphasis on the idea that 'We National Socialists alone have power. It is *our* revolution.' Hitler is the absolute master."[195]

Is it appropriate to call what happened in Germany between February and July 1933 a revolution? The National Socialist leadership, above all Hitler and Goebbels, were not the only ones to use this term as a matter of course. The Nazis' conservative coalition partners also employed it. In late March, Papen told the German-American Chamber of Commerce in New York that the "national revolution," whose goal was "to liberate Germany from grave Communist danger and to cleanse the governmental administration of inferior elements," had been carried out with "impressive orderliness."[196] In April, a close relative of Hindenburg, Lieutenant General Karl von Fabeck, proclaimed: "We are still in the middle of the national revolution, but it is victorious across the board."[197] Even critics and sceptics saw the overwhelming dynamics of change as revolutionary. "Only now . . . has the revolution truly begun," noted the writer Erich Ebermayer on 28 February, the day after the Reichstag fire.[198] Count Harry Kessler in turn characterised the situation in March as a "counter-revolution."[199]

Compared with contemporaries, historians have been more reticent about using the term "revolution" in conjunction with the Nazi consolidation of power. There are good reasons for this. The word usually implies not only a radical political shake-up, but a fundamental remaking of society, for example the replacement of one set of social elites with another. By contrast, the Nazi consolidation of power in 1933 was characterised by an alliance between traditional elites in the military, major industry, large-scale agriculture and governmental bureaucracy, on the one hand, and the Nazi mass movement and its Führer on the other. Moreover, since the American and French Revolutions, the term usually has the positive connotation of an increase in liberty, justice and humanity. That was anything but the case under the Hitler regime. Despite its insistence on the pretence of "legality," the first months of the new government left no doubt as to its radically inhumane character, which was hostile towards all principles of democracy, the rule of law and morality. "This revolution boasts of its bloodlessness," Thomas Mann wrote on 20 April 1933, Hitler's forty-fourth birthday, "but it is the most hateful and murderous revolution that has ever been."[200] Sebastian Haffner also recognised early on that this six-month period in 1933 represented a break with civilisation, which drew its social energies from the Nazis' will to subject the entire German people to their power and reform it in line with Hitler's far-reaching racist and ideological programme.[201] In light of the regime's goal of totally dominating all aspects of life, the historian Hans-Ulrich Wehler proposed the term "totalitarian revolution," depicting a new type of political and social upheaval. This concept still seems best suited for comprehending the specific character of the systematic transformation Germany underwent in 1933.[202]

After monopolising political power, Hitler redefined certain key ideas. Revolution, he announced to his Reich governors on 6 July, could not be allowed to become a "constant state of affairs." The revolutionary "current," he proclaimed, had to be "redirected into the secure riverbed of evolution." Now that the goal of "external power" had been achieved, emphasis would switch to "people's education."[203] Goebbels repeated this idea in a radio address in the city of Königsberg: "We will only be satisfied when we know that the entire people understands us and recognises us as its highest advocate." The goal, Goebbels stated with utter frankness, was that "there should be only one opinion, one party and one faith in Germany."[204]

This meant that all sectors of cultural life were to be brought into line with Nazi ideas. In the first six months of Nazi rule, Goebbels oversaw a comprehensive change in personnel in German radio, the most important medium of political and ideological indoctrination. In so far as they were not simply banned, newspapers were softened up by economic pressure and subjected to government monitoring.

Some of the larger liberal newspapers like the *Frankfurter Zeitung* were granted a measure of freedom, but even this was constrained by daily governmental press instructions and editorial self-censorship. In the realms of music, film, theatre, the visual arts and literature, the process of Nazification ran parallel to the removal of Jews from these areas of cultural life: they were seen to personify the modernism so hated by the Nazis, and Hitler had constantly defamed them as advocates of "cultural Bolshevism" prior to 1933. It was particularly easy for the National Socialists to "cleanse" Germany's universities since German academics were conspicuously willing to bring themselves into line with the regime. The most repulsive manifestation of this attitude was the action "Contrary to the Ungerman Spirit"—the book burnings carried out by students, with the support of university administrations, on Berlin's Opernplatz and in most other German university towns on 10 May. As a result the very first year of the Nazi regime saw a mass exodus of artists, writers, scientists and journalists from which German intellectual and cultural life has never fully recovered.[205] The establishment of the Reich Cultural Chamber, which was inaugurated with Hitler in attendance at the Berlin Philharmonic Concert Hall in November 1933, completed the reshaping of the entire arena of German culture.[206] Anyone who wanted to work in film, music, theatre, journalism, radio, literature or the visual arts was required to be a member of one of the seven individual chambers that comprised this institution.

As total as the process of bringing society into line was, the success or failure of the regime depended on its ability to keep its promise to combat mass unemployment. In his very first radio address on 1 February, Hitler announced a "massive, blanket attack on unemployment" that was to overcome the problem "once and for all" within four years.[207] On 6 July as well, he told his regional representatives that creating jobs was decisive: "History will only measure us on how we tackle this task."[208] Multiple factors played into the hands of Hitler and his regime. By the time he came to power, economic recovery was already under way. The government also profited from job-creation measures taken under Papen and Schleicher that were only just beginning to bear fruit.[209] In terms of announcing employment initiatives of his own, Hitler was conspicuously low-key in the weeks leading up to the Reichstag election.

He enumerated the reasons for this in a cabinet meeting on 8 February: "The Reich government has to get 18–19 million voters behind it. There is no economic programme in the whole wide world capable of attracting the approval of such a large mass of voters."[210]

It was not until late May 1933 that the cabinet agreed on the Law for the Reduction of Unemployment. Known as the "First Reinhardt Programme" after Finance Ministry State Secretary Fritz Reinhardt, it allocated 1 billion reichsmarks for the creation of additional jobs. That sum was augmented by 500 million reichsmarks in the "Second Reinhardt Programme of September 1933," which particularly concerned restoration and renovation projects and sought to boost the construction industry.[211] The regime took other measures to ease the situation in the job market. The First Reinhardt Programme introduced interest-free "marriage loans" of up to 1,000 reichsmarks, which were contingent on newly-wed women leaving the workforce on the day of their wedding. Simultaneously the regime launched a campaign against the "double-earner syndrome" aimed at forcing women out of the labour market. The government subsidised emergency works projects and assigned jobless people to work in agriculture. It also expanded the Volunteer Labour Service, a state employment programme that had been introduced in the final years of the Weimar Republic. All these measures led to a great reduction in the numbers of people officially registered as unemployed. Between January 1933 and January 1934, the official number of jobless declined from 6 to 3.8 million people, although these figures were by no means completely reliable.[212] In any case, the regime seemed to be keeping its promise and tackling the unemployment problem head-on, and this impression no doubt played a major role in increasing the aura surrounding the man at the top.

Hitler was no expert on questions of economic policy, but he had enough of an understanding of the subject to know that populist rhetoric alone would be insufficient. Incentives were needed to stimulate a self-perpetuating economic recovery. However, among the measures designed to jump-start the economy and create new jobs, the role played by the construction of the autobahn was less important than later myths about the Nazi "economic miracle" would have it. In his opening speech at the International Motor Show on 11 February 1933, Hitler had announced "the commencement and completion of a large-scale roadworks plan." He proclaimed: "Just as horse-drawn traffic created paths and the railway system built the tracks it needed, motor-vehicle transport has to get the motorway it requires."[213] The idea was not fundamentally new. In the mid-1920s, an "Association for the Preparation of the Motorway Hanseatic Cities–Frankfurt–Basle" (Hafraba) had drawn up plans for an autobahn. Hitler had probably also read a pamphlet written by the Munich engineer Fritz Todt in late 1932 entitled "Road Construction and Management," in which the author had stressed the "strategic" importance of motorway construction and calculated that Germany needed 5,000 to 6,000 kilometres of high-speed roads.[214] In late March and early April, Hafraba's commercial director gave two talks about the planned project in the Reich Chancellery. The motoring fan Hitler seized upon the idea "with great enthusiasm" but insisted on aiming for a national motorway network instead of a single stretch of road: "It would be a great achievement if we succeeded in realising the network under our regime."[215] At a conference with leading industrialists on 29 May, Hitler reiterated his intention to support the construction of the autobahn with all the means at his disposal. Tackling "the problem in its entirety" was the main task, Hitler proclaimed, adding: "Traffic in the years to come will take place on the largest of streets."[216]

On 27 June, the Law for the Establishment of the Undertaking "Reich Autobahn" came into force. Three days later, Todt was appointed inspector general of German roadways. On 23 September, Hitler personally dug the first turf for the stretch of motorway between Frankfurt and Darmstadt—a gesture with the propaganda aim of suggesting the Führer was leading the way in what was called the "labour battle."[217] But the short-term effect on unemployment of building the autobahn was only marginal. In 1933, no more than 1,000 men were employed building the first stretch of motorway, and a year after Todt's appointment only 38,000 had been given work.[218] On the one hand, the number of newly registered cars almost doubled in 1933, compared with the previous year, and the number of people employed in the car industry had also grown substantially; on the other, compared with the United States, the level of car ownership in Germany was low. The main reason, as Hitler complained in a meeting to discuss the financing of the autobahn in September 1933, was that the German car industry had not adapted its production to reflect people's actual income. "They keep building cars that are too heavy and are a long way from realising the goal of a car ranging in price from 1,000 to 1,200 reichsmarks," Hitler said.[219] Thus it was that in 1934 the idea was born of producing an affordable small car, the *Volkswagen*—the people's car—that would be affordable to the working classes.[220]

The strongest long-term stimuli driving economic recovery and the decrease in unemployment came from the rearmament of Germany, which Hitler began pursuing immediately after being named Reich chancellor. As early as February 1933, Hitler was stressing to Germany's military and his cabinet that rearmament would be made an absolute priority. "Sums in the billions" would have to be found, Hitler declared, because "the future of Germany depends solely and alone on the reconstruction of the Wehrmacht."[221] Hitler did not think then that Reichsbank President Hans Luther was flexible enough to support accelerated rearmament with expansive monetary and credit policies, so in March 1933 he appointed Hjalmar Schacht to the post. This was also an expression of gratitude for the valuable services Schacht had rendered to the National Socialists before 1933.[222] The package of expenditures drawn up for the military totalled an astronomical 35 billion reichsmarks. The sum dwarfed that allocated for civilian job-creation measures and was to be placed at the government's disposal in annual instalments of 4.4 billion reichsmarks over the course of eight years.[223] To finance such expenses, Schacht came up with a deviously clever system for procuring money. In the summer of 1933, for the purpose of financing arms contracts, four large industrial and armaments companies—Gutehoffnungshütte, Krupp, Rheinstahl and Siemens—formed a dummy firm called Metallurgische Forschungsgesellschaft (Mefo—Metallurgic Research Society), which issued bills of exchange, guaranteed by the state and discounted by the Reichsbank, to the arms producers. The first Mefo bills were drawn in the autumn of 1933, but in line with the pace of rearmament the first major payments only began in April 1934.[224] That initiated a spiralling process of financing a rearmament industry on credit, which in the long term would have led to serious economic defaults.

"Never stand still—always move forwards!" That was Goebbels's concise formulation in November 1933 of the action-first principle that had guided the Nazis since they took power on 30 January.[225] The principle reflected Hitler's social Darwinist mantra that constant struggle would be the vital elixir of his movement. Like all charismatic leaders, Hitler faced the problem that his power, which he owed to an extreme and extraordinary situation, might wear thin over time and be subjected to a process of "normalisation."[226] Thus while the tempo of his power consolidation and development varied, things were never allowed to come to a standstill. Hitler may have made more progress and achieved easier triumphs than he had dared imagine in his wildest dreams, but he was still quite some way from being the "Führer" whose dictatorship was unquestioned. While their positions were growing weaker, he still had to take into consideration the power of the military and the Reich president. And above all, within the Nazi movement itself, the SA was becoming a problem.

When the Nazis had consolidated their power in the summer of 1933, the Brownshirts saw themselves robbed of their most important *raison d'être*: terrorising and neutralising the Nazis' political opponents. Consequently, in early August, Göring rescinded the decree from the preceding February which made the SA an auxiliary police force. Politically there was no point any more to the Brownshirts' violent activism, and the Nazi leadership viewed it as counter-productive. Many SA men were disappointed. They had hoped that when the party achieved power, their personal situation would change for the better overnight, and these people now felt that the "party bigwigs" and their "reactionary" supporters had cheated them of the spoils of victory.[227] Within the SA itself tensions were rising between the "old fighters" and new members who had joined the paramilitary group in hordes since the May 1933 moratorium on new NSDAP members. On 30 January 1933, the SA had fewer than 500,000 members. By the summer of 1934, that number—which now also included incorporated nationalist militias, above all the Stahlhelm—had risen to 4.5 million. This enormous influx of newcomers could hardly be integrated, and increased the potential for dissatisfaction.[228] Calls for a "second revolution" were growing.

In June 1933, SA Chief of Staff Ernst Röhm made reference to this negative mood in an article he published in the monthly journal *Nationalsozialistische Monatshefte*. The "national uprising," wrote Röhm, had thus far "only travelled part of the way up the path of German revolution." The SA, he asserted, "would not tolerate the German revolution falling asleep or being betrayed by non-fighters halfway towards its goal." At the end of his article, Röhm issued a direct threat to all "wimpy bourgeois souls"; he wrote, "Whether they like it or not, we will continue our fight. If they finally understand what is at stake, then with them! If they refuse to understand, then without them! And if need be, against them!"[229] With that the perennial structural problem in the relationship between the NSDAP and the SA had re-emerged. Röhm made it unmistakably clear that the SA did not want to be reduced to a mere recipient of commands from the party leadership. On the contrary, he laid claim to a position of power for himself and his organisation within the Third Reich. The mass influx of new SA members played into his hands since it added weight to his demands vis-à-vis the much smaller Reichswehr. Röhm envisioned transforming the SA into a kind of militia army, thereby challenging the regular army's monopoly on the right to weaponry and threatening to subordinate the Reichswehr to the SA. This was a prospect that alarmed both the military leadership and Hitler, who had concluded an alliance with Germany's generals in February 1933.

The problems presented by the SA were inseparably connected to the question of who would succeed Hindenburg. In early October 1933, the Reich president turned 86. It was obvious that he could die at any time. When the time came, Goebbels had insisted at a meeting on the Obersalzberg in late March, Hitler himself should succeed him. But Hitler was undecided. "He is not really up for it," Goebbels noted.[230] By July, having conferred with Reich Chancellery State Secretary Hans Heinrich Lammers, Goebbels had decided: "Hitler cannot tolerate a Reich president hanging over him, even as a figurehead. Both offices must be united in a single person." After a "long discussion about fundamental principles" on 24 August, Hitler and Goebbels agreed that the positions of Reich chancellor and Reich president should be merged.[231] Two days later, Hitler travelled to East Prussia to visit Hindenburg in Neudeck and take part in a celebration at the Tannenberg memorial on 27 August. He considered it "a blessing and gift of providence," Hitler proclaimed, to be able to express thanks to the field marshal "in the name of the German people . . . on the soil of the most glorious battlefield in the great war." Hitler also used the occasion to give Hindenburg title to the Prussian domains of Langenau and the Preussenwald forest and declare the Neudeck estate exempt from taxes.[232]

Hitler could only succeed Hindenburg with the support of the Reichswehr since the Reich president was the army's commander-in-chief. That alone was reason enough to keep Röhm in his place. But as always when faced with difficult decisions, Hitler played for time. Initially he tried to make Röhm more obedient with a combination of verbal attacks and solicitous gestures. On the one hand, in his speech to his Gauleiter on 6 July, he left no doubt that he would "drown, if necessary, in blood" any attempt at a "second revolution." On 28 September, he repeated this threat in front of the same audience. "He knew all too well that there were many dissatisfied creatures whose ambition could not be sated," one report of that speech read. "As a matter of course he could show no consideration for such ambitions. He would not sit back and watch the activities of such subjects for very much longer. At some point he would suddenly intervene."[233] On the other hand, in December, Hitler invited Röhm to join his cabinet as a minister without portfolio, the same distinction that Hess enjoyed. And on New Year's Eve, he sent a letter to his "dear chief of staff," gushing with thanks for the "eternal services" he had performed for "the National Socialist movement and the German people."[234]

Nonetheless in early 1934 it became increasingly clear that Hitler could not postpone a decision for much longer. The mood of dissatisfaction had spread beyond SA circles. The national euphoria of the first few months of the regime had yielded to a certain sobriety. Even Goebbels had to acknowledge: "Negative mood in broad circles because of grandiosity, price hikes, state intervention in agriculture, etc."[235] Workers were angry that food prices were rising while their wages stagnated. Farmers did not like the Hereditary Farm Law, which restricted their freedom in running their property. Middle-class retailers still felt subjected to unfair competition from large department stores. And economic recovery was not continuing as fast as many people had hoped. Disappointment at unfulfilled material desires was combined with increasing bitterness at corruption and nepotism. The latter was directed at party functionaries who had seized the moment to claim lucrative posts. Hitler himself was largely exempt from criticism, however. The reports of the SPD in exile in Prague, which were based on information from sources within Germany, recorded as typical the sentiments of a Munich resident: "Our Adolf is all right, but those around him are all complete scoundrels."[236]

Nor did the growing dissatisfaction escape the notice of foreign diplomats. It was unmistakable, reported the Danish envoy, Herluf Zahle, in April 1934, that "the enthusiasm greeting the government has cooled to some degree."[237] Jews who were being harassed in Germany took heart. "People are no longer as convinced that what's going on right now will last for ever," Victor Klemperer wrote in his diary in early February 1934. "There's a gnashing of teeth going through all too many classes, professions and faiths."[238] In fact, the dissatisfaction rarely went beyond general grumbling. But Goebbels took it seriously enough to launch a counter-offensive in May aimed at the "pessimists, moaners and critics."[239]

The decline in the public mood formed the background to the growing conflict between the Reich government and the military, on the one side, and the SA on the other. In a speech he gave to his Gauleiter in Berlin on 2 February 1934, Hitler once again attacked the SA leadership without naming any names. Only "fools" could maintain that the "revolution was not yet at an end," Hitler fumed, which was merely a way of trying "to put themselves in certain positions."[240] The day before, Röhm had sent Werner von Blomberg a letter in which he demanded that the SA take over the function of defending the country and that the Reichswehr be reduced to a mere training army.[241] The military leadership saw this as an open declaration of hostility and began to draft its own "Guidelines for Working with the SA," in which the Brownshirts were degraded to the role of offering preliminary military instruction and helping to monitor the Reich's borders. In a demonstration of loyalty towards the Nazi leadership, at a meeting of military commanders on 2 and 3 February, Blomberg announced that the Reichswehr would require officers to prove their Aryan heritage and would adopt the swastika as an official military emblem.[242]

The time had come for Hitler to make a decision, and he did. At a meeting with the heads of the Reichswehr and the leaders of the SA and SS on 28 February, he openly rejected Röhm's ideas. A militia of the sort suggested by the SA chief of staff, Hitler said, "was unsuitable even for the smallest national defensive action," to say nothing of the future war for "living space" he again put forward as a vision. For that reason, he was determined to raise "a people's army, built up on the foundations of the Reichswehr, of thoroughly trained soldiers equipped with the latest weaponry." The SA was to subordinate itself to his orders. There could be no doubt, Hitler concluded, that "the Wehrmacht is the only armed force of the nation."[243] Röhm pretended to give in, but that evening he vented his rage at the "ignorant private." He did not intend to stick to what had been agreed, Röhm raged. Hitler was "without loyalty" and had to be "sent on holiday at the very least," the SA leader was reported as saying. One of those present, SA Obergruppenführer Viktor Lutze, passed on these utterances to Hitler, who responded tellingly: "We will have to let this matter ripen."[244]

As early as January 1934, Hitler had ordered the first head of the Gestapo, Rudolf Diels—by Diels's own account—to collect incriminating material against the leaders of the SA. An identical order was issued to Reichswehr departments.[245] On 20 April, Göring appointed Heinrich Himmler, who had taken over the political crimes divisions in the police forces of almost all the German states in the preceding months, as the inspector of the Prussian Secret State Police. He and Reinhard Heydrich, who was made director of the State Police Office, moved from Munich to Berlin. The Gestapo now began to cooperate more intensely with the intelligence department in the Reichswehr Ministry, swapping information about the SA. The net around Röhm and his associates was gradually drawn tighter and tighter.[246]

In the battle for power that commenced with Röhm, Hitler had no qualms about publicising the former's homosexuality and using it as a weapon against him. In mid-May, he had a one-to-one discussion with Goebbels, after which the propaganda minister noted: "Complaint about Röhm and his personnel policies under paragraph 175. Revolting."[247] Previously Hitler had shielded Röhm from attacks on his well-known homosexual leanings. In a decree in early February 1931, Hitler had particularly emphasised that the SA "was not a moral institution for the education of well-born daughters but a band of rough-hewn fighters." Members' private lives were only an issue "if they ran truly contrary to the National Socialist world view."[248] Moreover, during the presidential elections in March 1932, when the left-wing *Welt am Montag* and *Münchener Post* newspapers published compromising letters written by the SA chief of staff, Hitler had sworn: "Lieutenant Colonel Röhm will remain my chief of staff. Even the dirtiest and most repulsive smear campaigns will not change that fact in the slightest."[249] In the spring and early summer of 1934, however, Hitler tried to use Röhm's homosexuality as a noose to hang him with.

In early June, it appeared as if the situation might relax somewhat. In a personal conversation, Hitler extracted from Röhm a promise to send the SA "on holiday" for the entire month of July and to take a cure himself at the Bad Wiessee spa on Tegernsee Lake. But this discussion was not a genuine attempt at reconciliation. Hitler continued to mistrust Röhm's intentions. Goebbels noted: "He no longer trusts the SA leadership. We all need to be on our toes. Let's not feel too secure."[250] Röhm, too, only pretended to be placated. At an evening of partying in the SA's main headquarters on Berlin's Standartenstrasse, Ernst Hanfstaengl witnessed the chief of staff, intoxicated, "cursing in the wildest fashion" the Reichswehr, which had drawn Hitler over to their side.[251]

But it was Franz von Papen, and not anything the SA did, who caused the situation to come to a dramatic head in June 1934. A group of young conservatives—led by Papen's speechwriter, Edgar Julius Jung, his press director, Herbert von Bose, and his personal assistant, Günther von Tschirschky—had coalesced around the vice-chancellor. They saw the tensions within the Nazi movement as a chance to curb Hitler's demands for absolute power and to steer the regime in the more moderate direction of a restored monarchy.[252] The ambitions of the Papen circle were no secret to the Nazi leadership. In April they began to suspect that Papen was positioning himself to succeed Hindenburg, who had contracted a bladder infection the previous month and would withdraw completely to his Neudeck estate that June.[253] Another thorn in the side of Hitler and his entourage was the fact that Papen's office was increasingly becoming a focal point for complaints about the regime's dictatorial exercise of power. "Papen is the true complaints office," Goebbels fumed on 13 June.[254]

Four days later, a talk by the vice-chancellor at the University of Marburg put the NSDAP leadership on a state of red alert. Not only did Papen criticise the cult of personality surrounding Hitler, arguing that "Great men are not made by propaganda but gain that status through their deeds." He also excoriated the regime's use of violence and unchecked radicalism. "It would be reprehensible to believe that a people could be unified through terror, which is always the product of bad conscience," Papen stated.

No people can afford constant revolt from below if it wants to survive the court of history. At some point the movement will have to end, and a fixed social structure, held together by an independent justice system and a universally accepted power of state, must come into existence. Nothing can be built with constant dynamism. Germany cannot be allowed to become a train speeding blindly ahead without anyone knowing where it is headed.

The government, Papen assured his audience, "knows all about the selfishness, lack of character, mendacity, non-chivalry and presumption that tries to spread under the cover of the German revolution."[255]

What Papen did not mention was that he himself bore considerable responsibility for the conditions he criticised. In the first months of the regime, he had not tried to restrain Hitler once, and even after his speech, he did not necessarily want a confrontation. Immediately after his talk, he sent Hitler a telegram that read: "In the venerable university of town of Marburg, I just went to bat for the unwavering and true continuation of your revolution and the completion of your work. In admiration and loyalty, your Papen."[256] But it did not fool anyone within the Nazi leadership. Goebbels seethed: "Papen gave a wonderful speech for gripers and critics. Entirely against us except for a few empty phrases. Who wrote it for him? Where is the scoundrel?"[257] It soon emerged that Edgar Julius Jung had written the talk. He was arrested on 26 June, and Goebbels censored the speech but not before it had been read out on the Reich radio station in Frankfurt.[258] Papen's supporters had also distributed an abridged version to the press, and news of disagreement within the regime spread like wildfire. "It seems that there's something like a mood of conflict in the upper spheres at the moment," wrote Theodor Heuss on 20 June. "A speech Papen held last Sunday in Marburg has been deemed unsuitable for printing . . ."[259] Foreign diplomats racked their brains as to what Papen's speech could mean. "The atmosphere was heavy and oppressive, like that ahead of an oncoming thunderstorm," recalled François-Poncet.[260]

After the ban on his speech, Papen had no other choice than to offer to quit, but Hitler—who, according to Goebbels, was "very enraged" by the Marburg speech and determined to "get his own back against Papen"—deemed the time not right for his vice-chancellor's resignation.[261] He asked Papen to wait until they had the chance to discuss the situation with Hindenburg. Papen agreed, writing to Hitler that he felt like "a soldier duty bound to your work." At the same time, he protested against Jung's arrest. "If someone has to go to jail for the Marburg speech," Papen wrote, "I stand at your disposal."[262] In reality, Hitler had no intention of going to Neudeck with Papen. Instead, on 21 June he travelled there alone and was relieved to discover that the Marburg speech had made no impression on Hindenburg. "Never had the old man been as friendly," Hitler reported after his visit.[263] At the same time, Defence Minister von Blomberg, who was also at Neudeck, had urged him once again to rein in the SA.[264]

From 23 to 26 June, Hitler retreated to the Obersalzberg, and it was there that he apparently made his final decision. With his unique instinct for power, Hitler realised that the time had come for a double blow—against the SA leadership clique and the "reactionaries" around Papen—to cut through the domestic political stalemate. Himmler and Heydrich's staff immediately set about concocting an opaque mixture of rumours, false reports and manipulated orders intended to suggest that an SA rebellion was nigh. At the same time, lists were drawn up of those to be arrested and executed. On 25 June, Himmler summoned SS leaders to Berlin, where they were informed about Röhm's imminent putsch and made preparations to put it down.[265] That same day, Hess gave a speech on Cologne radio, in which he threatened: "Woe to him who breaks his loyalty in the belief that he is serving the revolution by revolting. It's pathetic how some people think they've been chosen to help the Führer by organising revolutionary agitation from below."[266] As Erich Ebermayer noted in his diary, Hess's speech was cause for "great commotion and agitation—everyone knows that something's in the air."[267] On 27 June, Hitler met with Blomberg and the head of the minister's office at the Reichswehr Ministry, Walther von Reichenau, to assure himself of the military's support for the planned action. Local defence commandos were put on high alert, and on 29 June, Blomberg published an article in the *Völkischer Beobachter* in which he declared his loyalty to the Nazi regime, writing, "The Wehrmacht and the state are one."[268]

To preserve the illusion of normality and keep the SA leadership feeling secure, on 28 June Hitler went with Göring and Viktor Lutze to Essen to attend the wedding of Gauleiter Josef Terboven. Having received word that Hindenburg had granted Papen an audience on

30 June, he drew up a schedule for the purge. "I've had enough," Lutze recorded Hitler saying. "I'm going to set an example."[269] On the evening of 28 June, Röhm was instructed by telephone to summon all SA Obergruppenführer, Gruppenführer and inspectors to Bad Wiessee for a meeting with Hitler. While Göring flew back to Berlin to take care of the measures that had been prepared, Hitler spent the morning of 29 June, as planned, inspecting a Reich Labour Service camp in the town of Buttenberg in Westphalia. At the crack of dawn, he had called Goebbels and summoned him to Bad Godesberg. "It's getting started," the propaganda minister noted. "In God's name. Anything is better than this terrible waiting around. I'm ready."[270] When he arrived at the Rheinhotel Dreesen, he learned to his surprise that the purge would be directed not just against the "reactionaries" around Papen, but against "Röhm and his rebels" as well. "Blood will flow—everyone should know that rebellion will cost people their heads," Goebbels wrote. "I'm in agreement. If you're going to do it, then do it ruthlessly."[271]

In Bad Godesberg, Hitler received cooked-up reports about increasing unrest within the SA, and all the evidence suggests that, having made his irreversible decision, he worked himself up into an extraordinary psychological state. It is hardly plausible that he believed the transparently constructed lies about an imminent SA putsch, but in order to legitimise the purge he seized upon even the most ridiculous conspiracy theories. He told Goebbels, for instance, that there were "indications that Röhm was conspiring with François-Poncet, Schleicher and Strasser."[272] That evening, as word came in that individual SA men had been marauding around Munich and causing trouble, Hitler decided on the spot to fly to the Bavarian capital with his entire entourage. The three-engine Junkers 52 landed at 4 a.m. on Oberwiesenfeld, the precise location where, ten years previously, he had been forced into a humiliating retreat by Bavarian police and Reichswehr units. Now he had no reason to fear resistance from either of those quarters. At the airport, Hitler was received by Gauleiter Wagner, who briefed him on the situation. "He was extraordinarily agitated," aeroplane captain Baur observed. "He kept fidgeting around in the air with his riding crop, several times bringing it down on his own foot."[273]

From the airport Hitler had himself sped to the Bavarian Interior Ministry. There, he summoned Munich SA leaders August Schneidhuber and Wilhelm Schmid and tore their designations of rank from their uniforms with his own hands. "You are under arrest and will be shot," he snarled.[274] Without waiting for his bodyguards in the SS Leibstandarte Adolf Hitler to arrive, Hitler ordered three cars and had himself driven to Bad Wiessee. Most of the guests in the Pension Hanselbauer, where Röhm and his men were staying, were still asleep when the cars arrived at 6:30 a.m. Accompanied by two police officers with drawn pistols and whip in hand, Hitler stormed into the SA chief of staff's room and blurted out the words: "Röhm, you are under arrest!" Still half asleep, Röhm looked up from his pillows and replied, "Heil, my Führer." "You are under arrest," Hitler screamed again, turning around and leaving the room.[275] One by one the SA leaders were taken into custody. Among them was Breslau Police President Edmund Heines, who was found in bed with a young man—a discovery Nazi propaganda used in the days to come to depict the Bad Wiessee guest house as a den of homosexual iniquity.[276]

Those arrested were held in the guest house basement before being taken to Munich's Stadelheim prison. Hitler also returned to the Bavarian capital with his entourage, stopping the cars full of SA leaders driving in the other direction to what they thought was their meeting with the Führer and ordering them to join his motorcade. Police officers from the political crimes division stopped SA leaders in Munich's main train station, arresting those whose names were on the lists. They, too, were taken to Stadelheim.[277] Around noon, Hitler arrived at the Brown House and addressed a large number of party and SA leaders. He was still in a state of hysteria and, as one eyewitness reported, he spat out a ball of froth when he began speaking. His voice cracking with over-excitement, he accused the Röhm clique of the "greatest betrayal in world history." He also named Röhm's betrayer, Viktor Lutze, as the new SA chief of staff. That afternoon, Hitler ordered Sepp Dietrich to have six of the detained SA men, whose names he had marked on a list in green pencil and who included Schneidhuber, Schmid and Edmund Heines, liquidated by an SS commando. Röhm was initially spared. Apparently, Hitler was still somewhat hesitant about having his old comrade-in-arms murdered.[278]

That morning, Goebbels had already sent the agreed code word "Hummingbird" to Berlin, signalling to Göring that he should mobilise the execution commandos. Papen's colleagues Herbert von Bose and Edgar Julius Jung were shot. The vice-chancellor escaped with his life but was placed under house arrest. Also executed was the leader of the religious lay organisation "Catholic Action" and ministerial director of the Transport Ministry, Erich Klausener, who had been linked with the Papen circle. Former Chancellor Schleicher and his wife were killed in their home in Neubabelsberg, and the same fate befell Schleicher's associate General Ferdinand von Bredow a few hours later. He was taken from his Berlin apartment on the evening of 30 June and shot. At the same time, Nazi thugs throughout the Reich took the opportunity to settle old scores. Gregor Strasser was put to death in the basement of Gestapo headquarters. Gustav Ritter von Kahr and the editor-in-chief of the Catholic magazine *Der gerade Weg* (The Straight and Narrow), Fritz Gerlich, who was one of Hitler's most passionate critics, were both put to death in the Dachau concentration camp. Otto Ballerstedt, an early political rival who had succeeded in putting Hitler behind bars for a few weeks in 1922 after being physically attacked by him, was found dead from a bullet to the back of the head in the vicinity of Dachau. Father Bernhard Stempfle, an early confidant of Hitler's, was also executed—probably for knowing too much about the Führer's past. Such was the murderous zeal of the SS commandos that they did not always adequately check the identities of people they took into custody. Willi Schmid, for example, a music critic for the *Münchener Neueste Nachrichten*, fell victim to a case of mistaken identity. Ninety people are known to have been killed in what became known as the "Night of the Long Knives"—the actual number is likely twice that.[279] Goebbels was satisfied that everything had gone to plan, noting: "No mistakes other than Frau Schleicher also going down. A shame, but there's no changing that."[280]

Hitler returned to Berlin on the evening of 30 June. A delegation led by Göring, Himmler and Frick greeted him at Tempelhof Airport. "The sight of him was 'one-of-a-kind,'" reported one eyewitness. "Brown shirt, black tie, dark brown leather coat, high, black military boots, everything dark upon dark. Above it all, bare-headed, a chalk-white, sleepless, unshaven face which seemed to be sunken and swollen at the same time and from which a pair of extinguished eyes stared through some clotted strands of hair hanging down."[281] After the murderous release of the previous twenty-four hours, Hitler began to regain his inner balance. Christa Schroeder, who encountered him late at night in the Reich Chancellery, recalled him sitting next to her, breathing heavily and saying: "I've just had a bath and feel like I've been born again."[282] The following day, a Sunday, Hitler was already playing the role of the congenial, good-humoured host at a garden party in the Chancellery. That afternoon, he ordered the commandant of the Dachau concentration camp to call upon Röhm, who was imprisoned in Stadelheim, to shoot himself. When Röhm refused, he was executed.[283] "All revolutions devour their own children," the former SA chief of staff had told Hans Frank, who visited him a few hours before.[284]

Berlin was abuzz with the wildest rumours on 1 July. No one seemed to know exactly what had happened. That evening, Goebbels gave a radio address in which he talked about a "small clique of professional saboteurs" who had deserved no mercy. "We're cleaning house," he said. "A herd of pestilence, a herd of corruption and pathological symptoms of moral barbarism that appear in public life will be smoked out and eradicated down to the bone." The propaganda minister dwelt at length on the homosexuality of Röhm and his circle, accusing them of being about to "bring the entire party leadership under the suspicion of a contemptible and disgusting sexual abnormality."[285] At a cabinet meeting on 3 July, Hitler also used Röhm's "unhappy predilection" as an explanation for both "the inferior personnel in SA leadership positions" and his "wilful conflict with the Wehrmacht." Then he proceeded on to the heart of the conflict. Röhm wished to make the SA a "state within a state," Hitler explained. In a four-hour conversation, he, Hitler, had implored the former chief of staff to desist from this, but to no avail. Röhm had given him every assurance under the sun, but behind Hitler's back, he had done exactly the opposite. Hitler did not shy away from spinning a fairy tale about a coup d'état Röhm was planning with Schleicher, Gregor Strasser and the French embassy. With that, the condition of "high treason" had been fulfilled, Hitler claimed, and he had been forced to act immediately in order to "prevent a catastrophe." Hitler brushed aside any legal objections by arguing that this had been a "military mutiny" that did not admit of any trials or similar procedures. Although he had not personally ordered all the executions, he took full responsibility for them. They had "saved the lives of countless others," Hitler asserted, and "stabilised the authority of the Reich government for all time."

Hitler then presented the cabinet with a draft law that would legalise the series of murders *ex post facto*. "The measures taken on 30 June and 1 and 2 July to put down treasonous acts against the nation and states are a legal form of emergency government defence," the draft read. Justice Minister Franz Gürtner hastened to add that this was not tantamount to creating a new legal code, but merely confirmed the validity of the existing one. In the name of his cabinet colleagues, Werner von Blomberg thanked Hitler for his "decisive and courageous action, which has spared the German people a civil war."[286]

While the cabinet meeting was still in session, Papen, whose house arrest had just been lifted, appeared. "Completely broken," noted Goebbels. "Asked for leave to speak. We all expected him to resign."[287] But although two of his closest associates had been murdered, Papen did not consider for a moment breaking with Hitler. In a conversation with the Nazi leader on 4 July, the two men agreed that Papen would continue in the office of vice-chancellor until September and then join the diplomatic corps. In the days that followed, Papen complained that the situation was "completely unbearable" as long as he and his team were not rehabilitated and the confiscated files from his office returned. And he announced once again that he intended to travel to Neudeck to tender his resignation to Hindenburg. But he does not seem to have meant these very serious threats, and when Otto Meissner informed him that the Reich president was "very much in need of peace and quiet," he abandoned his plans. When Hitler told him in another conversation on 11 July that he intended to take public responsibility for everything associated with putting down the SA revolt, Papen replied: "You will allow me to say to you how great I find that in both a manly and human sense."[288] From a moral standpoint, Papen could not have sunk any lower.

Nor did Hindenburg—even though he had been on familiar terms with Kahr and had thanked him the preceding October for his "loyal birthday wishes"—have any qualms about sending Hitler a congratulatory telegram, in which he wrote, "You have saved the German people from a serious threat."[289] On the afternoon of 3 July, Hitler travelled to Neudeck where he gave Hindenburg a private half-hour lecture about the alleged "Röhm revolt." Hindenburg reiterated his blessings for the crimes being committed by the German government: "That's the right way to go. Nothing will happen without bloodshed."[290] After returning to Berlin, Hitler told Goebbels: "Hindenburg was smashing. The old man is really something."[291]

The initial uncertainty people felt when they heard the news of the murders on 30 June soon gave way to relief. The SA men, who had been so welcome when suppressing the political Left in early 1933, had used up all of their credit among the general populace with their disorderly conduct. The bloody excesses of the SS were excused because they had helped remove an unwanted source of disruption. Goebbels was probably exaggerating when he noted: "A limitless enthusiasm is passing through the country."[292] But it is true that, far from losing prestige, Hitler's reputation had improved. This is reflected in a number of Nazi Party reports on the mood within the population. Among the broad masses, and particularly among those who took a wait-and-see attitude towards the movement, Hitler has achieved a great victory with his decisive action—he is "not only admired; he is deified," read one report from a small industrial town in Upper Bavaria.[293] Immediately after the Night of the Long Knives, Luise Solmitz noted in her diary: "The personal courage, the decisiveness and effectiveness [Hitler] showed in Munich, that's unique."[294] Neither Solmitz nor the majority of the German people were bothered by the state planning and carrying out acts of murder—a clear indication of how dulled people's sense of right and wrong was after only one and a half years of Nazi rule.

In the first few days after 30 June, Hitler avoided appearing in public, although his propaganda minister urged him to in order to combat negative foreign press headlines. "Everywhere we're coming into discredit," Goebbels noted on 7 July. "High time for the Führer to speak."[295] The previous day Hitler had flown to Berchtesgaden to rest on the Obersalzberg. But by 9 July, he was already back in Berlin announcing that he wanted to issue an explanation in front of the Reichstag. He discussed the details with Goebbels the following day.[296] On the evening of 13 July, when Hitler approached the Reichstag podium, he initially seemed inhibited. "Pale as a corpse with tired facial features and a voice that was still hoarse," was how François-Poncet recalled him.[297] The atmosphere was tense. After all, there had been thirteen Reichstag deputies among the executed SA men. Papen, who had asked Hitler to be excused, was missing from the government bench,[298] and SS men in pith helmets had been posted next to the speaker's lectern and throughout the hall. In his two-hour speech, Hitler repeated the lies about a conspiracy between Röhm, Schleicher and Strasser he had told to his cabinet on 3 July, and he did not neglect to mention that "certain shared predilection" of the Röhm clique as a main motive for their "high treason." He talked about the "bitterest decisions" of his life, for which he assumed responsibility "before history." Hitler told his audience: "Mutinies are broken according to never-changing laws. If someone tries to criticise me for not enlisting the regular courts, I can only say: in that hour, I was responsible for the fate of the German nation and was therefore the supreme judge of the German people."[299]

The constitutional lawyer Carl Schmitt was tasked with providing academic justification for this twisted notion in an article in the legal journal *Deutsche Juristen-Zeitung*. He wrote: "The Führer is only protecting the law from the worst sort of abuse, if in a moment of danger he creates immediate law on the basis of his status as leader and supreme judge."[300] Hitler's speech to the Reichstag was well received not just by the Third Reich's star lawyer, but also by the German people. Nazi reports on the public mood concluded that the speech had had a "liberating effect."[301] "I wish you could have *heard* these words instead of merely reading them," Elisabeth Gebensleben wrote to her daughter. "The greatness, honesty and openness of such a man make you feel small."[302]

Nonetheless, no matter how loquacious and inventive Hitler often was when recalling earlier episodes in his life, from now on he maintained steely silence about the Night of the Long Knives, when his murderous side had been on clear display. The topic was absolutely taboo, even for his closest intimates. When Heinrich Hoffmann once tried to broach it, Hitler brusquely waved him off. "Not a single word more!" Hitler said in a tone of voice that brooked no contradiction.[303]

On 30 June 1934, the true criminal nature of the Nazi regime was revealed, but only a few observers inside and outside Germany were able to see it. "The horrible thing is that a European people has delivered itself up to such a band of lunatics and criminals and continues to tolerate them," Victor Klemperer complained in his diary.[304] Thomas Mann, who had left Germany in February for initial exile in Switzerland, saw all his dark premonitions confirmed. In comparison with the "dirty swindler and murderous charlatan" Hitler, Mann wrote, Robespierre was positively honourable. The circles around Hitler were little better than "gangsters of the lowest sort." The Nobel laureate went on: "In any case, after little more than a year, Hitlerism is proving to be what we always saw, recognised and deeply felt it to be: the absolute *nadir* of baseness, decadent stupidity and bloodthirsty humiliation—it is becoming clear that Hitlerism will continue, certainly and unerringly, to prove itself as precisely that."[305] Mann's judgement was not only on the mark. It was astonishingly prescient.

The Reichswehr leadership, by contrast, felt it had got what it wanted. Röhm had been dispensed with as a rival and the status of the Reichswehr as the only "weapons-bearer of the nation" had been explicitly confirmed. The fact that a former Reichswehr minister and a ranking general had fallen victim to the bloodthirsty "cleansing" did nothing to dampen the triumphant mood. The former state secretary in the Reich Chancellery, Erwin Planck, may have entreated Kurt von Hammerstein's successor as army chief of staff, General Werner von Fritsch, to rein in the regime's proclivity for violence—"If you look on without acting, sooner or later you'll suffer the same fate'[306]—but the Reichswehr leadership did not heed any such warnings. At a commanders' conference on 5 July, Blomberg declared that Hitler had acted in the interest of the Wehrmacht, and that the military was now obliged "to thank him with even greater fidelity and loyalty if possible."[307] Such kowtowing weakened the Reichswehr's position within the Hitler state. The military had become an accomplice to Hitler's criminal polices, and there was no turning back.

It was the SS, and not the military, that actually profited from the Night of the Long Knives. On 20 July, Hitler decreed that as a reward for the "great service performed in conjunction with the events of 30 June," the SS was to be separated from the SA and henceforth run as an autonomous organisation. Reichsführer-SS Himmler was put directly under Hitler's own authority.[308] In the years to follow, the power of the SS would constantly grow, whereas under Viktor Lutze's leadership, the SA gradually devolved into little more than a veterans' organisation for "old street fighters."[309]

In late July, Hindenburg's condition deteriorated dramatically. His death was only a matter of days away. On the morning of 1 August, Hitler travelled to Neudeck, where he found the dying man still conscious. "Recognised him briefly," Goebbels wrote after Hitler's return to Berlin. "Expressed thanks and love. And hallucinated about the Kaiser."[310] Hindenburg died in the early hours of 2 August. The previous evening, before his death was even confirmed, Hitler had presented his cabinet with the Law on the Head of State of the German Reich, which regulated the question of Hindenburg's successor in Hitler's favour. It united the offices of Reich president and chancellor and transferred the powers of the former to the "Führer and Reich chancellor," as Hitler now officially referred to himself. Although this clearly violated the provisions of the Enabling Act, which specified that the responsibilities of the Reich president remain untouched, the cabinet approved the new law. Moreover, without any prompting by Hitler, Blomberg announced his intention to have German soldiers swear an oath of loyalty to the new commander-in-chief as soon as Hindenburg had died.[311] On 2 August, members of the Wehrmacht were forced to recite: "I swear by God this holy oath that I will show absolute obedience to the Führer of the German Reich and People, Adolf Hitler, the commander-in-chief of the Wehrmacht, and that as a brave soldier I will be willing to sacrifice my life at any time for this oath."[312] It may be that the military leadership hoped such a display of loyalty would secure them a measure of autonomy. In fact their actions hastened the transformation of the army into a tool for Hitler to use at will.

In his cabinet meeting on 2 August, Hitler played the role of someone mourning for Hindenburg so convincingly that Goebbels wrote: "Everyone was very moved."[313] Hitler declared that he "had lost a paternal friend" and reminded everyone "that the current Reich government would not exist without the hallowed Reich president." Given the "greatness of the deceased," Hitler declared that the title Reich president would be retired for all eternity. And he announced that the people would be asked to vote on the new organisation of state leadership on 19 August.[314] Hindenburg had asked to be buried next to his deceased wife at his Neudeck estate. But the Nazi leadership ignored this final wish and organised a pompous state funeral inside the Tannenberg Memorial on 7 August. In his address, Hitler once again invoked the myth of the hero of the Great War, which he had so successfully exploited in the previous months. "Deceased field commander, enter now into Valhalla" were the words with which Hitler sent Hindenburg to his tomb.[315]

That evening, Berlin was rocked by the news that Hindenburg had left behind a political testament. There were fears it might contain something politically explosive,[316] so Hitler dispatched Papen to Neudeck to retrieve it. On 14 August, it was opened in the Reich Chancellery. It consisted of two documents: a longer one that was Hindenburg's political testament and a personal letter to Hitler in which Hindenburg pleaded for a restoration of the monarchy, once political circumstances allowed. Hitler kept the letter to himself—it has never been found—but he had the other document published on 15 August. Not only was its content harmless, it actually worked in Hitler's favour. Hindenburg expressed his gratitude at being allowed to witness "the hour of Germany's restrengthening" during the twilight of his life. "My Chancellor Adolf Hitler and his movement have made a decisive, historic step towards the great goal of restoring to the German people its inner unity above any differences of caste or class," Hindenburg had written. The president took his leave from life in hope that what had led to 30 January 1933 "will ripen into the absolute fulfilment and completion of the historic mission of our people."[317] The Nazis could hardly have wished for a better endorsement ahead of the 17 August plebiscite. On the eve of the poll, Hindenburg's son Oskar addressed the German people by radio, calling upon them to "approve the transferral of the office my father previously occupied as Reich president to the Führer and Reich chancellor."[318]

On 19 August, the official results were announced: 89.9 per cent had voted in favour, with voter turnout recorded at 95.7 per cent. Nonetheless Goebbels was disappointed: "I expected more," he wrote.[319] The result apparently reflected disappointment among parts of the populace at corruption among Nazi functionaries. One voter in Potsdam, for instance, had scrawled on his ballot paper: "For Hitler, Yes, for his Big Shots, No."[320] In Swiss exile, Thomas Mann was positively surprised: "Five million 'no' votes plus two million abstentions are a respectable national performance under the current circumstances."[321] Victor Klemperer took a similar view, even if he ultimately had to acknowledge that a vast majority of Germans had voted for the Führer and Reich chancellor: "Hitler is the clear victor, and there's no end in sight."[322]

The popular referendum of August 1934 completed Hitler's consolidation of power. Over the space of a few months, Hitler had succeeded in outmanoeuvring his conservative coalition partners and removing or neutralising all political opposition. Step by step, he had made himself into the lord and master of the German Reich and transformed Germany into a dictatorship. "One man has been given a power that no one now alive has ever possessed," wrote Denmark's ambassador in Berlin. "He is now more powerful than any monarch, more powerful than the president of the United States, and more powerful than Mussolini."[323] And now that his absolute domestic power was secured, Hitler could turn his attention to dismantling the system put in place by the Treaty of Versailles.

15

Eviscerating Versailles

"No one else has ever explained and written down what he intends to do more often than I have," Hitler stated in a speech on 30 January 1941. "And I have written over and over about the eradication of Versailles."[1] That was true. From the very start of his political career as a popular agitator in the autumn of 1919, Hitler left no doubt that he would seek to remove the constraints of the Treaty of Versailles should he achieve power. Revising the post–First World War geopolitical order was only the first step—not the ultimate goal—of Hitler's foreign policy. After being named chancellor, Hitler did not at all lose sight of one of the other core points of his programme, the conquest of "living space" in eastern Europe. He made that clear in his speech to Germany's army and navy commanders on 3 February 1933. By late January 1941, when Hitler commemorated the eighth anniversary of the Nazi "seizure of power" in Berlin's Sportpalast, the racist, annihilationist war Hitler had envisioned against the Soviet Union was soon to become reality. A little over a month before, on 18 December 1940, Hitler had signed Order 21, which launched Operation Barbarossa.

Nonetheless, in the first years of his regime, Hitler scrupulously avoided any public mention of his radical expansionist aims. The Third Reich's precarious international position forced him to manoeuvre carefully. It was logical to assume that France, in particular, would not simply accept German rearmament and might launch a preemptive military strike. The phase between "the theoretical recognition of Germany's equal military rights and the achievement of a certain level of armament" would be "the most difficult and dangerous one," Hitler explained at a meeting of the Committee for the Creation of Work on 9 February 1933, where he stressed that rearmament would be given "absolute priority."[2] In a confidential speech to select representatives of the press in April 1940, a few weeks before Germany's invasion of France, Goebbels frankly admitted how much the Nazi leadership had feared a pre-emptive French strike in the early phase of rearmament. "A French premier," Goebbels admitted, "should have said in 1933, as I certainly would have, had I been French premier: 'The author of *Mein Kampf*, which contains this and that, has become German chancellor. This man cannot be tolerated as a neighbour. Either he will have to disappear, or we will start marching." That would have been completely logical, but it was not done. They let us be, and we were able to proceed unhindered through the zone of risk."[3]

Hitler was at pains during the first phase of rearmaments to conceal his real intentions and placate the other European powers with concili- atory gestures. He repeatedly insisted that Germany only desired equal status within the community of nations, and that this was in the interest of world peace. These clichéd assurances of benevolence were completely calculated, as he admitted in a confidential speech to select members of the press in November 1938. The circumstances of the past few years, Hitler told them, meant that he had been forced to speak "almost exclusively" of peace: "It was only by constantly empha- sising Germany's peaceful desires and intentions that I was able, bit by bit, to liberate the German people and give them the arms that were the necessary precondition of the next step."[4] Hitler was essentially applying the same tactics of reassurance and deception that had worked so well with his conservative coalition partners in his "seizure of power" to the arena of foreign policy. And much like German conservatives, most foreign diplomats were mistaken in their appraisals of Hitler. They, too, thought that his compulsive need for action could be "tamed" by binding him in international treaties. In November 1933, Sir Eric Phipps, the new British ambassador in Berlin, declared that Hitler could not be treated simply as the author of *Mein Kampf* since to do that would have left no option other than a pre-emptive military strike. On the other hand, Hitler could not be ignored. Would it not be more advisable, Phipps reasoned, to tie down this terribly dynamic politician in an agreement that he himself had freely and proudly signed?[5]

Only a handful of foreign observers realised that Hitler would never be content with a mere revision of the Treaty of Versailles. One man who did was the U.S. consul general in Berlin, George S. Messersmith.

As early as May 1933, he warned that while the Hitler regime would probably desire peace in the next few years in order to consolidate its position, ultimately the "new Germany" would "strive in every way to impose its will on the rest of the world."[6]

One reason foreign politicians widely underestimated Hitler was the initial lack of personnel changes at the German Foreign Ministry after 30 January 1933. Baron Konstantin von Neurath stayed on as foreign minister at Hindenburg's express wish, as did Neurath's deputy, Bernhard von Bülow. Germany's ambassadors to the world's leading nations also retained their posts. The only one to leave the diplomatic service in the spring of 1933 was Germany's ambassador to the United States, Friedrich von Prittwitz und Gaffron.[7] The appearance was thus maintained that German foreign policy was still being determined by the Foreign Ministry, and that seemed to the rest of the world to be a guarantee of not just personnel but policy continuity. In early February, when Germany's ambassador to the Soviet Union, Herbert von Dirksen, reported the Moscow government's unease about the new Hitler government, Bülow told him:

> I think people there overestimate the effect of the change of government on German foreign policy. In government, the National Socialists are of course different people and pursue different policies than the ones they have previously supported. That is always the way it is, and all parties are the same . . . They, too, put their pants on one leg at a time.[8]

Just as, domestically, hopes that the responsibility of government would make Hitler and the Nazis more "moderate" quickly proved illusory, similar ideas also emerged as dangerously misjudged in the arena of foreign policy, even if it took longer for the mistake to become clear. In the first months of his regime, Hitler's emphasis was on consolidating and expanding his power domestically. Abroad he was content to take a back seat and let the career diplomats at the Foreign Ministry go about their business. That changed once Hitler had established his dictatorship. Increasingly he took the reins in dealing with other countries. "[Hitler is] entirely occupied with foreign policy," wrote Goebbels as early as March 1934.[9] Henceforth Hitler would determine the direction of all important decisions, and as he had in destroying the political Left and subjugating his conservative coalition partners, he

displayed a sure sense for his adversaries' weaknesses, boldly and unscrupulously exploiting them on what was for him new terrain. As a result
he needed only three years to engineer a succession of remarkable
coups that eviscerated the system put in place by the Treaty of Versailles.

A series of factors helped Hitler along, one of which was that the
Versailles system was already beginning to fall apart when he took
office. At the Lausanne Conference of June 1932, Papen had succeeded
in freeing Germany from the pressures of reparations payments,
reaping the fruit Brüning had sown before him. The Schleicher government, too, had achieved a spectacular foreign-policy triumph with the
Five-Power Declarations of 11 December 1932, which acknowledged
as a basic principle that the German Reich would be allowed to arm
itself like any other nation. While the declaration stipulated that the
details would be decided at a League of Nations arms conference in
Geneva, it was nonetheless apparent that German foreign policy had
gained far more leeway during the phase of presidentially appointed
governments than it had enjoyed in the Stresemann era.[10]

   This trend was encouraged by the effects of the Great Depression,
which caused Britain and France massive economic and social problems
and limited their ability to take action abroad.[11] Moreover, in the two
leading democratic nations of Europe, the trauma of the First World
War had given rise to powerful pacifist movements that rejected any
thought of another European war and restricted their respective
governments' ability to maintain their military strengths. Particularly
in Britain, many people thought that the Versailles system was unjust
and that Germany was owed something.[12] Hitler also profited from
the fear of communism rampant among western Europe's bourgeois
political elites. By casting himself as a radical vanguard opponent of
Bolshevik Russia, the Führer was able to overcome numerous doubts
about himself personally and his government.

   Additionally, what has often been called the "crisis of democracy" in
inter-war Europe put the wind in Hitler's sails. To a degree, Mussolini
had kicked off this trend with his "March on Rome" in October 1922
and his establishment of a Fascist regime in Italy. Only two of the new
nations formed after 1918–19, Finland and Czechoslovakia, had remained
democratic through the post-war years of crisis. All the others—the
Austrian Republic, Hungary, Croatia and Slovenia (as of 1929 the Kingdom

of Yugoslavia), Poland and the Baltic states—had sooner or later all become authoritarian regimes. Even states that had existed prior to 1918, including Romania, Bulgaria, Greece, Albania, Portugal and Spain were subjugated to "authoritarian transformation."[13] Hitler and National Socialism benefited from this general development. The regime they created, so it seemed at least, was part of the mainstream of the epoch.

Foreign Minister von Neurath articulated his ministry's future foreign policy for the first time at a cabinet meeting on 7 April 1933. The presentation was based on a lengthy memorandum which Bülow had produced in March. The primary goal was the complete eradication of the Treaty of Versailles, and the plan was to proceed in stages. First, Germany had to focus on rearming itself and regaining its economic strength, all the while taking care not to provoke a preemptive strike by France or Poland. The second phase aimed at "territorial revisions of borders," with the main aim being the redrawing of Germany's eastern border so as to regain the territory ceded to Poland in 1919. Further goals were pushing back the northern border in Schleswig and regaining the German-speaking parts of Belgium. Later aims included retaking Alsace-Lorraine, regaining Germany's former colonies or acquiring new ones, and merging with Austria. An understanding between Germany and France, Neurath said, was "as good as impossible," while an understanding with Poland was "neither feasible nor desirable," which meant that for the time being Germany had to stay on good terms with Russia. Moreover, Germany should pursue friendly relations with Britain and "the closest possible co-operation" with Italy and "wherever there are mutual interests." Neurath concluded that foreign conflicts had to be avoided "until we have completely regained our strength."[14] This long-term strategy developed by the top diplomats at the Foreign Ministry continued in the tradition of German imperialism—although, as soon became clear, it only partly conformed to Hitler's own ideas.

The Foreign Ministry, the Reichswehr and Hitler also agreed that Germany's accelerated rearmament had to be disguised and that foreign nations had to be deceived about the true intentions of German policy by demonstrative gestures of peace. That was the goal of Hitler's first major foreign-policy speech to the Reichstag on 17 May 1933. In it, he emphasised Germany's demands for equal status but rejected any hint of war or force:

No new European war would be able to replace the unsatisfactory conditions of today with anything better. On the contrary, neither politically nor economically could the use of violence call forth a better situation than the one we have now . . . It is the profound wish of the national government of the German Reich to work honestly and actively to prevent any non-peaceful developments.

Hitler also declared his respect for the national rights of other people, claiming that the idea of "Germanification" was alien to the National Socialists. This was an out-and-out lie. In his speech of 3 February to the German generals, he himself had called for the "ruthless Germanification" of the territories to be conquered in eastern Europe. Hitler also spoke with a forked tongue when he signalled German willingness to disarm during the very phase when the country was rearming itself to the teeth. Moreover, Hitler's assurances of his peaceful intentions always contained the calculated, implicit threat that Germany might withdraw from the Geneva Disarmament Conference and quit the League of Nations, should the country continue to be denied equal status.[15]

Hitler's "peace speech" hit its mark. In terms of foreign policy Hitler played the role of the moderate, conciliatory politician so convincingly that even the SPD Reichstag faction, decimated though it was by oppression, voted for the government's declaration. "Even our bitter enemy Adolf Hitler seemed moved for a moment," recalled SPD deputy Wilhelm Hoegner. "He stood up and applauded us."[16] The nationalist Elisabeth Gebensleben's admiration for Hitler knew no bounds after the speech. "This man is so excellent he could become the *leader* [Führer] *of the world*," she wrote to her daughter in Utrecht. "I'm proud again to be German, *boundlessly* proud." Her daughter wrote back that Dutch newspapers had been full of approval of Hitler's speech, adding that it "made up for much of the sympathy Germany had lost abroad in recent years."[17]

Indeed, the foreign reception of the speech was overwhelmingly positive. In London *The Times* wrote that for the first time the world had seen Hitler the statesman.[18] Count Harry Kessler, who himself found the speech "surprisingly moderate," reported on 18 May from Paris that it had put the French press in a bind. "They have to admit that there is nothing objectionable in it," he wrote.[19] By contrast,

Thomas Mann saw through the charade with unusual penetrating vision. "Hitler's speech in the Reichstag a complete pacific retreat— ridiculous," he remarked succinctly and correctly.[20]

At the Geneva disarmament negotiations, which resumed in February 1933, German and French interests collided head-on. The British government tried to mediate but hesitated, in deference to French demands for security, to give Germany full equality in terms of arming itself. By May, Blomberg and Neurath were determined to scupper the conference. Hitler, however, who was fully occupied with pushing forward his campaign to Nazify Germany and had no interest in foreign-policy disputes for the moment, reacted with greater tactical flexibility. He had the diplomat Rudolf Nadolny instruct the German delegation not to reject all offers of mediation on principle. While he was uninterested in a breakthrough in Geneva, Hitler wanted to avoid creating the impression that Germany was trying to sabotage the proceedings. Instead the blame was to fall on the other side. As Hitler's representative, Goebbels travelled to Geneva in September to take part in the annual meeting of the League of Nations as part of the German delegation. "Depressing" was his verdict. "An assemblage of the dead. Parliamentarianism of nations."[21] That October, when British Foreign Minister John Simon presented a revised disarmament plan that included a four-year trial period for Germany, in which German arms would have been internationally monitored, he gave the German delegation the pretext it wanted to abruptly quit the conference.[22]

On 13 October, Hitler informed his cabinet about his decision to "break up the conference" and announce Germany's withdrawal from the League of Nations the following day. This step was to be supported by a re-election of the Reichstag, which had only been in office since 5 March. This would give the German people, Hitler argued, the chance "to iden- tify itself through a plebiscite with the peace policies of the Reich govern- ment." In turn, the world could no longer "accuse Germany of aggressive politics." In the face of possible League of Nations sanctions, the main thing was "to keep our nerve and stay true to our principles."[23]

As Goebbels noted in his diary, Hitler "struggled long and hard with himself" before reaching this decision, since quitting the League of Nations was not without risk.[24] German rearmament was still in its early stages, and the Reich would hardly have been prepared for a military confrontation. Sanctions could also do real harm to the process of German economic recovery. At the very least, Germany faced the danger of diplomatic isolation. "Our departure from the community of nations that had been created with great difficulty over fifteen years is of massive import, the significance of which we cannot anticipate today," wrote Erich Ebermayer in Leipzig.[25] Kessler spoke of the "most portentous European event since the occupation of the Ruhr," adding that it "could within a short time lead to a blockade of Germany or perhaps even war."[26]

On the evening of 14 October, Hitler turned to the world in a radio address in which he used for the first time the double strategy that would be instrumental in a series of foreign-policy coups. On the one hand, he announced irrevocable decisions without regard for diplomatic niceties while, on the other hand, he deflected potential consequences with nebulous rhetoric, conciliatory gestures and seductive offers. "Both victors and vanquished," Hitler said, "will have to find their way back into the community of mutual understanding and trust." He particularly appealed to Germany's "perennial but venerable adversary," France. "It would be a huge event for all of humanity if these two people were able to ban violence once and for all from their mutual existence," Hitler intoned.[27] Goebbels was particularly enthused about this passage from Hitler's speech: "A hand extended to France. Really powerful. Well, he can do it like no one else."[28] Goebbels was right. In terms of lying and dissembling, no other European politician was a match for Hitler.

By 17 October, Hitler could reassure his cabinet: "Neither have threatening steps been taken against Germany not are they to be expected . . . The critical moment seems to have passed. The excitement will probably calm down shortly."[29] Goebbels, too, was relieved: "World echo fabulous. Better than I thought. The others are already looking for ways out. We have the upper hand again. Hitler's coup was daring but correct."[30] On 18 October, Hitler gave a lengthy interview to the correspondent of the *Daily Mail*, George Ward Price, in which he sought to dispel the worries of the British government and populace about Germany going it alone in foreign policy. Hitler stressed how happy he would be if Germany and Britain, which he characterised as related nations, rediscovered their former friendship. He also emphasised his desire for an honest agreement with

France and denied planning war against Poland. He did not rule out Germany rejoining the League of Nations, but only on the condition that it was recognised as a full equal. He also promised that Germany would honour all its agreements and treaties: "What we have signed up to we will fulfil to the best of our abilities."[31]

On 24 October, Hitler opened the campaign for the Reichstag election and the referendum on his foreign policy with a speech in Berlin's Sportpalast. With great pathos, he announced that he would "rather die" than sign anything he was convinced was not in the interest of the German people. "If I ever lose my way in this regard or if the German people should come to believe that it cannot stand behind my actions, it can have me executed," Hitler exclaimed. "I will stand calm and still."[32] During the days that followed, he flew from city to city—Hanover, Cologne, Stuttgart, Frankfurt am Main, Weimar, Breslau, Elbing and Kiel—as he had during the hotly contested elections of 1932. On his approach to Kiel on 6 November, Captain Hans Baur briefly lost his orientation, and Hitler's plane only just reached Travemünde airport.[33]

On 8 and 9 November, Hitler interrupted his election tour to celebrate the tenth anniversary of the 1923 putsch in Munich. On the evening of 8 November, he spoke in the Bürgerbräukeller, the spot where he had proclaimed a "national revolution" a decade earlier. Back then, he said, he had not acted rashly, but rather "on behalf of a higher power." It was down to the "wisdom of Providence" that the putsch had not succeeded, since the time had not been ripe. Nonetheless, it was then that the young National Socialist movement had gained the "heroism" that had led to the successful "rebellion" of 1933.[34] At noon on 9 November, a parade of the "old fighters" from the beer hall to the Feldherrnhalle underscored the mythic reinterpretation of the events of 1923. The ceremony would be repeated every year and became a fixed component of the Nazi holiday calendar.

"Hitler looked very pale," Goebbels noted after seeing his performance at the ceremony at the Feldherrnhalle.[35] What the chancellor had put himself through in the preceding weeks would have exhausted even a man of the strongest physical constitution. On 10 November, the day after the Munich festivities, he appeared before workers in the Berlin factory district of Siemensstadt, with Goebbels producing the accompanying radio report as he had in March. Hitler cleverly adapted to his audience by presenting a home-made legend about his childhood and passing himself off as a man of proletarian origins and sentiment. "In my youth, I was a worker like you," he told his audience. "I worked my way up by working hard, learning and, I can also say, by going hungry." He went on to brag about the government's initial successes in combating unemployment and reiterated his desire for peace: "I should not be accused of being insane enough to want war."[36]

It seems that the role of peace-loving labour leader allowed Hitler to score some points. Goebbels, in any case, wrote of the audience's reaction: "Great celebrations. Only workers. A year ago they would have struck us dead. The boss in his best form. Huge success. Hard to get out of the hall."[37] Victor Klemperer, who listened to the speech on the radio, had an entirely different reaction: "A largely hoarse, overly shouted, excitable voice, long passages in the self-pitying tone of a preaching sectarian . . . disordered but passionate. Every sentence was a lie, but I almost think an unconscious lie. The man is a narrow-minded fanatic. And he's learned nothing."[38] As accurate as Klemperer's assessment might have been, the fact that Hitler was an *arriviste* autodidact led even an educated and intelligent person like the Dresden professor to underestimate him. The same was doubly true of Count Harry Kessler, who noted in his diary in mid-October that Hitler was "ultimately nothing more than a hysterical, half-educated house painter, whose big mouth has earned him a position for which he is not qualified."[39]

On 12 November, 45 million Germans had their say on the question: "Do you, German man and German woman, approve of this policy of your Reich government and are you prepared to declare it to be your own view and your own will to solemnly profess your belief in it?" A total of 40.5 million (95.1 per cent) voted yes, 2.1 million (4.9 per cent) voted no, and 0.75 per cent of the ballots were declared invalid. In the Reichstag elections, the Nazi Party list received 39.6 million (92.2 per cent) valid and 3.4 million invalid votes.[40] The Nazi leadership celebrated this as a great triumph. "Moved, Hitler put his hands on my shoulders," noted Goebbels, who himself took most of the credit for the result. "It has been achieved. The German people are unified. Now we can confront the world."[41] Electoral approval may have been higher than expected, but the picture of a single unified people was propaganda. Klemperer, who had twice voted no, in so far as his non-Jewish wife turned in two empty ballots, concluded: "That was almost an act of bravery since the entire world expected that the ballots would not be secret."[42]

Indeed, there were so many irregularities in the election that the result can only be seen as a partially accurate reflection of the prevailing mood.[43] On the other hand, there is no denying that the vast majority of Germans willingly gave the Hitler regime their approval. In the estimation of the Swiss envoy in Berlin, Paul Dinichert, the broad masses of Germans voted yes to the question "because they believed that they had to defend 'German honour,' saw inequalities in disarmament as intolerable and never had much affection for the League of Nations, and also because the vast majority pins its hopes for a better future on Hitler, whom they regard as their saviour from political, social and economic misery."[44] Even the observers working for the SPD leadership in exile could not deny that "the mood of patriotism" had gained "the upper hand" among blue-collar workers.[45] Within Catholic and Social Democratic milieus, too, which had resisted National Socialism prior to 1933, Hitler's standing had demonstrably improved.

Within the cabinet, Papen took on the task of expressing positively Byzantine thanks to Hitler on behalf of the conservative ministers: "Everyone was completely bowled over by the unique, overwhelming expression of faith such as no nation ever before had given to its leader." In just nine months, Papen added, Hitler's "genius" had succeeded in converting "an internally divided people into a Reich unified by its hopes for and belief in the future."[46] What the vice-chancellor must have repressed at this point was his own dramatic loss of political influence, which meant that he could no longer serve as a counterweight to the Nazi leader and his lust for power. The fact that after Papen's encomium, the ministers all rose from their seats to honour the chancellor spoke louder than any words at how completely Hitler now dominated the cabinet. And in foreign-policy matters, too, he began increasingly to take the lead.

The next bombshell dropped on 26 January 1934 when the German Reich and Poland announced the conclusion of a non-aggression pact that was supposed to last for ten years and that required both sides to seek peaceful solutions to any conflicts of interest. The author of this coup was not the Foreign Ministry, but rather Hitler himself. In

488   HITLER: ASCENT 1889–1939

early May 1933, he had expressed his wish to the Polish envoy, Alfred Wysocki, "that both countries dispassionately take stock of and embrace their mutual interests."[47] The resulting exchange of ideas was intensified in the autumn of 1933. In late September Goebbels met with Polish Foreign Minister Józef Beck in Geneva. "He wants to break free from France and move towards Berlin," Goebbels noted. "These threads will continue to be pursued."[48] In mid-November, Hitler received and held lengthy talks with Poland's new ambassador to Germany, Józef Lipski. With that, the official negotiations that led to the non-aggression pact commenced between Berlin and Warsaw.[49]

Understandably, this spectacular development created a stir both inside and outside Germany. It represented a break with previous German foreign policy, which had never accepted the territorial concessions the Treaty of Versailles had forced Germany to make to Poland, in particular the creation of the Polish Corridor that separated East Prussia from the rest of the Reich. For this very reason, Neurath had rejected the idea of Germany's reaching any understanding with its eastern neighbour in the spring of 1933. Now Hitler appeared to have engineered just that. "A diplomatic miracle has occurred!" wrote Ebermayer in his diary. "Germany and Poland have reached an agreement!"[50]

Of course Hitler's change of tack was not motivated by a sudden fondness for the authoritarian regime of Marshal Józef Piłsudski. On the contrary, the German chancellor had weighed up the advantages of the non-aggression pact. On the one hand, it offered protection against a joint pre-emptive strike by Poland and France—a danger that Hitler's regime initially took very seriously.[51] "Ten years of calm, even with sacrifices," was how Hitler summarised his foreign policy in November 1933.[52] On the other hand, the agreement with Poland served Hitler as a welcome means of proving that he was the man of peace he constantly claimed to be. And that was exactly how foreign diplomats now saw him—British Ambassador Phipps called the non-aggression pact the "achievement of a great statesman."[53] Nevertheless, despite pledging not to resort to violence, Hitler had not accepted the territorial integrity of the Polish state. The pact was not a "Locarno for the east." For Hitler, the priority was to keep his eastern flank safe. The future would offer opportunities for redrawing Germany's borders there, even if Hitler was careful not to mention this in public.

On the contrary, in his speech to the Reichstag on the first anniversary of his coming to power, he touted the agreement with Poland as a new chapter in the history of the two peoples: "Germans and Poles will have to learn to live with the fact of their mutual existence. It is therefore more effective to shape a situation, which the previous thousand years could not eradicate and the years after us will not be able to either, in such a way that both nations can derive the greatest possible benefit from it."[54]

The pact chiselled away at France's security concept of a cordon sanitaire in eastern Europe. It also "resolutely reversed the ABCs of Germany's eastern European policy," as the historian Klaus Hildebrand put it. "Instead of pursuing, as it had previously, an anti-Polish policy together with the Soviet Union, Germany now pursued an anti-Soviet policy together with Poland."[55] The regime may have renewed the German–Soviet Neutrality and Non-aggression Pact of April 1926 on 5 May 1933, but Hitler also made it clear that closer ties to Poland implied distancing Germany from the Soviet Union. That meant that the ideological conflict with the wielders of power in Moscow would determine future German foreign policy. "The burdensome moments in our relations with Russia have always been greater than the fruitful ones," Hitler told his cabinet in late September 1933.[56] And in fact, German–Soviet relations markedly worsened throughout 1933 and 1934. The cooperation between the Reichswehr and the Red Army in the Weimar Republic was abruptly terminated and Soviet foreign policy now reorientated itself westwards, particularly towards France. In September 1934, the Soviet Union joined the League of Nations, after the United States had politically recognised the Communist government the preceding November.

One year after taking power, Hitler was now determining the direction and pace of German foreign policy. If the diplomats in the Foreign Ministry had reservations about the methods Hitler used, they still loyally served the new regime. "Our kind *must* support the new era," the ambitious young envoy Ernst von Weizsäcker said. "What would succeed it, were it to fail?" The "expertise" of career diplomats had to complement the "idealistic drive of the national revolution," Weizsäcker argued, in order to prevent unfortunate developments.[57] Yet although they so eagerly placed themselves at his disposal, Hitler thoroughly mistrusted the elites at the Foreign Ministry. He still felt the inferiority complex of an *arriviste* when confronted by experienced and usually very worldly civil servants. In Hitler's eyes, the career diplomats lacked agility, were plagued by doubts and stuck in their bureaucratic ways. For that reason, he began early on to promote a number of competing organisations that could pursue foreign policy independent of traditional diplomacy. One of them was the NSDAP Foreign Policy Office, which was founded on 1 April 1933 by Alfred Rosenberg, the chief Nazi ideologue and one of Hitler's main foreign-policy advisers. Others were the NSDAP Foreign Organisation under Ernst Wilhelm Bohle and Joachim von Ribbentrop's office, which as of 1934 functioned as Hitler's extended arm on foreign-policy matters.[58]

Although Hitler disliked reading diplomatic reports—studying documents was never his forte—his vast memory allowed him to get enough of a grasp of foreign policy to impress diplomats with his knowledge of details. After meeting the new man in charge of the Chancellery for the first time, Weizsäcker came away with a positive impression: "Hitler was very serious and introverted, without doubt far beyond all the others. Something like a metaphysical quality gives him his advantage."[59] French Ambassador André François-Poncet, whom Hitler first received in early April 1933, found the Führer "thoroughly polite, by no means self-conscious, but rather unconstrained, if somewhat reticent, almost cool." Hitler, François-Poncet wrote, expressed himself "clearly and decisively" and gave "the impression of being completely honourable."[60] Anthony Eden, the British government's expert on disarmament and later Britain's foreign secretary, was surprised when he first visited Berlin in February 1934 to find Hitler a charming conversational partner: measured, friendly, well prepared and open to counter-arguments. Hitler had "nothing Prussian" about him, Eden wrote, but was instead a "typical Austrian."[61] Hitler assured Eden that the German government did not have any "aggressive intentions." On the contrary, it was prepared to accept "every European combination that can be seen as a guarantee for the preservation of peace."[62]

But even in 1933 and 1934, there was reason to doubt Hitler's assurances. In Germany's relations with Austria, for example, the Nazi regime charted a course that was anything but conciliatory and moderate. The native Austrian Hitler had dreamed about creating a greater Germany ever since his years in Vienna, and on the very first page of *Mein Kampf* he had supported the return of German Austria "to the great motherland" since "the same blood . . . belongs in a joint empire."[63] After 30 January 1933, National Socialists in Austria sensed a change of fortunes. They began demanding that Austria be united with the Reich and received massive support from the German NSDAP. But their initiative was blocked when Austrian Chancellor Engelbert Dollfuss of the conservative Christian Social Party dissolved parliament in March 1933 and began creating an authoritarian, caste-based state that was soon described as "Austro-fascist." It insisted on its autonomy and looked to Fascist Italy and not Nazi Germany as a role model.

In early May 1933, in response to the increasingly subversive activities of Austrian Nazis, the Dollfuss regime prohibited them from wearing their brown uniforms in public. On 19 June, the party was officially banned. Hitler countered with what amounted to a ban on Germans travelling to Austria: any Germans wanting to visit their southern neighbour were required to pay a fee of 1,000 reichsmarks—a serious blow to Austrian tourism. "This measure is likely to lead to the collapse of the Dollfuss government and new elections," Hitler told his cabinet. "These new elections will bring Austria into line from within so that an external annexation will not be necessary."[64] He was wrong. The Austrian government reacted by introducing visa requirements for local border traffic, a move that primarily affected National Socialists commuting between the two countries. The Austrian chapter of the NSDAP led by National Inspector Theodor Habicht now went on the offensive and staged a number of attacks throughout the country.[65]

At this point Mussolini, who viewed German plans to incorporate Austria with great mistrust, offered protection for the Dollfuss regime. In a joint declaration on 17 February 1934, Italy, France and Britain pledged to ensure Austrian independence and territorial integrity. The following month, Italy, Austria and Hungary signed the "Rome Protocols," which mandated close, primarily economic, cooperation between the three countries. Nazi Germany's designs on its neighbour seemed to have been thwarted, and a gap had opened up between the Reich and Italy, Hitler's preferred ally.

Thus the first meeting between Hitler and Mussolini on 14 and 15 June 1934 in Venice—the first trip abroad by the new German head of state—took place under inauspicious circumstances. On Neurath's advice, the Führer wore civilian clothing, and he did not cut a good figure next to the uniformed Duce. Visibly uncomfortable and insecure, he looked "more like a subordinate than a partner," his photographer Heinrich Hoffmann recalled.[66] More than likely, Hitler's thoughts were distracted by the imminent domestic purge of Ernst Röhm and the SA. The two men held their political talks in private, after Mussolini, who knew some German, refused an interpreter, and they failed to reach agreement about the Austrian issue. Afterwards, Mussolini gave a less than flattering account of Hitler to his wife, calling the German chancellor a violent man incapable of self-control. "He is more mule-headed than intelligent," Mussolini said, "and nothing positive came from our discussion."[67]

Only six weeks after the Venice meeting, the situation came to a head when the Austrian National Socialists staged a putsch. On 25 July Viennese SS men forced their way into the Chancellery on Ballhausplatz, shot Dollfuss dead and took over the headquarters of the Austrian Broadcasting Service. But the attempted coup was ill-prepared, and the Austrian army was able to put it down, albeit at the cost of 200 casualties. Former Justice Minister Kurt von Schuschnigg formed a new government and had the putschists arrested.[68]

That day, Hitler was at the Wagner Festival in Bayreuth. There is no doubt that he not only knew of but had approved the attempted coup. On Sunday, 22 July, three days before the putsch, he had summoned Habicht, the Austrian SA leader Hermann Reschny and Franz Pfeffer von Salomon, the former head of the SA who had a post in the intermediary staff of the NSDAP in Berlin, to Bayreuth, where they discussed the details of the action. Prior to that, he had received Major General Walther von Reichenau, the head of the Wehrmacht office in the Reichswehr Ministry, which suggests that the German military was also in the know. Goebbels noted: "Sunday: with the Führer [are] Gen v. Reichenau, then Pfeffer, Habicht, Reschny. The Austrian question. Will it succeed? I'm very sceptical."[69]

On 25 July, a nervous jolt went through Hitler's immediate circle. Goebbels confided to his diary: "Alarm from Austria. Chancellery and the Broadcasting Service occupied. Much to do, major excitement, terrible waiting. I remain sceptical. Pfeffer utterly optimistic, as is Habicht. Wait and see!"[70] That evening, during a performance of *Rheingold* in the Bayreuth Festspielhaus, the first news arrived that the putsch had failed. "In turns, Schaub and Brückner ran between Hitler's box and the room in front of ours which had a telephone," Friedelind Wagner observed. "One received the news over the phone, while the other hastened to Hitler and whispered it in his ear." After the performance, Hitler accompanied the Wagners to the restaurant in the Festspielhaus, where he had some liver dumpling soup. "I have to hold out here for an hour and let people see me," he said. "Otherwise people will think I had something to do with this matter."[71] Indeed, Hitler and Goebbels had their hands full denying and concealing any connection with the putschists. Goebbels's diaries reveal the hectic atmosphere: "One report after another. Prop[aganda] Ministry working well. Foreign Ministry still asleep. German envoy recalled from Vienna. Committed a boundless stupidity. Got involved in domestic Austrian affairs. Border closed. Anyone crossing it will be arrested. No other choice."[72]

Around 2 a.m., Hitler woke up a completely uninitiated Papen in Berlin to inform him "in an extremely agitated voice" that he would have to go to Vienna as Germany's new envoy. The situation was "extraordinarily serious." In Papen's recollection, Hitler even referred to the Austrian situation as a "second Sarajevo." The vice-chancellor initially demurred, saying that after the events of 30 June he could hardly be expected to take over a new function within the government. Hitler plied him with pleas and flattery. Papen, he said, "was the only man who could bring this gnarled and dangerous situation back to normal." He could at least come to Bayreuth to discuss the issue face to face. Hitler would send his personal aeroplane to pick him up.[73]

It is possible that Papen overdramatised this early-morning telephone call in his memoirs, but he did arrive in Bayreuth early on 26 July and was immediately named special German envoy in Vienna. The previous envoy was recalled, and Theodor Habicht was summoned to Bayreuth to answer extremely angry accusations. Several days later the directorate of the Austrian NSDAP was dissolved. In Papen's estimation, Hitler was still in a state of hysteria on 26 July. He had good reason to be. After learning of Dollfuss's assassination, Mussolini had sent two army divisions to Italy's Austrian border near the Brenner Pass. This threatening gesture unleashed panic within the Führer's entourage. For a time, Goebbels even saw "the danger of an intervention by the major powers."[74]

Rightly, no one in Rome believed a word of the German government's declaration on 26 July that "no German office had any connection with these events."[75] The Italian press was full of angry attacks on the Reich, and Goebbels instructed German newspapers to fire back in kind. A war of words unfolded that would last for months. Mussolini expressed the anti-German mood on 6 September at the Fair of the Levant in Bari, declaring: "Thirty centuries of history allow us to look down with pity on certain theories beyond the Alps, put forth by the descendants of a people that at a time when Rome had Caesar, Virgil and Augustus did not even possess a written language with which to keep records of its existence."[76]

German–Italian relations had hit a low point. "It's all over with Italy," Goebbels complained on 30 July. "The same old disloyalty. The Führer has internally written [Italy] off . . . He has broken with Rome once and for all."[77] That same day, in a conversation with the chief of the general staff, Colonel General Ludwig Beck, State Secretary Bülow stated that no one in the world believed that Hitler had not been involved in the events of 25 July. The putsch, Bülow said, had been "staged with unbelievable carelessness," and Germany's foreign position was now "dismal." "Everything is at risk, in particular all our rearmament . . ." was Bülow's gloomy prediction. "All the major powers that matter are against us. France, which continues to represent a threat in the background, does not need to lift a finger to create a favourable situation for itself."[78]

For Hitler, the failed putsch and the international reaction to it was a major embarrassment and setback in his quest to fundamentally revise the post–First World War political order of Europe. The lesson he drew from it was that he had to be more careful on the issue of incorporating Austria into the Reich and wait for a more promising moment. He continued his strategy of numbing the vigilance of Europe's leading powers with assurances of his peaceful intentions while secretly pursuing his rearmament policies. "Keep our traps shut and keep rearming" was how Goebbels summarised his master's tactical restraint in the latter half of 1934. "We cannot provoke anyone right now. We have to be completely gentle and mild."[79] At a Reich governors' conference in early November, Hitler asserted that the foreign-policy situation had improved since the summer but remained somewhat precarious. "The Reich government has no interest in getting drawn into a war," he said. "If we are granted ten to twelve years of peace, the National Socialist reconstruction will be complete. Then war against Germany would represent a serious danger for any enemy."[80] The long-term goals of Hitler's foreign policy still went well beyond a mere revision of the Treaty of Versailles. He made this clear in a confidential talk with his propaganda minister on the evening of 26 July 1934, after he had calmed down from the agitation of the previous hours, and the tension had yielded to a kind of euphoria. "Hitler talked about the future," Goebbels recorded. "He wore the expression of a prophet. Germany as the master of the world. The mission of a century."[81]

With this remark, Goebbels unwittingly underlined one of the most bewildering contradictions of Hitler as a politician. As realistic as he was about the scope of his foreign policy in the first years of his regime, he increasingly ignored Bismarck's axiom that politics was the art of the possible. Germany's ambassador to Italy, Ulrich von Hassell, was always struck in his encounters with the Führer by the "puzzling proximity of clear-sighted, realistic thoughts and wild, confused constellations of ideas."[82] Following this logic, Hitler was both a realist and a fantasist, and this unusual combination made it equally difficult for admirers and adversaries to know what Hitler really thought.

A popular referendum in the Saar region in January 1935 gave Hitler the chance to erase the humiliation of July 1934. Under the Treaty of Versailles, the area had been placed under international administration for fifteen years, after which the populace was to decide whether it wanted to be part of Germany or France, or whether it wanted to remain under League of Nations control. Supporters and opponents of the "return home to the Reich" engaged in a bitter battle. Opponents, principally Social Democrats and Communists, campaigned under the slogan "Defeat Hitler in the Saar!" Meanwhile proponents also formed a unified block called the German Front, which consisted of the NSDAP and the remnants of the bourgeois parties.[83] They based their campaign on the appeal of nationalism—as well as the fact that economic recovery in Germany was progressing noticeably while France was only just beginning to feel the effects of the Great Depression. A German Front victory was preordained, but the margin of that triumph was a surprise. On 13 January, 90.8 per cent of voters in the Saar region opted to be reunited with the German Reich, 8.8 per cent preferred to maintain the status quo and only 0.4 per cent wanted to join France. The numbers indicated that the vast majority of the left-wing camp had defected to the "Back Home to the Reich" cause—a huge disappointment for the Social Democratic leadership in exile.[84] Klaus Mann, who had placed great faith in the referendum, found the results extremely sobering: "This is our worst political defeat since January 1933. It proves that the slogans of the Left have no appeal . . . For the foreseeable future, all hope is dead."[85]

Nazi propaganda wasted no time in interpreting the election results as a personal triumph for the Führer. "90.5 per cent for Hitler—extremely moving," noted Goebbels. "Telephoned the Führer. He's beaming with joy . . . Gradually we're escaping the dilemma. Our first major foreign-policy triumph."[86] To his cabinet Hitler gushed about the patriotism of the people in the Saar, declaring: "We cannot even begin to appreciate the foreign-policy significance of this event."[87] On 1 March, the day on which the Saar region was officially returned to the Reich, Hitler struck the pose of the liberator on the square in front of Saarbrücken city hall and celebrated an "act of compensatory justice" that would "finally" improve relations with France. "Because we want peace," Hitler declared, "we must hope that the great neighbouring people are willing and prepared to look for peace with us. It must be possible for two great peoples to reach out to one another and jointly combat the miseries that threaten to swamp Europe."[88] The enthusiasm of Hitler's audience seems to have been genuine, not staged. As Goebbels recorded: "The people on the square below reeled as if in a frenzy. The cries of 'Heil' sounded like a prayer. A province has been reconquered."[89]

By that point, Hitler was already plotting his next move. "Plans are churning within him," Goebbels wrote on 22 January 1935 after a long conversation with the Führer. "He's now completely occupied with foreign policy. And armaments. These are still the main problems. We have to become a power. Everything else will sort itself out."[90] Since being named chancellor, Hitler had accelerated the expansion of the army, navy and air force. It was his absolute priority, and after quitting the Geneva disarmament conference in the autumn of 1933, he had accelerated the process. By 1935, Germany's illegal rearmament had reached a point where it could hardly be concealed. The question was how to announce it publicly and make it seem legitimate without completely alienating the Western powers.

In the London communiqué of 3 February, the governments of Britain and France condemned Germany's unilateral arms build-up but also expressed their wish to resume negotiations over an arms treaty. Among other things, they suggested concluding a "Locarno for the east" and an international convention banning aerial warfare. The Reich government gave an evasive answer on 15 February. In lieu of negotiations with both countries, Germany proposed a bilateral exchange of opinion with the British government and invited Foreign Secretary John Simon and now Lord Privy Seal Anthony Eden to Berlin for talks on 7 March.[91] On 4 March, three days before the scheduled meeting, the British government published a White Paper announcing a 50 per cent increase in funding for the Royal Air Force within five years as a reaction to Germany's covert rearmament. The step outraged Berlin, and Hitler rescinded his invitation to the British politicians, although he did use the excuse of having lost his voice. Goebbels noted: "London has published a vile White Paper about German armaments as an excuse for a British arms build-up. As a result, the Führer went hoarse and cancelled the English visit."[92]

On 10 March, Göring gave an interview to George Ward Price in which he admitted for the first time the existence of a German air force. "The main thrust of our activities," he announced, "was not to create an offensive weapon capable of threatening other peoples but to set up a military aviation division strong enough to repel attacks on Germany at any time." At the same time he boasted to a Royal Air Force attaché that Germany already had 1,500 warplanes: in reality, the Luftwaffe had slightly over 800 aircraft in the spring of 1935.[93] A few days later, on 15 March, the French government presented parliament with a draft law to extend compulsory military service to two years. With that, Hitler had a welcome excuse to reintroduce compulsory military service in Germany, something he had decided upon on the Obersalzberg. He informed the ambassadors of France, Britain, Italy and Poland of this measure on the afternoon of 16 March. "His voice betrayed no signs of hoarseness," recalled François-Poncet. "He was very sure of himself and collected, earnest, pervaded by the solemnity of the hour."[94]

Initially, the government and the Reichswehr had no clear idea about the desirable future strength of the German armed forces. In a memorandum of 6 March 1935, Ludwig Beck, as head of the Army Office, had set the strength of Germany's peacetime army at twenty-three divisions, which was to be increased to thirty-six divisions within three to four years. The chief of army command, Werner von Fritsch, on the other hand, pleaded for a quicker expansion of the army.[95] On 13 March, Hitler summoned his Wehrmacht adjutant, Colonel Friedrich Hossbach, to Munich and confided in him that in the days to come he would "announce the reintroduction of compulsory military service and legally set the future parameters of the army." In response to a question by Hitler, Hossbach specified thirty-six divisions as "the ideal final future organisation of the army as desired by the army command." This meant that Germany would maintain a peacetime army of 550,000 men, five and a half times larger than the size of the Reichswehr as set out in the Treaty of Versailles. Hitler immediately adopted the figure without consulting either War Minister von Blomberg or Foreign Secretary von Neurath. Blomberg was horrified when he was informed of Hitler's decision on 15 March. He was afraid that the western European powers would not accept a unilateral abrogation of military agreements in the Treaty of Versailles, and especially not such a gigantic increase in the size of the German forces. He expressed his concerns "frankly and passionately" at a conference of the most important ministers that evening.[96]

But Hitler would not be swayed. Through the night, he himself composed a proclamation entitled "To the German people!" that would be issued on Saturday, 16 March. It stated, contrary to fact, that Germany had faithfully fulfilled its disarmament responsibilities while the victorious powers had continued to stockpile arms and boycotted all attempts to negotiate an international arms-limitation treaty. Hitler wrote: "Under these circumstances, the German government sees itself compelled to take the measures necessary to end the unworthy and dangerous, defenceless state of a great people and Reich." The Law for the Build-Up of the Wehrmacht announced both the reintroduction of compulsory military service and the expansion of the army to include thirty-six divisions.[97]

Blomberg, who had tried in vain that morning to get Hitler to abandon the idea of thirty-six divisions,[98] had given up his opposition in the meantime. At the cabinet meeting in the early afternoon of 16 March, Hitler's ministers were of one mind. "The Führer laid out the situation," Goebbels noted. "Extreme solemnity. Then he read out the proclamation together with the law. Everyone was profoundly moved. Blomberg stood up and thanked the Führer. For the first time, there was the salute of 'Heil' in this room. Versailles has been erased by a law. A historic hour . . . We are once again a major power."[99]

Hitler's weekend coup caused little worry among the German people. On the contrary, Germans were generally enthusiastic. "In Berlin, people fought over the special editions of the newspapers," François-Poncet observed. "Groups formed. People cried 'Bravo! Finally!' The masses assembled in front of the Chancellery and showered Hitler with ovations!"[100] In bourgeois nationalist circles, 16 March 1935 represented the day, as Luise Solmitz wrote in her diary, "that we have longed for since the disgrace of 1918." She added: "We would never have experienced Versailles if such actions had always been taken, such answers always given."[101] Hitler gained in stature even among the working classes. "All of Munich was on its feet," an observer for the Social Democratic leadership in exile reported. "You can force a people to sing, but you cannot force a people to sing with such enthusiasm . . . [Hitler has] picked up extraordinary ground among the people and is loved by many."[102] On 17 March, the traditional day for mourning the war dead, which had been renamed the "Heroes' Memorial Day," the regime celebrated its open violation of the Treaty of Versailles with an official act of state in Berlin's main opera house. With the last living Wilhelmine field marshal, August von Mackensen, at his side, and the current military leadership in tow, Hitler marched down Unter den Linden boulevard to the royal residence, where he inspected a military parade.[103]

The big question was how the Western powers would respond to Hitler's provocation. Detractors argued that if Hitler were not opposed energetically enough, he would think that "he could get away with anything and dictate the laws of Europe." François-Poncet wrote that he had "already been appeased far too much."[104] But Hitler's immediate circle felt that the risks were calculable. "A daring gambit," Goebbels admitted but then added: "You have to create a fait accompli. The others won't declare war. If they complain, we should stuff cotton in our ears."[105] By 18 March, Goebbels believed the critical time was over: "We're all very happy. The Führer can be proud. The worst has been overcome." William L. Shirer, the American foreign correspondent in Berlin, concurred that "Hitler had got away with it."[106] And in fact, Britain, France and Italy did nothing more than issue some half-hearted protests. The three nations met for a conference in the town of Stresa on Lake Maggiore from 11 to 14 April, at which they condemned the

German Reich's "unilateral abrogation of treaties" and guaranteed the European status quo. Mussolini issued a threat: "All bridges with Germany have been burned. If the country wants to work towards peace in Europe all the better. If not, we will smash it since we have now put ourselves completely on the side of the Western powers."[107] But these strong words notwithstanding, the "Stresa Front" showed cracks right from the start. The three countries did not agree on any concrete steps to be taken if Hitler continued to violate agreements, and they were far from willing to intervene militarily. Thus a relieved Goebbels wrote in his diary: "Communiqué Stresa. The same old song. Condemnation of German violation of treaties. That need not interest us as long as they do not attack. Anyway, keep on rearming."[108]

If truth be told, Britain had already abandoned the mutual defensive front. In a note of protest on 18 March, the British government had also asked, to astonishment in Berlin, whether Simon and Eden's visit might not be rescheduled for a later date. The Nazi regime happily took the hint, and on 25 March, only nine days after Germany's crass violation of the Treaty of Versailles, the two British politicians arrived in the German capital. Paul Schmidt served for the first time as an interpreter for Hitler, and his memoirs contain a highly revealing account of the course of the talks and the behaviour of the German chancellor.

Hitler received his visitors with ostentatious cordiality and was visibly at pains to create a relaxed atmosphere. Schmidt was astonished how different Hitler was in his role as a diplomatic negotiator from the image of the "raging demagogue" he presented at many of his public appearances. "He expressed himself clearly and articulately, seemed very confident of his arguments and was easy to understand and translate into English," Schmidt wrote.

> He seemed to know exactly what he wanted to say. He had an empty notepad on the desk in front of him during the entire negotiations, but he never used it. Nor did he have any notes with him. When he paused to search for the right way to phrase something, and I did not have to take notes, I had the chance to observe him closely. He had clear, blue eyes that he fixed penetratingly on whomever he was talking to . . . His face was lively when he began speaking of this or that important point. His nostrils quivered slightly with agitation when he described

the danger Bolshevism represented for Europe. He underscored his words with sudden, energetic motion of his right hand. Occasionally, he clenched his hand in a fist . . . That morning and during the entire negotiations with the Englishmen, I found him to be a man who represented his standpoint skilfully, intelligently and in keeping with the etiquette I was accustomed to in political talks. It was as if he had done nothing other than conduct such negotiations for years.

The only aspect of Hitler's behaviour that struck Schmidt as odd was the length at which he spoke. Hitler could not suppress his tendency to hold monologues, and the first morning session was taken up by him repeatedly invoking the supposed threat represented by Bolshevik Russia. When Eden asked about the basis of his fears, Hitler answered with the evasive remark that he had begun his political career "in the moment that the Bolsheviks had struck out for the first time against Germany." In the afternoon, the talks were more substantive. The British diplomats suggested the creation of an "eastern treaty" that would include Poland, the Soviet Union, Czechoslovakia, Finland, Estonia, Latvia and Lithuania as well as Germany. The mention of Lithuania brought a change over Hitler. "Suddenly he seemed to become someone else," Schmidt recalled.

In the time to come I often experienced him becoming unforeseeably emotional. His anger came with almost no warning. His voice got hoarse, and he started rolling his R's and clenching his fists, while his eyes flashed thunderbolts. "Under no circumstances will we reach agreement with a state that tramples on the German minority in the Memel region," he declared. Then as suddenly as this storm had arisen, it disappeared. From one second to the next, Hitler was once more the calm, polite negotiator he had been before the Lithuania intermezzo.

Schmidt's account is impressive evidence of how skilfully Hitler employed his talent as an actor in diplomatic negotiations. He could slip from one role to the next as if pressing a button.

Hitler made it clear to his British visitors that he preferred bilateral treaties to any collective agreements. For this reason, he was reluctant to accept their suggestion of creating a "Danube pact" that would preclude incorporating Austria into the Reich. He did not rule out

Germany returning to the League of Nations, but he insisted on the condition that Germany be given back all of its former colonies—a demand Simon and Eden could not accept. That evening, Foreign Secretary von Neurath, who had been a silent listener at the talks, hosted a dinner in the Reich president's palace in honour of the British diplomats. In attendance were Hitler, all of his ministers, many of their deputies and other high-ranking Nazi Party figures.

The second day of talks focused on the question of armaments. In response to the British protests against Germany's unilateral abrogation of the Treaty of Versailles, Hitler answered with a reference to the Battle of Waterloo in 1815. "When Blücher arrived to bring help," Hitler asked, "did Wellington first contact the Foreign Ministry to check whether Prussian troop strengths were in accordance with the applicable treaties?" This was an extremely dubious historical analogy, but it seems to have left Simon and Eden speechless. When asked about the German air force, Hitler responded after a bit of hesitation: "We have already reached parity with Great Britain." As Schmidt recalled, "I thought I could read dismayed surprise and scepticism about the accuracy of Hitler's statements in the faces of the British diplomats."

Towards the end of the talks, Hitler broached the idea of a German–British naval agreement, suggesting that he would be willing to limit German naval strength to 35 per cent of Britain's. The British diplomats did not respond to this idea, but neither did they reject it. Their unchanging friendly and relaxed demeanour had Schmidt asking himself whether Hitler's method of presenting his discussion partners with faits accomplis did not in fact get more done than the usual Foreign Ministry method of conducting negotiations. The British visit culminated with dinner in the Chancellery on the evening of 26 March. "Hitler occasionally seemed shy without being awkward," Schmidt recalled. "Whereas he had appeared during the day for the negotiations in a brown uniform with a red swastika armband on his left sleeve, he now wore a tuxedo, an outfit that seemed to rebel against him."[109] Although the parvenu had grown noticeably more self-confident, he still seemed hesitant in polite society.

The visit yielded no concrete results, but Hitler was satisfied. "He's in very good spirits," noted Goebbels on 27 March. "The Englishmen's visit has steeled his resolve even more."[110] Still, in the coming weeks, the Nazi leadership was not entirely convinced it was out of the danger zone. In early April, Goebbels found Hitler very earnest and pensive. "Foreign policy is torturing him," the propaganda minister noted. On 5 April, after a long talk with Hitler on a stroll around the Chancellery garden, Goebbels wrote:

> He does not think it will come to war. If it did, it would be horrible. We have no raw materials. Doing everything to escape this crisis. Stockpiling a great amount of arms. We have no choice but to hold our nerve . . . The Führer says we must all hope we're not attacked. Mussolini might do something rash. So take care and do not let anything provoke us.[111]

By late April, as it became clear that the threats from Stresa were empty, the mood changed. "Everything's brightening up," Goebbels noted on 5 May. "The Führer will prevail. The seeds he's sown will bear fruit in their own good time."[112]

Hitler had already decided to hold a second major "peace speech" on German foreign policy, which he worked on intensely until mid-May. He repeatedly went over the details with Goebbels and was convinced that it would be "a great success all around."[113] On the evening of 21 May, Hitler appeared before the Reichstag in top form. His speech was continually interrupted by frenetic applause from the more than 600 Nazi deputies. "A superb speaker," concluded William Shirer, who listened to it from the gallery with other foreign diplomats and journalists.[114] Hitler made a good impression when he declared: "National Socialist Germany wants peace from its deepest ideological convictions." He assured his listeners that he had no intention of "annexing or incorporating Austria," that with the status of the Saar region now determined Germany would present France with no more territorial demands, and that he would fulfil the promises made in the Locarno agreements as long "as the other parties to the pact abide by it." Furthermore, Hitler expressed his fundamental willingness to participate in a "system of collective cooperation to ensure peace in Europe" and to conclude non-aggression treaties with Germany's neighbours as he had already with Poland. In conclusion, he repeated the suggestion he had made to Simon and Eden of a bilateral agreement limiting Germany's naval strength: "The German government

has the honest intention to do everything it can to create and maintain a relationship with the British people and state that will for ever
prevent a repetition of the only conflict in history between our two
nations."[115]

The historian Klaus Hildebrand has called Hitler's address of 21 May
1935 "an especially infamous lesson in deception and lying,"[116] and
indeed no other single speech did more to pull the wool over people's
eyes inside and outside Germany concerning Hitler's real intentions.
Nazi reports about the public mood concluded unanimously that the
speech had met with an enthusiastic echo throughout the people.[117]
Even a committed Hitler adversary like Harry Kessler, who read the
transcript of the speech while in Palma de Mallorca, was positively
impressed for the first time by the Nazi leader: "You can think what
you want of him," he wrote, "but this speech is a great achievement
by a statesman. It is perhaps the greatest and most important speech
any German statesman has made since Bismarck."[118]

Nor did the speech fail to have the desired effect in London, as the
British government declared itself willing to start talks over the naval
agreement. On 1 June, Hitler named Joachim von Ribbentrop special
ambassador to Britain and put him in charge of negotiations. The reason
for the appointment was not just his experience abroad. Ribbentrop
behaved with an almost canine subservience to Hitler and was willing
to do anything to ingratiate himself to his idol. As the German ambassador to Italy, Ulrich von Hassell, described him: "With a worshipful
expression, he hung on Hitler's lips, constantly saying 'mein Führer'
and transparently parroting back everything Hitler said, which the latter
seemed not to notice."[119] Goebbels, perennially jealous of all rivals for
Hitler's favour, also made no secret of his antipathy for Ribbentrop: "A
vain blabbermouth. I cannot understand what Hitler sees in him."[120]

Negotiations commenced on 4 June, and immediately Ribbentrop
almost caused a diplomatic incident by categorically insisting that
the other side accept Germany's building up its navy to 35 per cent
of the British strength. "If the British government does not immediately accept this condition," he declared, "it makes no sense to continue
these negotiations." The visibly irritated British foreign secretary had
to remind his German colleague that issuing such an ultimatum
violated all diplomatic conventions and left the room with a "frosty"
goodbye. Nonetheless, the British did not break off the talks. After a

few days of mulling over the proposition, they accepted Ribbentrop's condition as the basis for further talks, which took place not in the Foreign Office, but in the historic boardroom of the British Admiralty.[121] The Anglo-German Naval Agreement was signed on 18 June. Hitler, who received word from Ribbentrop by telephone, called it the happiest day of his life.[122] In his eyes, Ribbentrop had passed his first test, which qualified him for high-level tasks within the foreign service. With the naval agreement, Hitler believed he had achieved one of the goals he had formulated all the way back in the 1920s: an alliance with Britain on the basis of a global political understanding. In Hitler's mind the agreement meant that the German Reich now had a free hand to pursue its hegemonic ambitions on the Continent, in return for acknowledging British supremacy at sea. "Huge success for the Führer's policy," Goebbels commented after the agreement was signed. "The first step towards good relations with England—the end result has to be an alliance. In five years, the time will have come."[123]

But the idea of allying itself with Nazi Germany was far from the minds of the British government. London's main priority was to avoid a ruinous naval arms race of the sort it had pursued with the Wilhelmine Empire before 1914. Britain saw the naval agreement not as a prelimi-nary stage to an alliance but as a step towards tying the Third Reich into a system of collective European security. But it came at a huge cost, since the agreement destroyed the already-fragile Stresa Front. Hitler had succeeded in overcoming Germany's international isolation, and he was determined to exploit this new situation. On 18 August 1935, he summarised his foreign-policy plans to a group of confidants:

An eternal alliance with England. A good relationship with Poland. Colonies within a limited scope. Eastward expansion. The Baltic states belong to us. Dominate the Baltic Sea. Approaching conflicts: Italy–Abyssinia–England and Japan–Russia. Probably in several years. Then our great historic hour will come. We must be ready. Grand prospects.[124]

Hitler's summary was prompted by Italy's looming war against Abyssinia. Mussolini had long been covetously eyeing the northern African empire, ruled by Haile Selassi I, which had joined the League of Nations in 1927. Conquering Abyssinia was a way of revenging Italy's defeat by the Ethiopians at Adua in 1896. It was also part of a larger imperial project intended to make Italy a major colonial power comparable to Britain and France. Essentially, Mussolini was aiming at a kind of latter-day Roman Empire. In January 1935, Il Duce confronted French Foreign Minister Pierre Laval, demanding Italy be given a free hand in Abyssinia. He received what amounted to a green light for a military occupation. London, by contrast, repeatedly warned Mussolini that war against a League of Nations member would have consequences. But Britain did nothing to hinder the transport of Italian troops across the Mediterranean.[125] On 3 October, they attacked Abyssinia without an official declaration of war. The operation quickly turned into one of the most horrifying colonial wars of recent history. The Italian air force attacked the civilian population, using shrapnel, incendiary and poison-gas bombs.[126] On 7 October, the League of Nations condemned Italy and imposed economic sanctions but took no military action.

Hitler immediately realised that Mussolini's war in Africa was a chance to drive a wedge between Italy and the Western powers and dissolve the Stresa Front once and for all. Officially, Germany remained neutral in the conflict, but secretly Berlin played both sides off against each other. That summer, Hitler agreed to Selassi's request for weapons.[127] At the same time, he helped Mussolini get around the League of Nations sanctions by exporting militarily relevant raw materials and products to Italy. The idea was to "let the war in Abyssinia sink its teeth in"[128] and to force Mussolini into a corner that might encourage him to change his foreign policy. "Europe is in motion again," Goebbels noted in mid-October. "If we're clever, we'll be the winners."[129]

In May, Mussolini had already communicated a clear message to Berlin: "The stance of the European powers towards us in the Abyssinian question will determine Italy's friendship or enmity."[130] Berlin interpreted this as an overture and closely monitored the situation. "Mussolini seems to have entangled himself in Abyssinia," Goebbels remarked. "He cordially received Hassell. He's seeking our friendship again."[131] That July, the Italian ambassador, Vittorio Cerruti, a critic of Hitler, was recalled and replaced by the Germanophile Bernardo Attolico.[132] The longer the war went on, the more Mussolini distanced himself from the Western powers and the more he protested his fondness of Hitler. "I was his friend even before he came to power," Mussolini claimed.[133] At the same time, Berlin began to take Italy's side more and more openly. On 5 December 1935, after lunching with Hitler at the Chancellery, Goebbels noted: "Conversation about Abyssinia/ Italy. Sympathies increasingly with Mussolini."[134]

In January 1936, Mussolini made the decisive advance. In conversation with Ulrich von Hassell he suggested "fundamentally improving German–Italian relations and settling the one quarrel, the Austrian issue." Austria had to remain nominally independent, the Italian leader insisted, but it could become a "virtual satellite of Germany." Mussolini also declared that the Stresa Front was "dead once and for all," which meant that Italy would not act in solidarity with France and Britain in case of future German treaty violations and would not take part in any sanctions against Nazi Germany.[135] These assurances were a direct encouragement for Hitler to prepare his next foreign-policy coup: the remilitarisation of the left bank of the Rhine River, which was forbidden by the treaties of Versailles and Locarno.

Hitler had long been toying with the idea of a surprise operation. On 20 January 1936, he informed his entourage over lunch at the Chancellery of his determination "to go after a sudden solution to the question of the [demilitarised] Rhineland zone," although not at the moment "so as not to give the others the opportunity to get out of the Abyssinian conflict."[136] Only one month later, however, Hitler seems to have made up his mind. He told Hassell, whom he received in his private Munich apartment on 14 February, of his conviction that "the right moment psychologically" had come for remilitarising the Rhineland. Originally he had planned to launch the operation in early 1937, but the propitious circumstances demanded immediate action. The Soviet Union, he said, "was only concerned with maintaining calm on its western border, England was in bad shape militarily and seriously burdened with other problems, and France was domestically divided." Hitler predicted that "no military action would be forthcoming after such a step by Germany— at the most there would economic sanctions, and these had become unpopular among the vassals of the great powers, who often served as punching bags."[137] Hassell came away with the impression that Hitler was "more than 50 per cent decided." But as he confided to his diary, the ambassador highly doubted "that it was worth the risk to bring forward an event which would probably happen in one or two years anyway."[138]

Hassell shared his doubts not only with Konstantin von Neurath, but several German military leaders. The army command had long regarded the remilitarisation of the Rhineland as necessary, but, as Werner von Fritsch told Hitler on 12 February, it should be done "without running any risk that the issue would lead to war."[139] In a further conference with Hassell, Neurath and Ribbentrop at midday on 19 February in the Chancellery, Hitler emphasised that in the long term "passivity could not be a policy" and that going on the offensive "was here, too, the better strategy." Ribbentrop hastened to agree, while Hassell and Neurath were apparently very cautious about expressing their doubts. Hitler also explained why he thought he had to hurry. On 11 February, the French government had passed on a mutual defence treaty agreed with the Soviet Union the previous year to the French parliament for ratification. The treaty, which was also controversial in France, offered the perfect pretext for the planned operation. "We should use the pact with the Russians as an excuse," Hassell summarised Hitler's argument. In order to deny the other side the chance to "brand our operation as an attack," he wanted to combine the remilitarisation of the Rhineland with a seemingly broad package of offers, including the establishment of a demilitarised zone on both sides of the Rhine, a guarantee of the territorial integrity of the Netherlands and Belgium, a three-powers aerial warfare treaty and a Franco-German non-aggression pact.[140]

Hitler's desire to proceed with the remilitarisation was also motivated by domestic issues. According to Security Service reports, the public mood had been worsening since the autumn of 1935. Parts of the populace were unhappy about Nazi attacks on the Churches and especially with the one-sided prioritisation of the arms build-up at the expense of private consumers. Food imports were cut in favour of raw materials imports, which was leading to shortages. Hitler needed a spectacular foreign-policy success to distract attention from these domestic shortcomings. "He senses a decline in popular approval of the regime," Neurath speculated in conversation with Hassell, "and is seeking a national cause to fire up the masses again, to stage the usual elections with a popular referendum, or one of the two, and then we get them on side again."[141]

But as always when faced with major decisions, Hitler hesitated to take the final plunge. "He's still brooding," Goebbels noted on 21 February. "Should he remilitarise the Rhineland? Difficult question . . . The Führer is about to forge ahead. He thinks and ponders, and then suddenly he acts."[142] On 28 February, the day after the lower chamber of the French parliament ratified the treaty with the Soviet Union, Hitler still appeared "undecided." During an overnight train journey to Munich on 28–29 February, Goebbels advised him to wait at least until the upper house of the French parliament had approved the deal. "Then we should grab the bull by the horns," Goebbels wrote. "A difficult and decisive choice faces us."[143]

Hitler finally made up his mind for good on 1 March. That noon, he visited Goebbels in his Munich hotel and once again ran through his reasoning. "He's now completely determined," Goebbels noted. "His face projected calm and resolve. Once again a critical moment has come that calls for action. The world belongs to the bold! He who dares nothing, gains nothing."[144]

Hitler informed the Wehrmacht leadership about his decision the following day. As in March 1935, the operation was scheduled for a weekend. On Saturday 7 March, the Reichstag was to be convened for a meeting at which Hitler would announce the remilitarisation. Then the Reichstag would be dissolved, and fresh elections called for 29 March. Preparations were to be kept top secret to ensure the operation was a surprise. In order not to raise suspicions, Reichstag deputies would be summoned to Berlin for a "social evening." Troop deployments were to be disguised by marches of the SA and the German Labour Front. "Everything must proceed with lightning speed," Goebbels wrote.[145]

On 4 March, as Hitler began dictating his address to the Reichstag, voices of warning issued from the Foreign Ministry—much to Goebbels's irritation. "From all sides, scaredy-cats are appearing disguised as cautioners," the propaganda minister noted. "Especially in the Foreign Ministry they exist in large clumps. They are incapable of any sort of bold decision."[146] In any case, once Hitler had made up his mind there was no changing it. On the evening of 6 March, he informed his cabinet about the operation for the first time. The Franco–Soviet mutual defence pact, he told his ministers, represented "an obvious violation of the Treaty of Locarno," and he had therefore decided "to occupy the demilitarised zone on the Rhine once more with German troops." Hitler added: "All preparations for this have been made. The German troops are already on the march."[147] "Everyone was initially shocked," Goebbels noted. "But there's no turning back."[148]

The following morning, German troops moved into the Rhineland to the cheers of residents of the region. At 10 a.m., Neurath sent the diplomatic representatives of France, Britain, Italy and Belgium a memorandum announcing the abrogation of the Treaty of Locarno after the Franco–Soviet mutual defence pact and calling for negoti- ations to create a demilitarised zone on both sides of Germany's western border, a twenty-five-year non-aggression pact between Germany and France and Belgium, and a treaty concerning aerial warfare. The German government also signalled its willingness to rejoin the League of Nations. In his memoirs, François-Poncet insight- fully characterised Hitler's *modus operandi* as "hitting his opponent in the face while at the same time saying 'What I suggest is peace.'"[149]

There was a feverish atmosphere in the Reichstag as Hitler approached the microphone around 12 a.m. William Shirer noticed that Reichswehr Minister von Blomberg looked pale as a ghost and kept nervously drumming his fingers on the armrest of his chair.[150] The only order of business on the agenda was the "receipt of a decla- ration by the Reich government." Hitler began with a series of digres- sive tirades about the unfairness of the Treaty of Versailles and its allegedly crass denial of equal status to Germany. Only towards the end of the speech did he raise his actual point. By concluding a mutual defence treaty with the Soviets, France had violated the spirit of the Treaty of Locarno so that Germany no longer felt bound by the agreement. He read out the memorandum that Neurath had sent to the ambassadors of signatory states and declared to frenetic applause: "In the interest of the most basic right of a people to secure its borders and maintain its ability to defend itself, the government of the German Reich has today restored its full and unlimited sovereignty in the demilitarised zone of the Rhineland."[151]

More than 20,000 troops had crossed the Rhine, but only 3,000 penetrated further inland. They were under strict orders to retreat if attacked by French troops. But the French general staff was hesitant to launch such an attack, believing that their troops were no match for the Wehrmacht. In reality, a single French division would have sufficed to thwart Hitler's gambit. The Führer was well aware of the risk he was taking and anxiously awaited the first responses to the operation. According to Schmidt and other sources, Hitler later described the forty-eight hours after German troops reoccupied the

Rhineland as the tensest period of his life. "If the French had invaded the Rhineland," Hitler said, "we would have had to retreat in humiliation and shame since the military forces at our disposal would not at all have been equal to even moderate resistance."[152]

From his exile in Küstnacht, Switzerland, Thomas Mann offered "fervent prayers" to heaven that someone "finally teach this monster a lesson that will finally dampen the foreign-policy impertinence of his worshippers."[153] But Hitler was once again successful with his tactic of simultaneously appearing conciliatory and presenting adversaries with faits accomplis. It was already clear by the evening of 7 March that protests would once more be the only response of the Western powers. "France wants to summon the League of Nations council— let it," Goebbels crowed. "It's not going to do anything. That's the main thing. Everything else does not matter . . . We're all swimming in glee. What a day! . . . The Führer is beaming . . . We've regained sovereignty over our own country."[154] The next day, the regime celebrated Heroes' Memorial Day, as it had the previous year. Shirer noted that the faces of Hitler, Goebbels and Blomberg were "all smiles" as they took their place in the royal box at the State Opera House.[155]

On 19 March, the council of the League of Nations met in London to condemn the German treaty violation. But this was an empty gesture, particularly as Anthony Eden said in his speech to the council that Germany's illegal behaviour represented "no threat to peace" and did not call for a counterstrike since French security was not affected.[156] Goebbels commented laconically: "In London we were unanimously taken to task. That was expected. Decisive is what comes next."[157] Not much, was the answer, aside from some empty diplomatic talk that changed nothing. Once again Hitler had led the Western powers around by the nose without any repercussions. France and Britain's refusal to punish a flagrant breach of contract undermined international confidence in their willingness to defend Germany's smaller neighbours in case of aggression and meant a serious loss of face for the League of Nations.

In Germany the remilitarisation of the Rhineland had initially occasioned fears of a new military escalation. Yet as soon as people realised that the West again would do nothing but issue verbal protests, Germany was swept by a wave of national euphoria. Admiration for Hitler's daring was mixed with relief that the enterprise had had a happy ending. "Hitler succeeds at everything, people say," reported Social Democratic observers. "Not entirely buried hopes that the regime might be toppled from outside Germany have once more been deeply disappointed."[158] Wherever the Führer appeared during the "election campaign" in the second half of March, he was venerated by the masses. His most triumphant appearance was at the concluding rally in Cologne on 28 March. The official results of the "election" gave Hitler's party list 98.8 per cent of the vote. Even if the election was probably manipulated to some degree, this was an astonishing vote of confidence for Hitler and his foreign policy. "Triumph upon triumph," gloated Goebbels. "We did not dare hope for this in our wildest dreams. We were all stunned. The Führer was very still and said nothing. He only laid his hand on my shoulder. There were tears in his eyes."[159]

Hitler had taken a huge gamble and won. The diplomats and military leaders who had warned him about the risks looked like timorous naysayers, and Hitler's immediate circle now registered a change in the way the Führer appeared and behaved. More than ever before, Otto Dietrich recalled, Hitler considered himself infallible and began to perceive objections and doubts as attacks upon the "sovereignty of his will."[160] Martha Dodd, the daughter of the American ambassador in Berlin, also noticed the transformation. Whereas Hitler had previously seemed modest, even shy, on social occasions, he now behaved as if he were the creator of the world and mankind.[161] Hitler's increasing overestimation of himself went hand in hand with his growing impatience to achieve his foreign-policy goals. In 1934, he had assumed that Germany would need ten years of peace to arm the Reichswehr so it would be combat-ready. Now he set much shorter deadlines.[162] His coup in the Rhineland reinforced his tendency to go for broke. "Neither threats nor warnings will make me stray from my path," he had announced in Munich on 14 March. "With the certainty of a sleepwalker, I am travelling the road Providence has sent me down."[163] Hitler's popularity was so great by this point that the majority of Germans did not bat an eyelid at such hubris.

16

Cult and Community

"It is the miracle of our age that you found me . . . among so many millions," Hitler proclaimed at the Nuremberg Party Conference on 3 September 1936. "And that I found you is Germany's great fortune." With these words Hitler sought to suggest a mystical unity between himself as Führer and his followers. In a speech to NSDAP political directors two days earlier, he had already struck a pseudo-religious tone: "Once in the days of yore, you heard the voice of a man, and it touched your hearts, it awakened you, and you followed it . . . When we meet here, we are suffused with wonder at our coming together. Not all of you can see me, and I cannot see all of you. But I can feel you, and you can feel me."[1]

Such messianic rhetoric appealed to the desire of Hitler's followers who looked up to him as their supposed saviour with an unprecedented willingness to believe. Much of the evidence suggests that the dictator also saw himself as such and believed what he told his vassals. Hitler quickly forgot that he owed his rise to power not to some miracle but to a unique constellation of political crises, and that at the precise moment when his bid for power was about to fail he had been heaved into the Chancellery by a sinister plot.

The suggestion of unity of *Volk und Führer*—the people and its leader—had an effect on Hitler's detractors as well as his supporters. By March 1937, Victor Klemperer had given up any hope for change, confiding to his diary: "Hitler does indeed seem to be his people's chosen one. Gradually I have come to believe that his regime will last for decades."[2] On the other hand, there were some dissenting voices who warned contemporaries not to be blinded by spectacles staged by the regime. The "impossibility of free speech" and the fear of being informed upon, wrote one of the SPD in exile's informants, led "the average observer to overestimate the extent and above all the solidity of the government's support."³ So how much support did Hitler really enjoy? How great was the consensus between the government and the people? Is it correct to describe the first years of the Third Reich as one of those rare historical moments when, to quote the historian Hans-Ulrich Wehler, "the leader's rule and popular opinion were in complete agreement"?⁴

Even during his meteoric rise, Hitler had profited from his image as a charismatic leader ascribed to him by his true-believing apostles Hess and Goebbels. He promised to overcome the very crisis that had borne him aloft, to restore domestic order after years of latent civil war, to establish an ethnic-popular community (*Volksgemeinschaft*) beyond political quarrels and class conflicts, and to lead Germany to a new era of national greatness. Hitler became a beacon of hope to millions of people disappointed by the Weimar Republic and embittered by the "dictates" of the Treaty of Versailles. Hitler knew that he would lose the aura of a saviour if he disappointed the expectations people had of him. Thus he did everything he could to encourage the belief that the new cabinet, in contrast to its predecessors, was decisively tackling Germany's most pressing problems, above all mass unemployment. Under the slogan of "national renewal," a mood of optimism was created, and a social dynamic set in motion, which gave the impression that "under this government things are looking up for Germany."⁵

The first signs of economic recovery in the spring of 1933 seemed to confirm this impression. Hitler was credited for his tireless energy in the "labour battle," and bourgeois circles also appreciated the fact that, at the same time, he brutally suppressed the political Left. "The thoughts and feelings of most Germans are completely dominated by Hitler," remarked Luise Solmitz a few days before the Reichstag election of 5 March. "His fame is shooting to the stars. He is the saviour in an evil, sad, German world." When she asked an acquaintance who had previously rejected National Socialism which party she intended to vote for, the woman answered: "Hitler of course! . . . We now have to support his cause with all means at our disposal!"⁶ This semi-legitimate election, which yielded a major success, if not an absolute majority, further boosted Hitler's status. "A powerful national enthusiasm" was how Elisabeth Gebensleben described the mood in a letter to her daughter, adding: "There has hardly been an emperor who was celebrated as greatly as Hitler is loved, honoured and admired." After the announcement that made 1 May a national holiday, Gebensleben asked herself how Hitler had succeeded in "welding together a people that was divided and miserable." Only a few days later, she enthused: "What people can boast of a man even vaguely comparable to him?"[7] In November 1933, the Swiss envoy in Berlin, Paul Dinichert, concluded: "Unlimited trust in the Führer has undoubtedly spread to broad segments of the people in the preceding few months. Everywhere, in all strata of the populace, you meet people who are completely subordinate and look up to him with the most profound admiration."[8]

No one could have foreseen how widespread the cultish worship of Hitler would become after only six months of his regime. Cities and communities made him an honorary citizen,[9] and streets and squares were named after him. In April 1933, Hamburg's Rathausplatz was rechristened Adolf Hitler Square. The intent was to symbolically commandeer public space and erase representatives of democratic traditions from Germany's collective memory.[10] Whole postal sacks full of fan mail arrived every day at the Chancellery, and Hitler's private office, which was directed by Martin Bormann's brother Albert, had to take on four additional employees. Ordinary people expressed their adulation of Hitler in countless poems. "O leader you, the tool / In God's hands to reverse our fate / Press boldly on / Behind you a cohesive front / Solidly one as if cast in ore / Man for man," wrote a Hitler admirer from the southern German town of Schöneich, who also thanked the "most honourable Reich chancellor" for the pleasure he derived from "studying your *Mein Kampf*."[11] The Chancellery was swamped by requests for Hitler to serve as godfather to newborn children. In November 1933, Hitler's chief assistant, Wilhelm Brückner, was forced to put a stop to it, writing to one applicant: "As much as the Führer welcomes the loyalty and affection expressed in such requests, he is incapable of satisfying all of them given their sheer number. He has therefore decided only to assume the role of godfather in very exceptional cases such as a family's seventh son or ninth child in total."[12]

The cultish worship of the Führer took on some fairly bizarre forms. The East Prussian village of Sutzken, for instance, requested permission to rename itself "Hitler Heights," and a Düsseldorf Nazi

Party member tried to name his daughter "Hitlerine." (The authorities suggested Adolfine as an alternative.) "Hitler oaks" were planted, "Hitler cakes" baked, and "Hitler roses" were bred. The Reich Association of Dog Owners applied for permission to mint a commemorative coin with the image of "our beloved Führer, who is himself a breeder and lover of pure-bred dogs." The senate of the Eberswalde Academy of Forestry awarded Hitler an honorary doctorate in recognition of his support "for the culture of our native soil, the promotion of the agricultural classes and the encouragement of timber cultivation and the timber industry"; Hitler refused to accept the honour as a matter of "principle."[13] A lively trade in Hitler busts developed, and the image of the Führer adorned beer steins, porcelain tiles, ashtrays, playing cards, fountain pens and other banal everyday objects. The selling of Hitler kitsch and devotional trifles grew so quickly that as early as April 1933 the government announced it was taking measures to rein in the commercial exploitation of the Führer's likeness.[14]

Such excesses of cultish worship, as laughable as they may appear today, were serious expressions of the intense, erotically charged connection between large segments of the German population and Hitler. The cultish worship of the Führer was by no means just the product of a clever campaign of manipulation. On the contrary, "ethnic comrades," male and female, fell over themselves to exalt Hitler, projecting all their hopes and desires onto the figure of the Führer and thereby divorcing their image of him even further from reality. The propagandistic staging of the Hitler myth and the eagerness of the masses to endorse and subjugate themselves to it encouraged one another.

Enthusiasm for Hitler reached an initial zenith on the occasion of his forty-fourth birthday on 20 April 1933. "In a unison of hearts scarcely imaginable a few weeks ago, the people declared its allegiance to Adolf Hitler as leader of the new Germany," wrote the *Münchener Neueste Nachrichten* newspaper. The countless messages of congratulation preserved in the files of the Führer's office suggest that the paper was not exaggerating. Goebbels captured the sentiment of the day in a congratulatory article in which he celebrated Hitler as "a man of very great stature" who exercised a "mysterious magic" over everyone who came in contact with him. Hitler, the propaganda minister claimed, had not changed through all the highs and lows of his career.

"The longer one knows him," Goebbels wrote, "the more one learns to appreciate and love him, and the more unreservedly one is prepared to devote oneself to his great cause."[15] Such encomia reflected a shift in public attitudes. Hitler was no longer the polarising leader of a political party, but a figure of integration who embodied national unity and a "people's chancellor" who stood above all quarrelling. Victor Klemperer, who carefully monitored the language used by the Third Reich, noted: "To be added next to *protective custody* in my lexicon is *people's chancellor*."[16]

Birthday gifts were piled high in the Great Hall of the Chancellery, where Bismarck had chaired the Berlin Congress of 1878, reminding Hitler's assistant Fritz Wiedemann of a "department store." "There was a bit of everything," Wiedemann recalled,

> from a valuable oil painting some industrialist had given him to a pair of woollen socks from some old lady . . . In total it was a collection of a few nice things and a whole lot of kitsch. But whether they were valuable or not, they were moving expressions of the admiration and love the broad masses of the people felt for this man.[17]

Popular Hitler worship was in evidence throughout the Third Reich. In cinemas, there would be cascades of applause whenever the weekly newsreels showed the Führer's image, as the Polish journalist Count Antoni Sobanski observed to his amazement in the spring of 1933.[18] Most people voluntarily adopted the "Heil Hitler" greeting, with increasing numbers meaning it sincerely, rather than simply going along with the crowd. In April 1933, Annemarie Köhler, the doctor from the town of Pirna to whom Klemperer entrusted his diary, wrote of how "fanatical" the staff at her hospital had become. "They sit around the radio," Köhler related. "When the 'Horst Wessel Song' is played . . . they all stand up and perform the raised-arm Nazi salute."[19] The salute became an inviolable custom in many National Socialist families. A letter to the "honorable Führer" from a family in Mannheim in March 1933 read: "Our little Rita would like to send her regards to the Führer with a Heil Hitler! For that reason, we have taken the liberty of enclosing a photo of her performing the German salute. She is ten months old and is the youngest of five. Whenever we show her a picture of Uncle Adolf, she immediately salutes."[20]

Images of Hitler hung not just in private dwellings and government offices. They were everywhere in the public sphere. During the popular referendums organised by the regime, there was no escaping Hitler's likeness. One SPD-in-exile observer wrote of the vote on 19 August 1934: "Hitler on all the billboards. Hitler in all the shop windows. Hitler indeed in every kind of window you can find. Every tram, every train, every car—Hitler looks out of every window."[21] Many Germans turned to the Chancellery to try to get a picture of their "beloved Führer" autographed. In August 1934, when Heinrich Himmler procured a picture with Hitler's personal dedication for his parents, the Himmler household in Munich was beside itself. Gebhard Himmler, Heinrich's father, reported: "Dear Mum was in ecstasy."[22]

The Obersalzberg became a destination for pilgrimages. Thousands of devotees made their way to Hitler's country retreat to try to get a glimpse of their hero. "The area around Wachenfeld house is constantly occupied by men and women admirers," the president of Upper Bavaria reported in August 1934. "Even on walks in isolated spots the Reich chancellor is pursued by a throng of intrusive admirers and inquisitive persons."[23] Wiedemann found that there was "something religious" about the processions of these pilgrims: "Silently they passed with an expression which made clear that this was one of the greatest moments of their lives."[24]

Wherever Hitler went in the first years of his rule, he was celebrated like a pop star. "Everywhere ovations for him . . . magnificent how the people are awakening!" Goebbels noted on 18 April 1933 after travelling with Hitler by car from Berchtesgaden to Munich.[25] Albert Speer's memoirs contain similar descriptions: "Two men from the military escort walked in front of the car, with three more on each side, as the car proceeded at a crawl through the pressing crowd. As I usually did, I sat right behind Hitler on the emergency seat, and I'll never forget the impact of the jubilations, the delirium that was expressed in so many of the faces."[26] There can be no doubt that such scenes of jubilation were not organised: they were spontaneous outbursts of quasi-religious faith in the man who was credited with the powers of a miracle healer.

An incident recorded by Fritz Wiedemann illustrates these pseudo-religious components of the admiration for Hitler. During a visit to Hamburg, the crowd forced its way through the military escort, and one man succeeded in grasping Hitler's hand. "He began dancing around as if mad and crying over and over, 'I touched his hand, I touched his hand,'" recalled Wiedemann. "If the man had declared that he had been lame and could now walk again, I would not have been surprised. The crowd would have definitely believed it."[27] William Shirer witnessed similar scenes of pseudo-religious ecstasy at the Nuremberg Party Conference in 1934, when Hitler appeared for a moment on the balcony of his hotel room above a thousand-strong crowd, consisting largely of women. "They reminded me of the crazed expressions I saw once in the back country of Louisiana on the faces of some Holy Rollers who were about to hit the trail," wrote Shirer. "They looked up at him as if he were a messiah, their faces transformed into something positively inhuman."[28]

There was no way such excessive and continual hero worship could fail to affect Hitler's self-image. "Only one German has ever been celebrated in this way—Luther!" he called out triumphantly to his entourage in the autumn of 1934, when his motorcade from Weimar to Nuremberg had trouble making its way through the masses of his admirers.[29] The dictator visibly enjoyed being the centre of such unusual public appreciation. The awkwardness he had displayed on public occasions at the start of his chancellorship evaporated, and he became increasingly confident, his sense of self-importance growing as he was borne on wave upon wave of approval. Before long, he was addicted to the thrill of popular admiration. It reinforced Hitler's belief that he had been chosen by Providence to carry out a historic mission.

Pro-Hitler euphoria was by no means restricted to middle-class circles. It also increasingly spread to the working classes. Key to this was the regime's success in fighting unemployment. Economic developments from 1933 were referred to as an economic miracle, and in fact the number of jobless in Germany declined far more quickly than in other industrialised nations at the time. By 1936, primarily thanks to accelerated rearmament, Germany had practically achieved full employment. The rapid economic recovery had been financed by massive deficit spending, the costs of which would only become apparent later.[30] But what mattered most to workers was that a feeling of social security had been restored after the traumatic years of the Depression. As an observer for the SPD in exile in Rhineland-Westphalia reported in March 1935: "Today, having been given jobs in the arms industry, people who were to the left of us and were even Communists, defend the system, saying, 'I don't care about the whys and wherefores. I've got work. That's something the others were never able to take care of.'"[31] Another such report from February 1936 quotes workers who used to be members of the SPD and of the Reich Banner: "You people always made socialist speeches, but the Nazis have given us jobs . . . I don't care whether I make grenades or build the autobahn. I just want to work. Why did you not take job creation seriously?"[32]

Hitler also increased his popularity among the working classes by taking nearly every opportunity to excoriate the lack of social respect for physical labour. "Honour labour and respect the worker!" he proclaimed at the main 1 May event in Berlin in 1933. Mental and physical labourers, he said, should never be pitted against one another: "That's why we will root out the conceit that causes some individuals to look down on their comrades who 'only' work with a lathe, a machine or a plough."[33] Hitler's message was that greater appreciation for physical labour would raise the social prestige of workers and break down stubborn social prejudices in society. Hitler's fondness for styling himself as a "labourer" was part of his campaign to court the working classes and win them over for his regime.

Observers from the SPD in exile had no choice but to acknowledge the success of this strategy. "Major segments of the working classes have lapsed into unquestioning deification of Hitler," one report from June/July 1934 noted ruefully. Workers were still "greatly obsessed with Hitlerism," a report from February 1935 read, and three months later another observer concluded that "those workers who were previously indifferent are today the most submissive followers of the system and the most fervent believers in the cult of Hitler."[34] These reports are all the more credible because they were made by opponents and not adherents of the regime. Thus it was not merely wishful thinking when Goebbels repeatedly noted in his diary that workers were the "most loyal" supporters of National Socialism.[35] The bloody purge of the SA in late June 1934 did nothing to diminish Hitler's popularity among the working classes. On the contrary, many workers approved of Hitler's "energetic" action. As one SPD report noted, "Hitler is a fellow who does nothing by half measures" was a widely held view.[36]

Nonetheless, the huge popularity Hitler enjoyed did not spill over to his party. With the sacrosanct Führer increasingly considered beyond banal everyday reality, criticism of aspects of the regime was concentrated on his subordinates. This mechanism became particularly apparent in the first half of 1934, a period when the public mood worsened. "Generally speaking, Adolf Hitler is exempt from criticism," an SPD report from Berlin concluded. "He is credited with having good intentions, and people do not think he can do anything about the corruption of his subordinates." The sentiment which one voter had scrawled upon an election ballot, "Yes to Adolf Hitler, but a thousandfold no to the brown bigwigs,"[37] was widespread. Hitler benefited from comparisons with many party functionaries who flaunted their newly won power and were easily corruptible. In contrast the Führer depicted himself as a "simple man of the people," someone with few personal needs who placed himself entirely at the service of the nation. "I am probably the only statesman in the world who does not have a bank account," he boasted in late March 1936 in a speech to the workers at the Krupp factory in Essen. "I have no stocks or shares in any company. I don't draw any dividends."[38] Very few people realised that the official image of Hitler's modest lifestyle had nothing to do with reality. Moreover, the mythology of the Führer served a compensatory function; it blunted dissatisfaction over the problems and shortcomings of the Third Reich by blaming them solely on Hitler's subordinates. If Hitler were aware of the problems, popular opinion ran, he would doubtless make sure they were alleviated.[39] "If only the Führer knew" already established itself as a figure of speech in the early years of the regime.[40]

Hitler was well aware of the growing gap between his own beatified status and the negative image of Nazi Party functionaries. In a speech to his political directors at the Nuremberg party rally in 1935, he lashed out at all those "who would distinguish between the Führer and his followers . . . who would say yes to the Führer but question the necessity of the party." Hitler told his audience: "For me, you are the political officers of the German nation and you are indivisible from me come what may."[41] But such assurances did nothing to change the fact that Hitler's popularity was far greater than the party's, and indeed to an extent came at the expense of the latter. Whereas the Führer received credit for all the regime's achievements, disgruntlement was aimed exclusively at the "little Hitlers," the Nazi Party's local leadership.

Hitler's reputation was based on Germany's unexpectedly rapid economic recovery and his spectacular foreign-policy triumphs. The Saar region referendum of January 1935 and the reintroduction of compulsory military service two months later generated enthusiasm far beyond National Socialist circles. "Hitler is a guy who does not take any guff, who has backbone and who does what he thinks is right and necessary," read one SPD-in-exile report.[42] Nazi propaganda gleefully seized and expanded upon such sentiments. On the occasion of his forty-sixth birthday in 1935, the Nazi press spokesman, Otto Dietrich, celebrated Hitler as the "most supreme leader," who had secured Germany's ability to defend itself with his "incomparable decisiveness." Goebbels added: "The entire people loves him, because it feels safe in his hands like a child in the arms of its mother . . . Just as we do, who are gathered close by him, so the last man in the farthest village says in this hour: 'What he was, he is, and what he is, he should remain: our Hitler.'"[43]

But in the autumn of 1935, discontent over shortages of goods and inflation were once again growing. An SPD report from Saxony read: "The power of the cult of Hitler is no longer unbroken. Doubts are beginning to gnaw at the Hitler myth." Another observer in Westphalia reported: "His star is beginning to fade."[44] When he tried to alert Hitler to the public unease, Fritz Wiedemann received a blunt rebuke. "The mood among the people is not bad—it is good," Hitler scolded him. "I know better . . . Spare me such things in future."[45] Yet in truth, the dictator, who had a fine instinct for changes in the public mood, was worried himself. As we have seen, the remilitarisation of the Rhineland in March 1936 served in part to distract from domestic difficulties. Once initial fears of a military response by the Western powers proved unfounded, this risky operation unleashed a new wave of enthusiasm for Hitler, which was reflected in the results of the popular referendum of 29 March 1936. "Again and again, Hitler seems like a man of great character," reported observers for the SPD in exile. "Again and again, people look up and admire the man credited with the monstrous achievements of National Socialist power and organisation."[46]

"He is an idol for every one of us," Goebbels noted in his diary in early October 1936, after Hitler had made another triumphant appearance at the harvest festival on Bückeberg Mountain.[47] By then the mythic status of the Führer was well established. Hitler represented the strongest point of connection between the government and the people, and those who staged the Hitler cult did everything to celebrate and deify this supposed bringer of light. The National Socialist calendar of holidays, patterned after the Christian one, offered them plenty of opportunities. It kicked off on 30 January, the anniversary of the Nazi "seizure of power." On 24 February, Hitler commemorated the proclamation of the party programme in 1920 with the old guard in Munich's Hofbräuhaus. On 16 March, the Heroes' Memorial Day—formerly the People's Day of Mourning—featured a ceremonial event in the Reichstag followed by a military parade. April the 20th was the Führer's birthday. The Day of National Labour—1 May—was staged as a celebration of the ethnic-popular community. It was followed by Mother's Day on the second Sunday in May, the summer solstice on 21 June and the harvest festival, the "day to honour our farmers," at Bückeberg Mountain near the town of Hameln in early October. The cycle of holidays ended on 9 November with the march of the "old fighters" from the Bürgerbräukeller to the Feldherrnhalle, where a commemorative ceremony was held for the "fallen warriors of the movement."[48]

But the undisputed high point of the National Socialist calendar was the Nuremberg party rally in early September. Hundreds of thousands of functionaries, SA, SS and Labour Service men, Hitler Youth and League of German Girls members gathered each year in the ancient city of the Holy Roman Empire of the German Nation for the party's "general roll call." This painstakingly organised series of events bore hardly any resemblance to a traditional party conference. The rallies were not held to discuss controversial issues—which did not exist anyway in a party ruled by an infallible leader—but rather to glorify the regime and, in particular, the man who headed it. Contemporaries saw the rallies as "the epitome of the Third Reich's glamour and power."[49] All means available were employed here to visually represent the movement's capacity for mobilisation, dynamics and solidarity.

The Nazis had initially staged their 1927 and 1929 party rallies in Nuremberg, although the city fathers had not been particularly keen to host the event. For Hitler, the location offered the chance to portray himself as the reviver of the old German Empire in front of an appropriately Romantic, medieval backdrop. From 1930 to 1932, with the Nazis battling for power, no rallies were held, and the decision to revive the spectacle after Hitler became chancellor was taken relatively late. "Nuremberg rally decided," noted Goebbels in late July 1933. "It will be really big."[50] Much of the four-day celebration seemed a bit improvised—not surprisingly given the lack of preparation time. SA Chief of Staff Ernst Röhm had a major place at Hitler's side and accompanied him step for step at the ceremony honouring the dead in Luitpoldhain Park. The next year, after Röhm and his followers had been liquidated, the ceremony changed. The SA no longer enjoyed a central role. Along with the Labour Service, the Reichswehr took part in the rally for the first time, underscoring its status, guaranteed by Hitler, as "the nation's sole bearer of arms."[51]

With the 1934 Nuremberg rally, the event took on its permanent form, except for a few minor amendments made in the following years. The duration was extended from four to first seven and then eight days, and each day had a specific theme. The course of events was by now "so well rehearsed that it proceeds like military mobilisation," Hess reported about the spectacle in 1937.[52] It began with Hitler's arrival in the city, either by specially chartered train or plane, and the trip to his hotel, the Deutscher Hof. William Shirer, who attended the 1934 rally, was initially unimpressed, writing: "He fumbled his cap with his left hand as he stood in his car acknowledging the delirious welcome with somewhat feeble salutes from his right arm."[53] In the afternoon, Hitler was received by Nuremberg's mayor, Willy Liebel, in the main town hall ballroom. In 1938, this ceremony had a special note in the form of insignia and jewellery from the Holy Roman Empire that had been brought from Vienna to Nuremberg after the *Anschluss*.[54] The first day of the rally concluded with a performance of Wagner's *Meistersinger von Nürnberg*, usually conducted by the director of the Berlin Philharmonic Orchestra, Wilhelm Furtwängler. "A fantastic cast and a great performance," noted Goebbels in September 1938. "Furtwängler is a musical genius. I sat right behind him and could observe him closely. What a man. The Führer, too, was boundless in his enthusiasm."[55]

On the morning of the second day, from the balcony of the Deutscher Hof, which was constantly surrounded by curiosity-seekers, the Nazi leader inspected the Hitler Youth as they marched by with their flags. After that the party congress was opened in the Luitpoldhalle. Hitler and his vassals marched into the auditorium to the strains of the

"Badenweiler March," a Bavarian military march, composed in honour of Germany's first victory over France in the First World War. One contemporary described the scene as follows: "The hall is decked out in white satin curtains, with the places for the guests of honour, the diplomatic corps, the orchestra and the choir decorated in deep red. A giant swastika surrounded by gold oak clusters on a black background dominates the space."[56] To music by Wagner, hundreds of standards, the "field banners of the movement," were brought into the hall, first and foremost the "blood banner" from the failed November putsch. For Shirer, the whole ceremony had "something of the mysticism and religious fervor of an Easter or Christmas mass in a great Gothic cathedral." After opening remarks by Rudolf Hess, who tried to outdo himself year after year in his hymns of praise for Hitler, and the subsequent ceremony in memory of the movement's "blood witnesses," Adolf Wagner—the Gauleiter of Munich-Upper Bavaria—read out the "Führer's proclamation." As Shirer noted, "Curiously, [he] has a voice and a manner of speaking so like Hitler's that some of the correspondents who were listening back at the hotel thought it *was* Hitler."[57] The evening featured a "culture conference" in the opera house, which was introduced by Alfred Rosenberg and concluded with a speech by Hitler. As of 1937, this ceremony included the presentation of a "National Prize for Art and Science," the Nazi Party's answer to the embarrassing awarding of the Nobel Peace Prize to the writer Carl von Ossietzky, who was imprisoned in Esterwegen concentration camp.[58]

The third day began with a march of Labour Service men to the Zeppelin Field. "Standing there in the early-morning sunlight which sparkled on their shiny spades, 50,000 of them, with the first thousand bared above the waist, suddenly made the German spectators go mad with joy when, without warning, they broke into a perfect goose-step," wrote Shirer, adding: "The goose-step has always seemed to me to be an outlandish exhibition of the human being in his most undignified and stupid state, but I felt for the first time this morning what an inner chord it strikes in the strange soul of the German people."[59] The high point of this event was a call-and-response from the choir, which ended with: "Let the work of our hands succeed / For every cut of the spade we take / Shall be a prayer for Germany."[60] After being addressed by Reich Labour Leader Konstantin Hierl and Hitler, the columns of workers marched through the city past the Deutscher Hof. The ceremony demanded stamina of both Hitler and the members of his entourage. "Four hours of marching," Goebbels carped. "The sun beating down. Barely endurable."[61] In 1937, with the introduction of a "Day of Community," the rhythm of marches and roll calls was interrupted by young women and men entertaining spectators at the Zeppelin Field with dances and athletic performances. In the evening, the Nazi political leaders marched by torchlight past the Deutscher Hof. "Watched from the Führer's balcony," Goebbels gushed. "A wonderful, colourful spectacle. All the Gaue led by the old Gauleiter."[62]

The fifth day commenced with special meetings of the party congress. The main attraction was the march of the political directors onto the Zeppelin Field. Since 1936, this was held in the evening, and Albert Speer had come up with a special idea. The moment that Hitler's arrival was announced, 130 spotlights positioned around the field were switched on. The beams of light reached up to eight kilometres into the night sky. "Now, in a heartbeat, the spotlights tear through the black sky beyond the ramparts," an official report on the rally excitedly described the spectacle. "Blue cords of light ascend to the heights. They make their way together, join with one another and form a dome of fluid light above the people's heads."[63]

In his memoirs, Speer called the "dome of light" his loveliest creation, and indeed the clever installation made a lasting impression even on foreign spectators. The British ambassador, Nevile Henderson, compared it to being in the interior of a cathedral made of ice.[64] To the sound of fanfares, Hitler, accompanied by Reich Organisational Director Robert Ley, strode through the broad centre aisle to the "Führer stage." When illuminated, it looked like an oversized altar, and upon it the high priest of the movement celebrated his mass. The elevation of Hitler to a charismatic saint and an enlightened messiah was never as palpable as in the liturgy of this night-time "hour of consecration." In 1936, Robert Ley called out: "We believe in Our Lord in heaven, who created us, who directs and protects us, and who sent you to us, my Führer, so that you could liberate Germany. That is what we believe, my Führer!"[65]

The sixth day belonged to the Hitler Youth and the League of German Girls. More than 50,000 boys and girls gathered in the morning on the main arena of the old sports stadium to pay tribute to the Führer. "No sooner did the command 'At ease' come than a thunderous roar of tens of thousands of voices went up," the official report from 1938 related. "Everyone was allowed to express what they felt. It was as though the air was vibrating."[66] Three years earlier, at the same site, Hitler had proclaimed his ideals for Germany's youth: "fast as greyhounds, tough as leather and hard as Krupp-forged steel."[67] Reich Youth Leader Baldur von Schirach swore an oath of loyalty to the Führer on behalf of the entire Hitler Youth, and after a short address by Hitler, Hess administered the oaths to be taken by all young people who aspired to join the party. The ceremony concluded with Hitler, Schirach and Hess walking through the ranks before driving in a car through the stadium, bathing in the applause from the stands.

On the morning of the seventh day, the SA and SS turned out for roll call in the expansive Luitpold Arena. "Heil, my men!" was Hitler's greeting. "Heil, my Führer!" came the answer from 100,000 throats.[68] This ceremony was rather problematic in 1934, since the Night of the Long Knives had taken place only a couple of months beforehand. "There was considerable tension in the stadium and I noticed that Hitler's own SS bodyguard was drawn up in force in front of him, separating him from the mass of the brown-shirts," wrote Shirer.[69] In subsequent years, the situation relaxed, and the ceremony in the Luitpoldarena, like the other rally events, followed a predetermined ritual. To the sounds of mournful music, and accompanied by SA Chief of Staff Lutze and Reichsführer-SS Himmler a respectful distance behind him, Hitler made his way across the "Street of the Führer" to the memorial monument, where he stood for a long time, silent, before the "blood banner." It was an image that more than any other symbolised the isolated special position of the charismatic leader among the rows and columns of his followers. Hitler then retraced his steps to the stage, followed by the bearers of the "blood banner." After an address in which he praised the SA and SS as the "best political fighting troops of the German people,"[70] and after the singing of the German national anthem, he consecrated the new standards of party formations by touching them with the "blood banner." "An almost religious ceremony with a fixed, never-changing tradition," commented Goebbels.[71] This was followed by an hours-long march past the Führer, standing in an open car, on Adolf-Hitler Platz.

The eighth and final day of the rally was dominated by Wehrmacht exercises. It began with a morning reveille and a trio of open-air concerts on Nuremberg's three largest squares. That afternoon, soldiers demonstrated the state of German armaments on Zeppelin Field in front of jam-packed stands and before the eyes of foreign diplomats and military attachés. "A grandiose picture of our Wehrmacht," wrote a satisfied Goebbels about the presentation in 1936. "All branches of the military get their due. Marvellous flying formations . . . tanks, artillery, cavalry . . . wonderful and a joy to behold."[72] In later years, this military spectacle was supposed to take place on the gigantic, specially designated field at one end of the rally grounds, but like the other grotesquely proportioned construction projects envisioned in Nuremberg, work was halted by the Second World War. The rally came to an end with a programmatic speech by Hitler. Around midnight, the Wehrmacht music corps and marching bands closed the ceremonies with a Grand Tattoo.

The centrepiece of the Nuremberg rallies was always Hitler. He was lead actor, master of ceremonies and high priest all rolled into one. The perfectly drilled choreography was focused exclusively around him. For the four to eight days of the rallies, he was utterly in his element. He held fifteen to twenty addresses, sometimes as many as four in one day. The rallies were the perfect opportunity to indulge his monomaniacal need to speak. He experienced the week-long event in a state of ecstasy, almost intoxication, and there was inevitably a feeling of emptiness when it was over. The day afterwards, he confessed in January 1942, more than three years after the final Nuremberg rally, had always had "something sad like when the decorations are taken down from the Christmas tree."[73] The Nuremberg rally in 1939, which was supposed to be held under the slogan "The Party Conference of Peace," was cancelled in late August amidst preparations to invade Poland.

On the other hand, the Nuremberg rallies were physically exhausting. Hitler later recalled that the hardest part had been standing at attention with a raised arm for hours as his followers marched past him: "A couple of times, I got dizzy."[74] At the end of every ceremony, Goebbels would find him lying exhausted on the sofa of his hotel room. "He has given everything he had," the propaganda minister noted in 1936. "He'll have to take a break."[75] That year was particularly trying since Hitler also had to attend a "Memorial Party Conference" in Weimar as well as the Olympic Summer Games in Berlin. His entourage pleaded with him to cancel the Nuremberg rally for that year, but he adamantly refused.[76]

After each rally, Hitler assembled his paladins for a post-mortem of the event. He handed out praise and criticism and made suggestions for the future. But he was unwilling to change the sequence of ceremonies once it had been set. While he was alive, he told Speer in 1938, the "form" had to become "an immutable rite." As he explained: "Then no one will be able to change it later. I am afraid that those who come after me will feel the urge to change things. Some future Führer of the Reich may not have my talents, but this framework will support him and give him authority."[77] Here, too, Hitler articulated fears that he would die young and that his work might not survive him. The consecration of rituals was his way of lending potential successors something of his own charisma and establishing the Third Reich for the long term.

The mass spectacle of the Nuremberg rallies had the desired effect on both German and foreign observers. The French ambassador, François-Poncet, who attended the 1937 rally, recalled:

> Amazing and indescribable was the atmosphere of general enthusiasm into which the ancient city was submerged, that unique intoxication that seized hundreds of thousands of men and women, the romantic excitement, mythic ecstasy, a kind of holy madness. During those eight days Nuremberg . . . was a city under a magic spell—one could almost say a city transported to an altogether different world.[78]

In retrospect, British Ambassador Henderson opined that no one could claim to be fully acquainted with the Nazi movement without having attended and soaked in the atmosphere of a Nuremberg rally.[79]

Even as sceptical an observer as William Shirer would write in late 1934: "You have to go through one of these to understand Hitler's hold on the people, to feel the dynamic in the movement he's unleashed and the sheer, disciplined strength that the German people possess."[80] The magical backdrop of Nuremberg had a particular effect on foreign journalists who would otherwise have been expected to maintain critical distance towards the spectacle. A *New York Times* report on the last day of the 1937 rally recorded foreign journalists from all over the world listening to Hitler's concluding speech in their hotel and all spontaneously performing the raised-arm German greeting and enthusiastically singing along with the German national anthem and the "Horst Wessel Song."[81] Both Germans and foreigners were taken in by the majestic surface of the Third Reich, so that they lost sight of the dark sides of the dictatorship.

From the very beginning, the Nazi leadership had tried to reach out to the greatest number of people possible with the mass spectacle in Nuremberg. The main means of doing so was radio broadcasts. Yet they were largely restricted to recordings of speeches and were unable to communicate much of the atmosphere. By 1935, listeners had begun to get tired of them. "The comprehensive coverage on radio and in newspapers did not truly captivate the masses even during the rally week," concluded a report from the Rhineland. "The people were indifferent."[82] It made sense to use the medium of film as a disseminator.

The NSDAP had the 1927 and 1929 Nuremberg rallies filmed, but the end results consisted of primitive, silent footage intended only for party initiates and never broadly distributed. Moreover, at that time Hitler was not yet the absolutely dominant figure of the event.[83] That changed after the "seizure of power," and for the "Party Rally of Victory." In 1933, a work of vastly superior quality was commissioned to allow cinema audiences the chance to "experience" the event. Leni Riefenstahl's hour had come.

The gifted young actress had established contact with Hitler in the spring of 1932 after attracting his attention in the lead role in her directorial debut, *The Blue Light*. By that autumn, she had become a regular guest at the Goebbelses' house, where she occasionally encountered Hitler. She knew that her career would benefit if the National Socialists came to power,[84] and in mid-May 1933 Goebbels proposed a collaboration. "In the afternoon Leni Riefenstahl," he noted. "She told of her plans. I suggested a Hitler film. She was very enthusiastic." In June, the two discussed the details, with the propaganda minister remarking, "She's the only one of the stars who understands us." By August the deal was done, and Riefenstahl was invited to lunch at the Chancellery—a sign of Hitler's special favour. "She's going to make our party rally film," Goebbels enthused.[85] The news was officially announced at the end of the month, only a few days before the Nuremberg rally. "At the express wish of the Führer," it read,

Fräulein Riefenstahl had been entrusted with the artistic direction of the party-rally film.[86]

The fact that an actress-turned-director and a non-party member was handed this project was a thorn in the side of the veteran Nazis at the film division of the Propaganda Ministry, in particular its director, Arnold Raether. Behind the scenes, there was intriguing and feuding aimed at calling Riefenstahl's competence into question. But as long as she enjoyed Hitler's favour, she had nothing to fear. And after her first Nuremberg rally film, which would bear the title *The Victory of Faith*, even the doubters in Hitler's entourage were convinced of her skill as a director.[87]

On her own initiative, Riefenstahl hired three gifted cameramen: Sepp Allgeier, Franz Weihmayr and Walter Frentz, the last of whom would become Hitler's preferred cameraman and play an important role during the Second World War.[88] Understandably, the young female director, who led her team with great self-confidence during the four days of filming, caused quite a stir in Nuremberg. After the rally was over, she retreated to edit her footage. Goebbels, with whom she conferred, was certain: "She will produce something worthwhile."[89] Riefenstahl's most original contribution was to break the static, somewhat monotonous sequence of speeches and marches by giving them a flowing rhythm, which made them more interesting. Disregarding the chronology of the rally, she recut the events into a suggestive series of visual images. She did without a voice-over, which was quite unusual for a documentary film, using only original statements by the speakers and the audience's reaction. The entire film was accompanied by a soundtrack by Herbert Windt, a mixture of Wagneresque passages, folk melodies and crisp marches.[90]

Nonetheless, *The Victory of Faith* was anything but perfect, partly because the director was still a novice editor, partly because she was forced in part to use conventional weekly newsreel footage. Some scenes were unintentionally funny, such as when Göring paraded past Hitler's limousine unaware that the Führer wanted to shake his hand, or when Baldur von Schirach accidentally brushed Hitler's uniform cap from the rostrum with his behind.[91] But the dictator had no objections when the film was shown to a select private audience in November 1933. "A fabulous SA symphony," remarked Goebbels. "Riefenstahl did a good job. She is absolutely shattered by the work.

Hitler moved. Should be a huge hit."[92] The film premiered on
1 December in the Ufa-Palast cinema in Berlin. The event was like a
state occasion. Taking part along with Hitler, Goebbels, Röhm and
Hess were other prominent government representatives including
Papen, Neurath, Frick and Blomberg. "When the final note had faded,
the visibly moved audience took to its feet and sang the 'Horst Wessel
Song' to express its connection with the Führer and the movement,"
reported *Lichtspielbühne* magazine. "But even then no one clapped.
There was a moment of solemn silence, after which the enthusiasm
was released in deafening ovations."[93] In the days that followed, Hitler's
entourage was subjected to repeated screenings of the film. Even
Goebbels got sick and tired. "Evening at home," he noted. "Führer . . .
party rally film. Soon I'll have had enough of it."[94]

The press also greeted *The Victory of Faith* warmly as a "document
of its time of incalculable value," a "cinematic oratorio" and an "Eroica
of the Nuremberg Rally." One publicity campaign asserted: "The
Führer has become Germany . . . [and] all of Germany shall now hear
him thanks to the miracle of this film."[95] Local NSDAP chapters were
instructed to cancel all other events on the day this "massively powerful
cinematic work" was shown so that the greatest number of party
members and people in general would be able to attend. With the
help of mobile film trucks, the film was also shown in rural areas that
did not have cinemas. As a result, as many as 20 million people were
said to have seen Leni Riefenstahl's directorial debut.[96]

But after six months the film was withdrawn from circulation. In
a number of shots, Röhm could be seen next to Hitler, and after
30 June 1934, he was *persona non grata* on the silver screen. Almost
all copies of the film were destroyed, most likely on Hitler's orders.
After 1945, the film was considered lost, until a copy was discovered
in the East German state archives in the 1980s.[97] The Nazis needed
a replacement film, and Riefenstahl was once again hired to direct
it. In late August 1934 as a "special representative of the NSDAP Reich
Direction," she signed a distribution agreement with Ufa.[98] A week
before the "Party Rally for Unity and Strength," she travelled to
Nuremberg to begin preparations for *Triumph of the Will*. The title
had been Hitler's idea.

Riefenstahl's second film was on an entirely different level in terms
of finances, personnel and technology. The director could draw on a

budget of 300,000 reichsmarks and a staff of 170 employees, including 18 cameramen. "Film towers," equipped with cameras, microphones and spotlights, were erected at high points on the Nuremberg party rally grounds. A lift was installed on a 28-metre-high mast in the Luitpoldarena so that an operator with a hand-held camera could get new perspectives on the gigantic marching grounds. Tracks were laid around the speakers' stage so that Hitler could be filmed at unprecedented proximity and from various camera angles. Ultimately 130,000 metres of film were developed. Working at the Geyer Film Copying works in Berlin, Riefenstahl eventually trimmed that down to 3,000 metres, yielding a 114-minute film.[99]

As in *The Victory of Faith*, the director did not use a voice-over and ignored the chronology of the rally, instead boiling the seven days down to three and a half.[100] In contrast to her first film, Hitler was the all-dominating main character this time. The entire narrative was focused on the expectations of spectators who cried out, "We want to see our Führer!" Even the opening credits were preparation for his appearance: "On 5 September 1934 / 20 years after the outbreak of the World War / 16 years after the beginning of Germany's suffering / 19 months after the beginning of Germany's rebirth / Adolf Hitler again flew to Nuremberg to inspect his true followers." The opening scene shows the Führer in his aeroplane descending towards Nuremberg like a saviour sent from heaven. Riefenstahl then staged Hitler's journey from the airport to his hotel as a secular version of Christ's entry into Jerusalem. Standing in an open Mercedes, Hitler receives the adulation of the masses. A camera mounted in the car filmed him from behind, against the sunshine, so that his head seems to be ringed by a halo. A skilled use of cuts and counter-cuts shows Hitler mostly filmed from below and his jubilant admirers mostly from above. The Führer and his followers—the great, godlike charismatic leader and the faithful masses who looked up to him—are combined in a mystic unity.[101]

In November 1934, Goebbels viewed the first excerpts from the film. "Afternoon with Leni Riefenstahl, magnificent shots from the rally film," he noted. "Leni has got talent. If she were a man!" Five months later, when the film was finally finished, Goebbels was no less enthusiastic: "A grandiose spectacle. In the final section perhaps a bit drawn-out, but otherwise a mind-shattering portrayal. Leni's masterpiece."[102] *Triumph of the Will* premiered on 28 March 1935, two weeks after the reintroduction of compulsory military service. For the "film event of the year," Albert Speer had dressed up the façade of the Ufa-Palast cinema and hung gigantic swastika flags all over it. An 8-metre-tall bronze Reich eagle was mounted above the entrance, which was illuminated by spotlights on the evening of the premiere. Once again party and government VIPs put in appearances, and after the frenetic applause had died down following the screening, Hitler presented the director with an enormous bouquet of lilacs.[103] The reviews in the Nazi and Nazified press read like hymns. "The greatest cinematic work we have ever seen," gushed the *Völkischer Beobachter*.[104] Cinemas reported record numbers of ticket sales in the first few weeks of the film's run, and *Triumph of the Will* became Germany's most-watched film that year. On 25 June 1935, Goebbels presented Riefenstahl with the National Film Prize. In his citation, the propaganda minister praised her work as "the great cinematic vision of the Führer, who appears in it for the first time with a previously unknown, visual urgency."[105]

In terms of its propaganda value for the regime, *Triumph of the Will* was *the* film about Hitler. As one latter-day scholar of Nazi film put it, "here Hitler was shown the way he wanted to be seen for all time."[106] The cult surrounding the Führer was also maintained in other visual media, for instance in Hoffmann's popular books of photography, *Youth around Hitler* (1935), *Hitler in His Mountains* (1935) and *Hitler beyond the Everyday Routine* (1937), which sought to present the dictator as a nature enthusiast, a caring head of state and a lover of children.[107] But more than any other work, Riefenstahl's second Nuremberg rally film created the dominant image of Hitler and his relationship to the German people, not just in Germany but abroad as well, where *Triumph of the Will* was also screened and awarded prizes. During the Second World War, excerpts from it would be used for anti-Nazi educational films in Anglo-Saxon countries.[108]

"One People—one Empire—one Leader": those who saw Riefenstahl's opus usually came away with the impression that this was not just a propaganda slogan, but reality in the Third Reich. But was it truly? Did the ideal of *Volksgemeinschaft*, the ethnic-popular community, really exist, or was it a deceptive illusion, a construct alien to reality? Prior to 1933, Hitler's promise to overcome party and class divisions had been one of his most persuasive campaign slogans, greatly

"Pillory parade" in Gelsenkirchen in August 1935

Hitler enters Berlin's Olympic Stadium, accompanied by members of the National and International Olympic Committees, 1 August 1936

The planned North–
South Axis in Berlin,
with the central station
and the triumphal arch
in the foreground and
the great, domed hall
in the background

Hitler, Albert Speer
and Ludwig Ruff
looking at blueprints
and models for the
Nuremberg rally site

Hitler's office in the New Reich Chancellery, 1939

The concealable window in the Great Hall at the Berghof

Left: Hitler and Eva Braun on the Obersalzberg, autumn 1938

Below: Group photo from the Berghof New Year's Eve party in 1938. Hitler is in the front row with Eva Braun to his left.

LBI / DZ

Above: Defaced
windows of Jewish-
owned businesses in
Berlin, June 1938

Right: Onlookers watch
as the Old Synagogue
in Essen burns,
9 November 1938

Left: Mussolini in Berlin
during his state visit,
27 September 1937

Below: Hitler speaks
from the balcony of
Vienna's Hofburg
Palace, 15 March 1938.

Top: Hitler at the German
Gymnastics and Sports
Festival in Breslau,
31 July 1938

Right: Czech president
Emil Hácha with Hitler
in his office at the New
Reich Chancellery,
15 March 1939

Top: A military parade
on Berlin's new East–West
Axis in honour of Hitler's
fiftieth birthday,
20 April 1939

Right: Hermann Göring
congratulates Hitler
in the name of the
assembled Nazi leaders
on his fiftieth birthday.

contributing to the attractiveness of Hitler and the National Socialist movement.[109] It enlisted people's desires for a stable social and political order, as free as possible from conflict, as an indispensable basis for German national renewal. After coming to power, Hitler always wove these leitmotifs into his speeches. The new government, he emphasised in his first radio address as chancellor on 1 February 1933, would attempt "to make our people conscious once again, across all castes and classes, of its ethnic and political unity and the corresponding responsibilities." The introduction of a universal compulsory labour service, he explained at the end of that month in an interview with the stringer for the Associated Press in Berlin, Louis P. Lochner, would help "bridge class divides." In Potsdam's Garrison Church on 21 March, he demanded that "a German people must once more coalesce from farmers, the middle classes and workers." And two days later, when the Enabling Act was introduced, he intoned that the "creation of a genuine ethnic-popular community, which would rise above the special interests and conflicts of castes and classes," was Germany's only way out of crisis. "The millions of people who are divided up into professions, who have been separated into artificial classes, who have been blinded by obscure caste thinking and class insanity and can no longer understand each other, will all have to find a way back to one another," he reiterated at the 1 May celebration on Berlin's Tempelhof Field.[110]

Like much of Hitler's political platform, the idea of ethnic-popular community was deliberately kept opaque and open to interpretation. When the writer Hanns Johst asked for a clearer definition of the idea in conversation with Hitler in January 1934, he received the nebulous answer: "Ethnic-popular community means the community of all productive labour, the unity of all life interests, the overcoming of the private bourgeoisie and mechanistic union-organised masses, the uncompromising identity of personal destiny and the nation, of the individual and the people."[111] What stood beyond all doubt was that the society Hitler envisioned would be forged along racist lines. The only people allowed to be "ethnic-popular comrades" were those "of German blood," as the first point in the NSDAP party programme of 1920 had declared. There was no place in the ethnic-popular community for Jewish Germans or other groups stigmatised as racially inferior. It was also clear that Hitler's promise to overcome class antagonism did not mean that he denied the existence of conflicts of economic interest and the need for them to be represented. It did mean that they were to remain subordinate to politics.[112]

From the very beginning, the Nazis were keen to court the working classes, which was not just the largest group of employed people but also the one that, prior to 1933, in so far as they were organised by the SPD or KPD, had proved most resistant to the lure of Nazi propaganda. Hitler knew that there was no way to realise his ethnic-popular community without them or against their will. The "German worker," he stressed in his speech at Berlin's Sportpalast on 10 February 1933, would in future no longer be an "alien" in the German Reich. On the contrary, "the gates would be opened" so that he could "join the German ethnic-popular community as a bearer of the German nation."[113] To this end, the regime pursued a carrot-and-stick strategy. The party violently broke up working-class political parties and union organisations on the one hand, while offering attractive opportunities for integration on the other. On 10 May 1933, in a speech at the founding of the German Labour Front, which replaced the forcibly disbanded unions, Hitler characterised himself as an "honest mediator for both sides," who would ensure the interests of business and labour were balanced.[114]

Nonetheless, the Law on the Ordering of National Labour, of January 1934, clearly privileged employers, transferring the Führer principle to the realm of business. At the head of the "company community" was the "company leader," with the workers defined as his "followers."[115] In return for their loss of the right to influence company decisions and negotiate wages, however, workers were offered a series of concessions. The German Labour Office made efforts to approve work conditions and relations. Factory canteens were established; sports facilities and swimming pools were built; measures were taken to reduce noise and improve air quality and hygiene; and green spaces were laid out around factories. These were all attempts to give workers a sense of the "dignity of labour." The historian Peter Reichel has offered a precise summary: "In reality, capitalist conditions of production were not changed. They were only differently interpreted and staged. Perception was to be changed, via a veil of beautiful illusion."[116] Men's social existence was not to determine their consciousness, as Marxist teaching had it: their consciousness was to determine their social being.

More important and successful in the long term was a German Labour Front subsidiary programme, the "Strength through Joy" initiative, which was founded in November 1933 and modelled after the *Opera Nazionale Dopolavoro* in Fascist Italy. Its goal was to improve leisure activities for workers as a means of boosting their productivity and willingness to assimilate into Nazi society. In a short time, it developed into a mammoth organisation with 7,000 paid employees and 135,000 volunteers. "Strength through Joy," said Robert Ley, the director of the Labour Front, in June 1938, "is the most concise formula for introducing the broad masses to National Socialism."[117] The leisure-time activities on offer included theatre and concert visits, exhibitions, tours of museums, tennis and riding lessons, adult education courses and even holidays. The latter were particularly popular. "For many people, 'Strength through Joy' is simply a travel agent that offers enormous advantages," an SPD-in-exile observer reported in February 1938.[118] Travelling presupposed that workers got paid holidays, and in fact after 1933, they usually enjoyed six to twelve days' annual leave. Between 1934 and 1938 an average of more than a million Germans took all-inclusive trips with "Strength through Joy" every year. An additional 5 million took part in weekend excursions or short trips of a day or two.[119]

Especially coveted were trips overseas, for which "Strength through Joy" had its own fleet of cruise ships, including the newly built MS *Wilhelm Gustloff* and MS *Robert Ley*. In contrast to conventional passenger ships, these vessels did not have different classes of cabins. "The difference between third-, second- and first-class quarters on big cruise ships were terrible and incomprehensible," Hitler opined in one of his monologues in his wartime headquarters, since they rendered differences in lifestyle visible for all to see. "This is one of the main things for the German Labour Front to take care of," he added.[120] In the classless society on board a state-sponsored cruise ship, people from various walks of life were supposed to come together in harmony and provide an example for the assimilation of workers into the ethnic-popular community. "Towards the sun—German workers travel to Madeira," promised one popular travel report.[121] Goebbels was enthusiastic: "This is also something wonderful. Workers who have left their hometowns travel across land and sea and are glad when they're back in Germany."[122]

Of course, there was a considerable gap between promises and reality. The holidaymakers aboard "Strength through Joy" ships were by no means a cross section of German society. Members of the middle classes, white-collar employees, civil servants, the self-employed and party functionaries were disproportionately represented, while workers remained in the clear minority.[123] The costs of a trip by sea to Madeira were still beyond the means of most working-class households. In the SPD reports, people repeatedly complained that the trips abroad were reserved for the "bigwigs" and were far too expensive for average earners.[124] On the other hand, there was growing appreciation of the leisure activities on offer, especially weekend and holiday trips within Germany. "'If it is that cheap, you might as well put your hand up.' That's what many workers are saying and taking part," reported one SPD observer.[125] In February 1938, it was reported that "Strength through Joy" had become very popular in Berlin: "The events address the desire of the little man who wants to let his hair down for once and experience the same things the 'big boys' enjoy. It is a clever speculation about the petit-bourgeois desires of the apolitical workers."[126] But the SPD-in-exile observers had to admit that even formerly committed Social Democrats were susceptible and that this was an effective form of propaganda: "At the very least, 'Strength through Joy' is a distraction that serves to cloud people's minds and works propagandistically on behalf of the regime."[127]

"Strength through Joy" planners were aware that, despite the publicity campaigns, a lot of holiday wishes remained unfulfilled. To alleviate the dissatisfaction, they turned their attention towards constructing gigantic holiday resorts and leisure facilities. The most prestigious enterprise was the "Strength through Joy" sea spa Prora on the Baltic Sea island of Rügen.[128] Construction began in 1936, and the six-storey apartment blocks were supposed to stretch for 4.5 kilometres and house 20,000 holidaymakers. A one-week stay was supposed to cost no more than 20 reichsmarks, affordable even for low-income workers. Hitler was enthralled by what he called the "biggest seaside resort on earth."[129] An SPD report in April 1939 admitted: "This building is one of the most effective advertisements for the Third Reich."[130] But the structure was never completed: work on it was suspended with the start of the Second World War.

The beginnings of mass tourism in the Third Reich were part of a larger project and an example of the vision of a Nazi leisure and consumer society. Hitler wanted the racially homogeneous ethnic-popular community to be characterised by high levels of consumption.[131] Yet as we have seen, in its early years the Hitler regime prioritised rearmament over the desires of private consumers. In keeping with this policy, wage and income rises were quite modest. Real wages for workers in Germany rose only slightly between 1933 and 1939, and this was largely due to an extension of working hours.[132] Against this backdrop, there is little evidence for the argument advanced by Götz Aly in his book *Hitler's Willing Beneficiaries* that the Nazi regime was a "dictatorship of favours" that primarily served the interests of the weaker members of society.[133]

The Nazi mass consumer society remained little more than a promise, a vision of things possibly yet to come. A taste of it was provided by a series of *Volksprodukte*—people's products—which were supposed to be made widely available as state-of-the-art technological items. First and foremost among them was the *Volksempfänger* (People's Receiver) radio. Bearing the model number VE 301—a nod to the "seizure of power" on 30 January—it was unveiled to the public, with Hitler in attendance, at the Berlin Radio Trade Fair in August 1933. Standardisation and serial mass production meant that the radio could be purchased for the sensationally low price of 76 reichsmarks—with instalment plans available for low-income consumers. In 1939, it was joined by a further model, the *Deutscher Kleinempfänger* (DKE—Small German Receiver), which cost only 35 reichsmarks.[134] The Nazis never achieved their stated goal of putting a radio in every German household, but the number of listeners jumped from 4.5 million in 1933 to more than 11 million by 1939: 57 per cent of all households owned a receiver.[135] In radio, the National Socialists had control over the most important means for manipulating the masses. But Goebbels was aware that the aggressive propaganda the regime had promulgated at the start of its reign would cause people to tune out in the long term. For that reason, by September 1933 he was already calling for more entertainment programming. "The programmes have to be relaxing," the propaganda minister demanded. "Party politics must be kept to a minimum."[136]

Hitler never offered an opinion about television, whose development was encouraged after 1933, but as a gadget enthusiast, he is likely to have been interested in it. "I openly admit that I'm a fool for technology," he said in February 1942. "Anyone who comes to me with some surprising technological innovation will have an advantage."[137] Goebbels, who recognised early on the potential of the new medium, kept him apprised about the progress being made in developing television. The propaganda minister repeatedly noted in his diary that television had a "great future" and that people were on the threshold of "revolutionary innovations."[138] In 1935, the first "television parlours" were established. But the technology was primitive, and there were not many programmes to watch. A mass-produced television comparable to the "people's receiver" was a long way off, even if the *Westdeutscher Beobachter* newspaper prophesied in a report on the Radio Trade Fair in 1938 that television would soon be as commonplace as radio.[139]

The Nazis were less successful with another *Volksprodukt*, the Volkswagen. As an automobile fanatic, the mass motorisation of German society was an ideal close to Hitler's heart. Just as the radio industry had succeeded in making an affordable "people's receiver," Hitler proclaimed at the International Motor Show in early March 1934, the automobile industry should do its part "to build a car that will attract a million new customers."[140] Hitler did not use the term, but the *Leipziger Neueste Nachrichten* was hardly putting words in his mouth when it ran the headline: "Create the German Volkswagen!"[141] The price for the new vehicle was supposed to be less than 1,000 reichsmarks—a sum that most carmakers felt was far too low to be profitable. Ferdinand Porsche, whom Hitler greatly respected and defended against resistance from the automotive industry, was commissioned to design the vehicle. At the 1936 International Motor Show, Hitler told carmakers that the automobile had to go from being a "luxury item for the few to a practical item for all." He would see the Volkswagen project through with "uncompromising determination," Hitler announced, and he had no doubt that the ingenious Porsche would bring the "costs for procuring, running and maintaining the vehicle into an acceptable relation with the income of the broad masses of our people."[142]

But the Reich Association of the Automobile Industry remained sceptical, so Hitler transferred responsibility for the project to Ley's German Labour Front. In late May 1937, the "Society for the Preparation for the German Volkswagen" was founded, and that summer it was decided to base the main factory near the town of Fallersleben.[143] When laying the foundation stone on 26 May 1938, Hitler once again aimed a barb at critics who had argued that it was impossible to produce an affordable motor vehicle for the masses. "I hate the word 'impossible,'" Hitler declared. "It has always been a mark of cowardly people, who do not dare to realise great ambitions." Hitler revealed that the new vehicle would be called the "Strength through Joy Car" and announced that he would build both "the most massive German automobile factory" and a "model German workers' city."[144]

The public response was extraordinary. Many Germans greeted the announcement of a car for the people as "a great, pleasant surprise," an SPD observer reported in April 1939. "A veritable 'Strength through Joy' psychosis has arisen. For a long time, the 'Strength through Joy Car' was one of the main topics of conversation among all social classes in Germany." The idea of an automobile for the masses temporarily pushed aside all domestic and international concerns. "The politician who promises everyone a car is, if the masses believe his promises, a man of the masses. As far as the 'Strength through Joy Car' is concerned, the German people believe Hitler's announcements."[145] To help people purchase the car, the "Strength through Joy" organisation set up a savings plan that had potential customers putting aside a minimum of 5 reichsmarks a month towards the 990 reichsmark price of the car. By late 1939, 270,000 people had signed on, and by the end of the war that number had risen to 340,000. But only 5 per cent of them came from the working classes. And they never got their cars. During the war, the Volkswagen factory mainly produced jeeps for the Wehrmacht.[146]

The gap between propaganda and reality was even more marked in the social welfare institution the National Socialists considered the epitome of a functioning ethnic-popular community: the "Winter Relief." In the summer of 1933, Hitler announced his intention to found a welfare programme for the needy. Private welfare organisations had already run a Winter Relief for those requiring help in the late Weimar Republic, but it had not been much of a success.[147] The Nazi regime approached the project with far greater élan. Under the slogan "Fighting Hunger and Cold," the government wanted to show that it was serious about its principle of "communal before individual benefit." Erich Hilgenfeldt, the Reich administrator of the National Socialist People's Welfare, the largest mass organisation after the German Labour Front, was charged with setting up the new entity.

On 13 September 1933, Hitler and Goebbels opened the first Winter Relief agency to great fanfare. With this measure, Hitler announced, he wanted to prove "that this ethnic-popular community is not just an empty concept, but is truly something alive." "International Marxist solidarity" had been broken, he added, so that it could be replaced with "the national solidarity of the German people."[148]

A satisfied Goebbels later noted: "Our action against hunger and cold has made a huge impression."[149] The first call for donations succeeded in raising 358 million reichsmarks—a figure that would be bettered year on year until it reached 680 million reichsmarks in 1939–40. In a speech about the Winter Relief in 1937, Hitler called it the "largest social welfare organisation of all time."[150] Members of almost all Nazi organisations worked as volunteers, collecting money street to street and door to door and selling badges and pins. On the first Sunday in December, the Day of National Solidarity, prominent representatives of the regime also took part. For Goebbels, who collected money in front of the luxury Hotel Adlon in Berlin, these occasions were "popular festivals." "Unbelievable," he wrote.

> Tens of thousands. A celebration and hullabaloo that was impossible to ignore. I was almost crushed to death. Twice I had to flee inside the hotel. The marvellous people of Berlin. They gave and gave. Most generously the poor. I got tears in my eyes . . . Reported to the Führer that evening . . . A huge triumph. I filled up 42 collection cans.[151]

On every first Sunday between October and March, the regime appealed to Germans to eat only stew and donate the money they saved to the Winter Relief. Hitler used his entire repertoire to make this sacrifice seem palatable to his "ethnic comrades":

> And even if others say: You know, I'd love to take part in Stew Sunday, but I have constant stomach trouble, and I don't see the point, since I'll donate ten pfennigs anyway. [We say:] no, my dear friend, we set it all up deliberately. On purpose. Especially for you who doesn't see the point, it is useful for us to point you back at least once in the direction of your people, to the millions of your ethnic comrades, who would be happy to eat nothing all winter but the stew that you eat perhaps once a month.[152]

Only stews were served at Sunday lunches in the Chancellery, and those at the table were called upon to donate money as well. "The number of guests shrank to two or three," Albert Speer recalled, "which led Hitler to talk sarcastically about some of his associates' willingness to make sacrifices."[153]

But the Winter Relief was a "voluntary" charity organisation in name only. Workers had to tolerate contributions—10 per cent of their income taxes from 1935—being directly deducted from their wages. Those who refused to donate could count on being sanctioned. In November 1935, a farmer in northern Bavaria who had declared that he had no extra money for the Winter Relief received a sharp rebuke from the local Nazi chapter, accusing him of being "unwilling to feel like a member of the German ethnic-popular community." He was threatened, should he not change his behaviour, with being brought to "where enemies of the state and parasites on the people are usually taken."[154] In the long run, the public grew disgruntled with being constantly called upon to make sacrifices and approached by collectors. Charity drives in the streets and door to door, one SPD observer reported in December 1935, had taken on the character of "organised highway robbery." By January 1938, another observer wrote, they had "practically become a levy that no one can avoid."[155] Rumours also began to circulate that donations were not truly going to the needy. People joked that the abbreviation for the Winter Relief, WHV (*Winterhilfswerk*) actually stood for *Wir hungen weiter* (we continue to starve) or *Waffenhilfswerk* (Weapons Assistance Fund).[156] There was some justification for the idea that the Winter Relief helped finance Hitler's plans for war. The putative charity helped the Nazi regime throttle its expenditures for social welfare programmes and invest the money saved in arms. The phrase "socialism in deeds," which Hitler and his vassals used to describe the Winter Relief, could hardly be taken at face value.

The same applied to Hitler's promise that within the ethnic-popular community every German would enjoy the same chances to better himself, so that in the end the best and brightest would rise to positions of leadership. The central task of government leadership, Hitler declared in his closing address at the Nuremberg rally in 1934, had to be to create the conditions for the "most gifted minds to be deservedly advantaged regardless of origin, titles, class and wealth."[157] In an interview with Louis P. Lochner, he said that he agreed with the American idea of not "reducing everyone to the same level," but rather maintaining the "ladder principle." "Everyone must get the chance to climb the ladder," he declared.[158] In early 1937, during an afternoon walk with Goebbels on the Obersalzberg, Hitler elaborated on his vision of the Nazi society of the future. Afterwards Goebbels noted: "The way to rise up must be available for everyone. Not bound to exams, but performance . . . The misery of testing must be done away with everywhere. A hierarchy of performance has to be created. Strictly organised. Wealth to be concentrated there. True socialism means clearing the way for the capable."[159]

In his monologues in his military headquarters during the Second World War, Hitler would repeatedly revisit the idea of "a clear path for the capable." The decisive thing, he asserted, was to ensure "that the gates were open for all gifted people." In order to do that, Hitler added, Germany would have to eradicate its overdependence on "evaluations and pieces of paper." He went on: "In my movement, I myself have had great experiences in the highest positions. I have the highest civil servants who are agricultural workers and have continued to prove themselves." Performance, Hitler said, should be the only qualification for military promotion. "If a person has the stuff to excel, I don't look at whether he comes from a proletarian background," Hitler explained, "nor do I prevent children of military families from proving their worth once more."[160]

But Hitler's egalitarian rhetoric was one thing, and social reality in the Third Reich another. On the one hand, members of previously disadvantaged social classes had better chances to work their way up the social ladder. The NSDAP and its subordinate organisations in particular, with their gigantic apparatus and the rapidly expanding armed forces after the reintroduction of compulsory military service, offered a host of new, well-paid posts. The promise that performance would outweigh social background and class especially appealed to the younger generation, whose career prospects had looked so bleak prior to 1933. The chance for young university graduates to advance their careers quickly and even occupy leading positions stimulated their desire to achieve and unleashed considerable social energy. The opportunity for upward social mobility accounted for a large amount of the Nazi Party's attractiveness as a "modernising" force.[161]

Still, none of that altered the basic structure of German society. Hitler was by no means the social revolutionary, as the odd historian has claimed.[162] Class hurdles and barriers were lowered, but they still existed, and by no means was there full equality of opportunity in the Third Reich. Nazi propaganda, however, was remarkably successful in communicating a "feeling of social equality," and this alone reinforced Hitler's perceived role as a messianic saviour and strengthened Germans' emotional attachment to his regime.[163]

Hitler's "ethnic-popular community," therefore, was not simply a chimera or a deceptive façade, but nor did it become social reality or challenge the status quo of wealth and property. In the words of two prominent German historians, its appeal was based on "the ideal it represented, not the recognition of social reality."[164] Moreover, the vision for the future it entailed was not that of a society where everyone was equal, but precisely the opposite: a society characterised by extreme inequalities resulting from the Nazis' biological, racist policies. The integration of "ethnic comrades" went hand in hand with the exclusion of those deemed "alien to the community."

The latter category included not only enemies of the regime and Jewish Germans, but in principle anyone who did not conform to racist Nazi standards, be they the physically and mentally disabled, "antisocials," alcoholics, homosexuals or gypsies. In so far as they were not "improvable," these groups were to be subjected to racial-hygienic "special treatment." In the second volume of *Mein Kampf*, Hitler had already specified the maintenance of "racial purity" as one of the main tasks of the "ethnic state." What he meant was that "only the healthy should bear children." To this end, the state was to call upon "the most modern medical assistance" in order that "everyone who is demonstrably sick or genetically burdened . . . be declared unfit and made incapable of reproduction." This was to be accompanied by the "systematic promotion of fertility among the healthiest bearers of our ethnic identity."[165] Hitler repeatedly returned to these demands in his speeches prior to 1933. At the 1929 Nuremberg rally, he cited the example of Sparta, the "clearest racial state in human history," which had "systematically enacted racial laws." He contrasted this with the "modern humanistic nonsense" of the health and social policies in the Weimar Republic, which "preserve weakness at the cost of those who are healthier." Hitler declared: "Slowly but surely we are breeding the weak and killing off the strong . . . The remaking of the ethnic-popular body is the greatest mission of National Socialism."[166]

This racist programme was anything but original. Hitler was reviving ideas that had been disseminated internationally in the 1890s, as the concept of eugenics was growing in popularity.[167] After the enormous bloodletting of the First World War, such notions had once again gained credence among some doctors, psychiatrists, scientists and politicians, including a few socialists. The idea that "the best" had fallen in the war while "the inferior" had survived and been fattened up by the social welfare state dominated the discussion of eugenics in the Weimar Republic. In 1920, the criminal law expert Karl Binding and the psychiatrist Alfred Hoche had published a pamphlet polemic-ally entitled "The Admission of the Destruction of Unfit Life," that called upon Germans to follow the Spartan example and kill sickly infants and old people. "In matters of life and death, sympathy is the least appropriate emotion towards the dead in spirit," the authors argued. "There is no sympathy without suffering."[168]

In July 1932, the Prussian Health Council debated a proposed law that would have cleared the way for the compulsory sterilisation of the so-called genetically ill. That same year, the organisation repre-senting German doctors lobbied for the introduction of eugenic ster-ilisation to combat "the deterioration of German genetic material" and to "relieve pressure on public funds."[169] Once the Nazis were in power, the advocates of racist eugenics received a green light for their plans. On 14 July 1933, Hitler's cabinet approved the Law for the Prevention of Genetically Ill Offspring, which for the first time legal-ised compulsory sterilisation on the grounds of so-called racial hygiene. When Papen argued against compulsory measures, saying that appeals could be made to those affected, he was coolly rebuked by Hitler. The operations foreseen by the law, Hitler argued, were "not only minor, but ethically unimpeachable if one considered that genetically ill people would continue to reproduce in considerable numbers while millions of healthy children remained unborn."[170] With an eye towards the ongoing negotiations over the concordat with the Catholic Church, the announcement of the law was postponed for eleven days; it took effect on 1 January 1934. In his address to the Reichstag on the first anniversary of the "seizure of power," Hitler spoke of "truly revolutionary measures" that had been taken against the "army of those whose genetic proclivities meant that they had been born on the negative side of ethnic-popular life."[171]

The law decreed that people "whose offspring were, on the basis of medical experience, deemed extremely likely to suffer from serious genetic physical and mental deficiencies" could be made "infertile via surgical operation." Genetic deficiencies in the sense of the law included imbecility, schizophrenia, manic-depressive conditions, falling sickness, Huntington's chorea, congenital blindness and deafness, major physical deformities and even alcoholism. An application for sterilisation could be made either by the persons concerned or their legal representatives, or by public doctors and the directors of hospitals, clinics and convalescent homes. Cases were decided upon by newly established genetic health courts consisting of a judge and two doctors.[172] The introduction of the law was accompanied by a nationwide publicity campaign promoting compulsory sterilisation as "an act of charity and caring."[173] The courts approved 90 per cent of the applications; 290,000–300,000 men and women were sterilised in this fashion before the start of the Second World War, roughly half on the basis of "congenital imbecility"—a very flexible concept.[174] Compulsory sterilisation gave the regime an instrument for extending its policies of racial hygiene to all sorts of marginalised groups and to punish various forms of behaviour that deviated from the social norm. Hans-Ulrich Wehler had correctly called this process a "dry run for the euthanasia programme" after 1939, whose deadly "expunging" was the extreme extension of this sort of "ethnic corpus" therapy.[175]

Germany's Jewish minority was the primary group excluded from the Nazi ethnic-popular community. Hitler set their legal and social marginalisation in motion with the nationwide boycott of Jewish businesses in late March 1933 and the discriminatory laws that followed one month later.[176] After that, however, the Nazi regime held back somewhat. Hitler enumerated the reasons why at a conference of his Reich governors in late September 1933. A transcript of the speech read:

> He as Reich chancellor would have preferred a gradually stricter treatment of Jews in Germany by creating a new citizenship law and then increasingly cracking down on Jews. But the Jewish-organised inter-

national boycott demanded the most vigorous response possible. Abroad people complained that Jews were being treated legally as second-class citizens . . . Since Jews had considerable influence abroad, it was prudent not to give them any material they could use as propaganda against Germany.[177]

But it was not just deference to foreign opinion that initially dissuaded Hitler from forcing through further anti-Jewish laws. Having announced the end of the revolutionary phase of his "seizure of power" in July 1933, he also wanted to rein in the violent excesses of the SA. The Third Reich's first waves of anti-Semitism petered out in the second half of 1933.[178]

Yet away from the public eye, Jews were still being forced out of German economic, social and cultural life. In the towns and villages of provincial Germany, the anti-Jewish boycott continued, and posters and signs reading "Jews unwelcome" or "No admissions for Jews" could be seen at taverns or at the entry to towns. Synagogues were attacked, Jewish graves were defaced, and the homes and businesses of Jews had their windows smashed on a daily basis. Jews were insulted, belittled and physically beaten on the streets. "All the Jewish residents who have not fled live in constant panic," read a Nazi report from the northern Bavarian town of Gunzenhausen, which had seen the outbreak of a fully fledged pogrom in March 1934.[179]

Such anti-Semitic violence offered radical party activists in provincial Germany an ideal environment to draw strict racial borders within local society, isolating their Jewish neighbours and stigmatising "ethnic comrades" who continued to frequent Jewish shops and maintain contact with Jews.[180] Local police officers were caught between a rock and a hard place, having to assert the state's monopoly on force on the one hand while risking unpopularity with the well-known leaders of anti-Semitic mobs on the other. If they intervened at all, it was mostly too late, and as a rule, they arrested the victims and not the perpetrators. "Fearful of the party, the local police authorities do not satisfactorily respond to attacks, which are especially prevalent before Christmas," the state police office in the region of Kassel reported in December 1934.[181]

In the spring of 1935, anti-Jewish agitation dramatically increased. Along with boycotts, local Nazi groups opened up a second battleground with a campaign against so-called "race defilers." Jewish men and non-Jewish women suspected of carrying on affairs were driven through the streets and subjected to public humiliation in "pillory parades."[182] In every corner of the Third Reich, copies of the rabidly anti-Semitic newspaper *Der Stürmer*, with its lurid reports of "race defilement," were publicly displayed in glass cases. Often they listed the names and addresses of "ethnic comrades" who still patronised Jewish businesses. "There are always crowds around the *Stürmer* cases," read a report from East Prussia to the Central Association of German Citizens of the Jewish Faith. "The newspaper and its pictures have a powerful effect on the public, terrifying old customers so that they no longer dare to enter [Jewish] businesses."[183] The pressure to break off social and commercial relationships with Jews was constantly ratcheted up, and few Germans had the courage to resist. For their part, many Jews tried to make themselves inconspicuous and avoided appearing in public. "It is no fun going out any more," the forcibly retired teacher Willy Cohn wrote from Breslau. "The repulsive articles in the *Stürmer* are everywhere. It is surprising that more doesn't happen considering how incited the populace is."[184]

This second wave of anti-Semitism in Germany was not ordered from above, but there are indications that it was entirely welcome to the Nazi leadership, including Hitler. It was a pressure valve for dissatisfaction among the party grass roots, in particular SA men frustrated by the Night of the Long Knives. Moreover, after the success of the Saar referendum in January and the unproblematic reintroduction of compulsory military service in March, the need to defer to foreign opinion decreased. Significantly, that April, Hitler rejected an appeal to ban signs reading "Jews forbidden," which were said to make a bad impression on foreign visitors. On the contrary, Hitler said that he had "nothing against such signs."[185] Not without reason, the most radical party activists believed that they were acting in Hitler's interests, even if the regime did not officially endorse the anti-Semitic violence. The opinion that "the Führer had two faces," wrote a Hessian senior official from Wiesbaden, was widespread within "low-ranking party offices." He believed that: "Certain ordinances, especially in the area of the Jewish question, had to be issued because of foreign opinion. But the Führer's true will was known to every genuine National Socialist from his world view, and the task was to carry out this will."[186] In May 1935, the Gestapo in the region of Münster reported that broad sections of the movement, especially the SA, thought that the time had come "to take care of the Jewish problem from the ground up" and that the government would "then follow."[187]

The Nazi press whipped up the anti-Semitic fervour, with Goebbels in the role of the ringleader. "Jewish question—take more of a lead," he noted in early May 1935. During a stroll down Berlin's Kurfürstendamm, he found himself angered by the number of Jews who still appeared in public. "Another veritable parade of Jews. That will have to be taken care of soon."[188] In the newspaper *Der Angriff*, he wrote: "Some people believe that we do not notice how Jewry is once more trying to spread out today across all our streets. The Jew had better respect the dictates of hospitality and not act as if he were our equal."[189]

But in the spring of 1935, it became clear that once unleashed, anti-Semitic violence could develop a dynamic of its own and spread beyond the control of party authorities. In late May in Munich, Nazi activists and SS men in civilian clothing descended upon Jewish businesses in the city, intimidating customers and employees, and forcing shop owners to close their doors. Passers-by who criticised what was going on were abused, and a few policemen physically attacked. "These conditions are intolerable," protested the Jewish lawyer Leopold Weinmann, who had witnessed several of the incidents, in a letter to the Reich Interior Ministry. "Surely a cultured tourist city like Munich cannot tolerate regularly recurring scenes straight out of the Wild West."[190]

In mid-July, there was also major anti-Semitic violence in Berlin. The starting point was a cinema on Kurfürstendamm where Jewish patrons had allegedly protested against the showing of the anti-Semitic Swedish film *Petterson and Brendel*. Goebbels, who was on holiday in the Baltic Sea resort of Heiligendamm and who discussed the matter intensely with Hitler from 12 to 14 July, remarked: "Telegram from Berlin: Jews demonstrating against an anti-Semitic film. The Führer has had enough . . . This is truly outlandish. Something will have to give soon."[191] On the evening of 15 July, as *Der Angriff* reported the next day, a mob assembled in front of the cinema in order to "express their dissatisfaction at the provocative behaviour of the Jewish cinemagoers."[192] Afterwards, the demonstrators moved on to nearby cafés and restaurants where they beat up Jewish patrons and passers-by. "The street echoed with countless repeated cries of 'The Jews are our misfortune!,'" wrote the reporter for the Swiss *Neue Zürcher Zeitung* newspaper.

> Several Jewish shops were demolished. In panicked terror, several figures that were difficult to identify in the light of the street lamps fled across the boulevard . . . Vendors of *Der Stürmer* appeared with thick bundles of the paper and did brisk business. Gradually the police dispersed the mob and restored the normal flow of traffic. By 12.30 in the morning the tumult was over.[193]

The unrest was replicated in many German cities and regions, accompanied by a frenetic anti-Semitic publicity campaign. "The anti-Jewish agitation has exceeded all bounds," noted Victor Klemperer in his diary in early August 1935. "It is much worse than during the first boycott. Here and there, there have been incipient pogroms. Everyone fears that they will be beaten to death before too long."[194] With violence threatening to get completely out of hand, the Nazi leadership decided that the time was ripe to draw in the reins. "Clear instructions from central administrative offices are needed as to what is allowed and what is not in the anti-Jewish wave of propaganda," the state police office of the region of Cologne was already demanding in June 1935. Otherwise, police officers, who "ultimately bore the entire weight of responsibility," could not count on adequate support when they intervened.[195]

On 4 August, at the Gau party conference in Essen, Interior Minister Frick announced comprehensive legal measures concerning the "Jewish question," explicitly coming out against street terror by radical party members.[196] Five days later, Hitler had his deputy Hess tell all party offices to prevent individual acts of violence against Jews in future.[197] These individual instances of persecution had served their purpose in so far as they had paved the way for a further tightening of anti-Semitic legislation. Speaking in the wake of the unrest in Berlin, the head of the Security Service of the SS, Reinhard Heydrich, made much the same point: "The racially inclined part of the German people believes that the measures taken thus far without fanfare against the Jews are insufficient and they are demanding a generally stricter approach."[198] A memo by the Security Service's "Department of Jewish Affairs" of 17 August seconded that sentiment, stating that "all major offices reject a solution to the Jewish question by acts of terror." Instead, the memo argued, it was necessary to proclaim "effective laws to show the people that the Jewish question is being resolved from above."[199]

The Gestapo and Security Service's "Jewish experts" shared this wish with Hjalmar Schacht, whom Hitler had made Reich economics minister in early August 1934 in addition to his duties as president of the Reichsbank. In May 1935 he had complained to Hitler about the "uncontrolled battle against individual Jews outside the law, indeed in contravention of government ordinances," warning that the international boycott was having a negative effect on the German economy.[200] In a speech in Königsberg on 10 August, which was broadcast on national radio, Schacht launched a remarkably direct attack on anti-Semitic rowdies in the NSDAP, calling them "people who heroically deface windows at night and put up posters calling any German who buys anything in a Jewish shop a traitor to his people."[201] But this criticism was by no means a rejection of the Nazis' racist anti-Jewish policies, as Schacht made clear two days later at a high-ranking meeting at the Economics Ministry, to which he invited Wilhelm Frick, Franz Gürtner, Schwerin von Krosigk, Reinhard Heydrich, Education Minister Bernhard Rust and Prussian finance minister Johannes Popitz.

There a determined Schacht demanded that the "current lawlessness and the illegal activity" be halted since it made it impossible for him "to solve the economic questions with which he was entrusted." At the same time, he stated for the record that he held the principles of the National Socialist programme to be "thoroughly correct" and felt that they "must be carried through by all means." Schacht declared: "I've lived for thirty years with Jews, and for thirty years I have taken money from them, not vice versa. Nonetheless, the current methods are intolerable. A system has to be introduced into the prevailing confusion, and before this system is put into practice, people must cease and desist from other measures." Frick agreed that the "Jewish question" could not be solved with "wild individual actions," but rather only "slowly but surely with legal means" until, in accordance with the party manifesto, "the alien Jewish organism has been expunged without exception from the German people." Frick announced that laws were being drawn up to "rein in the dominance of Jewish influence." Among them was a "law on race," which, as Gürtner elaborated, would prohibit marriage between Jews and Aryans. Heydrich, who spoke last, concurred with the earlier speakers that the unsatisfactory situation at present could only be cleared up through "legislative measures by the state that would gradually, step by step and upon orders by the Führer achieve the goal of expunging the Jewish influence without exception."[202]

In a letter of 9 September to the participants at the meeting, Heydrich once again detailed his proposals for "solving the Jewish question." He called for the Jews to be subjected to "foreigners' law" as a means of "separating them from the German ethnic-popular community" and of denying them freedom of mobility, thereby preventing "the tide of Jews moving to the big cities." "Mixed marriages" should be forbidden, and extramarital relations between Germans and Jews criminalised as acts of "racial defilement." Public contracts should no longer be awarded to Jews, and they should be prohibited from dealing in property. All of these measures, Heydrich wrote in summing up, would serve as an "incentive to emigrate."[203] That was the goal which the head of the Security Service was advocating in the mid-1930s. "Systematic mass murder," Heydrich's biographer Robert Gerwarth has concluded, "was at this point beyond the imagination of even Heydrich and his anti-Jewish 'theoretical pioneers.'"[204] The same seems to have been true of Hitler. Despite the homicidal fantasies he had committed to paper in *Mein Kampf,* his steadfast insistence of "removing" Jews from the German ethnic-popular community did not entail physically annihilating them, but rather pursuing their legal discrimination, social isolation and economic expropriation to the point that they would either live in Germany under pitiable conditions and in utter segregation—or, preferably, be forced to emigrate.

By late August 1935, a broad consensus had crystallised between the Nazi leadership, the relevant government ministries and the Gestapo and the Security Service as to how to proceed on the "Jewish question." The approval of the race laws at the Nuremberg rally in mid-September was no great surprise.[205] What was surprising was that Hitler staged the announcement in a manoeuvre reminiscent of his foreign-policy coups. Originally, the Reichstag, which was called to session for the first and only time in Nuremberg on 15 September, was only supposed to ratify a law making the swastika flag the Reich's official national banner, replacing the old black-white-and-red imperial flag. The background was an incident in New York, where anti-Nazi dock workers had forcibly lowered the swastika flag from the MS *Bremen*. They were arrested, but an American judge subsequently ordered their release and attacked the policies of the Third Reich. Hitler and Goebbels were livid. The propaganda minister noted: "Our answer: The Reichstag will convene in Nuremberg and declare the swastika banner to be our national flag. Hitler in full swing."[206]

But on the evening of 13 September, the fourth day of the Nuremberg rally, Hitler decided that the Reichstag session should ratify not just the Reich Flag Law, but also the "race law," which Frick and Gürtner had announced at the meeting of 20 August. Goebbels wrote: "In the evening palaver in the hotel. Consulted with the Führer about the new laws."[207] The reasons for Hitler's sudden decision are not entirely clear. Possibly, with pressure from below having built up for months, Hitler may have felt that the time was ripe to placate his radical party comrades with a decisive administrative step and thus tame their need for action. That would be in keeping with his tendency to postpone taking major decisions, only to then make up his mind in a flash without considering any arguments to the contrary. He knew that the preparations for the planned law were advanced, and in his eyes, the rally may have seemed like the perfect forum to pressure the ministerial bureaucrats to finish formulating it and to ensure that it was greeted with the maximum enthusiasm when announced.

Late on the evening of 13 September Ministerial Counsel Bernhard Lösener, the "Jewish expert" in the Reich Interior Ministry, was ordered by telephone to fly to Nuremberg the next morning with his colleague from the Central Division, Ministerial Counsel Franz Albrecht Medicus. There they were informed by State Secretaries Hans Pfundtner and Wilhelm Stuckart that Hitler had charged them the previous day with formulating a "Jewish law" that would prohibit marriages between Jews and Aryans, extramarital sexual relations between the two, and the employment of Aryan servant girls in Jewish households.[208] Over the course of the day, the bureaucrats came up with a number of versions, which Frick presented to Hitler, only to be sent back with orders for changes. The main issue was whether the law should only apply to "full Jews," or whether it was to include Jewish "half-breeds' as well. Finally, around midnight, Hitler ordered the bureaucrats to give him four variations by the following morning, ranging from a strict version A to intermediate versions B and C to a mild version D. To "round off the legislation," he also demanded a Reich Citizenship Law to be presented to him that very night. In his recollections from 1950, Lösener was still outraged at "Hitler's new mood" that had forced him and his colleagues to come up with the draft law under extreme pressure when they were "physically and mentally at the end of their strength."[209] In fact, this was anything but a spontaneous intervention by Hitler. On the contrary, the need for a new Reich citizenship law had been under discussion for months, and preparations were well advanced. It only made sense to introduce it together with the "race law." Goebbels emphasised the connection in his diary entry he wrote about a conference with Hitler during the night of 14–15 September: "Frick and Hess were still there. Thoroughly consulted about the laws. New citizenship law that strips Jews of citizenship . . . Jew law that prohibits Jewish marriages with Germans and a series of other intensifications. We're still adjusting it. But it will work."[210]

The ministerial bureaucrats only learned during the Reichstag session on 15 September that Hitler had opted for the mild version D, albeit having struck out the phrase "This law only applies to full Jews" with his own hand, yet in the official announcements of the law, presumably with an eye towards foreign reactions, the phrase was maintained.[211] The Law for the Protection of German Blood and German Honour prohibited marriage and sexual intercourse "between Jews and citizens of Germany or related blood." Jews were also banned from taking on non-Jewish female household employees under the age of 45 and from "flying the Reich and national flag or displaying the Reich colours." The Reich Citizenship Law read: "A Reich citizen can only be someone who is a national of German or related blood and who proves by his conduct that he is willing and suitable to loyally serve the German people and Reich." Only full Reich citizens were entitled to "full political rights as spelled out in laws." Jewish Germans would henceforth only be considered as members of "the Protective Association of the German Reich," to which they owed "special loyalty."[212]

In a short speech by his standards, in the auditorium of the Nuremberg Cultural Association, in which he asked the Reichstag deputies to ratify the law, Hitler let the tactically maintained mask of moderation drop and showed himself for what he truly was: a fanatic anti-Semite who was determined to enact the racist Nazi programme at all costs. He scathingly attacked Jews in Germany and abroad whom he accused of being "corrosive and pitting peoples against one another." He unapologetically declared that the victims of anti-Semitism in Germany had triggered the violence themselves. In numerous locations, Hitler contended, people had "bitterly complained about the provocative behaviour of individual members of this people." If such behaviour was not to lead "to unpredictable defensive reactions of the outraged populace . . . the only way was to legally regulate the problem." His government had been guided, Hitler claimed, by the idea that "a singular secular solution would perhaps create a level on which the German people might find a tolerable relationship to the Jewish people." Should this hope not materialise, Hitler threatened, the problem would be transferred to the National Socialist Party "for a definitive solution."[213] In other words, in that case the radical activists in the party would be given the green light to intensify the anti-Semitic pressure from below.

Hitler's claim that the Nuremberg Laws were an attempt to find a "tolerable relationship to the Jewish people" was a deliberate lie intended to lead the public astray. In his diary, Goebbels left no doubt that the laws of 15 September were aimed at segregating Jews from the majority of society and providing momentum for their further persecution. "Today was of secular significance," he wrote. "Jewry has suffered a heavy blow. We have dared become the first people in many hundreds of years to take the bull by the horns."[214] Ten days after the Reichstag had unanimously ratified the Nuremberg Laws, Walter Gross, the Reich director of the NSDAP Office for Racial Politics, told his local officials how Hitler wished them to be interpreted: "The ultimate goal . . . of the Third Reich's entire racial policy . . . is the displacement of everything Jewish in the sense of the excretion of an alien element."[215]

"If you followed the National Socialist movement attentively, you had to see these things coming," Willy Cohn commented after the ratification of the Nuremberg Laws. "In this respect they're extremely consistent."[216] Victor Klemperer, who was married to a non-Jewish German, confined himself to a bitter diary entry: "The disgust is enough to make you ill."[217] The Nazi press enthusiastically welcomed the new legislation. On 16 September, the *Westdeutscher Beobachter* led with the headline: "We profess our loyalty to the purity of the race!" In a cynical commentary, the editor-in-chief wrote: "The Jewish race should feel lucky for the generosity of an Adolf Hitler. Every other people would have deemed its corrupters fair game. Instead of an emergency law, however, Germany provides state protection and legal order."[218]

It seems that the reactions of the German populace to the Nuremberg Laws varied greatly. Gestapo reports initially asserted that the laws had been received with approval and satisfaction since they finally created "a situation of clarity" and would put an end to the "unsavoury individual actions" of previous months.[219] On the other hand, from heavily Catholic areas like the region of Aachen came reports that "the laws had not been greeted with unanimous applause."[220] SPD-in-exile observers even wrote that the laws had "been met with vigorous rejection within the populace" and had been interpreted "not as a sign of the strength of the National Socialist movement but as evidence of weakness."[221] At the same time, the observers could not deny that constant anti-Semitic propaganda had left its mark on the German working classes. "In general, one can say that the National Socialists have in fact succeeded in deepening the gap between the people and the Jews," one report from January 1936 read. "The sense that the Jews are a separate race is now very common."[222]

Because Hitler had rejected the proviso that the Nuremberg Laws should only apply to "full Jews," instructions on how the laws were to be enforced needed to answer the question of who was in fact affected. A bitter, extended quarrel arose between the Interior Ministry and representatives of the NSDAP. Whereas Wilhelm Stuckart and Bernhard Lösener felt that only people with more than two Jewish grandparents should be considered Jewish, party representatives led by the Reich Doctors' leader, Gerhard Wagner, insisted that the definition be expanded to included "quarter-Jews," defined as people with one Jewish grandparent.[223] Hitler initially avoided making a decision. Goebbels noted on 1 October: "Jewish question still not decided. We've debated for a long while, but the Führer is still unsure."[224] The argument continued throughout October and was increasingly focused round the status of "half-Jews," defined as people with two Jewish grandparents. At the last minute, Hitler cancelled a high-level meeting on 5 November intended to resolve the issue.[225] But there came a point when further delays were impossible. "The Führer wants a decision now," Goebbels noted on 7 November. "A compromise has to be reached anyway, and an absolutely satisfactory solution is impossible."[226]

The First Ordinance on the Reich Citizenship Law of 14 November ended the tug of war. The Interior Ministry had largely got its way on the question of who was to be defined as Jewish, as the ordinance stipulated: "A Jew is someone descended from at least three Jewish grandparents in the racial sense." "Half-Jews" were only to be treated as Jews if they were members of the Jewish religious community or married to a Jewish spouse.[227] Goebbels noted: "A compromise but the best one available. Quarter-Jews to us. Half-Jews only in exceptional cases. In God's name, let's have some peace. Announce it skilfully and discreetly in the press. Not too much hullaballoo."[228] The propaganda minister's reticence was understandable. The ordinance revealed the utter absurdity of trying to classify the population according to racist criteria. For example, "half-Jews" were defined as people who had "two Jewish grandparents in the racial sense." But since there was no way to determine legally the characteristics of the Jewish "race," religion had to be enlisted. The ordinance stated: "A grandparent is automatically considered fully Jewish if he or she belonged to the Jewish religious community." It would have been difficult to make the grotesque senselessness of Nazi racial legislation any more apparent.[229]

In the wake of the Nuremberg Laws, the petty, everyday war against Jews continued. But with the Olympics approaching, the Nazi regime had no interest in a repeat of the pogrom-like violence of the summer of 1935. A few days before the start of the Winter Olympics in Garmisch-Partenkirchen, Hess ordered the removal of all "signs with extremist content" so as to avoid "making a bad impression on foreign tourists."[230] The German press was instructed on 27 January 1936 not to report on "violent confrontations with Jews": "Such things should be scrupulously avoided, right on down to the local sections of newspapers, in order not to provide foreign propaganda with material it can use against the Winter Games."[231]

When Wilhelm Gustloff, the leader of the Swiss branch of the NSDAP, was shot dead in Davos by a Jewish medical student two days before the start of the Games, the Nazi leadership's reaction was muted. Goebbels's spontaneous reaction was: "The Jews will pay for this. We'll take major actions against this."[232] But Hitler restrained his propaganda minister. As would not be the case with Kristallnacht in November 1938, this time the regime made no attempt to use the assassination as an excuse to mobilise "popular anger" against the Jewish minority.[233] At Gustloff's funeral in the northern German city of Schwerin on 12 February, Hitler did launch some sharply worded attacks, however, claiming that the Davos killing was evidence of a "guiding hand" and the "hateful power of our Jewish enemies." He added: "We understand and register this declaration of war!"[234]

The International Olympic Committee had awarded Berlin the 1936 Summer Games in 1931, but a year later, when the Nazis became the strongest party in Germany, the IOC began to have reservations. Via an intermediary, the Belgian IOC president, Henri de Baillet-Latour, enquired at the Brown House how the National Socialists intended to stage the Games should they come to power. Hitler answered that he was looking forward to the Games with "great interest."[235] On 16 March 1933, the newly appointed chancellor received the president of the German National Olympic Committee, Theodor Lewald, and promised him support for the preparation of the Games "in every respect."[236] Hitler refused the offer of an honorary post with the committee, but he did take over symbolic patronage for the event after Hindenburg's death in November 1934.[237] In the meantime, the IOC had also awarded the Winter Games to Garmisch-Partenkirchen.

From the very beginning, Hitler recognised the opportunities that came with hosting the Olympics. They offered a unique chance to present the world with images of a reinvigorated but peaceful and cosmopolitan Germany. He and Goebbels saw absolutely eye to eye on this. The latter's ministry formed a "propaganda committee for the Olympic Games" in January 1934 to coordinate large-scale publicity campaigns in Germany and abroad. "The 1936 Olympics are going to be huge," Goebbels promised. "We're really going to beat the drum!"[238] The regime spared neither effort nor money to squeeze every last drop of prestige from the Games. On 5 October 1933, Hitler made an initial inspection of the site for the "Reich Sports Field" on Berlin's western fringe to get a picture of the location and the progress made in the preparations. He brusquely cancelled the plans of sports functionaries to expand the existing stadium, ordering the construction of a new, modern arena with a capacity of 100,000 spectators. It was a "Reich task," Hitler declared in notes taken by Lewald: "If you've invited the whole world as your guest, something grandiose and beautiful must be created . . . a few million more here or there make no difference."[239] The gigantic site was to be transformed into the largest sporting complex in the world, with numerous additional sites for competitions, an open-air stage, a "House of German Sports" and military marching grounds. The architect Werner March, who had constructed the models for Germany's application to the IOC, was commissioned to plan the entire project.[240]

Hitler enthusiastically followed construction progress, suggesting changes and occasionally criticising the design of the stadium, with which he was never completely satisfied.[241] It is pure legend, however, that he was so angry about March's plans that he threatened to cancel the Olympics, as Albert Speer later contended in his memoirs and as Joachim Fest naively passed on.[242] Speer, who was only at the beginning of his career as Hitler's favourite architect in 1933 and 1934, was likely disappointed by someone else being commissioned to build the Olympic Stadium.

A more serious threat to the 1936 Olympics was the international movement calling for a boycott that had formed shortly after Hitler had assumed power. The early anti-Semitic excesses of the Nazi regime occasioned outrage—particularly in the United States. By April 1933, the *New York Times* was already reporting that the Games could be cancelled because of the German government's campaign against the Jews.[243] The president of the American Olympic Committee, Avery Brundage, floated the idea of transferring the Games to Rome or Tokyo, or cancelling them altogether. The IOC was satisfied, however, when the German side declared that it would adhere to Olympic rules and Jewish Germans would not be excluded from any of the competitions. In June 1934, the German Olympic Committee nominated twenty-one Jewish athletes for the Olympic training camp, but in the end, only two token individuals—"half-Jews" under Nazi racial classification—were included in Germany's Olympic team: the ice hockey player Rudi Ball, who plied his trade in Italy, and fencer Helene Mayer, who won gold for Germany in 1928 and had lived in California since 1932. She would win the silver medal in Berlin.[244]

A cancellation of the Games or a boycott by a great sporting nation like the United States would have meant a significant loss of prestige, and Hitler was at pains to take the wind out of his critics' sails.[245] He was assisted in this by Theodor Lewald who, despite being regularly assailed in the Nazi press for his Jewish background, did everything in his power to reassure the foreign public and the IOC about the

National Socialists' intentions. In the summer of 1934, when Brundage travelled to Germany to get a picture of the situation of Jewish athletes, his host adroitly threw dust in his eyes. Upon returning to the US, Brundage became a steadfast advocate of United States participation in both the Winter and Summer Games.[246] Nonetheless, the anti-Semitic violence of the summer of 1935 and the Nuremberg Laws rekindled the debate about the Games in the United States. Advocates of a boycott seemed to gain the upper hand in the country's largest athletics association, the Amateur Athletic Union, with AAU President Jeremiah Mahoney telling Lewald in October 1935 that participation in the Games would amount to a tacit acknowledgement of "everything the swastika symbolised."[247] But Avery Brundage and his supporters managed to secure a slight majority at the AAU convention that December. Germany's sports functionaries and the leaders of the regime breathed a sigh of relief.[248]

Only two months later, on 6 February 1936, Hitler opened the Winter Games in the Garmisch-Partenkirchen ice hockey stadium in front of 60,000 spectators and more than 1,000 athletes from 28 countries. "Endless applause from the audience," noted Goebbels. "Almost all foreign athletes performed the Hitler salute when they marched past the Führer."[249] But the propaganda minister as well as most German people present mistook the traditional Olympic raised-right-arm salute for the Nazi "German greeting."[250] All in all the Nazi leadership was satisfied with the ten-day event, at which the Norwegian figure-skating gold medallist Sonja Henie had captured the hearts of the crowds. The test run for Berlin had been a success, and there had been no unwelcome incidents. "On the whole the Nazis have done a wonderful propaganda job," William Shirer admitted. "They've greatly impressed most of the visiting foreigners with the lavish but smooth way in which they've run the games and with their kind manners, which to us who came from Berlin of course seemed staged."[251]

After Garmisch-Partenkirchen, not even the remilitarisation of the Rhineland, which so blatantly belied Hitler's pretence of peacefulness, could endanger the Berlin Games. On the contrary, the ineffectual response of the Western allies to yet another German violation of international agreements weakened the position of those who favoured a boycott. Even France, the country that should have felt most threatened by the remilitarisation, never seriously considered withholding its athletes from the competition. The new Popular Front government under socialist premier Léon Blum approved the funds for the French Olympic team. The policy of appeasement also won out within the Olympic movement.

The Reich capital got a thorough makeover. "Berlin is being transformed into a true festival city," Goebbels noted on 24 July, a week before the start of the Games. "But there's still a lot to do." On 30 July, after a drive around the city to inspect things, he was satisfied: "Berlin is now ready. It is gleaming in its lightest vestments."[252] Banners and other symbols of the regime were everywhere, on public squares, office buildings and private houses. Signs refusing entry to Jews had been removed, and discriminatory labels on park benches painted over.[253] For two weeks, Der Stürmer was nowhere to be found at newspaper kiosks, and Der Angriff reminded its readers to be solicitous towards foreign visitors: "We must be more charming than the Parisians, easier-going than the Viennese, livelier than the Romans, more cosmopolitan than Londoners and more practical than New Yorkers."[254] An Olympic tourist guide presented Berlin as a vibrant world metropolis and as the headquarters of a confident nationalist government: "[Wilhelmstrasse] is home to the workplace of a man whom every visitor to Berlin would give his eye-teeth to see: Adolf Hitler."[255]

If it was raining slightly in Berlin on 1 August, the opening day of the eleventh Olympic Summer Games, it did nothing to dampen the "festival fever."[256] At 1 p.m., Hitler received the members of the International and German National Olympic Committees, thanking them for their work and declaring that the German Reich had "gladly and happily" taken on responsibility for hosting the competition in a form "befitting the great idea and traditions of the Olympic Games."[257] Undermining this sentiment was the fact that Hitler, after travelling the 15-kilometre stretch to the Reich Sports Field in an open car that afternoon, first stopped at the Bell Tower to inspect an honour guard of the army, navy and air force and then proceeded with Werner von Blomberg to the Langemarckhalle to commemorate Germany's fallen soldiers in the First World War. Only after that, at 4 p.m., did he lead a delegation of the IOC and the German National Olympic Committee into the Olympic Stadium, where he strode, frenetically cheered by 80,000 spectators, to his "Führer box." The strict choreography of the ceremony was interrupted for a moment, when a small girl—

the 5-year-old daughter of the general secretary of the German National Olympic Committee—ran up to Hitler, curtsied and gave him a bouquet of flowers. The scene was apparently unplanned, but Hitler, who gladly had his picture taken with children, must have liked it.[258]

After that the forty-nine participating nations paraded into the stadium. (The Soviet Union boycotted the event, and the country's civil war kept Spain out of the Games.) The French were greeted with particular applause when they walked past the Führer's box with arms raised, which the crowd again misinterpreted as the German greeting. By contrast, the British team declined to salute and was given a cool reception, which even Goebbels described as "somewhat embarrassing."[259] When all the teams had arrived in the oval arena, Hitler declared the Games open for competition. The Olympic flag was raised, thousands of doves flew towards the heavens which had cleared by now, and cannons fired a twenty-one-gun salute. An Olympic hymn especially composed by Richard Strauss was played. Then the final torchbearer ran into the stadium and lit the Olympic fire. Rudolf Ismayr, a gold-medal-winning weightlifter at the 1932 Games in Los Angeles, recited the Olympic oath, although he took hold of the swastika banner, not the five-ringed Olympic flag—the merging of Nazi elements into Olympic ritual could hardly have been more obvious.[260]

The entire opening ceremony was designed to focus on Hitler. Fanfares announced his arrival, and his way to the VIP box was musically accompanied by Wagner's "Homage March." The enthusiasm that greeted Hitler in the stadium was not lost on the foreign athletes. One female Olympian from Britain felt that it was as if God himself had descended from heaven.[261] That evening, the people of Berlin showered their leader with tempestuous ovations when he returned to Wilhelmstrasse. "Often on the balcony," noted Goebbels. "The masses were out of their heads. It was very moving. Girls were brought up and wept before the Führer. A beautiful and a great day. A victory for the German cause."[262]

Hitler attended almost every day of competition, and those who observed him up close were taken aback by his behaviour. The sporting spirit was alien to the leader of the Third Reich. If German athletes were beaten, his countenance immediately darkened. But if a German sportsman won, reported Martha Dodd, his enthusiasm knew no limits, and he would leap up from his seat with childish glee.[263] It is a legend, however, that he refused to shake hands with the black American sprinter Jesse Owens, who won four gold medals and became the star of the Games. After Hitler had congratulated the Finnish and German medal winners on the first day of competition in his box, Henri de Baillet-Latour pointed out that such a gesture violated the Olympic protocol, whereupon Hitler did not congratulate any of the winners.[264] Nevertheless, numerous sources show that Hitler and the other leading Nazis were not at all pleased about the multiple triumphs of a black American since they convincingly gave the lie to the doctrine of the superiority of the "white race." After the events of 4 August, Goebbels noted: "We Germans won one gold medal, and the Americans three, two of them by a Negro. That's a scandal. White people should be ashamed. But what does that matter over there in that country without culture."[265] When Baldur von Schirach suggested it would make an excellent impression abroad if Hitler were to receive Owens in the Chancellery, the dictator was outraged. "Do you truly believe that I will allow myself to be photographed shaking hands with a Negro?" Hitler yelled in Schirach's face.[266]

Hans Frank remembered Hitler being "passionately interested" in the Games and "always full of feverish suspense at who would win what medal."[267] In the end, Germany topped the medals table ahead of the United States with 33 gold, 26 silver and 30 bronze—an outcome Goebbels praised as being "the result of reawakened ambition." He added: "This Olympics is a very big breakthrough . . . we can once more be proud of Germany . . . The leading sports nation in the world. That is magnificent."[268]

Germany impressed the world not just with sporting successes, but also, as had been the case in Garmisch-Partenkirchen, with its perfect organisation and an accompanying programme that showcased the regime's best side to foreign visitors. In retrospect, Hitler's interpreter Paul Schmidt called the sixteen-day event an "apotheosis for Hitler and the Third Reich." In numerous conversations with foreigners, Schmidt observed that they encountered Hitler with "the highest interest—to say nothing of great admiration."[269] André François-Poncet made a similar observation:

> The power of attraction he emanates has an effect beyond the borders of his own country. Kings, princes and famous guests come to the

capital less to take in the upcoming Games than to meet this man, who seems destined to so greatly influence the future and who seems to hold the fate of the continent in his hands."[270]

Hitler's paladins fell over themselves trying to outdo one another with parties and receptions for international VIPs. Joachim von Ribbentrop, just named Nazi Germany's ambassador to Great Britain, invited more than 600 guests to dinner at his villa in the southern Berlin district of Dahlem on 11 August. Three days later, Göring hosted a huge garden party in the grounds of the new Aviation Ministry, and Goebbels topped everyone on 15 August, the day before the Olympics concluded, with an "Italian Night" on Pfaueninsel Island in the Havel River that was attended by more than 2,700 people. "Great fireworks," he noted. "A life as never before. Magical lighting . . . Partner dancing. An elegant picture . . . The nicest party we've ever hosted."[271]

The 1936 Olympic Summer Games were also a media spectacle. More than 1,800 journalists were accredited for the event, and 41 broadcasters from around the world had sent reporters, who worked in sound booths in the Olympic Stadium; 125 German photographers supplied national and international agencies with pictures. For the first time ever, a major sporting event was broadcast live on television on the "Paul Nipkow" station and 160,000 viewers were able to watch the competitions in "television parlours" in Berlin, Potsdam and Leipzig, although the quality of the broadcasts left much to be desired.[272]

The most lasting impression came from Leni Riefenstahl's documentary film about the Olympics, for which she had been commissioned in August 1935. Once again, Hitler's star director came up with a number of innovations. She attached hand cameras to balloons so as to capture a bird's-eye view of the stadium. Trenches inside the arena allowed cameramen to film the athletes from close proximity and unusual angles. Riefenstahl's footage not only cast an aesthetic eye on perfectly trained, mostly masculine bodies. It was also a homage to the "new Germany," which she depicted as the successor to Ancient Greece. Various sequences showed Hitler as a true sports lover rooting for Germany's athletes and celebrating their triumphs. The two-part film—entitled *Festival of Peoples* and *Festival of Beauty*—premiered in the Ufa-Palast cinema on 20 April 1938, Hitler's forty-ninth birthday. Like her Nuremberg rally films, it was valuable to the Nazis because it concealed the reality of the Third Reich behind the beautifully staged appearances of the peaceful Olympic Games. "One is carried away by the power, depth and beauty of this work," Goebbels enthused. "A masterful achievement by Leni Riefenstahl."[273]

Without doubt, the Olympic Games were a great propaganda triumph for the Nazi regime and did wonders for Hitler's international standing. Most of the foreign journalists and visitors were blinded by the welcoming atmosphere and the smooth organisation. The Nazis had "put up a very good front," William Shirer concluded.[274] Once the Games were over, everyday reality in the Third Reich, including the persecution of Jews, soon resumed. There was a common saying among party radicals and SA men: "Once the Games are history, we'll beat the Jews into misery."[275] Victor Klemperer, who saw through the false front of the Olympics better than most people, predicted an "explosion" at the next Nuremberg rally, in which people would take their pent-up desire for aggression out on Jews.[276] Indeed, at the rally in September 1936, Nazi leaders competed with one another to see who could deliver the most hateful anti-Semitic tirade. In his opening and concluding speeches, Hitler once again invoked the Jewish-Bolshevik "global peril." An "international Jewish revolutionary centre in Moscow," he claimed, "was trying to revolutionise Europe via radio broadcasts and thousands of money and agitation channels."[277] The wild demagogue of Munich's beer cellars in the 1920s once again broke through the façade of the statesman and "people's chancellor." "What the Party Conference of Honour brought forth . . . in paroxysms of Jew-baiting and insane lies exceeded the imagination," wrote the down-hearted Klemperer in his diary. "You constantly hope that voices of shame and fear would be raised and a protest from abroad would come . . . but no!" Instead, Klemperer was forced to record, "admiration for the Third Reich, for its culture, trembling fear in the face of its army and its threats."[278]

17

Dictatorship by Division, Architecture of Intimidation

"What does it feel like, Herr Reichskanzler, being a Reichskanzler?" Sefton Delmer asked Hitler in February 1933, shortly after he was named German chancellor. "Do you know, Mr. Delmer," Hitler answered. "I've made a great discovery. There's nothing to this business of governing. Absolutely nothing. It is all done for you . . . you just simply sign your name to what is put before you, and that is that."[1] If Hitler did in fact say what the British journalist wrote in his memoirs, it was one of his typical poses. The truth is that in the early months of his government, the new man in charge was very diligent about performing his duties as chancellor.

He would arrive in his office punctually at 10 a.m., consult with his most important aides and force himself to read documents.[2] He carefully prepared himself for cabinet meetings in an attempt to impress his conservative coalition partners with his knowledge of details.[3] Hitler had no experience whatsoever in administration, so especially at the start he depended on ministerial civil servants. On the evening of 29 January 1933, in the Hotel Kaiserhof, he allegedly offered the ministerial counsel of the Interior Ministry, Hans Heinrich Lammers, the post of state secretary in the Chancellery with the words that he himself "was no politician and did not know anything of this administration business." Hitler did not intend to change, but he also did not want to embarrass himself, so he felt he needed "a civil servant who knows his way around."[4]

The more invulnerable Hitler thought his power was, however, and the less heed he had to pay Hindenburg and his conservative coalition partners, the more he tried to duck the routine duties of his office. With visible pleasure he told those around him again and again how people had "tried to get him used to how civil servants worked" and how he had been "so occupied reading through files and going through current issues" that he had no time "to take a calm look at larger problems."[5] Albert Speer quoted Hitler once saying over lunch: "In the first few weeks, every minute detail was laid before me to decide. I found piles of files on my desk every day, and no matter how hard I worked, they never got any fewer. Until I radically put an end to such senselessness."[6]

When the ailing Hindenburg retreated to his East Prussian estate in the spring of 1934, Hitler's self-imposed discipline concerning work dissipated noticeably, and he no longer bothered to maintain regular office routines. When he hired his assistant Fritz Wiedemann a few days before Christmas in 1933, he told him that he initially had had "great respect" for ministerial civil servants, but had since come to see that "they only put on their pants one leg at a time."[7]

In a remarkably brief time, Hitler had learned how to use the bureaucratic apparatus for his own ends so that he no longer had to be constantly present in the Chancellery. That gave him the space to pursue his personal interests and proclivities. Once again he was beset by the restlessness that had driven him from one campaign event to the next during his "days of battle." One manifestation was an insatiable desire to travel. "I cannot imagine anything more terrible than to sit in an office day in, day out, and to spend my whole life poring over files," one of his domestic servants overheard him saying on one of his car journeys. "I am afraid of getting old and not being able to travel as I like."[8] One of his favourite destinations was Munich. Speer, who had become part of his entourage of close associates over the course of 1933 and 1934, noticed that Hitler always reverted to his bohemian ways when he visited the Bavarian capital: "Most of his time is spent strolling around aimlessly, visiting construction sites, artists' studios, cafés and restaurants."[9]

During the first year of his reign, Hitler lived in Berlin in the official state secretary's apartment on the fourth floor of the extension to the Chancellery in Wilhelmstrasse 78, which had been opened in 1930. He was unable to move immediately into the old Chancellery at Wilhelmstrasse 77, the former Radziwill family mansion in which Bismarck, his successors and the chancellors of the Weimar Republic had lived, because Hindenburg had been using it since the autumn of 1932 while the Reich president's palace was being renovated.[10] After Hindenburg moved out in the autumn of 1933 Hitler turned to his Munich architect, Paul Ludwig Troost, who had renovated the Brown House, and commissioned him to modernise and refurnish the apartment in the Chancellery. But Troost died suddenly on 21 January of the following year. "Irreplaceable loss," noted Goebbels. "The Führer crushed. No one can replace him."[11]

But a new favourite architect was waiting in the wings: 28-year-old Albert Speer. Himself the son of an architect from the southern German city of Mannheim, Speer grew up in an affluent family and followed in his father's footsteps, studying in Karlsruhe, Munich and Berlin. He joined the NSDAP in March 1931 after attending a Hitler speech in Berlin's Hasenheide Park. Shortly thereafter, he met Karl Hanke, the organisational director of the Berlin Gau, who gave him his first commissions, including the renovation of the new Gau headquarters on Vossstrasse. Speer demonstrated his talent for improvisation and theatricality when he designed the backdrop, bordered by gigantic swastika banners, for Hitler's inaugural 1 May address on Tempelhof Field.[12] He attracted Hitler's personal attention in the summer of 1933, when he renovated, in record time, the official apartment Goebbels had taken over from Alfred Hugenberg. Hitler now asked Speer to supervise the construction work at Wilhelmstrasse 77. The Führer visited the site almost daily to check on progress, insisting that the work be carried out quickly since the small state secretary's apartment on the top floor of the extension was unsuited to hosting official events.[13] Renovations were complete in May 1934, and Hitler was finally able to move in.

On the ground floor were the public rooms: an expansive foyer that hosted official receptions, a small salon looking out on the garden, leading to the left to a "music salon" that was also used to screen films in the evening, and to the right to the so-called Bismarck room, also called the smokers' salon, where Hitler's lunch and dinner guests congregated before meals. It was connected to the dining room, which in turn gave out onto a conservatory with a long row of windows, also looking out over the garden. Hitler's private quarters were on the first floor and consisted of a living room with library, an office, a bedroom and a bathroom. A portrait of Hitler's mother hung over the spartan iron bed. Next to the chancellor's suite, a guest room was set up for Eva Braun, but it was rarely used before 1939. The servants lived next to that. The so-called "stairway room" in front of the Führer's apartment served as a reception for Hitler's secretaries. This led via a corridor to the wing of the building that housed the offices of Hitler's assistants, Reich Press Spokesman Otto Dietrich and the commander of Hitler's bodyguard, SS Obergruppenführer Sepp Dietrich.[14]

Hitler had four personal assistants: his main assistant, Wilhelm Brückner, who had commanded the Munich SA regiment during the Beer Hall Putsch and who had begun serving Hitler personally in August 1930; Julius Schaub, who had also taken part in the putsch and who had shadowed Hitler like a second skin since 1925; Fritz Wiedemann, the retired sergeant who had been Hitler's commanding officer in the List Regiment in 1916 and 1917 and who began working in the chancellery in 1934; and Albert Bormann, Martin Bormann's younger brother, who ran Adolf Hitler's "private chancellery." Hitler also had three military aides who served as go-betweens with the armed forces: Colonel Friedrich Hossbach for the army (as of 1934), Lieutenant Captain Karl Jesko von Puttkamer for the navy (as of 1935) and Captain Nicolaus von Below for the air force (as of 1937). Three secretaries were also members of Hitler's personal staff: Johanna Wolf (since 1929), Christa Schroeder (since 1933) and Gerda Daranowski (since 1937). Hitler also had two manservants, Able Seaman Karl Krause (as of 1934) and the bricklayer and member of the SS Leibstandarte Adolf Hitler, Heinz Linge (as of 1935), both of whom were trained at Munich's Hotel College before entering Hitler's service. Building manager Arthur Kannenberg and his wife Frieda were responsible for running the Führer's household. Aeroplane captain Hans Baur and Hitler's chauffeur Julius Schreck (as of 1936 Erich Kempka) took care of travel security on journeys.[15]

As Heinz Linge later testified, Hitler was "difficult to predict" in his dealings with his servants.[16] Sometimes he was charming, enquiring about their personal welfare and pausing for chats, especially with his secretaries in the reception area. He rarely neglected to give Christmas and birthday gifts to members of his staff and friends and acquaintances from the "battle days."[17] If someone was ill, Hitler sent flowers or sometimes even delivered them in person. And if we believe Goebbels's diaries, Hitler was deeply affected by the death of his long-time chauffeur Schreck in 1936: "The Führer very depressed. It's hit him the hardest. He stayed at home all day."[18]

But these seeming gestures of caring were not necessarily motivated by pure altruism. In general, Hitler's treatment of his underlings was based on cold calculations of usefulness. Friedrich Hossbach related how every time he thought he saw "signs of true human intimacy," Hitler's behaviour would swing around radically the following day: "Then you thought that you were standing in front of an alien and completely changed person."[19] Karl Krause also recalled after the war that it became increasingly difficult to talk to Hitler on a personal level: "It was as though he were cut off. A high wall of isolation was erected."[20]

Hitler's scattershot working habits put a great deal of pressure on his staff. He kept no regular hours, so his aides and his secretaries were practically on call around the clock. His servants also suffered from his notorious impatience. Knotting Hitler's tie when he wore a dinner jacket was always a challenge. "It had to be done very quickly, in about twenty-five seconds, and it had to be done properly," Krause recalled. "Otherwise, he grew ill-tempered and started shifting his weight from one foot to the other."[21]

Hitler surrounded himself with people he knew and whose loyalty he trusted, which is why he disliked personnel changes in his entourage. If he had tired of an underling, however, the slightest excuse was enough to fire or banish him. Fritz Wiedemann, for instance, was sent off to San Francisco in January 1939 as a consul general.[22] And Hitler's long-time friend and foreign press secretary Ernst Hanfstaengl was shunted off in particularly brusque fashion in February 1937 after his falling from grace.

Hanfstaengl's crime—if we believe the accounts by Albert Speer and others—was that he once opined over a meal that he had shown just as much bravery as a civilian wartime internee in the United States as front-line soldiers had during the war. Hitler and Goebbels decided to teach him a lesson. Hanfstaengl was issued sealed orders, which he was only to open after the plane he was ordered to board had taken off. It contained instructions to fly to Spain and to parachute into republican territory to work there as an agent for Franco. Hanfstaengl frantically tried to convince the pilot to turn the plane around, but the latter calmly kept flying on. When the plane finally touched down,

Hanfstaengl recognised that he was in Leipzig, not Spain, and realised that he had been the victim of a cruel practical joke. He soon left Germany for Switzerland before heading on to London.[23]

Despite Hitler's aversion to schedules in his work and private life, something akin to a routine in the Chancellery was established in the years prior to 1939. In the morning, before Hitler got up, one of his servants had to place the latest newspapers and press agency reports on a stool in front of his bedroom door. Waking Hitler was a strange procedure. The servant would ring a bell three times, whereupon Hitler would ring back three times by pressing a button on his bedside table. Only then was the servant allowed to knock on the door and tell Hitler what time it was. Karl Krause would always know by the sound of his master's voice what sort of mood he was in. While the servant prepared Hitler's breakfast, which consisted of two cups of warm milk, as many as ten biscuits and half a bar of broken-up, dark chocolate, Hitler would take a bath, shave and get dressed. Hitler breakfasted standing up, scanning through the latest reports of the German News Agency. He would then also discuss the lunch menu and choose from three vegetarian meals on offer.[24]

After breakfast, Hitler went to his official office in the Chancellery extension, which Speer had moved from the front to the back of the building overlooking the garden to avoid the noise of the crowds who gathered every day on Wilhelmstrasse and chanted their desire to see the Führer. He did have Speer put a balcony on the front façade, upon which he would show himself to his admirers when he felt like it. "The window was too uncomfortable," he told Speer. "I could not be seen from all sides. After all, I could not lean out."[25] On the way from his private chambers to the chancellor's office, he would discuss whom he would receive that day with his anxiously waiting aides. The decision as to who would be admitted and who would be turned away was his alone, but it is scarcely credible that his decisions depended solely on "his mood and his feelings about the individuals in question," as Otto Dietrich contended.[26] One of his most impressive talents as an actor was his ability when receiving others to conceal his personal antipathies behind solicitous gestures. Once he had arrived at his office, Dietrich would give Hitler a summary of the morning papers, and Hans Heinrich Lammers would brief him about ongoing business.

After Hitler had unified the offices of chancellor and president, Otto Meissner would also be summoned to give a report, as was Goebbels's deputy at the Propaganda Ministry, Walther Funk. Following that Hitler usually held discussions with ministers, diplomats and other figures.[27]

These conferences typically lasted until 2 p.m., sometimes longer, so that lunch guests had to be prepared to wait. "Hitler was sovereign and unreliable about when he would appear," Speer recalled.

> Lunch was planned for 2 p.m., but it was usually 3 p.m. or even later before Hitler arrived. He entered as casually as a private figure. He would greet his guests with a handshake, and they would gather around him as he expressed his opinion about this or that current issue. With more privileged guests, he would enquire as to the health of the wife. Then the head of press would give him excerpts of the news, and he would sit down in a chair off to the side to read them.[28]

His guests were left standing around with growling stomachs for another fifteen to twenty minutes until a servant announced: "Lunch is served."[29] Then Hitler led everyone into the dining room—a large square space, with a round table in the middle with room for some fifteen people. There were four other tables for four to six people in the corners. Hitler always sat with his back to the window facing a large painting that hung above the sideboard: *Triumph of Music* by the Munich society painter Friedrich August von Kaulbach.[30]

Before entering the dining room, Hitler would decide who would be sitting to his right and left: this was an eagerly awaited decision since proximity to the Führer was a sign of prestige and importance. "All of his paladins stood on their toes and tried to make themselves as tall and wide as possible in the hope that the Führer's eye might fall upon them," recalled Ribbentrop's private secretary Reinhard Spitzy. "Hitler clearly enjoyed the situation and took his time. 'Yes,' he would say, 'I'd like to my right . . .'—pause—'. . . Dr. Goebbels, and to my left Herr von Ribbentrop, and then further to the right General X and to the left Gauleiter Y.'"[31] The rest of the guests took the places that were left over, and aides and less important individuals usually sat at the side tables. The guest lists varied quite a bit. Often they contained NSDAP Gauleiter in Berlin on business, and government ministers, ambassadors and business leaders were also invited.

Goebbels was there almost every day, and Speer and Otto Dietrich were also frequent guests. Göring, Hess and Himmler appeared far less frequently. Occasionally Magda Goebbels or Leni Riefenstahl were invited, but usually the company was exclusively male. The food was simple. Most days, there was soup, meat with vegetables and potatoes, and something sweet for dessert. Hitler ate his vegetarian meal and drank Fachinger mineral water. Guests were welcome to follow him in these habits, but few chose to.[32]

Hitler jokingly nicknamed his lunches the "Merry Chancellor Restaurant,"[33] but the atmosphere was hardly one of relaxed merriment. "The people at his table did not feel free," Dietrich remarked. "Amidst the atmosphere Hitler created, even the liveliest people became taciturn listeners . . . They were self-conscious and did not volunteer much of themselves, while Hitler spoke and put them under his spell with words and gestures he had practised thousandfold."[34] Since Hitler often talked about current issues, his lunches were, in Speer's words, a "great source of information" for his guests, without which they would "lack orientation."[35] When Hitler took an uncharacteristic break from lecturing the others, an embarrassed silence would descend. At such moments, Goebbels would jump in. The propaganda minister enjoyed playing the *maître de plaisir*, and he was invited so often because he knew how to liven things up, entertaining the guests with jokes and anecdotes while undermining his rivals for Hitler's favour with seemingly harmless little jibes. Not infrequently, he would make fun of one of the other guests and engage in some verbal sparring, which Hitler would follow with amusement, intervening only if things threatened to escalate into a genuine quarrel.[36]

After lunch, which lasted between thirty minutes and an hour, Hitler would ask individual guests to accompany him to the conservatory, where they continued this or that discussion. For the movers and shakers of the Third Reich, this was the best chance to get Hitler's ear in hopes of influencing a decision in their favour. Speer, for instance, eagerly seized such opportunities to discuss his construction plans. Often such discussions lasted until late in the afternoon. When the weather was fine, Hitler enjoyed walking up and down the garden with his guests. He always carried some nuts in his pockets to feed the squirrels.[37] Early on in his regime, Hitler would sometimes retire to the Hotel Kaiserhof, where a corner table was kept reserved for him, for late-afternoon tea. But he soon abandoned this habit because word of his presence there would quickly make the rounds and attract flocks of mostly older female admirers.[38]

Dinner was usually planned for 8 p.m. and was mostly restricted to a smaller circle, including Goebbels, Speer, and frequently Heinrich Hoffmann and Captain Baur. Often, not all of the seats at the main table were taken so that Hitler's aides hastily invited guests from the world of culture, above all actresses. Unlike lunch, the table talk focused on general topics rather than political issues. "Hitler enjoyed hearing about theatrical performances and society scandals," Speer recalled. "The pilot told flying stories, Hoffmann contributed anecdotes from Munich's art world . . . but mostly Hitler repeated tales from his past and told us about how he had become what he was."[39] During the meal, Hitler's servants would bring him a list of four to six German and foreign films. Hitler would then select one or two to be shown that evening.[40]

After dinner, Hitler and his guests would repair to the "music salon," where everything had been set up for the screening. "We all sat down in comfortable armchairs," Speer related. "Hitler unbuttoned his jacket and stretched out his legs. The light slowly dimmed while household servants and bodyguards entered though the rear door."[41] Hitler liked breezy entertainment. If a film featured one of his favourite actors— Emil Jannings, Heinz Rühmann, Henny Porten, Lil Dagover, Olga Chechova, Zarah Leander or Jenny Jugo—he would order a copy before it had premiered in the cinemas. If a film was not to his taste, he made no secret of it, bellowing, "Stop the projector! What nonsense! Put on the next one!"[42] Goebbels occasionally complained to his diary about this monotonous ritual, which he considered a waste of time. On the other hand, it was important for him to get Hitler's opinion so that he could intervene and, if necessary, have changes made to the film before its premiere.[43]

After the screening, everyone went into the smoking parlour. While by that point most of the guests had trouble concealing their fatigue, Hitler usually seemed astonishingly fresh, as if he had only just come to life. The company sat around the fireplace, drinks and sandwiches were brought, and there was a bit of chit-chat. It was during these hours that the dictator seemed most relaxed. The greatest fear of his aides was that late at night the conversation would turn to Hitler's favourite topics, his experiences in the First World War and the "days of struggle." Such reminiscing could go on until two or three in the morning. After his guests had finally left, Hitler and his aides would discuss the next day's schedule. Karl Krause would then present him with the latest news agency report and prepare a valerian tea with a small bottle of cognac on the side. It was supposed to help Hitler fall asleep more quickly.[44]

On some nights, though, Hitler would withdraw earlier to his chambers to read newspapers and magazines. "Flipping through the pages of periodicals was one of his favourite activities," Krause recalled. For relaxation, he even read through back issues. In December 1933, for example, he ordered Schaub to procure all the editions of the *Berliner Illustrierte Zeitung* (Berlin Illustrated Newspaper) published between 1914 and 1932. The directorship of the Ullstein publishing house was only too happy to oblige and wished the chancellor "several hours of pleasant leisure in a life full of strenuous work perusing an illustrated chronicle of twenty years of ever-changing German history."[45]

A weekly, as well as a daily, routine also crystallised during the early years of Hitler's regime. There was hardly a weekend when Hitler did not set off for Munich or the Obersalzberg. Since he usually left on Friday evening and returned during the course of Monday, that meant that appointments in the Chancellery were condensed into four days.[46] Hitler had three Junkers 52s managed by Baur at his disposal. They were supplemented in the spring of 1935 by two four-motor Condor aircraft, which could fly from Berlin to Munich in only one hour and thirty-five minutes. Until September 1937, if Hitler decided to travel by rail, an extra carriage was attached to the regular Berlin–Munich train. After that, Hitler would make use of a special train with ten to twelve carriages all for himself. The "Führer car" consisted of a mahogany-panelled salon where Hitler could congregate with his aides, a sleeping compartment with a bath, and sleeping berths for his servants. During Wehrmacht manoeuvres, his special train served as his "main headquarters." A motorcade stood ready for him wherever he chose to alight.[47]

For shorter trips, Hitler preferred to travel by car. He always chose the destination and frequently kept it a secret from his entourage until the last minute. Sometimes he himself could not decide where he wanted to go and flipped a coin. "Once the decision had been reached in this way, it was set in stone, and he abided by it," Dietrich recalled, adding that this was "Hitler's one concession to superstition."[48]

Nonetheless, even if the final destination was set, Hitler did not mind making the odd detour. He remained loyal to the same hotels: in Weimar the venerable Hotel Elephant on the central market square; in the Bavarian spa town of Berneck Bube's Hotel; in Nuremberg the Deutscher Hof; in Augsburg the Drei Mohren; in Frankfurt the Baseler Hof (where, he once sneered, there was always a Bible on his bedside table); in Hamburg the luxurious Hotel Atlantik on Alster Lake; in the Rhineland and Ruhr Valley the Rheinhotel Dreesen in Bad Godesberg; and later in Vienna the royal suite of the Hotel Imperial.[49] Led by the Führer's black Mercedes, there was always a veritable caravan of cars containing Hitler's bodyguards, officers of the criminal police, his aides and personal physician, his servants and one of his secretaries as well as a car full of luggage at the tail end.[50]

Always restless, Hitler eagerly exploited any opportunity for a change of scenery. "There were years when he could hardly stand to stay in one place or in one of his homes for more than three or four days," Dietrich recalled. "You could almost set your watch by when his entourage would get the order to pack up and move on."[51] The constant moving around was a nightmare for his servants since fifteen to twenty suitcases had to be packed at the drop of a hat, and departures could never go fast enough for their impatient master.[52]

The business of government continued while Hitler was on the go. If he was in Munich, urgent conferences were held in his private apartment on Prinzregentenstrasse or in the Brown House. If he was somewhere else, he constantly received reports and requests, in response to which he issued immediate instructions and orders. Dietrich saw this idiosyncratic "flying' form of government" as one of the special qualities of Hitler's style of rule.[53]

Even when he was working in the Chancellery, Hitler avoided writing down his orders. Instead, his commands were issued verbally and delivered on the spur of the moment. As a rule he considered his decisions carefully, but sometimes he took them on the spot, leaving his underlings with the unenviable task of translating hasty remarks into practical instructions and make sure they got where they needed to. Misunderstandings and misinterpretations were an inevitable part of this oral leadership style.[54] On the other hand, it also opened up considerable room for those around Hitler to exert an influence. Here, too, Goebbels achieved a certain mastery. At lunch, Dietrich observed, "he fed Hitler with entertaining catchwords, adopted and exaggerated his tendencies and seized opportunities to elicit verbal orders in his favour in a variety of areas."[55] Not only party bigwigs used this strategy. Ministers and state secretaries, who had increasing difficulty getting access to Hitler, tried to as well. If they succeeded in gaining his attention, they immediately tried to explain their problems to Hitler one-to-one and to draw him into statements that could be interpreted as "the Führer's will." The "art of the ministries," Ernst von Weizsäcker, who became state secretary in the Foreign Ministry in 1937, emphasised in his memoirs, "was to exploit the lucky hour or minute when Hitler, sometimes through a stray word, made a decision that could be passed on as 'Führer mandate.'"[56]

Hitler's non-bureaucratic, personalised style of rule encouraged underlings to push ahead with initiatives of their own in the hopes of anticipating the Führer's will. "The Führer can hardly order from above everything that he may want carried out at some point," Werner Willikens, state secretary in the Prussian Agriculture Ministry, told agricultural representatives of the German states in February 1934. Therefore, it was the duty of every individual to try to work towards the Führer.[57] Ian Kershaw rightly sees this idea of "working towards the Führer" as one of the keys for understanding the specific ways in which Nazi rule functioned. Those who wanted to get ahead in this system could not wait for orders from above, but rather had to antic- ipate the Führer's will and take action to prepare and promote what they thought to be Hitler's intentions. This not only explains why the regime was so dynamic but also why it became more and more radical. In competing for the dictator's favour, his paladins tried to trump one another with ever more extreme demands and measures.[58] Small-time and medium-level NSDAP functionaries—from the block wardens to the cell, local and district leaders—were also convinced that they were "working towards the Führer" when they harassed Jews and informed on putative "parasites on the people." They were not just the willing executioners of Hitler's ideological postulates: they drove racist policies forward.

After the Nazification of parties and associations, the unification of the offices of president and chancellor, and the self-subordination of the Reichswehr to their new commander-in-chief, Hitler had personally concentrated more power than any German ruler in history. "Responsible to no one and unable to be replaced, his position is comparable only with that of the crowned heads of state of the absolute monarchies of the past," read an SPD-in-exile report from July–August 1934.[59] In contrast to Fascist Italy, where Il Duce had to tolerate a king at his side, Nazi Germany had no institutions that could have developed into a counterweight to Hitler's stranglehold on power.[60] In his two-pronged stroke in June 1934, the dictator had eradicated SA unrest within his own movement and got rid of his critics and detractors among the conservatives. The "Führer state" was now solidly established, and in it Hitler's charismatic authority was the most important resource for ruling. The referendums he staged after major domestic and foreign-policy decisions confirmed his overwhelming popularity. Without Hitler as the "hub of the entire National Socialist system,"[61] and without the mythology of the Führer as an integrative framework, there is no explaining the regime's astonishing cohesive force. "Fundamental to National Socialism and its system of rule," argued the historian Karl-Dietrich Bracher, "was the fact that from the beginning to its extreme end, it stood and fell with this one man."[62] Decisions could only be made under the regime if they were derived from and thus sanctioned by the will of the Führer.

Nonetheless, it would distort the reality of the Third Reich to imagine it as a strictly governed central system in which the Führer determined everything. Hitler's marked aversion to bureaucratic procedures and his scattershot, impulsive style of rule made such a system impossible. He demanded of all his underlings that they spare him from unwelcome, banal, everyday details. "The best man is for me the one who burdens me the least by taking responsibility for himself ninety-five out of every one hundred decisions," Hitler declared in October 1941. "Of course there are always cases that I ultimately have to decide."[63] In other words, Hitler claimed the solitary right to decide only on fundamental issues, not on routine matters he considered ancillary; it was then that he made determined use of his function as a coordinator. However, because he was not prepared to clarify the boundaries between state administration and party organisations, bureaucratic structures and administrative rules and procedures began to corrode from within. Hitler gradually transferred to government the practice he had already used as party leader of blurring areas of responsibility and staffing offices doubly so as to encourage rivalries and protect his own power.[64] As a seemingly paradoxical result, a polycratic network of competing offices and portfolios developed alongside Hitler's monocratic dictatorship.[65] For example, as we have seen in the area of foreign policy, three organisations besides the Foreign Ministry were active: the NSDAP Foreign-Policy Office, the Foreign Organisation of the Party and Ribbentrop's office.[66] In the area of publicity, the president of the Reich press office and head of Eher publishers, Max Amann, fiercely battled for power with Press Secretary Dietrich and Propaganda Minister Goebbels.[67]

One of the first victims of the unregulated parallel existence of the Führer's absolute authority and a plurality of competing power centres was the principle of government by cabinet. In February and March 1933 the cabinet met thirty-one times, on average once every two days. After the Enabling Act emancipated Hitler as chancellor from the emergency decrees of the president, Hitler's interest in conferring with his cabinet declined noticeably. Between June and December 1933, the cabinet met twenty times, in all of 1934 nineteen times, in 1935 twelve times, in 1936 four times and in 1937 six times. Its final meeting took place on 5 February 1938.[68]

As meetings declined in frequency, their character also changed. "In the beginning, there were still lively discussions, but later Hitler's monologues took up more and more time," recalled Schwerin von Krosigk.[69] Gradually, the cabinet devolved into an organ for carrying out the Führer's will, and in October 1934, all of Hitler's ministers were required to swear an oath of loyalty to him personally. On the fourth anniversary of the appointment of the "cabinet of national concentration," on 30 January 1937, Hitler made all his ministers members of the NSDAP, in so far as they were not already, and awarded them the Golden Party Badge. Paul von Eltz-Rübenach alone refused to accept the accolade, citing the regime's hostility to the Catholic Church, which horrified the rest of the cabinet. "It was as if we were all struck lame," Goebbels noted. "No one had expected that. Göring, Blomberg and Neurath profoundly thanked the Führer . . . But the mood was ruined."[70] Eltz-Rübenach was forced to submit his resignation that very day, and his ministry was divided up: Julius Dorpmüller became Reich transport minister, and Wilhelm Ohnesorge became Reich postal minister.

Starting in the summer of 1933, a new legislative practice established itself which rendered cabinet consultations obsolete. Before a draft law was submitted to the Chancellery, the ministers concerned had to clear up all matters of potential disagreement. State Secretary Lammers would then send the law to cabinet members with a request to register any objections by a certain date. Only when this cycle of correspondence was complete would Lammers take the law to Hitler for signature. Hitler either accepted or rejected it—he showed little interest in any of the preliminaries.[71] As the cabinet declined in importance, Lammers gained more and more power since his new function as an intermediary between the ministers and Hitler put him in a key position. He was informed early on about what laws which ministers intended to formulate and could intervene in the approval process since he was able to influence Hitler depending on how he presented a given law. In November 1937, the dictator honoured the work of this senior civil servant by naming him a Reich minister, elevating him to the same level as the other cabinet members. In the last years of the regime, however, Lammers would lose a battle for power with Martin Bormann, who had become the director of the party chancellery and the "Führer's secretary" and who would regulate privileged access to the dictator in the Führer's main headquarters.[72]

The dissolution of conventional forms of government was accelerated by Hitler's tendency to appoint special agents to take care of what he considered the most urgent tasks. As a rule, they were responsible neither to the party nor to the government administration, but rather only to Hitler personally. Their authority was based solely on the Führer's faith in them. Hitler largely kept out of the inevitable ensuing rivalries and battles for responsibility between newly established special staffs, on the one hand, and ministries and party offices on the other. As a social Darwinist, he was guided by the idea that whoever was stronger, and therefore better, would prevail in the end. He was also convinced that this was the way to overcome bureaucratic limitations and create incentives for greater competition, which would lead to a more effective mobilisation of forces. Finally, he was also inspired by a Machiavellian strategy of divide and conquer, playing rivals off against one another, and so shielding himself against potential usurpers of his power.[73]

The first in this series of special agents was the engineer Fritz Todt, whom Hitler named general inspector for the German road system on 30 June 1933 with a mandate to build the German autobahn network. Eltz-Rübenach was forced to turn over his Department K (automobile and roads division) to Todt. When ministerial experts complained at a cabinet meeting on 23 November 1933, Hitler replied that a gigantic enterprise like the construction of the autobahn required the creation of a new institution. As soon as the new autobahn was complete, Hitler promised, this new institution would be incorporated back into the Transport Ministry.[74] But because the energetic Todt performed his duties to Hitler's great satisfaction, in December 1938 he was also named general agent for the regulation of the construction industry. The companies and projects he directed were the genesis of the Organisation Todt, whose first projects included the construction of the West Wall along the Reich's western border. It was the only special organisation in Nazi Germany to bear the name of its director.[75]

The development of the Labour Service was a further example of how Hitler prised areas of responsibility away from traditional governmental institutions and entrusted them to individuals. In the summer of 1931, Heinrich Brüning had introduced a volunteer labour service, nominating a Reich commissioner to direct it in July 1932. After Hitler became chancellor, the new labour minister, the head of the Stahlhelm, Franz Seldte, laid claim to this position. Hitler, however, gave the job of heading the service to former Colonel General Konstantin Hierl, whom he appointed to the rank of a Labour Ministry state secretary in early May 1933. The result was permanent friction between the labour minister and the "Reich labour leader," as Hierl started calling himself in November 1933, which Hitler put an end to in early July 1934 when he officially appointed Hierl Reich commissioner for the labour service. He was formally responsible to Frick's Interior Ministry, but de facto Hitler's support made him the director of a special office. With the introduction of mandatory labour service in 1935, it developed into a huge organisation that forced hundreds of thousands of young men and women between the ages of 18 and 25 to perform six months of "voluntary labour for the German people."[76]

Much the same as Hierl, Reich Youth Leader Baldur von Schirach sought to expand his organisation into a "superior Reich office" and transform the Hitler Youth into a mandatory state institution that would inculcate the National Socialist world view in all young males between the ages of 10 and 18. In late 1935, Hitler approved the basics of this plan. In the spring of 1936, Hans Heinrich Lammers passed on a draft Reich Youth Law to the relevant government offices, but it met with resistance. Education Minister Bernhard Rust protested against the idea of "separating the guidance of youth completely from the Reich's existing responsibility to educate young people." Finance Minister Schwerin von Krosigk objected to the creation of a "new, expensive apparatus separate from the general government administration," and Frick complained that "the establishment of a new Reich special administration disrupts the necessary organic unity between the state and its administration."[77] Apparently surprised by such stiff opposition, Hitler decided to delay the drafting of the law. It was not until October that Schirach was able to discuss the project with Hitler and get him to reaffirm his support. On 1 December 1936, the cabinet approved the Law Concerning the Hitler Youth that made enrolment in the organisation mandatory. Prior to that Hitler had urged his education minister not to voice his reservations in the cabinet meeting. Thanks to Hitler's support, Schirach triumphed over the ministries. Paragraph 3 of the law gave him and the leadership of the Reich Youth "the status of a superior Reich office based in Berlin" and made them responsible "directly to the Führer and Reich chancellor."[78]

The clearest and most significant example of what the historian Martin Broszat called the "amalgamation of party and state functions in a special organisation immediately under the Führer" was the creation of the SS power complex.[79] From their Bavarian springboard between the autumn of 1933 and the spring of 1934, Heinrich Himmler and Reinhard Heydrich gradually succeeded in taking over the political divisions of the police in all the German states. Only in Prussia did their urge for expansion meet with resistance—from State President and Interior Minister Göring. In April 1934, the two sides agreed that Himmler would become inspector of the Prussian secret police and Heydrich director of the Secret Police Office. Although formally that subordinated Himmler to Göring, in practice it gave the SS leadership control over the political police force. Prinz-Albrecht-Strasse 8, where the Gestapo had their headquarters, soon became synonymous with the National Socialist system of terror.[80]

The bloody purge of the SA leadership in the summer of 1934 represented a further strategic triumph for Himmler and Heydrich. The SS gained full independence from the SA, and the Security Service was acknowledged as the only official surveillance organ of the Nazi movement. Simultaneously, the SS assumed command over all of Germany's concentration camps. Theodor Eicke, previously the commandant of the Dachau camp, was named "inspector of concentration camps and leader of the SS security associations." He reported directly to Himmler. The Dachau system was a model copied throughout the Reich. The SS leadership rebuffed repeated complaints by Justice Minister Gürtner about the arbitrary use of protective custody and the high number of fatalities in the camps by claiming everything was being run in line with the Führer's will.[81]

But that did not by any means satisfy Himmler's ambitions. His next target was control over the entire police force, which he wanted to amalgamate into the SS. In conversation with Hitler on 18 October 1935, he succeeded in gaining the dictator's basic support for the idea, although it would take nine months for his plan to be realised. Wilhelm Frick as interior minister was dead set against police powers being taken away from his ministry. On the contrary, he wanted to reintegrate the political divisions of the police back into the police force as a whole and put concentration camps under normal state supervision. Here, too, battles between Hitler's paladins were decided in favour of whoever could claim to be carrying out a "task for the Führer." On 10 February 1936, Himmler achieved a partial victory with the Prussian Law Concerning the Gestapo, which confirmed the autonomy of the political police as a special institution. His decisive breakthrough followed on 17 June, when Hitler named him "Reichsführer-SS and head of the German police in the Interior Ministry," a title which also gave him the rank of state secretary. Frick had insisted on the phrase "in the Interior Ministry" as a qualifier, but it was illusory to think that Himmler could be kept on a leash. Nominally he was subordinate to Frick, but as Reichsführer-SS he was responsible only to Hitler and could go over the interior minister's head whenever he wanted.[82]

Hitler's order of 17 June 1936 was, in the words of Heydrich's biographer, the "cornerstone of a new type of apparatus for political repression," which knew no more legal limits, operating instead in a situation of permanent state-of-emergency rule.[83] The immediate result was the reorganisation of the police into two main departments along SS lines: the "Order Police" (gendarmerie and uniformed police) under SS Obergruppenführer Kurt Daluege, and the "Security Police" (Gestapo and criminal police) under Heydrich. Himmler and his underlings envisioned a comprehensive "state protection corps" that would pre-emptively intervene against putative dangers to the "German people and race." In the spring of 1936, Werner Best—Heydrich's deputy at the Secret Police Office—defined the political police in an "ethnic-popular Führer state" as "an institution . . . that carefully monitors the political health of the body of the German people and recognises in timely fashion every symptom of illness, identifying and employing appropriate means to eradicate the destructive bacilli, whether they be products of self-induced decay or intentional infection from without."[84]

Operating under the premise that they were carrying out racial-hygienic preventative measures, the police could extend their persecution of Jews, Communists and socialists to more and more "enemies of the state" and "parasites on the people." Their victims included Freemasons, politically active clergymen, Jehovah's Witnesses, gypsies, homosexuals, prostitutes, "antisocials," the "work-shy" and "habitual criminals." Nonetheless, recent historical research has contextualised the two-dimensional picture of an all-powerful, omnipresent secret police in the Third Reich: the Gestapo's efficiency depended on the participation of ordinary Germans who were willing to inform on people they did not like.[85]

At the same time they were intensifying their terror campaigns, Himmler and Heydrich pressed on with the amalgamation of the SS and the police. The process was completed on 27 September 1939, a few weeks before the beginning of the Second World War, with the founding of the Reich Security Main Office (RSHA). It combined the Security Police and the Security Service into one super-entity, which would become the central executive institution carrying out the National Socialist policies of annihilation during the war.[86]

In terms of accumulating posts and expanding his own responsibilities, there was no competing with Göring, who in fact dubbed himself "the Führer's first paladin." In addition to his position as Prussian state president and interior minister, Göring was named Reich aviation minister in May 1933. In May 1934 he had to yield the Prussian Interior

Ministry to Frick, but he was compensated for that in July, when he was appointed as the Reich forestry and hunting master in the newly created Reich Forestry Office.[87] Hitler occasionally made light of Göring's obsession with uniforms and glamour, but he valued the former military officer's political gravitas so much that in a secret decree in December 1934, he made Göring his successor. "Immediately after my death," Hitler ordered, "he is to have the members of the Reich government, the Wehrmacht and the formations of the SA and SS swear an oath of loyalty to himself personally."[88]

The most important instrument of personal power for the Reich's "second man" was the Luftwaffe, command of which he assumed in the rank of colonel in early March 1935 and whose expansion into a third and equal branch of the armed forces, alongside the army and navy, he oversaw. Göring sought to use this position to extend his influence upon economic and rearmament decisions. This put him on a collision course with Hjalmar Schacht, who had been named "general agent for the war economy" in the Reich Defence Law of May 1935.[89]

As an acknowledged expert on economic questions and as the financial architect of Germany's rearmament programme, Schacht had enjoyed Hitler's special regard in the early years of the regime. That gradually changed as the finance minister and Reichsbank president began to draw insistent attention to the potentially ruinous consequences of accelerated rearmament for the German economy. Indeed, the problems were impossible to ignore even as early as 1934. Lacking sufficient currency reserves, the Reich had increasing difficulties importing raw materials for the arms build-up and foodstuffs to feed the population. Schacht had been a dedicated adherent of rearmament for years before and after the Nazis' rise to power, he told Blomberg in December 1935, but his sense of duty required him "to point out the economic limits that constrain any such policy."[90] Schacht pursued a running feud in particular with Agriculture and Food Minister Walter Darré over the availability of foreign currency. A decision by Hitler was required, but as was so often the case, he let things slide—in part because his attention in the spring of 1936 was monopolised by his riskiest endeavour to date, the remilitarisation of the Rhineland. In a secret decree of 4 April 1936, however, he did name Göring "Reich agent for raw materials and foreign currency matters."[91]

Schacht initially welcomed the appointment, assuming that Göring would protect him against attacks from the party. That soon proved to be a capital mistake. Göring was anything but content to referee conflicts over foreign currency. As commander-in-chief of the Luftwaffe, he had a vested interest in accelerated rearmament, and he used his new "Führer mandate" to gain control over the entire military economy. In early May 1936, without informing the Economic Ministry or any other government institution, he set up a new, autonomous office called the Raw Materials and Currency Staff of State President Göring.[92] Hitler brusquely rejected Schacht's subsequent request to rein in Göring's authority over currency matters, saying he did not want anything more to do with the matter. Schacht, Hitler said, "should settle such issues with Göring" and forbade the economics minister from ever raising the topic with him again.[93] Goebbels, another enemy of the acid-tongued finance expert, noted with satisfaction: "Things won't go well for long with Schacht. He's not one of us with all his heart. The Führer is very angry with him."[94] Considering himself irreplaceable, Schacht had overestimated Hitler's support. For him, the ensuing struggle for power with Göring was a losing battle.

Schacht's and Göring's positions collided head on at a meeting of the Prussian Ministerial Council on 12 May 1936 to discuss the general economic situation and the financing of armaments. Schacht emphasised his "unshakeable loyalty to the Führer" but warned of the danger of inflation if the pace of rearmament were not decelerated. For the first time he also threatened to resign. Göring continued to insist on the primacy of the arms build-up and argued that the currency problem could be got round by extracting more domestic raw materials and using "replacement materials." "If we have war tomorrow," Göring said, "we'll have to help ourselves with replacement materials. Money will no longer play a role. If that's the case, we have to be prepared to create the conditions for it during peacetime."[95] It was clear right from the start, given Hitler's ideological premises and the political goals he derived from them, which side of this fundamental economic disagreement he would favour. In late August 1936, he wrote a lengthy secret memo concerning the future direction of economic policy. It adopted the essentials of Göring's position and concluded with a pair of unambiguous commands: "1. The German army must be capable of being deployed in four years. 2. The German economy must be capable of waging war in four years."⁹⁶

On 4 September, Göring used a ministerial council meeting declared as a "secret Reich matter" to reveal the content of Hitler's memo to Schacht, Blomberg and Krosigk. Göring interpreted it as a "general instruction," which he alone had been charged with executing. "Thanks to the genius of the Führer, seemingly impossible things have become reality within the shortest span of time," he responded when Schacht objected. "All measures are to be carried out as if we were under the immediate threat of war."⁹⁷ On 9 September 1936 Hitler announced the new "Four Year Plan" for the economy at the Nuremberg rally, and on 18 October, he officially named Göring "the agent of the Four Year Plan," giving him the authority to issue orders to all Reich and party offices.⁹⁸ Göring felt he had achieved his goals. Supported by a generous interpretation of the Führer's will, he had gained a nearly all-powerful position in the armaments economy. The "specialists" he recruited for his new office from the party, the military and the private sector—including Carl Krauch, an IG Farben board member and an expert in the production of synthetic fuels—allowed him to usurp major responsibilities from the Economics Ministry. Nonetheless, Schacht kept his position, and Hitler never thought of firing him. "The Führer is very sceptical about Schacht," Goebbels noted in mid-November 1936. "But he's not relieving him of his responsibilities for foreign-policy reasons."⁹⁹

It was more than just Schacht's reputation abroad, however, which inspired Hitler to retain him. He also seems to have wanted to keep Göring from getting *too* powerful. Schacht's dogged efforts to combat his rival's presumption were not unwelcome to their mutual boss. In any case, for months Hitler merely sat back and watched Göring and Schacht's battle for power simmer. In early July 1937, Göring concluded an agreement with Schacht in which both men agreed to carry out their respective tasks in "close cooperation with one another."¹⁰⁰ But the deal was not worth the paper it was written on, as became clear a few days later when Göring announced the creation of the "Reich Works for Ore-Mining and Steel-Making Hermann Göring" in the town of Salzgitter without previously informing the Economics Ministry about his plans. This affront was too much for Schacht. In an enraged letter to Göring, Schacht declared that he could no longer countenance such unilateral actions, writing that "in a totalitarian state it is impossible to conduct a split economic policy."[101]

In a conversation with Hitler on 11 August on the Obersalzberg, Schacht once more tendered his resignation, but the dictator again refused to let him go. Hitler appealed to Schacht to come to an understanding with Göring and take two months to think things over. Hitler only accepted Schacht's resignation in late November 1937, appointing Goebbels's deputy Walther Funk as his successor. Schacht remained at the helm of the Reichsbank, however. Although practically without power, he continued in that post until 20 January 1939, at which point Hitler dismissed him with the remark "You don't fit into the whole National Socialist framework."[102] What prompted Schacht's dismissal was a memo he had written on 7 January in which he again underscored, in dramatic words, the danger of inflation. "The unlimited swelling of state expenditures demolishes any attempt at an orderly budget," Schacht had warned. "It brings state finances to the brink of collapse and shakes the national bank and the currency."[103] The monetary doomsayer had exhausted Hitler's patience long before that, but the dictator wanted to avoid a public break and appointed Schacht minister without portfolio. Schacht had no scruples about enjoying the privileges associated with that title, including a healthy annual salary and an official chauffeured car.

The year-long power battles between Göring and Schacht are a classic example of Hitler's technique of promoting instead of mediating rivalries, leaving things up in the air and avoiding clear decisions as long as they did not impinge on his own authority as Führer. This style of rule was also evident in the distribution of tasks within the NSDAP directorship—another minefield of jealousy and rivalry. On 21 April 1933, he ordained Hess as his deputy and empowered him "to decide in my name on all questions of party direction."[104] Hess owed this promotion to the absolute loyalty he had shown to Hitler as his private secretary prior to 1933. The dictator could be sure that his deputy, who harboured only limited desires for power, was not a potential rival.[105] The extremely succinct decree making Hess the "Führer's deputy" put him in a superior position to other elite party circles. On the other hand, however, Hitler had intentionally stopped short of subordinating the Reich directors and Gauleiter to Hess's authority. The result was a constant tug of war for responsibility within the party. Hess's ability to survive had less to do with his own battling nature than with the persistence and tactical cleverness of Martin Bormann. Born in 1900 as the son of a postal worker, Bormann had joined a Freikorps paramilitary group in 1918 and had spent a year in jail for a politically motivated killing committed in the spring of 1923. After that, he had worked in the administration of the Weimar Gau, before taking over the "SA Insurance" at Munich party headquarters, an entity that he expanded into the "NSDAP Relief Fund." In early July 1933, the industrious but widely unknown Bormann was named "staff director of the deputy to the Führer" and received the rank of an NSDAP Reich director the following October.[106]

Hess and Bormann did not just have to deal with pushy Gauleiter who insisted on their independence and knew how to exploit their connections to Hitler to get decisions made in their favour. Another source of resistance to the deputy to the Führer's claim to party pre-eminence was Reich Organisational Director Robert Ley, who possessed enormous influence as the head of the German Labour Front. Ley enviously followed the establishment of Hess's staff, which laid claim to an increasing number of responsibilities that had formerly been his own. In the subsequent power struggle between Hess/Bormann and Ley, Hitler behaved as usual, telling the rivals to reach an understanding on their own. Only when this failed did he mediate a compromise—albeit one that did not clarify spheres of responsibility, but instead rather encouraged further rivalry.[107] As a result there existed, alongside the main personnel office of the Reich organisational director, the personnel office in the staff of the deputy to the Führer which became increasingly involved in filling lower-level party posts.

Over the years, the deputy to the Führer's staff created a parallel office for every area of the Reich Organisational Directorship, in what amounted to a never-ending feud. In June 1939, only a few weeks before the start of the Second World War, Ley lobbied for the Reich Organisational Directorship's responsibilities to be clearly limited to what they had been before the expansion of Hess's office. That was the only way, he argued, to avoid "the organisationally superfluous and now untenable doubling of personnel and budgetary work."[108] Bormann brusquely rejected this demand:

> It is beyond doubt that the Führer's responsibility is boundless. Equally beyond doubt is the fact that the deputy to the Führer represents him,

in so far as he wishes to be represented, in the entire realm of the party, so that the deputy's authority here is also fundamentally boundless. Any limitation of the responsibility of the deputy to the Führer is thus not only unnecessary, but . . . impossible.[109]

In this instance, too, the side that could claim to be doing the Führer's will on the basis of a commensurate mandate had more leverage in the struggle for power and influence.

Hitler's aversion to adopting definitive positions was even more apparent in the allocation of executive responsibilities between the state and the party. The Law for the Securing of Unity of Party and State of 1 December 1933 may have stipulated that the NSDAP, as "the bearer of the German idea of state after the triumph of the National Socialist revolution," was "indivisibly linked with the state."[110] But it was unclear what that meant in practice, and Hitler did not exactly clear up the issue when he proclaimed at the 1935 Nuremberg rally: "What can be solved by the state will be solved by the state. What the state because of its very nature is unable to solve will be solved by the movement. The state is after all only one of the organisations of ethnic-popular life."[111] The parallel existence and rivalries between local group leaders, district leaders, Gauleiter and the deputy to the Führer as a supreme party authority on the one hand, and chief administrative officers, senior civil servants, state governments and the Reich ministries on the other, generated permanent tension and friction. Hitler-appointed special representatives and their staffs succeeded in usurping a considerable amount of functions of state. As deputy to the Führer and—since 1 December 1933—minister without portfolio, Hess was even able to extend his power to the legislative process. On 27 July 1934, during a joint visit to the Wagner Festival in Bayreuth, he secured Hitler's signature on a decree that gave him the right to influence and monitor all legislative plans by the ministries. A further Führer decree in September 1935 required all government offices to submit the personnel files of all candidates for higher public office, whether promotions or new appointments, to Hess for prior approval.[112]

Hitler had little interest in a clear delineation of party and state spheres. Instead, he tended to blur responsibilities, as the institution of the Reich governors shows. The Second Law for Bringing the States into Line with the Reich of 7 April 1933 installed Reich governors—*Reichsstatthalter*—in all German states except Prussia. They were charged with "ensuring that the political direction determined by the Reich chancellor was maintained," but they were not supposed to be members of the respective state governments. On Hitler's recommendation over the course of May 1933, Hindenburg named Gauleiter as governors in almost all the states.[113] The Law for the Reconstruction of the Reich of 30 January 1934, which dissolved the sovereignty of the states in favour of the Reich, actually rendered the Reich governors superfluous. But instead of getting rid of them, Article 3 of the law subordinated them to the "supervision of the Reich interior minister."[114] The Gauleiter/governors resisted this idea, claiming the right to refer any difference of opinion between themselves and Reich or state ministers to the Führer for settlement. Wilhelm Frick, in turn, found that this contradicted "the idea of a central, unified leadership of the Reich by the Reich chancellor and the specialised ministers at his side" and demanded that Hitler put the Gauleiter/governors in their place. Hitler agreed in principle with Frick but wanted to make an exception "with questions of special political significance," as Hans Heinrich Lammers told the interior minister. Such a solution was in accordance with "the Reich chancellor's own understanding of his leadership."[115] That decision essentially voided Article 3 of the law. In keeping with his policy of divide and conquer, Hitler retained the role of the final arbiter.

In the autumn of 1934, in an attempt nonetheless to subjugate the Reich governors, whose actual power rested in the fact that they were Gauleiter, Frick planned a law that would have rescinded the decree of 7 April 1933 and unified the offices of Reich governor and state president. In their new office as "leaders of the state government," however, the Reich governors would be strictly bound to instructions from the Interior Ministry. Hitler approved of the basic idea but characteristically insisted on revoking the new regulation's general applicability. Paragraph 4 of the Reich Governors' Law of 30 January 1935 therefore read: "The Führer and Reich chancellor can charge the Reich governor with the leadership of the state government." The replacement of "must" with "can" gave Hitler the freedom to do as he wanted. Whereas he immediately named the Reich governors as the state presidents of Saxony and Hesse, he refused to take the same steps in Württemberg, Baden and Thuringia, although he had already signed the preliminary documents at Frick's request.[116]

The dualism of party and state remained unresolved. All of Frick's efforts to reorganise the states with a comprehensive "Reich reform" and rationalise administrative structures never got beyond the initial stages. They foundered on Hitler's aversion to committing himself. The Führer also scuppered Frick's plan to replace the Enabling Act, which expired on 31 March 1937, with a Law Concerning Reich Legislature that would have transformed the emergency arrangement into a permanent, legally normative procedure. He had "doubts whether the moment was right for instituting that sort of law," Hitler told his cabinet on 26 January 1937 to justify his decision to have the Enabling Act extended: "Only if a new basic law of state was short enough for schoolchildren to learn by heart, would it be advantageous to revise the whole procedure of the Reich legislature."[117] There was never any "new founding law of state," and the dictator never believed that there would be one. In his later monologues at the Führer's main headquarters, Hitler mocked the tendency of bureaucracies to put everything down in written rules: "Exception is a foreign word to them. That's why they lack the courage to take on large responsibilities." In this context, he dismissed the idea of unified laws for the entire Reich as a blind obsession. "Why not have a regulation for a part of the Reich?" he asked. The only thing that mattered to the leadership was to "maintain an overview of the activities of the administration and keep the strings of power in its own hands."[118] The characteristic nebulousness that ran through all levels and authorities in the Nazi system of rule was not the result of the incompetence of those in power: it reflected Hitler's desire politically to secure for himself the greatest possible room to manoeuvre and intervene wherever he saw fit.

The regime's departure from normative commitments bolstered not only radicalism but encouraged unprecedented degrees of corruption, patronage and outright embezzlement. In their first years in power, the National Socialists may never have tired of excoriating the alleged dishonesty of democratic politicians during the Weimar Republic, but they themselves flung the door to corruption wide open within their own ranks. This began with preferential treatment for long-standing party members in the procurement of jobs. Thanks to political favouritism, National Socialists poured into open positions in the civil service even though they sometimes lacked even the most basic qualifications.

Moreover, city utilities—water, gas and electricity companies—and former union-owned and union-affiliated institutions like the Volksfürsorge insurance company or the GEG consumer cooperative became, in the words of the historian Frank Bajohr, "job-creation entities for National Socialists."[119]

The sense of personal entitlement and privilege flourished most at the top levels of the regime. "The degree and extent of corruption in the ruling class is without parallel," complained Sebastian Haffner in 1940, looking back at the years 1933 to 1938, before he fled to Britain.[120] Hitler led his underlings by poor example. In October 1934, a conscientious auditor determined that the chancellor owed 405,494.40 reichsmarks in taxes for the fiscal year 1933–34 alone. Munich Superior Financial President Ludwig Mirre was hastily summoned to Berlin where the state secretary in the Finance Ministry, Fritz Reinhardt, informed him that Hitler was exempt from taxes "due to his constitutional status." In December, Mirre consequently instructed the head of Hitler's local tax office: "All tax notifications in so far as they concern an obligation on the part of the Führer are by definition null and void . . . with that the Führer is exempt from taxes!"[121] As an expression of gratitude for his "official help," Mirre received a monthly raise of 2,000 reichsmarks and was named president of the Reich Financial Court in April 1935.

The tax-exempt dictator also had a plethora of funds into which he could dip to reward favourites and loyal vassals or to finance his private art collection. Among them were the Reich chancellor's and (after Hindenburg's death) the Reich president's discretionary funds, with which he as the head of state could do as he pleased. Along with royalties from sales of Mein Kampf, which earned him 1–2 million reichsmarks a year, Hitler acquired another enviable source of income in 1937, when he was paid a percentage of the revenues brought in by stamps bearing his image. The annual resulting income was in the tens of millions—Reich Postal Minister Ohnesorge presented Hitler with a cheque every year on his birthday.[122] Even more lucrative was the "Adolf Hitler donation of the German economy," instituted in June 1933 at the suggestion of Gustav Krupp von Bohlen und Halbach. It had employers paying a quarterly tax-deductible donation of 0.5 per cent of their wage costs into a private account that Hitler could use as he saw fit. Hitler appointed Martin Bormann to manage this account, and he used it, for instance, to cover part of the costs of expanding Haus Wachenfeld into a stately Alpine residence, the Berghof.[123]

Most of Hitler's paladins followed the lead of their Führer and had themselves declared exempt from taxes, acquired luxurious homes and set up special funds, foundations and secret bank accounts shielded from any public financial scrutiny. Göring—the Third Reich's "second man"—may have been particularly conspicuous with his grandiose lifestyle, including his feudal estate "Carinhall" in Schorfheide, north of Berlin. But other leading figures in the regime were hardly slouches either when it came to unscrupulously abusing their positions for personal gain. Goebbels, one of the more vitriolic critics of "bigwigs" in the Weimar Republic, lived in splendid fashion in his villa on Schwanenwerder Island in Lake Wannsee and had a second home on Lake Bogensee, north of the capital. And despite bemoaning the corruption among the clique of Nazi leaders while writing his memoirs in Spandau prison, Albert Speer was a more-than-willing beneficiary of the system of patronage, concealing his rocketing income from the tax authorities and acquiring an estate in Oderbruch to go along with his large new house on Berlin's Lichtensteinallee.[124]

Functionaries lower in the party hierarchy, from the Gauleiter on down to the district and local leaders, exploited their respective networks in the same way as the top members of the regime. Wasting public resources, embezzlement, abuse of party funds, shameless greed and crass careerism were part of everyday reality.[125] There was "no combating it," Fritz Wiedemann reasoned in retrospect, because the Nazified press was not allowed to report on corruption and because Hitler covered up abuses committed by the party's old guard: "This plague ate its way from the top to the bottom. What was allowable for the bigwigs was also all right for the little guy."[126]

Along with flourishing corruption, another of the most striking characteristics of National Socialist rule was a feverish mania for massive construction projects. From the very beginning, Hitler thought in dimensions that went beyond anything that had previously existed. Size beyond all rational proportion, in Speer's interpretation of his logic, "would impress and intimidate the people and psychologically secure his own rule and that of his successors."[127] Nazi architecture was intended as a visual representation of the power of the Third Reich, which Hitler's genius had built up after a period of Germany's decline and which he had bestowed as a gift upon its people. The monumental projects he commissioned, Hitler told those attending the Nuremberg rally in 1937, were conceived neither for the year 1940 nor for the year 2000. "They are intended," Hitler said, "to cast their shadows like the cathedrals of our past into the millennia of the future."[128] One had to build "on as large a scale as technically possible," he declared on another occasion, "and for all of eternity!"[129]

By no means did such megalomaniacal visions first crystallise in Hitler's crude world view after 1933. On the contrary, they originated in ideas he had developed in the first volume of *Mein Kampf* while still an inmate in Landsberg. In that book, he had lamented that "today's big cities . . . do not have any landmarks that dominate the entire look of the city . . . and could be seen as emblems of an entire era." He contrasted this with the example of ancient and medieval cities, which contained monuments, be they the Acropolis or Gothic cathedrals, "constructed for eternity, not for the moment, because they were intended to reflect the greatness and significance of a society and not the wealth of an individual owner."[130]

At the time when Hitler wrote these words, he complained to his fellow inmate Hess "how few monumental structures we will leave to prosperity aside from a few commercial skyscrapers." There was "nothing comparable to our cathedrals that belonged to and unified the collective," Hitler carped, adding: "Here, too, Germany must take the lead." He then presented his astonished disciple with sketches for a gigantic domed building, which was to serve as a conference space for "great national celebration." Even if such an expensive project would not meet with general understanding, and narrow-minded philistines would complain, Hitler believed that "generations to come would understand it—man doesn't live from bread alone, and neither does the nation."[131] Hitler's belief in his political mission and his passion for monumental construction projects were intimately connected, and he continued to engage in wild architectural fantasies after being released from Landsberg. After a joint visit to Berlin in 1925, Hess wrote that the "tribune" dreamed of "further expanding" a city that he "absolutely adored." And in December 1928, Hess summarised Hitler's attitude: "Only a metropolis that overshadowed everything as an uncontested centre could overcome the [German] tendency towards atomisation and provincialism."[132]

Hitler also shared his architectural daydreaming with Goebbels. "He talks about the future architectural look of the country and is very much a master builder," gushed the latter in July 1926. In the years that followed, the Führer and his chief propagandist regularly gave themselves over to self-indulgent musings about the colossal structures they would build some day. "Hitler is developing fantastic plans for new architecture—he's a real humdinger," Goebbels enthused in October 1930. One year later, a few days before the meeting of the "National Opposition" in Bad Harzburg, he noted: "The boss is developing construction plans for Berlin. Fantastic, genius. For the millennia. An idea hewn in stone. At heart he's an artist."[133]

From very early on, Hitler made no secret of his intention to fundamentally remake the look of Germany's larger cities once he came to power. In a speech in Munich's Löwenbräukeller in early April 1929, Hitler said that he did not want to construct purpose-driven buildings like department stores, factories, skyscrapers and hotels in the Third Reich. Instead he aimed to create "documents of art and culture . . . to last for millennia." He proclaimed: "We see before us the ancient cities, the Acropolis, the Parthenon, the Colosseum, we see the cities of the Middle Ages with their gigantic cathedrals and . . . we know that people need this sort of focus if they are not to come undone."[134]

No matter how half-baked these plans were, Hitler set about trying to realise them immediately after taking power. In the night of 30–31 January 1933, he started talking about architecture in one of his never-ending monologues. For starters, he announced, he would have the Chancellery redesigned since in its current state it was nothing more than a "vulgar reception site."[135] At the leaders' conference in Munich in late April 1933, he proclaimed his intention to create "new unforgettable documents," which would make the German people the latest in a series of the "world's great cultural peoples." He added: "We are not working for the moment but for the judgement of millennia."[136] In the spring of 1934, when Speer introduced Hitler to his wife at an evening reception, the chancellor solemnly intoned, without a trace of irony: "Your husband will erect buildings for me, the like of which have not been created for four millennia."[137]

There has been a lot of speculation as to why Hitler was so enthralled with Speer in particular. If we believe Speer's own account, Hitler himself offered a plausible explanation: "I was looking for an architect to whom I could entrust my blueprints. He had to be young since, as you know, these plans stretch far into the future. I needed someone who could carry on after my death with the authority I invested in him."[138] But there was apparently more to it than that. With his typically keen eye for the strengths and weaknesses of other people, Hitler recognised not only Speer's architectural and organisational talent, but also the burning ambition concealed behind a cool, completely controlled exterior. Hitler may also have regarded the ambitious young architect as the embodiment of everything he had dreamed of becoming as a young man—as a kind of alter ego, albeit one that was "more effortless and secure thanks to his good social background."[139] In any case, Hitler treated Speer with more affection than any other member of his inner circle except Goebbels. There have been repeated speculations as to an "erotic element" in their relationship, but as is the case wherever Hitler's emotional life is concerned, there is no concrete evidence for the idea.[140]

For his part, as he wrote in his *Spandau Diaries*, Speer felt at home around and "honestly drawn to" Hitler.[141] Speer enjoyed being a favourite and receiving the patronage of such a powerful man, who opened up for him, although he was not yet 30, seemingly limitless opportunities in his profession. After 1945, when commenting on his role as Hitler's favourite architect, Speer would repeatedly insist that he had had no other choice but to seize this dream chance and conclude a Faustian bargain. Hitler had exercised a "suggestive and irresistible power" over him, Speer claimed, and the magnitude of the task he was given had caused an "intoxication" and "massive increase in self-worth" which he had soon needed "as an addict needs his drug."[142] But Speer was not nearly as emotionally dependent as he tried to suggest. Hitler did not need to do anything much to win him over: from the very start, Speer was obsessed by grotesquely proportioned construction projects. The extent of his fundamental agreement with the dictator's political and architectural ideas and the degree to which his behaviour was calculated to secure the latter's lasting favour can be seen in an article he wrote in 1936 entitled "The Führer's Buildings." It was no less sycophantically wordy than any of Goebbels's many paeans:

> It will go down as unique in the history of the German people that at the decisive turning point, its leader not only commenced the greatest

reordering of our politics and world view but also proceeded with superior expertise as a master builder to create structures of stone that will still serve as testaments of the political will and cultural ability of their great age thousands of years down the road.[143]

The pilot project for the new cooperative flurry between Hitler and Speer was Nuremberg, the home of the party rallies. In early 1934, Speer was commissioned to replace the provisional wooden stage on Zeppelin Field with gigantic stone terraces. Hitler was so pleased with Speer's design that in the autumn he put the architect in charge of the planning for the entire Nuremberg rally site.[144] Alongside the existing assembly buildings and marching ground—the Luitpoldhalle, the Luitpoldarena, the Old Stadium and Zeppelin Field—Speer was to construct a series of colossal buildings: the Congress Hall, the German Stadium and the March Field. A few months later, Hitler was able to present the Nuremberg mayor, Willy Liebel, with the first sketches. In late 1935, the Association for the Nuremberg Rally Site was founded to help realise these plans. Citing his Führer mandate, Speer had no trouble getting his way with this group. The tenth rally after the Nazi "seizure of power," September 1943, was set as the deadline for the entire site to be finished.[145] Hitler repeatedly travelled to Nuremberg to inspect progress. He also frequently studied Speer's blueprints in the Chancellery. "The Führer showed us plans for Nuremberg," Goebbels noted in December 1935. "Truly grand. A unique monumentality! Speer has done a good job."[146] Hitler was less interested in the financing of the project. When asked about who was going to pay for all the construction work, Goebbels recorded: "The Führer doesn't want to talk about money. Build, build! It will get paid for. Friedrich the Great did not worry about money when he built Sanssouci."[147]

Speer's plans combined existing and planned structures into an ensemble, connected by a 2-kilometre-long "Great Street" of granite. At its southern end was the March Field, a 1,050-metre-wide and 600-metre-long parade ground surrounded by stands for 160,000 spectators and crowned by a Goddess of Victory that would have been 14 metres higher than the Statue of Liberty.[148] The new Congress Hall on the northern end of the Great Street was to be based on plans by Nuremberg architect Ludwig Ruff, who had succeeded in winning

Hitler's approval for his designs in early June 1934. The building was conceived as the sacral centre of the rallies and would have accommodated 50,000 people. "The most monumental covered building since antiquity," Goebbels effused.[149] This, as Hitler declared when laying the foundation stone on 12 September 1935, was where "the elite of the National Socialist Reich" would meet annually for centuries to come. "And if the movement should ever fall silent," Hitler proclaimed, "this building will speak as a witness for centuries. In the middle of a sacred grove of ancient oak trees, people will admire this first giant among the monuments of the Third Reich with reverent amazement."[150]

Even more gigantically proportioned was the German Stadium, a horseshoe-shaped arena with a planned capacity of more than 400,000, which would have made it the largest sports arena in the world. It would have positively dwarfed the 80,000-plus-capacity Olympic Stadium in Berlin. At the foundation-laying ceremony on 9 September 1937, Hitler congratulated Speer in front of a group of Nazi grandees with the words: "This is the greatest day of your life!"[151] By that point at the very latest, the star architect could have been under no illusions about the political goals inherent in Hitler's concept of colossal architecture. It was a prelude to the campaigns of territorial expansion soon to commence, at the end of which the Third Reich would not only aim to have hegemony over Europe but dominance of the entire world.[152] In the spring of 1937, when Speer informed Hitler that oversized athletics fields did not conform to Olympic norms, the latter allegedly replied: "That's of no consequence. The Olympic Games will take place in Tokyo in 1940 and thereafter, they will take place in Germany, in this stadium, for all time. And we're the ones to determine how the athletics fields are to be measured."[153]

None of these colossal projects was ever completed. By the start of the Second World War, the German Stadium had not got beyond the excavation stage. On the March Field, only a few of the twenty-six travertine gate towers were finished, and the Congress Hall was still a torso, although its construction was most advanced and was allowed to continue for a while.[154] Still, even if Hitler had not unleashed war in 1939, the deadline for the inauguration of the facilities could hardly have been met.

The Nuremberg rally grounds were by no means the Nazis' only gigantic construction project. Munich, the "capital of the movement," was supposed to be fundamentally remade. Along with a new main train station, the city was to get a massive "pillar of the movement," designed by Hitler himself, that would have loomed over the twin towers of the Frauenkirche. True to his habit of dividing responsibilities and encouraging competition so as to encourage improvements in performance, in 1937 Hitler commissioned the Munich architect Hermann Giesler, and not Speer, to oversee this project. In the autumn of 1940, Giesler also received a commission to supervise the remaking of Linz, "the hometown of the Führer." Two monumental bridges over the Danube were planned there, as well as a "Gau forum" with a massive auditorium, a picture gallery and a retirement residence for Hitler. Hamburg was to receive a viaduct spanning the Elbe River that was intended to overshadow the Golden Gate Bridge. And a host of other German cities were also earmarked for epochal construction projects.[155]

But the Reich capital was the central focus of the planned construction. Berlin, Hitler declared in September 1933 to a delegation of city administrators headed by State Commissioner and later Lord Mayor Julius Lippert, "must be elevated in terms of culture and urban development so that it is capable of competing with capitals throughout the world."[156] To this end, he pledged to make 40 million reichsmarks per year available—that sum was increased to 60 million in July 1934. In the months that followed it emerged that the heart of the project was the construction of a North–South Axis. The space and railway tracks of the Potsdam and Anhalt train stations were to be sacrificed for two new rail stations at either end of the axis. In March 1934, Hitler shared his pet project with city fathers. In the vicinity of the southern train station, there should be "a gigantic triumphal arch dedicated to the unvanquished army in the Great War" and in the middle, not far from the Brandenburg Gate, there would be an enormous assembly hall capable of holding 250,000 people.[157] Not much progress was made on these plans, perhaps because Berlin administrators hesitated in the face of such a radical intervention in existing city structures, perhaps because Hitler himself could not decide who should be entrusted with such a project for posterity. "He did not know the right architect," Lippert reported him saying in late June 1935. "And he could not say whether Speer alone would be up to the job."[158]

In the spring of 1936, Hitler seems to have made up his mind, mentioning to Speer that he still had one commission, "the biggest of all," to hand out. Speer therefore was probably not surprised when Hitler summoned him a few months later and asked him to take charge of the entire redevelopment of the Reich capital. Hitler used the occasion, Speer recalled, to give him two sketches, one of the Victory Arch and the other of the massive, domed People's Hall. "I did these sketches ten years ago," Hitler said. "I always kept them because I knew that some day I would build them. And now we are going to do precisely that."[159] Speer, who had already followed Hitler's specifications in the expansion of the Nuremberg rally grounds, eagerly accepted his suggestions for triumphal monuments in Berlin. "With the Führer looking at plans for the reconstruction of Berlin with him and Speer," Goebbels noted in mid-December 1936. "A marvellous arrangement. Very large and monumental. Calculated for 20 years. With a gigantic street from south to north. The splendid new buildings will go there. With that Berlin elevated to the leading city in the world. The Führer thinks big and boldly. He's 100 years ahead of his time."[160] Goebbels was attributing work largely done by Speer to Hitler. There is considerable evidence that the privileged architect believed he could best fulfil the architectural obsessions of his patron by designing buildings that were even more overwhelming and super-dimensional than Hitler himself envisioned.[161]

On 30 January 1937, Hitler officially named Speer "general building inspector of the Reich capital," and the architect was given a new office in the Academy of Fine Arts on Pariser Platz, right in the city centre. Hitler could access it, away from the public eye, via the ministerial gardens.[162] Sometimes he arrived with his lunch guests in tow, but more often he showed up after lunch or late at night in the former academy exhibition space, where the model city was gradually taking shape. Hitler was particularly enamoured with the 1:10,000 scale model of the North–South Axis that could be separated into individual components and pulled on tables with wheels. Never, Speer recalled, did he experience Hitler "so lively, so spontaneous, so carefree" as in the hours the two of them spent bent over the blueprints, intoxicated by the colossal size of the buildings.[163] Speer's father had a different reaction one day when his famous son proudly showed him the models, exclaiming: "You two have gone completely mad!"[164]

And in fact the "gigantomania" of these plans exceeded everything previously built in history. The North–South Axis, intended as the jewel of the new Berlin, was supposed to be 120 metres wide and 7 kilometres long—far wider and longer than the Champs Elysées.[165] The main train station at the southern end of this boulevard was to contain four storeys connected by lifts and escalators and be considerably larger than New York's Grand Central Station. People exiting the station were supposed to be overwhelmed by the massive Victory Arch—170 metres wide, 119 metres deep and 117 metres high—compared to which the Arc de Triomphe would have looked like a toy.[166] The 80-metre-high arch would have magically directed the viewer's gaze to the 5-kilometre-distant People's or Great Hall, which was the most vivid example of the sheer insanity of the plans. It was designed to accommodate 150,000 to 180,000 people. With a height of 226 metres and a circumference of 250 metres, the interior would have been seven times the size of St. Peter's Basilica. On Hitler's forty-eighth birthday on 20 April 1937, Speer gave him a model of the structure. "We stayed up until 2 a.m. with the blueprints, giving free rein to our imaginations," noted Goebbels.[167]

Along with the Victory Arch and the People's Hall, a series of other prestige buildings were to line the boulevard: a Soldiers' Hall with a crypt housing the sarcophagi of famous German military leaders from the past and future; a Reich Marshal's Office for Göring, whose baroque stairwell, conceived as the largest in the world, was designed to match its future resident's predilection for luxury; and last but certainly not least, a Führer Palace for Hitler, a fortress-like building with bulletproof shutters and a steel entrance portal. "It cannot be ruled out that I may be compelled some day to take unpopular measures," Hitler told Speer. "Perhaps there will be an uprising. This eventuality has to be planned for . . . We must be able to defend the centre of the Reich like a fortress."[168] Such statements suggest the basic fears concealed behind Hitler's pomposity and self-deification. The oversized buildings were to be decorated with similarly monumental sculptures fashioned by Arno Breker, whose 1936 work *Decathlete* for the Reich Sport Field had found Hitler's favour and who quickly gained access to the inner circles of power.[169]

Hitler's megalomaniacal plans for Berlin can only be understood in conjunction with his hegemonic aspirations abroad. In a sense they anticipated architecturally what had yet to be conquered by martial expansion. "Do you understand now why we plan so big?" he asked Speer one day and provided the answer himself: "The capital of the Germanic Empire."[170] Nor did the dictator conceal his ambitions from Goebbels. Late one night in mid-March 1937, a few weeks after Speer's appointment as general building inspector, Hitler told his propaganda minister that he intended to incorporate Austria and Czechoslovakia into the Reich. "We need both to round off our territory," Goebbels reported Hitler saying. "And we'll get them . . . When their citizens come to Germany, they'll be crushed by the greatness and power of the Reich . . . Hence the Führer's gigantic construction plans. He'll never give them up."[171] In the early summer of 1939, after Hitler had concluded the first phase of this territorial expansion and was preparing the next one, he stood once again lost in thought before the architectural model and pointed to the swastika-bearing eagle that was to adorn the dome of the People's Hall. "We'll change that," he said. "The eagle won't be clutching a swastika. It will be clutching the globe!"[172] Speer was not surprised, still less horrified, by the megalomania of such imperialistic statements. On the contrary, it was the "whole point" of his buildings, as Speer told the British journalist Gitta Sereny in the late 1970s: "All I *wanted* was for this great man to dominate the globe."[173]

The new Berlin would be the capital of a future global empire—dictator and architect were in complete agreement about that. In his later monologues in his headquarters, Hitler repeatedly returned to their mutual flights of fancy. Anyone entering the Führer's Palace, he said, "should feel as though he were approaching the ruler of the world." Berlin, which as the capital of the world would be renamed Germania, would be comparable only with Babylon or Ancient Rome. "What is London, and what is Paris in comparison?" Hitler sneered.[174] Of course, it was advisable not to go public with such plans, and well into the late 1930s Hitler continued to present himself as a man of peace. The German public received only snippets of information about the massive planned transformation of Berlin. In January 1938, Speer told the German News Agency about the basic idea of a North–South Axis, which Hitler had agreed with local politicians as early as 1933, but he merely hinted at the colossal size of the construction projects. The same was true of the articles that appeared in various newspapers in 1938 and 1939. For instance in June 1938, Hitler insisted that Goebbels rewrite his speech marking the beginning of construction on the House of Tourism: "For the sake of caution, he doesn't want me talking too much about the monumentality of our architectural transformation."[175]

Speer set himself a deadline of 1950 for the completion of all construction projects. Hitler was in a hurry. "You have to do everything to get it all done while I'm still alive," Hitler told Speer during a picnic in the summer of 1936. "Only if I myself have spoken and ruled in them, will they be consecrated in the way my successors will need."[176] In June 1938, work on what Goebbels called "the greatest construction project of all time" commenced simultaneously at twelve sites. And it was no accident that the propaganda minister wrote in the same diary entry of his own goal: "expulsion of all Jews from Berlin."[177] The space occupied by the train tracks between Postdam and Anhalt train stations did not suffice to build the North–South Axis. Apartment blocks would have to be torn down, and replacement quarters found for tenants. In September 1938, Speer went on record at a meeting with city administrators about how he thought this should be done, suggesting that "the large apartments necessary should be freed up by compulsorily evicting Jews." Speer asked for the suggestion to be treated confidentially since he first wanted to "determine the Führer's view."[178] After the Kristallnacht pogrom on 9 November 1938, Speer took one important step towards achieving this goal. On 26 November, in his capacity as special agent for the Four Year Plan, Göring stipulated that the general building inspector had a "right of first purchase" after the "removal of Jews from apartments, stores and warehouses."[179] Thanks to his Führer mandate, Speer succeeded in pushing aside all competing claims.

With the start of the Second World War, work was suspended on all the construction sites. But on 25 June 1940, after the defeat of France, Hitler issued a decree reading: "Berlin must very soon, as the capital of a strong, new Reich, be reconfigured architecturally to express the magnitude of our victory."[180] With that, Speer's claims on "Jewish apartments" were reactivated. Hitler's star architect preferred to forget this after 1945, and he concealed it from Joachim Fest in their conversations. But since the 1980s, historians have uncovered the truth. Speer's ministry played a pioneering role in the identification of Berlin Jews and their deportation to the death camps.[181]

On numerous occasions between the late autumn of 1940 and the spring of 1941, Hitler had the model of the new Berlin exhibited in the Academy of Fine Arts. "You sensed him warming and he repeatedly said: 'Very nice, very nice,'" one of Speer's colleagues wrote about a Führer visit in mid-March 1941. "'Now everyone is surely convinced. In the face of such works are there any grumblers who are against the configuration of Berlin?' Speer answered in the negative." Hitler slapped his knees in joy at the model of the People's Hall, which Speer had made several metres taller. "The Führer asked: 'How high is the hall?' Speer: 'More than 300 metres. It's a question of honour that it's no smaller.' The Führer laughed and said that that was the right attitude. That was the way to think. 300 metres was the elevation of the Obersalzberg above Berchtesgaden."[182] At this point, when he was preparing what he believed would be a Blitzkrieg of destruction against the Soviet Union, Hitler felt like a certain victor. But Germany's unexpected military defeats in the autumn and winter of 1941 would fundamentally change the situation. Work on the construction sites was suspended until March 1943. As was the case in Nuremberg, none of the monumental structures in Berlin was ever completed.

Another building, the New Reich Chancellery on Vossstrasse, was completed before the start of the Second World War. If we were to credit Speer's account, Hitler commissioned the building in late January 1938. "In the times to come, I need to hold important conversations," Speer quoted Hitler as saying.

> For that I need large halls and ballrooms, with which I can impress minor potentates in particular . . . How long do you need? For the blueprints, the demolitions, and everything else? A year and a half or two years would be too long for me. Can you be finished by 10 January 1939? I'd like to hold the next diplomats' reception in the new Chancellery.[183]

But this account, like much of what Speer wrote in his memoirs, does not completely conform to reality. Hitler had already conducted discussions with city representatives in 1934 about the building of a new "residence" in keeping with his prestige. The property on Vossstrasse had been purchased in 1935, and the buildings on it demolished, including the Gau headquarters, which Speer had redesigned as recently as 1932. Plans for the New Chancellery were finished by mid-1937, and construction commenced in April 1938.[184]

Nonetheless, although much of the preliminary work had been done, the extremely tight deadline tested Speer's talent for improvisation and created special challenges for architects Karl Piepenburg and Walter Kühnell, who managed the building site. Four and a half thousand construction workers laboured around the clock in two shifts. "This is now . . . no longer an American tempo—it's a German tempo," Hitler praised the work at the roofing ceremony on 2 August 1938.[185] On 7 January 1939, Speer gave Hitler a tour of the nearly finished interior, and two days later, after the official handover, at a ceremony in front of 8,000 workers at the Sportpalast, the dictator celebrated the New Chancellery "as the first monument of the new, great German Reich."[186]

The 422-metre-long building took up the entire northern side of Vossstrasse. Visitors entered through the main entranceway on Wilhelmplatz into the "courtyard of honour" and from there via an external set of steps, flanked by two super-dimensional Arno Breker sculptures, into the building proper. Before they reached the reception hall, they had to pass through a series of spaces: an entrance hall, a mosaic-covered ballroom, a domed hall and, finally, a 146-metre marble gallery that was twice as long as the Hall of Mirrors in the Palace of Versailles, upon which it was modelled. Hitler liked the fact that foreign dignitaries had to walk such a long way, which he thought "gave them a sense of the power and dimensions of the German Reich."[187] Hitler's office, which was more the size of a throne room—27 metres long by 14.5 metres wide by 9.75 metres tall—was also designed to intimidate. He particularly loved an inlay depicting a half-drawn sword in his gigantic desk. "Very good," Hitler said. "When the diplomats who sit before me at this desk see that, it will put fear into them."[188] Less than six years later, the New Chancellery lay in ruins. Hitler's monstrous dream of a global Aryan empire and a "world capital Germania" had burst like the balloon in Charlie Chaplin's brilliant, prescient anti-Hitler satire *The Great Dictator*.

18

The Berghof Society and the Führer's Mistress

"Noon at the Obersalzberg," Goebbels noted on 17 July 1936, shortly after the Berghof was officially opened. "The Führer received us with great joy on the steps and showed us the new house with rooms for all of us. It's magnificent. Comfortable guest rooms. A wonderful hall. The whole thing is a unique mountain manor. You can relax here. The Führer is very happy. Here he feels at home."[1] In 1928, when Hitler rented Haus Wachenfeld for the first time, he secured a right of first refusal to purchase it. In September 1932, the owner, an affluent widow named Margarete Winter from the northern German town of Buxtehude, offered to sell it to him. In June 1933, shortly after he became chancellor, the titles to the house and its entire inventory were transferred to Hitler's name. When Albert Speer visited for the first time in the spring of 1934, he was less than impressed, however: "After Berchtesgaden, there was a steep mountain road full of potholes up to the Obersalzberg, where Hitler's comfortable little wooden house with its protruding roof and tiny rooms awaited. The furniture was old-fashioned German 'Vertiko' rustic and gave the living spaces something cosy and petit bourgeois."[2]

As Speer recalled, Hitler decided to expand his modest holiday home into an imposing mountain manor in the summer of 1935. The dictator himself made the initial sketches, on the basis of which architect Alois Degano from the village of Gmund on Tegernsee Lake drew up blueprints. Haus Wachenfeld was not torn down. Instead, walls on the ground and first floors were opened up, so that old parts of the structure could be integrated with the new ones, whose 17-metre gables and total length of 37 metres seemed very ostentatious in comparison. Construction work, which began in March 1936, was pushed through at an accelerated pace. The Berghof was inaugurated on 8 July, with the Berchtesgaden Christmas Marksmen marching by and firing their guns in salute.[3] Martin Bormann, in his role of staff director of the deputy to the Führer, had been invaluable in getting the project financed. In the process he gained a useful entrée to the dictator's private circles and exploited Hitler's trust to make himself indispensable. Even before construction had been completed, Bormann began buying up land, lot by lot, around the Berghof. Those who did not want to sell were subjected to massive pressure, including threats that their property would be confiscated and they themselves sent to a concentration camp. The old farmhouses were demolished. In their stead, Bormann had new buildings constructed: a barracks complex for a company of SS men; an agricultural estate that was to serve as a model farm; a greenhouse to provide the vegetarian Hitler with fresh fruit and vegetables all year round; a small tearoom at the Mooslahner Kopf peak a few hundred metres down the mountain from the Berghof proper; and a further tearoom (the most expensive and difficult of Bormann's projects) on the Kehlstein peak some 800 metres higher up.[4]

In the early years of the Third Reich, Hitler's admirers had been able to make pilgrimages to the Obersalzberg at will in hopes of glimpsing their idol up close. Hitler often took walks in the surrounding area, for instance to Hochlenzer, a small mountain restaurant where customers could enjoy the sun and a refreshing drink on wooden benches. But in 1936, the Obersalzberg was declared a "Führer protection zone" and completely sealed off with barbed wire. Special ID was required to enter it, and access to the core of the area was strictly monitored by the SS. That ruled out any accidental contact between Hitler and the public at large.[5]

The Obersalzberg remained a major construction site up until the start of the Second World War. "Small, idyllic paths through fields were turned into broad lanes and concrete roads," recalled Otto Dietrich. "Where previously teams of oxen had picturesquely gone on their way, there was now the constant din of gigantic trucks and diggers. Alpine pastures were buried under scree, and stretches of forest gave way to barracks and camps. The mountain stillness was shattered by the rumble of dynamite detonations."[6] In private, Hitler occasionally joked about Bormann's mania for building, jesting that his name was fitting since he was "boring holes in the mountains,"⁷ but he also appreciated his industrious underling's reliability. Bormann was like a wandering notebook, ever ready to record the Führer's every wish.

Bormann's rise to a central figure at the dictator's mountain court did not escape the notice of Hitler's entourage. Goebbels, who always wanted to see himself as Hitler's favourite and was thus particularly sensitive to rivals, wrote in late October 1936: "The Führer is very satisfied with Bormann. He possesses energy and discretion." After a visit to the Obersalzberg, Goebbels added: "Bormann works decisively and reliably up there. He's firmly in the saddle."⁸ In order to be at Hitler's side whenever required, Bormann himself purchased a villa on the Obersalzberg. Göring, too, built an atypically modest house there in 1934. Speer was not about to be outdone. In the early summer of 1937, he rented a farmhouse, which he converted into a family holiday home, and built an adjacent studio, where he could work on his architectural plans.⁹

Hitler's Alpine residence featured thirty rooms spread over three floors. The showpiece was the Great Hall and its gigantic retractable window looking out onto the Untersberg, where legend had it that the German emperor Friedrich Barbarossa was slumbering, waiting to return some day. In front of the window was a 6-metre-long marble table. Documents awaiting Hitler's signature were often spread out on it, as were architectural blueprints and later, during the Second World War, military maps. Beside the table was a similarly oversized globe whose symbolic significance in terms of the Nazis' emerging territorial designs was all too obvious. Two groups of chairs—one surrounding a coffee table near the window, and the other arranged around a fireplace on the far side of the room—completed the furnishings. They had been selected by Gerdy Troost, the widow of architect Paul Troost. Hitler thought highly of her, visiting her studio whenever he was in Munich. She was also responsible for the two Gobelin tapestries in the Great Hall which were more than just wall decoration. They also served a function in Hitler's nightly film screenings: one covered the small window to the projection room, the other the screen on the opposite wall.¹⁰

Hitler was especially proud of his collection of works by sixteenth-century Italian masters and nineteenth-century German artists on display in the Great Hall. They included *Venus and Amor* by Paris Bordone, *Roman Ruins Landscape* by Giovanni Paolo Pannini, *Madonna tondo* by Giuliano Bugiardini, *Eve and Her Son Abel* by Edward von Steinle, an exponent of the nineteenth-century Nazarene movement, and *The Arts in Service of Religion* by Moritz von Schwind. His favourite work was Anselm Feuerbach's *Nanna* portrait, which bore a certain similarity to Hitler's niece Geli Raubal. "Is not Nanna wonderful?" he told one of his secretaries. "I can't help looking at her over and over again. She has a marvellous spot above the fireplace. Her hand glows as if it was alive."[11] And, of course, the collection would not have been complete without a bronze bust of Richard Wagner by Arno Breker. It stood on a massive chest of drawers which housed the loudspeakers for Hitler's film screenings.

Separated from the Great Hall only by a heavy velvet curtain, the rustically furnished living room left over from Haus Wachenfeld was the only room that recalled the old house and emanated a certain cosiness. It was dominated by a large green ceramic stove, whose tiles had been handmade by the Munich artisan Sofie Stork, the fiancée of Hitler's main assistant, Wilhelm Brückner. During the winter months, in particular, guests liked sitting on its surrounding benches since the enormous Great Hall was always rather cold. To the right of the window was a large bookcase, containing, among other things, *Meyer's Conversational Lexicon*. Hitler enjoyed consulting its volumes whenever there was a disagreement, to prove to others how phenomenal his memory was and that he was right once again.[12]

An expansive hallway connected the living room with the dining room, which had hardwood floors and patterned pine panelling. A long dining-room table offered space for twenty-four people. One length of the room had a semicircular bay window, in front of which guests would breakfast while Hitler was still in bed.[13] Hitler's private quarters—an office, a bedroom and a bathroom—were located on the first floor. Next to his bedroom, separated from it only by a small space with two connecting doors, was Eva Braun's apartment, which consisted of a bedroom, a small living room and a bathroom. "Why did the housekeeper of the Berghof, as Eva Braun was introduced to us, need a special entrance to Hitler's bedroom?" wondered Rochus Misch, who was part of the Führer's escort command from 1940, in his memoirs. "Everyone imagined a reason."[14]

After becoming chancellor, Hitler had continued his relationship with the young woman from Munich. During his frequent visits to the Bavarian capital, they would meet in his private apartment on Prinzregentenstrasse. On 6 February 1933, for instance, he celebrated Braun's twenty-first birthday there, giving her jewellery.[15] When interviewed by U.S. investigators in 1945, Hitler's housekeeper Anni Winter testified that sometimes Braun had been taken home at night, and sometimes she had stayed in the apartment.[16] The pilot Hans Baur recalled surprising Hitler and Braun during a rendezvous in Hitler's apartment shortly before Christmas 1933. Braun, he wrote, blushed, while Hitler had been "somewhat embarrassed."[17] Apparently, in the early years of their affair, Hitler wanted to keep it secret from his entourage. This was confirmed by the clandestine manner in which Hitler had her brought to the Obersalzberg. Speer recalled that several hours after the official motorcade arrived, a small, hardtop Mercedes would pull up with Hitler's secretaries Johanna Wolf and Christa Schroeder. "They were usually accompanied by a simple girl," Speer recalled. "She was pleasant, more a breath of fresh air than a beauty, and was modest in manner. There was no sign that she was the ruler's mistress: Eva Braun."[18] Speer added that the astonishment was all the greater the first time Hitler and Braun disappeared together in the direction of the upstairs bedrooms. Most of the evidence, however, suggests that the dictator did not allow her to stay the night in Haus Wachenfeld but rather put her up with his other visitors in nearby guest houses.[19]

The woman who initially ran the household on the Obersalzberg was Hitler's no-nonsense half-sister Angela Raubal, and the copious receipts for goods and services she accumulated over the years attest to her attention to even the smallest details. A number of Munich businesses profited handsomely for her diligence in keeping up Hitler's mountain retreat, in particular the city's largest department store, Horn am Stachus, which supplied her with everything from blankets, tablecloths and pillows to deck chairs. From April 1933 to August 1934 Raubal spent almost 12,000 marks at Horn alone.[20] Angela Raubal felt a lively antipathy for Eva Braun, ignoring her wherever possible and addressing her, when it could not be avoided, only as "Fräulein." In the words of one of Braun's biographers, she saw the young woman from Munich as "a decorative doll craftily spinning her web to ensnare her brother, who was always naive and inexperienced around 'brazen hussies.'"[21] The two are often thought to have fallen out in 1935, but the first big quarrel actually occurred a year earlier at the Nuremberg rally. Raubal, Magda Goebbels and other prominent Nazi wives were not at all happy about Braun taking a seat on the VIP stand for the first time. They found that the young woman behaved "very conspicuously," although most probably the mere presence of the Führer's girlfriend was an eyesore to them. The women badmouthed her, and after the rally Raubal promptly told Hitler about the incidents on the stand. But instead of dropping Braun, Hitler flew into a rage, forbade anyone to meddle in his private affairs and ordered Raubal to quit the Obersalzberg immediately.[22]

The other women who had made derogatory remarks about Braun, including Henriette von Schirach, were also banned from Hitler's Alpine residence. The scandal even temporarily clouded Hitler's relationship with Magda Goebbels. In mid-October 1934, the wife of the propaganda minister cleared the air with Hitler in the Reich Chancellery. Goebbels noted:

> As I suspected, a huge bit of tittle-tattle staged by Frau von Schirach. You have to feel sorry for the Führer. Now he wants to withdraw entirely. Silly women's prattle. Nothing better to do. It makes my blood boil. Frau Raubal already sent back to Austria. No women any more in the Chancellery. That's the result of it.[23]

In April 1935, Goebbels met Raubal in Frankfurt am Main: "She told with tears in her eyes what happened in Nuremberg . . . Poor woman! I consoled her as much as I could."[24] But whereas Hitler's relationship with the Goebbelses soon returned to normal, Raubal remained *persona non grata*. In mid-November 1935, she came to Berlin, but was not admitted to see the chancellor. Over coffee at the Goebbelses' home, she bemoaned her fate. "She's to be pitied," wrote the propaganda minister. "It would be good if the Führer would accept her again. She's been punished enough."[25] In January 1936, Raubal married Professor Martin Hammitzsch, the director of the State Architectural Academy in Dresden. She was "completely happy," she wrote to Hess, especially since she had spoken to her half-brother while he was visiting the Saxon city.[26] But that was as far as their reconciliation went. Hitler remained reserved towards his half-sister and rarely saw her.[27]

By removing Raubal, Hitler signalled unmistakably to his entourage that anyone who dared meddle with his private life and speak ill of his mistress would fall from grace and lose power and influence. Eva Braun's position was thus cemented. Indeed, as one of Braun's biographers put it, she became "practically untouchable within the inner circle."[28] Yet Hitler remained unusually secretive about their relationship. When he was in Berlin, he played the role of the ascetic Führer, nobly sacrificing himself for the nation and forgoing any sort of personal happiness. Even Goebbels fell for this pose. "He told me about his lonely, joyless private life," he noted in his diary in late January 1935. "Without women, without love, still consumed by memories of Geli. I was deeply moved. He's such a fine man."[29]

Since Hitler left his inner circle in the dark as to the precise nature of his relationship with Braun, it is doubly difficult for historians to put together a halfway reliable picture of it. The lack of authentic historical documents in particular is frustrating. In her final letter from the Chancellery in Berlin on 23 April 1945, Eva Braun ordered her sister Gretl to destroy all her private correspondence, especially her business letters. "An envelope addressed to the Führer to be found in the safe of the bunker"—likely the bunker in the small Munich villa at Wasserburgerstrasse 12 which Hitler purchased for Braun in 1936—was also to be destroyed. "Please do not read it," Braun told her sister. "I would ask you pack the Führer's letters and my answers to them (blue leather-bound portfolio) and perhaps bury them. Please do not destroy them."[30] Braun's most recent biographer, Heike Görtemaker, has speculated that Julius Schaub, who arrived at the Berghof on 25 April 1945, burned this correspondence along with other private Hitler documents before Gretl Braun could take them to safety.[31] But that would assume that the correspondence was in fact kept at the Berghof and not at Wasserburgerstrasse. It is possible that Gretl Braun ignored her sister's instructions and destroyed all the material. In any case, no letter from Eva Braun to Hitler or vice versa has ever been found.

That gives all the more significance to a twenty-two-page excerpt from Braun's diary covering 6 February to 28 May 1935. The authenticity of this document—which was found by American soldiers after the war together with films and photo albums and brought to the National Archives in Washington—is by no means beyond question. Braun's older sister, Ilse Fucke-Michels, confirmed that the pages were genuine when asked by the American journalist Nerin E. Gun, who first published them.[32] Werner Maser, who published facsimiles in 1973, also trusted their provenance.[33] By contrast, in 2003 the historian Anton Joachimsthaler claimed that a simple handwriting test proved that the diary excerpt was a fake: "Numerous documents show that between the ages of seventeen and thirty-three Eva Braun wrote an idiosyncratic, angular, left-leaning hand in Latin letters, which by no means conforms to the flowing, right-leaning diaries in traditional German Sütterlin script."[34] This is a serious objection, and as long as we have no authenticated example of Braun's writing in Sütterlin, doubts must remain. Görtemaker, however, tends towards considering the diaries authentic, arguing that, where Hitler's visits to Munich are concerned, they correspond exactly to Goebbels's diary entries and contain no internal inconsistencies.[35]

If we assume that the excerpts did indeed come from Braun's diary, what do they reveal about her relationship with Hitler? First and foremost they tell of the emotional ups and downs of a young woman uncertain about the true feelings of her much older lover. "I turned 23 today," Braun wrote on 6 February 1935. "But that does not necessarily mean I'm a happy 23. At the moment, I'm definitely not." Hitler had stayed in Berlin and had his assistant Schaub bring her a bouquet of flowers and a congratulatory telegram. Braun felt neglected, but she tried to keep up her spirits: "Do not give up hope. Soon I'll have to have learned how to be patient."[36] Just twelve days later she seems completely transformed. Hitler had "quite unexpectedly" come to Munich, and the two had spent an "enchanting evening" together. On this occasion, Hitler seems to have promised her that he would buy her a "little house" and that she would no longer have to work in Heinrich Hoffmann's photo studio. "I'm so endlessly happy that he loves me so and pray that he always does," she wrote.[37]

On 2 March, Braun also met Hitler in Prinzregentenstrasse, where she spent "a couple of wonderful hours." Subsequently her lover allowed her to amuse herself at a carnival ball in the city. But Hitler failed to keep an appointment to meet her the following day, and she waited in vain for news from him: "Maybe he wanted to meet alone with Dr. G[oebbels], who's also in the city, but he could have let me know. It was like sitting on red-hot coals at work with Hoffmann. I thought he'd arrive any minute." That evening Hitler left Munich without saying goodbye. Braun was left racking her brains about what she had done to make him treat her so thoughtlessly.[38] The inconstancy of the relationship seems to have taken a toll on Braun's nerves. "If only I'd never come into contact with him," she wrote on 11 March. "I'm desperate. He only needs me for certain purposes. Otherwise it's impossible [to understand]." A few days later, though, she herself dismissed this diary remark as "foolish."[39]

Occasionally, Braun's complaints about Hitler's unreliability were tempered by flashes of understanding. Once she wrote, "Actually it's self-evident that he has no great interest in me right now after having so much to do politically."[40] In fact, during the period covered by the diary excerpt, Hitler was preoccupied by his next foreign-policy moves. On 16 March, he announced the reintroduction of compulsory military service, and on 23 March, he held his talks with the British politicians John Simon and Anthony Eden in Berlin. He would have had scant time for his mistress in Munich. Late that month, he did invite her out for dinner at the Four Seasons Hotel in the Bavarian capital. Numerous people seem to have been in attendance, and Braun found out that in company Hitler treated her very differently—as if they hardly knew one another—than he did in the familiar confines of Prinzregentenstrasse. "I sat next to him for three hours and was hardly able to exchange a single word with him," she complained. "When we parted he gave me, as he has done once before, an envelope full of money." This businesslike gesture might be an indication of how little attention Hitler paid to his girlfriend's feelings. Braun was hurt: "It would have been nice if he'd written a goodbye or something nice. That would have made me happy."[41] Her status as a mistress, who was not allowed to appear as such in public, could not have been made any clearer.

Hitler kept his distance from Munich in April and May 1935. "Love seems to have been crossed off his programme at the moment," Braun wrote in late April.[42] She was also plagued by jealousy after Hoffmann's wife had cattily remarked that Hitler had found a "replacement" for her. "She's called Valkyrie and looks the part, including her legs," Braun wrote. "And he likes such dimensions."[43] The woman in question was Valkyrie Unity Mitford, a young British aristocrat who had come to Munich in October 1934, ostensibly to learn German, but whose main interest was meeting the dictator, whom she revered. In February 1935, she succeeded in attracting Hitler's attention in his favourite restaurant, the Osteria Bavaria. Since then, she had been part of Hitler's entourage and accompanied the dictator on trips. She was spotted at party rallies and at the Bayreuth festival. Hitler's assistants nicknamed her "Unity Mitfahrt"—Unity Along-for-the-Ride. Her closeness to the leaders of the Nazi regime was evident in the fact that Goebbels himself hosted her sister Diana's wedding to the British fascist leader, Oswald Mosley, in his house in Berlin in October 1936, with Hitler in attendance. "A matter that has to be kept top secret," noted the propaganda minister.[44] In terms of appearance, Eva Braun and Unity Mitford were very different. Braun was small, delicate and brunette. Mitford was almost six foot tall, athletic and had light blond hair and blue eyes—closer to Hitler's stated feminine ideal. But the dictator was not interested in her physical charms. He used his connection to her to gain information about the attitudes of the British upper classes and get messages passed on to Britain.[45] The two were never intimate.

Eva Braun thus had no reason for jealousy. Nor was there any truth to the rumour of an affair between Hitler and the beautiful Baroness Sigrid von Laffert, the niece of the *salonnière* and Nazi patroness Victoria von Dirksen.[46] There were other reasons why Hitler paid so little attention to his mistress in April and May 1935. Not only was he very busy; he also had health problems. He had been suffering for months from hoarseness, the result of years of straining his voice, and feared he might have throat cancer like Kaiser Friedrich III, who had died of the disease after only ninety-nine days on the throne in 1888. On 23 May, the director of the ear, nose and throat division at Berlin's Charité hospital, Professor Carl von Eicken, operated on Hitler. A polyp removed from his vocal cords proved benign. But the chancellor had to rest his voice. He did not fully recover until late June 1935.[47]

Hitler does not seem to have told Braun a thing about his illness, and she interpreted his lengthy silence as a sign that he had turned his back on her. "Is this the mad love he always assured me of, if he does not have a friendly word for me in three months?" she asked on 28 May. That day, she decided for the second time to end her life, this time by taking an overdose of sleeping pills. "I've decided on 35 pills," she wrote. "This time it's going to be 'dead certain.'"[48] But whether Braun truly meant to kill herself is even less certain than in her first suicide attempt in 1932. In the 1960s, Ilse Fucke-Michels told Nerin E. Gun of finding her sister "deeply unconscious" in their parents' apartment on the night of 28–29 May 1935 and of administering first aid. Afterwards, she called a doctor she could trust to be discreet and tore the pages from this period from Eva Braun's diary. She said she later returned them to her sister, who kept them in a safe place. But Fucke-Michels is the only witness to this incident, and even she voiced suspicions during the interview that her sister might have "staged her suicide a bit."[49]

We do not know whether Hitler, who on 27 May travelled to Munich for a few days to rest his voice,[50] ever learned of these events. One indication that he did might be the fact that in August 1935 Eva and her younger sister Gretl moved into a three-room apartment at Widenmayerstrasse 42, which Hitler had Hoffmann rent for them. It was only five minutes away from Hitler's own apartment on Prinzregentenstrasse. Apparently the dictator wanted to signal how important his relationship with his mistress was: he probably also wanted to get Braun out from under the thumb of her domineering father.[51] A short time later, Hitler had Hoffmann buy the villa at Wasserburgerstrasse 12 in the exclusive Bogenhausen district. Eva and Gretl Braun moved in there in March 1936. In September 1938, the titles for the house were transferred to Eva Braun, "private secretary in Munich."[52] With that, Hitler kept his promise to procure her a house of her own and make her financially independent, even if she was officially still in Hoffmann's employ.[53]

From the outside, the two-storey house looked fairly inconspicuous, but it was decorated with luxurious furniture, fine carpets and valuable oil paintings in keeping with Braun's status as the mistress of the most powerful man in Europe.[54] To avoid publicity, however, Hitler rarely visited Wasserburgerstrasse. As soon as he arrived in Munich, he would call his housekeeper, Anni Winter, ordering her to tell him the latest Munich gossip and get Braun on the telephone. The Führer's mistress would then get into her small Mercedes, a further status-symbol gift from Hitler, and have herself driven over to Prinzregentenstrasse.[55] When Hitler was not in Munich, she enjoyed inviting friends to her house for lively parties.[56]

On the Obersalzberg, her second home, Braun soon grew into the role of the woman of the house involuntarily vacated by Angela

Raubal. But she did not have to run the household. That responsibility fell to others: first Else Enders, who had previously worked in the Osteria Bavaria; from 1936 onwards a couple named Herbert and Anne Döhring; and during the Second World War, Willi and Gretel Mittelstrasser. On special occasions, the Chancellery building manager Arthur Kannenberg and his wife were also summoned to provide support.[57]

The privileged status Braun enjoyed at the Berghof was clearly underscored for everyone who worked there by the fact that her private quarters were next to Hitler's own and had separate access to them. Nonetheless, everything possible was done to prevent the news that the Führer had a mistress from getting beyond his inner circle. Both the service personnel and Hitler's guests had to swear to keep this fact confidential. "See nothing, hear nothing, say nothing" was the order of the day, Hitler's manservant Heinz Linge recalled.[58] Anna Mittelstrasser, a cousin of the Berghof manager who began work as a maid there in May 1941, was instructed on her first day: "Everything you now know, everything you see here and everything you hear here must stay here. You aren't allowed to say anything. Not to anybody. Never . . . Is that clear? And especially nothing about the Führer and Eva Braun."[59]

In January 1937, Reinhard Spitzy, secretary to the German ambassador to Britain, Joachim von Ribbentrop, got a big surprise while visiting the Berghof for the first time. Hitler and Ribbentrop were pacing around the Great Hall, lost in conversation, when the heavy velvet curtain in front of the living room opened, and a young woman announced that they should sit down to dine. The guests could no longer be kept waiting. "It was like being hit by lightning," Spitzy reported. "Who would dare to speak to the Führer like that? Who was this woman? Where did she come from?" After the meal, Spitzy put these questions to Wilhelm Brückner and was told: "Our Führer also has a right to a private life, and I would advise you never to tell anyone about what you have seen and heard in this regard . . . It would be best for you yourself to forget it. Otherwise . . ." The threat was unmistakable, and Spitzy "loyally joined the conspiracy of silence," as he put it in his memoirs.[60]

In addition to a gagging order on staff and guests, a series of other measures were taken to try to keep Hitler and Braun's liaison a secret.

During official receptions and visits by foreign guests, Braun would withdraw to her private quarters.[61] Albert Speer remarked that Hitler apparently considered Braun "only partially suitable for polite society."[62] But Speer misunderstood what was likely the primary motivation for Hitler—wanting to keep his private life out of the public eye in order to maintain the myth of the Führer sacrificing himself day and night for his people. That was the main reason Braun was not allowed to appear at Hitler's side at public events. She travelled to the Nuremberg rallies with Heinrich Hoffmann's party or with other members of Hitler's entourage, and she never stayed in the same hotel as Hitler.[63] There was only one published press photo showing the two of them together. It was taken during the 1936 Winter Olympics in Garmisch-Partenkirchen and shows Braun sitting two rows behind the dictator. Anyone who did not know better would never conclude from looking at the image that the two were involved in an intimate relationship.[64] And when Hitler went abroad, for instance during his state visit to Italy in May 1938, she—unlike the wives of the other high-ranking Nazi officials—travelled separately from the inner circle and never took part in official functions.[65]

Yet despite all the secrecy, there were many rumours about the Führer's alleged mistress. His assistant Nicolaus von Below, who met Braun when he visited the Berghof for the first time in November 1937, remembered that Hitler's private life had been a "topic of conversation" when he was subsequently invited to the home of War Minister von Blomberg. Hans Baur also recalled that Munich was full of gossip about Hitler being involved in "hanky-panky" with Braun.[66] In the autumn of 1937, a Czech newspaper published a photo of Braun taken in Berchtesgaden with the caption "Hitler's paramour." A friend of the Braun family had bought the paper while on a business trip to Vienna and showed it to Eva's father Friedrich, who accused his daughter of immoral behaviour.[67] But the German public took no notice of this publication. Only a small circle of people knew about Eva Braun's true status. Most Germans remained unaware that Hitler had a mistress until the end of the Second World War.[68]

The character of Hitler's relationship with Braun remained opaque even within his most intimate circles. Officially she was part of the Berghof staff, working as his "private secretary," and when others were present, Hitler tended to treat her with "awkwardly maintained distance," strictly avoiding any displays of intimacy or tenderness.[69] Like everyone else at the Berghof, Braun addressed Hitler as "my Führer," while he referred to her towards others as "Fräulein Braun" or Fräulein Eva," only occasionally calling her his "Tschapperl," an Austrian word meaning "small, cutely naive child." Initially, the two used the formal form of address "Sie" when others were around, although they gradually adopted the informal "du" in front of other Berghof regulars.[70] "If you were not in the know," Below observed, "it was almost impossible to tell that Braun and Hitler had a special relationship with one another."[71]

It is no wonder that after 1945 speculations were rampant about Hitler and Braun's sex life. Even people who claimed to have known Hitler well disagreed radically. Contemporary eyewitnesses can hardly be trusted on this issue, however, and historians are well advised to view their statements with extreme scepticism. Albert Speer, for instance, contradicted himself on a number of occasions. At his first interrogation at Kransberg Castle in the summer of 1945, he testified that Braun was Hitler's true love and that the Führer had always been faithful to her. "She meant a great deal to him," Speer said, "and he spoke of her with enormous respect and inner admiration."[72] But in Spandau prison in March 1949, Speer already voiced doubts as to whether Hitler was "even capable of honest feelings of friendship, gratitude and loyalty" towards Braun.[73] In his memoirs, published in 1969, three years after his release from prison where he'd written much of them, Speer's doubts had become certainties. Speer depicted Hitler as an emotionally raw, ruthless despot who had, in Braun's presence, made statements like: "Very intelligent people should make sure they get a primitive, stupid woman."[74] In conversation with Joachim Fest, who assisted him with publishing his memoirs, Speer offered a very simple explanation for Hitler's relationship with Braun: Hitler had "kept" her "exclusively for certain biological needs . . . so to speak for the regulation of his hormones."[75] But Speer gave no indication of why he was so certain.

If there was anyone close to Hitler who knew about sexual relations between him and Eva Braun, it would have been the Berghof staff: the couples who managed the place, the servants and the maids. But when they were questioned after the war, their answers were contradictory. House manager Herbert Döhring testified that neither he nor his wife had "gone out of their way to inspect the bed sheets," but that they would have seen indications, had there been intimate contact between Hitler and Braun. The relationship was not even a "true friendship," Döhring asserted, but rather an "amiable acquaintance."[76] Heinz Linge, by contrast, had no doubts that Hitler loved Braun and that the two had been intimate. He even maintained that he had once seen them in a "deep embrace."[77] Gretel Mittelstrasser, the wife of Döhring's successor, also assumed that Hitler and his girlfriend slept together. She even told her niece Anna, the maid, that she had procured medications so that Braun could delay her period when the Führer came to the Berghof.[78]

There is a fair amount of evidence to suggest that, behind his façade of inhuman inapproachability, Hitler maintained a normal romantic relationship with Braun. But there is no saying for sure, and biographers should beware of titillating readers with through-the-keyhole fantasies. "The duty of the chronicler must halt before and respect the most personal spheres of a human being," as Otto Dietrich once remarked.[79]

There is one definitive indication that Braun occupied an important position in Hitler's private life and was more than mere "decoration" or a "shield to ward off other female advances."[80] On 2 May 1938, seemingly concerned that something could happen to him on his imminent trip to Italy, Hitler personally wrote out his will and testament. It began by specifying that "Fräulein Eva Braun of Munich" was in case of his death to receive "1,000 marks a month, or 12,000 annually, for the rest of her life." His half-sister Angela Raubal and his sister Paula, who were to receive the same amount, were mentioned second and third.[81]

Who was admitted to the Berghof society and who was not? The most important criterion for inclusion was not party rank, but Hitler's personal likes and dislikes, and this depended, among other things, on how well a given individual got on with Eva Braun and accepted her role at the mountain manor. At the Berghof, Hitler wanted to surround himself with people—men and women in equal numbers— in whose presence he felt at ease and in whose company he could relax. In contrast to the Chancellery in Berlin, the Berghof circle on the Obersalzberg was far more familial, which was down primarily to the greater presence of the female element.[82]

That explains why Göring, although he too owned a house in the vicinity, was not part of the Berghof circle. He appeared at official events, but Hitler had no private contact with him. The same was true of Himmler: Hitler valued him as the unscrupulous organiser of a Reich-wide apparatus of terror and repression, but in private he also made fun of the Reichsführer-SS's cultish worship of everything Germanic.[83] The situation was no different with Ribbentrop, whom Hitler made Reich foreign minister in 1938 but whom he consciously kept at a distance from the Berghof. By contrast, Ribbentrop's liaison to Hitler, Walter Hewel, was invited to the Berghof because Hitler liked him personally.[84]

Hess only appeared at the Berghof in his official function. He had lost the exclusive position he enjoyed prior to 1933 as Hitler's private secretary when he became deputy to the Führer. His place was taken by Bormann, who had earned the dictator's favour with his tireless work on the construction on the Obersalzberg and his discreet handling of all the financial issues connected with it. He further ingratiated himself with Hitler by paying special attention to Braun, a point upon which, as Otto Dietrich noted, Hitler was "extraordinarily sensitive."[85] Bormann was Hitler's constant shadow at the Berghof, while his wife Gerda, who was the daughter of the "uppermost party judge" Walter Buch and whom he kept regularly pregnant, was only allowed to visit as a guest by her power-hungry husband.[86] Goebbels's situation was rather in-between. He and Magda were frequently invited to the Obersalzberg for private visits, but unlike in Berlin, here they were not part of Hitler's standard entourage. Most of their visits only lasted a few days, and during that time they were housed a short distance from the Berghof in the Bechsteins' villa, which had been used since 1935 as a guest house for Nazi elites.[87]

Albert and Margarete Speer, on the other hand, were regular, priv-ileged guests. The architect had gone to the Obersalzberg with Hitler as early as 1933, and after introducing Hitler to his wife, who appar-ently found the dictator's favour, the couple was accepted into the Berghof circle.[88] It was Hitler's express wish that the Speers buy a house on the Obersalzberg, and on special occasions, such as the Führer's birthday, their children, dressed in their Sunday best, were allowed to come along and present Hitler with bouquets of flowers. Hitler did his best with the children and tried to engage with them in "friendly, paternal fashion," Speer recalled, but he never found the "right wholehearted manner" and soon turned his back on them "after a few words of praise."[89]

The Speers were especially solicitous of Eva Braun. They took her skiing, which Hitler greeted with a furrowed brow as he feared that there would be an accident. Hitler hated snow anyway. "The cold, lifeless element was deeply foreign to his nature," wrote Speer. "The mere sight of snow made him act irritated."[90] In his memoirs, Speer claimed to have befriended Braun, the "unhappy woman . . . who doted on Hitler," because he felt sorry for her. But Heike Görtemaker has rightly questioned this idea. Like Bormann, Speer realised early on what an important role Braun played in Hitler's life, and he knew that he could deepen his connection with the Führer if he maintained friendly relations with her.[91]

Karl and Anni Brandt were close friends of the Speers. It was the wife in this case who had brought her husband into the Berghof circle. Competing under her maiden name, Anni Rehborn, she had been one of the most famous female swimmers of the 1920s, winning several German championships in the 100-metre freestyle and the 100-metre backstroke and setting numerous records. Hitler, whom she first met in 1927 or 1928, immediately liked her. In the early 1930s, she introduced him to her fiancé, then an assistant physician in the Bergmannsheil Clinic in the mining city of Bochum. Both joined the NSDAP, and in June 1933, Hitler invited them to the Obersalzberg.[92] When, on 15 August 1933, Wilhelm Brückner got in a car accident near the village of Reit im Winkel, Karl Brandt happened to be travelling in the car directly behind him. The young surgeon administered first aid, drove Brückner, who had a serious head injury, to the hospital in nearby Traunstein and operated on him himself.[93] Hitler was impressed and offered the physician the chance to become a member of his personal staff, accompanying him on trips so that he could receive immediate medical attention should he be the victim of an accident or assassination attempt. That new status automatically made the Brandts members of the Berghof circle. Karl and Anni Brandt's wedding in Berlin in March 1934 was attended by Hoffmann, Brückner, Hitler, Goebbels and Göring. In July 1934, Hitler invited the couple for the first time to the Bayreuth festival.[94]

On the Obersalzberg, the Brandts rented a suite in the Bechsteins' villa so as to be permanently contactable by Hitler. They shared the

Speers' enthusiasm for sports, and that also gave them something in common with Braun, whom they included in their joint activities. Brandt and Speer were uncannily similar. Both were young men— around thirty—who personally owed their meteoric careers to Hitler. Both were good-looking with engaging personalities, entirely unlike the coarse "old fighters." Both were very competent in their areas of expertise, extremely ambitious and willing to follow Hitler without scruple. It was no accident that with the start of the Second World War Hitler charged Brandt with carrying out his forced euthanasia programme.

Brandt was not the only physician in Hitler's entourage. In the spring of 1936, Hanskarl von Hasselbach, an NSDAP member since 1932, was hired as Hitler's second travelling doctor. He was a university friend of Brandt and transferred with him in November 1933 from Bochum to the university clinic in Berlin. He remained a member of Hitler's entourage, even if his relationship with the Führer was more remote than his colleague's.[95]

Another doctor appeared over the course of 1936. Fifty-year-old Theodor Morell ran a practice, frequented above all by screen and stage stars, near the Memorial Church on Berlin's Kurfürstendamm. His patients included Hoffmann, who recommended him to Hitler. During the tense months after the remilitarisation of the Rhineland, Hitler suffered from stomach complaints and eczema on his legs. Among other things, Morell prescribed Mutaflor capsules to restore Hitler's intestinal bacteria, and the treatment was a success. A former ship's doctor, Morell seems to have known how to exploit Hitler's hypochondria to ingratiate himself. In any case, Hitler swore by Morell's abilities, remarking privately: "He saved my life! Wonderful, how he helped me!"[96] As of 1937, Morell and his wife, the actress Johanna "Hanni" Moller, were an integral part of the Berghof society. The couple were also clever enough to court Braun's favour, and she smoothed their way.[97] Towards Hitler, Morell acted like a selfless assistant whose only wish "was to keep Germany's greatest man free of physical complaints for a long time."[98] In reality, he not only craved attention but had an excellent head for business. He exploited his privileged status of "the Führer's personal physician" for material gain, for instance in the form of lucrative shares in pharmaceutical companies.

Otherwise, the corpulent new arrival did not have many friends within the Berghof circle. Karl Brandt in particular was none too pleased about the appearance of a rival, whom he considered a loud-mouth and a quack.[99] But as long as Morell enjoyed Hitler's favour, he could feel secure. As a gesture of his appreciation in December 1938, Hitler appointed him a professor, and he told members of his entourage to consult his personal physician at the first sign of any complaint. Braun was also a patient of Morell, even though, if we believe Speer's memoirs, she once complained after an examination how "disgustingly dirty" he was.[100] Morell's body odour was no secret to Hitler either, but he answered jibes on that score from his entourage by saying that Morell was not there "to be smelled" but to keep him healthy.[101]

The only one of Hitler's old pals from Munich to become a regular at the Berghof was Heinrich Hoffmann. He usually visited with his second wife, Erna Gröbke, the daughter of a classical singer from the northern German city of Schwerin, whom he had married in April 1934. Hoffmann was a welcome guest not only as the man who visually documented the Third Reich and as a kind of court prankster. He also advised Hitler on art and purchased paintings for him. In June 1937, Hitler charged him with selecting the pictures to appear in the Great German Art Exhibition in Munich's House of German Art, after sacking the twelve-head-strong panel of judges whose work had displeased him. Assisted by Gerdy Troost and House of German Art Director Karl Kolb, he also curated exhibitions in the years that followed as the Führer's personal agent. Hitler appointed him a professor in July 1938.[102]

Hoffmann particularly enjoyed playing jokes on Morell and exposing him wherever possible to ridicule. For Hitler's personal physician, the photographer was "the evil spirit of the company at table."[103] Hitler had a soft spot for Hoffmann and ignored the fact that his old ally was a bit too fond of alcohol. The dictator's enormous faith in him was reflected in the fact that he asked Hoffmann to handle the finances for renting the apartment for Eva Braun and later purchasing her house. Hoffmann set up a small darkroom at the Berghof for her, and the Führer's mistress turned into a passionate amateur photographer and maker of home movies. Armed with a 16-millimetre Agfa-Movex camera, Braun made numerous films that, together with photos taken by cameraman Walter Frentz, provide an intimate look at everyday Berghof life. Occasionally Hoffmann bought photographs from his former employee, paying—no doubt on instructions from Hitler—relatively large sums of money for them.[104]

As a kind of compensation for not being allowed to appear at official functions, Hitler permitted Braun to invite guests of her own to the Obersalzberg, and rooms were set aside for that purpose. Among them were her constant companion and sister Gretl, who had begun working for Hoffmann as a clerk in 1932, her oldest and best friend, Herta Scheider (née Ostermeier), and Marianne (Marion) Schönmann (née Petzl), whose mother, the opera singer Maria Petzl, Hitler had heard perform during his days in Vienna. "With her lively manners and witty charm, she was typically Viennese," wrote Karl Brandt of Marion Schönmann in his essay "The Women around Hitler" in August 1945, and that explains the attention the dictator paid to this friend of Braun in particular. Hitler and Braun were among the small number of guests when Schönmann married a Munich construction magnate in August 1937.[105]

Also visible on the wedding photo was Sofie Stork, who remained part of the Berghof society even after breaking off her engagement to Brückner in 1936. She and Braun had become friends soon after she visited Haus Wachenfeld for the first time, and Stork made the intertitles for Braun's colour films. The ever-lively "Störklein" (Little Stork) or "Charly," as she was nicknamed, was a fixture at the Berghof New Year's Eve parties. She was very close to Hitler's assistant Fritz Wiedemann, and Hitler, too, appreciated the gifted artisan, bailing her out with considerable sums of money when her father's fishing tackle shop on Munich's Residenzstrasse got into financial difficulties.[106]

The regulars were complemented by occasional visitors. Hoffmann sometimes brought along the "old fighter" and Hitler's long-term friend Hermann Esser, who served as Bavarian economics minister from 1933 to 1935 and became president of the Reich Committee for Tourism in 1936. His wife was also friends with Braun. Speer was sometimes accompanied by his friend, the sculptor Arno Breker, and his wife Minima, a Greek woman with a sharp tongue with whom Hitler enjoyed joking. Also visiting every once in a while were NSDAP Reich Treasurer Franz Xaver Schwarz and his wife, and Daimler-Benz Director Jakob Werlin, who had known Hitler since the 1920s.[107]

Finally, to complete the picture, several members of Hitler's staff were also members of the Berghof circle. They included Reich Press Spokesman Otto Dietrich, the commander of Hitler's SS bodyguards, Sepp Dietrich, and Hitler's personal assistants Wilhelm Brückner and Julius Schaub. His secretaries Johanna Wolf, Christa Schroeder and Gerda Daranowski also took part in the Berghof social life, but there was a fine dividing line between them and the actual guests.[108] Among the military aides, 29-year-old Colonel Nicolaus von Below enjoyed Hitler's particular affection. He and his attractive 19-year-old wife Maria were popular guests and were close to the Speers and the Brandts.[109]

In retrospect, Speer described the "never-changing daily routine" on the Obersalzberg and among the "never-changing circle around Hitler" as "tiresome" and "boring." After a few days, Speer claimed, he felt "exhausted," and his only memories were of a "strange emptiness."[110] The question is why Speer so doggedly tried to stay in Hitler's presence if he found being at the Berghof such a waste of time. "How can you forget how excited we all were?" Maria von Below chastened Speer after reading the Obersalzberg chapter in his memoirs. "And how many moments there were when we were happy?"[111] Margarete Speer too told Gitta Sereny that she had found life in Hitler's circle fascinating. Hitler was "always very gallant to women, very Austrian," Frau Speer said.[112] Her husband's memoirs did not square with her own memories, and she angrily told him: "Life has not left me much! And now you've ruined what remained."[113] It is likely that after 1945 the women felt under less pressure to justify themselves and reinterpret their experience in the Berghof society.

As in the Chancellery, daily life at the Berghof followed a set pattern. In the morning, an almost ghostly silence lay upon the Alpine residence. With Hitler still sleeping, his guests tiptoed their way to breakfast. They were not allowed to take a bath since the pipes ran past the walls of his bedroom, and the dictator might have been disturbed by the sound of the running water. The only audible activity was in the utility rooms and the annexe, where Hitler's assistants stayed.[114]

Hitler usually got up late, and before the start of the Second World War he dressed in civilian clothing. After a quick breakfast, meetings were held between 11 a.m. and 2 p.m. in the Great Hall. During that time, guests would socialise on the terrace.[115] In Spandau prison, Speer looked back:

We would stand around casually on the terrace, while the ladies lay on the plaited wicker deck chairs with the cushions patterned in dark red squares. Like at a spa hotel, they sunned themselves. Braun was a modern woman. Servants in uniform, SS men chosen from Sepp Dietrich's bodyguards, offered drinks in practised, almost conspiratorial fashion: champagne, vermouth and soda, and fruit juices. At some point, Hitler's manservant would come and announce that the Führer would appear in ten minutes after repairing upstairs for a short while to recover from a long discussion. Lunch was by that point usually more than an hour overdue ... At the news of Hitler's imminent arrival, conversation hushed and no one laughed any more. Eva Braun would take her film camera from her deck chair and, accompanied by Negus, a Scotch terrier named after the emperor of Abyssinia, prepare to film Hitler's appearance.[116]

As soon as Hitler arrived, the atmosphere changed drastically. The guests suddenly tensed up and tried visibly to make a good impression. To protect his face from the sun, Hitler usually wore a velour hat, and his overall appearance had "something civilian, even sedate."[117] He kissed the hands of the ladies, including his secretaries, and shook hands with his other guests, asking everyone how they felt. After around half an hour, the servant announced that lunch was served, and Hitler would take the arm of one of the ladies whom he had selected to sit next to them. Eva Braun followed him. As of 1938, she was led to the table by Bormann, which underscored both her status as the lady of the house and Bormann's newly acquired influence in Hitler's court. The rest of the guests, men and women mixed, filed in behind them.[118]

The seating order was predetermined. Hitler took his place in the middle of the rectangular table across from the row of windows, with the lady of his choice to his right, Braun to his left and Bormann next to her. Seated across from Hitler was the guest of honour or, in the absence of one, another of the ladies. Hitler placed great emphasis on flower arrangements. The china was by Rosenthal, and the cutlery bore Hitler's monogram. Meals were served by SS men in white waistcoats and black trousers.[119] Speer's mother, who was invited to the Berghof a number of times in 1939, scoffed: "How nouveau riche it all is. Even how the meals are served is impossible, and the table decorations are coarse. Hitler was terribly nice, but it's a world for parvenus."[120] The food served was as simple as in the Chancellery. Even during official state visits, there was never more than a starter, a main course and dessert, although the guests did get to enjoy the fresh vegetables delivered every day from Bormann's greenhouse.

Unlike lunches in the Chancellery, the conversation tended to avoid politics. Hitler was an attentive listener to his female guests. "He was very warm, very personal," recalled Maria von Below. "With me, or Margarete Speer or Anni Brandt, he would ask about the children, be quite interested, I thought, in little stories about them, respond with laughter or understanding nods."[121] He enjoyed playing the Viennese charmer, showering the women with compliments and telling them about practical jokes he had played in school or amusing incidents from the "years of struggle." He also lectured about the health benefits of vegetarianism and his favourite dishes, such as the bread dumplings with sorrel sauce his mother had made for him. Rarely could he suppress his tendency to make fun of underlings who were not present, imitating their gestures and speech. Occasionally he would tease people at the table, putting them in a difficult position since they did not dare respond in kind. In the early years, Braun took little part in the conversation. Later, when she was more self-confident and comfortable in her role, she sometimes interrupted her lover's monologues and drew his attention to how late it was getting.[122]

Lunch usually lasted one hour. After Hitler rose from the table and kissed the ladies' hands in farewell, there were further meetings. Following that, hosts and guests took a ritual walk to the tearoom down on the Mooslahnerkopf. It was the only time that the Führer took in some fresh air.[123] Even at a casual pace, it took a mere twenty minutes to get there. Hitler would don a gigantic peaked cap, put on his badly fitting khaki windbreaker, take his walking stick and leash and lead the group, with his German shepherd at his side. He would summon one of the guests to walk beside him, which was considered a special honour, for a private chat about political matters. The entourage, including his assistants and secretaries, walked behind them in single file. Security men brought up the rear. Once at the tearoom, Hitler would pause on the viewing plateau, always using the same words to praise the view, which stretched all the way down to Salzburg.

The tearoom was a round stone building and consisted, aside from the kitchen and staff rooms, of a single, large room with comfortable armchairs, grouped around a round table: six large windows gave out in all directions. Hitler took his place in an armchair in front of the fireplace, with Braun to his left. Servants poured coffee and offered various cakes. Hitler preferred tea or hot chocolate and enjoyed freshly baked apple cake.[124] Conversation was usually laboured. Hoffmann would try to amuse the company by telling jokes, at Hitler's prompting. Occasionally Hitler himself would nod off in the middle of one of his monologues. Everyone else present would act as if they did not notice and continue to converse in hushed tones. At around 6 p.m., the group would set off back to the Berghof. Hitler usually had himself driven in an open-top Volkswagen convertible: everyone else went on foot. Hitler would then retreat to his private quarters before dinner, while his guests used their free time to attend to personal matters.[125]

The evening meal, which customarily began at 8:30 p.m., followed the same procedure as lunch, but the ladies appeared in formal wear and tastefully made-up. Hitler, who hated make-up,[126] would occasionally make a critical remark about the "war paint," but Braun did not let herself be deterred. The fashion-conscious young woman from Munich changed her clothes several times a day and made an impression with her evening elegance. After dinner, Hitler held further conferences in the Great Hall. From one minute to the next, his demeanour would change. His posture would stiffen, and the charismatic Führer would take the place of the congenial master of the house. His guests amused themselves playing ninepins in the basement or waited around the green-tiled stove in the living room for Hitler's monologue to come to an end. Braun, who shared Hitler's passion for cinema, always knew which new films had been sent down to the Berghof by the Propaganda Ministry and would choose one or two for the evening. If nothing new was available, she could always have recourse to the Berghof's film library, which contained thirty classic movies and eighteen Mickey Mouse cartoons Goebbels gave Hitler for Christmas in 1937. As was the case in the Chancellery, the staff and bodyguards were allowed to attend the screenings. The two Gobelin tapestries were rolled up, Hitler and Braun would take their places in the front row, and everyone else would sit down behind them. Only after the outbreak of the Second World War did Hitler depart from this ritual, saying that it was impossible for him to watch films at a time "when the German people were making so many sacrifices."[127]

"Shall we sit by the fireplace for a bit?" Hitler would ask when the screenings were over. Not infrequently, what was conceived as a short chat turned into a meeting that lasted well beyond midnight, with Hitler himself monopolising the conversation. Sometimes, however, Hitler fell into a brooding silence, fiddling around in the coals with his poker. The guests almost gave a sigh of relief when someone suggested music. Hitler had a large collection of records in a chest in the front part of the Great Hall, and Bormann would operate the phonograph. The repertoire was nearly always the same: works by Wagner, particularly the "Liebestod" from *Tristan and Isolde*, which Hitler said he wanted to be played in his "final hour," the symphonies of Bruckner and Beethoven, Franz Léhar operettas and songs by Richard Strauss and Hugo Wolf. Many an hour passed in this way, and Otto Dietrich could not remember Hitler ever asking if any of his guests felt tired and wished to retire for the night. "Listening to him and keeping him company until he thought he could fall asleep was the tribute he adamantly demanded of his guests," Dietrich recalled.[128] At some point, Hitler and Braun would whisper a few words to one another, she would withdraw to her private quarters on the first floor, and he would follow a short time later. No sooner had the two of them disappeared, than the atmosphere became more relaxed. For a little while things became lively, until everyone went to bed, and stillness descended upon the Berghof until the following morning.

Parties were rare. Hitler usually spent Christmas alone in Munich. On Christmas Eve in 1937, much to the surprise of his manservant Karl Krause, he ordered a taxi and had himself chauffeured aimlessly around the city for three hours.[129] On Boxing Day he usually travelled to the Obersalzberg, where he customarily spent the New Year season and "did not want to be disturbed."[130] But the manor was always a hive of activity on New Year's Eve. "The house is full beyond capacity," Gretl Braun wrote from the Berghof on 31 December 1938 to Fritz Wiedemann, who—much to her regret and that of Sofie Stork—could not be present. "More than thirty people are here, and I wonder how things will turn out. The hairdressers are under siege by the women, and the gentlemen are looking forward to their tuxedos."[131] After dinner there were fireworks ordered by Hitler and prepared by Kannenberg. Following that the dictator decamped to the Great Hall to receive New Year's congratulations from his guests and the staff. It was one of the few occasions when he relaxed his self-imposed prohibition on alcohol. With a sour expression on his face, he sipped at his champagne glass and toasted the New Year with his entourage. He took part in the traditional German custom of melting lead and auguring the future from the abstract figures that resulted. He begrudgingly posed for the obligatory group photo and autographed his guests' place cards. "Usually it was quite a lot of fun, but only after Hitler had left," Hoffmann recalled. "He almost always withdrew shortly after midnight."[132] Eva Braun was usually very reserved whenever Hitler was at the Berghof, but her behaviour changed immediately as soon as he left. "You could still see his limousine making its way down the serpentine roads, when the first preparations for amusements were made," recalled one of the bodyguards. "Although she had been as strict as a governess only moments before, she suddenly turned everything on its head. She became cheerful, cheerful and relaxed, almost childish."[133]

After the war, almost all of the members of the Berghof circle swore that politics had played no role whatsoever on the Obersalzberg and that no one ever talked about it. In August 1945, Karl Brandt wrote that Hitler "had wanted to be a private citizen there and maintain his private, personal relationships and inclinations."[134] Otto Dietrich, on the other hand, contradicted that claim, arguing that Hitler was incapable of distinguishing between public and private life: "He carried out business in the middle of his private life, and he lived out his private life in the middle of his business and the exercise of his leadership."[135] Dietrich correctly highlighted one of Hitler's fundamental qualities. Life on the Obersalzberg was characterised by the mingling of the two spheres, something expressed in the fact that there was no division between public and private areas at the Berghof.

Hitler's Alpine residence was not just a place of rest and relaxation or a private refuge from the stage of major politics. It was there that he withdrew to collect himself and plan his next steps when faced with crucial decisions. "When I go to the mountains, it's not just because of the beauty of the landscape," he explained in January 1942. "My imagination is much livelier there. I'm removed from all the trivia and am able to see: this or that is better, this or that is right, this or that will lead to success."[136] Not only did Hitler's decisions ripen at the Berghof; his mountain manor was also where he wrote his speeches for the Nuremberg rallies every year in late August and early September and where he received his most important foreign visitors, such as former British Prime Minister David Lloyd George in early September 1936. "They [the Germans] should thank God they have such a great leader," Lloyd George is alleged to have said after his three-hour meeting with Hitler.[137] The Duke and Duchess of Windsor were likewise impressed after visiting the German dictator at the Berghof in late October 1937, and Hitler was apparently flattered that the former British monarch had paid him his respects. He had "rarely seen the Führer so relaxed and animated as during that visit," Fritz Wiedemann later recalled.[138] But the Obersalzberg was also the site of dramatic political confrontations in advance of Hitler's foreign-policy coups. It was there that Austrian Chancellor Kurt von Schuschnigg was subjected to extortionate pressure on 12 February 1938, a few weeks before the amalgamation of Austria into the Third Reich, and it was there that Hitler invited British Prime Minister Neville Chamberlain for a first visit on 15 September 1938, at the height of the Sudentenland crisis. The idea, as Below put it, was to "receive him in an environment that played to the English love of country life."[139]

The Berghof was therefore both Hitler's personal retreat and a second power centre alongside the Chancellery in the Third Reich. This double function was the reason that in early 1936 Hitler ordered the construction of a field office of the Chancellery north-west of Berchtesgaden, only six kilometres away from the Obersalzberg. The topping-out ceremony took place in January 1937. Once it was completed the business of government ran smoothly. Thanks to modern communications and the governmental airport in Reichenhall-Berchtesgaden, Hitler was fully connected with the outside world and reachable at any time in his seemingly remote Alpine retreat. Nonetheless, even Hans Heinrich Lammers, the head of the Chancellery, could be refused permission to speak to Hitler for days at a time when the Führer was at the Berghof.[140]

Precisely because the personal and the political were intermingled, the impression that the Berghof circle was apolitical cannot be accurate. In mid-July 1937, for instance, Goebbels noted that those visiting the Obersalzberg had "passionately discussed" Britain's role in the world over lunch.[141] It is also known that Marion Schönmann, Eva Braun's friend, was a frank woman who openly criticised many of the political measures taken after the *Anschluss* in Austria.[142] The image of Braun as the apolitical, naive mistress of the Führer has also been revealed as a deliberate distortion by Speer and other members of the Berghof society in order to claim ignorance after the war about the criminal nature of Hitler's dictatorship.[143] Braun was by no means the dumb blonde observers long mistook her for. She was a modern young woman who knew quite well what she was getting into with Hitler and who herself helped bolster the mythic aura of the Führer with the photos she gave to Hoffmann and her home movies, which she made for posterity. Like the others who were part of the Berghof circle, she shared Hitler's racist political beliefs and knew all too well about the exclusion and persecution of the Jews. The fact that few, if any, words were wasted on anti-Semitism does not mean that the Berghof society objected to it in any way. The same is true of the regime's campaign against the Churches, which was initiated by none other than Hitler himself.

19

Hitler and the Churches

"The war will run its course, and then I will see it as my life's work to sort out the problem with the Churches," Hitler said over lunch at his main headquarters in mid-December 1941, by which point it was clear that Germany would not achieve a Blitzkrieg victory against the Soviet Union. "Only then will the German nation be safe. I do not care in the slightest about articles of faith, but I'm not having clerics sticking their noses in worldly affairs. This organised lie has to be broken in such a way that the state becomes the absolute master." He added: "When I was young, my view was: use dynamite! Today I see that you can't rush things. It has to rot away like a gangrenous limb. We need to get to the point where only idiots stand behind the pulpit and only old women sit in front of it, and the healthy youths are with us."[1]

These statements were anything but exceptional. On the contrary, they expressed Hitler's deep-seated enmity towards Christianity. The Christian Churches were the only institutions in the "Führer state" that escaped National Socialism's claims on total ideological power. Hitler wanted to subjugate the Churches to his will, reducing them to a shadow of themselves, but he postponed the attack until after the war had been successfully concluded. "In the long term, National Socialism and the Churches won't be able to coexist," he proclaimed in another of his monologues.[2]

At the same time, however, Hitler realised that he could not achieve this goal by using brute force. A certain tactical flexibility was needed, since the Christian Churches remained influential in German society. "It makes no sense to artificially create further difficulties," he admitted. "The cleverer we act, the better."[3] The dictator wanted to avoid an all-out war on the Christian faith and Christian culture at all costs. He remembered all too well Bismarck's failed "cultural struggle"—the

Kulturkampf—against the Catholic Church, and he thought that the time was wrong, at least in 1941, to engage in a battle against the Churches. "The best thing is to let Christianity gradually fade out," he said in October of that year. "A long phase-out has something conciliatory. The dogma of Christianity will collapse in the face of science."[4]

The same ambivalence had characterised Hitler's behaviour prior to 1933. On the one hand, he staged National Socialism as a secular religion, presenting himself as a messianic leader sent by the Almighty to deliver the German people from all evil. His own sanctification went hand in hand with the stylisation of his followers into "disciples," who unconditionally submitted to the Führer and who were willing, if necessary, to lay down their lives for him. Hitler constantly invoked the idea that faith could move mountains, and he rarely missed an opportunity to inject Christian phrases and notions, in pseudo-liturgical fashion, into his speeches.[5] Particularly in his Christmas addresses, he liked to cite Jesus as a model for himself and his followers. Just as the Christian saviour, whip in hand, had driven the usurers from the temple, Hitler promised, he would expel "international Jewish finance capital" from Germany.[6]

On the other hand, however, Hitler saw his movement as religiously neutral and equally far removed from both of the main Christian faiths. Article 24 of the party programme stipulated: "The party as such represents the standpoint of positive Christianity without declaring its allegiance to any particular confession."[7] Political parties had nothing to do with religious problems, Hitler had written in *Mein Kampf*, while conversely religions should not meddle in "political party nonsense." He added: "The mission of the movement is not that of a religious reformation, but rather the political reorganisation of our people." Hitler was enough of a realist to see that he could never come to power without support from Christian voters. Extending a hand to them in *Mein Kampf*, he described the "two religious confessions as equally valuable pillars for the continued existence of our people."[8]

For that reason, when the party was reconstituted in 1925, Hitler vehemently resisted all attempts to pursue religious quarrels. Attacks on Christian communities and institutions were expressly prohibited. In 1928, the Gauleiter of Thuringia, Arthur Dinter, who violated this prohibition by promoting the formation of a new ethnic-popular religion, was fired from his post and kicked out of the NSDAP.[9] In 1930, Alfred Rosenberg was forced to publicly identify his book *The Myth of the Twentieth Century*—a synthesis of neopagan beliefs circulating among the Far Right—as "a personal confession" that had nothing to do with the party.[10] Even as late as 1942 in his military headquarters, Hitler distanced himself from Rosenberg's work, which he claimed to have only read "bits of."[11]

After coming to power as chancellor, Hitler initially posed as a Christian statesman who wanted nothing more than to cooperate with Germany's two main Churches in carrying out the country's "national rebirth." "At no point during his rule did Hitler invoke God as often and passionately as during the first eight weeks," the historian Klaus Scholder has correctly asserted. "Never again did he give himself over to Christian figures of speech or appropriate Christian sites and attributes as greatly as in this period."[12] In his very first official declaration on 1 February 1933, he promised that Christianity "as the basis of our entire morality" would enjoy the "committed protection" of his nationalist government.[13] In his speech on the Enabling Act on 23 March, he took a further step towards the Churches. The new government, Hitler assured them, "considered the two Christian confessions as factors of paramount importance for preserving our identity as a people" and would leave their traditional rights untouched.[14] This declaration was directed primarily at the Catholic Centre Party, whose support he needed to get the necessary two-thirds majority for the Enabling Act in the Reichstag.

Prior to 1933, German Catholics had been relatively resistant to Hitler's lures. Beginning in September 1930, Catholic bishops had constantly warned against the teachings of National Socialism in their pastoral letters, and even as late as August 1932, with Hitler on the threshold of power, the German Bishops' Conference in Fulda reiterated their rejection of Nazi ideology and declared that Catholics were "not allowed" to be members of the NSDAP.[15] The Reichstag election of 5 March 1933 confirmed the solidity of political Catholicism, as the Centre Party and its Bavarian sister party, the BVP, only suffered small losses. Hitler considered prising apart Catholic resistance one of the most urgent tasks of the early phase of his rule.[16] He achieved an initial success on 28 March, when the Catholic bishops responded to his seemingly conciliatory attitude with an equally conciliatory declaration. "Without revoking our earlier rejection of certain religious and ethical errors," it read, "the episcopate believes it can conclude that the general prohibitions and warnings are no longer needed." This was followed by an appeal to "loyalty towards legitimate authority and a conscientious fulfilment of civic duty."[17] With that, the ban on Catholics being National Socialists was lifted. Among pious Catholics too, enthusiasm for Hitler and his "national uprising" grew. "The cassock-wearers are very small and crawl before us," Goebbels boasted.[18]

Hitler, who grew up in a Catholic environment and never officially left the Catholic Church, maintained a lifelong respect for the power of the institution and its thousands of years of tradition. He coveted an agreement with the Vatican along the lines of the Lateran Accords Mussolini had concluded in 1929. Such an agreement was a way of reaching a modus vivendi with Catholic clergymen, and it was also a method of undermining political Catholicism. The traditional constituencies of the Centre Party and the BVP, Hitler told his cabinet on 7 March 1933, could only be conquered "when the Curia abandons the two parties."[19] It only took a few months for the negotiations that Franz von Papen, at Hitler's request, began conducting on 10 April with Cardinal State Secretary Eugenio Pacelli, the former papal nuncio in Germany, to yield concrete results. A treaty between the National Socialist government and the Holy See was drawn up on 8 July, the signing ceremony took place on 20 July, and the concordat took effect on 10 September.[20] It prohibited Catholic clergymen from engaging in any kind of political activity, which essentially meant that the Catholic Church was abandoning the Centre Party and the BVP. The two parties subsequently decided to dissolve. In return, the Nazi regime agreed to guarantee Catholics' freedom to practise their religion, to protect Catholic lay organisations and to allow Catholic schools and religious instruction.

The conclusion of Nazi Germany's first international treaty gave the regime legitimacy and represented a personal triumph for Hitler. The fact that agreement with the Curia had been reached so much more quickly than even he himself had thought possible on 30 January, Hitler told his cabinet on 14 July 1933, was "such an indescribable success that all critical objections must be withdrawn in the face of it." Hitler also saw the agreement as "creating a chance and a sphere of trust that will be particularly significant in the more important fight against international Jewry."[21] Letters of gratitude from Catholic clergymen poured into the Chancellery. Munich's Cardinal Michael Faulhaber, for instance, was fulsome in his praise of Hitler. "What the old parliaments and parties failed to achieve in sixty years, your statesman's foresight has turned into reality, to the benefit of world history, in six months," the cardinal wrote on 24 July. "For Germany's reputation in East and West and before the entire world, this handshake with the Pope, the greatest moral authority in world history, is a gigantic achievement and an immeasurable blessing." Nonetheless, Faulhaber did not neglect to insist "that the articles of the concordat must go beyond just words on paper" and that subordinated religious authorities not be relegated "too much in the shadow of the statesmanlike greatness of the Führer."[22]

The bishops were to be sorely disappointed on precisely this score. The concordat had barely been signed when violations of its spirit and letter started occurring. In many places in Germany, party functionaries and police began targeting Catholic associations. There were bans and attempts to intimidate the Catholic press. Catholic civil servants were fired, and Catholic youth organisations were disbanded and their assets confiscated. Complaints and protests were slow to materialise. Neither Cardinal Pacelli nor the German episcopate wanted to endanger the agreement reached with the Nazi regime.[23] Nonetheless, Cardinal Faulhaber did voice disappointment in his sermons between the first Advent weekend and New Year's Eve. He rejected the Nazis' contempt for the Old Testament and distanced himself from their racist beliefs. "We should never forget that we were not saved by German blood," he preached. "We were saved thanks to the precious blood of our crucified Lord."[24] Such sentiments did not go unnoticed among the Nazi leadership. "The preachers are trying to stir people up against us!" Goebbels noted in late December 1933. "Beware!"[25]

Catholic dignitaries were put on high alert in late January 1934, when Hitler charged Rosenberg with "monitoring all aspects of ideological training and education by the party and Nazified associations." The author of *The Myth of the Twentieth Century* was considered the embodiment of all the NSDAP's anti-clerical tendencies. In February, the Vatican blacklisted that book, and in the pastoral letters of Easter 1934 the faithful were urged to fight against the "new paganism."[26] Yet the debate about Rosenberg's anti-Christian theses had an unwelcome side effect for the Catholic clergy. Interest in the book rose, and it became the second-biggest bestseller in the Third Reich after *Mein Kampf*. "Rosenberg's 'Myth' is doing brisk business," complained

Goebbels, who deeply hated the editor in chief of the *Völkischer Beobachter*. "The Churches are creating propaganda for it."[27]

Among the casualties of the Night of the Long Knives on 30 June 1934 were two prominent Catholics: Erich Klausener, the director of Catholic Action, one of the most important Catholic lay organisations, and Fritz Gerlich, the publisher of the Catholic weekly *Der gerade Weg* (The Straight and Narrow). In July 1932, the latter had subjected Hitler's movement to a scathing analysis in an article under the headline "National Socialism is a Plague." Gerlich had written:

> National Socialism . . . means hostility towards our foreign neighbours, a reign of terror domestically, civil war and wars between peoples. National Socialism means lies, hatred, fratricide and boundless misery. Adolf Hitler is preaching the legitimacy of lying. It is time for those of you who have fallen for the swindle of this power-mad individual to wake up![28]

Hitler's thugs took brutal revenge for these courageous words, and the Catholic bishops held their tongues. In fact, along with Protestant leaders and a large section of the public, they were relieved that Hitler had seemingly reined in the radicals in the SA.[29]

Hitler's dealings with the Protestant Church seem to have been relatively easy right from the start. Prior to 1933, the NSDAP had been most popular and celebrated their biggest electoral triumphs in the Protestant sections of Germany. The receptivity of nationalist Protestants to Hitler's ethnic-popular agenda was particularly evident in the "Faith Movement of German Christians." In June 1932, this organisation publicly demanded that the structure of the Church "be adapted to the natural conditions ordained by God and . . . still recognisable today . . . in ethnic identity and race." The German Christians added: "On the basis of this insight, we call for a battle to create a truly German Church. Only genuine German Christians belong to its community. Every German by blood belongs to it . . . but baptised Jews do not." In the spirit of "positive Christianity," the German Christians proclaimed their belief in "an affirmative, racially appropriate faith in Christ that accords with the German spirit of Luther and his heroic piety."[30] In Church elections in Prussia in November 1932, these "brown Christians," who occasionally referred to themselves as "Jesus Christ's SA," won a third of all seats.

In some regions of East Prussia and Pomerania they took almost 50 per cent of the vote.[31]

Thus it comes as no great surprise that the vast majority of Protestant leaders welcomed the political caesura of early 1933. In his Easter missive, the senior diocesan administrator in Prussia proclaimed himself in agreement with all his Protestant brethren in his "joy at the uprising of the most profound strengths of our nation to patriotic awareness, true ethnic community and religious renewal."[32] Few within the Protestant camp refused to be blinded in this fashion. One of them was the historian Friedrich Thimme, who in a letter from mid-February 1933 demonstrated rare prescience about the true nature of Hitler and his henchmen: "To my mind, everyone who believes in their grand promises and indeed their Christian beliefs is a fool. You should recognise them by the fruit of their deeds, and those fruits are murder, manslaughter, violence of every sort and ruthless careerism." In the same breath, Thimme branded the attitude of the Protestant Church "towards this organised hatred, murder and forced expulsion" as "simply shameful."[33] "How can God's blessing be upon a movement that is a slap in the face to the simplest and clearest tenets of Christianity?" he asked in May 1933. "The Church has an absolute duty to repeatedly raise a voice of caution and warning about all the injustice coming down from above."[34] And in November 1934, Thimme wrote to the British historian George Peabody Gooch: "I cannot approve in any way of raising the purported Aryan race to the status of an idol and driving Jews, among whom I have many highly intelligent friends, from all positions of authority, making life in Germany almost impossible for them."[35] But Thimme's voice was an exception to the rule among Protestants. Typical was the general superintendent of Kurmark, Otto Dibelius, who wrote in a church newsletter about the anti-Jewish boycott of 1 April 1933 that the Reich government "had admitted that in the stormy first days of the great transformation there has also been transgression. Things like this can and will happen in such times."[36]

Hitler wanted to amalgamate the twenty-eight regional Protestant Churches into a single Reich Church that could serve as a counterweight to the Catholic Church. For this aim, he could count on the support of the German Christians. On 25 April 1933, he appointed the sycophantic Königsberg military chaplain Ludwig Müller as his "representative on matters concerning the Protestant Church" and charged him with finishing plans for the Reich Church as soon as possible.[37] On 11 July, the new Church constitution was signed by the chosen representatives of the regional Protestant Churches, and on 14 July, it was approved by Hitler's cabinet. It proclaimed the amalgamation of all regional Churches into a "unified German Protestant Church" headed by a Reich bishop to be named by a national synod. New elections for the Church bodies were scheduled for 23 July.[38]

The German Christians enjoyed massive help from the regime in the run-up to this election. On the eve of the vote, in an address from Bayreuth broadcast on all German radio stations, Hitler came out in clear support of the religious movement. Under these circumstances it is hardly astonishing that the Protestant Church elections were a huge triumph for the German Christians, who ended up winning around 70 per cent of the vote.[39] Müller's election as Reich bishop at the first national synod in Luther's home city of Wittenberg on 27 September was a mere formality: he had achieved all his goals. As his post-war biographer has noted: "As Prussian state bishop and German Reich bishop, he was undoubtedly the most important figure in the Church hierarchy of German Protestantism."[40]

But before the synod could meet, resistance began to form. The impetus was provided by the Berlin pastor Martin Niemöller, a former U-boat commander and Freikorps paramilitary, who initially had high hopes for Hitler and the new regime but quickly grew disenchanted. On 21 September 1933, he sent a letter to pastors throughout Germany, calling on them to join together to form a "Pastors' Emergency League." The basic principles articulated in the letter included the duty to "perform one's pastoral duties solely according to the Holy Scripture and the creeds of the Reformation as the correct interpretation of Scripture." It also clearly rejected the "application of the Aryan paragraphs within the Church of Jesus Christ." By the end of the year, 6,000 pastors had pledged their support. For that reason, the historian James Bentley has rightly argued that Niemöller laid the cornerstone for Church opposition to Hitler.[41] The Pastors' Emergency League gained valuable momentum after a mass event held by the German Christians in Berlin's Sportpalast on 13 November turned into a "fiasco beyond compare."[42] To the frenetic applause of an audience of 20,000, the evening's main speaker, Berlin Gau church administrator Reinhold Krause, demanded nothing less than "the completion of Martin Luther's ethnic-popular mission with a second German reformation." This "new ethnic Church" would create space for the entire breadth of 'racially appropriate spiritual life." The first step was the "liberation of Church services and confessional matter from everything un-Germanic," including the Old Testament with its "Jewish profit morality" and its "stories of livestock traders and pimps." Having picked up a head of steam, Krause went on to insist that the New Testament be cleansed of "all obviously distorted and superstitious anecdotes" and that the faithful reject "the whole scapegoat and inferiority theology of the rabbi Paul."[43] Such ideas barely differed from Rosenberg's notion of a racial religion, and there was immediate resistance not only from the circles associated with the Emergency League but from moderate German Christians as well. Reich Bishop Müller was forced to remove Krause from his Church office and suspend the implementation of the Aryan paragraph.[44]

Hitler was extremely irritated at the conflicts following the Sportpalast event, interpreting Müller's response as a sign of weakness. At a reception on 29 November, the Führer informed Müller that he did not intend to intervene in the Church quarrel: the Reich bishop would have to solve his difficulties on his own.[45] It was the first step towards Hitler distancing himself from his former protégé, whom he saw as increasingly ill-suited for achieving the ultimate aim of a unified Protestant Church strictly loyal to the regime. Hitler left no doubt as to where his true sympathies lay at lunch in the Chancellery in early December 1933, where according to Goebbels he "really laid into" the Churches. He said he "now saw through the pasty-faced preachers and Reich Bishop Müller. The most upstanding of the lot is Krause, who at least does not conceal his disgust at the Jewish swindle that is the Old Testament."[46]

Müller used draconian methods to defend himself against his critics. In early January 1934, he proclaimed an "Ordinance Concerning the Restoration of Orderly Relations in the German Protestant Church," which prohibited any mention of conflicts and announcements on political matters pertaining to the Church during religious services. This gagging order was the least-effective means imaginable of silencing dissenting clergymen. Instead, it provoked further passionate protest. The Reich bishop, his detractors claimed, was threatening to bring down violence upon everyone "who for the sake of their conscience and their congregations was unable to keep silent about what the Church is going through at present."[47]

Contrary to his previously stated intention to stay out of the internal conflict within the Protestant Church, Hitler now declared himself willing to mediate between the German Christians and their opponents. He received both sides in the Chancellery on the afternoon of 25 January 1934, but the meeting was anything but what the leaders of the Church opposition, which included the bishops Theophil Wurm, August Marahrens and Hans Meiser, had anticipated. Right from the start and to everyone's surprise, Hitler turned the floor over to Göring, who read out the transcript of a telephone call made by Martin Niemöller that morning, which had been listened in on by the Gestapo. During the call, the Berlin clergyman had made a number of disparaging remarks about a conversation between Hitler and Hindenburg ahead of the meeting of Church leaders. Instead of protesting against such police-state surveillance, the dissenting bishops were utterly cowed. Years later, in his monologues in his military headquarters, Hitler still recalled with glee how the delegates of the Protestant Church had been so terrified by the reading out of the transcript that they "shrunk in terror" until they were barely visible.[48]

Niemöller kept his cool, however. He confirmed that these had been his words but sought to explain to Hitler that the Pastors' Emergency League's struggle was directed not against the Third Reich but rather for its welfare. Visibly irritated, the dictator shot back: "Leave concerns about the Third Reich to me, and focus your concerns on the Church." In the end, the Church leaders had to swear to Hitler that they would work together with Bishop Müller in the future. In a declaration at the end of the meeting, they reaffirmed their "unconditional loyalty to the Third Reich and its Führer" and their severest condemnation of "all critical machinations directed against the state, the people and the movement."[49] Müller's position was shored up in the short term, while the Church leaders' self-abasing declaration weakened the Emergency League. But Hitler never forgot that Niemöller alone dared stand up to him, and the pastor became the object of hateful persecution by the Führer and his henchmen. In a discussion with Himmler and Goebbels in late April, Hitler ordered them to take up battle against the Pastors' Emergency League. "It's going to be a witch-hunt," Goebbels noted. "Poor pastoral scum. We'll behave like Christians."[50]

But even a repressive crackdown could not restore calm within the Protestant Church. Müller's attempt to employ dictatorial means to

Nazify the regional Churches called forth resistance and attracted sympathy to the intra-Church opposition.[51] In late May 1934, 139 delegates met for the first "Confessional Synod of the German Protestant Church" in Wuppertal-Barmen. They agreed on a declaration, largely composed by the theologian Karl Barth, whose famous first thesis staked out the greatest imaginable distance from the German Christians: "We reject the false teaching that the Church can and must acknowledge, beyond the word of God, other events and powers, figures and truths as God's revelation." The Barmen Declaration of 31 May, as the historian Klaus Scholder has remarked, was without doubt the most significant event in what became known as the "Church Struggle": "Thanks to its plain language, its biblical reasoning and its unambiguous character as a confession of faith, it did not just reach theologians and pastors, but had a profound effect within congregations. It remained the *cantus firmus* of the Confessional Church even when its voice was almost drowned out."[52] The first Confessing Synod was followed by a second one in Niemöller's home district of Berlin-Dahlem in October 1934. It appointed a governing council to direct the activities of the Confessing Church and called upon "Christian congregations, pastors and Church councils" throughout Germany "to refuse to take any further instructions from the leadership of the Reich Church or any of its organs."[53]

By the autumn of 1934 it was obvious that Müller had not succeeded in ending the disagreements. In late October, Hitler surprisingly refused to meet him and forgave the southern German bishops Wurm and Meiser, who had been disciplined by the Reich bishop, summoning them to Berlin together with Marahrens, the bishop of Hanover. In a two-hour conversation on 30 October, he told them that he no longer had any interest in Church affairs—an unmistakable signal that Müller had fallen from grace.[54] But the three bishops were disappointed by the fact that Hitler did not, as they had expected, make it explicit that the Reich bishop's time was up. Even though Hitler disparaged Müller privately, saying that "he was neither a tactician nor a man of principles and was soft inside and hard externally, rather than vice versa,"[55] the dictator was not prepared to abandon him entirely. For his part, despite his obvious loss of influence, Müller refused to resign. Henceforth his popular nickname "Reibi" (for Reich bishop) became "Bleibi"—he who insists on staying.[56]

★

The Nazi regime's battle against the Churches caused great unease among Protestants and Catholics alike, but for most religious people it did not result in silent inner rejection of the regime—let alone open political opposition. On the contrary, all the evidence suggests that people blamed the regime's anti-clerical policies and harassment on ideological agitators like Alfred Rosenberg. Hitler's personal popularity remained unaffected. Here, too, he was a master of disguise, presenting himself as a person and a politician who maintained firm religious beliefs and was committed to defending the values of Christianity against fanatics within his own party. The willingness of the leaders of both confessions to declare their loyalty to and their respect for the Führer also served to divert the dissatisfaction of religious segments of the populace away from the man at the top and onto local party radicals.[57]

After the attempt to Nazify the Churches and get them to submit to the authority of the regime had failed, the Nazi leadership searched for a new strategy. In July 1935, Hitler put former Prussian Minister of Justice Hanns Kerrl in charge of Church affairs, which had previously been handled by the Ministries of the Interior and Culture. As the director of the newly established Reich Church Ministry, Kerrl had carte blanche to issue decrees affecting religion. He set up a Reich Church committee as well as local committees to act as go-betweens between Church and state and to mediate conflicts within the Protestant Church. It was necessary, Kerrl told the Nazi Gauleiter and Reich governors in early August 1935, "to identify those forces within the Christian Churches which affirmed the state and were permeated by National Socialism, and to preserve them in Church life."[58]

Hitler's goal in changing his policy towards the Churches was twofold. On the one hand, he wanted to remove them as much as possible from public life. On the other, he wished to de-escalate the conflicts or at least to avoid an open confrontation, which would have further depressed the worsening popular mood in the summer and autumn of 1935. "He's monitoring the decline in mood very carefully," noted Goebbels on 14 August. "He wants to make peace with the Churches. At least for the time being."[59] Nonetheless, in a pastoral letter read from pulpits only a few days later, Catholic bishops reaffirmed their Church's claim to have a public role and sharply condemned the regime's repressive policies. In a memorandum to Hitler, they may have stressed their "affirmative attitude towards the state." But they also expressed their "deep concerns in the face of the increasingly vocal attacks upon Christianity and the Church."[60]

Hitler was enraged and, together with Goebbels, pondered how to respond. "The Führer considers the question of Catholicism as very serious," Goebbels wrote in early September 1935. "Should he allow it to come to a head right now? I hope not. Later would be better. First we need some foreign-policy successes."[61] In his opening address of the Nuremberg rally on 11 September, Hitler proclaimed that he had "no intention of tolerating the continued or renewed politicisation of the confessions through the back door." He promised that he would lead a determined battle "to keep our public life free of those priests who took up the wrong jobs, since they should have become politicians and not ministers."[62]

In a series of trials in 1935 and 1936, the regime tightened the screws. Catholic priests and members of monastic orders were accused of sexually abusing children and youths and of violating the state's strict rules concerning foreign currency. The resulting trials before the regional court in Koblenz, which had been prepared with the intensive help of the state police, went on until late July 1936, when Hitler ordered them to be suspended.[63] The reason for his change of heart was the outbreak of the Spanish Civil War, which opened up the possibility of the regime and the Catholic Church burying the hatchet and forming a "unified anti-Bolshevist front." Nonetheless, although German bishops took a clear anti-Bolshevik stance in their pastoral letter of 19 August 1936, they also continued to insist that the "throttling" of Church life in Germany, in violation of the concordat, would have to stop before any agreement could be reached.[64]

In conversation with Goebbels in late October 1936, Hitler confirmed his intention to reach at least a temporary truce with Catholicism so that he could take on Bolshevism. "He intends to speak to Faulhaber," noted Goebbels.[65] On 4 November, the dictator received the cardinal on the Obersalzberg. Over the course of their three-hour talk, Hitler laid out the nightmare scenario of Bolshevism threatening all of Europe and called upon the Catholic Church to support him in his battle, telling Faulhaber: "Either nationalism and religion will triumph together, or they will both be destroyed." Hitler promised to "let bygones be bygones" and "get rid of all the minor issues that disrupted our peaceful cooperation." It was his "deepest wish," he said, to reach agreement with the Church. And once again Hitler's combination of the carrot and the stick had its desired effect. "The Führer has command over diplomatic and social formalities like a born sovereign," Faulhaber wrote in a confidential report about the meeting. "Without doubt the Reich chancellor lives a life of faith. He recognises Christianity as the architect of Western culture."[66]

For his part, Hitler told Goebbels that he had "really lit a fire" under the cardinal. Faulhaber, he said, had been "quite puny, babbling about dogma or something." Hitler had presented him with a clear choice: "War or reconciliation. There is nothing else. The Church has to come out in support of us, without reservations."[67] But Germany's Catholic bishops were not about to subjugate themselves unconditionally. In their pastoral letter at Christmas 1936, they declared themselves willing to support the regime in its "historic fight to defend us against Bolshevism," but repeated their demand that the rights given to them by the concordat be respected. Hitler vented his irritation at the bishops' intransigence during a long conversation about religion over lunch on the Obersalzberg in early January 1937. "Once again, the Catholic bishops have attacked us in a pastoral letter," he complained. "If the gods want to punish someone, they first blind him." Hitler also made it unmistakably clear that his public declarations concerning the value of the Christian Churches were mere lip service. "The Führer thinks Christianity is ripe for demise," Goebbels noted. "It may take a long time, but it will come."[68]

Hitler's anti-Catholicism was only reinforced on 30 January 1937 when, as we have seen, the strictly Catholic Postal and Transport Minister Paul von Eltz-Rübenach refused to accept the Golden Party Badge or be inducted into the NSDAP, with the explanation that the Nazis were "repressing the Church." Hitler and Goebbels were outraged. "That's the Catholics for you," the propaganda minister fumed. "They take orders from somewhere higher than the fatherland—the only, truly saving Church."[69] In the days that followed, Hitler also raved against the Churches: "They have learned nothing and will never learn. The most terrible institution imaginable. Without mercy and justice. You cannot make any compromises with them. If you do you are lost."[70] After Faulhaber delivered another critical sermon in Munich, Goebbels demanded: "We have to read these preachers the Riot Act. They have to be made to bend under the power of the state. Before that happens, there'll be no peace."[71]

Conferring with a small circle about the issue in late February 1937, Hitler delivered a fundamental philippic against Christianity and the Churches. Goebbels summed up the Führer's views:

> The Führer explained Christianity and Christ. Christ, too, was against global Jewish dominance. The Jews crucified him for that. But Paul falsified his teachings and in so doing undermined Ancient Rome. The Jew in Christianity. Marx used socialism to do the same to the German idea of community. But that does not mean that we should not be socialists.[72]

The idea of Jesus as Aryan and Paul as a Jewish agent who falsified Christ's teaching and diverted Christianity down a disastrous path was by no means original. It was an amalgamation of notions long current among ethnic-chauvinist circles. Hitler seems to have adopted them less from Alfred Rosenberg's *The Myth of the Twentieth Century* than from Houston Stewart Chamberlain's *The Foundations of the Nineteenth Century*.[73]

But Hitler's relationship towards such ideas was purely opportunistic. "We do not want to battle against Christianity—on the contrary, we have to declare ourselves to be the only true Christians," Goebbels recorded him saying. "This means that we have to throw the entire weight of the party at the saboteurs. Christianity is the slogan under which we will eradicate the preachers, just as socialism was the one under which we destroyed the Marxist bigwigs."[74] Although Hitler allowed his followers to worship him in cultish fashion, and although he enjoyed playing the high priest at the Nuremberg rallies, he consistently refused to portray himself as the founder of a religion. In a speech to the Gauleiter on 12 March 1937, he spoke out against the notion of "forming new religions," stating that National Socialism was "still too young." This was a clear rejection of Rosenberg's ideas. Moreover, he still wanted to avoid an open break with the Catholic Church. "In the battle against the Churches he quotes Schlieffen: 'victories with great dimensions or small victories,'" Goebbels noted. "And with good reason he does not want any ordinary victories. You can kill an adversary with silence or with blows. Onwards!"[75]

The next shock in this unresolved situation was the papal encyclical "With Burning Anxiety." Faulhaber had written the first draft, which was then edited by Cardinal Pacelli and approved by Pope Pius XI. Clandestine couriers brought the document to Germany, where it was printed and read out from pulpits on Palm Sunday, 21 March 1937. The encyclical excoriated the "open and concealed violence" against the Church in Germany. The articles of the concordat were being violated, the document complained, and the pressure being applied to the faithful was "both illegal and inhuman." The encyclical once again highlighted the incompatibility between the Christian faith and National Socialist teachings: "Whoever removes race or a people or a form of government, those who exercise power or any other basic foundations of human society . . . from the secular scale of values, and makes them the highest norm of religious values too, worshipping them in idolatrous fashion, is wrong and is falsifying the divinely ordained order of things."[76]

The evening before the encyclical was read out, Reinhard Heydrich informed Goebbels about its existence. "It's a provocation in the true sense of the word," the propaganda minister noted, although he advised the head of the Gestapo to "play dead" and ignore it rather than react harshly. "Economic pressure instead of arrests," Goebbels wrote. "Confiscation and prohibition of the Church newsletters that publish this bit of impudence. Otherwise keep your nerve and wait until the hour comes to shake off these provocateurs."[77] But ignoring the encyclical was not good enough for Hitler. In early April 1937, he phoned Goebbels from the Obersalzberg. "He wants to move against the Vatican," Goebbels noted. "The preachers do not realise how patient and mild we've been. Now they're going to become acquainted with our strictness, severity and determination."[78] On 6 April, Hitler ordered Justice Minister Gürtner to restart and prioritise the sexual abuse trials, which had been suspended the previous July.[79] They were accompanied by a frenzied anti-Catholic press campaign directed by Goebbels. "Heavy artillery is being deployed," he noted in late April. "One wink from me, and a diabolical concert has commenced. The preachers will be squirming now."[80]

Once again, Hitler was satisfied with his propaganda minister's work, and the latter registered with pleasure: "The Führer is becoming more and more radical on the Church issue . . . [He knows] no mercy any more . . . We're going to smoke out this band of pederasts."[81] In his annual 1 May speech, Hitler also took aim squarely: "If they try to usurp rights that exclusively belong to the state with letters, encyclicals and the like, we will force them back into the spiritual and ministerial activity that is rightfully theirs." In a reference to the pederasty trials, Hitler declared: "It is not appropriate for these quarters to criticise the morality of a state when they have more than reason enough to be concerned about their own morality."[82]

The low point of the defamation campaign was a speech by Goebbels in Berlin's Deutschlandhalle arena on 28 May. He had discussed the content of the speech for days with Hitler—indeed, the Führer even dictated several key passages himself, which was unprecedented. "Very cutting and drastic," Goebbels confided to his diary. "I would not have gone that far."[83] The speech was broadcast on all of Germany's radio stations, and German newspapers received the transcript an hour before Goebbels began speaking, along with instructions to print it "as prominently as possible."[84] Goebbels pulled out all the demagogic stops, referring to a "general decline in morals such as had hardly been known throughout civilised history to such a horrible and outrageous extent." "Animalistic sexual degeneracy was widespread among the Catholic clergy," Goebbels raged, and the entire brotherhood was covering up this "filth." Everywhere "sex offenders in priestly robes" were pursuing their "repulsive urges." This "sexual pestilence," Goebbels concluded, "must be removed by the roots."[85] After the speech, which drew standing ovations from more than 20,000 party members, Goebbels hurried back to the Führer in the Chancellery. "He shook my hand," Goebbels related. "He listened to the entire speech on the radio and told me that he couldn't sit still for a moment."[86]

In the days that followed this mass event, Hitler continued to vent his hatred to his entourage. "The Führer is raging against the preachers," Goebbels noted.[87] The propaganda minister constantly fanned the flames while the Gestapo took care to suppress any contrary opinions in the Catholic press and strictly monitored the sermons of Catholic clergymen. "In Germany, the pious Catholic is subject to emergency law," complained the bishop of Berlin, Konrad von Preysing. "He is forced to endure mockery and scorn, constraint and pressure without being able to defend himself, while the enemies of the Church enjoy freedom of speech, the freedom to attack and the freedom to scoff."[88]

But the trials ended in disappointment for the regime. In many cases, judges acquitted the defendants or only handed down light sentences. "The courts are failing to do their job," an outraged Goebbels complained in early July 1937. "They're only giving these preachers laughably tiny fines or a few days in jail for the worst sorts of crimes against the state. We need to take this to a special court."[89] Goebbels was able to convince Hitler of this too.[90] Nonetheless, in late July, the dictator told his justice minister to suspend the trials again, and although Goebbels repeatedly lobbied for their resumption, Hitler stuck by this decision. He may have assured Goebbels in December 1937 that he was only waiting for the right moment to "reopen the spigot with the preacher trials," but as the propaganda minister noted, "right now he wants peace and quiet on the Church issue."[91] Most likely, the change of course was related to the regime's transition, which we will examine below, from a policy of overturning the Treaty of Versailles to one of aggressive foreign expansion. In this phase, in which Hitler decided to realise his foreign-policy ambitions, it would not have seemed advisable to further ratchet up tension with the Vatican or the Catholic clergy in Germany.[92]

Furthermore, Hitler had likely realised that he would not be able to subjugate the Churches to his rule in the short term. He was going to have to be patient. He described his plans for the future to a small circle after a cabinet meeting on 11 May 1937:

> We will have to bend the Churches to our will and make them serve us. The vow of celibacy must be eradicated. Church assets must be confiscated, and no one should be allowed to study theology before the age of twenty-four. With that, we will rob them of their next generation. The monastic orders will have to be dissolved. In this way, and only in this way, will we be able to break them down. It will take decades. But then we will have them eating out of our hands.[93]

Hitler also refused to let things come to a complete head with the Protestant opposition. In late 1936, it gradually became clear that Hanns Kerrl's experimental attempts to make peace between the German Christians and the Confessing Church had failed. In January 1937, Hitler gave him a dressing-down over lunch in the Chancellery, taking "a hard line against the Churches." The "primacy of the state" had to be enforced "by all means," Hitler declared, dismissing Kerrl's policies as "too soft."[94] On 12 February, the Reich Church committee, the central body for restoring the unity of the Protestant Church, resigned en masse. Without consulting his ministerial colleagues, Kerrl therefore announced a decree that would have subjected the Church to increased state monitoring. Hitler was enraged by his underling going it alone, and refused to allow the decree to be made public. He also ordered Kerrl, Frick, Hess, Himmler, Goebbels and Deputy Interior Minister Wilhelm Stuckart to the Obersalzberg on 15 February to discuss the Church issue. "The Führer wants a clear line," Goebbels noted. "Kerrl made a huge mistake not consulting us."[95]

Goebbels travelled to the meeting by night train with Himmler and Stuckart, which gave them plenty of time to agree upon a mutual position. All three concurred that strict state regulation of the sort Kerrl envisioned would only create "martyrs." They also emphasised a fundamental long-term difference: "Kerrl wants to preserve the Church while we want to liquidate it."[96] The conference on the Obersalzberg lasted seven full hours, which indicated the significance Hitler attached to it. He sharply criticised Kerrl's ideas, saying that they amounted to making him a "summus episcopus" and that they could only be enforced violently. In view of the expected "great global struggle," Germany "did not need a battle over the Churches." After a long debate, Goebbels made a suggestion he had discussed previously with Himmler and Stuckart: "Either a separation of Church and state—for which in my opinion it is too early—or fresh elections of a constitutional synod, complete withdrawal of the party and state in this matter, entirely free proportional representation, and lucrative salaries for the synod delegates. In a year, they will come begging the state to save them from themselves." Hitler adopted the suggestion, according to Goebbels, "eagerly." The details were discussed, and the plan was approved by everyone present, including Kerrl. "A historic day," Goebbels crowed. "A turning point in the Church quarrel."[97]

Hitler's decree was announced in the evening papers, where it created a stir. It read: "After the Reich Church committee failed to produce an agreement between the groups within the German Protestant Church, the Church shall now autonomously and completely freely give itself a new constitution and, with it, a new order." The Reich Church minister was empowered "to prepare the election of a general synod for this purpose and take all necessary accompanying steps."[98] The following day, Goebbels called a press conference on the topic of "the Führer's step towards making peace on the Church issue."[99]

But any progress was mere propaganda. It soon became clear that the Church elections were only going to cause further unease instead of encouraging agreement between the opposing Protestant factions. Parts of the Confessing Church even threatened to boycott the elections, and in late 1937 preparations for them were halted. It was one of the rare occasions when a decree by Hitler simply came and went with no results.[100] For a time, the dictator considered forcibly separating Church and state, an idea supported by Kerrl, who, as Goebbels put in, had undergone a "remarkable about-turn."[101] But this plan, too, was abandoned. In December 1937, Hitler expressed his concern that "Protestantism would be completely destroyed, and we would have no counterweight any more to the Vatican."[102] Fundamental decisions on the Church issue were postponed amid intensifying preparations to go to war, and Kerrl was explicitly "prohibited from instituting any reforms."[103] Nonetheless this latest volte-face did not end the persecution of prominent representatives of the Confessing Church.

On 1 July 1937, on Hitler's orders, Martin Niemöller was arrested. Again and again he had condemned the Nazis' totalitarian world view in his sermons and read out lists of names of affected pastors.[104] "Pastor Niemöller finally arrested," noted Goebbels. "Small mention of this in the press. The thing now is to break him so that he can't believe his eyes or ears. We must never let up."[105] The propaganda minister and the Führer were in total agreement on this point. In December 1937, while the two were travelling together to attend Erich Ludendorff's funeral in Munich, Hitler confirmed: "[Niemöller] will not be released until he has been broken. Opposition to the state will not be tolerated."[106]

But Niemöller's trial, which began on 7 February 1938 and was closed to the public, ended as a defeat for the regime. Niemöller and his defence emphasised his nationalist past. The defendant described not only his sacrifices as a submarine commander in the First World War, but also his activities as a Freikorps member after 1918 and his early sympathies for the post-war German nationalist movement. A series of respected character witnesses testified on his behalf, assuring the court of the pastor's patriotic beliefs. In the end, Niemöller was sentenced to seven months in prison and fined 2,000 marks. But since he had already spent eight months in investigative custody in solitary confinement in a Berlin prison, he was considered to have served his sentence.[107]

Goebbels, who followed all phases of the trial with growing anger, was livid at the verdict, which was a de facto acquittal. He raged: "That takes the cake. I'm only going to give the press a brief announcement. The Führer will order Himmler to have this guy immediately taken to Oranienburg." While foreign journalists waited outside the courtroom for Niemöller to appear, Gestapo agents hurried him out a side entrance and took him to the Sachsenhausen concentration camp near the town of Oranienburg. "There he'll only be able to serve God by working and looking deep within himself," Goebbels noted.[108] The day after the verdict, Hitler expounded about "the case of Niemöller" over lunch in the Chancellery: "He's in the right place in a concentration camp. It will be quite some time before he gets out. That's how it is now for all enemies of the state. Anyone who thinks kindly old Hitler is a weakling will get acquainted with the hard-nosed Hitler."[109] And indeed Niemöller remained incarcerated, first in Sachsenhausen and as of 1941 in Dachau, as Hitler's "personal prisoner" until the demise of the Third Reich.

Aside from the spectacular trial of Niemöller, however, the ceasefire that Hitler ordered on the Church front in late 1937 held throughout 1938 and the first half of 1939. While he was redirecting his foreign policy towards a war of expansion, Hitler had no use for a major conflict with Germany's two main Churches. "The boss knows all too well that the Church issue is very touchy and could have very negative effects domestically in case of war," Hitler's secretary Christa Schroeder wrote in a letter to a friend.[110] The Nazis' final reckoning with the Churches was thus put off until after the war. The regime behaved quite differently concerning the "Jewish question." On that issue, 1938 was the decisive milestone on a path towards removing Jews entirely from Germany. In early December, when Hanns Kerrl made a renewed attempt to subjugate the Protestant Church to state control, Hitler— as Goebbels noted—ordered him to "back off." The propaganda minister added: "First things first, and now's the time for us to solve the Jewish question."[111]

20

Prelude to Genocide

"The final goal of our overall policy is clear to all of us," Hitler explained to NSDAP regional directors at the Nazi educational camp Ordensburg Vogelsang on 29 April 1937 about how he intended to proceed against Jews.

> With me the main thing is never to take a step that I may have to withdraw or that will damage us. You know, I always go to the extreme of what I feel I can risk but no further. You have to have a nose for what you can and cannot do. In a struggle against an enemy as well.[1]

The recording of this secret speech was interrupted at this point by cheers and applause. Hitler continued:

> I do not intend to immediately challenge my enemy to a physical fight. I do not say "Fight!" because I believe in fighting for fighting's sake. I say "I want to destroy you. And now, I'll ask my wits to help me to manoeuvre you into such a corner that you cannot lash out at me because you would suffer a fatal blow to the heart." That's how it is done.[2]

Hitler had raised his voice to maximum volume so that the words "That's how it is done" positively exploded from his lips in what Saul Friedländer called an "orgiastic spasm." It earned him frenetic applause from his audience.

Nonetheless, even when he seemed to be losing rhetorical self-control, Hitler knew exactly what he was saying. In fact, he was precisely describing his method for achieving all of his ends after he became chancellor. Just as he had always gone to the limit of what he could get away with in foreign policy, he gradually, step by step, worked his way towards radical measures of persecution in his anti-Jewish policies. In the spring of 1935, he gave the signal to start tightening the thumbscrews, whereas in the Olympic year of 1936, he ordered them relaxed somewhat. Even if his paladins fell over one another trying to "work towards the Führer" by suggesting their own initiatives to achieve his anti-Jewish aims,[3] it was ultimately Hitler who made the final decisions and upon whom everything depended. He always made sure that he pulled the strings and determined when action would be taken. Yet despite showing tactical flexibility, he never lost sight of his "final goal"—the eradication of European Jews. In the beginning, however, "eradication" meant displacement and not mass murder. In later November 1937, after a long discussion with Hitler about the "Jewish question," Goebbels noted: "Jews must leave Germany and all of Europe. That will take a while, but it will and must happen. The Führer is utterly decided on that."[4]

In the first half of 1937, Nazi domestic policy focused on the Churches. In the second half of that year, Hitler's concluding speech at the Nuremberg rally on 13 September introduced a new, radicalised phase of the persecution of the Jews. As he had the previous year, Hitler invoked the spectre of the "global peril" of "Jewish Bolshevism." But in 1937, he combined his attacks with enraged rants against the "Jewish race," which he tar-brushed as "inferior through and through." Because this race was incapable of any sort of cultural or creative productivity, Hitler claimed, it had to pursue the "imminent extinction of the heretofore upper intellectual classes of other peoples" in order to establish a domination spanning the globe. "In the current Soviet Russia of the proletariat," Hitler claimed, "more than 80 per cent of leading positions were occupied by Jews." The fact that in his show trials of 1936 and 1937, Stalin also had Jewish Communists like Karl Radek killed, something which, a puzzled Goebbels noted in his diary,[5] did not seem to have disturbed Hitler. He merely repeated, using nearly identical turns of phrase, what he had said in his speech "Why are we anti-Semites?" from 1920—a revealing example of the continuing of his paranoid hatred. It was no accident that he repeatedly referred to the German revolution of 1918 and 1919 as a purported Jewish grab for power: "Who were the leaders of our Bavarian Soviet republic? Who were the leaders of Spartacus? Who were the true money men and leaders of our Communist Party? . . . They were Jews and Jews only!"[6]

Hitler's diatribe had the desired effect. In the free city of Danzig, where the Nazis, led by Gauleiter Albert Forster, had succeeded in bringing all institutions into line politically, there was major anti-Semitic violence in late October 1937.[7] At the same time, a new wave of anti-Jewish boycotts began in many parts of the Third Reich. They were aimed at forcing Jews to stop doing business and thus increasing the pressure on them to emigrate. "The campaign of economic destruction against Jews in Germany is being pursued with extreme severity," the Breslau teacher Willy Cohn wrote on 26 October. "The pressure to sell businesses is growing from day to day."[8] The removal of Hjalmar Schacht as economics minister in late November got rid of a further obstacle to economically plundering Jews.[9] In an article in late January 1938, the German correspondent of the Swiss *Neue Zürcher Zeitung* remarked that the "elimination of the Jewish element in all branches of the economy . . . had been pursued for some time now with increasing virulence." The policy of "Aryanisation," he added, was "depriving Jews of every basis of existence."[10] Of the approximately 50,000 Jewish businesses in Germany before the Nazis came to power, only 9,000—including 3,600 in Berlin—still existed by the summer of 1939.[11]

Those forced to sell their business usually only received a fraction of the true value. And those who decided to emigrate had to pay a series of fees, including a "tax for fleeing the Reich," which meant that not much remained of their former assets. A new economic start abroad was made that much more difficult. In a letter to his local chamber of commerce in April 1938, one Munich businessman who identified himself as a National Socialist and an admirer of Hitler was "so disgusted by the brutal measures and the way Jews were coerced" that he refused to serve as an adviser for further Aryanisation of Jewish businesses. "As an old-fashioned, upright and honest merchant," he wrote, he could no longer stand back and watch "how shamelessly many 'Aryan' businessmen, entrepreneurs, etc. . . . try to get their claws on Jewish businesses, factories, etc. for a pittance." He added: "To me these people are like vultures, with runny eyes and tongues lolling out, swooping down upon the Jewish cadaver."[12] But voices like this one were the absolute exception. A good many Germans enriched themselves at Jews' expense, unscrupulously exploiting the desperate situation into which a harassed and persecuted minority had been forced.

This wave of plunder was accompanied by a furious anti-Jewish smear campaign. On 8 November 1937, Julius Streicher and Goebbels opened an exhibition entitled "The Eternal Jew"—the German equivalent of the Wandering Jew—at Munich's German Museum. It was intended to enlighten visitors about the "deleterious effect of Jewry all over the world." An SPD-in-exile observer reported that "large yellow posters scream out announcements of the exhibition throughout the streets, and everywhere you can see the face of the Eternal Jew." The exhibition, the observer predicted, would hardly fail to have the desired effect on ill-informed museum-goers since truth and lies had been "combined so cleverly" that the "lies will necessarily appear to be true."[13]

As of the autumn of 1937, the ever more severe execution of anti-Jewish policies was directly connected with the regime's transition to a foreign policy of aggressive expansionism. Hitler and his underlings largely ceased showing the sort of regard for foreign opinion that had previously encouraged them to maintain a degree of moderation. By then Jews' economic position in Germany had been so undermined that there was little need to fear their final removal from commercial life would damage the German economy.[14] On the contrary, the complete Aryanisation of Jewish assets promised relief for the Reich's tight financial situation. The monies generated by plundering Jews could be used to finance armaments and preparations for war.

The amalgamation of Austria into the Reich in March 1938 noticeably radicalised the persecution of Jews. In 1933, over half a million Jews lived in Germany. By late 1937, 152,000 had emigrated, while 363,000 were still sticking it out in the country.[15] All at once, 190,000 Austrian Jews were added to that number, and that rise, in the short term, seemed like a setback to German authorities' efforts to get as many Jews as possible to leave the country. In fact, however, the *Anschluss* provided a new dynamic to the process of "de-Jewification." It would reach a temporary zenith in the Kristallnacht pogrom on 9 and 10 November 1938. In the initial hours after German troops entered Austria, the violence against Jews on the streets of Vienna exceeded anything that had occurred in the "old Reich" after 1933. "That evening, all hell broke loose," the dramatist Carl Zuckmayer recalled.

The underworld opened its gates and released its most base, most horrible and most filthy spirits. The city was transformed into a nightmare vision of Hieronymus Bosch. Lemurs and half-demons seemed to have hatched from squalid eggs and crawled from dank holes in the ground. The air was filled with a constant piercing, wild, hysterical screaming.[16]

For days Austrian Nazis and their sympathisers vented their pent-up anti-Semitic aggression on Viennese Jews, who were humiliated and abused in every way imaginable in front of salacious onlookers. "University professors were made to scrub the streets with their bare hands, and pious old men with white beards were forced into temples and compelled to perform leg squats and yell 'Heil Hitler' in unison," the Viennese author Stefan Zweig recorded in his autobiography. "Innocent people were herded together on the street like rabbits and taken to sweep the grounds of SA barracks. All the hateful, sick, dirty fantasies that had been conceived in nocturnal orgies of the imagination were rampantly visible on the streets in broad daylight."[17] The uncontrolled terrorising of Jews reached such proportions that on 17 March Reinhard Heydrich threatened Gauleiter Josef Bürckel, who had been appointed Reich commissioner and made responsible for integrating Austria into the Reich, that he would arrest any Nazis who took part in "undisciplined" attacks.[18] But it still took a while for the waves of violence to ebb. "On the streets today gangs of Jews, on their hands and knees scrubbing the Schuschnigg signs off the sidewalks, with jeering storm troopers standing over them and taunting crowds around them," wrote William Shirer on 22 March.[19] In late April, the Italian ambassador in Vienna, Ubaldo Rochira, still reported renewed anti-Jewish attacks. In one of the large streets of the second district, he wrote, "around a hundred Jews had been forced to walk on all fours or crawl in the dust." The ambassador was surprised at the virulence of the anti-Semitism he encountered in all classes of the Viennese population, from intellectuals to ordinary workers.[20]

Panicked, many Viennese Jews immediately sought to leave Austria, and the number of suicides shot up dramatically.[21] Within a short span of time, Germany's special anti-Semitic laws were extended to the newly acquired part of the Reich. Within the space of a few months the process of Aryanisation, which had been in the hands of a so-called "Assets Office" in Vienna since May 1938, was also completed.[22] To step up the pace with which Austrian Jews were driven from their home country, a "Central Office for Jewish Emigration" was set up in the former Rothschild Palace under the directorship of Adolf Eichmann, a member of the Jewish Office in the Reich Security Main Office (Division II 112). This committed anti-Semite and dutiful bureaucrat developed an efficient procedure for pushing through Jewish emigration. It allowed applicants to be processed quickly in the same building almost in the manner of a conveyor belt. Eichmann had the assets of wealthy members of Vienna's Jewish community confiscated, using them to finance the emigration of poorer Jews. By May 1939, 100,000 Jews—more than half of Austria's Jewish population—had left the country. The "Vienna model" was so successful that it served as the basis for similar initiatives in the "old Reich."[23]

"Since the amalgamation of Austria, the fate of German Jews has entered a new stage," an SPD-in-exile observer commented in July 1938.

> The National Socialists have concluded from their experiences in Austria that rapidly pursuing anti-Jewish persecution does no harm to the system, and that unleashing the anti-Semitic instincts in the ranks of their members and tolerating open pogroms do not cause any economic difficulties or any loss of prestige in the world at large. Guided by this conception . . . the regime is ruthlessly applying the Viennese methods to the older parts of the Reich.[24]

Beginning in the spring of 1938, one discriminatory law followed another, all aimed at destroying the economic existence of Jews in the "Greater German Reich" and making their lives as difficult as possible. Jewish families were denied income tax deductions for children (1 February); Jewish business people were not allowed to compete for public contracts (1 March); and Jewish communities lost their legal status as public bodies (28 March). Especially pernicious was the decree of 26 April that required Jews to declare all of their assets in excess of 5,000 marks by 30 June. "What is the point of this ordinance?" asked Victor Klemperer, who filled out the form on 29 June. "We are used to living in this condition of having no rights and in expectation of the next outrage. It hardly ruffles our feathers."[25]

On 6 July, a new addendum to the trade laws forbade Jews from engaging in various professions, including property, marriage-brokering and door-to-door sales. In late July, Jewish doctors had their licences revoked. An ordinance on 17 August required Jewish men and women to go by first names contained on a list or add "Israel" or "Sara" to their own names. "If the lists had been drawn up under other circumstances," Saul Friedländer has remarked, "they could have served as evidence of the intellectual constitution of bureaucratic fools."[26] The lists had been compiled by the ministerial official at the Interior Ministry and legal commentator on the Nuremberg Laws, Hans Globke, who like so many other Nazis was allowed to continue his career after the war.[27]

Once again, administrative measures "from above" and violence "from below" combined to hasten radicalisation. Anti-Semitic rioting broke out in many parts of the "old Reich" in the spring of 1938 in the wake of the pogrom in Vienna.[28] As he had in 1935, Goebbels seized the initiative. In late April, he conferred with Berlin Police President Count Wolf-Heinrich von Helldorf about how to further ramp up anti-Jewish persecution. "Jewish businesses get combed out, and what happens? Jews open up a new swimming pool and a couple of new cinemas and cafés," Goebbels wrote in his diaries. "We're going to end the Jewish paradise in Berlin. Jewish businesses are going to be designated as such. In any case, we're now going to proceed more radically." Hitler declared himself in agreement with the idea but asked that concrete action only be undertaken after his trip to Italy in early May 1938.[29] At Helldorf's behest, the state police office in Berlin came up with a "Memorandum on the Treatment of Jews in the Reich Capital in all Areas of Public Life" on 17 May. It foresaw a host of discriminatory measures: from the introduction of special badges for Jews and the abolition of compulsory education for Jewish children to the visual identification of Jewish businesses and the establishment of segregated train carriages for Jews.[30]

The section of the Security Service responsible for Jewish affairs objected that "addressing the question of how to regulate the Jewish problem in Berlin independently of the Reich in its entirety is counter to our purposes."[31] But Goebbels insisted that the Reich capital had to lead the way. On 24 May, he once again conferred with Helldorf about the "Jewish question" in Berlin. "We want to force Jews out of economic and cultural life, indeed out of public life altogether,"

Goebbels wrote in his diary. "We have to start somewhere." Five days later he reassured himself of Hitler's support, and on 30 May he instructed the police president to "initiate the anti-Jewish programme."[32] On 31 May, Berlin police staged a large-scale raid on Kurfürstendamm and arrested 300 Jews, although most of them were released the following day. Goebbels was indignant, writing: "I'm going to kick up a storm as never before." In a speech to police officers on 10 June, he tried to win them over to his line: "I'm rebelling. Against every form of sentimentality. The watchword is not the law, but harassment. The Jews leave Berlin. And the police are going to help me."[33]

Beginning on 11 June, anti-Jewish activities were reported in most Berlin districts. "Starting late Saturday afternoon, groups of civilians, consisting usually of two or three men, were to be observed painting on the windows of Jewish shops the word 'JUDE' in large red letters, as well as the Star of David and caricatures of Jews," relayed the U.S. ambassador in Berlin, Hugh R. Wilson, to his secretary of state. "The painters in each case were followed by large groups of spectators who seemed to enjoy the proceedings enormously."[34] Wilson understood this action as an organised attempt to identify all Jewish businesses, and he remarked that it went further than anything which had happened since 1933. The excesses reached their temporary zenith on 20 and 21 June. The journalist Bella Fromm, who would emigrate a few weeks later to the United States, wrote in her diary:

> The entire Kurfürstendamm was full of graffiti and posters . . . In the district [behind Alexanderplatz] where the small Jewish shops are located, the SA went on a particularly terrible rampage. Everywhere you could see repulsive, bloodthirsty drawings of Jews beheaded, hanged or hacked to bits, accompanied by disgusting slogans. Windows had been smashed, and "plunder" from poor little shops lay scattered on the pavements and in the gutters.[35]

The corresponding report of the responsible Security Service officer noted laconically: "The operation was carried out with permission from local Berlin police authorities."[36] But the Berlin police did not just sit on their hands. As part of a large-scale operation targeting so-called "antisocials," they arrested some 1,500 Jews in mid-June 1938;

most of them were taken to Buchenwald concentration camp near Weimar. Goebbels was satisfied, writing: "Helldorf is now proceeding radically on the Jewish question. The party is helping him. Many arrests . . . We will make Berlin Jew-free. I'm not going to let up."[37]

But on 22 June, from the Obersalzberg, Hitler ordered an immediate stop to the operation. Goebbels, who gave a virulently anti-Semitic speech in Berlin's Olympic Stadium to celebrate the summer solstice that evening,[38] had to retreat. The anti-Semitic campaign in Berlin had created an enormously negative echo in the foreign press at a point where international tensions were rising daily because of the "Sudetenland crisis" provoked by the Nazi regime. Hitler thus decided for tactical reasons to temporarily put a lid on anti-Jewish activism.[39] He had not given up his ultimate goal, of course, and Hitler and Goebbels reached a mutual understanding during the Wagner Festival in Bayreuth on 24 June 1938. Goebbels noted: "The main thing is that the Jews will be forced out. In ten years they must be completely removed from Germany. But in the short term we want to keep the rich ones as collateral."[40]

In late June Wolf-Heinrich von Helldorf issued to all Berlin police officers "Guidelines for the Treatment of Jews and Jewish Affairs," in which he drew on the lessons from the operation in June. The goal, he wrote, was "to cause Jews to emigrate and not just to harass them randomly without any hope of achieving this end."[41] All Berlin police officers were called upon to "free Berlin from Jews and in particular the Jewish proletariat as much as possible." A catalogue encompassing seventy-six points described in detail how officers could put pressure on the defamed minority in daily life without exceeding the limits of the discriminatory laws already in place. "Helldorf has given me a list of the measures taken against Jews in Berlin," Goebbels noted, pleased with the work of the police president. "They are rigorous and comprehensive. In this way we'll be able to drive the Jews from Berlin in the foreseeable future."[42]

But there was an internal contradiction within the policy of forcibly driving away Jews. By doing everything in its power to rob Jews of the basis of their economic existence, the Nazi regime restricted their ability to emigrate. "While Jews are quickly being transformed into a proletarian community, which will soon be dependent on public welfare," reported Argentina's ambassador to Germany, Eduardo Labougle Carranza, in August 1938, "it is growing more difficult for them to emigrate, especially where money is concerned."[43] At Security Service headquarters, the dilemma was no secret either. One could no longer ignore, read a report for the months of April and May 1938, "that the chances for emigration have decreased just as much as the pressure to emigrate has grown." The increasing exclusion of Jews from economic life, the report added, was causing a reduction in income to Jewish communities and aid organisations, which came up with most of the money used to pay for Jewish emigration.[44]

To make matters worse, the readiness of Western countries to take in Jews was by no means rising as quickly as the persecution of Jews in Germany was intensifying. At a conference called in the French spa town of Evian on the initiative of U.S. President Franklin D. Roosevelt in July 1938, none of the thirty-two participating countries was willing to significantly raise its quotas for German-Jewish immigration. In this regard they played right into the hands of Nazi propaganda. "No one wants them," jeered the *Völkischer Beobachter*.[45] In his concluding speech at the Nuremberg rally in 1938, Hitler made fun of the hypocrisy of Western democracies that complained, on the one hand, about the "boundless cruelty" with which the Third Reich was trying to "rid itself of its Jewish element" while shrinking back, on the other, from the burdens connected with accepting such a large number of Jewish immigrants. "Plenty of morality," Hitler scoffed, "but no help at all."[46]

The experts in the Security Service envisioned Jewish emigration to Palestine as the solution to the situation, but the Nazi leadership saw itself facing the dilemma that if it encouraged Zionist activities, it might help create a new centre of "global Jewry," whose alleged power the regime was trying to break. In June 1937, Foreign Minister von Neurath told the German embassy in London in no uncertain terms: "The formation of a Jewish state or a state apparatus run by Jews under a British mandate is not in German interests."[47] One year later, while the conference in Evian was going on, Alfred Rosenberg published an editorial in the *Völkischer Beobachter* with the headline "Where to with the Jews?" It summarised the mains points of the debate. First: "Palestine is out of the question as a large centre for immigration." Second: "The states of the world do not consider themselves in a position to take in the Jews of Europe." Third: "We will have to look around for a closed territory not settled by Europeans."[48] In this context, in the spring of 1938, the island of

Madagascar off the eastern coast of Africa began to play a role in Hitler's calculations. On 11 April, Goebbels noted: "Talked for a long time over breakfast. Discussed the Jewish question. The Führer wants to drive the Jews entirely out of Germany. To Madagascar or somewhere like it. Correct! He's convinced that they originated in a former penal colony. It's possible. A people condemned by God."[49]

The idea was not new in itself. In the 1880s, one of the pioneers of popular anti-Semitism, the orientalist Paul de Lagarde, had advocated resettling Jews on Madagascar in conjunction with German expansion in eastern Europe, and since the 1920s, this "solution to the Jewish question" had been propagated by anti-Semites in various countries. In June 1926, for instance, the *Völkischer Beobachter* ran a front-page article by Englishman Henry Hamilton Beamish, who wrote: "Where is the paradise granted to the Jews, where they can live in happiness and peace, keep themselves pure and pursue . . . their ideals? It's Madagascar." The cynicism of Beamish's appeal was difficult to top since both he and the other advocates of the idea knew that conditions on the island were so forbidding that the majority of Jews deported there would die. The SS hate newspaper *Der Stürmer* openly acknowledged the genocidal aspect of the Madagascar idea in the 1930s. Its New Year's edition in 1938 opened with the headline "Madagascar" and a caricature of a horrified Jew with his back pressed to a globe. The caption read: "He sees the end coming."[50]

Hitler had not reached a decision—Goebbels's words "Madagascar or someplace like it" suggest that the dictator was considering a number of options—but it is clear that he considered it an absolute necessity to drive all Jews from Germany. In mid-August 1938, he told a small circle that the Nuremberg Laws were "actually too humane." As his army attaché recalled: "He was considering the use of additional laws to so restrict Jewish life in Germany that the vast majority of the Jewish population simply would not want to stay in Germany. That would be the best way of getting rid of them."[51] In late September 1938, with the threat of a large-scale European military conflict over the "Sudeten question" temporarily averted by the Munich Agreement, new anti-Semitic unrest flared up. The fear of war that had taken hold of many parts of the German populace that spring vented itself in heightened aggression towards the Jewish minority. In numerous places, particularly in southern and central Germany, synagogues and Jewish institutions were attacked. The violence had "a semi-pogrom character," according to a Security Service report in October 1938. Many party activists were convinced that the "moment of finally liquidating the Jewish question had come."[52] Presciently, Willy Cohn wrote in his diary on 4 November 1938: "I think the remaining Jews in Germany are in for some very tough times."[53] The pogrom throughout the Reich a few days later hardly came from nowhere. It was the culmination of the anti-Semitic violence that had grown ever more radical over the course of 1938. Once again it was Hitler who gave the decisive signal for Germans to give free rein to their hatred and destructive desires.

On 7 November, 17-year-old Herschel Grynszpan, a Jew who had grown up in Germany but who was a Polish citizen, shot and seriously injured the legation secretary of the German embassy in Paris, Ernst von Rath. The attack was an act of revenge. In late October, German police and SS men had rounded up some 17,000 Polish Jews who lived in the Third Reich and taken them to Germany's Polish border. Among the people deported, who had to exist for days under pitiful conditions in no man's land between the two countries, were Grynszpan's parents and siblings. "My heart bleeds when I think of our tragedy," Grynszpan wrote in a message to his uncle. "I had to protest in a way that the whole world would hear."[54]

Grynszpan's act of desperation gave the Nazi regime a welcome excuse to strike a coordinated blow against German Jews and what property they had left. Goebbels in particular saw a chance to repair his personal relationship with the Führer, which had been damaged in the previous months by his love affair with the Czech actress Lida Baarova, by demonstrating his exceptional zealotry.[55] On the evening of 7 November, the Propaganda Ministry instructed the press to report very extensively on the attack and to publish editorials making clear that it "would have to have the most serious consequences for Jews in Germany."[56] On 8 November, the *Völkischer Beobachter* published an editorial with the headline "The Criminals" that all but came out and called directly for a pogrom:

> It is clear that the German people will draw its conclusions from this latest deed. It cannot be that within our borders hundreds of thousands of Jews still dominate whole commercial streets, populate places of

amusement and pocket the rent of German tenants as "foreign" property owners while their racial comrades abroad call for war upon Germany and gun down German civil servants.[57]

On the morning of 9 November, news agencies reported that Rath would die any minute. In Berlin, the young journalist Ruth Andreas-Friedrich registered "a fearful pressure in the air like before a thunderstorm."[58]

During the nights of 7–8 November and 8–9 November, there had already been anti-Jewish outbursts in the city of Kassel and surrounding areas. They had been organised by local NSDAP functionaries who believed they were acting on behalf of the regime by taking the initiative. "In the state of Hesse there were large-scale anti-Semitic events," Goebbels noted. "Synagogues have been burned down. If we can only unleash popular anger now."[59] That required an unambiguous expression of will by Hitler, which Goebbels did not yet have. In his traditional speech at Munich's Bürgerbräu beer cellar on the evening of 8 November on the anniversary of the 1923 putsch, Hitler did not mention the attack in Paris. But his unusual silence did not mean that he wanted to play down the matter. On the contrary, it was a clear indication that he was up to something.[60] Unlike in the aftermath of the attack on Wilhelm Gustloff in early February 1936, when Hitler had forbidden anti-Semitic violence with an eye towards the Winter Olympics, this time he was determined to lash out at the Jews. But he wanted to wait until Rath died. In the night of 7–8 November, he sent his personal physician Karl Brandt to Paris, together with the head of the Munich Surgical Clinic, Georg Magnus. Both examined Rath and kept Hitler regularly informed about his condition.[61]

Ernst von Rath died around 4:30 p.m. on the afternoon of 9 November, and the news of his death was communicated to Hitler by telephone in his private apartment in Munich's Prinzregentenstrasse.[62] The dictator thus had sufficient time to form a clear idea of how to proceed before he headed off at 6 p.m. for the annual commemorative ceremony with the "old fighters" in the ballroom of Munich's City Hall. As the historian Richard Evans has shown, the events that followed that evening were a drama carefully staged by Hitler and Goebbels.[63] Around 9 p.m., over dinner, Hitler was brought a telegram relaying the news of Rath's death. Hitler feigned surprise, appeared shaken and immediately began talking agitatedly to Goebbels, who sat next to him. Goebbels's diary entry for this date is extremely terse but still makes it clear that this was the moment when Hitler gave the green light for the Kristallnacht pogrom. Goebbels noted: "He decided to let the demonstrations go on. Withdraw the police. The Jews will be allowed to feel the anger of the people. That is only correct. I immediately gave the relevant orders to the police and the party."[64]

Immediately after his conversation with Goebbels, and without giving his customary speech, Hitler left the event and returned to Prinzregentenstrasse. Apparently he wanted to avoid being directly connected with the events to come. Goebbels spoke in his stead. The wording of his speech was not recorded, but the effect it was meant to have was clear from a report published by the Supreme Party Court a few months later. All party leaders had understood the message "to be that to outsiders the party should not appear to be the originator of the demonstrations but that in reality it should organise and carry them out."[65] Goebbels himself noted about the reception of his speech: "Frenetic applause. Everyone ran to the telephone. Now the people will act."[66] This turn of phrase was typical of the central conceit that the Kristallnacht pogrom was an expression of popular fury—which helped the actual instigators, Hitler and Goebbels, remain in the shadows. In keeping with this, the Gauleiter and SA Gruppenführer who had assembled in Munich passed on instructions to subordinate offices throughout the Reich. The commands were then smoothly transferred to district and town directors.

Among the "old fighters" celebrating in the Bürgerbräu beer cellar were thirty-nine members of the "Storm Troop Adolf Hitler," which had been run as a veterans' organisation after its ban in 1924. A short time after Goebbels's incendiary speech, they were on a rampage through Munich's streets, destroying a number of businesses and setting fire to the Ohel Jakob Synagogue in Herzog-Rudolf-Strasse. (The city's main synagogue on Herzog-Max-Strasse had already been torn down in June.) Goebbels, who accompanied the Gauleiter of Munich and Upper Bavaria, Adolf Wagner, to Gau headquarters on Prannerstrasse, was able to inspect the destruction with his own eyes. "The storm troop went about its work," he noted. "And it was very thorough." One of the vandals was Hitler's personal assistant Julius

Schaub. "Schaub shifted into high gear," Goebbels remarked. "His storm-trooper background was reawakened."[67]

Before he administered the traditional midnight oath of loyalty to new SS recruits, Hitler agreed with Heinrich Himmler that the SS would not participate in the pogrom. Reinhard Heydrich called the head of the Berlin Gestapo, Heinrich Müller, who sent a memo informing all state police offices that "very soon operations against Jews, especially against their synagogues, will be taking place throughout Germany." The operations were "not to be disturbed," but "plundering and other special excesses were to be stopped." Moreover, the Gestapo was to take 20,000–30,000 Jews around the Reich into custody.[68] Goebbels's diary makes it clear that these orders went directly back to Hitler himself.[69] In an urgent telegram that went out at 1:20 a.m., Heydrich added specifics to Müller's instructions: "Only such measures as do not entail any danger to German lives or property are to be taken." Rioters were only allowed to destroy, but not plunder, Jewish businesses. Archival material from all synagogues and official Jewish sites was to be confiscated and handed over to local Security Service offices. The police and the Security Service in all districts were instructed to take into custody as many Jews, especially the better off, as there was space to hold them: "After their detention has been completed, contact needs to be established with the responsible concentration camps to quickly accommodate the Jews."[70]

In the meantime the pogrom had already commenced in many parts of the Reich. Everywhere SA men and party activists, mostly out of uniform, marched with canisters of petrol to the nearest synagogues, where they ransacked and set fire to the buildings. As ordered, local police did nothing, and fire brigades only intervened to prevent the flames from spreading to neighbouring buildings. At the same time, other troops of thugs attacked Jewish businesses, throwing their goods out on the street and smashing windows, so that the following morning the pavements glistened with broken glass; Berliners thus coined the euphemistic phrase "Reich Crystal Night" to describe the pogrom. Other vandals forced their way into Jewish families' houses, smashed the furniture and abused the inhabitants. There had not been such a massive outbreak of unfettered anti-Semitic violence in Germany since the Middle Ages.[71]

On the morning of 10 November, Goebbels conferred with Hitler about how to proceed. "To keep going or put a stop to it?" he noted. "That's the question now." The two men agreed to halt the "operation," at least temporarily. "If we allow it to continue, there is the danger of a mob forming," Goebbels wrote, explaining their decision.[72] On Hitler's order, he wrote a text "strictly calling upon" the German populace to "desist from all further demonstrations and acts of retribution in any form against Jewry." Goebbels promised: "Jewry will be given the ultimate answer to the Jewish assassination in Paris in the form of legislation and ordinances."[73] Hitler approved the text that noon in Osteria Bavaria.[74] The message was broadcast in the afternoon on German radio and was published on the front pages of newspapers the following day. Simultaneously, Goebbels ordered the press to be judicious in reporting the pogrom. German newspapers were not to run front-page headlines or pictures of the events.[75] That evening, in a speech to press representatives in the new "Führer Building" on Königsplatz, Hitler did not mention the events of the previous night at all. On 17 November, he took part in a memorial ceremony for Ernst von Rath in Düsseldorf, but unlike at Wilhelm Gustloff's funeral two and a half years previously, he chose not to speak. This was intended to maintain the illusion that he had had nothing to do with the pogrom.[76]

A report published by the Jewish division of the Reich Security Main Office on 7 December 1938 put the number of Jews killed at thirty-six. The figure was later revised upwards to ninety-one. In fact, the number was considerably higher, if suicides and those who died in or en route to concentration camps are included. More than 1,000 synagogues and prayer rooms were set on fire, and 7,000–7,500 Jewish businesses were ransacked and plundered. The damage done in the violence was estimated at around 50 million reichsmarks.[77]

Even worse than the material damage was the humiliation and harassment Jews suffered. Just as in Vienna the previous March and April, Jews were subject to an "explosion of sadism."[78] They were forced to kneel in front of synagogues and sing religious songs, dance or prostrate themselves and kiss the ground, while SA men punched and kicked them. In many places, Jewish men were herded through the streets in broad daylight before being taken away to concentration camps amidst jeers and insults from local officials, SA and SS men and Hitler Youths. Large crowds usually watched the demeaning spectacle.

"They stood packed together and watched us pass," a Jewish department store owner from the city of Hanau recalled. "Hardly anyone said anything, and only a few people laughed. You could see pity and horror in many people's faces."[79]

In total more than 30,000 Jews were arrested and taken to Dachau, Buchenwald and Sachsenhausen concentration camps, where they were subjected to horrific mistreatment by SS guards. As soon as they arrived, kicks and blows rained down upon them. Many were forced to run to the point of exhaustion around camp grounds or to stand at attention for hours in the November cold, without being allowed to move. "It was a chain of endless physical and emotional suffering," one of the misfortunates wrote about the reality of Buchenwald.

> The first days were the worst. They deprived us of water. Water was scarce to begin with, and they did not give us any at all. Your mouth completely dried out, your throat burned and your tongue literally stuck to your gums. When they handed out bread on the third day, I could not choke it down because I did not have any saliva in my mouth. Nights were terrible. People became hysterical and broke down. One man screamed that people were trying to kill him. Another gave a kind of sermon. A third babbled something about waves of electricity. There was screaming, crying, praying, cursing, coughing, dust, filth and a horrible stench. It was as if all hell had broken loose.[80]

Most of the detainees were released after a few weeks if they promised to immediately begin making plans to leave Germany. They also had to promise not to tell anyone about what they had experienced in the camps. But much of the truth seeped out. "The terrified hints and fragments of stories from Buchenwald are horrific," Victor Klemperer noted in early December 1938. "Despite the gagging order, people say that you won't return from that place a second time—ten to twenty people die there every day anyway."[81]

The night of 9–10 November 1938 was a complete shock for Jews still living in Germany. "In terms of suffering, privation, humiliation and terror, nothing that had happened previously could compare with this night," recalled Hugo Moses, a former Oppenheim Bank employee.[82] All of a sudden the pogrom had made Jews realise that they were without legal protection of any kind. They could be beaten, robbed and killed without the custodians of law and order lifting a finger or the perpetrators being threatened with any form of punishment. A line had been crossed: Germany had left the community of civilised nations. "We'll never again return to this country if we get out alive," the Berlin doctor Hertha Nathorff wrote in her diary one week after Kristallnacht.[83]

Although the Nazi Party press never ceased depicting the pogrom as a spontaneous expression of popular outrage, it was clear to everybody that this was a fictional narrative. Given the fact that the violence had obviously been organised, a state police office in Bielefeld concluded in late November 1938, the constant repetition of the propaganda version of events was "almost laughable."[84] In its report in November, the Reich Security Main Office also stated: "The people who carried out the operation generally were the party's political organisers, members of the SA and the SS, and individual members of the Hitler Youth."[85] Foreign observers saw the participation of young people as a particularly bad sign. It revealed "the moral demise of the young generation of Germans who are capable of all sorts of attacks and violence if ordered to carry them out by the party," the Polish consul general in Leipzig reported.[86] In some places, ordinary citizens had joined in with the SA troups, encouraging the perpetrators of violence and sometimes getting directly involved. But in general, the Security Service observed that "the civilian population was only very slightly involved in the operation."[87]

So what did the German people think about the pogrom of November 1938? Did they approve of or reject what had happened? It is difficult to arrive at a clear answer since there was no public sphere in Germany in which people could freely articulate their opinions and attitudes. "If we could only find out who was for it and who was against it!" Ruth Andreas-Friedrich wrote after witnessing a silent crowd looking at the smouldering ruins of the synagogue in Berlin's Fasanenstrasse on 10 November.[88] On 14 November, the Argentinian ambassador to Germany reported: "It cannot be determined what people's inner feelings about the events were since it is publicly known that the regime does not permit or tolerate criticism of the actions of party members and those working for them."[89] Publicly announcing one's disgust would have been risky since there were enough people in the general populace whose loyalty to the regime made them only too happy to turn others in to the Gestapo.[90] On 12 November, the Italian consul general in Innsbruck wrote that the population was "deeply outraged" at the pogrom, but was "very cautious about voicing opinions since word has it that three Aryans were taken off to the Dachau concentration camp at night for openly expressing their disapproval."[91]

Drawing on information gathered throughout the Reich, the SPD-in-exile reports concluded that the "excesses were strongly condemned by the vast majority of the German people."[92] But of course the information collected by people trusted by the SPD tended to come from former Social Democratic circles and probably only reflected the views of part of the populace. Still, foreign observers like the American consul general in Stuttgart, Samuel W. Honacker, also found that around 80 per cent of Germans disagreed with the violent operation while only 20 per cent had expressed satisfaction with it.[93] Even reports made by local officials, mayors and Gestapo offices spoke of "widespread disagreement" with the "operation" of 9–10 November and of a "generally quite unpropitious" effect on the popular mood. Even party members had rejected it, although they were "extraordinarily careful with their criticism lest they be branded Jew-lovers."[94]

Given all of these indications, it is fairly safe to say that the majority of the German populace reacted negatively to the Kristallnacht pogrom, although their public rejection of the violence was largely based not on empathy with the Jews but rather on their dismay at the destruction of valuable commodities. "On the one hand, we save toothpaste tubes and tin cans," complained an NSDAP member from the city of Duisburg, "and on the other houses are destroyed, and windows are smashed."[95] Significantly, Hitler as the main instigator again remained exempt from criticism. Various reports registered remarks such as "The Führer surely did not intend this."[96] The dictator's strategy of passing himself off as the disengaged statesman far above any such unpleasantness, while delegating responsibility to his underlings, was a complete success. On 26 November the temporary British consul general reported from Munich: "A childlike faith in the Führer and the conviction that he had nothing to do with the 'Pogrom' subsists, but criticism can be heard of other Party leaders, especially Goebbels, Himmler, Göring and von Schirach."[97]

There were isolated cases of neighbours and friends showing solidarity with those being persecuted and trying to help them, but they
were the exceptions. As a rule, people expressed sympathy with the
victims and outrage at the perpetrators only in private. On 24 November,
the Freiburg historian Gerhard Ritter wrote in a letter to his mother
that what he had seen in the previous few weeks was "the most
shameful and terrible spectacle that has happened in very many years."
Nonetheless, Ritter, a conservative patriot, hoped that those responsible would have "an internal change of heart and a return to being
calm."[98] Ulrich von Hassell, whom Hitler had removed from his post
as German ambassador to Italy at the beginning of the year, noted
on 25 November that he was "still under the burdensome impression
of the vile persecution of Jews." There was no doubt, he added, that
"this was an officially organised tempest against the Jews unleashed
at one and the same hour of the night throughout Germany—a true
scandal!"[99] Like Ritter and Hassell, many Germans seem to have felt
ashamed that the barbaric excesses of 9–10 November could have
happened in their ostensibly civilised nation. The Swiss consul general
in Cologne reported being asked by people from all walks of life in
the days following the pogrom: "What do you say to these terrible
events?" Every one of them, the consul continued, had added: "It
makes you ashamed to be German."[100]

Nonetheless, people's rejection of the pogrom did not worry the
regime because it remained in the private sphere. Nowhere was there
vocal public protest, not even within the Churches, as might have
been expected.[101] That being the case, Hitler and his henchmen could
consider Kristallnacht a success. They had unleashed anti-Semitic
violence against the Reich's Jewish minority on a previously unprecedented scale without encountering any resistance. That was a clear
sign that the majority of Germans had accepted the exclusion of Jews
from the "ethnic-popular community," even if they had reservations
about open brutality. As Richard Evans has rightly concluded, the
National Socialists now knew that they could do whatever they wanted
to Jews, and no one would stop them.[102]

As far as further action on the "Jewish question" was concerned, Hitler
set the agenda at a noon meeting with Goebbels in the Osteria Bavaria
on 10 November. "His views are radical and aggressive," Goebbels noted
afterwards. "The Führer wants to move on to extremely strict measures

against the Jews. They will have to repair their businesses themselves. Insurance companies will pay them nothing. The Führer then wants to gradually confiscate the businesses and give their former owners certificates, which we can devalue at any time."[103] On 11 November, Hitler instructed Göring, as the head of the Four Year Plan, to convene a conference in order to "centrally summarise the decisive steps."[104]

The conference took place the following day between 11 a.m. and 2:30 p.m. in the Aviation Ministry. Hundreds of civil servants, ministers and state secretaries took part, including Wilhelm Frick, his deputy Wilhelm Stuckart, Interior Ministry "race expert" Bernhard Lösener, Foreign Ministry Political Division Director Ernst Woermann, and his "Jewish expert" Emil Schumburg; Goebbels, Finance Minister von Krosigk, Justice Minister Gürtner, Economics Minister Funk and his ministerial director and the director of the division for economic organisation and Jewish affairs, Rudolf Schmeer; as well as Reinhard Heydrich, Kurt Daluege and Adolf Eichmann as representatives of the Security Service and the police. Minister for Economics, Labour and Finances Hans Fischböck and Reich Commissioner Josef Bürckel attended from Austria.

The detailed protocol of the conference has been preserved almost in its entirety. It is a horrific document—not only for the pitilessness with which the participants pursued their ideas to their logical conclusions, but also for the completely unrestrained language, free from any sort of moral scruple, that they used. "I would have preferred it if you had killed 200 Jews and not destroyed so many things of value," Göring declared after a representative of the German insurance industry, Eduard Hilgard, had broken down the damage done during Kristallnacht into individual categories. Citing the list drawn up by Berlin's police president the previous June, Goebbels suggested a whole series of harassment initiatives aimed at forcing Jews "from every corner of the public sphere," where they were behaving "provocatively." For example, Jews could be banned from attending cultural events. They would only be allowed to travel in segregated train carriages. They could be prohibited from public swimming pools and other leisure facilities and be banned from setting foot in a "German forest." "Today, there are packs of them running around in [Berlin's] Grunewald [forest]," Goebbels added. Göring suggested that one could

perhaps set aside a "certain section" of forest for Jews and proposed
that his forestry expert Friedrich Alpers "could see to it that animals
that resembled Jews—elk have such hooked noses—were brought and
settled there." Heydrich suggested that for the rest of the time they
spent in Germany, Jews be required to wear a "distinguishing badge"—
an idea that would be first realised with the introduction of the
notorious yellow star in September 1941. Göring supported the creation
of ghettos within cities so as to completely isolate Jews. Heydrich
rejected this idea, arguing that ghettos were "perennial hiding places
for criminals . . . impossible to keep under police surveillance." At the
end of the conference, during which conservative ministers and ministerial civil servants uttered not a single word of disapproval or moderation, Göring summed up the results: "This will work. These swine
won't be so quick to commit a second murder. And I have to say it
again. I would not want to be a Jew in Germany."[105]

The most immediate result of the conference was that that very
day Jews were required to pay an "atonement contribution" of one
billion reichsmarks for the Paris assassination. In addition, as of
1 January 1939, they were prohibited from running businesses or working
as tradesmen and required to pay for all the damage to their businesses
and residences during the pogrom themselves. The sums due to them
from insurance policies were confiscated by the Reich. "In any case,
it's now tabula rasa," wrote a happy Goebbels. "The radical opinion
has emerged victorious."[106] A Finance Ministry decree of 21 November
1938 required Jews to pay out to the state 20 per cent of their assets in
four instalments by August 1939. A further Finance Ministry edict
of 3 December established the regulations for the Aryanisation by
administrators of those Jewish businesses that still existed and required
Jews to turn over stocks and bonds, jewellery and art to state depots.[107]
With that, the Nazis had got their hands on nearly all of the Jewish
people's wealth. The "atonement contribution" alone increased Reich
revenue by 6 per cent in one fell swoop, offering noticeable relief to
Germany's state finances, which accelerated rearmament had left
extraordinarily tight.[108] "The benefits from all Aryanisation must exclusively go to the finance minister and not any other individual in the
Reich," Göring stressed at a speech to Gauleiter, senior municipal
officials and Reich governors on 6 December. Otherwise it would be
impossible to carry out the Führer's armaments programme.[109]

There were waves upon waves of discriminatory laws and edicts. On 15 November, the Education Ministry ordered all Jewish pupils to be thrown out of German schools since it was "intolerable" for German pupils to sit in the same classroom with Jews after "the ruthless assassination in Paris."[110] On 28 November, the Interior Ministry gave senior municipal officials the right to declare certain districts off-limits to Jews and to restrict their access to public spaces—a first step towards ghettoisation.[111] On 3 December, Jews had their driving licences revoked on the orders of Himmler as Reichsführer-SS and head of the German police. Five days later, Jews were banned from university libraries. These two prohibitions hit Victor Klemperer particularly hard. Previously he had enjoyed driving around the environs of Dresden with his wife—"it was a bit of freedom and life"—and even after his dismissal as a professor, he had been allowed to do research in Dresden's university library. Now he could do neither.[112]

"One step at a time," noted Goebbels, speaking for both himself and Hitler. "We're not going to ease up until we've got rid of them."[113] On 20 December, the Labour Ministry decreed that "all unemployed, able-bodied Jews" should be required to do forced labour. On 23 February 1939, the Transport Ministry prohibited Jews from using sleeper or dining cars on trains, and on 30 April, Jews were stripped of most of the rights they enjoyed under tenant-protection laws.[114]

At the conference of 12 November 1938, Heydrich had already suggested using the Viennese model to force Jews to emigrate, since Austria had succeeded in "forcing out" 50,000 Jews within a short span of time.[115] Göring agreed, and on 24 January 1939, he established a "Central Office for Jewish Emigration" in Berlin. Heydrich was put in charge, and with that he became one of the key figures in the Third Reich's "Jewish policy."[116] As much as officials insisted, on the one hand, that Jews emigrate, the more they did, on the other, to make this more difficult by inventing bureaucratic formalities and harassment. "Not only were there hefty fees to pay, so that the assets you still had were practically worthless," remembered a Jewish department store owner from Hanau, who emigrated in April 1939.

> You had to run around endlessly and go through all sorts of drudgery to collect all the necessary forms. You had to go to the passport office, the police, customs, the currency office, the city treasury, the emigrants'

advisory office, the registrar's office and other places. And you had to
return everywhere three times, even if all you wanted was the simplest
of forms.[117]

Despite all the obstacles, 115,000 German Jews succeeded in emigrating
between 10 November 1938 and the start of the Second World War in
early September 1939. That meant that in total 400,000 Jews had left
the Reich, excluding Austria, since the National Socialists came to
power.[118]

Those who stayed behind were completely marginalised and pauper-
ised. "There is no Jewish life any more," wrote Fritz Goldberg, a
former assistant theatre director in Berlin who would get out of
Germany in the nick of time in the summer of 1939. "There is only
a host of frightened, hunted people who have no houses of worship,
who are banned from entering any café, public square or hospital,
who can no longer attend any places of amusement and whose entire
belongings have been stolen and destroyed."[119] By the end of the year,
the Nazi leadership was already dropping dark hints as to what they
intended to do with the "broken rest" of the Jews who stayed in
Germany.[120] If in the "foreseeable future" the Reich became involved
in a "foreign-policy conflict," Göring had announced at the conference
of 12 November, there would have to be "a major reckoning with the
Jews."[121] On 24 November 1938, Hitler received South African Defence
and Economics Minister Oswald Pirow at the Berghof. On that occasion, he declared that it was his "unshakeable will" to solve the "Jewish
problem" before too long. This, Hitler declared, was not just a German,
but a European problem. Half cynically and half threateningly, he
added: "What do you think would happen to Jews in Germany,
Mr. Pirow, if I withdrew my protective hand from them? The world
cannot imagine it."[122]

On 30 January 1939, in his speech to the Reichstag on the sixth anniversary of taking power, which was also broadcast on radio, Hitler
publicly emphasised for the first time his determination to "deport
the Jews." Europe, he declared, would "never settle down before the
Jewish question is solved." There were enough "settlement areas" in
the world, the dictator declared, most likely referring to the Madagascar
idea. "The opinion that the Jews are a people destined by God to exist

to a large extent off the body and the labour of other peoples must be thrown out once and for all." Such statements remained within the framework of what Hitler had repeatedly said throughout 1938. What followed went further. In his life, Hitler claimed, he had been "a prophet often enough" and had mostly been "laughed at." But he now offered a further prophesy: "If international finance Jewry inside and outside Europe once again succeeds in plunging various peoples into a world war, the result will not be the Bolshevisation of the world and the triumph of Jewry, but the annihilation of the Jewish race in Europe."[123]

This speech has been interpreted as evidence that Hitler was already envisioning the "final solution"—the physical destruction of Jews. Yet at the time of the speech, Hitler probably intended his threat as a way of increasing pressure upon German Jews to emigrate and upon Western governments to relax their restrictive immigration policies.[124] With this in mind, Foreign Ministry State Secretary Ernst von Weizsäcker had declared on 15 November 1938 to the Swiss ambassador in Paris that "Jews are going to have to be deported since there is no way they can remain in Germany. But Weizsäcker had added: "If, however, no country can be found to accept them, sooner or later they will face complete destruction."[125]

But there was more to Hitler's declarations that German Jews would be annihilated than just tactics. On the contrary, they were embedded in a broader plan for the future. By the winter of 1938/9, it was already apparent that the aggressive expansionism of the Nazi regime would lead, sooner or later, to military hostilities in Europe. In the event that this conflict developed, as it had in 1914–1918, into a "world war" involving the United States, "international finance Jewry" was to be blamed. In this sense, Hitler's threats had an all-too-real, sinister core. If they fell into the hands of Himmler and his henchmen, Jews living in Europe had to reckon with the worst—being murdered.[126] In his declaration of 30 January 1939, Hitler was testing the waters for an extreme solution to the "Jewish question." It was no accident that he would repeatedly refer back to his earlier "prophecy" in 1941 and 1942 as the genocide of Jews got under way.

21

The Way to War

"The time for surprises is over," Hitler declared in his Reichstag speech on 30 January 1937, four years after taking power. "As a nation of equal status Germany is conscious of its European responsibility, and will work loyally towards solving the problems that beset us and other nations."[1] The dictator would have had good reason to manoeuvre Germany into quieter water when it came to foreign policy. The triumphs his regime had achieved during its first years were impressive enough. Step by step, Hitler had freed Germany from the constraints of the Treaty of Versailles and re-established its ability to pursue its own foreign-policy aims. By simultaneously posing as a man of peace and presenting them with faits accomplis, he had repeatedly duped and outmanoeuvred the Western powers. Exploiting an international constellation of circumstances that was extraordinarily favourable to the Third Reich, he had pushed through an accelerated rearmament programme without provoking a feared military intervention by the Versailles signatories. After that he was out of the danger zone. Germany once again had the most modern and powerful military on the European continent. "Today we have once again become a global power," Hitler announced on 20 February 1937 at the annual celebration of the Nazi Party's founding in the Hofbräuhaus.[2]

Yet the dictator was by no means content with what he had achieved, although in the spring of 1937 he forwent the sort of spectacular foreign-policy coups he had engineered in the preceding two years. "April has come and no Hitler surprise this spring yet," a somewhat astonished William Shirer remarked.[3] But behind this seeming restraint, a transition had begun from a policy of dismantling the Treaty of Versailles to one of expanding Germany's territory. From the very beginning, Hitler had left no doubt in private that the evisceration of the Versailles Treaty was only a preliminary goal. The ultimate aim of all his plans remained the conquest of "living space" in eastern Europe. In early June 1936, after a long conversation with Hitler about foreign policy, Goebbels noted:

> The Führer sees conflict in the East coming. Japan will batter Russia. And this colossus will begin to wobble. Then our hour will be at hand. Then we will have to gain enough territory for the next one hundred years. Hopefully, we'll be ready then, and the Führer will still be alive.[4]

Of course, such thoughts were kept confidential. While remaining on the lookout for opportunities to advance his aggressive aims, Hitler depicted himself in Germany and abroad as a politician of peace. A characteristic manifestation of this was the agreement reached between the Third Reich and Austria on 11 July 1936. In the public part of the treaty, the German government acknowledged "the full sovereignty of the federal state of Austria and the basic principle of non-intervention in its internal affairs." In return, Vienna promised to orient its foreign policy around the fact that "Austria saw itself as a German state." In the secret part of the treaty, Austria agreed to declare a generous political amnesty for imprisoned Austrian Nazis and to give "political responsibility to representatives of the so-called 'national opposition.'"[5] Austrian Chancellor Kurt von Schuschnigg believed that these concessions would ensure his country's independence. Hitler saw the agreement as a lever to help Austrian National Socialists achieve power from within, since as he told a group of Austrian Nazis around this time, his other foreign-policy initiatives were such that he could not bear the "burden of Austria" at the time. "I need two more years to start pursing my policies," he instructed them. "Within that time, the party in Austria is to maintain its discipline."[6]

Yet only two weeks after the signing of the German–Austrian accord, Hitler made a decision that completely contradicted his rhetoric of peace. In February 1936, Spain's Frente Popular (Popular Front) had emerged as narrow winners in that country's national election. On 17 July, military officers in the Spanish protectorate of Morocco, led by General Francisco Franco, revolted against the legitimate democratic government. The putschists lacked the means of transport needed to bring rebel troops to the Spanish mainland, so Franco turned to Hitler and Mussolini for help. Two members of the NSDAP Foreign Organisation in Spanish Morocco, Adolf Langenheim and Johannes Bernhardt, offered their services as go-betweens. On the evening of 24 July they arrived in Berlin, accompanied by a Spanish officer. The Foreign Ministry coolly rejected these emissaries, but Rudolf Hess directed them to Hitler, who as always at this time of year was attending the Wagner Festival in Bayreuth.[7]

News of the Spanish military revolt had reached Bayreuth on 19 July. "Hopefully they'll blast the Reds to pieces," Goebbels commented.[8] In the days that followed the Nazi leadership tried to get an overview of the situation. Hitler even asked 16-year-old Wolfgang Wagner to bring him his school atlas so he could look up where Tetúan, the capital of Spanish Morocco, was located.[9] The reports gradually drifting in suggested that the military revolt was not doing particularly well and that the republicans controlled the majority of Spain. On 25 July, the German ambassador in Madrid warned that civil war was imminent and laid out the consequences of a republican victory. Domestically, he wrote, a republican triumph "would establish Marxist rule in Spain in the long term, with the danger of a Spanish soviet regime." In terms of foreign policy, Spain would be "ideologically and materially bound to the Franco-Russian bloc."[10] On the evening of 25 July, after taking in a performance of *Siegfried*, Hitler received Franco's emissaries for lengthy discussions, after which he agreed to give them the support they requested. As a first measure, the military rebels received twenty Junkers 52 military transport aircraft, as well as six fighter planes to protect them, and anti-aircraft artillery. This military hardware allowed Franco to fly Spain's African army of around 13,500 men, which he commanded, from Tetúan to Seville.

Hitler made this decision without consulting the Foreign Ministry and over the initial reservations of Göring and Ribbentrop, who both feared that it would lead to international complications. There has been much speculation about Hitler's motivations, and it seems as though they combined power politics and ideology. With a Popular Front government under the socialist Léon Blum in power in France since June 1936, Hitler saw his fears of a "global Bolshevik threat" confirmed. "If they truly succeed in creating a Communist Spain, it is only a matter of time, given the current situation in France, that

that country too will be Bolshevised, and then Germany can 'pack it in,'" he told Ribbentrop, explaining his decision. "Wedged in between the powerful Soviet bloc in the east and a strong Spanish–French Communist bloc in the west, we could hardly do anything if Moscow decided to move against Germany."[11] By contrast, if he succeeded in helping Franco to victory, the chances were good that the Third Reich would gain Spain as an ally and would be able to squeeze France from both sides. An even more important factor seems to have been Hitler's desire to use a joint operation in Spain to better relations with Fascist Italy. Two further considerations appealed to Göring. Deployment in Spain was the perfect test run for the new Luftwaffe. And as the man responsible for the Four Year Plan, Göring had a profound interest in gaining access to militarily important raw materials in Spain like iron ore and pyrite.[12]

To reduce the risk of foreign-policy complications, Hitler sought to maintain the pretence of non-interference throughout the entire conflict. Initially the German regime seems to have assumed that it could limit its engagement in terms of both time and resources. The day after Hitler's decision, Goebbels noted: "We're going to involve ourselves a little in Spain. Aeroplanes, etc . . . Invisibly. Who knows what it's good for?"[13] But over the following weeks, Nazi Germany expanded its military involvement. The Third Reich did not just provide weapons, munitions and other vital war materiel. In late October 1936, a Luftwaffe combat unit that would become the Condor Legion, consisting of 6,500 men under the command of Major General Hugo Sperrle, was deployed to Spain. They were responsible, among other things, for the air raids on the small Basque city of Guernica on 26 April 1937, which killed more than 1,600 people and wounded 900 others. The regime in Berlin denied any involvement, but the evidence left no doubt about German responsibility for the attack. Guernica became a symbol for the horrors of modern aerial warfare and the subject of Pablo Picasso's famous painting, which was exhibited for the first time in the Spanish pavilion at the 1937 Paris World Fair.[14]

Only a few weeks after the Guernica massacre, there was a further major incident. On 29 May 1937, Spanish republican aircraft attacked the German warship MS *Deutschland*, which was lying at anchor in Ibiza. Twenty-three seamen were killed and seventy wounded. The following evening Hitler summoned Werner von Blomberg, Konstantin von Neurath, Erich Raeder, Göring and Goebbels to the Chancellery. "With the Führer until 3 a.m.," noted Goebbels. "He paced up and down with long strides, gnashing his teeth in anger."[15] In the heat of the moment, Hitler wanted to bomb Valencia, but he changed his mind and ordered the warship MS *Admiral Scheer*, which was also deployed in the Mediterranean, to bombard the port of Almería. Twenty-one people died and many others were injured in the attack; numerous buildings were also destroyed. "The Führer is quite pleased with the result," Goebbels wrote on 1 June. Two days later, he noted: "The Führer is still suffused by Almería . . . The first demonstration of power in the new Reich. A warning signal for all enemies of the Reich."[16] The Hitler regime used the attack on the MS *Deutschland* to suspend Germany's participation in the military non-intervention negotiations taking place in London at the time, which had only been for show to begin with. On 17 June, the bodies of the casualties from the MS *Deutschland* were brought back to Wilhelmshaven and buried at a pompous ceremony with Hitler in attendance.[17]

The Spanish Civil War lasted longer than the Nazi leadership had anticipated. By the end of 1936, Spanish nationalist troops had conquered almost half of the country, but republican forces, bolstered by volunteers from throughout Europe, the International Brigades, put up fierce resistance and were repeatedly able to halt their enemies' advances. "In Spain, things aren't really moving forward," Goebbels noted in July 1937. "The Führer no longer believes in a fascist Spain. Franco is a general without any movement behind him."[18] But although Hitler also complained about Franco's military acumen, the protracted fighting in Spain was hardly unwelcome since it diverted the attention of the world's great powers towards the European periphery and expanded Germany's room to manoeuvre in the middle of the Continent.

German intervention in Spain further cemented ties with Italy, which had already become closer because of Hitler's support for Mussolini's Abyssinian adventure. "The German–Italian barometer is rising quickly," Germany's ambassador in Rome, Ulrich von Hassell, reported in late July 1936. "I feel as lucky as Polycrates."[19] At secret conferences, the two countries coordinated their military assistance for Franco. With a contingent of 80,000 men, Italy was far more heavily involved than Germany. "Cooperation between the two secret allies is very close, although hardly simple given the [need for] secrecy," Hassell wrote.[20] Italian–German diplomatic contact also increased, and Mussolini approved of the German–Austrian agreement. In September 1936, Reich Minister Hans Frank issued an invitation by Hitler to Il Duce and his son-in-law Count Ciano, the new Italian foreign minister, to visit Germany.

On 21 October, Ciano arrived with a huge delegation in Berlin. There, on the second day of his visit, he signed a protocol, prepared by diplomats, in which Germany and Italy promised to cooperate in their fight against communism, to recognise the Franco government and to coordinate their interests along the Danube.[21] Three days later, Hitler received Ciano at the Berghof. The Italian foreign minister told him in Mussolini's name that Il Duce "had always had the warmest sympathies for him," whereupon the flattered German dictator replied that Mussolini was for him "the first statesman in the world with whom no one could compare in the slightest." In a two-hour conversation in his first-floor office, Hitler advanced the idea of a German–Italian alliance that would either make Britain change its course or be capable of subduing it. In three, four or at the latest five years, Hitler explained, Germany would be ready for war. No conflicts of interest, he added, existed between his nation and Ciano's, since Italy's future rested on the Mediterranean, while Germany demanded a free hand in eastern Europe and around the Baltic Sea.[22] After the meeting, Hitler led his Italian visitors to the gigantic window in the Great Hall with its majestic view of the Austrian Alps. "From here," he said, "I have to view a part of my German homeland, Austria, through a telescope!"[23]

This was Hitler's way of telling the Italians that he had by no means given up his ambitions concerning the country of his birth, but that did nothing to dampen Mussolini's satisfaction with the first Italian state visit to Germany since the Dollfuss murder. On 1 November 1936, Il Duce celebrated the new German–Italian mutual understanding in a speech at the Piazza del Duomo in Milan. "The line connecting Berlin and Rome is not a partition," he declared. "On the contrary, it is an axis around which all European nations can rotate, if they possess the will for cooperation and peace."[24] That was the birth of the term "Axis" in the world's political vocabulary. But the will to peace was the last thing that connected the two new allies: they were united by their desire to unhinge the European status quo. As the two opposing blocs, the Western democracies and the dictatorial Axis powers, became more and more established, Mussolini would grow ever more dependent on Germany, which was economically and militarily far more powerful than Italy.

Hitler had posited an alliance with Italy as a desirable goal in both *Mein Kampf* and his "Second Book" of 1928. His other coveted ally was Britain, but after the Anglo-German Naval Agreement of 1935, German–British relations had stalled, although Hitler still made a number of overtures. In early February 1936, he granted former British Aviation Minister Lord Londonderry a two-hour audience in the Chancellery, in which he revealed that he wanted to "live in a relationship of close friendship with England." Hitler wooed: "How often did I say to myself as a common soldier in the world war, when I faced English troops, that it is insane to fight against these men who could be members of our own people." That should never be allowed to happen again, Hitler insisted, despite the differences between the two countries, for instance over the return of Germany's former colonies.[25] In a gushing letter thanking Hitler for his hospitality, Lady Londonderry wrote: "To say that I was deeply impressed is not adequate. I am amazed. You and Germany remind me of the book of Genesis in the Bible."[26]

Nonetheless, such expressions of Hitler admiration in aristocratic circles hardly reflected official British policy, which continued to pursue a balance of power in Europe and preferred to see the Third Reich bound in a system of collective treaties rather than bilateral Anglo-German agreements. In May 1936, the press attaché at the German embassy in London, Fritz Hesse, wrote that it would be incorrect "if people on the Continent assumed that Great Britain were willing to give up the policies of collective security and the League of Nations."[27] Still, Hitler clung to his preferred foreign-policy constellation. After Joachim von Ribbentrop became German ambassador in August 1936 following the death of Leopold von Hoesch, Hitler told him: "Ribbentrop, bring me an alliance with England!"[28] The problem was that there was hardly anyone less suitable to achieving this aim than the vain diplomatic amateur, who was soon nicknamed "von Brickendrop." In October 1936, having barely arrived in London, Ribbentrop made a most undiplomatic speech in which he laid his

cards on the table. "How about . . . just giving Germany a free hand
in the east?" he said. "Bolshevism is a global plague that must be
eradicated anyway, and Germany's eye is trained on Russia. In return
for a free hand in the east, Hitler would be prepared to conclude every
sort of alliance with England."[29] No British government would have
been willing to give Hitler a free hand in eastern Europe, which would
have essentially meant German hegemony over the entire Continent.

Hitler was already growing frustrated with the British by November
1936. "The Führer complains a lot about England," Goebbels noted.
"It keeps refusing and refusing. Its leadership has no instincts."[30] Hitler's
attitudes were fed by reports from Ribbentrop, who could scarcely
conceal his growing aversion to the British establishment. The anti-
British faction in the Reich leadership was further strengthened by
the crisis in the royal family that saw the Germanophile Edward VIII
abdicate the throne in December 1936 in order to be able to marry
the twice-divorced American Wallis Simpson. Hitler repeatedly stressed
that he thought this was a great loss. "I am sure that with him we
could have achieved permanent cordial relations with England," he
told Albert Speer. "With him everything would have been different."[31]
The hospitality with which Hitler received the Duke of Windsor and
his wife on the Obersalzberg in October 1937 expressed his special
regard for Edward. But Hitler also clearly did not understand the
British political system. He seems to have assumed that the king could
have changed the country's foreign policy by decree.

Although Hitler did not abandon the idea of an alliance with Great
Britain, he began looking around for alternatives. Here, Japan came
into view. On 25 November 1936 in Berlin, Nazi Germany signed an
anti-Communist agreement with the Asian power. Its published section
bound the signatories to "keep one another informed about the activities of the Communist International, consult about the necessary
measures for defence and carry them out in close cooperation." Third
parties were to be invited "to take defensive measures in the spirit of
this treaty and sign on to it." In a secret addendum, Germany and
Japan assured one another of neutrality in the case of an unprovoked
attack or threat by the Soviet Union. In addition, the two sides pledged
not to conclude political agreements with Moscow "in contradiction
of the spirit of this pact without the other's permission."[32] Ribbentrop,
in particular, had pushed for the anti-Communist treaty and had

deliberately gone over the heads of the Foreign Ministry, which traditionally favoured good relations with China.[33] In late October 1936, he secured Hitler's agreement for the pact. Goebbels, who was spending time on the Obersalzberg, noted: "He just signed a treaty with Japan. Alliance against Bolshevism. When it's published in three weeks, it will change the entire situation. The seeds we planted are starting to grow."[34] But Goebbels overestimated the impact of the arrangement. Berlin and Tokyo never cooperated closely with one another. The new connection was, in the words of the historian Theo Sommer, "a hesitant alliance—an international peck on the cheek between two very unequal brothers who felt hardly any need to act in solidarity with one another."[35]

There was a deceptive calm over Europe for the whole of 1937. Hitler used the respite to decide upon his next foreign-policy moves. Goebbels's diaries reveal how, parallel to the intensification of anti-Semitic measures at home, Hitler gradually became more radical in trying to realise his ambitions abroad. In late January 1937, while delivering a broad summary of his foreign policy over lunch in the Chancellery, Hitler expressed his hope that Germany would have "six years yet" before the decisive battle. But he added that he would not fail "to seize an auspicious chance should it happen to arise."[36] One month later, he reiterated that he expected "a major world conflict in five to six years," but he now spoke more universally of reversing the relations of power that had dominated Europe since the end of the Thirty Years War in 1648. "In fifteen years, he will have destroyed the Peace of Westphalia," Goebbels noted. "He's developing fantastic prospects for the future. Germany will either triumph in the coming battle or cease to exist." Victory or death—that had been the slogan of the Wilhelmine elites in Germany in the First World War, and the former private who had become the most powerful man in Europe still subscribed to this all-or-nothing perspective. For that, Goebbels admired him blindly: "As always, his foresight is enormous and brilliant. He sees history with the prophetic vision of an oracle."[37]

As we have seen, Hitler's foreign ambitions were inseparably connected to the monumental construction projects in Berlin that began to take shape in the spring of 1937 when Speer was made general building inspector of the Reich capital. In mid-March, while fawning

with Goebbels over his plans for the future world capital "Germania,"
he named the first two objects of his expansionist desires. "He talked
of Austria and Czechoslovakia," the propaganda minister noted. "We
need both to round off our territory. And some day we'll get them."[38]
Hitler did not specify when he intended to swallow up these two
countries, but neither did he conceal the fact that, given Germany's
accelerated rearmament, the time would come sooner rather than
later. "The Führer is once again unfolding the entire miracle of
rearmament," Goebbels wrote on 10 April. "We're now almost totally
secure in the west . . . He has achieved a miracle thanks to a bold
gambit. The military leaders back then did not understand this at all.
For that reason the miracle is all the greater."[39] In early August 1937,
after Japan declared war on China, Hitler unambiguously came out
in favour of his partner in the anti-Communist pact. "China is militarily
inadequate," Goebbels quoted Hitler proclaiming. "They'll take a
beating from Japan. That's good because Japan will keep our backs
free against Moscow." According to Goebbels's diaries, Hitler then
immediately proceeded to speak of his own ambitions:

> Some day, the Führer will make *tabula rasa* in Austria . . . He'll throw
> everything into it. This state is not a real state at all. Its people belong
> to us, and it will come to us . . . And the land of Czechs is no state
> either. Some day it will be overrun as well.[40]

Over the course of 1937, while Hitler's next foreign-policy aims gradually crystallised, he gave up on his idea of an international political
deal with Britain. Lord Philip Lothian, Lloyd George's former private
secretary and the future British ambassador to the United States, was
under no illusions about the new atmosphere in Berlin when he visited
the city in early May. Hitler and Göring, he reported, had complained
that Britain was the country that ultimately prevented Germany from
achieving its rightful position in the world and asked why Britain was
pursuing an "anti-German" rather than a "British" foreign policy.[41] In
Hitler's egocentric view such "British" foreign policy obviously had to
adjust itself to German ideas about the distribution of global power.
In late May, Neville Chamberlain took over the leadership of the government from fellow Conservative Stanley Baldwin, but that did little to
raise spirits in Berlin. The new British ambassador, Nevile Henderson,

was considered more amenable to Germany than his predecessor, Eric Phipps,[42] but that did not seem to promise change in Great Britain's basic attitude towards Germany. Chamberlain's policy of appeasement was aimed at gaining time to close the armaments gap with the Third Reich. Chamberlain wanted to keep the peace in Europe for as long as possible by pacifying the German dictator with concessions and keeping his larger expansionist aims in check. Never for a moment did the British prime minister consider giving Hitler a free hand in eastern Europe.[43] But he would fool himself about Hitler's willingness to come to any sensible compromise and to abide by agreements.

By early June 1937, Hitler may still have declared that "everything's up in the air in London," but in reality he had given up on his fantasy of an Anglo-German alliance. Over lunch at the Chancellery, he mocked Britain's global status. "He considers it very weakened," Goebbels wrote. "The empire is stagnating, if indeed it is not already in decline." As of the summer of 1937, Hitler increasingly began to put his faith in the Berlin–Rome axis. "He's now counting on Mussolini," a sceptical Goebbels noted. "Perhaps too much. We should not completely forget England."[44] The Italian dictator requited German advances in kind. In the early days of June, during a visit by German Minister of War von Blomberg, Il Duce announced that he wanted to pay a state visit to Germany that autumn,[45] and on 4 September, the press office of the German Foreign Ministry announced that the trip was officially planned. "The upcoming visit by Mussolini is creating a massive stir throughout the entire world," wrote Goebbels, who would be occupied by it for the next two weeks. "And rightly so! This is an event of extensive significance."[46]

At 10 a.m. on 25 September, Mussolini's personal train arrived at Munich's central station. He was received by Hitler personally and a large entourage in uniform, in the midst of whom Goebbels felt "entirely naked."[47] The host warmly shook both of his visitor's hands and accompanied him to the Prinz Carl Palais, where Il Duce was staying. A little later, Mussolini was invited to Hitler's private apartment for an hourlong chat. The interpreter Paul Schmidt—rendered superfluous because the Italian leader insisted, as he had previously in Venice, on speaking German—had the opportunity to observe and compare the two dictators. "Hitler sat at the table slightly slumped," Schmidt recalled:

When he got more animated, the lock of hair so popular among caricaturists would fall down from his rather large forehead in front of his
face, which gave him something disorderly and bohemian . . . Across
from him, Mussolini made a totally different impression. Sitting bolt
upright, his body stiff and rocking back and forth slightly at the hips
whenever he spoke, the man with the head of Caesar seemed the paradigm of Ancient Rome, with a prominent forehead, a broad mouth and
a broad square chin protruding in a slightly cramped way . . . In Munich,
too, I found myself impressed by Mussolini's concise, crystal-clear formulations of his thoughts. He never said a word too many, and everything
that came out of his mouth could have been immediately published.
The difference in how the two men laughed was also interesting. Hitler's
laughter always had an undertone of mockery and sarcasm, betraying
traces of past disappointment and suppressed ambition. By contrast,
Mussolini was able to laugh his head off without constraint. It was a
liberating laugh demonstrating that the man had a sense of humour.[48]

Mussolini named Hitler "an honourary corporal in the Fascist militia,"
and that afternoon Hitler repaid the favour by awarding Il Duce the
Grand Cross of the Order of the German Eagle and the Golden Party
Badge. He also insisted on giving Mussolini a personal tour of the
exhibition in the House of German Art.[49] But Hitler's primary agenda
was to impress upon his Italian visitor the military strength his regime
had achieved. That evening the two men boarded their personal trains
to travel to a series of Wehrmacht manoeuvres taking place in
Mecklenburg in northern Germany. The following day, they visited the
Krupp factories. "A triumphal ride without compare through Essen,"
Goebbels noted. "Hundreds of thousands turned out, Mussolini
completely bowled over. Celebration and enthusiasm like never before."[50]
But that was overshadowed by the reception that the people of
Berlin gave Mussolini on the afternoon of 27 September. Even the
two men's entry into the Reich capital was specially staged. Shortly
before reaching the outlying district of Spandau, Hitler's train appeared
next to Mussolini's. The two then travelled parallel to one another
until just before the station on Heerstrasse, when Hitler's train abruptly
accelerated so that he reached the station first and was able to greet
his fellow dictator on the platform. "Just like in the fairy tale of the
hedgehog and hare," commented Schmidt.[51] The theatre set designer

Benno von Arent had transformed key points in the capital's city centre—the Brandenburg Gate, Pariser Platz and Wilhelmstrasse—into stage spectacles replete with "pylons, fasces, giant eagles, swastikas, flagpoles, and large numbers of nested or artfully knotted flags in Italian and German colours."[52] That evening Hitler hosted a gala dinner in Mussolini's honour at the Chancellery. In his toast, he praised Il Duce as "the brilliant creator of Fascist Italy, the founder of a new empire." Mussolini returned the compliment by calling Hitler "the warrior who restored to the German people the consciousness of their own greatness."[53]

On 28 September, Mussolini visited the Zeughaus Military History Museum in Berlin and Friedrich the Great's grave and the Garrison Church in Potsdam, before dining with Göring at his estate in Schorfheide. But the high point of his visit was an evening rally at the Olympic Stadium and the Maifeld parade grounds, which drew hundreds of thousands of Berliners. After Goebbels's introduction, Hitler took to the microphone to praise all the permanent qualities that Fascist Italy and Nazi Germany shared. Mussolini gave his response in German, but his heavy accent made him difficult to understand.[54] Moreover, during his speech, a serious thunderstorm opened up and deluged the stadium. For André François-Poncet, it was "a harbinger of the torrents of blood that would soon flood Europe."[55] But the French ambassador's judgement was informed by hindsight. At the time ordinary Berliners saw the situation less dramatically, cracking jokes that played on the similarities between the word Duce and *Dusche*, the German word for shower.[56]

On the morning of 29 September, the last day of Mussolini's visit, Hitler had ordered a parade of all branches of the Wehrmacht. Mussolini was so taken with the soldiers' goose-stepping that he introduced it to the Italian army as the *passo romano*.[57] In the afternoon, Hitler accompanied his departing guest to the Lehrter Bahnhof train station. "Everything was full of gravity and melancholy," Goebbels wrote melodramatically. "These two great men belong at one another's side. Then the train pulled out of the station. Mussolini waved for a long time."[58] That evening, according to Winifred Wagner, Hitler was "very happy about how the entire visit had gone."[59] When Hans Frank, who had accompanied Mussolini through Germany, phoned to say that Il Duce had crossed the border near Kiefersfelden, Hitler acted relieved and, contrary to his usual teetotalling ways, drank a glass of sparkling wine to celebrate "everything having come off so marvellously."[60] Mussolini too was pleased with his visit and told his wife: "The organisation is fantastic, and the German people have an unusually great character. With these trump cards, Hitler can dare to do anything."[61]

Nonetheless, the concrete results of the visit were meagre. Hitler and Mussolini hardly had any opportunity for serious talks during their five days together, and the Italian dictator had responded evasively when pressed on the Austria issue.[62] The final outcome was little more than a promise to cooperate more closely in the future. On 6 November 1937, Italy joined the anti-Communist pact, and a few weeks later it quit the League of Nations. What was more important was that, in contrast to their meeting in Venice in 1934, Hitler and Mussolini had grown closer. "Thank God, this time they also got along personally," Goebbels noted.[63] And despite numerous disappointments to come, the Führer continued to feel an atypical affection for Il Duce in later years. In his later monologues in his military headquarters, Hitler called Mussolini a "man of outstanding proportions, a historic phenomenon," and expressed his admiration for "everything he's achieved in Italy." On one occasion Hitler, who rarely showed his emotions, confessed: "This mighty figure—I really do like him personally!"[64]

Even during his rise to power, Hitler had repeatedly articulated his fear that he might die young, and the impatience with which he pursued his goals had its roots in this anxiety. In the autumn of 1937, as he was shifting his foreign policy from undermining the Treaty of Versailles to expansionism, he became obsessed with the idea that he had no time to lose. In late October, in a secret meeting with Nazi Party propaganda directors, Hitler was quoted as saying that "as best as anyone could tell, he did not have long to live since people in his family never reached old age." It was thus necessary "to take care of the problems (living space!) that need to be resolved as quickly as possible so that it happens within my lifetime." Hitler combined this statement with a reference to the uniqueness of his charismatic authority. Only he was capable of solving these problems, he said: "Later generations won't be able to."[65]

The anxiety plaguing Hitler now led him to share the foreign-policy ideas he had developed in constant back and forth with Goebbels with the regime's military and political leadership as well. At 4:15 p.m. on the afternoon of 5 November 1937, he convened a conference in the Chancellery that included Werner von Blomberg, the commanders of the three branches of the armed forces, Werner von Fritsch, Erich Raeder and Hermann Göring, Foreign Minister Konstantin von Neurath and his Wehrmacht assistant Friedrich Hossbach, who drew up the only surviving minutes of the meeting. It would be a key document at the Nuremberg Trials to prove that the primary defendants had conspired to destroy peace in Europe.[66] What had prompted the conference was a conflict between the army, the navy and the air force for scarce raw materials. Raeder in particular accused Göring of exploiting his position as the head of the Four Year Plan to promote the expansion of the Luftwaffe at the cost of the German navy. In conjunction with Raeder, Blomberg decided to end the long-simmering conflict by enlisting Hitler to make a decision.[67]

But as always when there were rivalries between departments and competition for preferment among his paladins, Hitler avoided making decisions. Instead, he used the opportunity to hold a more-than-two-hour monologue "informing the gentlemen in attendance about the developmental possibilities and necessities of our foreign-policy situation." Hitler explicitly ordered that his statements be regarded as "his will and testament in case he should pass away."[68] He then reiterated what he had told his military leadership all the way back on 3 February 1933 about Germany's future. The 85 million Germans with their "self-contained racial core," he said, "had a right to a much larger living space." Resolving this situation was the central task of German foreign policy. After he had discarded various alternatives for territorial expansion, Hitler had decided on the following to ensure that the German people could feed itself: "The necessary space for this will have to be found in Europe and not, as in liberal, capitalist views, by exploiting colonies . . . Areas containing lots of raw materials were better located in direct proximity to the Reich and not overseas." The dictator left his listeners in no doubt that "every territorial gain will entail breaking others' resistance and incurring risks."

Hitler's remarks contained nothing new for his military leaders in terms of the necessity of "gaining a larger living space," although they probably had not fully realised how serious Hitler was. But the heads of the armed forces certainly pricked up their ears during the second part of Hitler's monologue when he laid out how he saw the European balance of power in the autumn of 1937. For the first time, Hitler spoke of Germany confronting "its two worst enemies, England and France, which regarded a German colossus in Central Europe as a thorn in their sides." Here Hitler was drawing the consequences from his failed efforts to reach an understanding with Great Britain. As he had in his private conversations with Goebbels, Hitler spoke less than respectfully about his potential enemies. The British empire, he said, was rotting away and "impossible to maintain in the long run in terms of power politics." France, too, had been weakened by "domestic political difficulties." Nonetheless, he acknowledged that the "path of violence" he pondered going down was "never without risk." Here he invoked the wars of Friedrich the Great and those of Bismarck, which had unified Germany. They, too, Hitler claimed, had been an "unprecedented risk."

As his choice of historical role models shows, Hitler was prepared to go all out. The final section of his monologue was devoted to the questions of when and how. The dictator sketched out three scenarios. The latest possible time for Germany to launch an attack was between 1943 and 1945 (case 1). After that, Hitler said, "things would have changed to our disadvantage" since the other powers would have closed the gap in military strength with Germany. As an additional argument, Hitler referred to "the fact that the movement and its leader are growing older," again playing on his fears that he might die young. Should he still be alive, it was "his irrevocable will that the question of German living space be solved by 1943 to 1945 at the latest." But it might become necessary to act earlier if the social tensions within France "grew into a domestic crisis" (case 2), or if France should become embroiled in a war with another country so that "it could not take on Germany" at the same time (case 3). In all three cases, the initial goal would be to "subjugate the Czechs and Austria and to head off threats of a potential attack against Germany's flanks." The dictator had shown his hand, specifying the most immediate targets for German expansion, which he had mulled over all that spring. To forestall possible objections from his military commanders, he told them that Britain and France had "most probably already written off the Czechs and got used to the idea . . . that Germany would one day settle this issue." And if Britain did not participate in a war against Germany, France would not either.

Hitler's views were driven by military politics as much as by strategy. Amalgamating Czechoslovakia and Austria would free up fighting forces "for others purposes" in the event of war and allow the Reich to raise twelve additional divisions. With reference to Germany's involvement in the Spanish Civil War, Hitler declared that the Reich had no interest in a rapid victory by Franco. For Germany, it would be better if the conflict dragged on and ratcheted up tensions in the Mediterranean, which could potentially lead to war between Italy and France. If this scenario (case 3) materialised, as Hitler thought it might in the course of 1938, Germany would have to seize the chance "to take care of the Czech and Austrian question." As he had in his previous "weekend coups," Hitler counted on the element of surprise. A German attack against Czechoslovakia, he said, would have to be "quick as lightning."

A two-hour discussion followed, which Hossbach only recorded cursorily in his transcript. The military leaders expressed concerns. They had nothing against an *Anschluss* of Austria and an annexation of Czechoslovakia. In typical Wilhelmine fashion, they saw German hegemony in Central Europe as a worthwhile goal, even if they did not share Hitler's racist belief in the need for "living space." But they worried that Hitler's impatience would spark new European hostilities and inevitably lead to a second world war. Fritsch and Blomberg were of one mind that "England and France must not emerge as our enemies." Even in the event of a Franco-Italian war, Fritsch pointed out, France would still be capable of concentrating large numbers of forces on Germany's western front. Blomberg drew attention to the fact that the West Wall, Germany's series of western fortifications, was far from complete and that Czech fortifications would hinder German advances "in the extreme." Neurath objected that "a Franco-Italian conflict was by no means as imminent as the Führer seemed to assume."

Hossbach's report does not say how Hitler reacted to these objections, but apparently he merely reassured his audience "that he was convinced England would not take part in any war and did not believe that France would commence hostilities." It was exactly this optimistic prognosis that led to the criticism of the military leaders. Yet despite his scepticism, Blomberg was in no way prepared to oppose Hitler's wishes. On the contrary, in early December he issued the "First Supplement to the Order on Unified Preparation for War of the

Wehrmacht of 24 June 1937," which reflected the ideas Hitler had put forward the previous month. It read: "If Germany has attained full military readiness in all areas, the military preconditions will have been laid to wage an offensive war against Czechoslovakia and to bring the solution of the German space problem to a successful conclusion, even if one or another of the major powers attacks us."[69] Blomberg was, of course, mistaken if he truly believed that the annexation of Czechoslovakia would resolve "Germany's space problem" as Hitler saw it. For Hitler, such an annexation was only the first stage in a war for living space encompassing all of eastern Europe.

Despite Blomberg's compliance, Hitler must have sensed that parts of the Wehrmacht leadership still had serious reservations about his risky strategy. Fritsch's first reaction to Hitler's revelation was to cancel a multi-week holiday in Egypt that he had planned for some time, but Hitler succeeded in reassuring him "that the chance of conflict cannot be regarded as that imminent." The relationship between the Führer and the commander of the army had by no means been irreparably ruptured, as some historians have contended,[70] but it had noticeably cooled. Moreover, Hitler seems to have been particularly disappointed by Neurath's attitude, which reminded him of the reservations German diplomats had expressed ahead of the remilitarisation of the Rhineland in March 1936. Neurath would testify before the Nuremberg War Crimes Tribunal that in mid-January 1938 he had warned Hitler that "his policies would necessarily lead to a world war" and "that many of his plans could be realised, albeit more slowly, through peaceful means." But the dictator, Neurath testified, had simply replied that he was "running out of time."[71] Whatever the truth may have been, Hitler must have known that his plans would not attract the sort of unconditional support from military leaders and top diplomats to which he believed himself entitled. What could be more logical, especially after he had got rid of Hjalmar Schacht, than to grind down the last remaining pillars of his conservative coalition partners? And chance now gave Hitler the opportunity for a major clear-out among the upper echelons of both the military and the Foreign Ministry.

The beginning was a marital scandal. In September 1937, while strolling through Berlin's Tiergarten park, War Minister von Blomberg met a woman thirty-five years his junior named Margarethe Gruhn. The

60-year-old general field marshal, who had been widowed eight years previously, immediately fell in love, but Gruhn came from lowly circumstances, and Blomberg needed Hitler's permission to marry her. On the occasion of the state funeral for Erich Ludendorff on 22 December 1937 in Munich, the field marshal asked for the Führer's approval, introducing his fiancée as a "stenographer" and a "girl of the people." Hitler and Göring agreed to act as witnesses at the wedding—in the interest, they later claimed, of combating class conflicts and social prejudice.[72] The civil marriage ceremony took place on 12 January 1938 with only Hitler, Göring, Blomberg's five children from his first marriage and the mother of the bride in attendance. Not even Fritsch and Raeder were invited. The newly-weds embarked on their honeymoon immediately after the ceremony. The newspapers ran a brief announcement: "On Wednesday 12 January, Reich Minister of War General Field Marshal von Blomberg wed Fräulein Gruhn. The Führer and Colonel General Göring served as witnesses."[73]

But soon after the wedding, rumours began to surface about the young spouse's former life. Prostitutes reportedly told each other: "It's nice that one of us can rise in the world like this." In fact, Gruhn had come under the scrutiny of Berlin's vice squad several years previously. Around Christmas 1931, she had posed for pornographic photos and had been officially registered as a prostitute the following year. In December 1934, one of her customers had reported her to the police for allegedly stealing his gold watch. Berlin Police President Wolf-Heinrich von Helldorff got wind of these extremely embarrassing stories, and on 21 January 1938, he presented General Wilhelm Keitel, the head of the Wehrmacht office in the War Ministry, with the prostitute registration card and a mugshot of Margarethe Gruhn. Because Keitel had not met Blomberg's wife, he sent Helldorff to Göring, who confirmed the woman's identity. "This is a catastrophe," Göring allegedly said.[74]

On the evening of 24 January, when Hitler returned to Berlin from a three-day visit in Munich, Göring was waiting for him at the entrance to the Chancellery. The two immediately withdrew to Hitler's private quarters, where Göring showed the Führer Gruhn's file, including the pornographic photos. Hitler was shocked—not because the obscene images offended his prudishness,[75] but because he immediately realised that the scandal would reflect badly on him if it became public. As he had been a witness at the marriage, he now had good reason to fear that he would become the object of mockery inside and outside Germany. For two days, Hitler completely retreated from the public eye, conducting all meetings in his private quarters and not even appearing at mealtimes as usual. "His behaviour gave the Chancellery an uncanny atmosphere," recalled his assistant Below. "In the general absence of any information, everyone there felt edgy, worried and afraid."[76]

All the members of Hitler's entourage who saw him during this time confirmed that he was not acting: the scandal had shaken him to the core. In addition to worrying about a loss of prestige, he felt disappointed in his minister of war, whom he had trusted deeply. His personal assistant Fritz Wiedemann recalled: "He paced up and down in his room, a broken man, his hands behind his back, shaking his head and muttering: 'If a German field marshal can marry a whore then anything is possible in this world.'"[77] Goebbels, who arrived at the Chancellery at noon on 25 January, tried in vain to lift Hitler's spirits. "A tense mood," the propaganda minister noted. "Unpleasant situation with Blomberg. Still not cleared up. The Führer is very sombre and sad."[78] That morning, Hitler had held a private discussion with Friedrich Hossbach about the affair. Blomberg had put him in a "most difficult position," Hitler said, by concealing his wife's true past. As much as he regretted "having to lose such a loyal colleague," he concluded, Blomberg's position had become "untenable."[79]

Hitler ordered Göring to confront Blomberg with Gruhn's file in the War Ministry and to get him to declare the wedding null and void. It was the only way, Hitler said, to avert a scandal. But to Göring's and Hitler's astonishment, Blomberg rejected this suggestion. His love for his wife knew no bounds, he told Keitel. His decision was likely made easier by the fact that Göring had already informed him that he could not stay on in his post regardless of whether he separated from his wife or not. On the morning of 27 January, Hitler received the field marshal, who appeared in civilian clothing, for one final audience. He and his wife immediately travelled abroad so that his dismissal would attract as little notice as possible. Hitler gave him 50,000 marks' worth of foreign currency to underwrite the extended trip.[80]

But the troubled times were not over. Hot on the heels of the Blomberg affair followed an even more serious incident in which Werner von

Fritsch was accused of being a homosexual. Later, on the evening of his forty-ninth birthday in April 1938, Hitler would tell his assistant Gerhard Engel, "The thing with Fritsch would have never got rolling, if the minister of war had not played a dirty trick on him," adding that his trust in his generals had suffered a "major blow."[81] Historians long thought that Fritsch fell victim to a deliberate intrigue ordered by Hitler, but it appears that Hitler was telling the truth as far as he knew it to Engel.[82] Just as the Nazi leader had been surprised by the truth about Blomberg's wife, he does not seem to have harboured any intention of getting rid of the other main sceptic from the November meeting. However, with characteristic cunning, he did take the bull by the horns and turn an unpleasant surprise to his own advantage. André François-Poncet later remarked that the Blomberg–Fritsch double scandal was a fascinating case study "for anyone interested in the role that imponderables play in history."[83]

On the evening of 24 January, Hitler was still in shock at Göring's information about Blomberg's wife and pondering how to react when he suddenly recalled an incident from 1936. That summer, Heinrich Himmler had shown him a police file casting suspicion upon Fritsch of having had sex with a rent boy named Otto Schmidt, who had subsequently tried to blackmail him. At the time an outraged Hitler had refused to open an investigation and ordered the file to be destroyed. But now, already made mistrustful by Blomberg's behaviour, Hitler began to worry that there might have been something to the story. In any case, he wanted to be certain before he promoted Fritsch, the highest-ranking officer in the army, to the post of war minister as Blomberg's successor, so he ordered the Gestapo to reconstruct the police file. That did not prove very difficult since Reinhard Heydrich, defying Hitler's original order, had kept the most important parts of the file in a safe. The police report about Fritsch was on Hitler's desk the following evening.[84]

On the morning of 25 January, after informing him of the Blomberg affair and swearing him to secrecy, Hitler told Hossbach about the accusations against Fritsch. Hossbach recalled Hitler saying: "The colonel general will have to go since he is compromised by his homosexuality. He [Hitler] had the evidence in his hands and had possessed it for some years."[85] Hossbach was horrified. His only explanation for the situation was that Hitler was sick of the army commander and wanted an excuse to get rid of him. Convinced of Fritsch's innocence, he asked for permission to question the colonel general himself. Hitler categorically refused. Nonetheless, late the following evening, Hossbach drove to Fritsch's official apartment at Bendlerstrasse 25 and acquainted him with the accusations. "A filthy, rotten lie" was Fritsch's response.[86] The following morning, Hossbach informed Hitler about his act of disobedience. As far as he could tell, the Führer seemed to take the news "completely calmly." Indeed, Hossbach described him as being relieved when he heard his account of how the army commander had reacted. "If that's so, everything would be fine, and Fritsch could become minister," Hitler apparently said.[87]

But here Hitler proved to be a master actor yet again. In reality, he was seething at his underling's disobedience, and it must have taken all of his self-control to conceal his true feelings. The dictator was anything but relieved. On the contrary, the mood in the Chancellery on 26 January was one of impending catastrophe. "The worst crisis of the regime since the Röhm affair," Goebbels noted. "I'm completely shattered. The Führer looks like a corpse. I feel most sorry for him. I find Blomberg's behaviour incomprehensible . . . And now Fritsch is a Paragraph 175 case. He gave me his word of honour that it's not true. But who can believe it?"[88]

Both Hossbach and Fritsch believed that the whole affair was a sinister intrigue perpetrated by the Wehrmacht leadership. They doubted that the witness in question even existed and demanded that Fritsch be allowed to confront him. After some hesitation, Hitler agreed. When Fritsch, dressed in civilian clothing to avoid attracting attention, arrived that night at the Chancellery, Hossbach greeted him with the news that the witness was already there. The day before, four Gestapo officials had travelled to the Börgermoor penal camp in north-western Germany to collect the convicted blackmailer Otto Schmidt and take him to Berlin. "I want to see the swine!" Fritsch exclaimed and stormed up to the first-floor library where he was to meet with Hitler and Göring.[89]

The dictator got straight to the point, saying that he wanted to hear the truth. If Fritsch admitted to having a homosexual relationship, he would be sent on a long holiday like Blomberg, and that would be the end of it. The colonel general once again protested his innocence— but he made a crucial mistake. Ever since Hossbach had told him about the accusations levelled against him, he had racked his brains about where they might have come from. He recalled that in 1933 and 1934, as part of the Winter Relief campaign, he had treated an unemployed Hitler Youth to lunch, which they had regularly taken together in his private apartment. As Fritsch related this story at length to Hitler, it truly awakened the Führer's mistrust. Fritsch was allowed to read his police file, and while he was doing so, Schmidt was brought into the room, where he exclaimed, "Yes, he's the one!" Fritsch protested that he had never seen Schmidt in his life, giving Hitler his word of honour. But astonishingly the German head of state chose to believe a small-time criminal over the highest-ranking German military officer. Fritsch was ordered to submit to Gestapo interrogation the following day. He left the Chancellery, outraged at how he had been treated. That very evening he sent Hitler a letter stating: "Until the restoration of my honour, which has been besmirched, it is impossible for me to carry out any of my official duties."[90]

Fritsch was interrogated in the Gestapo headquarters in Berlin on the morning of 27 January, and he was forced to confront the witness against him for a second time. Despite intensive cross-examination, Schmidt stuck to his story, while the colonel general asserted his innocence with equal vigour. Ultimately it was one man's word against the other's. "Who knows what's right and what's wrong here?" noted Goebbels. "In any case, the situation is impossible. The investigations will continue. But it looks as though Fritsch will have to go."[91] Hitler, who, Goebbels found, had grown "haggard and grey," cancelled both his traditional speech to the Reichstag on 30 January and a planned cabinet meeting. On 28 January, Hossbach was brusquely dismissed. Hitler could not forgive him for disobeying orders.[92]

Since the Gestapo investigations had failed to establish any clarity, Hitler charged Justice Minister Gürtner with preparing a judicial report on the Fritsch case. "A devilish situation," Goebbels opined, adding that however it ended, the damage had been done.[93] By the end of January, the report, which had been prepared by Gürtner's personal adviser, Senior Governmental Counsel Hans von Dohnanyi, was ready. It was devastating for Fritsch since it concluded that the accusations raised against him "had not yet been conclusively refuted." The superficially harmless story involving the Hitler Youth was regarded as an "incriminating moment." On the other hand, the report also stated that the "decision over guilty or innocent would remain a matter for a judge's verdict." Gürtner did succeed in getting a regular trial scheduled in front of the Reich War Court.[94] For his part, Hitler was now completely convinced of Fritsch's guilt. "Fritsch has been unmasked as a 175er," Goebbels quoted him saying on 31 January. "While the incident may lie three years in the past, the Führer believes that it did happen. Fritsch denies everything, but that's what these people always do. He too will have to go."[95] On 3 February, Fritsch was ordered to submit his immediate resignation. After everything the army commander had gone through with Hitler in the past few days, Fritsch was glad to comply. "It is impossible for me to work with this man," he wrote.[96]

Who would succeed Blomberg and Fritsch? Although he had already seized a plethora of offices and responsibilities, Göring would have liked to get his hands on the War Ministry, but Hitler gruffly rejected the idea. "He does not even know a thing about the Luftwaffe," Hitler told Fritz Wiedemann. "Even I have a better understanding of it!"[97] In his final audience on 27 January, when asked to suggest someone to replace him, Blomberg spontaneously broached the idea of Hitler taking command of the Wehrmacht personally. That afternoon, Goebbels suggested the same, even going a step further than the general field marshal by proposing that the War Ministry should be disbanded in favour of separate army and navy ministries. "That would be the most logical solution," Goebbels argued.[98] Hitler immediately adopted the idea and began discussions with Keitel on 27 January about the Wehrmacht's future organisational structure.

As Goebbels put it, the most delicate question raised by the Blomberg–Fritsch affair was: "How to tell the people?"[99] Aside from a couple of rumours, nothing about what had happened had become public, and not even the nosiest foreign correspondents had got wind of the scandals. In these critical days, Hitler appeared like anything but an energetic, decisive Führer. "From everything I saw and heard, I concluded that Hitler did not know what to do," Below recalled. "He seemed undecided and summoned one adviser after the next to discuss the situation."[100] This is another indication that there had been no predetermined plan to topple the military leaders. Goebbels was growing impatient with Hitler's hesitation: "Things can't go on like this. Something has to happen. The Führer says he'll resolve the issue this week. It's high time. It's wearing us all out."[101]

On 31 January, after much deliberation, Hitler finally reached a decision. The departures of Blomberg and Fritsch should be presented as part of a comprehensive change of personnel at the top of the Wehrmacht and the Foreign Ministry so as to prevent any speculation about the real background of their two cases. "In order to make the whole thing opaque, there's to be a general reshuffle," Goebbels noted after a two-hour discussion with the dictator in his private office in the Chancellery. This solution had two advantages for Hitler. It allowed him to reshape the leadership of both the Wehrmacht and the Foreign Ministry according to his own wishes, and it gave him a plausible explanation for the departure of Germany's two highest-ranking military leaders. "I hope the real reasons for the dismissals get completely lost amidst the major personnel reshuffle," Goebbels commented.[102] It took Hitler a few days to think through all of his new appointments and clear up the details in discussions with his advisers. On the evening of 4 February, German radio listeners were advised to keep their ears to their wireless sets: an important announcement was imminent. At 11 p.m., a long communiqué from the Reich government announcing the changes in leadership was read out. Most Germans, however, learned of the news the next day in the papers, many of which published special editions. The central message was: "The most intense concentration of all power in the hands of the Führer."[103]

Hitler now personally became commander-in-chief of the Wehrmacht. The War Ministry was dissolved, replaced by the Wehrmacht Supreme Command with Wilhelm Keitel at its head as a Reich minister subordinate only to the Führer. Artillery General Walther von Brauchitsch was named Fritsch's successor as supreme commander of the army. Göring, whose own ambitions had been disappointed, was compensated with the title of general field marshal. Twelve mostly older generals were sent into retirement, while numerous commanders were transferred. At the Foreign Ministry, Neurath had to give way to Ribbentrop. Hitler promoted the latter against the advice of Goebbels, who considered Ribbentrop a "zero" and claimed to have said as much openly to the Führer.[104] In compensation, Neurath was made director of a "privy cabinet council," a newly created body that was supposed to advise Hitler but that in fact never met. Several of Germany's major ambassadorships were also reallocated. Ulrich von Hassell, Herbert von Dirksen and Franz von

Papen were recalled from Rome, Tokyo and Vienna respectively. Several weeks after being made the director of the political division, Ernst von Weizsäcker succeeded Neurath's son-in-law Hans Georg von Mackensen, who was made German ambassador to Italy, in the post of state secretary in the Foreign Ministry. Finally, Walther Funk was officially named economics minister, replacing Hjalmar Schacht, who had resigned in November 1937.[105]

The Nazi leadership's strategy of obfuscation worked. "The foreign press is full of wild speculations," Goebbels registered. "But they're completely in the dark concerning the bigger picture. Hopefully, things will stay that way. In any case, we seem to have hit our mark."[106] In the early afternoon of 5 February, Hitler summoned his generals to explain his decisions. He summarised the two scandals, read significant excerpts from the police files and also cited the devastating report by the Justice Ministry. The military leaders were stunned by the revelations, and none of them raised any objections to the new commander-in-chief.[107] Around 8 p.m., the cabinet convened for what would be its final meeting ever. Hitler spoke for an hour, his voice, as Goebbels described it, "sometimes choked with tears." As was so often the case, it is difficult to tell whether his emotion was genuine. He paid tribute to Blomberg and Fritsch's achievements in building up the Wehrmacht, lavished words of "highest praise and almost admiration" for Neurath, and asked his ministers to keep quiet about the drama that had played out behind the scenes. "Thank God, the people do not know anything about this and would not believe it if they did," Hitler said. "For that reason, the strictest discretion. We all need to stick to the words of the communiqué and nip any rumours in the bud."[108] That very evening, Hitler left Berlin for the Obersalzberg to recover from the excitement of the past two weeks.

As he had during the Night of the Long Knives three and a half years earlier, Hitler had succeeded in freeing himself from a critical situation in one fell swoop and emerging all the more powerful from it, although this time no blood had been shed. For that reason, with some justification, 4 February had been called a "dry 30 June."[109] But whereas in 1934 Hitler had subjugated the discontented wing of the SA with the help of the military, in 1937 he placed the military under his control by assuming the role of commander-in-chief. The supreme commander of the Wehrmacht, Keitel, was blindly loyal to Hitler. And with the appointment of Ribbentrop, the top job in the Foreign Ministry was now held by a reliable party member. With that the personnel was in place at all levels for the transition to a foreign policy of aggression.

On 10 March 1938, the main hearing in the Fritsch case began before the Reich War Court. It was chaired by Göring and ended on 18 March with a full acquittal. It turned out that the defendant had been mistaken for a former cavalry captain, also named Fritsch, who immediately confessed that he too had been blackmailed by Schmidt. When pressed by Göring, Schmidt finally admitted that he had lied.[110] Hitler took his time in reacting to the verdict. It was not until 30 March that he had a handwritten note delivered to Fritsch. "With a heart full of gratitude," he wrote disingenuously, he had confirmed the court's verdict, adding: "As terrible a burden as this horrible accusation must have been to you, all the more did I suffer under the thoughts that it unleashed."[111] But when Fritsch insisted that his honour be publicly restored, Hitler fell silent. It took a further three months for the Führer to admit that he had made mistakes. The admission came at a meeting of military leaders in the northern German town of Barth on 13 June, but Hitler still refused to publicly rehabilitate Fritsch, citing the fact that the Sudeten crisis was coming to a head as an excuse. As a small conciliatory gesture, Fritsch was put in charge of the same artillery regiment he had commanded in the past. He would be killed near Warsaw on 22 September 1939 during Germany's invasion of Poland.[112] Blomberg, on the other hand, was never accepted back into the military. He and his wife survived the war in the southern German spa town of Bad Wiessee. There he was taken prisoner by American soldiers and died in a Nuremberg prison in March 1946, shunned by his fellow officers.[113]

Even in the midst of resolving the Fritsch–Blomberg crisis, Hitler kept his sights trained on his next foreign-policy coup. "The Führer wants to divert the spotlight from the Wehrmacht and keep Europe guessing," noted Colonel Alfred Jodl, a close associate of Wilhelm Keitel, on 31 January. "Schuschnigg should not be allowed to gain confidence. He should tremble in fear."[114] The German–Austrian agreement of July 1936 had not, as expected, bound the Alpine republic to the Third Reich, and Austrian Chancellor von Schuschnigg had repeatedly put off fulfilling his pledge to give members of the "nationalist opposition" limited political authority. With that, he gave Austrian Nazis a pretence to agitate with increasing impatience for a share of power and ultimately for the amalgamation of Austria into Germany. These aims attracted vigorous support from Göring, who as the head of the Four Year Plan cast a greedy eye upon Austria's large iron ore reserves. The *Anschluss* would relieve the Third Reich's problems with raw materials and foreign currency, and Austria would serve as a bridgehead for further German expansion in southern Europe.[115]

During a visit to Rome in January 1937, Göring had broached the amalgamation idea to Mussolini but had, in Ambassador Hassell's words, "met with considerable coolness."[116] In April he tried again, this time coming straight out and declaring that "the *Anschluss* must and will come—nothing can stop it." According to the interpreter present, in response Mussolini "energetically shook his head."[117] Italy was obviously not yet ready to hand Germany a carte blanche where Austria was concerned. Even during his state visit to Berlin in late September, Mussolini still tried to duck the issue. Yet although ordered by Hitler to exercise restraint, Göring insisted on showing Mussolini a map depicting Austria as part of Germany when the latter visited his Carinhall manor on 28 September. Mussolini did not react, and Göring mistakenly interpreted that as a sign of acceptance. Göring showed the state secretary of the Austrian Foreign Ministry, Guido Schmidt, the same map when he visited Carinhall in November:[118] the leadership in Vienna was thus under no illusions as to the direction of German foreign policy. All Kurt von Schuschnigg and his government could do was to buy time with tactical manoeuvring.

As we know from his conversations with Goebbels, Hitler decided in the spring of 1937 to resolve the "Austrian question" as soon as the opportunity presented itself. Beginning that July, under the code name "Operation Otto," the German military drew up plans for an intervention. On 19 November, during a visit of the Lord Privy Seal and soon-to-be British foreign minister, Lord Halifax, Hitler declared that "a closer connection between Austria and the Reich had to be created under all circumstances." Halifax declared that the British government was prepared to discuss all contentious issues as long as no violence was used. Hitler responded with visible irritation to Great Britain's adamant refusal to allow him a free hand on the Continent. "How different this agitated, angry Hitler was from the calm, model chancellor who had sat across from Simon and Anthony Eden two years previously," the interpreter Paul Schmidt noted. "His triumphal tone of voice alone would have signalled to a neutral observer that the times had changed. The Hitler of 1937 no longer carefully felt his way forward like the Hitler of 1935. He was clearly convinced of his own strength and others' weakness."[119] The following day in Munich, Hitler described Halifax as "a cold fish" and "tough as leather," adding that their four-hour talk had been an "exercise in futility."[120] Nonetheless, he was given the impression that London would not stand in the way of a non-violent solution to the Austrian issue.

In early 1938, the domestic situation in Austria began to heat up. After searching the apartment of an Austrian Nazi, police found plans to force an amalgamation with Germany that spring. Acts of provocation and sabotage were to increase tensions to the point that the Wehrmacht would have a pretence for intervening militarily.[121] On 6 February, having been fired as German ambassador to Austria only two days previously, Franz von Papen travelled to the Berghof for a final audience with Hitler. He found the dictator in a "distracted, almost exhausted" state. Hitler's countenance only brightened when Papen told him that Schuschnigg had requested a face-to-face meeting with the Führer. Immediately Hitler sensed an opportunity and asked Papen to temporarily continue to perform his ambassadorial duties and to arrange a meeting with Schuschnigg. "I would be delighted to see him here," Hitler said, "in order to openly discuss everything."[122]

The meeting was scheduled for 12 February. From the very beginning, Hitler had no interest in an open exchange of opinions. Indeed, the meeting was a perfidious attempt at strong-arming the less powerful leader. To create a suitably threatening, military atmosphere, he ordered Wilhelm Keitel, General Walther von Reichenau and the first commander of the Condor Legion, General Hugo Sperrle, to the Obersalzberg.[123] Schuschnigg, who was accompanied only by State Secretary Guido Schmidt and an assistant, was received at the border near Salzburg by Papen and then taken to Hitler's mountain residence. The dictator greeted his guests with "great politeness" at the foot of the steps and immediately led the Austrian chancellor up to his first-floor office for a one-to-one chat.[124] But hardly had the doors closed behind the two men than Hitler tried to force Schuschnigg into a rhetorical corner. In his memoirs, published in 1946, Schuschnigg could still quote from memory his host's enraged monologues, during which he could hardly get a word in edgeways.[125]

Hitler brusquely dismissed Schuschnigg's assurance that his government still took the July 1936 agreement very seriously and was interested in "clearing up the remaining difficulties and misunderstandings." Austria, Hitler began, was not pursuing "German policies." Indeed, he fumed, the story was one of "constant betrayal of the people." Hitler threatened: "This historical nonsense has to come to a long-overdue end. And I assure you, Herr von Schuschnigg: I am completely committed to putting an end to everything." Hitler referred to his "historic mission," which Providence had given him and which suffused his entire being: "My task was preordained. I have taken the most difficult path any German has ever had to take, and I have achieved more in German history than any German was ever destined to achieve." Hitler then openly spoke of military intervention: "Surely you do not think you could put up even half an hour's resistance? Who knows? Maybe I'll be in Vienna tomorrow morning like a spring storm. Then you'll see!" Hitler claimed that he was in complete agreement with Italy on the issue, and that Britain and France "would not lift a finger for Austria." After two hours the meeting ended with an ultimatum: "Either we find a solution," Hitler told Schuschnigg, "or things will have to take their course . . . I only have time until this afternoon. And when I tell you that, you would be well advised to believe me. I do not bluff."

Over lunch in the dining room, Hitler abruptly switched roles and played the solicitous host. He told Schuschnigg, who sat directly across from him, about his love for cars and his architectural projects. He bragged that in Hamburg he had commissioned the world's biggest bridge and skyscrapers full of new offices: "When they set foot on German soil, Americans should see that construction here is bigger and better than in the United States."[126] Around 2 p.m., Hitler withdrew, and his guests were asked to be patient until talks resumed. This was a favourite trick of Hitler for softening up interlocutors. After a few hours, the new Foreign Minister von Ribbentrop and Papen appeared with a typed list of two pages which presented the German demands: freedom of action for Hitler's supporters in Austria; the post of interior minister for the National Socialist Arthur Seyss-Inquart; a general amnesty or suspended sentences for all imprisoned Austrian Nazis; and close coordination of Austrian foreign, economic and military policies with the Third Reich.[127] Schuschnigg and Schmidt were horrified. Contrary to all of Papen's assurances, the demands called

Austrian sovereignty into question. It was particularly difficult for them to accept the idea of Seyss-Inquart as interior minister, which would have put him in charge of the police.

In his second round of talks with Hitler, Schuschnigg pointed out that according to his country's constitution, only the Austrian president was allowed to name ministers or issue amnesties. Whereupon Hitler flung open the door and yelled for Keitel to come to him. Schuschnigg was sent outside to wait, while Keitel asked what the Führer required of him. "Nothing at all," answered Hitler, laughing. "I just wanted you up here."[128] This cheap bit of theatre was intended to impress upon the Austrians that Hitler was serious about his threats of military intervention. And the spectacle worked. After Papen made a few insignificant alterations to the text, Schuschnigg signed a pledge to start addressing the demands in three days' time. He respectfully declined Hitler's invitation to stay for dinner. The drive back to Salzburg was a sombre one, with Papen only interrupting the silence to say: "That's the way the Führer is sometimes. You've now experienced it for yourselves. But the next time you come, you'll be able to talk a lot more easily. The Führer can be unusually charming."[129] To amuse his dinner guests that night, Hitler acted out how he had "demolished" the Austrian chancellor.[130] And after Schuschnigg implemented the German demands and reconstituted his government on 15 February, within the agreed three days, he recounted what had happened at the Berghof: "He put Schuschnigg under pressure," Goebbels recorded. "Threatened with cannons. And Paris and London would not come to his rescue. Then Schuschnigg caved in completely. A little man. One-third of a Brüning."[131]

Schuschnigg hoped that the concessions would preserve a remnant of Austria's autonomy. But for Hitler the Berchtesgaden agreement meant that he could push ahead with the final phase of his plan to amalgamate Germany's southern neighbour. On 16 February, the new Austrian Interior Minister Seyss-Inquart was summoned to Berlin to receive instructions from the Führer. "It's the moment of truth," Goebbels observed. "Everything is fair game now."[132] On 20 February, Hitler gave the speech to the Reichstag in the Kroll Opera House that was originally planned for 30 January. For the first time, it was broadcast live on Austrian radio, and listeners were especially curious what he would say about Austria. As was his wont, Hitler pursued a carrot-and-stick strategy. On the one hand, he lamented the destiny of more than 10 million Germans who allegedly suffered from discrimination in Austria and Czechoslovakia: "In the long term it is intolerable for a self-respecting world power to be aware that ethnic comrades are being made to suffer greatly for their affection and loyalty to the people as a whole, its destiny and its view of the world." On the other hand, he expressed gratitude to Schuschnigg for the "great understanding and warm-hearted willingness" with which he had tried to find a joint way of resolving the problems. Hitler sought to portray his strong-arm tactics of 12 February as an organic extension of the agreement of July 1936, indeed as a "contribution to European peace." Few radio listeners were likely aware of how shamelessly the Führer was lying.[133]

In a speech to Austrian National Socialists on 26 February, Hitler was far more frank. The Berchtesgaden agreement went so far, he declared, that "the Austria issue would automatically be resolved if it were fully implemented." As Hitler's Austria expert Wilhelm Keppler recorded his words: "If it can at all be avoided, he did not wish there to be a violent solution since the dangers posed from abroad were decreasing year by year, as our military might is increasing more and more."[134] Thus the dictator does not seem to have regarded the amalgamation of Austria as imminent. But then everything happened more quickly than expected. On 9 March, Schuschnigg announced that he was calling a popular referendum in four days, under the slogan of "For a free, German, independent, social, Christian and unified Austria!"[135] This surprising move was intended to beat Hitler at his own game, since the German dictator had publicly stated on 12 February that a majority of Austrians would be on his side if a plebiscite were held.[136] But Schuschnigg had made a fatal mistake by scheduling the vote at such short notice, which fed suspicions of electoral manipulation. Moreover, the announcement that only voters over the age of 24 would be eligible to cast ballots directly challenged Hitler, since Austrian National Socialism drew its strongest support from younger generations. Schuschnigg's decision thus unintentionally hastened what he was trying to prevent. "The bomb of a popular referendum was bound to explode in his hand," Count Ciano quipped.[137]

The Nazi leadership in Berlin was dumbfounded by the news from Vienna, and Hitler was initially unsure how to respond. He ordered Wilhelm Keppler to travel to the Austrian capital to check out the situation for himself. On the evening of 9 March, Goebbels, who was hosting a reception for the editors-in-chief of German newspapers, was summoned to Hitler's side at the Chancellery. Göring, who had for months been playing a leading role in the *Anschluss* question, was already there. "Schuschnigg is trying a dirty trick," the propaganda minister was told. "He's trying to make fools of us." But Hitler and his advisers were uncertain which of two strategies to pursue. Either they could call upon Austrian Nazis to boycott the poll, which would have made it a farce, or they could declare that Schuschnigg had violated the Berchtesgaden agreement, which would be effective propaganda, and intervene militarily. During the night of 9–10 March, those assembled leaned towards military intervention. Goebbels recorded the dramatic process by which a decision was reached:

> Consulted with the Führer until 5 a.m. He thinks the hour is at hand. He just wants to sleep on it for a night. Italy and England won't do anything. France maybe but probably not. The risk is not as great as with the reoccupation of the Rhineland . . . We're drawing up detailed plans for the operation. If it comes to pass, it will be short and drastic. The Führer is in full swing. A wonderful battle mood.[138]

After the remilitarisation of the Rhineland in April 1936, Count Harry Kessler had characterised the secret of Hitler's success as his "intuitive, lightning-quick understanding of situations from which he equally quickly and suddenly draws conclusions."[139] This was precisely how the *Anschluss* of Austria now proceeded. After some initial hesitation, Hitler recognised that Schuschnigg had given him a unique opportunity he could not afford to miss. On 10 March he issued the orders for Operation Otto, declaring that "if other means failed to achieve the desired ends, the intention is to move into Austria with armed forces." It was crucial, however, that "the entire operation proceeds without violence in the form of a peaceful incursion welcomed by the people."[140] That morning Goebbels found Hitler hunched over maps: "He was brooding. March is a heady month. But it's also always been the Führer's lucky one." Around noon, the propaganda minister was once more summoned to the Chancellery: "The die has been cast. We're going in on Saturday (12 March). Immediately proceed on all the way to Vienna . . . The Führer himself will travel to Austria. Göring and I are to remain in Berlin. In eight days, Austria will be ours."[141]

The Chancellery was a hive of activity on the morning of 11 March as, one after another, the political and military leaders of the Third Reich and their entourages arrived. Unusually early for him, at 8 a.m., Hitler conferred with Goebbels. Together they dictated the text for the flyers that would be dropped by plane over Austria. "Heated, incendiary language," Goebbels remarked. "But it was fun."[142] After that was done, Hitler tried to make preparations to present the operation diplomatically. Prince Philipp of Hesse, the son-in-law of the Italian king, was dispatched to Rome with a personal message from Hitler to Mussolini justifying intervention in Austria as an "act of national self-defence." "You, too, Your Excellency, would not act any differently, if the destiny of the Italians were at stake," Hitler had written.[143] Ribbentrop was in London at the time and one of his underlings, Reinhard Spitzy, was flown immediately across the Channel to get the German foreign minister's assessment of the probable British reaction.[144] Around 10 a.m., an ultimatum was issued to the Austrian government. It was given until 5 p.m. to postpone the popular referendum, and Schuschnigg was to resign and name Arthur Seyss-Inquart his successor. In the early afternoon, around 2:45 p.m., Schuschnigg agreed to postpone the plebiscite but refused to resign.[145]

In this critical phase, Göring seized the initiative. Even in front of the Nuremberg War Crimes Tribunal, he still boasted, not without reason, that it had been less the Führer than he himself who had "set the tempo." Indeed, Göring added, he had "even overlooked reservations by the Führer and forced things along."[146] He spent the day constantly on the phone, issuing instructions to Seyss-Inquart, Keppler and the representatives of Germany's embassy in Vienna. "Most of these telephone calls," recalled an amazed Nicolaus von Below later, "took place in the presence of a larger audience."[147] At 3:45 p.m. Seyss-Inquart reported that Schuschnigg had set off to submit his resignation to the Austrian president, Wilhelm Miklas, whereupon Berlin issued a new ultimatum: by 7:30 there had to be a new cabinet under Seyss-Inquart. But Miklas still refused to appoint the Austrian Nazi, and he stuck by that refusal even after the military attaché to the German embassy, Lieutenant General Wolfgang Muff, acting on Göring's orders, threatened that German troops massing on the border would enter Austria if Miklas did not relent.

Around 8 p.m., Schuschnigg addressed the Austrian people over the radio to explain the reasons for his resignation. He was yielding to violence, he said, and the army had been instructed to withdraw without resistance when the Wehrmacht marched in. A short time later, Seyss-Inquart took over the microphone to say that he was still in office as interior minister and would maintain security. Although Austrian National Socialists were preparing to take power all around the country, at 8:45 p.m. Hitler still issued an order to the Wehrmacht to enter Austria the following day. A short time later, Göring dictated to Keppler the text of a telegram that Seyss-Inquart was to send to Berlin. It contained a request by the "provisional Austrian government" to the German government to support it in its attempt to "restore calm and order in Austria" and to send troops "as soon as possible" to this end. But Seyss-Inquart hesitated, so Keppler saw to it himself that the fake cry for help was delivered to Berlin. "With that we have authorisation," Goebbels commented.[148] Late that evening Prince Philipp of Hesse passed on the reassuring news from Rome that Mussolini had "reacted quite calmly to the whole affair." A visibly relieved Hitler responded: "Please tell Mussolini that I will never forget this . . . Never, never, never, come what may."[149] Moreover, Ribbentrop's report, which Spitzy brought with him from London, left little doubt that Britain would remain inactive as well.[150] By around midnight, when Miklas relented and named Seyss-Inquart Austrian chancellor, his action no longer had any influence on the course of events.

At 5:30 a.m. on 12 March, German troops marched into Austria. Nowhere did they encounter resistance. On the contrary, the soldiers were welcomed. At noon, Goebbels read out over the radio a proclamation of the Führer that justified the intervention as a response to an alleged violation of the Berchtesgaden agreement: "Summoned by the new National Socialist government in Vienna, [the Wehrmacht] will guarantee that within a short span of time the Austrian people will be given the opportunity in a genuine popular referendum to determine its future and shape its destiny."[151] Hitler had flown to Munich that morning, where a motorcade of Mercedes was already waiting at Oberwiesenfeld Airport. Around 4 p.m., they crossed into Austria near

Braunau, Hitler's birthplace. The 120-kilometre drive to Linz took four hours, since the cars had trouble passing through the crowds of cheering onlookers. It was already dark when Hitler arrived in the city. Among the few people who had mixed feelings on this occasion was the 66-year-old doctor Eduard Bloch. "The weak boy whom I had treated so often and had not seen for thirty years stood in a car," Bloch said in an interview in 1941, by which time he was in exile in New York. "He smiled, waved and gave the Nazi salute to the people who crowded the street. Then for a moment he glanced up at my window. I doubt that he saw me but he must have had a moment of reflection. Here was the home of the noble Jew who had diagnosed his mother's fatal cancer . . . It was a brief moment."[152]

From the balcony of the town hall, Hitler made a brief speech that was repeatedly interrupted by applause. In it, he invoked the Providence that had taken him "from this city to the leadership of the Reich" and charged him with "restoring his precious homeland to the German Reich."[153] Following that, he and his entourage decamped to the Weinzinger Hotel by the Danube, where people congregated in front of the building until early in the morning. Hitler repeatedly greeted these admirers until his security guards finally asked him to go to bed and get some rest.[154] Originally Hitler had no plans to immediately complete the amalgamation of Austria. But in the night of 12–13 March, overwhelmed by his triumphal journey, he decided that he would not settle for any "half-measures." State Secretary Wilhelm Stuckart was summoned to Linz to draw up the requisite legal ordinances. While the lawyers ironed out the details, Hitler travelled to Leonding and laid flowers upon his parents' graves. That evening, he signed the Law on the Reunification of Austria with the German Reich. The first article declared unequivocally: "Austria is a territory of the German Reich." Its second article set 10 April as the date for a "free and secret referendum open to all Austrian men and women of the age of twenty or older."[155]

On the morning of 14 March, Hitler travelled on to Vienna, the city he had left twenty-five years earlier as a completely unknown "art painter" who despaired of his future. In the Austrian capital, too, an ecstatic reception awaited him. The city's church bells rang when he entered Vienna from the direction of Schönbrunn. During his entire stay in the capital, Hitler "glowed," to use Fritz Wiedemann's phrase,[156]

and it is easy to imagine how satisfied he must have felt. The same
scenes of hysterical enthusiasm as had taken place in Linz now played
themselves out in front of the Hotel Imperial where he stayed.[157] The
next morning, hundreds of thousands of people converged on
Heldenplatz in front of the Hofburg Palace for a "liberation celebration." From the palace balcony, Hitler made what he described as the
"greatest announcement of triumph" in his life: "As the Führer and
chancellor of the German nation and empire, I announce to posterity
the entry of my homeland into the German Reich."[158] The euphoria
at the unification of Austria with Germany almost obscured the hatred
and violence simultaneously being visited upon Vienna's Jewish citizens. This was the dark side of the *Anschluss*, and it cast a shadow
upon everything to come.

   That afternoon, Hitler visited the grave of his niece Geli Raubal in
Vienna's central cemetery. He went alone ahead of his entourage and
spent a long time at the grave, Nicolaus von Below reported.[159] After
the parade, Hitler received the Archbishop of Vienna, Cardinal
Theodor Innitzer, in the Hotel Imperial. The dictator bowed deeply—
a calculated gesture that said nothing about his true religious dispos-
ition—and the cardinal offered a Nazi salute and assured the Führer
that Austrian Catholics would work vigorously for "the project of
German reconstruction."[160] Around 5 p.m., Hitler flew back to Munich,
and when he returned to the German capital the following day,
the people of Berlin treated him to a triumphant reception that, in the
words of Goebbels, who was never at a loss for superlatives, "overshadowed everything previous." The propaganda minister gushed:
"[Hitler passed] through an immeasurable human guard of honour . . .
The cries of celebration nearly burst your eardrums. You had it ringing
in your ears for hours afterwards. It was a singing, jubilant city."[161]

This new foreign-policy triumph took Hitler to the peak of his popularity. People of all walks of life now admired him. The Wagner family
was particularly enthusiastic. "How unique and unparalleled is this
deed of our Führer," gasped Winifred Wagner's assistant Lieselotte
Schmidt, adding: "He is more than a statesman . . . he is an executor
of a higher will, a genius before whom everyone ultimately will have
to bow."[162] Ernst von Weizsäcker, the state secretary designate in the
Foreign Ministry, who travelled to Vienna with Ribbentrop on

14 March, saw that date "as the most significant since 18 January 1871"—the day on which the Wilhelmine Empire had been founded. He was especially impressed by Hitler's ability "to seize an opportunity by the scruff of the neck."[163] The reaction of the conservative historian Gerhard Ritter was much the same, although he otherwise had a detached relationship to the Nazi regime. "I completely admire the mastery of the actor who knows how to stage everything," Ritter wrote in a letter to his brother in April 1938. "It is the first time that my admiration is without reservation!"[164]

For the Hamburg teacher Luise Solmitz, the *Anschluss* was the fulfilment of "my old German dream," made possible by "a man who fears nothing, knows no compromises, hindrances or difficulties." She wrote this in her diary despite the fact that she was stigmatised by the regime for having married a Jewish husband. "One must recall that one is excluded from the people's community oneself like a criminal or degraded person," she wrote.[165] Willy Cohn in Breslau, who personally suffered the many indignities inflicted upon Jews in Germany, likewise had ambiguous feelings. "It is hard to resist the sense of momentous events," he wrote on 13 March, adding the next day: "You have to admire the energy with which all this has been carried out . . . We Jews in Germany are not supposed to share the exuberance of this national uprising, but we do nonetheless."[166] By contrast, Victor Klemperer in Dresden did not get caught up in the jubilations. "The monstrous act of violence represented by the annexation of Austria," he noted, "the monstrous increase in power both domestically and abroad, the trembling defenceless fear of England and France. We won't live to see the end of the Third Reich."[167] Thomas Mann, in March 1938 on a reading tour of the United States, also remained deaf to the patriotic hullaballoo. "The monster is speaking today in Vienna," he wrote. "He won't do that without 'adeptness,' and he will try to calm things." But Mann was mistaken about the reaction of the Western powers: "At least apathy in Europe is not as hopeless as it seems. The consequences of this disgusting coup are unforeseeable. The shock is deep, and the lesson learned effective."[168] In fact, the British and French governments offered nothing more than verbal protests.

Reports by SPD-in-exile observers initially talked about widespread fears among the German population that a new war might be at hand.

On the morning of 12 March, citizens of Munich panicked and began stockpiling goods. "There were queues in front of shops," one observer wrote. "Bakeries were completely sold out and had to close early."[169] As it became clear that the Western powers were not going to intervene, and special radio reports relayed news of the enthusiastic receptions for Hitler in Linz and Vienna, the mood swung round: "At that point, you suddenly noticed a massive enthusiasm and joy over this triumph," another observer reported from Saxony. "The jubilations no longer knew any bounds. Even sectors that had been reserved towards Hitler or rejected him got carried away and conceded that he was a fine and clever statesman who would restore Germany's greatness and reputation after the defeat of 1918."[170] Among old and committed Social Democrats who remained immune to Nazi propaganda there was hopelessness and resignation. "Hitler succeeds at everything," an observer from the Rhineland Palatinate wrote. "He can do what he wants because everyone gives in to him. His domestic deceptions have also proven effective abroad. Here, too, Hitler has found his Hugenbergs."[171]

Hitler remained in a state of euphoria for days after his most impressive coup to date. On the evening of 18 March, he gave a speech in the Kroll Opera House detailing the events that had led up to the Reich swallowing Austria. At the end, he declared the Reichstag dissolved and announced the election on 10 April of "new representatives for Greater Germany" in conjunction with the referendum in Austria.[172] A few days later he paid a private visit to Bayreuth. "From two to six I had him all to myself, and everything was calm—it was all too nice since he could touch on very personal things with me that had moved his heart in Braunau and Linz," Winifred Wagner wrote in a letter to a friend. Hitler gave Wagner a detailed account of how everything had come so "suddenly" and "unexpectedly," and she happily noted "how fresh and well he looked," adding "that it makes you glad about this triumph."[173]

On 25 March, Hitler hit the campaign trail in Königsberg. He could hardly have suspected that the poll would be his last. Once again, he put himself through a demanding schedule. After Königsberg, he spoke in Leipzig, Berlin, Hamburg, Cologne, Frankfurt am Main, Stuttgart and Munich. From 3 to 9 April, he continued on to Graz, Klagenfurt, Innsbruck, Salzburg, Linz and Vienna in Austria. In the end he was exhausted, and his voice was completely hoarse and required treatment by his personal physician Morell.[174] Hitler only anticipated getting 80 per cent of the Austrian vote, so he was surprised when 99.75 per cent voted for amalgamation into Germany—a better result than in the old parts of the Reich (99.08 per cent). "A great celebration for the nation," Goebbels commented. "Germany has conquered an entire country by the ballot box."[175] Of course not everyone who voted yes was a committed Hitler supporter. Many Austrians cast their ballots opportunistically or out of fear. "No one believes that these were secret elections, and everyone is trembling," wrote Klemperer.[176] At the same time, the dictator's prestige was bolstered even further. Never was the consensus about Hitler's regime greater than in the spring of 1938.

The addition of Austria also strengthened the Reich's economic and military position. Austrian iron reserves could now be exploited for the German rearmament programme, and a huge steel-processing facility, the Hermann Göring Works, was built on the outskirts of Linz. Germany also got its hands on 1.4 billion reichsmarks' worth of gold and currency reserves, and masses of jobless Austrians, many of whom were highly qualified, relieved the tight German labour market. Incorporating the Austrian army, the Bundesheer, increased the strength of the Wehrmacht by 1,600 officers and 60,000 regular soldiers. Moreover, the Reich's strategic position had improved since it could now put pressure on Czechoslovakia from two sides.[177]

Two months previously, Hitler had had difficulty extracting himself from the Blomberg–Fritsch affair. Now he was riding on a wave of popular approval. Once again, he had used a foreign-policy triumph to ease domestic troubles. And once more, his instincts had led him to act at precisely the right moment. For four weeks after German troops entered Austria, he was celebrated like a god by cheering masses. It is no wonder, then, that he became ever more convinced of his own greatness and began losing touch with reality. In his speeches, he increasingly referred to Providence choosing him as its instrument. His sense of self-importance, which had already been greatly bolstered by his successful gamble in remilitarising the Rhineland in 1936, began increasingly to take on a nearly pathological character. Even Nicolaus von Below, who later admitted to being an "unconditional Hitler admirer" in the spring of 1938, was unsettled by the fact that Hitler began to talk incessantly in private about the historic mission he still had to fulfil. "Except for him there was no one now or in the near future ... who could perform the tasks facing the German people," Below quoted him saying.[178] And there was no doubt about which task was next on Hitler's agenda.

"People generally believe that Czechoslovakia will be up next," observers reported to the SPD leadership in exile in Prague.[179] In fact, only a few days after the *Anschluss*, Hitler set his sights on his next target for expansion. "Now it's the Czechs' turn," he told Goebbels on the evening of 19 March. "Without hesitation at the next opportunity."[180] On 28 March, the dictator received the leader of the Sudeten German Party, Konrad Henlein, in Berlin and informed him of his decision to "resolve" the Czechoslovakian issue in the not-too-distant future. He also instructed Henlein as to tactics to bring about that result, telling him that the Sudeten Germans should "always demand so much that they can never be satisfied."[181]

Along with Slovaks, Hungarians and Poles, the 3.5 million Sudeten Germans were one of the largest minorities in Czechoslovakia which, unusually for a state formed after the First World War, had remained a democracy despite post-war political crises and the Great Depression. Although they enjoyed full rights as citizens, many Sudeten Germans felt disadvantaged, and they were particularly hard hit by unemployment. Demanding economic improvements and regional autonomy, a protest movement coalesced around the Sudeten German Homeland Front, which was founded by Henlein in 1933 and renamed the Sudeten German Party two years later. Voices calling for amalgamation into the German Reich quickly became louder and louder. On 19 November 1937, Henlein wrote to Hitler, declaring that "It is practically impossible ... for Czechs and Germans to reach agreement and the Sudeten German question can only be resolved by the Reich."[182] After the *Anschluss*, the slogan "Back home to the Reich" became popular among Sudeten Germans, and Hitler used it as dynamite with which to demolish Czechoslovakia. The hatred for Czechs he had nurtured in his Vienna years re-emerged in full force. In conversation with Goebbels, he dismissed them as "impudent, mendacious, craven and subservient."[183]

On 21 April, Hitler and Wilhelm Keitel explored the possibilities for moving militarily against Czechoslovakia. The resulting plan was code-named "The Green Scenario." Hitler did not want a "sudden, out-of-the blue attack for no reason." Instead, military action was to be

preceded by "a period of diplomatic confrontations that would gradually intensify and lead to war." But Hitler did not entirely rule out
the possible need for "a lightning strike on account of some incident."[184]
And the manifesto that the Sudeten German Party agreed on in the
spa town of Karlsbad (today's Karlovy Vary) on 24 April made it clear
how such incidents could be staged. The party demanded the recognition of the Sudeten Germans as a "legal entity" with complete
autonomy, and called for reparations for all the economic damage they
had suffered since 1918 and "complete liberty to declare their allegiance
to German ethnic identity and the German world view"—that is,
National Socialism.[185] Following Hitler's instructions, Henlein had made
the sort of extreme demands that the Czech government could never
concede. This tactic instantly ratcheted up tensions and kicked off a
war of nerves that would determine the fate of Czechoslovakia.

Before Hitler further escalated the crisis, however, he paid his
promised return visit to Mussolini in Italy. On 2 May, three chartered
trains stood ready in Berlin's Anhalter Station to transport the
500-strong travelling party that included half of the Reich government,
high-ranking party functionaries, generals, diplomats, journalists and
the wives of Nazi VIPs. Eva Braun boarded almost unnoticed in
Munich and travelled not with the official delegation, but with the
Brandts, the Morells and the wife of the owner of the Rheinhotel
Dreesen—all familiar faces at the Berghof. We do not know whether
she even saw Hitler on the seven-day state trip.[186] The following
evening, the trains arrived in Rome, where they were greeted by King
Victor Emmanuel III, Mussolini and Count Ciano. The Italians had
done everything in their power to outdo the pomp of Mussolini's
visit to Germany the previous autumn. Four-horse carriages were
waiting in front of the train station to convey the guests, to the
applause of thousands of Romans, through the festively decorated
and brightly lit city to their accommodations.[187]

Hitler entered the eternal city not with Mussolini but with the king,
since, as the Italian head of state, Victor Emmanuel was his official
host. For that reason, the German dictator and the closest members
of his entourage stayed in the Quirinal Palace, the king's residence in
the capital, while most of the remaining visitors had to make do
with the Grand Hotel Plaza. Eva Braun stayed in the Hotel Excelsior,
away from all the others.[188] Hitler had difficulty adapting to the protocol

that had the diminutive king and not Il Duce playing the leading role, and the stiff-necked court ceremonies irritated him right from the start. The aristocratic members of the court made it abundantly clear that they considered him a parvenu, treating him with a pompous arrogance that pricked his most sensitive spot, his inferiority complex. "This entire horde of royal flunkies should be taken out and shot. It's revolting," wrote Goebbels, no doubt expressing what Hitler felt too. "How they treat us like parvenus! An outrage and a provocation."[189]

Hitler reacted increasingly sensitively to what he perceived as his supercilious treatment and Mussolini's undignified relegation to second-fiddle status. Already at the state banquet hosted by Victor Emmanuel on the evening of 4 May at the palace, Hitler had trouble controlling his temper. He was seated to the left of the queen. "The two of them did not say a word to one another during the entire meal," Fritz Wiedemann noted.[190] Afterwards Hitler could no longer hold his tongue: "It terrible how this great man, Il Duce, is treated by royal society. Did you see that he was seated all the way down at the far end of the table, behind the youngest princesses?"[191] Of course, the Italians also hoped to impress their German visitors with the progress they had made on the military front. On 5 May, Hitler, Mussolini, Victor Emmanuel and the crown prince boarded the warship MS *Cavour* in Naples to watch naval manoeuvres. The highlight was an exercise in which one hundred submarines simultaneously submerged and then, as if obeying some secret command, surfaced with equal precision a short time later.[192]

But Hitler remained irritable, and that evening he exploded at Ribbentrop and the head of the Foreign Ministry protocol department, Vicco von Bülow-Schwante. The spark that lit the fuse was comparatively harmless. After Hitler had donned his hated tuxedo for a special performance of the opera *Aida*, he was supposed to inspect a military parade with the king. He wanted to change into his uniform, and twenty minutes had been allocated in the strictly planned programme to that end. But suddenly an assistant to the king appeared and announced that they were behind schedule and that they needed to go outside immediately. Hitler was forced to inspect the troops at the royally attired king's side with his tuxedo tails flapping in the wind. "An unusually comic sight," Wiedemann reported. "The German Führer and Reich chancellor looked like an insane head waiter. It was all the more comic as you could see that he realised what a ridiculous figure he was cutting."[193] Hitler was seething with rage, and on the trip back to Rome he levelled bitter accusations at Ribbentrop. The foreign minister, in turn, immediately fired his head of diplomatic protocol.

Hitler had further reason to get upset at a military parade the following morning, when the Italian troops performed the *passo romano*, modelled on the German goose-step. The grandstand only contained enough chairs for the members of the Italian royal court and their German state guest, so that Mussolini had to stand. "That made me so angry I almost caused a public scandal," Hitler told his secretary Christa Schroeder.[194] In the afternoon, the Governor of Rome, Prince Colonna, held a reception. Several hundred guests attended, and the royal court turned up in its entirety. Hitler had the unpleasant task of opening the polonaise with the queen on his arm through an honour guard of guests, some of whom fell to their knees, while others kissed the hem of the queen's dress. "When Hitler noticed this, he went red in the face," his pilot Hans Baur remarked. "He positively dragged the queen forward to get through the long rows of guests as quickly as possible. The way he looked, we thought he was going to have a stroke."[195] That evening, Hitler complained that people had "stared at him as if he were an exotic animal." He simply could not warm to the "ceremonies of court lackeys."[196]

To a degree, Hitler's intemperate reaction recalled his behaviour in Munich salons in the early 1920s. Bavarian high society had also treated the ambitious beer-cellar rabble-rouser as a curiosity, and he had concealed his insecurities with eccentric poses. He had, of course, acquired many social graces since becoming chancellor, and he was no longer uncomfortable during official receptions or talks with career diplomats. Moreover, his successes had increased his self-confidence. Nonetheless, he felt ill at ease in the royal court in Rome, not just because he sensed the tacit antipathy its members maintained towards him, but also because he did not know how to react. There was nothing in his regular repertoire that allowed him to master unfamiliar situations like being dropped in amongst Italy's *grandezza*. Even at a point when his popularity had reached unprecedented heights in his home country and he was deified like no German politician before or since, his visit to Italy revealed that he still lived in fear of looking laughable. His megalomania was the flipside of his deep feelings of inferiority.

Hitler's mood only improved when Mussolini devoted his full attention to him, away from the disruptive presence of the king and his court. Together they jointly visited a major archaeological exhibition about the Roman emperor Augustus, and on 7 May Il Duce hosted a gala dinner in honour of his guest at the Palazzo Venezia. There, they once again exchanged assurances of their mutual regard and of the eternal friendship of their two peoples. Hitler declared that he saw "the natural border of the Alps between the two countries as inviolable," signalling that he had no territorial designs on southern Tyrol.[197] To conclude Hitler's visit, the two dictators travelled to Florence on 9 May, where they decamped at the Palazzo Pitti and visited the Uffizi Gallery. Years later in the monologues he held in his wartime headquarters, Hitler still rhapsodised about the magic of Rome, Florence and the Tuscan and Umbrian countryside: "How I wish I could travel around like an unknown painter in Italy!"[198] Around midnight on 9 May, Mussolini accompanied Hitler to the train station, taking his leave with the words: "Now no power in the world can divide us!"[199]

In a memorandum to Germany's foreign embassies, Ribbentrop deemed Hitler's visit to Italy a great success. The Berlin–Rome axis, he wrote, had proved a "reliable component in our general policy," and the friendship between Hitler and Mussolini had been "further deepened."[200] Although the hectic agenda had left hardly any time for serious political discussions, the German side had read into certain statements by their Italian counterparts a willingness not to put any obstacles in Germany's way should it decide to move against Czechoslovakia. "Mussolini is not interested in our intentions concerning Czechoslovakia," wrote State Secretary von Weizsäcker. "He is prepared to stand back and watch what we do there."[201]

Nonetheless, Hitler retained a deep-seated aversion to Italian high society and the Italian aristocracy. He told a small circle in the Chancellery that he had never seen "so many degenerate fools, mindless parrots and old frumps at the same time in one place." He characterised the polonaise in the palace as "the worst trial of martyrdom he had ever been through" and described the "thick as a pig" Italian queen as the "mutton thief from Montenegro," as the army attaché Gerhard Engel recalled: "He said that women had surrounded him and had almost put out his eyes with their wine glasses. Nothing should be left undone to support Mussolini in his battle against this corrupt society."[202] Hitler repeatedly expressed his satisfaction that he had never listened to those who had tried to talk him into a restoration of the monarchy in Germany. He even praised the "old middle-of-the-road Social Democrats" for doing away with the "spectre of the monarchy" in 1918 and suggested that their pensions should be increased.[203]

Hitler only remained in Berlin for a single day after returning from Italy. On 11 May he flew to Munich and withdrew for the next two weeks to the Obersalzberg.[204] During this time, Nazi propaganda whipped up the anti-Czech mood, and tensions increased in the Sudeten German regions of Czechoslovakia. On 20 May, worried about concentrations of German troops on their border, the Czech government ordered a partial mobilisation of the country's armed forces. France reaffirmed its commitment to come to Czechoslovakia's aid in case of a German attack, and Britain warned the Third Reich that it also would not stand by and do nothing. Hitler's government in Berlin saw itself compelled to offer reassurances that it had no intentions of invading Germany's neighbour.[205]

But the "weekend crisis" of 20 and 21 May did not bring an end to the tensions. As soon as London and Paris were convinced that Germany did not in fact intend to attack, and that the Czechs had unnecessarily dramatised the situation, the mood turned against Prague. Hitler, on the other hand, was enraged that the foreign press wrote of Germany backing down and suffering a diplomatic defeat. Far from encouraging a more prudent course, therefore, the May crisis made him all the more aggressive. On 26 May he returned to Berlin. Goebbels, who saw him on the morning of 28 May, noted: "He's brooding about what decision to make. That usually goes on for a while. But once he's made up his mind, he'll make sure his will is carried out."[206] By that afternoon, the dictator knew what he wanted to do. In the conservatory of the Chancellery, he told the leaders of the Wehrmacht and the Foreign Ministry: "It is my iron will that Czechoslovakia disappear from the map." No matter what threatening gestures they made, Hitler asserted, the Western powers were unlikely to intervene. Britain still needed time to build up its military, France would not act independently of Britain, and Italy was indifferent. So the chances of keeping the conflict local, Hitler concluded, were good.[207]

The revised orders for the Green Scenario on 30 May directly reflected Hitler's instructions. "It is my irrevocable decision to break up Czechoslovakia through military action," he said. "The task of waiting for the right time, in military and political terms, to carry this out falls to the political leadership." He ordered the Wehrmacht to make all the necessary preparations by 1 October.[208] After that point, as he made clear in a supplemental order on 18 June, Hitler wanted to be able "to exploit every favourable circumstance for achieving this end."[209]

The military leaders present at the meeting on 28 May did not raise any objections. Even Army Chief of the General Staff Ludwig Beck stayed silent: Nicolaus von Below described him maintaining a "face of stone" throughout the meeting.[210] However, Beck did express his reservations in a series of memoranda to Army Commander-in-Chief von Brauchitsch in late May and June. Like most of Germany's military leadership, Beck supported the idea of the Reich expanding its power; he had welcomed the *Anschluss* and had nothing in principle against the division of Czechoslovakia. But he feared that the way Hitler was proceeding would compel the Western allies to intervene, and he felt that Germany was insufficiently prepared for the protracted war that would inevitably come about.[211]

When informed by Brauchitsch about Beck's concerns, Hitler heaped scorn upon the chief of the general staff, calling him "an officer who is still stuck on the idea of an army of 100,000 men and for whom the desk chair is more important than the trenches." He had nothing against Beck personally, he said, but he had no use for people who did not share his convictions, so Beck's days were numbered.[212] Beck enjoyed little support within the military leadership and even among those who worked under him. A simulation of war which the general staff conducted in the second half of June concluded that an offensive against Czechoslovakia would only last a few days and that German troops could be redeployed to the western front more quickly than Beck thought. Increasingly, Beck found himself pegged as an "unconvincing Cassandra."[213]

In a further major memorandum of 15–16 July, Beck made a last-ditch effort to win over Brauchitsch, stating flat-out: "The prospect of destroying Czechoslovakia with military force without alerting England and France does not exist for the foreseeable future." The conflict, Beck argued, would "automatically expand into a European or world war, which as far as anyone could predict would end in a general catastrophe and not just a military defeat for Germany." The chief of staff called upon Brauchitsch to dissuade Hitler of the idea of a violent resolution of the Czech question "until the military situation has changed decisively."[214] In a presentation he gave to Brauchitsch, Beck went even further and mooted the idea of a collective resignation among military leaders in an attempt to get Hitler to abandon his risky policies of conflict. "Soldiers' obedience reaches its limits when their knowledge, their conscience and their sense of responsibility forbids them to carry out an order," Beck declared. "Extraordinary times demand extraordinary measures."[215] But neither Brauchitsch nor the majority of Germany's military leaders had the slightest inclination to rebel in a way that was utterly atypical of Prussian officers. That became clear at a meeting of high-ranking military leaders on 4 August. Most of the participants were critical of Hitler's plans for war, but no one said a single word about coming together to resist them.[216]

Hitler got wind of the meeting and immediately summoned Walther von Brauchitsch to the Berghof. Hitler was already convinced that there were too many doomsayers among his military leadership. "Our generals in Berlin of course once more have their pants full," he had scoffed in late July in Bayreuth.[217] He read Brauchitsch the Riot Act, raising his voice so much that the guests taking some fresh air on the terrace below Hitler's office decided they would be best advised to go inside. In his many years of service to Hitler, Nicolaus von Below recalled, this was "the only time he had got that loud during a conversation with a general."[218]

On 10 August, Hitler ordered the heads of the general staff of the armies and army groups earmarked for mobilisation to come to the Berghof. Most of them were younger generals, and for many it was the first time that they had met their supreme commander in person. Hitler put on a completely different persona to the one he had presented to Brauchitsch. Before lunch, he talked to them casually, "expressing moderate, sensible views, calm in tone and open to objections—in short, he was playing the role of a man you could talk to, and not that of the wild dictator," Fritz Wiedemann reported.[219] In an afternoon speech that went on for hours, Hitler tried to win the officers' support for his plans, but in the following discussion he encountered both reservations and approval. In the days that followed, according to Gerhard Engel, his disappointment expressed itself in "a long critical litany about the lukewarm, nerveless leaders of the army."[220]

Hitler suspected that Beck was behind the resistance, and he interpreted the latter's memorandum of 15–16 July, which Brauchitsch brought to his attention, as confirmation of that belief. In his diary, Hitler's military attaché described the dictator's reaction:

> He said people were trying to sabotage his work. Instead of the general staff being glad that it could work in line with its very own way of thinking, it refused any thought of war ... It was high time for the chief of staff to disappear ... It was a scandal that he now sat in the chair once occupied by Moltke. Moltke had to be restrained by Bismarck. Now the situation was the exact opposite.[221]

On 15 August, in a speech in Jüterbog to his commanding generals, Hitler rejected Beck's ideas in no uncertain terms. Three days later, after Brauchitsch had declined to defend him, Beck submitted his resignation. Hitler accepted it after three further days, but insisted that the resignation initially be kept secret because of the tense foreign-policy situation. On 1 September, Quartermaster General and Artillery General Franz Halder was named Beck's successor.[222]

In early August 1938, the British government sent Lord Walter Runciman to Prague to try to get the Czechoslovakian government and the Sudeten German Party to come to an agreement. "Runciman's whole mission stinks," wrote William Shirer. "He says he has come here to mediate between the Czech government and the Sudeten Party of Konrad Henlein. But Henlein is not a free agent. He cannot negotiate. He is completely under the orders of Hitler."[223] Although Prague yielded to British pressure and made one concession after another, even going as far as accepting nearly all the demands in the Sudeten Party's Karlsbad manifesto, the representatives of the German minority always found a pretext to demand more and more. Hitler, of course, was not interested in a peaceful settlement. In early June he had told Goebbels to ramp up anti-Czech propaganda: "We have to keep on stirring up trouble and rebellion. Never let them relax."[224]

That entire summer, German newspapers published reports about alleged "atrocities" carried out by Czechs against Sudeten Germans, stoking popular anger.

In mid-July, Fritz Wiedemann made an unofficial trip to London with a message from Hitler to Lord Halifax. Wiedemann was to tell the British foreign secretary that Britain was showing too little regard for Germany's interests and should learn to accept "German existential necessities." The Führer was "still quite embittered" about the British government's behaviour in the "weekend crisis" and dismayed about the British press's criticism of him. And Hitler formulated his central message in unmistakable terms: "The Sudeten German question must be resolved one way or the other. If the Czechs do not give in, one day it will be solved with violence." Halifax received Wiedemann on 18 July in his private apartment. When the foreign minister asked for a written statement to confirm that Germany planned no violent measures against Czechoslovakia, Wiedemann answered, as instructed: "You will not be getting this declaration." The trip did nothing to relax the tension, even though Halifax did articulate the hope that he would some day greet the Führer side by side with the king of England at Buckingham Palace.[225]

In July, as he did every year, Hitler attended the Wagner Festival in Bayreuth, but this time he was preoccupied by thoughts of the imminent military conflict. He inspected the latest designs of fortifications for the West Wall on Germany's border and made sketches of how he wanted them built.[226] Over lunch he declared: "I want to finally get a good night's sleep. That's why I've ordered the construction of fortifications that will prevent the enemy from invading from the west. Germans shall be able to sleep peacefully again." Minister Hanns Kerrl, one of the lunch guests, was craven enough to respond: "My Führer, the German people will always sleep peacefully as long as you're alive."[227] On 31 July, Hitler interrupted his visit for a day to attend the German Gymnastics and Sports Festival in Breslau. There, Sudeten Germans marched by the VIP stand, shouting "Back home to the Reich!," Goebbels noted. "The people yelled, cheered and cried. The Führer was deeply moved. When the hour is at hand, there will be a true storm."[228]

But Hitler still had not set a date for attacking Czechoslovakia. "The Führer is still brooding over the Prague question," Goebbels wrote on 10 August. "In his mind's eye he's already solved it and divided [the country] up into new Gaue."[229] Apparently at this point Hitler still thought that it would take some time to move against Prague. Eight days later, Goebbels summarised Hitler's thoughts on the western fortifications as: "By the first frost, they'll be finished. Then we'll be unassailable from the west, and France will no longer be able to do anything. With that, the solution of our central European problems can begin to ripen. In any case, we'll have our back free."[230] From 27 to 29 August, Hitler, Keitel and Jodl went on an inspection tour of Germany's western border. In Aachen, in the salon carriage of Hitler's special train, the commander of Army Group 2, Colonel General Wilhelm Adam, reported that only a third of the fortifications would be completed by the end of October. When Adam proceeded to express his opinion that the Western powers would not sit back and do nothing if Germany attacked Czechoslovakia, Hitler went into a rage. "We have no time to listen to this stuff any longer," he fumed. "The English have no army reserves, and the French are facing massive domestic problems. They'll be wary of taking us on." Adam responded coolly that there was no need then for further discussion and suggested they go out into the field. As was so often the case when someone stood up to him, Hitler regained his composure on the spot, and the inspection continued.[231]

Hitler also radiated optimism among those closest to him. "He does not think London will intervene and he's determined to act," wrote Goebbels, who had been invited to spend a couple of days on the Obersalzberg in late August.

> He knows what he wants and is taking a direct route towards his goal.
> At the slightest provocation, he intends to solve the Czech question . . .
> The whole thing will have to be rolled out as quickly as possible. You
> always have to take a large risk, if you want to make a large gain.[232]

Goebbels no doubt wrote these words in his diary with an eye towards it being published at a later date; at the time Hitler hardly behaved with that sort of directness on the Sudeten German issue. On the contrary, he continually vacillated between cold-hearted determination and indecision. In late August at the Berghof, he declined to receive the German ambassador to Britain, Herbert von Dirksen, who brought a message from British Prime Minister Neville Chamberlain.[233] On 2 September, when he was visited by Konrad Henlein, Hitler made no bones about the fact that he was considering a military solution, but he was still undecided as to when the attack should be launched. The two men agreed to let the Czechs "stew in their own juices" in the hope that they would gradually "soften up."[234] Nonetheless, his fundamental decision in late May to destroy Czechoslovakia in the foreseeable future put Hitler under pressure to act. The day after Henlein's visit, Hitler summoned Brauchitsch and Keitel to the Berghof, where 1 October was provisionally set as a date for the attack.[235]

Meanwhile, fear of a new war was growing within the German population, to a far greater extent than it had during the *Anschluss* of Austria. In contrast to the spring, when tension had given way to euphoria within the space of a few days, the Sudeten crisis went on for months. The increasingly shrill anti-Czech propaganda rebounded against the regime. Instead of creating sympathy for the allegedly persecuted Sudeten Germans, it stoked fears that this time there would be no way to resolve the issue without violence. Local Nazi reports spoke of a "war psychosis," and SPD-in-exile observers described much the same. One of them wrote:

> People fear that war will come and it will be Germany's downfall. Nowhere can any enthusiasm for war be felt . . . No one in the working classes (and very few from other social ranks) thinks that the Sudetenland is so important that Germany must have it at all costs. If war comes, it will be most unpopular in Germany.[236]

The Nazi Party conference of 1938, with its theme of "Greater Germany," was also dominated by the Sudeten German issue. Late in the evening of 9 September, after the political directors had turned out for a roll call, there was a discussion in Hitler's hotel about the operation plan for the Green Scenario. Walther von Brauchitsch and Franz Halder had been specifically summoned to Nuremberg. Hitler had suggested making territorial inroads by sending strong armoured divisions deep into Czechoslovakia and thereby bringing about a speedy outcome, and he was shocked that his generals had not followed this idea. He criticised "the wasting of time" and came straight out and demanded that attack plans be "amended to conform to his wishes." Brauchitsch and Halder yielded and tried to mollify their commander-in-chief with declarations of loyalty. Nonetheless, afterwards Hitler complained about "fear and cowardice in the army." In the best of all worlds, he said, he would have turned his armies over to his Gauleiter: "They have faith, while the army commanders do not."[237]

Hitler's concluding speech at the rally on 12 September was highly anticipated. As was his wont, he began by recalling the "days of struggle" before proceeding to his main topic: the "unbearable" fate of Sudeten Germans in Czechoslovakia. The German Reich, he declared, would "no longer accept further oppression against and persecution of three and a half million Germans." He then issued a threat to the Western democracies: if they were to deny the Sudeten Germans the right of self-determination, it would have "severe consequences." Hitler also warned Czechoslovakian President Eduard Beneš: "The Germans in Czechoslovakia are neither defenceless nor have they been abandoned."[238] For Goebbels, the Führer was "at the height of his rhetorical powers," while Shirer remarked: "I have never heard Hitler quite so full of hate, his audience quite so on the borders of bedlam."[239] It did not take long for the speech to have an echo. There was a wave of protests and confrontations in the Sudeten German territories, whereupon the government in Prague imposed martial law there. "Things are developing the way we wished," noted Goebbels with satisfaction."[240]

Then, on 14 September, something no one in the Nazi leadership had anticipated happened. Neville Chamberlain requested a meeting with Hitler, in an attempt to jointly find a peaceful way out of the crisis. Hitler could hardly reject the request without appearing in German and international public opinion like the warmonger he truly was, so he invited Chamberlain to come to the Berghof the following day. On the morning of 15 September, the almost-70-year-old British prime minister got on a plane for the first time in his life. He was accompanied by his close adviser Sir Horace Wilson and the director of the Central Europe division in the Foreign Office, William Strang. The British delegation was received by Joachim von Ribbentrop at Oberwiesenfeld airport in Munich, and they travelled on to Berchtesgaden by chartered train. Not coincidentally, military transports rolled down the tracks next to the train for the entire journey.

They provided a martial backdrop to the British government's struggle to preserve peace.[241]

Chamberlain arrived at the Berghof shortly after 5 p.m. Hitler welcomed him on the front steps. After greeting one another, they took tea in the Great Hall. To relax the awkward atmosphere, Chamberlain steered the conversation towards the paintings of which the art lover Hitler was so proud.[242] At the prime minister's request, the subsequent talks were held one-to-one in Hitler's office. As had also been the case with Kurt von Schuschnigg in February, Ribbentrop was made to wait in the anteroom. The interpreter Paul Schmidt was thus the only other witness to Hitler and Chamberlain's dramatic three-hour discussion. Hitler began calmly but grew increasingly excitable as he levelled more and more severe accusations against the government in Prague. When Chamberlain said that he was willing to discuss all German complaints as long as Hitler ruled out the use of force, Hitler responded: "Violence? Who's talking about violence here? Herr Beneš uses violence against my countrymen in the Sudetenland . . . I'm not willing to accept it any longer . . . In the short term, I'm going to solve this problem myself, one way or the other." The composed Chamberlain responded that if Hitler had irrevocably decided to move against Czechoslovakia, he need not have let him come to Berchtesgaden and that it would perhaps be better if he left since there seemed to be no point to his visit.

Schmidt had the impression that a critical point had been reached and that the question of war or peace was on a knife-edge. But to his amazement, Hitler changed roles. From one moment to the next, he transformed himself from a hot-headed, unpredictable megalomaniac into a rational, reasonably arguing negotiation partner. "If you agree that the principle of self-determination is the basis of the Sudeten question," Hitler proposed, "we can then talk about how this principle can be put into practice." Chamberlain responded that he would first have to consult his cabinet and suggested another meeting. The two men parted with Hitler assuring Chamberlain that he would not use force against Czechoslovakia in the meantime.[243]

Hardly had Chamberlain departed than Hitler informed Ribbentrop and Weizsäcker about how the talks had gone. "He clapped his hands like someone celebrating a particularly pleasurable success," Weizsäcker recalled. "He felt he had manoeuvred this dried-up civilian into a corner."[244] If he recognised the principle of self-determination, Chamberlain would have to be willing to support the cession of Sudeten territories to Germany. If the Czechs refused, Hitler believed, there were no further obstacles to a German military attack. If, contrary to expectations, the Czechs accepted this loss of territory, he could claim it as a victory and proceed with the ultimate destruction of Czechoslovakia at a later point, possibly the following spring.[245]

In the meantime, the situation in the Sudetenland became more and more tense. On the day of Chamberlain's visit Konrad Henlein issued a statement declaring that it was "ultimately impossible" for Sudeten Germans to remain in Czechoslovakia due to the "irreconcilable will for destruction" of the government in Prague. The declaration ended with the slogan: "We want to return home to the Reich."[246] Two days later, on orders from Berlin, a Sudeten German paramilitary unit was established, whose main task was to foment further unrest and stage acts of provocation. At the same time Goebbels stepped up his propaganda campaign against what he called "Czech terror," writing that "The mood must be brought to a boil."[247] The military planning of an attack against Czechoslovakia also continued. The main thing, Hitler told Goebbels, who had hurried to the Obersalzberg, was to keep their nerve: "We're already halfway to winning the war."[248]

Chamberlain was anything but impressed by Hitler's appearance. "He looks entirely undistinguished," the British prime minister wrote to his sister on 19 September. "You would never notice him in a crowd and would take him for the house painter he once was." But he also wrote in that same letter that he believed Hitler was a man of his word—a grievous error, as he would soon discover.[249] After his cabinet agreed to back him, Chamberlain agreed a joint line with France towards Prague. On 19 September, the British and French governments sent Beneš identical letters demanding that Czechoslovakia cede all territories with a German population of more than 50 per cent in return for guarantees of its new borders. Initially the government in Prague refused, but on 21 September it yielded to Western pressure.

Ahead of his second meeting with Chamberlain in Bad Godesberg, Hitler settled on a negotiating position that was as extreme as possible. "The Führer intends to present Chamberlain with clear demands," noted Goebbels on 22 September.

We get to draw the demarcation line as generously as possible. This area will be immediately vacated by the Czechs. The German Wehrmacht will march in. Everything within eight days. It will take that long to march in. If the other side is not happy with our [new] border, then a plebiscite in the entire area. That's to happen before Christmas . . . If Chamberlain demands new negotiations at a later date, then the Führer no longer feels bound by any prior agreements and can act as he wishes.[250]

At noon on 22 September, Chamberlain's plane landed in Cologne. He was housed with his delegation in the Hotel Petersberg, a short way up from Königswinter, and that afternoon Hitler received him in the Hotel Dreesen on the other side of the Rhine. This time the prime minister had brought along an interpreter of his own, Ivone Kirkpatrick, to avoid any misunderstandings.[251] Chamberlain was confident going into the negotiations. He had already secured the agreement of France and the Czechoslovakian government that the Sudeten territories would be ceded to Germany, thereby fulfilling Hitler's central demand. It was only reasonable to expect that the parties would reach quick agreement on this basis. He was therefore unpleasantly surprised when Hitler revealed that, "after the developments of the past few days," he could no longer accept this deal. "All at once, Chamberlain sat bolt upright in his chair," Paul Schmidt reported. "His face flushed in anger at the refusal and the lack of recognition of his effort." Hitler then presented a map with the new demarcation line and demanded that the occupation of the territories to be ceded "happen immediately." Chamberlain objected that this was a completely new demand that went beyond what they had agreed in Berchtesgaden, but Hitler remained adamant, declaring that he could no longer tolerate the persecution of Sudeten Germans by the Czechs. He also rejected the proposal for an international guarantee of Czech independence, arguing that Polish and Hungarian demands on Czech territory would also have to be settled soon. As the first round of negotiations concluded, the British contingent was left quite dispirited.[252]

The following day, Chamberlain did not appear for the scheduled continuation of talks. Instead he sent a letter that declared Hitler's new demands incompatible with principles previously agreed upon.

If German troops immediately advanced into the Sudetenland, the government in Prague would have no choice other than to order their troops to resist. The impact of the letter in the Hotel Dreesen was, in Schmidt's words, "like a bomb" had been dropped.[253] The German delegation grew edgy. William Shirer, who had the chance to observe Hitler up close in the hotel garden, was struck by "ugly black patches under his eyes" and a nervous twitching of his right shoulder, concluding: "I think the man is on the edge of a nervous breakdown."[254] Nonetheless, in the response which his interpreter delivered that afternoon, Hitler stuck to his demands. The negotiations seemed to have reached a complete impasse. "The whole situation is so tense it's coming apart at the seams," noted Goebbels.[255] But again Chamberlain proved conciliatory, offering to serve as a mediator between Berlin and Prague and asking for the new German demands to be collected in a memorandum. He would travel to Hitler's hotel on the other side of the Rhine to pick them up and get clarifications from Hitler.[256]

Around eleven that night, negotiations resumed with a wider circle of participants. On the German side Joachim von Ribbentrop, Ernst von Weizsäcker and the director of the legal department in the Foreign Ministry, Friedrich Gaus, took part. Horace Wilson and Ambassador Henderson represented Britain alongside Chamberlain. Schmidt translated the finished memorandum word for word. Hitler had not yielded an inch on the cardinal question and was still demanding that the withdrawal of Czechoslovakian forces from the Sudeten territory designated on his map begin on the morning of 26 September. It was to be concluded by 28 September, whereupon the area was to be ceded to Germany. The Czech government was being handed a deadline of four days. That was tantamount to an "ultimatum" for Chamberlain, who accused Hitler of failing to support even in the slightest his efforts to preserve peace.[257] Once again the negotiations were in danger of collapsing.

At this moment, one of Hitler's assistants brought the news that Beneš had ordered the general mobilisation of Czechoslovakia's armed forces. "Dead silence descended upon the room," Paul Schmidt recalled. "You could hear a pin drop." As though this bombshell had brought him to his senses, Hitler suddenly became more conciliatory. In a soft voice he reiterated his commitment not to take military action against Czechoslovakia as long as negotiations were ongoing and declared his

willingness to extend the deadline for evacuation by two days, until
1 October. He amended the memorandum in his own hand and made
some corrections to soften the wording. For his part, Chamberlain
stuck to his promise to pass on the document to the Czechoslovakian
government. Thus when the two sides took leave of one another on
24 September the atmosphere was not unfriendly. Hitler once again
displayed his charm, thanking Chamberlain profusely for his efforts to
preserve peace and assuring him that "the Sudeten question would be
the last major problem he saw himself compelled to resolve."[258]

But during a long walk with Goebbels though the Chancellery
garden on the afternoon of 25 September, Hitler made it clear how
much such assurances were worth. "He does not think that Beneš
will give in," Goebbels noted. "But terrible justice will be meted out
upon him if he does not. On 27 or 28 September, the deployment of
troops will be complete . . . And then we'll mobilise. That will be so
lightning-quick that the world will see it as a miracle." Hitler therefore
had by no means abandoned the plan of destroying Czechoslovakia
with a sudden military invasion. "The radical solution is the best one,"
Goebbels added. "Otherwise we'll never get rid of this matter."[259]

In fact, in a personal message to Hitler delivered by Horace Wilson
on the afternoon of 26 September, Chamberlain reported that the
government in Prague had rejected the memo as "fully unacceptable."
Although Hitler could hardly have been surprised by the news and,
in light of what he told Goebbels the day before, perhaps even
welcomed it, he nonetheless reacted with agitation. He jumped up
from his seat, yelling, "There is no point in negotiating any further."
He ran to the door as if he were about to quit the room and had to
be coaxed into listening as the message was read out in full. Afterwards,
Schmidt recalled, "he had a fit of a magnitude I never heard before
or after in a diplomatic discussion." Wilson repeatedly asked Hitler
to calm down, which only encouraged more outbreaks of fury.[260]

It seems as though Hitler's rage was not play-acted. As he had done
in the attempted putsch of 1923 and the Night of the Long Knives in
1934, he had likely worked himself up into an extraordinary psychological condition as the Sudeten crisis inexorably moved towards
a conclusion. In this state, in the evening of 26 September, he gave a
speech at Berlin's Sportpalast, by the end of which he was, in William
Shirer's words, "shouting and shrieking in the worst state of excitement

I have ever seen him in."²⁶¹ He began with an overview of his efforts for "practical policies of peace" in Europe, mentioning the German–Polish non-aggression pact, the naval agreement with Britain, his renunciation of Alsace-Lorraine, German friendship with Italy and the peaceful *Anschluss* of Austria. "And now we stand before the final problem that must and will be solved!" he shouted. "It is the last territorial demand I will make on Europe, but it is a demand upon which I will not yield and that I will, God willing, see fulfilled." He wildly lambasted Beneš, accusing the Czech president of waging a "war of extinction" against Germans in Czechoslovakia and declaring that "the time has come to talk in plain language." He had made Beneš an offer in his memorandum of 23 September, Hitler claimed, adding: "The decision is now in his hands." He then levelled a barely veiled threat: "War or peace. Either he can accept this offer and give Germans their freedom, or we will take this freedom ourselves! . . . We are determined. Herr Beneš now has the choice!"²⁶²

Shirer, who was sitting in the gallery directly above Hitler, remarked: "All during his speech he kept cocking his shoulder, and the opposite leg from the knee down would bounce up." For the first time, the American journalist thought that the Führer had "completely lost control of himself." After the speech, when Goebbels swore an oath of loyalty to the Führer and declared that "a November 1918" would never be repeated, Hitler could not hold himself back. "He leapt to his feet and with a fanatical fire in his eyes that I shall never forget brought his right hand, after a grand sweep, pounding down on the table and yelled with all the power in his mighty lungs: 'Ja!,'" wrote Shirer. "Then he slumped into his chair exhausted."²⁶³

The following morning Hitler was still in a state of agitation veering between euphoria and hysteria. Around noon, Horace Wilson appeared with another letter from Chamberlain. Britain, the prime minister wrote, would guarantee that Czechoslovakia honoured its commitment to evacuate the Sudetenland, if Germany would forgo using violence. Hitler refused even to consider the offer, insisting categorically that his memorandum had to be accepted by 2 p.m. on 28 September. Otherwise, the Wehrmacht would march into the Sudetenland on 1 October. He repeatedly threatened to "crush the Czechs," rolling his R's for dramatic effect. Whereupon Wilson calmly declared that he had also been instructed to communicate a further message from the prime minister. If France's obligations put it in a position where it had to directly engage in hostilities against Germany, the United Kingdom would consider itself bound to support France. Seemingly untouched by the significance of this statement, an enraged Hitler shot back: "If France and England want to start a fight, they should go ahead. It does not matter to me at all. I'm prepared for all eventualities."[264] With that the discussion was over. Wilson flew back to London that afternoon.

But Hitler was not nearly as indifferent to Chamberlain's warning as he pretended. In the days following the Bad Godesberg meeting, Hitler had assumed the British were "bluffing."[265] Now there was no longer any doubt that a German attack upon Czechoslovakia would mean war with both Britain and France. Facing this scenario, Hitler was unsure, even if he tried to conceal that fact from his entourage. In a conversation with Goebbels at noon on 27 September, he played the role of the steel-nerved statesman, pursuing his goal with the single-mindedness of a sleepwalker. His leading admirer was swept away—or at least pretended to be in his diary: "His hand did not tremble for a moment. A great genius walks among us . . . You simply have to serve him with profound faith."[266]

However, an incident in the centre of Berlin in the late afternoon of 27 September must have made an impression on Hitler. A motorised army division rolled down Wilhelmstrasse on its way to the Czech border in what was no doubt a demonstration of the Wehrmacht's military readiness. But pedestrians reacted quite differently than the crowds in the Sportpalast had, hurrying to the next underground station to avoid having to witness the spectacle. The few hundred people who had assembled on Wilhelmplatz stood in complete silence. When Hitler then briefly appeared on his balcony at the Chancellery, there were no cheers, and he quickly went back inside.[267] There was an unquestionable lack of enthusiasm among the public at large for another war, and for the first time, major doubts arose about Hitler's qualities as a statesman. Contemporary observers even talked about a crisis of trust between the people and their Führer.[268] This did not escape Goebbels's notice. Several days later, the propaganda minister admitted that the military division's passage through the centre of Berlin "had served to establish clarity about the mood of the people, and it was against war."[269]

On the evening of 27 September, Hitler seemed to have come to his senses and reconciled himself to the idea of a diplomatic solution that would hand him the risk-free triumph of amalgamating the Sudetenland, while only temporarily postponing his actual goal of destroying Czechoslovakia. He sent a conciliatory letter to Chamberlain, writing that he left it up to the British prime minister whether he thought it was worth continuing his efforts to bring the government in Prague "to reason at the final hour."[270] It was unclear whether Chamberlain would be willing to act as a mediator again, and Hitler kept the military option open for the more likely scenario that the prime minister refused to continue his mission. Around midnight, he repeated to Ernst von Weizsäcker that he wanted to "obliterate" the Czech state. As Weizsäcker wrote in a letter: "It will take a miracle to preserve peace."[271]

Ulrich von Hassell called 28 September "a critical day of the highest order."[272] The tension could be felt that morning in all of Europe's capitals. Only a few hours remained until Hitler's ultimatum elapsed. Nothing seemed capable of interrupting the momentum towards war. The Chancellery was a hive of activity, just as it had been on 11 March before the *Anschluss*. Ministers, military officers, high-ranking party functionaries and their staffs were standing and sitting around everywhere. Hitler, who was in an "extremely agitated, nervous mood," went from one group to the next, lecturing them. "There were many miniature Sportpalast speeches that morning," recalled Paul Schmidt.[273]

Shortly after 11 a.m., Hitler received the French ambassador, one of the few foreign diplomats he respected and whose opinion he valued. André François-Poncet urgently warned Hitler against the illusion that the conflict with Czechoslovakia could be localised. "If you attack this country, you will set all of Europe aflame . . ." Hitler was told. "Why do you want to take this risk, seeing that you can get your fundamental demands fulfilled without war?" Schmidt felt he could see in Hitler's face "how the scales gradually tipped towards peace." Unlike the previous day, Hitler did not blow his top, but rather patiently listened to François-Poncet's arguments.[274]

It was Mussolini's intervention, however, which finally tipped the balance. Around 11:40 a.m., the Italian ambassador, Bernardo Attolico, appeared at the Chancellery and announced breathlessly that he had an urgent message to convey from Il Duce. Hitler was summoned from his conversation with François-Poncet. The British government, Attolico announced, had asked via its ambassador if Italy would be willing to mediate. Mussolini had agreed to do so and therefore requested that the German government postpone mobilising its troops for twenty-four hours. Hitler briefly considered the request and then accepted Il Duce's suggestion. Only two hours before the German ultimatum was set to expire, the immediate threat of war had been removed.[275] At 12:15 p.m., when British Ambassador Henderson arrived at the Chancellery, he could sense that the atmosphere had changed. Henderson delivered Chamberlain's answer to Hitler's letter of the previous evening. The British prime minister suggested coming to Germany with the leaders of France and Italy for a conference to find a peaceful solution to the crisis. After Attolico had attested to Mussolini's willingness, Hitler agreed.[276] That afternoon, invitations were issued for a conference in Munich the following day.

On the evening of 28 September, Hitler travelled in a chartered train to the Bavarian capital. The following morning he went to Kufstein, where he boarded Mussolini's train, and the two dictators agreed a joint negotiating strategy. At the same time, French Prime Minister Edouard Daladier and Chamberlain landed at Oberwiesenfeld airport and were given a friendly welcome by Munich crowds on the way to their hotel.[277] In the early afternoon, the conference was opened in the "Führerbau" on Königsplatz. Taking part, in addition to the four heads of government, were Joachim von Ribbentrop, Count Ciano, Horace Wilson and the state secretary in the French Foreign Ministry, Alexis Léger. Göring, Weizsäcker, the ambassadors of Britain, France and Italy as well as expert lawyers, assistants and secretaries also joined the proceedings. Hitler was polite and solicitous, but he obviously felt uncomfortable. His face was pale, and his movements were agitated. Unable to speak any foreign languages, he stuck by Mussolini's side during the conference breaks, talking in German with him. Indeed, Hitler seemed positively fixated on the self-confident Italian leader. "When Il Duce laughed so did he; when Il Duce knitted his brow so did he," recalled François-Poncet. "I will never forget the scenes of imitation."[278]

One after another, the four heads of government stated their views. All of them stressed that they wanted to find a peaceful solution. "The atmosphere was one of general amicability interrupted only by several enraged attacks by Hitler on Beneš and some spirited rebuttals by Daladier," recalled Schmidt.[279] In the end Mussolini presented a written proposal. He was not the author, however: the document had been drawn up by Göring, Neurath and Weizsäcker, who had bypassed the warmongering Ribbentrop and given it directly to the Italian ambassador for transmission to Rome.[280] The document, which merged the demands from the German memorandum with British and French suggestions, formed the basis of the Munich Agreement, which the four leaders signed in the early hours of 30 September. It specified that the German army would begin occupying the Sudetenland on 1 October, and that the process would be completed in stages by 10 October. An international committee was to be formed consisting of representatives from Germany, Great Britain, France, Italy and Czechoslovakia. Popular referendums were to be held in disputed areas before the definitive borders of Czechoslovakia were set. Sudeten German political prisoners were to be granted amnesty. Moreover, in a separate declaration, Britain and France guaranteed the integrity of the remaining Czechoslovak state. Germany and Italy pledged to join the agreement as soon as the question of the country's Polish and Hungarian minorities was settled.[281] Before sunrise, Chamberlain and Daladier informed two representatives from Czechoslovakia, who had not been permitted to attend the conference, about its final outcome. William Shirer described Daladier as a "completely beaten and broken man."[282] To keep the peace and buy time, and in response to pressure from Britain, the French government had abandoned its commitment to its ally Czechoslovakia. By contrast, the mood in Berlin was euphoric. "We've achieved everything we set out to according to our little plan," Goebbels commented. "The big plan cannot be realised due to the prevailing circumstances at the moment. We walked a narrow tightrope over a dizzying abyss. Now we have solid ground under our feet again. That's a nice feeling."[283]

Hitler, however, was anything but euphoric. "Pale and ill-tempered" was how Paul Schmidt described him when the Führer received Chamberlain in his private apartment on 30 September. While the British prime minister cheerfully expounded on the new perspectives the Munich Agreement opened up for the Anglo-German relationship, Hitler sat there distracted, uncharacteristically hardly saying a word. In conclusion, Chamberlain took out a communiqué he had written that expressed the wish of both peoples never to "go to war with one another again" and to consult with one another to "remove possible sources of difference." Hitler silently signed it.[284] The next day he told Goebbels that he had not wanted to rebuff Chamberlain but did not believe that the document was "meant seriously by the other side."[285] In reality, Hitler never considered abandoning his war plans for a second. The reason for his bad mood was that he had failed to achieve his "big solution"—the break-up of Czechoslovakia. Hitler may have told his military attachés directly after Chamberlain's visit that in the short term he was not thinking of "any steps that could be politically dangerous" and that "we first must digest what we've won." But he was already beginning to look towards his next target for expansion after Czechoslovakia, as was revealed in his remark: "When the time is right, we'll soften up Poland using the tried and tested methods."[286] As time passed, Hitler began increasingly to view the Munich Agreement as a setback that had disrupted his timetable.[287]

Hitler's mood would hardly have improved when he learned that the German people had showered Chamberlain with ovations as he travelled in an open car through the streets of Munich. As Schmidt noted, the enthusiasm for Chamberlain carried an "undertone of criticism of Hitler" as the one who had led the world to the brink of a major war.[288] Relief that armed conflict had been averted was palpable everywhere, and only hardcore Hitler admirers such as the Wagners ascribed this fact to the Führer's "genius."[289] Reports by SPD-in-exile observers told a quite different story. They too described an overwhelming public feeling of joy that an international affair had once again ended happily, but they warned that this was not a lasting peace, but a "temporary ceasefire that will only last a few months or one or two years at the most." One report from south-western Germany read: "Despite the great triumph Hitler has achieved, the enthusiasm even among the most fanatical supporters of the regime is not as great as it was with the annexation of Austria."[290]

Hitler was deeply disappointed by the popular longing for peace that manifested itself in the days surrounding the Munich Agreement. "There is no way I can wage war with this people," he is said to have complained.[291] He drew his own conclusions from the pacificist mood of the population in a confidential speech to selected representatives of the press on 10 November 1938. His years of peaceful rhetoric, he said, had led to the false conclusion that the regime wanted to preserve peace "under all circumstances." It was therefore necessary to "recalibrate the German people psychologically and make it clear that there were things which, should they not be achieved by peaceful means, would have to be pushed through by force."[292]

The Munich Agreement was also a major setback for those who opposed Hitler. They had hoped that the Western powers would finally stand up and resist Hitler's campaign of aggression, and they were commensurately disappointed. The agreement, observers for the SPD in exile concluded, "has shaken to the core the opposition's faith in the ultimate triumph of what's right and the restoration of honesty and trust in the world."[293] This was true not only for Social Democrats and Communists but also for those conservative nationalist circles which had formed a conspiratorial group in response to the looming threat of war. Much remains unclear about the "September conspiracy," as the movement has been termed by historians, since most of what we know rests on individuals' statements after the Second World War, which may not be reliable. It seems that the movement consisted of a loose-knit network of people and groups with extremely diverse interests and ideas.[294] There were high-ranking military and govern-mental officials like Franz Halder and Ernst von Weizsäcker, whose activities were aimed not at overthrowing Hitler, but rather preventing a major European war, which they were convinced would end cata-strophically for Germany.[295] Then there was a group around Lieutenant-Colonel Hans Oster in the counter-intelligence department of the Wehrmacht Supreme Command and Interior Ministry official Hans Gisevius who wanted to use the Sudetenland crisis as a springboard for deposing the regime. We can only speculate about how far any plans for a coup d'état may have progressed and whether they would have had any chance of success. In any case, when Hitler followed Mussolini's suggestion and moderated his demands on 28 September, the rug was pulled from under their feet.[296]

In private, Hitler left no doubt that he considered Czechoslovakian cession of the Sudetenland only an interim solution. On 2 October, only three days after the Munich Agreement was signed, he discussed the situation with Goebbels, who noted: "His determination to oblit-erate the Czechs is unbroken."[297] In early October, Hitler travelled twice to the Sudetenland, inspecting the Czech defensive fortifications that had been handed over to the Wehrmacht without a fight. On 9 October, in a prominent speech in the western German city of Saarbrücken, he once again adopted a more aggressive tone towards Britain. While conceding that Chamberlain was prepared to reach an agreement, the situation would change immediately if power fell to politicians like Winston Churchill, whose explicit goal, Hitler claimed, was to "immediately unleash a new world war." Great Britain, he said, should cast off "certain airs from the Versailles epoch," adding, "We are no longer going to tolerate such schoolmarmish, patronising behaviour." This was not the only remark that showed how deeply irked Hitler was by the Munich Agreement. He also criticised indirectly the German people's predisposition towards peace. There were "weaklings" at home too, he hissed, who had not understood that "a difficult choice must be made."[298] The dictator was thinking, among others, of his military attaché Fritz Wiedemann. In late October he told Goebbels that Wiedemann would have to go since he had "not held up or kept his nerve during the crisis," adding, "Such people are useless when things come to a crunch."[299] As we have seen, Wiedemann would be sent to San Francisco as a consul general in January 1939. The former Economics Minister Hjalmar Schacht offered him consolation, saying that for him it had been a "great boon . . . to be able to see things from the outside for a while." In a letter to Wiedemann, Schacht wrote: "Things are developing with increasing speed thanks to the dynamism of the 'movement.' Be careful what you say. People here pay attention to every word."[300]

On 14 October, the publisher Hugo Bruckmann celebrated his seventy-fifth birthday, and Hitler personally presented his former patron with a large bouquet of flowers and chatted with him for one and a half hours, reliving old memories. "He was very personable and pleasant," the Bruckmanns told Ulrich von Hassell. "But everything he said clearly suggested that he had not got over the intervention of the [Western] powers and would have preferred his war. He was particularly angry at England—that was the reason for his incomprehensibly coarse speech in Saarbrücken."[301] This was not the only statement of its kind in Munich around this time, and it shows that Hitler was already plotting his next foreign-policy adventure. "[Hitler will] only remain calm for a little while," the former Economics Minister Kurt Schmitt opined. "He cannot help but cast his eye upon his next strategic move."[302]

Never stop—that was the law by which the National Socialist movement and its charismatic Führer operated and which gave the process
of coming to and consolidating power its irresistible dynamic. After
the great foreign-policy triumphs of 1938, Hitler never for a moment
considered taking an extended break and being satisfied with what he
had achieved, as Bismarck had done after 1871. He constantly needed
new victories to compensate for nascent popular dissatisfaction and
to bolster his own prestige. As a result, he was willing to take ever
greater risks, and his fear that he would die young lent further urgency
and impatience to his expansive activism. Hitler both drove events and
was himself a driven man. Thus on 21 October, he issued instructions
to the Wehrmacht concerning the destruction of the "remnants" of
Czechoslovakia. German plans were geared even in peacetime towards
"a sudden attack . . . so that the Czechs have no chance to organise
any sort of defence." The goal was "to rapidly occupy the country
and seal off Czech from Slovak territory."[303]

Foreign policy took a back seat in November and December 1938,
as the Nazi leadership concentrated on the Kristallnacht pogrom and
its aftermath. In late November, news that Berlin and Paris had come
to an agreement created a bit of a stir. The initiative had come from
French Foreign Minister Georges Bonnet, who sought some sort of
conciliation with France's increasingly threatening neighbour in the
wake of the Munich Agreement. On 6 December, Ribbentrop and
Bonnet signed a declaration in which France and Germany promised
to maintain "peaceful and neighbourly relations" and recognise their
mutual border. But lacking any specific commitments, this agreement
was not worth any more than the Anglo-German declaration of
30 September.[304]

In early February 1939, after his speech to the Reichstag on the
anniversary of taking power, Hitler withdrew to the Obersalzberg
with the express intent of pondering his next foreign-policy moves.
"Perhaps it will be the Czechs' turn again," Goebbels speculated. "That
problem has only been half solved."[305] On 10 February, Hitler returned
to Berlin to speak to army commanders in the Kroll Opera House.
The transcript of this speech, which was meant to be confidential, is
an enlightening document. Hitler spelled out his plans for the future
with rare openness. He began by criticising "certain Wehrmacht
circles" for adopting "a wait-and-see, if not sceptical attitude" towards

his risky policy on the Sudetenland. For that reason, Hitler said, he felt it necessary to let the officer corps in on the "internal reasons" that motivated his action. All of his foreign-policy moves since 1933, Hitler claimed, had followed a predetermined plan and were anything but spontaneous reactions to various situations. The triumphs of 1938 were by no means the final fulfilment of his ambition, but merely "a step along a long path, to which we have been predestined, gentlemen, and whose necessity I now want to briefly explain."

At this point Hitler revealed to his officer corps what he had told his top military leaders on 3 February 1933 and 5 November 1937. As the "strongest people not just in Europe but practically the entire word," Hitler said, the 85 million Germans, all members of a highly civilised race, had a right to greater space in order to preserve their standard of living. "I have taken it upon myself to solve the German question," Hitler declared, "that is, the German problem of [not having enough] space. You should be aware that as long as I live this thought will dominate my entire existence." He would never "shrink back even from the most extreme measures," Hitler added, and he expected his officer corps to stand behind with "trusting faith." Without explicitly naming the Soviet Union, he told his army commanders: "The next struggle will be a war purely of world views, a war between peoples and races."[306] The response to these revelations was apparently mixed. Hitler's attaché Gerhard Engel described the reaction as "partly enthusiastic and partly very sceptical."[307]

To start with, however, Hitler set about capturing what had escaped his clutches in the autumn of 1938. His preparations for the annexation of the remaining Czech territory were twofold. On the one hand, he came up with a variety of excuses for delaying the acknowledgement of Czech sovereignty guaranteed under the Munich Agreement; on the other, he encouraged separatist Slovaks to break away from what was left of Czechoslovakia. When negotiations between Prague and Bratislava over Slovak autonomy broke down, the new Czechoslovakian president, Emil Hácha, dismissed the local Slovakian government under Father Jozef Tiso, a German ally, and sent troops into Slovakia. "This is a launching pad," noted Goebbels with glee. "Now we can get a complete solution to the problem we were only half able to solve in October." At noon on 10 March, Hitler summoned Goebbels, Ribbentrop and Keitel to the Chancellery. "Decision: on Wednesday,

15 March, we'll invade and destroy the entire monstrous construct that is Czechoslovakia," Goebbels wrote. "The Führer is crowing with delight. The outcome is dead certain."[308] The Wehrmacht was issued its orders on 12 March. "The people are completely calm," Goebbels noted. "No one knows or suspects anything."[309]

On the afternoon of 13 March, Jozef Tiso arrived in Berlin at the Nazi government's request. Hitler informed him that Germany was about to occupy Czech territory and told him to proclaim Slovakian independence immediately. Otherwise, Hitler threatened, he would abandon Slovakia to its fate—that is, give Hungarian troops massing on the border carte blanche to invade.[310] On 14 March, the parliament in Bratislava declared Slovakia an independent state. At noon that day, as Hitler and Goebbels were discussing the details for what would become the "Reich Protectorate of Bohemia and Moravia," news arrived that Hácha had requested an audience with Hitler. Hitler agreed to meet the Czechoslovakian president but also informed the Wehrmacht leadership that the scheduled invasion would proceed no matter the circumstances.[311] That evening, accompanied by Czech Foreign Minister František Chvalkovský, Hácha arrived at Anhalter station in Berlin. The guard of honour on hand to welcome him was nothing but a façade. Hitler had no intention of negotiating in good faith. His goal was complete Czech capitulation, and he employed the same tactics of wearing down his opponent that he had used against Kurt von Schuschnigg. He kept his visitors waiting for hours in the Adlon Hotel, while he watched a movie at the Chancellery.[312]

It was past midnight when Hácha and Chvalkovský were led through the long hallways and reception rooms of the Reich Chancellery to Hitler's gigantic office, which was only dimly lit by several standing lamps.[313] To put additional pressure on his visitors, Hitler had a large group of underlings in attendance. Alongside Göring, Keitel and Ribbentrop, there were Ernst von Weizsäcker, Otto Meissner, Press Spokesman Otto Dietrich and the interpreter Paul Schmidt; also present was the SS officer and Foreign Ministry State Secretary Walter Hewel, who took the minutes of the meeting.[314] What ensued was the political equivalent of a scene from a gangster film without parallel in recent diplomatic history. Hácha had hoped to preserve at least partial Czech independence, but Hitler made it brutally clear right from the outset that there was no room for compromise. He rattled off a litany of supposed Czech affronts, claimed that the new Czech government was still animated by the "spirit of Beneš" and announced his intention to turn the remaining Czech territory into a German protectorate: at 6 a.m., the Wehrmacht would be invading. Hácha could do his people "one final service" by phoning his minister of war with the order not to resist German troops. "Hácha and Chvalkovský sat frozen in their seats," Schmidt recalled.[315] While an underling tried to establish a telephone connection with Prague, Göring threatened an aerial bombardment of that city if German demands were not met. That was apparently too much for the Czech president, who collapsed. Hitler's personal doctor Theodor Morell was called to give the only-semi-conscious Hácha an injection.[316]

Hácha recovered sufficiently to confer with his foreign minister in a separate room and issue the orders demanded to Prague via telephone. Around 4 a.m., he and Chvalkovský signed a declaration, presented to them by Hitler, in which the Czech president "entrusted the fate of the Czech people and country to the hands of the Führer of the German Reich." At this point, the minutes read, "The Führer accepted this declaration and expressed his commitment to take the Czech people under the protection of the German Reich and to guarantee an autonomous development of its ethnic-popular life in keeping with its particular characteristics."[317] None of the Germans present, including Weizsäcker, raised a word of objection to the treatment of the Czech delegation, which violated the basic conventions of diplomacy and common decency. On the contrary, in his 1950 memoirs, Weizsäcker still had the audacity to accuse Hácha of being complicit in the "seemingly legal beginning of Hitler's march on Prague."[318] This top diplomat also shared the Führer's racist prejudices against the Czechs. "They were never pleasant: outside the Reich border they were lice in the fur and inside, scabies under the skin," Weizsäcker remarked one day after the unscrupulous coercion of Hácha, which he euphemistically called a "memorable late-night act of negotiation led by the Führer using the whole range of tactics."[319]

Hitler himself was "overjoyed" and self-satisfied by the "greatest stroke of political genius of all time."[320] He demanded that his two secretaries Christa Schroeder and Gerda Daranowski, who had spent the night in a room next to Hitler's office, each give him a kiss on the cheek, saying: "This is the best day of my life . . . I will go down in history as the greatest German ever."[321] In the small hours German troops crossed the Czech border, and by 9 a.m. the first units had reached Prague, where they were greeted not with cheers, but with silence and choked-back anger. Around noon, Hitler boarded a train for the Bohemian town of Ceská Lípá, from where he travelled the remaining 100 kilometres to Prague in his three-axle Mercedes limousine. It was snowing heavily, so the city's inhabitants barely noticed him arriving at the Hradschin Castle, the office of the Czech president. Nothing had been prepared for his arrival, so his adjutants were sent out to procure some ham, sausage and beer.[322]

That night, assisted by Frick and Stuckart, Hitler issued a decree establishing the Reich Protectorate of Bohemia and Moravia. It granted Czechs a measure of autonomy.[323] Hitler named former Foreign Minister von Neurath as "Reich Protector." As a member of the old conservative elites, he was considered a moderate, and thus his appointment served to camouflage the fact that the Czechs were being subjected to German occupation.[324] At the same time, at Jozef Tiso's request, Slovakia was also placed under German protection, and German troops advanced to Bratislava. On the afternoon of 16 March, Hitler left Prague, returning to Berlin on 19 March via Brünn, Linz and Vienna. Goebbels had once again succeeded in mobilising thousands of people in the capital to turn out and cheer the Führer as he drove from the Görlitzer station to the Chancellery. "We have a week behind us that out of all the astonishing events we have experienced thus far has probably brought the most astonishing thing of all," former Reich negotiator and museum director Rudolf Buttmann noted in his diary. Hitler's "great statesmanship" had once again led to a "massive increase in power" without bloodshed. "He is always lucky," an acquaintance told Buttmann in the street.[325]

But such sentiments did not reflect the mood of the entire population. The annexation of the remnants of the Czech state was anything but universally welcomed. Many people remembered Hitler promising in his Sportpalast speech on 26 September that the Sudetenland would be his last territorial demand, asking "Was this really necessary?"[326] The executive committee of the SPD in exile, which had been forced to relocate from Prague to Paris, spoke on the basis of reports from within Germany of widespread "concern that with its latest 'victory'

Germany had taken another step towards a major war and another defeat."[327]

The significance of the destruction of Czechoslovakia for Hitler's war plans was considerable. The German Reich gained not only the largest Czechoslovakian armaments facilities, the Skoda factories in Pilsen and Prague; it also acquired enough weapons and supplies to outfit twenty further divisions. In addition to industrial resources, the German war effort gained access to Czechoslovakian copper, nickel, lead, aluminium, zinc and tin. The door was also wide open for Germany to penetrate the Danube and Balkan region economically. And in terms of military strategy, the Reich was now better positioned to launch campaigns to conquer further "living space in the east."[328]

On the evening of 15 March, Hitler was convinced that "in a fortnight, no one will be talking about this any more,"[329] but he was fundamentally mistaken. Hitler's seizure of Prague was a wake-up call to leaders in London, where the British government realised that it had been duped and that Hitler's promises were not worth the paper they were written on. The policy of appeasement and the idea that Hitler could be restrained by treaties and conciliation were revealed as utterly misguided. Ambassador Henderson was withdrawn from Berlin until further notice,[330] and in a speech in Birmingham on 17 March, Chamberlain announced an about-turn in British policy. The prime minister accused Hitler of crassly violating the principle of national self-determination that he himself had always invoked, concluding his address by asking: "Is this in fact a step towards trying to dominate the world by force?"[331]

The Nazi leadership did not take seriously the protests from London, which the French government seconded. "This is just hysterical, after-the-fact wailing that leaves us entirely cold," Goebbels scoffed.[332] Indeed, Hitler thought that he could exploit the situation to stage his next foreign-policy coup. On 20 March, Ribbentrop summoned Lithuanian Foreign Minister Joseph Urbsys, who was visiting Berlin, and demanded the immediate return of the Klaipeda Region, known in Germany as the Memel Territory, a part of East Prussia that had been put under French control after the First World War and was subsequently annexed by Lithuania in 1923. Two days later, the Lithuanian council of ministers approved the handover, and that afternoon Hitler boarded the battleship MS *Deutschland* in the port of

Swinemünde. Around midnight, Ribbentrop announced the signing of a treaty reuniting the Memel Territory with the Reich. Hitler declared a corresponding law the following morning while still on board the ship. "You live in a great age," he declared to his manservant Heinz Linge. "We now take care of little matters like this on the side."[333] At 2 p.m., Hitler disembarked at the port of Memel and gave a short speech from the balcony of the city's main theatre, in which he welcomed "our old German racial comrades as the newest citizens of our Greater German Empire."[334] That same evening he departed the city, and by noon on 24 March he was back in Berlin.

The amalgamation of the Memel Territory was the last foreign triumph Hitler would achieve without bloodshed. In the night of 21–22 March, while awaiting the decision of the Lithuanian government, he held a long conversation with Goebbels in the Chancellery about his future foreign policy. "He wants to calm things down a bit so that we regain trust," Goebbels reported in his diary.[335] Should Hitler have said anything of the kind, he was doubly deceiving himself. On the one hand, as we have seen, neither the Nazi system of rule nor Hitler's own personality allowed for any periods of extended peace and quiet. Less than three days after their conversation, Goebbels once again found him pondering how he could "solve the question of Danzig," or Gdansk, which had been declared a free city after the First World War. "He intends to apply some pressure on Poland and hopes that Poland responds," Goebbels noted.[336] With that, there was no more doubt about the next target of Hitler's free-flowing aggression. And Hitler also deceived himself about the possibility of regaining the trust of the Western powers, which he had forfeited once and for all by breaking the Munich Agreement. He had removed the mask of the peace-loving politician who only wanted to revise the status quo, and everyone could now see the brutal nature of his regime, which demanded unlimited expansion. The real problem, as British Foreign Secretary Lord Halifax put it at a cabinet meeting on 18 March, was Germany's drive for world domination, which it was in the interests of all states to resist.[337] On 31 March, Britain and France issued a statement guaranteeing the independence of Poland. The two sides of what in a few months would become the Second World War had been formed.

With the Kristallnacht pogrom the preceding November, Hitler had broken with all norms of civilisation. Now, by marching on Prague, he had crossed a comparable line in foreign policy. Ulrich von Hassell was right when he diagnosed this as "a first case of open hubris, a violation of all boundaries and also of all standards of decency."[338] There was no going back. On 15 March, Hitler believed he was at the zenith of his unprecedented career, but in reality his descent had already begun. He had gone down a path that would lead to his own demise. "That day," as François-Poncet aptly put it, "his fate was sealed."[339]

Of course, contemporary observers had to have a particularly keen eye to see the seeds of future catastrophe within Hitler's triumphs.[340] On 20 April 1939, as Germany's dictator celebrated his fiftieth birthday, the shadows of nemesis were far off in the future. Goebbels once again did his utmost to encourage cultish worship of the Führer. "The creator of Greater Germany is fifty years old," wrote Victor Klemperer. "Two days of lavish special editions of the newspapers. People falling over themselves to deify him."[341] Goebbels had begun preparing this event the previous summer. Then, in early December, Hitler had mentioned in passing that he did not wish for any particular festivities on his birthday, which Goebbels interpreted as an order to halt the preparations.[342] But the propaganda minister must have realised that Hitler had not wanted to be taken at his word. In terms of sheer volume, the programme that he came up with in January and which Hitler approved went beyond any previous festivities marking the Führer's birthday. Several days before the big event Goebbels noted drily: "A lot of work with the Führer's birthday. This time it is truly going to be celebrated."[343]

The press was issued detailed instructions about how the man at the top was to be honoured. Journalists were told not to write about "his childhood, his family or his private life" as "unbelievable amounts of nonsense have been published on these three subjects in the past." By contrast, they were encouraged to spill lots of ink about Germany's political turnaround and the political career of Adolf Hitler, and newspapers were instructed to publish large-scale, beautifully designed special editions.[344] The unusual significance of Hitler's fiftieth birthday as the ceremonial high point of the year was underscored when, at short notice, Wilhelm Frick declared 20 April 1939 a national holiday. That allowed large numbers of Germans from every corner of the Reich to take part in the festivities.

A radio address by Goebbels broadcast on all stations in Germany at 6:30 p.m. on 19 April kicked off the official programme. In his customary Byzantine style, the propaganda minister lauded Hitler as a "man of historic stature," whom the German people willingly and obediently followed in everything he undertook. "Like a miracle," Goebbels declared, Hitler had found a "basic solution to a central European question previously regarded as nearly insoluble." He called Hitler's forced break-up of Czechoslovakia an act of "peace based on practical reality."[345] At seven that evening, the entire NSDAP leadership—1,600 people in total—offered their congratulations in the Mosaic Hall of the Chancellery. Hess reassured the Führer of the unconditional loyalty of his vassals, should the "conflict-mongers of the world take things to the extreme," and presented Hitler with the gift of fifty original letters written by his hero Friedrich the Great.[346] These were only one of the many presents that lay stacked upon tables in the same Chancellery hall where Bismarck had convened the Berlin Congress in 1878. Many of them were kitsch, but some gifts—for instance, works by two of Hitler's favourite painters, Franz von Defregger and Carl Theodor von Piloty—were quite valuable. The economics minister and Reichsbank president, Walther Funk, outdid everyone else with his present for the art lover Hitler: *Venus in Front of the Mirror* by Titian.[347]

The main spectacle on the eve of Hitler's birthday was the dedication of the East–West Axis, the first major stretch of the new traffic system envisioned for the makeover of the capital. Accompanied by Albert Speer, Hitler drove down the broad, 7-mile road in an open car, where hundreds of thousands of Berliners had responded to Goebbels's call to turn out and form a guard of honour. "A celebration without compare," a satisfied Goebbels noted. "The street was bathed in a fairy-tale glow. And an unprecedented atmosphere. The Führer beamed with glee."[348] Shortly after 10 p.m. at the Wehrmacht's Grand Tattoo, fifty members of the "old guard" from each of the Gaue paraded by torchlight down Wilhelmstrasse. The Führer greeted the columns of Brownshirts from the Chancellery balcony.

At midnight, Hitler accepted the congratulations and gifts of his inner entourage. He seemed especially taken by the 4-metre-high model of the gigantic triumphal arch that Speer had had installed in the hall on Pariser Platz. "Visibly moved, he gazed for a long time at the model that physically manifested the dream of his younger years,"

Speer recalled. "Completely overcome, he shook my hand without saying a word, before telling the other guests in a euphoric voice about the significance of this structure for the future history of the Reich."[349] Almost compulsively, Hitler returned to stare at the model numerous times that night, abandoning himself to his fantastical vision of the future "world capital Germania."

The festivities continued the following morning with a concert by the band of the SS Leibstandarte in the Chancellery garden. The doyen of the diplomatic corps, the Papal nuncio Monsignor Cesare Orsenigo, led the ranks of those congratulating Hitler on his birthday. He was followed by the Reich Protector of Bohemia and Moravia, Konstantin von Neurath, with Emil Hácha in his wake, Jozef Tiso, members of the Reich government and the heads of the Wehrmacht. Symbolically for Hitler's immediate plans was the fact that he received the Gauleiter of Danzig, Albert Forster, who brought along a document naming Hitler an honorary citizen of the city intended as a "sign of its profound blood relation" to the German people.[350]

At 11 a.m., the Wehrmacht commenced its parade up and down the East–West Axis. It lasted four hours and aimed at illustrating the military strength the Reich had built up. All Wehrmacht formations took part, and the most modern weaponry, particularly tanks and heavy artillery, was put on display. A grandstand had been erected in front of Berlin's Technical University, where Hitler inspected the parade from under a canopy with a throne and the Führer's banner. "I always wonder where he gets his strength," Christa Schroeder wrote in a letter to a friend. "To stand there and greet people for four hours is damn taxing. We all felt dead tired just watching him."[351]

At Hitler's behest, Ribbentrop had invited 150 prominent foreign guests whom he sought to impress with such a display of military force. Absent from the grandstand, however, were the ambassadors of Britain and France, who had been recalled after Hitler's violation of the Munich Agreement. The United States had withdrawn its ambassador in November 1938 after the Kristallnacht pogrom. After the parade, Hitler invited his foreign guests to take tea with him, the Reich ministers, the Reich directors of the Nazi Party and the military leadership at the Chancellery.[352]

The German newsreels covering the week from 16 to 23 April were devoted exclusively to Hitler's fiftieth birthday. Twelve cameramen had shot more than 10,000 metres of film, which had been edited down to the standard newsreel length of 546 metres. The military parade, praised by the narrator as "the greatest military display of the Third Reich," was the centrepiece of the reports. No doubt this emphasis was intended to get the populace psychologically used to war, as Hitler had called for in his speech to the officer corps on 10 November 1938. Hitler no longer presented himself in the guise of the infallible statesman, but in the martial pose of a field commander who was displaying the fearsome might of his military machine to the eyes of an astonished world.[353]

Goebbels was extremely satisfied with how the two-day festivities had gone. "The Führer was celebrated by the people," he wrote, "as no mortal man before him has ever been celebrated."[354] SPD-in-exile observers had a more nuanced view of the event. If you looked at the amount of effort that went into the birthday, they wrote, you might easily think that Hitler's popularity was on the rise. "But anyone who really knows the people," opined one observer, "knows that a lot, if not all of this, is just show." Even the readers of the Nazified press were under no illusions about the fact that "Hitler's foreign-policy star is on the wane and the system is heading towards a second world war that seems lost right from the start." The observers concluded that "the paralysing fear of war hung over all the bannered splendour and celebratory din." But they hastened to add that this did not mean that the German people's faith in the Führer was "extinguished." On the contrary, it was "alive and well in broad swathes of the populace."[355] Ultimately Hitler's popularity was due to his aura as someone who always managed to maintain peace despite all his risky manoeuvres. When he unleashed world war at the start of September 1939 and when it became apparent in the winter of 1941–42 that, despite Germany's lightning-quick early triumphs, the conflict was turning into a military catastrophe, the myth surrounding the Führer would begin to decay, at first slowly but then faster and faster.

Notes

Introduction

1. In Thomas Mann, *An die gesittete Welt: Politische Schriften und Reden im Exil*, Frankfurt am Main, 1986, p. 253f.
2. Norbert Frei, *1945 und wir: Das Dritte Reich im Bewusstsein der Deutschen*, Munich, 2005, p. 7.
3. Jens Jessen, "Gute Zeiten für Hitler," *Die Zeit*, 11 Oct. 2012; *idem*, "Was macht Hitler so unwiderstehlich?," *Die Zeit*, 23 Sept. 2004.
4. Konrad Heiden, *Adolf Hitler: Das Zeitalter der Verantwortungslosigkeit. Eine Biographie*, Zurich, 1936; *idem*, *Adolf Hitler: Ein Mann gegen Europa. Eine Biographie*, Zurich, 1937; Alan Bullock, *Hitler: A Study in Tyranny*, London, 1990 (first published 1952); Joachim Fest, *Hitler*, Frankfurt am Main, Berlin and Vienna, 1973; Ian Kershaw, *Hitler 1889–1936: Hubris*, London, 1998; *idem*, *Hitler 1936–1945: Nemesis*, London, 2000. In addition, Sebastian Haffner's essay *Anmerkungen zu Hitler* is consistently thought-provoking.
5. Heiden, *Adolf Hitler: Ein Mann gegen Europa*, p. 267.
6. Heiden, *Adolf Hitler: Das Zeitalter der Verantwortungslosigkeit*, p. 6.
7. See Rainer Zitelmann, "Hitlers Erfolge: Erklärungsversuche in der Hitler-Forschung," *Neue Politische Literatur*, 27 (1982), pp. 47–69, at p. 47 f.; John Lukacs, *Hitler: Geschichte und Geschichtsschreibung*, Munich, 1997, p. 20f.; Ulrich Nill, "'Reden wie Lustmorde': Hitler-Biographen über Hitler als Redner," in Josef Kopperschmidt (ed.), *Hitler als Redner*, Munich, 2003, pp. 29–37, at pp. 35–7.
8. Thea Sternheim, *Tagebücher 1903–1971. Vol. II: 1925–1936*, eds. Thomas Ehrsam und Regula Wyss, Göttingen, 2002, p. 664 (entry for 31 Oct. 1935). In a letter to Konrad Heiden, Thea Sternheim wrote that he was the first to say "decisive words on these matters." She added: "How marvellous to see such a finely honed rapier gleaming." Ibid., pp. 665f. (entry for 4 Nov. 1935).
9. Harry Graf Kessler, *Das Tagebuch. Vol. 9: 1926–1937*, ed. Sabine Gruber and Ulrich Ott, with Christoph Hilse and Nadin Weiss, Stuttgart, 2010, p. 663 (entry for 14 April 1936).
10. See Ernst Schulte Strathaus, expert on cultural questions in the staff of the Führer's deputy, to Gerhard Klopfer, 5 Oct. 1936, requesting "that the Gestapo and the Security Service collect information on the writer Konrad Heiden." BA Berlin-Lichterfelde, NS 26/45.
11. See Lukacs, *Hitler*, p. 22f.; Gerhard Schreiber, *Hitler: Interpretationen 1923–1983: Ergebnisse, Methoden und Probleme der Forschung*, Darmstadt, 1984, pp. 312–14.
12. Bullock, *Hitler*, p. 382. Bullock revised his position in later works, in particular his double biography *Hitler and Stalin: Parallel Lives*, London, 1991.

13 Hermann Rauschning, *Die Revolution des Nihilismus*, Zurich, 1938, p. 56. Rauschning repeated this assessment when he published his conversations with Hitler (*Gespräche mit Hitler*, Zurich, 1940). Bullock and Fest saw this book as a major source, while Kershaw doubted its authenticity. See Kershaw, *Hitler: Hubris*, p. xiv. The present volume also does not use this source. On the question of the authenticity of *Gespräche mit Hitler*, see Jürgen Hensel and Pia Nordblom (eds.), *Hermann Rauschning: Materialien und Beiträge zu einer politischen Biographie*, Osnabrück, 2003, pp. 151ff.

14 Eberhard Jäckel, *Hitlers Weltanschauung: Entwurf einer Herrschaft* (1969), revised edition, Stuttgart, 1981. Jäckel's investigation had been triggered by the British historian Hugh Trevor-Roper's remark that Hitler's world view had been fixed from 1923 at the latest, and was afterwards expressed "absolutely clear and consequential" in his actions. Quoted in ibid., p. 19.

15 Eberhard Jäckel, "Rückblick auf die sogenannte Hitler-Welle," *Geschichte in Wissenschaft und Unterricht*, 28 (1977), pp. 695–710, at p. 706.

16 Karl-Dietrich Bracher, "Hitler—die deutsche Revolution: Zu Joachim Fests Interpretation eines Phänomens," *Die Zeit*, 12 Oct. 1973. Bracher, who published major works on the demise of the Weimar Republic, the rise of the Nazis and the Hitler dictatorship in the 1950s and 60s, himself helped pave the way for a more intense, critical investigation of the formation, structure and consequences of National Socialism and the Third Reich. See Karl-Dietrich Bracher, *Die Auflösung der Weimarer Republik* (1955), 3rd revised edition, Villingen, 1960; idem, Wolfgang Sauer and Gerhard Schulz, *Die nationalsozialistische Machtergreifung: Studien zur Errichtung des totalitären Herrschaftssystems in Deutschland 1933/34* (1960), new edition, Frankfurt am Main and Vienna, 1974; idem, *Die deutsche Diktatur: Entstehung, Struktur, Folgen* (1969), 7th edition, Cologne, 1993.

17 Theodor Schieder, "Hitler vor dem Gericht der Weltgeschichte," *Frankfurter Allgemeine Zeitung*, 27 Oct. 1973.

18 Fest, *Hitler*, p. 22. See also ibid., p. 216: "Hitler's rise to the point where he exercised an almost magical hold on people's imaginations is unthinkable without the coincidence of an individual and a social-pathological situation."

19 Ibid., p. 1035.

20 See Hermann Graml, "Probleme einer Hitler-Biographie: Kritische Bemerkungen zu Joachim C. Fest," *Vierteljahrshefte für Zeitgeschichte*, 22 (1974), pp. 76–92, at pp. 83, 88; Hannes Heer, *"Hitler war's": Die Befreiung der Deutschen von ihrer Vergangenheit*, Berlin, 2005, p. 33f.

21 See Fest, *Hitler*, p. 291f.

22 See Volker Ullrich, "Speers Erfindung," *Die Zeit*, 4 May 2005; idem, "Die Speer-Legende," *Die Zeit*, 23 Sept. 1999. The correspondence preserved in the Koblenz Federal Archive (N1340/17, 1340/53, 1340/54) reveals how closely Speer, Fest and the publisher Jobst Wolf Siedler worked together. The author plans to publish a separate study dedicated to this topic.

23 Klaus Hildebrand, "Hitler: Rassen- und Weltpolitik. Ergebnisse und Desiderata der Forschung," *Militärgeschichtliche Mitteilungen*, 19/1 (1976), pp. 207–24, at p. 213.

24 These became available in an edition prepared by the Munich Institute for Contemporary History from the 1980s.

25 Kershaw, *Hitler: Hubris*, pp. xii, xxvi, xxix (quotation on p. xxvi).

26 So Norbert Frei in his review "Dem Führer entgegenarbeiten," *Neue Zürcher Zeitung*, 6 Oct. 1998.

27 Kershaw, *Hitler: Hubris*, pp. 529–31. See also ibid., pp. 436–7: "Remarkable in the seismic upheavals of 1934–4 was not how much, but how little, the new chancellor needed to do to bring about the extension and consolidation of his power."

28 Klaus Hildebrand, "Nichts Neues über Hitler: Ian Kershaws zünftige Biographie über den deutschen Diktator," *Historische Zeitschrift*, 270 (2000), pp. 389–97, at p. 392.

29   See the author's reviews of Kershaw's two volumes: "Volk und Führer," *Die Zeit*, 8 Oct. 1998; "Die entfesselten Barbaren," *Die Zeit*, 19 Oct. 2000.

30   Frank Schirrmacher, "Wir haben ihn uns engagiert," *Frankfurter Allgemeine Zeitung*, 6 Oct. 1998.

31   Numerous books have been published that provide new insight into Hitler's personality and certain phases of his life—or at least promise to do so—the complete titles of which can be found in the bibliography. Claudia Schmölders' "physiognomic biography," *Hitlers Gesicht* (2000); Lothar Machtan's controversial revelatory study about Hitler's alleged homosexuality, *Hitlers Geheimnis* (2001); Birgit Schwarz's ground-breaking work about Hitler's views on art, *Geniewahn: Hitler und die Kunst* (2009); Timothy W. Ryback's research into Hitler's library and his reading habits, *Hitler's Private Library* (2009); Dirk Bavendamm's portrayal of his early years, *Der junge Hitler* (2009); Thomas Weber's investigation into Hitler's experiences in the First World War, *Hitler's First War* (2010); Ralf Georg Reuth's attempt to explain the origins of Hitler's anti-Semitism, *Hitlers Judenhass* (2009); Othmar Plöckinger's pathbreaking studies about Hitler's "formative years" in Munich from 1918 to 1920 (2013) and the history of *Mein Kampf* (2006); Ludolf Herbst's thesis about the creation of a German messiah, *Hitlers Charisma* (2010); Mathias Rösch's examination of *Die Münchner NSDAP 1925–1933* (2002); Andreas Heusler's history of the Brown House, *Wie München zur "Hauptstadt der Bewegung" wurde* (2008); and Sven Felix Kellerhoff's and Thomas Friedrich's investigation into Hitler's relationship with the capital, *Hitlers Berlin* (2003) and *Die missbrauchte Hauptstadt* (2007). Hitler's private life too has attracted increased attention over the last decade, from Anton Joachimsthaler's documentation *Hitlers Liste* (2003), which attempts to shed light on his personal relationships by investigating the list of gifts presented by Hitler in 1935/6, to Brigitte Hamann's research into Hitler's relationship with the Wagner family, *Winifred Wagner und Hitlers Bayreuth* (2002) and with the Linz doctor Eduard Bloch, *Hitlers Edeljude* (2008); Wolfgang Martynkewicz's portrait of Munich publishers and early Hitler supporters Hugo und Elsa Bruckmann, *Salon Deutschland* (2009); Anna Maria Sigmund's reconstruction of the triangular relationship between Hitler, his niece Geli Raubal and his driver Emil Maurice, *Des Führers bester Freund* (2003); to Heike B. Görtemaker's meticulously researched biography, *Eva Braun: Ein Leben mit Hitler* (2010), which explodes numerous myths surrounding the Führer's lover. In addition, we have Ulf Schmidt's medical-historical study, *Hitlers Arzt Karl Brandt* (2009), Jürgen Trimborn's studies on Hitler's favourite sculptor, *Arno Breker: Der Künstler und die Macht* (2011) and his star director, *Leni Riefenstahl: Eine deutsche Karriere* (2002); Karin Wieland's dual biography, *Dietrich & Riefenstahl: Der Traum von der neuen Frau* (2011); and Timo Nüsslein's portrait of Hitler's first architect, *Paul Ludwig Troost, 1878–1934* (2012). At the same time a wealth of biographies has been published of leading figures in the Weimar Republic and the Nazi regime, which also shed light on Hitler and his rule. These include Wolfram Pyta's broad canvas, *Hindenburg: Herrschaft zwischen Hohenzollern und Hitler* (2007), as well as Stefan Krings on Hitler's press spokesman Otto Dietrich (2010); Ernst Piper on Hitler's chief ideologue Alfred Rosenberg (2005); Robert Gerwarth on the head of the Reich Security Main Office, Reinhard Heydrich (2011); Dieter Schenk on Hitler's chief lawyer and later general governor of occupied Poland, Hans Frank (2006); Hans Otto Eglau on Hitler's sponsor, the industrialist Fritz Thyssen (2003); Christopher Kopper on Hitler's banker, Hjalmar Schacht (2006); Kirstin A. Schäfer on "Hitlers first field marshal," Werner von Blomberg (2006); Klaus-Jürgen Müller on Major-General Ludwig Beck (2008); and Johannes Leicht on Heinrich Class, chairman of the Pan-Germanic League. In addition there have been numerous monographs and essays on particular aspects of the Third Reich, which have enriched our understanding of the foundation and functioning of the Nazi Regime. I shall mention here only Götz Aly's provocative study *Hitlers Volksstaat* (2005); Adam Tooze's history of the Nazi economy, *The*

Wages of Destruction (2007); Wolfgang König's investigation of the National Socialist consumer society, *Volkswagen, Volksempfänger, Volksgemeinschaft* (2004); Markus Urban's portrayal of the party rallies, *Die Konsensfabrik* (2007); the surprise bestseller by Eckart Conze, Norbert Frei, Peter Hayes und Moshe Zimmermann about the history of the Foreign Office, *Das Amt und die Vergangenheit* (2010); Frank Bajohr's enlightening research into corruption in the Nazi era, *Parvenüs und Profiteure* (2001); and Michael Wildt's ground-breaking investigations into the leadership of the Reich Security Main Office, *Generation des Unbedingten* (2002) and the violence directed against Jews in the German provinces, *Volksgemeinschaft als Selbstermächtigung* (2007). The concept of *Volksgemeinschaft* (ethnic community) in particular has been debated extensively by historians in recent years. It is therefore not surprising that the German Historical Museum in 2010 showed an exhibition on the connection between ethnic community and crime; the exhibition catalogue, edited by Hans-Ulrich Thamer and Simone Erpel, was published as *Hitler und die Deutschen: Volksgemeinschaft und Verbrechen*. On the concept of *Volksgemeinschaft* see also the collection of essays edited by Frank Bajohr and Michael Wildt, *Volksgemeinschaft: Neue Forschungen zur Gesellschaft des Nationalsozialismus* (2009). Last but not least, with his trilogy *The Coming of the Third Reich* (2004), *The Third Reich in Power* (2006) and *The Third Reich at War* (2009), the British historian Richard J. Evans has given us the most comprehensive history of National Socialism to date, which deserves to be called the standard work on the subject.

One of the main sources for the present volume was the 1980 volume of Hitler's collected notes, *Sämtliche Aufzeichnungen 1905–1924*, ed. Eberhard Jäckel and Axel Kuhn, and the subsequent 13-volume edition of Hitler's speeches, writings and decrees, *Reden, Schriften, Anordnungen—1925–1933*, completed by the Munich Institute for Contemporary History in 2003. Both editions demonstrate conclusively how early Hitler's obsessive world view developed and how consistent it remained; see Wolfram Pyta, "Die Hitler-Edition des Instituts für Zeitgeschichte," *Historische Zeitschrift*, 281 (2005), pp. 383–94. It would be welcome if the Institute were to bring out a likewise thoroughly edited volume of direct Hitler source material for the period 1933–1945. Until that happens, historians will have to rely on Max Domarus's collection of Hitler's speeches and proclamations, *Reden und Proklamationen*, which is less than satisfactory in a number of respects. Particularly crucial for the present volume were the files of Reich Chancellery, published by the Historical Commission of the Bavarian Sciences together with the German Federal Archive as *Akten der Reichskanzlei: Die Regierung Hitler*. Kershaw had no access to vols. 2–6, edited by Friedrich Hartmannsgruber and covering the years 1934 to 1939, which appeared between 1999 and 2012. One major source, which has never been fully analysed, are the diaries of Joseph Goebbels, edited by Elke Fröhlich and commissioned by the Munich Institute for Contemporary History. They have only been available to scholars since 2006. Although stylised and written with an eye towards posterity, the diaries, given the proximity of Goebbels to his Führer, contain important insights into Hitler's thinking and motivation. They also yield a surprisingly vivid depiction of Hitler the private person. On the value of the diaries as historical source material see Angela Hermann, *Der Weg in den Krieg 1938/39. Studien zu den Tagebüchern von Joseph Goebbels*, Munich 2011, pp. 1–11. For criticism of the Munich edition, albeit exaggerated, see Bernd Sösemann, *Alles nur Propaganda? Untersuchungen zur revidierten Ausgabe der sogenannten Goebbels-Tagebücher des Münchner Imstituts für Zeitgeschichte*, in *Jahrbuch der Kommunikationsforschung*, 10 (2008), pp. 52–76. Just as valuable a source as the writings of Hitler's allies are those of his contemporaries in general, both admirers and detractors. The latter category includes Thomas Mann, Victor Klemperer, Thea Sternheim, Theodor Heuss, Sebastian Haffner and Count Harry Kessler, whose diaries only appeared in their entirety with the publication in 2010 of vol. 9, covering the period 1926–1937. Another important source are the reports made by foreign diplomats from ten different countries published by Frank Bajohr und Christoph Strupp of the Hamburg Institute for Contemporary History in 2011 under the title *Fremde Blicke auf das "Dritte Reich."*

In addition to consulting published source material the author also carried out substantial research of his own at the Federal Archive Berlin-Lichterfelde, the Federal Archive Koblenz, the Munich Institute for Contemporary History, the main Bavarian State Archive and the Bavarian State Library in Munich, and the Swiss Federal Archive in Bern. The author was surprised how much there was still to discover there, even though Hitler's life is considered one of the most thoroughly researched subjects in history.

32 Cited in Andreas Hillgruber, "Tendenzen, Ergebnisse und Perspektiven der gegenwärtigen Hitler-Forschung," *Historische Zeitschrift*, 226 (1978), pp. 600–21, at p. 612.

33 Kershaw, *Hitler: Hubris*, p. xxiv. See also Kershaw's interview with Franziska Augstein and Ulrich Raulff: "In gewisser Weise war er der Mann ohne Eigenschaften," *Frankfurter Allgemeine Zeitung*, 1 Oct. 1998: "Above all I wanted to specify the context in which he was able to function, that is, in which a person of his limited abilities was able to rise to positions of ever-greater power."

34 Kershaw, *Hitler: Hubris*, p. xii.

35 James P. O'Donnell, "Der grosse und der kleine Diktator," *Der Monat*, 30 (1978), pp. 51–62, at p 61. In conversation with the American historian Harold Deutsch on 11 May 1950, Hitler's former military adjutant, Gerhard Engel, remarked: "Just think how many faces Hitler had. He was one of the most elegant actors ever seen in the history of the world . . . Compared with him . . . a man like Mussolini was a mere amateur, despite his Caesar-like gestures." IfZ Munich, ZS 222, vol. 2.

36 Fest, *Hitler*, p. 29.

37 Schwerin von Krosigk to Georg Franz, 13 July 1962; BA Koblenz, N 1276/42.

38 Heiden, *Adolf Hitler: Der Mann gegen Europa*, p. 213. See also ibid., p. 214: there Heiden writes that the subjugator of men was "one of the unhappiest people in his private life."

39 Bullock, *Hitler*, p. 380; Fest, *Hitler*, pp. 714, 718.

40 Kershaw in "In gewisser Weise war er der Mann ohne Eigenschaften." See also Kershaw, *Hitler*, vol. 1, p. xxv: the "black hole" of Hitler the private individual.

41 Hans Mommsen, interviewed by Ulrich Specks, "Ein Mann ohne Privatsphäre," *Frankfurter Rundschau*, 10 Oct. 2001.

42 See the *Bild-Zeitung* headline of 21 Aug. 2004: "Darf man ein Monster als Menschen zeigen?" See also "Der Film *Der Untergang* zeigt ihn als Menschen. Darf man das?," *Tagesspiegel*, 11 Sept. 2004.

43 Albert Speer, *Spandauer Tagebücher* (1975), Berlin and Munich, 2002, p. 63 (entry for 10 Feb. 1947).

44 Leni Riefenstahl, letter to Albert Speer, 8 Jun. 1976; BA Koblenz, N 1340/49.

45 Fest, *Hitler*, p. 697 ff.

46 Stefan Zweig, *Die Welt von Gestern: Erinnerungen eines Europäers*, Stuttgart and Hamburg, p. 415.

47 Kershaw in "In gewisser Weise war er der Mann ohne Eigenschaften."

48 Sebastian Haffner coined the phrase in *Geschichte eines Deutschen: Die Erinnerungen, 1914–1933*, Stuttgart and Munich, 2000, p. 88.

49 Rudolf Augstein, "Hitler oder die Sucht nach Vernichtung der Welt," *Der Spiegel*, no. 38, 1973, pp. 63–86, at p. 63.

50 Eberhard Jäckel, "Hitler und die Deutschen: Versuch einer geschichtlichen Erklärung," in *Geschichte und Gegenwart: Festschrift für Karl-Dietrich Erdmann*, ed. Hartmut Boockmann, Kurt Jürgensen and Gerhard Stoltenberg, Münster, 1980, pp. 351–64, at p. 364.

1 *The Young Hitler*

1   Adolf Hitler, *Monologe im Führerhauptquartier 1941–1944: Die Aufzeichnungen Heinrich Heims*, ed. Werner Jochmann, Hamburg, 1980, p. 357 (dated 21 Aug. 1942).

2   See Dirk Bavendamm, *Der junge Hitler: Korrekturen einer Biographie 1889–1914*, Graz, 2009, p. 54.

3   See Anna Maria Sigmund, *Diktator, Dämon, Demagoge: Fragen und Antworten zu Adolf Hitler*, Munich, 2006, p. 125f. (on p. 124 see the facsimile of the legal documents dated 16 Oct. 1876); Guido Knopp, *Geheimnisse des "Dritten Reiches,"* Munich, 2011, pp. 25–9. The facsimile of the parish register was first published in Franz Jetzinger, *Hitlers Jugend: Phantasien, Lügen und Wahrheit*, Vienna, 1956, p. 16.

4   For a summarised discussion of the possible motives see Ian Kershaw, *Hitler 1889–1936: Hubris*, London, 1998, pp. 5–9.

5   Particularly Werner Maser, *Adolf Hitler: Legende—Mythos—Wirklichkeit*, 12th edition, Munich and Esslingen, 1989, p. 36. Following this, Wolfgang Zdral, *Die Hitlers: Die unbekannte Familie des Führers*, Frankfurt am Main and New York, 2005, p. 19f.

6   *Bayerischer Kurier*, 12 March 1932; BA Berlin-Lichterfelde, NS 26/13. The special edition of the *Wiener Sonn- und Montagszeitung* with the headline "Hitler heisst Schücklgruber" in BA Berlin-Lichterfelde, NS 26/17.

7   Hans Frank, *Im Angesicht des Galgens: Deutung Hitlers und seiner Zeit auf Grund eigener Erlebnisse und Erkenntnisse*, Munich and Gräfelfing, 1953, p. 330f. For the history of the speculation about Hitler's Jewish grandfather also see Brigitte Hamann, *Hitlers Wien: Lehrjahre eines Diktators*, Munich and Zurich, 1996, pp. 69–72; Knopp, *Geheimnisse des "Dritten Reiches,"* pp. 18–20. For a genealogical tree see ibid., pp. 16–18.

8   See Maser, *Adolf Hitler*, pp. 27–30.

9   August Kubizek, *Adolf Hitler: Mein Jugendfreund*, Graz and Göttingen, 1953, p. 59.

10   Statement of Herr Hebestreit, a customs officer in Braunau, from 21 June 1940; BA Berlin-Lichterfelde, NS 26/17a.

11   See Franziska Hitler's marriage license and death certificate in BA Berlin-Lichterfelde, NS 26/17a. Next to nothing is known about Klara Pölzl's childhood and youth. See Bavendamm, *Der junge Hitler*, p. 78f.

12   Petition reprinted in Zdral, *Die Hitlers*, p. 24f.

13   Facsimile of birth and baptism certificate in Kubizek, *Adolf Hitler*, p. 49.

14   See Anton Joachimsthaler, *Korrektur einer Biographie: Adolf Hitler 1908–1920*, Munich, 1989, p. 31; Christa Schroeder, *Er war mein Chef: Aus dem Nachlass der Sekretärin von Adolf Hitler*, ed. Anton Joachimsthaler, 3rd edition, Munich and Vienna, 1985, pp. 213f.; Olaf Rose (ed.), *Julius Schaub: In Hitlers Schatten*, Stegen, 2005, p. 337 ff.

15   On this source material see Bavendamm, *Der junge Hitler*, pp. 21–4; Ludolf Herbst, *Hitlers Charisma: Die Erfindung eines deutschen Messias*, Frankfurt am Main, 2010, p. 64f.; Othmar Plöckinger, "Frühe biographische Texte zu Hitler: Zur Bewertung der autobiographischen Texte in *Mein Kampf*," in *Vierteljahrshefte für Zeitgeschichte*, 58 (2010), pp. 93–114.

16   Adolf Hitler, *Mein Kampf. Vol. 1: Eine Abrechnung*, 7th edition, Munich, 1933, p. 1.

17   See Marlies Steinert, *Hitler*, Munich, 1994, p. 24; Hitler, *Mein Kampf*, p. 135: "My youthful German was the dialect that Lower Bavaria speaks—I could never forget it or learn Viennese jargon."

18   See, for example, *Monologe*, p. 26 (dated 27/28 Sept. 1941), p. 171 (dated 3/4 Jan. 1942).

19   See Jetzinger, *Hitlers Jugend*, pp. 63f., 122–4.

20   See Zrdal, *Die Hitlers*, pp. 30f.

21   Quoted in Kershaw, *Hitler: Hubris*, p. 13. Hitler told his friend Kubizek that conflicts "often ended with his father beating him." Kubizek, *Adolf Hitler*, p. 55. See also Albert Speer, *Erinnerungen*, Frankfurt am Main and Berlin, 1993, p. 138. Hitler once bragged to his secretary Christa Schröder that he had taken 32 blows without uttering the slightest gasp of pain (*Er war mein Chef*, p. 63). Compare this with Bavendamm, *Der junge Hitler*, pp. 114f.

22 See Bradley F. Smith, *Adolf Hitler: His Family, Childhood and Youth*, Stanford, 1967, pp. 43–5. In August 1942, Hitler recalled that "his old man was a passionate beekeeper," adding that he had been "repeatedly stung to the point that he [Hitler] had almost died," *Monologe*, p. 324 (dated 3 Aug. 1942).

23 See Frank, *Im Angesicht des Galgens*, p. 332. Hitler is said to have confided: "That was the most horrible shame I have ever felt. Oh, Frank, I know what a devil alcohol is! In my youth, it was my worst enemy—even worse than my father." But there are reasons to doubt the truth of this statement. See Jetzinger, *Hitlers Jugend*, pp. 93f.; Bavendamm, *Der junge Hitler*, p. 101.

24 *Die Tagebücher von Joseph Goebbels. Part 1: Aufzeichnungen 1923–1941*, ed. Elke Fröhlich, Munich, 1998–2006, vol. 2, p. 336 (entry for 9 Aug. 1932). See also ibid., p. 199 (entry for 20 Jan. 1932): "Hitler told moving stories of his childhood. Stories about his strict father and loving mother."

25 Quoted in Hamann, *Hitlers Wien*, p. 16; see Smith, *Adolf Hitler*, p. 51; on his half-brother Alois Hitler and his son William Patrick see Knopp, *Geheimnisse des "Dritten Reiches*," pp. 31–8, 55–70.

26 Kubizek, *Adolf Hitler*, p. 53.

27 Among others, Alice Miller, *Am Anfang war Erziehung*, Frankfurt am Main, 1980; following on, Christa Mulack, *Klara Hitler: Muttersein im Patriarchat*, Rüsselsheim, 2005, p. 51; for critics of the psychoanalytical interpretations see Wolfgang Michalka, "Hitler im Spiegel der Psycho-Historie: Zu neueren interdisziplinären Deutungsversuchen der Hitler-Forschung" in *Francia*, 8 (1980), pp. 595–611; Gerhard Schreiber, *Hitler: Interpretationen 1923–1983. Ergebnisse, Methoden und Probleme der Forschung*, Darmstadt, 1984, pp. 316–27; Kershaw, *Hitler: Hubris*, pp. 606–7 n63.

28 Otto Wagener, *Hitler aus nächster Nähe: Aufzeichnungen eines Vertrauten 1929–1932*, ed. Henry A. Turner, Frankfurt am Main, Berlin and Vienna, 1978, p. 425.

29 Goebbels, *Tagebücher*, part 1, vol. 1, p. 390 (entry for 22 July 1938).

30 Hitler, *Mein Kampf*, p. 6. See Hitler, *Monologe*, p. 375 (dated 29 Aug. 1942): "I spent a lot of time in my school years outside." In a letter to his childhood friend Fritz Seidl in Graz on 16 Oct. 1923, Hitler recalled "our sunny days as young scallywags we idled away together with others," BA Berlin-Lichterfelde, NS 26/14; reprinted in Adolf Hitler, *Sämtliche Aufzeichnungen 1905–1924*, ed. Eberhard Jäckel with Axel Kuhn, Stuttgart, 1980, no. 585, p. 1038. See Goebbels, *Tagebücher*, part 1, vol. 6, p. 49 (entry for 19 Aug. 1938): "He told stories about his youth in Leonding and Lambach. It was a happy time for him."

31 BA Berlin-Lichterfelde, NS 26/17a.

32 Hitler, *Monologe*, p. 281 (dated 17 Feb. 1942). See Goebbels, *Tagebücher*, part 1, vol. 3/2, p. 299 (entry for 20 Dec. 1936): "We talked about Karl May and his adventurous life. The Führer loves reading his books."

33 Albert Speer, *Spandauer Tagebücher*, Munich, 2002, p. 523 (entry for 5 May 1960). On his reading of Karl May, see Smith, *Adolf Hitler*, pp. 66f.; Hamann, *Hitlers Wien*, pp. 21, 544–8; Bavendamm, *Der junge Hitler*, pp. 359–76.

34 Hitler, *Mein Kampf*, p. 3. See Otto Dietrich, *12 Jahre mit Hitler*, Munich, 1955, p. 166: "In his own telling, even as a boy, Hitler was a wild and hard-to-tame youth."

35 Joachim Fest, *Hitler: Eine Biographie*, Frankfurt am Main, Berlin and Vienna, 1973, p. 37. According to the school register, Hitler attended the *Volksschule* in Leonding from 27 Feb. 1899 until he transferred to the *Realschule* in Linz on 17 Sept. 1900; BA Berlin-Lichterfelde, NS 26/65.

36 Published in Jetzinger, *Hitlers Jugend*, pp. 105f. In a letter to a former colleague on 28 April 1935, Heumer described how the assessment had come to pass. After the November 1923 putsch, Angela Raubal had given him a letter from Hitler's lawyer Lorenz Roder requesting an "objective characterization" of Hitler as a school pupil in order to "combat certain rumour in the hostile press." BA Koblenz, N 1128/30.

37 Hitler, *Mein Kampf*, p. 6.

38   See Smith, *Adolf Hitler*, pp. 69f.; Bavendamm, *Adolf Hitler*, p. 133.

39   Hitler, *Mein Kampf*, p. 7.

40   Ibid., p. 16. Klara Hitler's death announcement in BA Berlin-Lichterfelde, NS 26/17.

41   See Jetzinger, *Hitlers Jugend*, pp. 124–9; Smith, *Der junge Hitler*, p. 94.

42   Transcript made by Dr. Leopold Zaumer from Weitra on 16 and 23 Oct. 1938 of statements made by Marie Koppensteiner and Johann Schmidt, both children of Theresia Schmidt, née Pölzl; BA Berlin-Lichterfelde, NS 26/17a. In April 1938, the city of Weitra made Hitler an honorary citizen, pointing out that the Hitler and Pölzl family homes were only four kilometres away in the town of Spital: "Close family members of the Führer and Reich chancellor live here. The Führer and Reich chancellor also spent some time in his youth here." BA Berlin-Lichterfelde, NS 51/80.

43   Goebbels, *Tagebücher*, part 1, vol. 5, p. 331 (entry for 3 June 1938).

44   "Unser Führer Adolf Hitler als Student in Steyr von seinem einstigen Lehrer Gregor Goldbacher Prof. i. R."; BA Berlin-Lichterfelde, NS 26/17a.

45   Hitler, *Monologe*, p. 170 (dated 8 and 9 Jan. 1942); see also ibid., p. 376 (dated 29 Aug. 1942): "At least half of my professors had mental problems." See also *Hitlers Tischgespräche im Führerhauptquartier*, ed. Henry Picker, Stuttgart, 1976, p. 217 (dated 12 April 1942): "He said he had mostly unpleasant memories of the teachers who had run through his young life." See Gustav Keller, *Der Schüler Adolf Hitler: Die Geschichte eines lebenslangen Amoklaufs*, Münster, 2012, p. 110. The author—an educational psychologist—sees Hitler's poor performance in school as "the decisive trigger of his terrible psychological mis-development." It led to an inferiority complex for which Hitler tried to compensate with his "exaggerated desire for acknowledgement and power." Yet Keller's thesis that "Hitler ran amok for his entire life until finally committing suicide" is far too simplistic (quotations on pp. 3, 118, 121).

46   Hitler, *Mein Kampf*, p. 12. For L. Poetsch see Bavendamm, *Der junge Hitler*, pp. 136–41. In a letter dated 20 June 1929, Poetsch informed Hitler that his first name was Leopold and not Ludwig, as the first three editions of *My Struggle* had read: "Do not hold it against your old teacher, who remembers his former pupil fondly, if he takes the liberty to write to you," Poetsch gushed. On 2 July 1929, Hitler wrote back to express his gratitude: "They [the lines you wrote] immediately called up memories of my youth and the hours I spent with a teacher to whom I owe countless things and who partly paved the path I've travelled down." Hitler, *Reden, Schriften, Anordnungen— Februar 1925 bis Januar 1933. Vol. 3, Part 2: März 1929–Dezember 1929*, ed. and with notes by Klaus A. Lankheit, Munich, New Providence, London and Paris, 1994, no. 46, p. 279 with n2.

47   See Evan Burr Bukey, *"Patenstadt des Führers": Eine Politik- und Sozialgeschichte von Linz 1908–1945*, Frankfurt am Main and New York, 1993, p. 16.

48   Hitler, *Mein Kampf*, p. 16.

49   See Kubizek, *Adolf Hitler*, p. 23; Hamann, *Hitlers Wien*, pp. 40f.

50   Kubizek dates the beginnings of his friendship with Hitler as "All Saints' Day 1904" (p. 20). But Jetzinger has proven that the two boys met one another in the autumn of 1905; *Hitlers Jugend*, pp. 137, 141.

51   See Hamann, *Hitlers Wien*, p. 77–83 and subsequently, Kershaw, *Hitler: Hubris*, p. 21f. In the late 1930s the main NSDAP archive in Munich charged the journalist Renato Attilo Bleibtreu with locating material relating to Hitler's youth. He visited August Kubizek, who had been forced to give up his musical career after the First World War and become a local official in the town of Eferding near Linz. Bleibtreu noted: "If Kubitscheck [*sic*] can write down his recollections of Hitler in the same manner he tells them, they will be one of the most important holdings in the archive." BA Berlin-Lichterfelde, NS 26/17a. For Renato Bleibtreu see Brigitte Hamann, *Hitlers Edeljude: Das Leben des Armenarztes Eduard Bloch*, Munich and Zurich, 2008, pp. 339–49.

52   Kubizek, *Adolf Hitler*, pp. 34f.

53   See Claudia Schmölders, *Hitlers Gesicht: Eine physiognomische Biographie*, Munich, 2001, pp. 7, 9, 62f., 104, 182.

54   Kubizek, *Adolf Hitler*, p. 26.

55   Ibid., p. 27.

56   Hitler, *Mein Kampf*, p. 15. During a visit to Linz in April 1943, Hitler gave his companions a tour of the city theatre. Albert Speer wrote: "Visibly moved, he showed us the cheap seat in the uppermost rows where he had sat when he saw *Lohengrin*, *Rienzi* and other operas for the first time." Speer, *Spandauer Tagebücher*, p. 259 (entry for 14 Jan. 1951).

57   Thomas Mann, "Versuch über das Theater" in *Essays I: 1883–1914*, Frankfurt am Main, 2002, p. 139.

58   Kubizek, *Adolf Hitler*, p. 101.

59   Quoted in Jetzinger, *Hitlers Jugend*, p. 132.

60   Cf. *Rienzi* episode in Kubizek, *Adolf Hitler*, pp. 133–42 (quotations on pp. 140f. and 142). Speer related Hitler saying about the *Rienzi* overture in the summer of 1938: "Listening to this divinely blessed music as a young man in the Linz theatre, it occurred to me that I too would be able to unify the German Reich and make it great." *Spandauer Tagebücher*, p. 136, entry for 7 Feb. 1948. On Hitler's encounter with Kubizek on 3 Aug. 1939 in Bayreuth see Brigitte Hamann, *Winifred Wagner oder Hitlers Bayreuth*, Munich and Zurich, 2002, pp. 390–2. Bavendamm (*Der junge Hitler*, p. 282) uncritically accepts Kubizek's account, writing that as early as 1905, inspired by *Rienzi*, "Hitler believed in his political 'mission.'" Jochen Köhler advances a similar view when he writes of Hitler's "mystical initiation"; *Wagners Hitler: Der Prophet und sein Vollstrecker*, Munich, 1997, p. 35.

61   Kubizek, *Adolf Hitler*, p. 117.

62   Cf. "Stefanie" episode in Kubizek, *Adolf Hitler*, pp. 76–89: discussed in Jetzinger, *Hitlers Jugend*, pp. 142–8; Anton Joachimsthaler, *Hitlers Liste: Ein Dokument persönlicher Beziehungen*, Munich, 2003, pp. 48–52. See Goebbels, *Tagebücher*, part I, vol. 2/3, p. 81 (entry for 13 Dec. 1932): "Hitler told us about the great love of his youth. It's moving how he worships women." Ibid., vol. 5, p. 331 (entry for 3 June 1938): "The Führer talked of his childhood and his first love in Linz." Lothar Machtan dismisses Kubizek's account as a manoeuvre intended to distract from the homosexual overtones of his friendship with Hitler but he offers little proof for this view; *Hitlers Geheimnis: Das Doppelleben eines Diktators*, Berlin, 2001, pp. 47–57. We cannot, of course, rule out that there was a homosexual component in this "youthful bond," as Kubizek characterized his relationship to Hitler. On close male relationships at the turn of the century, see Claudia Bruns, *Politik des Eros: Der Männerbund in Wissenschaft, Politik und Jugendkultur 1880–1934*, Cologne, Weimar and Vienna, 2008.

63   Hitler, *Mein Kampf*, p. 18.

64   Facsimile in Kubizek, *Adolf Hitler*, p. 192. For the four postcards, ibid., pp. 146–9; Jetzinger, *Hitlers Jugend*, pp. 151–5; printed in Hitler, *Sämtliche Aufzeichnungen*, nos 3–6, p. 44f. In the mid 1970s, Paula Kubizek stated that she still possessed cards and letters from Hitler and was leaving them to her sons. "I don't want them to be sold," she said. "They should stay in the family." Paula Kubitschek (*sic*) to Henriette von Schirach, 10 Nov. 1976; BayHStA Munich, Nl H. v. Schirach 3.

65   Kubizek, *Adolf Hitler*, p. 145.

66   Hamann, *Hitlers Edeljude*, p. 81.

67   Compare the hospital operations record from 1907 and the notes made by the doctor, Karl Urban, from 16 Nov. 1938; BA Berlin-Lichterfelde, NS 26/65 and NS 26/17a.

68   Hamann, *Hitlers Wien*, p. 52.

69   Hitler, *Mein Kampf*, pp. 18f.

70   Ibid., p. 19.

71   Kubizek, *Adolf Hitler*, pp. 166f.; Hamann, *Hitlers Wien*, p. 54.

72   Eduard Bloch, "Erinnerungen an den Führer und dessen verewigte Mutter" (Nov. 1938); BA Berlin-Lichterfelde, NS 26/65. See also Eduard Bloch on Renato Bleibtreu, 8 Nov. 1938; ibid.

73   Kershaw, *Hitler: Hubris*, pp. 12, 24.

74   Rudolph Binion advances this thesis in ". . . *dass ihr mich gefunden habt": Hitler und die Deutschen*, Stuttgart, 1978, p. 38.

75   Hamann, *Hitlers Edeljude*, p. 69. At the start of 1908, Hitler sent Bloch a letter wishing him a happy new year, signed "In continuing gratitude, Adolf Hitler." See Bleibtreu's report, BA Berlin-Lichterfelde, NS 26/17a.

76   Hamann, *Hitlers Edeljude*, p. 261.

77   Kubizek, *Adolf Hitler*, p. 176.

78   See Hamann, *Hitlers Wien*, pp. 58, 85. Maser argues for the idea of Hitler as "a man of wealth," *Adolf Hitler*, p. 83.

79   Hamann, *Hitlers Wien*, pp. 59–62. This correspondence was discovered amidst the effects of Johanna Motloch and confiscated by the Gestapo. Martin Bormann presented Hitler with copies of the letters in Oct. 1942. He described Hitler's reaction to Heinrich Himmler: "The Führer was very moved by the memory of what he had experienced in the past." Ibid., p. 590n193.

80   *Hitlers Tischgespräche*, p. 276 (dated 10 May 1942); see also *Monologe*, p. 120 (dated 15/16 Jan. 1942).

81   See Hamann, *Hitlers Edeljude*, p. 94.

82   See Zdral, *Die Hitlers*, pp. 52, 203–6.

83   Hamann, *Hitlers Wien*, p. 63; Hitler, *Sämtliche Aufzeichnungen*, no. 9, p. 47.

2 *The Vienna Years*

1   Adolf Hitler, *Mein Kampf. Vol. 1: Eine Abrechnung*, 7th edition, Munich, 1933, p. 137.

2   Stefan Zweig, *Die Welt von Gestern: Erinnerungen eines Europäers*, Stuttgart and Hamburg, p. 27.

3   Cf. Carl E. Schorske, *Wien: Geist und Gesellschaft im Fin de Siècle*, Munich, 1994.

4   See Brigitte Hamann, *Hitlers Wien: Lehrjahre eines Diktators*, Munich and Zurich, 1996, pp. 135–50.

5   Hitler, *Mein Kampf*, pp. 22f.; see August Kubizek, *Adolf Hitler: Mein Jugendfreund*, Graz and Göttingen, 1953, p. 202.

6   See Hamann, *Hitlers Wien*, pp. 398, 439.

7   See ibid., pp. 467–9.

8   See Julia Schmidt, *Kampf um das Deutschtum: Radikaler Nationalismus in Österreich und dem Deutschen Reich 1890–1914*, Frankfurt am Main and New York, 2009.

9   Quoted in Franz Herre, *Jahrhundertwende 1900: Untergangsstimmung und Fortschrittsglauben*, Stuttgart, 1998, p. 190.

10   Hitler, *Mein Kampf*, p. 20.

11   Kubizek, *Adolf Hitler*, p. 224f.

12   See ibid., p. 226f.

13   Hitler, *Mein Kampf*, pp. 36f.; see *Hitlers Tischgespräche im Führerhauptquartier*, ed. Henry Picker, Stuttgart, 1976, p. 133 (entry for 13 March 1942): "He said that he always starts with the end, then browses through some sections in the middle, and only reads the whole book if his initial impression was positive." For Hitler's reading habits see Timothy W. Ryback, *Hitler's Private Library: The Books That Shaped His Life*, London, 2009, p. 114f.

14   Adolf Hitler, *Monologe im Führerhauptquartier 1941–1944: Die Aufzeichnungen Heinrich Heims*, ed. Werner Jochmann, Hamburg, 1980, p. 380 (dated 1 Sept. 1942).

15   Kubizek, *Adolf Hitler*, p. 232; see *Monologe*, p. 224 (dated 24/25 Jan. 1942): "How I enjoyed all those Wagner performances after the turn of the century! Those of us who were his loyal fans were known as Wagnerians."

16   See Kubizek, *Adolf Hitler*, pp. 229, 234; Hamann, *Hitlers Wien*, pp. 91–5; Dirk Bavendamm, *Der junge Hitler: Korrekturen einer Biographie 1889–1914*, Graz, 2009, pp. 333–6.

17   Based on Birgit Schwarz, *Geniewahn: Hitler und die Kunst*, Vienna, Cologne and Weimar, 2009, pp. 21ff. ("Hitlers Lieblingsmaler" chapter).

18   Heinrich Hoffmann, *Hitler wie ich ihn sah: Aufzeichnungen seines Leibfotographen*, Munich and Berlin, 1974, p. 29. See transcript of a conversation with Heinrich Hoffmann from 5 Dec. 1953: "Hitler said it was his fondest dream to own one of Grützner's works." IfZ, Munich, ZS 71. Further, Hamann, *Hitlers Wien*, p. 103; Albert Speer, *Erinnerungen: Mit einem Essay von Jochen Thies*, Frankfurt am Main and Berlin, 1993, pp. 56f.

19   *Hitlers Tischgespräche*, p. 146 (dated 27 March 1942). See Otto Wagener, *Hitler aus nächster Nähe: Aufzeichnungen eines Vertrauten 1929–1932*, ed. Henry A. Turner, Frankfurt am Main, Berlin and Vienna, 1978, p. 461: "Stuff like this bears no resemblance whatsoever to painting. It is merely the mental excrement of a sick mind."

20   See Schwarz, *Geniewahn*, pp. 82f.

21   Kubizek, *Adolf Hitler*, pp. 206f. For Ringstrasse see Philipp Blom, *Der taumelnde Kontinent: Europa 1900–1914*, Munich, 2008, p. 71.

22   See Kubizek, *Adolf Hitler*, p. 197; Joachim Fest, *Hitler: Eine Biographie*, Frankfurt am Main, Berlin and Vienna, 1973, p. 53.

23   See Kubizek, *Adolf Hitler*, pp. 239–49; Hamann, *Hitlers Wien*, pp. 96–8. On piano lessons see Josef Prewratsky-Wendt, "Meine Erinnerungen an meinen Klavierschüler Adolf Hitler!" from 17 Nov. 1938; BA Berlin-Lichterfelde, NS 26/65. The piano teacher, who also gave Kubizek lessons, described Hitler as a "likeable, almost shy young man . . . serious and calm, of medium build."

24   Thomas Mann, *An die gesittete Welt: Politische Schriften und Reden im Exil*, Frankfurt am Main, 1986, p. 256.

25   Kubizek, *Adolf Hitler*, pp. 199f.

26   Hitler, *Mein Kampf*, p. 83.

27   Kubizek, *Adolf Hitler*, pp. 290f.

28   See Hitler, *Mein Kampf*, p. 10. On the "German School Association" see Schmid, *Kampf um das Deutschtum*, pp. 30ff.

29   Hitler, *Mein Kampf*, p. 106. See also Hitler, *Monologe*, p. 379 (dated 1 Sept. 1942): "I didn't fall under Vienna's spell because I was very strict about my patriotic German convictions." Building on such sentiments, Bavendamm argues that Hitler believed from his earliest days that he was on a nationalist mission. The young Hitler, Bavendamm writes, "never lost sight of the ultimate goal of a greater German Reich with himself as its leader." *Der junge Hitler*, p. 218.

30   Hitler, *Mein Kampf*, p. 107.

31   See Hamann, *Hitlers Wien*, pp. 337, 349, 362.

32   Hitler, *Mein Kampf*, p. 128.

33   Ibid., p. 109.

34   Hitler, *Monologe*, p. 153 (dated 17 Dec. 1941).

35   See Hamann, *Hitlers Wien*, p. 429.

36   Hitler, *Monologe*, p. 153 (dated 17 Dec. 1941). For Lueger's "city revolution" see John W. Boyer, *Karl Lueger 1844–1910: Christlichsoziale Politik als Beruf. Eine Biographie*, Vienna, Cologne and Weimar, 2010, p. 181ff.

37   See Hitler, *Mein Kampf*, pp. 132f.

38   See Kubizek, *Adolf Hitler*, pp. 208–16.

39   Ibid., pp. 296f.

40   Hitler, *Mein Kampf*, p. 43.

41   Kubizek, *Adolf Hitler*, p. 296.
42   Hitler's letters to Kubizek, 21 July and 17 Aug. 1908 in Kubizek, *Adolf Hitler*, pp. 308f., 310f.; also published in Adolf Hitler, *Sämtliche Aufzeichnungen 1905–1924*, ed. Eberhard Jäckel with Axel Kuhn, Stuttgart, 1980, nos 13, 14, pp. 49–51.
43   Kubizek, *Adolf Hitler*, p. 312.
44   See also Franz Jetzinger, *Hitlers Jugend: Phantasien, Lügen und Wahrheit*, Vienna, 1956, p. 218; Hamann, *Hitlers Wien*, p. 196.
45   *Hitlers Tischgespräche*, p. 276 (dated 10 May 1942).
46   See also Bradley F. Smith, *Adolf Hitler: His Family, Childhood and Youth*, Stanford, 1967, pp. 112f.; Hamann, *Hitlers Wien*, p. 196. In June 1938, Hitler told Goebbels that "he left home at the age of seventeen and didn't get back in touch until 1922." *Die Tagebücher von Joseph Goebbels. Part 1: Aufzeichnungen 1923–1941*, ed. Elke Fröhlich, Munich, 1998–2006, vol. 5, p. 331 (entry for 3 June 1938).
47   Hitler, *Monologe*, p. 317 (dated 11/12 March 1942).
48   Hitler, *Mein Kampf*, pp. 40–2.
49   For a debunking of his claims of working on a building site see Hamann, *Hitlers Wien*, pp. 206–11.
50   See copies of the registration cards in BA Berlin-Lichterfelde, NS 26/17a. For Hitler's changing job descriptions see Anton Joachimsthaler, *Korrektur einer Biographie: Adolf Hitler 1908–1920*, Munich, 1989, p. 32.
51   A letter from Hitler to the Linz municipal authorities, 21 Jan. 1914; Jetzinger, *Hitlers Jugend*, pp. 262–4 (quotation on p. 263); also published in Hitler, *Sämtliche Aufzeichnungen*, no. 19, pp. 53–5.
52   Ian Kershaw, *Hitler: Hubris*, p. 52. After the *Anschluss* of Austria in 1938, Viennese newspapers ran articles on a flat in Simon-Denk-Strasse 11 in which he apparently lived in 1909; see Hamann, *Hitlers Wien*, pp. 206–8. But there is no evidence that Hitler lived there other than a photograph held by the Austrian National Library that bears the inscription: "The house in Vienna's District 9, Simon-Denk-Gasse 11, where Hitler lived as a lodger from 16 September to November 1909." Sigmund sees this as the "missing link" in Hitler's whereabouts during the fall of 1909 without engaging with Hamann's assertions to the contrary; Anna Maria Sigmund, *Diktator, Dämon, Demagoge: Fragen und Antworten zu Adolf Hitler*, Munich, 2006, p. 157f.
53   See also Kubizek, *Adolf Hitler*, pp. 186, 203.
54   Reinhold Hanisch, "Meine Begegnung mit Hitler" (1939); BA Berlin-Lichterfelde, NS 26/64 (the spelling errors have been corrected); published in Joachimsthaler, *Korrektur*, pp. 49f. (quotation on p. 49). A longer, three-part version of "I was Hitler's Buddy" appeared in *New Republic*, 5, 12, and 19 April 1939, pp. 239–42, 270–2, 297–300. On the credibility of this source see Hamann, *Hitlers Wien*, pp. 264–71.
55   Joachimsthaler, *Korrektur*, p. 49. When asked what he was waiting for, Hitler is said to have responded: "I don't know myself." Hanish remarked: "I have never seen such helpless resignation to bad luck." Hanisch, "I was Hitler's Buddy," p. 240.
56   See also Smith, *Adolf Hitler*, p. 132; Hamann, *Hitlers Wien*, p. 227.
57   See also Hamann, *Hitlers Wien*, pp. 229–34; Hertha Hurnaus et al. (eds), *Haus Meldemannstrasse*, Vienna, 2003 (foreword by Brigitte Hamann), pp. 5–7.
58   Hitler, *Mein Kampf*, p. 35; see also Hitler, *Monologe*, p. 316 (entry for 10/11 March 1942): "In my youth, I was a bit of an oddball who preferred to be alone rather than needing company."
59   Kubizek, *Adolf Hitler*, p. 275.
60   This is the view put forward in Lothar Machtan, *Hitlers Geheimnis: Das Doppelleben eines Diktators*, Berlin, 2001. Compare with Hamann, *Hitlers Wien*, p. 515.
61   See Kubizek, *Adolf Hitler*, p. 286: "As he often told me, he worried about becoming infected."
62   Quotation from Hamann, *Hitlers Wien*, p. 523.

63   See also Kershaw, *Hitler: Hubris*, p. 44f.
64   On this see Joachim Radkau, *Das Zeitalter der Nervosität: Deutschland zwischen Bismarck und Hitler*, Munich and Vienna, 1998.
65   Hanisch, "I was Hitler's Buddy," p. 299.
66   See the two facsimiles of the "Meldezettel für Unterpartei" in *Haus Meldemannstrasse*, pp. 6f.
67   Transcript of Hitler's testimony from 5 Aug. 1910; first published in Jetzinger, *Hitlers Jugend*, p. 224. Hanisch later denied the accusation that he had cheated Hitler, saying that following the latter's instructions, he had sold the picture for 12 Kronen, of which he had given Hitler 6 Kronen. Undated record from Reinhold Hanisch in BA Berlin-Lichterfelde, NS 26/64.
68   See Hamann, *Hitlers Wien*, pp. 249f., 507–10.
69   Transcript from the Linz district council from 4 May 1911; published in Jetzinger, *Hitlers Jugend*, p. 226.
70   Karl Honisch, "Wie ich im Jahre 1913 Adolf Hitler kennenlernte"; BA Berlin-Lichterfelde, NS 26/17a; published in Joachimsthaler, *Korrektur*, pp. 51–8. On 31 May 1939, Honisch sent his reminiscences to the NSDAP main archive with the commentary: "As requested, I have written everything down as thoroughly as possible. It should come as no surprise that I have forgotten a lot since twenty-six years have passed in the meantime." BA Berlin-Lichterfelde, NS 26/17a.
71   Joachimsthaler, *Korrektur*, p. 54 (Joachimsthaler's misreadings have been corrected).
72   Ibid., p. 55.
73   Ibid., p. 56.
74   Ibid., p. 56f.
75   See Kubizek, *Adolf Hitler*, p. 113: "To the best of my recollection, Hitler was already a committed anti-Semite when he came to Vienna." Disagreeing with this: Hamann, *Hitlers Wien*, p. 82.
76   Hitler, *Mein Kampf*, p. 69. See also Hitler's letter to an unknown "Herr Doktor" of 29 Nov. 1921: "Within the space of a year the harshest sort of reality made me, who had been raised in a rather cosmopolitan family, into an anti-Semite." Hitler, *Sämtliche Aufzeichnungen*, no. 325, p. 525. See also Hitler's testimony to Munich Court I on 26 Feb. 1924: "I came to Vienna as a cosmopolitan and left it as an absolute anti-Semite and the mortal enemy of the entire Marxist world view." *Der Hitler-Prozess 1924*, ed. and annotated by Lothar Gruchmann and Reinhold Weber with Otto Gritschneder, part 1, Munich, 1997, p. 20. See also Adolf Hitler, *Reden, Schriften, Anordnungen—Februar 1925 bis Januar 1933. Vol. 3: Zwischen den Reichstagswahlen Juli 1928–September 1930. Part 2: März 1929–Dezember 1929*, ed. Klaus As Lankheit, Munich, 1994, doc. 62, p. 341 (entry for 3 Aug. 1929): "I had been aware of the threat represented by Jews since I was eighteen and read whatever I could find on the subject."
77   Fest, *Hitler*, p. 64. Bullock sees the roots of Hitler's anti-Semitism in his "tortured sexual jealousy." Alan Bullock, *Hitler: A Study in Tyranny*, London, 1990, p. 39f. Haffner writes that Hitler "carried around his anti-Semitism from the very beginning like a congenital hunchback"; Sebastian Haffner, *Anmerkungen zu Hitler*, 21st edition, Munich, 1978, p. 15.
78   On what follows see Hamann, *Hitlers Wien*, pp. 239–42, 426–503; and subsequently, although partly a qualification of Hamann's theories, Kershaw, *Hitler: Hubris*, pp. 60–7. Critical of this theory is Ralf Georg Reuth, *Hitlers Judenhass: Klischee und Wirklichkeit*, Munich and Zurich, 2009, pp. 21–30, but his attempt to stylise Hitler into a "friend to Jews" (p. 28) is misleading. Before Brigitte Hamann, John Toland questioned Hitler's assertion that he had become an anti-Semite in Vienna. Toland argued that Hitler's anti-Jewish prejudice was probably fairly typical for the time and place and that he had become a hardcore anti-Semite at some later juncture. John Toland, *Adolf Hitler: Volume 1*, New York, 1976, p. 48f.

NOTES TO PAGES 44–50

79 Still of fundamental importance is Peter G. J. Pulzer, *Die Entstehung des politischen Antisemitismus in Deutschland und Österreich 1867–1914*, Gütersloh, 1964; new edition with a research report, Göttingen, 2004.

80 Hamann, *Hitlers Wien*, p. 404f.; for Lueger's anti-Semitism see Boyer, *Karl Lueger*, pp. 89ff.

81 On Guido List and Lanz von Liebenfels see Hamann, *Hitlers Wien*, pp. 293–319.

82 Wilfried Daim, *Der Mann, der Hitler die Ideen gab: Jörg Lanz von Liebenfels*, new and revised edition, Vienna, 1994.

83 Quoted in Hamann, *Hitlers Wien*, p. 499.

84 Hanisch, "I was Hitler's Buddy," p. 271. See also Franz Jetzinger, "Meine Erlebnisse mit Hitler Dokumenten," notes dated 12 July 1953: "There is hardly a trace of anti-Jewish hatred in his periods in Linz and Vienna." IfZ München, ZS 325.

85 Hamann, *Hitlers Wien*, p. 498.

86 For a summary see ibid., pp. 239–41.

87 Konrad Heiden, *Adolf Hitler: Das Zeitalter der Verantwortungslosigkeit: Eine Biographie*, Zurich, 1936, p. 28.

88 Recording of the owner of Kafee Kubata, Marie Wohlrabe, from 11 June 1940, and statements of the woman serving at the till, Maria Fellinger, on 17 June 1940; BA Berlin-Lichterfelde, NS 26/17a. Analysed in Kershaw, *Hitler: Hubris*, p. 620f.n87.

89 See Hamann, *Hitlers Wien*, p. 568.

90 For Rudolf Häusler's biography see ibid., pp. 566–8; Machtan, *Hitlers Geheimnis*, pp. 67ff.

91 Facsimile of the registration form in Joachimsthaler, *Korrektur*, p. 17.

92 Hitler, *Mein Kampf*, p. 138.

93 See David Clay Large, *Where Ghosts Walked: Munich's Road to the Third Reich*, New York and London, 1997, pp. 3–42.

94 See Schwarz, *Geniewahn*, pp. 70f.

95 Hitler, *Mein Kampf*, p. 139.

96 Erich Mühsam, *Unpolitische Erinnerungen: Mit einem Nachwort von Hubert van den Berg*, Hamburg, 1999, p. 89.

97 Hitler, *Monologe*, p. 115 (dated 29 Oct. 1941). For Heilmann & Littmann see Schwarz, *Geniewahn*, pp. 76f.

98 Hans Schirmer's report reprinted in Joachimsthaler, *Korrektur*, pp. 84f.; see further reports from the NSDAP main archive by people who bought paintings in Munich on pp. 85–9.

99 On Hitler's escape from registering for the draft, see the description and documents in Jetzinger, *Hitlers Jugend*, pp. 253–65.

100 First published in ibid., pp. 262–4 (see p. 273 for the facsimile of the letter); also in Hitler, *Sämtliche Aufzeichnungen*, no. 20, pp. 53–5. On the attempt by the SS to gain possession of Hitler's military record after the *Anschluss*, see Franz Jetzinger, "Meine Erlebnisse mit Hitler-Dokumenten."

101 Jetzinger, *Hitlers Jugend*, p. 265.

102 Quoted in Joachimsthaler, *Korrektur*, pp. 78f.

3 The Experience of War

1 Adolf Hitler, *Mein Kampf. Vol. 1: Eine Abrechnung*, 7th edition, Munich, 1933, p. 179. See Hitler's explanation from 14 April 1926: "I wore a soldier's grey uniform for almost six years. Of my time on Earth, these six years will remain not only my most eventful but also my most cherished years." Adolf Hitler, *Reden, Schriften, Anordnungen—Februar 1925 bis Januar 1933. Vol. 1: Die Wiedergründung der NSDAP Februar 1925–Juni 1926*, ed. and annotated Clemens Vollnhals, Munich, London, New York and Paris 1992, no. 123, p. 383.

2   This is also quite rightly emphasised in Ian Kershaw, *Hitler 1889–1936: Hubris*, London, 1998, p. 73. Thomas Weber's contrary thesis—that the First World War did not form Hitler but rather that he remained fully open and malleable—is unconvincing; Thomas Weber, *Hitler's First War: Adolf Hitler, the Men of the List Regiment, and the First World War*, Oxford and New York, pp. 254, 345. After he was shunted off as a consul general to San Francisco in January 1939, Hitler's former adjutant Fritz Wiedemann used the trans-Atlantic crossing aboard the MS *Hamburg* to jot down his key memories. Wiedemann summarised what Hitler had said upon appointing him before Christmas in 1933: "Emphasised importance of war and revolution for own development. Said, 'Otherwise I would have likely made an excellent architect.'" BA Koblenz, N 1720/4.

3   Hitler, *Mein Kampf*, p. 174.

4   Kurt Riezler, *Tagebücher, Aufsätze und Dokumente*, ed. and introduced Karl Dietrich Erdmann, Göttingen 1972, p. 183 (entry for 7 July 1914). On the German Reich leadership's risky politics during the July 1914 crisis see Volker Ullrich, *Die nervöse Grossmacht: Aufstieg und Untergang des deutschen Kaiserreichs 1871–1918*, Frankfurt am Main, 1997, pp. 250–63.

5   Hitler, *Mein Kampf*, p. 176. Later, with an eye towards the outbreak of the First World War, Hitler declared: "The most devastating thing for the German government is not that it did not want war, but that in fact it was manoeuvred into war against its own volition." Adolf Hitler, *Reden, Schriften, Anordnungen—Februar 1925 bis Januar 1933. Vol. 2: Vom Weimarer Parteitag bis zur Reichstagswahl Juli 1926–Mai 1928. Part 1: Juli 1926–Juli 1927*, ed. and annotated Bärbel Dusik, Munich, London, New York and Paris, 1992, no. 104, p. 256 (dated 17 April 1927).

6   First reprinted in Egmont Zechlin, "Bethmann Hollweg, Kriegsrisiko und SPD," in *Der Monat*, no. 208 (1966), p. 32.

7   See *Das Hitler-Bild: Die Erinnerungen des Fotografen Heinrich Hoffmann*, ed. Joe J. Heydecker, St. Pölten and Salzburg, 2008, p. 49. This is a reprint of a series based on audio recordings that appeared, starting in November 1954, in *Münchner Illustrierte* magazine.

8   Quoted in Anton Joachimsthaler, *Korrektur einer Biographie: Adolf Hitler 1908–1920*, Munich, 1989, p. 101.

9   When Hitler happened to see the photo at Hoffmann's studio, he reportedly remarked: "I too was in that crowd!" Hoffmann promptly enlarged the image and succeeded in locating Hitler. The photographer later recalled: "The photo quickly became world-famous. There was hardly a newspaper in Germany or abroad that did not publish it. We had to make thousands and thousands of prints to satisfy the demand." Heydecker, *Hoffmann- Erinnerungen*, p. 50. See also, Heinrich Hoffmann, *Hitler wie ich ihn sah: Aufzeichnungen seines Leibfotografen*, Munich and Berlin, 1974, pp. 32f. Recently the authenticity of the photographs has been doubted: see Sven Felix Kellerhof, "Berühmtes Hitler-Foto möglicherweise gefälscht," in *Die Welt*, 14 Oct. 2010. On Hoffman's darkroom see Rudolf Herz, *Hoffmann & Hitler: Fotografie als Medium des Führer-Mythos*, Munich, 1994, p. 26ff.; Heike B. Görtemaker, *Eva Braun: Leben mit Hitler*, Munich, 2010, pp. 14ff.

10   Hitler, *Mein Kampf*, p. 177.

11   Stefan Zweig, *Die Welt von Gestern: Erinnerungen eines Europäers*, Stuttgart and Hamburg, p. 254.

12   Erich Mühsam, *Tagebücher 1910–1924*, ed. and with an afterword by Chris Hirte, Munich, 1994, pp. 101, 109 (entries for 3/4 and 11 Aug. 1914).

13   Quoted in Bernd Ulrich and Benjamin Ziemann (eds), *Frontalltag im Ersten Weltkrieg: Wahn und Wirklichkeit*, Frankfurt am Main, 1994, p. 31. See also Benjamin Ziemann, *Front und Heimat: Ländliche Kriegserfahrungen in Bayern 1914–1923*, Essen, 1997, pp. 41ff.

14   Richard J. Evans (ed), *Kneipengespräche im Kaiserreich: Die Stimmungsberichte der Hamburger Politischen Polizei 1892–1914*, Reinbek by Hamburg, 1989, p. 415 (dated 24 and 29 July 1917).

15   Thomas Mann, "Gedanken im Kriege," in *Essays II: 1914–1916*, ed. and with critical commentary by Hermann Kurzke, Frankfurt am Main, 2002, p. 32.
16   Hitler, *Mein Kampf*, p. 177.
17   See ibid., p. 179.
18   See the detailed account in Joachimsthaler, *Korrektur*, pp. 102–9, which is based on research done by Bavarian officials in 1924.
19   See ibid., p. 113.
20   See ibid., p. 114; Weber, *Hitler's First War*, pp. 21–4; Fritz Wiedemann, *Der Mann, der Feldherr werden wollte: Erlebnisse und Erfahrungen des Vorgesetzten Hitlers im 1. Weltkrieg und seines späteren persönlichen Adjutanten*, Velbert and Kettwig, 1964, p. 18.
21   Hitler to A. Popp, 20 Oct. 1914; Adolf Hitler, *Sämtliche Aufzeichnungen 1905–1924*, ed. Eberhard Jäckel with Axel Kuhn, Stuttgart, 1980, no. 24, p. 59.
22   Hitler, *Mein Kampf*, p. 180.
23   Hitler to A. Popp, 20 Oct. 1914; Hitler, *Sämtliche Aufzeichnungen*, no. 24, p. 59.
24   Ibid., no. 25, p. 59.
25   Adolf Hitler, *Monologe im Führerhauptquartier 1941–1944: Die Aufzeichnungen Heinrich Heims*, ed. Werner Jochmann, Hamburg, 1980, pp. 407f. (dated 23 March 1944). See *Die Tagebücher von Joseph Goebbels. Part 1: Aufzeichnungen 1923–1941*, ed. Elke Fröhlich, Munich, 1998–2006, vol. 5, p. 253 (entry for 10 April 1938): "The Führer told of how the song 'Die Wacht am Rhein' had moved him when he crossed over [the river] for the first time in October 1914."
26   Hitler to J. Popp, 3 Dec. 1914; Hitler, *Sämtliche Aufzeichnungen*, no. 26, p. 60.
27   Based on John Horne and Alan Kramer, *Deutsche Kriegsgreuel 1914: Die umstrittene Wahrheit*, Hamburg 2004, pp. 65–72.
28   See Joachimsthaler, *Korrektur*, p. 120.
29   Hitler to E. Hepp, 5 Feb. 1915; Hitler, *Sämtliche Aufzeichnungen*, no. 30, pp. 64–9.
30   Hitler's account tallies with the numbers in the official regiment history. Its fighting strength had decreased to a mere 750 men and non-commissioned officers and 4 officers. This means that of the regiment's 3,000 soldiers, around 70 per cent fell or were wounded in battle. See Fridolin Solleder (ed.), *Vier Jahre Westfront: Geschichte des Regiment List RIR 16*, Munich, 1932, p. 60. See Weber, *Hitler's First War*, pp. 48f.
31   Hitler, *Mein Kampf*, p. 130f. See also a letter by Rudolf Hess from 29 June 1924: "Yesterday, the tribune told stories from 1914 that were so vivid and fascinating that I felt overwhelmed." BA Bern, Nl Hess; quoted in Othmar Plöckinger, *Geschichte eines Buches: Adolf Hitlers "Mein Kampf" 1922–1945*, Munich, 2006, p. 48.
32   R. Hess to I. Pröhl, 29 June 1924; Rudolf Hess, *Briefe 1908–1933*, ed. Rüdiger Hess, Munich and Vienna, 1987, p. 342.
33   Hitler to J. Popp, 26 Jan. 1915; Hitler, *Sämtliche Aufzeichnungen*, no. 29, p. 63.
34   See Wiedemann, *Der Mann*, p. 24; Balthasar Brandmayer, *Zwei Meldegänger*, Bruckmühl, 1932, p. 48.
35   Hitler to J. Popp, 3 Dec. 1914; Hitler, *Sämtliche Aufzeichnungen* no. 26, p. 60.
36   The incident is described in Hitler's letter to E. Hepp, 22 Jan. 1915; ibid., no. 27, p. 68.
37   Hitler to J. Popp, 3 Dec. 1914; ibid., no. 26, p. 61.
38   Hitler to J. Popp, 26 Jan. 1915; ibid., no. 29, pp. 63f.
39   Hitler to E. Hepp, 5 Feb. 1915; ibid., no. 30, pp. 68f.
40   Quoted in Michael Jürgs, *Der kleine Frieden im Grossen Krieg. Westfront 1914: Als Deutsche, Franzosen und Briten gemeinsam Weihnachten feierten*, Munich, 2003, p. 43.
41   Ibid., p. 87. See Weber, *Hitler's First War*, p. 61.
42   Statement by Heinrich Lugauer, a runner in RIR. 16, on 5 Feb. 1940; BA Berlin-Lichterfelde, NS 26/47. See Weber, *Hitler's First War*, p. 63.
43   Hitler, *Monologe*, p. 46 (entry for 24/25 July 1941). See ibid., p. 71 (entry for 25/26 Sept. 1941): "I'm infinitely grateful that I experienced the war as I did." Goebbels,

Tagebücher, part 1, vol. 2/1, p. 203 (entry for 21 July 1930): "Boss told us about the war. It's his favourite topic and one that never runs dry."

44 Adolf Hitler, *Reden, Schriften, Anordnungen—Februar 1925 bis Januar 1933. Vol. 3: Zwischen den Reichstagswahlen Juli 1928–September 1930. Part 3: Januar 1930–September 1930*, ed. Christian Hartmann, Munich, 1994, doc. 116, p. 430 (dated 16 Sept.1930). See Otto Wagener, *Hitler aus nächster Nähe: Aufzeichnungen eines Vertrauten 1929–1932*, ed. Henry A. Turner, Frankfurt am Main, Berlin and Vienna, 1978, p. 142: Wagener recounts Hitler saying that, after reading a book on the Battle of the Somme, he only then fully understood "why someone would lie in a dirty hole and hold out." See also Hess, *Briefe*, p. 263 (dated Aug. 1920): "From the very beginning to the end of the war, Hitler was on the frontlines as a common soldier."

45 See Weber, *Hitler's First War*, pp. 99–101, 283. Hitler immediately sued the *Echo der Welt* for defamation. In its judgment of 9 March 1932, the Hamburg State Court ruled that the defendant was prohibited from portraying Hitler's wartime service in a way that "suggested the plaintiff had tried to shirk his duties as a soldier." BA Berlin-Lichterfelde, NS 26/17a.

46 Ferdinand Widmann to A. Hitler, 9 March 1932; BA Berlin-Lichterfelde, NS 26/18.

47 Statement by Heinrich Lugauer on 5 Feb. 1940; BA Berlin-Lichterfelde, NS 26/47. Further statements by Wilhelm Hansen, Hans Raab and Hans Bauer in ibid. In March 1933, the *Berner Tageblatt* newspaper published an article, "written by a German academic," which read: "He [Hitler] was always prepared to do difficult duties. I often experienced how the runners disagreed about whose turn it was when one of them was called by the regimental office . . . It was always Hitler who stole away and voluntarily delivered the message." *Berner Tageblatt*, 23 March 1933; BA Berlin-Lichterfelde, R 43 II/959.

48 Transcript by Friedrich Petz from 1922; quoted in Joachimsthaler, *Korrektur*, p. 160f. See the similar verdicts of the regimental commander Major Baron Anton von Tabeuf in February 1922 (ibid., p. 169) and his deputy Baron von Godin in July 1918 (ibid., p. 175f.) In 1931, the last commander of the regiment, Maximilian Baligand, dedicated a copy of the regimental history to "his brave runner, the honorable former private Adolf Hitler with gratitude and in memory of serious but great times in the past." Timothy W. Ryback, *Hitler's Private Library: The Books That Shaped His Life*, London, 2009, p. 14.

49 Wiedemann added: "On the field of battle, he proved his worth as a courageous and particularly reliable runner, who deserved his Iron Cross, First Class and who was put forward for that honour numerous times, before he actually received it." BA Koblenz, N 1720/4. See also Wiedemann, *Der Mann*, pp. 25, 85.

50 See Weber, *Hitler's First War*, pp. 293f., 321–5, 341f.

51 Ibid., pp. 105f, 345.

52 Stefan Ernstling, *Der phantastische Rebell: Alexander Moritz Frey oder Hitler schiesst dramatisch in die Luft*, Zurich, 2007, p. 52.

53 Wiedemann, *Der Mann*, p. 26. See Fritz Wiedemann's statement from 1 July 1947; Robert M. W. Kempner, *Das Dritte Reich im Kreuzverhör: Aus den unveröffentlichten Vernehmungsprotokollen des Anklägers in den Nürnberger Prozessen*, Munich, 2005, p. 92 ("not leadership material").

54 Max Amann's questioning in Nuremberg on 5 Nov. 1947; Joachimsthaler, *Korrektur*, p. 160.

55 Hitler, *Mein Kampf*, p. 181.

56 Hess, *Briefe*, p. 342 (dated 29 June 1924). For the phenomenon of fear in the First World War, see Susanne Michl and Jan Plamper, "Soldatische Angst im Ersten Weltkrieg," *Geschichte und Gesellschaft*, 35.2 (2009), pp. 209–48.

57 Hitler, *Mein Kampf*, p. 181.

58 Hitler, *Monologe*, p. 75 (dated 27/28 Sept. to 9 Oct. 1941).

59   Ibid., p. 296 (dated 24/25 Feb. 1942). In the spring of 1926, Hitler underlined a passage from Ernst Jünger's book *Feuer und Blut* (*Fire and Blood*) that described this side of the experience of war. See Ryback, *Hitler's Private Library*, pp. 82–4.

60   Hitler, *Monologe*, p. 71 (dated 25/26 Sept. 1941).

61   Max Amann's questioning in Nuremberg on 5 Nov. 1947; Joachimsthaler, *Korrektur*, p. 158.

62   Brandmayer, *Zwei Meldegänger*, p. 103.

63   See Werner Maser, *Adolf Hitler: Legende—Mythos—Wirklichkeit*, 12th edition, Munich and Esslingen, 1989, pp. 315, 598–628. For a critical perspective see Joachimsthaler, *Korrektur*, pp. 161–4; Guido Knopp, *Geheimnisse des "Dritten Reiches,"* Munich, 2011, pp. 268–76.

64   See Lothar Machtan, *Hitlers Geheimnis: Das Doppelleben eines Diktators*, Berlin, 2001, pp. 81ff. Machtan largely based his assertions on later testimony by Hans Mend, the List Regiment's equestrian orderly, but Mend was a known liar and psychopath. See Joachimsthaler, *Korrektur*, pp. 143f.; Weber, *Hitler's First War*, pp. 137–9.

65   See Joachimsthaler, *Korrektur*, pp. 144f.; Weber, *Hitler's First War*, p. 317.

66   See Weber, *Hitler's First War*, p. 139f.

67   Examples in Joachimsthaler, *Korrektur*, pp. 128, 160; Claudia Schmölders, *Hitlers Gesicht: Eine physiognomische Biographie*, Munich, 2000, pp. 11–13. See also Joachim Fest, *Hitler: Eine Biographie*, Frankfurt am Main, Berlin and Vienna, 1973, p. 104; Weber, *Hitler's First War*, p. 139.

68   Hitler, *Monologe*, p. 219 (dated 22/23 Jan. 1942).

69   Hitler, *Mein Kampf*, p. 182.

70   Max Amann's questioning in Nuremberg on 5 Nov. 1947; Joachimsthaler, *Korrektur*, p. 159.

71   Brandmayer, *Zwei Meldegänger*, pp. 66–8.

72   Hitler to E. Hepp, 5 Feb. 1915; Hitler, *Sämtliche Aufzeichnungen*, no. 30, p. 69.

73   Hitler, *Monologe*, p. 411 (dated 19 May 1944). See Otto Dietrich, *12 Jahre mit Hitler*, Munich, 1955, p. 164. Hans Frank, *Im Angesicht des Galgens: Deutung Hitlers und seiner Zeit auf Grund eigener Erlebnisse und Erkenntnisse*, Munich and Gräfelfing, 1953, p. 46: "I had a well-thumbed paperback copy of *The World as Will and Representation* in my knapsack." On the topic of Hitler reading Schopenhauer, see Birgit Schwarz, *Geniewahn: Hitler und die Kunst*, Vienna, Cologne and Weimar, 2009, pp. 51–3, who asserts that Schopenhauer's idea of genius supported Hitler's view of himself as an artist. By contrast Ryback (*Hitler's Private Library*, p. 104) doubts that Hitler ever read Schopenhauer during the war. Reports from his former regimental comrades confirm that Hitler spent every free minute reading. See Heinrich Lugauer's statement of 5 Feb. 1940 and Hans Bauer's of 15 Feb. 1940; BA Berlin-Lichterfelde, NS 26/47.

74   See John Keegan, *The Face of Battle: A Sturdy of Agincourt, Waterloo and the Somme*, London, 1978, pp. 204ff; Gerhard Hirschfeld, Gerd Krumeich and Irina Renz (eds): *Die Deutschen an der Somme 1914–1918: Krieg, Besatzung, Verbrannte Erde*, Essen, 2006, pp. 79ff.

75   Quoted in Hirschfeld *et al.*, *Die Deutschen an der Somme*, p. 147. Hitler, too, described the Battle of the Somme as "more hell than war"; *Mein Kampf*, p. 209.

76   Wiedemann, *Der Mann*, p. 29.

77   Hitler, *Monologe*, p. 172 (dated 3/4 Jan. 1942).

78   Hitler, *Mein Kampf*, p. 210.

79   Ibid., p. 210. See Hitler's testimony in front of Munich Court I on 26 Feb. 1924: "Whereas we had previously showed absolute obedience at the front, it more or less dissolved in the field hospital." *Der Hitler-Prozess 1924*, ed. and annotated by Lothar Gruchmann and Reinhold Weber with Otto Gritschneder, part 1, Munich, 1997, p. 21. On "self-mutilation," see Ulrich and Ziemann, *Frontalltag*, pp. 151–3.

80 Hitler, *Mein Kampf*, p. 211.

81 Ingo Materna and Hans-Joachim Schreckenbach (eds) with Bärbel Holtz, *Berichte des Berliner Polizeipräsidenten zur Stimmung und Lage der Bevölkerung in Berlin 1914–1918*, Weimar, 1987, no. 175, p. 156. For background see Volker Ullrich, "Kriegsalltag: Zur inneren Revolutionierung der wilhelminischen Gesellschaft," in Wolfgang Michalka (ed.), *Der Erste Weltkrieg: Wirkung—Wahrnehmung—Analyse*, Munich and Zurich, 1994, pp. 603–21.

82 Hitler, *Mein Kampf*, p. 211.

83 Quoted in Ziemann, *Front und Heimat*, p. 274.

84 W. Rathenau to W. Schwaner, 4 Aug. 1916; *Walther Rathenau, Briefe. Vol. 2: 1914–1922*, ed. Alexander Jaser, Clemens Picht and Ernst Schulin, Düsseldorf, 2006, p. 1552.

85 Quoted in Volker Ullrich, "'Drückeberger': Die Judenzählung im Ersten Weltkrieg," in Julius H. Schoeps and Joachim Schlör (eds), *Antisemitismus: Vorurteile und Mythen*, Munich and Zurich, 1995, p. 214.

86 Hitler, *Mein Kampf*, p. 211. See Hitler's speech on 29 Feb. 1928: "For four years, these people avoided serving at the front." Adolf Hitler, *Reden, Schriften, Anordnungen—Februar 1925 bis Januar 1933. Vol. 2: Vom Weimarer Parteitag bis zur Reichstagswahl Juli 1926–Mai 1928. Part 2: August 1927–Mai 1928*, ed. and annotated Bärbel Dusik, Munich, 1992, no. 237, pp. 701f.

87 Hitler, *Mein Kampf*, pp. 211f.

88 See John Toland, *Adolf Hitler: Volume 1*, New York, 1976, pp. 70. Reuth's assumption that during the war Hitler had been completely free of anti-Jewish sentiment seems rather implausible; Ralf Georg Reuth, *Hitlers Judenhass: Klischee und Wirklichkeit*, Munich and Zurich, 2009, pp. 35–43. But that does not mean that he despised Jews. Weber (*Hitler's First War*, p. 237) also asserts that in early 1917 Hitler was "no committed, avowed anti-Semite."

89 Wiedemann, *Der Mann*, pp. 33f.

90 Hitler to K. Lanzhammer, 19 Dec. 1916; www.europeana1914–1918.eu. Facsimile in *Süddeutsche Zeitung*, 3 May 2012. Hitler to B. Brandmayer, 21 Dec. 1916; Hitler, *Sämtliche Aufzeichnungen* no. 44, p. 78.

91 Wiedemann, *Der Mann*, p. 30. In August 1938, Professor Max Unold contacted Wiedemann and informed him: "Some time ago, I found the enclosed notebook from the war and discovered that as a corporal in my replacement battalion in Munich in 1917, I had none other than Adolf Hitler in my quarters." According to Unold's notes, the battalion was quartered in a school on Munich's Luisenstrasse in February and March of 1917. M. Unold to F. Wiedemann, 18 Aug. 1938; BA Koblenz, N 1720/8.

92 Hitler, *Monologe*, p. 57 (dated 8/9–10/11 Aug. 1941).

93 See the entry "Tank" (author: Gerhard P. Gross) in Gerhard Hirschfeld, Gerd Krumeich and Irina Renz (eds) with Markus Pöhlmann, *Enzyklopädie Erster Weltkrieg*, Paderborn, 2003, pp. 917–19.

94 Hitler prepared himself by reading Max Osborn's book on Berlin, which appeared as vol. 43 of the series *Berühmte Kunststätten* im Leipziger Verlag E. A. Seemann; he had purchased it in November 1915 in Tournes. Ryback, *Hitler's Private Library*, pp. 7f, 18–22.

95 Hitler to E. Schmidt, 6 Oct. 1917; Hitler, *Sämtliche Aufzeichnungen*, no. 50, p. 82. See also Hitler's Berlin visits between 1916 and 1918, Thomas Friedrich, *Die missbrauchte Hauptstadt: Hitler und Berlin*, Berlin, 2007, pp. 11–27; Sven Felix Kellerhoff, *Hitlers Berlin: Geschichte einer Hassliebe*, Berlin and Brandenburg, 2005, pp. 17–20.

96 Hitler to M. Amann, 8, 11, and 12 Oct. 1917; Hitler, *Sämtliche Aufzeichnungen*, nos 51–53, pp. 82f.

97 Volker Ullrich, *Kriegsalltag: Hamburg im Ersten Weltkrieg*, Cologne, 1982, pp. 85–92 (quotation on p. 87).

98 *Berichte des Berliner Polizeipräsidenten*, no. 242, p. 213.

99   Ullrich, *Kriegsalltag*, p. 126. For a case study of the strike in Jan. 1918, *idem*, "Der Januarstreik 1918 in Hamburg, Kiel und Bremen: Eine vergleichende Studie zur Geschichte der Streikbewegungen im Ersten Weltkrieg," in *Zeitschrift für Hamburgische Geschichte*, (1985), pp. 45–74.

100   Quoted in Bernd Ulrich, *Die Augenzeugen: Deutsche Feldpostbriefe in Kriegs- und Nachkriegszeit 1914–1933*, Essen, 1997, p. 74n104; Ulrich and Ziemann, *Frontalltag*, p. 196.

101   Hitler, *Mein Kampf*, pp. 213, 217.

102   *Berichte des Berliner Polizeipräsidenten*, no. 270, p. 240.

103   See Joachimsthaler, *Korrektur*, p. 172; Weber, *Hitler's First War*, p. 209.

104   Hitler, *Monologe*, p. 152 (dated 10/11 Nov. 1941). For the awarding of the Iron Cross, First Class see Joachimsthaler, *Korrektur*, p. 173; Weber, *Hitler's First War*, p. 215. By contrast Othmar Plöckinger (*Unter Soldaten und Agitatoren: Hitlers prägende Jahre im deutschen Militär 1918–1920*, Paderborn, 2013, p. 16f.) doubts that Gutmann played a role in Hitler's commendation since he was not a member of the regiment at the time when Hitler was put forward for or awarded the Iron Cross. See ibid., p. 18, for a facsimile of the list of recorded soldiers in Hitler's regiment on 4 Aug. 1918.

105   Quoted in Ulrich and Ziemann, *Frontalltag*, p. 204.

106   Hitler, *Monologe*, p. 100 (dated 21/22 Oct. 1941). See Weber, *Hitler's First War*, pp. 218, 219.

107   Hitler, *Mein Kampf*, p. 221.

108   For a summary see Hans-Joachim Neumann and Henrik Eberle, *War Hitler krank? Ein abschliessender Befund*, Bergisch-Gladbach, 2009, pp. 42–8.

109   Hitler to an unknown "Herr Doktor," 29 Nov. 1921; Hitler, *Sämtliche Aufzeichnungen*, no. 325, p. 526. Facsimile in Joachimsthaler, *Korrektur*, pp. 92–4. See Hitler's testimony in front of Munich Court I, 26 Feb. 1924: "For a short time, I was completely blind and didn't think I would ever be able to see again . . . Over the course of my treatment, my condition improved to the point that when I was released from the field hospital I could at least read large headlines." *Der Hitler-Prozess 1924*, vol. 1, p. 19.

110   This is suggested in Bernhard Horstmann, *Hitler in Pasewalk: Die Hypnose und ihre Folgen*, Düsseldorf, 2004 (quotation on p. 113).

111   Quoted in Uwe Lohalm, *Völkischer Radikalismus: Die Geschichte des Deutschvölkischen Schutz- und Trutzbundes 1919–1923*, Hamburg, 1970, p. 53.

112   Hitler, *Mein Kampf*, pp. 221–5. See also Hitler's testimony in front of Munich Court I, 26 Feb. 1924: "On 9 November (1918) it became clear to me, and that night I made my decision: the vacillations in my life between whether to go into politics or remain an architect came to an end. That night I decided that, if I got my vision back, I would turn to politics." *Der Hitler-Prozess 1924*, p. 21.

113   Ernst Deuerlein, *Hitler: Eine politische Biographie*, Munich, 1969, p. 40.

4 *The Leap into Politics*

1   Adolf Hitler, *Monologe im Führerhauptquartier 1941–1944: Die Aufzeichnungen Heinrich Heims*, ed. Werner Jochmann, Hamburg, 1980, p. 234 (dated 25/26 Jan. 1942).

2   See Anton Joachimsthaler, *Korrektur einer Biographie: Adolf Hitler 1908–1920*, Munich, 1989, p. 187; Othmar Plöckinger, *Unter Soldaten und Agitatoren: Hitlers prägende Jahre im deutschen Militär 1918–1920*, Paderborn, 2013, p. 29.

3   See Bernhard Grau, *Kurt Eisner 1867–1919: Eine Biographie*, Munich, 2001, pp. 343ff.

4   Wilhelm Herzog, *Menschen, denen ich begegnete*, Bern and Munich, 1959, pp. 67f.

5   See Grau, *Kurt Eisner*, pp. 388ff.

6   Michael Epkenhans, "'Wir als deutsches Volk sind doch nicht klein zu kriegen . . .': Aus den Tagebüchern des Fregattenkapitäns Bogislav von Selchow 1918/19," in *Militärgeschichtliche Mitteilungen*, 55 (1996), p. 202.

7   Quoted in Joachimsthaler, *Korrektur*, p. 190. In November 1929, Hitler declared: "I did not support that revolution for a second." Adolf Hitler, *Reden, Schriften, Anordnungen—Februar 1925 bis Januar 1933. Vol. 3, Part 2: März 1929–Dezember 1929*, ed. and annotated by Klaus A. Lankheit, Munich, New Providence, London and Paris, 1994, doc. 93, p. 436. Joachim Riecker (*Hitlers 9. November: Wie der Erste Weltkrieg zum Holocaust führte*, Berlin, 2009, p. 49) offers no evidence for his statement that Hitler "was initially positive towards the revolution."

8   Adolf Hitler, *Mein Kampf. Vol. 1: Eine Abrechnung*, 7th edition, Munich, 1933, p. 226.

9   Franz J. Bauer (ed.): *Die Regierung Eisner 1918/19: Ministerratsprotokolle und Dokumente*, Düsseldorf, 1987, no. 40b, p. 246 (dated 3 Jan. 1919). The *Münchener Neueste Nachrichten* newspaper wrote of a "dance pandemic"; quoted in Martin H. Geyer, *Verkehrte Welt: Revolution, Inflation und Moderne. München 1914–1924*, Göttingen, 1998, p. 72. On the phenomenon of the "dance craze" during the November revolution, see also Volker Ullrich, *Die Revolution von 1918/19*, Munich, 2009, pp. 42f.

10   Hitler, *Mein Kampf*, p. 226. On the stay in Traunstein and the date of the return to Munich, see Plöckinger, *Unter Soldaten und Agitatoren*, pp. 34–6 (page 33 contains a photo of Hitler together with Ernst Schmidt in the Traunstein training camp).

11   See ibid., pp. 37–41.

12   Quoted in Friedrich Hitzer, *Anton Graf Arco: Das Attentat auf Kurt Eisner und die Schüsse im Landtag*, Munich, 1988, p. 391.

13   Quoted in Michaela Karl, *Die Münchner Räterepublik: Porträts einer Revolution*, Düsseldorf, 2008, p. 108.

14   Ralf Höller, *Der Anfang, der ein Ende war: Die Revolution in Bayern 1918/19*, Berlin, 1999, p. 193.

15   Harry Graf Kessler, *Das Tagebuch. Vol 7: 1919–1923*, ed. Angela Reinthal with Janna Brechmacher and Christoph Hilse, Stuttgart, 2007, p. 222 (entry for 5 April 1919).

16   On the Freikorps of Ritter von Epp, see the brochure and newspaper clipping collection in BA Koblenz, N 1101/34. Upon Epp's discharge from the Reichswehr in October 1923, Bavarian state premier Eugen von Knilling thanked the general for his "courageous intervention in liberating Munich from the hands of Bolshevism." Knilling went on: "Your services are part of history and represent an honourable page that shines out from the darkness of recent years." E. v. Knilling to Ritter von Epp, 31 Oct. 1923; BA Koblenz, N 1101/43a.

17   Erich Mühsam, *Tagebücher 1910–1924*, ed. and with an afterword by Chris Hirte, Munich, 1994, p. 191 (entry for 7 May 1919).

18   Konrad Heiden, *Adolf Hitler: Das Zeitalter der Verantwortungslosigkeit. Eine Biographie*, p. 64. In his 1933 autobiography, *Eine Jugend in Deutschland*, Ernst Toller reported that during a period of incarceration, a fellow prisoner told of meeting Hitler in a Munich barracks in the first months of the republic. "Back then, Hitler declared he was a Social Democrat," the man allegedly said. Ernst Toller, *Prosa, Briefe, Dramen, Gedichte*, Reinbek bei Hamburg, 1961, p. 165.

19   See Joachimsthaler, *Korrektur*, p. 204, who puts the vote in mid-February 1919. Ralf Georg Reuth (*Hitlers Judenhass: Klischee und Wirklichkeit*, Munich and Zurich, 2009, p. 89) reaches a similar conclusion, writing that the "government soldier Adolf Hitler" was an "adherent of Social Democracy" in late February and March 1919. Plöckinger (*Unter Soldaten und Agitatoren*, pp. 42–6) correctly rejects this assertion as untenable.

20   Bauer, *Die Regierung Eisner*, introduction, p. lxi.

21   Hitler, *Monologe*, p. 248 (dated 1 Feb. 1942).

22   Joachim Fest, *Hitler: Eine Biographie*, Frankfurt am Main, Berlin and Vienna, 1973, p. 123. Ian Kershaw, *Hitler 1889–1936: Hubris*, London, 1998, p. 120, also writes of "sheer opportunism." Ludolf Herbst (*Hitlers Charisma: Die Erfindung eines deutschen Messias*, Frankfurt am Main, 2010) characterises Hitler's stance as "wait and see" (p. 96) adding, "Hitler skilfully manoeuvred his way through a political difficult time" (p. 99).

23   See Ralf Georg Reuth, *Hitler: Eine Biographie*, Munich and Zurich, 2003, p. 78f.; Thomas Weber, *Hitler's First War: Adolf Hitler, the Men of the List Regiment, and the First World War*, Oxford and New York, p. 251. Contrary to this, Plöckinger (*Unter Soldaten und Agitatoren*, p. 43) describes Hitler's participation in the funeral procession as "less than likely."

24   Quoted in John Toland, *Adolf Hitler: Volume 1*, New York, 1976, p. 85.

25   See Joachimsthaler, *Korrektur*, p. 213f.; Plöckinger, *Unter Soldaten und Agitatoren*, p. 48f. Reuth's idea that Hitler became "a functionary in the gears of global Communist revolution" (*Hitlers Judenhass*, p. 94) is completely off-base.

26   Hitler, *Mein Kampf*, p. 226. Plöckinger expresses well-founded doubts about this version in *Unter Soldaten und Agitatoren*, pp. 57, 64f.

27   Hitler, *Mein Kampf*, p. 227.

28   Quoted in Joachimsthaler, *Korrektur*, p. 214. See also the investigating committee's report about Georg Dufter dated 4 June 1919 in Plöckinger, *Unter Soldaten und Agitatoren*, pp. 344f.

29   See Plöckinger, *Unter Soldaten und Agitatoren*, p. 100.

30   Joachimsthaler, *Korrektur*, p. 225.

31   Hellmuth Auerbach, "Hitlers politische Lehrjahre und die Münchner Gesellschaft 1919–1923," in *Vierteljahrshefte für Zeitgeschichte*, 25 (1977), p. 18.

32   As found in Karl Mayr's anonymous article in the U.S. magazine *Current History*, "I was Hitler's Boss: By a former officer of the Reichswehr," Nov. 1941, p. 193. For a critical perspective see Plöckinger, *Unter Soldaten und Agitatoren*, p. 102n11.

33   Ernst Deuerlein, "Hitlers Eintritt in die Politik und die Reichswehr," in *Vierteljahrshefte für Zeitgeschichte*, 7 (1959), p. 179.

34   See Plöckinger, *Unter Soldaten und Agitatoren*, pp. 103f., 108. Here the author corrects the position he previously held: see Othmar Plöckinger, "Adolf Hitler als Hörer an der Universität München im Jahr 1919: Zum Verhältnis zwischen Reichswehr und Universität," in Elisabeth Kraus (ed.), *Die Universität München im Dritten Reich: Aufsätze*, vol. 2, Munich, 2008, pp. 13–47.

35   The programme for the first course can be found in Deuerlein, "Hitlers Eintritt," doc. 2, pp. 191f. For the third course's speakers see Plöckinger, *Unter Soldaten und Agitatoren*, pp. 108–10.

36   Diary of Gottfried Feder, vol. 1 (entries for 6 June and July 1919), IfZ München, ED 874. For Feder's theories see Reuth, *Hitlers Judenhass*, pp. 158–61; Plöckinger, *Unter Soldaten und Agitatoren*, pp. 263–5.

37   Hitler, *Mein Kampf*, p. 229.

38   Karl Alexander von Müller, *Mars und Venus: Erinnerungen 1914–1918*, Stuttgart, 1954, p. 338.

39   Ibid., pp. 338f. See also Müller's notes, "Berührungen mit der NSDAP," about the two lectures, Karl Mayr and his "curious protégé"; BayHStA München, Nl K. A. v. Müller 101.

40   Hitler, *Mein Kampf*, p. 243. For something similar see Adolf Hitler, *Reden, Schriften, Anordnungen—Februar 1925 bis Januar 1933. Vol. 4: Von der Reichstagswahl bis zur Reichspräsidentenwahl Oktober 1930–März 1932. Part 2: Juli 1931–Dezember 1931*, ed. Christian Hartmann, Munich, 1996, doc. 80, p. 250 (entry for 4 April 1931).

41   Deuerlein, "Hitlers Eintritt," doc. 4, p. 196f.; see Plöckinger, *Unter Soldaten und Agitatoren*, pp. 113–19 (see p. 120 for a facsimile of the handwritten list of participants in Walther Bendt's "educational commando").

42   See Plöckinger, *Unter Soldaten und Agitatoren*, pp. 123f.

43   Hitler, *Mein Kampf*, p. 235.

44   Orderly Lorenz Frank on 23 Aug. 1919 in Deuerlein, "Hitlers Eintritt," doc. 9, p. 200. Other voices in Plöckinger, *Unter Soldaten und Agitatoren*, p. 128.

45   Report by First Lieutenant Bendt on 21 Aug. 1919 in Deuerlein, "Hitlers Eintritt," doc. 7, p. 199.

46   See Plöckinger, *Unter Soldaten und Agitatoren*, pp. 194ff., 210ff.
47   Quoted in Dirk Walter, *Antisemitische Kriminalität und Gewalt: Judenfeindschaft in der Weimarer Republik*, Bonn, 1999, p. 55.
48   Quoted in Plöckinger, *Unter Soldaten und Agitatoren*, p. 330.
49   *Münchener Neueste Nachrichten* from 14 Nov. 1919; quoted in Hans-Günter Richardi, *Hitler und seine Hintermänner: Neue Fakten zur Frühgeschichte der NSDAP*, Munich, 1991, p. 81.
50   For the anti-Semitic pamphlets available in libraries and reading rooms for troops see Plöckinger, *Unter Soldaten und Agitatoren*, pp. 218ff, 251ff.
51   Report by First Lieutenant Bendt dated 21 Aug. 1919; Deuerlein, "Hitlers Eintritt," doc. 7, p. 199. In Landsberg Prison in June 1924, Hitler told Rudolf Hess that he had "only arrived at his current stance on the Jewish question after some serious internal conflicts." Rudolf Hess, *Briefe 1908–1933*, ed. Rüdiger Hess, Munich and Vienna, 1987, pp. 334f. (dated 11 June 1924).
52   A. Gemlich to Captain Mayr, 4 Sept. 1919; Deuerlein, "Hitlers Eintritt," doc 10a, pp. 201f.
53   Hitler to A. Gemlich, 16 Sept. 1919; Deuerlein, "Hitlers Eintritt," doc. 12, pp. 203–5; also reproduced in Adolf Hitler, *Sämtliche Aufzeichnungen 1905–1924*, ed. Eberhard Jäckel with Axel Kuhn, Stuttgart, 1980, no. 61, pp. 88–90. Plöckinger (*Unter Soldaten und Agitatoren*, p. 143) correctly concludes that in his answer Hitler "did not advance any original positions, but merely summarised views and ideas that were already widespread in anti-Semitic circles." On the interpretation of the "Gemlich letter," see also ibid., pp. 332–8.
54   See Walter, *Antisemitische Kriminalität*, pp. 34f.
55   See Plöckinger, *Unter Soldaten und Agitatoren*, pp. 257, 334f.
56   Hitler to A. Gemlich, 16 Sept. 1919; Deuerlein, "Hitlers Eintritt," doc. 12, p. 204. See also Hitler's contribution to a discussion at an NSDAP meeting on 6 April 1920: "We do not want to be the sort of emotional anti-Semites who create a pogrom mood. We are filled with the uncompromising determination to grasp this evil by the roots and tear it out in its entirety (enthusiastic applause)." Ibid. no. 91, p. 119.
57   Captain Mayr to A. Gemlich, 17 Sept. 1919; Deuerlein, "Hitlers Eintritt," doc. 11, p. 202f. Against the background of these remarks it is all the more astonishing that Karl Mayr would get close to the SPD in 1923 and later collaborate with the Reich Banner Black-Red-Gold. See Othmar Plöckinger, "Frühe biographische Texte zu Hitler: Zur Bewertung der autobiographischen Texte in *Mein Kampf*," in *Vierteljahrshefte für Zeitgeschichte*, 58 (2010), p. 99n25.
58   Hitler, *Mein Kampf*, p. 236.
59   See Plöckinger, *Unter Soldaten und Agitatoren*, pp. 144, 147–51.
60   See Auerbach, "Hitlers politische Lehrjahre," p. 8f.; Werner Maser, *Die Frühgeschichte der NSDAP: Hitlers Weg bis 1924*, Frankfurt am Main and Bonn, 1965, pp. 146–8; Reginald Phelps, "Before Hitler came: Thule Society and Germanen Orden," in *Journal of Modern History*, 35 (1963), pp. 245–61; Hermann Gilbhard, *Die Thule-Gesellschaft: Vom okkulten Mummenschanz zum Hakenkreuz*, Munich, 1994.
61   See Dirk Stegmann, "Zwischen Repression und Manipulation: Konservative Machteliten und Arbeiter- und Angestelltenbewegung 1910–1918: Ein Beitrag zur Vorgeschichte der DAP/NSDAP," in *Archiv für Sozialgeschichte*, 12 (1972), p. 385ff.; Maser, *Frühgeschichte*, pp. 142–6.
62   From February to August 1919, between 10 and 38 people took part in DAP members' meetings. See Anton Joachimsthaler, *Hitlers Weg begann in München 1913–1923*, Munich, 2000, p. 251.
63   Hitler, *Mein Kampf*, pp. 237f.
64   See Plöckinger, *Unter Soldaten und Agitatoren*, p. 151f.

65   Georg-Franz Willing, *Die Hitler-Bewegung: Der Ursprung 1919–1922*, Hamburg and
      Berlin, 1962, p. 66. On the differing records of this remark see Kershaw, *Hitler:
      Hubris*, p. 643n79.
66   Hitler, *Mein Kampf*, p. 241.
67   See Fest, *Hitler*, p. 170. According to a statement by Hans Georg Grassinger, the
      operational manager of the *Münchener Beobachter* and one of the founders of the
      German Socialist Party (DSP), which evolved out of the Thule Society, Hitler offered
      to work for the DSP and the newspaper in the fall of 1919, but there was no position
      for him. Testimony by Hans Georg Grassinger, 19 Dec. 1951; IfZ München, ZS 50.
68   Hitler, *Mein Kampf*, p. 243. In an article in the *Illustrierter Beobachter* newspaper on
      3 Aug. 1929, Hitler recalled the "unbelievably tiny beginnings" of the movement.
      Hitler, *Reden, Schriften, Anordnungen*, vol. 3, part 2, doc. 62, pp. 336–41 (quote on
      p. 336).
69   Hitler, *Mein Kampf*, p. 244.
70   See Plöckinger, *Unter Soldaten und Agitatoren*, p. 157.
71   See the report by Michael Lotter, secretary of the DAP in the NSDAP-Hauptarchiv,
      dated 17 Oct. 1941; Joachimsthaler, *Hitlers Weg*, p. 257 (see p. 258 for a facsimile of the
      membership card); in addition, A. Drexler in an unsent letter to Hitler from Jan. 1940:
      Ernst Deuerlein (ed.), *Der Aufstieg der NSDAP in Augenzeugenberichten*, Munich, 2nd
      edition, 1976, pp. 97f.
72   Hitler, *Mein Kampf*, p. 390. Over lunch at the Reich Chancellery in December
      1936, Hitler told stories "from the first party meetings" for which he himself
      "typed up and distributed flyers." *Die Tagebücher von Joseph Goebbels. Part 1:
      Aufzeichnungen 1923–1941*, ed. Elke Fröhlich, Munich, 1998–2006, vol. 3/2, pp. 274f.
      (entry for 3 Dec. 1936).
73   Hitler, *Mein Kampf*, p. 390. See the advertisement in the *Münchener Beobachter* in
      Plöckinger, *Unter Soldaten und Agitatoren*, p. 158f.
74   Max Amann's questioning in Nuremberg on 5 Nov. 1947; Joachimsthaler, *Hitlers
      Weg*, p. 264.
75   PND report on the DAP meeting of 13 Nov. 1919; Hitler, *Sämtliche Aufzeichnungen*,
      no. 66a, p. 93. Also in Deuerlein, "Hitlers Eintritt," doc. 14, pp. 205–7.
76   *Münchener Beobachter*, 19 Nov. 1919; Hitler, *Sämtliche Aufzeichnungen*, no. 66b, p. 94.
77   See Plöckinger, *Unter Soldaten und Agitatoren*, pp. 160–3, 169.
78   Report on the DAP meeting of 10 Dec. 1919; Deuerlein, "Hitlers Eintritt," doc. 16,
      pp. 209f.; Hitler, *Sämtliche Aufzeichnungen*, no. 69b, pp. 98f.
79   PND report on the DAP meeting of 16 Jan. 1919; Hitler, *Sämtliche Aufzeichnungen*,
      no. 73, p. 105.
80   See an outline of the DAP leadership structure of Dec. 1919 in Hitler, *Sämtliche
      Aufzeichnungen*, no. 68, p. 95; facsimile in Joachimsthaler, *Hitlers Weg*, p. 266.
81   A reprint of the 25-point programme, etc. in Deuerlein (ed.), *Der Aufstieg der NSDAP*,
      pp. 108–12.
82   PND report on the DAP meeting of 24 Feb. 1920; Hitler, *Sämtliche Aufzeichnungen*,
      no. 83a, p. 110.
83   Ibid.; see also Plöckinger, *Unter Soldaten und Agitatoren*, p. 176.
84   Hitler, *Mein Kampf*, p. 406. See Hitler's article on the second anniversary of 24 Feb.
      1920 in the *Völkischer Beobachter*: "When I finally adjourned the meeting at 10:30
      p.m., we were not the only ones who had the feeling that a wolf had been born
      that was destined to attack the herd of seducers and betrayers of the people."
      Hitler, *Sämtliche Aufzeichnungen*, no. 363, p. 584.
85   *Münchener Neueste Nachrichten*, 25 Feb. 1920; quoted in Hans-Günter Richardi, *Hitler
      und seine Hintermänner: Neue Fakten zur Frühgeschichte der NSDAP*, Munich, 1991,
      pp. 116f.; *Völkischer Beobachter*, 28 Feb. 1920; Hitler, *Sämtliche Aufzeichnungen*, no. 83b,
      p. 111.
86   See the entry in Hitler's military pay-book; BayHStA München, Nl Adolf Hitler.

5 *The King of Munich*

1   Adolf Hitler, *Monologe im Führerhauptquartier 1941–1944: Die Aufzeichnungen Heinrich Heims*, ed. Werner Jochmann, Hamburg, 1980, p. 209 (dated 16/17 Jan. 1942); see ibid., p. 147 (dated 30 Nov. 1941): "In hindsight, this was the time of the most beautiful struggle."

2   Ibid., p. 173 (dated 3/4 Jan. 1942).

3   Ibid., pp. 209f. (dated 16/17 Jan. 1942).

4   See David Clay Large, *Where Ghosts Walked: Munich's Road to the Third Reich*, New York and London, 1997, p. 231; Andreas Heusler, *Das Braune Haus: Wie München zur "Hauptstadt der Bewegung" wurde*, Munich, 2008, pp. 201f.

5   On the Kapp Putsch and its consequences see Heinrich August Winkler, *Weimar 1918–1933: Die Geschichte der ersten deutschen Demokratie*, Munich, 1993, pp. 122ff.

6   See Dirk Walter, *Antisemitische Kriminalität und Gewalt: Judenfeindschaft in der Weimarer Republik*, Bonn, 1999, pp. 64f.

7   Bogislav von Selchow to Escherich, 24 June 1922; BayHStA München, Nl Escherich 47. On "Organisation Consul" and the attacks it carried out, see Martin Sabrow, *Der Rathenau-Mord: Rekonstruktion einer Verschwörung gegen die Republik von Weimar*, Munich, 1994.

8   See Bruno Thoss, *Der Ludendorff-Kreis 1919–1923: München als Zentrum der mitteleuropäischen Gegenrevolution*, Munich, 1978.

9   Large, *Where Ghosts Walked*, p. 126.

10 *Der Hitler-Prozess 1924*, ed. and annotated by Lothar Gruchmann and Reinhold Weber with Otto Gritschneder, part 2, Munich, 1997, p. 447.

11 Adolf Hitler, *Mein Kampf. Vol. 1: Eine Abrechnung*, 7th edition, Munich, 1933, p. 403.

12 *Hitlers Tischgespräche im Führerhauptquartier*, ed. Henry Picker, Stuttgart, 1976, p. 160 (dated 19 March 1942).

13 Quoted in Werner Maser, *Die Frühgeschichte der NSDAP: Hitlers Weg bis 1924*, Frankfurt am Main and Bonn, 1965, p. 256.

14 Hitler, *Mein Kampf*, pp. 560f.

15 See Reginald H. Phelps, "Hitler als Parteiredner im Jahre 1920," in *Vierteljahrshefte für Zeitgeschichte*, 11 (1963), p. 284. See also Rudolf Hess to Milly Kleinmann, 11 April 1921: "[Hitler] speaks regularly; on Monday evenings to a small private circle, and every eight to fourteen days publicly." BA Bern, Nl Hess, J1.211-1989/148, 27. Hitler's postcard to "Frau Regierungsrat" Dora Lauböck, Rosenheim, from Vienna, undated (Oct. 1920): "Yesterday spoke here for the first time with great success. Today, it's Leopoldstadt's turn." IfZ München, ED 100/86.

16 Hitler, *Mein Kampf*, p. 544.

17 Hitler to G. Seifert, 27 Oct. 1921; Adolf Hitler, *Sämtliche Aufzeichnungen 1905–1924*, ed. Eberhard Jäckel with Axel Kuhn, Stuttgart, 1980, no. 309, p. 509. Figures from Kurt Pätzold and Manfred Weissbecker, *Geschichte der NSDAP 1920–1945*, Cologne, 1998, pp. 27, 54.

18 See Ernst Hanfstaengl, *Zwischem Weissem und Braunem Haus: Erinnerungen eines politischen Aussenseiters*, Munich, 1970, pp. 86f.

19 John Toland, *Adolf Hitler: Volume 1*, New York, 1976, p. 112.

20 For the typical course of a meeting see Hanfstaengl, *Zwischen Weissem und Braunem Haus*, pp. 37–9; Hanfstaengl's note "ad A. H., Dez.1922": "The conclusion culminated in a rallying cry, a slogan. The spoken word as weapon." BSB München, Nl Hanfstaengl Ana 405, Box 25.

21 In Marlies Steinert, *Hitler*, Munich, 1994, p. 125.

22 Hanfstaengl, *Zwischen Weissem und Braunem Haus*, p. 84.

23 Ibid., p. 85.

24 Ibid., p. 41. See Franz Pfeffer von Salomon's notes of 19 Aug. 1964. Salomon believed that Hitler's secret was that he expressed "what was already present deep down,

fermenting and boiling and waiting to be put in the right words." IfZ München, ZS 177. Josef Kopperschmidt also saw the most important factor in Hitler's success as a mass public speaker as the "rhetorical principle of connection," i.e. the ability to connect with people's existing hopes and fears. Josef Kopperschmidt (ed.), *Hitler der Redner*, Munich, 2003, p. 18.

25   Hans Frank, *Im Angesicht des Galgens: Deutung Hitlers und seiner Zeit auf Grund eigener Erlebnisse und Erkenntnisse*, Munich and Gräfelfing, 1953, pp. 39f. See Dieter Schenk, *Hans Frank: Hitlers Kronjurist und Generalgouverneur*, Frankfurt am Main, 2006, pp. 48f.

26   Konrad Heiden, *Adolf Hitler: Das Zeitalter der Verantwortungslosigkeit. Eine Biographie*, Zurich, 1936, pp. 100f.

27   Hitler, *Sämtliche Aufzeichnungen*, no. 223, p. 367 (dated 21 April 1921). On 9 January 1922, Hitler concluded a speech at an NSDAP meeting in Munich with the words: "So help me God! Amen." Ibid., no. 341, p. 544.

28   Kurt Lüdecke, *I Knew Hitler: The Story of a Nazi who Escaped the Blood Purge*, London, 1938, pp. 22f. On Lüdecke see Lothar Machtan, *Hitlers Geheimnis: Das Doppelleben eines Diktators*, Berlin, 2001, pp. 302ff.

29   Joachim Fest, *Hitler: Eine Biographie*, Frankfurt am Main, Berlin and Vienna, 1973, p. 217.

30   Karl Alexander von Müller, *Im Wandel einer Welt: Erinnerungen. Vol. 3: 1919–1932*, ed. Otto Alexander von Müller, Munich, 1966, pp. 144f.

31   See Ernst Deuerlein, "Hitlers Eintritt in die Politik und die Reichswehr," in *Vierteljahrshefte für Zeitgeschichte*, 7 (1959), p. 190; Ludolf Herbst, *Hitlers Charisma: Die Erfindung eines deutschen Messias*, Frankfurt am Main, 2010, p. 119.

32   See the first prototypes of the swastika flag drawn by First Treasurer Rudolph Schüssler in 1920–1 in BA Berlin-Lichterfelde, NS 26/2559. See Karl-Heinz Weissmann, *Das Hakenkreuz: Symbol eines Jahrhunderts*, Schnellrode, 2006.

33   See Tilman Allert, *Der deutsche Gruss: Geschichte einer unheilvollen Geste*, Berlin, 2005.

34   See Hellmuth Auerbach, "Hitlers politische Lehrjahre und die Münchner Gesellschaft 1919–1923," in *Vierteljahrshefte für Zeitgeschichte*, 25 (1977), p. 19. On the early agitation of the NSDAP see also the undated notes by Rudolf Hess (August 1920): "Red has been chosen for good reason. Those workers who have not yet been won over are outraged by the misuse, in their eyes, of their beautiful colour red for 'reactionary' purposes." BA Bern, Nl Hess, J1.211-1989/148, 27.

35   Hitler, *Sämtliche Aufzeichnungen*, no. 16, p. 127 (dated 24 April 1920), no. 100, p. 131 (dated 11 May 1920), no. 91, p. 119 (dated 6 April 1920).

36   Ibid., no. 435, p. 752 (dated 3 Dec. 1922).

37   Ibid., no. 185, p. 297 (dated 17 Jan. 1921).

38   Ibid., no. 248, p. 411 (dated 24 May 1931). See ibid., no. 377, p. 611 (dated 12 April 1922): November 1918 was "no achievement, but rather the beginning of our collapse."

39   Ibid., no. 96, p. 128 (dated 27 April 1920), no. 120, p. 162 (dated 15 July 1920), no. 405, p. 692 (dated 18 Sept. 1922). Joachim Riecker (*Hitlers 9. November: Wie der Erste Weltkrieg zum Holocaust führte*, Berlin, 2009, p. 97) sees the agitator's "unquenchable thirst to avenge and erase [German] defeat in the First World War" as his most important source of motivation. But Riecker's attempt to draw direct connections from this to the Holocaust is misguided.

40   Ibid., no. 93, p. 124.

41   See Boris Barth, "Dolchstosslegende und Novemberrevolution," in Alexander Gallus (ed.), *Die vergessene Revolution*, Göttingen, 2010, p. 133.

42   Hitler, *Sämtliche Aufzeichnungen*, no. 147, p. 236 (dated 22 Sept. 1920). For the above quotes see ibid., no. 108, p. 143 (dated 11 June 1920), no. 126, p. 169 (dated 1 Aug. 1920), no. 141, p. 225 (dated 5 Sept. 1920). As early as late 1919, Hitler wrote a pamphlet with the polemical title "The Forced Peace of Brest-Litovsk and the Peace of Reconciliation and Understanding of Versailles?" (ibid., no. 72, pp. 101–4), which

was widely distributed among soldiers stationed in Munich. See Othmar Plöckinger, *Unter Soldaten und Agitatoren: Hitlers prägende Jahre im deutschen Militär 1918–1920*, Paderborn, 2013, pp. 166f.

43 Hitler, *Sämtliche Aufzeichnungen*, no. 249, p. 412 (dated 26 May 1921), no. 252, p. 417 (dated 29 May 1921), no. 315, p. 515 (dated 11 Nov. 1921).

44 Ibid., no. 224, p. 368 (dated 24 April 1921).

45 Ibid., no. 227, p. 374 (dated 3 May 1921).

46 Ibid., no. 368, p. 590 (dated 1 March 1922). See ibid., no. 383, p. 638 (dated 5 May 1922): "But Rathenau perpetrated his biggest swindle in Genoa when he tossed Germany's assets into the Entente's insatiable maw."

47 See ibid., no. 103, p. 137 (dated 31 May 1920), no. 108, p. 144 (dated 11 June 1920), no. 197, p. 318 (dated 13 Feb. 1921).

48 Ibid., no. 252, p. 414 (dated 29 May 1921); no. 264, p. 444 (dated 20 July 1921).

49 Ibid., no. 138, p. 212 (dated 25 Aug. 1920).

50 Ibid., no. 141, p. 233 (dated 5 Sept. 1920). See ibid., no. 147, p. 234 (dated 22 Sept. 1920), no. 205, p. 336 (dated 6 March 1921), no. 412, p. 708 (dated 25 Oct. 1922).

51 Ibid., no. 1239, p. 217 (dated 25 Aug 1920).

52 Ibid., no. 129, p. 176 (dated 7 Aug. 1920).

53 Ibid., no. 160, pp. 250, 254 (dated 26 Oct. 1920).

54 Ibid., no. 140, p. 220 (dated 31 Aug. 1920).

55 Ibid., no. 96, p. 127 (dated 27 April 1920), no. 203, p. 333 (dated 6 March 1921).

56 Ibid., no. 101, p. 134 (dated 19 May 1920).

57 Ibid., no. 96, p. 127 (dated 27 April 1920), no. 187, p. 300 (dated 27 Jan. 1921).

58 Ibid., no. 239, p. 394 (dated 15 May 1921).

59 Ibid., no. 305, p. 505 (dated 21 Oct. 1921), no. 405, p. 692 (dated 18 Sept. 1922).

60 The writer Carl Zuckmayer, who attended a Hitler event in the autumn of 1923, was struck by the "numbing hammering of repeated phrases in a certain contagious rhythm." Zuckmayer concluded: "This was practiced and skilled, and it possessed a terrifying, primitive, barbaric effectiveness." *Als wär's ein Stück von mir*, Frankfurt am Main, 1966, pp. 384f.

61 Hitler, *Mein Kampf*, p. 198.

62 See Martin H. Geyer, *Verkehrte Welt: Revolution, Inflation und Moderne. München 1914–1924*, Göttingen, 1998, pp. 96f.

63 See Steinert, *Hitler*, p. 125.

64 Fritz Stern, *Kulturpessimismus als politische Gefahr: Eine Analyse nationaler Ideologie*, new edition, Stuttgart, 2005, is still the standard on this topic; Kurt Sontheimer, *Antidemokratisches Denken in der Weimarer Republik: Die politischen Ideen des deutschen Nationalismus zwischen 1918 und 1933*, Munich, 1968 (student's edition).

65 Quoted in Auerbach, *Hitlers politische Lehrjahre*, p. 26.

66 See Reginald H. Phelps, "Hitlers 'grundlegende' Rede über den Antisemitismus," in *Vierteljahrshefte für Zeitgeschichte*, 16 (1968), pp. 390–420 (text of the speech on pp. 400–20). Also reprinted in Hitler, *Sämtliche Aufzeichnungen*, no. 136, pp. 184–204.

67 For the source material see Phelps, "Hitlers 'grundlegende' Rede," pp. 395–9. In a letter to Theodor Fritsch on 28 Oct. 1930, Hitler claimed to have "intensively studied the *Handbook on the Jewish Question* in his early years in Vienna." Adolf Hitler, *Reden, Schriften, Anordnungen—Februar 1925 bis Januar 1933. Vol. 4: Von der Reichstagswahl bis zur Reichspräsidentenwahl Oktober 1930–März 1932. Part 1: Oktober 1930–Juni 1931*, ed. Constantin Goschler, Munich, 1993, doc. 32, p. 133.

68 Cited in Phelps, "Hitlers 'grundlegende' Rede," p. 400.

69 Hitler, *Sämtliche Aufzeichnungen*, no. 273, p. 452 (dated 12 Aug. 1921).

70 Ibid., no. 275, p. 458 (dated 19 Aug. 1921).

71 Ibid., no. 171, p. 273 (dated 3 Dec. 1920), no. 285, p. 471 (dated 8 Sept. 1921), no. 585 (dated 23 Feb. 1922), no. 223, p. 366 (dated 21 April 1921).

72   Heinrich Heim to Fritz von Trützschner, 12 Aug. 1920; BA Berlin-Lichterfelde, NS 26/18. On 3 Nov. 1943, an employee at the NSDAP Archive added the following note: "The letter to Herr von Trützschner was written in 1920 by today's Ministerial Council Heim (Party Chancellery) and returned as undeliverable. It was given to me unopened by Party Comrade Heim for the Party Archive. The letter contains an extraordinarily interesting characterisation of the Führer and his stance back then on the Jewish question." On Heinrich Heim's biography, see Werner Jochmann's introduction in *Monologe*, pp. 11f. See also the exchange between Rudolf Hess and Heim in 1936/38 in BA Bern, Nl Hess, J1.211-1993/300, Box 7.

73   Karl Mayr to Wolfgang Kapp, 24 Sept. 1920; Erwin Könnemann and Gerhard Schulze (eds), *Der Kapp-Lüttwitz-Ludendorff-Putsch: Dokumente*, Munich, 2002, p. 526. In a letter of 11 Dec. 1920 to the Pan-Germanic leaders Heinrich Class and Ernst Bang, Munich Police President Ernst Pöhner recommended Hitler as "a first-rate organisational and agitating force," who had become known as "the best speaker of the National Socialist German Workers Party in all of Bavaria." Quoted in Johannes Leicht, *Heinrich Class 1868–1953: Die politische Biographie eines Alldeutschen*, Paderborn, 2012, p. 288.

74   Klaus Gietinger, *Der Konterrevolutionär Waldemar Pabst: Eine deutsche Karriere*, Hamburg, 2009, p. 220.

75   Hanfstaengl, *Zwischen Weissem und Braunem Haus*, p. 50. See also the characterisation of Hitler: "A powerful forehead, blue eyes, the entire head like that of a bull and a voice with a wonderful everyday tone as well." Adolf Hitler, *Reden, Schriften, Anordnungen—Februar 1925 bis Januar 1933. Vol. 3: Zwischen den Reichtagswahlen Juli 1928–September 1930. Part 2: März 1929–Dezember 1929*, ed. Klaus A. Lankheit, Munich, 1994, doc. 62, p. 342.

76   Margarete Plewnia, *Auf dem Weg zu Hitler: Der "völkische" Publizist Dietrich Eckart*, Berlin, 1970, p. 67.

77   Transcript of the testimony from 15 Nov. 1923 in BA Berlin-Lichterfelde, NS 26/2180. See Hermann Esser's testimony for Ralph Engelmann, 5 March 1970: "Eckart regarded Hitler as the only man capable of making a popular movement into something huge. He knew exactly that Hitler was the sort of speaker these masses needed." BayHStA München, Nl Esser.

78   Fest, *Hitler*, p. 196.

79   Hitler, *Monologe*, p. 208 (dated 16/17 Jan. 1942).

80   For the acquisition of the *Völkischer Beobachter* see Drexler's note from 1940, reprinted in Ernst Deuerlein (ed.), *Der Aufstieg der NSDAP in Augenzeugenberichten*, Munich, 2nd edition, 1976, pp. 128f.; transcript of a conversation with Hans Georg Grassinger, the operations manager, on 19 Dec. 1951; IfZ München, ZS 50.

81   Hitler, *Sämtliche Aufzeichnungen*, no. 175, pp. 277f. (dated 18 Dec. 1920).

82   Timothy W. Ryback, *Hitler's Private Library: The Books That Shaped His Life*, London, 2009, p. 29.

83   Hitler, *Mein Kampf*, p. 781.

84   Christa Schroeder, *Er war mein Chef: Aus dem Nachlass der Sekretärin von Adolf Hitler*, ed. Anton Joachimsthaler, 3rd edition, Munich and Vienna, 1985, p. 65. *Die Tagebücher von Joseph Goebbels. Part 1: Aufzeichnungen 1923–1941*, ed. Elke Fröhlich, Munich, 1998, vol. 4, p. 51 (entry for 15 March 1937): "The Führer . . . talked about Dietrich Eckart. What a gentleman!"

85   Hitler, *Monologe*, p. 161 (dated 28/29 Dec. 1941), p. 208 (dated 16/17 Jan. 1942).

86   Transcript of a conversation with Mathilde Scheubner-Richter on 9 July 1952; IfZ München, ZS 292. For further information, see also Ernst Piper, *Alfred Rosenberg: Hitlers Chefideologe*, Munich, 2005, pp. 57ff.; Gerd Koenen, *Der Russland-Komplex: Die Deutschen und der Osten 1900–1945*, Munich, 2005, pp. 266–8.

87   Cited in this order in Hitler, *Sämtliche Aufzeichnungen*, no. 106, p. 140 (dated 6 June 1920), no. 124, p. 166 (dated 27 July 1920), no. 197, p. 319 (dated 13 Feb. 1921), no. 72, p. 451 (dated 4 Aug. 1921), no. 352, p. 560 (dated 30 Jan. 1922).

88 Rudolf Hess, *Briefe 1908–1933*, ed. Rüdiger Hess, Munich and Vienna, 1987, p. 264 (dated 14 Sept. 1920), p. 267 (dated 11 April 1921). After the first meeting with the "tribune" he had become "an enthusiastic follower within minutes," Hess wrote to Ilse Pröhl on 10 July 1924 from Landsberg prison; BA Bern, Nl Hess, J1.211-1989/148, 33. For Hess's participation in putting down the Soviet Republic see his letter to his parents, dated 18 May 1919; Hess, *Briefe 1908–1933*, pp. 240–2; BA Bern, Nl Hess, J1.211-1989/148, 21. On his close relationship with Karl Haushofer see Hess's letters to his parents, dated 19 May 1921 and 8 May 1923; BA Bern, Nl Hess, J1.211-1989/148, 27, 31.

89 Unpublished memoirs of Gustav Ritter von Kahr, p. 877; BayHStA München, Nl Kahr 51.

90 R. Hess to Kahr, 17 May 1921; Deuerlein, *Aufstieg*, pp. 32–134 (quote on p. 133).

91 See Albrecht Tyrell, *Vom "Trommler" zum "Führer": Der Wandel von Hitlers Selbstverständnis zwischen 1919 und 1924 und die Entwicklung der NSDAP*, Munich 1975, pp. 72–89 (on DSP), pp. 95–109 (on the merger of the parties).

92 Hitler, *Sämtliche Aufzeichnungen*, no. 129, pp. 173–9, no. 132, p. 181 (dated 8 Aug. 1920).

93 Tyrell, *Vom "Trommler" zum "Führer*," p. 100.

94 Ibid., p. 99.

95 Quoted in ibid., p. 109. In conversation on 31 Oct. 1951, Gerhard Rossbach described his first impression of Hitler with the words: "A pathetic civilian with a badly knotted tie who had nothing but art on his mind and always showed up late. Brilliant speaker with great powers of suggestion." IfZ München, ZS 128.

96 For a summary of the contents, see Tyrell, *Vom "Trommler" zum "Führer*," pp. 111–16. Dickel was an adherent of Otto Damaschke's ideas for land reform and had established a housing project for workers in the moorlands near Augsburg, which he named Dickelsmoor. See Franz Maria Müller, "Wie Hitler Ausburg eroberte. Erlebnisbericht aus der Frühzeit der nationalsozialistischen Bewegung" (undated, post-1945); IfZ München, MS 570.

97 Tyrell, *Vom "Trommler" zum "Führer*," pp. 119f.

98 Ibid., pp. 121f.

99 Hitler, *Sämtliche Aufzeichnungen*, no. 338, p. 539 (dated 5 Jan. 1922). For Hitler's hatred towards education professionals see Otto Wagener, *Hitler aus nächster Nähe: Aufzeichnungen eines Vertrauten 1929–1932*, ed. Henry A. Turner, Frankfurt am Main, Berlin and Vienna, 1978, p. 57.

100 Ian Kershaw, *Hitler 1889–1936: Hubris*, London, 1998, p. 163.

101 Hitler, *Sämtliche Aufzeichnungen*, no. 262, pp. 436–8 (dated p. 438).

102 Quoted in Tyrell, *Vom "Trommler" zum "Führer*," p. 128. Committee member Benedict Angermeier resigned in protest over Hitler being named NSDAP party chairman. See the testimony of his sons Paul and Kurt Angermeier, 22 Jan. 1952; IfZ München, ZS 20.

103 Reprinted in Deuerlein, *Aufstieg*, pp. 138–40.

104 Quoted in Maser, *Frühgeschichte*, p. 276.

105 On the party conference of 29 July 1921 see Hitler, *Sämtliche Aufzeichnungen*, no. 269, pp. 447–9, no. 270, pp. 449f. NSDAP Vice-Chairman Oskar Körner reported on 4 Aug. 1921 to Gustav Seifert (Hanover): "All existing misunderstandings within the party, which were caused by external elements, have been completely eradicated." IfZ München, MA 736/141.

106 On the party charter of 29 July 1921 see Tyrell, *Vom "Trommler" zum "Führer*, pp. 132–50.

107 Quoted in Maser, *Frühgeschichte*, p. 280.

108 Quoted in ibid., p. 281.

109 See Emil Maurice's affidavit on 16 March 1946; IfZ München, ZS 270. On the creation of the SA see Peter Longerich, *Die braunen Bataillone: Geschichte der SA*, Munich, 1989, pp. 22–5. The founding proclamation is reprinted in Deuerlein, *Aufstieg*, p. 144.

110 On Röhm see Longerich, *Die braunen Bataillone*, pp. 15–22.

111   Hitler, *Sämtliche Aufzeichnungen*, no. 301, p. 499 (dated 5 Oct. 1921).

112   On the violent attacks on Jews in Munich see Walter, *Antisemitische Kriminalität*, pp. 97ff.

113   Hitler, *Monologe*, pp. 122f. (dated 2 Nov. 1941). See also ibid., p. 146 (dated 30 Nov 1941): "I could only use people who knew how to brawl."

114   See a report on this meeting in Deuerlein, *Aufstieg*, pp. 145f.

115   Rudolf Hess to Klara and Fritz Hess dated 7 July 1922; Hess, *Briefe*, p. 291.

116   Deuerlein, *Aufstieg*, p. 147.

117   Hitler, *Mein Kampf*, pp. 563–7 (quote on p. 567). See also the report on the meeting in Hitler, *Sämtliche Aufzeichnungen*, no. 316, pp. 515–17 (dated 12 Nov. 1921).

118   Fest, *Hitler*, p. 211.

119   Large, *Where Ghosts Walked*, p. 144f. See also the Austrian consul general to Munich's report in Deuerlein, *Aufstieg*, pp. 153f.

120   Hitler, *Sämtliche Aufzeichnungen*, no. 399, p. 679 (dated 16 Aug. 1922). A further demonstration planned for 25 Aug. on Königsplatz was banned. See diaries of G. Feder, vol. 4 (entry for 25 Aug. 1923); IfZ München, ED 874.

121   Hitler, *Mein Kampf*, p. 615. See also Hitler, *Monologe*, pp. 144f (entry for 30 Nov. 1941): "As soon as we were outside, we gave them such a hiding that the street was clear within ten minutes."

122   See the overview provided in Maser, *Frühgeschichte*, pp. 320f.

123   See Auerbach, "Hitlers Lehrjahre," p. 36; Pätzold and Weissbecker, *Geschichte der NSDAP*, p. 67; Deuerlein, *Aufstieg*, p. 157.

124   See Michael H. Kater, "Zur Soziologie der frühen NSDAP," in *Vierteljahrshefte für Zeitgeschichte*, 19 (1971), pp. 124–59 (these figures on p. 139).

125   See Heusler, *Das Braune Haus*, p. 120.

126   Hitler, *Sämtliche Aufzeichnungen*, no. 116, p. 156 (dated 3 June 1920). See also *Tischgespräche*, p. 204 (dated 8 April 1942): "The entire initial years of the time of struggle were aimed at winning over workers for the NSDAP."

127   Notes by Rudolf Hess, "Der Nationalsozialismus in München" (undated, 1922); BA Berlin-Lichterfelde, NS 6/71.

128   From the transcript of the Reicherts' daughter Antonie Reichert's questioning on 20 June and 9 Sept. 1952; IfZ München 287; see Hanfstaengl, *Zwischen Weissem und Braunem Haus*, p. 53.

129   See Toland, *Adolf Hitler: Volume 1*, p. 142f. (based on Helene Hanfstaengl's recollections).

130   See Hanfstaengl, *Zwischen Weissem und Braunem Haus*, pp. 42f.; David G. Maxwell, "Ernst Hanfstaengl—Des 'Führers' Klavierspieler," in Ronald Smelser, Enrico Syring and Rainer Zitelmann (eds), *Die braune Elite II: 21 weitere biographische Skizzen*, Darmstadt, 1993, pp. 137–49. Peter Conradi's biography, *Hitlers Klavierspieler: Ernst Hanfstaengl—Vertrauter Hitlers, Verbündeter Roosevelts*, Frankfurt am Main, 2007, is little more than a paraphrasing of Hanfstaengl's memoirs.

131   Hanfstaengl, *Zwischen Weissem und Braunem Haus*, p. 52.

132   Ibid., pp. 52f. For further books in Hitler's library at the Thierschstrasse residence, among them Einhart's *German History* (the pseudonym of Pan-German Heinrich Class), see Ryback, *Hitler's Private Library*, pp. 49–51. Antonie Reichert said that Hitler owned "a lot of architectural literature" as well as a gramophone and a collection of Richard Wagner records; IfZ München, ZS 287.

133   Hanfstaengl, *Zwischen Weissem und Braunem Haus*, p. 55

134   Hitler, *Sämtliche Aufzeichnungen*, no. 188, p. 303 (dated 27 Jan. 1921). See also Heiden, *Hitler: Das Zeitalter der Verantwortungslosigkeit*, p. 109; Maser, *Frühgeschichte*, pp. 282–4. Less enlightening is Wulf C. Schwarzwäller, *Hitlers Geld: Vom armen Kunstmaler zum millionenschweren Führer*, Vienna, 1998, pp. 32f.

135   On 12 April 1923, during the period of hyper-inflation, the Willi Bruss Bank in Berlin transferred to Hitler's account a "donation in support of your anti-Semitic efforts"

of 200,000 reichsmarks. BA Koblenz, N 112 8/7. See also documents concerning further donations in 1923. The chairman of the Pan-Germanic League, Heinrich Class, gave 3,000 marks in August 1920 and also supported Hitler financially in the years that followed. See Leicht, *Heinrich Class*, pp. 286f.

136   Handwritten letter from Hermine Hoffmann to Hitler; BA Koblenz, N 1128/5. On 11 July 1938, Hermine Hoffmann's 81st birthday, Hitler visited her in Solln, bringing flowers and liqueur. See the daily notes of SS Untersturmführer Max Wünsche, 11 July 1938; BA Berlin-Lichterfelde, NS 10/125. See also Hitler, *Monologe*, p. 315, dated 10/11 March 1942): "Of all my maternal friends, only old Mrs. Hoffmann was unfailingly solicitous." On Hitler's relationship with Hermine Hoffmann, see also Martha Schad: "Above all, his eyes are extraordinarily compelling." "Freundinnen und Verehrerinnen," in, Ulrike Leutheusser (ed.), *Hitler und die Frauen*, Munich, 2003, pp. 30–2; Anton Joachimsthaler, *Hitlers Liste: Ein Dokument persönlicher Beziehungen*, Munich, 2003, pp. 130–5.

137   Hitler's postcards to Dora and Theodor Lauböck in BA Berlin-Lichterfelde, NS 26/1242 and IfZ München, ED 100/86. Also reprinted in Hitler, *Sämtliche Aufzeichnungen*, no. 152, p. 248, no. 156, p. 246, no. 304, p. 503, no. 373, p. 598. The Lauböcks also maintained a relationship with Hitler's sister, Paula. See the undated postcard from Dora Lauböck to Hitler with a handwritten postscript from Paula Hitler; BA Berlin-Lichterfelde, NS 26/1242. On Christmas 1922 see the entry in the guest book; IfZ München ED 100/86; also in Joachimsthaler, *Hitlers Liste*, p. 219. On Fritz Lauböck's employment as Hitler's private secretary see his records on incoming and outgoing letters between May and the end of Oct. 1923; BA Koblenz, N 1128/29. On 17 April 1937 Fritz and Dora Lauböck gave their collected documents and papers to the Hauptarchiv der NSDAP; BA Berlin-Lichterfelde, NS 26/1242.

138   See for example the payment reminder from the Munich printers M. Müller & Sohn to the *Völkischer Beobachter*, Franz Eher Nachf., 22 May 1923. According to it, the newspaper's account was 73 million marks in the red and had therefore exceeded its credit of 30 million by 43 million marks. That very day, the business director of the *Beobachter*, Josef Pickl, asked Hitler for help in raising a large sum of money to pay off its debts. BA Koblenz, N 1128/6 and N 1128/8.

139   See Gottfried Grandel to Hitler, 27 Oct. 1920 (on the financial situation of the *Völkischer Beobachter*); BA Koblenz, N 1128/2; Franz Maria Müller, "Wie Hitler Augsburg eroberte" (undated, post-1945); IfZ München, MS 570.

140   Emil Gansser to Karl Burhenne, 8 March 1922, with enclosed note on the Hitler movement; BA Berlin-Lichterfelde, NS 26/1223.

141   See the invitation to Hitler's talk dated 26 May 1922 from E. Gansser; BA Berlin-Lichterfelde, NS 26/1223. For the content of the talk see Hitler, *Sämtliche Aufzeichnungen* no. 387, pp. 642f. See also Wilhelm Weicher's recollections, "Wie ich Adolf Hitler kennenlernte," in *Der Türmer 36* (April 1934): "A lot of prophets stood up to speak in those heady days. I heard most of them, but none captivated me as much as Adolf Hitler." BA Berlin-Lichterfelde, NS 26/1223; Hanfstaengl's note on a telephone call with Emil Gansser in the spring of 1923; BSB München, Nl Hanfstaengl Ana 405, Box 25. On Hitler's entrance see Henry A. Turner, *Die Grossunternehmer und der Aufstieg Hitlers*, Berlin, 1986, p. 68f.

142   See ibid., pp. 70f; on Richard Franck see Hitler, *Monologe*, p. 208 (dated 16/17 Jan. 1942), p. 257 (dated 3 Feb. 1942).

143   Quoted in Brigitte Hamann, *Winifred Wagner oder Hitlers Bayreuth*, Munich and Zurich, 2002, p. 75. On Hitler's trip to Switzerland in the summer of 1923 see Raffael Scheck, "Swiss Funding for the Early Nazi Movement," in *Journal of Modern History*, 91 (1999), pp. 793–813; Alexis Schwarzenbach, "Zur Lage in Deutschland: Hitlers Zürcher Rede vom 30 Aug. 1923," in *Traverse* 2006/1, pp. 178–89. On Rudolf Hess's stay in Switzerland in the spring of 1922 see his letters to Ilse Pröhl, dated 17 March and 4 April 1922; BA Bern, Nl Hess, J1.211-1989/148, 29. In Oct. 1922 Hess and Dietrich

Eckart accepted an invitation to the Willeses' country house near Zurich; Hess to Ilse Pröhl, 31 Oct. 1922; ibid. Hitler only told Hess of his own journey to Switzerland when they were imprisoned together at Landsberg: "It was a pleasure to hear him talk so excitedly of his impressions of his first journey outside Germany and Austria." Hess to Ilse Pröhl, 18 May 1924; BA Bern, Nl Hess, J1.211-1989/148, 33. Hitler's passport, issued on 13 Aug. 1923, stamped with the date of entry into Switzerland of 26 Aug. 1923; BayHStA München, Nl Adolf Hitler. In his communications with Ralph Engelmann of 5 March 1970, Hermann Esser confirmed that Emil Gansser had established connection to Switzerland; BayHStA München, Nl Esser.

144   Hanfstaengl's unpublished memoirs, p. 32; BSB München, Nl Hanfstaengl Ana 405, Box 47. See also Hanfstaengl, *Zwischen Weissem und Braunem Haus*, p. 99: "Like a will-o'-wisp, he appears first here, then there, only to disappear a moment later."

145   Gottfried Feder to "my dear Herr Hitler," 10 Aug. 1923 (which ended: "With a heartfelt greeting of Heil and in full confidence"); IfZ München, ED 100/86.

146   Hanfstaengl, *Zwischen Weissem und Braunem Haus*, p. 44.

147   Large, *Where Ghosts Walked*, p. 154. See Markus Schiefer, "Vom 'Blauen Bock' in die Residenz—Christian Weber," in Marita Krauss (ed.), *Rechte Karrieren in München: Von der Weimarer Zeit bis in die Nachkriegsjahre*, Munich, 2010, pp. 152–65 (particularly pp. 155f.).

148   Martin Broszat, *Der Staat Hitlers: Grundlegung und Entwicklung seiner inneren Verfassung*, Munich, 1969, p. 66. See Hanfstaengl's note "A. H.—Stammcafé Heck"; BSB München, Nl Hanfstaengl Ana 405, Box 26.

149   Hanfstaengl, *Zwischen Weissem und Braunem Haus*, p. 88.

150   Quoted in Auerbach, "Hitlers politische Lehrjahre," p. 35. See the transcript of an interrogation of Göring on 20 July 1945, who claimed that Hitler had particularly welcomed him "since he always wanted to have a young officer respected throughout the nation in the ranks of the movement." IfZ München, ZS 428. For Göring's biography see Alfred Kube, *Pour le mérite und Hakenkreuz: Hermann Göring im Dritten Reich*, Munich, 1986, pp. 4–8.

151   See Hamann, *Winifred Wagner*, pp. 73f.; Large, *Where Ghosts Walked*, p. 151f; Hanfstaengl, *Zwischen Weissem und Braunem Haus*, pp. 48f.; Schad, "Freundinnen und Verehrerinnen," pp. 38–43; Joachimsthaler, *Hitlers Liste*, pp. 68–71.

152   Müller, *Im Wandel einer Welt*, p. 129. See also the recording by Karl Alexander von Müller "Meine Beziehungen zur NSDAP" (undated, post-1945); BayHStA München, Nl K. A. v. Müller 7. Among those who attended the Munich historian's lectures in 1922–3 were Göring, Hess and Ernst Hanfstaengl.

153   See Wolfgang Martynkewicz, *Salon Deutschland: Geist und Macht 1900–1945*, Berlin, 2009; Miriam Käfer, "Hitlers frühe Förderer aus dem Grossbürgertum: Das Verlegerehepaar Elsa und Hugo Bruckmann," in Krauss (ed.), *Rechte Karrieren in München*, pp. 72–9. On Elsa Bruckmann's anti-Semitic views see her letter to Karl Alexander von Müller dated 20 March 1929, in which she denigrated the German Cultural Association as a "culturally Jewified" antithesis of the ethnic-chauvinistic Fighting Association for German Culture. BayHStA München, Nl K. A. v. Müller 246.

154   See Martynkewicz, *Salon Deutschland*, pp. 382, 387, 408.

155   *Herbst 1941 im "Führerhauptquartier": Berichte Werner Koeppens an seinen Minister Rosenberg*, ed. and annotated Martin Vogt, Koblenz, 2002, p. 1 (dated 6 Sept. 1941). See also the telegram from Hitler offering condolences to Elsa Bruckmann; BSB München, Bruckmanniana Suppl. Box 4; quoted in Käfer, "Frühe Förderer," p. 74.

156   Fest, *Hitler*, p. 197.

157   Hitler told his secretary Christa Schroeder that he often felt like "an ape in a zoo"; Schroeder, *Er war mein Chef*, p. 69.

158   Hamann, *Winifred Wagner*, pp. 83f.; see also Hitler, *Monologe*, p. 224 (dated 24/25 Jan. 1942): "When I entered Wahnfried for the first, I was so moved!"

159 Hamann, *Winifred Wagner*, p. 85.
160 H. St. Chamberlain to Hitler, Bayreuth, 7 Oct. 1923; the dictated letter signed by Chamberlain in BA Koblenz, N 1128/16. See Hamann, *Winifred Wagner*, p. 82.
161 Hess, *Briefe*, p. 275 (entry for 3 July 1921).
162 Hanfstaengl, *Zwischen Weissem und Braunem Haus*, pp. 36, 86f.
163 Machtan, *Hitlers Geheimnis*, p. 146. See Albert Krebs, *Tendenzen und Gestalten der NSDAP: Erinnerungen aus der Frühzeit der Partei*, Stuttgart, 1959, p. 133, who emphasises Hitler's ability to "adapt himself to various people and groups."
164 *Tischgespräche*, p. 181 (dated 3 April 1942). See also Hitler, *Monologe*, pp. 204f. (dated 16/17 Jan. 1942): "No pictures of me existed. Those who didn't know me had no idea what I looked like."
165 See Rudolf Herz, *Hoffmann & Hitler: Fotografie als Medium des Führer-Mythos*, Munich, 1994, pp. 92f. (on p. 93 see a reproduction of the page from *Simplizissimus*); Claudia Schmölders, *Hitlers Gesicht: Eine physiognomische Biographie*, Munich, 2000, pp. 46–8, 54.
166 On the incident see Hanfstaengl, *Zwischen Weissem und Braunem Haus*, pp. 74f.; Herz, *Hoffmann & Hitler*, pp. 93f.; Pahl's account in Thomas Friedrich, *Die missbrauchte Hauptstadt: Hitler und Berlin*, Berlin, 2007, p. 61.
167 Quoted in Friedrich, *Die missbrauchte Hauptstadt*, p. 62. See also *Das Hitler-Bild: Die Erinnerungen des Fotografen Heinrich Hoffmann*, ed. Joe J. Heydecker, St. Pölten and Salzburg, 2008, pp. 27–36 ("Mein Kampf um das erste Hitler-Bild").
168 On Heinrich Hoffmann's biography see Herz, *Hoffmann & Hitler*, pp. 26–34; Heike B. Görtemaker, *Eva Braun: Leben mit Hitler*, Munich, 2010, pp. 15f.; Heinrich Hoffmann, *Hitler wie ich ihn sah: Aufzeichnungen seines Leibfotografen*, Munich and Berlin, 1974, pp. 7–17 (foreword by Henriette Hoffmann).
169 Harry Graf Kessler, *Das Tagebuch. Vol. 7: 1919–1923*, ed. Angela Reinthal with Janna Brechmacher and Christoph Hilse, Stuttgart, 2007, p. 567 (entry for 29 Oct. 1922) On the legendary "March on Rome" see Hans Woller, *Geschichte Italiens im 20. Jahrhundert*, Munich, 2010, pp. 92f.
170 Hitler, *Sämtliche Aufzeichnungen*, no. 419, p. 726, no. 422, p. 728. See also *Monologe*, p. 43 (dated 21/22 July 1941): "The March on Rome in 1922 was a turning point of history. The mere fact that they were able to do that gave us a powerful boost."
171 Quoted in Maser, *Frühgeschichte*, p. 356. See Herbst, *Hitlers Charisma*, p. 144. On 18 Sept. 1923 the *Berliner Dienst* concluded that in a comparison between Hitler and Mussolini "the German Mussolini was no copy of the Italian, unable to stand on his own two feet." BA Koblenz, N 1128/12.
172 See Ludolf Herbst, *Hitlers Charisma: Die Erfindung eines deutschen Messias*, Frankfurt am Main, 2010, p. 139; Auerbach, "Hitlers politische Lehrjahre," p. 24; Kershaw, *Hitler: Hubris*, p. 182f.
173 R. Hess to K. A. v. Müller, 23 Feb. 1923; BayHStA München, Nl. K. A. v. Müller 19/1. The letter also contained an invitation to attend Hitler's speech to university students in the Löwenbräukeller on 26 Feb. The manuscript of the prize-winning essay, which Hess claimed had been written "a couple of hours before the deadline," is reprinted in Bruno Hipler, *Hitlers Lehrmeister: Karl Haushofer als Vater der NS-Ideologie*, St. Ottilien, 1996, pp. 221–6 (quotations on pp. 222, 225). See also Hess's description of Hitler's appearance in Zirkus Krone, which emphasised his "unbending, iron-hard dictator's skull." "Der Nationalsozialismus in München" (undated, 1922); BA Berlin-Lichterfelde, NS 6/71.
174 Quoted in Plewnia, *Auf dem Weg zu Hitler*, p. 90.
175 These and other congratulatory letters and telegrams to Hitler in BA Koblenz, N 1128/7. Even among respectable middle-class audiences in Munich's Hofgarten, Hanfstaengl observed "a certain aggressive admiration for the events south of the Alps, the élan of Mussolini's fascist movement and the new Italy." Hanfstaengl recorded statements like: "Indeed, we need someone like that at the top—a

Renaissance man and a power politician, someone without scruples." "Der Ruf nach dem Borgia Typ"; BSB München, Nl Hanfstaengl Ana 405, Box 25.

176   On Max Weber's concept of charismatic leadership, see the penetrating analysis in Herbst, *Hitlers Charisma*, pp. 11–57.

177   See ibid., especially pp. 137ff.

178   See Hans-Ulrich Wehler, *Deutsche Gesellschaftsgeschichte 1914–1949*, Munich, 2003, pp. 559–61. On the origins of the Führer cult also see Ian Kershaw, *The Hitler Myth: Image and Reality in the Third Reich*, Oxford, 1987, pp. 21–31.

179   Max Maurenbrecher, "Adolf Hitler," in *Deutsche Zeitung*, 10 Nov. 1923; reprinted in Joachim Petzold, "Class und Hitler: Über die Förderung der frühen Nazibewegung durch den Alldeutschen Verband und dessen Einfluß auf die nazistische Ideologie," in *Jahrbuch für Geschichte* 21 (1980), pp. 284f. Further, see André Schlüter, *Moeller van den Bruck: Leben und Werk*, Cologne, Weimar and Vienna, 2010, p. 299n80. In his speech to the Nationale Klub 1919 in Berlin on 29 May 1922, Hitler stressed that he "considered himself to be only the drummer for the movement of national liberation." Hitler, *Sämtliche Aufzeichnungen*, no. 387, p. 643.

180   Hitler, *Sämtliche Aufzeichnungen*, no. 436, p. 754 (dated 4 Dec. 1922).

181   Herz, *Hoffmann & Hitler*, pp. 99f. (on pp. 98f. see the first three photographs). See also Hanns Hubert Hofmann, *Der Hitler-Putsch: Krisenjahre deutscher Geschichte 1920–1924*, Munich, 1961, p. 74, who emphasises that even before 1923 Hitler had already begun to "feel his way around in the role of messiah."

182   Deuerlein, *Aufstieg*, p. 139.

183   Hanfstaengl, *Zwischen Weissem und Braunem Haus*, p. 63; Richard Wagner, *Lohengrin*, ed. Egon Voss, Stuttgart, 2001, p. 21. See Hanfstaengl's note: "You couldn't find out anything about his previous life: the official hour of his birth was the outbreak of the world war in 1914, about which he never tired of talking." BSB München, Nl Hanfstaengl Ana 405, Box 25.

184   Hitler to an unknown "Herr Doktor," 29 Nov. 1921; original with Hitler's hand-written corrections in BA Koblenz, N 1128/24; reprinted in Hitler, *Sämtliche Aufzeichnungen*, no. 325, pp. 525–7. See Othmar Plöckinger, "Frühe biographische Texte zu Hitler: Zur Bewertung der autobiographischen Texte in *Mein Kampf*," in *Vierteljahrshefte für Zeitgeschichte*, 58 (2010), pp. 95f.

185   *Kölnische Zeitung*, 8 Nov. 1922: "Ein Abend bei Adolf Hitler"; BA Berlin-Lichterfelde, NS 26/1223.

186   Müller, *Im Wandel einer Welt*, p. 145.

187   Margarete Vollerthun to Hitler, 27 Feb. 1923; BA Koblenz, N 1128/5.

188   Detlev Clemens, *Herr Hitler in Germany: Wahrnehmungen und Deutungen des Nationalsozialismus in Grossbritannien 1920 bis 1939*, Göttingen and Zurich, 1996, pp. 46f., 54, 60. For the American perspective see Sander A. Diamond, *Herr Hitler: Amerikas Diplomaten, Washington und der Untergang Weimars*, Düsseldorf, 1985, pp. 53f.; report by Truman Smith, military attaché to the U.S. embassy, of 25 Nov. 1922; copy in BSB München, Nl Hanfstaengl Ana 405, Box 25.

189   Wartime comrade Wackerl, Munich, to Hitler, 19 April 1923; BA Koblenz, N 1128/7.

6 Putsch and Prosecution

1   Adolf Hitler, *Monologe im Führerhauptquartier 1941–1944: Die Aufzeichnungen Heinrich Heims*, ed. Werner Jochmann, Hamburg, 1980, p. 171 (dated 3/4 Jan. 1942).

2   Cited in David Clay Large, *Where Ghosts Walked: Munich's Road to the Third Reich*, New York and London, 1997, p. 189. See also the "obituary" for the NSDAP in the *Frankfurter Zeitung* from 10 Nov. 1923 in Philipp W. Fabry, *Mutmassungen über Hitler: Urteile von Zeitgenossen*, Königstein im Taunus, 1979, p. 25. "If ridiculousness were

fatal, Hitler would be long dead," wrote the *Vossische Zeitung* on 9 Nov. 1931; BA Berlin-Lichterfelde, NS 26/87.

3   See Ludolf Herbst, *Hitlers Charisma: Die Erfindung eines deutschen Messias*, Frankfurt am Main, 2010, pp. 212f. See also Sabine Behrenbeck, *Der Kult um die toten Helden: Nationalsozialistische Mythen, Riten und Symbole 1923 bis 1945*, Vierow bei Greifswald, 1996, p. 299ff.

4   G. Escherich to Herrn Elvers, 28 March 1923; BayHStA München, Nl Escherich 47. For context see Heinrich August Winkler, *Weimar 1918–1933: Die Geschichte der ersten deutschen Demokratie*, Munich, 1993, pp. 188ff.

5   Adolf Hitler, *Sämtliche Aufzeichnungen 1905–1924*, ed. Eberhard Jäckel with Axel Kuhn, Stuttgart, 1980, no. 456, pp. 781, 783, 784. See ibid., no. 460, p. 792; no. 463, pp. 800f.

6   Sebastian Haffner, *Geschichte eines Deutschen: Die Erinnerungen 1914–1933*, Stuttgart and Munich, 2000, p. 61. See also Martin H. Geyer, *Verkehrte Welt: Revolution, Inflation und Moderne. München 1914–1924*, Göttingen, 1998, pp. 382ff.

7   See Ulrich Linse, *Barfüssige Propheten: Erlöser der zwanziger Jahre*, Berlin, 1983.

8   Ernst Deuerlein (ed.), *Der Hitler-Putsch: Bayerische Dokumente zum 8./9. November 1923*, Stuttgart, 1962, doc. 3, p. 164 (dated 8 Sept. 1923).

9   Notes by Rudolf Hess, entitled "The party above all parties," early 1923; BA Bern, Nl Hess, J1.211-1989/148, 31. Transcript of a conversation with Maria Endres on 11 Dec. 1951; IfZ München, ZS 33. For figures see Kurt Pätzold and Manfred Weissbecker, *Geschichte der NSDAP 1920–1945*, Cologne, 1998, p. 72. The circulation of the *Völkischer Beobachter* mirrored the number of party members. It increased from c.13,000 in January 1923 to 24,000 in July 1923. See the statistics compiled by Lauböck Sr, in BA Koblenz, N 1128/19.

10   Harry Graf Kessler, *Das Tagebuch. Vol. 7: 1919–1923*, ed. Angela Reinthal with Janna Brechmacher and Christoph Hilse, Stuttgart, 2007, p. 570 (entry for 9 Nov. 1922).

11   Quoted in Large, *Where Ghosts Walked*, pp. 161.

12   Quotation in in Ernst Deuerlein (ed.), *Der Aufstieg der NSDAP in Augenzeugenberichten*, Munich, 2nd edition, 1976, pp. 160f.

13   Lawyer and NSDAP member Dr. Richard Dingeldey's records of the conversation between Nortz and Hitler on 29 Jan. 1923; BA Berlin-Lichterfelde, NS 26/385. See also Interior Minister Dr. Schweyer to the Munich Police Directorship, 24 Jan. 1923; ibid.

14   Report by Police President Nortz to the public prosecutor at the Munich District Court I with reference to Adolf Hitler, 9 Feb. 1923; BA Berlin-Lichterfelde, NS 26/385. On the discussion between Hitler and Kahr see unpublished memoirs of Gustav Ritter von Kahr, p. 1174; BayHStA München, Nl Kahr 51. According to Kahr, Hitler declared: "I'm not that stupid to destroy the work I've done this far with an attempted putsch. I give you my word of honour that I'm not contemplating a putsch."

15   Karl Alexander von Müller heard the conversations in the Löwenbräukeller and made notes that same night. Shorthand notes and photocopy in BayHStA München, Nl. K. A. v. Müller 19/1. See also Karl Alexander von Müller, *Im Wandel einer Welt: Erinnerungen. Vol. 3: 1919–1932*, ed. Otto Alexander von Müller, Munich, 1966, pp. 145f.; in addition see the meeting reports in Hitler, *Sämtliche Aufzeichnungen*, nos. 467–478, pp. 805–18. The enormous red placard that invited people to the twelve gatherings in BA Koblenz, N 1128/28.

16   Wolfgang Benz, *Politik in Bayern 1913–1933: Berichte des württembergischen Gesandten Karl Moser von Filseck*, Stuttgart, 1971, pp. 120f. See also *Vorwärts*, 28 Jan. 1923: "Hitler diktiert—Schweyer pariert"; and *Frankfurter Zeitung*, 31 Jan. 1923: "Der Held Hitler"; BA Berlin-Lichterfelde, NS 26/386.

17   *Der Hitler-Prozess 1924*, ed. and annotated by Lothar Gruchmann and Reinhold Weber in collaboration with Otto Gritschneder, part 2, Munich, 1997, p. 738.

18   Memorandum on the purpose and task of the Working Association of Patriotic Fighting Organisations (with handwritten amendments by Hitler), 19 April 1923; BA Koblenz, N 1128/4. Reprinted in Hitler, *Sämtliche Aufzeichnungen*, no. 515, pp. 902–5 (quote on p. 905). On the above see Peter Longerich, *Die braunen Bataillone: Geschichte der SA*, Munich, 1989, pp. 33f.

19   Josef Karl Fischer to Escherich, 15 April 1923; BayHStA München, Nl Escherich 47.

20   Quotes in the following, respectively: bookshop owner Hans Goltz to Hitler, 2 May 1923; BA Koblenz, N 1128/8; Dr. Paula Wack to Hitler, 29 April 1923; BA Koblenz, N 1128/7; "A true supporter" to Hitler, 4 Nov. 1923; BA Koblenz, N 1128/14. On the attacks in the autumn of 1923 see Dirk Walter, *Antisemitische Kriminalität und Gewalt: Judenfeindschaft in der Weimarer Republik*, Bonn, 1999, pp. 115–19.

21   Hitler, *Sämtliche Aufzeichnungen*, no. 520, p. 913 (dated 26 April 1923); no. 522, p. 917 (dated 30 April 1923). See also the order issued to the leaders of the fighting associations on 30 April 1923, which stipulated: "Army weapons will be taken along as a form of self-defence in case of emergency." BA Berlin-Lichterfelde, NS 26/104. Rudolf Hess told his parents on 8 May 1923: "The fact that we suddenly have weapons is coming to many as a complete shock." BA Bern, Nl Hess, J1.211-1989/148, 31.

22   Deuerlein, *Aufstieg*, pp. 170–3 (quote on p. 171). See also the final report on the events by the Munich Police Directorship (police commando) from 30 April and 1 May 1923, and also the letter from Police President Nortz to Public Prosecutor Dresse with reference to the 1 May 1923 attacks, 23 May 1923; BA Berlin-Lichterfelde, NS 26/104.

23   Hitler, *Monologe*, p. 250 (dated 1 Feb. 1942). In his memoirs (p. 1183), Gustav von Kahr remarked that "after this embarrassment—for a time at least—Hitler became entirely meek and mild." BayHStA München, Nl Kahr 51.

24   Hitler, *Sämtliche Aufzeichnungen*, no. 523, p. 918 (dated 1 May 1923).

25   Escherich's diary for 22 Feb. and 1 May 1923; BayHStA München, Nl Escherich 10. "Escherich und der Nationalsozialismus," interview with the *Allgäuer Zeitung* dated 10 May 1923; BA Koblenz, N 1128/3. In an enraged letter to Escherich, Göring protested in the name of all military officers in the NSDAP against being called "desperados." Ibid.

26   Quoted in Large, *Where Ghosts Walked*, p. 170.

27   Lothar Gruchmann, "Hitlers Denkschrift an die bayerische Justiz vom 16. Mai 1923: Ein verloren geglaubtes Dokument," in *Vierteljahrshefte für Zeitgeschichte*, 39 (1991), pp. 305–28 (Hitler's memorandum pp. 323–8). On Gürtner's appointment to Bavarian minister of justice see BA Koblenz, N 1530/20.

28   Hitler, *Monologe*, p. 204 (dated 16/17 Jan. 1942); see ibid., p. 207: "Yes, I am deeply connected to this mountain." On Hitler's time on the Obersalzberg in 1923, see the Munich police transcript of Dietrich Eckart's interrogation on 15 Nov. 1923; BA Berlin-Lichterfelde, NS 26/2180: Ulrich Chaussy, *Nachbar Hitler: Führerkult und Heimatzerstörung am Obersalzberg*, 6th revised and extended edition, Berlin, 2007, pp. 27ff.

29   Rudolf Hess, *Briefe 1908–1933*, ed. Rüdiger Hess, Munich and Vienna, 1987, p. 299 (dated 15 July 1923).

30   Joachim Fest, *Hitler: Eine Biographie*, Frankfurt am Main, Berlin and Vienna, 1973, p. 247.

31   Hess, *Briefe*, p. 299 (dated 15 July 1923). See also Hitler's letter to Walter Riehl, the National Socialist leader in Vienna, of 5 July 1923, in which the former writes of "being interrupted two or three times a week to hold lectures." Hitler, *Sämtliche Aufzeichnungen*, no. 543, p. 943. By contrast, in a letter to Hitler dated 28 Aug. 1923, Emil Maurice expressed concern "that something isn't right here . . . You've been conspicuously quiet recently—the opposite of the way you used to live." Quoted in Anna Maria Sigmund, *Des Führers bester Freund: Adolf Hitler, seine Nichte Geli Raubal und der "Ehrenarier" Emil Maurice—Eine Dreiecksbeziehung*, Munich, 2003, p. 47.

32 Sebastian Haffner, *Geschichte eines Deutschen: Die Erinnerungen 1914–1933*, Stuttgart, 2000, p. 63. See also Eugeni Xammar, *Das Schlangenei: Berichte aus dem Deutschland der Inflationsjahre 1922–1924*, Berlin, 2007, pp. 122f. (dated 19 Oct. 1923). Escherich's recollections of the months from June to October 1923 provide an insightful look at how the German currency and the German economy plummeted; BayHStA München, Nl Escherich 10.

33 Quoted in Longerich, *Die braunen Bataillone*, p. 38; Harold J. Gordon, *Hitlerputsch 1923: Machtkampf in Bayern 1923–1924*, Frankfurt am Main, 1971, p. 219.

34 See Winkler, *Weimar*, pp. 202–10.

35 Deuerlein, *Der Hitler-Putsch*, no. 6, p. 170.

36 *Der Hitler-Prozess*, part 1, pp. 37, 266. See Kahr, memoirs, p. 1009: according to this source, Ludendorff had been actively and eagerly cooperating with Hitler since 1922; BayHStA München, Nl Kahr 51. According to the testimony of Karl Kriebel on 17 June 1952, his brother Hermann Kriebel served "as a middleman between Hitler and Ludendorff on numerous occasions." IfZ München, ZS 256. Hess first told his parents about his contact with Ludendorff in a letter dated 22 Sep. 1920; BA Bern, Nl Hess, J1.211-1989/148, 25.

37 Quoted in Gordon, *Hitlerputsch 1923*, pp. 193f. On the founding of the Patriotic Fighting Association see the letters by former Captain Weiss from 17 Sept. 1923; BA Berlin-Lichterfelde, NS 26/3. In addition see the diaries of G. Feder, vol. 5 (entry for 25 Sept. 1923); IfZ München, ED 874.

38 *Der Hitler-Prozess*, Part 1, p. 190.

39 BA Koblenz, N 1128/2. The quoted letters to Hitler, along with many others from the autumn of 1923 are collected in BA Koblenz, N 1128/12, N 1128/13, N 1128/14, N 1128/15: BA Berlin-Lichterfelde, NS 26/1, NS 26/2, NS 26/2a, NS 26/3.

40 Hitler, *Sämtliche Aufzeichnungen*, no. 566, pp. 1002, 1004.

41 Hess, *Briefe*, pp. 303f. (dated 16 Sept. 1923). See Rudolf Olden, *Hitler*, Amsterdam, 1935; new edition, Hildesheim, 1981, p. 88: "Sooner or later, the moment comes when the speaker is overcome with spirit, and something unknown and undefinable bursts out of him, sobbing, screaming and gurgling."

42 Ibid., p. 304 (dated 16 Sept. 1923).

43 Hitler to Kahr, 27 Sept. 1923; Hitler, *Sämtliche Aufzeichnungen*, no. 573, p. 1017.

44 Ibid., no. 581, pp. 1028f. (dated 7 Oct. 1923); no. 583, pp. 1932, 1034 (dated 14 Oct. 1923). In conversation with the head of the Bavarian crown prince's cabinet, Count von Soden, on 26 Sept. 1923, Scheubner-Richter also declared: "There is no enthusiasm within the fighting associations for Herr von Kahr since he is a man of half-measures." Kahr, memoirs, p. 1252; BayHStA München, Nl. Kahr 51.

45 See Gordon, *Hitlerputsch 1923*, pp. 206–9. In his diary, Franz Ritter von Epp expressed his outrage at the "thunderbolt" Seeckt hurled at Lossow: "The entire grit this government lacks towards the outside, it tries to display towards its own people . . . Cowardly and craven without, brutal within." Political diary of Ritter von Epp, vol. 1 (entry for 20 Oct. 1923); BA Koblenz, N 1101/22.

46 See Kahr, memoirs, pp. 1293ff. ("The longing for a directory for the Reich"); BayHStA München, Nl Kahr 51. On the autumn 1923 plans to form a "directory" see Walter Mühlhausen, *Friedrich Ebert 1871–1925: Reichspräsident der Weimarer Republik*, Bonn, 2006, pp. 681ff.

47 *Der Hitler-Prozess*, part 3, p. 788.

48 Deuerlein, *Der Hitler-Putsch*, doc. 16, pp. 186f.

49 Hitler, *Sämtliche Aufzeichnungen*, no. 589, p. 1043 (dated 23 Oct. 1923); no. 592, pp. 1049f. (dated 30 Oct. 1923). See Rudolf Hess to Karl Haushofer, 6 Oct. 1923: "The convalescence of the whole must proceed from Bavaria outwards; the Bavarians as the most German of Germans." BA Koblenz, N 1122/15.

50 *Der Hitler-Prozess*, part 4, p. 1587. See also ibid., part 3, p. 1199: "A man who is capable of something has the goddamned duty and responsibility to see it through."

51   Ibid., part 3, p. 659 (Seisser statement).
52   Quoted in Gordon, *Hitlerputsch 1923*, p. 231.
53   Seisser's report on the meeting in Berlin, 3 Nov. 1923; Deuerlein, *Der Hitler-Putsch*, doc. 79, pp. 301–4 (quotation on p. 303). Escherich also noted in Berlin on 3 Nov. 1923: "The general view is that a national dictatorship will have to follow in the next few days. Hopefully this will be possible by legal means." BayHStA München, Nl Escherich 10. On 11 March 1923, at the behest of Lossow, Hitler had met with Seeckt. After Hitler had held a one-and-a-half-hour monologue about his plans to topple the government in Berlin, it ended with Seeckt abruptly remarking: "From this day forth, Mr. Hitler, we have nothing more to say to each other." Report written down from memory by Seeckt's assistant, Colonel Hans Harald von Selchow, on 15 Oct. 1956; IfZ München, ZS 1900.
54   *Der Hitler-Prozess*, part 1, p. 78 (Friedrich Weber's statement on Bund Oberland); part 2, p. 772 (Lossow's statement).
55   Ibid., part 1, p. 44. See also Rudolf Hess's records from 9 April 1924, stating that Hitler had "the definite impression" that the triumvirate would "always shy back from taking the final step" and that "it would never be taken, if he himself didn't act." Hess, *Briefe*, p. 318.
56   Fritz Lauböck to Otto Weber (Lübeck), 28 Sept. 1923; BA Koblenz, N 1128/1. On the rumours about the reinstatement of the Bavarian monarchy see Adolf Schmalix to Christian Weber, 20 Sept. 1937; BA Berlin-Lichterfelde, NS 26/1267.
57   Ernst Hanfstaengl, *Zwischem Weissem und Braunem Haus: Erinnerungen eines politischen Aussenseiters*, Munich, 1970, p. 120.
58   *Der Hitler-Prozess*, part 1, p. 212.
59   Heinrich Hoffmann and Dietrich Eckart, for instance, were not informed. Both only learned of the "national revolution" in the Bürgerbräukeller on the night of 9 Nov. See Heinrich Hoffmann's manuscript for the court proceedungs of January 1947, pp. 10f.; IfZ München, MS 2049; transcript of Dietrich Eckart's questioning on 15 Nov. 1923; BA Berlin-Lichterfelde, NS 26/2180.
60   *Der Hitler-Prozess*, part 1, p. 114 (Pöhner's statement).
61   Hess, *Briefe*, p. 310 (dated 16 Nov./4 Dec. 1923). During the preceding weeks Hess spent most of his time with his mother in Reicholdsgrün, studying economics. His former "mood of storm and stress" was "quite muted," he wrote in a letter to his friend Professor Karl Haushofer in mid-September 1923. It felt good, he wrote, to "relax from all the external agitation." In early October, he said that he had no intention of returning to Munich, writing, "I'm waiting to be summoned." R. Hess to K. Haushofer, 13 Sept., 6 Oct. 1923; BA Koblenz, N 1122/15. See also Hess to Ilse Pröhl, 27 Sep., 1 Oct., 24 Oct. 1923; BA Bern, Nl Hess, J1.211-1989/148, 31. Accordug to these letters, Hess travelled to Munich "at the last moment," at the end of October.
62   Hanfstaengl, *Zwischen Weissem und Braunem Haus*, p. 129. Gottfried Feder also first received the order to be at the Bürgerbräukeller at 9 p.m. on 8 Nov. Notes on "November 1923," in G. Feder's diaries, vol. 5; IfZ München, ED 874.
63   Hofmann, *Der Hitler-Putsch*, p. 160.
64   Konrad Heiden, *Adolf Hitler: Das Zeitalter der Verantwortungslosigkeit. Eine Biographie*, Zurich, 1936, p. 156.
65   See Hess, *Briefe*, p. 311 (dated 16 Nov./4 Dec. 1923).
66   *Der Hitler-Prozess*, part 1, p. 50.
67   Müller, *Im Wandel einer Welt*, p. 161. See Kahr, memoirs, p. 1353; BayHStA München, Nl Kahr 51.
68   Indictment from 8 Jan. 1924; *Der Hitler-Prozess*, part 1, p. 309.
69   Kahr, memoirs, pp. 1354f.; BayHStA München, Nl Kahr 51. See *Der Hitler-Prozess*, part 2, p. 749 (Lossow's statement).
70   Quotes from, respectively, *Der Hitler-Prozess*, part 3, p.795 (Kahr's statement); part 1, p. 51 (Hitler's statement), p. 310 (indictment); part 2, p. 750 (Lossow's statement);

part 1, p. 310 (indictment), p. 115 (Pöhner's statement), p. 310 (indictment). See Kahr, memoirs, pp. 1355f.; BayHStA München, Nl Kahr 51.

71 Müller, *Im Wandel einer Welt*, p. 162.

72 On Göring's entrance see *Der Hitler-Prozess*, part 2, pp. 597, 620, 631, 634.

73 Müller, *Im Wandel einer Welt*, pp. 162f.; *Der Hitler-Prozess*, part 1, p. 311 (indictment).

74 Kahr, memoirs, pp. 1345f.; BayHStA München, Nl Kahr 51. In Munich in the spring of 1924, rumours swirled that Ludendorff had summoned his old confidant from the world war, Colonel Max Bauer, to the city on 8 Nov. 1923, but Bauer had refused to come and warned Ludendorff against the planned undertaking. As rumour had it, a letter to that effect had been confiscated when authorities had searched Ludendorff's home, but prosecutors had decided not to use it. Political diary of Ritter von Epp, vol. 1 (entry for 27 April 1924); BA Koblenz, N 1101/22.

75 Quotes from, respectively, *Der Hitler-Prozess*, part 1, p. 311 (indictment); part 3, p. 796 (Kahr's statement); part 1, p. 53 (Hitler's statement). See Kahr, memoirs, pp. 1357f; Bay HstA München, Nl Kahr 51.

76 Quotes from, respectively, *Der Hitler-Prozess*, part 3, p. 797 (Kahr's statement); Müller, *Im Wandel einer Welt*, p. 164; *Der Hitler-Prozess*, part 1, pp. 311f. (indictment); Müller, *Im Wandel einer Welt*, p. 164; *Der Hitler-Prozess*, part 1, p. 312 (indictment). See Kahr, memoirs, pp. 1359f.; BayHStA München, Nl Kahr 51

77 *Der Hitler-Prozess*, part 1, p. 53.

78 See Hofmann, *Der Hitler-Putsch*, p. 169; *Der Hitler-Prozess*, part 1, p. 279: Ludendorff said that he had been unable to believe "that the gentlemen would go back on their word." According to testimony by Mathilde Scheubner-Richter on 9 July 1952, Ludendorff visited her two days after the failed putsch and cried like a small child, saying: "Noble lady, it is the end of Germany, if German officers break their word to another German officer." IfZ München, ZS 292.

79 See Peter Longerich, *Heinrich Himmler: Biographie*, Munich, 2008, pp. 76f.

80 *Der Hitler-Prozess*, part 2, p. 756 (Lossow's statement).

81 Ibid., p. 757; see Kahr, memoirs, pp. 1367f.; BayHStA München, Nl. Kahr 51.

82 Text in Hitler, *Sämtliche Aufzeichnungen*, no. 597, p. 1056.

83 *Der Hitler-Prozess*, part 3, p. 873 (Seisser's statement).

84 *Der Hitler-Prozess*, part 2, pp. 662f. (retired Major Alexander Siry's statement).

85 See the report by the Spanish journalist Eugeni Xammar, who was present in the Bürgerbräukeller on 8 Nov.: "Der Putsch als Spektakel" (*Das Schlangenei*, pp. 134–8).

86 For details see Walter, *Antisemitische Gewalt*, pp. 120–36; further, see the indictment against forty members of Stosstrupp Hitler, dated 29 April 1924, reprinted in Hans Kallenbach, *Mit Adolf Hitler auf Festung Landsberg*, Munich, 1933, pp. 16–29.

87 Detlev Clemens, *Herr Hitler in Germany: Wahrnehmungen und Deutungen des Nationalsozialismus in Grossbritannien 1920 bis 1939*, Göttingen and Zurich, 1996, p. 80.

88 See Gordon, *Hitlerputsch 1923*, p. 241; Walter, *Antisemitische Gewalt*, p. 114. On 13 Nov. 1923, the widow Elly von der Pfordten wrote to Karl Alexander von Müller with the request: "Should you be able with the help of Engineer F(eder) to tell me more about my husband's final moments, I would be very grateful. Every word is important to me." BayHStA München, Nl K. A. v. Müller 19/1.

89 Hanfstaengl's note; BSB München, Nl Hanfstaengl Ana 405, Box 25; *Der Hitler-Prozess*, part 3, p. 1203.

90 Recorded as "November 1923" in G. Feder's diaries, vol. 5; IfZ München, ED 874. The quote is from Hofmann, *Der Hitler-Putsch*, p. 194

91 *Der Hitler-Prozess*, part 1, p. 282 (Ludendorff's statement).

92 See ibid., p. 57 (Hitler's statement): "Herr Ludendorff in particular took the standpoint that we had to try to go into the city ourselves, even if it were our last move, and attempt to get public opinion on our side." See notes of a conversation with Karl Kriebel from 17 June 1952; IfZ München, ZS 258.

93   *Der Hitler-Prozess* part 1, p. 58. See also ibid., p. 230 (Kriebel's statement); part 2, p. 400 (Brückner's statement). On the role of Rossbach and the Infantry School see the transcript of a conversation with Gerhard Rossbach, dated 31 Oct. 1951; IfZ München, ZS 128.

94   See Hanfstaengl, *Zwischen Weissem und Braunem Haus*, p. 143. Text in David Jablonski, *The Nazi Party in Dissolution: Hitler and the Verbotszeit 1923–1925*, London, 1989, p. 29. That morning, the *Münchener Neueste Nachrichten* (9 Nov. 1923) ran a headline reading, "National Directorship to be Instituted." Six days earlier, the *Münchener Zeitung* (3 Nov. 1923) had already run the headline "Hitler's Putsch—Kahr's Rape" and published Kahr's contrary appeal. Copies of the newspapers in BayHStA München, Nl K. A. v. Müller 19/2.

95   See the report by Police First Lieutenant Baron von Godin, 10 Nov. 1923; Deuerlein, *Der Hitler-Putsch*, doc. 97, pp. 330f.

96   For the following quotations see also Anna Maria Sigmund, "Als Hitler auf der Flucht war," in *Süddeutsche Zeitung*, 8 and 9 Nov. 2008 (based on the unpublished memoirs of Helene Hanfstaengl).

97   See the report dramatising his wife's memoirs in Hanfstaengl, *Zwischen Weissem und Braunem Haus*, p. 6.

98   Deuerlein, *Der Hitler-Putsch*, doc. 118, p. 372 (dated 13 Nov. 1923). See also the recollections of the Uffinger police constable Georg Schmiedel in "Ich verhaftete Adolf Hitler!," in the *Weilheimer Tageblatt*, 10 Dec. 1949; BSB Müchen, Nl Hanfstaengl Ana 405, Box 40; further, the half-monthly report of the Weilheim Police Directorship from 30 Nov. 1923; BA Berlin-Lichterfelde, NS 26/66.

99   On Hitler's arrival in jail, see the description of former prison official Franz Hemmerich "Die Festung Landsberg am Lech 1920–1945," written in 1970, pp. 3f.: "A couple of strands of hair hung down into his face, pale and sunken from stress and sleepless nights, out of which a pair of hard eyes stared out into the void." IfZ München, ED 153; Otto Lurker, *Hitler hinter Festungsmauern: Ein Bild aus trüben Tagen*, Berlin, 1933, pp. 4–6 (on p. 65 see the protective custody order from 11 Nov. 1923).

100   See Gordon, *Der Hitlerputsch*, pp. 416–23. On Hess see Hess to his parents, 21 Dec. 1923, 2 April 1924; BA Bern, Nl Hess, J1.211-1989/148, 31, 33; Hess, *Briefe*, p. 322 (dated 11 May 1924). On Feder, see "Promemoria 1923/24," in G. Feder's diaries, vol. 6; IfZ München, ED 874.

101   Quoted in Gordon, *Der Hitlerputsch*, p. 313.

102   Clemens, *Herr Hitler in Germany*, p. 80. See Kahr, memoirs, pp. 1376f.; BayHStA München, Nl Kahr 51. In a conversation with Ritter von Epp, Minister President Knilling described Kahr as "the most hated man in Munich." Political diary of Ritter von Epp, vol. 1 (entry for 10 Nov. 1923); BA Koblenz, N 1101/22.

103   Karl Alexander von Müller to Paul Nikolaus Cossmann, 13 Nov. 1923; BayHStA München, Nl K. A. v. Müller 19/1. For the course of the mass event at Munich University on 12 Nov. 1923 see Deuerlein, *Der Hitler-Putsch*, doc. 113, pp. 357f.; Anton Schmalix to Christian Weber, 20 Sept. 1937; BA Berlin-Lichterfelde, NS 26/1267. On the students' mood see Albrecht Haushofer in retrospect to Rudolf Hess, 29 March 1935; BA Koblenz, N 1122/957.

104   See Winkler, *Weimar*, pp. 241ff.

105   Memoirs of Franz Hemmerich, p. 13; IfZ München, ED 153. See ibid., pp. 9–15: According to these sources, Hitler began his hunger strike several days after being brought to Landsberg and held out for ten days.

106   Otto Gritschneder, *Bewährungsfrist für den Terroristen Adolf H.: Der Hitler-Putsch und die bayerische Justiz*, Munich, 1990, p. 35. See also Ott's report in the *Bayernkurier*, 3 Nov. 1973, reprinted in Werner Maser, *Adolf Hitlers "Mein Kampf": Geschichte, Auszüge, Kommentare*, 9th edition, Esslingen, 2001, pp. 18–20. Anton Drexler too claimed that he—together with attorney Lorenz Roder—had convinced Hitler to end his hunger

strike after thirteen days. Anton Drexler to Felix Danner, 5 Jan. 1934; BA Berlin-Lichterfelde, NS 26/2012.

107   Hess, *Briefe*, p. 313 (dated 16 Nov./4 Dec. 1923).

108   Quoted in John Toland, *Adolf Hitler: Volume 1*, New York, 1976, p. 192. On 23 Nov. one of Hitler's early visitors, the Sudeten German National Socialist Hans Knirsch, reported: "He still has no use of his arm." Othmar Plöckinger, *Geschichte eines Buches: Adolf Hitlers "Mein Kampf" 1922–1945*, Munich, 2006, p. 32.

109   See Brigitte Hamann, *Winifred Wagner oder Hitlers Bayreuth*, Munich and Zurich, 2002, pp. 86–100 (quotations on pp. 90, 91, 96f., 97, 99, 94).

110   Report by deputy state prosecutor Dr. Ehard, 14 Dec. 1923, on interrogating Hitler during the previous days; *Der Hitler-Prozess*, part 1, pp. 299–307 (quotation on pp. 299f.).

111   Ibid., p. 307.

112   See the reports by the *Münchener Neuesten Nachrichten*, 27 Feb. 1924 and the *München-Augsburger Abendzeitung*, 27 Feb. 1924; BA Berlin-Lichterfelde, NS 26/1928c and NS 26/1928d. On the run-up to the trial, see Wilhelm Frick to his sister Emma, 12 Feb. 1924. Frick wrote that "the trial is attracting massive public interest—the unintended result is European fame." BA Koblenz, N 1241/7.

113   Hanfstaengl, *Zwischen Weissem und Braunem Haus*, p. 156.

114   *München-Augsburger Abendzeitung*, 27 Feb. 1924; *Münchener Zeitung*, 26 Feb. 1924; *Münchener Neueste Nachrichten*, 27 Feb. 1924; BA Berlin-Lichterfelde NS 26/1928e, NS 26/1928b, NS 26/1928d.

115   Indictment from 8 Jan. 1924; *Der Hitler-Prozess*, part 1, pp. 308–22 (quotation on p. 324).

116   Ibid., pp. 60f.

117   Kahr, memoirs, p. 1450; BayHStA München, Nl Kahr 51. The quote is from Friedrich Hitzer, *Anton Graf Arco: Das Attentat auf Eisner und die Schüsse im Landtag*, Munich, 1988, p. 313. On Neidhardt see Bernhard Huber, "Georg Neidhardt—nur ein unpolitischer Richter?," in Marita Krauss (ed.), *Rechte Karrieren in München: Von der Weimarer Zeit bis in die Nachkriegsjahre*, Munich, 2010, pp. 95–111.

118   *Der Hitler-Prozess*, part 2, pp. 738f. See the political diary of Ritter von Epp, vol. 1 (entry for 12 March 1924): "From the trial: Lossow snd Seisser getting the job done. Kahr is collapsing." BA Koblenz, N 1101/22.

119   See *Der Hitler-Prozess*, part 3, pp. 1034, 1088.

120   Quoted in Deuerlein, *Aufstieg*, p. 205. See also the *Bayerischer Kurier* report, which concluded that "in terms of content" the trial was like "a rabble-rousing meeting of ethnic chauvinists"; ibid., p. 228. The Social Democratic newspaper *Münchener Post* (29 Feb. 1924) wrote that the proceedings were "increasingly taking on comedic qualities." BA Berlin-Lichterfelde, NS 26/1928a.

121   *Der Hitler-Prozess*, part 4, pp. 1591f.; Rudolf Hess called Hitler's concluding statement "probably one of the best and most powerful speeches he's ever given." Hess, *Briefe*, p. 317 (dated 2 April 1924).

122   *Der Hitler-Prozess*, part 4, p. 1593.

123   See the exact wording of the court's verdict in Gritschneder, *Bewährungsfrist*, pp. 67–94. Gottfried Feder was "deeply shaken" by the court's ruling. G. Feder's diaries, vol. 5 (entry for 1 April 1924); IfZ Munich, ED 874.

124   Extract from the report by the *Münchener Neueste Nachrichten* in *Der Hitler-Prozess*, part 4, pp. 1597–9 (quotation on p. 1599).

125   Quoted in Large, *Where Ghosts Walked*, p. 194; see Clemens, *Herr Hitler in Germany*, p. 88.

126   *Die Weltbühne*, (10 April 1924), p. 466 (reprint 1978).

127   Gritschneder, *Bewährungsfrist*, p. 92.

128   See Andreas Heusler, *Das Braune Haus: Wie München zur "Hauptstadt der Bewegung" wurde*, Munich, 2008, p. 105.

129 In comparison, see Ian Kershaw, *Hitler 1889–1936: Hubris*, London, 1998, pp. 223ff., who asserts that Hitler first presented himself as the "Führer" during his Landsberg incarceration. Likewise Herbst, *Hitlers Charisma*, pp. 178ff.

130 Hitler, *Monologe*, p. 262 (dated 3/4 Feb. 1942). See also Hitler's speech in Weimar on 20 Oct. 1926, in which he said that he had no intention to take a step like the one he had back in 1923. Adolf Hitler, *Reden, Schriften, Anordnungen—Februar 1925 bis Januar 1933. Vol. 2: Vom Weimarer Parteitag bis zur Reichstagswahl Juli 1926–Mai 1928. Part 1: Juli 1926–Juli 1927*, ed. and annotated Bärbel Dusik, Munich, London, New York and Paris, 1992, no. 39, p. 79.

131 Sebastian Haffner, *Germany: Jekyll & Hyde—Deutschland von innen betrachtet*, Berlin, 1996, p. 21. See also *idem, Anmerkungen zu Hitler*, 21st edition, Munich, 1978, p. 9. Fest (*Hitler*, p. 282), also speaks of a "veritably suicidal make-up."

132 See Johannes Kunisch, *Friedrich der Grosse: Der König und seine Zeit*, Munich, 2004, pp. 173, 209, 368, 373, 407.

133 In an essay that served as a preliminary version of his account of the Hitler putsch in the third volume of his memoirs, Karl Alexander von Müller noted: "There were already signs that should have given us pause for thought: the ruthlessness with which he broke his word to Kahr and Lossow; the wild yet cold-blooded gamble of a putsch that could have resulted in a blood-bath; and the even riskier move of ordering a march through the city, which indeed cost a number of people their lives, while he fled." BayHStA München, Nl K. A. v. Müller 101.

134 *Der Hitler-Prozess*, part 2, p. 738.

135 Only in a letter at the end of February 1924 did Rudolf Hess consider whether it would not have been wiser "to delay the operation, not to do things too hastily . . . But it's of course easy to recognise in hindsight that there was still time!" Hess to Ilse Pröhl, 28 February 1924; BA Bern, Nl Hess, J1.211-1989/148, 33.

7 *Landsberg Prison and* Mein Kampf

1 Hans Frank, *Im Angesicht des Galgens: Deutung Hitlers und seiner Zeit auf Grund eigener Erlebnisse und Erkenntnisse*, Munich and Gräfelfing, 1953, pp. 46f.

2 Konrad Heiden, *Adolf Hitler: Das Zeitalter der Verantwortungslosigkeit. Eine Biographie*, Zurich, 1936, p. 188.

3 Adolf Hitler, *Sämtliche Aufzeichnungen 1905–1924*, ed. Eberhard Jäckel with Axel Kuhn, Stuttgart, 1980, no. 636, p. 1232. See Rudolf Hess, *Briefe 1908–1933*, ed. Rüdiger Hess, Munich and Vienna, 1987, p. 317 (dated 2 April 1924). In the six months he still had to serve, wrote Hess, Hitler "will have the chance to further edify and educate himself in peace."

4 Adolf Hitler, *Monologe im Führerhauptquartier 1941–1944: Die Aufzeichnungen Heinrich Heims*, ed. Werner Jochmann, Hamburg, 1980, p. 262 (dated 3/4 Feb. 1942).

5 Ibid., p. 49 (dated 27/28 July 1941). See Hess, *Briefe*, p. 391 (dated 8 March 1928). Hess quotes Hitler saying that his enemies would have every reason to regret imprisoning him: "Here he had time to collect himself and arrive at some fundamental conclusions."

6 Hitler, *Monologe*, p. 262 (dated 3/4 Feb. 1942).

7 Hess, *Briefe*, p. 338 (dated 18 June 1924). See also Rudolf Hess to Heinrich Heim, 16 July 1924. Hess wrote that it was not until Landsberg that he "first completely comprehended the massive importance" of Hitler as a person; BA Berlin-Lichterfelde, NS 6/71. In a speech after being released from Landsberg in November 1924, the law student Hermann Fobke declared: "I would like it if you too would recognise that this man justifies the faith we put in him, namely that he can be the leader who takes us on the path to our ultimate goal: a free, ethnically based Greater Germany." BA Berlin-Lichterfelde, NS 26/901.

8   Carl von Ossietzky, *Sämtliche Schriften. Vol. 2: 1922–1924*, ed. Bärbel Boldt, Dirk
      Grathoff and Michael Sartorius, Reinbek bei Hamburg, 1994, p. 335.
9   Ernst Hanfstaengl, *Zwischen Weissem und Braunem Haus: Erinnerungen eines politischen
      Aussenseiters*, Munich, 1970, p. 157. See Hanfstaengl's unpublished memoirs, p. 122:
      "You could have opened a flower shop, a vegetable shop and a wine store with all
      the stuff that piled up." BSB München, Nl Hanfstaengl Ana 405, Box 47.
10   Otto Lurker, *Hitler hinter Festungsmauern: Ein Bild aus trüben Tagen*, Berlin, 1933, p. 20.
      See Franz Hemmrich's memoirs, pp. 49f.; IfZ München, ED 153.
11   Ernst Deuerlein (ed.), *Der Aufstieg der NSDAP in Augenzeugenberichten*, Munich, 2nd
      edition, 1976, p. 232.
12   Lurker, *Hitler hinter Festungsmauern*, pp. 57f.; for the visitor list see Ernst Piper, *Alfred
      Rosenberg: Hitlers Chefideologe*, Munich, 2005, p. 101; Othmar Plöckinger, *Geschichte
      eines Buches: Adolf Hitlers "Mein Kampf" 1922–1945*, Munich, 2006, p. 33.
13   BA Berlin-Lichterfelde NS 10/123, with the handwritten addition "To the Führer
      from his old fellow traveller in the struggle, Elsa Bruckmann, 24 September '34."
14   See Lurker, *Hitler hinter Festungsmauern*, pp. 18, 21; Hans Kallenbach, *Mit Adolf Hitler
      auf Festung Landsberg*, Munich, 1933, p. 82. Franz Hemmrich's memoirs, p. 32; IfZ
      München, ED 153. For Hitler's predilection for Bavarian traditional dress see Hitler,
      Monologe, pp. 282f. (dated 17 Feb. 1942).
15   Hess, *Briefe*, p. 326 (dated 18 May 1924); see also ibid., pp. 323f. (dated 16 May 1924):
      "He looks better now that he's well-fed and there's no chance for him to run willy-
      nilly from one meeting to another until deep into the night."
16   See the register of prisoners in Landsberg in BA Berlin-Lichterfelde, NS 26/66;
      Kallenbach, *Mit Adolf Hitler auf Festung Landsberg*, pp. 55f.; Lurker, *Hitler hinter
      Festungsmauern*, p. 32; Franz Hemmrich's memoirs, pp. 24, 26; IfZ München, ED
      153.
17   Kallenbach, *Mit Adolf Hitler auf Festung Landsberg*, p. 45.
18   Hanfstaengl, *Zwischen Weissem und Braunem Haus*, p. 157; see Kallenbach, *Mit Adolf
      Hitler auf Festung Landsberg*, pp. 66f. According to Franz Hemmrich's memoirs (p. 32),
      Hitler served as a referee and donated books and tobacco as prizes for the winners;
      IfZ München, ED 153. On the sports competitions see also Rudolf Hess's letter to
      his father Fritz Hess; BA Bern, Nl Hess, JI.211-1989/148, 33.
19   Kallenbach, *Mit Adolf Hitler auf Festung Landsberg*, p. 77.
20   Ibid., pp. 115–17; see also Lurker, *Hitler hinter Festungsmauern*, p. 55.
21   Hanfstaengl, *Zwischen Weissem und Braunem Haus*, p. 156; see Hess, *Briefe*, p. 323
      (dated 16 May 1924): "The treatment is beyond reproach, the absolute definition of
      'honourable.'" See also Hitler, *Monologe*, p. 113 (29 Oct. 1941): "None of the prison
      guards ever insulted us."
22   Quoted in Plöckinger, *Geschichte eines Buches*, p. 30n6.
23   Kallenbach, *Mit Adolf Hitler auf Festung Landsberg*, p. 117.
24   See Plöckinger, *Geschichte eines Buches*, p. 26. An issue of "The Landsberg Honorary
      Citizen" with the subtitle "Gazette of the Prisoners of Landsberg am Lech" in BA
      Berlin-Lichterfelde, NS 26/92. See also Lurker, *Hitler hinter Festugsmauern*, p. 35;
      Kallenbach, *Mit Adolf Hitler auf Festung Landsberg*, p. 113.
25   Hitler, *Monologe*, p. 113 (dated 29 Oct. 1941).
26   Hess, *Briefe*, p. 344 (dated 5 July 1924).
27   See David Jablonsky, *The Nazi Party in Dissolution: Hitler and the Verbotszeit 1923–1925*,
      London, 1989, pp. 28ff.
28   See Piper, *Rosenberg*, p. 97.
29   As in Alan Bullock, *Hitler: A Study in Tyranny*, London, 1990, p. 122. Ian Kershaw,
      Hitler 1889–1936: Hubris, London, 1998, pp. 225f., disagrees, stressing Hitler's belief
      in Rosenberg's loyalty as a main motive. Piper (*Rosenberg*, pp. 97f.) agrees.
30   Albrecht Tyrell, *Führer befiehl . . . Selbstzeugnisse aus der "Kampfzeit" der NSDAP:
      Dokumentation und Analyse*, Düsseldorf, 1969, doc. 22a, pp. 72f. See also party

leadership of the NSDAP ("Rolf Eidhalt") to the local Straubing chapter on 5 Dec. 1923, stating that the character of the movement as a "secret organisation" would free local chapters of "lukewarm members just going along for the ride." BA Berlin-Lichterfelde, NS 26/89.

31 Speech by Hermann Fobke in Göttingen in Nov. 1924; BA Berlin-Lichterfelde, NS 26/901. See Hess, *Briefe*, p. 324 (dated 16 May 1924): "Of course we miss him on the outside, his unifying personality and the authority which makes small-time blow-hards give in." See also Wolfgang Horn, *Der Marsch zur Machtergreifung: Die NSDAP bis 1933*, Düsseldorf, 1980, p. 174.

32 Hanfstaengl, *Zwischen Weissem und Braunem Haus*, p. 159.

33 See Jablonsky, *The Nazi Party in Dissolution*, p. 54; Tyrell, *Führer befiehl*, p. 68; Horn, *Der Marsch zur Machtergreifung*, pp. 177f.

34 Tyrell, *Führer befiehl*, doc. 31, pp. 81–3 (quote on p. 82). See ibid., doc. 23, pp. 73f.

35 See Martin H. Geyer, *Verkehrte Welt: Revolution, Inflation und Moderne. München 1914–1924*, Göttingen, 1998, pp. 355f.; Jablonsky, *The Nazi Party in Dissolution*, pp. 82f.; Horn, *Der Weg zur Machtergreifung*, pp. 178f.

36 See Horn, *Der Weg zur Machtergreifung*, pp. 163, 184; Piper, *Rosenberg*, pp. 104f.

37 For the results of the Reichstag elections see Tyrell, *Führer befiehl*, doc. no. 25, p. 76; for the electoral pact ibid., doc. 24b, p. 75. Gottfried Feder travelled to Landsberg on 9 May, where Hitler was "very charming and warm" and congratulated him on the election. G. Feder's diaries, vol. 5 (entry for 9 May 1924); IfZ München, ED 874.

38 See Jablonsky, *The Nazi Party in Dissolution*, pp. 86f.; Kershaw, *Hitler: Hubris*, p. 229. By contrast, in an "open letter to Herr von Graefe" on 17 March 1926, Hitler clearly contended that he had been against the merger from the very beginning: "To me during my imprisonment, the thought that my marvellous popular movement could be handed over to a clique of parliamentarians was worse than the lack of liberty itself." Adolf Hitler, *Reden, Schriften, Anordnungen—Februar 1925 bis Januar 1933. Vol. 1: Die Wiedergründung der NSDAP Februar 1925–Juni 1926*, ed. and annotated Clemens Vollnhals, Munich, London, New York and Paris, 1992, no. 111, pp. 343f.

39 G. Feder's diaries, vol. 5 (entry for 24 May 1924); IfZ München, ED 874. Full text of the declaration of 26 May 1924 in Horn, *Der Marsch zur Machtergreifung*, p. 187.

40 Tyrell, *Führer befiehl*, doc. 27, pp. 77f.

41 See Jochen Haupt's pamphlet "Über die organisatorischen Massnahmen zur Fortsetzung der nationalsozialistischen Parteiarbeit in Norddeutschland," in Werner Jochmann, *Nationalsozialismus und Revolution: Ursprung und Geschichte der NSDAP in Hamburg 1922–1933. Dokumente*, Frankfurt am Main, 1963, doc. 16, pp. 69–72.

42 Hitler, *Sämtliche Aufzeichnungen*, no. 636, p. 1232.

43 Rudolf Hess to Wilhelm Sievers, 11 May 1925; reprinted in Henrik Eberle (ed.), *Briefe an Hitler: Ein Volk schreibt seinem Führer. Unbekannte Dokumente aus Moskauer Archiven—zum ersten Mal veröffentlicht*, Bergisch-Gladbach, 2007, pp. 56f. In contrast, Hermann Fobke, another former Landsberg inmate, told an audience in Göttingen in Nov. 1924 "that today Hitler is still the committed anti-parliamentarian he always was." BA Berlin-Lichterfelde, NS 26/901.

44 Jochmann, *Nationalsozialismus und Revolution*, doc. 20, pp. 77f. (quote on p. 78). Also in Hitler, *Sämtliche Aufzeichnungen*, no. 647, pp. 1238f. On 19 June, after visiting Landsberg, Gottfried Feder wrote that Hitler was "depressed," adding "he wants to withdraw entirely from the movement and has to work, that is, write to earn money." G. Feder's diaries, vol. 6 (entry for 19 June 1924); IfZ München, ED 874. In a letter to Albert Stier on 23 June 1924, Hitler reiterated his decision to resign the party leadership; Tyrell, *Führer befiehl*, doc. 28, p. 78; also in Hitler, *Sämtliche Aufzeichnungen*, no. 649, pp. 1239f.

45 Hermann Fobke to Ludolf Haase, 23 June 1924; Jochmann, *Nationalsozialismus und Revolution*, doc. 26, pp. 90–2 (quote on p. 91). See Rudolf Hess to Heinrich Heim, 16 July 1924. Hitler, wrote Hess, did not want to take responsibility "for what is

happening on the outside without his knowledge and in part against his will." On the other hand, according to Hess, Hitler was "convinced he could get everything back on track soon after he was freed." BA Berlin-Lichterfelde, NS 6/71.

46 Quoted in Deuerlein, *Aufstieg*, pp. 235f.; see Emil Maurice to Adolf Schmalix, 19 July 1924; BA Berlin-Lichterfelde, NS 26/1267; Jablonsky, *The Nazi Party in Dissolution*, pp. 96–8.

47 Deuerlein, *Aufstieg*, p. 236.

48 Confidential report about the Weimar conference by Adalbert Volck, a lawyer from Lüneburg, 20 July 1924; Jochmann, *Nationalsozialismus und Revolution*, doc. 30, pp. 98–102 (quote on p. 101). See Jablonsky, *The Nazi Party in Dissolution*, pp. 103ff.

49 G. Feder's diaries, vol. 6 (entry for 14 Aug. 1924); IfZ München, ED 874. See Kershaw, *Hitler: Hubris*, p. 233f.; Horn, *Der Marsch zur Machtergreifung*, p. 192; Piper, *Rosenberg*, pp. 108f.

50 Hermann Fobke to Adalbert Volck, 29 July 1924; Jochmann, *Nationalsozialismus und Revolution*, doc. 33, pp. 122–4 (quote on p. 123); see ibid., doc. 37, p. 133; doc. 51, p. 165 ("position of strict neutrality").

51 Hess, *Briefe*, p. 349 (dated 17 Aug. 1924).

52 Hanfstaengl, *Zwischen Weissem und Braunem Haus*, p. 166. See Hanfstaengl's unpublished memoirs, p. 128: "His healthy political instincts told him to let the various groups fight it out and stay in the background himself for the time being." BSB München, Nl Hanfstaengl Ana 405, Box 47.

53 See Bullock, *Hitler*, pp. 126f.; Fest, *Hitler*, p. 316.

54 *Der Hitler-Prozess 1924*, ed. and annotated by Lothar Gruchmann and Reinhold Weber with Otto Gritschneder, part 1, Munich, 1997, p. 299. See Hitler's letter to Adolf Vogl, 10 Jan. 1924: "I am expressing my resentment in what I'm writing to justify myself, the first part of which I hope will outlive the trial and me." Hitler, *Sämtliche Aufzeichnungen*, no. 604, p. 1060.

55 Franz Hemmrich's memoirs, p. 35; IfZ München, ED 153.

56 See Plöckinger, *Geschichte eines Buches*, pp. 21f.

57 See Wolfgang Horn, "Ein unbekannter Aufsatz Hitlers aus dem Frühjahr 1924," in *Vierteljahrshefte für Zeitgeschichte*, 16 (1968), pp. 280–94. See Plöckinger, *Geschichte eines Buches*, pp. 23–6.

58 Hitler, *Sämtliche Aufzeichnungen*, no. 636, pp. 1232f. On 12 May 1924, Hitler told something similar to a delegation of National Socialist deputies from Salzburg: "At the moment he was writing a book . . . in which he will settle the scores with the critics who emerged after 8 Nov." Quoted in Plöckinger, *Geschichte eines Buches*, p. 34.

59 See Plöckinger, *Geschichte eines Buches*, pp. 38, 42–8 (on p. 39 see also the catalogue's title page with a photograph of Hitler). See also Timothy W. Ryback, *Hitler's Private Library: The Books That Shaped His Life*, London, 2009, p. 66.

60 See Plöckinger, *Geschichte eines Buches*, p. 49; based on it, Ryback, *Hitler's Private Library*, p. 67. On the autobiographical sections of *Mein Kampf* see Othmar Plöckinger, "Frühe biographische Texte zu Hitler: Zur Bewertung der autobiographischen Texte in *Mein Kampf*," in *Vierteljahrshefte für Zeitgeschichte*, 58 (2010), pp. 112f. Plöckinger has shown that Hitler basically only recapitulated and embellished those details of his biography that were already known in ethnic-chauvinistic circles.

61 Hess, *Briefe*, pp. 341f. (dated 29 June 1924). For more on this see Chapter 3, p. 56.

62 Hess, *Briefe*, p. 346 (entry for 23 July 1923). The first sentence quoted, which is missing in the Wolf Rüdiger Hess edition, in BA Bern, Nl Hess, J1.211-1989/148, 33.

63 Otto Lurker, *Hitler hinter Festungsmauern: Ein Bild aus trüben Tagen*, Berlin, 1933, p. 56. For a critical perspective on this legend see Plöckinger, *Geschichte eines Buches*, p. 122. Also Florian Beierl and Othmar Plöckinger, "Neue Dokumente zu Hitlers Buch 'Mein Kampf,'" in *Vierteljahrshefte für Zeitgeschichte*, 57 (2009), pp. 261–95 (in particular pp. 273, 278f.).

64 See the details provided by Ilse Hess on 28 Dec. 1952 and 29 June 1965 in Werner Maser, *Adolf Hitlers "Mein Kampf": Geschichte, Auszüge, Kommentare*, 9th edition, Esslingen, 2001, p. 29. Further, Olaf Rose (ed.), *Julius Schaub: In Hitlers Schatten*, Stegen, 2005, p. 59. On Hitler's working methods see Beierl and Plöckinger, "Neue Dokumente," pp. 276ff. Both Rudolf Hess and prison guard Franz Hemmrich bear witness to Hitler setting out his initial thoughts by hand. Plöckinger, *Geschichte eines Buches*, p. 153; Franz Hemmrich's memoirs, pp. 35f.; IfZ München, ED 153.

65 Hess, *Briefe*, p. 347 (dated 24 July 1924). See also ibid., p. 349 (dated 17 Aug. 1924): "My daily routine begins as follows—at 5 a.m., I get up and make cups of tea for Hitler (who is writing his book) and myself."

66 Ibid., p. 347 (dated 4 Aug. 1924). In his letter to Heinrich Heim dated 16 July 1924 Hess announced that Hitler's book should be appearing in the autumn. BA Berlin-Lichterfelde, NS 6/71.

67 Hermann Fobke to Eduard Heinze, a National Socialist in Stettin, 23 Aug. 1924; Plöckinger, *Geschichte eines Buches*, p. 55. See also Hermann Fobke to Adalbert Volck, 29 July 1924; Jochmann, *Nationalsozialismus und Revolution*, doc. 33, p. 124.

68 Leybold's report from 15 Sept. 1924; Deuerlein, *Aufstieg*, p. 238.

69 See Anna Maria Sigmund, *Des Führers bester Freund: Adolf Hitler, seine Nichte Geli Raubal und der "Ehrenarier" Emil Maurice—eine Dreiecksbeziehung*, Munich, 2003, p. 71. In contrast, Franz Hemmrich (memoirs, p. 57) asserts that the Munich censors gave the manuscript of *Mein Kampf* back to Hitler; IfZ München, ED 153.

70 Hanfstaengl, *Zwischen Weissem und Braunem Haus*, pp. 161f.

71 On this see Plöckinger, *Geschichte eines Buches*, pp. 67ff.

72 Ibid., pp. 76–8, 86–9.

73 Ibid., pp. 68, 71f., 85, 151. There is no evidence for the common claims that either Father Bernhard Stempfle, the editor in chief of the *Miesbacher Anzeiger*, or Hanfstaengl helped edit the manuscript. See ibid., pp. 129f., 133–41. Hanfstaengl's unpublished memoirs, pp. 141f.; BSB München, Ana 405, Box 47. In early March 1925, Stolzing-Cerny gave Gottfried Feder page proofs of *Mein Kampf* with passages relating to Feder. "Quite wonderful," he commented. G. Feder's diaries, vol. 6 (entry for 5 March 1925); IfZ München, ED 74.

74 See Plöckinger, *Geschichte eines Buches*, p. 120: Also Wolfgang Martynkewicz, *Salon Deutschland: Geist und Macht 1900–1945*, Berlin, 2009, pp. 424f. (Letter from Elsa Bruckmann to her husband dated 26 Sept. 1924); Hitler, *Monologe*, p. 206 (dated 16/17 Jan. 1942).

75 Hess, *Briefe*, p. 370 (dated 24 Oct. 1926). Among other things, Hess now also put together the running heads, as Stolzing-Cerny had got things "terribly wrong" in the first volume. Hess to his father Fritz Hess, 24 Oct. 1926; BA Bern, Nl Hess, J1.211-1989/148, 36.

76 Ibid., p. 346 (dated 23 July 1924). See ibid., p. 349 (dated 17 Aug. 1924): "Its publication will be a severe blow for his enemies."

77 For the figures see Plöckinger, *Geschichte eines Buches*, pp. 177–82.

78 Rudolf Hess to his father Fritz Hess, 19 April 1933; BA Bern, Nl Hess, J1.211-1989/148, 51. The time-consuming corrections to the "people's edition" were made by Rudolf and Ilse Hess. See Rudolf Hess to his parents, 16 April 1930; BA Bern, Nl Hess, J1.211-1989/148, 45. On what follows see Plöckinger, *Geschichte eines Buches*, pp. 182–8, 407–13, 432–40.

79 Frank, *Im Angesicht des Galgens*, p. 46. See also Otto Wagener, *Hitler aus nächster Nähe: Aufzeichnungen eines Vertrauten 1929–1932*, ed. Henry A. Turner, Frankfurt am Main, Berlin and Vienna, 1978, p. 415.

80 See Ryback, *Hitler's Private Library*, p. 77f. For example, Emil Maurice received the tenth copy of the luxury edition of 1925, limited to 500 copies, with the dedication: "For my loyal and upstanding shield bearer." Sigmund, *Des Führers bester Freund*, pp. 72f. (see p. 73 for the facsimile of the dedication). During the 1925 Wagner Festival in Bayreuth, Hitler also presented Winifred Wagner with a freshly printed,

personally dedicated copy of the first volume. See Brigitte Hamann, *Winifred Wagner oder Hitlers Bayreuth*, Munich and Zurich, 2002, p. 142.

81   Hitler, *Mein Kampf. Vol. 1: Eine Abrechnung*, 7th edition, Munich, 1933, pp. 231f.

82   On the style of the book, see Fest, *Hitler*, pp. 291–3. The cultured Fest does not conceal his contempt for the "half-educated" Hitler. In a similar vein, see Bullock, *Hitler*, p. 122; Ralf Georg Reuth, *Hitler: Eine Biographie*, Munich and Zurich, 2003, p. 172. According to Hess, Hitler remarked in Landsberg: "Nobody should write in German unless he has read Schopenhauer, with his beautifully clear style." BA Bern, Nl Hess, J1.211-1989/148, 33. There is no evidence of a "clear style" in *Mein Kampf*, however.

83   Lurker, *Hitler hinter Festungsmauern*, p. 52; Franz Hemmrich's (memoirs, p. 28) wrote that Hitler's cell increasingly came to resemble a "small study." IfZ München, ED 153. In November 1937, Rudolph Schüssler claimed that in 1924 he had delivered "the most significant material from the Sternecker period," which formed the basis of *Mein Kampf*, in two large packages to Landsberg. See Ernst Schulte-Strathaus, Central Party Archive employee, to staff director Martin Bormann, 27 Nov. 1937; BA Berlin-Lichterfelde, NS 10/55.

84   Otto Strasser, *Hitler und ich*, Konstanz, 1948, p. 78. See Ryback, *Hitler's Private Library*, p 69. The Bruckmanns sent the Chamberlain books to the prison, see Martynkewicz, *Salon Deutschland*, p. 410. On the influence of Paul de Lagarde on Hitler see Ulrich Sieg, "Ein Prophet nationaler Religion: Paul de Lagarde und die völkische Bewegung," in Friedrich Wilhelm Graf (ed.), *Intellektuellen-Götter*, Munich, 2009, pp. 1–19.

85   See Ryback, *Hitler's Private Library*, pp. 66–71 (quote on p. 71). On Ford also see Reuth, *Hitler*, pp. 174f.

86   See Timothy Ryback, *Hitlers Bücher: Seine Bibliothek—sein Denken*, Cologne, 2010, pp. 126–49 (chapter not included in the earlier English and American editions).That Hitler had read the work of Madison Grant is confirmed by his speech in Zirkus Krone on 6 April 1927; Adolf Hitler, *Reden, Schriften, Anordnungen—Februar 1925 bis Januar 1933. Vol. 2: Vom Weimarer Parteitag bis zur Reichstagswahl Juli 1926–Mai 1928. Part 1: Juli 1926–Juli 1927*, ed. and annotated Bärbel Dusik, Munich, London, New York and Paris, 1992, no. 99, p. 236.

87   See Ryback, *Hitler's Private Library*, p. 114f; Wagener, *Hitler aus nächster Nähe*, p. 149. For a selection of Hitler's reading see Chapter 2, p. 32.

88   See also the analysis of Eberhard Jäckel, still the standard on the subject, in *Hitlers Weltanschauung: Entwurf einer Herrschaft*, Stuttgart, 1981. See also Barbara Zehnpfennig, *Hitlers "Mein Kampf": Eine Interpretation*, 2nd edition, Munich, 2002, which endeavours to make "something comprehensible" out of the text (p. 32).

89   Hitler, *Mein Kampf*, p. 372.

90   Ibid., pp. 312, 314, 316.

91   Quotations in ibid., pp. 372, 317, 422.

92   Ibid., p. 317.

93   Hitler, *Sämtliche Aufzeichnungen*, no. 654, p. 1242.

94   Hitler, *Mein Kampf*, pp. 69f.

95   Saul Friedländer, *Das Dritte Reich und die Juden: Die Jahre der Verfolgung 1933–1939*, Munich, 1998, pp. 87ff., particularly pp. 104, 113f.

96   See the overview in Jäckel, *Hitlers Weltanschauung*, p. 69.

97   Hitler, *Mein Kampf*, p. 772. See Hitler's speech at Zirkus Krone, 13 April 1927; Hitler, *Reden, Schriften, Anordnungen*, vol. 2, part 1, no. 104, pp. 259f.

98   See Hess, *Briefe*, p. 345 (dated 10 July 1924). But Bruno Hipler, *Hitlers Lehrmeister: Karl Haushofer als Vater der NS-Ideologie*, St. Ottilien, 1996, pp. 159, 207, completely exaggerates the situation when he calls Haushofer the "spiritual father" of the Nazi world view and the "inspiration" behind *Mein Kampf*. For a critical perspective see Plöckinger, *Geschichte eines Buches*, pp. 144f. See also Karl Lange, "Der Terminus 'Lebensraum' in Hitlers *Mein Kampf*," in *Vierteljahrshefte für Zeitgeschichte*, 13 (1965), pp. 426–37.

99   See Axel Kuhn, *Hitlers aussenpolitisches Programm*, Stuttgart, 1970, p. 115. While in Landsberg, Hitler read Haushofer's 1913 book about Japan, *Dai Nihonaus*, which uses the example of Japan to illustrate the necessity of war for survival among peoples. See Hess, *Briefe*, p. 328 (dated 19 May 1924). On the content of the book see Hippler, *Hitlers Lehrmeister*, pp. 29ff.

100   Hitler, *Mein Kampf*, p. 154.

101   Ibid., pp. 739, 742.

102   Ibid., p. 743.

103   Victor Klemperer, *LTI: Notizbuch eines Philologen*, 24th edition, fully revised, ed. and annotated Elke Fröhlich, Stuttgart, 2010, p. 34. See also Joachim Riecker, *Hitlers 9. November: Wie der Erste Weltkrieg zum Holocaust führte*, Berlin, 2009, p. 87: "There are few politicians who, before taking power, so openly described their fundamental convictions and allowed such a free view into their emotional lives as Adolf Hitler."

104   See Karl Lange, *Hitlers unbeachtete Maximen: Mein Kampf und die Öffentlichkeit*, Stuttgart, 1968, pp. 30, 144–7.

105   Strasser, *Hitler und ich*, pp. 79f.

106   Plöckinger, *Geschichte eines Buches*, p. 362. See also, critically, Michael Wildt, *Geschichte des Nationalsozialismus*, Göttingen, 2008, p. 37.

107   Quoted in Plöckinger, *Geschichte eines Buches*, pp. 225–7.

108   Hellmut von Gerlach, "Duell Hitler-Schleicher," in *Die Weltbühne*, 14 June 1932, p. 875 (reprinted 1978). See Plöckinger, *Geschichte eines Buches*, pp. 228–40.

109   See Plöckinger, *Geschichte eines Buches*, pp. 405f., 424–9, 443f.

110   See Hess, *Briefe*, p. 351 (dated 20 Aug. 1924): "He's as impatient as a child for his release on 1 Oct."

111   Hitler, *Sämtliche Aufzeichnungen*, no. 26, p. 1270. On the relationship between Hitler and Werlin see Eberhard Reuss, *Hitlers Rennschlachten: Die Silberpfeile unterm Hakenkreuz*, Berlin, 2006, pp. 40–5. Also, Hitler, *Monologe*, p. 259 (dated 3/4 Feb. 1942): "The first thing I bought after being released from prison on 20 Dec. 1924 was a Mercedes compressor."

112   Franz Hemmrich's memoirs, p. 37; IfZ München, ED 153.

113   Deuerlein, *Aufstieg*, pp. 238f.

114   Otto Gritschneder, *Bewährungsfrist für den Terroristen Adolf H.: Der Hitler-Putsch und die bayerische Justiz*, Munich, 1990, pp. 101f.

115   Ibid., pp. 103–7, 114–18. In late Sep. 1924 Justice Minister Gürtner also officially protested against the "conditional pardon" issued to Hitler and Kriebel, arguing that both were suspected of maintaining "contact with dissolved organisations." BayHStA München, Nl Held 727.

116   Hermann Fobke to Ludolf Haase, 2 Oct. 1924; Jochmann, *Nationalsozialismus und Revolution*, doc. 48, p. 157.

117   See Alfons Probst (member of the state assembly) to State President Held, 22 Sept. 1924, on the memo dated 16 Sept. 1924 from Ministerial Councillor Josef Pultar, secretary to the president of the Austrian National Council in Vienna; BayHStA München, Nl Held 731. Report of the *Regensburger Anzeiger*, 7 Nov. 1924, "Hitlers Staatsangehörigkeit (mit hs. Zusatz des Sohnes von Held)"; ibid., Nl Held 730. See also Deuerlein, *Aufstieg*, p. 239f.; Donald Cameron Watt, "Die bayerischen Bemühungen um Ausweisung Hitlers 1924," in *Vierteljahrshefte für Zeitgeschichte*, 6 (1958), pp. 270–80.

118   Hitler, *Sämtliche Aufzeichnungen*, no. 664, pp. 1246f. (entry for 16 Oct. 1924). See Hess, *Briefe*, p. 353 (dated 14 Oct. 1924): Austria "has revoked the tribune's citizenship . . . We are rejoicing!"

119   See Plöckinger, *Geschichte eines Buches*, pp. 74f.; Franz Jetzinger, *Hitlers Jugend: Phantasien, Lügen und Wahrheit*, Vienna, 1956, pp. 279f. (see p. 272 for the facsimile of Hitler's application, dated 7 April 1925).

120   See Gritschneder, *Bewährungsfrist*, pp. 119–30. The telegram from the Bavarian state prosecutor to the management of Landsberg Prison, dated 20 Dec. 1924, in BA Berlin-Lichterfelde NS 26/67.

121   G. Feder's diaries, vol. 6 (entry for 8 Dec. 1924): "Heavy defeat" for the National Socialists; IfZ München, ED 874.

122   Maria Hof to State President Held, 16 Dec. 1924; BayHStA München, Nl Held 729.

123   Hitler, *Monologe*, p. 260 (dated 3/4 Feb. 1942). On 18 Nov. 1938, Hitler visited Landsberg and had his assistant Brückner present gifts to two guards, whom he still recognised. Daily diaries of Max Wünsche, dated 18 Nov. 1938; BA Berlin-Lichterfelde, NS 10/125.

124   Hess, *Briefe*, p. 359 (entry for 20 Dec. 1924). According to Rudolf Buttmann's diary, entry for 20 Dec. 1924, Director Leybold refused Strasser admittance to the facility, citing Hitler's wish that there be no "leaving ceremonies"; BayHStA München, Nl Buttmann 82.

125   See Rudolf Buttmann's diary entry about a conversation at the Bechsteins' house in Berlin on 19 June 1925, in which Hitler articulated "his disappointment with Ludendorff since he let the three of them escape during the night of 8/9 Nov. 1923"; BayHStA München, Nl Buttmann 82.

126   Hess, *Briefe*, p. 357 (dated 11 Dec. 1924).

127   See Heinrich Hoffmann, *Hitler wie ich ihn sah: Aufzeichnungen seines Leibfotographen*, Munich and Berlin, 1974, pp. 41f.; *Das Hitler-Bild: Die Erinnerungen des Fotografen Heinrich Hoffmann*, ed. Joe J. Heydecker, St. Pölten and Salzburg, 2008, pp. 61f.; Rudolf Herz, *Hoffmann & Hitler: Fotografie als Medium des Führer-Mythos*, Munich, 1994, p. 95.

128   Hitler, *Monologe*, p. 260 (dated 3/4 Feb. 1942).

129   Martynkewicz, *Salon Deutschland*, pp. 409–11.

130   Hanfstaengl, *Zwischen Weissem und Braunem Haus*, pp. 163f. See also the account of Christmas Eve in Hanfstaengl's unpublished memoirs, pp. 128f.; BSB München, Nl Hanfstaengl Ana 405, Box 47.

131   First newsletter to local group leaders and VB representatives in Bavaria, 31 Dec. 1924; BA Berlin-Lichterfelde, NS 26/88.

132   Emil Hamm to Hermann Fobke, 11 Jan. 1925; Plöckinger, *Geschichte eines Buches*, p. 65.

133   BayHStA München, Nl Held 730. See Adalbert Volck to Hermann Fobke, 15 Jan. 1925: "Hitler has to step up before the end of the year. Now those who are indecisive and complaining are doing the talking." BA Berlin-Lichterfelde, NS 26/899.

8   *Führer on Standby*

1   Ernst Hanfstaengl, *Zwischen Weissem und Braunem Haus: Erinnerungen eines politischen Aussenseiters*, Munich, 1970, p. 167. Hanfstaengl originally wrote in his unpublished memoirs (p. 125): "The next time I'm not going to fall off the high wire." BSB München, Nl Hanfstaengl Ana 405, Box 47.

2   Adolf Hitler, *Reden, Schriften, Anordnungen—Februar 1925 bis Januar 1933. Vol. 1: Die Wiedergründung der NSDAP Februar 1925–Juni 1926*, ed. and annotated Clemens Vollnhals, Munich, 1992, doc. 50, p. 99 (dated 12 June 1925).

3   Ibid., doc. 51, p. 102 (dated 14 June 1925). See ibid., doc. 54, p. 105 (dated 5 July 1925), doc. 55, p. 116 (dated 8 July 1925): "That is why this city is holy ground for me and the movement."

4   See Peter Longerich, *Deutschland 1918–1933: Die Weimarer Republik*, Hannover, 1995, pp. 16off., 231ff.; Heinrich August Winkler, *Weimar 1918–1933: Die Geschichte der ersten deutschen Demokratie*, Munich, 1993, pp. 306ff.

5   On what follows see Peter Gay, *Weimar Culture: The Outside as Insider*, new edition, New York, 2002; Ursula Büttner, *Weimar: Die überforderte Republik 1918–1933*, Stuttgart, 2008, p. 298ff.; Peter Hoeres, *Die Kultur von Weimar: Durchbruch der Moderne*, Berlin-Brandenburg, 2008, pp. 84ff.

6   Sebastian Haffner, *Geschichte eines Deutschen: Die Erinnerungen 1914–1933*, Stuttgart and Munich, 2000, p. 72; see Jürgen Peter Schmied, *Sebastian Haffner: Eine Biographie*, Munich, 2010, p. 30.

7   *Bayerischer Anzeiger*, 21 Jan. 1925; BayHStA München, Nl Held 730.

8   Rudolf Hess, *Briefe 1908–1933*, ed. Rüdiger Hess, Munich and Vienna, 1987, p. 364 (dated 2 March 1925). See G. Feder's diaries, vol. 7 (entry for 13 March 1925): "Hitler in Berlin . . . Full of confidence a[nd] strength." IfZ München, ED 874. Rudolf Hess had been released from Landsberg prison on 30 Dec. 1924, and through Karl Haushofer found part-time employment at the "German Academy." A position of trust at Hitler's side seemed more appealing, however, not least because it was better paid. Rudolf Hess to Klara Hess, 11 Jan. 1925; BA Bern, Nl Hess, J1.211-1989/148, 31.

9   Otto Strasser, *Hitler und ich*, Konstanz, 1948, p. 82. The previous quote in *Bayerischer Anzeiger*, 9 Jan. 1925; BayHStA München, Nl. Held 730. According to Gregor Strasser, Pöhner had arranged for Hitler to have access to Held at a meeting of the People's Bloc (Völkischer Block) parliamentary fraction to the Bavarian Landtag. Diary of R. Buttmann, entry for 12 Jan. 1925; BayHStA München, Nl Buttmann 82.

10   Hitler, *Reden, Schriften, Anordnungen*, vol. 1, doc. 1 and 2, pp. 1–6 (quote on p. 3). Hitler sent Gregor Strasser an advance copy of the statement with the note: "Only now is he once again a political somebody." Diary of R. Buttmann, entry for 26 Feb. 1925; BayHStA München, Nl Buttmann 82.

11   Hitler, *Reden, Schriften, Anordnungen*, vol. 1, doc. 4, pp. 7–9 (quote on p. 9).

12   Ibid., doc. 6, pp. 14–28 (quotes on pp. 20, 21, 27). Gottfried Feder characterised Hitler's speech as a "masterly mix of the purest demagoguery . . . and the purest patriotism." G. Feder's diaries, vol. 7 (entry for 27 Feb. 1925); IfZ München, ED 874.

13   Hess, *Briefe*, p. 363 (dated 2 March 1925); see diary of R. Buttmann, entry for 27 Feb. 1925; BayHStA München, Nl Buttmann 82; Brigitte Hamann, *Winifred Wagner oder Hitlers Bayreuth*, Munich and Zurich, 2002, pp. 134f.

14   See Mathias Rösch, *Die Münchner NSDAP 1925–1933: Eine Untersuchung zur inneren Struktur der NSDAP in der Weimarer Republik*, Munich, 2002, pp. 170–4. On the foundation of the Nazi faction of the Bavarian Landtag see Rudolf Buttmann's diary entries for 22 Sept., 24 Sept., 27 Sept. 1925; BayHStA München, Nl Buttmann 83. For more on Buttmann's role see Susanne Wanninger, "Dr. Rudolf Buttmann— Parteimitglied Nr. 4 und Generaldirektor der Münchner Staatsbibliothek," in Marita Krauss (ed.), *Rechte Karrieren in München: Von der Weimarer Zeit bis in die Nachkriegsjahre*, Munich, 2010, pp. 80–94. The local chapters of the National Socialist Working Association in northern Germany subordinated themselves to the reconstituted NSDAP in late February 1925. See the circular from Ludolf Haase dated 28 Feb. 1925; BA Berlin-Lichterfelde, NS 26/899.

15   Hitler, *Reden, Schriften, Anordnungen*, vol. 1, doc. 6, p. 20.

16   Karl Alexander von Müller, *Im Wandel einer Welt: Erinnerungen*, ed. Otto Alexander von Müller, Munich, 1966, p. 301. See Wolfgang Martynkewicz, *Salon Deutschland: Geist und Macht 1900–1945*, Berlin, 2009, pp. 412–14; Miriam Käfer, "Hitlers frühe Förderer aus dem Grossbürgertum: Das Verlegerehepaar Elsa und Hugo Bruckmann," in Krauss (ed.), *Rechte Karrieren in München*, p. 63.

17   Hitler, *Reden, Schriften, Anordnungen*, vol. 1, doc. 6, p. 28n9.

18   Ibid., doc. 14–16, pp. 40–7; doc. 19–39, pp. 52–72 (quote on p. 59).

19   Ibid., doc. 40, p. 73 (dated 4 April 1925).

20   Hanfstaengl, *Zwischen Weissem und Braunem Haus*, p. 180. In his unpublished memoirs, Hanfstaengl quotes Hitler saying with satisfaction: "Finally we're rid of him." BSB München, Nl Hanfstaengl Ana 405, Box 47. See the interview with Hermann Esser dated 13 March 1964, vol. 1: "Hitler was naturally happy as a lark. For him that was the end of the matter." BayHStA München, Nl Esser.

21   Escherich's diaries, looking back at April 1925; BayHStA München, Nl Escherich 12.

22 Hitler, *Reden, Schriften, Anordnungen*, vol. 1, doc. 42, pp. 76f. (dated 28 April 1925). See also Rudolf Hess to his parents, 24 April 1925: "Many obstacles will now be removed for the tribune, and that might even be decisive." BA Bern, Nl Hess, J1.211-1989/148, 35.

23 See Bettina Amm, *Die Ludendorff-Bewegung: Vom nationalsozialistischen Kampfbund zur völkischen Weltanschauungssekte*, Hamburg, 2006.

24 Hitler, *Reden, Schriften, Anordnungen*, vol. 1, doc. 4, p. 9. On what follows see Peter Longerich, *Die braunen Bataillone: Geschichte der SA*, Munich, 1989, pp. 45–52; Transcript of an interview with Franz Pfeffer von Salomon dated 20 Feb 1953; IfZ München, ZS 177.

25 R. Buttmann's diaries, entry for 21 Feb. 1925; BayHStA München, Nl Buttmann 82. On what follows see Udo Kissenkoetter, *Gregor Strasser und die NSDAP*, Stuttgart, 1978, pp. 16–22: idem, "Gregor Strasser," in Ronald Smelser and Rainer Zitelmann (eds), *Die Braune Elite: 22 biographische Skizzen*, Darmstadt, 1989, pp. 273ff.

26 Gregor Strasser to Joseph Goebbels, 11 Nov. 1925; Albrecht Tyrell, *Führer befiehl . . . Selbstzeugnisse aus der "Kampfzeit" der NSDAP: Dokumentation und Analyse*, Düsseldorf, 1969, doc. 46, p. 115.

27 Ibid., doc. 50a, p. 121.

28 See Hinrich Lohse, "Der Fall Strasser," undated memorandum (*c.* 1952); IfZ München, ZS 265. Figures from Ian Kershaw, *Hitler 1889–1936: Hubris*, London, 1998, p. 270.

29 Quoted in Ralf Georg Reuth, *Goebbels*, Munich and Zurich, 1990, pp. 76f.; see also Peter Longerich, *Joseph Goebbels: A Biography*, London, 2015, pp. 3ff. See *Die Tagebücher von Joseph Goebbels. Part 1: Aufzeichnungen 1923–1941*, ed. Elke Fröhlich, Munich, 1998, vol. 1, p. 108 (entry for 20 March 1924): "Hitler is an idealist who's full of enthusiasm. When I read his speeches, I'm buoyed by them and allow them to carry me to the stars."

30 Goebbels, *Tagebücher*, part 1, vol. 1, p. 353 (entry for 11 Sept. 1925).

31 Ibid., p. 344 (entry for 21 Aug. 1925).

32 According to Hermann Fobke's report on the founding of the Working Association Northwest, dated 11 Sept. 1925; Werner Jochmann, *Nationalsozialismus und Revolution: Ursprung und Geschichte der NSDAP in Hamburg 1922–1933. Dokumente*, Frankfurt am Main, 1963, doc. 66, pp. 207–11 (quote on p. 209).

33 Ibid., doc. 67, p. 213. See also Gerhard Schildt, "Die Arbeitsgemeinschaft Nord-West: Untersuchungen zur Geschichte der NSDAP 1925/26," diss. Freiburg, 1964, pp. 105–14.

34 Goebbels, *Tagebücher*, part 1, vol. 1/1, p. 365 (entry for 14 Oct. 1925). On the Gauleiter convention in Weimar on 12 July 1925 see ibid., p. 326 (entry for 14 July 1925); G. Feder's diaries, vol. 7 (entry for 12 July 1925); IfZ München, ED 874.

35 Goebbels, *Tagebücher*, part 1, vol. 1/1, p. 375 (entry for 6 Nov. 1925). On 20 Nov. 1925, Hitler and Goebbels met again at an event in Plauen and once again Goebbels noted: "He greeted and welcomed me like an old friend. How I like him! What a fellow!" ibid., p. 379 (entry for 23 Nov. 1925).

36 Extract from Strasser's draft manifesto in Tyrell, *Führer befiehl*, doc. 49a, p. 119; reprinted in full in Reinhard Kühnl, "Zur Programmatik der nationalsozialistischen Linken: Das Strasser-Programm von 1925/26," in *Vierteljahrshefte für Zeitgeschichte*, 14 (1966), pp. 317–33.

37 See Tyrell, *Führer befiehl*, doc. 48, pp. 117–19.

38 See Schildt, "Arbeitsgemeinschaft," pp. 140–53. Feder's appearance was by no means a surprise, in contrast to how Goebbels depicted it in his diaries (part 1, vol. 1/1, p. 48, entry for 25 Jan. 1926). Feder had told Goebbels he would be coming in a letter on 23 Dec. 1925; see Longerich, *Goebbels*, p. 65.

39 Adolf Hitler, *Monologe im Führerhauptquartier 1941–1944: Die Aufzeichnungen Heinrich Heims*, ed. Werner Jochmann, Hamburg, 1980, p. 259 (dated 3/4 Feb. 1942). See ibid., p. 307 (dated 28 Feb./1 March 1942). See also Hamann, *Winifred Wagner*, pp. 138–42; Elsa Bruckmann to Hitler, Bayreuth, 26 July 1925; copy in BA Koblenz, N 1128/30.

At an NSDAP event in Bayreuth on 29 July 1925, Hitler declared that "even as a young man, he had wanted to attend the Wagner festival, and now his wish had come true." Hitler, *Reden, Schriften, Anordnungen*, vol. 1, doc. 58, p. 139.

40 See the diary entries of Rudolf Buttmann, who visited Hitler three times in Berchtesgaden in Sept. 1925. On 25 Sept., Alfred Rosenberg—the editor in chief of the *Völkischer Beobachter*—complained that he had not seen Hitler for three months. "Important letters are still going unanswered," Rosenberg fretted. On the evening of 26 Sept., Hitler went to Nuremberg before heading to a "German Day" in neighbouring Fürth the following day. Buttmann held his first conference with Hitler in the party's Munich headquarters on 14 Oct. On 18 Dec. Hitler declared that he would remain in Munich until April to "take care of organisational work." See Buttmann's diary entries for 4, 9, 11, 18, 25, 26, 27 Sept., 14 Oct., 18 Dec. 1925; BayHStA München, Nl Buttmann 83.

41 Hitler, *Reden Schriften Anordnungen*, vol. 1, doc. 74, p. 175.

42 See Gregor Strasser to Joseph Goebbels, 8 Jan. 1926. Strasser wrote that Feder had received the draft manifesto and would try to "warm Hitler up for it." Jochmann, *Nationalsozialismus und Revolution*, doc. 71, p. 220. On 30 Jan. 1926, after the second Hanover conference, Feder told Hitler and Hess about Strasser's "ambush." Hitler agreed with Feder's "annihilating criticism" of Strasser's draft programme. G. Feder's diaries, vol. 8 (entry for 30 Jan. 1926); IfZ München, ED 874. See also R. Buttmann to his wife, 11 Feb. 1926: "Strasser has drawn up a draft platform . . . that is said to be terrible." BayHStA München, Nl Buttmann 63,2.

43 Goebbels, *Tagebücher*, part 1, vol. 1/2, p. 52 (entry for 6 Feb. 1926).

44 Ibid., p. 53 (entry for 11 Feb. 1926).

45 Hitler, *Reden, Schriften, Anordnungen*, vol. 1, doc. 101, pp. 294–6 (dated 14 Feb. 1926); Hinrich Lohse, "Der Fall Strasser," undated memorandum (*c.* 1952); IfZ München, ZS 265. Buttmann, who only grudgingly participated in the Bamberg conference and had driven back to Munich that evening with Strasser and Esser, noted that, in particular, Hitler had rejected "Strasser's support for the whole business of seizing aristocratic property and his foreign policy fantasies." See R. Buttmann's diary entry for 14 Feb. 1926; BayHStA München, Nl Buttmann 83: R. Buttmann to his wife, 11 Feb. 1926; ibid., Nl Buttmann 63,2. On the Bamberg conference see Schildt, "Arbeitsgemeinschaft," pp. 155–65.

46 Goebbels, *Tagebücher*, part 1, vol. 1/2, p. 55 (entry for 15 Feb. 1926).

47 Ibid., p. 55 (entry for 15 Feb. 1926). G. Feder's diaries, vol. 8 (entry for 14 Feb. 1926): "Hitler took him to task sentence by sentence." IfZ München, ED 874.

48 BA Berlin-Lichterfelde, NS 26/900; see also Jochmann, *Nationalsozialismus und Revolution*, doc. 74, p. 225 (entry for 5 March 1926).

49 See Joachim Fest, *Hitler: Eine Biographie*, Frankfurt am Main, Berlin and Vienna, 1973, p. 342.

50 Adolf Hitler, *Reden, Schriften, Anordnungen—Februar 1925 bis Januar 1933. Vol. 2: Vom Weimarer Parteitag bis zur Reichstagswahl Juli 1926–Mai 1928. Part 1: Juli 1926–Juli 1927*, ed. and annotated Bärbel Dusik, Munich, 1992, doc. 29, p. 64. See Udo Kissenkoetter, *Gregor Strasser und die NSDAP*, Stuttgart 1978, p. 31.

51 Interview with Hermann Esser dated 16 March 1964, vol. 1; BayHStA München, Nl Esser.

52 For the following quotes see Goebbels, *Tagebücher*, part 1, vol. 1/2, pp. 71–3 (entry for 13 April 1926).

53 Ibid., p. 76 (entry for 19 April 1926).

54 Ibid., p. 96 (entry for 16 June 1926).

55 Ibid., pp. 111f. (entries for 23 and 24 July 1926). In December 1926, Hitler gave Goebbels "the very first copy" of the second volume of *Mein Kampf*. Goebbels read it on his return trip to Berlin "with feverish anticipation." He wrote: "The real Hitler just as he is! I sometimes almost cried out in joy." Ibid., p. 159 (entry for 12 Dec. 1926).

56 Ibid., p. 89 (entry for 24 May 1926): "He heaps praise on me in public." On the party conference of 22 May 1926 see Hitler, *Reden, Schriften, Anordnungen*, vol. 1, doc. 143–146, pp. 428–65 (quotations on pp. 437, 461, 464, 441, 444).

57 Goebbels, *Tagebücher* part 1, vol. 1/2, p. 103 (entry for 6 July 1926). On the party rally in Weimar on 3 and 4 July 1926 see Hitler, *Reden, Schriften, Anordnungen*, vol. 2, part 1, doc. 3–7, pp. 4–25; diaries of G. Feder, vol. 8 (entries for 3/4 July 1926); IfZ München, ED 874. According to Buttmann, the Hitler greeting was trotted out for the first time in Weimar. R. Buttmann's diary entry for 4 July 1926; BayHStA Müchen, Nl Buttmann 83. See also Volker Mauersberger, *Hitler in Weimar: Der Fall einer deutschen Kulturstadt*, Berlin, 1999, pp. 222–8.

58 Quoted in Wolfgang Horn, *Der Marsch zur Machtergreifung: Die NSDAP bis 1933*, Düsseldorf, 1980, p. 276.

59 Figures from Ernst Deuerlein (ed.), *Der Aufstieg der NSDAP in Augenzeugenberichten*, Munich, 2nd edition, 1976, pp. 254, 291; Kershaw, *Hitler: Hubris*, pp. 690–1n250; Ludolf Herbst, *Hitlers Charisma: Die Erfindung eines deutschen Messias*, Frankfurt am Main, 2010, p. 224.

60 Rösch, *Die Münchner NSDAP*, pp. 213, 529. See also Andreas Heusler, *Das Braune Haus: Wie München zur "Hauptstadt der Bewegung" wurde*, Munich, 2008, pp. 110, 123. These sources belie Hitler's contention at an NSDAP event on 13 April 1926 "that the party experienced continuous, major growth in membership both within Munich and without." Hitler, *Reden, Schriften, Anordnungen*, vol. 1, doc. 123, p. 375.

61 See Rösch, *Die Münchner NSDAP*, pp. 206f., 210f., 530.

62 R. Buttmann to his wife, 3 Feb. 1927; BayHStA München, Nl Buttmann 63,2. See Goebbels, *Tagebücher* part 1, vol. 1/2, p. 179 (entry for 5 Feb 1927): "Hitler is said to be furious with me. We'll see."

63 On the election results see Jürgen Falter, Thomas Lindenberger and Siegfried Schumann, *Wahlen und Abstimmungen in der Weimarer Republik: Materialien zum Wahlverhalten 1919–1931*, Munich, 1986, pp. 98, 108, 111.

64 Hess, *Briefe*, p. 375 (dated 23 Jan. 1927). See also Rudolf Hess to Ilse Pröhl, 23 Jan. 1927: ". . . the tribune is convinced that this year will be the big year. He was glowing again today: 'Hess, you will see that I'm not mistaken!!!'" BA Bern, Nl Hess, J1.211-1989/148, 39. In Nov. 1925 Hitler declared he had a "feeling" that the movement would make a "mighty leap" in 1926. R. Buttmann's diary for 14 Nov. 1925; BayHStA München, Nl Buttmann 83.

65 Quoted in David Clay Large, *Where Ghosts Walked: Munich's Road to the Third Reich*, New York and London, 1997, p. 215.

66 Theodor Heuss, *Politik: Ein Nachschlagewerk für Theorie und Praxis*, Halberstadt, 1927, p. 138; quoted in Rösch, *Die Münchner NSDAP*, p. 533.

67 Detlev Clemens, *Herr Hitler in Germany: Wahrnehmungen und Deutungen des Nationalsozialismus in Grossbritannien 1920 bis 1939*, Göttingen and Zurich, 1996, p. 118.

68 Deuerlein, *Aufstieg*, pp. 269–79 (quotes on pp. 270, 271, 272). On the "long wait" for Hitler see the diaries of R. Buttmann, entry for 9 March 1925; BayHStA München, Nl Buttmann 83. The *Völkischer Beobachter* of 11 March 1927 carried a relatively short report on the meeting because the stenographer had lost her notes (Hitler, *Reden, Schriften, Anordnungen*, vol. 2, part 1, doc. 884, pp. 179–81). See also Konrad Heiden, *Adolf Hitler: Das Zeitalter der Verantwortungslosigkeit. Eine Biographie*, Zurich, 1936, p. 226.

69 For the figures see Hitler, *Reden, Schriften, Anordnungen*, vol. 2, part 1, doc. 94, 96, 99, pp. 221, 227, 235. The quote in ibid., p. 235n3.

70 Ibid., doc. 94, 121, pp. 252, 371 (dated 16 Dec. 1925 and 11 April 1926).

71 Ibid., doc. 128, p. 397 (dated 17 April 1926).

72 Ibid., doc. 48, 94, pp. 87, 250.

73 Ibid., vol. 2, part 1, doc. 104, p. 265 (dated 13 April 1927); Adolf Hitler, *Reden, Schriften, Anordnungen—Februar 1925 bis Januar 1933. Vol. 2: Vom Weimarer Parteitag bis zur*

Reichstagswahl Juli 1926–Mai 1928. Part 2: August 1927–Mai 1928, ed. and annotated Bärbel Dusik, Munich, 1992, doc. 258, pp. 779, 789 (dated 17 April 1928).

74   Ibid., vol. 1, doc. 112, p. 354 (dated 18 March 1926); vol. 2, part 2, doc. 199, p. 560 (dated 27 Nov. 1927), doc. 224, p. 654 (dated 26 Jan. 1928); Adolf Hitler, *Reden, Schriften, Anordnungen—Februar 1925 bis Januar 1933. Vol. 3: Zwischen den Reichstagswahlen Juli 1928–September 1930. Part 1: Juli 1928–Februar 1929*, ed. Bärbel Dusik and Klaus A. Lankheit with Christian Hartmann, Munich, 1993, p. 21 (dated 13 July 1928): "Look at our culture: Negro dancing, the jimmy [i.e. shimmy], jazz bands, pathetic cubism, Dadaism, butchered literature, wretched theatre, terrible cinema, cultural devastation as far as you can see."

75   Ibid., vol. 1, doc. 61, p. 145 (dated 15 Aug. 1925).

76   Ibid., vol. 1, doc. 26, p. 57 (dated 25 March 1925), doc. 145, p. 475 (dated 22 May 1926); vol. 2, part 1, doc. 152, p. 395 (dated 26 June 1927). On the crass anti-Semitism Goebbels propagated in *Der Angriff*, which began appearing weekly in 1927, see Longerich, *Goebbels*, pp. 90–2. Goebbels's hate campaign was directed above all against Berlin Police Vice President Dr. Bernhard Weiss, who was defamed as "Isidor Weiss." See Dietz Bering, *Kampf um Namen: Bernhard Weiss gegen Joseph Goebbels*, Stuttgart, 1991, p. 241ff.

77   Hitler, *Reden, Schriften, Anordnungen*, vol. 2, part 1, doc. 146, p. 369 (dated 13 June 1927); vol. 2, part 2, doc. 235, p. 674 (dated 24 Feb. 1928).

78   Ibid., vol. 1, doc. 103, pp. 297–330 (quotes on pp. 298, 315, 318, 319f., 325). See Werner Jochmann, *Im Kampf um die Macht: Hitlers Rede vor dem Hamburger Nationalklub von 1919*, Frankfurt am Main, 1960; Manfred Asendorf, "Hamburger Nationalklub, Keppler-Kreis, Arbeitsstelle Schacht und der Aufstieg Hitlers," in *1999: Zeitschrift für Sozialgeschichte des 19. und 20. Jahrhunderts*, 2 (1987), pp. 106–50, particularly pp. 107–13; see also Kershaw, *Hitler: Hubris*, pp. 286f. Hitler also avoided any anti-Semitic statements and held "a moderate and tedious speech" when addressing Rhineland industrialists in the Hotel Düsseldorfer Hof in Königswinter on 1 Dec. 1926. Notes of Wilhelm Breucker dated 22 Oct. 1956; IfZ München, ZS 1193.

79   Hitler, *Reden, Schriften, Anordnungen*, vol. 2, part 1, doc. 80, p. 158 (dated 20 Feb. 1927). The above quotations ibid., doc. 94, p. 225 (dated 30 March 1927); doc. 62, p. 111 (dated 1 Jan. 1927).

80   Ibid., vol. 1, doc. 57, p. 136 (dated 15 July 1925), doc. 78, p. 202 (dated 8 Oct. 1925), doc. 147, p. 466 (dated 30 May 1926).

81   Ibid., vol. 2, part 2, doc. 168, p. 495 (dated 21 Aug. 1927).

82   Ibid., vol. 1, doc. 94, p. 240 (dated 16 Dec. 1925); vol. 2, part 1, doc. 7, pp. 19f. (dated 4 July 1926).

83   Ibid., vol. 2, part 1, doc. 83, p. 167 (dated 6 March 1927); doc. 102, p. 247 (dated 9 April 1927).

84   Ibid., vol. 2, part 2, doc. 197, p. 559 (dated 24 Nov. 1927); doc. 230, p. 662 (dated 1 Feb. 1928).

85   Ibid., vol. 1, doc. 136, p. 418 (dated 22 April 1926); doc. 94, p. 261 (dated 16 Dec. 1925).

86   Tyrell, *Führer befiehl*, pp. 168–73 (quotation on p. 173).

87   Goebbels, *Tagebücher*, part 1, vol. 1/3, p. 103 (entry for 16 Oct. 1928).

88   Hitler, *Reden, Schriften, Anordnungen*, vol. 1, doc. 78, pp. 199, 203 (dated 28 Oct. 1925).

89   Hanfstaengl, *Zwischen Weissem und Braunem Haus*, p. 190.

90   Hitler, *Reden, Schriften, Anordnungen*, vol. 1, doc. 92, p. 237 (dated 12 Dec. 1925); vol. 2, part 1, doc. 59, p. 106 (dated 18 Dec. 1926). See ibid., vol. 3, part 1, doc. 65, p. 350 (dated 11 Dec. 1928): "We intend to wage this struggle exactly the way the Prince of Peace has taught us." At an SS meeting in Munich on 5 Dec. 1930 Hitler declared that in their political activities National Socialists "advocate principles for which Christ was once born and for which he was persecuted and crucified by the Jews." Adolf Hitler, *Reden, Schriften, Anordnungen—Februar 1925 bis Januar 1933. Vol. 4: Von der Reichstagswahl bis zur Reichspräsidentenwahl Oktober 1930–März 1932. Part 1: Oktober 1930–Juni 1931*, ed. Constantin Goschler, Munich, 1993, doc. 38, p. 149.

91   Ibid., vol. 1, doc. 18, p. 51 (dated 22 May 1925); vol. 2, part 2, doc. 190, p. 544 (dated
      9 Nov. 1927), doc. 278, p. 844 (dated 19 May 1928).
92   Ibid., vol. 1, doc. 129, p. 398 (dated 7 April 1926); vol. 2, part 1, doc. 140, p. 341 (dated
      3 June 1927). For the idea of National Socialism as a political religion see Michael
      Burleigh, *The Third Reich: A New History*, London, 2000, pp. 114–20; Herbst, *Hitlers
      Charisma*, pp. 196–8, 207. On Hitler's appropriation of Christianity see Michael
      Rissman, *Hitlers Gott: Vorsehungsglaube und Sendungsbewusstsein eines deutschen
      Diktators*, Zurich and Munich, 2001, pp. 29–33.
93   Hitler, *Reden, Schriften, Anordnungen*, vol. 1, doc. 1, p. 3 (dated 26 Feb. 1925).
94   Ibid., vol. 2, part 2, doc. 183, p. 515 (dated 30 Sept. 1927).
95   Tyrell, *Führer befiehl*, doc. 78d, pp. 203–5 (quote on p. 204). Also in Hitler, *Reden,
      Schriften, Anordnungen*, vol. 3, part 1, doc. 4, pp. 23–6.
96   Hess, *Briefe*, p. 386 (dated 20 Nov. 1927).
97   Tyrell, *Führer befiehl*, no. 65, pp. 169, 171. See also Hitler, *Reden, Schriften, Anordnungen*,
      vol. 2, part 1, doc. 159, pp. 414f.
98   Ibid., vol. 1, doc. 159, p. 482 (dated 24 June 1926). On the "Woltereck case" see Rösch,
      Die Münchner NSDAP, p. 206.
99   Hitler, *Reden, Schriften, Anordnungen*, vol. 2, part 1, doc. 130, p. 321. On the Munich
      SA rebellion see Rösch, *Die Münchner NSDAP*, pp. 157–65.
100   Hess, *Briefe*, p. 375 (dated 23 Jan. 1927). See Otto Wagener, *Hitler aus nächster Nähe:
      Aufzeichnungen eines Vertrauten 1929–1932*, ed. Henry A. Turner, Frankfurt am Main,
      Berlin and Vienna, 1978, p. 44; Tyrell, *Führer befiehl*, p. 148.
101   Hanfstaengl, *Zwischen Weissem und Braunem Haus*, p. 182.
102   Rudolf Herz, *Hoffmann & Hitler: Fotografie als Medium des Führer-Mythos*, Munich,
      1994, pp. 162–9 (quote on p. 163). See Claudia Schmölders, *Hitlers Gesicht: Eine physio-
      gnomische Biographie*, Munich, 2000, p. 106.
103   Tyrell, *Führer befiehl*, doc. 57b, p. 156 (dated 3 July 1926). In a letter to Rudolf Hess's
      fiancée Ilse Pröhl, dated 16 Nov. 1927, Goebbels reported about a meeting with
      Hitler in Nuremberg the previous day: "What a man he is! I'm almost envious that
      you can be at his side all the time. We can all be proud of him." BA Bern, Nl Hess,
      J1.211-1993/300, Box 5. See Goebbels, *Tagebücher*, part 1, vol. 1/2, p. 291 (entry for 16
      Nov. 1927): "He is fabulously clear in his vision." On Goebbels's propagation of the
      Führer cult see Thomas Friedrich, *Die missbrauchte Hauptstadt: Hitler und Berlin*,
      Berlin, 2007, pp. 200–4.
104   Hess, *Briefe*, p. 386 (dated 20 Nov. 1927).
105   Hitler, *Reden, Schriften, Anordnungen*, vol. 2, part 2, doc. 166, pp. 485–7 (quotation
      on p. 486).
106   Report by the Reich Commissioner for Public Order on the NSDAP rally in
      Nuremberg on 19–21 Aug. 1927; Deuerlein, *Aufstieg*, pp. 279–85 (quotation on p. 280).
      See G. Feder's diaries, vol. 9 (entry for 21 Aug. 1927): "The entire SA paraded by.
      Decorated with flowers, they cheered the Führer. Hitler must have felt that this was
      a great hour." IfZ München, ED 874. Similar, Goebbels, *Tagebücher*, part 1, vol. 1/2,
      p. 258 (entry for 22 Aug. 1927). The programme for the rally is in BA Berlin-Lichterfelde,
      NS 26/390.
107   Daniel Siemens, *Horst Wessel: Tod und Verklärung eines Nationalsozialisten*, Berlin,
      2009; p. 72.
108   Tyrell, *Führer befiehl*, doc. 68d, p. 185.
109   Hitler, *Reden, Schriften, Anordnungen*, vol. 2, part 2, doc. 181, p. 514, doc. 216, p. 595,
      doc. 264, p. 794.
110   Rudolf Hess to his parents, 9 June 1925; BA Bern, Nl Hess, J1.211-1989/148, 35. See
      Hitler, *Reden, Schriften, Anordnungen*, vol. 1, doc. 52, p. 103; ibid., doc. 135, p. 416
      (dated 22 April 1926).
111   Ibid., vol. 2, part 2, doc. 11/12, p. 583 (dated 2 Jan. 1928). On Strasser's party reform
      see Kissenkoetter, *Gregor Strasser und die NSDAP*, pp. 34–40.

112   On this framework see Herbst, *Hitlers Charisma*, pp. 244f.; Rösch, *Die Münchner NSDAP*, pp. 133–7. On the Fighting League for German Culture see Martynkewicz, *Salon Deutschland*, pp. 439ff.

113   On the concept of the "war youth generation" see Ulrich Herbert, "'Generation der Sachlichkeit': Die völkische Studentenbewegung der frühen zwanziger Jahre," in Frank Bajohr, Werner Johe and Uwe Lohalm (eds), *Zivilisation und Barbarei: Die widersprüchlichen Potentiale der Moderne*, Hamburg, 1991, pp. 115–44.

114   For more on Himmler and the development of the SS see Peter Longerich, *Heinrich Himmler: Biographie*, Munich, 2008, pp. 18–125.

115   See Stefan Frech, *Wegbereiter Hitlers? Theodor Reismann-Grone: Ein völkischer Nationalist 1863–1949*, Paderborn, 2009, pp. 263–7, 285f. On Hitler's speech of 18 June 1926, see Hitler, *Reden, Schriften, Anordnungen*, vol. 1, doc. 157, pp. 478–89 (quotation on p. 480). See Goebbels, *Tagebücher*, part 1, vol. 1/2, p. 97 (entry for 19 June 1926): "Yesterday Hitler spoke to industrialists in Essen. Fabulous! . . . Hitler is up to all his tasks."

116   Hess, *Briefe*, p. 380 (dated 27 April 1927). On Hitler's speech of 27 April 1927 see Hitler, *Reden, Schriften, Anordnungen*, vol. 2, part 1, doc. 112, pp. 285f.

117   Hitler, *Reden, Schriften, Anordnungen*, vol. 2, part 2, doc. 174, pp. 501–9 (quotations on pp. 508, 505). Further, see Henry A. Turner, *Die Grossunternehmer und der Aufstieg Hitlers*, Berlin, 1986, pp. 113–15; Martynkewicz, *Salon Deutschland*, pp. 435–7; Käfer, "Hitlers frühe Förderer," pp. 64f. Later Hitler reported that after their conversation Kirdorf had "paid almost all the party's debts and got it back on its feet." Albert Speer, *Spandauer Tagebücher*, Munich, 2002, p. 123 (entry for 20 Oct. 1947). See Goebbels, *Tagebücher*, part 1, vol. 3/2, p. 252 (entry for 15 Nov. 1936).

118   Quoted in Turner, *Grossunternehmer*, p. 111. In a letter to his son Hermann on 29 Nov. 1927, Reusch wrote: "I cannot say that I discovered much intellectual about [Hitler's ideas]." Christian Marx, *Paul Reusch und die Gutehoffnungshütte: Leitung eines deutschen Grossunternehmens*, Göttingen, 2013, p. 321.

119   Rudolf Hess to his parents, 14 Dec. 1927; BA Bern, Nl Hess, J1.211-1989/148, 39.

120   Kirdorf to Hitler, 8 Aug. 1929; quoted in Dirk Stegmann, "Zum Verhältnis von Grossindustrie und Nationalsozialismus 1930–1933," in *Archiv für Sozialgeschichte*, 13 (1973), pp. 399–482 (quotation on p. 414). In a letter congratulating Kirdorf on his 87th birthday on 8 April 1934, Hitler thanked him again for his contribution to the "revival of our German people and empire." BA Berlin-Lichterfelde, NS 10/123. When Kirdorf died on 13 July 1938, Hitler took part in his funeral. See daily diaries of Max Wünsche, dated 13, 14 and 16 July 1938; BA Berlin-Lichterfelde, NS 10/125.

121   Hitler, *Reden, Schriften, Anordnungen*, vol. 2, part 2, doc. 209, p. 587. See Goebbels, *Tagebücher*, part 1, vol. 1/2, p. 301 (entry for 12 Dec. 1927): "The boss was generally in good spirits. The cause is coming along well on all fronts."

122   R. Buttmann's diary entry for 4 Jan. 1928; BayHStA München, Nl Buttmann 85.

123   Hitler, *Reden, Schriften, Anordnungen*, vol. 2, part 2, doc. 272, pp. 836f. (dated 14 May 1928).

124   Goebbels, *Tagebücher*, part 1, vol. 1/2, p. 368 (entry for 13 May 1928).

125   On the results of the Reichstag election see Peter D. Stachura, "Der kritische Wendepunkt? Die NSDAP und die Reichstagswahlen vom 20. 5. 1928," in *Vierteljahrshefte für Zeitgeschichte*, 26 (1978), pp. 66–99 (tables on pp. 84f.).

126   Hitler, *Reden, Schriften, Anordnungen*, vol. 2, part 2, doc. 279, p. 847 (dated 20 May 1928). See Hess, *Briefe*, pp. 392f. (dated 28 June 1928): "What is better, stronger and more powerful has prevailed because of natural selection and now exists as a single party with an ethnic orientation."

127   Deuerlein, *Aufstieg*, p. 293; Goebbels, *Tagebücher*, part 1, vol. 1/2, p. 373 (entry for 21 May 1928).

128   See Longerich, *Goebbels*, p. 100. On the temporary ban between May 1927 and April 1928 see ibid., pp. 104–9. On the development of the Berlin NSDAP under

the leadership of Goebbels see Andreas Wirsching, *Vom Weltkrieg zum Bürgerkrieg? Politischer Extremismus in Deutschland und Frankreich 1918–1933/39: Berlin und Paris im Vergleich*, Munich, 1999, pp. 437–54; Friedrich, *Die missbrauchte Hauptstadt*, pp. 160ff.

129　R. Buttmann's diary entries for 4 and 10 July 1928; BayHStA München, Nl Buttmann 85. On the election results in Munich see Rösch, *Die Münchner NSDAP*, pp. 227, 534.

130　Quoted in Richard J. Evans, *The Coming of the Third Reich*, London, 2004, p. 209; see Stachura, "Wendepunkt," p. 93.

131　Hitler, *Reden, Schriften, Anordnungen*, vol. 2, part 2, doc. 203, pp. 570–82.

132　Ibid., vol. 2, part 2, doc. 254, pp. 771f. (dated 13 April 1928).

133　Hitler, *Monologe*, pp. 206f. (dated 16/17 Jan. 1942). On the dating of the rental agreement see Anton Joachimsthaler, *Hitlers Liste: Ein Dokument persönlicher Beziehungen*, Munich, 2003, pp. 285, 288f. Ulrich Chaussy, *Nachbar Hitler: Führerkult und Heimatzerstörung am Obersalzberg*, 6th revised and extended edition, Berlin, 2007, p. 46, erroneously gives spring 1927 as the date. Elsa Bruckmann, Winifred Wagner and Helene Bechstein helped with the furnishing of the Wachenfeld guesthouse. See Joachimsthaler, *Hitlers Liste*, p. 124; Käfer, "Hitlers frühe Förderer," p. 59. Helene Bechstein shared Hitler's preference for the Obersalzberg. On 27 July 1926 she told Rudolf Hess that she was delighted that "Wolf" was able to relax there for a few days: "Hopefully he will find a house up there someday. I won't give up on that plan." BA Bern, Nl Hess, J1.211-1993/300, Box 2. In Feb. 1927 the Bechsteins bought a house for themselves on the Obersalzberg from an industrialist from Fürth; see Joachimsthaler, *Hitlers Liste*, p. 87f.

134　Hitler, *Reden, Schriften, Anordnungen—Februar 1925 bis Januar 1933. Vol. 6: Register, Karten, Nachträge*, ed. Katja Klee, Christian Hartmann and Klaus A. Lankheit, Munich, 2003, doc. 8, pp. 325f. (dated 17 May 1926). See Othmar Plöckinger, *Geschichte eines Buches: Adolf Hitlers "Mein Kampf" 1922–1945*, Munich, 2006, pp. 159f.; Timothy W. Ryback, *Hitler's Private Library: The Books That Shaped His Life*, London, 2009, pp.79–84; Heimo Schwilk, *Ernst Jünger: Ein Jahrhundertleben*, Munich and Zurich, 2007, p. 289.

135　Quoted in Martynkewicz, *Salon Deutschland*, p. 425.

136　Gerhard L. Weinberg (ed.), *Hitlers Zweites Buch: Ein Dokument aus dem Jahr 1928*, Stuttgart, 1961. Reprinted in Hitler, *Reden, Schriften, Anordnungen—Februar 1925 bis Januar 1933. Vol. 2 A: Aussenpolitische Standortbestimmung nach der Reichstagswahl Juni–Juli 1928*, ed. und annotated Gerhard L. Weinberg, Christian Hartmann and Klaus A. Lankheit, Munich, 1995.

137　Hess, *Briefe*, p. 392 (dated 28 June 1928). See the letter from Winifred Wagner dated 24 June 1928: "Wolf is in Berchtesgaden writing a new book, which I'm to receive as a birthday present. Hess, who knows about these things, thinks very highly of it." Hamann, *Winifred Wager*, pp. 165f.

138　Adolf Hitler, *Die Südtiroler Frage und das Deutsche Bündnisproblem*, Munich, 1926; reprinted in Hitler, *Reden, Schriften, Anordnungen*, vol. 1, doc. 100, pp. 269–93.

139　See the introduction by Gerhard L. Weinberg in Hitler, *Reden, Schriften, Anordnungen*, vol. 2A, pp. XVIf.; Kershaw, *Hitler: Hubris*, p. 291.

140　Hitler, *Reden, Schriften, Anordnungen*, vol. 2A, quotations on pp. 10f., 19, 60, 66, 119, 183.

141　Ibid., vol. 2, part 1, doc. 2, pp. 11–22. See Goebbels, *Tagebücher*, part 1, vol. 1/3, p. 53 (entry for 14 July 1928).

142　See Plöckinger, *Geschichte eines Buches*, p. 163. In July 1929 Goebbels noted: "He's writing a new book about foreign policy." Goebbels, *Tagebücher*, part 1, vol. 1 /3, p. 281 (entry for 5 July 1929).

143　See the introduction by Gerhard L. Weinberg in Hitler, *Reden, Schriften, Anordnungen*, vol. 2A, pp. xxIf.; Ryback, *Hitler's Private Library*, p. 92.

144　Albert Speer, *Erinnerungen: Mit einem Essay von Jochen Thies*, Frankfurt am Main and Berlin, 1993, p. 100.

145   Hitler, *Reden, Schriften, Anordnungen*, vol. 3, part 1, doc. 15, pp. 52f. (dated 2 Sept. 1928).

146   Goebbels, *Tagebücher*, part 1, vol. 1/3; p. 75 (entry for 1 Sept. 1928).

147   Tyrell, *Führer befiehl*, doc. 74, p. 196 (dated 29 March 1926).

148   Ibid., doc. 82, pp. 211–13 (quotations on pp. 211, 212). It is uncertain whether the letter was sent or not. See ibid., p. 211n31.

149   Ibid., doc. 98, p. 254. See Otto Erbersdobler's answers to a questionnaire from A. Tyrell, July 1968; IfZ München, ZS 1949.

150   See Hitler, *Reden, Schriften, Anordnungen*, vol. 1, doc. 50, p. 100: "The art of leadership consists of the leader taking the people in their current form as his material and deploying them where they are best deployed."

151   Albert Krebs, *Tendenzen und Gestalten der NSDAP: Erinnerungen aus der Frühzeit der Partei*, Stuttgart, 1959, pp. 127f. See Gregor Strasser's similar statements in Wagener, *Hitler aus nächster Nähe*, pp. 127f.

152   Krebs, *Tendenzen und Gestalten*, pp. 128f.

153   Longerich, *Deutschland 1918–1933*, p. 254; Winkler, *Weimar*, p. 352.

154   See Rudolf Heberle, *Landbevölkerung und Nationalsozialismus: Eine soziologische Untersuchung der politischen Willensbildung in Schleswig-Holstein 1918 bis 1932*, Stuttgart, 1963, pp. 124ff., 156ff.; Gerhard Stoltenberg, *Politische Strömungen im schleswig-holsteinischen Landvolk 1918–1933*, Düsseldorf, 1962, pp. 110ff.; Stephanie Merkenich, *Grüne Front gegen Weimar: Reichsland-Bund und agrarischer Lobbyismus 1918–1933*, Düsseldorf, 1998, pp. 247ff.

155   Adolf Hitler, *Reden, Schriften, Anordnungen—Februar 1925 bis Januar 1933. Vol. 3: Zwischen den Reichstagswahlen Juli 1928–September 1930. Part 2: März 1929–Dezember 1929*, ed. Klaus A. Lankheit, Munich, 1994, doc. 14, p. 120 (dated 23 March 1920). See ibid., doc. 3, p. 36 (dated 6 March 1929): "What we had been preaching for years, now became reality."

156   Evans, *The Coming of the Third Reich*, p. 211.

157   See the results in Tyrell, *Führer befiehl*, p. 381.

158   Hitler, *Reden, Schriften, Anordnungen*, vol. 3, part 1, doc. 52, pp. 245–53 (dated 20 Nov. 1928).

159   Hess, *Briefe*, p. 393 (dated 24 Oct. 1928).

160   Deuerlein, *Aufstieg*, pp. 299–301. See also Hitler's account of the trip, in which he gleefully noted "how greatly our National Socialist idea has taken form and shape in people's heads here." Hitler, *Reden, Schriften, Anordnungen*, vol. 3, part 2, doc. 9 and 10, pp. 105–14 (quotation on p. 111).

161   Goebbels, *Tagebücher*, part 1, vol. 1/3, p. 247 (entry for 14 May 1929).

162   G. Feder's diaries, vol. 11 (entry for 25 June 1929): "Glorious election victory in Coburg. 13 of 25 seats!"; IfZ München, ED 874. On the election results see Falter et al., *Wahlen und Abstimmungen*, pp. 98, 108, 111. See also Evans, *The Coming of the Third Reich*, p. 211.

163   Hitler's call of 1 March 1929 for the party rally in Hitler, *Reden, Schriften, Anordnungen*, vol. 3, part 2, doc. 1, pp. 3–7 (quotation on p. 5). See also Rudolf Hess to his parents, 21 May 1929: "This time it will be a magnificent occasion!" BA Bern, Nl Hess, J1.211-1989/148, 43.

164   Hitler, *Reden, Schriften, Anordnungen*, vol. 3, part 1, doc. 67, pp. 357–60 (quotations on pp. 358, 359). See also Otto Wagener's report, who had taken part in a rally for the first time. Wagener, *Hitler aus nächster Nähe*, pp. 9–21; Goebbels, *Tagebücher*, part 1, vol. 1/3, pp. 293–9 (entries for 1–6 Aug. 1929). The day's programme is in BA Berlin-Lichterfelde, NS 26/391.

165   See Longerich, *Die braunen Bataillone*, pp. 94f. According to testimony by Walter Stennes on 29 July 1968, the SA could "hardly be preserved" at that point. Stennes said that Hitler had been "desperate and pale as a sheet" and claimed that only intervention by himself and Salomon von Pfeffer had prevented a catastrophe. IfZ München, ZS 1147.

166   According to sworn testimony by Prince August Wilhelm on 16 May 1947, he was
       accepted into the NSDAP in April 1930 and into the SA in December 1931. IfZ
       München, ZS 1318. See also Lothar Machtan, *Der Kaisersohn bei Hitler*, Hamburg,
       2006, pp. 165–7, 171.

167   Goebbels, *Tagebücher*, part 1, vol. 1/3, p. 295 (entry for 3 Aug. 1929).

168   See Winkler, *Weimar*, pp. 347f.; Longerich, *Deutschland 1918–1933*, pp. 251f.

169   See Hitler, *Reden, Schriften, Anordnungen*, vol. 3, part 2, doc. 50, pp. 290–2 (dated
       9 July 1929), doc. 55, p. 303 (dated 25 July 1929), doc. 56, pp. 304f. (dated 25 July
       1929). See also Klaus Wernecke (with Peter Heller), *Der vergessene Führer: Alfred
       Hugenberg—Pressemacht und Nationalsozialismus*, Hamburg, 1982, pp. 147ff. On
       Hugenberg's media empire see Heidrun Holzbach, *Das "System Hugenberg": Die
       Organisation bürgerlicher Sammlungspolitik vor dem Aufstieg der NSDAP*, Stuttgart,
       1981, pp. 259ff.

170   Goebbels, *Tagebücher*, part 1, vol. 1/3, p. 285 (entry for 12 July 1929).

171   Ibid., p. 281 (entry for 5 July 1929). See Longerich, *Goebbels*, pp. 113–16.

172   Hitler, *Reden, Schriften, Anordnungen*, vol. 3, part 2, doc. 88, pp. 411–20.

173   On the election results see Falter *et al.*, *Wahlen und Abstimmungen*, pp. 90, 111.

174   Harry Graf Kessler, *Das Tagebuch. Vol. 9: 1926–1937*, ed. Sabine Gruber and Ulrich
       Ott with Christoph Hilse and Nadin Weiss, Stuttgart, 2010, p. 264 (entry for 3 Oct.
       1929), p. 268 (entry for 7 Oct. 1929). See also Jonathan Wright, *Gustav Stresemann
       1878–1929: Weimars grösster Staatsmann*, Munich, 2006.

175   See Hanfstaengl, *Zwischen Weissem und Braunem Haus*, p. 231; Heike B. Görtemaker,
       Eva Braun: Leben mit Hitler, Munich, 2010, p. 53. On Hugo Bruckmann's help with
       renting the apartment see Joachimsthaler, *Hitlers Liste*, pp. 112–15. After visiting
       Prinzregentenstrasse on 10 April 1930, Winifred Wagner reported that Hitler had
       beamed "like a child." See Hamann, *Winifred Wagner*, p. 181. The Reichert family,
       with whom Hitler had lodged on Thierschstrasse, also moved to Prinzregentenstrasse;
       there they lived in a small apartment on the third floor. Anni Winter, the wife of
       Ritter von Epp's former manservant Georg Winter, became Hitler's housekeeper.
       In early December 1933, the landlord assured Hitler that he intended neither to
       raise the rent nor to sell the apartment: Hugo Schühle to Hitler, 1 Dec. 1933; BA
       Berlin-Lichterfelde, NS 10/123. In 1935, Hitler bought the whole building, at which
       point the Reicherts moved out. That meant that Hitler had the third floor all to
       himself. See transcript of an interview with Anni Winter (undated, post-1945); IfZ
       München, ZS 194.

9 *Dark Star Rising*

1   Letter from Hitler to a German living abroad, 2 Feb. 1930; Fritz Dickmann, "Die
       Regierungsbildung in Thüringen als Modell der Machtergreifung: Ein Brief Hitlers
       aus dem Jahr 1930," in *Vierteljahrshefte für Zeitgeschichte*, 14 (1966), pp. 454–65 (quota-
       tion on p. 464). Also reprinted in Adolf Hitler, *Reden, Schriften, Anordnungen—Februar
       1925 bis Januar 1933. Vol. 3: Zwischen den Reichtagswahlen Juli 1928–September 1930.
       Part 3: Januar 1930–September 1930*, ed. Christian Hartmann, Munich, 1994, doc. 11,
       pp. 59–64.

2   See Harold James, *Deutschland in der Weltwirtschaftskrise 1924–1936*, Stuttgart, 1988,
       pp. 65ff.

3   Hans-Ulrich Wehler, *Deutsche Gesellschaftsgeschichte 1914–1949*, Munich, 2003, p. 259.
       On the extent of unemployment see Heinrich August Winkler, *Der Weg in die
       Katastrophe: Arbeiter und Arbeiterbewegung in der Weimarer Republik 1930 bis 1933*, Berlin
       and Bonn, 1987, pp. 23f.

4   See Wehler, *Deutsche Gesellschaftsgeschichte*, pp. 553–61, 571f.

5   See Ludwig Richter, *Die Deutsche Volkspartei 1918–1933*, Düsseldorf, 2002, pp. 595ff.

6   See Heinrich August Winkler, *Weimar 1918–1933: Die Geschichte der ersten deutschen Demokratie*, Munich, 1993, p. 372; see also Karl-Dietrich Bracher's classic study, *Die Auflösung der Weimarer Republik: Eine Studie zum Problem des Machtverfalls in der Demokratie*, Villingen, 1955, 3rd revised and expanded edition, 1960, pp. 296ff.

7   See Wolfram Pyta, *Hindenburg: Herrschaft zwischen Hohenzollern und Hitler*, Munich, 2007, pp. 555–75.

8   See Eberhard Kolb, *Die Weimarer Republik*, 2nd edition, Munich, 1988, pp. 125f.

9   *Die Tagebücher von Joseph Goebbels. Part 1: Aufzeichnungen 1923–1941*, ed. Elke Fröhlich, Munich, 1998, vol. 2, p. 120 (entry for 30 March 1930).

10   Ibid., p. 124 (entry for 4 April 1930). See ibid., p. 131 (entry for 13 April 1930).

11   Hitler, *Reden, Schriften, Anordnungen*, vol. 3, part 3 doc. 31, pp. 146f.

12   Dickmann, "Regierungsbildung," pp. 461, 462. On the game of poker Hitler played with the formation of the Thuringia state government see Volker Mauersberger, *Hitler in Weimar: Der Fall einer deutschen Kulturstadt*, Berlin, 1999, pp. 237–55; Martin Broszat, *Die Machtergreifung: Der Aufstieg der NSDAP und die Zerstörung der Weimarer Republik*, Munich, 1984, pp. 103–7.

13   See Mauersberger, *Hitler in Weimar*, pp. 262–80 (quotation on p. 270). For election results for Weimar see ibid., p. 242.

14   Hitler to Frick, 2 April 1931; Adolf Hitler, *Reden, Schriften, Anordnungen—Februar 1925 bis Januar 1933. Vol. 4: Von der Reichstagswahl bis zur Reichspräsidentenwahl Oktober 1930–März 1932. Part 1: Oktober 1930–Juni 1931*, ed. Constantin Goschler, Munich, 1993, doc. 78, pp. 245f.

15   See Patrick Moreau, "Otto Strasser—Nationaler Sozialismus versus National- sozialismus," in Ronald Smelser and Rainer Zitelmann (eds), *Die Braune Elite: 22 biographische Skizzen*, Darmstadt, 1989, pp. 286–98. For greater detail see *idem*, *Nationalsozialismus von links: Die "Kampfgemeinschaft Revolutionärer Nationalsozialisten" und die "Schwarze Front" Otto Strassers 1930–1935*, Stuttgart, 1985.

16   Goebbels, *Tagebücher*, part 1, vol. 2/1, p. 71 (entry for 24 Jan. 1930).

17   Ibid., p. 111 (entry for 16 March 1930). See ibid., p. 119 (entry for 28 March 1930): "I don't believe a word he says any more. He doesn't dare move against Strasser. What will happen later if he has to rule Germany as its dictator?"

18   See Daniel Siemens, *Horst Wessel: Tod und Verklärung eines Nationalsozialisten*, Berlin, 2009, pp. 129ff. The quotation in Goebbels, *Tagebücher*, part 1, vol. 2/1, p. 94 (entry for 23 Feb. 1930).

19   Goebbels, *Tagebücher*, part 1, vol. 2/1, p. 144 (entry for 28 April 1930).

20   Otto Strasser, *Hitler und ich*, Konstanz, 1948, pp. 129–47 (quotations on pp. 137, 138, 144). The report is based on Otto Strasser's notes immediately after the conversa- tion. Albert Krebs quotes a similar statement by Hitler: "Socialism? What is socialism? If people have enough to eat and can amuse themselves, that is socialism." Albert Krebs, *Tendenzen und Gestalten der NSDAP: Erinnerungen aus der Frühzeit der Partei*, Stuttgart, 1959, p. 143.

21   Goebbels, *Tagebücher*, part 1, vol. 2/1, p. 162 (entry for 22 May 1930).

22   See Jürgen Falter, Thomas Lindenberger and Siegfried Schumann, *Wahlen und Abstimmungen in der Weimarer Republik: Materialien zum Wahlverhalten 1919–1931*, Munich, 1986, p. 108.

23   Hitler, *Reden, Schriften, Anordnungen*, vol. 3, part 3, doc. 67, pp. 249f. (dated 30 June 1930).

24   Goebbels, *Tagebücher*, part 1, vol. 2/1, p. 188 (entry for 1 July 1930).

25   Gregor Strasser to Rudolf Jung, 22 July 1930; Albrecht Tyrell, *Führer befiehl . . . Selbstzeugnisse aus der "Kampfzeit" der NSDAP: Dokumentation und Analyse*, Düsseldorf, 1969, doc. 136, pp. 332f.; see Hinrich Lohse, "Der Fall Strasser," undated memorandum (c.1952); IfZ München, ZS 265; Moreau, "Otto Strasser," pp. 290ff.

26   See Bracher, *Auflösung*, pp. 335–40; Winkler, *Weimar*, pp. 378–81; Kolb, *Die Weimarer Republik*, p. 126.

27   See Gerhard Paul, *Aufstand der Bilder: Die NS-Propaganda vor 1933*, Bonn, 1990, pp. 90–2 (quotations on pp. 91, 92).

28   Goebbels, *Tagebücher*, part 1, vol. 2/1, p. 236 (entry for 11 Sept. 1930).

29   Quotations from the following: Hitler, *Reden, Schriften, Anordnungen*, vol. 3, part 3, doc. 87, pp. 325, 329 (dated 12 Aug. 1930); doc. 81, pp. 295f. (dated 3 Aug. 1930); doc. 76, p. 280 (dated 18 July 1930); doc. 90, p. 357 (dated 18 Aug. 1930); doc. 86, p. 322 (dated 10 Aug. 1930); doc. 110, p. 140 (dated 10 Sept. 1930); doc. 90, p. 359 (dated 18 Aug. 1930).

30   For example, see Wehler, *Deutsche Gesellschaftsgeschichte*, p. 569; Ian Kershaw, *Hitler 1889–1936: Hubris*, London, 1998, p. 330; Ralf Georg Reuth, *Hitler: Eine Biographie*, Munich and Zurich, 2003, p. 228; Joachim Fest, *Hitler: Eine Biographie*, Frankfurt am Main, Berlin and Vienna, 1973, p. 459; John Toland, *Adolf Hitler: Volume 1*, New York, 1976, p. 253.

31   Quotations in Hitler, *Reden, Schriften, Anordnungen*, vol. 3, part 3, doc. 76, pp. 277, 279 (dated 18 July 1930); doc. 77, pp. 285, 289 (dated 24 July 1930); doc. 82, p. 299 (dated 5 Aug. 1930); doc. 86, p. 316 (dated 10 Aug. 1930); doc. 108, p. 391 (dated 8 Sept. 1930).

32   Quotations in ibid., vol. 3, part 3, doc. 87, p. 322 (dated 12 Aug. 1930); doc. 90, p. 345 (dated 18 Aug. 1930); doc. 86, p. 311 (dated 10 Aug. 1930); doc. 90, p. 351 (dated 18 Aug. 1930); doc. 92, p. 364 (dated 21 Aug. 1930).

33   Ibid., vol. 3, part 3, doc. 109, pp. 394–407 (quotation on p. 407).

34   Ibid., vol. 3, part 3, doc. 107, pp. 387, 388 (dated 7 Sept. 1930).

35   Rudolf Hess, *Briefe 1908–1933*, ed. Rüdiger Hess, Munich and Vienna, 1987, p. 405 (dated 10 Sept. 1930); see Adolf Hitler, *Monologe im Führerhauptquartier 1941–1944: Die Aufzeichnungen Heinrich Heims*, ed. Werner Jochmann, Hamburg, 1980, p. 170 (dated 3/4 Jan. 1942). According to Hanfstaengl (*Zwischen Weissem und Braunem Haus: Erinnerungen eines politischen Aussenseiters*, Munich, 1970, p. 207) Hitler said before the election that he would have been satisfied with forty.

36   Hitler, *Reden, Schriften, Anordnungen*, vol. 3, part 3, doc. 116, p. 420 (dated 16 Sept. 1930).

37   See Falter *et al.*, *Wahlen und Abstimmungen*, pp. 71f.

38   See Jürgen Falter, *Hitlers Wähler*, Munich, 1991, pp. 98ff, particularly pp. 366ff. For a summary see Michael Wildt, *Geschichte des Nationalsozialismus*, Göttingen, 2008, pp. 58–64; Winkler, *Weimar*, pp. 389f.; Broszat, *Machtergreifung*, pp. 113–17.

39   Goebbels, *Tagebücher*, part 1, vol. 2/1, pp. 239f. (entries for 15 Sept. and 16 Sept. 1930).

40   Harry Graf Kessler, *Das Tagebuch. Vol. 9: 1926–1937*, ed. Sabine Gruber and Ulrich Ott with Christoph Hilse and Nadin Weiss, Stuttgart, 2010, pp. 375, 377 (entry for 15 Sept. 1930).

41   Victor Klemperer, *Leben sammeln, nicht fragen wozu und warum: Tagebücher 1925–1932*, ed. Walter Nowojski, Berlin, 1996, p. 659 (entry for 15 Sept. 1930).

42   Thea Sternheim, *Tagebücher. Vol. 2: 1925–1936*, ed. and selected Thomas Ehrsam and Regula Wyss, Göttingen, 2002, p. 296 (entry for 15 Sept. 1930), p. 298 (entry for 20 Sept. 1930).

43   Bella Fromm, *Als Hitler mir die Hand küsste*, Berlin, 1993, p. 35 (dated 14 Oct. 1930).

44   *Frankfurter Zeitung*, 15 Sept. 1930; quoted in Ernst Deuerlein (ed.), *Der Aufstieg der NSDAP in Augenzeugenberichten*, Munich, 2nd edition, 1976, p. 318.

45   Carl von Ossietzky, "Vor Sonnenuntergang," in *Die Weltbühne*, 16 Sept. 1930, pp. 425–7 (quotation on p. 426). Also in *idem*, *Sämtliche Schriften. Vol. 5: 1929–1930*, ed. Bärbel Boldt, Ute Maack and Günther Nickel, Reinbek bei Hamburg, 1994, pp. 445–8.

46   "Quietus," "Die Zukunft des Nationalsozialismus," in *Die Weltbühne*, 23 Sept. 1930, pp. 477–80 (quotation on p. 477).

47   Kessler, *Das Tagebuch*, vol. 9, p. 377 (entry for 18 Sept. 1930).

48   Quoted in Deuerlein, *Aufstieg*, p. 320.

49   Julius Curtius, *Sechs Jahre Minister der deutschen Republik*, Heidelberg, 1948, pp. 170f.; see Andreas Rödder, *Stresemanns Erbe: Julius Curtius und die deutsche Aussenpolitik 1929–1931*, Paderborn, 1996, p. 96.

50   Detlev Clemens, *Herr Hitler in Germany: Wahrnehmungen und Deutungen des Nationalsozialismus in Grossbritannien 1920 bis 1939*, Göttingen and Zurich, 1996, pp. 161f. (quotation on p. 162).

51   Ibid., pp. 163–6 (quotations on pp. 165, 166f.). An excerpt from the Rothermere article is also in Deuerlein, *Aufstieg*, pp. 322f. See also Brigitte Granzow, *A Mirror of Nazism: British Opinion and the Emergence of Hitler 1929–1933*, London, 1964, pp. 101ff.; Ian Kershaw, *Making Friends with Hitler: Lord Londonderry and Britain's Road to War*, London, 2005, p. 58.

52   Hitler, *Reden, Schriften, Anordnungen*, vol. 3, part 3, doc. 115, p. 419.

53   Pyta, *Hindenburg*, p. 589. On the SPD's policy of tolerance see Winkler, *Weimar*, pp. 394–6; Kolb, *Weimarer Republik*, p. 127; Bracher, *Auflösung*, pp. 370f.

54   On the talks between Brüning and Hitler on 5 Oct. 1930 see Heinrich Brüning, *Memoiren 1918–1934*, Stuttgart, 1970, pp. 192–6 (quotations on pp. 194, 195, 196). See also Herbert Hömig, *Brüning: Kanzler in der Krise der Republik. Eine Weimarer Biographie*, Paderborn, 2000, pp. 204–8; Gerhard Schulz, *Von Brüning zu Hitler: Der Wandel des politischen Systems in Deutschland 1930–1933*, Berlin and New York, 1992, pp. 179–82; Winkler, *Weimar*, pp. 393f. On how the talks came about see Krebs, *Tendenzen und Gestalten*, pp. 141–3.

55   Goebbels, *Tagebücher*, part 1, vol. 2/1, p. 255 (entry for 6 Oct. 1930).

56   Krebs, *Tendenzen und Gestalten*, p. 141 writes that Hitler could only free himself from his feelings of inferiority vis-à-vis Brüning by developing a "hate complex." See also Kershaw, *Hitler: Hubris*, p. 339.

57   Hess, *Briefe*, p. 495 (dated 24 Oct. 1930).

58   Hanfstaengl, *Zwischen Weissem und Braunem Haus*, p. 209.

59   Hitler, *Reden, Schriften, Anordnungen*, vol. 3, part 3, doc. 124, p. 452n2. For the interviews see ibid., doc. 124, pp. 452f (*Daily Mail*, 25 Sept. 1930); doc. 127, pp. 461–8 (*Gazzetta del Popolo*, 29 Sept. 1930); vol. 4, part 1, doc. 1, pp. 3f. (*The Times*, 2 Oct. 1930); doc. 2, pp. 4–9 (Hearst press, 4 Oct. 1930).

60   Goebbels, *Tagebücher*, part 1, vol. 2, 1, p. 264 (entry for 18 Oct. 1930). Quotations from Thomas Mann, "Deutsche Ansprache: Ein Appell an die Vernunft," Berlin, 1930; reprinted in *idem, Gesammelte Werke in Einzelbänden: Von deutscher Republik*, Frankfurt am Main, 1984, pp. 294–314. See Thomas Mann, *Briefe III: 1924–1932*, selected and ed. Thomas Sprecher, Hans R. Vaget and Cornelia Bernini, Frankfurt am Main, 2011, p. 491 (dated 29 Oct. 1930) and commentary pp. 516–18. See also Klaus Harpprecht, *Thomas Mann: Eine Biographie*, Reinbek bei Hamburg, 1995, pp. 664–7; Winkler, *Weimar*, p. 391; David Clay Large, *Where Ghosts Walked: Munich's Road to the Third Reich*, New York and London, 1997, p. 222.

61   Friedrich Meinecke, "Nationalsozialismus und Bürgertum," in *Kölnische Zeitung*, 21 Dec. 1930; quoted in Kurt Sontheimer, *Antidemokratisches Denken in der Weimarer Republik: Die politischen Ideen des deutschen Nationalismus zwischen 1918 und 1933*, Munich, 1968 (student's edition), pp. 293f.

62   Sebastian Haffner, *Geschichte eines Deutschen: Die Erinnerungen 1914–1933*, Stuttgart and Munich, 2000, pp. 88f.

63   Alongside Sontheimer's classic study, *Antidemokratisches Denken*, see the concise and hard-hitting analysis in Wehler, *Deutsche Gesellschaftsgeschichte*, pp. 486–93. See also Reinhard Mehring, *Carl Schmitt: Aufstieg und Fall. Eine Biographie*, Munich, 2009, pp. 247ff; Heimo Schwilk, *Ernst Jünger: Ein Jahrhundertleben*, Munich and Zurich, 2007, pp. 340ff.; André Schlüter, *Möller van den Bruck: Leben und Werk*, Cologne, Weimar and Vienna, 2010, pp. 287ff.; Detlef Felken, *Oswald Spengler: Konservativer Denker zwischen Kaiserreich und Diktatur*, Munich, 1988.

64   Bernd Sösemann (ed.), *Theodor Wolff: Der Journalist. Berichte und Leitartikel*, Düsseldorf, 1993, p. 273 (dated 14 Sept. 1930).

65   Ossietzky, *Sämtliche Schriften*, vol. 5, pp. 435f. (quotation on p. 435).

66 Ossietzky, "Brüning darf nicht bleiben," in ibid., pp. 450–4 (quotation on p. 453). See also Hans-Erich Kaminski, "Die Rechte soll regieren," in *Die Weltbühne*, 23 Sept. 1930, pp. 470–3.

67 Ossietzky, *Sämtliche Schriften*, vol. 5, pp. 447, 453, 455. Kurt Tucholsky ridiculed Hitler in similar fashion, calling him "an upstart Mongolian," a "house painter" and a "man with a beery vocal organ." Philipp W. Fabry, *Mutmassungen über Hitler: Urteile von Zeitgenossen*, Königstein im Taunus, 1979, p. 63. On *Die Weltbühne*'s underestimation of Hitler see Alexander Gallus, *Heimat "Weltbühne": Eine Intellektuellengeschichte im 20. Jahrhundert*, Göttingen, 2012, p. 55.

68 Ernst Toller, "Reichskanzler Hitler," in *Die Weltbühne*, 7 Oct. 1930. See Richard Dove, *Ernst Toller: Ein Leben für Deutschland*, Göttingen, 1993, pp. 179f.

69 Hanfstaengl, *Zwischen Weissem und Braunem Haus*, p. 214; see Hans Frank, *Im Angesicht des Galgens: Deutung Hitlers und seiner Zeit auf Grund eigener Erlebnisse und Erkenntnisse*, Munich and Gräfelfing, 1953, pp. 84–6.

70 Hitler, *Reden, Schriften, Anordnungen*, vol. 3, part 3, doc. 123, pp. 434–57 (quotations on pp. 434, 439, 438f., 440, 444, 445, 441).

71 Richard Scheringer, *Das grosse Los: Unter Soldaten, Bauern und Rebellen*, Hamburg, 1959, p. 236; see Ralf Georg Reuth, *Goebbels*, Munich and Zurich, 1990, p. 176.

72 Complete version of the memorandum in Robert W. Kempner (ed.), *Der verpasste Nazi-Stopp: Die NSDAP als staats- und republikfeindliche, hochverräterische Verbindung. Preußische Denkschrift von 1930*, Frankfurt am Main, Berlin and Vienna, 1983, pp. 17–135 (quotations on pp. 135, 117).

73 Quoted in Schulz, *Von Brüning zu Hitler*, p. 160.

74 See Johannes Hürter, *Wilhelm Groener: Reichswehrminister am Ende der Weimarer Republik 1928–1932*, Munich, 1993, pp. 270, 284–92; Schulz, *Von Brüning zu Hitler*, pp. 157–60.

75 Goebbels, *Tagebücher*, part 1, vol. 2, 1, p. 327 (entry for 18 Jan. 1931).

76 Kessler, *Das Tagebuch*, vol. 9, p. 385 (entry for 13 Oct. 1930).

77 See Dirk Walter, *Antisemitische Kriminalität und Gewalt: Judenfeindschaft in der Weimarer Republik*, Bonn, 1999, pp. 209–11; Thomas Friedrich, *Die missbrauchte Hauptstadt: Hitler und Berlin*, Berlin, 2007, pp. 254–60. On 14 Oct. 1930, Thea Sternheim noted: "National Socialist rowdies have smashed the windows of downtown Jewish businesses as the inaugural act of the pogrom carefully prepared by their press." *Tagebücher*, vol. 2, p. 299. See Goebbels, *Tagebücher*, part 1, vol. 2/1, p. 260 (entry for 14 Oct. 1930).

78 Hitler, *Reden, Schriften, Anordnungen*, vol. 4, part 1, doc. 7, p. 19 (International News Service, 14 Oct. 1930); see also ibid., doc. 8, p. 22f. (*The Times*, 14 Oct. 1930).

79 The transcript of the Reichstag session of 18 Oct. 1930 is reprinted in Klaus Schönhoven and Jochen Vogel (eds), *Frühe Warnungen vor dem Nationalsozialismus: Ein historisches Lesebuch*, Bonn, 1998, pp. 115–24 (quotation on p. 115).

80 See Martin Döring, *"Parlamentarischer Arm der Bewegung": Die Nationalsozialisten im Reichstag der Weimarer Republik*, Düsseldorf, 2001, pp. 271–6.

81 Goebbels, *Tagebücher*, part 1, vol. 2/1, p. 298, p. 301 (entries for 6 and 10 Dec. 1930). See Reuth, *Goebbels*, p. 182f.; Peter Longerich, *Joseph Goebbels: A Biography*, London, 2015, pp. 140f.; Friedrich, *Die missbrauchte Hauptstadt*, pp. 271–6. Thea Sternheim quoted the Jewish gallery owner and art dealer Alfred Flechtheim as saying: "You shouldn't provoke the people! Get rid of the film!" She commented: "If Jews are that cowardly, pogroms will happen." *Tagebücher*, vol. 2, pp. 311f. (entry for 8 Dec. 1930).

82 Quoted in Döring, *"Parlamentarischer Arm,"* p. 279.

83 On the atmosphere of latent civil war during the final years of the Weimar Republic, see Dirk Blasius, *Weimars Ende: Bürgerkrieg und Politik 1930–1933*, Frankfurt am Main, 2008, pp. 22ff.; Andreas Wirsching, *Vom Weltkrieg zum Bürgerkrieg? Politischer Extremismus in Deutschland und Frankreich 1918–1933/39: Berlin und Paris in Vergleich*, Munich, 1999, pp. 575ff.

84   See Peter Longerich, *Die braunen Bataillone: Geschichte der SA*, Munich, 1989, pp. 116ff.
85   As in Hitler's letter to Interior Minister Groener, 14 Nov. 1931; Adolf Hitler, *Reden, Schriften, Anordnungen—Februar 1925 bis Januar 1933: Vol. 4: Von der Reichstagswahl bis zur Reichspräsidentenwahl Oktober 1930–März 1932. Part 2: Juli 1931–Dezember 1931*, ed. Christian Hartmann, Munich, 1996, doc. 71, pp. 198–203 (quotation on p. 200). See also Hitler's letter to Brüning of 13 Dec. 1931, in which he writes of "pure self-defence . . . against the terror of Communist murderers." Ibid., doc. 94, p. 271.
86   See Goebbels, *Tagebücher*, part 1, vol. 2/1, p. 230 (entry for 1 Sept. 1930): "At 2 a.m. a telegram from Berlin. SA stormed and destroyed headquarters." On the first Stennes revolt see Longerich, *Die braunen Bataillone*, pp. 102–4; idem, *Goebbels*, pp. 134–7; Wirsching, *Vom Weltkrieg zum Bürgerkrieg?*, pp. 459f.
87   Hitler, *Reden, Schriften, Anordnungen*, vol. 3, part 3, doc. 100, pp. 378f. (entry for 1 Sept. 1930).
88   Goebbels, *Tagebücher*, part 1, vol. 2/1, p. 231 (entry for 3 Sept. 1930).
89   See Longerich, *Die braunen Bataillone*, pp. 81 ff., 115ff.
90   Hitler, *Reden, Schriften, Anordnungen*, vol. 4, part 1, doc. 59, pp. 200f.
91   Goebbels, *Tagebücher*, part 1, vol. 2/1, p. 357 (entry for 4 March 1931). See ibid., p. 373 (entry for 28 March 1931: "Something foul in the SA again. Stennes isn't letting up.").
92   Hitler, *Reden, Schriften, Anordnungen*, vol. 4, part 1, doc. 67, pp. 229f. (dated 7 March 1931).
93   Goebbels, *Tagebücher*, part 1, vol. 2/1, p. 377 (entry for 2 April 1931). Hitler's order of 30 March 1931 in Hitler, *Reden, Schriften, Anordnungen*, vol. 4, part 1, doc. 72, pp. 236f.
94   Quoted in Kershaw, *Hitler: Hubris*, p. 349.
95   Hitler, *Reden, Schriften, Anordnungen*, vol. 4, part 1, doc. 79, pp. 246–8 (quotation on p. 247).
96   Ibid., doc. 80, pp. 248–58 (quotations on pp. 254, 255, 256, 258). In an angry letter of 13 April 1931 to Julius Friedrich Lehmann, the Pan-Germanic League's main publisher, Hitler complained about the reporting on the Stennes affair in the *Deutsche Zeitung* newspaper, which he accused of maliciously taking up a position against him. Not even the "Jewish press," fumed Hitler, had behaved "so disgracefully" in this case (ibid., doc. 93, pp. 290–2). On 21 April 1931, the chairman of the Pan-Germanic League, Heinrich Class, sent Hugenberg a copy of the letter, which, as he noted showed "the putative saviour of Germany at the apex of megalomania, hotheadedness, impoliteness and lack of judgement." Class asked: "What will become of this?" BA Koblenz, N 1231/36.
97   Goebbels, *Tagebücher*, part 1, vol. 2/1, p. 387 (entry for 17 April 1930).
98   Deuerlein, *Aufstieg*, pp. 345, 366. See also Hess, *Briefe*, p. 406 (dated 24 Oct. 1930).
99   See Andreas Heusler, *Das Braune Haus: Wie München zur "Hauptstadt der Bewegung" wurde*, Munich, 2008, pp. 132–8; Hitler's call to members of 26 May 1930 in Hitler, *Reden, Schriften, Anordnungen*, vol. 3, part 3, doc. 50, pp. 207–9.
100 Timo Nüsslein, *Paul Ludwig Troost, 1878–1934*, Vienna, Cologne and Weimar, 2012, pp. 69f. On the relationship between Hitler and Troost see ibid., pp. 66–76.
101 Goebbels, *Tagebücher*, part 1, vol. 2/1, p. 202 (entry for 20 July 1930), p. 280 (entry for 12 Nov. 1930), p. 353 (entry for 26 Feb. 1931). See Nüsslein, *Paul Ludwig Troost*, pp. 103f.; Heusler, *Das Braune Haus*, pp. 142f.
102 Hitler, *Reden, Schriften, Anordnungen*, vol. 4, part 1, doc. 61 (dated 21 Feb. 1931), pp. 206–18 (quotation on p. 214).
103 Hess, *Briefe*, pp. 408f. (dated 10 March 1930). On the renovations see Nüsslein, *Paul Ludwig Troost*, pp. 82–7; Heusler, *Das Braune Haus*, pp. 146f.
104 Frank, *Im Angesicht des Galgens*, pp. 93f.; see also Heusler, *Das Braune Haus*, pp. 159f. In an interview dated 13 March 1964, vol. 2, Hermann Esser said that more or less all meetings in the Brown House were carried out standing; BayHStA München, Nl Esser. In his testimony from July 1968, Stennes confirmed that part of Hitler's nature was "to plan things such that no one knows which direction he's headed in

and only he himself was acquainted with all his contacts." IfZ München, ZS 1147. On the furnishing of Hitler's office see Birgit Schwarz, *Geniewahn: Hitler und die Kunst*, Vienna, Cologne and Weimar, 2009, pp. 118f.

105 Goebbels, *Tagebücher*, part 1, vol. 2/1, p. 163 (entry for 24 May 1930), p. 353 (entry for 26 Feb. 1931). See also ibid., p. 202 (entry for 20 July 1930): "Horrible middle-of-the-road cretins"; p. 371 (25 March 1931): "Horrible to see him mingling with these philistines"; p. 394 (28 April 1931): "The people surrounding Hitler. Gruesome!"; p. 153 (12 May 1930): "The most primitive company."

106 See Stefan Krings, *Hitlers Pressechef Otto Dietrich 1897–1952: Eine Biographie*, Göttingen, 2010, pp. 103–5.

107 Heusler, *Das Braune Haus*, pp. 156f.

108 Erich Mühsam, "Jedem das Seine," in *Die Welt am Montag*, 1 June 1931; reprinted in idem, *Ein Lesebuch: Sich fügen heisst lügen*, ed. Marlies Fritzen, Göttingen, 2003, pp. 244f.

109 See Hans Otto Eglau, *Fritz Thyssen: Hitlers Gönner und Geisel*, Berlin, 2003, pp. 127f.

110 See ibid., pp. 87, 96, 105, 108, 117, 122–7; Henry A. Turner, *Die Grossunternehmer und der Aufstieg Hitlers*, Berlin, 1986, pp. 177, 180, 184f. In a letter of 30 Dec. 1931, Thyssen informed Hugenberg that he was "friends with Göring." BA Koblenz, N 1231/39. On Göring's role as Hitler's representative in Berlin, see the transcript of his testimony from 20 July 1945: "The Führer entrusted me with this office because back then I was the only one in the party with enough contacts to represent the party in society." IfZ München, ZS 428.

111 See Christopher Kopper, *Hjalmar Schacht: Aufstieg und Fall von Hitlers mächtigstem Bankier*, Munich and Vienna, 2006, pp. 173–7.

112 Fromm, *Als Hitler mir die Hand küsste*, p. 32 (dated 12 Feb. 1930).

113 Kopper, *Hjalmar Schacht*, p. 189.

114 Hjalmar Schacht, *76 Jahre meines Lebens*, Bad Wörishofen, 1953, p. 351. See Kopper, *Hjalmar Schacht*, pp. 188f. On the role of Stauss see Turner, *Grossunternehmer*, pp. 174f. Hitler had spoken with Stauss in Göring's apartment as early as the end of September 1930. See Goebbels, *Tagebücher*, part 1, vol. 1/2, p. 251 (entry for 30 Sept. 1930).

115 Goebbels, *Tagebücher*, part 1, vol. 2/1, p. 319 (entry for 6 Jan. 1931).

116 Schacht, *76 Jahre*, p. 351. On the meeting of 5 Jan. 1931 see also Kopper, *Hjalmar Schacht*, pp. 189–91; Eglau, *Fritz Thyssen*, pp. 120–2; Turner, *Grossunternehmer*, p. 176.

117 Schacht, *76 Jahre*, p. 352.

118 Otto Wagener, *Hitler aus nächster Nähe: Aufzeichnungen eines Vertrauten 1929–1932*, ed. Henry A. Turner, Frankfurt am Main, Berlin and Vienna, 1978, p. 398.

119 Goebbels, *Tagebücher*, part 1, vol. 2/1, p. 327 (entry for 18 Jan. 1931); Hess, *Briefe*, pp. 405f. (dated 24 Oct. 1930).

120 See, for example, Carl von Ossietzky: "In his early years, Adolf Hitler may have acted out of a genuine ignorance. Today he's only a creature of industry." *Sämtliche Schriften*, vol. 5, p. 435 (dated 9 Sept. 1930). Kurt Hiller wrote in *Die Weltbühne*, 23 Sept. 1930, p. 468: "National Socialism has been bought off by the industrialists who act according to the principle 'divide and conquer' and fragment the proletariat into warring factions."

121 See Turner, *Grossunternehmer*, pp. 139–53.

122 See Kolb, *Die Weimarer Republik*, p. 122.

123 See Turner, *Grossunternehmer*, pp. 157, 164. In a parliamentary faction meeting in June 1929, Göring sneered to Feder: "You know yourself that your economic policies aren't binding for the party." G. Feder's diaries, vol. 11 (entry for 4 June 1929); IfZ München, ED 874.

124 Turner, *Grossunternehmer*, p. 165.

125 Wagener, *Hitler aus nächster Nähe*, p. 443.

126 See Turner, *Grossunternehmer*, p. 160. The meeting was arranged by Admiral Magnus von Levetzow, Kaiser Wilhelms II's political attaché, who had been a follower of the Nazi movement since September 1930. See Gerhard Granier, *Magnus von Levetzow:*

Seeoffizier, Monarchist und Wegbereiter Hitlers: Lebensweg und ausgewählte Dokumente, Boppard am Rhein, 1982, pp. 153f.

127 Stefan Frech, *Wegbereiter Hitlers? Theodor Reismann-Grone: Ein völkischer Nationalist, 1863–1949,* Paderborn, 2009, p. 288.

128 Hitler, *Reden, Schriften, Anordnungen,* vol. 3, part 3, doc. 36, pp. 141–4 (quotation on p. 144). See Turner, *Grossunternehmer,* pp. 10f.; Manfred Asendorf, "Hamburger Nationalklub, Keppler-Kreis, Arbeitsstelle Schacht und der Aufstieg Hitlers," in *1999: Zeitschrift für Sozialgeschichte des 19. und 20. Jahrhunderts,* 2 (1987), pp. 123–6.

129 Goebbels, *Tagebücher,* part 1, vol. 2/1, pp. 366, 371 (entries for 17 and 25 March 1931). Comment about Repuke quoted in Dirk Stegmann, "Zum Verhältnis von Grossindustrie und Nationalsozialismus 1930–1933," in *Archiv für Sozialgeschichte* 13 (1973), p. 419. See also Turner, *Grossunternehmer,* pp. 168f.; Longerich, *Goebbels,* p. 144.

130 See Wagener, *Hitler aus nächster Nähe,* pp. 478–80; Turner, *Grossunternehmer,* p. 172.

131 See Stegmann, "Zum Verhältnis," pp. 418f.; Turner, *Grossunternehmer,* pp. 178, 181f.

132 See Oron James Hale, "Adolf Hitler: Taxpayer," in *American Historical Review,* 60 (1955), pp. 830–42; Turner, *Grossunternehmer,* pp. 185f.

133 See Turner, *Grossunternehmer,* pp. 186f.; see also *Hitlers Tischgespräche im Führerhauptquartier,* ed. Henry Picker, Stuttgart, 1976, p. 423 (dated 6 July 1942); Hanfstaengl, *Zwischen Weissem und Braunem Haus,* p. 216.

134 See Turner, *Grossunternehmer,* pp. 187f.; see also Hitler's statement dated 7 April 1932 in Adolf Hitler, *Reden, Schriften, Anordnungen—Februar 1925 bis Januar 1933. Vol. 5: Von der Reichspräsidentenwahl bis zur Machtergreifung April 1932–Januar 1933. Part 1: April 1932–September 1932,* ed. Klaus A. Lankheit, Munich, 1996, doc. 19, pp. 36f. On Hitler's new Berlin residence see Friedrich, *Die missbrauchte Hauptstadt,* pp. 291–4.

135 Winkler, *Weimar,* p. 421.

136 Thea Sternheim, *Tagebücher,* vol. 2, p. 362 (entry for 13 July 1931). See Goebbels, *Tagebücher,* part 1, vol. 2/2, p. 57 (entry for 15 July 1931): "Danatbank is closing its counters. Panic on the markets and in the economy. A giant scandal."

137 See Falter *et al., Wahlen und Abstimmungen,* pp. 100, 94, 95.

138 Goebbels, *Tagebücher,* part 1, vol. 2/1, p. 328 (entry for 18 Jan. 1931), p. 407 (entry for 17 May 1931).

139 Hitler, *Reden, Schriften, Anordnungen,* vol. 4, part 2, doc. 12, pp. 39f. (dated 21 July 1931).

140 Ibid., doc. 20, pp. 65–7 (quote on p. 66). The previous quote in ibid., p. 67n15.

141 Goebbels, *Tagebücher,* part 1, vol. 2/2, pp. 73f. (entry for 10 Aug. 1931).

142 See Walter, *Antisemitische Kriminalität und Gewalt,* pp. 211–21 (quotations on pp. 213, 218); Wirsching, *Vom Weltkrieg zum Bürgerkrieg?,* pp. 463f.; Friedrich, *Die missbrauchte Hauptstadt,* pp. 319–25.

143 Hitler, *Reden, Schriften, Anordnungen,* vol. 5, part 2, doc. 31, pp. 104–6 (quotation on pp. 105f.) and report by the Munich police headquarters on Hitler's speech in ibid., p. 106n16.

144 Hess, *Briefe,* p. 414 (dated 9 Sept. 1931).

145 Astrid Pufendorf, *Die Plancks: Eine Familie zwischen Patriotimus und Widerstand,* Berlin, 2006, p. 252. On Hindenburg's plans in the autumn of 1931 see Pyta, *Hindenburg,* pp. 629f. See also Brüning, *Memoiren,* p. 386, who wrote that Hindenburg spoke generally on 13 Sept. 1931 about the need to "move more to the right."

146 Goebbels, *Tagebücher,* part 1, vol. 2/2, p. 116 (entry for 5 Oct. 1931). See Longerich, *Goebbels,* p.162f.

147 Quoted in Deuerlein, *Aufstieg,* p. 355. See Thilo Vogelsang, *Reichswehr, Staat und NSDAP: Beiträge zur deutschen Geschichte 1930–1932,* Stuttgart, 1962, pp. 135–7. See also *Die Deutschnationalen und die Zerstörung der Weimarer Republik: Aus dem Tagebuch von Reinhold Quaatz 1928–1933,* ed. Hermann Weiss and Paul Hoser, Munich, 1989, p. 157 (entry for 20 Oct. 1931): "Schleicher characterised Hitler precisely as a dreamer and an unstable character, even if full of patriotic desires."

148 Brüning, *Memoiren*, p. 391. See Hömig, *Brüning: Kanzler in der Krise*, pp. 397f.

149 On Hitler's meeting with Hindenburg of 10 Oct. 1931 see Pyta, *Hindenburg*, pp. 634–7. Further, Hitler, *Monologe*, p. 211 (dated 18 Jan. 1942): "I immediately crossed the bridge to becoming a soldier, but it was a huge challenge to cross the bridge into politics."

150 Brüning, *Memoiren*, p. 391; Ernst von Weizsäcker, *Erinnerungen*, Munich, 1950, p. 103; see Hömig, *Brüning: Kanzler in der Krise*, p. 398.

151 Pyta, *Hindenburg*, p. 1014n43 und p. 634.

152 Goebbels, *Tagebücher*, part 1, vol. 2/2, p. 121 (entry for 12 Oct. 1931). Hitler told Magnus von Levetzow that his "general estimation of the old man" was that he was "an unimportant but not unlikeable figure." Granier, *Magnus von Levetzow*, p. 311 (dated 14 Oct. 1932). By contrast, among party comrades, Hitler supposedly described Hindenburg as "a trembling old man unable to take a leak." Krebs, *Tendenzen und Gestalten*, p. 34.

153 See Richter, *Deutsche Volkspartei*, pp. 713ff.; Reinhard Neebe, *Grossindustrie, Staat und NSDAP 1930–1933*, Göttingen, 1981, pp. 99–110; Winkler, *Weimar*, pp. 430f.

154 Hitler, *Reden, Schriften, Anordnungen*, vol. 4, part 2, doc. 46, pp. 134–59 (quotations on pp. 143, 152). See also Hitler to Brüning, 13 Dec. 1931, Ibid., doc. 94, pp. 264–92 (particularly p. 287).

155 See Schacht, *76 Jahre meines Lebens*, pp. 367f.; Kopper, *Hjalmar Schacht*, pp. 191–4.

156 Turner, *Grossunternehmer*, p. 220. See also Erich von Gilsa to Paul Reusch, 13 Oct. 1931: "Noticeably, none of the true leaders of industry were present." Schulz, *Von Brüning zu Hitler*, p. 559n825.

157 Goebbels, *Tagebücher*, part 1, vol. 2/2, p. 121 (entry for 12 Oct. 1931).

158 Hitler to Franz Seldte, 2 Dec. 1931; Hitler, *Reden, Schriften, Anordnungen*, vol 4, part 2, doc. 82, pp. 226–31 (quotation on p. 228). See Otto Schmidt-Hannover, *Umdenken oder Anarchie: Männer—Schicksale—Lehren*, Göttingen, 1959, p. 182, where Hitler in Bad Harzburg is described as "cocky and scatterbrained . . . like a cross between a prima donna and a Napoleon imitator." On how the Harzburg rally came about and the events of the day, see the recent account by Larry Eugene Jones, "Nationalists, Nazis, and the Assault against Weimar: Revisiting the Harzburg Rally of October 1931," in *German Studies Review*, 29 (2006), pp. 483–94 (particularly p. 488).

159 Hitler, *Reden, Schriften, Anordnungen*, vol. 4, part 2, doc. 43 and 44, pp. 123–32 (quotation on p. 130). See Goebbels, *Tagebücher*, part 1, vol. 2/2, p. 122 (entry for 12 Oct. 1931), who described Hitler as "pale as a ghost" and "in bad form" but still "miles above everyone else."

160 *Vossische Zeitung*, 28 Oct. 1931; BA Berlin-Lichterfelde, NS 26/87. In a letter to Otto Schmidt-Hannover on 3 January 1932, Hugenberg complained about "the ugly game that the National Socialists are playing with their former allies." BA Koblenz, N 1231/39.

161 On a car trip to the wedding of Magda and Joseph Goebbels on 19 Dec. 1931, Hitler told Victoria von Dirksen, an aristocrat who sympathised with the National Socialists, that he needed to assume power as soon as possible, which was "why he was looking around in all directions for allies." He added that he would reach agreement with Hugenberg "when the moment was right." See the letter from DNVP Press Officer Hans Brosius to Hugenberg (based on statements by Dirksen), 23 Dec. 1931; BA Koblenz, N 1231/192. On the role of the Dirksen Salon as a go-between connecting the traditional aristocracy and National Socialism, see Stephan Malinowski, *Vom König zum Führer: Sozialer Niedergang und politische Radikalisierung im deutschen Adel zwischen Kaiserreich und NS-Staat*, Berlin, 2003, pp. 554f.

162 Hitler, *Reden, Schriften, Anordnungen*, vol. 4, part 2, doc. 48, pp. 159–64 (quotation on p. 160).

163 Goebbels, *Tagebücher*, part 1, vol. 2/2, p. 128 (entry for 19 Oct. 1931).

164 Deuerlein, *Aufstieg*, pp. 361f. On the "Boxheim documents" see Ulrich Herbert, *Best: Biographische Studien über Radikalismus, Weltanschauung und Vernunft 1903–1989*, Bonn 1996, pp. 112–19. See also Bracher, *Auflösung*, pp. 431–5; Schulz, *Von Brüning zu Hitler*, pp. 604–8; Winkler, *Weimar*, pp. 433f.

165 Quoted in Herbert, *Best*, p. 116.

166 Thea Sternheim, *Tagebücher*, vol. 2, p. 379 (entry for 27 Nov. 1931).

167 Quoted in Schulz, *Von Brüning zu Hitler*, p. 608.

168 Report in *The Times* of 5 Dec. 1931 on Hitler's press conference; Hitler, *Reden, Schriften, Anordnungen*, vol. 4, part 2, doc. 83, pp. 231–5. See ibid., doc. 91, pp. 256–9 (Hitler's article of 11 Dec. 1931, originally conceived to be a speech on American radio).

169 Hanfstaengl, *Zwischen Weissem und Braunem Haus*, p. 258. See Hanfstaengl's unpublished memoirs, p. 205: "He came in and spoke brilliantly, clearly, rationally and utterly convincingly." BSB München, Nl Hanfstaengl Ana 405, Box 47.

170 Hubert R. Knickerbocker, *Deutschland so oder so?*, Berlin, 1932, pp. 207f. See also the report by Sefton Delmer, the Berlin correspondent for the *Daily Express*, on his first meeting with Hitler in May 1931. Sefton Delmer, *Die Deutschen und ich*, Hamburg, 1963, pp. 114–18, particularly p. 116.

171 Frederic M. Sackett to Henry L. Stimson, 7 Dec. 1931; quoted in Hitler, *Reden, Schriften, Anordnungen*, vol. 4, part 2, doc. 85, p. 239n4.

172 Dorothy Thompson, *Kassandra spricht: Antifaschistische Publizistik 1932–1942*, Leipzig and Weimar, 1988, pp. 41–3.

173 Klaus Mann, *Der Wendepunkt: Ein Lebensbericht*, Frankfurt am Main, 1963, pp. 228f. Mann remembered the meeting happening "around a year before Hitler came to power," that is in early 1932. His diary, however, gives the date as 14 July 1932: "At the very next table Adolf Hitler in the stupidest sort of company. His inferiority is strikingly obvious. Extremely talentless. The fascination he exerts is the biggest embarrassment in history." Klaus Mann, *Tagebücher 1931 bis 1933*, ed. Joachim Heimannsberg, Peter Laemmle and Winfried F. Schoeller, Munich, 1989, p. 64. See Uwe Naumann (ed.), *"Ruhe gibt es nicht, bis zum Schluss." Klaus Mann, 1906–1949: Bilder und Dokumente*, Reinbek bei Hamburg, 1999, p. 132.

174 Theodor Heuss, *Hitlers Weg: Eine historisch-politische Studie über den Nationalsozialismus*, 6th edition, Stuttgart, Berlin and Leipzig, 1932 (quotations on pp. 103, 131, 105, 138, 148f., 99, 100). In late October 1931, Heuss sent the manuscript (minus the final chapter) to the Union Deutsche Verlagsgesellschaft publishers in Stuttgart. By 19 Dec., the proof corrections were finished. "It is entirely without polemic—an empirical study spiced up with a lot of irony," Heuss wrote to his friend Friedrich Mück in Heilbronn on 21 Dec. 1931. Theodor Heuss, *Bürger der Weimarer Republik: Briefe 1918–1933*, ed. Michael Dorrmann, Munich, 2008, no. 186, pp. 431–3, no. 193, pp. 447–53 (quotation on pp. 450f.). For a facsimile of the first edition, see p. 451. On 25 Jan. 1932, Goebbels noted: "Read Theodor Heuss's pamphlet 'Hitlers Weg' [Hitler's Way]. Better late than never. Not completely stupid. He knows a lot about us. Exploits this somewhat unfairly. But it's a critique you don't have to be ashamed of." Goebbels, *Tagebücher*, part 1, vol. 2/2, p. 203. See also Peter Merseburger, *Theodor Heuss: Der Bürger als Präsident. Biographie*, Munich, 2012, pp. 279–85.

175 Klemperer, *Tagebücher 1925–1932*, p. 739 (entry for 25 Dec. 1931); Kessler, *Das Tagebuch*, vol. 9, p. 400 (entry for 31 Dec. 1931).

10 Hitler and Women

1 Brigitte Hamann, *Winifred Wagner oder Hitlers Bayreuth*, Munich and Zurich, 2002, p. 210.

2 Konrad Heiden, *Adolf Hitler: Das Zeitalter der Verantwortungslosigkeit. Eine Biographie*, Zurich, 1936, p. 303.

3 For a summary see Hans-Joachim Neumann and Henrik Eberle, *War Hitler krank? Ein abschliessender Befund*, Bergisch-Gladbach, 2009, pp. 52–60; see also Heinz Linge, *Bis zum Untergang: Als Chef des Persönlichen Dienstes bei Hitler*, ed. Werner Maser, Munich, 1982, p. 94; Werner Maser, *Adolf Hitler: Legende—Mythos—Wirklichkeit*, 12th edition, Munich and Esslingen, 1989, pp. 323f.; Gustav Keller, *Der Schüler Adolf Hitler: Die Geschichte eines lebenslangen Amoklaufs*, Münster, 2012, p. 25, repeats the story of the bitten penis without discussion. On the tale that Hitler had lost a testicle after being wounded at the beginning of October 1916, see Thomas Weber, *Hitler's First War: Adolf Hitler, the Men of the List Regiment, and the First World War*, Oxford and New York, 2010. pp. 154f.

4 Ernst Hanfstaengl, *Zwischen Weissem und Braunem Haus: Erinnerungen eines politischen Aussenseiters*, Munich, 1970, pp. 183f. In his unpublished memoirs (p. 3), Hanfstaengl writes that Hitler was, "in the medical sense, impotent" and lived in a "sexual no man's land." Hitler has "no normal sex life," he added (p. 42); BSB München, Nl Hanfstaengl Ana 405, Box 47. In an interview on 28 Oct. 1951, Hanfstaengl contended that Hitler had had a sexual relationship with Rudolf Hess. IfZ München, ZS 60.

5 See Guido Knopp, *Hitler: Eine Bilanz*, Berlin, 1995, pp. 140f.

6 Lothar Machtan, *Hitlers Geheimnis: Das Doppelleben eines Diktators*, Berlin, 2001, p. 7. The theory of Hitler's repressed homosexuality has also been put forward in Manfred Koch-Hillebrecht, *Homo Hitler: Psychogramm eines Diktators*, Munich, 1999, pp. 249, 406.

7 Lothar Machtan, "Was Hitlers Homosexualität bedeutet: Anmerkungen zu einer Tabugeschichte," in *Zeitschrift für Geschichtswissenschaft*, 51 (2003), pp. 334–51 (quotations on pp. 337, 336). In contrast, see Heiden, *Hitler: Das Zeitalter der Verantwortungslosigkeit*, p. 353, who rejected assertions that Hitler was homosexual as a "fanciful combination that can be disproven by pure, empirical facts."

8 Christa Schroeder, *Er war mein Chef: Aus dem Nachlass der Sekretärin von Adolf Hitler*, ed. Anton Joachimsthaler, 3rd edition, Munich and Vienna, 1985, pp. 153, 152, 155. See also Hanfstaengl, *Zwischen Weissem und Braunem Haus*, p. 61, who cited Eva Braun as saying: "Believe me, he's an absolute eunuch and not a man, despite his constant desires." See also Harry Graf Kessler, *Das Tagebuch. Vol. 9: 1926–1937*, ed. Sabine Gruber and Ulrich Ott with Christoph Hilse and Nadin Weiss, Stuttgart, 2010, p. 631 (entry for 28 Jan. 1935): "Hitler is said most probably to be neither hetero- nor homosexual, but rather a eunuch who has no sexual feelings." (Kessler's statement was based on remarks by Hermann Keyserling.)

9 Joachim Fest, *Hitler: Eine Biographie*, Frankfurt am Main, Berlin and Vienna, 1973, p. 448. See also Helm Stierlin, "Anziehung und Distanz: Hitler und die Frauen aus der Sicht des Psychotherapeuten," in Ulrike Leutheusser (ed.), *Hitler und die Frauen*, Munich, 2003, p. 264. Stierlin asserts that "the erotic needs and sexual energy that were blocked in his private self were allowed to express themselves all the more wildly in his public self."

10 Guido Knopp, *Hitlers Frauen und Marlene*, Munich, 2001, p. 37.

11 Adolf Hitler, *Monologe im Führerhauptquartier 1941–1944: Die Aufzeichnungen Heinrich Heims*, ed. Werner Jochmann, Hamburg, 1980, pp. 230f. (dated 25/26 Jan. 1941); also for the following quote. See Karl Wilhelm Krause, *10 Jahre Kammerdiener bei Hitler*, Hamburg, 1949, p. 43: "Often during his excursions, he would exclaim: 'My God is that a beautiful girl (a beautiful woman).'"

12 Schroeder, *Er war mein Chef*, p. 152.

13 See Brigitte Hamann, *Hitlers Wien: Lehrjahre eines Diktators*, Munich and Zurich, 1996, pp. 517–19.

14 Joachim Radkau, *Das Zeitalter der Nervosität: Deutschland zwischen Bismarck und Hitler*, Munich and Vienna, 1998, p. 147.

15 See above, p. 61. Speer recalled Hitler's close circle of intimates noticing that he "never broached sexual topics or told dirty jokes." Speer to Joachim Fest, 13 Sept. 1969; BA Koblenz, N 1340/17.

16 See Maser, *Adolf Hitler*, p. 315.

17 Ernst Deuerlein (ed.), *Der Aufstieg der NSDAP in Augenzeugenberichten*, Munich, 2nd edition, 1976, p. 139.

18 Heiden, *Hitler: Das Zeitalter der Verantwortungslosigkeit*, p. 355. A relationship between Hitler and Jenny Haug was also confirmed by Maria Enders, an employee in the NSDAP offices, in a conversation on 11 Dec. 1951; IfZ München, ZS 33.

19 See Martha Schad, "'Das Auge war vor allen Dingen ungeheuer anziehend': Freundinnen und Verehrerinnen," in Ulrike Leutheusser (ed.), *Hitler und die Frauen*, Munich, 2003, pp. 30–55; Anton Joachimsthaler, *Hitlers Liste: Ein Dokument persönlicher Beziehungen*, Munich, 2003, pp. 63–135.

20 Hitler, *Monologe*, p. 316 (dated 10/11 March 1942).

21 Hamann, *Winifred Wagner*, p. 139; see Schad, "Freundinnen und Verehrerinnen," p. 40. All the same, Hitler still sent "Fräulein Bechstein" a birthday telegram in June 1938. Daily diaries of Max Wünsche dated 23 June 1938; BA Berlin-Lichterfelde, NS 10/125.

22 Hamann, *Winifred Wagner*, p. 148.

23 Deuerlein, *Aufstieg*, p. 238. The prison guard Franz Hemmrich also recalled (p. 44) Hitler being "extremely indifferent" to the female sex: "He treated them with charming politeness but without the slightest hint of salaciousness in either his words or his gaze." IfZ München, ED 153.

24 *Hitlers Tischgespräche im Führerhauptquartier*, ed. Henry Picker, Stuttgart, 1976, p. 145 (dated 27 March 1942). In a conversation about the "women's question" in July 1924 in Landsberg, Hitler declared: "Women have no place in the political representation of the people. Politics is an exclusively male domain, especially in those areas where the logical extension of politics means that men will have to shed their blood." Rudolf Hess, *Briefe 1908–1933*, ed. Rüdiger Hess, Munich and Vienna, 1987, p. 345 (dated 10 July 1924). See diaries of G. Feder, vol. 11 (entry for 1 Nov. 1929); IfZ München, ED 874.

25 Hitler, *Monologe*, pp. 315f. (dated 10/11 March 1942); p. 310 (dated 1 March 1942). See also *Hitlers Tischgespräche*, p. 273 (dated 8 March 1942): "Marriage, as Hitler sees it, is . . . a task in which career battles are the job of the man, and the household order, the sanctuary from which the struggle for survival is launched, is the woman's role."

26 Hess, *Briefe*, p. 332 (dated 8 June 1924). According to testimony by the highest party judge of the NSDAP, Walter Buch, on 1 May 1947, even before 9 Nov. 1923 Hitler had declared: "I cannot marry. My wife will be Germania." IfZ München, ZS 805. Hitler seems to have seen his sister Paula on rare occasions. Gottfried Feder confirms her presence in Munich in February 1923: diaries, vol. 5 (entry for 8 Feb. 1923); IfZ München, ED 874.

27 R. Buttmann's diary for 23 Dec. 1924; BayHStA München, Nl Buttmann 82; Adolf Hitler, *Reden, Schriften, Anordnungen—Februar 1925 bis Januar 1933. Vol. 1: Die Wiedergründung der NSDAP Februar 1925–Juni 1926*, ed. and annotated Clemens Vollnhals, Munich, London, New York and Paris, 1992, doc. 8, p. 32.

28 Schroeder, *Er war mein Chef*, p. 153.

29 Anna Maria Sigmund, *Des Führers bester Freund: Adolf Hitler, seine Nichte Geli Raubal und der "Ehrenarier" Emil Maurice—Eine Dreiecksbeziehung*, Munich, 2003, p. 94.

30 "Hitlers unbekannte Geliebte: Ein Bericht von Gunter Peis," in *Stern*, 13 June 1959, pp. 28–34.

31 On what follows see Peis, "Hitlers unbekannte Geliebte," on which was based Anna Maria Sigmund, "Marie Reiter," in *idem.*, *Die Frauen der Nazis: Die drei Bestseller vollständig aktualisiert in einem Band*, Munich, 2005, pp. 673–729; Schad "Freundinnen und Verehrerinnen," pp. 69–79.

32 Hitler, *Monologe*, p. 230 (dated 25/26 Jan. 1942).

33 See above, pp. 263f.

34 Henriette von Schirach, *Frauen um Hitler*, Munich, 1983, pp. 244f.

35 Machtan, *Hitlers Geheimnis*, p. 180.

36   Hitler, *Monologe*, p. 208 (dated 16/17 Jan. 1942).
37   Sigmund, "Maria Reiter," p. 694. Hitler's postcards and letters are reprinted in full in Anna Maria Sigmund, *Die Frauen der Nazis*, vol. 3, Munich, 2002, pp. 11ff.; see Joachimsthaler, *Hitlers Liste*, pp. 187–96. The authenticity has been assured. A graphology report can be found in the appendix of the *Stern* report of 13 June 1959.
38   Sigmund, "Maria Reiter," p. 698.
39   Heiden, *Hitler: Das Zeitalter der Verantwortungslosigkeit*, p. 357. See Schroeder, *Er war mein Chef*, p. 156 ("the only woman he ever loved"); *Das Hitler-Bild: Die Erinnerungen des Fotografen Heinrich Hoffmann*, ed. Joe J. Heydecker, St. Pölten and Salzburg, 2008, p. 77 ("Hitler's great love"); Fest, *Hitler*, p. 447 ("his one great love"); Ian Kershaw, *Hitler 1889–1936: Hubris*, London, 1998, p. 352 ("Hitler, for the first and only time in his life . . . became emotionally dependent on a woman"); Ronald Hayman, *Hitler & Geli*, London, 1997, p. 3 ("Geli was the crucial woman in Hitler's life, more important than Eva Braun").
40   For biographical details see Anna Maria Sigmund, "Geli Raubal," in: *idem, Die Frauen der Nazis*, vol. 1, Vienna, 1998, pp. 131ff.; *idem.; Des Führers bester Freund*, pp. 23ff.
41   Memoirs of Franz Hemmrich, p. 44; IfZ München, ED 153.
42   Quoted in Sigmund, *Des Führers bester Freund*, p. 101.
43   Hess, *Briefe*, p. 385 (dated 17 Sept. 1927). Hitler, Angela Raubal and Geli Raubal added greetings on a postcard sent by Rudolf Hess to Ilse Pröhl from the Sächsische Schweiz on 2 Sept. 1929; BA Bern, Nl Hess, J1.211-1989/148, 39. See *Die Tagebücher von Joseph Goebbels. Part 1: Aufzeichnungen 1923–1941*, ed. Elke Fröhlich, Munich, 1998, vol. 1/2, p. 258 (entry for 22 Aug. 1927): "I'm getting to know the boss's relatives. Likeable people just like him"; p. 260 (entry for 24 Aug. 1927): "Took my leave of the boss and his sweet niece Geli." See ibid., p. 267 (entries for 8 and 10 Sept. 1927).
44   H. v. Schirach, *Frauen um Hitler*, p. 46. On Geli Raubal's outward appearance see also Hayman, *Hitler & Geli*, pp. 102–4; Baldur von Schirach, *Ich glaubte an Hitler*, Hamburg, 1967, p. 107.
45   Heinrich Hoffmann, *Hitler wie ich ihn sah: Aufzeichnungen seines Leibfotografen*, Munich and Berlin, 1974, p. 124; see H. v. Schirach, *Frauen um Hitler*, p. 50. Gottfried Feder confirmed that Hitler's niece had been at the Osteria Bavaria for the first time on 10 Nov. 1927; G. Feder's diaries, vol. 10; IfZ München, ED 874.
46   H. v. Schirach, *Frauen um Hitler*, pp. 55–9 (quotation on p. 58).
47   Ibid., p. 61; see Sigmund, *Des Führers bester Freund*, pp. 125f.
48   Geli Raubal to Emil Maurice, 24 Dec. 1927; partially reprinted in Sigmund, "Geli Raubal," in *Die Frauen um Hitler*, vol. 1, pp. 140f. (see p. 141 for a facsimile of the letter).
49   See Sigmund, *Des Führers bester Freund*, pp. 127–9 (see p. 128 for a facsimile of a reference signed by Hitler, which gives the leaving date of Jan. 1928). See also IfZ München, ZS 290.
50   Nerin E. Gun, *Eva Braun-Hitler: Leben und Schicksal*, Velbert und Kettwig, 1968, p. 24.
51   Quoted in Sigmund, *Des Führers bester Freund*, p. 127.
52   H. v. Schirach, *Frauen um Hitler*, p. 51. In 1929 Hanfstaengl observed Geli Raubal and Hitler taking in a performance at Munich's Residenztheater together. They behaved like a "romantic couple," Hanfstaengl noted. Note by Hanfstaengl "Geli & A. H."; BSB München, Nl Hanfstaengl Ana 405, Box 26.
53   See Goebbels, *Tagebücher*, part 1, vol. 1/3, p. 52 (entry for 13 July 1928); p. 54 (entry for 15 July 1928).
54   Ibid., p. 123 (entry for 15 Nov. 1928). See ibid., p. 124 (entry for 17 Nov. 1928), p. 126 (entry for 19 Nov. 1928). About Hitler's performance at the Sportpalast Rudolf Hess wrote to his parents on 21 Nov. 1928: "You cannot imagine what the meeting was like—18,000 people and the boss's oratory has rarely been as captivating." BA Bern, Nl Hess, J1.211-1989/148, 41.

55   See Sigmund, *Des Führers bester Freund*, pp. 154, 159.

56   Goebbels, *Tagebücher*, part 1, vol. 1/3, p. 295 (entry for 2 Aug. 1929).

57   Gun, *Eva Braun-Hitler*, p. 24.

58   Hoffmann, *Hitler wie ich ihn sah*, p. 124. See also an interview with Hermann Esser, dated 18 March 1964, vol. 1, who claimed that it was obvious that "Hitler was very attached to her, to say nothing of being in love." BayHStA München, Nl Esser.

59   Goebbels, *Tagebücher*, part 1, vol. 1/3, pp. 105f. (entry for 19 Oct. 1928). On the rumours see also Schirach, *Ich glaubte an Hitler*, p. 105; Joachimsthaler, *Hitlers Liste*, p. 323.

60   Ralf Georg Reuth (ed.), *Joseph Goebbels Tagebücher. Vol. 1: 1924–1929*, Munich and Zurich, 1992, p. 428 (entry for 22 Nov. 1929). See Goebbels, *Tagebücher*, part 1, vol. 2/1, p. 68 (entry for 20 Jan. 1930): "He's not working very much . . . And then there are the women, the women."

61   Hanfstaengl, *Zwischen Weissem und Braunem Haus*, p. 233. See also Hanfstaengl's unpublished memoirs, p. 198, where he claims that Hitler's relationship "had directed his male libido into the proper channel for the first and only time in his life." BSB München, Nl Hanfstaengl Ana 405, Box 47.

62   Schroeder, *Er war mein Chef*, p. 153. Henriette von Schirach was also convinced that "there were no intimate relations between the two." Quoted in Knopp, *Hitler: Eine Bilanz*, p. 144. See Joachimsthaler, *Hitlers Liste*, p. 327.

63   Transcript of a conversation with Adolf Vogl and his wife on 2 Jan. 1952; IfZ München, ZS 167; see Hanfstaengl, *Zwischen Weissem und Braunem Haus*, pp. 235f.; Sigmund, *Des Führers bester Freund*, p. 144. In October 1923, the lawyer Richard Dingeldey invited Hitler to dinner on Franz-Joseph-Strasse 37. Also on the guest list were "our common friends Herr and Frau Vogl" and the Wagner scholar and musical director Alfred Lorenz. See R. Dingeldey to "my most esteemed Herr Hitler," 10 Oct. 1923; BA Koblenz, N 1128/15.

64   See Hamann, *Winifred Wagner*, p. 185; Sigmund, *Des Führers bester Freund*, p. 146: Goebbels, *Tagebücher*, part 1, vol. 2/1, p. 202 (entry for 20 July 1930).

65   See Otto Wagener, *Hitler aus nächster Nähe: Aufzeichnungen eines Vertrauten 1929–1932*, ed. Henry A. Turner, Frankfurt am Main, Berlin and Vienna, 1978, p. 98.

66   See the bill issued by Rich & Söhne, Munich for "1 pair of snake leather shoes (cost 33 marks)," which Geli Raubal had purchased on 14 July 1931. The head of the company wrote: "My dear Herr Hitler! In accordance with your order, which we greatly value, we present you with a bill for the shoes purchased by your niece and send our fond regards with a Heil!" BA Berlin-Lichterfelde, NS 26/2557.

67   Olaf Rose (ed.), *Julius Schaub: In Hitlers Schatten*, Stegen, 2005, p. 107.

68   Hoffmann, *Hitler wie ich ihn sah*, pp. 125f. (quotation on p. 126). See also H. v. Schirach, *Frauen um Hitler*, pp. 62–4.

69   H. v. Schirach, *Frauen um Hitler*, p. 64.

70   Rose, *Julius Schaub*, p. 108. Schaub gives the date as 18 Sept., which cannot be correct as Geli Raubal spent that evening locked in her room.

71   See Gun, *Eva Braun-Hitler*, p. 21; Sigmund, *Des Führers bester Freund*, p. 170.

72   Heydecker, *Hoffmann-Erinnerungen*, p. 78. See Hoffmann, *Hitler wie ich ihn sah*, p. 128. On the morning of 19 Sept., Hess called Goebbels and told him: "Geli shot herself last night. What a terrible blow! I don't dare to speculate about her motives. How will the boss get over it?" Goebbels, *Tagebücher*, part 1, vol. 2/2, p. 103 (entry for 20 Sept. 1931).

73   Sigmund, *Des Führers bester Freund*, pp. 203–5 (see p. 204 for a facsimile of the speeding ticket).

74   See ibid., pp. 174f.

75   Ibid., pp. 170f. See *idem*, "Geli Raubal," in *Die Frauen der Nazis*, vol. 1, p. 149.

76   Statements from Georg Winter, Anni Winter, Maria Reichert and Anna Kirmair are part of the final report from the Munich police dated 28 Sept. 1931; reprinted in Sigmund, "Geli Raubal," in *Die Frauen der Nazis*, vol. 1, pp. 148f.; see also *idem*., *Des Führers bester Freund*, pp. 171–3.

77   Hitler's statement from 19 Sept. 1931; reprinted in Sigmund, *Des Führers bester Freund*, pp. 175f.; see *idem*, "Geli Raubal," in *Die Frauen der Nazis*, vol. 1, pp. 150, 154.

78   *Münchener Post*, 21 Sept. 1931; for further examples of press commentary, see *Regensburger Echo*, 25 Sept. 1931 ("Tragedy in Munich's Bogenhausen"), *Freistaat*, 22 Sept. 1931 ("Hitler's family drama"), *Fränkische Tagespost*, 21 Sept. 1931 ("Suicide in Hitler's apartment") in BA Berlin-Lichterfelde, NS 26/13.

79   See Sigmund, *Des Führers bester Freund*, pp. 179f.; *idem*, "Geli Raubal," in *Die Frauen der Nazis*, vol. 1, p. 151.

80   Adolf Hitler, *Reden, Schriften, Anordnungen—Februar 1925 bis Januar 1933. Vol. 4: Von der Reichstagswahl bis zur Reichspräsidentenwahl Oktober 1930–März 1932. Part 2: Juli 1931–Dezember 1931*, ed. Christian Hartmann, Munich, 1996, doc. 36, pp. 109–11.

81   On the rumours see Sigmund, *Des Führers bester Freund*, p. 203; Gun, *Eva Braun-Hitler*, pp. 27f.; Hanfstaengl, *Zwischen Weissem und Braunem Haus*, p. 242. The story of Geli's pregnancy can be traced back to Bridget Hitler, the first wife of Hitler's half-brother, Alois; see Michael Unger (ed.), *The Memoirs of Bridget Hitler*, London, 1979, pp. 70–7. The claim that Hitler was the murderer was spread by Otto Strasser, who heard it from his brother Paul, who himself heard it from his brother Gregor, murdered in 1934; Otto Strasser, *Hitler und ich*, Konstanz, 1948, pp. 236–8.

82   See Hamann, *Winifred Wagner*, p. 211; interview with Hermann Esser on 20 March 1964, vol. 1; BayHStA München, Nl Esser; Sigmund, *Des Führers bester Freund*, pp. 184f. Leo Raubal also called his sister's death "a mystery" in an interview of 22 March 1971; IfZ München, ZS 2239. Adolf Vogl considered it "out of the question" that Geli Raubal could have committed suicide. IfZ München, ZS 167.

83   H. v. Schirach, *Frauen um Hitler*, p. 67; see Gun, *Eva Hitler-Braun*, p. 21.

84   See Hayman, *Hitler & Geli*, p. 145. See also O. Strasser, *Hitler und ich*, p. 97. Strasser, however, merely writes of "extravagant wishes" that "the imagination of a healthy man would hardly believe possible."

85   Hanfstaengl, *Zwischen Weissem und Braunem Haus*, pp. 233, 238. See the very similar account in Hanfstaengl's unpublished memoirs, pp. 189, 192; BSB München, Nl Hanfstaengl Ana 405, Box 47.

86   Hanfstaengl, *Zwischen Weissem und Braunem Haus*, p. 234. See Hayman, *Hitler & Geli*, p. 154, who uncritically accepts Hanfstaengl's version. The nude portraits, which as late as 1998 Anna Maria Sigmund reprinted and described as genuine ("Geli Raubal," in *Die Frauen der Nazis*, vol. 1, p. 144), were in fact fakes by forger Konrad Kujau. Sigmund corrected her mistake in 2003 in her book *Des Führers bester Freund* (pp. 208f.).

87   Gun, *Eva Braun-Hitler*, p. 28. See Heydecker, *Hoffmann-Erinnerungen*, p. 79. Gun and Hoffmann rely on an anecdote told by Anni Winter. According to Winter, before Geli Raubal locked herself in her room, she had discovered a letter from Eva Braun while tidying up Hitler's chamber. In it, Braun thanked Hitler for inviting her out to the theatre. But it was no secret to Raubal that Hitler had been meeting up with Heinrich Hoffmann's assistant for some time. As far as we can tell, Raubal did not see Braun as a rival. See also Rose, *Julius Schaub*, p. 103, who writes of a fleeting meeting between the two at the 1930 Oktoberfest. Gunter Peis ("Die unbekannte Geliebte") emphasises Raubal's "jealousy of Mimi Reiter," who claimed to have slept with Hitler in the summer of 1931 (see above p. 275). More recently Peter Longerich (*Joseph Goebbels: A Biography*, London, 2015, p. 160) has insinuated that there might have been a connection between Hitler's interest in Magda Goebbels (p. 285) and Raubal's suicide.

88   As in the statement by Emil Maurice dated 5 June 1945; quoted in Sigmund, *Des Führers bester Freund*, p. 186.

89   Hoffmann, *Hitler wie ich ihn sah*, pp. 130–4; see Hoffmann's manuscript for his court trial (January 1947), p. 14: Hoffmann claimed that Hitler shut himself away for ten

days, which is manifestly untrue; IfZ München, MS 2049; Gun, *Eva Braun-Hitler*, p. 22; Otto Dietrich, *12 Jahre mit Hitler*, Munich, 1955, p. 198 (from a statement by Gregor Strasser); Hans Frank, *Im Angesicht des Galgens: Deutung Hitlers und seiner Zeit auf Grund eigener Erlebnisse und Erkenntnisse*, Munich and Gräfelfing, 1953, pp. 97f. (from a statement by Rudolf Hess); Karl Alexander von Müller, *Im Wandel einer Welt: Erinnerungen. Vol. 3: 1919–1932*, ed. Otto Alexander von Müller, Munich, 1966, p. 307. Elsa Bruckmann is quoted as saying that Hitler was "utterly broken and spent several hours sobbing in incomprehension."

90   Fest, *Hitler*, p. 445. See also Kershaw, *Hitler: Hubris*, p. 354: "He seemed to be on the verge of a nervous breakdown. He spoke of giving up politics and finishing it all."

91   Hitler, *Reden, Schriften, Anordnungen*, vol. 4, part 2, doc. 37, pp. 111–15. See Goebbels, *Tagebücher*, part 1, vol. 2/2, p. 107 (entry for 25 Sept. 1931): "Early yesterday: picked up the boss. Looked haggard and pale as chalk . . . He didn't say much. Not a word about Geli."

92   See Sigmund, *Des Führers bester Freund*, pp. 193–5; Goebbels, *Tagebücher*, part 1, vol. 2/2, p. 211 (entry for 5 Feb. 1932), p. 366 (entry for 19 Sept. 1932); Hoffmann, *Hitler wie ich ihn sah*, p. 133. Hitler hired the florist Karl A. Rolleder in Vienna to maintain Raubal's grave, although he neglected to pay the bill for the plants, bouquets, cleaning and upkeep of his niece's final resting place. The florist was forced to send Hitler a reminder, asking the latter to not take it amiss if he "permitted himself to recall the outstanding sums." Karl A. Rolleder to Hitler, 5 Nov. 1931, 22 Feb. 1932; BA Berlin-Lichterfelde, NS 26/2557.

93   Goebbels, *Tagebücher*, part 1, vol. 2/2, p. 135 (entry for 27 Oct. 1931). See ibid., p. 154 (entry for 22 Nov. 1931): "The boss talked about women whom he loves a lot. About the special one he has yet to find . . . About Geli, whom he lost and for whom his heart pines. He was very emotional. We all like him so very much. He's so selfless." See also Görtemaker, *Eva Braun*, pp. 54–6.

94   Wagener, *Hitler aus nächster Nähe*, p. 358. See Hoffmann, *Hitler wie ich ihn sah*, p. 117.

95   Hess, *Briefe*, p. 415 (dated 9 Nov. 1931).

96   See above pp. 7f. and below pp. 380f. See also the justified criticism from Görtemaker, *Eva Braun*, pp. 10f.

97   Fest, *Hitler*, p. 446.

98   H. v. Schirach, *Frauen um Hitler*, p. 73; Hoffmann's manuscript for his court trial (January 1947), p. 14: "With the death of his niece, a piece of Hitler's humanity was dead and buried as well. He became a different person." IfZ München, MS 2049; see Marlies Steinert, *Hitler*, Munich, 1994, p. 252; Kershaw, *Hitler: Hubris*, p. 354.

99   Goebbels, *Tagebücher*, part 1, vol. 2/2, p. 85 (entry for 26 Aug. 1931); p. 91 (entry for 4 Sept. 1931). On Hitler's meeting with Magda Quant in Hotel Kaiserhof see Wagener, *Hitler aus nächster Nähe*, pp. 376–8.

100   Goebbels, *Tagebücher*, part 1, vol. 2/2, pp. 98, 100 (entries for 14 and 16 Sept. 1931).

101   See Longerich, *Goebbels*, p. 159.

102   Goebbels, *Tagebücher*, part 1, vol. 2/2, p. 200 (entry for 20 Jan. 1932). Among the women that the Goebbelses invited to social events in order to introduce them to Hitler was the singer and actress Gretl Slezak, the daughter of celebrated tenor Leo Slezak, whom a youthful Hitler had admired at the Linz Stadttheater in the role of Lohengrin. See Goebbels, *Tagebücher*, part 1, vol. 2/2, p. 247 (entry for 22 March 1932); p. 271 (entry for 30 April 1932); vol. 2/3, p. 63 (entry for 20 Nov. 1932), p. 75 (entry for 6 Dec. 1932). See also Schroeder, *Er war mein Chef*, pp. 159–62; Sigmund, *Des Führers bester Freund*, pp. 272f.; Joachimsthaler, *Hitlers Liste*, pp. 489–96.

103   Leni Riefenstahl, *Memoiren*, Munich, 1987, p. 214: On the meeting with Hitler in May 1932 see ibid., pp. 157–60. See Jürgen Trimborn, *Riefenstahl: Eine deutsche Karriere*, Berlin, 2002, pp. 129–33; Karin Wieland, *Dietrich & Riefenstahl: Der Traum von der neuen Frau*, Munich, 2011, pp. 176–8. In early Nov. 1932, Leni Riefenstahl paid Hitler a visit in Hotel Kaiserhof. "She's very enthusiastic about us," noted Goebbels, *Tagebücher*, part 1, vol. 2/3, p. 50 (entry for 3 Nov. 1932).

104   See Görtemaker, *Eva Braun*, pp. 39–43; Anna Maria Sigmund, "Eva Braun," in *idem, Die Frauen der Nazis*, vol. 1, pp. 159ff.

105   Hoffmann, *Hitler wie ich ihn sah*, p. 135.

106   Gun, *Eva Braun-Hitler*, pp. 46f.; for a critical perspective on Gun's portrayal see Görtemaker, *Eva Braun*, pp. 19–21.

107   See Görtemaker, *Eva Braun*, pp. 21–3; H. v. Schirach, *Frauen um Hitler*, p. 224; Gun, *Eva Braun-Hitler*, pp. 49f.

108   Schroeder, *Er war mein Chef*, p. 156. The NSDAP treasurer, Franz Xaver Schwarz, also said during questioning on 21 July 1945 that the relationship between Hitler and Eva Braun had been "purely platonic"; IfZ München, ZS 1452.

109   H. v. Schirach, *Frauen um Hitler*, p. 226.

110   See Gun, *Eva Braun-Hitler*, p. 55; Maser, *Adolf Hitler*, p. 322, who relies on a statement by Anni Winter from 1969. During her internment together with Christa Schroeder in Augsburg in 1945, Winter told of how Eva Braun began paying weekend visits half a year after Raubal's suicide. "Every Saturday," Winter said, "she appeared with a little suitcase at the apartment on Prinzregentenplatz." Schroeder, *Er war mein Chef*, pp. 234f.

111   Görtemaker, *Eva Braun*, p. 52. Upon examining the photos of the 1938 Munich Conference, which showed Daladier, Mussolini and Chamberlain in Hitler's apartment, Eva Braun allegedly told her best friend Herta Schneider (née Ostermeier): "If Chamberlain only knew the history of this sofa." Gun, *Eva Braun-Hitler*, p. 55.

112   Wagener, *Hitler aus nächster Nähe*, p. 99.

113   Richard Wagner, *Rienzi, der Letzte der Tribunen: Grosse tragische Oper in fünf Akten. Nach der Originalpartitur* ed. Egon Voss, Stuttgart, 2010, pp. 59f.; see also Hanfstaengl's note, "Rienzi—A. H."; BSB München, Nl Hanfstaengl Ana 405, Box 25.

114   Wagener, *Hitler aus nächster Nähe*, p. 358.

115   Gun, *Eva-Braun-Hitler*, p. 57. See Fritz Wiedemann, *Der Mann, der Feldherr werden wollte: Erlebnisse und Erfahrungen des Vorgesetzten Hitlers im 1. Weltkrieg und seines späteren persönlichen Adjutanten*, Velbert and Kettwig 1964, p. 70.

116   Gun, *Eva Braun-Hitler*, p. 56. See Görtemaker, *Eva Braun*, pp. 59–62, who discusses the question of when the attempt would have happened, and considers the beginning of Nov. 1932 as the most likely date.

117   Hoffmann, *Hitler wie ich ihn sah*, p. 137; see Hoffmann's manuscript for his court trial (January 1947), p. 22; IfZ München, MS 2049.

118   Schroeder, *Er war mein Chef*, p. 164; Joachimsthaler, *Hitlers Liste*, pp. 441f. On the question of motives see Görtemaker, *Eva Braun*, pp. 62f.

119   Hanfstaengl, *Zwischen Weissem und Braunem Haus*, p. 287; see also Hanfstaengl's unpublished memoirs, p. 236: "Hitler was at his most mild . . . It was the last time I experienced him in such a relaxed mood." BSB München, Nl Hanfstaengl Ana 405, Box 47.

11 *Bids and Bluffs*

1   Joseph Goebbels, *Vom Kaiserhof zur Reichskanzlei*, Munich, 1934, p. 20. On the later changes to the diary see Peter Longerich, *Joseph Goebbels: A Biography*, London 2015, pp. 192.

2   Otto Dietrich, *Mit Hitler in die Macht: Persönliche Erlebnisse mit meinem Führer*, 2nd edition, Munich, 1934 (quotations on pp. 15, 36, 58, 80). See Stefan Krings, *Hitlers Pressechef Otto Dietrich 1897–1952: Eine Biographie*, Göttingen, 2010, pp. 267f.

3   See *Die Tagebücher von Joseph Goebbels. Part 1: Aufzeichnungen 1923–1941*, ed. Elke Fröhlich, Munich, 1998, vol. 2, p. 186 (entry for 1 Jan. 1932): "The new year must bring the decision."

4   Leopold Schwarzschild, *Chronik eines Untergangs: Deutschland 1924–1939*, ed. Andreas P. Wesemann, Vienna, 2005, p. 232. See Golo Mann, *Erinnerungen und Gedanken: Eine Jugend in Deutschland*, Frankfurt am Main, 1986, p. 442.

5   Adolf Hitler, *Reden, Schriften, Anordnungen—Februar 1925 bis Januar 1933. Vol. 4: Von der Reichstagswahl bis zur Reichspräsidentenwahl Oktober 1930–März 1932. Part 3: Januar bis März 1932*, ed. Christian Hartmann, Munich, 1997, doc. 1, pp. 3–10 (quotations on pp. 4, 5).

6   Ibid., doc. 2, pp. 11–13 (quotation on p. 12).

7   Rudolf Hess, *Briefe 1908–1933*, ed. Rüdiger Hess, Munich and Vienna, 1987, p. 413 (dated 3 Sept. 1931).

8   See Hitler to Karl Haniel, 25 Jan. 1932; Hitler, *Reden, Schriften, Anordnungen*, vol. 4, part 3, doc. 13, pp. 69f.

9   Ibid., doc. 15, pp. 74–110 (quotations on pp. 81, 88, 106, 109). On Hitler's appearance before the Düsseldorf Industrial Club see Henry A. Turner, *Die Grossunternehmer und der Aufstieg Hitlers*, Berlin, 1986, pp. 260–71; Gustav Luntowski, *Hitler und die Herren an der Ruhr: Wirtschaftsmacht und Staatsmacht im Dritten Reich*, Frankfurt am Main, 2000, pp. 43–6; Volker Ackermann (ed.), *Treffpunkt der Eliten: Die Geschichte des Industrie-Clubs Düsseldorf*, Düsseldorf, 2006, pp. 128–39.

10   Dietrich, *Mit Hitler in die Macht*, pp. 46–9.

11   See Turner, *Grossunternehmer*, pp. 268f.; Luntowski, *Hitler und die Herren an der Ruhr*, pp. 46f.; Ackermann, *Treffpunkt der Eliten*, pp. 127f.; Krings, *Hitlers Pressechef*, pp. 148f.

12   See Turner, *Grossunternehmer*, p. 265.

13   See Hans Otto Eglau, *Fritz Thyssen: Hitlers Gönner und Geisel*, Berlin, 2003, p. 134. In a letter to Hugenberg on 20 Jan. 1932, which was sent from the Park Hotel in Düsseldorf, Thyssen announced he was resigning his membership in the DNVP. On 28 Jan. 1932, Thyssen added that he never deceived Hugenberg about the fact that he would only be a member of the party "as long as it was committed to cooperating with Hitler." BA Koblenz, N 1231/39.

14   Dietrich, *12 Jahre mit Hitler*, Munich, 1955, pp. 185f. See Krings, *Hitlers Pressechef*, p. 149n216, who quotes from the unpublished section of his memoirs: "I noticed that relatively minor sums were coming in. There were a couple of cheques for a few thousand marks, but relative to Hitler's expectations, the overall results were scant, which made him voice his disappointment."

15   See Turner, *Grossunternehmer*, pp. 274f.; Eglau, *Fritz Thyssen*, p. 135.

16   See Heinrich Brüning, *Memoiren 1918–1934*, Stuttgart, 1970, pp. 451, 500; Heinrich August Winkler, *Weimar 1918–1933: Die Geschichte der ersten deutschen Demokratie*, Munich, 1993, p. 444; Wolfram Pyta, *Hindenburg: Herrschaft zwischen Hohenzollern und Hitler*, Munich, 2007, pp. 645–50.

17   Quoted in Johannes Hürter, *Wilhelm Groener: Reichswehrminister am Ende der Weimarer Republik 1928–1932*, Munich, 1993, pp. 322f. In late January 1932, after negotiations had broken down, Groener described Hitler as a "visionary and idol of stupidity" and a "jester of the masses" who should be kept away from political power "at all costs." Ibid., p. 324.

18   See Hitler to Brüning, 12 Jan., 15 Jan., 25 Jan. 1932; Hitler, *Reden, Schriften, Anordnungen*, vol. 4, part 3, doc. 6, pp. 11–13; doc. 8, pp. 34–44; doc. 12, pp. 58–68. Rudolf Hess thought it was "utterly brilliant" how Hitler "turned the tables" with regard to Hindenburg's candidature. Rudolf Hess to Klara Hess, 15 Jan. 1932; BA Bern, Nl Hess, J1.211-1989/148, 49. In a letter to Brüning of 11 Jan. 1932 Hugenberg said the DNVP would refuse to support an extension of Hindenburg's term of office. BA Koblenz, N 1231/36.

19   Goebbels, *Tagebücher*, part 1, vol. 2/2, p. 199 (entry for 20 Jan. 1932).

20   Ibid., p. 205 (entry for 28 Jan. 1932), p. 207 (entry for 30 Jan. 1932).

21   Ibid., p. 209 (entry for 3 Feb. 1932).

22   Brüning, *Memoiren*, p. 519.

23   Hermann Pünder, *Politik in der Reichskanzlei: Aufzeichnungen aus den Jahren 1929–1932*, ed. Thilo Vogelsang, Stuttgart, 1961, p. 144 (entry for 15 Feb. 1932). See Pyta, *Hindenburg*, pp. 658–63.

24   Goebbels, *Tagebücher*, part 1, vol. 2/2, p. 225 (entry for 23 Feb. 1932).

25   A copy of the contract of employment prepared between the Free State of Braunschweig and the writer Adolf Hitler in BA Koblenz, N1128/27. For documentation surrounding Hitler's citizenship see Rudolf Morsey, "Hitler als Braunschweigischer Regierungsrat," in *Vierteljahrshefte für Zeitgeschichte*, 8 (1960), pp. 419–48; see also Gunnhild Ruben, *"Bitte mich als Untermieter bei Ihnen anzumelden!"*: *Hitler und Braunschweig 1932–1935*, Norderstedt, 2004, pp. 42–52.

26   Morsey, "Hitler als Braunschweigischer Regierungsrat," p. 442.

27   Goebbel, *Tagebücher*, part 1, vol. 2/2, p. 228 (entry for 26 Feb. 1932). See also ibid., p. 230 (entry for 1 March 1932): "He'll have to present himself as 'Government Counsel Hitler.' Well, well." At Baldur von Schirach's wedding with Henriette Hoffmann on 31 March 1932, where Hitler and Röhm served as best men, he signed the registry as "Government Counsel Hitler." Note by Henriette von Schirach, *"76 Jahre Leben in Deutschland"* (1989); BayHStA München, Nl. H. v. Schirach 3.

28   Heinrich August Winkler, *Der Weg in die Katastrophe: Arbeiter und Arbeiterbewegung in der Weimarer Republik 1930 bis 1933*, Berlin and Bonn, 1987, pp. 512f. On the clashes over the candidacy within the political Right, see Volker R. Berghahn, "Harzburger Front und die Kandidatur Hindenburgs für die Präsidentschaftswahlen 1932," in *Vierteljahrshefte für Zeitgeschichte*, 13 (1965), pp. 64–82.

29   Thea Sternheim, *Tagebücher. Vol. 2: 1925–1936*, ed. and selected Thomas Ehrsam and Regula Wyss, Göttingen, 2002, p. 394 (entry for 16 Feb. 1932).

30   Quoted in Klaus Schönhoven and Jochen Vogel (eds), *Frühe Warnungen vor dem Nationalsozialismus: Ein historisches Lesebuch*, Bonn, 1998, pp. 245f.; see Martin Döring, *"Parlamentarischer Arm der Bewegung": Die Nationalsozialisten im Reichstag der Weimarer Republik*, Düsseldorf, 2001, pp. 322f.; Winkler, *Weimar*, p. 446.

31   Goebbels, *Tagebücher*, part 1, vol. 2/2, p. 226 (entry for 24 Jan. 1932).

32   Ibid., pp. 230f. (entry for 1 March 1932); see Gerhard Paul, *Aufstand der Bilder: Die NS-Propaganda vor 1933*, Bonn, 1990, pp. 95f.

33   Hitler, *Reden, Schriften, Anordnungen*, vol. 4, part 3, doc. 29, pp. 138–44 (quotation on p. 142).

34   Goebbels, *Tagebücher*, part 1, vol. 2/2, p. 229 (entry for 28 Feb. 1932).

35   Quoted in Hitler, *Reden, Schriften, Anordnungen*, vol. 4, part 3, doc. 32, p. 153n1.

36   Quoted in ibid., doc. 34, p. 166n1.

37   Hitler to Hindenburg, 28 Feb. 1932; ibid., doc. 30, pp. 145–50 (quotation on p. 147).

38   Ibid., doc. 39, p. 191; see ibid., doc. 29, p. 144; doc. 32, pp. 160f.; doc. 35, p. 172; doc. 36, p. 181; doc. 41, p. 199; doc. 43, p. 202; doc. 45, p. 214. On this element of Hitler's election strategy see also Pyta, *Hindenburg*, p. 671f.

39   Hitler, *Reden, Schriften, Anordnungen*, vol. 4, part 3, doc. 32, p. 157; see ibid., doc. 34, p. 169; doc. 36, p. 179; doc. 39, p. 191; doc. 41, p. 199; doc. 43, p. 201; doc. 45, p. 213.

40   Quoted in Wolfgang Horn, *Der Marsch zur Machtergreifung: Die NSDAP bis 1933*, Düsseldorf, 1980, p. 347n66; see Paul, *Aufstand der Bilder*, p. 97.

41   Goebbels, *Tagebücher*, part 1, vol. 2/2, p. 235 (entry for 6 March 1932).

42   Ibid., p. 237 (entry for 9 March 1932). See also ibid., p. 241 (entry for 13 March 1932): "Hitler just called from Nuremberg. Everyone is confident of victory. He is too." On 29 Feb. 1932, Wilhelm Frick had written to his sister Emma: "We'll have to use all our strength if we're to be victorious. Our prospects are quite good." BA Koblenz, N 1241/7.

43   Hitler, *Reden, Schriften, Anordnungen*, vol. 4, part 3, doc. 46, pp. 219–22 (particularly pp. 219f.).

44   See Jürgen Falter, Thomas Lindenberger and Siegfried Schumann, *Wahlen und Abstimmungen in der Weimarer Republik: Materialien zum Wahlverhalten 1919–1931*, Munich, 1986, p. 46.

45   See Horn, *Der Marsch zur Machtergreifung*, p. 349; Winkler, *Weimar*, p. 449.

46   Goebbels, *Tagebücher*, part 1, vol. 2/2, pp. 241f. (entry for 14 March 1932).

47   Hitler, *Reden, Schriften, Anordnungen*, vol. 4, part 3, doc. 47, pp. 223–5 (quotations on pp. 224, 225).

48   Dietrich, *Mit Hitler in die Macht*, pp. 62f.

49   Ernst Hanfstaengl, *Zwischen Weissem und Braunem Haus: Erinnerungen eines politischen Aussenseiters*, Munich, 1970, p. 271.

50   Hitler, *Reden, Schriften, Anordnungen*, vol. 4, part 3, doc. 50, pp. 239–45 (quotations on p. 239).

51   See Wolfgang Stribrny, "Der Versuch einer Kandidatur des Kronprinzen Wilhelm bei der Reichspräsidentenwahl 1932," in *Geschichte in der Gegenwart: Festschrift für Kurt Kluxen*, Paderborn, 1972, pp. 199–210; Willibald Gutsche, *Ein Kaiser im Exil: Der letzte deutsche Kaiser Wilhelm II in Holland*, Marburg, 1991, pp. 138–40. On this episode see also Pyta, *Hindenburg*, pp. 674–8; Gerhard Granier, *Magnus von Levetzow: Seeoffizier, Monarchist und Wegbereiter Hitlers. Lebensweg und ausgewählte Dokumente*, Boppard am Rhein, 1982, pp. 173f.; Goebbels, *Tagebücher*, part 1, vol. 2/2, p. 252 (entry for 31 March 1932), p. 253 (entry for 1 April 1932). Heinrich Class, the chairman of the Pan-Germanic League, also called upon the ultra-nationalists to vote "unanimously" for Hitler in the run-off election: Class to Hugenberg, 19 March 1932; BA Koblenz, N 1231/36. In a lengthy letter to Hitler on 20 March 1932, Hugenberg justified his decision to remain passive in the run-off election by claiming that Hitler's candidacy had no chance of success and by citing the NSDAP's repeated violations of cooperative agreements reached in Bad Harzburg. BA Koblenz, N 1231/37. See also Hugenberg to Crown Prince Wilhelm, 27 April 1932; ibid.

52   Hitler, *Reden, Schriften, Anordnungen*, vol. 4, part 3, doc. 59, pp. 258–61 (quote on p. 258).

53   Goebbels, *Tagebücher*, part 1, vol. 2/2, p. 243 (entry for 16 March 1932), p. 246 (entry for 21 March 1932).

54   Dietrich, *Mit Hitler in die Macht*, p. 70; see Krings, *Hitlers Pressechef*, p. 119. "To his great regret" Hess did not accompany Hitler on his "flying tour" because the Führer wanted him "to keep an eye on things" at Munich party headquarters. Ilse Hess to the parents of Rudolf Hess, 9 May 1932; BA Bern, Nl Hess, J1.211-1989/148, 49.

55   Adolf Hitler, *Reden, Schriften, Anordnungen—Februar 1925 bis Januar 1933. Vol. 5: Von der Reichspräsidentenwahl bis zur Machtergreifung April 1932–Januar 1933. Part 1: April 1932–September 1932*, ed. Klaus A. Lankheit, Munich, 1996, doc. 7, pp. 20f.; see Goebbels, *Tagebücher*, part 1, vol. 2/2, p. 255 (entry for 5 April 1932).

56   See the apt analysis in Paul, *Aufstand der Bilder*, pp. 204–10 (quotation on p. 208).

57   Brigitte Hamann, *Winifred Wagner oder Hitlers Bayreuth*, Munich and Zurich, 2002, p. 214. See also Rudolf Hess to his parents, 23 Aug. 1928: "He has a great aversion to flying . . . He has a strong feeling that one day something will happen to him when he's flying." BA Bern, Nl Hess, J1.211-1989/148, 41. See Hess, *Briefe*, p. 418 (dated 4 May 1932); Adolf Hitler, *Monologe im Führerhauptquartier 1941–1944: Die Aufzeichnungen Heinrich Heims*, ed. Werner Jochmann, Hamburg, 1980, pp. 191f. (dated 9/10 Jan. 1942). In Hans Baur's account (*Ich flog Mächtige der Erde*, Kempten im Allgäu, 1956, p. 81), Hitler's "lack of faith in air travel" came from his first-ever flight around the time of the Kapp Putsch, during which the pilot had to make an emergency landing.

58   See Dietrich, *Mit Hitler in die Macht*, pp. 79–82.

59   Sefton Delmer, *Die Deutschen und ich*, Hamburg, 1963, pp. 146–8. See Hanfstaengl's unpublished memoirs, p. 212: "Hitler usually took the left- or right-hand front seat and dozed off, or pretended to. Or he would stare silently out the window or at a map. When people tried to attract his attention, he would bury himself in a newspaper or some notes." BSB München, Nl Hanfstaengl Ana 405, Box 47.

60   See ibid., p. 151; see Hitler, *Reden, Schriften, Anordnungen*, vol. 5, part 1, p. 270n2. On the margins of a campaign event in Gera on 26 July 1932, Hitler's entourage also "lashed out at the crowd in a number of places."

61   Ibid., doc. 8, pp. 21–5 (quotation on p. 23).

62   See the bills from 1 Sept. to 4 Sept. 1931, 10 Sept. to 13 Sept. 1931, 3 Dec. to 6 Dec. 1931, 10 Dec. to 13 Dec. 1931, 2 March 1932, 21 March to 22 March 1932, 28 April to 2 May 1932; BA Berlin-Lichterfelde, NS 26/2557. For the article in *Welt am Montag* see Hitler, *Reden, Schriften, Anordnungen*, vol. 5, part 1, doc. 11, pp. 27f.n12.

63   See the speech in Schwenningen, 9 April 1932: ibid., doc. 28, p. 47. See ibid., doc. 25, pp. 42f. (dated 8 April 1932); doc. 20, p. 38 (dated 7 April 1932). Hitler's declaration of 7 April 1932: ibid., doc. 19, pp. 36f. See also the affidavit by Rudolf Hess on 13 April 1932; BA Berlin-Lichterfelde, NS 26/328; Goebbels, *Tagebücher*, part 1, vol. 2/2, p. 253 (entry for 2 April 1932): "The Hitler bill for 4,000 marks at the Kaiserhof is an unpleasant matter. Of course it's fake. I'm going to read them the Riot Act. The Kaiserhof will give in."

64   Falter *et al.*, *Wahlen und Abstimmungen*, p. 46; Winkler, *Weimar*, p. 453.

65   Sternheim, *Tagebücher*, vol. 2, p. 399 (entry for 11 April 1932).

66   Goebbels, *Tagebücher*, part 1, vol. 2/2, p. 259 (entry for 10 April 1932). See also Hitler's public declaration on 10 April 1932, in which he claimed that "a great victory has been achieved." Hitler, *Reden, Schriften, Anordnungen*, vol. 5, part 1, doc. 30, p. 49; and Hitler's interview with Sefton Delmer from 10 April 1932: "'It is a great victory for us,' he said to me, his eyes shining with delight." Ibid., doc. 33, p. 51.

67   Goebbels, *Tagerbücher*, part 1, vol. 2/2, p. 260 (entry for 12 April 1932).

68   Hitler, *Reden, Schriften, Anordnungen*, vol. 5, part 1, doc. 39, p. 62n2.

69   Ibid., doc. 45, p. 75 (dated 18 April 1932); doc. 57, p. 91 (dated 22 April 1932).

70   Falter *et al.*, *Wahlen und Abstimmungen*, pp. 101, 91, 113, 94, 89. The architect Troost noted in his diary on 27 April 1932: "[Hitler] arrived in a fine mood, overjoyed at his success in the local elections." Timo Nüsslein, *Paul Ludwig Troost 1878–1934*, Vienna, Cologne and Weimar, 2012, p. 103.

71   Goebbels, *Tagebücher*, part 1, vol. 2/2, pp. 267f. (entry for 25 April 1932).

72   Pyta, *Hindenburg*, p. 683.

73   See Brüning, *Memoiren*, pp. 541f.; Pyta, *Hindenburg*, p. 687.

74   Hitler, *Reden, Schriften Anordnungen*, vol. 4, part 3, doc. 52, pp. 246–51; doc. 53, p. 251–3 (quotation on p. 252).,

75   See Hürter, *Wilhelm Groener*, pp. 339–45; Winkler, *Weimar*, pp. 449f., 454; Dirk Blasius, *Weimars Ende: Bürgerkrieg und Politik 1930–1933*, Frankfurt am Main, 2008, pp. 39–41.

76   Harry Graf Kessler, *Das Tagebuch. Vol. 9: 1926–1937*, ed. Sabine Gruber and Ulrich Ott with Christoph Hilse and Nadin Weiss, Stuttgart, 2010, p. 410 (entry for 16 April 1932). Similarly, the Foreign Office declared after Hitler's retreat, "Hitler's bark is worse than his bite." Detlev Clemens, *Herr Hitler in Germany: Wahrnehmungen und Deutungen des Nationalsozialismus in Grossbritannien 1920 bis 1939*, Göttingen and Zurich, 1996, p. 223.

77   Peter Longerich, *Die braunen Bataillone: Geschichte der SA*, Munich, 1989, p. 154. See Goebbels, *Tagebücher*, part 1, vol. 2/2, p. 261 (entry for 15 April 1932): "The ban on the SA is a done deal. But we'll get through it."

78   Hitler, *Reden, Schriften, Anordnungen*, vol. 5, part 1 doc. 36, pp. 54–6 (quotation on p. 56). See Hitler's interview with the *Evening Standard*, 18 April 1932: "The prohibition of the storm troops cannot last for ever; it is only a temporary measure." Ibid., doc. 37, pp. 57–59 (quotation on p. 57).

79   See Hürter, *Wilhelm Groener*, pp. 345f.; Winkler, *Weimar*, p. 455; Pyta, *Hindenburg*, p. 688.

80   See Pyta, *Hindenburg*, pp. 688f.; Hürter, *Wilhelm Groener*, pp. 344, 348; Martin Broszat, *Die Machtergreifung: Der Aufstieg der NSDAP und die Zerstörung der Weimarer Republik*, Munich, 1984, p. 140. On Schleicher's loss of support for Groener, see Brüning, *Memoiren*, p. 547; Pünder, *Politik in der Reichskanzlei*, p. 118 (dated 11 April 1932). Brüning saw Schleicher's manoeuvring as "a horrible violation of the trust of his superior Groener."

81 Goebbels, *Tagebücher*, part 1, vol. 2/2, p. 271 (entry for 29 April 1932), p. 274 (entry for 5 May 1932), p. 276 (entry for 9 May 1932).

82 Ibid., p. 276 (entry for 9 May 1932).

83 See Brüning, *Memoiren*, p. 586; Pyta, *Hindenburg*, p. 694.

84 Theodor Heuss to Reinhold Meier, 14 May 1932; Theodor Heuss, *Bürger der Weimarer Republik: Briefe 1918–1933*, ed. Michael Dorrmann, Munich, 2008, p. 465. See Pünder, *Politik in der Reichskanzlei*, p. 120 (dated 10 May 1932); Brüning, *Memoiren*, p. 587.

85 Goebbels, *Tagebücher*, part 1, vol. 2/2, p. 279 (entry for 12 May 1932).

86 See Hürter, *Wilhelm Groener*, p. 351.

87 Pünder, *Politik in der Reichskanzlei*, p. 123 (dated 15 May 1932).

88 Goebbels, *Tagebücher*, part 1, vol. 2/2, pp. 281, 283, 284, 285.

89 Ibid., p. 288 (entry for 25 May 1932).

90 Note by Meissner dated 14 June 1932; Walther Hubatsch, *Hindenburg und der Staat: Aus den Papieren des Generalfeldmarschalls und Reichspräsidenten von 1878 bis 1934*, Göttingen, 1966, pp. 327f.; see also Otto Meissner, *Staatssekretär unter Ebert, Hindenburg, Hitler*, Hamburg, 1950, pp. 223f.; Pyta, *Hindenburg*, p. 695; Winkler, *Weimar*, pp. 467f.

91 Pünder, *Politik in der Reichskanzlei*, p. 126 (dated 26 May 1932). See Meissner's note of 14 June 1932; Hubatsch, *Hindenburg und der Staat*, p. 328.

92 Note by Meissner dated 14 June 1932; Hubatsch, *Hindenburg und der Staat*, p. 329. See Pyta, *Hindenburg*, pp. 696f.

93 See Brüning, *Memoiren*, pp. 601f.; Meissner, *Staatssekretär*, pp. 226f.

94 Pünder, *Politik in der Reichskanzlei*, p. 129 (dated 29 May 1932).

95 Goebbels, *Tagebücher*, part 1, vol. 2/2, p. 293 (entry for 31 May 1932).

96 Kessler, *Das Tagebuch*, vol. 9, p. 427 (entry for 30 May 1932).

97 Winkler, *Weimar*, p. 472.

98 See memorandum from Meissner dated 30 May 1932; Thilo Vogelsang, *Reichswehr, Staat und NSDAP: Beiträge zur deutschen Geschichte 1930–1932*, Stuttgart, 1962, pp. 458f.

99 Goebbels, *Tagebücher*, part 1, vol. 2/2, p. 293 (entry for 30 May 1932).

100 Falter *et al.*, *Wahlen und Abstimmungen*, pp. 100, 98.

101 Goebbels, *Tagebücher*, part 1, vol. 2/2, p. 297 (entry for 6 June 1932). See ibid., p. 308 (entry for 24 June 1932): "We have to divorce ourselves from the Papen cabinet and go into the campaign free and unattached." In late June 1932, in a conversation with the editor-in-chief of the *Rheinisch-Westfälische Zeitung*, Eugen Mündler, Gregor Strasser voiced his concern that "the Nazis could be blamed for the mistakes of the Papen cabinet and suffer during the campaign." Mündler to Justice Minister Franz Gürtner, 21 June 1932; BA Koblenz, N 1530/22.

102 Lutz Schwerin von Krosigk in a letter dated 12 Feb. 1971; BA Koblenz, N 1276/23. See Joachim Petzold, *Franz von Papen: Ein deutsches Verhängnis*, Munich and Berlin, 1995, p. 63. When asked by a journalist on 30 May, "Who will you appoint as chancellor, General?" Schleicher supposedly answered, "I've got someone fine in mind—you'll be amazed."

103 See Winkler, *Weimar*, pp. 479f.; Pyta, *Hindenburg*, pp. 706–8; Petzold, *Franz von Papen*, pp. 66f.

104 Franz von Papen, *Der Wahrheit eine Gasse*, Munich, 1952, p. 195. On the date see Goebbels, *Tagebücher*, part 1, vol. 2/2, p. 294 (entry for 1 June 1932).

105 *Akten der Reichskanzlei: Weimarer Republik. Das Kabinett von Papen 1. Juni bis 3. Dezember 1932. Vol. 1: Juni bis September 1932*, ed. Karl-Heinz Minuth, Boppard am Rhein, 1989, no. 18, pp. 54 and 55n10.

106 Kessler, *Das Tagebuch*, vol. 9, p. 446 (entry for 21 June 1932), pp. 461f. (entry for 12 July 1932).

107 Ibid., p. 465 (entry for 18 July 1932), See Léon Schirmann, *Altonaer Blutsonntag 17. Juli 1932: Dichtungen und Wahrheit*, Hamburg, 1994.

108 Papen to Kerrl, 6 June 1932; *Das Kabinett von Papen*, vol. 1, no. 10, pp. 22f.

109 Goebbels, *Tagebücher*, part 1, vol. 2/2, p. 297 (entry for 6 June 1932). See ibid., p. 298 (entry for 7 June 1932): "We'll stay in opposition until we achieve total power. I talked to Hitler on the phone, and he shares my opinion entirely."

110 Cabinet meeting of 11 July 1932; *Das Kabinett von Papen*, vol. 1, no. 57, pp. 204–8 (quotations on pp. 205, 207).

111 See cabinet meeting of 16 July 1932; ibid., no. 63, p. 240.

112 Notes by Hirtsiefer and Severing dated 20 July 1932; ibid., no. 69b, pp. 259–62 (quotation on p. 260).

113 Prussian Government to the Reich Chancellor, 20 July 1932; ibid., no. 71, pp. 263f.

114 Goebbels, *Tagebücher*, part 1, vol. 2/2, p. 324 (entry for 21 July 1932).

115 See Peter Lessmann, *Die preussische Schutzpolizei in der Weimarer Republik: Streifendienst und Strassenkampf*, Düsseldorf, 1989, pp. 367–70.

116 Quoted in Winkler, *Der Weg in die Katastrophe*, p. 671.

117 Goebbels, *Tagebücher*, part 1, vol. 2/2, p. 324 (entry for 20 July 1932).

118 Karl-Dietrich Bracher, *Die Auflösung der Weimarer Republik: Eine Studie zum Problem des Machtverfalls in der Demokratie*, Villingen, 1955, p. 390.

119 See Winkler, *Weimar*, pp. 529f.

120 Hitler, *Reden, Schriften, Anordnungen*, vol. 5, part 1, doc. 84, p. 156.

121 Paul, *Aufstand der Bilder*, pp. 100f.

122 Text in Hitler, *Reden, Schriften, Anordnungen*, vol. 5, part 1, doc. 109, pp. 216–19. On sales see ibid., p. 216n1.

123 See ibid., doc. 122, p. 241n1; Dietrich, *Mit Hitler in die Macht*, pp. 109f.; Baur, *Ich flog Mächtige der Erde*, p. 88.

124 Hitler, *Reden, Schriften, Anordnungen*, vol. 5, part 1, doc. 126, p. 246n1.

125 Ibid., doc. 141, p. 268n4.

126 Hanfstaengl, *Zwischen Braunem und Weissem Haus*, pp. 266f.; Hanfstaengl's unpublished memoirs, p. 216; BSB München, Nl Hanfstaengl Ana 405, Box 47. See also Dietrich, *Mit Hitler in die Macht*, pp. 74f.: "From car to aeroplane, from aeroplane to car, from car into hotel . . . And repeat day after day."

127 Hitler, *Reden, Schriften, Anordnungen*, vol. 5, part 1, doc. 148, p. 276; see ibid., doc. 129, p. 249 (dated 21 July 1932, Göttingen): "I can only say that, yes, it is my life's goal to destroy and eliminate these 30 parties"; doc. 151, p. 278 (dated 28 July 1932, Aachen); doc. 158, p. 285 (dated 29 July 1932, Radolfzell); doc. 159, p. 289 (dated 30 July 1932, Kempten).

128 Quotations in ibid., doc. 112, pp. 224f. (dated 15 July 1932, Tilsit); doc. 113, p. 230 (dated 15 July 1932, Gumbinnen); doc. 118, p. 234 (dated 17 July 1932, Königsberg); doc. 121, p. 239 (dated 19 July 1932, Cottbus).

129 Ibid., doc. 112, p. 227.

130 Ibid., doc. 123, p. 244.

131 Ibid., doc. 111, p. 222 (dated 15 July 1932).

132 Ibid., doc. 163, p. 294 (dated 31 July/1 Aug. 1932).

133 *Die Deutschnationalen und die Zerstörung der Weimarer Republik: Aus dem Tagebuch von Reinhold Quaatz 1928–1933*, ed. Hermann Weiss and Paul Hoser, Munich, 1989, p. 199 (entry for 1 Aug. 1932). On the result for 31 July 1932, see Falter *et al.*, *Wahlen und Abstimmungen*, pp. 41, 44.

134 Kessler, *Das Tagebuch*, vol. 9, p. 479 (entry for 31 July 1932).

135 Goebbels, *Tagebücher*, part 1, vol. 2/2, p. 330 (entry for 1 Aug. 1932). See ibid., p. 331 (entry for 2 Aug. 1932): "We must gain power. And rule, show what we can do . . . Tolerating another government is deadly. Hitler sees things this way too."

136 Ibid., p. 332 (entry for 3 Aug. 1932).

137 Ibid., p. 332 (entry for 4 Aug. 1932).

138 Ibid., p. 333 (entry for 5 Aug. 1932). Baldur von Schirach (*Ich glaubte an Hitler*, Hamburg, 1967, p. 136) quoted Hitler as saying: "I want total power, now or never."

139   According to a draft letter by Schleicher to the *Vossische Zeitung* dated 30 Jan. 1934; Thilo Vogelsang, "Zur Politik Schleichers gegenüber der NSDAP 1932," in *Vierteljahrshefte für Zeitgeschichte*, 6 (1958), pp. 86–118 (quotation on p. 89).

140   Goebbels, *Tagebücher*, part 1, vol. 2/2, p. 334 (entry for 7 Aug. 1932).

141   Ibid., p. 337 (entry for 11 Aug. 1932).

142   Kessler, *Das Tagebuch*, vol. 9, p. 488 (entry for 10 Aug. 1932).

143   Ibid., p. 488 (entry for 11 Aug. 1932).

144   Goebbels, *Tagebücher*, part 1, vol. 2/2, p. 338 (entry for 12 Aug. 1932).

145   Notes by Meissner dated 11 Aug. 1932; Hubatsch, *Hindenburg und der Staat*, pp. 335–8 (quotation on p. 336).

146   Quoted in Pyta, *Hindenburg*, p. 717.

147   Cabinet meeting on 10 Aug. 1932; *Das Kabinett von Papen*, vol. 1, no. 99, pp. 377–86 (quotations on pp. 379, 385f.).

148   Goebbels, *Tagebücher*, part 1, vol. 2/2, p. 339 (entry for 13 Aug. 1932).

149   See Pünder, *Politik in der Reichskanzlei*, p. 139 (dated 13 Aug. 1932).

150   On the course of the conversation see Papen, *Der Wahrheit eine Gasse*, pp. 222f. (quotations on p. 223); Goebbels, *Tagebücher*, part 1, vol. 2/2, p. 340: Schleicher and Papen whispered in Hitler's ear "as though he were a sick horse," trying to get him to accept the vice-chancellorship. "They're trying to wear us down," Goebbels wrote. "That's out of the question. Hitler is refusing . . . Papen wants to inform Hindenburg." See also Pünder, *Politik in der Reichskanzlei*, p. 139 (dated 13 Aug. 1932).

151   Goebbels, *Tagebücher*, part 1, vol. 2/2, p. 340 (entry for 14 Aug. 1932).

152   Memorandum from Meissner dated 13 Aug. 1932; first printed in Vogelsang, *Reichswehr, NSDAP und Staat*, pp. 479f.; also in Hubatsch, *Hindenburg und der Staat*, pp. 338f.; *Das Kabinett von Papen*, vol. 1, no. 101, pp. 391f. According to Meissner's notes entitled "Hitlers Aufstieg zur Macht und seine Regierungszeit 1932–1935" (undated, post 1945), Hindenburg declared at the end of this conversation that he now had a better opinion of Hitler: "He's fiery and passionate, but he's a patriotic man with big plans and the best intentions." IfZ München, ZS 1726. See also Meissner, *Staatssekretär*, pp. 239–41; Winkler, *Weimar*, pp. 510f.; Pyta, *Hindenburg*, pp. 719f.

153   This was also Goebbels's opinion, *Tagebücher*, part 1, vol. 2/2, p. 340 (entry for 14 Aug. 1932): "Hitler has been lured into a trap with Hindenburg."

154   Minutes of the talks dated 13 Aug. 1932, signed by Hitler, Frick and Röhm; BA Berlin-Lichterfelde, NS 51/222; reprinted in *Das Kabinett von Papen*, vol. 1, no. 102, pp. 393–6 (quotation on p. 395). Also in Hitler, *Reden, Schriften, Anordnungen*, vol. 5, part 1, doc. 167, pp. 300–2.

155   The official communiqué reprinted in *Das Kabinett von Papen*, vol. 1, doc. 101, p. 392n5.

156   Pünder, *Politik in der Reichskanzlei*, p. 141 (dated 18 Aug. 1932). See Papen, *Der Wahrheit eine Gasse*, p. 224.

157   Minutes signed by Hitler, Frick and Röhm dated 13 Aug. 1932; *Das Kabinett von Papen*, vol. 1, doc. 102, pp. 393f.

158   Alan Bullock, *Hitler: A Study in Tyranny*, London, 1990, p. 222. See Konrad Heiden, *Adolf Hitler: Das Zeitalter der Verantwortungslosigkeit. Eine Biographie*, Zurich, 1936, p. 300: "In front of the eyes of the entire German people, Hitler ascended the steps of power, and before those same eyes, he tumbled back down them."

159   Hitler, *Reden, Schriften, Anordnungen*, vol. 5, part 1, doc. 180, pp. 330–7 (quotation on pp. 330f.). See Ralf Georg Reuth, *Hitler: Eine Biographie*, Munich and Zurich, 2003, p. 274.

160   Goebbels, *Tagebücher*, part 1, vol. 2/2, p. 341 (entry for 14 Aug. 1932).

161   Hanfstaengl, *Zwischen Weissem und Braunem Haus*, p. 279.

162   Hitler, *Reden, Schriften, Anordnungen*, vol. 5, part 1, doc. 172, pp. 313–15 (quotation on p. 314: "He was bitter over his rebuff last Saturday by President von Hindenburg"). Joachim von Ribbentrop, who visited the Obersalzberg in August 1932, found Hitler "full of fury with Herr von Papen and the entire government in Berlin." Joachim

von Ribbentrop, *Zwischen London und Moskau: Erinnerungen und letzte Aufzeichnungen*, ed. Annelies von Ribbentrop, Leoni am Starnberger See, 1961, p. 36.

163   Hitler, *Reden, Schriften, Anordnungen*, vol. 5, part 1, doc. 173, pp. 173f.

164   On the series of violent attacks from August 1932 see Richard Bessel, *Political Violence and the Rise of Nazism: The Storm Troopers in Eastern Germany 1925–1934*, New Haven, 1984, pp. 87ff.; Dirk Walter, *Antisemitische Kriminalität und Gewalt: Judenfeindschaft in der Weimarer Republik*, Bonn, 1999, pp. 237–40; Blasius, *Weimars Ende*, p. 84; Longerich, *Die braunen Bataillone*, pp. 156f.

165   Kessler, *Das Tagebuch*, vol. 9, p. 480 (entry for 1 Aug. 1932).

166   Cabinet meeting of 9 Aug. 1932; *Das Kabinett von Papen*, vol. 1, no. 98, pp. 374–7 (quotation on pp. 374f.). See Winkler, *Weimar*, p. 508; Blasius, *Weimars Ende*, p. 87.

167   See the documentation in Paul Kluke, "Der Fall Potempa," in *Vierteljahrshefte für Zeitgeschichte*, 5 (1957), pp. 279–97; see also Richard Bessel, "The Potempa Murder," in *Central European History*, 10 (1977), pp. 241–54.

168   Hitler, *Reden, Schriften, Anordnungen*, vol. 5, part 1, doc. 174, p. 317. See also Hitler's telegram of 23 Aug. 1932, ibid., doc. 175, pp. 318–20; Goebbels, *Tagebücher*, part 1, vol. 2/2, p. 346 (entry for 24 Aug. 1932): "Major storm of protest because of the death sentence. Hitler has issued a sharply worded call to arms . . . Things at a boil everywhere."

169   Quoted in Winkler, *Weimar*, pp. 513f.; see Goebbels, *Tagebücher*, part 1, vol. 2/2, p. 346: "A sharply worded essay: 'The Jews are to blame.' It will do the job."

170   Quoted in Reuth, *Hitler*, p. 273. See also Heiden, *Hitler: Das Zeitalter der Verantwortungslosigkeit*, p. 300: "A cry of outrage is going through the general public. That went too far!"

171   Kessler, *Das Tagebuch*, vol. 9, p. 496 (entry for 28 Aug. 1932).

172   See Kluke, "Der Fall Potempa," pp. 285f.; Blasius, *Weimars Ende*, p. 95. Hitler had already announced the pardons of the Potempa murderers in a speech at Zirkus Krone in Munich on 9 Sept. 1932; Hitler, *Reden, Schriften, Anordnungen*, vol. 5, part 1, doc. 183, p. 347.

173   Schacht to Hitler, 29 Aug. 1932; Hess, *Briefe*, pp. 420f.

174   Goebbels, *Tagebücher*, part 1, vol. 2/2, p. 348 (entry for 26 Aug. 1932).

175   Brüning, *Memoiren*, p. 623. On the contact between the Centre and Nazi parties see Herbert Hömig, *Brüning: Politiker ohne Auftrag. Zwischen Weimarer und Bonner Republik*, Paderborn, 2005, pp. 31–5.

176   Goebbels, *Tagebücher*, part 1, vol. 2/2, p. 348 (entry for 26 Aug. 1932).

177   See Brüning, *Memoiren*, p. 624; Hömig, *Brüning: Politiker ohne Auftrag*, p. 34.

178   Hugenberg to Albert Vögler, 19 Aug. 1932; BA Koblenz, N 1231/39. In late August, rumours started circulating in Hugenberg's party that a "cabinet of Schleicher (Chancellor)-Brüning-Strasser" was already a "done deal." Quaatz, *Die Deutschnationalen und die Zerstörung der Weimarer Republik*, p. 201 (dated 27 Aug. 1932).

179   See Winkler, *Weimar*, pp. 515f.

180   Cabinet meeting of 10 Aug. 1932; *Das Kabinett von Papen*, vol. 1, no. 99, p. 382. See also Eberhard Kolb and Wolfram Pyta, "Die Staatsnotstandsplanung unter den Regierungen Papen und Schleicher," in Heinrich August Winkler (ed.), *Die deutsche Staatskrise 1930–33*, Munich, 1992, pp. 155–81.

181   Memorandum by Meissner dated 30 Aug. 1932; Hubatsch, *Hindenburg und der Staat*, pp. 339–43; also in *Das Kabinett von Papen*, vol. 1, no. 120, pp. 474–9.

182   Hitler, *Reden, Schriften, Anordnungen*, vol. 5, part 1, doc. 176, pp. 320–2 (quotation on p. 320).

183   Quoted in Döring, *Parlamentarischer Arm*, p. 335 (also the previous quote). See Quaatz, *Die Deutschnationalen und die Zerstörung der Weimarer Republik*, p. 202 (dated 30 Aug. 1932): "Nazis very well-behaved in order to convince Hindenburg of a 'functioning Reichstag.' No socialists in the presidium since the Centre has moved to the right!"

184   Goebbels, *Tagebücher*, part 1, vol. 2/2, p. 354 (entry for 1 Sept. 1932).

185   Ibid., p. 359 (entry for 9 Sept. 1932), p. 361 (entry for 11 Sept. 1932). See Pyta, *Hindenburg*, p. 736.
186   Brüning, *Memoiren*, p. 625.
187   Hitler, *Reden, Schriften, Anordnungen*, vol. 5, part 1, doc. 178, pp. 325–9 (quotations on pp. 328f.). See Goebbels, *Tagebücher*, part 1, vol. 2/2, p. 355: "Sportpalast full beyond capacity. Hitler almost consumed with ovations. He spoke better than ever. A sharply worded final reckoning with Papen and the reactionaries. Storms of enthusiasm. This speech will work miracles."
188   Hitler, *Reden, Schriften, Anordnungen*, vol. 5, part 1, doc. 180, pp. 330–7 (quotations on pp. 331, 335).
189   Ibid., doc. 183, pp. 339–50 (quotation on p. 350). See Goebbels, *Tagebücher*, part 1, vol. 2/2, p. 358: "In the evening Zirkus Krone. Hitler really went after Papen. Thunderous ovations from the more than capacity house."
190   Papen, *Der Wahrheit eine Gasse*, p. 235. On the Reichstag session of 12 Sept. 1932 see Döring, *Parlamentarischer Arm*, pp. 337–44; Winkler, *Weimar*, pp. 522f.
191   Goebbels, *Tagebücher*, part 1, vol. 2/2, p. 362 (entry for 13 Sept. 1932). See Pünder, *Politik in der Reichskanzlei*, p. 145 (dated 13 Sept. 1932): "The only positive is the vast majority for a vote of no confidence."
192   Kessler, *Das Tagebuch*, vol. 9, p. 502 (entry for 13 Sept. 1932).
193   See the cabinet meetings of 14 and 17 Sept. 1932; *Das Kabinett von Papen*, vol. 2, no. 141, pp. 576–83, no. 146, p. 599.
194   Pünder, *Politik in der Reichskanzlei*, p. 149 (dated 8 Oct. 1932).
195   Goebbels, *Tagebücher*, part 1, vol. 2/2, p. 372 (entry for 28 Sept. 1932), p. 373 (entry for 29 Sept. 1932).
196   See Longerich, *Die braunen Bataillone*, pp. 159f.; Horn, *Der Marsch zur Machtergreifung*, pp. 357f.
197   Goebbels, *Tagebücher*, part 1, vol. 2/3, p. 38 (entry for 16 Oct. 1932).
198   See Turner, *Grossunternehmer*, pp. 354–8.
199   Hitler, *Reden, Schriften, Anordnungen*, vol. 5, part 1, doc. 193 (dated 24 Sept. 1932), pp. 362–5 (quotation on p. 363). See also Goebbels, *Tagebücher*, part 1, vol. 2/3, p. 30 (entry for 2 Oct. 1932): "Hitler very optimistic. Probably too much."
200   Adolf Hitler, *Reden, Schriften, Anordnungen—Februar 1925 bis Januar 1933. Vol. 5: Von der Reichspräsidentenwahl bis zur Machtergreifung April 1932–Januar 1933. Part 2: Oktober 1932–Januar 1933*, eds Klaus A. Lankheit and Christian Hartmann, Munich, 1998, doc. 5, pp. 13–15 (quotation on p. 15). See also ibid., doc. 4, pp. 10f. (interview with the Italian newspaper *Il Trevere* from 4 Oct. 1932): "We are neither impatient nor fearful nor nervous because we know that the 6 November elections will necessarily go our way."
201   Goebbels, *Tagebücher*, part 1, vol. 2/2, p. 363 (entry for 14 Sept. 1932).
202   Von Hassell's notes on his discussions with Hitler in Ulrich von Hassell, *Römische Tagebücher und Briefe 1932–1938*, ed. Ulrich Schlie, Munich, 2004, p. 217.
203   Paul, *Aufstand der Bilder*, p. 105.
204   Hitler, *Reden, Schriften, Anordnungen*, vol. 5, part 2, doc. 54, p. 146 (dated 1 Nov. 1932, Karlsruhe); doc. 22, p. 77 (dated 18 Oct. 1932, Elbing).
205   Ibid., doc. 56, p. 168 (dated 3 Nov. 1932, Hanover). See ibid., doc. 25, p. 85 (dated 19 Oct. 1932, Breslau), "The only thing that tempts me is leadership itself, genuine power, and nothing else."
206   Ibid., doc. 6, p. 16 (dated 11 Oct. 1932, Günzburg); doc. 21, p. 73 (dated 17 Oct. 1932, Königsberg); doc. 16, p. 61 (dated 16 Oct. 1932, Coburg).
207   See Paul, *Aufstand der Bilder*, p. 106; Ian Kershaw, *Hitler 1889–1936: Hubris*, London, 1998, p. 389.
208   Heiden, *Hitler: Das Zeitalter der Verantwortungslosigkeit*, p. 302. Kessler, *Das Tagebuch*, vol. 9, p. 513 (entry for 11 Oct. 1932) reported Nazi sympathisers saying that Hitler's behaviour had shown that he and the party were "pursuing politics for reasons of prestige and elevating the party above the nation."

209 Quotations in Hitler, *Reden, Schriften, Anordnungen*, vol. 5, part 2, doc. 12, p. 77 (dated 18 Oct. 1932, Elbing); doc. 10, p. 23 (dated 13 Oct. 1932, Nuremberg); doc. 21, p. 75 (dated 17 Oct. 1932, Königsberg), doc. 47, p. 133 (dated 30 Oct. 1932, Essen).

210 Goebbels, *Tagebücher*, part 1, vol. 2/2, p. 370 (entry for 25 Sept. 1932).

211 Ibid., vol. 2/3, p. 51 (entry for 5 Nov. 1932). On the Berlin public transport strike see Winkler, *Der Weg in die Katastrophe*, pp. 765–73.

212 Excerpts from the diary of Luise Solmitz, 4 Jan. 1932–5 March 1933; Werner Jochmann, *Nationalsozialismus und Revolution: Ursprung und Geschichte der NSDAP in Hamburg 1922–1933. Dokumente*, Frankfurt am Main, 1963, p. 416 (dated 6 Nov. 1932).

213 Falter *et al.*, *Wahlen und Abstimmungen*, pp. 41, 44.

214 Quoted in Bernd Sösemann, *Das Ende der Weimarer Republik in der Kritik demokratischer Publizisten*, Berlin, 1976, p. 164.

215 Goebbels, *Tagebücher*, part 1, vol. 2/3, p. 49 (entry for 1 Nov. 1932), p. 53 (entry for 7 Nov. 1932).

216 Hitler, *Reden, Schriften, Anordnungen*, vol. 5, part 2, doc. 61, pp. 185f. (entry for 6 Nov. 1932).

217 See Goebbels, *Tagebücher*, part 1, vol. 2/3, p. 54 (entry for 8 Nov. 1932): "Yesterday: rotten mood in the Gau"; p. 56 (entry for 11 Nov. 1932) "Bitter mood."

218 Ibid., p. 54 (entry for 9 Nov. 1932).

219 Papen to Hitler, 13 Nov. 1932; *Das Kabinett von Papen*, vol. 2, no. 214, p. 952n2. See Papen, *Der Wahrheit eine Gasse*, p. 240.

220 Goebbels, *Tagebücher*, part 1, vol. 2/3, p. 57 (entry for 12 Nov. 1932), p. 58 (entry for 13 Nov. 1932).

221 Hitler to Papen, 16 Nov. 1932, Hitler, *Reden, Schriften, Anordnungen*, vol. 5, part 2, doc. 65, pp. 188–93 (quotation on p. 190); also in *Das Kabinett von Papen*, vol. 2, no. 214, pp. 952–6. See Goebbels, *Tagebücher*, part 1, vol. 2/3, p. 61 (entry for 17 Nov. 1932): "Hitler sent a letter cancelling talk with Papen. Letter makes a big impression."

222 Cabinet meeting on 17 Nov. 1932; *Das Kabinett von Papen*, vol. 2, no. 215, pp. 956–60 (quotations on pp. 957, 960). See Papen, *Der Wahrheit eine Gasse*, p. 241.

223 Kessler, *Das Tagebuch*, vol. 9, p. 529 (entry for 18 Nov. 1932).

224 Winkler, *Der Weg in die Katastrophe*, p. 790.

225 Kessler, *Das Tagebuch*, vol. 9, p. 531 (entry for 19 Nov. 1932).

226 Meissner's minutes on Hugenberg's reception, 18 Nov. 1932; *Das Kabinett von Papen*, vol. 2, no. 217, pp. 973f. (quotation on p. 974).

227 Meissner's minutes on the meeting between Hindenburg and Dingeldey, 18 Nov. 1932; ibid., no. 219, pp. 977–9 (quotation on p. 978).

228 Meissner's minutes on the meeting between Kaas and Schäffer, 18 and 19 Nov. 1932; ibid., no. 218, pp. 975–7 (quotation on p. 976); no. 223, pp. 987f.

229 Goebbels, *Tagebücher*, part 1, vol. 2/3, pp. 62f. (entry for 19 Nov. 1932).

230 Meissner's minutes on the meeting between Hindenburgs and Hitler, 19 Nov. 1932; Hubatsch, *Hindenburg und der Staat*, pp. 350–2; also in *Das Kabinett von Papen*, vol. 2, no. 222, pp. 984–6 (quotations on pp. 984n3, 985, 986). On the idea of an enabling law see Pyta, *Hindenburg*, pp. 754f.

231 Goebbels, *Tagebücher*, part 1, vol. 2/3, p. 63 (entry for 20 Nov. 1932), p. 64 (entry for 21 Nov. 1932).

232 Meissner's minutes on the meeting between Hindenburgs and Hitler, 21 Nov. 1932; Hubatsch, *Hindenburg und der Staat*, pp. 352–6; also in *Das Kabinett von Papen*, vol. 2, doc. 224, pp. 988–92 (quotations on pp. 988, 990, 992). Hitler's letter to Hindenburg dated 21 Nov. 1932 also in Hitler, *Reden, Schriften, Anordnungen*, vol. 5, part 2, doc. 67, pp. 194–7.

233 See Hitler to Meissner, 21 Nov. 1932; Hitler, *Reden, Schriften, Anordnungen*, vol. 5, part 2, doc. 68, pp. 197–9; Meissner to Hitler, 22 Nov. 1932; *Das Kabinett von Papen*, vol. 2, no. 225, pp. 992, 994. See Meissner, *Staatssekretär*, pp. 248f.

234 Hitler to Meissner, 23 Nov. 1932; Hitler, *Reden, Schriften, Anordnungen*, vol. 5, part 2, doc. 69, pp. 199–205 (quotation on p. 204): Meissner to Hitler, 24 Nov. 1932; *Das Kabinett von Papen*, vol. 2, no. 227, pp. 998–1000 (quotation on p. 999).

235 Goebbels, *Tagebücher*, part 1, vol. 2/3, p. 67 (entry for 25 Nov. 1932), p. 68 (entry for 26 Nov. 1932).

236 Text of the petition in Eberhard Czichon, *Wer verhalf Hitler zur Macht? Zum Anteil der deutschen Industrie an der Zerstörung der Weimarer Republik*, Cologne, 1967, no. 10, pp. 69f.

237 Hjalmar Schacht to Hitler, 12 April 1932; BA Berlin-Lichterfelde, NS 51/46. On the "Keppler Circle" see Turner, *Grossunternehmer*, pp. 293–301; Dirk Stegmann, "Zum Verhältnis von Grossindustrie und Nationalsozialismus 1930–1933," in *Archiv für Sozialgeschichte* 13 (1973), pp. 426–8.

238 On the signatories of the petition see Turner, *Grossunternehmer*, p. 365; Stegmann, "Zum Verhältnis von Grossindustrie und Nationalsozialismus," pp. 434f.; Petzold, *Franz von Papen*, pp. 119f.; Asendorf, *Hamburger Nationalklub*, p. 146.

239 Schacht to Hitler, 12 Nov. 1932; Czichon, *Wer verhalf Hitler zur Macht?*, p. 64.

240 Vögler to Schröder, 21 Nov. 1932; ibid., p. 72.

241 Cabinet meeting of 25 Nov. 1932; *Das Kabinett von Papen*, vol. 2, no. 232, pp. 1013–17 (quotation on p. 1014).

242 Diary entries by Hans Schäffer dated 26 Nov. 1932; *Das Kabinett von Papen*, vol. 2, no. 234, pp. 1025f.

243 See Winkler, *Weimar*, pp. 547–53. See Goebbels, *Tagebücher*, part 1, vol. 2/3, p. 70 (entry for 29 Nov. 1932): "Papen seems on the out. Schleicher at the fore again . . . Searching for a tolerating majority. Won't find one with us."

244 Goebbels, *Tagebücher*, part 1, vol. 2/3, p. 70 (entry for 28 Nov. 1932).

245 Hitler's interview in the *Daily Express*, 27 Nov. 1932; Hitler, *Reden, Schriften, Anordnungen*, vol. 5, part 2, doc. 73, pp. 213f.; Delmer, *Die Deutschen und ich*, p. 174.

246 Hitler, *Reden, Schriften, Anordnungen*, vol. 5, part 2, doc. 74, pp. 214f. (dated 30 Nov. 1932); see Goebbels, *Tagebücher*, part 1, vol. 2/3, p. 71 (entry for 1 Dec. 1932): "Meissner has invited the boss to visit the old man . . . A new 13 August is in the works. The decision: Hitler won't go."

247 Memorandum by Meissner on the meetings with Hindenburg on 1 and 2 Dec. 1932; Hubatsch, *Hindenburg und der Staat*, pp. 266f.; see also Papen, *Der Wahrheit eine Gasse*, pp. 243–5. On Schleicher's "vertical front" idea see Axel Schildt, *Militärdiktatur auf Massenbasis? Die Querfrontkonzeption der Reichswehrführung um General Schleicher am Ende der Weimarer Republik*, Frankfurt am Main and New York 1981.

248 Papen, *Der Wahrheit eine Gasse*, p. 245.

249 Schwerin von Krosigk's diary notes on the cabinet meeting of 2 Dec. 1932; *Das Kabinett von Papen*, vol. 2, no. 239b, pp. 1036–8.

250 Papen, *Der Wahrheit eine Gasse*, p. 250.

251 Goebbels, *Tagebücher*, part 1, vol. 2/3, p. 72 (entry for 2 Dec. 1932).

252 See a critical appraisal of the source in Longerich, *Goebbels*, pp. 194f.

253 Goebbels, *Tagebücher*, part 1, vol. 2/3, p. 75 (entry for 5 Dec. 1932): "Makes me want to vomit"; p. 76 (entry for 7 Dec. 1932): "Almost a 40 per cent decline in Thuringia since 31 July."

254 Quoted in Eberhard Kolb, "Die Weimarer Republik und das Problem der Kontinuität vom Kaiserreich zum 'Dritten Reich,'" in idem., *Umbrüche deutscher Geschichte 1866/71–1918/19–1929/33: Ausgewählte Aufsätze*, eds Dieter Langewiesche and Klaus Schönhoven, Munich, 1993, p. 367.

255 Report by the Munich police, 30 Dec. 1932; quoted in Henry A. Turner, *Thirty Days to Power: January 1933*, London, 1996, p. 58. On the NSDAP crisis see Hans Frank, *Im Angesicht des Galgens: Deutung Hitlers und seiner Zeit auf Grund eigener Erlebnisse und Erkenntnisse*, Munich and Gräfelfing, 1953, p. 107; Mathias Rösch, *Die Münchner*

NSDAP 1925–1933: Eine Untersuchung zur inneren Struktur der NSDAP in der Weimarer Republik, Munich, 2002, pp. 370f., 427f., 431.

256 Goebbels, *Tagebücher*, part 1, vol. 2/2, p. 310 (entry for 28 June 1932), p. 355 (entry for 2 Sept. 1932), p. 356 (entry for 4 Sept. 1932).

257 August Heinrichsbauer to Gregor Strasser, 20 Sept. 1932; BA Berlin-Lichterfelde, NS 51/222. See also Eugen Mündler to Franz Gürtner, 21 June 1932, who wrote that Gregor Strasser was well liked in industrialist circles because he was considered "an honest, straight-forward person." BA Koblenz, N 1530/22.

258 Goebbels, *Tagebücher*, part 1, vol. 2/3, p. 55.

259 Ibid., p. 71 (entry for 1 Dec. 1932).

260 See ibid., p. 75 (entry for 6 Dec. 1932).

261 Hitler, *Reden, Schriften, Anordnungen*, vol. 5, part 2, doc. 84, pp. 247–9 (quotations on pp. 248, 249).

262 Goebbels, *Tagebücher*, part 1, vol. 2/3, p. 75 (entry for 6 Dec. 1932).

263 Quoted in Udo Kissenkoetter, *Gregor Strasser und die NSDAP*, Stuttgart, 1978, p. 203. The original resignation letter has not been preserved, only a handwritten draft, which is part of the estate of Strasser's deputy, Paul Schulz. Ibid., p. 172. For more on the Strasser crisis see Peter Stachura, *Gregor Strasser and the Rise of Nazism*, London, 1983, pp. 103ff.

264 Hinrich Lohse, "Der Fall Strasser," undated memorandum (c.1952); IfZ München, ZS 265.

265 Ibid.; see Goebbels, *Tagebücher*, part 1, vol. 2/3, p. 77 (entry for 9 Dec. 1932): "Inspectors visiting Hitler. All very downcast but none with Strasser." Otto Wagener recalled Hitler preparing himself by reading Marc Antony's speech from Shakespeare's *Julius Caesar*. Note by Martin Broszat on a meeting with Otto Wagener, 5 Feb. 1960; IfZ München, ZS 1732.

266 Ibid., p. 78 (entry for 9 Dec. 1932). See also Leni Riefenstahl's account, for once credible, who visited Hitler in the Hotel Kaiserhof on 8 Dec. 1932; Leni Riefenstahl, *Memoiren*, Munich, 1987, p. 186. On the article in the *Täglichen Rundschau* see Kissenkoetter, *Gregor Strasser und die NSDAP*, p. 73.

267 Hitler's order from 9 Dec. 1932; Hitler, *Reden, Schriften, Anordnungen*, vol. 5, part 2, doc. 86, p. 251.

268 See Kissenkoetter, *Gregor Strasser und die NSDAP*, p. 177.

269 See Goebbels, *Tagebücher*, part 1, vol. 2/3, p. 78 (entry for 10 Dec. 1932): "Feder has tripped himself up. Asks for a sabbatical in a letter that goes to the press before it goes to Hitler. That can't be topped. Everyone outraged." In early January 1933, Otto Engelbrecht, the NSDAP district and regional director in Murnau, reported back to the party leadership about a conversation with Feder on 30 Dec. 1932. He quoted Feder as saying that he, "like Strasser, had long realised that the movement had passed its zenith. For that reason, it had been unwise to refuse to join the government." BA Berlin-Lichterfelde, NS 51/222.

270 Goebbels, *Tagebücher*, part 1, vol. 2/3, p. 79 (entry for 10 Dec. 1932).

271 Ibid., p. 81 (entry for 13 Dec. 1932).

272 Ibid., p. 80 (entry for 11 Dec. 1932).

273 Hitler, *Reden, Schriften, Anordnungen*, vol. 5, part 2, doc. 89, pp. 253–8 (quotation on p. 256).

274 Ibid., doc. 92, pp. 259–61 (quotation on p. 260).

275 Goebbels, *Tagebücher*, part 1, vol. 2/3, p. 79 (entry for 11 Dec. 1932), p. 85 (entry for 17 Dec. 1932), p. 87 (entry for 22 Dec. 1932).

276 Ibid., p. 89 (entry for 24 Dec. 1932). See ibid., p. 90 (entry for 25 Dec. 1932): "The main thing is that the movement sticks together. It is our ultimate source of consolation."

277 *Akten der Reichskanzlei: Weimarer Republik. Das Kabinett von Schleicher 3. Dezember 1932 bis 20. Januar 1933*, ed. Anton Golecki, Boppard am Rhein, 1986, no. 16, p. 57. At a

meeting of the steering committee of the Pan-Germanic League on 10–11 Dec. 1932 in Berlin, Heinrich Class opined that "the role of the NSDAP has basically been played out even if it continues to have millions of supporters in the years to come." Rainer Hering, *Konstruierte Nation: Der Alldeutsche Verband 1890–1939*, Hamburg, 2003, pp. 484f.; see Johannes Leicht, *Heinrich Class 1968–1953: Die politische Biographie eines Alldeutschen*, Paderborn, 2012, p. 387.

278   Quoted in Kolb, *Umbrüche deutscher Geschichte*, p. 369.

279   Quoted in Reuth, *Hitler*, p. 285.

280   Quoted in Kolb, *Umbrüche deutscher Geschichte*, p. 368.

281   Thomas Mann, *Briefe III: 1924–1932*, selected and ed. Thomas Sprecher, Hans R. Vaget and Cornelia Bernini, Frankfurt am Main, 2011, p. 673 (dated 22 Dec. 1932). Thomas Mann's son, Golo Mann, felt similar; see Tilmann Lahme, *Golo Mann: Biographie*, Frankfurt am Main, 2009, p. 87.

282   Memorandum by Malcolm Christie dated 19 Dec. 1932; Clemens, *Herr Hitler in Germany*, p. 246.

283   Quoted in Joachim Fest, *Hitler: Eine Biographie*, Frankfurt am Main, Berlin and Vienna, 1973, p. 495. In a confidential note on 12 Jan. 1933, an advisor to the Italian consulate in Berlin, Vincenzo Cionnardi, offered a different view: "It is true that there's lots of talk about the collapse of the party and the end, sooner or later, of the movement. But this has less to do with reality than with the hopes and expectations of the other parties and various segments of society that fear Hitler might come to power." Frank Bajohr and Christoph Strupp (eds), *Fremde Blicke auf das "Dritte Reich": Berichte ausländischer Diplomaten über Herrschaft und Gesellschaft in Deutschland 1933–1945*, Göttingen, 2011, p. 352.

284   Jochmann, *Nationalsozialismus und Revolution*, pp. 419f.

285   Heuss, *Bürger der Weimarer Republik*, p. 536 (dated 29 Dec. 1932). On Bosch's position at the end of 1932 see Joachim Scholtyseck, *Robert Bosch und der liberale Widerstand gegen Hitler 1933 bis 1945*, Munich, 1999, p. 113.

286   Carl von Ossietzky, "Wintermärchen," *Die Weltbühne*, 3 Jan. 1933; in *idem*, *Sämtliche Schriften*. Vol. 6: *1931–1933*, eds Gerhard Kraiker, Günther Nickel, Renke Siems and Elke Suhr, Reinbek bei Hamburg, 1994, pp. 437–43 (quotations on pp. 437, 440).

287   Ernst Deuerlein (ed.), *Der Aufstieg der NSDAP in Augenzeugenberichten*, Munich, 2nd edition, 1976, p. 411.

288   Quoted in Turner, *Thirty Days to Power*, p. 29.

12 *Month of Destiny: January 1933*

1   Heinrich Brüning, *Memoiren 1918–1934*, Stuttgart, 1970, p. 648. Albert Speer also said that in the winter of 1933–34 Hitler repeatedly talked of having been faced with "very difficult situations, which he had always escaped due to a favourable turn of events." Albert Speer, *Erinnerungen: Mit einem Essay von Jochen Thies*, Frankfurt am Main and Berlin, 1993, p. 54.

2   Brigitte Hamann, *Winifred Wagner oder Hitlers Bayreuth*, Munich and Zurich, 2002, pp. 229f.

3   See *Die Tagebücher von Joseph Goebbels. Part 1: Aufzeichnungen 1923–1941*, ed. Elke Fröhlich, Munich, 1998, vol. 2/3, p. 93 (entry for 30 Dec. 1932).

4   Ibid., p. 94 (entry for 31 Dec. 1932).

5   Adolf Hitler, *Reden, Schriften, Anordnungen—Februar 1925 bis Januar 1933. Vol. 5: Von der Reichspräsidentenwahl bis zur Machtergreifung April 1932–Januar 1933. Part 2: Oktober 1932–Januar 1933*, eds Klaus A. Lankheit and Christian Hartmann, Munich, 1998, doc. 107, pp. 297–311 (quotations on pp. 298, 299, 310f.).

6   Leopold Schwarzschild, *Chronik eines Untergangs: Deutschland 1924–1939*, ed. Andreas P. Wesemann, Vienna, 2005, p. 243. See Schwerin von Krosigk to Holm Eggers,

21 Aug. 1974, who wrote that "the influence Papen had exercised over the old gentleman" had been decisive: "In a sense, he guaranteed that the matter would turn out well." BA Koblenz, N 1276/42.

7   Konrad Heiden, *Adolf Hitler: Das Zeitalter der Verantwortungslosigkeit. Eine Biographie*, Zurich, 1936, p. 315.

8   See Wolfram Pyta, *Hindenburg: Herrschaft zwischen Hohenzollern und Hitler*, Munich, 2007, p. 791. For an example of the earlier depiction of Hindenburg see Joachim Fest, *Hitler: Eine Biographie*, Frankfurt am Main, Berlin and Vienna, 1973, p. 502; in Fest's view, Hindenburg was "exhausted, confused and not always capable of maintaining an overview."

9   Karl-Dietrich Bracher, *Die Auflösung der Weimarer Republik: Eine Studie zum Problem des Machtverfalls in der Demokratie*, Villingen, 1955, p. 691.

10 Keppler to Schröder, 19 Dec. 1932; Eberhard Czichon, *Wer verhalf Hitler zur Macht? Zum Anteil der deutschen Industrie an der Zerstörung der Weimarer Republik*, Cologne, 1967, pp. 74–6 (quotation on p. 75). On the circumstances surrounding the meeting see also the transcript of Kurt von Schröder's questioning on 18 June 1947; IfZ München, ZS 557.

11 Heinrich Muth, "Das 'Kölner Gespräch' am 4. Januar 1933," in *Geschichte in Wissenschaft und Unterricht*, 37 (1986), pp. 463–80, 529–41 (quotation on p. 531).

12 Keppler to Schröder, 26 Dec. 1932; Czichon, *Wer verhalf Hitler zur Macht?* pp. 76f. See also Franz von Papen, *Der Wahrheit eine Gasse*, Munich, 1952, p. 254.

13 On Hitler's and Papen's motives, see Henry A. Turner, *Thirty Days to Power: January 1933*, London, 1996, pp. 42f.

14 On the conspiratorial circumstances surrounding the meeting see Otto Dietrich, *Mit Hitler in die Macht: Persönliche Erlebnisse mit meinem Führer*, 2nd edition, Munich, 1934, pp. 169f.; Turner, *Thirty Days to Power*, p. 38.

15 On the course and content of the conversation see the affidavit by Kurt von Schröder dated 21 July 1947; Czichon, *Wer verhalf Hitler zur Macht?*, pp. 77–9 (quotation on p. 78); Papen, *Der Wahrheit eine Gasse*, pp. 255f.; Turner, *Thirty Days to Power*, pp. 44f.; Joachim Petzold, *Franz von Papen: Ein deutsches Verhängnis*, Munich and Berlin, 1995, pp. 138–40. For a critical perspective on the sources see Muth, "Das 'Kölner Gespräch,'" pp. 533–6.

16 Keppler to Schröder, 6 Jan. 1933; Schacht to Schröder, 6 Jan. 1933; Czichon, *Wer verhalf Hitler zur Macht?*, pp. 79f.

17 Goebbels, *Tagebücher*, part 1, vol. 2/3, p. 103 (entry for 10 Jan. 1933).

18 See Turner, *Thirty Days to Power*, p. 47; see also Papen's letter to Ferdinand von Bredow dated 31 Oct. 1933; Irene Strenge, *Ferdinand von Bredow: Notizen vom 20. 2. 1933 bis 31. 12. 1933. Tägliche Aufzeichnungen vom 1. 1. 1934 bis 28. 6. 1934*, Berlin, 2009, p. 175n1 (entry for 23 Oct. 1933).

19 Hitler, *Reden, Schriften, Anordnungen*, vol. 5, part 2, doc. 116, p. 332n1. Further press commentary in n2.

20 Ibid., doc. 116, p. 332.

21 Goebbels, *Tagebücher*, part 1, vol. 2/3, p. 100 (entry for 7 Jan. 1933). See also ibid., p. 101 (entry for 8 Jan. 1933): "The press is still buzzing with [the news of] the Hitler–Papen meeting." For the reporting of the *Tägliche Rundschau*, see Petzold, *Franz von Papen*, pp. 140–2.

22 Quoted in Turner, *Thirty Days to Power*, p. 50.

23 See ibid., p. 71; Papen, *Der Wahrheit eine Gasse*, pp. 255, 260f. During a conversation with BVP Chairman Schäffer on 10 Jan. 1933, Schleicher was "quite dismayed" at the meeting between Papen and Hitler, who was "obviously trying to get access to the old man, even though the latter can't stand him." Schäffer's diary dated 10 Jan. 1933; quoted in Astrid Pufendorf, *Die Plancks: Eine Familie zwischen Patriotimus und Widerstand*, Berlin, 2006, p. 305.

24 Otto Meissner, *Staatssekretär unter Ebert, Hindenburg, Hitler*, Hamburg, 1950, p. 261.

25 See Pyta, *Hindenburg*, p. 780.
26 Goebbels, *Tagebücher*, part 1, vol. 2/3, p. 103 (entry for 10 Jan. 1933).
27 *Akten der Reichskanzlei: Weimarer Republik. Das Kabinett von Schleicher 3. Dezember 1932 bis 20. Januar 1933*, ed. Anton Golecki, Boppard am Rhein, 1986, no. 25, pp. 101–17 (quotations on pp. 109, 106). See Henry A. Turner, *Die Grossunternehmer und der Aufstieg Hitlers*, Berlin, 1986 pp. 370f.; Heinrich August Winkler, *Weimar 1918–1933: Die Geschichte der ersten deutschen Demokratie*, Munich, 1993, pp. 562f. On 21 Dec. 1932, Hugenberg informed Schleicher about "the concerns . . . we have in relation to the great economic challenges of the moment and the danger of slipping back into parliamentary procedure." BA Koblenz, N 1231/38.
28 See Turner, *Thirty Days to Power*, p. 83; Winkler, *Weimar*, pp. 558f.
29 See Meissner, *Staatssekretär*, pp. 251f.; Winkler, *Weimar*, pp. 569f. In a cabinet meeting on 16 Jan. 1933 Schleicher expressed his doubts as to whether Strasser "would bring many followers with him." *Das Kabinett von Schleicher*, no. 56, p. 233.
30 *Das Kabinett von Schleicher*, no. 50, pp. 206–8; no. 51, pp. 208–14. See Papen, *Der Wahrheit eine Gasse*, p. 261 (dated 12 Jan. 1933): "As we're hearing, the presentations of the National Board of the Reich Landowners' Association, when they were received by Hindenburg yesterday, made a deep impression upon him."
31 *Das Kabinett von Schleicher*, no. 51, p. 214n116. See Bernd Hoppe, "Von Schleicher zu Hitler: Dokumente zum Konflikt zwischen dem Reichslandbund und der Regierung Schleicher in den letzten Wochen der Weimarer Republik," in *Vierteljahrshefte für Zeitgeschichte*, 45 (1997), pp. 629–57; Stephanie Merkenich, *Grüne Front gegen Weimar: Reichsland-Bund und agrarischer Lobbyismus 1918–1933*, Düsseldorf, 1998, pp. 316f.
32 Goebbels, *Tagebücher*, part 1, vol. 2/3, p. 106 (entry for 15 Jan. 1933); idem, *Vom Kaiserhof zur Reichskanzlei*, Munich, 1934, p. 241.
33 See Turner, *Thirty Days to Power*, pp. 112f; Pyta, *Hindenburg*, p. 770.
34 *Das Kabinett von Schleicher*, no. 56, p. 234n15; ibid., no. 25, p. 103.
35 Statement from the DNVP Reichstag faction dated 21 Jan. 1933 (with Hugenberg's handwritten draft) in BA Koblenz, N 1231/38. In mid-December 1932, the conservative nationalist politician and agricultural estate owner Ewald von Kleist-Schmenzin called for a war against the government, proclaiming "Schleicher must go in favour of an authoritarian state leadership." The cabinet was only presidential in name, Kleist-Schmenzin sneered, since "in reality Schleicher was dependent on parties and groups and changed his policies if he met any opposition from them." BA Koblenz, N 1231/37.
36 See Wolfgang Michalka, "Joachim von Ribbentrop: Vom Spirituosenhändler zum Aussenminister," in Ronald Smelser and Rainer Zitelmann (eds), *Die Braune Elite: 22 biographische Skizzen*, Darmstadt, 1989, pp. 201–11. On the meeting of 10/11 Jan. 1933, see Joachim von Ribbentrop, *Zwischen London und Moskau: Erinnerungen und letzte Aufzeichnungen*, ed. Annelies von Ribbentrop, Leoni am Starnberger See, 1961, pp. 36–8. On Hitler's visit to the opera, see Hitler, *Reden, Schriften, Anordnungen*, vol. 5, part 2, doc. 126, p. 346. See also Goebbels, *Tagebücher*, part 1, vol. 2/3, p. 103 (entry for 11 Jan. 1933): "Hitler intends to talk to Papen late this evening. On tenterhooks." When interrogated on 11 Sept. 1946, Ribbentrop testified that Wilhelm Keppler had asked him to make his house in the Berlin district of Dahlem available for Papen and Hitler's talks; IfZ München, ZS 1357.
37 Goebbels, *Tagebücher*, part 1, vol. 2/3, p. 105 (entry for 13 Jan. 1933); Ribbentrop, *Zwischen London und Moskau*, p. 38.
38 Quoted in Jutta Ciolek-Kümper, *Wahlkampf in Lippe: Die Wahlkampfpropaganda der NSDAP zur Landtagswahl am 15. Januar 1933*, Munich, 1976, p. 153. See also *Hitlers Tischgespräche im Führerhauptquartier*, ed. Henry Picker, Stuttgart, 1976, p. 325 (dated 21 May 1942): "He campaigned in the Lippe election with particular energy and using every ounce of his personality."
39 Ciolek-Kümper, *Wahlkampf in Lippe*, p. 147.

40   See ibid., pp. 164f.

41   Quotations in Hitler, *Reden, Schriften, Anordnungen*, vol. 5, part 2, doc. 114, p. 328 (dated 4 Jan. 1933, Bösingfeld), doc. 125, p. 344 (dated 9 Jan. 1933, Lage), doc. 127, p. 350 (dated 11 Jan. 1933, Lemgo), doc. 120, p. 377 (dated 6 Jan. 1933, Horn), doc. 117, p. 333 (dated 5 Jan. 1933, Leopoldshöhe).

42   Goebbels, *Tagebücher*, part 1, vol. 2/3, p. 105 (entry for 13 Jan. 1933).

43   Dietrich, *Mit Hitler in die Macht*, p. 176. On the occasion of Grevenburg's 400th anniversary during New Year 1937/38, Baron von Oeynhausen had a plaque mounted in the inner courtyard. As he wrote to Hitler, it was intended to recall that the Führer had "honoured" Grevenburg by residing there and "organising and leading the campaign that culminated with victory in Lippe on 15 Jan. and the historical turning point for Germany's destiny on 30 Jan." Baron von Oeynhausen to Hitler, 15 Dec. 1937. Wiedemann responded in Hitler's name on 27 Dec. 1937; BA Koblenz, N 1720/8.

44   Goebbels, *Tagebücher*, part 1, vol. 2/3, p. 105 (entry for 13 Jan. 1933). See ibid., p. 98 (entry for 4 Jan. 1933); p. 99 (entry for 5 Jan. 1933); pp. 105f. (entry for 14 Jan. 1933): "Speaking of Strasser. He's about to betray us to Schleicher . . . A base plot"; p. 106 (entry for 15 Jan. 1933): "Strasser wants to join the cabinet as vice-chancellor! Traitor!"

45   See Ernst Deuerlein (ed.), *Der Aufstieg der NSDAP in Augenzeugenberichten*, Munich, 2nd edition, 1976, p. 415.

46   Quoted in Ciolek-Kümper, *Wahlkampf in Lippe*, p. 273.

47   Quoted in Turner, *Thirty Days to Power*, p. 65.

48   Goebbels, *Tagebücher*, part 1, vol. 2/3, p. 107 (entry for 16 Jan. 1933).

49   Quoted in Ciolek-Kümper, *Wahlkampf in Lippe*, pp. 279f.

50   Goebbels, *Tagebücher*, part 1, vol. 2/3, p. 108 (entry for 17 Jan. 1933). According to an account by another participant, Hitler declared that the change in power was just around the corner and no one could stop him taking "Bismarck's seat." Hinrich Lohse, "Der Fall Strasser," undated memorandum (c.1952); IfZ München, ZS 265.

51   See Goebbels, *Tagebücher*, part 1, vol. 2/3, p. 112 (entry for 22 Jan. 1933), p. 115 (entry for 25 Jan. 1933).

52   Keppler to Schröder, 19 Jan. 1933; Muth, "Das 'Kölner Gespräch,'" p. 538.

53   Hugenberg to Hitler, 28 Dec. 1932; BA Koblenz, N 1231/37. See Larry Eugene Jones, "'The Greatest Stupidity of My Life': Alfred Hugenberg and the Formation of the Hitler Cabinet, January 1933," in *Journal of Contemporary History*, 27 (1992), pp. 63–87 (at p. 70).

54   *Die Deutschnationalen und die Zerstörung der Weimarer Republik: Aus dem Tagebuch von Reinhold Quaatz 1928–1933*, ed. Hermann Weiss and Paul Hoser, Munich, 1989, p. 223 (entry for 17 Jan. 1933). See also Goebbels, *Tagebücher*, part 1, vol. 2/3, p. 109 (entry for 18 Jan. 1933): "Hitler was with Hugenberg. But without success."

55   Ribbentrop, *Zwischen London und Moskau*, p. 39 (dated 18 Jan. 1933).

56   Papen to Springorum, 20 Jan. 1933; Muth "Das 'Kölner Gespräch,'" p. 538. On 7 Jan. 1933 Papen met with Springorum, Krupp, Vögler and Reusch in Dortmund to exchange opinions. We do not know the details of their discussions. See Petzold, *Franz von Papen*, pp. 144–6. Apparently, Papen gave the others the impression that Hitler no longer wanted the chancellorship and would be satisfied with a junior position in a coalition. See Christian Marx, *Paul Reusch und die Gutehoffnungshütte: Leitung eines deutschen Grossunternehmens*, Göttingen, 2013, pp. 324f.

57   Goebbels, *Tagebücher*, part 1, vol. 2/3, pp. 109f. (entry for 19 Jan. 1933), p. 110 (entry for 20 Jan. 1933). See Turner, *Thirty Days to Power*, p. 78. On the film *The Rebel*, see Siegfried Kracauer, *Von Caligari zu Hitler: Eine Geschichte des deutschen Films*, vol. 2, ed. Karsten Witte, Frankfurt am Main, 1979, pp. 275f.; 567–9.

58   Goebbels, *Tagebücher*, part 1, vol. 2/3, p. 112 (entry for 22 Jan. 1933).

59   Hitler, *Reden, Schriften, Anordnungen*, vol. 5, part 2, doc. 143, p. 375n2.

60   Ibid., pp. 375–87 (quotations on pp. 381, 375, 378, 387). See Goebbels, *Tagebücher*, part 1, vol. 2/3, p. 111 (entry for 21 Jan. 1933): "Hitler entered to gigantic celebrations and spoke marvellously . . . Never-ending ovations. Hitler is quite a fellow."

61   Hitler, *Reden, Schriften, Anordnungen*, vol. 5, part 2, doc. 145, pp. 389f. On the cult of Horst Wessel see Daniel Siemens, *Horst Wessel: Tod und Verklärung eines Nationalsozialisten*, Berlin, 2009, pp. 131ff.

62   Goebbels, *Tagebücher*, part 1, vol. 2/3, p. 113 (entry for 23 Jan. 1933).

63   Quoted in Heinrich August Winkler, *Der Weg in die Katastrophe: Arbeiter und Arbeiterbewegung in der Weimarer Republik 1930 bis 1933*, Berlin and Bonn, 1987, p. 838.

64   See Ribbentrop, *Zwischen London und Moskau*, p. 39 (dated 22 Jan. 1933); Turner, *Thirty Days to Power Weg*, p. 112.

65   See Pyta, *Hindenburg*, p. 787; Turner, *Thirty Days to Power*, p. 115. The blackmail theory is advanced, among others, in Fest, *Hitler*, p. 501. In May 1942, Hitler himself recalled "unreservedly laying out the political situation as he understood it and openly declaring that every further week of waiting would be a lost one." *Hitlers Tischgespräche*, p. 325 (dated 21 May 1942).

66   See Papen, *Der Wahrheit eine Gasse*, p. 265.

67   Goebbels, *Tagebücher*, part 1, vol. 2/3, p. 114 (entry for 25 Jan. 1933).

68   See Ribbentrop, *Zwischen London und Moskau*, p. 39 (dated 22 Jan. 1933).

69   Ibid., p. 39 (dated 23 Jan. 1933).

70   Goebbels, *Tagebücher*, part 1, vol. 2/3, p. 114 (entry for 25 Jan. 1933).

71   Ribbentrop, *Zwischen London und Moskau*, p. 39 (dated 24 Jan. 1933). See Goebbels, *Tagebücher*, part 1, vol. 2/3, pp. 116f. (entry for 26 Jan. 1933): "The Harzburg Front re-emerging. Frick and Göring negotiating."

72   Quaatz, *Die Deutschnationalen und die Zerstörung der Weimarer Republik*, p. 224 (dated 21 Jan. 1933).

73   Goebbels, *Tagebücher*, part 1, vol. 2/3, p. 112 (entry for 22 Jan. 1933).

74   Cabinet meeting of 16 Jan. 1933; *Das Kabinett von Schleicher*, no. 56, pp. 230–8.

75   Meissner's notes on Schleicher's reception from Hindenburg on 23 Jan. 1933; ibid., no. 65, pp. 284f.

76   See Winkler, *Weimar*, pp. 578, 581; Turner, *Thirty Days to Power*, pp. 100f.; Merkenich, *Grüne Front gegen Weimar*, p. 318.

77   Winkler, *Weimar*, p. 582.

78   Braun to Schleicher, 28 Jan. 1933; *Das Kabinett von Schleicher*, no. 73, pp. 311f.

79   Kaas to Schleicher, 26 Jan. 1933; ibid., no. 70, pp. 304f.

80   Cabinet meeting of 28 Jan. 1933; ibid., no. 71, pp. 306–10.

81   Ibid., no. 77, p. 317. See Goebbels, *Tagebücher*, part 1, vol. 2/3, p. 118 (entry for 29 Jan. 1933): "Breaking news: Schleicher has just stepped down. So we've toppled him! More quickly than I thought . . . The old man practically chucked him out. A just punishment for this latter-day Fouché."

82   Kessler, *Das Tagebuch*, vol. 9, p. 535 (entry for 28 Jan. 1933).

83   Ribbentrop, *Zwischen London und Moskau*, p. 40 (dated 27 Jan. 1933). On the talks between Hitler and Hugenberg on 27 Jan. 1933 see Turner, *Thirty Days to Power*, p. 138; Jones, "Hugenberg and the Hitler Cabinet," p. 73. Goebbels, *Tagebücher*, part 1, vol. 2/3, p. 117 (entry for 28 Jan. 1933): "Hitler spoke with Hugenberg who is being intransigent, insisting on Schmidt as Hitler's state secretary, Brosius as his press spokesman and the subordination of the Berlin police to the Reichswehr. Impossible demands. Infuriating." See also Quaatz, *Die Deutschnationalen und die Zerstörung der Weimarer Republik*, p. 228 (concerning 28 Jan. 1933): "Hugenberg suggested 'neutralising' the police, something Hitler heatedly rejected"; Otto Schmidt-Hannover, *Umdenken oder Anarchie: Männer—Schicksale—Lehren*, Göttingen, 1959, pp. 332f.

84   Goebbels, *Tagebücher*, part 1, vol. 2/3, p. 118 (entry for 29 Jan. 1933).

85   On the rumours of a Papen cabinet see Kessler, *Das Tagebuch*, vol. 9, p. 533 (entry for 25 Jan. 1933), p. 534 (entry for 27 Jan. 1933).

86 Ribbentrop, *Zwischen London und Moskau*, p. 41 (dated 27 Jan. 1933).

87 Papen, *Der Wahrheit eine Gasse*, pp. 269f.

88 Schwerin von Krosigk's diary on the events in Berlin between 23 and 28 Jan. 1933; *Das Kabinett von Schleicher*, no. 77, p. 318.

89 See Turner, *Thirty Days to Power*, pp. 143f. According to Schmidt-Hannover (*Umdenken oder Anarchie*, p. 340), Blomberg was "the joker added at the last minute to the contest for governmental power." On Blomberg's appointment see Kirstin A. Schäfer, *Werner von Blomberg: Hitlers erster Feldmarschall. Eine Biographie*, Paderborn, 2006, pp. 97–100.

90 Goebbels, *Tagebücher*, part 1, vol. 2/3, p. 118 (entry for 29 Jan. 1933).

91 See Papen, *Der Wahrheit eine Gasse*, pp. 271f.; Ribbentrop, *Zwischen London und Moskau*, p. 42 (dated 29 Jan. 1933); Turner, *Thirty Days to Power*, pp. 145f.

92 See Theodor Duesterberg's unpublished memoirs, pp. 173, 179; BA Koblenz, N 1377/44.

93 Theodor Duesterberg, *Der Stahlhelm und Hitler*, Wolfenbüttel and Hanover, 1949, pp. 38f. See also Theodor Duesterberg's memorandum, "Die Regierungsbildung am 30. Januar 1933," dated 27 April 1946 (which erroneously dates the meeting as 26 Jan.). Afterwards Duesterberg declared: "If you go to bed with an anaconda, you can't complain if you wake up with your legs broken. The hour will come, Herr Privy Counsellor, in which you'll have to flee through the garden in the middle of the night in your underpants." IfZ München, ZS 1700. Repeated verbatim in Duesterberg's memoirs, p. 188; BA Koblenz, N 1377/44.

94 Quaatz, *Die Deutschnationalen und die Zerstörung der Weimarer Republik*, p. 229 (dated 29 Jan. 1933).

95 Goebbels, *Tagebücher*, part 1, vol. 2/3, p. 119 (entry for 30 Jan. 1933).

96 Hammerstein's notes from 28 Jan. 1935; Bracher, *Die Auflösung der Weimarer Republik*, pp. 733f.; Kurt Freiherr von Hammerstein, *Spähtrupp*, Stuttgart, 1963, pp. 49f. Contrary to this see Hans Magnus Enzensberger, *Hammerstein oder Der Eigensinn: Eine deutsche Geschichte*, Frankfurt am Main, 2008, pp. 101–7, who suggests that Hammerstein did not want to prevent a Papen–Hugenberg cabinet so much as to keep Hitler from attaining power.

97 Hammerstein's notes from 28 Jan. 1935; Bracher, *Die Auflösung der Weimarer Republik*, p. 734; Hammerstein, *Spähtrupp*, pp. 55f.

98 Goebbels, *Tagebücher*, part 1, vol. 2/3, p. 119 (entry for 30 Jan. 1933).

99 *Hitlers Tischgespräche*, p. 327 (dated 21 May 1942); see Goebbels, *Tagebücher*, part 1, vol. 2/3, p. 119 (entry for 30 Jan. 1933): "Called Helldorf. He's taking measures with Police Major Wecke."

100 See Turner, *Thirty Days to Power*, pp. 150–2; Meissner, *Staatssekretär*, pp. 268f.

101 Wieland Eschenhagen (ed.), *Die "Machtergreifung": Tagebuch einer Wende nach Presseberichten vom 1. Januar bis 6. März 1933*, Darmstadt and Neuwied, 1982, pp. 86f.

102 *Das Kabinett von Schleicher*, no. 46, p. 232.

103 See Goebbels, *Tagebücher*, part 1, vol. 2/3, p. 119 (entry for 30 Jan. 1933).

104 Duesterberg, *Der Stahlhelm und Hitler*, p. 40; see Duesterberg, "Die Regierungsbildung am 30. Januar 1933"; IfZ München, ZS 1700; Duesterberg's memoirs, p. 189, BA Koblenz, N 1377/44; Turner, *Thirty Days to Power*, p. 155.

105 Duesterberg, *Der Stahlhelm und Hitler*, pp. 40f.; see Duesterberg, "Die Regierungsbildung am 3. Januar 1933"; IfZ München, ZS 1700; Duesterberg's memoirs, pp. 190f.; BA Koblenz, N 1377/44. See also Papen, *Der Wahrheit eine Gasse*, pp. 275f.; Meissner, *Staatssekretär*, pp. 269f.; Turner, *Thirty Days Power*, pp. 156f.

106 Schwerin von Krosigk's diaries on the events of 29 and 30 Jan. 1933; *Das Kabinett von Schleicher*, no. 79, pp. 320–3 (quotation on p. 323).

107 Goebbels, *Tagebücher*, part 1, vol. 2/3, p. 120 (entry for 31 Jan. 1933).

108 Ibid., p. 120 (entry for 31 Jan. 1933). On Hitler's reception at the Hotel Kaiserhof see also Hanfstaengl, *Zwischen Weissem und Braunem Haus*, p. 288; Hanfstaengl's unpublished memoirs, p. 238: "'Now we're at our destination,' he announced with

euphoric exaltation. All of us, waiters and maids included, gathered around him and tried to shake his hand"; BSB München, Nl Hanfstaengl Ana 405, Box 47.

109   Hitler, *Reden, Schriften, Anordnungen*, vol. 5, part 2, doc. 150, pp. 296–8.

110   Kessler, *Das Tagebuch*, vol. 9, p. 537 (entry for 30 Jan. 1933). See Duesterberg's memoirs, p. 192: "There was an undeniable, massive tumult of excitement almost everywhere in Berlin during this mild winter night." BA Koblenz, N 1377/44.

111   Heinrich Hoffmann, *Hitler wie ich ihn sah: Aufzeichnungen seines Leibfotographen*, Munich and Berlin, 1974, p. 49.

112   Quoted in Lothar Machtan, *Der Kaisersohn bei Hitler*, Hamburg, 2006, p. 279. See Geoffrey Verhey, *Der "Geist von 1914" und die Erfindung der Volksgemeinschaft*, Hamburg, 2000, pp. 362f.

113   See Hans Frank, *Im Angesicht des Galgens: Deutung Hitlers und seiner Zeit auf Grund eigener Erlebnisse und Erkenntnisse*, Munich and Gräfelfing, 1953, p. 129.

114   Goebbels, *Tagebücher*, part 1, vol. 2/3, p. 121 (entry for 31 Jan. 1933).

115   Ibid., p. 120 (entry for 31 Jan. 1933). See Frank, *Im Angesicht des Galgens*, p. 111: "Fantastically splendid, unforgettable, magnificent hours!"

116   Rudolf Hess, *Briefe 1908–1933*, ed. Rüdiger Hess, Munich and Vienna, 1987, pp. 424f. (dated 31 Jan. 1933). On the headed paper Hess had crossed out "The Chancellor" and added by hand: "The day after Adolf Hitler came to power"; BA Bern, Nl Hess, J1.211-1989/148, 51.

117   E. Krogmann's diary from 30 Jan. 1933; quoted in Karl Heinz Roth, "Ökonomie und politische Macht: Die 'Firma Hamburg' 1930–1945," in Angelika Ebbinghaus and Karsten Linne (eds), *Kein abgeschlossenes Kapitel: Hamburg im "Dritten Reich,"* Hamburg, 1997, p. 15. Heinrich Himmler's mother Anna was also "moved with joy that your desire, which we all shared, has been fulfilled and your Führer has achieved this hard-won victory." Anna Himmler to Heinrich Himmler, 31 Jan. 1933; BA Koblenz, N 1126/13.

118   L. Solmitz's diary from 30 Jan. 1933; Werner Jochmann, *Nationalsozialismus und Revolution: Ursprung und Geschichte der NSDAP in Hamburg 1922–1933. Dokumente*, Frankfurt am Main, 1963, p. 73.

119   Lutz Graf Schwerin von Krosigk, *Es geschah in Deutschland: Menschenbilder unseres Jahrhunderts*, Tübingen and Stuttgart, 1951, p. 147.

120   Ewald von Kleist-Schmenzin, "Die letzte Möglichkeit: Zur Ernennung Hitlers zum Reichskanzler am 30. Januar 1933," in *Politische Studien*, 10 (1959), p. 92. See Turner, *Thirty Days to Power*, pp. 147f.

121   Quoted in Gerhard Ritter, *Carl Goerdeler und die deutsche Widerstandsbewegung*, Stuttgart, 1954, pp. 65f. See Jones, "Hugenberg and the Hitler Cabinet," p. 63.

122   Quoted from the report of 1958 by the Munich Institute for Contemporary History, for example in Deuerlein, *Der Aufstieg*, p. 418. In comparison see Fritz Tobias, "Ludendorff, Hindenburg, Hitler: Das Phantasieprodukt des Ludendorff-Briefes vom 30. Januar 1933," in Uwe Backes, Eckhard Jesse and Rainer Zitelmann, *Die Schatten der Vergangenheit: Impulse zur Historisierung des Nationalsozialismus*, Frankfurt am Main and Berlin, 1992, pp. 319–43. Further, Lothar Gruchmann, "Ludendorffs 'prophetischer' Brief an Hindenburg vom Januar/Februar 1933: Eine Legende," in *Vierteljahrshefte für Zeitgeschichte*, 47 (1999), pp. 559–62. Ludendorff's letters to Hindenburg from 25 Aug. and 18 Nov. 1933, in which he protested against the loss of rights, are reprinted in Henrik Eberle (ed.), *Briefe an Hitler: Ein Volk schreibt seinem Führer: Unbekannte Dokumente aus Moskauer Archiven—zum ersten Mal veröffentlicht*, Bergisch-Gladbach, 2007, pp. 189f.

123   See Manfred Nebelin, *Ludendorff: Diktator im Ersten Weltkrieg*, Munich, 2011, pp. 9f., 17. On the "reconciliation" between Hitler and Ludendorff see Goebbels, *Tagebücher*, part 1, vol. 4, pp. 74, 82 (entries for 1 April and 6 April 1937). On Hitler's reaction to the death of Ludendorff see ibid., vol. 5, p. 64 (entry for 22 Dec. 1937). In early 1941, Hitler ordered that the house where Ludendorff was born, on the estate of

Kruszewnia near Posen, be preserved as a monument in honour of the general's "undying services." Wehrmacht Adjutant Schmundt to Lammers, 27 Jan. 1941; BA Berlin-Lichterfelde, R 43 II/985.

124 Kessler, *Das Tagebuch*, vol. 9, p. 538 (entry for 31 Jan. 1933), p. 539 (entry for 6 Feb. 1933). The *Tägliche Rundschau* was of the same opinion on 31 Jan. 1933: "The Harzburger, and not Herr Hitler, are the true victors." Quoted in Petzold, *Franz von Papen*, p. 160.

125 *Vossische Zeitung*, 30 Jan. 1933. Quoted in Dirk Blasius, "30. Januar 1933: Tag der Machtergreifung," in Dirk Blasius and Wilfried Loth (eds), *Tage deutscher Geschichte im 20. Jahrhundert*, Göttingen, 2006, p. 51. See also *Berliner Tageblatt*, 30 Jan. 1933; Eschenhagen, *Die "Machtergreifung,"* p. 96.

126 Quoted in Saul Friedländer, *Das Dritte Reich und die Juden: Die Jahre der Verfolgung 1933–1939*, Munich, 1998, vol. 1, p. 27. See ibid. for the statements by the Association's board on 30 Jan. 1933: "Today in particular the old saying applies: wait and see." See also Avraham Barkai, *Der Centralverein deutscher Staatsbürger jüdischen Glaubens 1893–1938*, Munich, 2002, pp. 271f.

127 Willy Cohn, *Kein Recht, nirgends: Tagebuch vom Untergang des Breslauer Judentums 1933–1941*, ed. Norbert Conrads, Cologne, Weimar and Berlin, 2006, vol. 1, pp. 6f. (entries for 30 and 31 Jan. 1933).

128 Josef and Ruth Becker (eds), *Hitlers Machtergreifung: Dokumente vom Machtantritt Hitlers, 30. Januar 1933 bis zur Besiegelung des Einparteienstaats 14. Juli 1933*, Munich, 1983, p. 34. See Winkler, *Der Weg in die Katastrophe*, p. 868.

129 See Winkler, *Der Weg in die Katastrophe*, pp. 868, 757–9.

130 Peter Jahn (ed.), *Die Gewerkschaften in der Endphase der Republik 1930–1933*, Cologne, 1988, doc. 170, p. 831.

131 Sebastian Haffner, *Geschichte eines Deutschen: Die Erinnerungen 1914–1933*, Stuttgart and Munich, 2000, pp. 105f.

132 See Turner, *Thirty Days to Power*, p. 159.

133 Thea Sternheim, *Tagebücher. Vol. 2: 1925–1936*, ed. and selected Thomas Ehrsam and Regula Wyss, Göttingen, 2002, p. 470 (entry for 30 Jan. 1933).

134 Klaus Mann, *Tagebücher 1931 bis 1933*, ed. Joachim Heimannsberg, Peter Laemmle and Winfried F. Schoeller, Munich, 1989, p. 113 (entry for 30 Jan. 1933). The Leipzig writer and close associate of Klaus Mann Erich Ebermayer was also "stunned" by Hitler's appointment as chancellor: "It's as though there's a dark shadow upon the world. As though something terrible, irreparable and fateful has happened." Erich Ebermayer, *Denn heute gehört uns Deutschland . . . Persönliches und politisches Tagebuch*, Hamburg and Vienna, 1959, p. 11 (entry for 30 Jan. 1933).

135 Sefton Delmer, *Die Deutschen und ich*, Hamburg, 1963, p. 178.

136 Detlev Clemens, *Herr Hitler in Germany: Wahrnehmungen und Deutungen des Nationalsozialismus in Grossbritannien 1920 bis 1939*, Göttingen and Zurich, 1996, pp. 252–5 (quotation on p. 254).

137 See Claus W. Schäfer, *André François-Poncet als Botschafter in Berlin 1931–1938*, Munich, 2004, pp. 163–8.

138 Paul Dinichert to Councillor Guiseppe Motta, 2 Feb. 1933; Frank Bajohr and Christoph Strupp (eds), *Fremde Blicke auf das "Dritte Reich": Berichte ausländischer Diplomaten über Herrschaft und Gesellschaft in Deutschland 1933–1945*, Göttingen, 2011, pp. 354f.

139 See the thoughtful observations in Heinrich August Winkler, *Musste Weimar scheitern? Das Ende der ersten Republik und die Kontinuität der deutschen Geschichte*, Munich, 1991.

140 In Fritz Wiedemann's recollection, in his "table talks" during the 1930s Hitler enjoyed mocking "the Bavarian government . . . that had sent him for a time to Landsberg Prison and then released him, instead of liquidating him." Wiedemann added: "He left no doubt that, if the positions had been reversed, he would have 'cracked down

ruthlessly' without any false sentimentality." Fritz Wiedemann, *Der Mann, der Feldherr werden wollte: Erlebnisse und Erfahrungen des Vorgesetzten Hitlers im 1. Weltkrieg und seines späteren persönlichen Adjutanten*, Velbert and Kettwig 1964, p. 55.

141   See Heinrich August Winkler, "Die abwendbare Katastrophe: Warum Hitler am 30. Januar 1933 Reichskanzler wurde," in *idem, Auf ewig in Hitlers Schatten? Anmerkungen zur deutschen Geschichte*, Munich, 2007, pp. 93–104 (at p. 95).

142   On the alternative of a military dictatorship under Schleicher see Turner, *Thirty Days to Power*, pp. 170–2. In comparison, Hans-Ulrich Wehler, *Deutsche Gesellschaftsgeschichte 1914–1949*, Munich, 2003, p. 587, considered the Nazi regime "as the only remaining response to the crisis of state."

143   Veit Valentin, *Geschichte der Deutschen*, Berlin, 1947; new edition, Cologne, 1991, p. 593.

144   Eberhard Jäckel, *Das deutsche Jahrhundert: Eine historische Bilanz*, Stuttgart, 1996, pp. 151ff, taking a firm stance against Fritz Fischer, *Hitler war kein Betriebsunfall: Aufsätze*, Munich, 1993, pp. 174–81. See the sharp but relevant criticism of Jäckel by Heinrich August Winkler, "Triumph des Zufalls?," in *Historische Zeitschrift* 268 (1999), pp. 681–8.

145   Adolf Hitler, *Monologe im Führerhauptquartier 1941–1944: Die Aufzeichnungen Heinrich Heims*, ed. Werner Jochmann, Hamburg, 1980, p. 155 (dated 17/18 Dec. 1941).

13   *Hitler as Human Being*

1   Otto Dietrich, *12 Jahre mit Hitler*, Munich, 1955, p. 15.

2   Ernst Hanfstaengl, *Zwischen Weissem und Braunem Haus: Erinnerungen eines politischen Aussenseiters*, Munich, 1970, p. 217. See also Hanfstaengl's note "ad A. H.— Charakterisierung": "Basically you can only pin down his essence indirectly, that is, by comparing him with other contemporaries." BSB München, Nl Hanfstaengl Ana 405, Box 25.

3   Albert Speer, *"Alles was ich weiss": Aus unbekannten Geheimdienstprotokollen vom Sommer 1945*, ed. Ulrich Schlie, Munich, 1999, p. 50.

4   André François-Poncet, *Als Botschafter in Berlin 1931–1938*, Mainz, 1947, p. 356.

5   Otto Meissner, *Staatssekretär unter Ebert, Hindenburg, Hitler*, Hamburg, 1950, p. 615.

6   Ian Kershaw, *Hitler 1889–1936: Hubris*, London, 1998, p. 340. On this connection, see above pp. 7f. Furthermore, see Dirk van Laak, "Adolf Hitler," in Frank Möller (ed.), *Charismatische Führer der deutschen Nation*, Munich, 2004, p. 157, who claims that Hitler had "practically no private life."

7   Hanfstaengl, *Zwischen Weissem und Braunem Haus*, p. 335.

8   Konrad Heiden, *Adolf Hitler: Das Zeitalter der Verantwortungslosigkeit. Eine Biographie*, Zurich, 1936, pp. 330, 333.

9   Dietrich, *12 Jahre mit Hitler*, pp. 15, 24f.

10   Albert Speer, *Erinnerungen: Mit einem Essay von Jochen Thies*, Frankfurt am Main and Berlin, 1993, p. 37; *idem, Spandauer Tagebücher*, Munich, 2002, p. 634 (entry for 4 May 1965); see also the corrected manuscript of the *Erinnerungen* (second edition), chapter 1, on "Hitler's Qualities": "He could be kindly yet at the same time pitiless and unjust. He might appear loyal and honest and simultaneously amoral. Those around him saw him as a benevolent patriarch, but he could commit crimes with infernal determination." BA Koblenz, N 1340/384. On Hitler's "many faces" see François-Poncet, *Als Botschafter in Berlin*, pp. 356f.

11   Hanfstaengl, *Zwischen Weissem und Braunem Haus*, p. 218.

12   Joachim Scholtyseck, *Der Aufstieg der Quandts: Eine deutsche Unternehmerdynastie*, Munich, 2011, pp. 265f. The banker Eduard Heydt felt much the same way. To Count Harry Kessler he described Hitler "as the proverbial 'amiable fellow' of the minor civil servant type who by no means made a deep impression when you spoke with

him." Harry Graf Kessler, *Das Tagebuch. Vol. 9: 1926–1937*, ed. Sabine Gruber and Ulrich Ott with Christoph Hilse and Nadin Weiss, Stuttgart, 2010, p. 399 (entry for 12 Dec. 1931).

13 Sefton Delmer, *Die Deutschen und ich*, Hamburg, 1963, p. 115.

14 Dorothy Thompson, *Kassandra spricht: Antifaschistische Publizistik 1932–1942*, Leipzig and Weimar, 1988, p. 41. See Bella Fromm, *Als Hitler mir die Hand küsste*, Berlin, 1993, p. 111 (dated 30 March 1933): "An average-looking man of small stature."

15 William S. Shirer, *Berliner Tagebuch: Aufzeichnungen 1934–41*, transcribed and ed. Jürgen Schebera, Leipzig and Weimar 1991, p. 23 (entry for 4 Sept. 1934). See François-Poncet, *Als Botschafter in Berlin*, p. 146, on being received by Hitler on 8 April 1933: "When I observed him up close in moments of calm, I was struck by . . . how average and unimpressive his facial features are, although I reminded myself that it's precisely this insignificance that appeals to the masses who celebrate and find their own reflection in him."

16 Lutz Graf Schwerin von Krosigk, *Es geschah in Deutschland: Menschenbilder unseres Jahrhunderts*, Tübingen and Stuttgart, 1951, p. 193.

17 Hanfstaengl, *Zwischen Weissem und Braunem Haus*, p. 83. See Hanfstaengl's unpublished memoirs, p. 63: "'Don't worry,' he said. 'I'm not creating a new fashion. In time, people will come to imitate me.'" BSB München, Nl Hanfstaengl Ana 405, Box 47. Rudolf Hess's mother too disliked Hitler's moustache. Hess promised that he would read her letter to Hitler. "But it won't make the slightest difference," Hess wrote. "He is the most stubborn person I know!" Rudolf Hess to his parents, 9 June 1925; BA Bern, Nl Hess, J1.211-1989/148, 35.

18 Christa Schroeder, *Er war mein Chef: Aus dem Nachlass der Sekretärin von Adolf Hitler*, ed. Anton Joachimsthaler, 3rd edition, Munich and Vienna, 1985, p. 72.

19 Klaus Mann, *Der Wendepunkt: Ein Lebensbericht*, Frankfurt am Main, 1963, p. 228.

20 Speer, *Spandauer Tagebücher*, p. 40 (entry for 30 Nov. 1946).

21 Karl Alexander von Müller, *Mars und Venus: Erinnerungen 1914–1918*, Stuttgart, 1954, p. 338. Theodor Duesterberg wrote in his unpublished memoirs (p. 189) of "peculiar wolf eyes." BA Koblenz, N 1377/47.

22 Brigitte Hamann, *Winifred Wagner oder Hitlers Bayreuth*, Munich and Zurich, 2002, p. 209.

23 Otto Wagener, *Hitler aus nächster Nähe: Aufzeichnungen eines Vertrauten 1929–1932*, ed. Henry A. Turner, Frankfurt am Main, Berlin and Vienna, 1978, p. 43; see also ibid., p. 56, where Wagener stressed "his large bottomless eyes." After the Second World War, the cook on the Obersalzberg, Therese Linke, also recalled Hitler's "very strong handshake" and his "compelling gaze." Linke added: "It always made you feel so strange." IfZ München, ZS 3135.

24 Schroeder, *Er war mein Chef*, p. 71.

25 Peter Sprengel, *Gerhart Hauptmann: Bürgerlichkeit und grosser Traum. Eine Biographie*, Munich, 2012, p. 669.

26 Heiden, *Hitler: Das Zeitalter der Verantwortungslosigkeit*, p. 336.

27 Martha Dodd, *Nice to meet you, Mr. Hitler! Meine Jahre in Deutschland 1933 bis 1937*, Frankfurt am Main, 2005, p. 77.

28 H. St. Chamberlain to Hitler, 7 Oct. 1923; BA Koblenz, N 1128/16.

29 Schwerin von Krosigk, *Es geschah in Deutschland*, p. 193. See also Schwerin von Krosigk's notes on Hitler's personality (*c*.1945), in which he writes of "the fineness and beauty of his hands, which were surely the hands of an artist"; IfZ München, ZS 145, vol. 5. H(ubert) R. Knickerbocker, *Deutschland so oder so?*, Berlin, 1932, p. 207, also described Hitler as having the "hands of an artist."

30 Quoted in Rüdiger Safranski, *Ein Meister aus Deutschland: Heidegger und seine Zeit*, Munich and Vienna, 1994, p. 274.

31 Quoted in Claudia Schmölders, *Hitlers Gesicht: Eine physiognomische Biographie*, Munich, 2000, p. 60.

32 Sönke Neitzel, *Abgehört: Deutsche Generäle in britischer Gefangenschaft, 1942–1945*, Berlin, 2005, doc. 3, p. 92.

33 Thomas Mann, "Bruder Hitler" (1939) in *An die gesittete Welt: Politische Schriften und Reden im Exil*, Frankfurt am Main, 1986, p. 255. Heinrich Class wrote in his unpublished memoirs of Hitler's "hysterical eloquence." Johannes Leicht, *Heinrich Class, 1968–1953: Die politische Biographie eines Alldeutschen*, Paderborn, 2012, p. 288.

34 Heiden, *Hitler: Das Zeitalter der Verantwortungslosigkeit*, p. 331.

35 Otto Strasser, *Hitler und ich*, Konstanz, 1948, p. 85. See also Ernst Niekisch, "Hitler—ein deutsches Verhängnis" (1931), in *idem*, *Politische Schriften*, Cologne and Berlin, 1965, pp. 21f., who describes Hitler as the "biggest demagogue" Germany ever produced: "He was instinctively driven to the element he made his very own—the mass event." Or as Veit Valentin (*Geschichte der Deutschen*, Berlin, 1947; new edition, Cologne, 1991, p. 594) succinctly put it: "Adolf Hitler is German genius in the form of a demagogue."

36 Schwerin von Krosigk, *Es geschah in Deutschland*, p. 194; see Schwerin von Krosigk to Fred L. Casmir, 11 Aug. 1960: "Hitler had an intuition for what moved people internally and expressed it succinctly. His listeners felt understood and were swept away, melting into one with the speaker." BA Koblenz, N 1276/40.

37 Knickerbocker, *Deutschland so oder so?*, p. 206.

38 Rudolf Hess, *Briefe 1908–1933*, ed. Rüdiger Hess, Munich and Vienna, 1987, p. 355 (dated 27. Nov. 1924). In his account of a three-hour-long speech by Hitler in Nuremberg on 3 Dec. 1928 Rudolf Hess reported that the senior civil servant who monitored the meeting for the police had "thrown all caution to the winds" and joined in the applause. At the end, "out of sheer excitement," he had shaken Julius Streicher's hand and "declared his faith in the tribune." Rudolf Hess to Ilse Hess, 4 Dec. 1928; BA Bern, Nl Hess, J1.211-1989/148, 41.

39 Golo Mann, *Erinnerungen und Gedanken: Eine Jugend in Deutschland*, Frankfurt am Main, 1986, p. 382. See Schwerin von Krosigk to Fred L. Casmir: "Even those who didn't want to fall under the spell of [Hitler's] magic had to fight against his elixir." BA Koblenz, N 1276/40. On Golo Mann's opposition to National Socialism prior to 1933 see Tilmann Lahme, *Golo Mann: Biographie*, Frankfurt am Main, 2009, pp. 70–3.

40 Hanfstaengl, *Zwischen Weissem und Braunem Haus*, p. 36. See Hans Frank, *Im Angesicht des Galgens: Deutung Hitlers und seiner Zeit auf Grund eigener Erlebnisse und Erkenntnisse*, Munich and Gräfelfing, 1953, p. 39: "His vocal organ sometimes sounded hoarse and switched strangely with drastic contrasts in volume. Sentences that began calmly would suddenly leap impressively in tone at a certain word or when they came to their conclusion." As he was still speaking without microphone, at larger meetings Hitler was forced to talk so loudly that he sometimes lost his voice. Rudolf Hess told Ilse Pröhl about one such incident, at the exhibition hall in Essen, in a letter of 29 April 1927; BA Bern, Nl Hess, J1.211-1989/148, 39.

41 Baldur von Schirach, *Ich glaubte an Hitler*, Hamburg, 1967, p. 20.

42 Schwerin von Krosigk, *Es geschah in Deutschland*, p. 220. See Hanfstaengl's unpublished memoirs, p. 60: "He had marked theatrical abilities and also a sharp comic eye." BSB München, Nl Hanfstaengl Ana 405, Box 47. On Hitler's acting talents see also Heinz Schreckenberg, *Hitler: Motive und Methoden einer unwahrscheinlichen Karriere. Eine biographische Studie*, Frankfurt am Main, 2006, pp. 100–7.

43 Albert Krebs, *Tendenzen und Gestalten der NSDAP: Erinnerungen aus der Frühzeit der Partei*, Stuttgart, 1959, p. 133.

44 Schwerin von Krosigk to Fred L. Casmir, 11 Aug. 1960; BA Koblenz, N 1276/40.

45 Frank Bajohr and Christoph Strupp (eds), *Fremde Blicke auf das "Dritte Reich": Berichte ausländischer Diplomaten über Herrschaft und Gesellschaft in Deutschland 1933–1945*, Göttingen, 2011, p. 436. On the different roles which Hitler played during his speeches, see Gudrun Brockhaus, *Schauder und Idylle: Faschismus als Erlebnisangebot*, Munich, 1999, p. 226.

46   Robert Coulondre, *Von Moskau nach Berlin: Erinnerungen des französischen Botschafters*, Berlin, 1950, p. 310. After their meeting, Coulondre asked: "What kind of a person is this infernal Hitler really?"

47   Krebs, *Tendenzen und Gestalten*, p. 133.

48   Levetzow to Donnersmarck, 20 Nov. 1931; Gerhard Granier, *Magnus von Levetzow: Seeoffizier, Monarchist und Wegbereiter Hitlers. Lebensweg und ausgewählte Dokumente*, Boppard am Rhein, 1982, p. 316. Hermine had already read the second volume of *Mein Kampf* by the beginning of 1927. The themes had "interested her very much," she wrote to Elsa Bruckmann on 10 Feb. 1927; Miriam Käfer, "Hitlers frühe Förderer aus dem Grossbürgertum: Das Verlegerehepaar Elsa und Hugo Bruckmann," in Marita Krauss (ed.), *Rechte Karrieren in München: Von der Weimarer Zeit bis in die Nachkriegsjahre*, Munich, 2010, p. 61.

49   Delmer, *Die Deutschen und ich*, p. 117; see Dietrich, *12 Jahre mit Hitler*, p. 245; Lothar Machtan, *Der Kaisersohn bei Hitler*, Hamburg, 2006, pp. 220 ff., 309ff.

50   Prince August Wilhelm to Rudolf Hess, 21 Sep. 1934; BA Bern, Nl Hess, J1.211-1993/300, Box 1. On Hitler's contempt for the Hohenzollern see, for example, *Die Tagebücher von Joseph Goebbels. Part 1: Aufzeichnungen 1923–1941*, ed. Elke Fröhlich, Munich, 1998, vol. 2/3, pp. 181 (entry for 5 May 1933), 331 (entry for 6 Dec. 1933). After Hitler and Göring had visited the royal castle, the crown princess is supposed to have told the servants to "open the windows [and air the place out]." Hitler later heard of this, which only bolstered his antipathy towards the crown prince and princess. Wiedemann, individual recollections, San Francisco, 28 March 1939, BA Koblenz, N 1740/4

51   See Hanfstaengl, *Zwischen Weissem und Braunem Haus*, p. 226; Duesterberg memoirs, p. 189; BA Koblenz, N 1377/47.

52   Krebs, *Tendenzen und Gestalten*, pp. 148, 135.

53   Ernst von Weizsäcker, *Erinnerungen*, Munich, 1950, p. 199.

54   Speer, *Spandauer Tagebücher*, p. 634 (entry for 4 May 1965).

55   Schroeder, *Er war mein Chef*, p. 67. See Frank, *Im Angesicht des Galgens*, p. 95: "a master of imitating the way other people talked." After Hindenburg's death, Hitler enjoyed imitating his deep voice. See Henrik Eberle and Mathias Uhl (eds), *Das Buch Hitler: Geheimdossier des NKWD für Josef W. Stalin aufgrund der Verhörprotokolle des Persönlichen Adjutanten Hitlers, Otto Günsche, und des Kammerdieners Heinz Linge, Moskau 1948/49*, Bergisch Gladbach, 2005, pp. 49f.

56   Krebs, *Tendenzen und Gestalten*, p. 129.

57   Goebbels, *Tagebücher*, part 1, vol. 3/2, p. 300 (entry for 21 Dec. 1936). Hitler also often performed his impressions in Wagner's company. See Hamann, *Winifred Wagner*, pp. 313, 387.

58   Speer, *Spandauer Tagebücher*, p. 199 (entry for 3 March 1947).

59   Hanfstaengl, *Zwischen Weissem und Braunem Haus*, p. 165.

60   Hanskarl Hasselbach, one of Hitler's personal physicians, testified after the war that Hitler had possessed "a phenomenal memory in all areas," such as he "had never encountered in any other human being." IfZ München, ZS 242. See also Robert Ley, "Gedanken um den Führer" (1945): "Adolf Hitler had a powerful concentration like no other—his memory never deserted him." BA Koblenz, N 1468/4.

61   See Fritz Wiedemann, *Der Mann, der Feldherr werden wollte: Erlebnisse und Erfahrungen des Vorgesetzten Hitlers im 1. Weltkrieg und seines späteren persönlichen Adjutanten*, Velbert and Kettwig 1964, pp. 78f.

62   See Hanskarl von Hasselbach's memorandum: "Hitlers Kenntnisse und geistige Fähigkeiten" (27 Sept. 1945); BA Koblenz, N 1128/33; Nicolaus von Below, *Als Hitlers Adjutant 1937–45*, Mainz, 1980, p. 150.

63   See Heinrich Hoffmann, *Hitler wie ich ihn sah: Aufzeichnungen seines Leibfotografen*, Munich and Berlin, 1974, p. 160; Karl Wilhelm Krause, *10 Jahre Kammerdiener bei*

Hitler, Hamburg, 1949, pp. 46f. Hitler acquired the 1933 navy calendar from Franz Eher Verlag in October 1932. See the receipt in BA Berlin-Lichterfelde, NS 26/2557.

64   On this see Manfred Koch-Hillebrecht, *Homo Hitler: Psychogramm eines Diktators*, Munich, 1999, pp. 93ff. ("Hitler als Eidetiker").

65   Schroeder, *Er war mein Chef*, p. 76.

66   Wagener, *Hitler aus nächster Nähe*, p. 149.

67   See Hanfstaengl, *Zwischen Weissem und Braunem Haus*, p. 45; Schroeder, *Er war mein Chef*, p. 76.

68   Dietrich, *12 Jahre mit Hitler*, p. 165. See Hanfstaengl, *Zwischen Weissem und Braunem Haus*, p. 55.

69   Hess, *Briefe*, p. 267 (dated 11 April 1921), p. 324 (dated 16 May 1924).

70   Wagener, *Hitler aus nächster Nähe*, p. 80.

71   Goebbels *Tagebücher*, part 1, vol. 2/3, p. 55 (entry for 9 Nov. 1932). See ibid., vol. 2/2, p. 361 (entry for 11 Sept. 1932), vol. 3/1, p. 386 (entry for 27 Feb. 1936), vol. 3 /2, p. 133 (entry for 17 July 1936). See Wilhelm Brückner's memorandum of August 1945: "A. H. a brilliant mind, who autodidactically acquired fantastic knowledge in all areas as a youth." IfZ München, ED 100/43.

72   Karl Alexander von Müller, *Im Wandel einer Welt: Erinnerungen. Vol. 3: 1919–1932*, ed. Otto Alexander von Müller, Munich, 1966, pp. 302f.; see also the note from K. A. v. Müller: "Encountered Hitler repeatedly at the Bruckmanns. He had an immense but completely arbitrarily collected corpus of knowledge." BayHStA München, Nl K. A. v. Müller 101.

73   Hess, *Briefe*, p. 346 (dated 23 July 1924). Rudolf Hess to his parents, 29 April 1927; BA Bern, Nl Hess, J1.211-1989/148, 39.

74   See Schwerin von Krosigk's essay on Hitler's personality (*c*.1945); IfZ München, ZS 145, vol. 5; transcript of an interview with Heinrich Hoffmann dated 5 Dec. 1953; IfZ München, ZS 71.

75   Wagener, *Hitler aus nächster Nähe*, p. 57. Müller (*Im Wandel einer* Welt, p. 303) wrote of a "Caliban-esque fury against the 'arrogance of the educated.'" In conversation with Hans Frank, Hitler expressed his utter contempt for "the entire contradictory pretensions of professors and university priests" (*Im Angesicht des Galgens*, p. 47).

76   Wiedemann, *Der Mann*, p. 194

77   Hitler to W. Poppelreuther, 4 July 1932; BA Berlin-Lichterfelde R 43 II/959. Hitler raised no objections to this letter being reprinted in Poppelreuther's book, *Hitler, der politische Psychologe* (1933). Lammers to W. Poppelreuther, 10 Nov. 1933; ibid.

78   Speer, *Spandauer Tagebücher*, p. 523, entry for 3 May 1960.

79   Hanfstaengl, *Zwischen Weissem und Braunem Haus*, pp. 174, 176.

80   See Wagener, *Hitler aus nächster Nähe*, pp. 180–2; Hanfstaengl, *Zwischen Weissem und Braunem Haus*, pp. 175f.

81   Transcript of an interview with Mathilde Scheubner-Richter dated 9 July 1952; IfZ München, ZS 292.

82   Schirach, *Ich glaubte an Hitler*, p. 31.

83   Hanfstaengl, *Zwischen Weissem und Braunem Haus*, p. 49. See interview with Hermann Esser dated 16 March 1964, vol. 1: one of Hitler's "passions," which he never lost, was for black patent leather shoes. BayHStA München, Nl Esser.

84   Hess, *Briefe*, p. 299 (dated 15 July 1923).

85   See Rudolf Herz, *Hoffmann & Hitler: Fotografie als Medium des Führer-Mythos*, Munich, 1994, pp. 104–6.

86   See Hoffmann, *Hitler, wie ich ihn sah*, pp. 196f.

87   See ibid., p. 197; Heinz Linge, *Bis zum Untergang: Als Chef des Persönlichen Dienstes bei Hitler*, ed. Werner Maser, Munich, 1982, p. 67.

88   Hanfstaengl, *Zwischen Weissem und Braunem Haus*, p. 174. See Hanfstaengl's unpublished memoirs, p. 143; BSB München, Nl Hanfstaengl Ana 405, Box 47.

89 Fromm, *Als Hitler mir die Hand küsste*, p. 91 (dated 10 Feb. 1933). See also Duesterberg's memoirs, p. 197: "The new Reich chancellor struck me as being like an 'apprentice waiter' helping out in a borrowed tuxedo in a second-rate establishment . . . It was hard to suppress my laughter." BA Koblenz, N 1337/44. See also Dodd, *Nice to meet you, Mr. Hitler!*, p. 77, who wrote of Hitler's hesitancy whenever he was around his diplomatic corps.

90 Facsimile of the handwritten letter in Anton Joachimsthaler, *Hitlers Liste: Ein Dokument persönlicher Beziehungen*, Munich, 2003, p. 362. For the Napoleon quote see Volker Ullrich, *Napoleon*, Reinbek bei Hamburg, 2004, p. 144. Here, too, Goebbels served as his master's mouthpiece. On 21 Feb. 1936, after Hitler had once again spoken at length about the beginnings of the movement, Goebbels noted: "His life truly is a tale of adventure." *Tagebücher* part 1, vol. 3/1, p. 383.

91 Schroeder, *Er war mein Chef*, p. 55; see also Krause, *10 Jahre Kammerdiener*, pp. 29f.; Linge, *Bis zum Untergang*, p. 107.

92 See, for example, Goebbels, *Tagebücher*, part 1, vol. 3/2, p. 280 (entry for 6 Dec. 1936), vol. 4, p. 49 (entry for 13 March 1937), vol. 5, p. 374 (entry for 9 July 1938).

93 Quoted in Leicht, *Heinrich Class*, p. 288.

94 Delmer, *Die Deutschen und ich*, p. 116.

95 Ulrich von Hassell, *Römische Tagebücher und Briefe, 1932–1938*, ed. Ulrich Schlie, Munich, 2004, p. 216. See Rudolf Diels, *Lucifer ante portas . . . Es spricht der erste Chef der Gestapo*, Stuttgart, 1950, p. 57: "Even when he was talking to a single individual, he spoke as if he were addressing tens of thousands of people. Even in one-on-one conversations, he lapsed into the gestures of a mass orator."

96 See Wagener, *Hitler aus nächster Nähe*, p. 72.

97 Dietrich, *12 Jahre mit Hitler*, p. 160; see Goebbels, *Tagebücher*, part 1, vol. 2/3, p. 293 (entry for 17 March 1933): "Hitler palavered. That's when he feels most comfortable." See also the note by Blomberg: "When he's talking to one or two other people, he actually only ever holds monologues." Kirstin A. Schäfer, *Werner von Blomberg: Hitlers erster Feldmarschall. Eine Biographie*, Paderborn, 2006, p. 119f.

98 Goebbels, *Tagebücher*, part 1, vol. 2/1, p. 203 (entry for 21 July 1930), p. 285 (entry for 19 Nov. 1930), vol. 2/2, p. 225 (entry for 13 Feb. 1932), vol. 2/3, p. 221 (entry for 5 July 1933), vol. 3/2, p. 188 (entry for 20 June 1936), p. 318 (entry for 6 Jan. 1937): "Yesterday evening, the Führer spoke at length of the war. That's his element."

99 Schlie, *Albert Speer*, p. 51; see Speer, *Spandauer Tagebücher*, p. 21 (entry for 11 Oct. 1946).

100 Goebbels, *Tagebücher*, part 1, vol. 1/3, p. 272 (entry for 22 June 1929), vol. 2/1, p. 325 (entry for 15 Jan. 1931). See ibid., vol. 3/2, p. 151 (entry for 7 Aug. 1936): "When I speak to him alone, he talks to me like a father. That's when I like him best."

101 Ibid., vol. 3/1, p. 181 (entry for 8 Feb. 1935), vol. 3/2, p. 219 (entry for 21 Oct. 1936).

102 Müller, *Im Wandel einer Welt*, p. 304. See also ibid., p. 301: there was a "terrible alien air" around Hitler that "separated him from all others." See also the testimony of his secretary Johanna Wolf on 1 July 1947: "I don't know if he was friends with anyone. He was very reserved." Robert M. W. Kempner, *Das Dritte Reich im Kreuzverhör: Aus den unveröffentlichten Vernehmungsprotokollen des Anklägers in den Nürnberger Prozessen*, Munich, 2005, p. 54.

103 Speer, *Erinnerungen*, p. 114.

104 Ribbentrop, *Zwischen London und Moskau*, pp. 48, 45.

105 According to Franz Xaver Schwarz, the NSDAP treasurer, Hitler was on informal terms with Streicher, Kriebel, Esser, Röhm and Christan Weber. He later withdrew the use of "du" with Esser. IfZ München, ZS 1452.

106 O. Strasser, *Hitler und ich*, p. 93.

107 See Wiedemann, *Der Mann*, p. 55. On the reunion see also Thomas Weber, *Hitler's First War: Adolf Hitler, the Men of the List Regiment, and the First World War*, Oxford, 2010, pp. 260ff. Hitler seems not to have answered an invitation to all former

members of the regiment to celebrate a joint Christmas party in 1934; BA Berlin-Lichterfelde, NS 51/74. But he did make a generous donation so that 210 former "List men" could visit the graves of their fallen comrades in France and Belgium in July 1938. Hitler was presented with a photo album of that trip for his fiftieth birthday on 20 April 1939. BA Koblenz, N 1720/7.

108   Goebbels, *Tagebücher*, part 1, vol. 2/1, p. 371 (entry for 25 March 1931).

109   See Speer, *Erinnerungen*, p. 57.

110   Below, *Als Hitlers Adjutant*, pp. 35, 135.

111   Handwritten letter from Helene Bechstein to Hitler, 21 April 1933; BA Berlin-Lichterfelde, NS 10/123.

112   She complained in a letter dated 21 April 1933 about the poor treatment of the leader of the National Socialist Women's League, Elsbeth Zander, by Robert Ley; ibid. See also Joachimsthaler, *Hitlers Liste*, pp. 92f. On Hitler's birthday visit see Helene Bechstein to Rudolf Hess, 29 May 1936: "Wolf" had spoiled her, and "now that she was on her own, such attention being paid to her was twice as agreeable." BA Bern, Nl Hess, J1.211-1993/300, Box 2.

113   See the exuberant thank you letters from Hugo and Elsa Bruckmann dated 4 Oct. 1934; BA Berlin-Lichterfelde, NS 10/123.

114   Elsa Bruckmann to Georg Karo, 27 March 1934; BSB München, Bruckmanniana Suppl. Box 7; quoted in Käfer, *Hitlers frühe Förderer*, p. 70.

115   Wagener, *Hitler aus nächster Nähe*, p. 128. See Konrad Heiden, *Adolf Hitler: Ein Mann gegen Europa*, Zurich, 1937, pp. 207f., who writes of Hitler's "fundamental lack of love and emotional connection"; Alan Bullock, *Hitler: A Study in Tyranny*, London, 1990, p. 380 ("a man who admitted no loyalties"); Joachim Fest, *Hitler: Eine Biographie*, Frankfurt am Main, Berlin and Vienna, 1973, pp. 714 ("lack of social connections"), 716 ("impoverishedness in human relationships"); Ian Kershaw, *Hitler 1936–1945: Nemesis*, London, 2000], p. 34 ("cut off from any meaningful personal relationship").

116   Speer, *Erinnerungen*, p. 56. See Hoffmann's manuscript for his court trial (January 1947), p. 12; IfZ München, MS 2049; transcript of an interview with Heinrich Hoffmann dated 5 Dec. 1953; IfZ München, ZS 71; Heike B. Görtemaker, *Eva Braun: Leben mit Hitler*, Munich, 2010, pp. 24f. See also Goebbels, *Tagebücher*, part 1, vol. 3/1, p. 92 (entry for 12 Aug. 1934): "Spent the evening at the Hoffmanns. The Führer read aloud parodies in Munich dialect. Very droll"; p. 378 (entry for 1 Feb. 1936): "Had coffee with Hoffmann. The Führer very relaxed."

117   Speer, *Erinnerungen*, p. 164. See Eva Rieger, *Friedelind Wagner: Die rebellische Enkelin Richard Wagners*, Munich and Zurich, 2012, p. 53; Below, *Als Hitlers Adjutant*, p. 25: "He felt at home at Winifred Wagner's. He enjoyed his life as a private person. He didn't feel that sort of friendship with any other family and addressed them familiarly, which was a rarity for Hitler."

118   Hamann, *Winifred Wagner*, pp. 143, 314. See ibid., pp. 146, 209; Rieger, *Friedelind Wagner*, p. 53.

119   See Dietrich, *12 Jahre mit Hitler*, p. 247; Peter Longerich, *Joseph Goebbels: A Biography*, London, 2015, pp. 252f., 361.

120   Goebbels, *Tagebücher*, part 1, vol. 3/1, p. 106 (entry for 15 Sept. 1934), vol. 3/2, p. 356 (entry for 2 Feb. 1937). See ibid., p. 135 (entry for 20 July 1936): "He loves Helga as if she were his own child."

121   Ibid., p. 299 (entry for 20 Dec. 1936).

122   On the Baarova affair see Longerich, *Goebbels*, pp. 391–6.

123   See, for example, the postcards sent by Rudolf Hess to Ilse Pröhl from Hamburg (2 March 1926), Leipzig (4 March 1926), Essen (18 June 1926), Osnabrück (19 June 1926), Nuremberg (2 Aug. 1926), Detmold (25 Nov. 1926), Essen (26 and 27 April 1927), Hildesheim (30 April 1927), Leipzig (5 Sept. 1927). On most of these cards Hitler had added greetings with his own hand. BA Bern, Nl Hess, J1.211-1989/148, 37, 39. On the wedding, see Hess, *Briefe*, pp. 389f. (dated 14 Jan. 1928); Ilse Hess to

the parents of Rudolf Hess, 15 Jan. 1928; BA Bern, Nl Hess, J1.211-1989/148, 41. A printed wedding card in BA Koblenz, N 1122/15.

124 Hamann, *Winifred Wagner*, p. 165.

125 See Hanfstaengl, *Zwischen Weissem und Braunem Haus*, pp. 83f.

126 Speer, *Erinnerungen*, p. 136. See also Franz Pfeffer von Salomon's statement dated 20 Feb. 1953: Hitler preferred to appoint people "who had something to hide or a weak point which he could use to apply the emergency brakes if he felt it necessary." IfZ München, ZS 177.

127 See Hanskarl Hasselbach's memorandum "Hitler's knowledge of human nature"; BA Koblenz, N 1128/33; Wilhelm Brückner's memorandum of August 1945; IfZ München, ED 100/43.

128 Richard Walter Darré, Notes 1945–1948, p. 181; IfZ München, ED 110, vol. 1.

129 Heiden, *Hitler: Das Zeitalter der Verantwortungslosigkeit*, p. 210. See Hanskarl Hasselbach's memorandum "Hitler's knowledge of human nature," which quoted the dictator as saying that he only needed a brief moment "to say what sort of a person a given individual was and how he could best use that person." BA Koblenz, N 1128/33.

130 Speer, *Spandauer Tagebücher*, p. 278 (entry for 14 March 1952); see Below, *Als Hitlers Adjutant*, p. 34.

131 Krebs, *Tendenzen und Gestalten*, p. 127; see Wagener, *Hitler aus nächster Nähe*, p. 170; Schwerin von Krosigk, essay on Hitler's personality; IfZ München, ZS 145, vol. 5.

132 See Hanfstaengl, *Zwischen Weissem und Braunem Haus*, pp. 63, 68.

133 Wagener, *Hitler aus nächster Nähe*, pp. 75, 252.

134 Speer, corrected manuscript of *Erinnerungen* (second version), chapter 1; BA Koblenz, N 1340/384.

135 Goebbels, *Tagebücher*, part 1, vol. 1/3, p. 208 (entry for 20 March 1929).

136 Schroeder, *Er war mein Chef*, p. 75. See Hanfstaengl, *Zwischen Weissem und Braunem Haus*, p. 134: "Wild horses could not get it out of Hitler if he did not want to say something."

137 Wagener, *Hitler aus nächster Nähe*, p. 168.

138 Ibid., p. 82.

139 Krebs, *Tendenzen und Gestalten*, p. 135. See Speer, *Erinnerungen*, p. 111: "In general, self-control was one of Hitler's most notable qualities."

140 Schirach, *Ich glaubte an Hitler*, p. 49.

141 Schwerin von Krosigk to Fred L. Casmir, 11 Aug. 1960; BA Koblenz, N 1276/40. See also Hess, *Briefe*, p. 396 (dated 18 Dec. 1928) who writes of "this hot head who could also be so cool, sober and calculating."

142 Speer, *Spandauer Tagebücher*, p. 133 (entry for 20 Dec. 1947).

143 Speer, *Erinnerungen*, p. 114. On Hitler's "threatening stare" see also Koch-Hillebrecht, *Homo Hitler*, pp. 324f.

144 Schwerin von Krosigk, essay on Hitler's personality; IfZ München, ZS 145, vol. 5. On Hitler's suggestive effect on Blomberg see Schäfer, *Werner von Blomberg*, pp. 115f.

145 Speer, corrected manuscript of *Erinnerungen* (second version), chapter 1; BA Koblenz, N 1340/384.

146 Hess, *Briefe*, p. 425 (dated 31 Jan. 1933).

147 Hanfstaengl, *Zwischen Weissem und Braunem Haus*, pp. 102, 223. See Hanfstaengl's unpublished memoirs, p. 181: "Hitler never overcame his coffeehouse habits or his congenital inability to keep to an orderly daily working rhythm . . . He showed up announced or unannounced and kept others waiting for hours." BSB München, Nl Hanfstaengl Ana 405, Box 47.

148 Schirach, *Ich glaubte an Hitler*, pp. 53f.; see Frank, *Im Angesicht des Galgens*, pp. 93f., on Hitler's inability to work systematically; interview with Hermann Esser dated 13 March 1964, vol. 2: "Hitler never really sat down at his desk in either the Brown House in Munich or the Reich Chancellory." BayHStA München, Nl Esser.

149 Wagener, *Hitler aus nächster Nähe*, p. 266. See Hanfstaengl's note about the "ink-shy Hitler": "If he wrote down anything, it was noted on long loose sheets of paper— in pencil and in the form of bullet points." BSB München, Nl Hanfstaengl Ana 405, Box 25.

150 Goebbels, *Tagebücher*, part 1, vol. 2/2, p. 247 (entry for 23 March 1932). See also ibid., p. 245 (entry for 19 March 1932): "Hitler constantly has new ideas. But it's impossible to work with him and be scrupulous about details."

151 Wiedemann's memorandum "Preparation for speeches"; BA Koblenz, N 1720/4.

152 Schroeder, *Er war mein Chef*, pp. 78–81. See Johanna Wolf's statement dated 1 July 1947; Kempner, *Das Dritte Reich im Kreuzverhör*, p. 55; Krause, *10 Jahre Kammerdiener*, pp. 42f.; Linge, *Bis zum Untergang*, pp. 111f.

153 See Wiedemann, shorthand notes, 25 Feb. 1939; BA Koblenz, N 1720; Friedrich Hossbach (*Zwischen Wehrmacht und Hitler 1934–1938*, 2nd revised edition, Göttingen, 1965, p. 20) described Hitler's life as vacillating "between a maximum need for activity and capability and an idleness that verged on apathy."

154 Goebbels, *Tagebücher*, part 1, vol. 2/1, p. 186 (entry for 29 June 1930). See also ibid., vol. 2/2, p. 224 (entry for 22 Feb. 1932).

155 See Speer, *Spandauer Tagebücher*, p. 354 (entry for 8 Dec. 1953); Schirach, *Ich glaubte an Hitler*, p. 235.

156 Dietrich, *12 Jahre mit Hitler*, p. 28.

157 Schlie, *Albert Speer*, p. 40. See Speer, corrected manuscript of *Erinnerungen* (second version), chapter 1: "Those around him spoke reverently of an antenna that allowed him to sense particular conditions and relationships." BA Koblenz, N 1340/384.

158 Goebbels, *Tagebücher*, part 1, vol. 2/2, p. 210 (entry for 3 Feb. 1932). See ibid., vol. 2/3, p. 160 (entry for 1 April 1933): "Hitler has the finest instincts I've ever experienced."

159 Wagener, *Hitler aus nächster Nähe*, p. 251.

160 Goebbels, *Tagebücher*, part 1, vol. 2/3, p. 76 (entry for 7 Dec. 1932). See ibid., vol. 3/2, p. 257 (entry for 19 Nov. 1936): "He has a soft spot for artists because he's an artist himself."

161 Schlie, *Albert Speer*, p. 55. See Ribbentrop, *Zwischen London und Moskau*, p. 46.

162 Hess, *Briefe*, p. 327 (dated 18 May 1924). In June 1924 Hitler asked his landlady Frau Reichert in a handwritten note, which Hess included with the letter he sent to his fiancée, to hand over to "Fräulein Pröhl" his "history of architecture in four volumes," recognisable by its blue boards. BA Bern, Nl Hess, J1.211-1989/148, 33

163 Ibid., pp. 395f. (dated 18 Dec. 1928). See also ibid., p. 369 (dated 7 Feb. 1925).

164 Schlie, *Albert Speer*, p. 166. See also below, pp. 597ff.

165 Hitler to Countess de Castellance, Ségur, 19 April 1934; BA Berlin-Lichterfelde, NS 10/123.

166 See transcript of an interview with Anni Winter (undated); IfZ München, ZS 194.

167 See the receipts in BA Berlin-Lichterfelde, NS 26/2557; NS 10/120. See Wiedemann's memorandum "Architektur," in which he said that Hitler got "the greatest pleasure" from visitors bringing him books about the architectural works of the world's great cities. BA Koblenz, N 1720/4.

168 *Hitlers Tischgespräche im Führerhauptquartier*, ed. Henry Picker, Stuttgart, 1976, p. 146 (dated 27 March 1942). See also Gerhard Engel, *Heeresadjutant bei Hitler 1938–1943*, ed. and annotated Hildegard von Kotze, Stuttgart, 1974, pp. 34 (dated 20 Aug. 1938), 48 (dated 8 April 1939).

169 Adolf Hitler, *Monologe im Führerhauptquartier 1941–1944: Die Aufzeichnungen Heinrich Heims*, ed. Werner Jochmann, Hamburg, 1980, p. 400 (dated 13 June 1943); see Schlie, *Speer*, p. 57.

170 See Birgit Schwarz, *Geniewahn: Hitler und die Kunst*, Vienna, Cologne and Weimar, 2009, pp. 103–5.

171 See ibid., pp. 105ff.

172 Goebbels, *Tagebücher*, part 1, vol. 3/1, p. 233 (entry for 19 May 1935); see Engel, *Heeresadjutant bei Hitler*, p. 33 (dated 28 Aug. 1938).

173 Goebbels, *Tagebücher*, vol. 4, p. 235 (entry for 27 July 1937). Albert Speer confirmed that Hitler considered Wagner "the greatest artist Germany ever produced." A. Speer to Joachim Fest, 13 Sept. 1969; BA Koblenz, N 1340/17.

174 Hans Severus Ziegler, *Adolf Hitler aus dem Erleben dargestellt*, Göttingen, 1964, p. 171. See Hamann, *Winifred Wagner*, pp. 231ff.; Bernd Buchner, *Wagners Welttheater: Die Geschichte der Bayreuther Festspiele zwischen Kunst und Politik*, Darmstadt, 2013.

175 See Rieger, *Friedelind Wagner*, p. 89.

176 See Goebbels, *Tagebücher*, part 1, vol. 3/1, pp. 357 (entry for 1 Jan. 1936), 386 (entry for 27 Feb. 1936); vol. 5, p. 96 (entry for 14 Jan. 1938). See also Wiedemann's memorandum "Musik"; BA Koblenz, N 1720/4; Speer, *Erinnerungen*, pp. 144f.

177 Hanfstaengl, *Zwischen Weissem und Braunem Haus*, pp. 103f.; see Hanfstaengl's unpublished memoirs, p. 79: "What a classic example of discipline it is when a father is prepared to condemn his son to death. Great deeds demand hard measures." BSB München, Nl Hanfstaengl Ana 405, Box 47. On the film *Fridericus Rex* see Siegfried Kracauer, *Von Caligari zu Hitler: Eine Geschichte des deutschen Films*, vol. 2, ed. Karsten Witte, Frankfurt am Main, 1979, pp. 124–6.

178 Hess, *Briefe*, p. 371 (dated 24 Oct. 1926).

179 Goebbels, *Tagebücher*, part 1, vol. 2/2, p. 210 (entry for 3 Feb. 1932). On *Girls in Uniform* see Kracauer, *Von Caligari bis Hitler*, pp. 237–40.

180 Goebbels, *Tagebücher*, part 1, vol. 2/2, p. 211 (entry for 4 Feb. 1932).

181 See above p. 359.

182 Hitler, *Monologe*, p. 192 (dated 9/10 Jan. 1942). See also Werner Koeppen's reports, p. 51 (dated 3 Oct. 1941): "The Führer regards the automobile as the most wonderful of humanity's inventions as long as it's truly used for fun." Hitler was a member of the General German Automobile Club. See the membership cards for 1926/27 to 1930/31 in BayHStA München, Nl Adolf Hitler. Receipts for garages, petrol, car accessories and other things for 1931/32 in BA Berlin-Lichterfelde, NS 26/2557.

183 Schirach, *Ich glaubte an Hitler*, p. 61; see Olaf Rose (ed.), *Julius Schaub: In Hitlers Schatten*, Stegen, 2005, p. 69.

184 Hess, *Briefe*, p. 339 (dated 16 June 1924). On Hitler's admiration for the production capacity of the American automobile industry see Rainer Zitelmann, *Hitler: Selbstverständnis eines Revolutionärs*, 2nd revised and expanded edition, Stuttgart, 1989, pp. 352f., 356f.

185 See Eberhard Reuss, *Hitlers Rennschlachten: Die Silberpfeile unterm Hakenkreuz*, Berlin, 2006, pp. 45f.

186 See the facsimile of Hitler's letter to director Wilhelm Kissel dated 13 May 1932; Rose, *Julius Schaub*, pp. 70–2.

187 Quoted in Reuss, *Hitlers Rennschlachten*, p. 51.

188 Daimler-Benz AG to the Reich chancellor's office, 14 June 1933; BA Berlin-Lichterfelde, NS 10/119. See the Daimler-Benz book, *Ein Rüstungskonzern im "Tausendjährigen Reich,"* ed. Hamburger Stiftung für Sozialgeschichte des 20. Jahrhunderts, Nördlingen, 1987, pp. 123ff.

189 See Julius Schreck, "Mit dem Führer auf Reisen": Beitrag für das Reemtsma-Album "Adolf Hitler" (1936); BA Berlin-Lichterfelde, NS 10/121; Rose, *Julius Schaub*, p. 69.

190 Rudolf Hess to his parents, 7 July 1925; BA Bern, Nl Hess, J1.211-1989/148, 35. Dietrich, *12 Jahre mit Hitler*, p. 190. See Rudolf Hess to his parents, 21 Sept. 1935: before 1933, Hitler could not bear it "if there was another car in front of him for a considerable amount of time or if he was overtaken by another car." BA Bern, Nl Hess, J1.211-1989/148, 55.

191 Goebbels, *Tagebücher*, part 1, vol. 1/3, p. 175 (entry for 28 Jan. 1929).

192 Ibid., vol. 2/3, p. 236 (entry for 28 July 1933). See Dietrich, *12 Jahre mit Hitler*, pp. 161, 208.

193   Hanfstaengl, *Zwischen Weissem und Braunem Haus*, p. 80; see Hanfstaengl's unpublished memoirs, p. 60; BSB München, Nl Hanfstaengl Ana 405, Box 47.

194   Wagener, *Hitler aus nächster Nähe*, p. 100.

195   Meissner, *Staatssekretär*, p. 616. See Speer, *Spandauer Tagebücher*, p. 158 (entry for 5 May 1948): "Right up until the end there was something ascetic in Hitler's private life"; Frank, *Im Angesicht des Galgens*, p. 95: "Wherever he went, he lived as simply as imaginable . . . His asceticism was genuine and not put on."

196   Speer, *Spandauer Tagebücher*, p. 140 (entry for 15 Feb. 1947).

197   Schirach, *Ich glaubte an Hitler*, p. 128.

198   Speer, *Erinnerungen*, p. 123.

199   See the receipts for 1933/34 in BA Berlin-Lichterfelde, NS 10/115 und NS 10/119.

200   See Krause, *10 Jahre Kammerdiener*, p. 24.

201   See Hitler, *Monologe*, p. 99 (entry for 21/22 Oct. 1941); Wiedemann, *Der Mann*, p. 134; Linge, *Bis zum Untergang*, p. 108.

202   See Wiedemann's shorthand notes dated 25 Feb. 1939: "I am the only head of state who doesn't have a bank account." BA Koblenz, N 1740/4.

203   See the files in BA Berlin-Lichterfelde, NS 26/2557, NS 10/115, NS 10/116, NS 10/119, NS 10/120; Brückner's notebook from 1935, which has an appendix containing a detailed breakdown of all expenditure. BA Berlin-Lichterfelde, NS 26/1209. See also Dietrich, *12 Jahre mit Hitler*, p. 210; Schroeder, *Er war mein Chef*, p. 72; Rose, *Julius Schaub*, p. 135; Krause, *10 Jahre Kammerdiener*, p. 45.

204   Max Domarus, *Hitler: Reden und Proklamationen 1932–1945. Vol. 1: Triumph. Part 1: 1932–1934*, Munich, 1965, p. 200. The wages were transferred to a fund to benefit those left behind by deceased SA men and police. See Schwerin von Krosigk to Staatssekretär Lammers, 15 March 1933; BA Berlin-Lichterfelde, NS 10/115.

205   See Guido Knopp, *Geheimnisse des "Dritten Reiches,"* Munich, 2011, pp. 177f.

206   Wagener, *Hitler aus nächster Nähe*, pp. 358, 362; transcript of an interview with Anni Winter (undated); IfZ München, ZS 194.

207   Hanfstaengl, *Zwischen Weissem und Braunem Haus*, p. 164. See Hitler, *Monologe*, p. 218 (dated 22 Jan. 1942): Hitler said that when he was still eating meat, he had "sweated tremendously" during his speeches and needed to drink six bottles of water to get through them. "When I became a vegetarian," he asserted, "I only had to take a sip of water now and again."

208   Schirach, *Ich glaubte an Hitler*, p. 129; see Dietrich, *12 Jahre mit Hitler*, p. 219.

209   Delmer, *Die Deutschen und ich*, p. 152.

210   Hanfstaengl, *Zwischen Weissem und Braunem Haus*, p. 44

211   Schirach, *Ich glaubte an Hitler*, p. 67.

212   See Ulf Schmidt, *Hitlers Arzt Karl Brandt: Medizin und Macht im Dritten Reich*, Berlin, 2009, p. 137; Hans-Joachim Neumann and Henrik Eberle, *War Hitler krank? Ein abschliessender Befund*, Bergisch-Gladbach, 2009, pp. 110, 223f.

213   Speer, *Erinnerungen*, p. 138. See Theodor Duesterberg, *Der Stahlhelm und Hitler*, Wolfenbüttel and Hannover, 1949, p. 99: "It was not his thing to laugh at himself." See Goebbels, *Tagebücher*, part 1, vol. 2/3, p. 236 (entry for 27 July 1933): "Long dinner with the Führer. We laughed about Schaub's fiasco until our cheeks started to hurt."

214   See *Tischgespräche*, p. 181 (dated 3 April 1942); Fest, *Hitler*, p. 709; Paul Schmidt, *Statist auf diplomatischer Bühne 1923–45: Erlebnisse des Chefdolmetschers im Auswärtigen Amt mit den Staatsmännern Europas*, Bonn, 1950, p. 366.

215   Goebbels, *Tagebücher*, part 1, vol. 1/2, p. 189 (entry for 25 Feb. 1927). See also Hitler's letter to Arthur Dinter dated 25 July 1928, in which he said that at the age of 39 he had "at most 20 years" to achieve what he had set out to do. Albrecht Tyrell, *Führer befiehl . . . Selbstzeugnisse aus der "Kampfzeit" der NS DAP: Dokumentation und Analyse*, Düsseldorf, 1969, no. 78d, p. 205.

216 See Schirach, *Ich glaubte an Hitler*, pp. 114f. On Hitler's stomach cramps see Goebbels, *Tagebücher*, part 1, vol. 1/3, p. 150 (entry for 23 Dec. 1928), pp. 168f. (entry for 20 Jan. 1929).

217 Krebs, *Tendenzen und Gestalten*, pp. 136f.; see also Richard Walter Darré, Notes 1945–1948, p. 34. Darré characterised Hitler as being obsessed with the "conviction that he had to achieve everything he believed destiny had charged him with before he died." Darré added: "That meant he was always in a kind of rush, which of course also affected the people around him and his subordinates." IfZ München, ED 110, vol. 1.

218 Speer, *Erinnerungen*, p. 120. Heinrich Hoffmann recorded Hitler saying: "If some people think I insist too much on my plans being carried out quickly, I can only say that I sense I won't live to be very old. That makes me try to complete all of my plans. After me, no one will be able to complete them." *Das Hitler-Bild: Die Erinnerungen des Fotografen Heinrich Hoffmann*, ed. Joe J. Heydecker, St. Pölten and Salzburg, 2008, pp. 150f.; See Dietrich, *12 Jahre mit Hitler*, p. 140.

219 Transcript of an interview with Hanskarl von Hasselbach 1951/52; IfZ München, ZS 242.

220 See Rose, *Julius Schaub*, p. 112; Dietrich, *12 Jahre mit Hitler*, p. 218; Hanfstaengl, *Zwischen Weissem und Braunem Haus*, p. 284. See Rudolf Hess to his parents, 19 Dec. 1933: "Astonishingly the Führer is very well—despite the incredible strain he is under . . ." BA Bern, Nl Hess, J1.211-1989/148, 51.

221 Hamann, *Winifred Wagner*, pp. 325f.

222 Wagener, *Hitler aus nächster Nähe*, p. 199.

223 See Wiedemann, *Der Mann*, p. 85; Krause, *10 Jahre Kammerdiener*, p. 38. On the safety precautions for Hitler and the Reich Chancellery see official instructions in BA Berlin-Lichterfelde, R 43 II/1104a.

224 Krause, *10 Jahre Kammerdiener*, pp. 40f. On Schreck's pistols see Carl Walther Waffenfabrik, Zella-Mehlis, to SS-Oberführer Schreck, 4 Dec. 1935; BA Berlin-Lichterfelde, NS 10/121.

225 Speer, *Spandauer Tagebücher*, p. 29 (entry for 1 Nov. 1946).

226 Schroeder, *Er war mein Chef*, p. 73.

227 Speer, *Spandauer Tagebücher*, p. 140 (entry for 15 Feb. 1947). See Schroeder, *Er war mein Chef*, p. 73; Schirach, *Ich glaubte an Hitler*, pp. 114f.

228 Goebbels, *Tagebücher*, part 1, vol. 5, p. 358 (entry for 24 June 1938); Max Wünsche's daily diaries from 22 June 1938. On the following day Adjutant Schaub telephoned Schmeling and afterwards reported back to Hitler; BA Berlin-Lichterfelde, NS 10/125. The film of the boxing match was banned by the Propaganda Ministry, with the explicit approval of Hitler. Ibid. dated 14 July 1938. On Schmeling's reception at the Reich Chancellery see Max Schmeling, *Erinnerungen*, Frankfurt am Main, Berlin and Vienna, 1977, pp. 262f., 361–5.

229 Speer, *Erinnerungen*, p. 57.

230 Dietrich, *12 Jahre mit Hitler*, p. 151.

231 Goebbels, *Tagebücher*, part 1, vol. 2/2, p. 251 (entry for 29 March 1932).

232 Quoted in Schmölders, *Hitlers Gesicht*, p. 61.

233 Kessler, *Das Tagebuch*, vol. 9, p. 601 (entry for 6 July 1933).

14 *Totalitarian Revolution*

1 Baldur von Schirach, *Ich glaubte an Hitler*, Hamburg, 1967, p. 168.

2 Theodor Heuss to Peter Rassow, 7 Feb. 1933; Theodor Heuss, *In der Defensive: Briefe 1933–1945*, ed. Elke Seefried, Munich, 2009, pp. 109f.

3 Quoted in Josef and Ruth Becker (eds), *Hitlers Machtergreifung: Dokumente vom Machtantritt Hitlers—30. Januar 1933 bis zur Besiegelung des Einparteienstaats 14. Juli 1933*, Munich, 1983, p. 297. Typical of the attitudes of the conservative ministers in the

cabinet was a statement by Schwerin von Krosigk in a letter to former Reich Chancellor Hans Luther on 16 April 1952: "Before National Socialism came to power, I had great respect for its idealistic goals, serious reservations about its methods and rowdy representatives, and fond hopes that it would 'shed its skin.'" BA Koblenz N 1276/23. On the process of disillusionment for the German nationalists see Hermann Beck, *The Fateful Alliance: German Conservatives and Nazis in 1933. The "Machtergreifung" in New Light*, New York and Oxford, 2008, pp. 124ff., 133ff., 228ff.

4   Quoted in Becker, *Hitlers Machtergreifung*, p. 217.

5   See Richard Walter Darré, Notes 1945–1948, p. 42: "Nothing could be further from the truth than the belief that there had been a plan from the very start for the whole development of the Third Reich." Darré added that Hitler had acted "as an ingenious tactician reacting to the moment." IfZ München, ED 110, vol. 1. See also Hans-Ulrich Thamer, *Verführung und Gewalt: Deutschland 1933–1945*, Berlin, 1986, p. 232; Hans-Ulrich Wehler, *Deutsche Gesellschaftsgeschichte 1914–1949*, Munich, 2003, p. 606.

6   Victor Klemperer, *Ich will Zeugnis ablegen bis zum letzten: Tagebücher 1933–1941*, ed. Walter Nowojski with Hadwig Klemperer, Berlin, 1995, p. 9 (entry for 10 March 1933). In April 1933, during a conversation about "the horrendous situation in Germany," the Franco-American publisher Jacques Schiffrin said that he could not understand how "there was no resistance anywhere from anyone." Count Harry Kessler remarked, "I couldn't give him an explanation either." Harry Graf Kessler, *Das Tagebuch. Vol. 9: 1926–1937*, ed. Sabine Gruber and Ulrich Ott with Christoph Hilse and Nadin Weiss, Stuttgart, 2010, p. 555 (entry for 5 April 1933).

7   Sebastian Haffner, *Geschichte eines Deutschen: Die Erinnerungen 1914–1933*, Stuttgart and Munich, 2000, pp. 145–8, 152, 176–8.

8   Cabinet meeting on 30 Jan. 1933; *Akten der Reichskanzlei: Die Regierung Hitler. Part 1: 1933/34. Vol. 1: 30 Januar bis 31 April 1933*, ed. Karl-Heinz Minuth, Boppard am Rhein, 1983, no. 1, pp. 1–4 (quotations on p. 2).

9   See Rudolf Morsey, "Hitlers Verhandlungen mit der Zentrumsführung am 31. 1. 1933," in *Vierteljahrshefte für Zeitgeschichte*, 9 (1961), pp. 182–94.

10   Cabinet meeting on 3 Jan. 1933; *Die Regierung Hitler*, part 1, vol. 1, no. 2, pp. 5–8 (quotations on p. 6)

11   Hindenburg's decree dated 1 Feb. 1933; ibid., no. 3, p. 10n6. No one insisted on written confirmation of Hitler's assurance that the make-up of the cabinet would not change regardless of the outcome of the election. When Schwerin von Krosigk protested to Papen, the latter replied that "you can't begin cooperating with an act of mistrust." Schwerin von Krosigk to Holm Eggers, 21 Aug. 1974; BA Koblenz, N 1276/42.

12   Hjalmar Schacht, *Abrechnung mit Hitler*, Hamburg, 1948, p. 31; see also Hjalmar Schacht, *76 Jahre meines Lebens*, Bad Wörishofen, 1953, p. 379: "My impression was that Hitler was weighed down by the burden of responsibility placed upon him."

13   Government appeal to the German people, 1 Feb. 1933; Max Domarus, *Hitler: Reden und Proklamationen 1932–1945. Vol. 1: Triumph. Part 1: 1932–1934*, Munich, 1965, pp. 191–4.

14   Quoted in Hans Magnus Enzensberger, *Hammerstein oder Der Eigensinn: Eine deutsche Geschichte*, Frankfurt am Main, 2008, p. 114.

15   Hitler's speech to military commanders has survived in three forms: 1. notes of Lieutenant General Curt Liebmann; first reprinted in Thilo Vogelsang, "Neue Dokumente zur Geschichte der Reichswehr 1930–1933," in *Vierteljahrshefte für Zeitgeschichte*, 2 (1954), pp. 397–439 (text on pp. 434f.); 2. notes of General Horst von Mellenthin; first reprinted in Carl Dirks and Karl-Heinz Janssen, *Der Krieg der Generäle: Hitler als Werkzeug der Wehrmacht*, Berlin, 1999, pp. 232–6; 3. a transcript, probably made by one of Hammerstein's daughters, which was sent by KPD agents to Moscow on 14 Feb.; reprinted in Andreas Wirsching, "'Man kann nur Boden germanisieren': Ein neue Quelle zu Hitlers Rede vor den Spitzen der Reichswehr am 3. Februar 1933," in *Vierteljahrshefte für Zeitgeschichte*, 49 (2001), pp. 517–50 (text on pp. 545–8). Liebmann's notes are the most extensive, which is why they are the source for all further quotes, unless otherwise noted.

16   Mellenthin's notes read: "Marxism must be pulled up by the roots and eradicated"; Dirks and Janssen, *Der Krieg der Generäle*, p. 235. The Hammerstein transcript reads: "Our goal is the subjugation of Marxism by any means necessary." Wirsching, "Eine neue Quelle," p. 547.

17   In the Hammerstein transcript, the language of this passage is sharper: "The army will then be capable of conducting an active foreign policy, and the goal of increasing the German people's living space will be reached through military force. The goal will probably be the East. Nonetheless, it is impossible to Germanicise the populations of land that has been annexed or conquered. You can only Germanicise territory. As Poland and France have done, several million people will have to be ruthlessly expelled." Wirsching, "Eine neue Quelle," p. 547.

18   Klaus-Jürgen Müller, *Generaloberst Ludwig Beck: Eine Biographie*, Paderborn, 2008, pp. 101, 103.

19   Raeder's statement before the Nuremberg military court; reprinted in Wirsching, "Eine neue Quelle," p. 548f. (quotation on p. 549).

20   *Die Regierung Hitler*, part 1, vol. 1, no. 17, p. 51 (dated 8 Feb. 1933). On the relationship between Hitler and the military leadership during the early phase of the regime, see Klaus-Jürgen Müller, *Armee und Drittes Reich 1933–1939: Darstellung und Dokumente*, Paderborn, 1987, pp. 51f.

21   *Die Regierung Hitler*, part 1, vol. 1, no. 3, p. 9 (dated 1 Feb. 1933).

22   *Die Tagebücher von Joseph Goebbels. Part 1: Aufzeichnungen 1923–1941*, ed. Elke Fröhlich, Munich, 1998, vol. 2/3, p. 122 (entry for 3 Feb. 1933), p. 213 (entry for 4 Feb. 1933).

23   Reprinted in Bernd Sösemann, with Marius Lange, *Propaganda: Medien und Öffentlichkeit in der NS-Dikatur*, Stuttgart, 2011, vol. 1, no. 53, pp. 95–9. See *Die Regierung Hitler*, part 1, vol. 1, no. 9, pp. 29f. (dated 2 Feb. 1933), no. 11, pp. 34f. (dated 3 Feb. 1933).

24   Goebbels, *Tagebücher*, part 1, vol. 2/3, p. 123 (entry for 4 Feb. 1933). On the election campaign of February/March 1933 see Gerhard Paul, *Aufstand der Bilder: Die NS-Propaganda vor 1933*, Bonn, 1990, pp. 111–13.

25   Quoted in Becker, *Hitlers Machtergreifung*, pp. 57–60 (quote on p. 59).

26   Goebbels, *Tagebücher*, part 1, vol. 2/3, p. 126 (entry for 11 Feb. 1933).

27   Domarus, *Hitler*, vol. 1, part 1, pp. 203–8.

28   Goebbels, *Tagebücher*, part 1, vol. 2/3, p. 127 (entry for 11 Feb. 1933).

29   Erich Ebermayer, *Denn heute gehört uns Deutschland . . . Persönliches und politisches Tagebuch*, Hamburg and Vienna, 1959, pp. 21f. (entry for 11 Feb. 1933).

30   Jesko von Hoegen, *Der Held von Tannenberg: Genese und Funktion des Hindenburg-Mythos*, Cologne, Weimar and Vienna, 2007, pp. 378–80.

31   Papen to Hugenberg, 12 Feb. 1933; BA Koblenz, N 1231/38. On the origins of the "Battle Front Black, White and Red" see Beck, *The Fateful Alliance*, pp. 93f.

32   Hoegen, *Der Held von Tannenberg*, p. 382. See Wolfram Pyta, *Hindenburg: Herrschaft zwischen Hohenzollern und Hitler*, Munich, 2007, p. 817.

33   The content of the meeting, according to the report by the leader of the Berlin offices of Gutehoffnungshütte, Martin Blank, to Paul Reusch, 21 Feb. 1933, reprinted in Dirk Stegmann, "Zum Verhältnis von Grossindustrie und Nationalsozialismus 1930–1933," in *Archiv für Sozialgeschichte*, 13 (1973), pp. 477–80. See also Fritz Springorum to Paul Reusch, 21 Feb. 1933, ibid., pp. 480f.; Henry A. Turner, *Die Grossunternehmer und der Aufstieg Hitlers*, Berlin, 1986, pp. 393–5; Joachim Petzold, *Franz von Papen: Ein deutsches Verhängnis*, Munich and Berlin, 1995, pp. 170–3. On Gustav Krupp's position see Harold James, *Krupp: Deutsche Legende und globales Unternehmen*, Munich, 2011, pp. 196–9. On the 75:25 split there followed a disagreement as not all donors wanted "Battle Front Black, White, Red" to receive a quarter of the money. See Hugenberg to Schacht, 2 March 1933; Schacht to Hugenberg, 3 March 1933; BA Koblenz, N 1231/38.

34   Goebbels, *Tagebücher*, part 1, vol. 2/3, p. 133 (entry for 21 Feb. 1933).

35   Ibid., p. 130 (entry for 16 Feb. 1933). See Martin Broszat, *Der Staat Hitlers: Grundlegung und Entwicklung seiner inneren Verfassung*, Munich, 1969, pp. 90–5.

36   Directive from Göring dated 17 Feb. 1933; Becker, *Hitlers Machtergreifung*, pp. 74f.

37   Kessler, *Das Tagebuch*, vol. 9, p. 542 (entry for 17 Feb. 1933).

38   Broszat, *Der Staat Hitlers*, p. 95.

39   See Heinrich August Winkler, *Der Weg in die Katastrophe: Arbeiter und Arbeiterbewegung in der Weimarer Republik 1930 bis 1933*, Berlin and Bonn, 1987, p. 879; Joachim Fest, *Hitler: Eine Biographie*, Frankfurt am Main, Berlin and Vienna, 1973, p. 541. On SA terror attacks against the left see Richard J. Evans, *The Coming of the Third Reich*, London, 2004, pp. 317–21.

40   Kessler, *Das Tagebuch*, vol. 9, p. 444 (entry for 19 Feb. 1933). See ibid., p. 544 (entry for 20 Feb. 1933), p. 545 (entry for 22 Feb. 1933).

41   On the controversy over the Reichstag fire see, most recently, Sven Felix Kellerhoff, *Der Reichstagsbrand: Die Karriere eines Kriminalfalles*, Berlin, 2008. When all the arguments are considered, the thesis that van der Lubbe acted alone is the most plausible. In the summer of 1945, in the Mondorf internment camp near Luxembourg, Schwerin von Krosigk asked Göring who had been responsible for the Reichstag fire, saying "You can tell *me* the truth." Göring responded that he would have been proud if he had "set the Reichstag ablaze," but "unfortunately he was completely innocent." Schwerin von Krosigk to Fritz Tobias, 27 Jan. 1970; BA Koblenz, N 1276/40; see also Schwerin von Krosigk to Heinrich Fraenkel, 20 Jan. 1975; ibid.

42   See Ernst Hanfstaengl, *Zwischen Weissem und Braunem Haus: Erinnerungen eines politischen Aussenseiters*, Munich, 1970, pp. 294f.; Goebbels, *Tagebücher*, part 1, vol. 2/3, p. 137 (entry for 28 Feb. 1933): "Hanfstaengl called with the news: the Reichstag is burning. What an imagination [I thought]. But it was true."

43   Rudolf Diels, *Lucifer ante portas . . . Es spricht der erste Chef der Gestapo*, Stuttgart, 1950, p. 194. Göring said to Papen: "This can only be a Communist attack on our new government!" Franz von Papen, *Der Wahrheit eine Gasse*, Munich, 1952, p. 302. Sefton Delmer (*Die Deutschen und ich*, Hamburg, 1963, p. 190) also quoted Göring telling Hitler that the fire was "definitely the work of the Communists."

44   Goebbels, *Tagebücher*, part 1, vol. 2/3, p. 137 (entry for 28 Feb. 1933).

45   Diels, *Lucifer ante portas*, p. 194.

46   Delmer, *Die Deutschen und ich*, p. 191.

47   Goebbels, *Tagebücher*, part 1, vol. 2/3, p. 137 (entry for 28 Feb. 1933).

48   André François-Poncet, *Als Botschafter in Berlin 1931–1938*, Mainz, 1947, p. 95.

49   See Thamer, *Verführung und Gewalt*, p. 254; Evans, *The Coming of the Third Reich*, pp. 334f.

50   Cabinet meeting on 28 Feb. 1933; *Die Regierung Hitler*, part 1, vol. 1, no. 32, pp. 128–31 (quotation on pp. 128, 129).

51   Reprinted in Becker, *Hitlers Machtergreifung*, pp. 107f.; Sösemann, *Propaganda*, vol. 1, pp. 105f. See the comprehensive analysis by Thomas Raithel and Irene Strenge, "Die Reichstagsbrandverordnung: Grundlegung der Diktatur mit den Instrumenten des Weimarer Ausnahmezustands," in *Vierteljahrshefte für Zeitgeschichte*, 48 (2000), pp. 413–60.

52   Karl-Dietrich Bracher, Wolfgang Sauer and Gerhard Schulz, *Die nationalsozialistische Machtergreifung: Studien zur Errichtung des totalitären Herrschaftssystems in Deutschland 1933/34*, 2nd revised edition, Cologne and Opladen 1962, p. 82.

53   Ernst Fraenkel, *Der Doppelstaat: Recht und Justiz im "Dritten Reich,"* Frankfurt am Main and Cologne, 1974, p. 26. See Norbert Frei, *Der Führerstaat: Nationalsozialistische Herrschaft 1933 bis 1945*, new and expanded edition, Munich, 2001, p. 51.

54   See Pyta, *Hindenburg*, p. 814.

55   Becker, *Hitlers Machtergreifung*, p. 117.

56   François-Poncet, *Als Botschafter in Berlin*, p. 21. See also Papen's comment to Cardinal Michael Faulhaber, 1 March 1933: "The National Socialists are all keyed up right now, but after the elections, they'll calm down." Becker, *Hitlers Machtergreifung*, pp. 113f.

57   Werner Jochmann, *Nationalsozialismus und Revolution: Ursprung und Geschichte der NSDAP in Hamburg 1922–1933. Dokumente*, Frankfurt am Main, 1963, p. 425.

58   Hedda Kalshoven, *Ich denk so viel an Euch: Ein deutsch-holländischer Briefwechsel 1920–1949*, Munich, 1995, p. 169 (dated 10 March 1933).

59   Quoted in Ian Kershaw, *The Hitler Myth: Image and Reality in the Third Reich*, Oxford, 1987, p. 52.

60   Becker, *Hitlers Machtergreifung*, pp. 116f.

61   Kessler, *Das Tagebuch*, vol. 9, p. 550 (entry for 5 March 1933).

62   See Jürgen Falter, Thomas Lindenberger and Siegfried Schumann, *Wahlen und Abstimmungen in der Weimarer Republik: Materialien zum Wahlverhalten 1919–1931*, Munich, 1986, pp. 41, 44.

63   Ebermayer, *Denn heute gehört uns Deutschland*, p. 35 (dated 5 March 1933). See Kesssler, *Das Tagebuch*, vol. 9, p. 350 (entry for 6 March 1933): "Despite unprecedented pressure and the complete paralysis of their propaganda, the Social Democrats only lost 100,000 votes and the KPD only one million. That's an amazing and admirable demonstration of the indomitability of the 'Marxist Front.'"

64   Goebbels, *Tagebücher*, part 1, vol. 2/3, p. 141 (entry for 6 March 1933).

65   Sackett's report to Foreign Minister Hull, 9 March 1933; Becker, *Hitlers Machtergreifung*, p. 135.

66   Goebbels, *Tagebücher*, part 1, vol. 2/3, p. 138 (entry for 2 March 1933) See also Schwerin von Krosigk's recording for a BBC programme on German history between 1918 and 1933 (1966): "In the first time Hitler in fact seemed to be a man whom one could get on. He was very polite; when things were discussed in the cabinet he kept to the subject; he did not mind contradiction and he did not interfere with the work of the ministries." BA Koblenz, N 1276/37.

67   Schwerin von Krosigk, essay on Hitler's personality (c.1945); Ifz München, ZS 145, vol. 5; see also Lutz Graf Schwerin von Krosigk, *Es geschah in Deutschland: Menschenbilder unseres Jahrhunderts*, Tübingen and Stuttgart, 1951, p. 199.

68   Cabinet meeting on 7 March 1933; *Die Regierung Hitler*, part 1, vol. 1, no. 44, pp. 159–66 (quotations on pp. 160, 161).

69   Cabinet meeting on 11 March 1933; ibid., no. 56, pp. 193–5.

70   Goebbels, *Tagebücher*, part 1, vol. 2/3, p. 145 (entry for 12 March 1933), p. 147 (entry for 15 March 1933).

71   Quoted in Peter Longerich, *Joseph Goebbels: A Biography*, London, 2015, p. 212.

72   Cabinet meeting on 7 March 1933; *Die Regierung Hitler*, part 1, no. 44, p. 160.

73   Goebbels, *Tagebücher*, part 1, vol. 2/3, p. 142 (entry for 8 March 1933), p. 143 (entry for 9 March 1933).

74   See Volker Ullrich, "Wohlverhalten um jeden Preis: Die 'Machtergreifung' in Hamburg und die Politik der SPD," in Angelika Ebbinghaus and Karl-Heinz Roth (eds), *Grenzgänge: Heinrich Senfft zum 70. Geburtstag*, Lüneburg, 1999, pp. 303–18; Ursula Büttner, "Der Aufstieg der NSDAP," in *Hamburg im "Dritten Reich,"* ed. Forschungsstelle für Zeitgeschichte in Hamburg, Göttingen, 2005, pp. 59–62.

75   See Broszat, *Der Staat Hitlers*, pp. 135–7; Thamer, *Verführung und Gewalt*, p. 260; Frei, *Der Führerstaat*, pp. 55f.

76   G. Heim to Hindenburg, 10 March 1933; *Die Regierung Hitler*, part 1, vol. 1, no. 54, pp. 190f. On the fall of Bavaria see Falk Wiesemann, *Die Vorgeschichte der national-sozialistischen Machtübernahme in Bayern 1932/33*, Berlin, 1975.

77   See Peter Longerich, *Heinrich Himmler: Biographie*, Munich, 2008, pp. 159f.; Robert Gerwarth, *Reinhard Heydrich: Biographie*, Munich, 2011, pp. 89ff .

78   Domarus, *Hitler*, vol. 1, part 1, p. 222; See David Clay Large, *Where Ghosts Walked: Munich's Road to the Third Reich*, New York and London, 1997, p. 237.

79 *Die Regierung Hitler*, part 1, vol. 1, no. 80, p. 276 (dated 31 March 1933), no. 93, p. 312 (dated 7 April 1933). See Broszat, *Der Staat Hitlers*, pp. 143f.; Frei, *Der Führerstaat*, p. 57. In a letter to Interior Minister Frick on 29 March 1933, Hugenberg protested that the drive to "disable the Communists" was being used to undermine the position of the DNVP in the state parliaments. Hugenberg wrote of his impression that "our agreement that the fresh election, which I never wanted, would not impact on any of the parties involved was increasingly being pushed into the background." BA Koblenz, N 1231/36.

80 Rumbold to Foreign Secretary Simon, 12 April 1933; Becker, *Hitlers Machtergreifung*, p. 228. See Broszat, *Der Staat Hitlers*, p. 145; Frei, *Der Führerstaat*, p. 58.

81 Klemperer, *Tagebücher 1933–1941*, p. 8 (entry for 10 March 1933).

82 Diels, *Lucifer ante portas*, p. 255. On the SA violence after 5 March see Thamer, *Verführung und Gewalt*, pp. 264–6; Peter Longerich, *Die braunen Bataillone: Geschichte der SA*, Munich, 1989, pp. 168–71; Evans, *The Coming of the Third Reich*, pp. 346–8.

83 Kessler, *Das Tagebuch*, vol. 9, p. 552 (entry for 8 March 1933). See Klemperer, *Tagebücher 1933–1941*, p. 9 (entry for 10 March 1933): "No one dares to say anything. Everyone's afraid."

84 Heuss, *In der Defensive*, pp. 118f. (dated 14 March 1933).

85 Domarus, *Hitler*, vol. 1, part 1, pp. 219, 221.

86 Hitler to Papen, 11 March 1933; *Die Regierung Hitler*, part 1, vol. 1, no. 58, pp. 204–8. By contrast, immediately after 30 Jan. 1933, Hitler and Papen interacted "in a manner that could hardly have been more cordial." Duesterberg's memoirs, p. 197; BA Koblenz, N 1377/47.

87 From recent literature see Robert Sigel, "Das KZ Dachau und die Konstituierung eines rechtsfreien Raumes als Ausgangspunkt des nationalsozialistischen Terrorsystems," in Andreas Wirsching (ed.), *Das Jahr 1933: Die nationalsozialistische Machtergreifung und die deutsche Gesellschaft*, Göttingen, 2009, pp. 156–68; Ludwig Eiber, "Gewalt im KZ Dachau: Vom Anfang eines Terrorsystems," in ibid., pp. 169–81. See also Wolfgang Benz and Barbara Distel, *Der Ort des Terrors: Geschichte der nationalsozialistischen Konzentrationslager. Vol. 2: Frühe Lager*, Munich, 2005, pp. 233–74.

88 Jochmann, *Nationalsozialismus und Revolution*, p. 431.

89 Haffner, *Geschichte eines Deutschen*, p. 225.

90 Goebbels, *Tagebücher*, part 1, vol. 2/3, p. 134 (entry for 24 Feb. 1933).

91 See Armin Nolzen, "Der 'Führer' und seine Partei," in Dietmar Süss and Winfried Süss (eds), *Das "Dritte Reich": Eine Einführung*, Munich, 2008, pp. 56f.

92 Ebermayer, *Und heute gehört uns Deutschland*, p. 34 (dated 5 March 1933). See the report by the U.S. Consul General in Berlin, George S. Messersmith, 25 April 1933: "One of the most extraordinary features of the situation to an objective observer, is the fact that so many clear-thinking and really well-informed persons appear to have lost their balance and are actively approving of measures and policies which they previously condemned as fundamentally dangerous and unsound." Frank Bajohr and Christoph Strupp (eds), *Fremde Blicke auf das "Dritte Reich": Berichte ausländischer Diplomaten über Herrschaft und Gesellschaft in Deutschland 1933–1945*, Göttingen, 2011, pp. 369f. (quotation on p. 370).

93 Goebbels, *Tagebücher*, part 1, vol. 2/3, p. 223 (entry for 7 July 1933). See also Frank Bajohr, "Ämter, Pfründe, Korruption: Materielle Aspekte der nationalsozialistischen Machtergreifung," in Wirsching (ed.), *Das Jahr 1933*, pp. 185–99.

94 Bella Fromm, *Als Hitler mir die Hand küsste*, Berlin, 1993, p. 131 (dated 21 May 1933).

95 Delmer, *Die Deutschen und ich*, p. 179.

96 Antoni Graf Sobanski, *Nachrichten aus Berlin 1933–1936*, Berlin, 2007, p. 31.

97 See *Die Regierung Hitler*, part 1, vol. 1, no. 192, p. 658 (entry for 13 July 1933).

98 Ibid., no. 56, p. 195n10 (entry for 11 March 1933). Goebbels commented: "A fantastic boost to our prestige!" Goebbels, *Tagebücher*, part 1, vol. 2/3, p. 144 (entry for 12 March 1933).

99   Ebermayer, *Denn heute gehört uns Deutschland*, p. 75 (dated 9 May 1933). See ibid., p. 86 (dated 16 May 1933). In May 1933, when Ebermayer's books were banned, everyone distanced themselves from him as if he were "a leper." "It's incomprehensible how cowardly people are," Ebermayer complained.

100 See Haffner, *Geschichte eines Deutschen*, pp. 197–204.

101 See Goebbels, *Tagebücher*, part 1, vol. 2/3, p. 148 (entry for 17 March 1933): "Discussed the plan for 21 March. It will be huge"; p. 149 (entry for 18 March 1933): "The entire Potsdam celebration is ready. It will be huge and classic."

102 On the following see Klaus Scheel, *Der Tag von Potsdam*, Berlin, 1993; Hoegen, *Der Held von Tannenberg*, pp. 384–93; Pyta, *Hindenburg*, pp. 820–4.

103 See Goebbels, *Tagebücher*, part 1, vol. 2/3, p. 152 (entry for 21 March 1933).

104 François-Poncet, *Als Botschafter in Berlin*, p. 108.

105 See Pyta, *Hindenburg*, p. 822.

106 Reprinted in Walther Hubatsch, *Hindenburg und der Staat: Aus den Papieren des Generalfeldmarschalls und Reichspräsidenten von 1878 bis 1934*, Göttingen, 1966, p. 374. Goebbels commented: "The old man is like a stone memorial. He read out his message. Succinctly and imperiously." *Tagebücher*, part 1, vol. 2/3, p. 153 (entry for 23 March 1933).

107 Heuss, *In der Defensive*, p. 126 (dated 22 March 1933).

108 Domarus, *Hitler*, vol. 1, part 1, pp. 226–8.

109 Goebbels, *Tagebücher*, part 1, vol. 2/3, p. 153 (entry for 23 March 1933).

110 Pyta, *Hindenburg*, p. 824. Heinrich Brüning (*Memoiren 1918–1934*, Stuttgart, 1970, p. 657) also recalled that Hindenburg occasionally wiped a tear from his eye with his brown gloves."

111 Kalshoven, *Ich denk so viel an Euch*, pp. 182f. (dated 22 March 1933).

112 Ebermayer, *Und heute gehört uns Deutschland*, pp. 46f. (dated 21 March 1933). See Duesterberg's memoirs, p. 205: "Even otherwise clear-eyed people were swept away, intoxicated." BA Koblenz, N 1377/47.

113 Pyta, *Hindenburg*, p. 824. See also Wolfram Pyta, "Geteiltes Charisma: Hindenburg, Hitler und die deutsche Gesellschaft im Jahre 1933," in Wirsching (ed.), *Das Jahr 1933*, pp. 47–69 (at p. 54).

114 Schirach, *Ich glaubte an Hitler*, p. 168. See also Hans Frank, *Im Angesicht des Galgens: Deutung Hitlers und seiner Zeit auf Grund eigener Erlebnisse und Erkenntnisse*, Munich and Gräfelfing, 1953, p. 129, who quoted Hitler saying on 30 Jan. 1933 that he hoped he would be able to "win over" Hindenburg.

115 Goebbels, *Tagebücher*, part 1, vol. 2/3, p. 131 (entry for 17 Feb. 1933). See Brüning, *Memoiren*, p. 650, who wrote that by mid-February 1933 the news from the Hindenburg residence was that "the Reich President's previous rejection of Hitler had turned into incipient fondness." On 12 March 1933, Hindenburg wrote to his daughter: "The patriotic upswing is pleasing. May God preserve our unity." Pyta, *Hindenburg*, p. 808.

116 *Hitlers Tischgespräche im Führerhauptquartier*, ed. Henry Picker, Stuttgart, 1976, p. 328 (dated 21 May 1942). On the change in the relationship between Hitler and Hindenburg see also Otto Dietrich, *12 Jahre mit Hitler*, Munich, 1955, p. 41; Friedrich Hossbach, *Zwischen Wehrmacht und Hitler 1934–1938*, 2nd revised edition, Göttingen, 1965, p. 12; Schwerin von Krosigk, in his essay on Hitler's personality (*c*.1945) wrote that Hitler and Hindenburg had initially treated one another with "great reserve," but that "a relationship of great mutual respect and deep trust" had grown over the course of one-and-a-half years of working together. IfZ München, ZS 145, vol. 5.

117 Papen, *Der Wahrheit eine Gasse*, pp. 295, 309.

118 Meissner's minutes on Schäffer's meeting with the Reich president, 17 Feb. 1933; *Die Regierung Hitler*, part 1, vol. 1, no. 23, pp. 87–90 (quotations on p. 89). Meissner sent his minutes to State Secretary Lammers in the Reich Chancellory with the message: "I allow myself . . . to emphasise that the Reich president defended the Reich

chancellor against certain contentions made by State Secretary Schäffer with great warmth and vigour." Ibid., p. 87n1. In a letter to Reichstag Deputy Ritter von Lex on 15 March 1933, Schäffer denied—"categorically on my word of honour"—having made derogatory remarks about Hitler during the audience with Hindenburg on 17 Feb. He also pointed out that as early as Nov. 1932 he had offered "a very positive personal opinion of the Reich chancellor." Ritter von Lex passed the letter to Hitler on that very day. BA Berlin-Lichterfelde, NS 1/123.

119 *Hitlers Tischgespräche*, p. 329 (dated 21 May 1942).

120 Goebbels, *Tagebücher*, part 1, vol. 2/3, p. 153 (entry for 23 March 1933).

121 Pyta, *Hindenburg*, p. 825. In a handwritten note on 30 Jan. 1934 Hindenburg expressed to Hitler his "sincere respect for your passionate work and your great achievements." Deutsches Nachrichtenbüro no. 207 dated 30 Jan. 1934; BA Berlin-Lichterfelde, R 43 II/959.

122 Pyta, "Geteiltes Charisma," p. 61.

123 Thamer, *Verführung und Gewalt*, p. 272.

124 Cabinet meeting on 15 March 1933; *Die Regierung Hitler*, part 1, vol. 1, no. 60, pp. 212–17 (quotations on pp. 214, 216).

125 Cabinet meeting on 20 March 1933; ibid., no. 68, pp. 238–40. See Thamer, *Verführung und Gewalt*, pp. 274f.; Frei, *Der Führerstaat*, pp. 61f.

126 Text in Rudolf Morsey (ed.), *Das "Ermächtigungsgesetz" vom 24. März 1933: Quellen zur Geschichte und Interpretation des "Gesetzes zur Behebung der Not von Volk und Reich,"* new revised and expanded edition, Düsseldorf, 2010, no. 34, pp. 70f.

127 Wilhelm Hoegner, *Der schwierige Aussenseiter: Erinnerungen eines Abgeordneten, Emigranten und Ministerpräsidenten*, Munich, 1959, p. 92.

128 Domarus, *Hitler*, vol. 1, part 1, pp. 229–37; excerpts in Morsey, *Das "Ermächtigungsgesetz,"* no. 28, pp. 50–6.

129 See Carl Severing, *Mein Lebensweg: Vol. 2*, Cologne, 1950, pp. 384f.

130 Morsey, *Das "Ermächtigungsgesetz,"* pp. 43, 57, 82. See Brüning, *Memoiren*, pp. 656, 658f.; see also Josef Becker, "Zentrum und Ermächtigungsgesetz," in *Vierteljahrshefte für Zeitgeschichte*, 9 (1961), pp. 195–210.

131 Domarus, *Hitler*, vol. 1, part 1, pp. 239–41; excerpts in Morsey, *Das "Ermächtigungsgesetz,"* no. 30, pp. 58–60.

132 See Friedrich Stampfer, *Erfahrungen und Erkenntnisse*, Cologne, 1957, p. 268; Fest, *Hitler*, p. 562; Winkler, *Der Weg in die Katastrophe*, p. 905.

133 Goebbels, *Tagebücher*, part 1, vol. 2/3, p. 154 (entry for 25 March 1933).

134 Domarus, *Hitler*, vol. 1, part 1, pp. 242–6; excerpts in Morsey, *Das "Ermächtigungsgesetz,"* no. 30, pp. 60–3.

135 See Morsey, *Das "Ermächtigungsgesetz,"* no. 30, pp. 63–6.

136 Frei, *Der Führerstaat*, p. 61.

137 Cabinet meeting on 24 March 1933; *Die Regierung Hitler*, part 1, vol. 1, no. 72, p. 248.

138 See Thamer, *Verführung und Gewalt*, pp. 279–82; Broszat, *Der Staat Hitlers*, p. 117; Pyta, *Hindenburg*, p. 826.

139 Goebbels, *Tagebücher*, part 1, vol. 2/3, p. 154 (entry for 25 March 1933). See Schwerin von Krosigk to Lutz Böhme, 8 May 1975: "The law was one step, but probably also the most important on the path of legality, towards converting political power into the absolute rule of a *single* man." BA Koblenz, N 1276/42.

140 See Saul Friedländer, *Das Dritte Reich und die Juden: Die Jahre der Verfolgung 1933–1939*, Munich, 1998, vol. 1, pp. 30f.; Peter Longerich, *Politik der Vernichtung: Eine Gesamtdarstellung der nationalsozialistischen Judenverfolgung*, Munich and Zurich, 1998, pp. 26–30; Michael Wildt, *Volksgemeinschaft als Selbstermächtigung: Gewalt gegen Juden in der deutschen Provinz 1919 bis 1939*, Hamburg, 2007, pp. 107ff., 115ff. See also the documents in Otto Dov Kulka and Eberhard Jäckel (eds), *Die Juden in den geheimen Stimmungsberichten 1933–1945*, Düsseldorf, 2004, doc. 1–6, pp. 45–9.

141 Quoted in Wildt, *Volksgemeinschaft als Selbstermächtigung*, p. 108.

142 See the article in the *New York Times* of 27 March 1933; reprinted in *Die Verfolgung und Ermordung der europäischen Juden durch das nationalsozialistische Deutschland 1933–1945. Vol. 1: Deutsches Reich 1933–1937*, ed. Wolf Gruner, Munich, 2008, doc. 14, pp. 92–7.

143 See Eckart Conze, Norbert Frei, Peter Hayes and Moshe Zimmermann, *Das Amt und die Vergangenheit: Deutsche Diplomaten im Dritten Reich und in der Bundesrepublik*, Munich, 2010, pp. 25–9.

144 Goebbels, *Tagebücher*, part 1, vol. 2/3, p. 156 (entry for 27 March 1933). See *ibid*, p. 157 (entry for 28 March 1933): "I dictated a strongly worded appeal to counteract the horrific campaign by the Jews. The mere announcement of this appeal caused that *mishpoke* to buckle. This is the way to deal with them."

145 Reprinted in *Die Verfolgung und Ermordung der europäischen Juden*, vol. 1, doc. 17, pp. 100–4 (quotations on pp. 102f.).

146 Cabinet meeting on 29 March 1933; *Die Regierung Hitler*, part 1, vol. 1, no. 78, pp. 270f.

147 Cabinet meeting on 31 March 1933; ibid., no. 80, pp. 276f.

148 Quoted in Gianluca Falanga, *Mussolinis Vorposten in Hitlers Reich: Italiens Politik in Berlin 1933–1945*, Berlin, 2008, p. 27.

149 Haffner, *Die Geschichte eines Deutschen*, pp. 154f.

150 Ibid., p. 138.

151 Rumbold's report to Foreign Secretay Simon, 13 April 1933; Becker, *Hitlers Machtergreifung*, p. 232. See also the report from U.S. Consul General George S. Messersmith of 3 April 1933: "The boycott was not generally popular with the German people according to the best information which the Consulate General can secure up to this time . . . This is no indication that the feeling against the Jews has in any sense died down, but merely that the popular opinion does not approve of a measure which even the man in the street realizes may be destructive of the internal economic life and seriously affect Germany's foreign trade." Bajohr and Strupp (eds), *Fremde Blicke auf das "Dritte Reich,"* p. 364.

152 For a summary of the public's reaction see Hannah Ahlheim, *"Deutsche, kauft nicht bei Juden!" Antisemitischer Boykott in Deutschland 1924 bis 1935*, Göttingen, 2011, pp. 254–62.

153 Klemperer, *Tagebücher 1933–1941*, p. 15 (entry for 30 March 1933). See Willy Cohn, *Kein Recht, nirgends: Tagebuch vom Untergang des Breslauer Judentums 1933–1941*, ed. Norbert Conrads, Cologne, Weimar and Berlin, 2006, p. 25 (entry for 1 April 1933): "the Dark Ages." Kurt F. Rosenberg: *"Einer, der nicht mehr dazugehört": Tagebücher 1933–1937*, ed. Beate Meyer and Björn Siegel, Göttingen, 2012, p. 89 (entry for 1 May 1933): "Is that the people of poets and thinkers? We were proud to be part of it and give it our strength and best intentions."

154 Kessler, *Das Tagebuch*, vol. 9, p. 554 (entry for 1 April 1933). In a letter of 1 April 1933 Theodor Heuss called the "boycott" on the streets of Berlin "nothing other than shameful"; *In der Defensive*, p. 132.

155 See Longerich, *Politik der Vernichtung*, pp. 39–41; Wildt, *Volksgemeinschaft als Selbstermächtigung*, pp. 158ff.

156 Text in *Die Verfolgung und Ermordung der europäischen Juden*, vol. 1, doc. 29, pp. 130–4.

157 Hindenburg to Hitler, 4 April 1932; Hubatsch, *Hindenburg und der Staat*, pp. 375f.

158 Hindenburg to Prince Carl of Sweden, 26 April 1933; *Die Regierung Hitler*, part 1, vol. 1, no. 109, pp. 391f.; see *Hitlers Tischgespräche*, p. 330 (dated 21 May 1942).

159 Hitler to Hindenburg, 5 April 1933; Hubatsch, *Hindenburg und der Staat*, pp. 376–8.

160 See Longerich, *Politik der Vernichtung*, p. 41–5; Friedländer, *Das Dritte Reich und die Juden*, vol. 1, pp. 40–3.

161 Harold James, "Die Deutsche Bank und die Diktatur 1933–1945," in Lothar Gall *et al.*, *Die Deutsche Bank 1870–1995*, Munich, 1995, p. 337. See Friedländer, *Das Dritte Reich und die Juden*, vol. 1, p. 46.

162 On the following see Volker Ullrich, "Anpassung um jeden Preis? Die Kapitualition der deutschen Gewerkschaften 1932/33," in Inge Marssolek and Till Schelz-Brandenburg

(eds), *Soziale Demokratie und sozialistische Theorie: Festschrift für Hans-Josef Steinberg zum 60. Geburtstag*, Bremen, 1995, pp. 245–55.

163 Peter Jahn (ed.), *Die Gewerkschaften in der Endphase der Republik 1930–1933*, Cologne, 1988, doc. 189, pp. 865–7.

164 Ibid., doc. 197, pp. 881f.

165 Leipart to Hindenburg, 10 March 1933; *Die Regierung Hitler*, part 1, vol. 1, no. 53, pp. 188f. On SA violence against unions see Michael Schneider, *Unterm Hakenkreuz: Arbeiter und Arbeiterbewegung 1933 bis 1939*, Bonn, 1999, pp. 61–5.

166 Cabinet meeting on 24 March 1933; *Die Regierung Hitler*, part 1, vol. 1, no. 72, p. 252. See Goebbels, *Tagebücher*, part 1, vol. 2/3, p. 155 (entry for 25 March 1933): "I managed to get 1 May approved as a national holiday. The cabinet gave me a mandate to see that it is put into practice. I'm going to make it huge." On 7 April 1933, the cabinet passed a draft law concerning the "The Holiday of National Labour." See *Die Regierung Hitler*, no. 93, pp. 311f.

167 Goebbels, *Tagebücher*, part 1, vol. 2/3, p. 170 (entry for 18 April 1933).

168 Jahn, *Die Gewerkschaften in der Endphase der Republik*, doc. 206, pp. 898–200.

169 Ibid., doc. 204, p. 897.

170 See Goebbels, *Tagebücher*, part 1, vol. 2/3, p. 177 (entry for 30 April 1933): "Tempelhof. Gigantic facilities. Unprecedented. This will be a unique mass event." On the May 1933 holiday see Peter Fritzsche, *Wie aus Deutsche Nazis wurden*, Zurich and Munich, 1999, pp. 229ff.

171 Domarus, *Hitler*, vol. 1, part 1, pp. 259–64.

172 Goebbels, *Tagebücher*, part 1, vol. 2/3, p. 179 (entry for 2 May 1933); François-Poncet, *Als Botschafter in Berlin*, pp. 115f.

173 Goebbels, *Tagebücher*, part 1, vol. 2/3, p. 179 (entry for 3 May 1933).

174 See Ronald Smelser, *Robert Ley: Hitlers Mann an der "Arbeitsfront,"* Potsdam, 1989, pp. 134ff.

175 See Broszat, *Der Staat Hitlers*, pp. 185–90; Frei, *Der Führerstaat*, p. 74.

176 Goebbels, *Tagebücher*, part 1, vol. 2/3, p. 200 (entry for 3 June 1933).

177 *Die Regierung Hitler*, part 1, vol. 1, no. 165, pp. 575–7. On the end of the SPD see Erich Matthias, "Die Sozialdemokratische Partei Deutschlands," in *idem* and Rudolf Morsey (eds), *Das Ende der Parteien 1933*, Düsseldorf, 1960, pp. 168–75, 180–7; Winkler, *Der Weg in die Katastrophe*, particularly pp. 915–18; 923–5, 929–49.

178 Quoted in Winkler, *Der Weg in die Katastrophe*, p. 947. On the "Köpenick Blood Week" see Richard J. Evans, *The Third Reich in Power*, London, 2005, p. 21.

179 Goebbels, *Tagebücher*, part 1, vol. 2/4, p. 213 (entry for 23 June 1933).

180 On the end of the German State Party and the German People's Party see Erich Matthias and Rudolf Morsey, "Die Deutsche Staatspartei," in *idem*, *Das Ende der Parteien*, pp. 65–72; Ludwig Richter, *Die Deutsche Volkspartei 1918–1933*, Düsseldorf, 2002, pp. 801–20.

181 Goebbels, *Tagebücher*, part 1, vol. 2/3, p. 176 (entry for 28 April 1933), p. 212 (entry for 22 June 1933). On 7 Nov. 1935, Hitler declared the Stahlhelm, which had continued to exist as a "traditional association," dissolved. See the draft of the letter (with Hitler's handwritten corrections) in BA Berlin-Lichterfelde, NS 10/123. See also the minutes of the meeting between Hitler and Seldte in Haus Wachenfeld on 12 Aug. 1935 with reference to the future of the Stahlhelm; BA Berlin-Lichterfelde, NS 10/30.

182 Minutes of Hindenburg's meeting with Hugenberg and Winterfeld, 17 May 1933; BA Koblenz, N 1231/38. On the attacks on DNVP centres see Beck, *The Fateful Alliance*, pp. 228–43.

183 Cabinet meeting on 27 June 1933; *Die Regierung Hitler*, part 1, vol. 1, no. 170, p. 601. On Hugenberg's resignation and the dissolution of the German National Front see Beck, *The Fateful Alliance*, pp. 283–93.

184 Kessler, *Das Tagebuch*, vol. 9, p. 596 (entry for 28 June 1933).

185 Hugenberg to Hitler, 13 Sept. 1933; Hitler to Hugenberg, 24 Dec. 1933; Hugenberg to Hitler, 26 Jan. 1934; BA Koblenz, N 1231/37.

186 *Die Regierung Hitler*, part 1, vol. 1, no. 170, p. 601; no. 175, p. 609.

187 Goebbels, *Tagebücher*, part 1, vol. 2/3, p. 217 (entry for 28 June 1933), p. 218 (entry for 29 June 1933).

188 See ibid., p. 219 (entry for 1 July 1933): "Centre Party wants to dissolve, but only under the same conditions as the DNVP. Rejected. The party should be broken!" On the end of the Centre Party see Rudolf Morsey, "Die deutsche Zentrumspartei," in Matthias and Morsey, *Das Ende der Parteien*, pp. 377–404; Winfried Becker, "Die Deutsche Zentrumspartei gegenüber dem Nationalsozialismus und dem Reichskonkordat 1930–1933," in *Historisch-Politische Mitteilungen*, 7 (2000), pp. 1–37.

189 See Martina Steber, ". . . dass der Partei nicht nur äussere, sondern auch innere Gefahren drohen": Die Bayerische Volkspartei im Jahr 1933," in Wirsching (ed.), *Das Jahr 1933*, pp. 70–91.

190 Cabinet meeting on 14 July 1933; *Die Regierung Hitler*, part 1, vol. 1, no. 193, pp. 661f. Wording in Sösemann, *Propaganda*, vol. 1, p. 133.

191 Swiss chargé d'affaires Hans Frölicher to Federal Counsellor Giuseppe Motta, 7 July 1933; Bajohr and Strupp (eds), *Fremde Blicke auf das "Dritte Reich,"* p. 382.

192 Report by François-Poncet to Foreign Minister Paul Boncour, 4 July 1933; Becker, *Hitlers Machtergreifung*, pp. 365f.

193 Heuss, *In der Defensive*, p. 163 (entry for 25 June 1933). See Rosenberg, *Tagebücher 1933–1937*, p. 97 (entry for 7 May 1933): "Everything is in flux. One event follows the next. No one knows what tomorrow will look like."

194 Haffner, *Geschichte eines Deutschen*, p. 186.

195 Klemperer, *Tagebücher 1933–1941*, p. 39 (entry for 9 July 1933).

196 *Die Regierung Hitler*, part 1, vol. 1, no. 75, pp. 260f.

197 Quoted in Pyta, "Geteiltes Charisma," p. 57.

198 Ebermayer, *Denn heute gehört uns Deutschland*, p. 33 (dated 28 Feb. 1933).

199 Kessler, *Das Tagebuch*, vol. 9, p. 551 (entry for 7 March 1933).

200 Thomas Mann, *Tagebücher 1933–1934*, ed. Peter de Mendelssohn, Frankfurt am Main, 1977, p. 52 (entry for 20 April 1933).

201 See Haffner, *Geschichte eines Deutschen*, particularly pp. 139f.

202 Wehler, *Deutsche Gesellschaftsgeschichte 1914–1949*, pp. 601–3. See also Horst Möller, "Die nationalsozialistische Machtergreifung: Konterrevolution oder Revolution?," in *Vierteljahrshefte für Zeitgeschichte*, 31 (1983), pp. 25–51. Möller (p. 50) also sees the "ambition to control broad areas of the total reality of life in the Nazi state" as an indication of the regime's "revolutionary character."

203 Domarus, *Hitler*, vol. 1, part 1, p. 286. See also minutes of the Reich governors' conference on 6 July 1933 (probably based on the notes by Reich Governor Ritter von Epp) in *Die Regierung Hitler*, part 1, vol. 1, no. 180, pp. 629–36: "Revolution cannot be a permanent state . . . further development must take the form of evolution" (p. 631). See also Hitler's decree about the powers of Reich Governor Ritter von Epp of 6 July 1933; BA Koblenz, N 1101/95.

204 Becker, *Hitlers Machtergreifung*, p. 340.

205 See the excellent account in Evans, *The Coming of the Third Reich*, pp. 392–440 ("Hitler's Cultural Revolution").

206 See Goebbels, *Tagebücher*, part 1, vol. 2/3, p. 316 (entry for 16 Nov. 1933); Ebermayer, *Denn heute gehört uns Deutschland*, pp. 203f. (dated 16 Nov. 1933); Evans, *The Third Reich in Power*, pp. 138f.

207 Domarus, *Hitler*, vol. 1, part 1, p. 193

208 *Die Regierung Hitler*, part 1, vol. 1, no. 180, p. 632.

209 See also Christoph Buchheim, "Das NS-Regime und die Überwindung der Weltwirtschaftskrise in Deutschland," in *Vierteljahrshefte für Zeitgeschichte*, 56 (2008), pp. 381–414, particularly pp. 383–9.

210 *Die Regierung Hitler*, part 1, vol. 1, no. 17, p. 55 (dated 8 Feb. 1933). On Hitler's caution regarding economic policy during the first months of his chancellorship see Detlev Humann, *"Arbeitsschlacht": Arbeitsbeschaffung und Propaganda in der NS-Zeit 1933–1939*, Göttingen, 2011, pp. 58ff.

211 See Buchheim, "Das NS-Regime und die Überwindung der Weltwirtschaftskrise," pp. 390f.; Evans, *The Third Reich in Power*, p. 330; Humann, *"Arbeitsschlacht,"* pp. 75–8.

212 See Buchheim, "Das NS-Regime und die Überwindung der Weltwirtschaftskrise," pp. 392–5; Evans, *The Third Reich in Power*, pp. 330f; Humann, *"Arbeitsschlacht,"* pp. 118ff., 152ff., 242ff., 366ff., 428ff. On the unreliability of the statistics see ibid., pp. 624ff.

213 Domarus, *Hitler*, vol. 1, part 1, pp. 208f.

214 See *Die Regierung Hitler*, part 1, vol. 1, p. xliii (introduction); no. 92, p. 308n7 (dated 6 April 1933). See also Adam Tooze, *The Wages of Destruction: The Making and Breaking of the Nazi Economy*, London, 2006, pp. 46f.

215 Report by Hafraba's commercial director Hof on a meeting with Hitler, 6 April 1933; *Die Regierung Hitler*, part 1, vol. 1, no. 92, pp. 306–11 (quotations on pp. 308f., 310).

216 Meeting with leading industrialists, 29 May 1933; ibid., no. 147, pp. 506–27 (quote on p. 511).

217 See Goebbels, *Tagebücher*, part 1, vol. 2/3, p. 275 (entry for 24 Sept. 1933). On "labour battle" propaganda see Humann, *"Arbeitsschlacht,"* p. 635ff.

218 See Tooze, *The Wages of Destruction*, p. 47.

219 *Die Regierung Hitler*, part 1, vol. 2, no. 211, p. 741 (dated 18 Sept. 1933). See Evans, *The Third Reich in Power*, pp. 327f.

220 See Hans Mommsen and Manfred Grieger, *Das Volkswagenwerk und seine Arbeiter im Dritten Reich*, Düsseldorf, 1996, pp. 56ff.

221 *Die Regierung Hitler*, part 1, vol. 1, no. 19, p. 62 (dated 9 Feb. 1933). See above p. 417.

222 See Christopher Kopper, *Hjalmar Schacht: Aufstieg und Fall von Hitlers mächtigstem Bankier*, Munich and Vienna, 2006, pp. 205–9. In a letter to the editor of the weekly newspaper *Die Zeit* on 20 July 1948, Theodor Duesterberg, the former second-in-command of the Stahlhelm, accused Schacht of being, next to Papen, "the man most responsible for helping Hitler gain power during Hindenburg's lifetime." Duesterberg also wrote that he could not believe that "such a respected newspaper" would defend Schacht. BA Koblenz, N 1377/27.

223 Tooze, *The Wages of Destruction*, pp. 53f.

224 See Kopper, *Hjalmar Schacht*, pp. 269f.; Tooze, *The Wages of Destruction*, pp. 54, 62; Evans, *The Third Reich in Power*, p. 345.

225 Goebbels, *Tagebücher*, part 1, vol. 2/3, p. 313 (entry for 13 Nov. 1933). See also Hitler's address to the second meeting of the General Council for the Economy, 20 Sept. 1933: "Those who rest, rust. Those who stand still, fall." *Die Regierung Hitler*, part 1, vol. 2, no. 214, p. 810.

226 See Wehler, *Deutsche Gesellschaftsgeschichte 1914–1949*, pp. 646f.; Ludolf Herbst, *Hitlers Charisma: Die Erfindung eines deutschen Messias*, Frankfurt am Main, 2010, pp. 22f.; 259f.; Dirk van Laak, "Adolf Hitler," in Frank Möller (ed.), *Charismatische Führer der deutschen Nation*, Munich, 2004, pp. 162f.

227 See Longerich, *Die braunen Bataillone*, pp. 188–91.

228 See ibid., pp. 183f.

229 Becker, *Hitlers Machtergreifung*, pp. 327–30 (quotations on p. 329). See also Röhm's memo of 30 May 1933, in which he refers to the danger that "the SA and SS could be reduced to the role of mere propaganda troops." BA Berlin-Lichterfelde, NS 26/328.

230 Goebbels, *Tagebücher*, part 1, vol. 2/3, p. 156 (entry for 27 March 1933).

231 Ibid., p. 230 (entry for 19 July 1933), pp. 252f. (entry for 25 Aug. 1933).

232 Domarus, *Hitler*, vol. 1, part 1, pp. 293f. See "Zeitfolge für den Besuch des Herrn Reichskanzlers und des Herrn Preussischen Ministerpräsidenten in Neudeck und

die Tannenbergfeier am 27. August 1933" in BA Berlin-Lichterfelde R 43 II/971. For the memorial ceremony, participants were ordered to wear "dark coattails with a dark top hat or other dark hat," and for the dinner with Hindenburg "a tuxedo with medals." On 25 April 1934 Hitler thanked Hindenburg for the best wishes and flowers on his birthday and told the Reich president how happy he was "to be allowed to do what I can to rebuild the Reich in peacetime under the greatest field marshal of the world war." See the draft of the letter (with Hitler's handwritten corrections) and the final version, BA Berlin-Lichterfelde, NS 10/123.

233 *Die Regierung Hitler*, part 1, vol. 1, no. 180, p. 631; part 1, vol. 2, no. 222, p. 868.

234 Draft of the letter (with Hitler's handwritten amendments) in BA Berlin-Lichterfelde NS 10/123.

235 Goebbels, *Tagebücher*, part 1, vol. 2/3, p. 309 (entry for 8 Nov. 1933).

236 *Deutschland-Berichte der Sozialdemokratischen Partei Deutschlands (Sopade) 1934–1940*, ed. Klaus Behnken, Frankfurt am Main, 1980, 1 (1934), p. 101; see also pp. 9–13, 99–103 for further pieces of evidence for the change of national mood in the spring and early summer of 1934. See Frei, *Der Führerstaat*, pp. 9–17; Thamer, *Verführung und Gewalt*, pp. 327f.; Ian Kershaw, *The Hitler Myth: Image and Reality in the Third Reich*, Oxford, 1987, pp. 21–31.

237 Report by envoy Herluf Zahle dated 16 April 1934; Bajohr and Strupp (eds), *Fremde Blicke auf das "Dritte Reich,"* p. 403. See also the report by John C. White from the U.S. embassy, 26 April 1933, in which he talks of "increasing discontent with present conditions." Ibid., p. 403.

238 Klemperer, *Tagebücher 1933–1941*, p. 86 (entry for 7 Feb. 1934). See Irene Strenge, *Ferdinand von Bredow: Notizen vom 20. 2. 1933 bis 31. 12. 1933. Tägliche Aufzeichnungen vom 1. 1. 1934 bis 28. 6. 1934*, Berlin, 2009, p. 223 (entry for 26 March 1934): "Everywhere's there's complaining . . . There's a lot of unhappiness in the air"; ibid., p. 230 (entry for 25 May 1934): "Nowhere is there any joy, unhappiness everywhere . . . everyone sees this coming to a bad end."

239 Goebbels, *Tagebücher*, part 1, vol. 3/1, p. 39 (entry for 24 April 1934), p. 48 (entry for 13 May 1934).

240 Longerich, *Die braunen Bataillone*, p. 203.

241 See ibid., p. 204.

242 See Müller, *Armee und Drittes Reich*, pp. 57, 64; doc. 57, pp. 192–5. See also Kirstin A. Schäfer, *Werner von Blomberg: Hitlers erster Feldmarschall. Eine Biographie*, Paderborn, 2006, pp. 123f., 136; Immo von Fallois, *Kalkül und Illusion: Der Machtkampf zwischen Reichswehr und SA während der Röhm-Krise 1934*, Berlin, 1994, pp. 106–12.

243 Müller, *Armee und Drittes Reich*, doc. 58, p. 195; Schäfer, *Werner von Blomberg*, p. 137.

244 See Bracher et al., *Die nationalsozialistische Machtergreifung*, p. 944; Heinz Höhne, *Mordsache Röhm: Hitlers Durchbruch zur Alleinherrschaft 1933–1934*, Reinbek, 1984, p. 206. Hanfstaengl encountered "an enraged, hollering, drunken Röhm" on the street, bellowing the "foulest curses I've ever heard." Hanfstaengl's unpublished memoirs, p. 306; BSB München, Nl Hanfstaengl, Ana 405, Box 47.

245 See Diels, *Lucifer ante portas*, pp. 379–82; Longerich, *Die braunen Bataillone*, p. 208; Fallois, *Kalkül und Illusion*, p. 125.

246 See Longerich, *Heinrich Himmler*, pp. 178, 181f.; Gerwarth, *Reinhard Heydrich*, pp. 101f., 104f.

247 Goebbels, *Tagebücher*, part 1, vol. 3/1, p. 49 (entry for 15 May 1934).

248 Adolf Hitler, *Reden, Schriften, Anordnungen—Februar 1925 bis Januar 1933. Vol. 4: Von der Reichstagswahl bis zur Reichspräsidentenwahl Oktober 1930–März 1932. Part 1: Oktober 1930–Juni 1931*, ed. Constantin Goschler, Munich, 1993, doc. 54, p. 183. See Lothar Machtan, *Hitlers Geheimnis: Das Doppelleben eines Diktators*, Berlin, 2001, pp. 208f. As early as February 1927, Hitler had expressed concern about the "175ers in the party." R. Buttmann's diary dated 14 Feb. 1927; BayHStA München, Nl Buttmann 83.

249 Adolf Hitler, *Reden, Schriften, Anordnungen—Februar 1925 bis Januar 1933. Vol. 5: Von der Reichspräsidentenwahl bis zur Machtergreifung April 1932–Januar 1933. Part 1: April 1932–September 1932*, ed. Klaus A. Lankheit, Munich, 1996, doc. 15, p. 32. See Machtan, *Hitlers Geheimnis*, pp. 217–28; Susanne zur Nieden, "Aufstieg und Fall des virilen Männerhelden: Der Skandal um Ernst Röhm und seine Ermordung," in *idem* (ed.), *Homosexualität und Staatsräson: Männlichkeit, Homophobie und Politik in Deutschland 1900–1945*, Frankfurt am Main 2005, pp. 147–75.

250 Goebbels, *Tagebücher*, part 1, vol. 3/1, p. 57 (entry for 3 June 1934).

251 Hanfstaengl, *Zwischen Weissem und Braunem Haus*, pp. 340f. In a confidential letter of 12 June 1934, Hermann Höfle—a former member of the Epp Freikorps who had taken part in the 1923 putsch—had warned Röhm against "intrigues" directed against him from within the Reichswehr. Höfle encouraged Röhm to get Hitler to "take an uncompromising public stand for the SA in the presence of all the army's generals and important officials." BA Berlin-Lichterfelde, NS 26/328.

252 See Frei, *Der Führerstaat*, pp. 25–7; Longerich, *Die braunen Bataillone*, p. 212; Thamer, *Verführung und Gewalt*, p. 326.

253 See Goebbels, *Tagebücher*, part 1, vol. 3/1, p. 51 (entry for 21 April 1934): "Papen would like to assume Hindenburg's position when the old man dies. Out of the question." On Hindenburg's illness and withdrawal to Neudeck, see Pyta, *Hindenburg*, p. 836. In Neurath's papers is a handwritten note by Hindenburg dated 12 May 1934: "Please have Herr von Neurath come between 5 and 5:30 p.m. or tomorrow between 12 and 12:30 a.m." Neurath noted: "The last time I was summoned to listen to Hindenburg." BA Koblenz, N 1310/96. As late as 12 March 1934 Rudolf Hess had reported on a great feast at Hindenburg's residence: "The old man is still surprisingly hale and hearty; he played the host until it was almost midnight." Rudolf Hess to Fritz Hess, 12 March 1934; BA Bern, Nl Hess, J1.211-1989/148, 53.

254 Goebbels, *Tagebücher*, part 1, vol. 3/1, p. 62 (entry for 16 June 1934). See ibid., p. 60 (entry for 9 June 1934) "A republican office for complaints in its purest form."

255 Petzold, *Franz von Papen*, pp. 211–17 (quotations on p. 215f.). The text of the Marburg speech is also in Edmund Forsbach, *Edgar Jung: Ein konservativer Revolutionär*, Pfullingen, 1984, pp. 154–74.

256 The original telegram in BA Berlin-Lichterfelde, R 43 II/971; with a handwritten addendum from the Reich Chancellery switchboard: "Opened and read on 20 May on behalf of Martin Bormann."

257 Goebbels, *Tagebücher*, part 1, vol. 3/1, p. 65 (entry for 18 June 1934).

258 See Frei, *Der Führerstaat*, pp. 28f. On 17 June 1934 Herbert von Bose sent three copies of the speech to the Ministry for Propaganda with the request to transmit it to the press; BA Berlin-Lichterfelde, NS 10/50.

259 Heuss, *In der Defensive*, pp. 236f. (dated 20 June 1934).

260 François-Poncet, *Als Botschafter in Berlin*, p. 187. See Strenge, *Ferdinand von Bredow*, p. 235 (dated 24 June 1934): "Everyone asked himself: what does Papen want? Who does he have behind him? What's Hitler stance toward him? . . . There's something undetermined and indeterminable in the air." On the mood in June 1934 see also Klemperer, *Tagebücher 1933–1941*, p. 116 (entry for 13 June 1934): "Everywhere there is uncertainty, things bubbling under the surface, secrets. Day in, day out, we wait." See also Martha Dodd, *Nice to meet you, Mr. Hitler! Meine Jahre in Deutschland 1933 bis 1937*, Frankfurt am Main, 2005 p. 153, who writes of an "electrically charged" atmosphere ahead of 30 June: "Everyone could sense something in the air but no one knew what."

261 Goebbels, *Tagebücher*, part 1, vol. 3/1, p. 65 (entry for 18 June 1934).

262 Papen to Hitler, 27 June 1934; BA Lichterfelde, NS 10/50. See Papen, *Der Wahrheit eine Gasse*, pp. 349f.

263 Hans-Günther Seraphim (ed.), *Das politische Tagebuch Alfred Rosenbergs aus den Jahren 1934/35 und 1939/40*, Göttingen, 1956, p. 31. See Pyta, *Hindenburg*, p. 845.

264 See Höhne, *Mordsache Röhm*, p. 238.

265 See ibid., pp. 239–43. On 29 June, while visiting Ribbentrop's home, Himmler declared that Röhm was a "dead man." Joachim von Ribbentrop, *Zwischen London und Moskau: Erinnerungen und letzte Aufzeichnungen*, ed. Annelies von Ribbentrop, Leoni am Starnberger See, 1961, p. 52.

266 Quoted in Longerich, *Die braunen Bataillone*, p. 212.

267 Ebermayer, *Denn heute gehört uns Deutschland*, p. 326 (dated 27 June 1934).

268 Frei, *Der Führerstaat*, p. 30; on the military's preparation for the action against the SA see Fallois, *Kalkül und Illusion*, pp. 134–9.

269 Quoted in Höhne, *Mordsache Röhm*, p. 256.

270 Goebbels, *Tagebücher*, part 1, vol. 3/1, p. 71 (entry for 29 June 1934).

271 Ibid., p. 72 (entry for 1 July 1934). On the sombre mood at the dinner table in Hotel Dreesen see Hans Baur, *Ich flog Mächtige der Erde*, Kempten in Allgäu, 1956, p. 119.

272 Goebbels, *Tagebücher*, part 1, vol. 3/1, p. 72 (entry for 1 July 1934).

273 Baur, *Ich flog Mächtige der Erde*, p. 119. According to Wilhelm Brückner, Reichswehr officers told Hitler that "armed Munich SA men had turned out for roll call" at the airport. The situation was described as "very threatening." Memorandum by Wilhelm Brückner dated 28 May 1949; IfZ München, ED 100/43.

274 Höhne, *Mordsache Röhm*, p. 267.

275 Report from Hitler's chauffeur Erich Kempka; quoted in Evans, *The Third Reich in Power*, pp. 32.; see also the transcript of an interview with Erich Kempka dated 25 March 1952; IfZ München, ZS 253.

276 See Longerich, *Die braunen Bataillone*, p. 217; Frei, *Der Führerstaat*, p. 32. See Goebbels, *Tagebücher*, part 1, vol. 3/1, p. 72 (entry for 1 July 1934): "Heines is pathetic. [Caught] with a boy of pleasure."

277 See Höhne, *Mordsache Röhm*, p. 269.

278 See ibid., pp. 271–4. Facsimile of the list in Otto Gritschneder, *'Der Führer hat Sie zum Tode verurteilt . . .": Hitlers "Röhm-Putsch'-Morde vor Gericht*, Munich, 1993, p. 28. See Frank, *Im Angesicht des Galgens*, pp. 148–51. Frank claimed that it was thanks to his own intervention that not more people were executed in Stadelheim.

279 See the list of the murdered in Gritschneder, *"Der Führer,"* pp. 60–2. On Fritz Gerlich see Rudolf Morsey (ed.), *Fritz Gerlich—ein Publizist gegen Hitler: Briefe und Akten 1930–1934*, Paderborn, 2010, pp. 36–9. On Ballerstedt see his sister-in law's memorandum (undated) in BayHStA München, Nl Ballerstedt. On Bredow see Strenge, *Ferdinand von Bredow*, p. 238.

280 Goebbels, *Tagebücher*, part 1, vol. 3/1, p. 72 (entry for 1 July 1934).

281 Hans Bernd Gisevius, *Adolf Hitler: Versuch einer Deutung*, Munich, 1963, p. 291.

282 Christa Schroeder, *Er war mein Chef: Aus dem Nachlass der Sekretärin von Adolf Hitler*, ed. Anton Joachimsthaler, 3rd edition, Munich and Vienna, 1985, p. 51.

283 See Gritschneder, *"Der Führer,"* pp. 32–6.

284 Frank, *Im Angesicht des Galgens*, p. 149.

285 Quoted in Machtan, *Hitlers Geheimnis*, pp. 244f. See Goebbels, *Tagebücher*, part 1, vol. 3/1, p. 73 (entry for 4 July 1934).

286 Cabinet meeting on 3 July 1934; *Die Regierung Hitler*, part 1, vol. 2, no. 375, pp. 1354–8.

287 Goebbels, *Tagebücher*, part 1, vol. 3/1, p. 74 (entry for 4 July 1934).

288 Papen to Hitler, 10 July, 12 July 1934; BA Berlin-Lichterfelde, NS 10/50. See also Petzold, *Franz von Papen*, pp. 226–9, who has consulted further documents held in the special archives in Moscow, Papen papers.

289 Domarus, *Hitler*, vol. 1, part 1, p. 405; Kahr, memoirs, pp. 1091ff. (on Hindenburg's visit to Kahr's house at the end of August/beginning of September 1920); BayHStA München, Nl Kahr 51; Hindenburg's telegram to Kahr, 23 Oct. 1933; ibid., Nl Kahr 16.

290 According to Hitler's communication to the mayor of Hamburg, Krogmann, 18 Aug. 1934; Pyta, *Hindenburg*, p. 849. According to Wilhelm Brückner, Hindenburg had told Hitler: "If you want to create history, you also have to take measures that

will make bloodshed unavoidable." Memorandum by Wilhelm Brückner dated 28 May 1949; IfZ München, ED 10/43. See also chauffeur Erich Kempka's questioning on 26 Sept. 1945; IfZ München, ZS 253; Hossbach, *Zwischen Wehrmacht und Hitler*, p. 50.

291 Goebbels, *Tagebücher*, part 1, vol. 3/1, p. 76 (entry for 6 July 1934).

292 Ibid., p. 73 (entry for 4 July 1934).

293 Quoted in Kershaw, *The Hitler Myth*, p. 88. Further examples on pp. 110–13. See also *Deutschland-Berichte der Sopade*, 1 (1934), pp. 197–200. Foreign diplomats reached a similar verdict. See U.S. Consul Ralph C. Busser's report from Leipzig dated 19 July 1934, and Charles M. Hathaway's from Munich dated 20 July 1934; Bajohr and Strupp (eds), *Fremde Blicke auf das "Dritte Reich*," pp. 412f., 414f.

294 Luise Solmitz's diary, 30 June 1934; quoted in Evans, *The Third Reich in Power*, p. 39.

295 Goebbels, *Tagebücher*, part 1, vol. 3/1, p. 76 (entry for 7 July 1934).

296 See ibid., pp. 77f. (entry for 11 July 1934).

297 François-Poncet, *Als Botschafter in Berlin*, p. 190.

298 Papen to Hitler, 13 July 1934; BA Berlin-Lichterfelde, NS 10/50. After the speech, Papen wrote to Hitler that he felt the "urge, as in January 1933, to shake your hand and thank you for everything you have given anew to the German people by crushing the insipient second revolution and proclaiming immutable principles of statesmanship." Papen to Hitler, 14 July 1934; ibid.

299 Domarus, *Hitler*, vol. 1 part 1, pp. 410–24 (quotations on pp. 415, 421, 424).

300 Quoted in Reinhard Mehring, *Carl Schmitt: Aufstieg und Fall. Eine Biographie*, Munich, 2009, p. 352.

301 Kershaw, *The Hitler Myth*, p. 89; see *Deutschland-Berichte der Sopade*, 1 (1934), pp. 201f.

302 Kalshoven, *Ich denk so viel an Euch*, p. 236 (entry for 14 July 1934).

303 Heinrich Hoffmann, *Hitler wie ich ihn sah: Aufzeichnungen seines Leibfotografen*, Munich and Berlin, 1974, p. 72. See Olaf Rose (ed.), *Julius Schaub: In Hitlers Schatten*, Stegen, 2005, p. 140; Wilhelm Brückner told criminal investigators in Traunstein on 25 June 1952 that in his presence Hitler "had never talked to anyone ever again about this action"; IfZ München, ED 100/43.

304 Klemperer, *Tagebücher 1933–1941*, p. 122 (entry for 14 July 1934).

305 Mann, *Tagebücher 1933–1945*, pp. 458 (entry for 4 July 1934), 462 (entry for 7 July 1934), 463 (entry for 8 July 1934). See Thea Sternheim, *Tagebücher. Vol. 2: 1925–1936*, ed. and selected Thomas Ehrsam and Regula Wyss, Göttingen, 2002, p. 589 (entry for 5 July 1934): "Germany is being systematically destroyed by the bloodhound and petty bourgeois Adolf Hitler. The German as the world's nightmare and scum."

306 Quoted in Astrid Pufendorf, *Die Plancks: Eine Familie zwischen Patriotimus und Widerstand*, Berlin, 2006, p. 373.

307 Liebmann's notes, 5 July 1934; Frei, *Der Führerstaat*, p. 39. See Blomberg's edict to the military, 1 July 1934; Müller, *Armee und Drittes Reich*, pp. 206f. See also Schäfer, *Werner von Blomberg*, p. 141; Fallois, *Kalkül und Illusion*, pp. 150–4.

308 See Longerich, *Heinrich Himmler*, p. 184; Frei, *Der Führerstaat*, p. 40.

309 See Longerich, *Die braunen Bataillone*, pp. 220–4.

310 Goebbels, *Tagebücher*, vol. 3/1, p. 87 (entry for 2 Aug. 1934).

311 Cabinet meeting on 1 Aug. 1934 (9:30 p.m.); *Die Regierung Hitler*, part 1, vol. 2, no. 382, pp. 1384f.

312 Quoted in Fallois, *Kalkül und Illusion*, p. 162. See Schäfer, *Werner von Blomberg*, pp. 151–5.

313 Goebbels, *Tagebücher*, part 1, vol. 3/1, p. 88 (entry for 4 Aug. 1933). Schwerin von Krosigk (essay on Hitler's personality, *c.* 1945) wrote that at the subsequent cabinet meeting it was apparent that the death of the "old man" hit Hitler "very hard." Hitler, Krosigk recalled, had been "visibly moved" as he told of his final visit to Neudeck; IfZ München, ZS 145, vol. 5. Oskar von Hindenburg thanked Hitler in a telegram on 2 Aug. 1934 for the "warm words" about the death of his father; BA Berlin-Lichterfelde NS 10/123.

314 Cabinet meeting on 2 Aug. 1934; *Die Regierung Hitler*, part 1, vol. 2, no. 383, pp. 1386–8.

315 Domarus, *Hitler*, vol. 1, part 1, p. 438. See Hoegen, *Der Held von Tannenberg*, pp. 411–14.

316 See Goebbels, *Tagebücher*, part 1, vol. 3/1, p. 90 (entry for 8 Aug. 1934): "High alert on account of an alleged political testament made by the old man, perhaps written by Papen? . . . Decision: political testament will be treated as of concern only to the Führer and the government."

317 Reprinted in Hubatsch, *Hindenburg und der Staat*, pp. 380–3 (quotations on pp. 382f.) On the story of Hindenburg's testament see Pyta, *Hindenburg*, pp. 864–7.

318 Hoegen, *Der Held von Tannenberg*, p. 420.

319 Goebbels, *Tagebücher*, part 1, vol. 3/1, p. 95 (entry for 20 Aug. 1934).

320 Quoted in Kershaw, *The Hitler Myth*, p. 68. On coercion of voters and voting fraud in connection with the election of 19 Aug. 1934, see *Deutschland-Berichte der Sopade*, 1 (1934), pp. 282–7, 347–9.

321 Mann, *Tagebücher 1933–1934*, p. 510 (entry for 20 Aug. 1934).

322 Klemperer, *Tagebücher 1933–1941*, pp. 137f. (entry for 21 Aug. 1934).

323 Danish ambassador Herluf Zahle, 4 Aug. 1934; Bajohr and Strupp (eds), *Fremde Blicke auf das "Dritte Reich*, p. 417.

15 Eviscerating Versailles

1 Max Domarus, *Hitler: Reden und Proklamationen 1932–1945. Vol. 2: Untergang. Part 2: 1941–1945*, Munich, 1965, p. 1659.

2 *Akten der Reichskanzlei: Die Regierung Hitler. Part 1: 1933/34. Vol. 1: 30 Januar bis 31 April 1933*, ed. Karl-Heinz Minuth, Boppard am Rhein, 1983, no. 19, pp. 62f.

3 Goebbels's confidential speech of 5 April 1940 to members of the German press, quoted in Rainer F. Schmidt, *Die Aussenpolitik des Dritten Reiches 1933–1939*, Stuttgart, 2002, p. 11.

4 Wilhelm Treue, "Rede Hitlers vor der deutschen Presse (10 November 1938)," in *Vierteljahrshefte für Zeitgeschichte*, 6 (1958), p. 182. See Domarus, *Hitler*, vol. 1, part 2, p. 974.

5 Eric Phipps's report of 21 Nov. 1933; *Documents of British Foreign Policy 1919–1939 (DBFP)*, London, 1947–1984, 2nd series 1929–1938, vol. 6, no. 60, pp. 90f., quoted in Detlev Clemens, *Herr Hitler in Germany: Wahrnehmungen und Deutungen des Nationalsozialismus in Grossbritannien 1920 bis 1939*, Göttingen and Zurich, 1996, p. 350. In an article in the *Daily Mail* on 2 Nov. 1933, editor Ward Price answered the question "Can We Trust Hitler?" in the affirmative, calling Hitler an honest man who wanted to redirect the energy and enthusiasm of Germany's youth toward domestic goals. Wolff's Telegraphisches Büro no. 2765, dated 2 Nov. 1933; BA Berlin-Lichterfelde, R 43 II/959.

6 George S. Messersmith's report of 9 May 1933; Frank Bajohr and Christoph Strupp (eds), *Fremde Blicke auf das "Dritte Reich": Berichte ausländischer Diplomaten über Herrschaft und Gesellschaft in Deutschland 1933–1945*, Göttingen, 2011, p. 372.

7 On the continuity of personnel in the German Foreign Ministry see Eckart Conze, Norbert Frei, Peter Hayes and Moshe Zimmermann, *Das Amt und die Vergangenheit: Deutsche Diplomaten im Dritten Reich und in der Bundesrepublik*, Munich, 2010, pp. 31–41.

8 *Akten der deutschen Auswärtigen Politik 1918–1945 (ADAP)*. Series C: 1933–1937, Göttingen, 1971–1981, vol. 1, part 1, no. 10, pp. 20f. See Klaus Hildebrand, *Das vergangene Reich: Deutsche Aussenpolitik von Bismarck zu Hitler 1871–1945*, Stuttgart, 1995, pp. 578, 580f.

9 *Die Tagebücher von Joseph Goebbels. Part 1: Aufzeichnungen 1923–1941*, ed. Elke Fröhlich, Munich, 1998, vol. 2/3, p. 386 (entry for 16 March 1934).

10   See Hildebrand, *Das vergangene Reich*, pp. 550–2, 556; see also Schmidt, *Die Aussen-politik des Dritten Reiches*, p. 31; Hans-Ulrich Thamer, *Verführung und Gewalt: Deutsch-land 1933–1945*, Berlin, 1986, pp. 312, 314.

11   For a summary see Heinrich August Winkler, *Geschichte des Westens. Vol. 2: Die Zeit der Weltkriege 1914–1945*, Munich, 2011, pp. 577–602.

12   See Schmidt, *Die Aussenpolitik des Dritten Reiches*, pp. 40–2; Bernd-Jürgen Wendt, *Grossdeutschland: Aussenpolitik und Kriegsvorbereitung des Hitler-Regimes*, Munich, 1987, p. 84.

13   See the excellent account in Winkler, *Geschichte des Westens*, vol. 2, pp. 332–404.

14   Bülow's memorandum of 13 March 1933 is reprinted and annotated in Günter Wollstein, "Eine Denkschrift des Staatssekretärs Bernhard von Bülow vom März 1933: Wilhelminische Konzeption der Aussenpolitik zu Beginn der nationalsozialis-tischen Herrschaft," in *Militärgeschichtliche Mitteilungen*, 1 (1973), pp. 77–94. Extensive detail on its contents in Wendt, *Grossdeutschland*, pp. 72–9. Neurath's presentation in *Die Regierung Hitler*, part 1, vol. 1, no. 93, pp. 313–18.

15   Max Domarus, *Hitler: Reden und Proklamationen 1932–1945. Vol. 1: Triumph. Part 1: 1932–1934*, Munich, 1965, pp. 270–9 (quotations on p. 273).

16   Wilhelm Hoegner, *Flucht vor Hitler: Erinnerungen an die Kapitulation der ersten deutschen Republik 1933*, Frankfurt am Main, 1982, p. 203. See Goebbels, *Tagebücher*, part 1, vol. 2/3, p. 188 (entry for 18 May 1933): "The declaration of confidence from the entire house, including the SPD, accepted. Afterwards I was with the Führer. Everyone is happy."

17   Hedda Kalshoven, *Ich denk so viel an Euch: Ein deutsch-holländischer Briefwechsel 1920–1949*, Munich, 1995, pp. 201f.

18   Quoted in Josef and Ruth Becker (eds), *Hitlers Machtergreifung: Dokumente vom Machtantritt Hitlers. 30. Januar 1933 bis zur Besiegelung des Einparteienstaats 14. Juli 1933*, Munich, 1983, p. 309. The Danish ambassador in Berlin reported that the chancellor's statements had "undeniably been characterised by heartfelt moderation." Bajohr and Strupp (eds), *Fremde Blicke auf das "Dritte Reich,"* p. 376.

19   Harry Graf Kessler, *Das Tagebuch. Vol. 9: 1926–1937*, ed. Sabine Gruber and Ulrich Ott with Christoph Hilse and Nadin Weiss, Stuttgart, 2010, pp. 596f. (entry for 17 May 1933). See ibid., p. 571 (entry for 20 May 1933): "You can sense how uncom-fortable the French are with Hitler's speech. Their entire diplomatic position is under threat."

20   Thomas Mann, *Tagebücher 1933–1934*, ed. Peter de Mendelssohn, Frankfurt am Main, 1977, p. 88 (entry for 18 May 1933).

21   Goebbels, *Tagebücher* part 1, vol. 2/3, p. 276 (entry for 25 Sept. 1933).

22   On the Geneva disarmament negotiations see Hans-Adolf Jacobsen, *National-sozialistische Aussenpolitik 1933–1939*, Frankfurt am Main and Berlin, 1968, pp. 396–9; Schmidt, *Die Aussenpolitik des Dritten Reiches*, pp. 142–52; Wendt, *Grossdeutschland*, pp. 91–3.

23   Cabinet meeting on 13 Oct. 1933; *Die Regierung Hitler*, part 1, vol. 2, no. 230, pp. 903–6 (quotation on pp. 904, 905).

24   Goebbels, *Tagebücher*, part 1, vol. 2/3, p. 290 (entry for 12 Oct. 1933). See ibid., p. 288: "The boss is struggling with the most difficult decisions." See also Rudolf Hess to his aunt Emma Rothacker in Zurich, 30 Oct. 1933: "The last big foreign policy deci-sion was of course very difficult for the Führer. He arrived at it after many sleep-less nights, as he saw no other way for us." BA Bern, Nl Hess, J1.211-1993/300, Box 4.

25   Erich Ebermayer, *Denn heute gehört uns Deutschland . . . Persönliches und politisches Tagebuch*, Hamburg and Vienna, 1959, p. 184 (entry for 15 Oct. 1933).

26   Kessler, *Das Tagebuch*, vol. 9, p. 608 (entry for 14 Oct. 1933).

27   Domarus, *Hitler*, vol. 1, part 1, pp. 308–14 (quotations on pp. 309, 312).

28   Goebbels, *Tagebücher*, part 1, vol. 2/3, p. 292 (entry for 16 Oct. 1933).

29   Cabinet meeting on 17 Oct. 1933; *Die Regierung Hitler*, part 1, vol. 2, no. 231, p. 908.

30   Goebbels, *Tagebücher*, part 1, vol. 2/3, p. 293 (entry for 17 Oct. 1933).

31   Domarus, *Hitler*, vol. 1, part 1, pp. 318–23 (quotations on pp. 319, 321, 320, 322).

32   Ibid., pp. 323f. See Goebbels, *Tagebücher*, part 1, vol. 2/3, p. 299 (entry for 25 Oct. 1933): "He spoke fabulously, especially at the end. Marvellous ovations. People were beside themselves. A good start."

33   See Hans Baur, *Ich flog Mächtige der Erde*, Kempten im Allgäu, 1956, pp. 108–10.

34   Domarus, *Hitler*, vol. 1, part 1, p. 326.

35   Goebbels, *Tagebücher*, part 1, vol. 2/3, p. 310 (entry for 9 Nov. 1923).

36   Domarus, *Hitler*, vol. 1, part 1, p. 330.

37   Goebbels, *Tagebücher*, part 1, vol. 2/3, p. 311 (entry for 11 Nov. 1933).

38   Victor Klemperer, *Ich will Zeugnis ablegen bis zum letzten: Tagebücher 1933–1941*, ed. Walter Nowojski with Hadwig Klemperer, Berlin, 1995, pp. 67f. (entry for 11 Nov. 1933).

39   Kessler, *Das Tagebuch*, vol. 9, p. 609 (entry for 15 Oct. 1933).

40   See Domarus, *Hitler*, vol. 1, part 1, p. 331.

41   Goebbels, *Tagebücher*, part 1, vol. 2/3, p. 313 (entry for 13 Nov. 1933).

42   Klemperer, *Tagebücher 1933–1941*, p. 68 (entry for 14 Nov. 1933).

43   See *Die Regierung Hitler*, part 1, vol. 2, no. 243n1, pp. 939f. See also Norbert Frei, *Der Führerstaat: Nationalsozialistische Herrschaft 1933 bis 1945*, new and expanded edition, Munich, 2001, p. 94.

44   Dinichert to Federal Counsellor Giuseppe Motta, 17 Nov. 1933; Bajohr and Strupp (eds), *Fremde Blicke auf das "Dritte Reich,"* pp. 391f.

45   Bernd Stöver, *Volksgemeinschaft im Dritten Reich: Die Konsensbereitschaft der Deutschen aus der Sicht sozialistischer Exilberichte*, Düsseldorf, 1993, p. 178.

46   *Die Regierung Hitler*, part 1, vol. 2, no. 243, pp. 339–41.

47   Official communiqué dated 3 May 1933; ibid. part 1, vol. 1, no. 107, p. 382n4.

48   Goebbels, *Tagebücher*, part 1, vol. 2/3, p. 277 (entry for 27 Sept. 1933).

49   See Jacobsen, *Nationalsozialistische Aussenpolitik*, pp. 403–6; Gerhard L. Weinberg, *The Foreign Policy of Hitler's Germany. Vol. 1: Diplomatic Revolution in Europe 1933–1936*, London, 1970, pp. 184–94.

50   Ebermayer, *Denn heute gehört uns Deutschland*, p. 248 (entry for 28 Jan. 1934). See Irene Strenge, *Ferdinand von Bredow: Notizen vom 20. 2. 1933 bis 31. 12. 1933. Tägliche Aufzeichnungen vom 1. 1. 1934 bis 28. 6. 1934*, Berlin, 2009, p. 218 (dated 28 Jan. 1934): "Not a bad gambit."

51   See cabinet meeting on 25 April 1933; *Die Regierung Hitler*, part 1, vol. 1, no. 107, p. 381.

52   Goebbels, *Tagebücher*, part 1, vol. 2/3, p. 317 (entry for 17 Nov. 1933).

53   Phipps to Simon, 31 Jan. 1934; *DBFP 1919–1939*, 2nd series, vol. 6, p. 365; see Schmidt, *Die Aussenpolitik des Dritten Reiches*, p. 157.

54   Domarus, *Hitler*, vol. 1, part 1, p. 357.

55   Hildebrand, *Das vergangene Reich*, p. 586.

56   Speech to his cabinet on 26 Sept. 1933; *Die Regierung Hitler*, part 1, vol. 1, no. 218, p. 838. See also Bülow's memorandum of 26 Sept. 1933; *ADAP, Series C*, vol. 1, part 2, no. 457, pp. 839f.: "He said that it was only natural for a sharp antagonism to persist between Germany and Russia, but that he didn't support breaking off German–Russian relations or giving the Russians any pretence for doing so."

57   *Die Weizsäcker-Papiere 1933–1950*, ed. Leonidas Hill, Frankfurt am Main, Berlin and Vienna, 1974, pp. 70, 76 (dated 30 March 1033, end of Aug. 1933). See Conze et al., *Das Amt und die Vergangenheit*, pp. 69f.

58   See Jacobsen, *Nationalsozialistische Aussenpolitik*, pp. 45ff., 90ff., 252ff.; Schmidt, *Die Aussenpolitik des Dritten Reiches*, pp. 60, 65–70.

59   *Die Weizsäcker-Papiere 1933–1950*, p. 74 (dated 6 Aug. 1933).

60　André François-Poncet, *Als Botschafter in Berlin 1931–1938*, Mainz, 1947, p. 146. After visiting Berlin in May 1934, King Boris of Bulgaria stated: "I have seen many great dictators, but none of them were as proper and upstanding as Hitler!" German embassy in Sofia to Foreign Minister von Neurath, 24 May 1934; BA Koblenz, N 1310/10.

61　Anthony Eden, *Angesichts der Diktatoren: Memoiren 1923–1938*, Cologne and Berlin, 1964, p. 88; R. R. James, *Anthony Eden*, London, 1988, p. 135; See Schmidt, *Die Aussenpolitik des Dritten Reiches*, p. 23.

62　Conversation between Hitler and Lord Eden, 20 Feb. 1934; *Die Regierung Hitler*, part 1, vol. 2, no. 305, pp. 1143–9 (quotation on p. 1149). See also Hitler's letter to Lord Rothermere dated 2 March 1934 (with Hitler's handwritten corrections), in which he expressed his longing for "an honest understanding between the peoples of Europe" and invited Rothermere to visit Germany. BA Berlin-Lichterfelde, NS 10/123. Rothermere, the owner of the *Daily Mail*, had written an op-ed piece supporting the Nazi regime in July 1933. In December 1934, he was one of the guests of honour at an evening gala in the Chancellery. See Ian Kershaw, *Making Friends with Hitler: Lord Londonderry and Britain's Road to War*, London, 2005, pp. 59. In a letter from May 1935, after Germany had re-introduced universal conscription, Hitler assured the press baron as to his "abiding determination . . . to make a historical contribution towards re-establishing good and lasting relations between the two Germanic nations" (ibid., p. 82). The letter was apparently preceded by another Rothermere visit to Berlin. On 28 April 1935 Wilhelm Brückner's notebook read: "Rothermere—Boss"; BA Berlin-Lichterfelde, NS 26/1209. On Rothermere's visit to the Obersalzberg at the beginning of January 1937 see Goebbels, *Tagebücher*, part 1, vol. 3/2, p. 320 (entry for 8 Jan. 1937).

63　Adolf Hitler, *Mein Kampf. Vol. 1: Eine Abrechnung*, 7th edition, Munich, 1933, p. 3.

64　Cabinet meeting on 26 May 1933; *Die Regierung Hitler*, part 1, vol. 1, no. 142, p. 493. See Goebbels, *Tagebücher*, part 1, vol. 2/3, p. 194 (entry for 27 May 1933): "1,000 marks set as fee for a visa. That will topple Dollfuss."

65　See Jacobsen, *Nationalsozialistische Aussenpolitik*, pp. 406–8; Hildebrand, *Das vergangene Reich*, p. 594; Schmidt, *Die Aussenpolitik des Dritten Reiches*, p. 163. On "Austro-Fascism" see Ernst Hanisch, *Der lange Schatten des Staates: Österreichische Gesellschaftsgeschichte im 20. Jahrhundert*, Vienna, 1994, pp. 310–15.

66　Heinrich Hoffmann, *Hitler wie ich ihn sah: Aufzeichnungen seines Leibfotografen*, Munich and Berlin, 1974, p. 61. A collection of newspaper cuttings on Hitler's visit to Venice, with countless press photographs, in BA Koblenz, N 1310/56.

67　Walter Rauscher, *Hitler und Mussolini: Macht, Krieg und Terror*, Graz, Vienna and Cologne, 2001, pp. 213f.; see also Gianluca Falanga, *Mussolinis Vorposten in Hitlers Reich: Italiens Politik in Berlin 1933–1945*, Berlin, 2008, pp. 46f.

68　See Kurt Bauer, *Elementar-Ereignis: Die österreichischen Nationalsozialisten und der Juli-Putsch 1934*, Vienna, 2003.

69　Goebbels, *Tagebücher*, part 1, vol. 3/1, p. 83 (entry for 24 July 1934). See Peter Longerich, *Joseph Goebbels: A Biography*, London, 2015, p. 268; Kurt Bauer, "Hitler und der Juliputsch 1934 in Österreich: Eine Fallstudie zur nationalsozialistischen Aussenpolitik in der Frühphase des Regimes," in *Vierteljahrshefte für Zeitgeschichte*, 59 (2011), pp. 193–227 (particularly pp. 208–13).

70　Goebbels, *Tagebücher*, part 1, vol. 3/1, p. 84 (entry for 26 July 1934).

71　Friedelind Wagner, *Nacht über Bayreuth*, 3rd edition, Cologne, 1997, pp. 159f.; see Brigitte Hamann, *Winifred Wagner oder Hitlers Bayreuth*, Munich and Zurich, 2002, p. 286.

72　Goebbels, *Tagebücher*, part 1, vol. 3/1, p. 84 (entry for 26 July 1934).

73　Franz von Papen, *Der Wahrheit eine Gasse*, Munich, 1952, p. 379f.

74　Goebbels, *Tagebücher*, part 1, vol. 3/1, p. 85 (entry for 28 July 1934).

75　Rauscher, *Hitler und Mussolini*, p. 214.

76　Jens Petersen, *Hitler–Mussolini: Die Entstehung der Achse Berlin–Rom 1933–1936*, Tübingen, 1973, p. 370. See Falanga, *Mussolinis Vorposten*, pp. 50f.

77 Goebbels, *Tagebücher*, part 1, vol. 3/1, p. 86 (entry for 30 July 1934).

78 Colonel General Beck's notes on a statement by Bülow on foreign policy, 30 July 1934; reprinted in Klaus-Jürgen Müller, *Armee und Drittes Reich 1933–1939: Darstellung und Dokumente*, Paderborn, 1987, pp. 280f.; see also Klaus-Jürgen Müller, *Generaloberst Ludwig Beck: Eine Biographie*, Paderborn, 2008, pp. 145f.

79 Goebbels, *Tagebücher*, part 1, vol. 3/1, p. 145 (entry for 30 Nov. 1934), p. 164 (entry for 6 Jan. 1935).

80 *Die Regierung Hitler* , vol. 2, part 1, no. 33, pp. 135f. (dated 1 Nov. 1934).

81 Goebbels, *Tagebücher*, part 1, vol. 3/1, p. 85 (entry for 28 July 1934).

82 Ulrich von Hassell, *Römische Tagebücher und Briefe 1932–1938*, ed. Ulrich Schlie, Munich, 2004, p. 118 (dated 17 Jan. 1936).

83 See Patrick von zur Mühlen, *"Schlagt Hitler an der Saar!": Abstimmungskampf, Emigration und Widerstand im Saargebiet 1933–1945*, Bonn, 1979; Gerhard Paul, *"Deutsche Mutter—heim zu Dir!": Warum es misslang, Hitler an der Saar zu schlagen. Der Saarkampf 1933 bis 1945*, Cologne, 1984.

84 See Stöver, *Volksgemeinschaft im Dritten Reich*, pp. 179f.; *Deutschland-Berichte der Sopade*, 2 (1935), p. 151.

85 Klaus Mann, *Tagebücher 1934 bis 1935*, ed. Joachim Heimannsberg, Peter Laemmle and Winfried F. Schoeller, Munich, 1989, p. 92 (entry for 15 Jan. 1935). On Golo Mann's disappointment see Tilmann Lahme, *Golo Mann: Biographie*, Frankfurt am Main, 2009, pp. 114f. Count Harry Kessler noted: "A very surprising result and a great triumph for Hitler, whose position is much stronger both domestically and abroad." *Das Tagebuch*, vol. 9, p. 629 (entry for 15 Jan. 1935).

86 Goebbels, *Tagebücher*, part 1, vol. 3/1, p. 168 (entry for 16 Jan. 1935).

87 Cabinet meeting on 24 Jan. 1935; *Die Regierung Hitler*, vol. 2, part 1, no. 84, p. 322.

88 Domarus, *Hitler*, vol. 1, part 2, pp. 484–8 (quotation on p. 485).

89 Goebbels, *Tagebücher*, part 1, vol. 3/1, p. 193 (entry for 2 March 1935).

90 Ibid., p. 171 (entry for 22 Jan. 1935).

91 See François-Poncet, *Als Botschafter in Berlin*, pp. 228f.; Domarus, *Hitler*, vol. 1, part 2, pp. 481f.; Heinz Höhne, *Die Zeit der Illusionen: Hitler und die Anfänge des Dritten Reiches 1933–1936*, Düsseldorf, Vienna and New York, 1991, pp. 295f.

92 Goebbels, *Tagebücher*, part 1, vol. 3/1, p. 194 (entry for 6 March 1935). See ibid., p. 197 (entry for 10 March 1935): "The English have lost out. Revenge for the white paper. Cheers, Sir John Simon!"

93 See Höhne, *Zeit der Illusionen*, p. 298; Schmidt, *Die Aussenpolitik des Dritten Reiches*, p. 169; Goebbels, *Tagebücher*, part 1, vol. 3/1, p. 199 (entry for 14 March 1935): "Göring interview. Official announcement about our air forces . . . It's out in the open now, and the sky won't fall in."

94 François-Poncet, *Als Botschafter in Berlin*, p. 232.

95 See Müller, *Generaloberst Ludwig Beck*, pp. 202–5; Ian Kershaw, *Hitler 1889–1936: Hubris*, London, 1998, pp. 548f.

96 See Friedrich Hossbach, *Zwischen Wehrmacht und Hitler 1934–1938*, 2nd revised edition, Göttingen, 1965, pp. 81–3.

97 Domarus, *Hitler*, vol. 1, part 2, pp. 491–5 (quotation on p. 494).

98 See Goebbels, *Tagebücher*, part 1, vol. 3/1, p. 201 (entry for 18 March 1935): "The Führer battled Blomberg over the number of divisions. He got his way: thirty-six." In August 1942 Hitler recalled: "That was a battle I had with good old Fritsch the day universal conscription was re-introduced. Thirty-six divisions were drawn up!" Adolf Hitler, *Monologe im Führerhauptquartier 1941–1944: Die Aufzeichnungen Heinrich Heims*, ed. Werner Jochmann, Hamburg, 1980, p. 343, dated 16 Aug. 1942. Hitler likely confused Fritsch with Blomberg here.

99 Goebbels, *Tagebücher*, part 1, vol. 3/1, p. 201 (entry for 18 March 1935). See Wilhelm Brückner's notebook dated 16 March 1935: "1.30 cabinet meeting. Universal conscription announced." BA Berlin-Lichterfelde, NS 26/1209. No minutes of the cabinet

meeting seem to have been produced—at least there are none included in *Akten der Reichskanzlei: Die Regierung Hitler*, vol. 2, part 1.

100   François-Poncet, *Als Botschafter in Berlin*, p. 234.

101   Quoted in Richard J. Evans, *The Third Reich in Power 1933–1939*, London, 2005, p. 627. On 15 April 1935, a confectioner from Düsseldorf wrote to Hitler: "This hour has brought a lot of joy to us as former frontline soldiers. It touched every true German soldier's heart." BA Berlin-Lichterfelde, NS 51/75.

102   *Deutschland-Berichte der Sopade*, 2 (1935), p. 279; see Ian Kershaw, *The Hitler Myth: Image and Reality in the Third Reich*, Oxford, 1987, pp. 71. See also the report by the American consul general in Stuttgart, Samuel W. Honacker, dated 3 May 1935, stating that the re-introduction of compulsory military service was "enthusiastically received by the overwhelming part of the population." Bajohr and Strupp (eds), *Fremde Blicke auf das "Dritte Reich,"* p. 426.

103   See Joachim Fest, *Hitler: Eine Biographie*, Frankfurt am Main, Berlin and Vienna, 1973, p. 637; Kershaw, *Hitler: Hubris*, pp. 693f.; William S. Shirer, *Berliner Tagebuch: Aufzeichnungen 1934–41*, transcribed and ed. Jürgen Schebera, Leipzig and Weimar, 1991, pp. 35f. (entry for 17 March 1935).

104   François-Poncet, *Als Botschafter in Berlin*, p. 235. See also Thomas Mann, *Tagebücher 1935–1936*, ed. Peter de Mendelssohn, Frankfurt am Main, 1978, p. 59 (entry for 17 March 1935) "The challenge is brutal. But it's too late. We've already allowed too much to happen."

105   Goebbels, *Tagebücher*, part 1, vol. 3/1, p. 200 (entry for 16 March 1935), pp. 201–2 (entry for 18 March 1935), p. 202 (entry for 20 March 1935) "I believe we'll survive," Hitler remarked to Alfred Rosenberg around this time. Hans-Günther Seraphim (ed.), *Das politische Tagebuch Alfred Rosenbergs aus den Jahren 1934/35 und 1939/40*, Göttingen, 1956, p. 76.

106   Shirer, *Berliner Tagebuch*, p. 35 (entry for 16 March 1935). See Klemperer, *Tagebücher 1933–1941*, p. 190 (entry for 23 March 1935): "Hitler has declared the reintroduction of universal conscription. Abroad there have been some half-hearted protests, but people have swallowed this fait accompli. The result: Hitler's regime is more stable than ever."

107   Quoted in Petersen, *Hitler–Mussolini*, p. 400; see also Falanga, *Mussolinis Vorposten*, p. 57.

108   Goebbels, *Tagebücher*, part 1, vol. 3/1, p. 218 (entry for 15 April 1935). See ibid., p. 219 (entry for 17 April 1935): "The only answer is to arm ourselves and act like good sports."

109   All quotations in Paul Schmidt, *Statist auf diplomatischer Bühne 1923–45: Erlebnisse des Chefdolmetschers im Auswärtigen Amt mit den Staatsmännern Europas*, Bonn, 1950, pp. 293–303. On the talks in Berlin on 25/26 March 1935 see also Goebbels, *Tagebücher*, part 1, vol. 3/1, pp. 206–8 (entries for 26 and 28 March 1935). From the British perspective, see Eden, *Angesichts der Diktatoren*, pp. 167–76. In contrast to the spring of 1934, Hitler made a negative impression on Eden, who found him more authoritarian and less eager to please (p. 168).Hitler gave a full report on the talks to his cabinet on 29 March 1935; *Die Regierung Hitler*, vol. 2, part 1, no. 132, p. 490.

110   Goebbels, *Tagebücher*, part 1, vol. 3/1, p. 208 (entry for 28 March 1935).

111   Ibid., p. 211 (entry for 3 April 1935), p. 212 (entry for 5 April 1935).

112   Ibid., p. 226 (entry for 5 May 1935).

113   Ibid., p. 235 (entry for 21 May 1935). See ibid., p. 227 (entry for 5 May 1935), p. 229 (entry for 9 May 1935), p. 230 (entry for 11 May 1935), p. 231 (entry for 13 May 1935), p. 232 (entry for 15 May 1935), p. 233 (entry for 19 May 1935).

114   Shirer, *Berliner Tagebuch*, p. 42 (entry for 21 May 1935). See Goebbels, *Tagebücher*, part 1, vol. 3/1, p. 236 (entry for 23 May 1935): "The Führer was in top form."

115   Domarus, *Hitler*, vol. 1, part 2, pp. 505–14 (quotations on pp. 506, 507, 511, 512, 513).

116   Hildebrand, *Das vergangene Reich*, p. 599.

117   Kershaw, *Der Hitler-Mythos*, pp. 125f.

118   Kessler, *Das Tagebuch*, vol. 9, p. 640 (entry for 25 May 1935). See ibid., p. 640 (entry for 26 May 1935): "You can't deny that Hitler showed nerve and leadership ability here."

119   Hassell, *Römische Tagebücher und Briefe*, p. 127.

120   Goebbels, *Tagebücher*, part 1, vol. 2/3, p. 359 (entry for 20 Jan. 1934).

121   On the British–German talks see Schmidt, *Als Statist*, pp. 311–15 (quotations on pp. 311, 312); see also Joachim von Ribbentrop, *Zwischen London und Moskau: Erinnerungen und letzte Aufzeichnungen*, ed. Annelies von Ribbentrop, Leoni am Starnberger See, 1961, pp. 61–3.

122   Ribbentrop, *Zwischen London und Moskau*, p. 64. See also Goebbels, *Tagebücher*, part 1, vol. 3/1, p. 249 (entry for 19 June 1935): "The Führer is completely happy. Huge success for Ribbentrop and all of us."

123   Goebbels, *Tagebücher*, part 1, vol. 3/1, p. 250 (entry for 21 June 1935). See ibid., p. 249 (entry for 19 June 1935): "We're getting close to our goal of an alliance with England. The key is to keep working, doggedly and tirelessly." On 4 Feb. 1936, Hitler received the former air minister Lord Londonderry in the Chancellery and played the role of the good host. "It was almost as though the suitor Hitler were wooing prudish Britannia," recalled Hitler's interpreter Schmidt. *Als Statist*, p. 355. On Londonderry's visit to Berlin see Kershaw, *Making Friends with Hitler*, pp. 132–40.

124   Goebbels, *Tagebücher*, part 1, vol. 3/1, p. 279 (entry for 19 Aug. 1935).

125   See Petersen, *Hitler–Mussolini*, pp. 377–9; Hans Woller, *Geschichte Italiens im 20. Jahrhundert*, Munich, 2010, pp. 144f.; Winkler, *Geschichte des Westens*, vol. 2, pp. 708–11.

126   See Aram Mattioli, *Experimentierfeld der Gewalt: Der Abessinienkrieg und seine internationale Bedeutung 1935–1941*, Zurich, 2005; further, *idem*, "Entgrenzte Kriegsgewalt: Der italienische Giftgaseinsatz in Abessinien 1935–1936," in *Vierteljahrshefte für Zeitgeschichte*, 51 (2003), pp. 311–38.

127   On 17 July 1935, a representative of the Ethiopian king appeared in Berlin and asked Germany, under strict confidentiality, "to immediately arm the king's troops so that they could put up as much resistance as possible to the Italians." Neurath suggested that Hitler grant that request and give the king weapons worth 3 million marks. Bülow to Neurath, 18 July 1935; Neurath to Hitler, 20 July 1935; BA Koblenz, N 1310/10.

128   Marie-Luise Recker, *Die Aussenpolitik des Dritten Reiches*, Munich, 1990, p. 12.

129   Goebbels, *Tagebücher*, part 1, vol. 3/1, p. 313 (entry for 19 Oct. 1935).

130   Quoted in Falanga, *Mussolinis Vorposten*, p. 62.

131   Goebbels, *Tagebücher*, part 1, vol. 3/1, p. 232 (entry for 15 May 1935).

132   See Falanga, *Mussolinis Vorposten*, pp. 62–4.

133   Esmonde M. Robertson, "Hitler und die Sanktionen des Völkerbunds," in *Vierteljahrshefte für Zeitgeschichte*, 26 (1978), pp. 237–64 (quotation on p. 254). See Schmidt, *Die Aussenpolitik des Dritten Reiches*, p. 189; Rauscher, *Hitler und Mussolini*, p. 234.

134   Goebbels, *Tagebücher*, part 1, vol. 3/1, p. 341 (entry for 6 Dec. 1935).

135   Hassell to Foreign Ministry, 6 Jan. 1936; Esmonde M. Robertson, "Zur Wiederbesetzung des Rheinlands 1936," in *Vierteljahrshefte für Zeitgeschichte*, 10 (1962), pp. 178–205 (at pp. 188–90). See Petersen, *Hitler–Mussolini*, pp. 466–71.

136   Goebbels, *Tagebücher*, part 1, vol. 3/1, p. 366 (entry for 21 Jan. 1936). As early as mid-December 1935, after talking to Hitler, Britain's ambassador Phipps had noted that the chancellor probably intended to remilitarise the Rhineland as soon as an opportunity presented itself. See Kershaw, *Making Friends with Hitler*, p. 134. See Neurath's minutes of the talks on 13 Dec. 1935; *ADAP*, Series C, vol. 4, part 2, no. 462; see also the cabinet meeting on 13 Dec. 1935: *Die Regierung Hitler*, vol. 2, part 2, no. 281, p. 987; Goebbels, *Tagebücher*, part 1, vol. 3/1, p. 347 (entry for 15 Dec. 1935).

137   Hassell's notes of 14 Feb. 1936; reprinted in Robertson, "Zur Wiederbesetzung des Rheinlands," pp. 192f.

138   Hassell, *Römische Tagebücher und Briefe*, p. 126 (dated 23 March 1936). According to Hassell's notes, Hitler declared at the beginning of the meeting: "I've summoned you to discuss a decision I'm about to take that will perhaps be significant for Germany's entire future!" ibid.

139   Hossbach, *Zwischen Wehrmacht und Hitler*, p. 84.

140   Hassell's minutes of the Berlin talks of 19 Feb. 1936; reprinted in Robertson, "Zur Wiederbesetzung des Rheinlands," pp. 194–6. See Hassell, *Römische Tagebücher und Briefe*, pp. 127f. (dated 23 Feb. 1936).

141   Hassell, *Römische Tagebücher und Briefe*, p. 127 (dated 23 Feb. 1936). See Robertson, "Zur Wiederbesetzung des Rheinlands," p. 203.

142   Goebbels, *Tagebücher*, part 1, vol. 3/1, p. 383 (entry for 21 Feb. 1936).

143   Ibid., pp. 388f. (entry for 29 Feb. 1935).

144   Ibid., vol. 3/2, p. 30 (entry for 2 March 1936).

145   Ibid., p. 31 (entry for 4 March 1936). According to Goebbels's notes, Blomberg, Fritsch, Raeder and Ribbentrop took part in the meeting alongside him.

146   Ibid., p. 33 (entry for 6 March 1936).

147   *Akten der Reichskanzlei: Die Regierung Hitler. Vol. 3: 1936*, ed. Friedrich Hartmannsgruber, Munich, 2002, no. 39, p. 165.

148   Goebbels, *Tagebücher*, part 1, vol. 3/2, p. 35 (entry for 8 March 1935).

149   François-Poncet, *Als Botschafter in Berlin*, p. 257. The memorandum is reprinted in *ADAP*, Series C, vol. 5/1, enclosure to no. 3, pp. 14–17. See also Claus W. Schäfer, *André François-Poncet als Botschafter in Berlin 1931–1938*, Munich, 2004, pp. 255–8.

150   Shirer, *Berliner Tagebuch*, p. 56 (entry for 7 March 1936).

151   Domarus, *Hitler*, vol. 1, part 2, pp. 583–97 (quotation on p. 594). On the reaction of the deputies, see Shirer's vivid description: "Now the six hundred deputies, personal appointees all of Hitler, little men with big bodies and bulging necks and cropped hair and pouched bellies and brown uniforms and heavy boots, little men of clay in his fine hands, leap to their feet like automatons . . . Their hands are raised in slavish salute, their faces now contorted with hysteria, their mouths wide open, shouting, shouting, their eyes, burning with fanaticism, glued on the new god, the Messiah." *Berliner Tagebuch*, p. 57 (entry for 7 March 1936).

152   Schmidt, *Als Statist*, p. 320. Hans Frank, *Im Angesicht des Galgens: Deutung Hitlers und seiner Zeit auf Grund eigener Erlebnisse und Erkenntnisse*, Munich and Gräfelfing, 1953, p. 211, remembered a similar statement when travelling with Hitler from Cologne to Berlin at the end of the month: "I've never had to withstand the sort of fear I have in these past days of the Rhineland action. If the French had been serious about their threats, it would have been a massive political defeat for me . . . Am I glad [they weren't], thank God! How happy I am that everything went smoothly!" In January 1942, Hitler recalled: "If another man had been in my place on 13 [*sic*] March, he would have lost his nerve! It was only my stubbornness and audacity that got us through." Hitler, *Monologe*, p. 140, dated 27 Jan. 1942. On Hitler's nervousness in the days following 7 March, see Albert Speer, *Erinnerungen: Mit einem Essay von Jochen Thies*, Frankfurt am Main and Berlin, 1993, pp. 85f.; Hossbach, *Zwischen Wehrmacht und Hitler*, p. 20.

153   Thomas Mann, *Tagebücher 1935–1936*, p. 272 (entry for 11 March 1936). See also Lahme, *Golo Mann*, p. 107

154   Goebbels, *Tagebücher*, part 1, vol. 3/2, p. 36 (entry for 8 March 1936).

155   Shirer, *Berliner Tagebuch*, p. 59 (entry for 8 March 1936).

156   Quoted in Schmidt, *Die Aussenpolitik des Dritten Reiches*, p. 201.

157   Goebbels, *Tagebücher*, part 1, vol. 3/2, p. 46 (entry for 21 March 1936).

158   *Deutschland-Berichte der Sopade*, 3 (1936), p. 460. See Kershaw, *The Hitler Myth*, pp. 126–9.

159 Goebbels, *Tagebücher*, part 1, vol. 3/2, p. 52 (entry for 31 March 1936). A detailed survey of Hitler's campaign trail in March 1936 and of the programme of the rallies in BA Berlin-Lichterfelde, NS 10/125.

160 Otto Dietrich, *12 Jahre mit Hitler*, Munich, 1955, p. 45.

161 Martha Dodd, *Nice to meet you, Mr. Hitler! Meine Jahre in Deutschland 1933 bis 1937*, Frankfurt am Main, 2005, p. 232.

162 In a top-level meeting in the Chancellery on 26 Nov. 1935, Hitler said that he could not tell how long German rearmament would last, but that it would probably take "3 to 4 years." *Die Regierung Hitler*, vol. 2, part 2, no. 267, p. 948.

163 Domarus, *Hitler*, vol. 1, part 2, p. 606. On the change in the way Hitler saw himself during the year of 1936, see Kershaw, *Hitler: Hubris*, pp. 590f; Thamer, *Verführung und Gewalt*, p 540; Wendt, *Grossdeutschland*, pp. 105, 110; Evans, *The Third Reich in Power*, p. 637.

16 Cult and Community

1   Max Domarus, *Hitler: Reden und Proklamationen 1932–1945. Vol. 1: Triumph. Part 2: 1935–1938*, Munich, 1965, pp. 643, 641.

2   Victor Klemperer, *Ich will Zeugnis ablegen bis zum letzten: Tagebücher 1933–1941*, ed. Walter Nowojski with Hadwig Klemperer, Berlin, 1995, p. 340 (entry for 27 March 1937); see ibid., p. 373 (entry for 17 Aug. 1937): "I'm increasingly coming to believe that Hitler truly embodies the soul of the German people, that he truly is Germany and that for that reason he will rightfully persist in the future."

3   *Deutschland-Berichte der Sozialdemokratischen Partei Deutschlands (Sopade) 1934–1940*, ed. Klaus Behnken, Frankfurt am Main, 1980, 2 (1935), p. 653 (dated 15 June 1935).

4   Hans-Ulrich Wehler, *Deutsche Gesellschaftsgeschichte 1914–1949*, Munich, 2003, p. 676. In his notes "Thoughts concerning the Führer," written in his Nuremberg jail cell in 1945, Robert Ley concluded: "If a people and its leader ever truly became one, it was Adolf Hitler and the German people." BA Koblenz, N 1468/4.

5   According to Leipzig anatomist Hermann Voss, quoted in Götz Aly, *Hitlers Volksstaat: Raub, Rassenkrieg und nationaler Sozialismus*, Frankfurt am Main, 2005, p. 49.

6   Werner Jochmann, *Nationalsozialismus und Revolution: Ursprung und Geschichte der NSDAP in Hamburg 1922–1933. Dokumente*, Frankfurt am Main, 1963, pp. 426 (dated 28 Feb. 1933), 427 (dated 1 March 1933). See also the letter from Hess's parents to Rudolf and Ilse Hess, early May 1933: "[Hitler's] name is now on everybody's lips as the saviour of Germany and thus of the whole world." BA Bern, Nl Hess, J1.211-1989/148, 51.

7   Hedda Kalshoven, *Ich denk so viel an Euch: Ein deutsch–holländischer Briefwechsel 1920–1949*, Munich, 1995, pp. 169 (dated 10 March 1933), 197 (dated 4 May 1933), 199 (dated 17 May 1933). The Hamburg banker Cornelius von Berenberg-Gossler confided to his diary that the notoriously reserved inhabitants of the city were "blindly in love with Hitler." Cited in Frank Bajohr, "Die Zustimmungsdiktatur: Grundzüge national-sozialistischer Herrschaft in Hamburg," in Angelika Ebbinghaus and Karsten Linne (eds), *Kein abgeschlossenes Kapitel: Hamburg im "Dritten Reich,"* Hamburg, 1997, p. 108.

8   Paul Dinichert to Federal Counsellor Giuseppe Motta, 17 Nov. 1933; Frank Bajohr and Christoph Strupp (eds), *Fremde Blicke auf das "Dritte Reich": Berichte ausländischer Diplomaten über Herrschaft und Gesellschaft in Deutschland 1933–1945*, Göttingen, 2011, p. 392. "The press worships Hitler like a combination of God and His prophets," noted Victor Klemperer, *Tagebücher 1933–1941*, p. 54 (entry for 6 Sept. 1933).

9   For example see the municipality of Wackerberg bei Tölz, 10 May 1933: Beatrice und Helmut Heiber (eds), *Die Rückseite des Hakenkreuzes: Absonderliches aus den Akten des Dritten Reiches*, Munich, 1993, p. 126; Quedlingburg, 20 April 1933: Henrik Eberle (ed.), *Briefe an Hitler: Ein Volk schreibt seinem Führer. Unbekannte Dokumente aus Moskauer*

Archiven—zum ersten Mal veröffentlicht, Bergisch-Gladbach, 2007, p. 264; the Assocation of Thuringian Towns, 18 April 1933; the town Werl, 26 April 1933; Bremen, 8 May 1933: BA Berlin-Lichterfelde, R 43 II/959; Berlin and Munich: *Die Tagebücher von Joseph Goebbels. Part 1: Aufzeichnungen 1923–1941*, ed. Elke Fröhlich, Munich, 1998, vol. 2/4, part 3, p. 315 (entry for 15 Nov. 1933). For Hitler's further honorary citizenships between 1935 and 1938 see BA Berlin-Lichterfelde, NS 51/79. In a public announcement of 22 May 1933, the Führer's office asked for understanding that it could not immediately answer "the great number of requests that arrived every day for Hitler to accept honorary citizenships and certificates thereof." BA Berlin-Lichterfelde, NS 51/80.

10   See Axel Schildt: "Jenseits der Politik? Aspekte des Alltags," in *Hamburg im "Dritten Reich*," p. 250; Hans-Ulrich Thamer and Simone Erpel, *Hitler und die Deutschen: Volksgemeinschaft und Verbrechen. Katalog zur Ausstellung im Deutschen Historischen Museum in Berlin*, Dresden, 2010, p. 210.

11   Eberle (ed.), *Briefe an Hitler*, pp. 129f. See ibid. pp. 130f., 132, 135, 163–5 for further examples.

12   Ibid., pp. 141f.

13   Heiber (ed.), *Die Rückseite des Hakenkreuzes*, pp. 12, 119–26. Headteacher of the Eberswalde Academy of Foresty to Hitler, 8 April 1933, and answer from Lammers, 27 April 1933; BA Berlin-Lichterfelde R 43 II/959.

14   See Thamer and Erpel, *Hitler und die Deutschen*, pp. 208, 225.

15   Quotation from the *MNN* in Ian Kershaw, *The Hitler Myth: Image and Reality in the Third Reich*, Oxford, 1987, p. 58. See Rudolf Hess to Fritz Hess, 19 April 1933: "All day long the people are queueing in the Reich Chancellory to add their birthday congratulations to the books on display there. The love of the people and their reverence is unbelievable." BA Bern, Nl Hess, J1.211-1989/148, 51. Messages for Hitler's birthday in 1933 in BA Berlin-Lichterfelde, NS 51/72. Similar in tone were the greetings for New Year 1934/35; ibid., NS 51/73 und NS 51/74. Goebbels's article "Unser Hitler!" for Wolff's Telegraphisches Büro, 19 April 1933; BA Berlin-Lichterfelde R 43 II/959.

16   Klemperer, *Tagebücher 1933–1941*, p. 37 (entry for 17 June 1933). On the shift in public attitudes towards Hitler see Kershaw, *The Hitler Myth*, p. 59; Rudolf Herz, *Hoffmann & Hitler: Fotografie als Medium des Führer-Mythos*, Munich, 1994, pp. 202ff.

17   Fritz Wiedemann, *Der Mann, der Feldherr werden wollte: Erlebnisse und Erfahrungen des Vorgesetzten Hitlers im 1. Weltkrieg und seines späteren persönlichen Adjutanten*, Velbert and Kettwig 1964, pp. 92f.; see Christa Schroeder, *Er war mein Chef: Aus dem Nachlass der Sekretärin von Adolf Hitler*, ed. Anton Joachimsthaler, 3rd edition, Munich and Vienna, 1985, pp. 92f.; Heinrich Hoffmann, *Hitler wie ich ihn sah: Aufzeichnungen seines Leibfotographen*, Munich and Berlin, 1974, p. 198.

18   Antoni Graf Sobanski, *Nachrichten aus Berlin 1933–1936*, Berlin, 2007, p. 89. See Martha Dodd, *Nice to meet you, Mr. Hitler! Meine Jahre in Deutschland 1933 bis 1937*, Frankfurt am Main, 2005, p. 233.

19   Klemperer, *Tagebücher 1933–1941*, p. 21 (entry for 10 April 1933).

20   Eberle (ed.), *Briefe an Hitler*, pp. 159f.

21   *Deutschland-Berichte der Sopade*, 1 (1934), p. 275. In a decree on 25 Sept. 1933, Interior Minister Frick ordered that public offices only hang up pictures of the Führer "that do not give cause for concern about how he is presented or artistically depicted." BA Berlin-Lichterfelde, R 43 II/959.

22   Gebhard Himmler to Heinrich Himmler, 30 Aug. 1934, with the addition from his mother Anna Himmler: "You can't imagine how happy we are about the picture of our beloved Führer." BA Koblenz, N 1126/13. See the similar reaction of Rudolf Hess's mother after she was sent a picture "of our beloved Führer" with the handwritten dediction, "To Herr and Frau Hess, dear parents of my oldest and most loyal comrade in arms, with heartfelt devotion, Ad. Hitler." Klara Hess to Rudolf Hess, 4 Jan. 1934; BA Bern, Nl Hess, J1.211-1989/148, 53.

23   Kershaw, *The Hitler Myth*, p. 60.

24 Wiedemann, *Der Mann*, p. 80; see Goebbels, *Tagebücher*, part 1, vol. 2/3, p. 252: "People stood around and waited for hours"; vol. 3/1, p. 100 (entry for 2 Sept. 1934): "First the people down below marched past him. It was moving. What trust [they have!"; see ibid., vol. 4, pp. 215, 217 (entries for 11 and 13 July 1937).

25 Goebbels, *Tagebücher*, part 1, vol. 2 /3, p. 170 (entry for 18 April 1933); see ibid., p. 192 (entry for 23 May 1933): Kiel; p. 232 (entry for 22 July 1933): Bayreuth Festival; p. 238 (entry for 31 July 1933): Stuttgart Gymnastics Festival; p. 259 (entry for 2 Sept. 1933): Nuremberg Party Conference; vol. 3/1, p. 54 (entry for 28 May 1934): Dresden; p. 94 (entry for 18 Aug. 1934): Hamburg.

26 Albert Speer, *Erinnerungen: Mit einem Essay von Jochen Thies*, Frankfurt am Main and Berlin, 1993, p. 61. See Otto Dietrich, *12 Jahre mit Hitler*, Munich, 1955, p. 183, on the "indescribable scenes" surrounding Hitler's journeys in peace time.

27 Wiedemann, *Der Mann*, p. 81. The Jewish lawyer Kurt F. Rosenberg from Hamburg concluded that "one cannot overstate the religious needs of the people as one of the forces driving the new movement in Germany." Kurt F. Rosenberg: *"Einer, der nicht mehr dazugehört": Tagebücher 1933–1937*, ed. Beate Meyer and Björn Siegel, Göttingen, 2012, p. 257 (entry for 16 March 1935).

28 William S. Shirer, *Berliner Tagebuch: Aufzeichnungen 1934–41*, transcribed and ed. Jürgen Schebera, Leipzig and Weimar, 1991, p. 24 (entry for 4 Sept. 1934). On the occasion of his 44th birthday, three sisters from the city of Halle wrote to Hitler that the moment they first caught sight of him was "the greatest of our lives thus far." They had sensed, they wrote, how "everyone alive and breathing was drawn to you as though attracted by a magnetic force." BA Berlin-Lichterfelde, NS 51/72.

29 Speer, *Erinnerungen*, p. 79. Hess testified that for Hitler, alongside Friedrich the Great and Richard Wagner, Luther was "the greatest German": "All those revolutionary, tough and fearless spirits that overcome the world are of his kind." Rudolf Hess to Klara Hess, 21 Jan. 1927; BA Bern, Nl Hess, J1.211-1989/148, 39.

30 For a summary see Wehler, *Deutsche Gesellschaftsgeschichte 1914–1949*, pp. 709–11 ("Was there a National Socialist economic miracle?")

31 *Deutschland-Berichte der Sopade*, 2 (1935), p. 283.

32 Ibid., 3 (1936), p. 157.

33 Domarus, *Hitler*, vol. 1, part 1, pp. 260, 262. See countless other examples in Rainer Zitelmann, *Hitler: Selbstverständnis eines Revolutionärs*, 2nd revised and expanded edition, Stuttgart, 1989, pp. 190–6.

34 *Deutschland-Berichte der Sopade*, 1 (1934), p. 197; 2 (1935), pp. 24, 422.

35 Goebbels, *Tagebücher*, part 1, vol. 3/1, p. 341 (entry for 6 Dec. 1935). See ibid., vol. 3/2, pp. 40 (entry for 13 March 1936), 94 (entry for 30 May 1936). Further, Hans Frank, *Im Angesicht des Galgens: Deutung Hitlers und seiner Zeit auf Grund eigener Erlebnisse und Erkenntnisse*, Munich and Gräfelfing, 1953, p. 198.

36 *Deutschland-Berichte der Sopade*, 1 (1934), pp. 198, 200.

37 Ibid., 1 (1934), pp. 10f. In early June 1934, the Gestapo in Kassel reported: "As unshakable as people's trust in the Führer may be, there is also some strong criticism of the lower party organs and particular local conditions." Thomas Klein (ed.), *Die Lageberichte der Geheimen Staatspolizei über die Provinz Hessen-Nassau*, Cologne and Vienna, 1986, vol. 1, p. 102.

38 Domarus, *Hitler*, vol. 1, part 2, p. 613. See Michael Burleigh, *The Third Reich: A New History*, London, 2000, p. 246.

39 *Deutschland-Berichte der Sopade*, 2 (1935), p. 152.

40 Ibid., 2 (1935), p. 758: "Sayings like 'If the Führer only knew . . . he wouldn't put up with this' were common." Further examples in Frank Bajohr, "Ämter, Pfründe, Korruption," in Andreas Wirsching (ed.), *Das Jahr 1933: Die nationalsozialistische Machtergreifung und die deutsche Gesellschaft*, Göttingen, 2009, pp. 196, 199n52. On the compensatory function of the mythology of the Führer see Kershaw, *The Hitler Myth*, pp. 83, 96–104.

41   Domarus, *Hitler*, vol. 1, part 2, p. 529.
42   *Deutschland-Berichte der Sopade*, 2 (1935), p. 277; see ibid., p. 410: "There is no doubt that the constant drum-beating about equality, honour and German liberty has had an effect and caused confusion even deep within the ranks of the formerly Marxist working classes."
43   Kershaw, *The Hitler Myth*, p. 73; see Goebbels, *Tagebücher*, part 1, vol. 2/3, p. 37 (entry for 22 April 1934): "The people is indivisibly at Hitler's side. No human being has ever enjoyed this sort of trust."
44   *Deutschland-Berichte der Sopade*, 2 (1935), pp. 904, 1018.
45   Wiedemann, *Der Mann*, p. 90.
46   *Deutschland-Berichte der Sopade*, 3 (1936), p. 281.
47   Goebbels, *Tagebücher*, part 1, vol. 3/2, p. 203 (entry for 5 Oct. 1936).
48   See Karlheinz Schmeer, *Die Regie des öffentlichen Lebens im Dritten Reich*, Munich, 1956, pp. 68-116.
49   Hans-Ulrich Thamer, "Faszination und Manipulation: Die Nürnberger Reichsparteitage der NSDAP," in Uwe Schultz (ed.), *Das Fest: Eine Kulturgeschichte von der Antike bis zur Gegenwart*, Munich, 1988, pp. 352-68 (quotation on p. 353).
50   Goebbels, *Tagebücher*, part 1, vol. 2/3, p. 237 (entry for 29 July 1933).
51   See Markus Urban, *Die Konsensfabrik: Funktion und Wahrnehmung der NS-Reichsparteitage 1933-1941*, Göttingen, 2007, pp. 61f.
52   Rudolf Hess to his parents, 21 Sept. 1937; BA Bern, Nl Hess, J1.212-1989/148, 59. On what follows see Schmeer, *Die Regie*, pp. 109-16; Thamer, 'Faszination und Manipulation," pp. 360-3; Peter Reichel, *Der schöne Schein des Dritten Reiches: Faszination und Gewalt des Faschismus*, Munich, 1991, pp. 126-34; Siegfried Zelnhefer, *Die Reichsparteitage der NSDAP: Geschichte, Struktur und Bedeutung der grössten Propagandafeste im nationalsozialistischen Feierjahr*, Nuremberg, 2002, pp. 91-113; *idem*, "Rituale und Bekenntnisse: Die Reichsparteitage der NSDAP," in Centrum Industriekultur Nürnberg (ed.), *Kulissen der Gewalt: Das Reichsparteitagsgelände in Nürnberg*, Munich, 1992, pp. 91-3. The running order of the 1938 party rally is given in detail in Yvonne Karow, *Deutsches Opfer: Kultische Selbstauslöschung auf den Reichsparteitagen der NSDAP*, Berlin, 1994, pp. 209-81.
53   Shirer, *Berliner Tagebuch*, p. 23 (entry for 4 Sept. 1934).
54   See Goebbels, *Tagebücher*, part 1, vol. 6, p. 74 (entry for 6 Sept. 1938): "The Reich insignia have been transferred to Nuremberg and will now stay here."
55   Ibid. On Furtwängler's role in the Third Reich see Fred K. Prieberg, *Kraftprobe: Wilhelm Furtwängler im Dritten Reich*, Wiesbaden, 1986; Eberhard Straub, *Die Furtwänglers: Geschichte einer deutschen Familie*, Munich, 2007.
56   Karow, *Deutsches Opfer*, p. 214.
57   Shirer, *Berliner Tagebuch*, pp. 24f. (entry for 5 Sept. 1934).
58   See Urban, *Die Konsensfabrik*, pp. 142-4.
59   Shirer, *Berliner Tagebuch*, p. 26 (entry for 6 Sept. 1934).
60   Karow, *Deutsches Opfer*, p. 230.
61   Goebbels, *Tagebücher*, part 1, vol. 3/1, p. 292 (entry for 13 Sept. 1935).
62   Ibid., vol. 3/2, p. 180 (entry for 11 Sept. 1936).
63   Karow, *Deutsches Opfer*, p. 248. See Sobanski, *Nachrichten aus Berlin 1933-36*, p. 210 on the 1936 party rally: "The Führer proceeds ahead, and a miracle occurs. Everything turns bright. Suddenly, we are sitting under a dome of light, consisting of milky blue columns, separated by strips of deep-blue night and joining together overhead in a bright sapphire."
64   Nevile Henderson, *Fehlschlag einer Mission: Berlin 1937 bis 1939*, Zurich 1940, p. 80; Speer, *Erinnerungen*, p. 71; Joachim Fest, *Speer: Eine Biographie*, Berlin, 1999, pp. 74-6. See Goebbels, *Tagebücher*, part 1, vol. 4 (entry for 11 Sept. 1937): "In the evening a massive roll call of the party organisations on the Zeppelin Field: an incomparable bit of theatre. Wonderfully beautiful, illuminated by an endless dome of light."

65   Cited in Zelnhofer, 'Rituale und Bekenntnisse," p. 94.

66   Karow, *Deutsches Opfer*, p. 251.

67   Domarus, *Hitler*, vol. 1, part 2, p. 532.

68   Karow, *Deutsches Opfer*, p. 265.

69   Shirer, *Berliner Tagebuch*, p. 28 (entry for 9 Nov. 1934).

70   Karow, *Deutsches Opfer*, p. 266.

71   Goebbels, *Tagebücher*, part 1, vol. 4, p. 309 (entry for 13 Sept. 1937). According to Albert Speer, the idea of "the long march from the monument of honour to the grandstand" was Hitler's own and was planned by him in all its detail. Speer to Joachim Fest, 13 Sept. 1969; BA Koblenz, N 1340/17.

72   Ibid., vol. 3/2, p. 189 (entry for 15 Sept. 1936).

73   Adolf Hitler, *Monologe im Führerhauptquartier 1941–1944: Die Aufzeichnungen Heinrich Heims*, ed. Werner Jochmann, Hamburg, 1980, p. 225 (dated 24/25 Jan. 1942). See also Unity Mitford (on her see below pp. 616f.) to her sister Diana, 19 Sept. 1935: "He (Hitler) said he felt terribly flat now that all it's over, & that it was so depressing driving away from Nürnberg." Charlotte Mosley (ed.), *The Mitfords: Letters between Six Sisters*, London, 2007, p. 54.

74   Hitler, *Monologe*, p. 225 (dated 24/25 Jan. 1942).

75   Goebbels, *Tagebücher*, part 1, vol. 3/2, p. 184 (entry for 15 Sept. 1936).

76   Ibid., pp. 151 (entry for 7 Aug. 1936), 153 (entry for 9 Aug. 1936): "The Führer refuses to give up the party rally. Well then, in God's name!"

77   Albert Speer, *Spandauer Tagebücher*, Munich, 2002, p. 403 (entry for 28 Nov. 1954). On Hitler's need for control when it came to the sequence of events at rallies, see also Urban, *Die Konsensfabrik*, pp. 151–8.

78   André François-Poncet, *Als Botschafter in Berlin 1931–1938*, Mainz, 1947, p. 273. See also François-Poncet's report on the 1935 rally, 19 Sept. 1935; Bajohr and Strupp (eds), *Fremde Blicke auf das "Dritte Reich,"* pp. 436f.

79   Henderson, *Fehlschlag einer Mission*, pp. 78f.

80   Shirer, *Berliner Tagebuch*, p. 28 (entry for 10 Sept. 1934).

81   Hamilton T. Burden, *Die programmierte Nation: Die Nürnberger Reichsparteitage*, Gütersloh, 1967, p. 212. See Bella Fromm, *Als Hitler mir die Hand küsste*, Berlin, 1993, p. 206 (entry for 11 Sept. 1934): "This mass event is a powerful, intoxicating poison. Not all foreigners are capable of keeping a clear head in the face of this overwhelming spectacle."

82   *Deutschland-Berichte der Sopade*, 2 (1935), p. 1019. On the radio broadcasts of the rallies see Urban, *Die Konsensfabrik*, pp. 189–208; Reichel, *Der schöne Schein des Dritten Reiches*, p. 135.

83   See Peter Zimmermann, "Die Parteitagsfilme der NSDAP und Leni Riefenstahl," in Peter Zimmermann and Kay Hoffmann (eds), *Geschichte des dokumentarischen Films in Deutschland. Vol. 3: "Drittes Reich" 1933–1945*, Stuttgart, 2005, pp. 511–13; Urban, *Die Konsensfabrik*, pp. 208–11.

84   See Karin Wieland, *Dietrich & Riefenstahl: Der Traum von der neuen Frau*, Munich, 2011, pp. 176–83, 294–6. The author corrects the thoroughly apologist account from Leni Riefenstahl's memoirs.

85   Goebbels, *Tagebücher*, part 1, vol. 2/3, pp. 188 (entry for 17 May 1933), 205 (entry for 12 June 1933), 254 (enry for 27 Aug. 1933).

86   Quoted in Wieland, *Dietrich & Riefenstahl*, p. 298.

87   See Speer, *Erinnerungen*, p. 71; Jürgen Trimborn, *Riefenstahl: Eine deutsche Karriere*, Berlin, 2002, pp. 178–81; Wieland, *Dietrich & Riefenstahl*, pp. 298–300.

88   See Wieland, *Dietrich & Riefenstahl*, pp. 301f.; on Walter Frentz see Hans Georg Hiller von Gaertringen (ed.), *Das Auge des Dritten Reiches: Hitlers Kameramann und Fotograf Walter Frentz*, Berlin, 2006, pp. 69ff.

89   Goebbels, *Tagebücher* , part 1, vol. 2/3, p. 265 (entry for 11 Sept. 1933).

90   See Mario Leis, *Leni Riefenstahl*, Reinbek bei Hamburg, 2009, pp. 64f.; Trimborn, *Riefenstahl*, pp. 189f.; Stephan Dolezel and Martin Loiperdinger, "Adolf Hitler in

Parteitagsfilmen und Wochenschau," in Martin Loiperdinger, Rudolf Herz and Ulrich Pohlmann (eds), *Führerbilder: Hitler, Mussolini, Roosevelt, Stalin in Fotografie und Film*, Munich, 1995, p. 84.

91 See Leis, *Leni Riefenstahl*, pp. 65f.; Trimborn, *Riefestahl*, p. 196.

92 Goebbels, *Tagebücher*, part 1, vol. 2/3, p. 325 (entry for 29 Nov. 1935).

93 Quoted in Wieland, *Dietrich & Riefenstahl*, p. 307. See Goebbels, *Tagebücher*, part 1, vol. 2/3, p. 328 (entry for 2 Dec. 1933): "The symphony of images came to a conclusion amidst endless cheers."

94 Goebbels, *Tagebücher*, part 1, vol. 2/3, p. 340 (entry for 19 Dec. 1933).

95 Rainer Rother, *Leni Riefenstahl: Die Verführung des Talents*, Berlin, 2000, p. 60; Zimmermann, *Die Parteitagsfilme der NSDAP*, p. 515.

96 See Trimborn, *Riefenstahl*, p. 192; Urban, *Die Konsensfabrik*, p. 214.

97 See Trimborn, *Riefenstahl*, pp. 194f.; Leis, *Leni Riefenstahl*, pp. 67f.

98 See Martin Loiperdinger, *Der Parteitagsfilm "Triumph des Willens" von Leni Riefenstahl*, Opladen, 1987, p. 45.

99 See Trimborn, *Riefenstahl*, pp. 212, 215; Leis, *Leni Riefenstahl*, pp. 70f.

100 See Loiperdinger, *Der Parteitagsfilm "Triumph des Willens,"* pp. 61–4; Leis, *Leni Riefenstahl*, pp. 72f.

101 See Loiperdinger, *Der Parteitagsfilm "Triumph des Willens,"* pp. 68–72; Leis, *Leni Riefenstahl*, pp. 74f.; Wieland, *Dietrich & Riefenstahl*, pp. 319–21; Rother, *Leni Riefenstahl*, p. 75; Zimmermann, *Die Parteitagsfilme der NSDAP*, pp. 519f.; Philipp Stasny, "Vom Himmel hoch: Adolf Hitler und die 'Volksgemeinschaft' in 'Triumph des Willens,'" in Thamer and Erpel, *Hitler und die Deutschen*, p. 86. A detailed analysis of the opening scenes and the religious connotations in Kristina Oberwinter, *"Bewegende Bilder": Repräsentation und Produktion von Emotionen in Leni Riefenstahls "Triumph des Willens,"* Berlin, 2007, pp. 35–49, 144–54.

102 Goebbels, *Tagebücher*, part 1, vol. 2/3, pp. 140 (entry for 22 Nov. 1934), 206 (entry for 26 March 1935). Hitler watched scenes from the film for the first time on 5 March 1935. Wilhelm Brückner noted on that date: "Leni Riefenstahl. Talented Lisl!" Notebook of W. Brückner from 1935; BA Berlin-Lichterfelde NS 26/1206.

103 See Trimborn, *Riefenstahl*, pp. 221f.; Wieland, *Dietrich & Riefenstahl*, p. 324; Oberwinter, *"Bewegende Bilder,"* p. 178. According to Riefenstahl (*Memoiren*, Munich, 1987, p. 232), she suffered "an attack of dizziness" when presented with the flowers.

104 Facsimile of the article in Loiperdinger, *Der Parteitagsfilm "Triumph des Willlens,"* p. 48.

105 Quoted in Oberwinter, *"Bewegende Bilder,"* p. 180. Riefenstahl sent Hitler a thank-you telegram reading: "This great award will give me the strength to create new contributions for you, my Führer, and your great work." Quoted in Wieland, *Dietrich & Riefenstahl*, p. 325.

106 As in Erwin Leiser, *"Deutschland erwache! Propaganda im Film des Dritten Reiches*, Reinbek bei Hamburg, 1978, p. 30. See Reichel, *Der schöne Schein des Dritten Reiches*, p. 138.

107 Here see Herz, *Hoffmann & Hitler*, pp. 225–9.

108 See Leis, *Leni Riefenstahl*, p. 76; Urban, *Die Konsensfabrik*, pp. 219f.

109 See Hans-Ulrich Thamer, "Nation als Volksgemeinschaft: Völkische Vorstellungen, Nationalsozialismus und Gemeinschaftsideologie," in Jörg-Dieter Gauger and Klaus Weigelt (eds), *Soziales Denken in Deutschland zwischen Tradition und Innovation*, Bonn, 1990, p. 113; Thomas Rohrkrämer, *Die fatale Attraktion des Nationalsozialismus: Über die Popularität eines Unrechtsregimes*, Paderborn 2013, pp. 178ff. On the ideas of *Volksgemeinschaft* gaining traction in the Weimar Republic, see Michael Wildt, "Die Ungleichheit des Volkes: 'Volksgemeinschaft' in der politischen Kommunikation der Weimarer Republik," in Frank Bajohr and Michael Wildt (eds), *Volksgemeinschaft: Neue Forschungen zur Gesellschaft des Nationalsozialismus*, Frankfurt am Main, 2009, pp. 24–40.

110 Quotations in Domarus, *Hitler*, vol. 1, part 1, pp. 192, 212, 227, 231, 260.

111 Ibid., vol. 1, part 2, p. 350.

112 See Thamer, "Nation als Volksgemeinschaft," p. 123; Zitelmann, *Hitler: Selbstverständnis eines Revolutionärs*, pp. 205f., 208f. On the opaqueness of Hitler's terminology see also Norbert Frei, "'Volksgemeinschaft': Erfahrungsgeschichte und Lebenswirklichkeit der Hitler-Zeit," in *idem, 1945 und wir: Das Dritte Reich im Bewusstsein der Deutschen*, Munich, 2005, pp. 110–12.

113 Domarus, *Hitler*, vol. 1, part 1, p. 206.

114 Ibid., p. 267.

115 See Hans-Ulrich Thamer, *Verführung und Gewalt: Deutschland 1933–1945*, Berlin, 1986, p. 499; Richard J. Evans, *The Third Reich in Power 1933–1939*, London, 2005, pp. 460f.

116 Reichel, *Der schöne Schein des Dritten Reiches*, p. 235. See also Michael Schneider, *Unterm Hakenkreuz: Arbeiter und Arbeiterbewegung 1933 bis 1939*, Bonn, 1999, pp. 225–7.

117 Quoted in *Deutschland-Berichte der Sopade*, 6 (1939), p. 463. See Evans, *The Third Reich in Power*, p. 466.

118 *Deutschland-Berichte der Sopade*, 5 (1938), p. 158.

119 Figures from Wolfgang König, *Volkswagen, Volksempfänger, Volksgemeinschaft: "Volksprodukte" im Dritten Reich. Vom Scheitern einer nationalsozialistischen Konsumgesellschaft*, Paderborn, 2004, pp. 192, 194.

120 Hitler, *Monologe*, p. 65 (dated 22/23 Sept. 1941).

121 Quoted in Schildt, "Jenseits der Politik?," in *Hamburg im "Dritten Reich,"* p. 284. See Hasso Spode, "'Der deutsche Arbeiter reist': Massentourismus im Dritten Reich," in Gerhard Huck (ed.), *Sozialgeschichte der Freizeit: Untersuchungen zum Wandel der Alltagskultur in Deutschland*, Wuppertal, 1980, pp. 281–306.

122 Goebbels, *Tagebücher*, part 1, vol. 3/2, p. 64 (entry for 19 April 1936). In his monologues in his military headquarters, Hitler announced: "Every worker will in future have a holiday, several days that belong to him alone. And once or twice in his life, he'll be able to go on a cruise." Hitler, *Monologe*, p. 73 (dated 27/28 Sept. 1941).

123 See König, *Volkswagen, Volksempfänger, Volksgemeinschaft*, pp. 203–5; Thamer, *Verführung und Gewalt*, p. 501; Evans, *The Third Reich in Power*, pp. 470f.

124 See *Deutschland-Berichte der Sopade*, 2 (1935), pp. 845f.; 3 (1936), pp. 882f., 884f.; 6 (1939), p. 474.

125 Ibid., 1 (1934), p. 523.

126 Ibid., 5 (1938), p. 172. See ibid., 6. (1939), p. 478, which cites workers who had yet to take part in them praising Hitler for "creating the wonderful Strength through Joy trips."

127 Ibid., 2 (1935), p. 1456.

128 See Jürgen Rostock and Franz Zadnicek, *Paradiesruinen: Das KdF-Seebad der Zwanzigtausend auf Rügen*, Berlin, 1995; further, König, *Volkswagen, Volksempfänger, Volksgemeinschaft*, pp. 208–15; Evans, *The Third Reich in Power*, pp. 469f.

129 Cited in König, *Volkswagen, Volksempfänger, Volksgemeinschaft*, p. 209. In July 1935, Hitler discussed plans for "a major working-class beach resort on a North Sea island" with Goebbels: "10,000 beds. 15 million. We'll get it done. We're both throbbing with enthusiasm." Goebbels, *Tagebücher*, part 1, vol. 3/1, p. 262 (entry for 15 July 1935).

130 *Deutschland-Berichte der Sopade*, 6 (1939), p. 469.

131 See König, *Volkswagen, Volksempfänger, Volksgemeinschaft*, pp. 18f.; see also Hans-Werner Niemann, "'Volksgemeinschaft' als Konsumgemeinschaft?," in Detlef Schmiechen-Ackermann (ed.), *"Volksgemeinschaft": Mythos, wirkungsmächtige soziale Verheissung oder soziale Realität im "Dritten Reich"? Zwischenbilanz einer Kontroverse*, Paderborn, 2012, pp. 87–109.

132 In particular see Rüdiger Hachtmann, *Industriearbeit im "Dritten Reich": Untersuchungen zu den Lohn- und Arbeitsbedingungen in Deutschland 1933–1945*, Göttingen, 1989; *idem,* "Lebenshaltungskosten und Realeinkommen während des 'Dritten Reiches,'" in

Vierteljahrsschrift für Sozial- und Wirtschaftsgeschichte, 75 (1988), pp. 32–73; Adam Tooze, *The Wages of Destruction: The Making and Breaking of the Nazi Economy*, London, 2006, pp. 141–3.

133   See Aly, *Hitler Volksstaat*, pp. 36f., 49ff.; for a critical perspective see Rüdiger Hachtmann, "Öffentlichkeitswirksame Knallfrösche: Anmerkungen zu Götz Alys 'Volksstaat,'" in *Sozial.Geschichte: Zeitschrift für historische Analyse des 20. und 21. Jahrhunderts*, 20 (2005), pp. 46–66.

134   See König, *Volkswagen, Volksempfänger, Volksgemeinschaft*, pp. 33ff.

135   See ibid., pp. 82f. Tooze, *The Wages of Destruction*, p. 148, also sees the radio as a product that boosted the German economy in the 1930s.

136   Goebbels, *Tagebücher*, part 1, vol. 2/3, p. 264 (entry for 9 Sept. 1933). See ibid., vol. 3/2, p. 330 (entry for 16 Jan. 1937): "Fewer plays and talking and more music and entertainment. The general tendency is to loosen things up!"

137   Hitler, *Monologe*, p. 275 (dated 9 Feb. 1942).

138   Hitler, Goebbels, *Tagebücher*, part 1, vol. 2/3, p. 251 (entry for 23 Aug. 1933); vol. 3/1, pp. 155 (entry for 19. Dec. 1934), 181 (entry for 8 Feb. 1935), 222 (entry for 25 April 1935); vol. 6, p. 35 (entry for 6 Aug. 1938).

139   Quoted in König, *Volkswagen, Volksempfänger, Volksgemeinschaft*, p. 103.

140   Domarus, *Hitler*, vol. 1, part 1, p. 370

141   Hans Mommsen and Manfred Grieger, *Das Volkswagenwerk und seine Arbeiter im Dritten Reich*, Düsseldorf, 1996, p. 60.

142   Domarus, *Hitler*, vol. 1, part 2, p. 577. See Goebbels, *Tagebücher*, part 1, vol. 3/1, p. 380 (entry for 17 Feb. 1936): "The Führer held a wonderful speech. Called for the Volkswagen. Excellent use of evidence." On F. Porsche and his relationship with Hitler see Mommsen and Grieger, *Das Volkswagenwerk*, pp. 71ff.; Tooze, *The Wages of Destruction*, pp. 153–5.

143   See Mommsen and Grieger, *Das Volkswagenwerk*, pp. 117ff., 133ff.

144   Domarus, *Hitler*, vol. 1, part 2, p. 868. In January 1937, Hitler had already consulted Goebbels about building a "gigantic factory for the Volkswagen . . . and in addition a model city. A massive project. The Führer is burning with enthusiasm." Goebbels, *Tagebücher*, part 1, vol. 3/2, p. 327 (entry for 13 Jan. 1937).

145   *Deutschland-Berichte der Sopade*, 6 (1939), p. 488. See ibid., p. 490.

146   See Mommsen and Grieger, *Das Volkswagenwerk*, pp. 189–201; König, *Volkswagen, Volksempfänger, Volksgemeinschaft*, pp. 178–81; Tooze, *The Wages of Destruction*, p. 156.

147   See Florian Tennstedt, "Wohltat und Interesse: Das Winterhilfswerk des Deutschen Volkes. Die Weimarer Vorgeschichte und ihre Instrumentalisierung durch das NS-Regime," in *Geschichte und Gesellschaft*, 13 (1987), pp. 157–80.

148   Domarus, *Hitler*, vol. 1, part 1, pp. 300f.

149   Goebbels, *Tagebücher*, part 1, vol. 2/3, p. 267 (entry for 14 Sept.1933).

150   Domarus, *Hitler*, vol. 1, part 2, p. 742.

151   Goebbels, *Tagebücher*, part 1, vol. 3/1, p. 151 (entry for 10 Dec. 1934). See ibid., p. 343 (entry for 9 Dec. 1935), vol. 3/2, p. 280 (entry for 7 Dec. 1936).

152   Domarus, *Hitler*, vol. 1, part 2, p. 545.

153   Speer, *Erinnerungen*, p. 134.

154   Herwart Vorländer, *Die NSV: Darstellung und Dokumentation einer nationalsozialistischen Organisation*, Boppard am Rhein, 1988, p. 50 (the letter reprinted in ibid., p. 230).

155   *Deutschland-Berichte der Sopade*, 2 (1935), p. 1422, 5 (1938), p. 77.

156   See Vorländer, *Die NSV*, p. 53.

157   Quoted in Zitelmann, *Hitler: Selbstverständnis eines Revolutionärs*, p. 132. On pp. 122ff. see numerous further references for the time prior to 1933.

158   Domarus, *Hitler*, vol. 1, part 1, p. 373 (dated 25 March 1934).

159   Goebbels, *Tagebücher*, part 1, vol. 3/2, p. 318 (entry for 6 Jan. 1937).

160   Quotations from Hitler, *Monologe*, pp. 72 (dated 27/28 Sept. 1941), 114 (dated 29 Oct. 1941), 120 (dated 1/2 Nov. 1941), 290 (dated 22 Feb. 1942).

161   On the longrunning debate on modernity and social mobility in National Socialism, triggered by David Schoenbaum's book *Die braune Revolution (Eine Sozialgeschichte des Dritten Reiches*, Cologne, 1968), see a summary in Michael Wildt, *Geschichte des Nationalsozialismus*, Göttingen, 2008, pp. 106–9. See also Wehler, *Deutsche Gesellschaftsgeschichte 1914–1949*, pp. 686–8, 771–3.

162   See Zitelmann, *Hitler: Selbstverständnis eines Revolutionärs*, pp. 38, 489–96.

163   Frei, "Volksgemeinschaft," pp. 114f.; see Rolf Pohl, "Das Konstrukt 'Volksgemeinschaft' als Mittel zur Erzeugung von Massenloyalität im Nationalsozialismus," in Schmiechen-Ackermann (ed.), *"Volksgemeinschaft*," pp. 69–84.

164   As in Bajohr and Wildt (eds), *Volksgemeinschaft*, p. 8. For a critical perspective see Hans Mommsen, "Der Mythos der Volksgemeinschaft," in *idem, Zur Geschichte Deutschlands im 20. Jahrhundert*, Munich, 2010, pp. 162–74. For a refined view see Ian Kershaw, "'Volksgemeinschaft': Potenzial und Grenzen eines neuen Forschungskonzepts," in *Vierteljahrshefte für Zeitgeschichte*, 59 (2011), pp. 1–17.

165   Adolf Hitler, *Mein Kampf. Vol. 1: Eine Abrechnung*, 7th edition, Munich, 1933, pp. 444–6.

166   Adolf Hitler, *Reden, Schriften, Anordnungen—Februar 1925 bis Januar 1933. Vol. 3: Zwischen den Reichstagswahlen Juli 1928–September 1930. Part 2: März 1929–Dezember 1929*, ed. Klaus A. Lankheit, Munich, 1994, doc. 64, pp. 348, 353 (dated 4 Aug. 1929).

167   See Gisela Bock, *Zwangssterilisation im Nationalsozialismus: Studien zur Rassenpolitik und Frauenpolitik*, Opladen, 1986, pp. 28–76.

168   Burleigh, *The Third Reich*, p. 350. See Wehler, *Deutsche Gesellschaftsgeschichte 1914–1949*, pp. 664–9; Wildt, *Geschichte des Nationalsozialismus*, pp. 110f.

169   Bock, *Zwangssterilisation*, p. 80.

170   *Akten der Reichskanzlei: Die Regierung Hitler. Part 1: 1933/34. Vol. 1: 30. Januar bis 30. April 1933*, ed. Karl-Heinz Minuth, Boppard am Rhein, 198, no. 193, pp. 664f.

171   Domarus, *Hitler*, vol. 1, part 1, p. 355.

172   See Bock, *Zwangssterilisation*, pp. 88, 182ff.

173   Ibid., p. 90.

174   Ibid., pp. 230–3. See Evans, *The Third Reich in Power*, p. 508.

175   Wehler, *Deutsche Gesellschaftsgeschichte 1914–1949*, p. 671; See Peter Longerich, *Politik der Vernichtung: Eine Gesamtdarstellung der nationalsozialistischen Judenverfolgung*, Munich and Zurich, 1998, pp. 60f.

176   See above pp. 441–4.

177   *Die Regierung Hitler*, part 1, vol. 2, no. 222, pp. 865f. In a memo to the Gauleiter on 12 Sept. 1933 Martin Bormann wrote: "For foreign policy reasons, we must immediately desist from anti-Jewish measures beyond those already taken." *Die Verfolgung und Ermordung der europäischen Juden durch das nationalsozialistische Deutschland 1933–1945. Vol. 1: Deutsches Reich 1933–1937*, ed. Wolf Gruner, Munich, 2008, doc. 76, p. 242.

178   See Longerich, *Politik der Vernichtung*, pp. 46–50.

179   Otto Dov Kulka and Eberhard Jäckel (eds), *Die Juden in den geheimen Stimmungsberichten 1933–1945*, Düsseldorf, 2004, no. 32, p. 75 (also numerous other documents). On antiSemitic violence in the provinces in 1933/4 see Michael Wildt, *Volksgemeinschaft als Selbstermächtigung: Gewalt gegen Juden in der deutschen Provinz 1919 bis 1939*, Hamburg, 2007, pp. 138ff.; Hannah Ahlheim, *"Deutsche, kauft nicht bei Juden!" Antisemitischer Boykott in Deutschland 1924 bis 1935*, Göttingen, 2011, pp. 318ff.

180   See Wildt, *Volksgemeinschaft als Selbstermächtigung*, particularly pp. 144, 172.

181   Kulka and Jäckel (eds), *Die Juden in den geheimen Stimmungsberichten 1933–1945*, no. 60, pp. 100f.

182   See Wildt, *Volksgemeinschaft als Selbstermächtigung*, pp. 225ff.; see Alexandra Przyrembel, *"Rassenschande": Reinheitsmythos und Vernichtungslegitimation im Nationalsozialismus*, Göttingen, 2003.

183   Quoted in Wildt, *Volksgemeinschaft als Selbstermächtigung*, p. 192; see also Ahlheim, "*Deutsche kauft nicht bei Juden!*," pp. 366f.

184   Willy Cohn, *Kein Recht, nirgends: Tagebuch vom Untergang des Breslauer Judentums 1933–1941*, ed. Norbert Conrads, Cologne, Weimar and Berlin, 2006, vol. 1, p. 259 (entry for 12 Aug. 1935); see Klemperer, *Tagebücher 1933–1941*, p. 192 (entry for 17 April 1935); Rosenberg, *Tagebücher 1933–1937*, pp. 264f. (entry for 4 March 1935), 282 (entry for 23 March 1935).

185   Fritz Wiedemann to Martin Bormann, 30 April 1935; IfZ München, ED 9.

186   Quoted in Wildt, *Volksgemeinschaft als Selbstermächtigung*, p. 272.

187   Kulka and Jäckel (eds), *Die Juden in den geheimen Stimmungsberichten 1933–1945*, no. 122, p. 138.

188   Goebbels, *Tagebücher*, part 1, vol. 3/1, pp. 229 (entry for 9 May 1935), 234 (entry for 19 May 1935).

189   *Der Angriff*, 1 July 1935; quoted in Longerich, *Politik der Vernichtung*, p. 86. See also Goebbels's speech of 11 May 1934: "They will be required to behave in Germany in a manner befitting guests." *Die Verfolgung und Ermordung der europäischen Juden*, vol. 1, doc. 117, p. 338.

190   L. Weinmann to Reich Interor Ministry, 26 May 1935; *Die Verfolgung und Ermordung der europäischen Juden*, vol. 1, doc. 168, pp. 440f.; see also the report of the Munich police dated 17 May 1935: Kulka and Jäckel (eds), *Die Juden in den geheimen Stimmungsberichten 1933–1945*, no. 121, p. 137. See also Wildt. *Volksgemeinschaft als Selbstermächtigung*, pp. 199f.; Longerich, *Politik der Vernichtung*, p. 84; Saul Friedländer, *Das Dritte Reich und die Juden: Die Jahre der Verfolgung 1933–1939*, Munich, 1998, vol. 1, pp. 154f.

191   Goebbels, *Tagebücher*, part 1, vol. 3/1, p. 262 (entry for 15 July 1935).

192   Quoted in Longerich, *Politik der Vernichtung*, p. 87.

193   *Neue Zürcher Zeitung*, 16 July 1935; *Die Verfolgung und Ermordung der europäischen Juden*, vol. 1, doc. 176, p. 452. See Goebbels, *Tagebücher*, part 1, vol. 3/1, p. 263 (entry for 19 July 1935); "Riots on Kurfürstendamm, Jews beaten up. Foreign press moaning on about a 'pogrom.'" On the "Kurfürstendamm riots" see Longerich, *Politik der Vernichtung*, pp. 86f.; Ahlheim, "*Deutsche kauft nicht bei Juden!*," pp. 387f.

194   Klemperer, *Tagebücher 1933–1941*, p. 212 (entry for 11 Aug. 1935).

195   Kulka and Jäckel (eds), *Die Juden in den geheimen Stimmungsberichten 1933–1945*, no. 133, p. 143.

196   See Longerich, *Politik der Vernichtung*, p. 95.

197   See ibid., p. 94.

198   Heydrich to Lammers, 16 July 1935; quoted in Werner Jochmann, "Die deutsche Bevölkerung und die nationalsozialistische Judenpolitik bis zur Verkündung der Nürnberger Gesetze," in *idem, Gesellschaftskrise und Judenfeindschaft in Deutschland 1870–1945*, Hamburg, 1988, p. 246.

199   Reprinted in Michael Wildt (ed.), *Die Judenpolitik des SD 1935 bis 1939: Eine Dokumentation*, Munich, 1995, doc. 2, pp. 69f.

200   Christopher Kopper, *Hjalmar Schacht: Aufstieg und Fall von Hitlers mächtigstem Bankier*, Munich and Vienna, 2006, pp. 277f.

201   Ibid., pp. 279f.; see Goebbels, *Tagebücher*, part 1, vol. 3/1, p. 280 (entry for 21 Aug. 1935): "Schacht held a provocative speech à la Papen in Königsberg."

202   Cabinet meeting on 20 Aug. 1935 (from the Gestapo report found in the special archives in Moscow); *Die Verfolgung und Ermordung der europäischen Juden*, vol. 1, doc. 189, pp. 471–8.

203   Heydrich to the participants in the high-ranking meeting at the Economics Ministry on 9 Sept. 1935; Wildt, *Die Judenpolitik des SD 1935–1939*, doc. 3, pp. 70–3.

204   Robert Gerwarth, *Reinhard Heydrich: Biographie*, Munich, 2011, p. 121.

205   The view that the Nuremberg Laws were improvised is based on recollections by Bernhard Lösener in 1950: "Das Reichsministerium des Innern und die Judengesetz-

gebung," in *Vierteljahrshefte für Zeitgeschichte*, 9 (1961), pp. 262–313. For a detailed critical perspective on the sources see Cornelia Essner, *Die "Nürnberger Gesetze" oder die Verwaltung des Rassenwahns 1933–1945*, Paderborn, 2002, pp. 113–34. See also Wildt, *Volksgemeinschaft als Selbstermächtigung*, p. 263.

206   Goebbels, *Tagebücher*, part 1, vol. 3/1, p. 290 (entry for 9 Sept. 1935). On the New York incident see David Bankier, *Die öffentliche Meinung im Hitler-Staat: Die "Endlösung" und die Deutschen*, Berlin, 1995, pp. 65f.

207   Goebbels, *Tagebücher*, part 1, vol. 3/1, p. 293 (entry for 15 Sept. 1935).

208   Lösener, "Das Reichsministerium des Innern und die Judengesetzgebung," p. 273.

209   Ibid., p. 209.

210   Goebbels, *Tagebücher*, part 1, vol. 3/1, p. 294 (entry for 15 Sept. 1935).

211   Lösener, "Das Reichsministerium des Innern und die Judengesetzgebung," p. 276. See Friedländer, *Das Dritte Reich und die Juden*, vol. 1, p. 165.

212   Text of the laws in *Die Verfolgung und Ermordung der europäischen Juden*, vol. 1, doc. 198/199, pp. 492–4.

213   Domarus, *Hitler*, vol. 1, part 2, pp. 536f.

214   Goebbels, *Tagebücher*, part 1, vol. 3/1, p. 294 (entry for 17 Sept. 1935).

215   *Die Verfolgung und Ermordung der europäischen Juden*, vol. 1, doc. 202, p. 502. According to Fritz Wiedemann, Hitler enumerated the goals of his "Jewish policies" at the 1935 Nuremberg Rally as: "exclusion from all professions, ghetto, confinement to a territory where they can behave as is the wont of their kind while the German people watches them as it would watch wild animals." Wiedemann's shorthand notes dated 25 Feb. 1939; BA Koblenz, N 1720/4.

216   Cohn, *Kein Recht, nirgends*, vol. 1, p. 276 (entry for 14 Sept. 1935).

217   Klemperer, *Tagebücher 1933–1941*, p. 219 (entry for 17 Sept. 1935).

218   Quoted in Peter Longerich, *"Davon haben wir nichts gewusst!" Die Deutschen und die Judenverfolgung 1933–1945*, Munich, 2006, p. 93.

219   As in the reports from Berlin and Koblenz from September 1935; quoted in Otto Dov Kulka, "Die Nürnberger Rassegesetze und die deutsche Bevölkerung im Lichte geheimer SS-Lage- und Stimmungsberichte," in *Vierteljahrshefte für Zeitgeschichte*, 32 (1984), p. 602.

220   Ibid., p. 603.

221   *Deutschlandberichte der Sopade*, 2 (1935), p. 1019.

222   Ibid., 3 (1936), p. 27. See ibid., p. 24: "The general consensus is that there is a 'Jewish question.'"

223   See Lösener, "Das Reichsministerium des Innern und die Judengesetzgebung," pp. 279f.

224   Goebbels, *Tagebücher*, part 1, vol. 3/1, p. 301 (entry for 1 Oct. 1935).

225   See Uwe Dietrich Adam, *Judenpolitik im Dritten Reich*, Königstein im Taunus, 1979, pp. 138–40.

226   Goebbels, *Tagebücher*, part 1, vol. 3/1, p. 324 (entry for 7 Nov. 1935).

227   Text in *Die Verfolgung und Ermordung der europäischen Juden*, vol. 1, doc. 210, pp. 521–3. Later Stuckart claimed that he had partially "defanged" the Nuremberg Laws. Schwerin von Krosigk to Hans Mommsen, 2 July 1968; BA Koblenz, N 1276/23.

228   Goebbels, *Tagebücher*, part 1, vol. 3/1, p. 329 (entry for 15 Nov. 1935). On the "delicate compromise" of 14 Nov. 1935 see Essner, *Die "Nürnberger Gesetze,"* pp. 171–3.

229   See Adam, *Judenpolitik*, p. 142; Longerich, *Politik der Vernichtung*, p. 113; Ian Kershaw, *Hitler 1889–1936: Hubris*, London, 1998, p. 572.

230   Quoted in Friedländer, *Das Dritte Reich und die Juden*, vol. 1, p. 133.

231   Gabriele Toepser-Ziegert (ed.), *NS-Presseanweisungen der Vorkriegszeit. Edition und Dokumentation: 1936, Vol. 4, Part 1*, Munich, 1993, p. 85 (dated 27 Jan. 1936).

232   Goebbels, *Tagebücher*, part 1, vol. 3/1, p. 376 (entry for 6 Feb. 1936).

233   See the report by the Bavarian police dated 1 March 1936: "The murder of National Socialist Regional Director Gustloff by the Jew Frankfurter did not lead to public

violence against Jews." Kulka and Jäckel (eds), *Die Juden in den geheimen Stimmungsberichten 1933–1945*, no. 204, p. 192.

234   Domarus, *Hitler*, vol. 1, part 2, pp. 574f.; see Goebbels, *Tagebücher*, part 1, vol. 3/1, p. 379 (entry for 14 Feb. 1936): "The Führer held a radical, strongly worded speech against the Jews. That is a good thing. It was broadcast on all stations."

235   Arnd Krüger, *Die Olympischen Spiele 1936 und die Weltmeinung: Ihre aussenpolitische Bedeutung unter besonderer Berücksichtigung der USA*, Berlin, 1972, p. 31.

236   Lewald to Lammers, 16 March 1933; *Akten der Regierung Hitler*, part 1, vol. 1, no. 66, p. 234n3.

237   Hitler to Lewald, 13 Nov. 1934; facsimile in Reinhard Rürup (ed.), *1936: Die Olympischen Spiele und der Nationalsozialismus*, Berlin, 1996, p. 51.

238   Goebbels, *Tagebücher*, part 1, vol. 2/3, p. 358 (entry for 16 Jan. 1934). See Rudolf Hess to his parents, 18 Dec. 1935: "The Olympic Games will show the new Germany at its most effective." BA Bern, Nl Hess, J1.211-1989/148, 55. In a letter to his father of 8 June 1936 Hess described the Olympics as "the first great representative opportunity for the new Reich"; BA Bern, Nl Hess, J1.211-1989/148, 57. On propaganda activities in the Olympic year and their effects see Ewald Grothe, "Die Olympischen Spiele von 1936: Höhepunkt der NS-Propaganda?," in *Geschichte in Wissenschaft und Unterricht*, 59 (2008), pp. 291–307.

239   Lewald to State Secretary Pfundtner, 5 Oct. 1933 with enclosed notes on Hitler's visit; *Die Regierung Hitler*, part 1, vol. 2, no. 226, pp. 893–5. See Goebbels, *Tagebücher*, part 1, vol. 2/3, p. 289 (entry for 11 Oct. 1933): "Discussion of the Olympics with the boss. New, magnificent stadium facility. The boss generous as always. That's how I like to see him." See also *Hitlers Tischgespräche im Führerhauptquartier*, ed. Henry Picker, Stuttgart, 1976, pp. 216f. (dated 12 April 1942).

240   On the details see Wolfgang Schäche and Norbert Szymanski, *Das Reichssportfeld: Architektur im Spanungsfeld von Sport und Macht*, Berlin-Brandenburg, 2001, pp. 76–103.

241   See Goebbels, *Tagebücher*, part 1, vol. 3/1, p. 130 (entry for 2 Nov. 1934): "[Hitler] complained about the construction of the stadium, which he rightfully thinks is not fit for purpose."

242   Speer, *Erinnerungen*, p. 94; Fest, *Speer*, pp. 81f.; Ian Kershaw is also uncritical in *Hitler 1936–1945: Nemesis*, London, 2000, p. 5f. Critical of Speer's contention are Schäche and Szymanski, *Das Reichssportfeld*, pp. 78–80; Armin Fuhrer, *Hitlers Spiele: Olympia 1936 in Berlin*, Berlin-Brandenburg, 2011, pp. 26f.

243   Quoted in Krüger, *Die Olympischen Spiele 1936*, pp. 46f.

244   See Fuhrer, *Hitlers Spiele*, pp. 44–8; Alexander Emmerich, *Olympia 1936: Trügerischer Glanz eines mörderischen Systems*, Cologne, 2011, p. 150.

245   On the attacks on Lewald in the press see Lewald to Lammers, 3 April 1933; *Die Regierung Hitler*, part 1, vol. 1, no. 84, pp. 284–6.

246   See Fuhrer, *Hitlers Spiele*, pp. 47f.; Emmerich, *Olympia 1936*, p. 53.

247   Quoted in Guy Walters, *Berlin Games: How Hitler Stole the Olympic Dream*, London, 2006, p. 53.

248   See Krüger, *Die Olympischen Spiele 1936*, pp. 163–6.

249   Goebbels, *Tagebücher*, part 1, vol. 3/1, p. 377 (entry for 8 Feb. 1936).

250   See Krüger, *Die Olympischen Spiele 1936*, p. 170; Fuhrer, *Hitlers Spiele*, pp. 65f.

251   Shirer, *Berliner Tagebuch*, p. 51 (from Februar 1936); see Goebbels, *Tagebücher*, part 1, vol. 3/1, p. 381 (entry for 17 Feb. 1936): "Everyone praises how we've organised things. It was indeed fantastic."

252   Goebbels, *Tagebücher*, part 1, vol. 3/2, pp. 138 (entry for 24 July 1936), 143 (entry for 30 July 1936). See Shirer, *Berliner Tagebuch*, p. 67 (entry for 27 July 1936): "Interest here is concentrated on the Olympic Games opening next week, with the Nazis outdoing themselves to create a favourable impression on foreign visitors."

253   See Fromm, *Als Hitler mir die Hand küsste*, p. 248 (entry for 23 July 1936); David Clay Large, *Berlin: Biographie einer Stadt*, Munich, 2002, p. 280.

254 Quoted in Richard Mandell, *Hitlers Olympiade: Berlin 1936*, Munich, 1980, p. 134.

255 Quoted in Large, *Berlin*, p. 280.

256 Goebbels, *Tagebücher*, part 1, vol. 3/2, p. 146 (entry for 18 Feb. 1936).

257 Domarus, *Hitler*, vol. 1, part 2, p. 632.

258 See Schäche and Szymanski, *Das Reichssportfeld*, pp. 107f.; Fuhrer, *Hitlers Spiele*, pp. 92f.

259 Goebbels, *Tagebücher*, part 1, vol. 3/2, p. 146 (entry for 2 Aug. 1936). See Fuhrer, *Hitlers Spiele*, pp. 93f.; François-Poncet, *Als Botschafter in Berlin*, p. 269.

260 See Fuhrer, *Hitlers Spiele*, pp. 94f.; Emmerich, *Olympia 1936*, pp. 132f.

261 Quoted in Walters, *Berlin Games*, p. 187.

262 Goebbels, *Tagebücher*, part 1, vol. 3/2, p. 146 (entry for 2 Aug. 1936).

263 Dodd, *Nice to meet you, Mr. Hitler!*, p. 234. See also François-Poncet, *Als Botschafter in Berlin*, p. 270; Fromm, *Als Hitler mir die Hand küsste*, p. 249 (entry for 15 Aug. 1936).

264 See Mandell, *Hitlers Olympiade*, pp. 203ff.; Large, *Berlin*, pp. 281f.; Kershaw, *Hitler: Nemesis*, p. 7.

265 Goebbels, *Tagebücher*, part 1, vol. 3/2, p. 149 (entry for 5 Aug. 1936).

266 Baldur von Schirach, *Ich glaubte an Hitler*, Hamburg, 1967, p. 218. See Speer, *Erinnerungen*, p. 86.

267 Frank, *Im Angesicht des Galgens*, p. 250; see Wiedemann, *Der Mann*, p. 209.

268 Goebbels, *Tagebücher*, part 1, vol. 3/2, pp. 147 (entry for 3 Aug. 1936), 161 (entry for 17 Aug. 1936).

269 Paul Schmidt, *Statist auf diplomatischer Bühne 1923–45: Erlebnisse des Chefdolmetschers im Auswärtigen Amt mit den Staatsmännern Europas*, Bonn, 1950, p. 330.

270 François-Poncet, *Als Botschafter in Berlin*, p. 267.

271 Goebbels, *Tagebücher*, part 1, vol. 3/2, pp. 160f. (entry for 16 Aug. 1936); see ibid., p. 158 (entry for 14 Aug. 1936); Joachim von Ribbentrop, *Zwischen London und Moskau: Erinnerungen und letzte Aufzeichnungen*, ed. Annelies von Ribbentrop, Leoni am Starnberger See, 1961, pp. 94f.

272 See Rürup (ed.), *1936: Die Olympischen Spiele und der Nationalsozialismus*, pp. 169–77; Fuhrer, *Hitlers Spiele*, pp. 133–9.

273 Goebbels, *Tagebücher*, part 1, vol. 5, p. 267 (entry for 21 Aug. 1938). On the Olympics film see Rother, *Leni Riefenstahl*, pp. 87–101; Wieland, *Dietrich & Riefenstahl*, pp. 329–46; Leis, *Leni Riefenstahl*, pp. 78–86; Fuhrer, *Hitlers Spiele*, pp. 127–33.

274 Shirer, *Berliner Tagebuch*, p. 68 (entry for 16 Aug. 1936) On the foreign echo see also Krüger, *Die Olympischen Spiele 1936*, pp. 206–15; Large, *Berlin*, pp. 280f.

275 Quoted in Krüger, *Die Olympischen Spiele 1936*, p. 229.

276 Klemperer, *Tagebücher 1933–1941*, pp. 291f.

277 Domarus, *Hitler*, vol. 1, part 2, pp. 638, 645f. See Friedländer, *Das Dritte Reich und die Juden*, vol. 1, p. 201.

278 Klemperer, *Tagebücher 1933–1942*, p. 305 (entry for 14 Sept. 1936). See Cohn, *Kein Recht, nirgends*, vol. 1, p. 353 (entry for 11 Sept. 1936); Thomas Mann, *Tagebücher 1937–1939*, ed. Peter de Mendelssohn, Frankfurt am Main, 1980, p. 38 (entry for 10 March 1937): "Why in God's name this prostration before something so obviously pathetic?"

17 Dictatorship by Division, Architecture of Intimidation

1 Sefton Delmer, *Die Deutschen und ich*, Hamburg, 1963, p. 182.

2 See Otto Dietrich, *12 Jahre mit Hitler*, Munich, 1955, pp. 39, 249.

3 See Lutz Graf Schwerin von Krosigk, *Es geschah in Deutschland: Menschenbilder unseres Jahrhunderts*, Tübingen and Stuttgart, 1951, p. 199.

4 Lammers's statement in the "Wilhelmstrasse trial" on 3 Sept. 1948; quoted in Dieter Rebentisch, "Hitlers Reichskanzlei zwischen Politik und Verwaltung," in *idem* and Karl Teppe (eds), *Verwaltung contra Menschenführung im Staat Hitlers*, Göttingen, 1986,

p. 68. See also sworn statement by Wilhelm Brückner, June 1954: "Hitler wanted a man who was not burdened from the start by party intrigues and who could bring a top level of judicial qualifications to the job." IfZ München, ED 100/43.

5   Friedrich Hossbach, *Zwischen Wehrmacht und Hitler 1934–1938*, 2nd revised edition, Göttingen, 1965, p. 43.

6   Albert Speer, *Erinnerungen: Mit einem Essay von Jochen Thies*, Frankfurt am Main and Berlin, 1993, p. 48.

7   Fritz Wiedemann, *Der Mann, der Feldherr werden wollte: Erlebnisse und Erfahrungen des Vorgesetzten Hitlers im 1. Weltkrieg und seines späteren persönlichen Adjutanten*, Velbert and Kettwig 1964, pp. 60f.

8   Karl Wilhelm Krause, *10 Jahre Kammerdiener bei Hitler*, Hamburg, 1949, p. 22. Otto Dietrich spoke in the questioning of 26 May 1947 of an "unbroken life of travel"; IfZ München, ZS 874. See Dietrich, *12 Jahre mit Hitler*, p. 161. On Hitler's "travel mania" see Joachim Fest, *Hitler: Eine Biographie*, Frankfurt am Main, Berlin and Vienna, 1973, pp. 612, 737; Marlies Steinert, *Hitler*, Munich, 1994, p. 123.

9   Speer, *Erinnerungen*, p. 59. See Wiedemann's shorthand notes dated 25 Feb. 1939: "Whenever he travelled from Berlin to Munich, his first stop was Troost's studio, then his own apartment, a meal in the Osteria, and the office for construction in the Bavarian Interior Ministry." BA Koblenz, N 1720/4. On Hitler's typical routine during his visits to Munich see also Max Wünsche's daily diaries dated 18 June, 25 June, 2 July, 6 July, 21 July 1938; BA Berlin-Lichterfelde, NS 10/125; Dietrich, *12 Jahre mit Hitler*, pp. 200–2.

10   See Hans Wilderotter, *Alltag der Macht: Berlin Wilhelmstrasse*, Berlin, 1998, p. 74.

11   *Die Tagebücher von Joseph Goebbels. Part 1: Aufzeichnungen 1923–1941*, ed. Elke Fröhlich, Munich, 1998, vol. 2/3, p. 360 (entry for 22 Jan. 1934). See Timo Nüsslein, *Paul Ludwig Troost 1878–1934*, Vienna, Cologne and Weimar, 2012, pp. 67f.; on the state funeral on 24 Jan. 1934, see ibid., pp. 160f. In September 1941, Hitler still described Troost as "the greatest architect of our time." Reports by Werner Koeppen, p. 1 (dated 6 Sept. 1941).

12   See Joachim Fest, *Speer: Eine Biographie*, Berlin, 1999, pp. 21–50.

13   Speer, *Erinnerungen*, p. 43. See Fest, *Speer*, p. 52.

14   See Nicolaus von Below, *Als Hitlers Adjutant 1937–45*, Mainz, 1980, p. 28; Krause, *10 Jahre Kammerdiener*, p. 34f.; Christa Schroeder, *Er war mein Chef: Aus dem Nachlass der Sekretärin von Adolf Hitler*, ed. Anton Joachimsthaler, 3rd edition, Munich and Vienna, 1985, pp. 59–61; Rochus Misch, *Der letzte Zeuge: "Ich war Hitlers Telefonist, Kurier und Leibwächter,"* Zurich and Munich, 2008, pp. 73–7; Steinert, *Hitler*, pp. 325f.

15   See Karl Brandt's testimony about Wihelm Brückner and Julius Schaub (20 Sept. 1945); BA Koblenz, N 1128/33; Below, *Als Hitlers Adjutant*, pp. 29f., 71, 90; Schroeder, *Er war mein Chef*, pp. 37, 42, 44f., 46, 53f.; Krause, *10 Jahre Kammerdiener*, pp. 23–7; Heinz Linge, *Bis zum Untergang: Als Chef des Persönlichen Dienstes bei Hitler*, ed. Werner Maser, Munich, 1982, pp. 24f.; Ernst Hanfstaengl, *Zwischen Weissem und Braunem Haus: Erinnerungen eines politischen Aussenseiters*, Munich, 1970, pp. 309f.; Olaf Rose (ed.), *Julius Schaub: In Hitlers Schatten*, Stegen, 2005, pp. 21, 51.

16   Linge, *Bis zum Untergang*, p. 59.

17   The list of gifts for the years 1935 and 1936 is reprinted in Anton Joachimsthaler, *Hitlers Liste: Ein Dokument persönlicher Beziehungen*, Munich, 2003, pp. 12–15. The thank you letter for the gift of flowers at New Year 1934 (from Victoria von Dirksen, Margarete Frick, Cornelia Popitz and others) in BA Berlin-Lichterfelde, NS 10/123. On Hitler's pleasure at giving gifts see Schoeder, *Er war mein Chef*, pp. 55f.; Dietrich, *12 Jahre mit Hitler*, p. 197.

18   Goebbels, *Tagebücher*, part 1, vol. 3/2, p. 85 (entry for 17 May 1936). See ibid., p. 85 (entry for 18 May 1936): "Sometimes the Führer is somewhere else entirely. He suffers greatly." Hitler attended Schreck's funeral in Münchel-Gräfelding on 19 May 1936, and he also saw to it that Schreck's gravestone was maintained. See BA Berlin-Lichterfelde, NS 10/121. See also Hanfstaengl's note about Schreck's burial: "A. H.

in a peaked cap like Puss in Boots with his Gauleiter, office directors and other brown armadillos crowding around him. Depressing! A pack of gangsters." BSB München, Nl Hanfstaengl Ana 405, Box 27.

19   Hossbach, *Zwischen Wehrmacht und Hitler*, p. 22. See Schwerin von Krosigk's essay on Hitler's personality (*c*.1945): "His benevolence can give way to an outbreak of anger or terrifying severity with surprising suddenness"; IfZ München, ZS 145, vol. 5.

20   Krause, *10 Jahre Kammerdiener*, p. 61.

21   Ibid., p. 27. On the above see Schroeder, *Er war mein Chef*, pp. 60, 83.

22   Wiedemann, *Der Mann*, pp. 235f.; see below p. 747.

23   On 23 June 1937, Hanfstaengl responded from London to the numerous congratulations and telegrams he had received on his fiftieth birthday the previous February; BSB München, Nl. Hanfstaengl Ana 405, Box 46. The Nazi leadership were concerned that Hanfstaengl might reveal intimate details from Hitler's inner circle and tried in vain to convince him to return to Germany. See sworn statements by Julius Schaub and Wilhelm Brückner from August 1949; IfZ München, ED 100/43; Speer, *Erinnerungen*, p. 141; Hanfstaengl, *Zwischen Weissem und Braunem Haus*, pp. 362ff.; Lothar Machtan, *Hitlers Geheimnis: Das Doppelleben eines Diktators*, Berlin, 2001, pp. 343ff. Further, Goebbels, *Tagebücher*, part 1, vol. 3/2, p. 368 (entry for 11 Feb. 1937), vol. 4, pp. 47 (entry for 12 March 1937), 53 (entry for 16 March 1937), 59 (entry for 20 March 1937), 91 (entry for 13 April 1937), 97 (entry for 16 April 1937), vol. 5, p. 105 (entry for 19 Jan. 1938). See also Hanfstaengl's correspondence with Lammers, Julius Streicher and Wilhelm Brückner in December 1937 concerning Kurt Lüdecke's book *I Knew Hitler*, which had been published the previous month by Charles Scribner in New York. Hanfstaengl demanded that Hitler personally rehabilitate him, threatening to reveal things "that might not be so pleasant for certain gentlemen." BA Berlin-Lichterfelde, R 43 II/889b. See the facsimile of a handwritten, threatening letter to Hitler on 12 Feb. 1939 in Machtan, *Hitlers Geheimnis*, pp. 351–3. In August 1939 "in the name of the Führer," Martin Bormann offered to give Hanfstaengl a "suitable position" and to take over all "financial responsibilities" arising from his exile, if he agreed to return to Germany. Hanfstaengl did not take up the offer. He demanded a written document in which Hitler assumed "ultimate responsibility" for the wrong that had been done to him, which the dictator refused to provide. See Bormann to Hanfstaengl, 15 Aug. 1939 and Hanfstaengl's answer on 18 Aug. 1939; BSB München, Nl Hanfstaengl, Ana 405, Box 40.

24   See Krause, *10 Jahre Kammerdiener*, pp. 12–14.

25   See Speer, *Erinnerungen*, p. 47; Wilderotter, *Alltag der Macht*, p. 72; Sven Felix Kellerhoff, *Hitlers Berlin: Geschichte einer Hassliebe*, Berlin and Brandenburg, 2005, p. 110.

26   Dietrich, *12 Jahre mit Hitler*, p. 152.

27   See Wiedemann, *Der Mann*, p. 68; Hanfstaengl, *Zwischen Weissem und Braunem Haus*, p. 311; Dietrich, *12 Jahre mit Hitler*, p. 152.

28   Speer, *Erinnerungen*, p. 132; see Baldur von Schirach, *Ich glaubte an Hitler*, Hamburg, 1967, p. 237.

29   Krause, *10 Jahre Kammerdiener*, p. 15.

30   See Birgit Schwarz, *Geniewahn: Hitler und die Kunst*, Vienna, Cologne and Weimar, 2009, pp. 138f. See that page for a photograph of the dining room and a reproduction of the painting.

31   According to the description by Ribbentrop's private secretary, Reinhard Spitzy, *So haben wir das Reich verspielt: Bekenntnisse eines Illegalen*, 2nd edition, Munich and Vienna, 1987, p. 125. See Wilderotter, *Alltag der Macht*, p. 124.

32   See Speer, *Erinnerungen*, p. 133; Dietrich, *12 Jahre mit Hitler*, pp. 252f.; Hanfstaengl, *Zwischen Weissem und Braunem Haus*, pp. 311f.; Wiedemann, notes on "daily life"; BA Koblenz, N 1720/4.

33   Speer, *Erinnerungen*, p. 133; see Henrik Eberle and Mathias Uhl (eds), *Das Buch Hitler: Geheimdossier des NKWD für Josef W. Stalin aufgrund der Verhörprotokolle des Persönlichen Adjutanten Hitlers, Otto Günsche, und des Kammerdieners Heinz Linge, Moskau 1948/49*, Bergisch Gladbach, 2005, p. 51.

34   Dietrich, *12 Jahre mit Hitler*, p. 253. The diplomat Ulrich von Hassell noted after a meal in the Reich Chancellery in 1936: "All in attendance hung on his every word and repeated what he said." Ulrich von Hassell, *Römische Tagebücher und Briefe 1932–1938*, ed. Ulrich Schlie, Munich, 2004, p. 144 (entry for 26 July 1936). See Wiedemann's shorthand notes dated 25 Feb. 1939: "The conversation at mealtimes was conducted almost exclusively by the Führer. The others listened and agreed. It was basically impossible to raise any objections no matter how well founded they might have been." BA Koblenz, N 1720/4.

35   Albert Speer, *"Alles was ich weiss": Aus unbekannten Geheimdienstprotokollen vom Sommer 1945*, ed. Ulrich Schlie, Munich, 1999, p. 39.

36   See Speer, *Erinnerungen*, p. 138; Dietrich, *12 Jahre mit Hitler*, pp. 253f.; Hanfstaengl, *Zwischen Weissen und Braunem Haus*, p. 318; Linge, *Bis zum Untergang*, pp. 105, 120f.; Heinrich Hoffmann, *Hitler wie ich ihn sah: Aufzeichnungen seines Leibfotografen*, Munich and Berlin, 1974, pp. 170f. See also Peter Longerich, *Joseph Goebbels: A Biography*, London, 2015, pp. 251f; Wilderotter, *Alltag der Macht*, pp. 124f.

37   See Speer, *Erinnerungen*, p. 142; Schlie (ed.), *Albert Speer*, p. 39; Krause, *10 Jahre Kammerdiener*, p. 16; Schroeder, *Er war mein Chef*, p. 74; Wiedemann, *Der Mann*, pp. 69f.; Hans Baur, *Ich flog Mächtige der Erde*, Kempten im Allgäu, 1956, pp. 98f.; Dietrich, *12 Jahre mit Hitler*, p. 248.

38   See Krause, *10 Jahre Kammerdiener*, p. 19; Wiedemann, *Der Mann*, p. 77; Hanfstaengl, *Zwischen Weissem und Braunem Haus*, pp. 334f.; Baur, *Ich flog Mächtige der Erde*, pp. 128f.

39   Speer, *Erinnerungen*, p. 143; see Below, *Als Hitlers Adjutant*, p. 33; Krause, *10 Jahre Kammerdiener*, p. 19.

40   See Krause, *10 Jahre Kammerdiener*, p. 19.

41   Speer, *Erinnerungen*, p. 143; see Below, *Als Hitlers Adjutant*, p. 33.

42   Krause, *10 Jahre Kammerdiener*, p. 20. For examples see also Max Wünsche's daily diaries dated 19 June 1938 (9 p.m.): "The Führer found the film *Capriccio* particularly bad (manure of the strongest sort)." BA Berlin Lichterfelde, NS 10/125. On Hitler's favourite actors see Speer, *Erinnerungen*, p. 49.

43   For example, see Goebbels, *Tagebücher*, part 1, vol. 2/3, pp. 332 (entry for 7 Dec. 1933), 377 (entry for 24 Feb. 1934), 384 (entry for 9 March 1934); vol. 3/1, pp. 35 (entries for 16 and 18 April 1934); 50 (entry for 19 May 1934). Max Wünsche's daily diaries dated 16 June 1938: "The Propaganda Ministry is to be informed as to the Führer's opinion every time he watches a film." BA Berlin-Lichterfelde, NS 10/125. See the reports filed by Hitler's assistants about his opinions in 1938 in BA Berlin-Lichterfelde, NS 10/44. For the 1936 list of films the Propaganda Ministry sent almost every day to Schaub or Wiedemann, see BA Berlin-Lichterfelde, NS 10/42.

44   Krause, *10 Jahre Kammerdiener*, p. 21; see Wiedemann's notes on "daily life"; BA Koblenz N 1740/4; Wiedemann, *Der Mann*, p. 78

45   Krause, *10 Jahre Kammerdiener*, p. 49; Dr. Eduard Stadtler to Hitler, 13 Dec. 1933; BA Berlin-Lichterfelde, NS 10/120.

46   See Hossbach, *Zwischen Wehrmacht und Hitler*, p. 17; Krause, *10 Jahre Kammerdiener*, p. 21.

47   See Baur, *Ich flog Mächtige der Erde*, pp. 124, 127f.; Krause, *10 Jahre Kammerdiener*, p. 22; Hossbach, *Zwischen Wehrmacht und Hitler*, p. 18; Below, *Als Hitlers Adjutant*, p. 39f.; Schroeder, *Er war mein Chef*, pp. 89, 345f.; Wiedemann, *Der Mann*, pp. 75f.

48   Dietrich, *12 Jahre mit Hitler*, p. 162; see note by Fritz Wiedemann (undated): "It's an utter fabrication that Hitler's decisions were influenced by astrology, horoscopes or other such superstitions. He loathed such things." BA Koblenz, N 1720/4.

49   See the hotel bills for 1931 and 1932 for the Hotels Elephant, Dreesen, Deutscher Hof, Hospiz Baseler Hof, Hospiz Viktoria, Bube's Hotel Pension in BA Berlin-Lichterfelde, NS 26/2557. Further, Dietrich, *12 Jahre mit Hitler*, pp. 163, 177, 179, 180, 184, 191, 194.

50   See ibid., pp. 182f.; Krause, *10 Jahre Kammerdiener*, p. 22. In a general directive to upper-level Reich offices on 11 March 1936, the Propaganda Ministry ordered that "no news may be given to the press about the Führer's travels or participation in events." Only the press division of the Reich government or the press office of the NSDAP were allowed to release such information. BA Berlin-Lichterfelde, R 43 II/976e.

51   Dietrich, *12 Jahre mit Hitler*, p. 162.

52   See Linge, *Bis zum Untergang*, p. 109; Krause, *10 Jahre Kammerdiener*, p. 29.

53   Dietrich, *12 Jahre mit Hitler*, p. 202.

54   See ibid., pp. 153, 251; Below, *Als Hitlers Adjutant*, pp. 32f.; Steinert, *Hitler*, pp. 326, 333; Ian Kershaw, *Hitler 1936–1945: Nemesis*, London, 2000, p. 33. During interrogation in 1945, Albert Speer spoke of "indeterminate form of command." Schlie (ed.), *Albert Speer*, p. 29.

55   Dietrich, *12 Jahre mit Hitler*, p. 253; see Hans Frank, *Im Angesicht des Galgens: Deutung Hitlers und seiner Zeit auf Grund eigener Erlebnisse und Erkenntnisse*, Munich and Gräfelfing, 1953, pp. 332f.

56   Ernst von Weizsäcker, *Erinnerungen*, Munich, 1950, pp. 201f.; see Wiedemann's shorthand notes of 25 Feb. 1939: "After one of his long lectures, it was very difficult, if not impossible, to get clear decisions." BA Koblenz, N 1720/4.

57   Kershaw, *Hitler: Hubris*, p. 578.

58   See ibid., pp. 665–7. In his memoirs Richard Walter Darré wrote of an "everyone-for-himself battle" that maintained "equilibrium between the dynamic strengths of the men involved in it" and thus served to stabilise Hitler's power. Diaries 1945–1946, pp. 58f.; IfZ München, ED 110, vol. 1.

59   *Deutschland-Berichte der Sopade*, 1 (1934), p. 356.

60   See Hans Mommsen, "Hitlers Stellung im nationalsozialistischen Herrschaftssystem," in Gerhard Hirschfeld and Lothar Kettenacker (eds), *Der "Führerstaat": Mythos und Realität*, Stuttgart, 1981, pp. 43–5.

61   As in Sebastian Haffner, *Germany: Jekyll & Hyde. Deutschland von innen betrachtet*, Berlin, 1996, p. 36.

62   Karl Dietrich Bracher, *Zeitgeschichtliche Kontroversen um Faschismus, Totalitarismus, Demokratie*, Munich, 1976, p. 85.

63   Adolf Hitler, *Monologe im Führerhauptquartier 1941–1944: Die Aufzeichnungen Heinrich Heims*, ed. Werner Jochmann, Hamburg, 1980, p. 82 (dated 14 Oct. 1941).

64   See Otto Dietrich's testimony of 20 Sept. 1947; IfZ München, ZS 874; Dietrich, *12 Jahre mit Hitler*, p. 129: "He systematically filled posts twice and assigned overlapping tasks without defining individual responsibilities."

65   See Mommsen, "Hitlers Stellung," p. 51; Hans-Ulrich Thamer, *Verführung und Gewalt: Deutschland 1933–1945*, Berlin, 1986, p. 340; Hans-Ulrich Wehler summarises the long-running debate among scholars on the monocracy or polyarchy of the NS system in *Deutsche Gesellschaftsgeschichte 1914–1949*, Munich, 2003, pp. 623–6.

66   See above p. 490.

67   See Stefan Krings, *Hitlers Pressechef Otto Dietrich 1897–1952: Eine Biographie*, Göttingen, 2010, pp. 222ff.

68   On what follows see Lothar Gruchmann, "Die 'Reichsregierung' im Führerstaat: Stellung und Funktion des Kabinetts im nationalsozialistischen Herrschaftssystem," in Günter Doeker and Winfried Steffani (eds), *Klassenjustiz und Pluralismus: Festschrift für Ernst Fraenkel zum 75. Geburtstag*, Cologne, 1973, pp. 187–223 (figures on p. 192). See also Martin Broszat, *Der Staat Hitlers: Grundlegung und Entwicklung seiner inneren Verfassung*, Munich, 1969, pp. 350f.; *Akten der Reichskanzlei: Die Regierung Hitler*,

Vol. 5 (1938), ed. Friedrich Hartmannsgruber, Munich, 2008, p. xvi. In November 1938, Hitler told Lammers he intended to convene the cabinet again between 10 and 15 Dec., but nothing came of it. Lammers to the Reich ministers, 26 Nov. 1938; BA Berlin-Lichterfelde, NS 10/25.

69   Schwerin von Krosigk to Lennart Westberg, 24 Feb. 1976; BA Koblenz, N 1276/36.

70   Cabinet meeting on 30 Jan. 1937, *Akten der Reichskanzlei: Die Regierung. Hitler, Vol. 4 (1937)*, ed. Friedrich Hartmannsgruber, Munich, 2005, no. 23, pp. 73f.; Goebbels, *Tagebücher*, part 1, vol. 3/2, p. 353 (entry for 21 Jan. 1937).

71   See Broszat, *Der Staat Hitlers*, pp. 358f.; Ian Kershaw, *Hitler: Profiles in Power*, revised edition, London, 2000, p. 113; Wilderotter, *Alltag der Macht*, pp. 215f.

72   See Kershaw, *Hitler: Profiles in Power*, p. 136; Wilderotter, *Alltag der Macht*, pp. 216–19; Wehler, *Deutsche Gesellschaftsgeschichte 1914–1949*, pp. 633, 635.

73   See Robert Ley, "Gedanken um den Führer" (1945): "The Führer loved to see two people competing for a single area [of responsibility]. He was convinced that got results." BA Koblenz, N 1468/4. See also Albert Speer under questioning in 1945: "He largely followed the ancient principle of divide and conquer." Schlie (ed.), *Albert Speer*, p. 34.

74   *Die Regierung Hitler*, part 1, vol. 2, no. 254, p. 972; see Broszat, *Der Staat Hitlers*, pp. 328–32.

75   On Organisation Todt see Franz W. Seidler, *Die Organisation Todt: Bauen für Staat und Wehrmacht 1938–1945*, Bonn, 1998.

76   See Detlev Humann, *"Arbeitsschlacht": Arbeitsbeschaffung und Propaganda in der NS-Zeit 1933–1939*, Göttingen, 2011, pp. 366–400; Broszat, *Der Staat Hitlers*, pp. 332–4.

77   *Akten der Reichskanzlei: Die Regierung Hitler, Vol. 3 (1936)*, ed. Friedrich Hartmannsgruber, Munich, 2002, no. 72, p. 263; no. 87, p. 313; no. 97, pp. 353f.

78   Text of the law in Bernd Sösemann, with Marius Lange, *Propaganda: Medien und Öffentlichkeit in der NS-Diktatur*, Stuttgart, 2011, vol. 1, no. 373, p. 445; see also *Die Regierung Hitler*, vol. 3, no. 194, p. 732; Broszat, *Der Staat Hitlers*, pp. 334–6.

79   Broszat, *Der Staat Hitlers*, p. 336.

80   See Peter Longerich, *Heinrich Himmler: Biographie*, Munich, 2008, pp. 165–78; Robert Gerwarth, *Reinhard Heydrich: Biographie*, Munich, 2011, pp. 95, 100–2.

81   See Broszat, *Hitlers Staat*, pp. 337–40; Kershaw, *Hitler: Profiles in Power*, p. 77; Norbert Frei, *Der Führerstaat: Nationalsozialistische Herrschaft 1933 bis 1945*, new and expanded edition, Munich, 2001, p. 139.

82   See Longerich, *Heinrich Himmler*, pp. 207–9; Gerwarth, *Reinhard Heydrich*, p. 113; Broszat, *Der Staat Hitlers*, pp. 341–3; Frei, *Der Führerstaat*, pp. 139f.

83   As in Gerwarth, *Reinhard Heydrich*, p. 113.

84   Quoted in Ulrich Herbert, *Best: Biographische Studien über Radikalismus, Weltanschauung und Vernunft 1903–1989*, Bonn 1996, p. 164. On the above see Longerich, *Heinrich Himmler*, p. 213.

85   See Robert Gellateley, *The Gestapo and German Society: Enforcing Racial Policy 1933–1945*, Oxford, 1992; *idem*, "'Allwissend und allgegenwärtig'? Entstehung, Funktion und Wandel des Gestapo-Mythos," in Gerhard Paul and Klaus-Michael Mallmann (eds), *Die Gestapo: Mythos und Realität*, Darmstadt, 2003, pp. 44–70.

86   See Michael Wildt, *Generation des Unbedingten: Das Führungskorps des Reichssicherheitshauptamtes*, Hamburg, 2002, pp. 251ff.; Carsten Dams and Michael Stolle, *Die Gestapo: Herrschaft und Terror im Dritten Reich*, Munich, 2008, pp. 28–31.

87   Alfred Kube, *Pour le mérite und Hakenkreuz: Hermann Göring im Dritten Reich*, Munich, 1989, pp. 27, 52, 66.

88   "Führer Decree" of 7 Dec. 1934; ibid., p. 72. On Hitler's criticism of Göring's lifestyle see Goebbels, *Tagebücher*, part 1, vol. 2/3, pp. 232 (entry for 22 July 1933), 269 (entry for 16 Sept. 1933), 294 (entry for 19 Oct. 1933), 299 (entry for 25 Oct. 1933). See also Below, *Als Hitlers Adjutant*, pp. 59f.

89   See Kube, *Pour le mérite und Hakenkreuz*, pp. 54f., 138.

90   Schacht to Blomberg, 24 Dec. 1935; quoted in Adam Tooze, *The Wages of Destruction: The Making and Breaking of the Nazi Economy*, London, 2006, p. 209.

91   See ibid., p. 251; Kube, *Pour le mérite und Hakenkreuz*, pp. 140f.; Christopher Kopper, *Hjalmar Schacht: Aufstieg und Fall von Hitlers mächtigstem Bankier*, Munich and Vienna, 2006, pp. 266f., 306.

92   See Kube, *Pour le mérite und Hakenkreuz*, pp. 142f.; Kopper, *Hjalmar Schacht*, p. 308.

93   According to Göring's memorandum to Krogmann; Carl Vincent Krogmann, *Es ging um Deutschlands Zukunft 1932–1939: Erlebtes täglich diktiert von dem früheren Regierenden Bürgermeister in Hamburg*, Leoni am Starnberger See, 1976, pp. 272f.

94   Goebbels, *Tagebücher*, part 1, vol. 3/2, p. 74 (entry for 3 Feb. 1936); see also ibid., p. 73 (entry for 2 May 1936): "The Führer came out vigorously against Schacht. He's now in for a hard time." Speer also remembered a loud altercation between Hitler and Schacht in 1936; Speer, *Erinnerungen*, p. 111.

95   Ministerial Council meeting with Göring, 12 May 1936; *Die Regierung Hitler*, vol. 3, no. 89, pp. 317–24 (quotation on p. 320). See also Göring to the ministerial council meeting on 27 May 1936: "All measures are to be considered from the perspective of how we can be certain of being able to wage war." Ibid., no. 93, pp. 339–44 (quotation on p. 340).

96   Wilhelm Treue, "Hitlers Denkschrift zum Vierjahresplan 1936," in *Vierteljahrshefte für Zeitgeschichte*, 3 (1955), pp. 184–210 (quotation on p. 210).

97   Ministerial council meeting with Göring, 4 Sept. 1936; *Die Regierung Hitler*, vol. 3, no. 138, pp. 500–4 (quotations on pp. 503, 504). Wiedemann quoted Göring as saying in late 1936: "My Führer, if I see things correctly, a major war within the next five years is unavoidable. You surely won't object if I subordinate all the measures I take to this perspective." Wiedemann, "Einzelerinnerungen," notes made in San Francisco, 28 March 1939; BA Koblenz, N 1720/4.

98   See Kube, *Pour le mérite und Hakenkreuz*, pp. 157f.; Tooze, *The Wages of Destruction*, p. 223.

99   Goebbels, *Tagebücher*, part 1, vol. 3/2, p. 252 (entry for 15 Nov. 1936). The propaganda minister was impatient with Hitler for delaying Schacht's dismissal: "I believe the Führer won't be able to avoid getting rid of him. So let's get on with it." Ibid., vol. 4, p. 58 (entry for 19 March 1937). For his sixtieth birthday on 22 Jan. 1937, Hitler gave Schacht a valuable painting by Spitzweg. Schacht thanked Hitler the following day in an effusive telegram: "Among the many considerations I received on the day, your expression of trust in me was my greatest honour and source of joy." BA Berlin-Lichterfelde, NS 10/34.

100   Kopper, *Hjalmar Schacht*, p. 323; see Kube, *Pour le mérite und Hakenkreuz*, p. 189.

101   *Die Regierung Hitler*, vol. 4, no. 124, p. 454n6. On Hermann Göring's creation of the Reich Works see Tooze, *The Wages of Destruction*, pp. 230–9.

102   On the discussion of 20 Jan. 1939 see Hjalmar Schacht, *76 Jahre meines Lebens*, Bad Wörishofen, 1953, pp. 495f.; Ulrich von Hassell, *Vom anderen Deutschland: Aus den nachgelassenen Tagebüchern 1938–1944*, Frankfurt am Main, 1964, pp. 41f. (entry for 25 Jan. 1939). See also Goebbels, *Tagebücher*, part 1, vol. 6, p. 233 (entry for 20 Jan. 1939); Kopper, *Hjalmar Schacht*, pp. 315–18.

103   Memorandum from the Reichsbank directorate to Hitler, 7 Jan. 1939; quoted in Kopper, *Hjalmar Schacht*, pp. 326f.

104   BA Berlin-Lichterfelde, NS 6/71; see Max Domarus, *Hitler: Reden und Proklamationen 1932–1945. Vol. 1: Triumph. Part 1: 1932–1934*, Munich, 1965, p. 257.

105   See Peter Longerich, *Hitlers Stellvertreter: Führung der Partei und Kontrolle des Staatsapparats durch den Stab Hess und die Partei-Kanzlei Bormanns*, Munich, 1992, p. 8; Peter Diehl-Thiele, *Partei und Staat im Dritten Reich: Untersuchungen zum Verhältnis von NSDAP und allgemeiner Staatsverwaltung. Studienausgabe*, Munich, 1971, p. 208.

106   See Longerich, *Hitlers Stellvertreter*, pp. 10f.; Diehl-Thiele, *Partei und Staat im Dritten Reich*, pp. 208f. For Martin Bormann's biography see Jochen von Lang, *Der Sekretär: Martin*

Bormann. Der Mann, der Hitler beherrschte, 3rd revised edition, Munich and Berlin, 1987; Volker Koop, Martin Bormann: Hitlers Vollstrecker, Vienna, Cologne and Weimar, 2012.

107   On the power struggle between Hess/Bormann and Ley see Longerich, Der Stellvertreter, pp. 14–16; Diehl-Thiele, Partei und Staat im Dritten Reich, pp. 209–12.

108   Ley to Hess, 20 June 1939; quoted in Diehl-Thiele, Staat und Partei im Dritten Reich, pp. 237f.

109   Bormann to Ley, 17 Aug. 1939; cited in ibid., p. 240.

110   Text of the law of 1 Dec. 1933 in Sösemann, Propaganda, vol. 1, no. 119, p. 167.

111   Quoted in Diehl-Thiele, Partei und Staat im Dritten Reich, p. 20.

112   See Longerich, Hitlers Stellvertreter, pp. 18–20; Diehl-Thiele, Partei und Staat im Dritten Reich, pp. 231–4.

113   See Diehl-Thiele, Partei und Staat im Dritten Reich, pp. 42–4. Text of the law of 7 April 1933 in Sösemann, Propaganda, vol. 1, no. 74, p. 119.

114   Text of the law of 30 Jan. 1934 in ibid., no. 138, p. 197. See Diehl-Thiele, Partei und Staat im Dritten Reich, p. 61; Broszat, Der Staat Hitlers, p. 151.

115   Frick to Lammers, 4 June 1934; Lammers to Frick, 27 June 1934; quoted in Diehl-Thiele, Partei und Staat im Dritten Reich, p. 69; see Broszat, Der Staat Hitlers, pp. 152f.

116   See Diehl-Thiele, Staat und Partei im Dritten Reich, pp. 70–3; Broszat, Der Staat Hitlers, p. 157. Text of the laws of 30 Jan. 1935 in Sösemann, Propaganda, vol. 1, no. 234, pp. 297f.

117   Die Regierung Hitler, vol. 4, no. 21, p. 68. See Broszat, Der Staat Hitlers, p. 361.

118   Hitler, Monologe, p. 50 (dated 1/2 Aug. 1941). On Hitler's aversion to bureaucrats see, for example, Goebbels, Tagebücher, part 1, vol. 5, p. 59 (entry for 18 Dec.1937): "Lawyers are a priori idiots."

119   Frank Bajohr, Parvenüs und Profiteure: Korruption in der NS-Zeit, Frankfurt am Main, 2001, pp. 21–9 (quotation on p. 27). See also idem, "Ämter, Pfründe, Korruption," in Andreas Wirsching (ed.), Das Jahr 1933: Die nationalsozialistische Machtergreifung und die deutsche Gesellschaft, Göttingen, 2009, p. 191. In a letter to Hitler on 4 Jan. 1935, a man from Leipzig complained that favouritism was shown to "old street fighters" when jobs were handed out. Without being a member of the party, it was impossible to get work. "This is a situation," the man wrote, "that the leading heads of the NSDAP used to condemn in the sharpest terms as the economy of socialist party membership." BA Berlin-Lichterfelde, NS 51/73.

120   Haffner, Germany: Jekyll & Hyde, p. 43.

121   Guido Knopp, Geheimnisse des "Dritten Reiches," Munich, 2011, pp. 146f. (see also the facsimile of the tax demand of 20 Oct. 1934). On Hitler's tax exemption see also Wulf C. Schwarzwäller, Hitlers Geld: Vom armen Kunstmaler zum millionenschweren Führer, Vienna, 1998, pp. 158–60.

122   See Gerd R. Ueberschär and Winfried Vogel, Dienen und Verdienen: Hitlers Geschenke an seine Eliten, Frankfurt am Main, 1999, pp. 39–52, 92; Speer, Erinnerungen, p. 100; Below, Als Hitlers Adjutant, p. 83.

123   See Schwarzwäller, Hitlers Geld, pp. 195–8; Knopp, Geheimnisse des "Dritten Reiches," pp. 178f.; Speer, Erinnerungen, pp. 100f.; Dietrich, 12 Jahre mit Hitler, p. 211; Koop, Martin Bormann, pp. 25, 34f.

124   See Bajohr, Parvenüs und Profiteure, pp. 62–70; Speer, Erinnerungen, p. 231.

125   See Hanfstaengl, Zwischen Weissem und Braunem Haus, p. 325: "By the summer of 1933 party comrades, whom I had visited for years in modest top-floor apartments, had moved into splendid, luxurious villas and were throwing their weight around as party big-wigs."

126   Wiedemann, Der Mann, p. 196. When Wiedemann spoke to Hitler in the summer of 1935 about the demoralising effects of rampant corruption, Hitler answered: "Oh, Wiedemann, people always think I can act completely freely and do whatever I please. But I'm only a human being who is driven by destiny, whose actions are in some respects prescribed." Wiedemann's shorthand notes dated 25 Feb. 1939; BA Koblenz, N 1720/4.

127 Albert Speer, *Spandauer Tagebücher*, Munich, 2002, p. 202 (entry for 16 March 1949).

128 Domarus, *Hitler*, vol. 1, part 2, p. 719 (dated 7 Sept. 1937).

129 Speech in the House of German Art in Munich, 10 Dec. 1938; ibid., p. 983. See Wiedemann, *Der Mann*, p. 88.

130 Adolf Hitler, *Mein Kampf. Vol. 1: Eine Abrechnung*, 7th edition, Munich, 1933, pp. 290f.

131 Rudolf Hess, *Briefe 1908–1933*, ed. Rüdiger Hess, Munich and Vienna, 1987, p. 327 (dated 18 May 1924). Even prior to the 1923 putsch, during a social event at the Scheubner-Richters, Hitler had effused about the construction projects he had in mind for Berlin. Transcript of an interview with Mathilde Scheubner-Richter dated 9 July 1952; IfZ München, ZS 292.

132 Hess, *Briefe*, p. 369 (dated 7 July 1925), p. 395 (dated 18 Dec. 1928).

133 Goebbels, *Tagebücher*, part 1, vol. 1/2, p. 113 (entry for 25 July 1926); vol. 2/1, p. 256 (entry for 9 Oct. 1930); vol. 2/2, pp. 116f. (entry for 5 Oct. 1931).

134 Adolf Hitler, *Reden, Schriften, Anordnungen—Februar 1925 bis Januar 1933. Vol. 3: Zwischen den Reichstagswahlen Juli 1928–September 1930. Part 2: März 1929–Dezember 1929*, ed. Klaus A. Lankheit, Munich, 1994, doc. 21, p. 192 (dated 9 April 1929).

135 Frank, *Im Angesicht des Galgens*, p. 130.

136 Domarus, *Hitler*, vol. 1, part 1, p. 257 (dated 22 April 1933).

137 Speer, *Erinnerungen*, p. 71; see also Speer, *Spandauer Tagebücher*, p. 135 (entry for 28 Dec. 1947): "He wanted to construct buildings for all eternity." An article prepared by the Propaganda Ministry for *Time* magazine about Hitler as the initiator of massive construction projects read: "National Socialism wants to build its own stone monuments to last for centuries, nay, millennia." Helmuth v. Feldmann to Wiedemann, 31 Jan. 1938 with the article enclosed; BA Koblenz, N 1720/6.

138 Speer, *Erinnerungen*, p. 44.

139 As in Fest, *Speer*, p. 63.

140 The theory of an erotic element to Hitler and Speer's relationship was first presented in Alexander Mitscherlich, "Hitler blieb ihm ein Rätsel: Die Selbstblendung Albert Speers," in Adalbert Reif, *Albert Speer: Kontroversen um ein deutsches Phänomen*, Munich, 1978, pp. 466f.; see also Fest, *Hitler*, p. 716; *idem*, *Speer*, p. 60; Gitta Sereny, *Albert Speer: His Battle with the Truth*, new edition, London, 1996, pp. 109, 138f. In a letter to Hannah Arendt on 5 Jan. 1971, Fest wrote: "No doubt there was a strong erotic component." Hannah Arendt and Joachim Fest, *Eichmann war von empörender Dummheit: Gespräche und Briefe*, eds Ursula Ludz and Thomas Wild, Munich and Zurich, 2011, p. 96.

141 Speer, *Spandauer Tagebücher*, p. 128 (entry for 10 Dec. 1947).

142 Ibid., p. 609 (entry for 19 Feb. 1964). The Faust/Mephisto analogy in Speer, *Erinnerungen*, p. 44. In his conversations with Fest, Speer repeatedly declared that he had fallen "head over heels" for Hitler. Joachim Fest, *Die unbeantwortbaren Fragen: Notizen über Gespräche mit Albert Speer zwischen 1966 und 1981*, Reinbek bei Hamburg, 2005, p. 30; see ibid., p. 196.

143 Albert Speer, "Die Bauten des Führers (1936)"; reprinted in Heinrich Breloer, with Rainer Zimmer, *Die Akte Speer: Spuren eines Kriegsverbrechers*, Berlin, 2006, pp. 41–8 (quotation on p. 41).

144 Speer, *Erinnerungen*, pp. 67f.; 77.

145 See Josef Henke, "Die Reichsparteitage der NSDAP in Nürnberg 1933–1938: Planung, Organisation, Propaganda," in *Aus der Arbeit des Bundesarchivs*, ed. Heinz Boberach and Hans Booms, Boppard, 1977, p. 496; Centrum Industriekultur Nürnberg (ed.), *Kulissen der Gewalt: Das Reichsparteitagsgelände in Nürnberg*, Munich, 1992, pp. 41f.

146 Goebbels, *Tagebücher*, part 1, vol. 3/1, p. 350 (entry for 19 Dec. 1935). On Hitler's visits to Nuremberg see Dietrich, *12 Jahre mit Hitler*, pp. 173f.; Henke, *Die Reichsparteitage*, pp. 406f.; Centrum Industriekultur (ed.), *Kulissen der Gewalt*, p. 45.

147 Goebbels, *Tagebücher*, part 1, vol. 4, p. 305 (entry for 10 Sept. 1937). Hitler told his finance minister Schwerin von Krosigk that while it was Krosigk's duty to voice his

concerns "he would never let his plans fail for lack of funds." Schwerin von Krosigk to Lennart Westberg, 24 Feb. 1976; BA Koblenz, N 1276/36.

148   See Speer, *Erinnerungen*, pp. 8of.; Fest, *Speer*, p. 83.

149   Goebbels, *Tagebücher*, part 1, vol. 3/2, p. 280. See Jost Dülffer, Jochen Thies and Josef Henke, *Hitlers Städte: Baupolitik im Dritten Reich. Eine Dokumentation*, Cologne and Vienna, 1978, pp. 223–8 (minutes of Professor Ruff's presentation of his plans for the Nuremberg Congress Hall to the Führer in the Reich Chancellery, 1 June 1934).

150   Domarus, *Hitler*, vol. 1, part 2, p. 527; see Goebbels, *Tagebücher*, part 1, vol. 3/1, p. 291 (entry for 13 Sept. 1935).

151   Speer, *Erinnerungen*, p. 82.

152   For this connection see Jochen Thies, *Architekt der Weltherrschaft: Die "Endziele" Hitlers*, Düsseldorf, 1976, particularly pp. 69, 103f.

153   Speer, *Erinnerungen*, p. 84.

154   See Centrum Industriekultur (ed.), *Kulissen der Gewalt*, pp. 44f.; Henke, *Die Reichsparteitage*, pp. 403f.

155   See Dülffer et al., *Hitlers Städte*, pp. 159ff., 191ff., 251ff.; Michael Früchtel, *Der Architekt Hermann Giesler: Leben und Werk 1898–1987*, Munich, 2008, pp. 145ff., 284ff.; Speer, *Fest*, pp. 118f.; for Hamburg see Goebbels, *Tagebücher*, part 1, vol. 3/2, p. 322 (entry for 9 Jan. 1937).

156   Report on the meeting in the Reich Chancellery, 19 Sept. 1933; Dülffer et al., *Hitlers Städte*, pp. 90–3 (quotation on p. 92).

157   Minutes of the meeting in the Reich Chancellery, 29 March 1934; ibid., pp. 97–9 (quotations on pp. 97, 99).

158   Minutes of the meeting in the Reich Chancellery, 28 June 1935; ibid., pp. 112–16 (quotation on p. 115). On Hitler's meetings with the Berlin city council between 1933 and 1935 see Kellerhoff, *Hitlers Berlin*, pp. 122–4; Thomas Friedrich, *Die miss-brauchte Hauptstadt: Hitler und Berlin*, Berlin, 2007, pp. 458–60. 464–9, 475f.

159   Speer, *Erinnerungen*, pp. 87f.; see Fest, *Die unbeantwortbaren Fragen*, pp. 31f.

160   Goebbels, *Tagebücher*, part 1, vol. 3/2, p. 253 (entry for 16 Nov. 1936). In a similar vein see ibid., pp. 317 (entry for 5 Jan. 1937), 343 (entry for 25 Jan. 1937).

161   According to Speer's memoirs, Hitler was initially "almost shocked" by the blueprints for the Great Hall and was sceptical about whether the dome could bear the weight it had to support. But when Speer assured him that the structural questions had been examined and the plans deemed sound, Hitler "enthusiastically approved" them. Fest, *Die unbeantwortbaren Fragen*, p. 79.

162   See Speer, *Erinnerungen*, p. 90; Fest, *Speer*, p. 95. On Speer's appointment see Goebbels, *Tagebücher*, part 1, vol. 3/2, p. 354 (entry for 31 Jan. 1937).

163   Speer, *Erinnerungen*, pp. 147d.; see Sereny, *Albert Speer*, pp. 144f. (recollections of Willi Schelkes and Rudolf Wolters, two of Speer's colleagues).

164   Speer, *Erinnerungen*, p. 148; see also *idem, Spandauer Tagebücher*, p. 551 (entry for 21 Jan. 1962); Sereny, *Albert Speer*, p. 158.

165   See Speer, *Erinnerungen*, pp. 89f.; Goebbels, *Tagebücher*, part 1, vol. 4, p. 52 (entry for 15 March 1937): "It will be a street of the most monumental proportions. We will immortalise ourselves in stone."

166   See Speer, *Erinnerungen*, pp. 149f.

167   Goebbels, *Tagebücher*, part 1, vol. 4, p. 100 (entry for 20 April 1937). See Speer, *Erinnerungen*, pp. 167f.; Hitler, *Monologe*, p. 101 (dated 21/22 Oct. 1941): "The Great Hall will be so large that it could swallow up St. Peter's Cathedral and the square in front."

168   Speer, *Erinnerungen*, pp. 171–4 (quotation on p. 173); see *idem, Spandauer Tagebücher*, p. 167 (entry for 24 Oct. 1948).

169   See Jürgen Trimborn, *Arno Breker: Der Künstler und die Macht. Die Biographie*, Berlin, 2011, pp. 144ff., 204ff.

170   Speer, *Erinnerungen*, p. 153.

171   Goebbels, *Tagebücher*, part 1, vol. 4, p. 52 (entry for 15 March 1937).

172   Speer, *Erinnerungen*, p. 175; see *idem, Spandauer Tagebücher*, p. 247 (entry for 2 Nov. 1950).

173   Sereny, *Albert Speer*, p. 186.

174   Hitler, *Monologe*, p. 101 (dated 21/22 Oct. 1941), p. 318 (dated 11/12 March 1942). On the renaming of Berlin as "Germania," see *Hitlers Tischgespräche im Führerhauptquartier*, ed. Henry Picker, Stuttgart, 1976, p. 366 (dated 8 June 1942).

175   Goebbels, *Tagebücher*, part 1, vol. 5, p. 345 (entry for 15 June 1938). On the above see the German News Agency, 27 Jan. 1938. The programme for the redesign of Berlin is reprinted in Dülffer et al., *Hitlers Städte*, pp. 134–41; see also the articles in *Deutsche Bauzeitung*, 2 Feb. 1938, in the weekly newspapers *Koralle*, 22 May 1938, and *Berliner Illustrierte*, 15 Dec. 1938, quoted in Friedrich, *Die missbrauchte Hauptstadt*, pp. 486–9.

176   Speer, *Spandauer Tagebücher*, p. 31 (entry for 1 Nov. 1946). See Schlie (ed.), *Albert Speer*, p. 57: "He always said his fondest wish was to see his construction projects completed." Hitler intended to celebrate completion in 1950 with a World Fair to be held at "a gigantic site along the River Havel." Goebbels, *Tagebücher*, part 1, vol. 4, p. 347 (entry for 7 Oct. 1937).

177   Goebbels, *Tagebücher*, part 1, vol. 5, p. 333 (entry for 4 June 1938).

178   Minutes of a meeting with the General Building Inspector on 14 Sept. 1938; reprinted in Breloer, *Die Akte Speer*, pp. 92–5 (quotations on pp. 93, 94). See Susanne Willems, *Der entsiedelte Jude: Albert Speers Wohnungsmarktpolitik für den Berliner Hauptstadtbau*, Berlin, 2000, pp. 71ff.

179   Willems, *Der entsiedelte Jude*, pp. 86f.

180   Facsimile of the decree of 15 June 1940 in Breloer, *Die Akte Speer*, p. 100. See Speer, *Erinnerungen*, pp. 188, 192.

181   See Schmidt, *Albert Speer*, pp. 199–206; Willems, *Der entsiedelte Jude*, pp. 158ff.; Breloer, *Die Akte Speer*, pp. 199–206.

182   Willi Schelkes, notes on a "visit from the Führer" dated 15 March 1941; reprinted in Breloer, *Die Akte Speer*, pp. 121–4 (quotations on pp. 122, 123, 124).

183   Speer, *Erinnerungen*, p. 116.

184   See Angela Schönberger, *Die Neue Reichskanzlei: Zum Zusammenhang von national-sozialistischer Ideologie und Architektur*, Berlin, 1981, pp. 37–44; Dietmar Arnold, *Neue Reichskanzlei und "Führerbunker": Legende und Wirklichkeit*, Berlin, 2005, pp. 62–7. On the demolition of the Gau headquarters see Goebbels, *Tagebücher*, part 1, vol. 5, pp. 41f. (entry for 8 Dec. 1937).

185   Hitler's speech at the topping-out ceremony of the New Chancellery, 2 Aug. 1938; Schönberger, *Die Neue Reichskanzlei*, pp. 177–82 (quotation on pp. 179f.).

186   Hitler's speech at the official opening of the New Chancellery, 9 Jan. 1939; ibid., pp. 183–6 (quotation on p. 186). On the opening celebrations see the German News Agency report of 9 Jan. 1939; BA Berlin-Lichterfelde, R 43 II/1054.

187   Speer, *Erinnerungen*, p. 117. On the rooms in the New Chancellery see the brochure, "Der Erweiterungsbau der Reichskanzlei: Einweihung am 9. Januar 1939," as well as Otto Meissner's instructions of 22 Feb. 1939 with reference to the description of the Führer's official rooms in the rebuilt Chancellery; BA Berlin-Lichterfelde, R 43 II/1054. See also Fest, *Speer*, pp. 144–6; Wilderotter, *Alltag der Macht*, pp. 310–12; Schönberger, *Die Neue Reichskanzlei*, pp. 87–114; Arnold, *Neue Reichskanzlei*, pp. 93–100. On the Breker sculptures see Trimborn, *Arno Breker*, pp. 222f.

188   Speer, *Erinnerungen*, p. 128.

18 The Berghof Society and the Führer's Mistress

1   *Die Tagebücher von Joseph Goebbels. Part 1: Aufzeichnungen 1923–1941*, ed. Elke Fröhlich, Munich, 1998, vol. 3/2, p. 132 (entry for 17 July 1936). See ibid., p. 123 (entry for

4 July 1936): "The Führer is happy because the Berghof is finished. I will be with him as of 15 July with my family."

2   Albert Speer, *Erinnerungen: Mit einem Essay von Jochen Thies*, Frankfurt am Main and Berlin, 1993, p. 59. On the purchase of Haus Wachenfeld see the title deeds of the Munich Notary's Office VI dated 26 June 1933 and Max Amann's letter to Julius Schaub, 28 May 1934; BA Berlin-Lichterfelde, NS 10/117. See also Anton Joachimsthaler, *Hitlers Liste: Ein Dokument persönlicher Beziehungen*, Munich, 2003, p. 294; Ulrich Chaussy, *Nachbar Hitler: Führerkult und Heimatzerstörung am Obersalzberg*, 6th revised and extended edition, Berlin, 2007, p. 44.

3   See Speer, *Erinnerungen*, p. 99; Chaussy, *Nachbar Hitler*, pp. 110f., 137; Joachimsthaler, *Hitlers Liste*, p. 304. See the architect Alois Degano's final bill of 17 July 1936; BA Berlin-Lichterfelde, NS 10/117.

4   For full details see Chaussy, *Nachbar Hitler*, pp. 94–107, 121–30; Otto Dietrich, *12 Jahre mit Hitler*, Munich, 1955, pp. 211–14; Speer, *Erinnerungen*, p. 98; Jochen von Lang, *Der Sekretär: Martin Bormann. Der Mann, der Hitler beherrschte*, 3rd revised edition, Munich and Berlin, 1987, pp. 102, 105f.; Volker Koop, *Martin Bormann: Hitlers Vollstrecker*, Vienna, Cologne and Weimar, 2012, pp. 27, 31, 33.

5   Handwritten memoirs of Therese Linke, cook on the Obersalzberg from 1933 to 1939 (undated, post-1945); IfZ München, ZS 3135. See Dietrich, *12 Jahre mit Hitler*, pp. 212f.; Christa Schroeder, *Er war mein Chef: Aus dem Nachlass der Sekretärin von Adolf Hitler*, ed. Anton Joachimsthaler, 3rd edition, Munich and Vienna, 1985, p. 175; Speer, *Erinnerungen*, pp. 60f., 98; Karl Wilhelm Krause, *10 Jahre Kammerdiener bei Hitler*, Hamburg, 1949, p. 40; Heike B. Görtemaker, *Eva Braun: Leben mit Hitler*, Munich, 2010, pp. 147.

6   Dietrich, *12 Jahre mit Hitler*, p. 212.

7   Ibid., p. 211. Hitler's servant Heinz Linge quoted the Führer saying of Bormann: "This mole has moved mountains overnight." Heinz Linge, *Bis zum Untergang: Als Chef des Persönlichen Dienstes bei Hitler*, ed. Werner Maser, Munich, 1982, p. 44.

8   Goebbels, *Tagebücher*, part 1, vol. 3/2, pp. 222 (entry for 22 Oct. 1936), 316 (entry for 5 Jan. 1937). On Bormann's rise see Robert Ley, "Gedanken um den Führer" (1945); BA Koblenz, N 1468/4; transcript of an interview with Nicolaus von Below dated 7 Jan. 1952; IfZ München, ZS 7.

9   See Horst Möller, Volker Dahm and Hartmut Mehringer (eds), *Die tödliche Utopie: Bilder, Texte, Dokumente. Daten zum Dritten Reich*, 3rdrd edition, Munich, 2001, pp. 42, 68; Chaussy, *Nachbar Hitler*, pp. 83f.; Gitta Sereny, *Albert Speer: His Battle with the Truth*, new edition, London, 1996, pp. 117f.; Margarete Nissen, *Sind Sie die Tochter Speer?*, Munich, 2005, p. 16.

10 See Speer, *Erinnerungen*, pp. 99f., 101f., 103f.; Dietrich, *12 Jahre mit Hitler*, p. 223; Schroeder, *Er war mein Chef*, pp. 176f.; Albert Speer, *"Alles was ich weiss": Aus unbekannten Geheimdienstprotokollen vom Sommer 1945*, ed. Ulrich Schlie, Munich, 1999, pp. 237f.; Joachim Fest, *Hitler: Eine Biographie*, Frankfurt am Main, Berlin and Vienna, 1973, pp. 713f., 722. For Gerdy Troost's biography and her role in the Third Reich see Timo Nüsslein, *Paul Ludwig Troost 1878–1934*, Vienna, Cologne and Weimar, 2012, pp. 175–83.

11 Traudl Junge, *Bis zur letzten Stunde: Hitlers Sekretärin erzählt ihr Leben*, Munich, 2002, p. 91. On Hitler's paintings in the Great Hall see Birgit Schwarz, *Geniewahn: Hitler und die Kunst*, Vienna, Cologne and Weimar, 2009, pp. 159–73.

12 See Schroeder, *Er war mein Chef*, p. 177; Junge, *Bis zur letzten Stunde*, pp. 67, 69f.; *Das Hitler-Bild: Die Erinnerungen des Fotografen Heinrich Hoffmann*, ed. Joe J. Heydecker, St. Pölten and Salzburg, 2008, p. 176; Joachimsthaler, *Hitlers Liste*, pp. 501, 503.

13 See Schroeder, *Er war mein Chef*, pp. 178f.; Junge, *Bis zur letzten Stunde*, pp. 67f.; Heinrich Hoffmann, *Hitler wie ich ihn sah: Aufzeichnungen seines Leibfotographen*, Munich and Berlin, 1974, p. 159; Speer, *Erinnerungen*, p. 102.

14   Rochus Misch, *Der letzte Zeuge: "Ich war Hitlers Telefonist, Kurier und Leibwächter,"* Zurich and Munich, 2008, p. 96. See also Anna Plaim and Kurt Kuch, *Bei Hitlers: Zimmermädchen Annas Erinnerungen*, Munich, 2005, pp. 38f.; Joachimsthaler, *Hitlers Liste*, p. 458.

15   See Nerin E. Gun, *Eva Braun-Hitler: Leben und Schicksal*, Velbert und Kettwig, 1968, p. 82.

16   Quoted in Görtemaker, *Eva Braun*, p. 92.

17   Hans Baur, *Ich flog Mächtige der Erde*, Kempten im Allgäu, 1956, p. 113.

18   Speer, *Erinnerungen*, p. 59.

19   Ibid.; contrary to this see Gun, *Eva Braun-Hitler*, p. 85; Schroeder, *Er war mein Chef*, p. 172; Joachimsthaler, *Hitlers Liste*, pp. 300, 442.

20   See the receipts in BA Berlin-Lichterfelde, NS 26/2557 (for 1932), NS 26/115 und NS 26/120 (for 1933/34).

21   As in Gun, *Eva Braun-Hitler*, pp. 91f.; see Schroeder, *Er war mein Chef*, p. 164; Joachimsthaler, *Hitlers Liste*, pp. 300, 442.

22   See, with the party rally in 1935 incorrectly dated, Schroeder, *Er war mein Chef*, p. 165; Ernst Hanfstaengl, *Zwischen Weissem und Braunem Haus: Erinnerungen eines politischen Aussenseiters*, Munich, 1970, p. 165; Joachimsthaler, *Hitlers Liste*, pp. 301f., 456f.; Görtemaker, *Eva Braun*, pp. 144f.; Guido Knopp, *Geheimnisse des "Dritten Reiches,"* Munich, 2011, p. 313. Gun (*Eva Braun-Hitler*, p. 94) does not discuss why Angela Raubal was removed from the Berghof. She also cites the wrong year, 1936.

23   Goebbels, *Tagebücher*, part 1, vol. 3/1, p. 122 (entry for 19 Oct. 1934). On 28 Aug. 1934, Joseph and Magda Goebbels, together with their daughter Helga, visited the Obersalzberg and met Frau Raubal, who was "very nice" to them. Ibid., p. 99 (29 Aug. 1934). In mid-October 1934, Goebbels wondered why Hitler was no longer inviting him and his wife to dinner: "We have the feeling that someone has turned him against us. That has hurt us both." Ibid., p. 119 (entry for 15 Oct. 1934).

24   Ibid., pp. 216f. (entry for 13 April 1935).

25   Ibid., p. 329 (entry for 15 Nov. 1935).

26   Angela Hammitzsch to Rudolf Hess, 22 May 1936; BA Bern, Nl Hess, J1.211-1993/300, Box 6. Hess invited Hitler's half-sister to stay with him when she came to Munich. Hess to Angela Hammitzsch, 22 June 1936; ibid. On Angela Raubal's wedding see Schroeder, *Er war mein Chef*, p. 165; Joachimsthaler, *Hitlers Liste*, p. 303.

27   See Goebbels, *Tagebücher*, part 1, vol. 4, p. 59 (entry for 19 March 1937): "Had a long talk with Frau Raubal. The Führer's reserve hurts a lot. Otherwise she's quite happy with her husband." In June 1937, Hitler and Goebbels met with Angela Hammitzsch in Dresden and had an "enjoyable lively evening." Ibid., p. 196 (25 June 1937). According to Therese Linke, Angela Raubal also spent a few days again on the Obersalzberg with her husband, presumably in the late 1930s; IfZ München, ZS 3135. Max Wünsche's appointment book contains an entry for Frau Hammitzsch's visit on 7 Oct. 1939. BA Berlin-Lichterfelde, NS 10/591.

28   As in Görtemaker, *Eva Braun*, p. 116; see Knopp, *Geheimnisse des "Dritten Reiches,"* pp. 313f.

29   Goebbels, *Tagebücher*, part 1, vol. 3/1, p. 177 (entry for 31 Jan. 1935). See ibid., p. 179 (entry for 4 Feb. 1935): "Long talk with the Führer. Personal things. He spoke of women, marriage, love and loneliness. I'm probably the only one he talks to like this."

30   Reprinted in Gun, *Eva Braun-Hitler*, pp. 190f.; facsimile of the letter ibid., between pp. 192 and 193. On the existence of the bunker in Wasserburgstrasse 12 see ibid., p. 121.

31   See Görtemaker, *Eva Braun*, pp. 101f.

32   Ilse Fucke-Michels to Nerin E. Gun, 8 April 1967; facsimile in Gun, *Eva Braun-Hitler*, p. 69.

33   Werner Maser, *Adolf Hitler: Legende—Mythos—Wirklichkeit*, 12th edition, Munich and
      Esslingen, 1989, pp. 332–75. Maser introduces the diary with the remark that it has
      "more to say about Hitler's relations with women than most substantial 'reports'
      and interpretations by 'initiated' observers and ostensibly well-informed biographers'
      (p. 331). Anna Maria Sigmund, too, sees the fragmentary diary as a "mirror of
      Eva Braun's psyche"; Anna Maria Sigmund, *Des Führers bester Freund: Adolf Hitler,
      seine Nichte Geli Raubal und der "Ehrenarier" Emil Maurice—Eine Dreiecksbeziehung*,
      Munich, 2003, p. 170.

34   Joachimsthaler, *Hitlers Liste*, p. 444; see also on p. 447 a sample of Eva Braun's
      handwriting. See also Eva Braun to Ilse Hess from the Obersalzberg, 2 Jan. [1938];
      BA Bern, Nl Hess, J2.211-1993/300, Box 2. Facsimile in Görtemaker, *Eva Braun*, p. 90.

35   See Görtemaker, *Eva Braun*, pp. 313f. (notes 119–22, 125, 131). Wilhelm Brückner's
      extremely terse entries in his notebook for the year 1935 support Eva Braun's claim.
      The notebook, which historians have yet to analyse thoroughly, is preserved at the
      Bundesarchiv Berlin-Lichterfelde, NS 26/1209.

36   Entry dated 6 Feb. 1935; Gun, *Eva Braun-Hitler*, pp. 70f.; Maser, *Adolf Hitler*, pp. 332–7.

37   Entry dated 18 Feb. 1935; Gun, *Eva Braun-Hitler*, pp. 73f.; Maser, *Adolf Hitler*, pp. 340–5.

38   Entry dated 4 March 1935; Gun, *Eva Braun-Hitler*, pp. 74f,; Maser, *Adolf Hitler*,
      pp. 344–51. On Goebbels's presence in Munich see Goebbels, *Tagebücher*, part 1, vol.
      3/1, pp. 193f. (entry for 4 March 1935).

39   Entry dated 11 March 1935; Gun, *Eva Braun-Hitler*, pp. 75f.; Maser, *Adolf Hitler*,
      pp. 352–7.

40   Entry dated 16 March 1935; Gun, *Eva Braun-Hitler*, p. 36; Maser, *Adolf Hitler*, pp. 356f.

41   Entry dated 1 April 1935; Gun, *Eva Braun-Hitler*, p. 76; Maser, *Adolf Hitler*, pp. 358f.
      Speer told Gitta Sereny that he also saw Eva Braun "blush deeply" over dinner at
      the Hotel Vier Jahreszeiten "when Hitler silently handed her an envelope as he
      passed." Braun later told Speer that there was money in the envelope and Hitler
      had also behaved like that on other occasions in public. Sereny, *Albert Speer*, p. 192f.
      In conversation with Joachim Fest, Speer said the incident happened in 1938;
      Joachim Fest, *Die unbeantwortbaren Fragen: Notizen über Gespräche mit Albert Speer
      zwischen 1966 und 1981*, Reinbek bei Hamburg, 2005, p. 84. It is possible that Speer's
      memory was faulty and that he recalled an incident in 1935 as recorded by Eva
      Braun in her "diary."

42   Entry dated 29 April 1935; Gun, *Eva Braun-Hitler*, p. 76; Maser, *Adolf Hitler*, pp. 360f.

43   Entry dated 10 May 1935; Gun, *Eva Braun-Hitler*, p. 77; Maser, *Adolf Hitler*, pp. 362f.

44   Goebbels, *Tagebücher*, part 1, vol. 3/2, p. 205 (entry for 6 Oct. 1936); see ibid., pp. 206
      (entry for 7 Oct. 1936): "The Führer is very moved." On Unity Mitford, see her
      letters to her sister Diana from 1935 to 1939, which she signed with "Heil Hitler,"
      in Charlotte Mosley (ed.), *The Mitfords: Letters between Six Sisters*, London, 2007,
      pp. 54–6, 63–5, 68f., 75f., 113, 116, 125–7, 128f., 130–2, 137; see also Joachimsthaler, *Hitlers
      Liste*, pp. 507–40; Knopp, *Geheimnisse des "Dritten Reiches,"* pp. 306–11.

45   See Nicolaus von Below, *Als Hitlers Adjutant 1937–45*, Mainz, 1980, p. 82. On 3 Sept.
      1939, after Britain declared war on Germany, Mitford tried to commit suicide. This
      took place in Munich and not, as is often claimed, on a park bench in the English
      Garden, but at Königinstrasse 15. She was taken to hospital, badly injured and with
      a bullet in her brain. Hitler paid for her treatment and visited Mitford in hospital
      on 8 Nov. 1939. In Dec. 1939, she was transferred to a clinic in Bern, and in January
      1940 she returned to England. She died on 28 May 1948 from the aftereffects of her
      attempted suicide. See Joachimsthaler, *Hitlers Liste*, pp. 534–40; Knopp, *Geheimnisse
      des "Dritten Reiches,"* p. 311.

46   See Görtemaker, *Eva Braun*, pp. 109–11. Sigrid von Laffert was also among the
      women who caught Hitler's eye. In a handwritten letter from the spa resort of Bad
      Doberan on 20 July 1934, she thanked Hitler "for the charmingly done-up hamper
      with its wonderful contents and for your kind lines . . . They made me hugely

happy." BA Berlin-Lichterfelde, NS 10/123. In Wilhelm Brückner's notebook for 1935, Laffert's birthday on 18 Jan. was explicitly noted. BA Berlin-Lichterfelde, NS 26/1209. Max Wünsche wrote on 16 June 1938 (7:30 p.m.): "Tea with Baroness Laffert." BA Berlin-Lichterfelde, NS 10/125. In July 1938, Hitler paid for an operation that Laffert required. See the exchange of letters between her and Fritz Wiedemann in BA Koblenz, N 1720/7. Max Wünsche's calendar shows visits by Sigrid von Laffert to Hitler for 13 Dec. and 19 Dec. 1939. BA Berlin-Lichterfelde, NS 10/591. Laffert married the diplomat Johann Bernhard von Welczek in December 1940. On Victoria von Dirksen and Sigrid von Laffert see Joachimsthaler, *Hitlers Liste*, pp. 203–12; Martha Schad, *Sie liebten den Führer: Wie Frauen Hitler verehrten*, Munich, 2009, pp. 55–77.

47   On 23 May 1935 Wilhelm Brückner just noted "Berlin Operation"; BA Berlin-Lichterfelde, NS 26/1209. On the operation see Hans-Joachim Neumann and Henrik Eberle, *War Hitler krank? Ein abschliessender Befund*, Bergisch-Gladbach, 2009, pp. 172f.; Ulf Schmidt, *Hitlers Arzt Karl Brandt: Medizin und Macht im Dritten Reich*, Berlin, 2009, pp. 133f.; Görtemaker, *Eva Braun*, p. 111. Goebbels, *Tagebücher*, part 1, vol. 3/1, p. 238 (entry for 27 May 1935): "Hitler can't speak at all. He's in treatment. He writes down what he wants to say"; p. 250 (21 June 1935): "He's completely recovered. We were afraid he had throat cancer. It was just a harmless growth. Thank, thank, thank God!" During the campaigns of 1932, having overtaxed his voice in the past, Hitler hired the opera singer Paul Stieber-Devrient to help him improve his breathing technique. See Werner Maser (ed.), *Paul Devrient: Mein Schüler Adolf Hitler: Das Tagebuch seines Lehrers*, Munich, 2003.

48   Entry dated 28 May 1935; Gun, *Eva Braun-Hitler*, p. 78; Maser, *Adolf Hitler*, pp. 368–75.

49   See Gun, *Eva Braun-Hitler*, pp. 78f.; Görtemaker, *Eva Braun*, p. 112.

50   Goebbels, *Tagebücher*, part 1, pp. 239 (entry for 29 May 1935), 242 (entry for 5 June 1935): "The Führer is staying in Munich." See also Wilhelm Brückner's diary entries between 27 May and 12 June 1935; BA Berlin-Lichterfelde, NS 26/1209.

51   See Görtemaker, *Eva Braun*, p. 112; Joachimsthaler, *Hitlers Liste*, pp. 424–6. In a letter to Hitler on 7 Sept. 1935 Friedrich Braun complained that his family had been "torn apart . . . because my two daughters Eva and Gretl have moved into an apartment you put at their disposal, and I as the head of the family have been presented with a fait accompli." Gun, *Eva Braun-Hitler*, pp. 87f.

52   See Görtemaker, *Eva Braun*, pp. 204f.; Joachimsthaler, *Hitlers Liste*, pp. 459–62; Gun, *Eva Braun-Hitler*, pp. 116f.

53   See Görtemaker, *Eva Braun*, p. 202; Hoffmann, *Hitler wie ich ihn sah*, p. 136.

54   On the furnishing of Eva Braun's villa see Gun, *Eva Braun-Hitler*, pp. 117–20; Sigmund, *Die Frauen der Nazis*, pp. 172f.

55   See Below, *Als Hitlers Adjutant*, pp. 81, 83; Henrik Eberle and Mathias Uhl (eds), *Das Buch Hitler: Geheimdossier des NKWD für Josef W. Stalin aufgrund der Verhörprotokolle des Persönlichen Adjutanten Hitlers, Otto Günsche, und des Kammerdieners Heinz Linge, Moskau 1948/49*, Bergisch Gladbach, 2005, pp. 62f.; Joachimsthaler, *Hitlers Liste*, p. 473. On Anni Winter's role see also Schlie (ed.), *Albert Speer*, p. 236.

56   See Anni Winter's statement dated 6 March 1948; cited in Joachimsthaler, *Hitlers Liste*, pp. 467f. Gun, *Eva Braun-Hitler*, pp. 119f., quotes a letter by Eva Braun from the spring of 1937: "I spend almost all my time with Liserl, Georg, Peppo, Toni and Röschen."

57   See Schroeder, *Er war mein Chef*, p. 167; Joachimsthaler, *Hitlers Liste*, pp. 302, 438; Görtemaker, *Eva Braun*, p. 194.

58   Linge, *Bis zum Untergang*, p. 74.

59   Plaim and Kuch, *Bei Hitlers*, p. 39.

60   Reinhard Spitzy, *So haben wir das Reich verspielt: Bekenntnisse eines Illegalen*, 2nd edition, Munich and Vienna, 198, p. 128.

61   See Julius Schaub's statement, quoted in Joachimsthaler, *Hitlers Liste*, p. 468; Baur, *Ich flog Mächtige der Erde*, p. 114; Gun, *Eva Braun-Hitler*, pp. 95, 130.

62   Speer, *Erinnerungen*, p. 106.

63   On the 1935 rally see Görtemaker, *Eva Braun*, pp. 113, 116; 1937 rally: ibid., pp. 139, 320 (note 38); 1938 rally: ibid., pp. 177f., 324 (note 48).

64   See ibid., p. 63.

65   See ibid., pp. 117, 123, 208–15.

66   Below, *Als Hitlers Adjutant*, pp. 50f.; Baur, *Ich flog Mächtige der Erde*, p. 114. The Bruckmanns were also aware of the existence of Hitler's "girlfriend." See Ulrich von Hassell, *Vom anderen Deutschland: Aus den nachgelassenen Tagebüchern 1938–1944*, Frankfurt am Main, 1964, p. 58 (entry for 22 July 1939).

67   See Gun, *Eva Braun-Hitler*, pp. 122f. In the second volume of his Hitler biography (*Adolf Hitler: Ein Mann gegen Europa*, Zurich, 1937, p. 191), Konrad Heiden also mentions Hitler having a "girlfriend in Munich, a Miss B., a photographer by trade."

68   See Gun, *Eva Braun-Hitler*, p. 125; Joachimsthaler, *Hitlers Liste*, p. 418.

69   As in Speer, *Erinnerungen*, p. 59.

70   See Joachimsthaler, *Hitlers Liste*, pp. 416, 470f.; Linge, *Bis zum Untergang*, pp. 65, 103; Speer, *Erinnerungen*, pp. 114f.; Krause, *10 Jahre Kammerdiener*, p. 45; Gun, *Eva Braun-Hitler*, pp. 129f., 160; Plaim and Kuch, *Bei Hitlers*, pp. 74f.

71   Below, *Als Hitlers Adjutant*, p. 50.

72   Schlie (ed.), *Albert Speer*, p. 59. Karl Brandt, Hitler's personal physician, wrote from Kransberg prison in August 1945: "Hitler and his Eva were quite deeply connected emotionally." Ibid., p. 228.

73   Albert Speer, *Spandauer Tagebücher*, Munich, 2002, p. 198 (entry for 3 March 1949).

74   Speer, *Erinnerungen*, p. 106.

75   Fest, *Die unbeantwortbaren Fragen*, p. 59.

76   Statement by Herbert Döhring, summer of 2001; quoted in Joachimsthaler, *Hitlers Liste*, p. 454.

77   Series of articles by Heinz Linge in the newspaper *Revue* (November 1955 to March 1956); here no. 45 (dated November 1955); collected in IfZ München, MS 396: see also Linge, *Bis zum Untergang*, pp. 64f., 68, 94.

78   See Plaim and Kuch, *Bei Hitlers*, pp. 75, 108; Knopp, *Die Geheimnisse des "Dritten Reiches,"* p. 317. When asked during his interrogation by Robert W. M. Kempner on 12 March 1947 whether Hitler had loved Eva Braun, Julius Schaub answered: "He liked her very much." When pressed whether this meant Hitler had loved her, Schaub answered: "He was very fond of her." IfZ München, ZS 137.

79   Dietrich, *12 Jahre mit Hitler*, p. 231.

80   As in Hanfstaengl, *Zwischen Weissem und Braunem Haus*, p. 359; statement by Christa Schroeder; quoted in Joachimsthaler, *Hitlers Liste*, pp. 454f.

81   Hitler's personal will and testament dated 2 May 1938; copy in BA Koblenz, N 1128/22; facsimile in Gun, *Eva Braun-Hitler*, after p. 128. On the fear Hitler could be assassinated on his trip to Italy, see also Rudolf Hess to Karl Haushofer, 20 April 1938: "One has to accept that destiny is immutable and hope that it still needs this man as a tool for achieving Greater Germany." BA Koblenz, N 1122/125.

82   See Schlie (ed.), *Albert Speer*, p. 59; Dietrich, *12 Jahre mit Hitler*, pp. 216f.; Hoffmann, *Hitler wie ich ihn sah*, p. 159; Fritz Wiedemann, *Der Mann, der Feldherr werden wollte: Erlebnisse und Erfahrungen des Vorgesetzten Hitlers im 1. Weltkrieg und seines späteren persönlichen Adjutanten*, Velbert and Kettwig 1964, p. 79; Misch, *Der letzte Zeuge*, p. 101; Wiedemann's shorthand notes dated 25 Feb. 1939: "Guests only close acquaintances and friends. The sort of comfortable country life." BA Koblenz, N 1720/4. Hermann Esser also later attested that the only friends invited to the Berghof were those "accepted by Eva Braun." Interview with Hermann Esser dated 3 April 1964; BayHStA München. Nl Esser.

83   See Goebbels, *Tagebücher*, part 1, vol. 3/1, p. 279 (entry for 21 Aug. 1935): "cultish nonsense"; Speer, *Erinnerungen*, p. 108; Wiedemann's notes dated 25 Feb. 1939: "He had less sympathy for Darré's cult of blood and soil and Himmler's worship of every-thing ancient Germanic, which he made fun of occasionally." BA Koblenz, N 1720/4.

84 See Speer, *Erinnerungen*, p. 111; Dietrich, *12 Jahre mit Hitler*, p. 217; Junge, *Bis zur letzten Stunde*, p. 77. On Hewel's role see Eckart Conze, Norbert Frei, Peter Hayes and Moshe Zimmermann, *Das Amt und die Vergangenheit: Deutsche Diplomaten im Dritten Reich und in der Bundesrepublik*, Munich, 2010, pp. 153f.; Enrico Syring, "Walter Hewel: Ribbentrops Mann beim 'Führer,'" in Ronald Smelser, Enrico Syring and Rainer Zitelmann (eds), *Die braune Elite II: 21 weitere biographische Skizzen*, Darmstadt, 1993, pp. 150–65.

85 Dietrich, *12 Jahre mit Hitler*, p. 216; see Görtemaker, *Eva Braun*, pp. 142f.

86 See Schlie (ed.), *Albert Speer*, pp. 81, 231; Linge, *Bis zum Untergang*, p. 138. On Martin und Gerda Bormann's children see Koop, *Martin Bormann*, pp. 185f.

87 See, for example, Goebbels, *Tagebücher*, part 1, vol. 4, p. 214 (entry for 10 July 1937): "We're staying at the Bechsteins' house and are very comfortable." See Joachimsthaler, *Hitlers Liste*, pp. 99f.

88 See Speer, *Erinnerungen*, p. 105; Sereny, *Albert Speer*, pp. 109f.; Görtemaker, *Eva Braun*, pp. 127–32.

89 Speer, *Erinnerungen*, p. 107; see also *idem*, *Spandauer Tagebücher*, p. 208 (entry for 19 June 1949). By contrast, Schwerin von Krosigk found that Hitler showed his "most human and attractive side" when he was around children. Krosigk wrote that his face, "which often looked so tense, as though it were covered by a mask," relaxed when he was in the presence of children and took on an "expression of true cordiality and benevolence." See Schwerin von Krosigk's essay on Hitler's personality (*c.* 1945); IfZ München, ZS 145, vol. 5. See also Sereny, *Albert Speer*, pp. 123f.; Nissen, *Sind Sie die Tochter Speer?*, p. 19.

90 Speer, *Spandauer Tagebücher*, p. 127 (entry for 18 Nov. 1947); see *idem*, *Erinnerungen*, p. 107; Nissen, *Sind Sie die Tochter Speer?*, p. 25 (Margarete Speer's note). On Hitler's dislike of snow and skiing see Rudolf Hess to his parents, 10 May 1937: "Now that at long last the warmth of spring has arrived, the Führer simply can't believe it that somebody voluntarily returns to the ice and snow." BA Bern, Nl Hess, 1.121-1989/148, 59.

91 Speer, *Erinnerungen*, p. 107; questioning it is Görtemaker, *Eva Braun*, pp. 131f. At the Berghof Speer was considered as "Eva Braun's actual confidante." Schlie (ed.), *Albert Speer*, p. 221.

92 See Schmidt, *Hitlers Arzt Karl Brandt*, pp. 89–92; Neumann and Eberle, *War Hitler krank?*, pp. 100f.; Schroeder, *Er war mein Chef*, p. 173; Görtemaker, *Eva Braun*, pp. 132f.

93 See Schmidt, *Hitlers Arzt Karl Brandt*, p. 93; Schroeder, *Er war mein Chef*, p. 174. See Goebbels, *Tagebücher*, part 1, vol. 2/3, p. 148 (entry for 17 Aug. 1933): "Brückner has had a serious car accident. Fractured skull and an injured arm. Extremely serious. Hospital in Traunstein. I called the Führer. He was deeply shaken."

94 See Görtemaker, *Eva Braun*, p. 134; Goebbels, *Tagebücher*, part 1, vol. 2/3, p. 386 (entry for 16 March 1934); Schmidt, *Hitlers Arzt Karl Brandt*, p. 95, falsely dates the wedding at the end of 1934.

95 See a summary of interviews with Hanskarl von Hasselbach during 1951 and 1952 in IfZ München, ZS 242; see also Neumann and Eberle, *War Hitler krank?*, pp. 103f.

96 Speer, *Erinnerungen*, p. 119. See Goebbels, *Tagebücher*, part 1, vol. 5, p. 102 (entry for 17 Jan. 1938): "Dr. Morell got him on his feet with a bacterial cure. I'm very happy about that." On Morell's role see the transcript of an interview with Anni Winter (undated): IfZ München, ZS 194; Ernst Günther Schenk, *Patient Hitler: Eine medizinische Biographie*, Düsseldorf, 1989, pp. 163f., 180; Neumann and Eberle, *War Hitler krank?*, pp. 90–3; Schmidt, *Hitlers Arzt Karl Brandt*, pp. 137–9.

97 In a letter in late August 1937 Eva Braun wrote that "Morell can be eternally grateful to me for being allowed to visit the mountain." Gun, *Eva Braun-Hitler*, p. 140. See Görtemaker, *Eva Braun*, pp. 177f.; Schlie (ed.), *Albert Speer*, p. 231. A special identification card was arranged for Frau Morell on 3 Jan. 1938, which allowed her to visit the Obersalzberg; IfZ München, F 123. Frau Morell's presence at lunch on the Berghof was attested to for 26 June and 4 July 1938 in Max Wünsche's daily diaries; BA Berlin-Lichterfelde, NS 10/125.

98   Morell to Hitler, 2 Feb. 1938; quoted in Beatrice und Helmut Heiber (eds), *Die Rückseite des Hakenkreuzes: Absonderliches aus den Akten des Dritten Reiches*, Munich, 1993, p. 50.

99   In remarks recorded in prison in September 1945, Brandt said he found it "incomprehensible" that Morell had been kept on so long as "the Führer's personal physician." Karl Brandt, "Theodor Morell" (19 Sept. 1945); BA Koblenz, N 1128/33.

100   Speer, *Erinnerungen*, p. 120. On Eva Braun's treatment by Morell see also the letter from Ilse Hess to Carla Leitgen, 3 Feb. 1938; quoted in Görtemaker, *Eva Braun*, p. 181.

101   Interview with Hanskarl von Hasselbach dated 1951/52; IfZ München, ZS 242.

102   See Sabine Brantl, *Haus der Kunst: München. Ein Ort und seine Geschichte im Nationalsozialismus*, Munich, 2007, pp. 81–4: Goebbels, *Tagebücher*, part 1, vol. 4, pp. 170f. (entry for 6 June 1937), 216 (entry for 12 July 1937). Max Wünsche's daily diaries dated 20 June, 10 July 1938; BA Berlin-Lichterfelde, NS 10/125. See also Görtemaker, *Eva Braun*, pp. 26f.; Below, *Als Hitlers Adjutant*, pp. 82f.

103   Theodor Morell to Hanni Morell, 28 May 1940; BA Koblenz, N 1348/6.

104   See Görtemaker, *Eva Braun*, p. 202; Joachimsthaler, *Hitlers Liste*, pp. 466f.; Hans Georg Hiller von Gaertringen (ed.), *Das Auge des Dritten Reiches: Hitlers Kameramann und Fotograf Walter Frentz*, Berlin, 2006, pp. 108–25.

105   See Joachimsthaler, *Hitlers Liste*, pp. 422f., 458, 462, 472, 502, 507–15 (see p. 515 for a photograph from the wedding on 7 Aug. 1937); Görtemaker, *Eva Braun*, pp. 70, 169f.; quotation in Schlie (ed.), *Albert Speer*, p. 229. Max Wünsche's daily diaries dated 2 July 1938 (7 p.m.): "Visit from Frau Marion Schönmann." BA Berlin-Lichterfelde NS 10/125.

106   See the exchange of letters between Sofie Stork and Fritz Wiedemann 1937–39 in BA Koblenz, N 1720/8. After the New Year's party of 1937–8, the clique of friends referred to one another as "Fifty Brother" and "Fifty Sister." On Sofie Stork see also Joachimsthaler, *Hitlers Liste*, pp. 497–506; Görtemaker, *Eva Braun*, pp. 168f.

107   See Görtemaker, *Eva Braun*, pp. 182–9, 199; Dietrich, *12 Jahre mit Hitler*, p. 217; interview with Hermann Esser dated 3 April 1964, vol. 2; BayHStA München, Nl Esser; Max Wünsche's daily diaries dated 22 June, 5 July, 6 July 1938; BA Berlin-Lichterfelde NS 10/125; Arno Breker, *Im Strahlungsfeld der Ereignisse: Leben und Wirken eines Künstlers. Porträts, Begegnungen, Schicksale*, Preussisch Oldendorf, 1972, p. 183; Jürgen Trimborn, *Arno Breker: Der Künstler und die Macht. Die Biographie*, Berlin, 2011, pp. 212f.

108   See Sereny, *Albert Speer*, p. 194; Schlie (ed.), *Albert Speer*, pp. 231–3; Speer, *Erinnerungen*, p. 114; Schmidt, *Hitlers Arzt Karl Brandt*, pp. 102f.

109   See Görtemaker, *Eva Braun*, pp. 160f.; Schlie (ed.), *Albert Speer*, p. 231; Below, *Als Hitlers Adjutant*, p. 96.

110   Speer, *Erinnerungen*, pp. 102, 105, 107. Joachim Fest does not challenge this description. See Fest, *Hitler*, p. 721; idem, *Speer*, pp. 140f. For a critical perspective on Speer's account see Görtemaker, *Eva Braun*, pp. 127, 129f., 161.

111   Sereny, *Albert Speer*, p. 112.

112   Ibid., p. 193.

113   Fest, *Die unbeantwortbaren Fragen*, p. 171.

114   See Gun, *Eva Braun-Hitler*, p. 105; Schroeder, *Er war mein Chef*, pp. 95f.; Baldur von Schirach, *Ich glaubte an Hitler*, Hamburg, 1967, p. 266; Junge, *Bis zur letzte Stunde*, pp. 69, 72; Plaim and Kuch, *Bei Hitlers*, p. 47.

115   See Speer, *Erinnerungen*, p. 102; Gun, *Eva-Braun-Hitler*, pp. 105f.; Dietrich, *12 Jahre mit Hitler*, p. 216; Below, *Als Hitlers Adjutant*, p. 97; Linge, *Bis zum Untergang*, p. 81; Wiedemann, notes on "daily life"; BA Koblenz, N 1720/4. Details on timings according to the daily diaries of Max Wünsche from 16 June to 20 Nov. 1938; BA Berlin-Lichterfelde, NS 10/125.

116   Speer, *Spandauer Tagebücher*, p. 204 (entry for 13 May 1949).

117   Ibid., p. 205.

118 See Gun, *Eva Braun-Hitler*, pp. 106f.; Schroeder, *Er war mein Chef*, p. 178; Junge, *Bis zur letzten Stunde*, pp. 73, 75; Speer, *Erinnerungen*, p. 102; Eberle and Uhl (eds), *Das Buch Hitler*, p. 201; Nissen, *Sind Sie die Tochter Speer?*, pp. 23f. (Margarete Speer's note).

119 See Dietrich, *12 Jahre mit Hitler*, p. 218; Schroeder, *Er war mein Chef*, p. 179; Speer, *Erinnerungen*, p. 102; Junge, *Bis zur letzten Stunde*, p. 75; Eberle and Uhl (eds), *Das Buch Hitler*, p. 202.

120 Speer, *Spandauer Tagebücher*, p. 206 (entry for 13 May 1949).

121 Sereny, *Albert Speer*, p. 435. See ibid., p. 153: those who sat next to Hitler at the lunch or dinner table had the feeling afterwards that "he had really wanted to know something about them—cared about them."

122 See Gun, *Eva Braun-Hitler*, p. 108; Junge, *Bis zur letzten Stunde*, pp. 77f.; Dietrich, *12 Jahre mit Hitler*, pp. 220f.; Speer, *Erinnerungen*, p. 108; Fest, *Die unbeantwortbaren Fragen*, p. 64; Schroeder, *Er war mein Chef*, pp. 181f.

123 The first walk to the little tearoom took place on 9 Aug. 1937. See excerpts from the notebook of the "private secretary" to Hitler (probably Julius Schaub) about his daily routine during the years 1934–1943; BA Berlin-Lichterfelde, NS 26/16.

124 See Speer, *Erinnerungen*, p. 103; Schroeder, *Er war mein Chef*, pp. 182–4; Junge, *Bis zur letzten Stunde*, pp. 78–80; Gun, *Eva Braun-Hitler*, pp. 109f.; Dietrich, *12 Jahre mit Hitler*, p. 222.

125 See Heydecker, *Hoffmann-Erinnerungen*, pp. 166f.; Speer, *Erinnerungen*, p. 103; Schroeder, *Er war mein Chef*, pp. 184–6; Junge, *Bis zur letzten Stunde*, pp. 81–3; Gun, *Eva Braun-Hitler*, pp. 110, 112f.

126 See Goebbels, *Tagebücher*, part 1, vol. 3/2, p. 102 (entry for 9 June 1936): "Spent a long time alone with the Führer. He doesn't like heavily made-up women. He thinks highly of Magda that she's remained such a clear-headed simple woman."

127 Junge, *Bis zur letzten Stunde*, p. 81. On the above see Gun, *Eva Braun-Hitler*, p. 114; Schroeder, *Er war mein Chef*, p. 186; Dietrich, *12 Jahre mit Hitler*, pp. 228f.; Goebbels, *Tagebücher*, part 1, vol. 5, p. 64 (entry for 22 Dec. 1937); Speer, *Erinnerungen*, pp. 104f.

128 Dietrich, *12 Jahre mit Hitler*, p. 230; see also Schroeder, *Er war mein Chef*, pp. 188–90; Hoffmann, *Hitler wie ich ihn sah*, p. 161; Gun, *Eva Braun-Hitler*, pp. 114f.; Junge, *Bis zur letzten Stunde*, pp. 88–94; Speer, *Erinnerungen*, pp. 104f. From June to November 1938 Hitler usually went to bed around midnight, although occasionally not until 1:30 a.m. Max Wünsche's daily diaries; BA Berlin-Lichterfelde, NS 10/125.

129 Krause, *10 Jahre Kammerdiener*, pp. 53–5. See also Leni Riefenstahl, *Memoiren*, Munich, 1987, p. 250 (for Christmas Eve 1935).

130 Martin Bormann to Wilhelm Brückner, 14 Dec. 1938; BA Berlin-Lichterfelde, NS 10/116.

131 Handwritten letter by Gretl Braun to Fritz Wiedemann (addressed to "Beloved 'Fifty Partner'"), 31 Dec. 1938; BA Koblenz, N 1720/6. In his return letter of 5 Jan. 1939 (which he began with "Dear Fifty Sister"), Wiedemann assured Braun that "he had thought intensely about the previous year's party on New Year's Eve" and hoped "equally intensely" that he would see her again.

132 Hoffmann, *Hitler wie ich ihn sah*, p. 119. See Schroeder, *Er war mein Chef*, p. 175; Gun, *Eva Braun-Hitler*, pp. 102–4 (description of the New Year's Eve 1938 festivities on the Obersalzberg by Ilse Braun). On Hitler's "particular passion for fireworks" see Albert Speer to Joachim Fest, 13 Sept. 1969; BA Koblenz, N 1340/17. Hanfstaengl spoke in a note about Hitler's "pyromaniacal tendency"; BSB München, Nl Hanfstaengl Ana 405, Box 25.

133 Misch, *Der letzte Zeuge*, p. 111; see Knopp, *Geheimnisse des "Dritten Reiches,"* pp. 317f.

134 Schlie (ed.), *Albert Speer*, p. 225.

135 Dietrich, *12 Jahre mit Hitler*, p. 150. In her essay "76 Jahre Leben in Deutschland" (1989) Henriette von Schirach describes the Berghof as the "stage of history"; BayHStA München, Nl H. v. Schirach 3.

136   Adolf Hitler, *Monologe im Führerhauptquartier 1941–1944: Die Aufzeichnungen Heinrich Heims*, ed. Werner Jochmann, Hamburg, 1980, p. 167 (dated 2/3 Jan. 1942). See Wiedemann's notes dated 25 Feb. 1939: "Without doubt, the Obersalzberg was the place where the Führer determined the main lines of his policy." BA Koblenz, N 1720/4.

137   Heydecker, *Hoffmann-Erinnerungen*, p. 85; Hoffmann, *Hitler wie ich ihn sah*, p. 58. When Lloyd George's daughter jokingly greeted him in from of the hotel in Berchtesgaden with "Heil Hitler!" the former British prime minister remarked in all seriousness that Hitler truly was a "great man." Paul Schmidt, *Statist auf diplomatischer Bühne 1923–45: Erlebnisse des Chefdolmetschers im Auswärtigen Amt mit den Staatsmännern Europas*, Bonn, 1950, p. 340.

138   Wiedemann, *Der Mann*, p. 157; see Schroeder, *Er war mein Chef*, pp. 192f.; Schmidt, *Als Statist auf diplomatischer Bühne*, p. 376; Hoffmann, *Hitler wie ich ihn sah*, pp. 58f.

139   Below, *Als Hitlers Adjutant*, p. 122.

140   See Lammers to Willhelm Brückner, Berchtesgaden, 21 Oct. and 25 Oct. 1938: Although Lammers insisted that he needed to get Hitler's signature on two important draft laws, he was only granted access to him on 31 Oct.; BA Berlin-Lichterfelde, R 43 II 886a. See also Görtemaker, *Eva Braun*, pp. 150–2, 154f. In late November, Lammers again requested an appointment, writing: "Since I only had the chance to speak to the Führer in the most urgent cases, and then only in limited fashion, this summer and autumn, the last time on 31 Oct., numerous matters have piled up and can no longer be put off. To take care of them I will need at least an hour." Lammers to Brückner, 22 Nov. 1938; BA Berlin-Lichterfelde, NS 10/25.

141   Goebbels, *Tagebücher*, part 1, vol. 4, p. 217 (entry for 13 July 1937); see also ibid., vol. 3/2, p. 317 (entry for 5 Jan. 1937): "Debates about Spain at table."

142   See Görtemaker, *Eva Braun*, pp. 170–2; Joachimsthaler, *Hitlers Liste*, pp. 512f. (Nicolaus von Below's and Herbert Döhring's statements); Below, *Als Hitlers Adjutant*, p. 97.

143   See Görtemaker, *Eva Braun*, pp. 77, 173f. See also the image of the "unpolitical" Eva Braun in Speer, *Erinnerungen*, p. 107; Dietrich, *12 Jahre mit Hitler*, p. 235; Joachimsthaler, *Hitlers Liste*, pp. 474f. (Herbert Döhring's statement); Schroeder, *Er war mein Chef*, p. 166.

19   Hitler and the Churches

1   Adolf Hitler, *Monologe im Führerhauptquartier 1941–1944: Die Aufzeichnungen Heinrich Heims*, ed. Werner Jochmann, Hamburg, 1980, p. 150 (dated 13 Dec. 1941); see also *Hitlers Tischgespräche im Führerhauptquartier*, ed. Henry Picker, Stuttgart, 1976, p. 80 (dated 13 Dec. 1941). Hitler said in February 1942 that by the age of fifteen at the latest he "didn't believe [in religion] any more." He added that only "a few stupid model students believed in so-called Communion." Hitler, *Monologe*, p. 288 (dated 20/21 Feb. 1942). Schwerin von Krosigk opined that it was the "very bigoted brand of Catholicism" in Austria which repelled the young Hitler and turned him against religion. Schwerin von Krosigk, essay on Hitler's personality, (c.1945); IfZ München, ZS 145, vol. 5. For a similar assessment see Hanskarl von Hasselbach "Hitlers Einstellung zum Christentum"; BA Koblenz, N 1128/33. By contrast, Friedrich Heer's thesis (*Der Glaube des Adolf Hitler: Anatomie einer politischen Religiosität*, Munich, 1968, 2nd edition, 1998) that Hitler was influenced by "specifically Catholic elements" seems rather implausible.

2   Hitler, *Monologe*, p. 40 (dated 11/12 July 1941).

3   Ibid., p. 108 (dated 25 Oct. 1941).

4   Ibid., p. 83 (dated 14 Oct. 1941).

5   See Michael Rissman, *Hitlers Gott: Vorsehungsglaube und Sendungsbewusstsein eines deutschen Diktators*, Zurich and Munich, 2001, pp. 30–3, 42–52.

6   For an analysis of Hitler's Christmas addresses see Friedrich Tomberg, *Das Christentum in Hitlers Weltanschauung*, Munich, 2012, pp. 118–20, 124–6, 128–31.

7   Walther Hofer (ed.), *Der Nationalsozialismus: Dokumente 1933–1945*, Frankfurt am Main, 2011, p. 30.

8   Adolf Hitler, *Mein Kampf. Vol. 1: Eine Abrechnung*, 7th edition, Munich, 1933, pp. 127, 379.

9   See above p. 206. See also Klaus Scholder, *Die Kirchen und das Dritte Reich. Vol. 1: Vorgeschichte und Zeit der Illusion 1918–1934*, Frankfurt am Main, Berlin and Vienna, 1977, pp. 116–22. Otto Erbersdobler, the Gauleiter of Lower Bavaria from 1929 to 1932, quotes Hitler saying in relation to Dinter: "We're politicians and not religious reformers. Those who feel called to become reformers should do so, but not in our party." IfZ München, ZS 1949.

10   Ernst Piper, *Alfred Rosenberg: Hitlers Chefideologe*, Munich, 2005, p. 185; see also Scholder, *Die Kirchen und das Dritte Reich*, vol. 1, p. 240.

11   *Tischgespräche*, p. 213 (dated 11 April 1942). See ibid., p. 416 (dated 4 July 1942), where Hitler states that he "always thought that it was a mistake for Rosenberg to get involved in a discussion with the Church."

12   Scholder, *Die Kirchen und das Dritte Reich*, vol. 1, p. 280; see Hans-Ulrich Wehler, *Deutsche Gesellschaftsgeschichte 1914–1949*, Munich, 2003, p. 798: "He successfully styled himself as a 'homo religiosus' in the highest office of state."

13   Max Domarus, *Hitler: Reden und Proklamationen 1932–1945. Vol. 1: Triumph. Part 1: 1932–1934*, Munich, 1965, p. 192.

14   Ibid., pp. 232f.

15   See Michael Hesemann, *Hitlers Religion: Die fatale Heilslehre des Nationalsozialismus*, Munich, 2004, pp. 363f.; John Cornwell, *Pius XII: Der Papst, der geschwiegen hat*, Munich, 1999, pp. 139–41.

16   See Scholder, *Die Kirchen und das Dritte Reich*, vol. 1, pp. 300, 303.

17   Cited in ibid., p. 320.

18   *Die Tagebücher von Joseph Goebbels. Part 1: Aufzeichnungen 1923–1941*, ed. Elke Fröhlich, Munich, 1998, vol. 2/3, p. 197 (entry for 4 June 1933).

19   *Akten der Reichskanzlei: Die Regierung Hitler. Part 1: 1933/34. Vol. 1: 30. Januar bis 30. April 1933*, ed. Karl-Heinz Minuth, Boppard am Rhein, 1983, no. 44, p. 160.

20   On the negotiations see Scholder, *Die Kirchen und das Dritte Reich*, vol. 1, pp. 487–511; Cornwell, *Pius XII*, pp. 175–87.

21   *Die Regierung Hitler*, part 1, vol. 1, no. 193, p. 683.

22   Quoted in Scholder, *Die Kirchen und das Dritte Reich*, vol. 1, p. 514.

23   See Cornwell, *Pius XII*, pp. 193–7; Richard J. Evans, *The Third Reich in Power 1933–1939*, London, 2005, pp. 241–3.

24   Scholder, *Die Kirchen und das Dritte Reich*, vol. 1, pp. 660f.

25   Goebbels, *Tagebücher*, part 1, vol. 2/3, p. 346 (entry for 27 Dec. 1933).

26   See Klaus Scholder, *Die Kirchen und das Dritte Reich. Vol. 2: Das Jahr der Ernüchterung 1934—Barmen und Rom*, Berlin, 1985, pp. 137f.

27   Goebbels, *Tagebücher*, part 1, vol. 3/2, p. 293 (entry for 16 Dec. 1936).

28   Quoted in Hesemann, *Hitlers Religion*, p. 370; see Rudolf Morsey (ed.), *Fritz Gerlich: Ein Publizist gegen Hitler. Briefe und Akten 1930–1934*, Paderborn, 2010, p. 30.

29   See John S. Conway, *Die nationalsozialistische Kirchenpolitik 1933–1945: Ihre Ziele, Widersprüche und Fehlschläge*, Munich, 1969, pp. 114f.; Cornwell, *Pius XII*, p. 203; Scholder, *Die Kirchen und das Dritte Reich*, vol. 2, pp. 253–9.

30   Quoted in Scholder, *Die Kirchen und das Dritte Reich*, vol. 1, p. 263. On the receptiveness of the Protestant social milieu to National Socialism, see the excellent study by Manfred Gailus, *Protestantismus und Nationalsozialismus: Studien zur nationalsozialistischen Durchdringung des protestantischen Sozialmilieus in Berlin*, Cologne, Weimar and Vienna, 2001, pp. 57ff.

31   See Scholder, *Die Kirchen und das Dritte Reich*, vol. 1, pp. 272f.

32 Quoted in ibid., p. 299. When the Enabling Act was passed on 23 March 1933, the head of the German Christians in Hesse-Nassau and Hesse-Darmstadt, Gustav Adolf Wilhelm Meyer, wrote to Hitler expressing his "most fervent thanks before God, who has thus far so visibly and wonderfully blessed your battle on behalf of Germany and who has now crowned it with majestic victory." BA Berlin-Lichterfelde, NS 51/45.

33 Annelise Thimme (ed.), *Friedrich Thimme 1868–1938: Ein politischer Historiker, Publizist und Schriftsteller in seinen Briefen*, Boppard am Rhein, 1994, pp. 320f. (dated 14 Feb. 1933).

34 Ibid., p. 333 (dated 25 May 1933).

35 Ibid., p. 340 (dated 4 Oct. 1933).

36 Quoted in Ernst Klee, *"Die SA Jesu Christi": Die Kirche im Banne Hitlers*, Frankfurt am Main, 1989, p. 31.

37 See Thomas Martin Schneider, *Reichsbischof Ludwig Müller: Eine Untersuchung zu Leben, Werk und Persönlichkeit*, Göttingen, 1993, pp. 105f.

38 See Gailus, *Protestantismus und Nationalssozialismus*, pp. 115f.; Schneider, *Reichsbischof Ludwig Müller*, p. 146; Scholder, *Die Kirchen und das Dritte Reich*, vol. 1, pp. 479–81.

39 See Scholder, *Die Kirchen und das Dritte Reich*, vol. 1, pp. 565–9. See a detailed analysis of the votes of the Berlin parishes in Gailus, *Protestantismus und Nationalsozialismus*, pp. 117–22.

40 As in Schneider, *Reichsbischof Ludwig Müller*, p. 152.

41 For the above quotes see James Bentley, *Martin Niemöller: Eine Biographie*, Munich, 1985, p. 93. On Niemöller's attitude in the first half of 1933 see ibid., p. 60.

42 Kurt Meier, *Kreuz und Hakenkreuz: Die evangelische Kirche im Dritten Reich*, Munich, 1992, p. 49.

43 Scholder, *Die Kirchen und das Dritte Reich*, vol. 1, pp. 703f.; Meier, *Kreuz und Hakenkreuz*, pp. 50f.

44 See Schneider, *Reichsbischof Ludwig Müller*, pp. 164f.; Bentley, *Martin Niemöller*, pp. 99f.

45 See Scholder, *Die Kirchen und das Dritte Reich*, vol. 1, p. 721, vol. 2, p. 14; Schneider, *Reichsbischof Ludwig Müller*, p. 168.

46 Goebbels, *Tagebücher*, part 1, vol. 2/3, p. 332.

47 Bentley, *Martin Niemöller*, pp. 105–7.

48 *Tischgespräche*, p. 204 (dated 7 April 1942); see Goebbels, *Tagebücher*, part 1, vol. 3/2, p. 363 (entry for 28 Jan. 1934): "[Hitler] is flogging the priests to the point of complete collapse."

49 On the meeting at the Chancellery on 25 Jan. 1934 see Scholder, *Die Kirchen und das Dritte Reich*, vol. 2, pp. 59–64; Bentley, *Martin Niemöller*, pp. 109–12; Meier, *Kreuz und Hakenkreuz*, pp. 60f.; Schneider, *Reichsbischof Ludwig Müller*, pp. 186, 191.

50 Goebbels, *Tagebücher*, part 1, vol. 3/1, p. 40 (entry for 28 April 1934).

51 See Schneider, *Reichsbischof Ludwig Müller*, pp. 191–3; Scholder, *Die Kirchen und das Dritte Reich*, vol. 2, pp. 75ff., 159ff.

52 Scholder, *Die Kirchen und das Dritte Reich*, vol. 2, p. 190 (quotations on p. 191).

53 Bentley, *Martin Niemöller*, pp. 137f.; on the Dahlem synod of 19–20 Oct. 1934, see also Scholder, *Die Kirchen und das Dritte Reich*, vol. 2, pp. 339–47.

54 See Bentley, *Martin Niemöller*, pp. 138f.; on the conversation of 30 Oct. 1934 see Scholder, *Die Kirchen und das Dritte Reich*, vol. 2, pp. 354f.; Gerhard Besier, *Die Kirchen und das Dritte Reich: Spaltungen und Abwehrkämpfe 1934–1937*, Berlin and Munich, 2001, pp. 19–21 (Besier's portrayal is markedly opposite to Scholder's).

55 Goebbels, *Tagebücher*, part 1, vol. 3/1, p. 126 (entry for 25 Oct. 1934).

56 Schneider, *Reichsbischof Ludwig Müller*, pp. 215f.

57 See Ian Kershaw, *The Hitler Myth: Image and Reality in the Third Reich*, Oxford, 1987, pp. 105–20.

58 Conway, *Die nationalsozialistische Kirchenpolitik*, pp. 149f.; on the establishment of the Reich Church Ministry see Schneider, *Reichsbischof Ludwig Müller*, pp. 218f.;

Meier, *Kreuz und Hakenkreuz*, pp. 129–33; Besier, *Die Kirchen und das Dritte Reich*, pp. 287ff.

59 Goebbels, *Tagebücher*, part 1, vol. 3/1, p. 278 (entry for 19 Aug. 1935). See also Hans Günter Hockerts, "Die Goebbels-Tagebücher 1932–1941: Eine neue Hauptquelle zur Erforschung der nationalsozialistischen Kirchenpolitik," in Dieter Albrecht, Hans Günter Hockerts, Paul Mikat and Rudolf Morsey (eds), *Politik und Konfession: Festschrift für Konrad Repken zum 60. Geburtstag*, Berlin, 1983, pp. 359–92.

60 Besier, *Die Kirchen und das Dritte Reich*, pp. 164f.; see Goebbels, *Tagebücher*, part 1, vol. 3/1, p. 285 (entry for 31 Aug. 1935): "Pastoral letter by the Catholic bishops. Very critical. But in the end a prayer for the government. Oh well. They pray, we act."

61 Goebbels, *Tagebücher*, part 1, vol. 3/1, p. 288 (entry for 6 Sept. 1935).

62 Domarus, *Hitler*, vol. 1, part 2, pp. 525f.

63 See Hans Günter Hockerts, *Die Sittlichkeitsprozesse gegen katholische Ordensangehörige und Priester 1936/1937: Eine Studie zur nationalsozialistischen Herrschaftstechnik und zum Kirchenkampf*, Mainz, 1971, pp. 63–6.

64 Ibid., p. 69; see Besier, *Die Kirchen und das Dritte Reich*, pp. 715f.

65 Goebbels, *Tagebücher*, part 1, vol. 3/2, p. 219 (entry for 21 Oct. 1936).

66 Ludwig Volk (ed), *Akten Kardinal Michael von Faulhabers 1917–1945. Vol. 2: 1935–1945*, Mainz, 1978, pp. 184–94. On Hitler's remarks to Faulhaber of 4 Nov. 1936 see Hockerts, *Die Sittlichkeitsprozesse*, pp. 70f.; Besier, *Die Kirchen und das Dritte Reich*, pp. 762–5.

67 Goebbels, *Tagebücher*, part 1, vol. 3/2, pp. 245 (entry for 10 Nov. 1936), 252 (entry for 15 Nov. 1936). See ibid., p. 240 (entry for 6 Nov. 1936): "The Vatican seems to have become very brittle. It will now have to decide whether it's for us or against us. War or peace. We're prepared whatever."

68 Ibid., p. 316 (entry for 5 Jan. 1937). On the Christmas 1936 pastoral letter see Besier, *Die Kirchen und das Dritte Reich*, pp. 773f.

69 Goebbels, *Tagebücher*, part 1, vol. 3/2, pp. 353f. (entry for 31 Jan. 1937).

70 Ibid., p. 365 (entry for 9 Feb. 1937). See also ibid., p. 362 (entry for 6 Feb. 1937): "The churches have ruined our morale and our courage. Above all by making death into fearsome horror. Antiquity knew none of that."

71 Ibid., p. 379 (entry for 18 Feb. 1937).

72 Ibid., p. 389 (entry for 23 Feb. 1937). See Hanskarl von Hasselbach's essay "Hitlers Einstellung zur Religion": "Hitler thinks that as a man from Galilee, Christ was of Aryan descent and that, with the exception of his ethical values, he was to be admired as a brilliant popular leader in the fight against the power and attacks by the demoralised Pharisees." BA Koblenz, N 1128/33.

73 See Piper, *Alfred Rosenberg*, pp. 189–91. On the possible influence of Nietzsche on Hitler's idea of Paul see Tomberg, *Das Christentum in Hitlers Weltanschauung*, pp. 14, 114, 152f.

74 Goebbels, *Tagebücher*, part 1, vol. 3/2, p. 389 (entry for 23 Feb. 1937).

75 Ibid., vol. 4, p. 49 (entry for 13 March 1937). See ibid., p. 166 (entry for 3 June 1937): "He expressed his gratitude for the role of the religious reformer." See also Schwerin von Krosigk, "Essay on Hitler's personality" (c.1945), who asserts that Hitler always resisted attempts within party circles "to found a new religion with him at its centre." IfZ München, ZS 145, vol. 5.

76 Dieter Albrecht (ed.), *Der Notenwechsel zwischen dem Heiligen Stuhl und der Deutschen Reichsregierung. Vol. 1: Von der Ratifizierung des Reichskonkordats bis zur Enzyklika "Mit brennender Sorge,"* Mainz, 1965, no. 7, pp. 404–43. On the origin of the encyclical and the reaction to it see Cornwell, *Pius XII*, pp. 219–21; Besier, *Die Kirchen und das Dritte Reich*, pp. 777ff.

77 Goebbels, *Tagebücher*, part 1, vol. 4, p. 62 (entry for 21 March 1937).

78 Ibid., p. 76 (entry for 2 April 1937).

79 Hockerts, *Die Sittlichkeitsprozesse*, p. 73.

80 Goebbels, *Tagebücher*, part 1, vol. 4, p. 116 (entry for 30 April 1937). See ibid., pp. 78 (entry for 4 April 1937), 83 (entry for 7 April 1937), 90 (entry for 13 April 1937), 115 (entry for 29 April 1937).

81 Ibid., pp. 86 (entry for 10 April 1937), 118 (entry for 1 May 1937).

82 Domarus, *Hitler*, vol. 1, part 2, p. 690. See Goebbels, *Tagebücher*, part 1, vol. 4, p. 120 (entry for 2 May 1937): "The Führer hit the mark as always . . . with a pointed attack on clergymen who meddle in politics, which was received with frenetic applause."

83 Goebbels, *Tagebücher*, part 1, vol. 4, p. 155 (entry for 28 May 1937). See ibid., p. 151 (entry for 26 May 1937).

84 Hockerts, *Die Sittlichkeitsprozesse*, p. 113.

85 Quotations in ibid., p. 114; Ralf Georg Reuth, *Goebbels*, Munich and Zurich, 1990, p. 361.

86 Goebbels, *Tagebücher*, part 1, vol. 4, p. 157 (entry for 29 May 1937).

87 Ibid., p. 164 (entry for 2 June 1937).

88 Quoted in Hockerts, *Die Sittlichkeitsprozesse*, p. 125.

89 Goebbels, *Tagebücher*, part 1, vol. 4, p. 209 (entry for 4 July 1937). See ibid., p. 229 (entry for 23 Sept. 1937).

90 See ibid., pp. 237 (entry for 28 July 1937): "The Führer wants to empower a special court for the preachers' trial. That's the only way to go!"; 255 (entry for 7 Aug. 1937): "He now finally, finally, wants to empower a special court."

91 Ibid., vol. 5, p. 66 (entry for 22 Dec. 1937).

92 See Hockerts, *Die Sittlichkeitsprozesse*, pp. 75–7.

93 Goebbels, *Tagebücher*, part 1, vol. 4, p. 135 (entry for 12 May 1937).

94 Ibid., vol. 3/2, p. 328 (entry for 14 Jan. 1937).

95 Ibid., p. 375 (entry for 15 Feb. 1937). On the resignation of the Reich Church Committee and Kerrl's attempted decree, see Besier, *Die Kirchen und das Dritte Reich*, pp. 631–40; Conway, *Die nationalsozialistische Kirchenpolitik*, pp. 221f.

96 Goebbels, *Tagebücher*, part 1, vol. 3/2, p. 375 (entry for 15 Feb. 1937).

97 Ibid., p. 376 (entry for 16 Feb. 1937).

98 Reprinted in Conway, *Die nationalsozialistische Kirchenpolitik*, p. 222.

99 Goebbels, *Tagebücher*, part 1, vol. 3/2, p. 376 (entry for 16 Feb. 1937).

100 See Meier, *Kreuz und Hakenkreuz*, p. 136.

101 Goebbels, *Tagebücher*, part 1, vol. 4, p. 238 (entry for 29 July 1937); see ibid., p. 191 (entry for 22 June 1937).

102 Ibid., vol. 5, p. 39 (entry for 7 Dec. 1937).

103 Ibid., vol. 5, p. 6 (entry for 22 Dec. 1937).

104 See Bentley, *Martin Niemöller*, pp. 155–61; Gailus, *Protestantismus und Nationalsozialismus*, pp. 306–8, 328–30.

105 Goebbels, *Tagebücher*, part 1, vol. 4, p. 208 (entry for 3 July 1937). See ibid., p. 209 (entry for 4 July 1937): "We have the swine now and we're not letting go of him."

106 Ibid., vol. 5, p. 65 (entry for 22 Dec. 1937). See ibid., p. 109 (entry for 21 Jan. 1938): "The Niemöller case: the Führer will never release him. That's the only correct thing to do."

107 See Bentley, *Martin Niemöller*, pp. 171–3.

108 Goebbels, *Tagebücher*, part 1, vol. 5, p. 185 (entry for 2 March 1938). For a view of the Niemöller trial through the eyes of Goebbels see ibid., pp. 136 (entry for 5 Feb. 1938), 142 (entry for 8 Feb. 1938), 166 (entry for 20 Feb. 1938), 172 (entry for 23 Feb. 1938), 179 (entry for 27 Feb. 1938).

109 Ibid., p. 187 (entry for 4 March 1938).

110 Christa Schroeder to Johanna Nusser, 21 April 1939; IfZ München, ED 524; reprinted in Christa Schroeder, *Er war mein Chef: Aus dem Nachlass der Sekretärin von Adolf Hitler*, ed. Anton Joachimsthaler, 3rd edition, Munich and Vienna, 1985, pp. 93–7 (quotation on p. 96).

111 Goebbels, *Tagebücher*, part 1, vol. 6, p. 215 (entry for 8 Dec. 1938).

20 *Prelude to Genocide*

1   Quoted in *Die Verfolgung und Ermordung der europäischen Juden durch das national-sozialistische Deutschland 1933–1945. Vol. 1: Deutsches Reich 1933–1937*, ed. Wolf Gruner, Munich, 2008, doc. 276, p. 658. The full text of the speech in Hildegard von Kotze and Helmut Krausnick (eds), *"Es spricht der Führer": 7 exemplarische Hitler-Reden*, Gütersloh, 1966, pp. 123–77.

2   See Saul Friedländer, *Das Dritte Reich und die Juden: Die Jahre der Verfolgung 1933–1939*, Munich, 1998, vol. 1, p. 206.

3   See Ian Kershaw, *Hitler 1936–1945: Nemesis*, London, 2000, pp. 42, 132.

4   *Die Tagebücher von Joseph Goebbels. Part 1: Aufzeichnungen 1923–1941*, ed. Elke Fröhlich, Munich, 1998, vol. 4, p. 429 (entry for 30 Nov. 1937).

5   Ibid., vol. 3/2, pp. 343 (entry for 25 Jan. 1937), 344f. (entry for 26 Jan. 1937), 346 (entry for 27 Jan. 1937): "The show trial is continuing in Russia. The Jews are eating themselves alive." On Radek's arrest and his trial, see Wolf-Dietrich Gutjahr, *Revolution muss sein: Karl Radek. Die Biographie*, Cologne, Weimar and Vienna, 2012, pp. 850–75.

6   Max Domarus, *Hitler: Reden und Proklamationen 1932–1945. Vol. 1: Triumph. Part 2: 1935–1938*, Munich, 1965, pp. 727–32 (quotations on pp. 728, 729f.). Excerpts also in *Die Verfolgung und Ermordnung der europäischen Juden*, vol. 1, doc. 295, pp. 698–707.

7   See Dieter Schenk, *Hitlers Mann in Danzig: Albert Forster und die NS-Verbrechen in Danzig-Westpreussen*, Bonn, 2000, p. 87. Goebbels, *Tagebücher*, part 1, vol. 4, pp. 376 (entry for 26 Oct. 1937), 381 (entry for 29 Oct. 1937).

8   Willy Cohn, *Kein Recht, nirgends: Tagebuch vom Untergang des Breslauer Judentums 1933–1941*, ed. Norbert Conrads, Cologne, Weimar and Berlin, 2006, vol. 1, p. 483 (entry for 26 Oct. 1937).

9   See Friedländer, *Das Dritte Reich und die Juden*, vol. 1, p. 257; *Deutschland-Berichte der Sozialdemokratischen Partei Deutschlands (Sopade) 1934–1940*, ed. Klaus Behnken, Frankfurt am Main, 1980, 5 (1938), p. 176.

10   *Die Verfolgung und Ermordung der europäischen Juden durch das nationalsozialistische Deutschland 1933–1945. Vol. 2: Deutsches Reich 1938–August 1939*, ed. Susanne Heim, Munich, 2009, doc. 6, pp. 91–3 (quotations on pp. 91, 92). On the wave of boycotts and the forced elimination of Jews from the economy, see Michael Wildt, *Volksgemeinschaft als Selbstermächtigung: Gewalt gegen Juden in der deutschen Provinz 1919 bis 1939*, Hamburg, 2007, pp. 299f.; Peter Longerich, *Politik der Vernichtung: Eine Gesamtdarstellung der nationalsozialistischen Judenverfolgung*, Munich and Zurich, 1998, pp. 118–29.

11   See Avraham Barkai, *Vom Boykott zur "Entjudung": Der wirtschaftliche Existenzkampf der Juden im Dritten Reich 1933–1945*, Frankfurt am Main, 1988, pp. 78–80; idem, "'Schicksalsjahr 1938': Kontinuität und Verschärfung der wirtschaftlichen Ausplünderung der deutschen Juden," in Walter H. Pehle (ed.), *Der Judenpogrom 1938: Von der "Reichskristallnacht" zum Völkermord*, Frankfurt am Main, 1988, pp. 94–117 (at p. 96). For an excellent case study see Frank Bajohr, *'Arisierung" in Hamburg: Die Verdrängung der jüdischen Unternehmer 1933–1945*, Hamburg, 1997, pp. 173ff.

12   Quoted in Barkai, *Vom Boykott zur "Entjudung*, p. 142; idem, "'Schicksalsjahr 1938,'" p. 107.

13   *Deutschland-Berichte der Sopade*, 5 (1938), pp. 195f.; see ibid., 4 (1937), p. 1567. See also Goebbels, *Tagebücher*, part 1, vol. 4, p. 398 (entry for 9 Nov. 1938); Friedländer, *Das Dritte Reich und die Juden*, vol. 1, pp. 274f.; on the anti-Semitic campaign in the press see Peter Longerich, *'Davon haben wir nichts gewusst!" Die Deutschen und die Judenverfolgung 1933–1945*, Munich, 2006, pp. 109f.

14   See Longerich, *Politik der Vernichtung*, p. 155.

15   On this see the statistical estimates of the SD-Hauptamt II 112 from 12 Nov. and 18 Nov. 1937; Otto Dov Kulka and Eberhard Jäckel (eds), *Die Juden in den geheimen Stimmungsberichten 1933–1945*, Düsseldorf, 2004, doc. 288, 289, pp. 245–7.

16　　Carl Zuckmayer, *Als wär's ein Stück von mir*, Frankfurt am Main, 1966, p. 71.

17　　Stefan Zweig, *Die Welt von Gestern: Erinnerungen eines Europäers*, Stuttgart and Hamburg, p. 27, p. 409. See also the depiction by Walter Grab, *Meine vier Leben: Gedächtniskünstler—Emigrant—Jakobinerforscher—Demokrat*, Cologne, 1999, pp. 56–8. See also the reports by David Schapira and Karl Sass on the mistreatment of Viennese Jews after the *Anschluss* in *Die Verfolgung und Ermordung der europäischen Juden*, vol. 2, doc. 17/18, pp. 113–23. For background see Gerhard Botz, *Nationalsozialismus in Wien: Machtübernahme, Herrschaftssicherung, Radikalisierung 1938/39*, revised and expanded edition, Vienna, 2008, pp. 126–36.

18　　See Robert Gerwarth, *Reinhard Heydrich: Biographie*, Munich, 2011, pp. 154f.; Friedländer, *Das Dritte Reich und die Juden*, vol. 1, p. 263.

19　　William S. Shirer, *Berliner Tagebuch: Aufzeichnungen 1934–41*, transcribed and ed. Jürgen Schebera, Leipzig and Weimar, 1991, p. 109 (entry for 23 March 1938).

20　　Report by Ubaldo Rochira from 26 April 1938; Frank Bajohr and Christoph Strupp (ed.), *Fremde Blicke auf das "Dritte Reich": Berichte ausländischer Diplomaten über Herrschaft und Gesellschaft in Deutschland 1933–1945*, Göttingen, 2011, pp. 481f.

21　　See Botz, *Nationalsozialismus in Wien*, pp. 137–45. See Goebbels, *Tagebücher*, part 1, vol. 5, p. 255 (entry for 23 March 1938): "Many Jewish suicides in Vienna."

22　　See Botz, *Nationalsozialismus in Wien*, pp. 313–24; Friedländer, *Das Dritte Reich und die Juden*, vol. 1, pp. 263f.

23　　See David Cesarani, *Adolf Eichmann: Bürokrat und Massenmörder. Biographie*, Berlin, 2002, pp. 89–101; Botz, *Nationalsozialismus in Wien*, pp. 332–42; Friedländer, *Das Dritte Reich und die Juden*, vol. 1, pp. 265f.; Michael Wildt (ed.), *Die Judenpolitik des SD 1935 bis 1939: Eine Dokumentation*, Munich, 1995, pp. 52–4.

24　　*Deutschland-Berichte der Sopade*, 5 (1938), pp. 732f. On Austria's role as a "test case for the persecution of Jews in the Reich" see Hans Mommsen, *Auschwitz: 17. Juli 1942. Der Weg zur europäischen "Endlösung der Judenfrage"*, Munich, 2002, pp. 76f.

25　　Victor Klemperer, *Ich will Zeugnis ablegen bis zum letzten: Tagebücher 1933–1941*, ed. Walter Nowojski with Hadwig Klemperer, Berlin, 1995, p. 412 (entry for 29 June 1938). Text of the decree in *Die Verfolgung und Ermordung der europäischen Juden*, vol. 2, doc. 29, pp. 139–41.

26　　Friedländer, *Das Dritte Reich und die Juden*, vol. 1, p. 276. Text of the decree in *Die Verfolgung und Ermordung der europäischen Juden*, vol. 2, doc. 84, pp. 269f. Victor Klemperer commented: "Five minutes ago, I read the law concerning Jewish first names. You'd have to laugh, if it didn't threaten to drive you mad." *Tagebücher 1933–1941*, p. 419 (entry for 24 Aug. 1938).

27　　In Oct. 1949, Globke was appointed ministerial director, and later he made it to state secretary in the chancellory under West Germany's first chancellor, Konrad Adenauer. See Jürgen Bevers, *Der Mann hinter Adenauer: Hans Globkes Aufstieg vom NS-Juristen zur Grauen Eminenz der Bonner Republik*, Berlin, 2009, pp. 28ff.

28　　See Wildt, *Volksgemeinschaft als Selbstermächtigung*, pp. 303–6.

29　　Goebbels, *Tagebücher*, part 1, vol. 5, p. 269 (entry for 23 April 1938).

30　　The memorandum is reprinted in Wolf Gruner, "'Lesen brauchen sie nicht zu können . . .': Die 'Denkschrift über die Behandlung der Juden in der Reichshauptstadt auf allen Gebieten des öffentlichen Lebens' vom Mai 1938," in *Jahrbuch für Antisemitismusforschung*, 4 (1995), pp. 305–41. See Wildt, *Die Judenpolitik des SD 1933–1938*, pp. 55f.; Longerich, *Politik der Vernichtung*, pp. 172f.

31　　Longerich, *Politik der Vernichtung*, p. 173.

32　　Goebbels, *Tagebücher*, part 1, vol. 5, pp. 317 (entry for 25 May 1938), 325 (entry for 30 May 1938), 326 (entry for 31 May 1938).

33　　Ibid., pp. 329 (entry for 2 June 1938), 340 (entry for 11 June 1938).

34　　Report by the U.S. ambassador in Berlin to his Secretary of State, 22 June 1938; *Die Verfolgung und Ermordung der europäischen Juden*, vol. 2, doc. 47, pp. 176–9 (quotations on pp. 177, 179). See the report by the Italian ambassador Bernardo

Attolico of 21 June 1938; Bajohr and Strupp (eds), *Fremde Blicke auf das "Dritte Reich,"* pp. 483f.

35 Bella Fromm, *Als Hitler mir die Hand küsste,* Berlin, 1993, p. 294 (entry for 28 June 1938). See also *Deutschland-Berichte der Sopade,* 5 (1938), pp. 755–61.

36 Report by the SD-Hauptamt II 112 dated 1 July 1938; Kulka and Jäckel (eds), *Die Juden in den geheimen NS-Stimmungsberichten 1933–1945,* no. 332, p. 278.

37 Goebbels, *Tagebücher,* part 1, vol. 5, p. 351 (entry for 19 June 1938). See further documents in Christian Faludi (ed.), *Die "Juni-Aktion" 1938: Eine Dokumentation zur Radikalisierung der Judenverfolgung,* Frankfurt am Main, 2013. On the so-called "antisocials" action running parallel see *Die Verfolgung und Ermordung der europäischen Juden,* vol. 2, doc. 39, pp. 160f.; Longerich, *Politik der Vernichtung,* pp. 175–7; Wildt, *Die Judenpolitik des SD 1933–1938,* p. 56.

38 Text in *Die Verfolgung und Ermordung der europäischen Juden,* vol. 2, doc. 48, pp. 180–2. See Goebbels, *Tagebücher,* part 1, vol. 5, p. 356 (entries for 22 and 23 June 1938).

39 See Longerich: *"Davon haben wir nichts gewusst!",* pp. 112–14; idem, *Joseph Goebbels: A Biography,* London, 2010, p. 383.

40 Goebbels, *Tagebücher,* part 1, vol. 5, p. 393 (entry for 25 July 1938).

41 Reprinted in *Die Verfolgung und Ermordung der europäischen Juden,* vol. 2, doc. 68, pp. 234–43 (quotation on p. 234). See Longerich, *Politik der Vernichtung,* pp. 182f.

42 Goebbels, *Tagebücher,* part 1, vol. 5, p. 396 (entry for 27 July 1938).

43 Eduardo Labougle to Foreign Minister José María Cantilo, 13 Aug. 1938; Bajohr and Strupp (eds), *Fremde Blicke auf das "Dritte Reich,"* p. 488,

44 Report by the SD-Hauptamt II 112 dated April and May 1938; Wildt, *Die Judenpolitik des SD 1933–1938,* doc. 29, p. 186.

45 Quoted in Friedländer, *Das Dritte Reich und die Juden,* vol. 1, p. 270.

46 Domarus, *Hitler,* vol. 1, part 2, p. 899.

47 Quoted in Wildt, *Die Judenpolitik des SD 1933–1938,* p. 42. See on pp. 40–5 the section "SD and Palestine."

48 Quoted in Longerich, *"Davon haben wir nichts gewusst!",* p. 115.

49 Goebbels, *Tagebücher,* part 1, vol. 5, p. 256 (entry for 11 April 1938); see ibid., pp. 269f. (entry for 23 April 1938): "The Führer wants to deport all of them. Negotiate with Poland and Romania. Madagascar would be most suitable for them." Hitler's manservant Karl Krause remembered British Prime Minister Neville Chamberlain asking during his visit to the Berghof in September 1938, "How does Herr Hitler intend to solve the Jewish question?" to which Hitler replied: "Britain's global empire has enough islands! Make one of them available! All the Jews in the world could congregate there." Karl Wilhelm Krause, *10 Jahre Kammerdiener bei Hitler,* Hamburg, 1949, p. 37.

50 See Magnus Brechtken, *"Madagaskar für die Juden": Antisemitische Idee und politische Praxis 1885–1945,* Munich, 1997, pp. 16f., 34f, 61f.

51 Gerhard Engel, *Heeresadjutant bei Hitler 1938–1943,* ed. and annotated Hildegard von Kotze, Stuttgart, 1974, p. 31 (dated 13 Aug. 1938).

52 Kulka and Jäckel (eds), *Die Juden in den geheimen NS-Stimmungsberichten 1933–1945,* no. 353, p. 297; Longerich, *Politik der Vernichtung,* pp. 193f.

53 Cohn, *Kein Recht nirgends,* vol. 2, p. 533 (entry for 4 Nov. 1938).

54 Quoted in Friedländer, *Das Dritte Reich und die Juden,* vol. 1, p. 290. See Trude Maurer, "Abschiebung und Attentat: Die Ausweisung der polnischen Juden und der Vorwand für die 'Kristallnacht,'" in Pehle (ed.), *Der Judenpogrom 1938,* pp. 52–73; Hermann Graml, *Reichskristallnacht: Antisemitismus und Judenverfolgung im Dritten Reich,* Munich, 1988, pp. 9–12. Conclusive evidence is lacking for the suggestion that the attack had homosexual undertones, as suggested by Hans-Jürgen Döscher, *"Reichskristallnacht": Die Novemberpogrome 1938,* Frankfurt am Main and Berlin, 1988, pp. 65f., 154ff.

55 On this see Ralf Georg Reuth, *Goebbels,* Munich and Zurich, 1990, pp. 348–51, 388–90; Longerich, *Joseph Goebbels,* pp. 391–6.

56   DNB circular, 7 Nov. 1938; *NS-Presseanweisungen der Vorkriegszeit: Edition und Dokumentation*, vol. 6, part 3, Munich, 1999, no. 3176, p. 1050. Also reprinted in Wolfgang Benz, "Der Novemberpogrom 1938," in *idem* (ed.), *Die Juden in Deutschland 1933–1945: Leben unter nationalsozialistischer Herrschaft*, Munich, 1998, p. 506.

57   Quoted in *Die Verfolgung und Ermordung der europäischen Juden*, vol. 2, introduction, p. 53. See Benz, "Der Novemberprogrom 1938," pp. 505f.; further voices from the press in Longerich, *"Davon haben wir nichts gewusst!"*, pp. 124f.

58   Ruth Andreas-Friedrich, *Der Schattenmann: Tagebuchaufzeichnungen 1938–1945*, Frankfurt am Main, 1983, p. 26 (entry for 9 Nov. 1938).

59   Goebbels, *Tagebücher*, part 1, vol. 6, p. 178 (entry for 9 Nov. 1938). On the outbursts in Hesse on 8/9 Nov. 1938 see Wildt, *Volksgemeinschaft als Selbstermächtigung*, pp. 320–4.

60   See Friedländer, *Das Dritte Reich und die Juden*, vol. 1, p. 193.

61   See Ulf Schmidt, *Hitlers Arzt Karl Brandt: Medizin und Macht im Dritten Reich*, Berlin, 2009, pp. 165f.; Döscher, *"Reichskristallnacht,"* p. 64; Goebbels, *Tagebücher*, part 1, vol. 6, p. 179 (entry for 10 Nov. 1938): "The condition . . . of Rath in Paris continues to be critical."

62   Nicolaus von Below, *Als Hitlers Adjutant 1937–1945*, Mainz, 1980, p. 136. Brandt's official telegram to Hitler with the news of the death arrived in Berlin at 6:20 p.m. Facsimile in Döscher, *"Reichskristallnacht,"* p. 74. See Goebbels, *Tagebücher*, part 1, vol. 6, p. 180 (entry for 10 Nov. 1938): "In the afternoon, the death of the German diplomat Rath was announced."

63   As in Richard J. Evans, *The Third Reich in Power 1933–1939*, London, 2005, pp. 581f. A "careful staging" is also spoken of in Uwe Dietrich Adam, "Wie spontan war der Pogrom?," in Pehle (ed.), *Der Judenpogrom 1938*, p. 92. See also Alan E. Steinweis, *Kristallnacht 1938: Ein deutscher Pogrom*, Stuttgart, 2011, pp. 47–53.

64   Goebbels, *Tagebücher*, part 1, vol. 6, p. 180 (entry for 10 Nov. 1938).

65   Report of the Supreme Party Court to Hermann Göring, 13 Feb. 1939; *Der Prozess gegen die Hauptkriegsverbrecher vor dem Internationalen Militärtribunal in Nürnberg (IMT)*, Nuremberg, 1947–9, vol. 32, doc. 3063-PS, p. 21. See Benz, *Der Novemberpogrom 1938*, p. 510.

66   Goebbels, *Tagebücher*, part 1, vol. 6, p. 180 (entry for 10 Nov. 1938).

67   Ibid., pp. 180f. (entry for 10 Nov. 1938). On the role of the "Storm Troop Adolf Hitler" see Angela Hermann, "Hitler und sein Stosstrupp in der 'Reichskristallnacht,'" in *Vierteljahrshefte für Zeitgeschichte*, 56 (2008), pp. 603–19, particularly pp. 611–17.

68   Text in *Die Verfolgung und Ermordung der europäischen Juden*, vol. 2, doc. 125, pp. 366f.; see Gerwarth, *Reinhard Heydrich*, p. 160.

69   Goebbels, *Tagebücher*, part 1, vol. 6, p. 181 (entry for 10 Nov. 1938): "The Führer has ordered that 25,000–30,000 Jews be immediately arrested. That will leave an impression."

70   Text in *Die Verfolgung und Ermordung der europäischen Juden*, vol. 2, doc. 126, pp. 367f.; see Gerwarth, *Reinhard Heydrich*, p. 160.

71   On what happened during the pogrom see Dieter Obst, *"Reichskristallnacht": Ursachen und Verlauf des antisemitischen Pogroms vom November 1938*, Frankfurt am Main, 1991, pp. 102ff.; Graml, *Reichskristallnacht*, pp. 22ff.

72   Goebbels, *Tagebücher*, part 1, vol. 6, pp. 181f. (entries for 10 and 11 Nov. 1938).

73   Quoted in Obst, *"Reichskristallnacht,"* p. 94.

74   See Goebbels, *Tagebücher*, part 1, vol. 6, p. 182 (entry for 11 Nov. 1938): "I reported to the Führer in the Osteria . . . With a few small amendments, the Führer approved my decree concerning the discontinuation of the campaigns."

75   Quoted in Longerich, *"Davon haben wir nichts gewusst!"*, p. 125. See pp. 126f. for reports from German newspapers. Further voices from the press in Benz, *Der Novemberpogrom 1938*, pp. 515–19.

76   Domarus, *Hitler*, vol. 1, part 2, pp. 973, 978. In response to critical remarks made by Winifred Wagner, Hitler answered: "Something like this had to happen to finally

drive the Jews from Germany." Hitler denied to the Wagner children that he had anything to do with the pogrom. Brigitte Hamann, *Winifred Wagner oder Hitlers Bayreuth*, Munich and Zurich, 2002, p. 380.

77 Report by the SD-Hauptamt II 112, 7 Dec. 1938; Kulka and Jäckel (eds), *Die Juden in den geheimen NS-Stimmungsberichten 1933–1945*, no. 356, pp. 304–9; Longerich, *Politik der Vernichtung*, pp. 203f.; Evans, *The Third Reich in Power*, pp. 585, 590; Hermann, "Hitler und sein Stosstrupp," pp. 608f.

78 As in Friedländer, *Das Dritte Reich und die Juden*, vol. 1, p. 299.

79 Ute Gerhardt and Thomas Karlauf (eds), *Nie mehr zurück in dieses Land: Augenzeugen berichten über die Novemberpogrome 1938*, Berlin, 2009, p. 139. For more on the demeaning rituals see Obst, "*Reichskristallnacht*," pp. 279–307. See also Wildt, *Volksgemeinschaft als Selbstermächtigung*, pp. 345f.; Longerich, *Politik der Vernichtung*, pp. 203f.; Evans, *The Third Reich in Power*, pp. 590f. The governmental president of Lower Bavaria and the Upper Palatinate wrote on 8 Dec. 1938: "On the morning of 10 November in Regensburg, prior to their deportation, the men were led in closed ranks through the city. They were forced to carry a sign that read 'The Jews are moving out.'" Kulka and Jäckel (eds), *Die Juden in den geheimen NS-Stimmungsberichten 1933–1945*, no. 377, p. 329.

80 Report by Karl E. Schwab; Gerhardt and Karlauf (eds), *Nie mehr zurück in dieses Land*, p. 142. See also ibid., pp. 163–88, for the report by Karl Rosenthal, Rabbi of the Berlin Reform Congregation. Further reports in Ben Barkow, Raphael Gross and Michael Lenarz (eds), *Novemberpogrom 1938: Die Augenzeugenberichte der Wiener Library*, London and Frankfurt am Main, 2008, pp. 485–654.

81 Klemperer, *Tagebücher 1933–1941*, p. 443 (entry for 6 Dec. 1938).

82 Gerhardt and Karlauf (eds), *Nie mehr zurück in dieses Land*, p. 37.

83 Ibid., p. 215. On experiencing the absolute violence and the absolute powerlessness see Wildt, *Volksgemeinschaft als Selbstermächtigung*, p. 347. See also Benz, *Der Novemberpogrom 1938*, p. 498 ("Rückfall in die Barbarei").

84 Kulka and Jäckel (eds), *Die Juden in den geheimen NS-Stimmungsberichten 1933–1945*, no. 369, p. 324.

85 Ibid., no. 356, pp. 304f.

86 Feliks Chiczewski to the Polish ambassador in Berlin, 12 Nov. 1938; Bajohr and Strupp (eds), *Fremde Blicke auf das "Dritte Reich,"* p. 503.

87 Kulka and Jäckel (eds), *Die Juden in den geheimen NS-Stimmungsberichten 1933–1945*, no. 356, p. 305.

88 Andreas-Friedrich, *Der Schattenmann*, p. 30 (entry for 10 Nov. 1938).

89 Eduardo Labougle to Foreign Minister José María Cantilo, 14 Nov. 1938; Bajohr and Strupp (eds), *Fremde Blicke auf das "Dritte Reich,"* p. 514.

90 See Dieter W. Röckenmaier, *Denunzianten: 47 Fallgeschichten aus den Akten der Gestapo im NS-Gau Mainfranken*, Würzburg, 1998. Further, Eric A. Johnson, *Der national-sozialistische Terror: Gestapo, Juden und gewöhnliche Deutsche*, Berlin, 2001, pp. 110ff.

91 Guido Romano on the political situation, 12 Nov. 1938; Bajohr and Strupp (eds), *Fremde Blicke auf das "Dritte Reich,"* p. 509.

92 *Deutschland-Berichte der Sopade*, 5 (1938), p. 1204. On the relativity of this statement see Longerich, *"Davon haben wir nichts gewusst!,"* p. 131.

93 Report by Samuel W. Honacker, 12 Nov. 1938; Bajohr and Strupp (eds), *Fremde Blicke auf das "Dritte Reich,"* p. 505.

94 See the reports in Kulka and Jäckel (eds), *Die Juden in den geheimen NS-Stimmungsberichten 1933–1945*, no. 358, p. 316; no. 359, p. 318; no. 363, p. 319; no. 368, p. 322; no. 369, p. 323; no. 376, p. 328; no. 385, p. 333; no. 313, p. 337.

95 Quoted in Hans Mommsen and Dieter Obst, "Die Reaktion der deutschen Bevölkerung auf die Verfolgung der Juden 1933–1943," in Hans Mommsen and Susanne Willems (eds), *Herrschaftsalltag im Dritten Reich: Studien und Texte*, Düsseldorf, 1988, p. 392. See Kulka and Jäckel (eds), *Die Juden in den geheimen NS-Stimmungs-berichten 1933–1945*, no. 376, p. 329; no. 387, p. 334; no. 395, p. 38.

96   Kulka and Jäckel (eds), *Die Juden in den geheimen NS-Stimmungsberichten 1933–1945*, no. 380, p. 331.

97   Report by Wolstan Weld-Forester, 24 Nov. 1938; Bajohr and Strupp (eds), *Fremde Blicke auf das Dritte Reich,"* p. 520.

98   Quoted in Christoph Cornelissen, *Gerhard Ritter: Geschichtswissenschaft und Politik im 20. Jahrhundert*, Düsseldorf, 2001, pp. 244f.

99   Ulrich von Hassell, *Vom anderen Deutschland: Aus den nachgelassenen Tagebüchern 1938–1944*, Frankfurt am Main, 1964, p. 26 (entry for 25 Nov. 1938).

100 Franz-Rudolf von Weiss to the Swiss envoy in Berlin, Hans Frölicher, 12/13 Nov. 1938; Bajohr and Strupp (eds), *Fremde Blicke auf das "Dritte Reich,"* p. 510. See similar reactions in Benz, *Der Novemberpogrom 1938*, p. 527; Mommsen and Obst, "Die Reaktion der deutschen Bevölkerung," p. 391; Gerhardt and Karlauf (eds), *Nie mehr zurück in dieses Land*, p. 90.

101 On the churches' position see Friedländer, *Das Dritte Reich und die Juden*, vol. 1, pp. 319f.

102 As in Evans, *The Third Reich in Power*, p. 589. See Frank Bajohr, "Vom antijüdischen Konsens zum schlechten Gewissen: Die deutsche Gesellschaft und die Judenverfolgung 1933–1945," in idem and Dieter Pohl, *Der Holocaust als offenes Geheimnis: Die Deutschen, die NS-Führung und die Alliierten*, Munich, 2006, pp. 37–43.

103 Goebbels, *Tagebücher*, part 1, vol. 6, p. 182 (entry for 11 Nov. 1938).

104 See Göring to the conference on 12 Nov. 1938; *Die Verfolgung und Ermordung der europäischen Juden*, vol. 2, doc. 146, p. 408.

105 Protocol of the conference on 12 Nov. 1938 in ibid., pp. 408–37 (quotations on pp. 421, 415f., 432f., 435).

106 Goebbels, *Tagebücher*, part 1, vol. 6, p. 185 (entry for 13 Nov. 1938). Text of the decrees in *Die Verfolgung und Ermordung der europäischen Juden*, vol. 2, doc. 142–144, pp. 403–5.

107 See Barkai, "'Schicksalsjahr 1938,'" pp. 115f.

108 See Götz Aly, *Hitlers Volksstaat: Raub, Rassenkrieg und nationaler Sozialismus*, Frankfurt am Main, 2005, p. 61.

109 Susanne Heim and Götz Aly, "Staatliche Ordnung und 'organische Lösung": Die Rede Hermann Görings 'über die Judenfrage' vom 6. Dezember 1938," in *Jahrbuch für Antisemitismusforschung*, 2 (1992), pp. 378–404 (quotation on p. 392).

110 Text of the decrees in *Die Verfolgung und Ermordung der europäischen Juden*, vol. 2, doc. 152, pp. 450f.

111 See Longerich, *Politik der Vernichtung*, pp. 213f.; Friedländer, *Das Dritte Reich und die Juden*, vol. 1, p. 307.

112 Klemperer, *Tagebücher 1933–1941*, pp. 442 (entry for 6 Dec. 1938), 449 (New Year's Eve 1938).

113 Goebbels, *Tagebücher*, part 1, vol. 6, p. 209 (entry for 4 Dec. 1938).

114 See Longerich, *Politik der Vernichtung*, p. 214. Text of the law of 30 April 1939 in *Die Verfolgung und Ermordung der europäischen Juden*, vol. 2, doc. 277, pp. 743–6.

115 Ibid., doc. 146, p. 431.

116 See Gerwarth, *Reinhard Heydrich*, p. 163. See also Gabriele Anderl, "Die 'Zentralstellen für jüdische Auswanderung' in Wien, Berlin und Prag: Ein Vergleich," in *Tel Aviver Jahrbuch für deutsche Geschichte*, 23 (1994), pp. 275–99. Text of Göring's orders of 24 Jan. 1939 in *Die Verfolgung und Ermordung der europäischen Juden*, vol. 2, doc. 243, pp. 656f.

117 Gerhardt and Karlauf (eds), *Nie mehr zurück in dieses Land*, p. 155. See also Klemperer, *Tagebücher 1939–1941*, p. 464 (entry for 6 March 1939): "Everyone is trying desperately to get out, but it's getting ever more difficult."

118 Figures in Evans, *The Third Reich in Power*, p. 599.

119 Gerhardt and Karlauf (eds), *Nie mehr zurück in dieses Land*, pp. 311f.

120 As per the chapter heading in Friedländer, *Das Dritte Reich und die Juden*, vol. 1, p. 329.

121 *Die Verfolgung und Ermordung der europäischen Juden*, vol. 2, doc. 146, p. 436.

122 Notes by Walter Hewel on the conversation between Hitler and Minister Pirow, 24 Nov. 1938; *Die Verfolgung und Ermordnung der europäischen Juden*, vol. 2, doc. 172, pp. 486–91 (quotations on p. 488). On the visit by Pirow see Brechtken, "*Madagaskar für die Juden*," pp. 199–202.

123 Domarus, *Hitler*, vol. 2, part 1, pp. 1047–67 (quotations on pp. 1057f.).

124 See Hans Mommsen, "Hitler's Reichstag Speech of 30 January 1939," in *History & Memory*, 9 (1997), pp. 147–61 (particularly pp. 148, 150f.).

125 Report by the Swiss ambassador in Paris, Walter Stücki, to the head of the Swiss Political Office, Giuseppe Motta, 15 Nov. 1938; *Die Verfolgung und Ermordnung der europäischen Juden*, vol. 2, doc. 151, pp. 447–50 (quotation on p. 449).

126 On this interpretation see Friedländer, *Das Dritte Reich und die Juden*, vol. 1, pp. 335–7; Evans, *The Third Reich in Power*, pp. 604f.; Kershaw, *Hitler: Nemesis*, pp. 152f. See also the intelligent analysis by Philippe Burrin, *Warum die Deutschen? Antisemitismus, Nationalsozialismus, Genozid*, Berlin, 2004, pp. 96–111.

21 *The Way to War*

1 Max Domarus, *Hitler: Reden und Proklamationen 1932–1945. Vol. 1: Triumph. Part 2: 1935–1938*, Munich, 1965, p. 668.

2 Ibid., p. 681.

3 William S. Shirer, *Berliner Tagebuch: Aufzeichnungen 1934–41*, transcribed and ed. Jürgen Schebera, Leipzig and Weimar, 1991, p. 73 (entry for 8 April 1937).

4 *Die Tagebücher von Joseph Goebbels. Part 1: Aufzeichnungen 1923–1941*, ed. Elke Fröhlich, Munich, 1998, vol. 3/2, p. 102 (entry for 9 June 1936).

5 Text in *Akten der deutschen Auswärtigen Politik 1918–1945 (ADAP), Series C 1933–1937*, Göttingen, 1971–1981, vol. 5, part 2, no. 446, pp. 703–7.

6 Quoted in Norbert Schausberger, "Österreich und die nationalsozialistische Anschlusspolitik," in Manfred Funke (ed.), *Hitler, Deutschland und die Mächte: Materialien zur Aussenpolitik des Dritten Reiches*, Düsseldorf, 1978, p. 740.

7 See also Hans-Henning Abendroth, "Deutschlands Rolle im Spanischen Bürgerkrieg," in ibid., pp. 471–88 (at pp. 472–4); see also Frank Schauff, *Der Spanische Bürgerkrieg*, Göttingen, 2006, pp. 67ff., 145ff.

8 Goebbels, *Tagebücher*, part 1, vol. 3/2, p. 135 (entry for 20 July 1936).

9 See Brigitte Hamann, *Winifred Wagner oder Hitlers Bayreuth*, Munich and Zurich, 2002, p. 321.

10 *ADAP, Series D*, vol. 3, no. 4, p. 8. See Abendroth, *Deutschlands Rolle im Spanischen Bürgerkrieg*, pp. 474f.

11 Joachim von Ribbentrop, *Zwischen London und Moskau: Erinnerungen und letzte Aufzeichnungen*, ed. Annelies von Ribbentrop, Leoni am Starnberger See, 1961, p. 89. Hitler made a similar argument in the cabinet meeting of 1 Dec. 1936; see Goebbels, *Tagebücher*, part 1, vol. 3/2, pp. 272f. (entry for 2 Dec. 1936)

12 See Alfred Kube, *Pour le mérite und Hakenkreuz: Hermann Göring im Dritten Reich*, Munich, 1989, pp. 165f.; on Hitler's motives see Carlos Collado Seidel, *Der Spanische Bürgerkrieg: Geschichte eines europäischen Konflikts*, Munich, 2006, pp. 91–5; Bernd-Jürgen Wendt, *Grossdeutschland: Aussenpolitik und Kriegsvorbereitung des Hitler-Regimes*, Munich, 1987, pp. 111f.; Klaus Hildebrand, *Das vergangene Reich: Deutsche Aussenpolitik von Bismarck zu Hitler 1871–1945*, Stuttgart, 1995, pp. 628f.; Hans-Ulrich Thamer, *Verführung und Gewalt: Deutschland 1933–1945*, Berlin, 1986, pp. 545–7.

13 Goebbels, *Tagebücher*, part 1, vol. 3/2, p. 140 (entry for 27 July 1936).

14 See Hugh Thomas, *Der Spanische Bürgerkrieg*, Frankfurt am Main, 1964, pp. 326–9; Richard J. Evans, *The Third Reich in Power 1933–1939*, London, 2005, p. 640.

15   Goebbels, *Tagebücher*, part 1, vol. 4, p. 160 (entry for 31 May 1937). See Shirer, *Berliner Tagebuch*, p. 75 (entry for 30 May 1937): "One informant tells me Hitler has been screaming with rage all day and wants to declare war on Spain. The army and navy are trying to restrain him."

16   Goebbels, *Tagebücher*, part 1, vol. 4, pp. 162 (entry for 1 June 1937), 165 (entry for 3 June 1937).

17   See ibid, p. 185 (entry for 18 June 1937); Domarus, *Hitler*, vol. 1, part 2, p. 701.

18   Goebbels, *Tagebücher*, part 1, vol. 4, p. 231 (entry for 24 July 1937). See ibid., p. 282 (entry for 26 Aug. 1937): "This Spanish conflict is gradually taking a heavy toll on his nerves." See also Henrik Eberle and Mathias Uhl (eds), *Das Buch Hitler: Geheimdossier des NKWD für Josef W. Stalin aufgrund der Verhörprotokolle des Persönlichen Adjutanten Hitlers, Otto Günsche, und des Kammerdieners Heinz Linge, Moskau 1948/49*, Bergisch Gladbach, 2005, p. 65, which quotes Hitler as saying: "In the military realm, Franco is completely incompetent. A typical sergeant and nothing more."

19   Ulrich von Hassell, *Römische Tagebücher und Briefe 1932–1938*, ed. Ulrich Schlie, Munich, 2004, p. 144 (entry for 26 July 1936).

20   Ibid., p. 164 (entry for 6 Dec. 1936).

21   *ADAP*, Series C, vol. 5, part 2, no. 624, pp. 1056–8.

22   Jens Petersen, *Hitler–Mussolini: Die Entstehung der Achse Berlin–Rom 1933–1936*, Tübingen, 1973, p. 491.

23   Quoted in Walter Rauscher, *Hitler und Mussolini: Macht, Krieg und Terror*, Graz, Vienna and Cologne, 2001, p. 241; see Gianluca Falanga, *Mussolinis Vorposten in Hitlers Reich: Italiens Politik in Berlin 1933–1945*, Berlin, 2008, p. 80.

24   Quoted in Petersen, *Hitler–Mussolini*, p. 492.

25   Paul Schmidt: *Statist auf diplomatischer Bühne 1923–45: Erlebnisse des Chefdolmetschers im Auswärtigen Amt mit den Staatsmännern Europas*, Bonn, 1950, pp. 335f.; see Ian Kershaw, *Making Friends with Hitler: Lord Londonderry and Britain's Road to War*, London, 2005, pp. 136–9.

26   Kershaw, *Making Friends with Hitler*, p. 145.

27   Josef Henke, *England in Hitlers politischem Kalkül*, Boppard am Rhein, 1973, p. 63.

28   Ribbentrop, *Zwischen London und Moskau*, p. 93.

29   Quoted in Wolfgang Michalka, *Ribbentrop und die deutsche Weltpolitik 1933–1940: Aussenpolitische Konzeptionen und Entscheidungsprozesse im Dritten Reich*, Munich, 1980, p. 121.

30   Goebbels, *Tagebücher*, part 1, vol. 3/2, p. 249 (entry for 13 Nov. 1936).

31   Albert Speer, *Erinnerungen: Mit einem Essay von Jochen Thies*, Frankfurt am Main and Berlin, 1993, p. 88; see Fritz Wiedemann, *Der Mann, der Feldherr werden wollte: Erlebnisse und Erfahrungen des Vorgesetzten Hitlers im 1. Weltkrieg und seines späteren persönlichen Adjutanten*, Velbert and Kettwig 1964, p. 152; Ribbentrop, *Zwischen London und Moskau*, p. 104; Henke, *England in Hitlers politischem Kalkül*, p. 67; Goebbels, *Tagebücher*, part 1, vol. 3/2, p. 278 (entry for 5 Dec. 1936): "The Führer is furious at the moral hypocrites . . . The Baldwin government is behaving atrociously."

32   On the origins and signing of the pact, the best survey of the subject still is Theo Sommer, *Deutschland und Japan zwischen den Mächten 1935–1940: Vom Antikominternpakt zum Dreimächtepakt*, Tübingen, 1962 , pp. 23–56 (see pp. 493–5 for the text of the pact and the secret addendum).

33   See Michalka, *Ribbentrop und die deutsche Weltpolitik*, p. 135.

34   Goebbels, *Tagebücher*, part 1, vol. 3/2, p. 218 (entry for 21 Oct. 1936).

35   As in Sommer, *Deutschland und Japan zwischen den Mächten*, p. 49.

36   Goebbels, *Tagebücher*, part 1, vol. 3/2, p. 349 (entry for 28 Jan. 1937).

37   Ibid., p. 389 (entry for 23 Feb. 1937).

38   Ibid., vol. 4, p. 52 (entry for 15 March 1937). In May 1937 Hassell learned from Neurath in Rome that "Hitler has written off Czechoslovakia. He's not trying to reach any

genuine understanding and instead envisions . . . the country being broken up."
Hassell, *Römische Tagebücher*, p. 199 (entry for 6 May 1937).

39   Goebbels, *Tagebücher*, part 1, vol. 4, p. 87 (entry for 10 April 1937).

40   Ibid., p. 247 (entry for 3 Aug. 1937). On the final day of the 1937 Nuremberg Rally, Hitler remarked to Goebbels: "Austria . . . will be resolved violently." Ibid., p. 312 (entry for 14 Sept. 1937).

41   Henke, *England in Hitlers politischem Kalkül*, p. 81.

42   See Goebbels, *Tagebücher*, part 1, vol. 4, p. 154 (entry for 28 May 1937).

43   For a broader assessment see Robert Alexander Clarke Parker, *Chamberlain and Appeasement: British Policy and the Coming of the Second World War*, London, 1993; see also Rainer F. Schmidt, *Die Aussenpolitik des Dritten Reiches 1933–1939*, Stuttgart, 2002, pp. 232–9.

44   Goebbels, *Tagebücher*, part 1, vol. 4, pp. 214 (entry for 10 July 1937), 217 (entry for 13 July 1937) 185 (entry for 18 June 1937).

45   See Falanga, *Mussolinis Vorposten*, p. 88.

46   Goebbels, *Tagebücher*, part 1, vol. 4, p. 296 (entry for 5 Sept. 1937). See ibid., pp. 315 (entry for 9 Sept. 1937), 318 (entry for 19 Sept. 1937), 321 (entry for 21 Sept. 1937), 322 (entry for 22 Sept. 1937), 324 (entry for 23 Sept. 1937).

47   Ibid., p. 328 (entry for 26 Sept. 1937).

48   Schmidt, *Statist auf diplomatischer Bühne*, pp. 365f.; Schmidt's characterisation is recognisably modelled on the account by André François-Poncet, *Als Botschafter in Berlin 1931–1938*, Mainz, 1947, pp. 299f.

49   See Domarus, *Hitler*, vol. 1, part 2, p. 734.

50   Goebbels, *Tagebücher*, part 1, vol. 4, p. 332 (entry for 28 Sept. 1937). See also Hans Frank, *Im Angesicht des Galgens: Deutung Hitlers und seiner Zeit auf Grund eigener Erlebnisse und Erkenntnisse*, Munich and Gräfelfing, 1953, pp. 269f.

51   Schmidt, *Statist auf diplomatischer Bühne*, p. 367.

52   Ibid., p. 368.

53   Domarus, *Hitler*, vol. 1, part 2, p. 735.

54   See ibid., pp. 737f., Rauscher, *Hitler und Mussoloni*, p. 248; Goebbels, *Tagebücher*, part 1, vol. 4, p. 334: "[Mussolini] speaks with a passionate accent . . . Sometimes he yells too much. But that doesn't prevent him from achieving an effect."

55   François-Poncet, *Als Botschafter in Berlin*, p. 310. Foreign Minister Ciano restricted his notes concerning the evening's mass ceremony to: "Lots of emotion and lots of rain." Galeazzo Ciano, *Tagebücher 1937/38*, Hamburg, 1949, p. 19.

56   Frank, *Im Angesicht des Galgens*, p. 271; see Nicolaus von Below, *Als Hitlers Adjutant 1937–45*, Mainz, 1980, p. 44.

57   See Rauscher, *Hitler und Mussolini*, p. 245.

58   Goebbels, *Tagebücher*, part 1, vol. 4, pp. 335f. (entry for 30 Sept. 1937).

59   Hamann, *Winifred Wagner*, p. 350. See also Goebbels, *Tagebücher*, part 1, vol. 4, p. 336 (entry for 30 Sept. 1937): "[Hitler] was happy everything went so well."

60   Frank, *Im Angesicht des Galgens*, p. 273.

61   Rauscher, *Hitler und Mussolini*, p. 248

62   Goebbels, *Tagebücher*, part 1, vol. 4, p. 332 (entry for 28 Sept. 1937): "Only Austria is still open. But he always skips over that."

63   Ibid., p. 329 (entry for 26 Sept. 1937); see Wiedemann, *Der Mann*, p. 133.

64   Adolf Hitler, *Monologe im Führerhauptquartier 1941–1944: Die Aufzeichnungen Heinrich Heims*, ed. Werner Jochmann, Hamburg, 1980, pp. 144 (dated 20 Nov. 1941), 246 (dated 31 Jan. 1942). See ibid., p. 44 (dated 21/22 July 1941). Wiedemann's notes "Stellung zu Italien" (position on Italy) read: "Mussolini and Hitler have so much in common in terms of their thinking and their past that a relationship of strong personal friendship and trust developed." BA Koblenz, N 1720/4.

65   Domarus, *Hitler*, vol. 1, part 2, p. 745.

66   On the question of the authenticity of Hossbach's protocol see Walter Bussmann, "Zur Entstehung und Überlieferung der 'Hossbach-Niederschrift,'" in *Vierteljahrshefte für Zeitgeschichte*, 16 (1968), pp. 373–8; Jonathan Wright and Paul Stafford, "Hitler, Britain and the Hossbach-Memorandum," in *Militärgeschichtliche Mitteilungen*, 46 (1987/2), pp. 77–123. See also Hossbach's notes on the history of its origins in Friedrich Hossbach, *Zwischen Wehrmacht und Hitler 1934–1938*, 2nd revised edition, Göttingen, 1965, pp. 189–92.

67   On the story behind the conference of 5 Nov. 1937 see Wendt, *Grossdeutschland*, pp. 11–14.

68   The Hossbach protocol is reprinted in Hossbach, *Zwischen Wehrmacht und Hitler*, pp. 181–9; Domarus, *Hitler*, vol. 1, part 2, pp. 748–745 (from which it is quoted here). For a detailed account of the contents see Wendt, *Grossdeutschland*, pp. 15–24.

69   Reprinted in *Der Prozess gegen die Hauptkriegsverbrecher vor dem Internationalen Militärtribunal in Nürnberg (IMT)*, Nuremberg, 1947–9, vol. 34, pp. 745ff.

70   As in Wendt, *Grossdeutschland*, p. 27. Contrary to this see Karl Heinz Janssen and Fritz Tobias, *Der Sturz der Generäle: Hitler und die Blomberg-Fritsch-Krise 1938*, Munich, 1994, p. 18.

71   *IMT*, vol. 16, pp. 640f.

72   See Janssen and Tobias, *Der Sturz der Generäle*, pp. 24–31. This account corrects earlier historical hypotheses that the Blomberg–Fritsch crisis was a plot hatched by Himmler, Heydrich and Göring. On this see Harold C. Deutsch, *Das Komplott oder die Entmachtung der Generale: Blomberg- und Fritsch-Krise. Hitlers Weg zum Krieg*, Zurich, 1974. On Blomberg's affair with Margarethe Gruhn see also Kirstin A. Schäfer, *Werner von Blomberg: Hitlers erster Feldmarschall. Eine Biographie*, Paderborn, 2006, pp. 175–7.

73   See Janssen and Tobias, *Der Sturz der Generäle*, pp. 38–42 (quotation on p. 41); Schäfer, *Werner von Blomberg*, pp. 178f.

74   See Janssen and Tobias, *Der Sturz der Generäle*, pp. 27f., 43–50 (quotations on pp. 45, 50); Schäfer, *Werner von Blomberg*, pp. 180f.

75   As in Janssen and Tobias, *Der Sturz der Generäle*, p. 51.

76   Below, *Als Adjutant Hitlers*, pp. 63f.

77   Wiedemann, *Der Mann*, p. 112; see also Goebbels, *Tagebücher*, part 1, vol. 5, p. 127 (entry for 1 Feb. 1938): "The Führer . . . shared his whole sorrow with me. Complained that his faith in humanity has been utterly shaken. Blomberg gets married to a whore and stays with her and abandons the state . . . The Führer trusted him blindly. That was a big mistake."

78   Goebbels, *Tagebücher*, part 1, vol. 5, p. 115 (entry for 26 Jan. 1938).

79   Hossbach, *Zwischen Wehrmacht und Hitler*, pp. 107f.

80   See Janssen and Tobias, *Der Sturz der Generäle*, pp. 53–5; Schäfer, *Werner von Blomberg*, pp. 187f.

81   Gerhard Engel, *Heeresadjutant bei Hitler 1938–1943*, ed. and annotated Hildegard von Kotze, Stuttgart, 1974, pp. 20f. (dated 26 April 1938).

82   See Janssen and Tobias, *Der Sturz der Generäle*, pp. 84f.

83   François-Poncet, *Als Botschafter in Berlin*, p. 291.

84   See Janssen and Tobias, *Der Sturz der Generäle*, pp. 86–97.

85   Hossbach, *Zwischen Wehrmacht und Hitler*, p. 108.

86   Ibid., pp. 108–10 (quotation on p. 110). See Janssen and Tobias, *Der Sturz der Generäle*, pp. 97–100.

87   Hossbach, *Zwischen Wehrmacht und Hitler*, p. 110.

88   Goebbels, *Tagebücher*, part 1, vol. 5, pp. 117f. (entry for 27 Jan. 1938).

89   Hossbach, *Zwischen Wehrmacht und Hitler*, p. 112; see Janssen and Tobias, *Der Sturz der Generäle*, pp. 91, 104.

90   Horst Mühleisen, "Die Fritsch-Krise im Frühjahr 1938: Neue Dokumente aus dem Nachlass des Generalobersten," in *Militärgeschichtliche Mitteilungen*, 56 (1997/2),

pp. 471–508, doc. 1. The above quotation is in Hossbach, *Zwischen Wehrmacht und Hitler*, p. 112. See Janssen and Tobias, *Der Sturz der Generäle*, pp. 104–8.

91 For the following quote see also Goebbels, *Tagebücher*, part 1, vol. 5, p. 119 (entry for 28 Jan. 1938). See also Janssen and Tobias, *Der Sturz der Generäle*, pp. 109–14.

92 See Goebbels, *Tagebücher*, vol. 5, p. 122 (entry for 29 Jan. 1938). On the tempestuous meeting see Hossbach, *Zwischen Wehrmacht und Hitler*, pp. 115–18.

93 Goebbels, *Tagebücher*, part 1, vol. 5, p. 124.

94 See Janssen and Tobias, *Der Sturz der Generäle*, pp. 116–23.

95 Goebbels, *Tagebücher*, part 1, vol. 5, p. 127 (entry for 1 Feb. 1938).

96 Janssen and Tobias, *Der Sturz der Generäle*, p. 140.

97 Wiedemann, *Der Mann*, p. 113. See Janssen and Tobias, *Der Sturz der Generäle*, pp. 125f.

98 Goebbels, *Tagebücher*, part 1, vol. 5, p. 119 (entry for 28 Jan. 1938). See Janssen and Tobias, *Der Sturz der Generäle*, pp. 126f.

99 Goebbels, *Tagebücher*, part 1, vol. 5, p. 119 (entry for 28 Jan. 1938).

100 Below, *Als Hitlers Adjutant*, p. 75.

101 Goebbels, *Tagebücher*, part 1, vol. 5, p. 125 (entry for 31 Jan. 1938).

102 Ibid., pp. 127f. (entry for 1 Feb. 1938).

103 Janssen and Tobias, *Der Sturz der Generäle*, p. 149; Domarus, *Hitler*, vol. 1, part 2, p. 782.

104 Goebbels, *Tagebücher*, part 1, vol. 5, p. 127 (entry for 1 Feb. 1938).

105 On the reshuffle of 4 Feb. 1938 see ibid., p. 137 (entry for 5 Feb. 1938); Below, *Als Hitlers Adjutant*, pp. 73f.; Otto Dietrich, *12 Jahre mit Hitler*, Munich, 1955, pp. 50f.; Janssen and Tobias, *Der Sturz der Generäle*, pp. 150f.; Eckart Conze, Norbert Frei, Peter Hayes and Moshe Zimmermann, *Das Amt und die Vergangenheit: Deutsche Diplomaten im Dritten Reich und in der Bundesrepublik*, Munich, 2010, pp. 124–6. Hassell was suspended by Neurath on 18 Jan. 1938. He suspected that a plot against him was the reason for his dismissal. See Hassell to Neurath, 24 Jan. 1938, and Neurath to Lammers, 26 Jan. 1938; BA Berlin-Lichterfelde, R 43 II/889b.

106 Goebbels, *Tagebücher*, part 1, vol. 5, p. 138 (entry for 6 Feb. 1938).

107 Janssen and Tobias, *Der Sturz der Generäle*, pp. 152f.; Below, *Als Hitlers Adjutant*, p. 79; Ian Kershaw, *Hitler 1936–1945: Nemesis*, London, 2000, p. 59.

108 Goebbels, *Tagebücher*, part 1, vol. 5, p. 140 (entry for 6 Feb. 1938). See also the expression of thanks from Hitler to Blomberg and Neurath in *Akten der Reichskanzlei: Die Regierung Hitler: Vols 2–6: 1934/35–1939*, ed. Friedrich Hartmannsgruber, Munich, 1999–2012, vol. 5, doc. 31, pp. 110f.

109 François-Poncet, *Als Botschafter in Berlin*, p. 295. In a telegram on 5 Feb. 1938, François-Poncet wrote of a "kind of second 30 June." Claus W. Schäfer, *André François-Poncet als Botschafter in Berlin 1931–1938*, Munich, 2004, p. 281.

110 Notes by lawyer Rüdiger Graf von der Goltz on the trial (written 1945/46); IfZ München, ZS 49. A detailed account of the trial in Janssen and Tobias, *Der Sturz der Generäle*, pp. 173–82.

111 Ibid., p. 183.

112 See ibid., pp. 237–9, 247–9.

113 See ibid., pp. 77–9; Schäfer, *Werner von Blomberg*, pp. 199ff.

114 IMT, vol. 28, p. 362.

115 See Schausberger, "Österreich und die nationalsozialistische Anschlusspolitik," pp. 470f.

116 Hassell, *Römische Tagebücher*, p. 173 (entry for 15 Jan. 1937). See Kube, *Pour le mérite und Hakenkreuz*, pp. 225–7.

117 Schmidt, *Statist auf diplomatischer Bühne*, p. 347; see Kube, *Pour le mérite und Hakenkreuz*, p. 230.

118 See Kube, *Pour le mérite und Hakenkreuz*, pp. 236f., 239.

119 Schmidt, *Statist auf diplomatische Bühne*, pp. 377f.

120 Goebbels, *Tagebücher*, part 1, vol. 4, p. 415 (entry for 21 Nov. 1937).

121 See Schausberger, "Österreich und die nationalsozialistische Anschlusspolitik," pp. 478f.

122 Franz von Papen, *Der Wahrheit eine Gasse*, Munich, 1952, p. 460; see Joachim Petzold, *Franz von Papen: Ein deutsches Verhängnis*, Munich and Berlin, 1995, p. 252.

123 See Below, *Als Hitlers Adjutant*, p. 84.

124 See Papen, *Der Wahrheit eine Gasse*, pp. 467f.

125 On what follows see Kurt von Schuschnigg, *Ein Requiem in Rot-Weiss-Rot*, Zurich, 1946, pp. 38–44.

126 Ibid., p. 45.

127 See *ADAP*, Series D, vol. 1, no. 295, pp. 423f.; Schuschnigg, *Ein Requiem*, pp. 46f.; Papen, *Der Wahrheit eine Gasse*, pp. 470f.

128 Papen, *Der Wahrheit eine Gasse*, p. 471; see IMT, vol. 10, pp. 567f.; Schuschnigg, *Ein Requiem*, p. 49.

129 Schuschnigg, *Ein Requiem*, pp. 51f.; see Papen, *Der Wahrheit eine Gasse*, p. 475.

130 Eberle and Uhl (eds), *Das Buch Hitler*, p. 72.

131 Goebbels, *Tagebücher*, part 1, vol. 5, p. 159 (entry for 16 Feb. 1938). See ibid., p. 157 (entry for 16 Feb. 1938): "He was very rigorous with Schuschnigg . . . Cannon always speak clearly."

132 Ibid., p. 161 (entry for 17 Feb. 1938).

133 Domarus, *Hitler*, vol. 1, part 2, pp. 801–3. See Goebbels, *Tagebücher*, part 1, vol. 5, p. 168 (entry for 21 Feb. 1938).

134 Memorandum by Wilhelm Keppler, Hitler's Austria expert, dated 28 Feb. 1938; *ADAP*, Series D, vol. 1, no. 328, p. 450; see Kube, *Pour le mérite und Hakenkreuz*, p. 243.

135 Schausberger, "Österreich und die nationalsozialistische Anschlusspolitik," p. 752.

136 See Schuschnigg, *Ein Requiem*, p. 41.

137 Ciano, *Tagebücher 1937/38*, p. 123 (entry for 10 March 1938).

138 Goebbels, *Tagebücher*, part 1, vol. 5, pp. 198f. (entry for 10 March 1938).

139 Harry Graf Kessler, *Das Tagebuch. Vol. 9: 1926–1937*, ed. Sabine Gruber and Ulrich Ott with Christoph Hilse and Nadin Weiss, Stuttgart, 2010, p. 663 (entry for 16 April 1936); see also Konrad Heiden, *Adolf Hitler: Ein Mann gegen Europa*, Zurich, 1937, p. 266: "The substance of Hitler's politics resides in his lightning quick reaction to circumstances."

140 Domarus, *Hitler*, vol. 1, part 2, p. 808.

141 Goebbels, *Tagebücher*, part 1, vol. 5, pp. 200f. (entry for 11 March 1938).

142 Ibid., p. 202 (entry for 12 March 1938).

143 *ADAP*, Series D, vol. 1, no. 352, p. 470.

144 See Reinhard Spitzy, *So haben wir das Reich verspielt: Bekenntnisse eines Illegalen*, 2nd edition, Munich and Vienna, 1987, pp. 233–8.

145 See Goebbels, *Tagebücher*, part 1, vol. 5, p. 202 (entry for 12 March 1938); IMT, vol. 16, pp. 360–2; Kershaw, *Hitler: Nemesis*, pp. 76f.

146 IMT, vol. 9, p. 333.

147 Below, *Als Hitlers Adjutant*, p. 90.

148 On the unfolding of events see the transcript of the telephone conversations in Schuschnigg, *Ein Requiem*, pp. 84–98; IMT, vol. 16, pp. 167f.; Goebbels, *Tagebücher*, part 1, vol. 5, p. 203 (entry for 12 March 1938); Schausberger, "Österreich und die nationalsozialistische Anschlusspolitik," pp. 754f.; Kershaw, *Hitler: Nemesis*, pp. 77f.

149 IMT, vol. 31, pp. 368f.; Domarus, *Hitler*, vol. 1, part 2, p. 813. See Ciano, *Tagebücher 1937/38*, p. 124 (entry for 12 March 1938).

150 See Spitzy, *So haben wir das Reich verspielt*, p. 238.

151 Domarus, *Hitler*, vol. 1, part 2, pp. 816f.; see Goebbels, *Tagebücher*, part 1, vol. 5, p. 205 (entry for 13 March 1938).

152 Brigitte Hamann, *Hitlers Edeljude: Das Leben des Armenarztes Eduard Bloch*, Munich and Zurich, 2008, pp. 259f.

153 Domarus, *Hitler*, vol. 1, part 2, p. 817.

154 See Christa Schroeder, *Er war mein Chef: Aus dem Nachlass der Sekretärin von Adolf Hitler*, ed. Anton Joachimsthaler, 3rd edition, Munich and Vienna, 1985, p. 85.

155 Domarus, *Hitler*, vol. 1, part 2, pp. 820f.; see Goebbels, *Tagebücher*, part 1, vol. 5, p. 208: "With that amalgamation is practically complete. It's a historic hour. Indescribable joy among all of us."

156 Wiedemann, *Der Mann*, p. 123.

157 See Below, *Als Hitlers Adjutant*, p. 93; Baldur von Schirach, *Ich glaubte an Hitler*, Hamburg, 1967, pp. 240f.; Schroeder, *Er war mein Chef*, p. 85; Heinrich Hoffmann, *Hitler wie ich ihn sah: Aufzeichnungen seines Leibfotographen*, Munich and Berlin, 1974, p. 97.

158 Domarus, *Hitler*, vol. 1, part 2, p. 824

159 Below, *Als Hitlers Adjutant*, p. 93.

160 See Domarus, *Hitler*, vol. 1, part 2, p. 825; Engel, *Heeresadjutant bei Hitler*, pp. 15f. (dated 14 March 1938); Hans Baur, *Ich flog Mächtige der Erde*, Kempten im Allgäu, 1956, p. 165; Spitzy, *So haben wir das Reich verspielt*, p. 248; Schirach, *Ich glaubte an Hitler*, p. 241.

161 Goebbels, *Tagebücher*, part 1, vol. 5, pp. 212 (entry for 16 March 1938), 214 (entry for 17 March 1938). See Below, *Als Hitlers Adjutant*, p. 94; Schroeder, *Er war mein Chef*, p. 86.

162 Hamann, *Winifred Wagner*, p. 354.

163 *Die Weizsäcker-Papiere 1933–1950*, ed. Leonidas Hill, Frankfurt am Main, Berlin and Vienna, 1974, p. 123 (dated 13 March and 15 March 1938).

164 Christoph Cornelissen, *Gerhard Ritter: Geschichtswissenschaft und Politik im 20. Jahrhundert*, Düsseldorf, 2001, p. 244; see also the historian Friedrich Meinecke to Hajo Holborn, 7 April 1938; Friedrich Meinecke, *Werke. Bd. VI: Ausgewählter Briefwechsel*, Stuttgart, 1962, p. 180.

165 Evans, *The Third Reich in Power*, p. 663.

166 Willy Cohn, *Kein Recht, nirgends: Tagebuch vom Untergang des Breslauer Judentums 1933–1941*, ed. Norbert Conrads, Cologne, Weimar and Berlin, 2006, vol. 1, pp. 523f. (entries for 13 March, 14 March 1938).

167 Victor Klemperer, *Ich will Zeugnis ablegen bis zum letzten: Tagebücher 1933–1941*, ed. Walter Nowojski with Hadwig Klemperer, Berlin, 1995, p. 399 (entry for 20 March 1938).

168 Thomas Mann, *Tagebücher 1937–1939*, ed. Peter de Mendelssohn, Frankfurt am Main, 1980, p. 188 (entry for 13 March 1938).

169 *Deutschland-Berichte der Sozialdemokratischen Partei Deutschlands (Sopade) 1934–1940*, ed. Klaus Behnken, Frankfurt am Main, 1980, 5 (1938), p. 258.

170 Ibid., pp. 263f.

171 Ibid., p. 262.

172 Domarus, *Hitler*, vol. 1, part 2, pp. 826–32.

173 Hamann, *Winifred Wagner*, p. 355; see Eva Rieger, *Friedelind Wagner: Die rebellische Enkelin Richard Wagners*, Munich and Zurich, 2012, p. 105.

174 See Spitzy, *So haben wir das Reich verspielt*, p. 254; Goebbels, *Tagebücher*, part 1, vol. 5, p. 252 (entry for 10 April 1938).

175 Goebbels, *Tagebücher*, part 1, vol. 5, p. 256 (entry for 11 April 1938). See ibid., p. 254 (entry for 10 April 1938); Domarus, *Hitler*, vol. 1, part 2, p. 850. Even after 1945, Hitler's adjutant Nicolaus von Below was convinced "that following the *Anschluss* there were no more than half a million eligibile voters in Germany who were against us" (*Als Hitlers Adjutant*, p. 96). The historian Hans-Ulrich Wehler agrees: "If there had been a free election monitored by the League of Nations, the result [of 99 per cent of the vote for the Nazis] would probably have been no different" (*Deutsche Gesellschaftsgeschichte 1914–1949*, p. 622). That is probably something of an exaggeration.

176 Klemperer, *Tagebücher 1933–1941*, p. 403 (entry for 10 April 1938).

177 On the advantages of the *Anschluss* see Wendt, *Grossdeutschland*, pp. 143f.; Thamer, *Verführung und Gewalt*, pp. 579f.; Schmidt, *Die Aussenpolitik des Dritten Reiches*, pp. 255f.; Evans, *The Third Reich in Power*, pp. 655f.; Adam Tooze, *The Wages of Destruction: The Making and Breaking of the Nazi Economy*, London, 2006, pp. 245–7.

178 Below, *Als Hitlers Adjutant*, pp. 95f.

179 *Deutschland-Berichte der Sopade*, 5 (1938), p. 268. See also Shirer, *Berliner Tagebuch*, p. 111 (entry for 14 April 1938).

180 Goebbels, *Tagebücher*, part 1, vol. 5, p. 222 (entry for 20 March 1938). See Speer, *Erinnerungen*, p. 123: "Shortly after the *Anschluss*, Hitler had a map of Central Europe brought out and privately showed a circle of keen listeners that Czechoslovakia was now trapped in a 'vise' from both sides."

181 Konrad Henlein's report on his meeting with the Führer on 28 March 1938; *ADAP*, Series D, vol. 2, no. 107, p. 158. See Goebbels, *Tagebücher*, part 1, vol. 5, p. 236 (entry for 29 March 1938): "The Führer spoke with Henlein. The plan is to constantly demand more than what Prague can give. Then the thing will start rolling."

182 Konrad Henlein to Neurath, 19 Nov. 1937, with a report for Hitler on current questions on German policy in the Czech Republic; *ADAP*, Series D, vol. 2, no. 23, pp. 40–51 (quotation on p. 41). For context see Ralf Gebel, *"Heim ins Reich": Konrad Henlein und der Reichsgau Sudetenland (1938–1945)*, Munich, 1999.

183 Goebbels, *Tagebücher*, part 1, vol. 5, p. 328 (entry for 1 June 1938)

184 Memorandum by Wehrmacht adjutant Rudolf Schmundt dated 22 April 1938: summary of the meeting between Hitler and Keitel on 21 April 1938; *ADAP*, Serise D, vol. 2, no. 133, p. 190.

185 Henlein's memorandum on the eight demands announced in Karlsbad on 24 April 1938; ibid., no. 135, p. 192.

186 See Heike B. Görtemaker, *Eva Braun: Leben mit Hitler*, Munich, 2010, pp. 214f. Contrary to Görtemaker's claim, Magda Goebbels did not take part in the trip. During her husband's visit to Italy she gave birth to her fifth child—a daughter, Hedda. See Goebbels, *Tagebücher*, part 1, vol. 5, p. 289 (entry for 6 May 1938).

187 See a description of the reception in Schmidt, *Statist auf diplomatischer Bühne*, p. 385; Spitzy, *So haben wir das Reich verspielt*, p. 263; Frank, *Im Angesicht des Galgens*, pp. 292f.

188 See Görtemaker, *Eva Braun*, pp. 214f.

189 Goebbels, *Tagebücher*, part 1, vol. 5, p. 290 (entry for 6 May 1938).

190 Wiedemann, *Der Mann*, p. 139. See Goebbels, *Tagebücher*, part 1, vol. 5, p. 288 (entry for 5 May 1938): "It was a cold, dead, empty occasion."

191 Frank, *Im Angesicht des Galgens*, p. 296. See Olaf Rose (ed.), *Julius Schaub: In Hitlers Schatten*, Stegen, 2005, p. 176; Schroeder, *Er war mein Chef*, p. 87.

192 See Schmidt, *Statist auf diplomatischer Bühne*, p. 386; Below, *Als Hitlers Adjutant*, p. 98; Wiedemann, *Der Mann*, pp. 140f.; Goebbels, *Tagebücher*, part 1, vol. 5, pp. 288f. (entry for 6 May 1938).

193 Wiedemann, *Der Mann*, p. 142. On the incident see also Wiedemann's notes entitled "individual recollections," San Francisco, 28 March 1939; BA Koblenz, N 1720/4; Spitzy, *So haben wir das Reich verspielt*, pp. 266f.; Rose, *Julius Schaub*, pp. 177f.; Schmidt, *Statist auf diplomatischer Bühne*, p. 386.

194 Schroeder, *Er war mein Chef*, p. 87.

195 Baur, *Ich flog Mächtige dieser Erde*, p. 162.

196 Below, *Als Hitlers Adjutant*, p. 99; Baur, *Ich flog Mächtige dieser Erde*, p. 163. See Goebbels, *Tagebücher*, part 1, vol. 5, p. 292 (entry for 7 May 1938): "The Führer is furious at this entire court herd."

197 Domarus, *Hitler*, vol. 1, part 2, pp. 859–61 (quotation on p. 861). See Goebbels, *Tagebücher*, part 1, vol. 5, p. 294 (entry for 8 May 1938): "Major conversations at table. Mussolini came out clearly on our side. The Führer solemnly guaranteed to respct the Brenner border."

198 Hitler, *Monologe*, p. 44 (dated 21/22 July 1941).

199   Ciano, *Tagebücher 1937/38*, p. 159 (entry for 9 May 1938). See Goebbels, *Tagebücher*, part 1, vol. 5, p. 297 (entry for 10 May 1938): "Very warm farewells between him and the Duce."

200   *ADAP, Series D*, vol. 1, no. 761, p. 899.

201   *Die Weizsäcker-Papiere 1933–1950*, p. 128 (dated 13 May 1938). See Goebbels, *Tagebücher*, part 1, vol. 5, p. 292 (entry for 7 May 1938): "Mussolini has given us an absolutely free hand."

202   Engel, *Heeresadjutant bei Hitler*, p. 23 (dated 22 May 1938).

203   Speer, *Erinnerungen*, p. 124; Frank, *Im Angesicht des Galgens*, pp. 296f. See Hitler, *Monologe*, p. 248 (dated 31 Jan. 1942): "We can't thank Noske, Ebert and Scheidemann enough for cleaning this up for us." See also Wiedemann's notes "Einstellung zu den Fürstenhäusern" (notes on attitude towards aristocratic houses); BA Koblenz, N 1720/4.

204   See Below, *Als Hitlers Adjutant*, p. 100; Goebbels, *Tagebücher*, part 1, vol. 5, pp. 302 (entry for 12 May 1938), 320 (entry for 27 May 1938).

205   For the details see Gerhard L. Weinberg, "The May Crisis, 1938," in *Journal of Modern History*, 29 (1957), pp. 213–25.

206   Goebbels, *Tagebücher*, part 1, vol. 5, p. 323 (entry for 29 May 1938).

207   On the conference of 28 May 1938 see Klaus-Jürgen Müller, *Generaloberst Ludwig Beck: Eine Biographie*, Paderborn, 2008, pp. 321f.; Below, *Als Hitlers Adjutant*, pp. 101f.; Wiedemann, *Der Mann*, pp. 126–8; Wiedemann's essay "Crisis of spring and summer 1938": "The time was set as not before the end of September and probably not until March 1939. Neurath responded to me: 'So now we have at least a year. A lot can happen in the meantime.'" BA Koblenz, N 1720/4.

208   *ADAP, Series D*, vol. 2, no. 221, pp. 281–5 (quotation on p. 282).

209   Ibid., no. 282, pp. 377–80 (quotation on p. 377).

210   Below, *Als Hitlers Adjutant*, p. 102.

211   See Müller, *Generaloberst Ludwig Beck*, pp. 313f., 324–32.

212   Engel, *Heeresadjutant bei Hitler*, p. 24 (dated May 1938); see ibid., p. 27 (dated 18 July 1938).

213   See Müller, *Generaloberst Ludwig Beck*, pp. 335–8 (quotation on p. 338).

214   Ibid., pp. 339f.

215   Ibid., pp. 342f.

216   Sworn statement by Colonel General Wilhelm Adam regarding the meeting on 4 Aug. 1938 (1947/48); IfZ München ZS 6. See also Müller, *Generaloberst Beck*, pp. 351–4.

217   Goebbels, *Tagebücher*, part 1, vol. 5, p. 393 (entry for 25 July 1938). See Engel, *Heeresadjutant bei Hitler*, p. 29 (entry for 2 Aug. 1938).

218   Below, *Als Hitlers Adjutant*, p. 112.

219   Wiedemann, *Der Mann*, p. 172.

220   Engel, *Heeresadjutant bei Hitler*, p. 32 (dated 17 Aug. 1938). On the speech of 10 Aug. 1938 see the transcript by General Gustav Adolf von Weitersheim dated 13 Feb. 1948; IfZ München, ZS 1655. Further, Below, *Als Hitlers Adjutant*, pp. 112f.; Müller, *Generaloberst Ludwig Beck*, p. 355.

221   Engel, *Heeresadjutant bei Hitler*, p. 33 (dated 20 Aug. 1938).

222   See Müller, *Generaloberst Ludwig Beck*, pp. 356–8; Christian Hartmann, *Halder: Generalstabschef Hitlers 1938–1942*, 2nd revised and expanded edition, Paderborn, 2010, pp. 62–4.

223   Shirer, *Berliner Tagebuch*, p. 118 (entry for 4 Aug. 1938).

224   Goebbels, *Tagebücher*, part 1, vol. 5, p. 331 (entry for 3 June 1938).

225   On the Wiedemann mission, see the guidelines issued by Hitler on 15 July 1938 and Wiedemann's memorandum for Ribbentrop about his conversation with Halifax on 18 July 1938; BA Koblenz, N 1720/3. That same day Wiedemann flew to Berchtesgaden to brief Hitler, but Hitler preferred to take a two-hour walk with Unity Mitford and only gave his adjutant five minutes. Wiedemann's essay "Crisis of spring and summer 1938"; BA Koblenz, N 1720/4. See also Wiedemann, *Der Mann*, pp. 159–67. Max Wünsche's daily diaries, 15 July, 19 July 1938; BA Berlin-Lichterfelde, NS 10/125.

226   See Engel, *Heeresadjutant bei Hitler*, p. 28 (dated August 1938).

227   Hamann, *Winifred Wagner*, p. 371.

228   Goebbels, *Tagebücher*, part 1, vol. 6, p. 29 (entry for 1 Aug. 1938). See also Unity Mitford's account in a letter to Diana Mitford, 4 Aug. 1938; Charlotte Mosley (ed.), *The Mitfords: Letters between Six Sisters*, London, 2007, pp. 130f.

229   Goebbels, *Tagebücher*, part 1, vol. 6, p. 39 (entry for 10 Aug. 1938).

230   Ibid., p. 49 (entry for 19 Aug. 1938). See ibid., p. 52 (entry for 21 Aug. 1938): "At the moment, his mind is completely occupied by military questions."

231   Sworn statement by Colonel General Wilhelm Adam regarding the Western border discussion with Hitler on 27 Aug. 1938 (1947/48); IfZ München, ZS 6; see also Anton Hoch and Hermann Weiss, "Die Erinnerungen des Generalobersten Wilhelm Adam," in Wolfgang Benz (ed.), *Miscellania: Festschrift für Helmut Krausnick zum 75. Geburtstag*, Stuttgart, 1980, p. 55.

232   Goebbels, *Tagebücher*, part 1, vol. 6, p. 68 (entry for 1 Sept., 2 Sept. 1938).

233   Dirksen to Wiedemann, 29 Aug. 1938, and Wiedemann's telegram to Dirksen, 1 Sept. 1938; BA Koblenz, N 1720/6. According to Max Wünsche's diary of 31 Aug. 193, Meissner was afterwards informed "that the Führer will not receive Envoy Dirksen (concerning information from Chamberlain)." BA Berlin-Lichterfelde, NS 10/125.

234   Goebbels, *Tagebücher*, part 1, vol. 6, p. 70 (entry for 3 Sept. 1938). See Helmuth Groscurth, *Tagebücher eines Abwehroffiziers 1938–1940*, eds Helmut Krausnick and Harold C. Deutsch, Stuttgart, 1970, pp. 111f. (entry for 4 Sept. 1938).

235   Schmundt's records from 4 Sept. 1938; IMT, vol. 25, pp. 404–69; ADAP, Series D, vol. 2, no. 424, pp. 546f.

236   *Deutschland-Berichte der Sopade*, 5 (1938), pp. 915f.; see Ian Kershaw, *The Hitler Myth: Image and Reality in the Third Reich*, Oxford, 1987, pp. 133f.; Evans, *The Third Reich in Power*, pp. 674f.

237   Engel, *Heeresadjutant bei Hitler*, pp. 36f. (dated 8 Sept., 10 Sept. 1938). See Below, *Als Hitlers Adjutant*, pp. 120f.

238   Domarus, *Hitler*, vol. 1, part 2, pp. 897–906 (quotations on pp. 901, 904, 905).

239   Goebbels, *Tagebücher*, part 1, vol. 6, p. 88 (entry for 13 Sept. 1938); Shirer, *Berliner Tagebuch*, p. 123 (entry for 12 Sept. 1938).

240   Goebbels, *Tagebücher*, part 1, vol. 6, p. 89 (entry for 14 Sept. 1938).

241   See Schmidt, *Statist auf diplomatischer Bühne*, pp. 394f.

242   See Birgit Schwarz, *Geniewahn: Hitler und die Kunst*, Vienna, Cologne and Weimar, 2009, p. 171.

243   Schmidt, *Statist auf diplomatischer Bühne*, pp. 395–8. On the events of the Chamberlain visit see also Max Wünsche's diary of 15 Sept. 1938: according to Wünsche, Chamberlain's plane took off at 10:15 a.m. and landed at 12:36 p.m. in Munich. At 4:05 p.m. his chartered train arrived in Berchtesgaden, and the British delegation got to the Berghof at 5:10 p.m. At 5:30 p.m, Hitler and Chamberlain's one-on-one talks commenced. The prime minister left at 8:10 p.m. BA Berlin-Lichterfelde, NS 10/125.

244   Ernst von Weizsäcker, *Erinnerungen*, Munich, 1950, p. 244.

245   *Die Weizsäcker-Papiere 1933–1950*, p. 143 (? Sept. 1938).

246   *ADAP*, Series D, vol. 2, no. 490, pp. 639f.

247   Goebbels, *Tagebücher*, part 1, vol. 6, p. 97 (entry for 18 Sept. 1938).

248   Ibid., p. 99 (entry for 19 Sept. 1938).

249   Chamberlain's letter to his sister, Ida, 19 Sept. 1938; Kershaw, *Hitler: Nemesis*, pp. 110, 112.

250   Goebbels, *Tagebücher*, part 1, vol. 6, p. 105 (entry for 22 Sept. 1938); see ibid., pp. 101 (entry for 20 Sept. 1938), 103 (entry for 21 Sept. 1938): "The Führer will show Chamberlain his map, and that will be it!"

251   See Nevile Henderson, *Fehlschlag einer Mission: Berlin 1937 bis 1939*, Zurich, 1940, pp. 174f.; Schmidt, *Statist auf diplomatischer Bühne*, p. 400.

252 Schmidt, *Statist auf diplomatischer Bühne*, pp. 400f.; see Alan Bullock, *Hitler: A Study in Tyranny*, London, 1990, pp. 457f. (according to Kirkpatrick); Goebbels, *Tagebücher*, part 1, vol. 6, p. 107 (entry for 23 Sept. 1938).

253 Schmidt, *Statist auf diplomatischer Bühne*, p. 402. Goebbels's contention that in his letter Chamberlain "had basically expressed his agreement with Hitler's demands" was apparently based on a willful misunderstanding. *Tagebücher*, part 1, vol. 6, p. 108 (entry for 24 Sept. 1938).

254 Shirer, *Berliner Tagebuch*, p. 133 (entry for 22 Sept. 1938).

255 Goebbels, *Tagebücher*, part 1, vol. 6, p. 109 (entry for 24 Sept. 1938).

256 See Henderson, *Fehlschlag einer Mission*, p. 178; Schmidt, *Statist auf diplomatischer Bühne*, p. 404.

257 Schmidt, *Statist auf diplomatischer Bühne*, pp. 404f.; see Goebbels, *Tagebücher*, part 1, vol. 6, pp. 109f. (entry for 24 Sept. 1938); Weizsäcker, *Erinnerungen*, p. 185.

258 Schmidt, *Statist auf diplomatischer Bühne*, pp. 405f.; see Bullock, *Hitler*, p. 460 (according to Kirkpatrick's notes).

259 Goebbels, *Tagebücher*, part 1, vol. 6, p. 113 (entry for 26 Sept. 1938).

260 Schmidt, *Statist auf diplomatischer Bühne*, p. 407; see Henderson, *Fehlschlag einer Mission*, p. 181; Bullock, *Hitler*, p. 461 (according to Kirkpatrick's notes).

261 Shirer, *Berliner Tagebuch*, p. 137 (entry for 26 Sept. 1938); see Groscurth, *Tagebücher eines Abwehroffiziers*, p. 124 (entry for 26 Sept. 1938): "A speech by the Führer in the evening. Terrible, ignoble bellowing."

262 Domarus, *Hitler*, vol. 1, part 2, pp. 923–32 (quotations on pp. 925, 927, 930, 932). Goebbels described Hitler's tirade as "a psychological masterpiece." *Tagebücher*, part 1, vol. 6, p. 166 (entry for 27 Sept. 1938).

263 Shirer, *Berliner Tagebuch*, pp. 137f. (entry for 26 Sept. 1938).

264 Schmidt, *Statist auf diplomatischer Bühne*, pp. 408f.; Henderson, *Fehlschlag einer Mission*, pp. 182f.; Bullock, *Hitler*, pp. 463f. (according to Kirkpatrick's notes).

265 See Goebbels, *Tagebücher*, part 1, vol. 6, p. 116 (entry for 27 Sept. 1938): "Question: are the English bluffing or are they serious? Answer: they're bluffing."

266 Ibid., p. 118 (entry for 28 Sept. 1938).

267 See Ruth Andreas-Friedrich, *Der Schattenmann: Tagebuchaufzeichnungen 1938–1945*, Frankfurt am Main, 1983, pp. 9–11 (entry for 27 Sept. 1938); Shirer, *Berliner Tagebuch*, pp. 138f. (entry for 27 Sept. 1938); Henderson, *Fehlschlag einer Mission*, pp. 183f.

268 See Kershaw, *The Hitler Myth*, pp. 135–7; Frank Bajohr and Christoph Strupp (ed.), *Fremde Blicke auf das "Dritte Reich": Berichte ausländischer Diplomaten über Herrschaft und Gesellschaft in Deutschland 1933–1945*, Göttingen, 2011, pp. 491f. Even a convinced Hitler supporter such as Ilse Hess was asking at the end of Sept. 1938, "whether in a couple of years the Sudetenland would have fallen into our laps like ripe fruit in any case, without our risking so much right now." But she added: "And the Führer knows what is right." Ilse Hess to Rudolf Hess, 28 Sept. 1938. BA Bern, Nl Hess, J1.211-1989/148, 61.

269 Goebbels, *Tagebücher*, part 1, vol. 6, p. 125 (entry for 2 Oct. 1938). In Wiedemann's recollection, Goebbels said over lunch at the Reich Chancellery on 28 Sept. 1938: "My Führer, you saw the division marching through Berlin. If you think the German people are ready for war, then you're fooling yourself." Wiedemann's shorthand notes, 25 Feb. 1939; BA Koblenz, N 1720/4.

270 Hitler to Chamberlain, 27 Sept. 1938; reprinted in Henderson, *Fehlschlag einer Mission*, pp. 343–6 (quotation on p. 346). See Bullock, *Hitler*, pp. 465f.; Schmidt, *Statist auf diplomatischer Bühne*, pp. 409f.

271 *Die Weizsäcker-Papiere*, p. 170 (notes from October 1939 with a look back at 1938/39), p. 144 (dated 27 Sept. 1938).

272 Ulrich von Hassell, *Vom anderen Deutschland: Aus den nachgelassenen Tagebüchern 1938–1944*, Frankfurt am Main, 1964, p. 19 (entry for 29 Sept. 1938); see Goebbels, *Tagebücher*, part 1, vol. 6, p. 119 (entry for 29 Sept. 1938): "Yesterday: dramatic day."

273 Schmidt, *Statist auf diplomatischer Bühne*, p. 410. The above quotation in Wiedemann, *Der Mann*, p. 178.

274 Schmidt, *Statist auf diplomatischer Bühne*, p. 411; see François-Poncet, *Als Botschafter in Berlin*, p. 333; Schäfer, *André François-Poncet als Botschafter in Berlin*, pp. 309f.

275 See Schmidt, *Statist auf diplomatischer Bühne*, pp. 411f.; see Falanga, *Mussolinis Vorposten*, pp. 107f.

276 See Henderson, *Fehlschlag einer Mission*, p. 187; Schmidt, *Statist auf diplomatischer Bühne*, p. 413; Falanga, *Mussolinis Vorposten*, p. 108.

277 See Below, *Als Hitlers Adjutant*, p. 128; Henderson, *Fehlschlag einer Mission*, pp. 189f.; François-Poncet, *Als Botschafter in Berlin*, p. 335.

278 François-Poncet, *Als Botschafter in Berlin*, pp. 336f. According to Weizsäcker, Hitler was "revolted by the whole conference . . . He was never one for *par inter pares*." *Die Weizsäcker-Papiere 1933–1950*, p. 172 (notes from October 1939).

279 Schmidt, *Statist auf diplomatischer Bühne*, p. 414.

280 See *Die Weizsäcker-Papiere 1933–1950*, pp. 171f. (notes from October 1939); Weizsäcker, *Erinnerungen*, pp. 188f.

281 Text of the Munich Agreement in Domarus, *Hitler*, vol. 1, part 2, pp. 942f.

282 Shirer, *Berliner Tagebuch*, p. 140 (entry for 30 Sept. 1938). On 1 Oct. 1938, Golo Mann wrote in his diary: "The end of France. The good people just don't realise that." Tilmann Lahme, *Golo Mann: Biographie*, Frankfurt am Main, 2009, p. 141.

283 Goebbels, *Tagebücher*, part 1, vol. 6, p. 122 (entry for 30 Sept. und 1 Oct. 1938).

284 Schmidt, *Statist auf diplomatischer Bühne*, p. 417; text of the communiqué in Domarus, *Hitler*, vol. 1, part 2, p. 946.

285 Goebbels, *Tagebücher*, part 1, vol. 6, p. 125 (entry for 2 Oct. 1938).

286 Engel, *Heeresadjutant bei Hitler*, p. 40 (dated 1 Oct. 1938).

287 Below, *Als Hitlers Adjutant*, p. 138.

288 Schmidt, *Statist auf diplomatischer Bühne*, pp. 417f.

289 Hamann, *Winifred Wagner*, p. 377.

290 *Deutschland-Berichte der Sopade*, 5 (1938), pp. 942, 943.

291 Erich Kordt, *Nicht aus den Akten . . . Die Wilhelmstrasse in Frieden und Krieg. Erlebnisse, Begegnungen und Eindrücke 1928–1945*, Stuttgart, 1950, p. 260.

292 Wilhelm Treue, "Rede Hitlers vor der deutschen Presse (10 November 1938)," in *Vierteljahrshefte für Zeitgeschichte*, 6 (1958), p. 182.

293 *Deutschland-Berichte der Sopade*, 5 (1938), pp. 393f.; see Mann, *Tagebücher 1937–1939*, p. 303 (entry for 2 Oct. 1938): "The better part of the world is in deep desperation."

294 See the convincing account by Müller, *Generaloberst Ludwig Beck*, pp. 366–8, which corrects previous research.

295 See Hartmann, *Halder*, pp. 101–15; Rainer A. Blasius, *Für Grossdeutschland gegen den Krieg: Ernst von Weizsäcker in den Krisen um die Tschechoslowakei und Polen 1938/39*, Cologne and Vienna, 1981, pp. 45, 55f.

296 See Gerd R. Ueberschär, "Die Septemberverschwörung 1938 und Widerstandsbewegungen bis zum Kriegsbeginn," in idem, *Für ein anderes Deutschland: Der deutsche Widerstand gegen den NS-Staat 1933–1945*, Frankfurt am Main, 2006, pp. 37f.

297 Goebbels, *Tagebücher*, part 1, vol. 6, p. 127 (entry for 3 Oct. 1939); see ibid., p. 139 (entry for 10 Oct. 1938): "The Führer wants to break up the Czechs, either by war or through peaceful means." Around the same time, Weizsäcker told Hassell that Hitler had said that "the Czech problem will have to be liquidated within a few months." Hassell, *Vom anderen Deutschland*, p. 21 (entry for 10 Oct. 1938).

298 Domarus, *Hitler*, vol. 1, part 2, pp. 954–6.

299 Goebbels, *Tagebücher*, part 1, vol. 6, p. 158 (entry for 24 Oct. 1938); see ibid., p. 234 (entry for 21 Jan. 1939): "Wiedemann is going to California as a consul general. He lost his nerve in the crisis."

300 Schacht to Wiedemann, 18 March 1939 (addressed from the Hotel Monte Verita in Ascona); BA Koblenz, N 1720/8. See ibid. for numerous further documents

expressing individuals' regrets that Wiedemann was leaving Hiter's service. On 23 Feb. 1939 Wiedemann set sail on the MS *Hamburg* from Bremen to New York.

301 Hassell, *Vom anderen Deutschland*, pp. 23f. (entry for 15 Oct. 1938).

302 Ibid., p. 24 (entry for 23 Oct. 1938). See also François-Poncet's view in Schäfer, *André François-Poncet als Botschafter in Berlin*, p. 311.

303 *ADAP*, Series D, vol. 4, no. 81, p. 90; also reprinted in Domarus, *Hitler*, vol. 1, part 2, pp. 960f.

304 Text of the declaration in Domarus, *Hitler*, vol. 1, part 2, p. 982. For the back story see Michalka, *Ribbentrop und die deutsche Weltpolitik*, pp. 259–64; Hildebrand, *Das vergangene Reich*, pp. 674f.

305 Goebbels, *Tagebücher*, part 1, vol. 6, p. 246 (entry for 1 Feb. 1939).

306 Text of the speech in Jost Dülffer, Jochen Thies and Josef Henke, *Hitlers Städte: Baupolitik im Dritten Reich. Eine Dokumentation*, Cologne and Vienna, 1978, pp. 289–313. See also the report of the 10 Feb. 1939 speech by General Hans Jordan (based on notes). The decisive passage read: "An officer shouldn't only be a 'soldier.' Today, wars between people are 'world-view wars.' For that reason, today's warrior has to be suffused by his world view." IfZ München, ED 57.

307 Engel, *Heeresadjutant bei Hitler*, p. 45 (dated 18 Feb. 1939).

308 Goebbels, *Tagebücher*, part 1, vol. 6, pp. 279f. (entry for 11 March 1939).

309 Ibid., p. 283 (entry for 13 March 1939).

310 See the minutes of State Secretary Hewel on the talks between Hitler and Tiso, 13 March 1939; *ADAP*, Series D, vol. 4, no. 202, pp. 212–14; Goebbels, *Tagebücher*, part 1, vol. 6, p. 285 (entry for 14 March 1938): Hitler told Tiso in no uncertain terms that "Slovakia's historical hour has come. If the Slovaks do nothing, they'll be swallowed by the Hungarians."

311 See Goebbels, *Tagebücher*, part 1, vol. 6, p. 286 (entry for 15 March 1938); Below, *Als Hitlers Adjutant*, p. 151.

312 See Below, *Als Hitlers Adjutant*, p. 152; Goebbels, *Tagebücher*, part 1, vol. 6, p. 287 (entry for 15 March 1938): "The Führer made them wait until midnight, which slowly but surely softened them up. That's what was done to us in Versailles."

313 See Schmidt, *Statist auf diplomatischer Bühne*, pp. 427, 429.

314 See Below, *Als Hitlers Adjutant*, p. 152.

315 Schmidt, *Statist auf diplomatischer Bühne*, pp. 429f.; see the minutes by State Secretary Hewel on the meeting of 15 March 1939; *ADAP*, Series D, vol. 4, no. 228, pp. 229–34.

316 See Schmidt, *Statist auf diplomatischer Bühne*, pp. 430f.; Speer, *Erinnerungen*, p. 130; Hoffmann, *Hitler wie ich ihn sah*, pp. 98f.; Goebbels, *Tagebücher*, part 1, vol. 6, p. 287 (entry for 15 March 1938): "Negotiations were conducted with raw bitterness. Hacha passed out once."

317 *ADAP*, Series D, vol. 4, no. 229, p. 235. Facsimile in Thamer, *Verführung und Gewalt*, p. 603.

318 Weizsäcker, *Erinnerungen*, p. 218.

319 *Die Weizsäcker Papiere 1933–1950*, p. 152 (dated 16 March 1939). See Conze et al., *Das Amt*, p. 135.

320 Goebbels, *Tagebücher*, part 1, vol. 6, p. 287 (entry for 15 March 1938).

321 Schroeder, *Er war mein Chef*, pp. 88, 322 See ibid., pp. 88f.; Eberle and Uhl (eds), *Das Buch Hitler*, p. 92; Below, *Als Hitlers Adjutant*, p. 153.

323 Text in Domarus, *Hitler*, vol. 2, part 1, pp. 1098–100.

324 See Conze et al., *Das Amt*, p. 135.

325 R. Buttmann's diaires dated 19 March 1939; BayHStA München, Nl Buttmann 89.

326 Below, *Als Hitlers Adjutant*, p. 156.

327 *Deutschland-Berichte der Sopade*, 6 (1939), p. 276. See ibid., pp. 278–86; Bajohr and Strupp (eds), *Fremde Blicke auf das "Dritte Reich,"* p. 528.

328 See Wendt, *Grossdeutschland*, pp. 166f.; Schmidt, *Die Aussenpolitik des Dritten Reiches*, pp. 311f.; Kershaw, *Hitler: Nemesis*, p. 165.

329 Erich Kordt, *Wahn und Wirklichkeit*, Stuttgart, 1947, p. 144.

330   See Henderson, *Fehlschlag einer Mission*, p. 246. Henderson only returned to Berlin on 25 April. Ibid., p. 254.

331   Domarus, *Hitler*, vol. 2, part 1, p. 1105.

332   Goebbels, *Tagebücher*, part 1, vol. 6, p. 292 (entry for 19 March 1939). See ibid., p. 293 (entry for 20 March 1939): "Rightly, the Führer doesn't take the protests in Paris and London at all seriously. They're a false alarm."

333   Eberle and Uhl (eds.), *Das Buch Hitler*, p. 95. Text of the treaty and the law regarding the reunion of the Memel Territory with the Reich in Domarus, *Hitler*, vol. 2, part 1, pp. 1110–2.

334   Ibid., pp. 1112f.

335   Goebbels, *Tagebücher*, part 1, vol. 6, p. 296 (entry for 23 March 1939). See ibid., p. 285 (entry for 4 March 1939), p. 286 (entry for 15 March 1939): "He intends to take a long break after this action is brought to a successful conclusion."

336   Ibid., p. 300 (entry for 25 March 1939).

337   Kershaw, *Hitler: Nemesis*, p. 174.

338   Hassell, *Vom anderen Deutschland*, p. 46 (entry for 22 March 1939).

339   François-Poncet, *Als Botschafter in Berlin*, p. 342.

340   See Sebastian Haffner, *Anmerkungen zu Hitler*, 21st edition, Munich, 1978, pp. 43f.

341   Klemperer, *Tagebücher 1933–1941*, p. 469 (entry for 20 April 1939).

342   Goebbels, *Tagebücher*, part 1, vol. 5, pp. 370 (entry for 6 July 1938), 381 (entry for 15 July 1938); vol. 6, pp. 58 (entry for 26 Aug. 1938), 208 (entry for 3 Dec. 1938).

343   Ibid., p. 318 (entry for 16 April 1939). On the Propaganda Ministry's preparations see Peter Bucher, "Hitlers 50. Geburtstag: Zur Quellenvielfalt im Bundesarchiv," in Heinz Boberach and Hans Booms (eds), *Aus der Arbeit des Bundesarchivs*, Boppard am Rhein, 1978, pp. 432–34; Kurt Pätzold, "Hitlers fünfzigster Geburtstag am 20. April 1939," in Dietrich Eichholtz and Kurt Pätzold (eds), *Der Weg in den Krieg: Studien zur Geschichte der Vorkriegsjahre 1935/36 bis 1939*, Cologne, 1989, pp. 321–4.

344   Press instruction of 3 March 1939; Hans Bohrmann (ed.), *NS-Presseanweisungen der Vorkriegszeit: Edition und Dokumentation*, vol. 6, part 1, Munich, 1999, p. 206; also reprinted in Bernd Sösemann, with Marius Lange, *Propaganda: Medien und Öffentlichkeit in der NS-Diktatur*, Stuttgart, 2011, vol. 1, no. 513, p. 548.

345   Quotations in Bucher, "Hitlers 50. Geburtstag," p. 434; Ralf Georg Reuth, *Goebbels*, Munich and Zurich, 1990, p. 410. See Goebbels, *Tagebücher*, part 1, vol. 6, p. 322 (entry for 20 April 1939).

346   Domarus, *Hitler*, vol. 2, part 1, p. 1144; Pätzold, "Hitlers fünfzigster Geburtstag," p. 327. As a further example for the rhapsodic homages addressed to Hitler, see Ritter von Epp's birthday wishes on 20 April 1939; BA Koblenz, N 1101/95.

347   See Schwarz, *Geniewahn*, p. 259. For the presents see the detailed list in BA Berlin-Lichterfelde, NS 51/77. See also Schroeder, *Er war mein Chef*, p. 94; Below, *Als Hitlers Adjutant*, p. 160; Speer, *Erinnerungen*, p. 164; Henrik Eberle (ed.), *Briefe an Hitler: Ein Volk schreibt seinem Führer. Unbekannte Dokumente aus Moskauer Archiven—zum ersten Mal veröffentlicht*, Bergisch-Gladbach, 2007, pp. 307–10.

348   Goebbels, *Tagebücher*, part 1, vol. 6, p. 322 (entry for 20 April 1939). See Peter Longerich, *Joseph Goebbels: A Biography*, London, 2015, pp. 417f.; Speer, *Erinnerungen*, p. 163; Below, *Als Hitlers Adjutant*, p. 160.

349   Speer, *Erinnerungen*, p. 163; see Below, *Als Hitlers Adjutant*, pp. 160f.; Joachim Fest, *Speer: Eine Biographie*, Berlin, 1999, p. 154.

350   Domarus, *Hitler*, vol. 2, part 1, p. 1145; see Bucher, "Hitlers 50. Geburtstag," p. 436; Dieter Schenk, *Hitlers Mann in Danzig: Albert Forster und die NS-Verbrechen in Danzig-Westpreussen*, Bonn, 2000, p. 108.

351   Christa Schroeder to Johanna Nusser, 21 April 1939; IfZ München, ED 524; reprinted in Schroeder, *Er war mein Chef*, p. 94. On the military parade see Below, *Als Hitlers Adjutant*, p. 161; Bucher, "Hitlers 50. Geburtstag," pp. 430f.; Pätzold, "Hitlers fünfzigster Geburtstag," pp. 331–3.

352   See Domarus, *Hitler*, vol. 2, part 1, p. 1146; Pätzold, "Hitlers fünfzigster Geburtstag," pp. 324f.; Bucher, "Hitlers 50. Geburtstag," p. 437.

353   See Fritz Terveen, "Der Filmbericht über Hitlers 50. Geburtstag: Ein Beispiel nationalsozialistischer Selbstdarstellung und Propaganda," in *Vierteljahrshefte für Zeitgeschichte*, 7 (1959), pp. 75–84 (particularly p. 82); Bucher, "Hitlers 50. Geburtstag," pp. 442–5. After the parade, Hitler supposedly said: "Gentlemen, today I won a great battle . . . without shedding a drop of blood." Arno Breker, *Im Strahlungsfeld der Ereignisse: Leben und Wirken eines Künstlers. Porträts, Begegnungen, Schicksale*, Preussisch Oldendorf, 1972, p. 136.

354   Goebbels, *Tagebücher*, part 1, vol. 6, p. 323 (entry for 21 April 1939).

355   *Deutschland-Berichte der Sopade*, 6 (1939), pp. 450, 442.

Bibliography

1. Primary Sources

1.1 Unpublished Sources

Bundesarchiv (BA) Berlin-Lichterfelde

Bestand NS 6 (NSDAP party office) 71; Bestand NS 10 (personal adjutancy of the Führer and Reich Chancellor) 25, 30, 34, 42, 44, 50, 55, 115, 116, 117, 119, 120, 121, 122, 123, 125, 591; Bestand NS 26 (principal NSDAP archive) 1, 2, 2a, 3, 11, 12, 13, 14, 16, 17, 17a, 18, 43a, 45, 47, 63, 64, 65, 66, 67, 78, 83, 87, 88, 89, 92, 100, 104, 114a, 126, 127, 328, 385, 386, 389, 390, 391, 593, 800, 897, 898, 899, 900, 901, 904, 1209, 1212, 1223, 1242, 1267, 1928a, 1928b, 1928c, 1928d, 2012, 2050, 2180, 2228, 2504, 2557, 2559; Bestand NS 51 (office of the Führer/Bouhler's department) 45, 46, 59, 60, 72, 73, 74, 75, 76, 77, 222; Bestand R 43 (New Reich Chancellery) II/886a, 888b, 889b, 957a, 959, 967e, 971, 974b, 985, 1052, 1054, 1104a

Bundesarchiv (BA) Koblenz

N 1101 (Nachlass Franz Ritter von Epp) 22, 34, 43a, 44, 45, 95; N 1122 (Nachlass Karl Haushofer) 15, 59, 125, 957; N 1126 (Nachlass Heinrich Himmler) 13, 17, 18; N 1128 (Nachlass Adolf Hitler) 1, 2, 3, 4, 5, 6, 7, 8, 9, 10, 11, 12, 13, 14, 15, 16, 17, 19, 22, 24, 27, 28, 29, 30, 33; N 1231 (Nachlass Alfred Hugenberg) 7, 36, 37, 38, 39, 88, 89, 192; N 1241 (Nachlass Wilhelm Frick) 3, 4, 7; N 1276 (Nachlass Lutz Graf Schwerin von Krosigk) 23, 36, 37, 40, 41, 42, 111, 112; N 1310 (Konstantin Freiherr von Neurath) 10, 56, 66, 74, 96, 137; N 1340 (Nachlass Albert Speer) 17, 39, 49, 53, 54, 55, 88, 132, 133, 134, 384; N 1348 (Nachlass Theodor Morell) 6; N 1377 (Nachlass Theodor Duesterberg) 27, 47, 48; N 1468 (Nachlass Robert Ley) 4; N 1530 (Nachlass Franz Gürtner) 20, 22; N 1720 (Nachlass Fritz Wiedemann) 3, 4, 6, 7, 8

Institut für Zeitgeschichte (IfZ) Munich

Bestand ED 9 (adjutancy of the Führer 1933–8); 57 (Hans Jordan's notes on Hitler's speech of 10 Feb. 1939); 100 (David Irving collection), vol. 43, 78, 86; 110 (Richard Walter Darré's diaries 1945–8, vol. 1); 153 (memoirs of prison guard Franz Hemmrich); 524 (Christa Schroeder's correspondence with Johana Nüsser 1939–42); 874 (Gottfried Feder's diaries 1919–29, vols 1–11)

Bestand MS 396 (Heinz Linge's series of articles in the *Revue* 1955/6); 570 (Franz Maria Müller: Wie Hitler Augsburg eroberte); 2049 (Heinrich Hoffmann's testimony of 1947)

Bestand F 123 (Theodor Morell collection)

Bestand MA 736/141

Bestand ZS 6 (Wilhelm Adam), 7 (Nicolaus von Below), 20 (Paul und Karl Angermeier), 29 (Adolf Dresler), 33 (Maria Enders), 49 (Rüdiger von der Goltz), 50 (Hans Georg Grassinger), 60 (Ernst Hanfstaengl), 71 (Heinrich Hoffmann), 128 (Gerhard Rossbach), 135 (Hjalmar Schacht), 137 (Julius Schaub), 145 (Lutz Schwerin von Krosigk), 167 (Adolf Vogl), 177 (Franz Pfeffer von Salomon), 191 (Fritz Wiedemann), 194 (Anni Winter), 200 (Paul und Kurt Angermeier), 242 (Hanskarl von Hasselbach), 253 (Erich Kempka), 258 (Karl Kriebel), 265 (Hinrich Lohse), 270 (Emil Maurice), 287 (Antonie Reichert), 292 (Mathilde Scheubner-Richter), 325 (Franz Jetzinger), 353 (Heinrich Lammers), 428 (Hermann Göring), 557 (Kurt von Schröder), 638 (Hans Baur), 805 (Walter Buch), 874 (Otto Dietrich), 1030 (Hermann Esser), 1147 (Walther Stennes), 1193 (Wilhelm Breucker), 1318 (Prinz August Wilhelm), 1357 (Joachim von Ribbentrop), 1433 (Paul Otto Schmidt), 1452 (Franz Xaver Schwarz), 1495 (Franz Seldte), 1551 (Oskar von Hindenburg), 1655 (Gustav Adolf von Wertersheim), 1700 (Theodor Duesterberg), 1726 (Otto Meissner), 1732 (Otto Wagener), 1770 (Werner Küchenthal), 1900 (Hans Harald von Selchow), 1949 (Otto Erbersdobler), 2209 (Hermann Buch), 2239 (Leo Raubal), 2240 (Christa Schroeder), 2250 (Max Wünsche), 2260 (Walter Frentz), 3135 (Therese Linke)

Bayerisches Hauptstaatsarchiv Munich

Nachlass Adolf Hitler; Nachlass Hermann Esser; Nachlass Henriette von Schirach 3, 4; Nachlass Rudolf Buttmann 63,2, 63,3, 82, 83, 84, 85, 89; Nachlass Gustav Ritter von Kahr 16, 51; Nachlass Karl Alexander von Müller 7, 19/1, 19/2, 101, 246; Nachlass Heinrich Held 724, 727, 729, 730, 731; Nachlass Georg Escherich 10, 11, 12, 47; Nachlass Otto Ballerstedt

Bayerische Staatsbibliothek Munich

Nachlass Ernst Hanfstaengl (Ana 405) Box 25, 26, 27, 40, 45, 46, 47

Schweizerisches Bundesarchiv Bern

Nachlass Rudolf Hess, Bestand J1.211
1989/148 (private correspondence of Rudolf Hess) 21, 25, 27, 29, 31, 33, 35, 37, 39, 41, 43, 45, 47, 49, 51, 53, 55, 57, 59, 61, 63
1993/300 (private correspondence of the Hess family) Boxes 1–7

1.2 *Published Sources*

Akten der deutschen Auswärtigen Politik 1918–1945. Serie C: 1933–1937, Bände 1 bis 6, Göttingen 1971–81, *Serie D: 1938–1939, Bände 1 bis 4*, Baden-Baden 1951–9
Akten der Reichskanzlei – Weimarer Republik. Das Kabinett Papen: 1. Juni bis 3. Dezember 1932. Vol. 1: Juni bis September 1932, Vol. 2: September bis Dezember 1932, ed. Karl-Heinz Minuth, Boppard am Rhein, 1989
Akten der Reichskanzlei – Das Kabinett Schleicher: 3. Dezember 1932 bis 20. Januar 1933, ed. Anton Golecki, Boppard am Rhein, 1986
Akten der Reichskanzlei – Die Regierung Hitler. Teil 1 und 2: 1933/34, ed. Karl-Heinz Minuth, Boppard am Rhein, 1983
Akten der Reichskanzlei – Die Regierung Hitler. Vol. 2–6: 1934/35–1939, ed. Friedrich Hartmannsgruber, Munich, 1999–2012
Bajohr, Frank and Christoph Strupp (eds), *Fremde Blicke auf das "Dritte Reich": Berichte ausländischer Diplomaten über Herrschaft und Gesellschaft in Deutschland 1933–1945*, Göttingen, 2011
Bauer, Franz J. (ed.), *Die Regierung Eisner 1918/19: Ministerratsprotokolle und Dokumente*, Düsseldorf, 1987
Becker, Josef and Ruth (eds), *Hitlers Machtergreifung: Dokumente vom Machtantritt Hitlers. 30. Januar 1933 bis zur Besiegelung des Einparteienstaats 14. 7. 1933*, Munich, 1983

Benz, Wolfgang (ed.), *Politik in Bayern 1913–1933: Berichte des württembergischen Gesandten Carl Moser von Filseck*, Stuttgart, 1971

Bohrmann, Hans (ed.), *NS-Presseanweisungen der Vorkriegszeit: Bände 1–6*, Munich, 1984–99

Breloer, Heinrich, with Rainer Zimmer, *Die Akte Speer: Spuren eines Kriegsverbrechers*, Berlin, 2006

Der Hitler-Prozess 1924, ed. and annotated by Lothar Gruchmann and Reinhold Weber, with Otto Gritschneder, 4 parts, Munich, 1997

Der Notenwechsel zwischen dem Heiligen Stuhl und der Deutschen Reichsregierung. Vol. 1: Von der Ratifizierung des Reichskonkordats bis zur Enzyklika "Mit brennender Sorge," ed. Dieter Albrecht, Mainz, 1965

Der Prozess gegen die Hauptkriegsverbrecher vor dem Internationalen Militärtribunal in Nürnberg (IMT), 42 vols, Nuremberg, 1947–9

Deuerlein, Ernst (ed.), *Der Aufstieg der NSDAP in Augenzeugenberichten*, 2nd edition, Munich, 1976

Deuerlein, Ernst (ed.), *Der Hitler-Putsch: Bayerische Dokumente zum 8./9. November 1923*, Stuttgart, 1962

Deuerlein, Ernst, "Hitlers Eintritt in die Politik und die Reichswehr," in *Vierteljahrshefte für Zeitgeschichte*, 7 (1959), pp. 177–227

Deutschland-Berichte der Sozialdemokratischen Partei Deutschlands (Sopade) 1934–1940, ed. Klaus Behnken, 7 vols, Frankfurt am Main, 1980

Die Verfolgung und Ermordung der europäischen Juden durch das nationalsozialistische Deutschland 1933–1945. Vol. 1: Deutsches Reich 1933–1937, ed. Wolf Gruner, Munich, 2008, *Vol. 2: Deutsches Reich 1938–August 1939*, ed. Susanne Heim, Munich, 2009

Die Weizsäcker-Papiere 1933–1950, ed. Leonidas Hill, Frankfurt am Main, Berlin and Vienna, 1974

Domarus, Max, *Hitler: Reden und Proklamationen 1932–1945. Vol. 1: Triumph, Pt 1: 1932–1934, Pt 2: 1935–1938. Vol. 2: Untergang, Pt 1: 1939–1940, Pt 2: 1941–1945*, Munich, 1965

Dülffer, Jost, Jochen Thies and Josef Henke, *Hitlers Städte: Baupolitik im Dritten Reich. Eine Dokumentation*, Cologne and Vienna, 1978

Eberle, Henrik (ed.), *Briefe an Hitler: Ein Volk schreibt seinem Führer. Unbekannte Dokumente aus Moskauer Archiven—zum erstenmal veröffentlicht*, Bergisch-Gladbach, 2007

Eberle, Henrik and Mathias Uhl (eds), *Das Buch Hitler: Geheimdossier des NKWD für Josef W. Stalin aufgrund der Verhörprotokolle des Persönlichen Adjutanten Hitlers, Otto Günsche, und des Kammerdieners Heinz Linge, Moskau 1948/49*, Bergisch Gladbach, 2005

Eschenhagen, Wieland (ed.), *Die "Machtergreifung": Tagebuch einer Wende nach Presseberichten vom 1. Januar bis 6. März 1933*, Darmstadt and Neuwied, 1982

Faludi, Christian (ed.), *Die "Juni-Aktion" 1938: Eine Dokumentation zur Radikalisierung der Judenverfolgung*, Frankfurt am Main, 2013

Heiber, Beatrice and Helmut (eds), *Die Rückseite des Hakenkreuzes: Absonderliches aus den Akten des Dritten Reiches*, Munich, 1993

Heim, Susanne and Götz Aly, "Staatliche Ordnung und 'organische Lösung': Die Rede Hermann Görings 'über die Judenfrage' vom 6. Dezember 1938," in *Jahrbuch für Antisemitismusforschung*, 2 (1992), pp. 378–404

Herbst 1941 im "Führerhauptquartier": Berichte Werner Koeppens an seinen Minister Rosenberg, ed. and annotated Martin Vogt, Koblenz, 2002

Hitler, Adolf, *Mein Kampf: Vol. 1: Eine Abrechnung: Vol. 2: Die nationalsozialistische Bewegung*, 7th/10th editions, Munich, 1933

Hitler, Adolf, *Monologe im Führerhauptquartier 1941–1945: Die Aufzeichnungen Heinrich Heims*, ed. Werner Jochmann, Hamburg, 1980

Hitler, Adolf, *Reden, Schriften, Anordnungen—Februar 1925 bis Januar 1933*, ed. Münchner Institut für Zeitgeschichte, 6 vols in 13 parts, Munich, 1992–2003

Hitler, *Sämtliche Aufzeichnungen 1905–1924*, ed. Eberhard Jäckel, with Axel Kuhn, Stuttgart, 1980

Hitlers Tischgespräche im Führerhauptquartier, ed. Henry Picker, 3rd completely revised and expanded edition, Stuttgart, 1976

Hubatsch, Walther, *Hindenburg und der Staat: Aus den Papieren des Generalfeldmarschalls und Reichspräsidenten von 1878 bis 1934*, Göttingen, 1966

Jahn, Peter (ed.), *Die Gewerkschaften in der Endphase der Republik 1930–1933*, Cologne, 1988

Jochmann, Werner, *Nationalsozialismus und Revolution: Ursprung und Geschichte der NSDAP in Hamburg, 1922–1933. Dokumente*, Frankfurt am Main, 1963

Kempner, Robert M. W. (ed.), *Der verpasste Nazi-Stopp: Die NSDAP als staats- und republikfeindliche hochverräterische Verbindung. Preussische Denkschrift von 1930*, Frankfurt am Main, Berlin and Vienna, 1983

Kempner, Robert M. W., *Das Dritte Reich im Kreuzverhör: Aus den unveröffentlichten Vernehmungsprotokollen des Anklägers in den Nürnberger Prozessen*, Munich, 2005

Kluke, Paul, "Der Fall Potempa," in *Vierteljahrshefte für Zeitgeschichte*, 5 (1957), pp. 279–97

Könnemann, Erwin and Gerhard Schulze (eds), *Der Kapp-Lüttwitz-Ludendorff-Putsch: Dokumente*, Munich, 2002

Kulka, Otto Dov and Eberhard Jäckel (eds), *Die Juden in den geheimen Stimmungsberichten 1933–1945*, Düsseldorf, 2004

Morsey, Rudolf, "Hitler als Braunschweigischer Regierungsrat," in *Vierteljahrshefte für Zeitgeschichte*, 8 (1960), pp. 419–48

Morsey, Rudolf, "Hitlers Verhandlungen mit der Zentrumsführung am 31. 1. 1933," in *Vierteljahrshefte für Zeitgeschichte*, 9 (1961), pp. 182–94

Morsey, Rudolf (ed.), *Das "Ermächtigungsgesetz" vom 24. März 1933: Quellen zur Geschichte und Interpretation des "Gesetzes zur Behebung der Not von Volk und Reich,"* revised and expanded edition, Düsseldorf, 2010

Neitzel, Sönke, *Abgehört: Deutsche Generäle in britischer Gefangenschaft 1942–1945*, Berlin, 2005

Phelps, Reginald H., "Hitler als Parteiredner im Jahre 1920," in *Vierteljahrshefte für Zeitgeschichte*, 11 (1963), pp. 274–330

Phelps, Reginald H., "Hitlers 'grundlegende' Rede über den Antisemitismus," in *Vierteljahrshefte für Zeitgeschichte*, 16 (1968), pp. 390–420

Robertson, Esmonde M., "Zur Wiederbesetzung des Rheinlands 1936," in *Vierteljahrshefte für Zeitgeschichte*, 10 (1962), pp. 178–205

Rürup, Reinhard (ed.), *1936—Die Olympischen Spiele und der Nationalsozialismus*, Berlin, 1996

Schönhoven, Klaus and Jochen Vogel (eds), *Frühe Warnungen vor dem Nationalsozialismus: Ein historisches Lesebuch*, Bonn, 1998

Schwarzenbach, Alexis, "'Zur Lage in Deutschland': Hitlers Zürcher Rede vom 18. August 1923," in *Traverse*, 1 (2006), pp. 176–89

Sösemann, Bernd (ed.), *Theodor Wolff: Der Journalist. Berichte und Leitartikel*, Düsseldorf, 1993

Sösemann, Bernd, *Propaganda: Medien und Öffentlichkeit in der NS-Diktatur*, with Marius Lange, 2 vols, Stuttgart, 2011

Tyrell, Albrecht, *Führer befiehl . . . Selbstzeugnisse aus der "Kampfzeit" der NSDAP: Dokumentation und Analyse*, Düsseldorf, 1969

Ulrich, Bernd and Benjamin Ziemann (eds), *Frontalltag im Ersten Weltkrieg: Wahn und Wirklichkeit*, Frankfurt am Main, 1994

Volk, Ludwig (ed.), *Akten Kardinal Michael von Faulhabers 1917–1945. Vol. 2: 1935–1945*, Mainz, 1978

Wildt, Michael (ed.), *Die Judenpolitik des SD 1935 bis 1939: Eine Dokumentation*, Munich, 1995

2. Diaries, Letters, Memoirs

Andreas-Friedrich, Ruth, *Der Schattenmann: Tagebuchaufzeichnungen 1938–1945*, Frankfurt am Main, 1998

Arendt, Hannah and Joachim Fest, *Eichmann war von empörender Dummheit: Gespräche und Briefe*, eds Ursula Ludz and Thomas Wild, Munich and Zurich, 2011

Barkow, Ben, Raphael Gross and Michael Lenarz (eds), *Novemberpogrom 1938: Die Augenzeugenberichte der Wiener Library*, London and Frankfurt am Main, 2008

Baur, Hans, *Ich flog Mächtige der Erde*, Kempten in Allgäu, 1956

Below, Nicolaus von, *Als Hitlers Adjutant 1937–1945*, Mainz, 1980

Brandmayer, Balthasar, *Zwei Meldegänger*, Bruckmühl, 1932

Breker, Arno, *Im Strahlungsfeld der Ereignisse: Leben und Wirken eines Künstlers. Porträts, Begegnungen, Schicksale*, Preussisch Oldendorf, 1972

Brockhaus, Gudrun, *Schauder und Idylle: Faschismus als Erlebnisangebot*, Munich, 1997

Brüning, Heinrich, *Memoiren 1918–1934*, Stuttgart, 1970

Ciano, Galeazzo, *Tagebücher 1937/38*, Hamburg, 1949

Cohn, Willy, *Kein Recht, nirgends: Tagebuch vom Untergang des Breslauer Judentums 1933–1941*, ed. Norbert Conrads, 2 vols, Cologne, Weimar and Berlin, 2006

Coulondre, Robert, *Von Moskau nach Berlin 1936–1939: Erinnerungen des französischen Botschafters*, Bonn, 1950

Curtius, Julius, *Sechs Jahre Minister der deutschen Republik*, Heidelberg, 1948

Das Hitler-Bild: Die Erinnerungen des Fotografen Heinrich Hoffmann, ed. Joe J. Heydecker, St. Pölten and Salzburg, 2008

Delmer, Sefton, *Die Deutschen und ich*, Hamburg, 1963

Die Deutschnationalen und die Zerstörung der Weimarer Republik: Aus dem Tagebuch von Reinhold Quaatz 1928–1933, eds Hermann Weiss and Paul Hoser, Munich, 1989

Die Tagebücher von Joseph Goebbels. Part 1: Aufzeichnungen 1923–1941, ed. Elke Fröhlich, 9 vols in 14 parts, Munich, 1998–2006

Diels, Rudolf, *Lucifer ante portas . . . Es spricht der erste Chef der Gestapo*, Stuttgart, 1950

Dietrich, Otto, *Mit Hitler in die Macht: Persönliche Erlebnisse mit meinem Führer*, 2nd edition, Munich, 1934

Dietrich, Otto, *12 Jahre mit Hitler*, Munich, 1955

Dodd, Martha, *Nice to meet you, Mr. Hitler! Meine Jahre in Deutschland 1933 bis 1937*, Frankfurt am Main, 2005

Duesterberg, Theodor, *Der Stahlhelm und Hitler*, Wolfenbüttel and Hannover, 1949

Ebermayer, Erich, *Denn heute gehört uns Deutschland . . . Persönliches und politisches Tagebuch*, Hamburg and Vienna, 1959

Eden, Anthony, *Angesichts der Diktatoren: Memoiren 1923–1938*, Cologne and Berlin, 1964

Engel, Gerhard, *Heeresadjutant bei Hitler 1938–1943*, ed. and annotated Hildegard von Kotze, Stuttgart, 1974

Epkenhans, Michael, "'Wir als deutsches Volk sind doch nicht klein zu kriegen . . .': Aus den Tagebüchern des Fregattenkapitäns Bogislav von Selchow 1918/19," in *Militärgeschichtliche Mitteilungen*, 55 (1996), pp. 165–224

François-Poncet, André, *Als Botschafter in Berlin 1931–1938*, Mainz, 1947

Frank, Hans, *Im Angesicht des Galgens: Deutung Hitlers unsd seiner Zeit auf Grund eigener Erlebnisse und Erkenntnisse*, Munich and Gräfelfing, 1953

Fromm, Bella, *Als Hitler mir die Hand küsste*, Berlin, 1993

Gerhardt, Ute and Thomas Karlauf (eds), *Nie mehr zurück in dieses Land: Augenzeugen berichten über die Novemberpogrome 1938*, Berlin, 2009

Goebbels, Joseph, *Vom Kaiserhof zur Reichskanzlei*, Munich, 1934

Groscurth, Helmuth, *Tagebücher eines Abwehroffiziers 1938–1940*, eds Helmut Krausnick and Harold C. Deutsch, Stuttgart, 1970

Haffner, Sebastian, *Geschichte eines Deutschen: Die Erinnerungen 1914–1933*, Stuttgart and Munich, 2000

Hammerstein, Kunrat Freiherr von, *Spähtrupp*, Stuttgart, 1963

Hanfstaengl, Ernst, *Zwischen Weissem und Braunem Haus: Erinnerungen eines politischen Aussenseiters*, Munich, 1970

Hanisch, Reinhold, "I was Hitler's Buddy," in *New Republic*, 5, 12, 19 April 1939, pp. 239–42, 270–2, 297–300

Hassell, Ulrich von, *Vom anderen Deutschland: Aus den nachgelassenen Tagebüchern 1938–1944*, Frankfurt am Main, 1964

Hassell, Ulrich von, *Römische Tagebücher und Briefe 1932–1938*, ed. Ulrich Schlie, Munich, 2004

Henderson, Nevile, *Fehlschlag einer Mission: Berlin 1937 bis 1939*, Zurich, 1940

Hess, Rudolf, *Briefe 1908–1933*, ed. Rüdiger Hess, Munich and Vienna, 1987

Heuss, Theodor, *Bürger der Weimarer Republik: Briefe 1918–1933*, ed. Michael Dorrmann, Munich, 2008

Heuss, Theodor, *In der Defensive: Briefe 1933–1945*, ed. Elke Seefried, Munich, 2009

"Hitlers unbekannte Geliebte: Ein Bericht von Gunter Peis," in *Stern*, 13 June 1959, pp. 28–34

Hoch, Anton and Hermann Weiss, "Die Erinnerungen des Generalobersten Wilhelm Adam," in Wolfgang Benz (ed.), *Miscellania: Festschrift für Helmut Krausnick zum 75. Geburtstag*, Stuttgart, 1980, pp. 32–62

Hoegner, Wilhelm, *Flucht vor Hitler: Erinnerungen an die Kapitulation der ersten deutschen Republik 1933*, Frankfurt am Main, 1982

Hoffmann, Heinrich, *Hitler wie ich ihn sah: Aufzeichnungen seines Leibfotografen*, Munich and Berlin, 1974

Hossbach, Friedrich, *Zwischen Wehrmacht und Hitler 1934–1938*, 2nd revised edition, Göttingen, 1965

Junge, Traudl, *Bis zur letzten Stunde: Hitlers Sekretärin erzählt ihr Leben*, Munich, 2002

Kallenbach, Hans, *Mit Adolf Hitler auf Festung Landsberg*, Munich, 1933

Kalshoven, Hedda, *Ich denk so viel an Euch: Ein deutsch-holländischer Briefwechsel 1920–1949*, Munich, 1995

Kessler, Harry Graf, *Das Tagebuch. Vol. 7: 1919–1923*, ed. Angela Reinthal, with Janna Brechmacher and Christoph Hilse; *Vol. 8: 1923–1926*, ed. Angela Rheinthal, Günter Riederer and Jörg Schuster, with Johanna Brechmacher, Christoph Hilse and Nadin Weiss; *Vol. 9: 1926–1937*, ed. Sabine Gruber and Ulrich Ott, with Chrisoph Hilse and Nadin Weiss, Stuttgart, 2007, 2009, 2010

Klemperer, Victor, *Leben sammeln, nicht fragen wozu und warum: Tagebücher 1918–1924, 1925–1932*, ed. Walter Nowojski, Berlin, 1996

Klemperer, Victor, *Ich will Zeugnis ablegen bis zum letzten: Tagebücher 1933–1941*, ed. Walter Nowojski, with Hadwig Klemperer, Berlin, 1995

Kordt, Erich, *Nicht aus den Akten . . . Die Wilhelmstrasse in Frieden und Krieg: Erlebnisse, Begegnungen und Eindrücke 1928–1945*, Stuttgart, 1950

Krause, Karl Wilhelm, *10 Jahre Kammerdiener bei Hitler*, Hamburg, 1949

Krebs, Albert, *Tendenzen und Gestalten der NSDAP: Erinnerungen aus der Frühzeit der Partei*, Stuttgart, 1959

Krogmann, Carl Vincent, *Es ging um Deutschlands Zukunft 1932–1939: Erlebtes täglich diktiert von dem früheren Regierenden Bürgermeister in Hamburg*, Leoni am Starnberger See, 1976

Kubizek, August, *Adolf Hitler: Mein Jugendfreund*, Graz and Göttingen, 1953

Linge, Heinz, *Bis zum Untergang: Als Chef des Persönlichen Dienstes bei Hitler*, ed. Werner Maser, Munich, 1982

Lösener, Bernhard, "Das Reichsministerium des Innern und die Judengesetzgebung," in *Vierteljahrshefte für Zeitgeschichte*, 9 (1961), pp. 262–313

Lüdecke, Kurt, *I Knew Hitler: The Story of a Nazi who Escaped the Blood Purge*, London, 1938

Lurker, Otto, *Hitler hinter Festungsmauern: Ein Bild aus trüben Tagen*, Berlin, 1933

Mann, Golo, *Erinnerungen und Gedanken: Eine Jugend in Deutschland*, Frankfurt am Main, 1986

Mann, Klaus, *Der Wendepunkt: Ein Lebensbericht*, Frankfurt am Main, 1963

Mann, Klaus, *Tagebücher 1931 bis 1933, 1934 bis 1935*, ed. Joachim Heimannsberg, Peter Laemmle and Wilfried F. Schoeller, Munich, 1989

Mann, Thomas, *Briefe III: 1924–1932*, selected and ed. Thomas Sprecher, Hans R. Vaget and Cornelia Bernini, Frankfurt am Main, 2011

Mann, Thomas, *Tagebücher 1933–1934, 1935–1936, 1937–1939*, ed. Peter de Mendelssohn, Frankfurt am Main, 1977, 1978, 1980

Maser, Werner (ed.), *Paul Devrient: Mein Schüler Adolf Hitler. Das Tagebuch seines Lehrers*, Munich, 2003

Meissner, Otto, *Staatssekretär unter Ebert, Hindenburg, Hitler*, Hamburg, 1950

Misch, Rochus, *Der letzte Zeuge: "Ich war Hitlers Telefonist, Kurier und Leibwächter,"* Zurich and Munich, 2008

Mosley, Charlotte (ed.), *The Mitfords: Letters between Six Sisters*, London, 2007

Mühsam, Erich, *Tagebücher 1910–1924*, ed. and with an afterword by Chris Hirte, Munich, 1994

Mühsam, Erich, *Unpolitische Erinnerungen: Mit einem Nachwort von Hubert van den Berg*, Hamburg, 1999

Müller, Karl Alexander von, *Mars und Venus: Erinerungen 1914–1918*, Stuttgart, 1954

Müller, Karl Alexander von, *Im Wandel einer Welt: Erinnerungen 1919–1932*, ed. Otto Alexander von Müller, Munich, 1966

Morsey, Rudolf (ed.), *Fritz Gerlich—ein Publizist gegen Hitler: Briefe und Akten 1930–1934*, Paderborn, 2010

Nissen, Margarete, *Sind Sie die Tochter Speer?*, Munich, 2005

Papen, Franz, *Der Wahrheit eine Gasse*, Munich, 1952

Plaim, Anna and Kurt Kuch, *Bei Hitlers: Zimmermädchen Annas Erinnerungen*, Munich, 2005

Pünder, Hermann, *Politik in der Reichskanzlei: Aufzeichnungen aus den Jahren 1929–1932*, ed. Thilo Vogelsang, Stuttgart, 1961

Rathenau, Walther, *Briefe. Pt 2: 1914–1922*, ed. Alexander Jaser, Clemens Picht and Ernst Schulin, Düsseldorf, 2006

Reuth, Ralf Georg (ed.), *Joseph Goebbels: Tagebücher 1924–1945*, 5 vols, Munich and Zurich, 1992

Ribbentrop, Joachim von, *Zwischen London und Moskau: Erinnerungen und letzte Aufzeichnungen*, ed. Annelies von Ribbentrop, Leoni am Starnberger See, 1961

Riefenstahl, Leni, *Memoiren*, Munich, 1987

Riezler, Kurt, *Tagebücher, Aufsätze und Dokumente*, ed. and introduced by Karl Dietrich Erdmann, Göttingen, 1972

Rose, Olaf (ed.), *Julius Schaub: In Hitlers Schatten*, Stegen, 2005

Rosenberg, Kurt F., *"Einer, der nicht mehr dazugehört": Tagebücher 1933–1937*, ed. Beate Meyer and Björn Siegel, Göttingen, 2012

Schacht, Hjalmar, *76 Jahre meines Lebens*, Bad Wörishofen, 1953

Scheringer, Richard, *Das grosse Los: Unter Soldaten, Bauern und Rebellen*, Hamburg, 1959

Schirach, Baldur von, *Ich glaubte an Hitler*, Hamburg, 1967

Schirach, Henriette von, *Frauen um Hitler*, Munich, 1983

Schmeling, Max, *Erinnerungen*, Frankfurt am Main, Berlin and Vienna, 1977

Schmidt, Paul, *Statist auf diplomatischer Bühne 1923–45: Erlebnisse des Chefdolmetschers im Auswärtigen Amt mit den Staatsmännern Europas*, Bonn, 1950

Schmidt-Hannover, Otto, *Umdenken oder Anarchie: Männer–Schicksale–Lehren*, Göttingen, 1959

Schroeder, Christa, *Er war mein Chef: Aus dem Nachlass der Sekretärin von Adolf Hitler*, ed. Anton Joachimsthaler, 3rd edition, Munich and Vienna, 1985

Schuschnigg, Kurt von, *Ein Requiem in Rot-Weiss-Rot*, Zurich, 1946

Schwerin von Krosigk, Lutz Graf, *Es geschah in Deutschland: Menschenbilder unseres Jahrhunderts*, Tübingen and Stuttgart, 1951

Seraphim, Hans-Günther (ed.), *Das politische Tagebuch Alfred Rosenbergs aus den Jahren 1933/34 und 1939/40*, Göttingen, 1956

Shirer, William S., *Berliner Tagebuch: Aufzeichnungen 1934–1941*, transcribed and ed. Jürgen Schebera, Leipzig and Weimar, 1991

Sobanski, Antoni Graf, *Nachrichten aus Berlin 1933–1936*, Berlin, 2007

Speer, Albert, *"Alles was ich weiss": Aus unbekannten Geheimdienstprotokollen vom Sommer 1945*, ed. Ulrich Schlie, Munich, 1999

Speer, Albert, *Erinnerungen: Mit einem Essay von Jochen Thies*, Frankfurt am Main and Berlin, 1993

Speer, Albert, *Spandauer Tagebücher: Mit einem Vorwort von Joachim Fest*, Munich, 2002

Spitzy, Reinhard, *So haben wir das Reich verspielt: Bekenntnisse eines Illegalen*, 2nd revised edition, Munich and Vienna, 1987

Stampfer, Friedrich, *Erfahrungen und Erkenntnisse*, Cologne, 1957

Sternheim, Thea, *Tagebücher. Vol. 2: 1925–1936*, ed. and selected Thomas Ehrsam and Regula Wyss, Göttingen, 2002

Strasser, Otto, *Hitler und ich*, Konstanz, 1948

Strenge, Irene, *Ferdinand von Bredow: Notizen vom 20. 2. 1933 bis 31. 12. 1933. Tägliche Aufzeichnungen vom 1. 1. 1934 bis 28. 6. 1934*, Berlin, 2009

Thimme, Annelise (ed.), *Friedrich Thimme 1868–1938: Ein politischer Historiker, Publizist und Schriftsteller in seinen Briefen*, Boppard am Rhein, 1994

Unger, Michael (ed.), *The Memoirs of Bridget Hitler*, London, 1979

(Wagener, Otto), *Hitler aus nächster Nähe: Aufzeichnungen eines Vertrauten 1929–1932*, ed. Henry A. Turner, Frankfurt am Main, Berlin and Vienna, 1978

Wagner, Friedelind, *Nacht über Bayreuth*, 3rd edition, Cologne, 1997

Weizsäcker, Ernst, *Erinnerungen*, Munich, 1950

Wiedemann, Fritz, *Der Mann, der Feldherr werden wollte: Erlebnisse und Erfahrungen des Vorgesetzten Hitlers im 1. Weltkrieg und seines späteren persönlichen Adjutanten*, Velbert and Kettwig, 1964

Zuckmayer, Carl, *Als wär's ein Stück von mir*, Frankfurt am Main, 1966

Zweig, Stefan, *Die Welt von gestern: Erinnerungen eines Europäers*, Stuttgart and Hamburg

3. Secondary Sources

Adam, Uwe Dietrich, *Judenpolitik im Dritten Reich*, Königstein im Taunus, 1979

Ahlheim, Hannah, *"Deutsche, kauft nicht bei Juden!": Antisemitischer Boykott in Deutschland 1924 bis 1935*, Göttingen, 2011

Allert, Tilman, *Der deutsche Gruss: Geschichte einer unheilvollen Geste*, Berlin, 2005

Aly, Götz, *Hitlers Volksstaat: Raub, Rassenkrieg und nationaler Sozialismus*, Frankfurt am Main, 2005

Anderl, Gabriele, "Die 'Zentralstellen für jüdische Auswanderung' in Wien, Berlin und Prag: Ein Vergleich," in *Tel Aviver Jahrbuch für deutsche Geschichte*, 23 (1994), pp. 279–99

Arnold, Dietmar, *Neue Reichskanzlei und "Führerbunker": Legende und Wirklichkeit*, Berlin, 2005

Asendorf, Manfred, "Hamburger Nationalklub, Keppler-Kreis, Arbeitsstelle Schacht und der Aufstieg Hitlers," in *1999. Zeitschrift für Sozialgeschichte des 19. und 20. Jahrhunderts*, 2 (1987), pp. 106–50

Auerbach, Helmuth, "Hitlers politische Lehrjahre und die Münchner Gesellschaft 1919–1923," in *Vierteljahrshefte für Zeitgeschichte*, 25 (1977), pp. 1–45

Bajohr, Frank, *"Arisierung" in Hamburg: Die Verdrängung der jüdischen Unternehmer 1933–1945*, Hamburg, 1997

Bajohr, Frank, *Parvenüs und Profiteure: Korruption in der NS-Zeit*, Frankfurt am Main, 2001

Bajohr, Frank and Michael Wildet (eds), *Volksgemeinschaft: Neue Forschungen zur Gesellschaft des Nationalsozialismus*, Frankfurt am Main, 2009

Bankier, David, *Die öffentliche Meinung im Hitler-Staat: Die "Endlösung" und die Deutschen*, Berlin, 1995

Barkai, Avraham, *Vom Boykott zur "Entjudung": Der wirtschaftliche Existenzkampf der Juden im Dritten Reich 1933–1945*, Frankfurt am Main, 1988

Barkai, Avraham, *Der Centralverein deutscher Staatsbürger jüdischen Glaubens 1893–1938*, Munich, 2002

Barth, Boris, "Dolchstosslegende und Novemberrevolution," in Alexander Gallus (ed.), *Die vergessene Revolution*, Göttingen, 2010, pp. 117–39

Bauer, Kurt, *Elementar-Ereignis: Die österreichischen Nationalsozialisten und der Juli-Putsch 1934*, Vienna, 2003

Bauer, Kurt, "Hitler und der Juliputsch 1934 in Österreich: Eine Fallstudie zur national-sozialistischen Aussenpolitik in der Frühphase des Regimes," in *Vierteljahrshefte für Zeitgeschichte*, 59 (2011), pp. 193–227

Bavaj, Riccardo, *Die Ambivalenz der Moderne im Nationalsozialismus: Eine Bilanz der Forschung*, Munich, 2003

Bavendamm, Dirk, *Der junge Hitler: Korrektur einer Biographie 1889–1914*, Graz, 2009

Beck, Hermann, *The Fateful Alliance: German Conservatives and Nazis in 1933. The "Machtergreifung" in New Light*, New York and Oxford, 2008

Becker, Josef, "Zentrum und Ermächtigungsgesetz," in *Vierteljahrshefte für Zeitgeschichte*, 9 (1961), pp. 195–210

Behrenbeck, Sabine, *Der Kult um die toten Helden: Nationalsozialistische Mythen, Riten und Symbole 1923 bis 1945*, Vierow bei Greifswald, 1996

Beierl, Florian and Othmar Plöckinger, "Neue Dokumente zu Hitlers Buch 'Mein Kampf,'" in *Vierteljahrshefte für Zeitgeschichte*, 57 (2009), pp. 261–95

Bentley, James, *Martin Niemöller: Eine Biographie*, Munich, 1985

Benz, Wolfgang (ed.), *Die Juden in Deutschland 1933–1945: Leben unter nationalsozialistischer Herrschaft*, Munich, 1998

Benz, Wolfgang, *Die Protokolle der Weisen von Zion: Die Legende von der jüdischen Weltverschwörung*, Munich, 2007

Benz, Wolfgang and Barbara Diestel, *Der Ort des Terrors: Geschichte der nationalsozialistischen Konzentrationslager. Vol. 2: Frühe Lager*, Munich, 2005

Besier, Gerhard, *Die Kirchen und das Dritte Reich: Spaltungen und Abwehrkämpfe 1934–1937*, Berlin and Munich, 2001

Berghahn, Volker R., *Der Stahlhelm: Bund der Frontsoldaten 1918–1935*, Düsseldorf, 1966

Berghahn, Volker R., "Harzburger Front und die Kandidatur Hindenburgs für die Präsidentschaftswahlen 1932," in *Vierteljahrshefte für Zeitgeschichte*, 13 (1965), pp. 64–82

Bering, Dietz, *Kampf um Namen: Bernhard Weiss gegen Joseph Goebbels*, Stuttgart, 1991

Bessel, Richard, *Political Violence and the Rise of Nazism: The Storm Troopers in Eastern Germany 1925–1934*, New Haven, 1984

Bessel, Richard, "The Potempa Murder," in *Central European History*, 10 (1977), pp. 241–54

Binion, Rudolph, "... dass ihr mich gefunden habt": *Hitler und die Deutschen*, Stuttgart, 1978

Blasius, Dirk, *Weimars Ende: Bürgerkrieg und Politik 1930–1933*, Frankfurt am Main, 2008

Blasius Rainer A., *Für Grossdeutschland gegen den Krieg: Ernst von Weizsäcker in den Krisen um die Tschechoslowakei und Polen 1938/39*, Cologne and Vienna, 1981

Blom, Philipp, *Der taumelnde Kontinent: Europa 1900–1914*, Munich, 2008

Bock, Gisela, *Zwangssterilisation im Nationalsozialismus: Studien zur Rassenpolitik und Frauenpolitik*, Opladen, 1986

Botz, Gerhard, *Nationalsozialismus in Wien: Machtübernahme, Herrschaftssicherung, Radikalisierung 1938/39*, revised and expanded edition, Vienna, 2008

Boyer, John W., *Karl Lueger 1844–1910: Christlichsoziale Politik als Beruf. Eine Biographie*, Vienna, Cologne and Weimar, 2010

Bracher, Karl-Dietrich, *Die Auflösung der Weimarer Republik: Eine Studie zum Problem des Machtverfalls in der Demokratie*, 3rd revised and expanded edition, Villingen, 1960

Bracher, Karl-Dietrich, *Die deutsche Diktatur: Entstehung, Struktur, Folgen*, 7th edition, Cologne, 1993

Bracher, Karl-Dietrich, Wolfgang Sauer and Gerhard Schulz, *Die nationalsozialistische Machtergreifung: Studien zur Errichtung des totalitären Herrschaftssystems in Deutschland 1933/34*, 2nd revised edition, Cologne and Opladen, 1962

Brantl, Sabine, *Haus der Kunst, München: Ein Ort und seine Geschichte im Nationalsozialismus*, Munich, 2007

Brechtken, Magnus, *"Madagaskar für die Juden": Antisemitische Idee und politische Praxis 1885–1945*, Munich, 1997

Breloer, Heinrich, *Speer und Er: Hitlers Architekt und Rüstungsminister*, Berlin, 2005

Breloer, Heinrich, *Unterwegs zur Familie Speer: Begegnungen, Gespräche, Interviews*, Berlin, 2005

Broszat, Martin, *Der Staat Hitlers: Grundlegung und Entwicklung seiner inneren Verfassung*, Munich, 1969

Broszat, Martin, *Die Machtergreifung: Der Aufstieg der NSDAP und die Zerstörung der Weimarer Republik*, Munich, 1984

Broszat, Martin, "Soziale Motivation und Führer-Bindung des Nationalsozialismus," in *Vierteljahrshefte für Zeitgeschichte*, 18 (1979), pp. 392–409

Bruns, Claudia, *Politik des Eros: Der Männerbund in Wissenschaft, Politik und Jugendkultur 1880–1934*, Cologne, Weimar and Vienna, 2008

Bucher, Peter, "Hitlers 50. Geburtstag," in Heinz Boberach and Hans Booms (eds), *Aus der Arbeit des Bundesarchivs*, Boppard am Rhein, 1978, pp. 423–46

Buchheim, Christoph, "Das NS-Regime und die Überwindung der Weltwirtschaftskrise in Deutschland," in *Vierteljahrshefte für Zeitgeschichte*, 56 (2008), pp. 381–414

Büttner, Ursula, *Weimar: Die überforderte Republik 1918–1933*, Stuttgart, 2008

Bukey, Evan Burr, *"Patenstadt des Führers": Eine Politik- und Sozialgeschichte von Linz 1908–1945*, Frankfurt am Main and New York, 1993

Bullock, Alan, *Hitler: A Study in Tyranny*, London, 1990

Bullock, Alan, *Hitler and Stalin: Parallel Lives*, London, 1991

Burden, Hamilton T., *Die programmierte Nation: Die Nürnberger Reichsparteitage*, Gütersloh, 1967

Burleigh, Michael, *The Third Reich: A New History*, London, 2000

Burrin, Philippe, *Warum die Deutschen? Antisemitismus, Nationalsozialismus, Genozid*, Berlin, 2004

Bussmann, Walter, "Zur Entstehung und Überlieferung der 'Hossbach-Niederschrift,'" in *Vierteljahrshefte für Zeitgeschichte*, 16 (1968), pp. 373–8

Centrum Industriekultur Nürnberg (ed.), *Kulissen der Gewalt: Das Reichsparteitagsgelände in Nürnberg*, Munich, 1992

Ceserani, David, *Adolf Eichmann: Bürokrat und Massenmörder. Biographie*, Berlin, 2002

Chaussy, Ulrich, *Nachbar Hitler: Führerkult und Heimatzerstörung am Obersalzberg*, 6th revised and expanded edition, Berlin, 2007

Ciolek-Kümper, Jutta, *Wahlkampf in Lippe: Die Wahlpropaganda der NSDAP zur Landtagswahl am 15. Januar 1933*, Munich, 1976

Clemens, Detlev, *Herr Hitler in Germany: Wahrnehmungen und Deutungen des Nationalsozialismus in Grossbritannien 1920 bis 1939*, Göttingen and Zurich, 1996

Conradi, Peter, *Hitlers Klavierspieler. Ernst Hanfstaengl: Vertrauter Hitlers, Verbündeter Roosevelts*, Frankfurt am Main, 2007

Conway, John S., *Die nationalsozialistische Kirchenpolitik 1933–1945: Ihre Ziele, Widersprüche und Fehlschläge*, Munich, 1969

Conze, Eckart, Norbert Frei, Peter Hayes and Moshe Zimmermann, *Das Amt und die Vergangenheit: Deutsche Diplomaten im Dritten Reich und in der Bundesrepublik*, Munich, 2010

Cornelissen, Christoph, *Gerhard Ritter: Geschichtswissenschaft und Politik im 20. Jahrhundert*, Düsseldorf, 2001

Cornwell, John, *Pius XII: Der Papst, der geschwiegen hat*, Munich, 1999

Czichon, Eberhard, *Wer verhalf Hitler zur Macht? Zum Anteil der deutschen Industrie an der Zerstörung der Weimarer Republik*, Cologne, 1967

Daim, Wilfried, *Der Mann, der Hitler die Ideen gab: Jörg Lanz von Liebenfels*, revised edition, Vienna, 1994

Dams, Carsten and Michael Stolle, *Die Gestapo: Herrschaft und Terror im Dritten Reich*, Munich, 2008

Deuerlein, Ernst, *Hitler: Eine politische Biographie*, Munich, 1969

Diamond, Sander A., *Herr Hitler: Amerikas Diplomaten, Washington und der Untergang Weimars*, Düsseldorf, 1985

Dickmann, Fitz, "Die Regierungsbildung in Thüringen als Modell der Machtergreifung: Ein Brief Hitlers aus dem Jahr 1930," in *Vierteljahrshefte für Zeitgeschichte*, 14 (1966), pp. 454–65

Diehl-Thiele, Peter, *Partei und Staat im Dritten Reich: Untersuchungen zum Verhältnis von NSDAP und allgemeiner Staatsverwaltung. Studienausgabe*, Munich, 1971

Dirks, Carl and Karl-Heinz Janssen, *Der Krieg der Generäle: Hitler als Werkzeug der Wehrmacht*, Berlin, 1999

Döring, Martin, *"Parlamentarischer Arm der Bewegung": Die Nationalsozialisten im Reichstag der Weimarer Republik*, Düsseldorf, 2001

Döscher, Hans-Jürgen, *"Reichskristallnacht": Die Novemberpogrome 1938*, Frankfurt am Main and Berlin, 1988

Eglau, Hans Otto, *Fritz Thyssen: Hitlers Gönner und Geisel*, Berlin, 2003

Emmerich, Alexander, *Olympia 1936: Trügerischer Glanz eines mörderischen Systems*, Cologne, 2011

Ernstling, Stefan, *Der phantastische Rebell: Alexander Moritz Frey oder Hitler schiesst dramatisch in die Luft*, Zurich, 2007

Essner, Cornelia, *Die "Nürnberger Gesetze" oder die Verwaltung des Rassenwahns 1933–1945*, Paderborn, 2002

Evans, Richard J., *The Coming of the Third Reich*, London, 2004

Evans, Richard J., *The Third Reich in Power 1933–1939*, London, 2005

Fabry, Philipp W., *Mutmassungen über Hitler: Urteile von Zeitgenossen*, Königstein im Taunus, 1979

Falanga, Gianluca, *Mussolinis Vorposten in Hitlers Reich: Italiens Politik in Berlin 1933–1945*, Berlin, 2008

Fallois, Immo von, *Kalkül und Illusion: Der Machtkampf zwischen Reichswehr und SA während der Röhm-Krise 1934*, Berlin, 1994

Falter, Jürgen, *Hitlers Wähler*, Munich, 1991

Falter, Jürgen, Thomas Lindenberger and Siegfried Schumann, *Wahlen und Abstimmungen in der Weimarer Republik: Materialien zum Wahlverhalten 1919–1931*, Munich, 1986

Felken, Detlef, *Oswald Spengler: Konservativer Denker zwischen Kaiserreich und Diktatur*, Munich, 1988

Fest, Joachim, *Hitler: Eine Biographie*, Frankfurt am Main, Berlin and Vienna, 1973

Fest, Joachim, *Speer: Eine Biographie*, Berlin, 1999

Fest, Joachim, *Die unbeantwortbaren Fragen: Notizen über Gespräche mit Albert Speer zwischen 1966 und 1981*, Reinbek bei Hamburg, 2005

Fischer, Fritz, *Hitler war kein Betriebsunfall: Aufsätze*, Munich, 1993, pp. 174–81

Forsbach, Edmund, *Edgar Jung: Ein konservativer Revolutionär*, Pfullingen, 1984

Forschungsstelle für Zeitgeschichte in Hamburg (ed.), *Hamburg im "Dritten Reich,"* Göttingen, 2005

Fraenkel, Ernst, *Der Doppelstaat: Recht und Justiz im "Dritten Reich,"* Frankfurt am Main and Cologne, 1974

Frech, Stefan, *Wegbereiter Hitlers? Theodor Reismann-Grone: Ein völkischer Nationalist 1863–1949*, Paderborn, 2009

Frei, Norbert, *Der Führerstaat: Nationalsozialistische Herrschaft 1933 bis 1945*, revised edition, Munich, 2001

Frei, Norbert, *1945 und wir: Das Dritte Reich im Bewusstsein der Deutschen*, Munich, 2005

Friedländer, Saul, *Das Dritte Reich und die Juden: Die Jahre der Verfolgung 1933–1939*, Munich, 1998

Friedrich, Thomas, *Die missbrauchte Hauptstadt: Hitler und Berlin*, Berlin, 2007

Fritzsche, Peter, *Wie aus Deutsche Nazis wurden*, Zurich and Munich, 1999

Früchtel, Michael, *Der Architekt Hermann Giesler: Leben und Werk 1898–1987*, Munich, 2008

Fuhrer, Armin, *Hitlers Spiele: Olympia 1936 in Berlin*, Berlin and Brandenburg, 2011

Funke, Manfred (ed.), *Hitler, Deutschland und die Mächte: Materialien zur Aussenpolitik des Dritten Reiches*, Düsseldorf, 1978

Gärtringen, Georg Hiller von (ed.), *Das Auge des Dritten Reiches: Hitlers Kameramann und Fotograf Walter Frentz*, Berlin, 2006

Gailus, Manfred, *Protestantismus und Nationalsozialismus: Studien zur nationalsozialistischen Durchdringung des protestantischen Sozialmilieus in Berlin*, Cologne, Weimar and Vienna, 2001

Gallus, Alexander, *Heimat "Weltbühne": Eine Intellektuellengeschichte im 20. Jahrhundert*, Göttingen, 2012

Gay, Peter, *Weimar Culture: The Outside as Insider*, new edition, New York, 2002

Gebel, Ralf, *"Heim ins Reich": Konrad Henlein und der Reichsgau Sudetenland 1938–1945*, Munich, 1999

Gellately, Robert, *The Gestapo and German Society: Enforcing Racial Policy 1933–1945*, Oxford, 1992

Gellately, Robert, *Lenin, Stalin und Hitler: Drei Diktatoren, die Europa in den Abgrund führten*, Bergisch-Gladbach, 2009

Gerwarth, Robert, *Reinhard Heydrich: Biographie*, Munich, 2011

Geyer, Martin H., *Verkehrte Welt: Revolution, Inflation und Moderne. Munich 1914–1924*, Göttingen, 1998

Gietinger, Klaus, *Der Konterrevolutionär Waldemar Pabst—eine deutsche Karriere*, Hamburg, 2009

Gilbhard, Hermann, *Die Thule-Gesellschaft: Vom okkulten Mummenschanz zum Hakenkreuz*, Munich, 1994

Görtemaker, Heike B., *Eva Braun: Leben mit Hitler*, Munich, 2010

Gordon, Harold J., *Hitlerputsch 1923: Machtkampf in Bayern 1923–1924*, Frankfurt am Main, 1971

Graml, Hermann, *Reichskristallnacht: Antisemitismus und Judenverfolgung im Dritten Reich*, Munich, 1988

Granier, Gerhard, *Magnus von Levetzow: Seeoffizier, Monarchist und Wegbereiter Hitlers. Lebensweg und ausgewählte Dokumente*, Boppard am Rhein, 1982

Granzow, Brigitte, *A Mirror of Nazism: British Opinion and the Emergence of Hitler 1929–1933*, London, 1964

Grau, Bernhard, *Kurt Eisner 1867–1919: Eine Biographie*, Munich, 2001

Gritschneder, Otto, *Bewährungsfrist für den Terroristen Adolf H: Der Hitler-Putsch und die bayerischen Justiz*, Munich, 1990

Gritschneder, Otto, *"Der Führer hat sie zum Tode verurteilt . . .": Hitlers "Röhm Putsch"-Morde vor Gericht*, Munich, 1993

Gross, Raphael, *Anständig geblieben: Nationalsozialistische Moral*, Frankfurt am Main, 2010

Grothe, Ewald, "Die Olympischen Spiele von 1936—Höhepunkt der NS-Propaganda?," in *Geschichte in Wissenschaft und Unterricht*, 59 (2008), pp. 291–307

Gruchmann, Lothar, "Die 'Reichsregierung' im Führerstaat: Stellung und Funktion des Kabinetts im nationalsozialistischen Herrschaftssystem," in Günter Doeker and Winfried Seffani (eds), *Klassenjustiz und Pluralismus: Festschrift für Ernst Fraenkel zum 75. Geburtstag*, Cologne, 1973, pp. 187–223

Gruchmann, Lothar, "Hitlers Denkschrift an die bayerische Justiz vom 16. Mai 1923: Ein verloren geglaubtes Dokument," in *Vierteljahrshefte für Zeitgeschichte*, 39 (1991), pp. 305–28

Gruchmann, Lothar, "Ludendorffs 'prophetischer' Brief an Hindenburg vom Januar/Februar 1933: Eine Legende," in *Vierteljahrshefte für Zeitgeschichte*, 47 (1999), pp. 559–62

Gruner, Wolf, "'Lesen brauchen sie nicht können . . .' Die 'Denkschrift über die Behandlung der Juden in der Reichshauptstadt auf allen Gebieten des öffentlichen Lebens' vom Mai 1938,'" in *Jahrbuch für Antisemitismusforschung*, 4 (1995), pp. 305–41

Gun, Nerin E., *Eva Braun-Hitler: Leben und Schicksal*, Velbert und Kettwig, 1968

Gutjahr, Wolf-Dietich, *Revolution muss sein: Karl Radek—die Biographie*, Cologne, Weimar and Vienna, 2012

Gutsche, Willibald, *Ein Kaiser im Exil: Der letzte deutsche Kaiser Wilhelm II in Holland*, Marburg, 1991

Hachtmann, Rüdiger, *Industriearbeit im "Dritten Reich": Untersuchungen zu den Lohn- und Arbeitsbedingungen in Deutschland 1933–1945*, Göttingen, 1989

Hachtmann, Rüdiger, "Öffentlichkeitswirksame Knallfrösche: Anmerkungen zu Götz Alys 'Volksstaat,'" in *Sozial.Geschichte. Zeitschrift für historische Analyse des 20. und 21. Jahrhunderts. N. F.*, 20, pp. 46–66.

Haffner, Sebastian, *Germany: Jekyll & Hyde. Deutschland von innen betrachtet*, Berlin, 1996

Haffner, Sebastian, *Anmerkungen zu Hitler*, 21st edition, Munich, 1978

Haidinger, Martin and Günther Steinbach, *Unser Hitler: Die Österreicher und ihr Landsmann*, Salzburg, 2009

Hale, Oron James, "Adolf Hitler Taxpayer," in *American Historical Review*, 60 (1955), pp. 830–42

Hamann, Brigitte, *Hitlers Wien: Lehrjahre eines Diktators*, Munich and Zurich, 1996

Hamann, Brigitte, *Hitlers Edeljude: Das Leben des Armenarztes Eduard Bloch*, Munich and Zurich, 2008

Hamann, Brigitte, *Winifred Wagner oder Hitlers Bayreuth*, Munich and Zurich, 2002

Harpprecht, Klaus, *Thomas Mann: Eine Biographie*, Reinbek bei Hamburg, 1995

Hartmann, Christian, *Halder: Generalstabschef Hitlers 1938–1942*, 2nd revised and updated edition, Paderborn, 2010

Hayman, Ronald, *Hitler & Geli*, London, 1997

Heberle, Rudolf, *Landbevölkerung und Nationalsozialismus: Eine soziologische Untersuchung der politischen Willensbildung in Schleswig-Holstein 1918–1932*, Stuttgart, 1963

Heer, Friedrich, *Der Glaube des Adolf Hitler: Anatomie einer politischen Religiosität*, 2nd edition, Esslingen and Munich, 1998

Heiden, Konrad, *Adolf Hitler: Das Zeitalter der Verantwortungslosigkeit. Eine Biographie*, Zurich, 1936

Heiden, Konrad, *Adolf Hitler: Ein Mann gegen Europa*, Zurich, 1937

Henke, Josef, *England in Hitlers politischem Kalkül*, Boppard am Rhein, 1973

Henke, Josef, "Die Reichsparteitage der NSDAP in Nürnberg 1933–1938: Planung, Organisation, Propaganda," in *Aus der Arbeit des Bundesarchivs*, ed. Heinz Boberach and Hans Booms, Boppard am Rhein, 1977, pp. 398–409

Hensel, Jürgen and Pia Nordblom (eds), *Hermann Rauschning: Materialien und Beiträge zu einer politischen Biographie*, Osnabrück, 2003

Herbert, Ulrich, "'Generation der Sachlichkeit': Die völkische Studentenbewegung der frühen zwanziger Jahre," in Frank Bajohr, Werner Johe and Uwe Lohalm (eds), *Zivilisation und Barbarei: Die widersprüchlichen Potentiale der Moderne*, Hamburg, 1991, pp. 115–41

Herbert, Ulrich, *Best: Biographische Studien über Radikalismus, Weltanschauung und Vernunft 1903–1989*, Bonn, 1996

Herbst, Ludolf, *Hitlers Charisma: Die Erfindung eines deutschen Messias*, Frankfurt am Main, 2010

Hering, Rainer, *Konstruierte Nation: Der Alldeutsche Verband 1890 bis 1939*, Hamburg, 2003

Hermann, Angela, *Der Weg in den Krieg 1938/39: Studien zu den Tagebüchern von Joseph Goebbels*, Munich, 2011

Hermann, Angela, "Hitler und sein Stosstrupp in der 'Reichskristallnacht,'" in *Vierteljahrshefte für Zeitgeschichte*, 56 (2008), pp. 603–19

Herre, Franz, *Jahrhundertwende 1900: Untergangsstimung und Fortschrittsglauben*, Stuttgart, 1998

Herz, Rudolf, *Hoffmann & Hitler: Fotografie als Medium des Führer-Mythos*, Munich, 1994

Hesemann, Michael, *Hitlers Religion: Die fatale Heilslehre des Nationalsozialismus*, Munich, 2004

Heusler, Andreas, *Das Braune Haus: Wie München zur "Hauptstadt der Bewegung" wurde*, Munich, 2008

Heuss, Theodor, *Hitlers Weg: Eine historisch-politische Studie über den Nationalsozialismus*, 6th edition, Stuttgart, Berlin and Leipzig, 1932

Hildebrand, Klaus, *Das vergangene Reich: Deutsche Aussenpolitik von Bismarck zu Hitler 1871–1945*, Stuttgart, 1995

Hildebrand, Klaus, *Das Dritte Reich*, 6th revised edition, Munich, 2003

Hipler, Bruno, *Hitlers Lehrmeister: Karl Haushofer als Vater der NS-Ideologie*, St. Ottilien, 1996

Hirschfeld, Gerhard, Gerd Krumeich and Irina Renz, with Markus Pöhlmann (eds), *Enzyklopädie Erster Weltkrieg*, Paderborn, 2003

Hirschfeld, Gerhard, Gerd Krumeich and Irina Renz (eds), *Die Deutschen an der Somme 1914–1918: Krieg, Besatzung, Verbrannte Erde*, Essen, 2006

Hitzer, Friedrich, *Anton Graf Arco: Das Attentat auf Eisner und die Schüsse im Landtag*, Munich, 1988

Hockerts, Hans Günter, *Die Sittlichkeitsprozesse gegen katholische Ordensangehörige und Priester 1936/37: Eine Studie zur nationalsozialistischen Herrschaftstechnik und zum Kirchenkampf*, Mainz, 1971

Hockerts, Hans Günter, "Die Goebbels-Tagebücher 1932–1941: Eine neue Hauptquelle zur Erforschung der nationalsozialistischen Kirchenpolitik," in Dieter Albrecht et al. (eds), *Politik und Konfession: Festschrift für Konrad Repgen zum 60. Geburtstag*, Berlin, 1983, pp. 359–92

Hoegen, Jesko von, *Der Held von Tannenberg: Genese und Funktion des Hindenburg-Mythos*, Cologne, Weimar and Vienna, 2007

Höhne, Heinz, *Mordsache Röhm: Hitlers Durchbruch zur Alleinherrschaft 1933–1934*, Reinbek, 1984

Höhne, Heinz, *Die Zeit der Illusionen: Hitler und die Anfänge des Dritten Reiches 1933–1936*, Düsseldorf, Vienna and New York, 1991

Höller, Ralf, *Der Anfang, der ein Ende war: Die Revolution in Bayern 1918/19*, Berlin, 1999

Hömig, Herbert, *Brüning: Kanzler in der Krise der Republik. Eine Weimarer Biographie*, Paderborn, 2000

Hömig, Herbert, *Brüning: Politiker ohne Auftrag. Zwischen Weimarer und Bonner Republik*, Paderborn, 2005

Hoeres, Peter, *Die Kultur von Weimar: Durchbruch der Moderne*, Berlin and Brandenburg, 2008

Hofmann, Hanns Hubert, *Der Hitler-Putsch: Krisenjahre deutscher Geschichte 1920–1924*, Munich, 1961

Holzbach, Heidrun, *Das "System Hugenberg": Die Organisation bürgerlicher Sammlungspolitik vor dem Aufstieg der NSDAP*, Stuttgart, 1981

Hoppe, Bernd, "Von Schleicher zu Hitler: Dokumente zum Konflikt zwischen dem Reichslandbund und der Regierung Schleicher in den letzten Wochen der Weimarer Republik," in *Vierteljahrshefte für Zeitgeschichte*, 45 (1997), pp. 629–57

Horn, Wolfgang, *Der Marsch zur Machtergreifung: Die NSDAP bis 1933*, Düsseldorf, 1980

Horn, Wolfgang, "Ein unbekannter Aufsatz Hitlers aus dem Frühjahr 1924," in *Vierteljahrshefte für Zeitgeschichte*, 16 (1968), pp. 280–94

Horne, John and Alan Kramer, *Deutsche Kriegsgreuel 1914: Die umstrittene Wahrheit*, Hamburg, 2004

Horstmann, Bernhard, *Hitler in Pasewalk: Die Hypnose und ihre Folgen*, Düsseldorf, 2004

Hürter, Johannes, *Wilhelm Groener: Reichswehrminister am Ende der Weimarer Republik 1928–1932*, Munich, 1993

Hüttenberger, Peter, *Die Gauleiter: Studie zum Wandel des Machtgefüges in der NSDAP*, Stuttgart, 1969

Humann, Detlev, *"Arbeitsschlacht": Arbeitsbeschaffung und Propaganda in der NS-Zeit 1933–1939*, Göttingen, 2011

Hurnaus, Hertha, et al. (eds), *Haus Meldemannstrasse*, Vienna, 2003

Industrie-Club e. V. Düsseldorf (ed.), *Treffpunkt der Eliten: Die Geschichte des Industrie-Clubs Düsseldorf. Texte und wissenschaftliche Bearbeitung von Volker Ackermann*, Düsseldorf, 2006

Jablonski, David, *The Nazi Party in Dissolution: Hitler and the Verbotszeit 1923–1925*, London, 1989

Jacobsen, Hans-Adolf, *Nationalsozialistische Aussenpolitik 1933–1939*, Frankfurt am Main and Berlin, 1968

Jäckel, Eberhard, *Hitlers Weltanschauung: Entwurf einer Herrschaft*, revised and expanded edition, Stuttgart, 1981

Jäckel, Eberhard, *Das deutsche Jahrhundert: Eine historische Bilanz*, Stuttgart, 1996

James, Harold, "Die Deutsche Bank und die Diktatur 1933–1945," in Lothar Gall et al., *Die Deutsche Bank 1870–1995*, Munich, 1995, pp. 315–408

James, Harold, *Krupp: Deutsche Legende und globales Unternehmen*, Munich, 2011

Janssen, Karl Heinz and Fritz Tobias, *Der Sturz der Generäle: Hitler und die Blomberg-Fritsch-Krise 1938*, Munich, 1994

Jetzinger, Franz, *Hitlers Jugend: Phantasien, Lügen und Wahrheit*, Vienna, 1956

Joachimsthaler, Anton, *Hitlers Liste: Ein Dokument persönlicher Beziehungen*, Munich, 2003

Joachimsthaler, Anton, *Hitlers Weg begann in München 1913–1923*, Munich, 2000

Joachimsthaler, Anton, *Korrektur einer Biographie: Adolf Hitler 1908–1920*, Munich, 1989

Jochmann, Werner, *Im Kampf um die Macht: Hitlers Rede vor dem Hamburger Nationalklub von 1919*, Frankfurt am Main, 1960

Jochmann, Werner, *Gesellschaftskrise und Judenfeindschaft in Deutschland 1870–1945*, Hamburg, 1988

Johnson, Eric J., *Der nationalsozialistische Terror: Gestapo, Juden und gewöhnliche Deutsche*, Berlin, 2001

Jones, Larry Eugene, "'The Greatest Stupidity of My Life': Alfred Hugenberg and the Formation of the Hitler Cabinet, January 1933," in *Journal of Contemporary History*, 27 (1992), pp. 63–87

Jones, Larry Eugene, "Nationalists, Nazis and the Assault against Weimar: Revisiting the Harzburg Rally of October 1931," in *German Studies Review*, 29 (2006), pp. 483–94

Käfer, Miriam, "Hitlers frühe Förderer aus dem Grossbürgertum: Das Verlegerehepaar Elsa und Hugo Bruckmann," in M. Krauss (ed.), *Rechte Karrieren in München*, pp. 52–79

Karl, Michaela, *Die Münchner Räterepublik: Porträts einer Revolution*, Düsseldorf, 2008

Karow, Yvonne, *Deutsches Opfer: Kultische Selbstauslöschung auf den Reichsparteitagen der NSDAP*, Berlin, 1994

Kater, Michael H., "Zur Soziologie der frühen NSDAP," in *Vierteljahrshefte für Zeitgeschichte*, 19 (1971), pp. 124–59

Keller, Gustav, *Der Schüler Adolf Hitler: Die Geschichte eines lebenslangen Amoklaufs*, Münster, 2010

Kellerhoff, Sven Felix, *Hitlers Berlin: Geschichte einer Hassliebe*, Berlin and Brandenburg, 2005

Kellerhoff, Sven Felix, *Der Reichstagsbrand: Die Karriere eines Kriminalfalles*, Berlin, 2008

Kershaw, Ian, *The Hitler Myth: Image and Reality in the Third Reich*, Oxford, 1987

Kershaw, Ian, *Hitler: Profiles in Power*, revised edition, London, 2000

Kershaw, Ian, *Hitler 1889–1936: Hubris, Hitler 1936–1945: Nemesis*, London, 1998, 2000

Kershaw, Ian, *Making Friends with Hitler: Lord Londonderry and Britain's Road to War*, London, 2005

Kershaw, Ian, "'Volksgemeinschaft': Potenzial und Grenzen eines neuen Forschungskonzepts," in *Vierteljahrshefte für Zeitgeschichte*, 59 (2001), pp. 1–17

Kettenacker, Lothar, "Hitler und die Kirchen: Eine Obsession mit Folgen," in Günther Heydemann and Lothar Kettenacker (eds), *Kirchen in der Diktatur: Drittes Reich und SED-Staat*, Göttingen, 1993, pp. 67–87

Kissenkoetter, Udo, *Gregor Strasser und die NSDAP*, Stuttgart, 1978

Klee, Ernst, *"Die SA Jesu Christi": Die Kirche im Banne Hitlers*, Frankfurt am Main, 1989

Klemperer, Victor, *LTI: Notizbuch eines Philologen*, 24th fully revised and expanded edition, ed. and annotated by Elke Fröhlich, Stuttgart, 2010

Knickerbocker, H(ubert) R., *Deutschland so oder so?*, Berlin, 1932
Knopp, Guido, *Hitler: Eine Bilanz*, Berlin, 1995
Knopp, Guido, *Geheimnisse des "Dritten Reiches,"* Munich, 2011
Koch-Hillebrecht, Manfred, *Homo Hitler: Psychogramm eines Diktators*, Munich, 1999
Koch-Hillebrecht, Manfred, *Hitler: Ein Sohn des Krieges. Fronterlebnis und Weltbild*, Munich, 2003
Koenen, Gerd, *Der Russland-Komplex: Die Deutschen und der Osten 1900–1945*, Munich, 2005
Köhler, Joachim, *Wagners Hitler: Der Prophet und sein Vollstrecker*, Munich, 1997
König, Wolfgang, *Volkswagen, Volksempfänger, Volksgemeinschaft: "Volksprodukte" im Dritten Reich. Vom Scheitern der nationalsozialistischen Konsumgesellschaft*, Paderborn, 2004
Kolb, Eberhard, *Die Weimarer Republik*, 2nd edition, Munich, 1988
Kolb, Eberhard and Wolfram Pyta, "Die Staatsnotstandsplanung unter den Regierungen Papen und Schleicher," in Heinrich August Winkler (ed.), *Die deutsche Staatskrise 1930–33*, Munich, 1992, pp. 155–81
Kolb, Eberhard, "Die Weimarer Republik und das Problem der Kontinuität vom Kaiserreich zum 'Dritten Reich,'" in *idem, Umbrüche deutscher Geschichte 1866/71–1918/19–1929/33: Ausgewählte Aufsätze*, eds Dieter Langewiesche and Klaus Schönhoven, Munich, 1993, pp. 359–72
Koop, Volker, *Martin Bormann: Hitlers Vollstrecker*, Vienna, Cologne and Weimar, 2012
Kopper, Christopher, *Hjalmar Schacht: Aufstieg und Fall von Hitlers mächtigstem Bankier*, Munich and Vienna, 2006
Kopperschmidt, Josef (ed.), *Hitler als Redner*, Munich, 2003
Kracauer, Siegfried, *Von Caligari zu Hitler: Eine psychologische Geschichte des deutschen Films*, Frankfurt am Main, 1979
Krauss, Marita (ed.), *Rechte Karrieren in München: Von der Weimarer Zeit bis in die Nachkriegsjahre*, Munich, 2010
Krings, Stefan, *Hitlers Pressechef Otto Dietrich 1897–1952: Eine Biographie*, Göttingen, 2010
Krüger, Arnd, *Die Olympischen Spiele 1936 und die Weltmeinung: Ihre aussenpolitische Bedeutung unter besonderer Berücksichtigung der USA*, Berlin, 1972
Kube, Alfred, *Pour le mérite und Hakenkreuz: Hermann Göring im Dritten Reich*, Munich, 1989
Kühnl, Reinhard, "Zur Programmatik der nationalsozialistischen Linken: Das Strasser-Programm von 1925/26," in *Vierteljahrshefte für Zeitgeschichte*, 14 (1966), pp. 317–33
Kuhn, Axel, *Hitlers aussenpolitisches Programm*, Stuttgart, 1970
Kulka, Otto Dov, "Die Nürnberger Rassegesetze und die deutsche Bevölkerung im Lichte geheimer SS-Lage- und Stimmungsberichte," in *Vierteljahrshefte für Zeitgeschichte*, 32 (1984), pp. 582–624
Laak, Dirk van, "Adolf Hitler," in Frank Möller (ed.), *Charismatische Führer der deutschen Nation*, Munich, 2004, pp. 149–69
Lahme, Tilmann, *Golo Mann: Biographie*, Frankfurt am Main, 2009
Lang, Jochen von, *Der Sekretär: Martin Bormann. Der Mann, der Hitler beherrschte*, 3rd revised edition, Munich and Berlin, 1987
Lange, Karl, *Hitlers unbeachtete Maximen: "Mein Kampf" und die Öffentlichkeit*, Stuttgart, 1968
Lange, Karl, "Der Terminus 'Lebensraum' in Hitlers 'Mein Kampf,'" in *Vierteljahrshefte für Zeitgeschichte*, 13 (1965), pp. 426–37
Large, David Clay, *Where Ghosts Walked: Munich's Road to the Third Reich*, New York, 1996
Large, David Clay, *Berlin: Biographie einer Stadt*, Munich, 2002
Leicht, Johannes, *Heinrich Class 1868–1953: Die politische Biographie eines Alldeutschen*, Paderborn, 2012
Leis, Mario, *Leni Riefenstahl*, Reinbek bei Hamburg, 2009
Leiser, Erwin, *'Deutschland erwache!" Propaganda im Film des Dritten Reiches*, Reinbek bei Hamburg, 1978
Lessmann, Peter, *Die preussische Schutzpolizei in der Weimarer Republik: Streifendienst und Strassenkampf*, Düsseldorf, 1989

Leutheusser, Ulrike (ed.), *Hitler und die Frauen*, Munich, 2003

Linse, Ulrich, *Barfüssige Propheten: Erlöser der zwanziger Jahre*, Berlin, 1983

Lohalm, Uwe, *Völkischer Radikalismus: Die Geschichte des Deutschvölkischen Schutz- und Trutzbundes 1919–1923*, Hamburg, 1970

Loiperdinger, Martin, *Der Parteitagsfilm "Triumph des Willens" von Leni Riefenstahl*, Oplasden, 1987

Longerich, Peter, *Die braunen Bataillone: Geschichte der SA*, Munich, 1989

Longerich, Peter, *Hitlers Stellvertreter: Führung der Partei und Kontrolle des Staatsapparats durch den Stab Hess und die Partei-Kanzlei Bormanns*, Munich, 1992

Longerich, Peter, *Deutschland 1918–1933: Die Weimarer Republik*, Hannover, 1995

Longerich, Peter, *Politik der Vernichtung: Eine Gesamtdarstellung der nationalsozialistischen Judenverfolgung*, Munich and Zurich, 1998

Longerich, Peter, *'Davon haben wir nichts gewusst!" Die Deutschen und die Judenverfolgung 1933–1945*, Munich, 2006

Longerich, Peter, *Heinrich Himmler: Biographie*, Munich, 2008

Longerich, Peter, *Goebbels: A Biography* London, 2015

Lukacs, John, *Hitler: Geschichte und Geschichtsschreibung*, Munich, 1997

Luntowski, Gustav, *Hitler und die Herren an der Ruhr: Wirtschaftsmacht und Staatsmacht im Dritten Reich*, Frankfurt am Main, 2000

Machtan, Lothar, *Hitlers Geheimnis: Das Doppelleben eines Diktators*, Berlin, 2001

Machtan, Lothar, "Was Hitlers Homosexualität bedeutet: Anmerkungen zu einer Tabugeschichte," in *Zeitschrift für Geschichtswissenschaft*, 51 (2003), pp. 334–51

Machtan, Lothar, *Der Kaisersohn bei Hitler*, Hamburg, 2006

Mandell, Richard, *Hitlers Olympiade: Berlin 1936*, Munich, 1980

Mann, Thomas, "Bruder Hitler (1939)," in *An die gesittete Welt: Politische Schriften und Reden im Exil*, Frankfurt am Main, 1986, pp. 253–60

Marks, Stefan, *Warum folgten sie Hitler? Die Psychologie des Nationalsozialismus*, Düsseldorf, 2007

Martynkewicz, Wolfgang, *Salon Deutschland: Geist und Macht 1900–1945*, Berlin, 2009

Marx, Christian, *Paul Reusch und die Gutehoffnungshütte: Leitung eines deutschen Grossunternehmens*, Göttingen, 2013

Maser, Werner, *Die Frühgeschichte der NSDAP: Hitlers Weg bis 1924*, Frankfurt am Main and Bonn, 1965

Maser, Werner, *Adolf Hitlers "Mein Kampf": Geschichte, Auszüge, Kommentare*, 9th edition, Esslingen, 2001

Maser, Werner, *Adolf Hitler: Legende–Mythos–Wirklichkeit*, 12th edition, Munich and Esslingen, 1998

Matthias, Erich and Rudolf Morsey (eds), *Das Ende der Parteien 1933*, Düsseldorf, 1960

Mattioli, Aram, *Experimentierfeld der Gewalt: Der Abessinienkrieg und seine internationale Bedeutung 1935–1941*, Zurich, 2005

Mauersberger, Volker, *Hitler in Weimar: Der Fall einer deutschen Kulturstadt*, Berlin, 1999

Mehring, Reinhard, *Carl Schmitt: Aufstieg und Fall*, Munich, 2009

Meier, Kurt, *Kreuz und Hakenkreuz: Die evangelische Kirche im Dritten Reich*, Munich, 1992

Mensing, Björn and Friedrich Prinz (eds), *Irrlicht im leuchtenden München? Der Nationalsozialismus in der "Hauptstadt der Bewegung,"* Regensburg, 1991

Merkenich, Stephanie, *Grüne Front gegen Weimar: Reichsland-Bund und agrarischer Lobbyismus 1918–1933*, Düsseldorf, 1998

Merseburger, Peter, *Theodor Heuss: Der Bürger als Präsident. Biographie*, Munich, 2012

Michalka, Wolfgang, *Ribbentrop und die deutsche Weltpolitik 1933–1940: Aussenpolitische Konzeptionen und Entscheidungsprozesse im Dritten Reich*, Munich, 1980

Miller, Alice, *Am Anfang war Erziehung*, Frankfurt am Main, 1980

Moeller, Horst, "Die nationalsoziaistische Machtergreifung: Konterrevolution oder Revolution?," in *Vierteljahrshefte für Zeitgeschichte*, 31 (1983), pp. 25–51

Mommsen, Hans, "Hitlers Stellung im nationalsozialistischen Herrschaftssystem," in
  Gerhard Hirschfeld and Lothar Kettenacker (eds), Der "Führerstaat": Mythos und Realität,
  Stuttgart, 1981, pp. 43–72
Mommsen, Hans and Susanne Willems (eds), Herrschaftsalltag im Dritten Reich: Studien
  und Texte, Düsseldorf, 1988
Mommsen, Hans and Manfred Krieger, Das Volkswagenwerk und seine Arbeiter im Dritten
  Reich, Düsseldorf, 1996
Mommsen, Hans, "Hitler's Reichstag Speech of 30 January 1939," in History & Memory,
  9 (1997), pp. 147–61
Mommsen, Hans, Zur Geschichte Deutschlands im 20. Jahrhundert, Munich, 2010
Moreau, Patrick, Nationalsozialismus von links: Die "Kampfgemeinschaft Revolutionärer
  Nationalsozialisten" und die "Schwarze Front" Otto Strassers 1930–1935, Stuttgart, 1985
Mühleisen, Horst, "Die Fritsch-Krise im Frühjahr 1938: Neue Dokumente aus dem Nachlass
  des Generalobersten," in Militärgeschichtliche Mitteilungen, 56 (1997), pp. 471–508
Mühlhausen, Walter, Friedrich Ebert 1871–1925: Reichspräsident der Weimarer Republik, Bonn,
  2006
Müller, Klaus-Jürgen, Armee und Drittes Reich 1933–1939: Darstellung und Dokumente,
  Paderborn, 1987
Müller, Klaus-Jürgen, Generaloberst Ludwig Beck: Eine Biographie, Paderborn, 2008
Mulack, Christa, Klara Hitler: Muttersein im Patriarchat, Rüsselsheim, 2005
Muth, Heinrich, "Das 'Kölner Gespräch' am 4. Januar 1933," in Geschichte in Wissenschaft
  und Unterricht, 37 (1986), pp. 463–80
Nebelin, Manfred, Ludendorff: Diktator im Ersten Weltkrieg, Munich, 2011
Neebe, Reinhard, Grossindustrie, Staat und NSDAP 1930–1933, Göttingen, 1981
Neliba, Günter, Wilhelm Frick: Eine politische Biographie, Paderborn, 1992
Neumann, Hans-Joachim and Henrik Eberle, War Hitler krank? Ein abschliessender Befund,
  Bergisch-Gladbach, 2009
Nieden, Susanne zur, "Aufstieg und Fall des virilen Männerhelden: Der Skandal um Ernst
  Röhm und seine Ermordung," in idem (ed.), Homosexualität und Staatsräson: Männlichkeit,
  Homophobie und Politik in Deutschland 1900–1945, Frankfurt am Main, 2005, pp. 147–75
Niekisch, Ernst, "Hitler—ein deutsches Verhängnis" (1931), in idem, Politische Schriften,
  Cologne and Berlin, 1965, pp. 19–62
Nüsslein, Timo, Paul Ludwig Troost 1878–1934, Vienna, Cologne and Weimar, 2012
Oberwinter, Kristina, "Bewegende Bilder": Repräsentation und Produktion von Emotionen in
  Leni Riefenstahls "Triumph des Willens," Berlin, 2007
Obst, Dieter, "Reichskristallnacht": Ursachen und Verlauf des antisemitischen Pogroms vom
  November 1938, Frankfurt am Main, 1991
O'Donnell, James P., "Der grosse und der kleine Diktator," in Der Monat, 30 (1978), pp. 51–62
Olden, Rudolf, Hitler, Amsterdam, 1935; new edition, Hildesheim, 1981
Ossietzky, Carl von, Sämtliche Schriften: Vol. 2: 1922–1924, ed. Bärbel Boldt, Dirk Grathoff
  and Michael Sartorius; Vol. 5: 1929–1930, ed. Bärbel Boldt, Ute Maack and Günther
  Nickel; Vol. 6: 1931–1933, ed. Gerhard Kraiker, Günther Nickel, Renke Siems and Elke
  Suhr, Reinbek bei Hamburg, 1994
Pätzold, Kurt, "Hitlers fünfzigster Geburtstag am 20. 4. 1939," in Dietrich Eichholtz and
  Kurt Pätzold (eds), Der Weg in den Krieg: Studien zur Geschichte der Vorkriegsjahre 1935/36
  bis 1939, Cologne, 1989, pp. 309–43
Pätzold, Kurt and Manfred Weissbecker, Geschichte der NSDAP 1920–1945, Cologne, 1998
Parker, Robert and Alexander Clarke, Chamberlain and Appeasement: British Policy and the
  Coming of the Second World War, London, 1993
Paul, Gerhard, "Deutsche Mutter—heim zu Dir!": Warum es misslang, Hitler an der Saar zu
  schlagen. Der Saarkampf 1933 bis 1945, Cologne, 1984
Paul, Gerhard, Aufstand der Bilder: Die NS-Propaganda vor 1933, Bonn, 1990
Paul, Gerhard and Klaus-Michael Mallmann (eds), Die Gestapo—Mythos und Realität,
  Darmstadt, 2003

Pehle, Walter H. (ed.), *Der Judenpogrom 1938: Von der "Reichskristallnacht" zum Völkermord*, Frankfurt am Main, 1988

Petersen, Jens, *Hitler–Mussolini: Die Entstehung der Achse Berlin–Rom 1933–1936*, Tübingen, 1973

Petzold, Joachim, "Class und Hitler: Über die Förderung der frühen Nazibewegung durch den Alldeutschen Verband und dessen Einfluss auf die nazistische Ideologie," in *Jahrbuch für Geschichte*, 21 (1980), pp. 247–88

Petzold, Joachim, *Franz von Papen: Ein deutsches Verhängnis*, Berlin, 1995

Phelps, Reginald H., "Before Hitler Came: Thule Society and Germanen Orden," in *Journal of Modern History*, 35 (1963), pp. 245–61

Piper, Ernst, *Alfred Rosenberg: Hitlers Chefideologe*, Munich, 2005

Plewnia, Margarete, *Auf dem Weg zu Hitler: Der "völkische" Publizist Dietrich Eckart*, Berlin, 1970

Plöckinger, Othmar, *Geschichte eines Buches: "Mein Kampf" 1922–1945*, Munich, 2006

Plöckinger, Othmar, *Unter Soldaten und Agitatoren: Hitlers prägende Jahre im deutschen Militär 1918–1920*, Paderborn, 2013

Plöckinger, Othmar, "Adolf Hitler als Hörer an der Universität Munich, im Jahr 1919: Zum Verhältnis zwischen Reichswehr und Universität," in Elisabeth Kraus (ed.), *Die Universität München im Dritten Reich: Aufsätze. Teil II*, Munich, 2008, pp. 12–47

Plöckinger, Othmar, "Frühe biographische Texte zu Hitler: Zur Bewertung der autobiographischen Texte in 'Mein Kampf,'" in *Vierteljahrshefte für Zeitgeschichte*, 58 (2010), pp. 93–114.

Przyrembel, Alexandra, *"Rassenschande": Reinheitsmythos und Vernichtungslegitimation im Nationalsozialismus*, Göttingen, 2003

Pufendorf, Astrid, *Die Plancks: Eine Familie zwischen Patriotismus und Widerstand*, Berlin, 2006

Pulzer, Peter G. J., *Die Entstehung des politischen Antisemitismus in Deutschland und Österreich 1867 bis 1914: Neuausgabe mit einem Forschungsbericht*, Göttingen, 2004

Pyta, Wolfram, *Hindenburg: Herrschaft zwischen Hohenzollern und Hitler*, Munich, 2007

Pyta, Wolfram, "Die Hitler-Edition des Instituts für Zeitgeschichte," in *Historische Zeitschrift*, 281 (2005), pp. 383–94

Radkau, Joachim, *Das Zeitalter der Nervosität: Deutschland zwischen Bismarck und Hitler*, Munich and Vienna, 1998

Raithel, Thomas and Irene Strenge, "Die Reichstagsbrandverordnung: Grundlegung der Diktatur mit den Instrumenten des Weimarer Ausnahmezustands," in *Vierteljahrshefte für Zeitgeschichte*, 48 (2000), pp. 413–60

Rauscher, Walter, *Hitler und Mussolini: Macht, Krieg und Terror*, Graz, Vienna and Cologne, 2001

Rauschning, Hermann, *Die Revolution des Nihilismus*, Zurich, 1938

Rebentisch, Dieter, "Hitlers Reichskanzlei zwischen Politik und Verwaltung," in idem and Karl Teppe (eds), *Verwaltung contra Menschenführung im Staat Hitlers*, Göttingen, 1986, pp. 65–99

Recker, Marie-Luise, *Die Aussenpolitik des Dritten Reiches*, Munich, 1990

Reichel, Peter, *Der schöne Schein des Dritten Reiches: Faszination und Gewalt des Faschismus*, Munich, 1991

Reif, Adalbert, *Albert Speer: Kontroversen um ein deutsches Phänomen*, Munich, 1978

Reuss, Eberhard, *Hitlers Rennschlachten: Die Silberpfeile unterm Hakenkreuz*, Berlin, 2006

Reuth, Ralf Georg, *Goebbels*, Munich and Zurich, 1990

Reuth, Ralf Georg, *Hitler: Eine Biographie*, Munich and Zurich, 2003

Reuth, Ralf Georg, *Hitlers Judenhass: Klischee und Wirklichkeit*, Munich and Zurich, 2009

Richardi, Hans-Günter, *Hitler und seine Hintermänner: Neue Fakten zur Frühgeschichte der NSDAP*, Munich, 1991

Richter, Ludwig, *Die Deutsche Volkspartei 1918–1933*, Düsseldorf, 2002

Riecker, Joachim, *Hitlers 9. November: Wie der Erste Weltkrieg zum Holocaust führte*, Berlin, 2009

Rieger, Eva, *Friedelind Wagner: Die rebellische Enkelin Richard Wagners*, Munich, 2012

Rissmann, Michael, *Hitlers Gott: Vorsehungsglaube und Sendungsbewusstsein eines deutschen Diktators*, Zurich and Munich, 2001

Robertson, Esmonde M., "Hitler und die Sanktionen des Völkerbunds," in *Vierteljahrshefte für Zeitgeschichte*, 26 (1962), pp. 237–64

Rödder, Andreas, *Stresemanns Erbe: Julius Curtius und die deutsche Aussenpolitik 1929–1931*, Paderborn, 1996

Rösch, Mathias, *Die Münchner NSDAP 1925–1933: Eine Untersuchung zur inneren Struktur der NSDAP in der Weimarer Republik*, Munich, 2002

Rostock, Jürgen and Franz Zadnicek, *Paradiesruinen: Das KDF-Seebad der Zwanzigtausaend auf Rügen*, Berlin, 1995

Roth, Karl Heinz, "Ökonomie und politische Macht: Die 'Firma Hamburg' 1930–1945," in Angelika Ebbinghaus and Kartsten Line (eds), *Kein abgeschlossenes Kapitel: Hamburg im "Dritten Reich,"* Hamburg, 1997, pp. 15–176

Rother, Rainer, *Leni Riefenstahl: Die Verführung des Talents*, Berlin, 2000

Ruben, Gunnhild, *"Bitte mich als Untermieter bei Ihnen anzumelden!" Hitler und Braunschweig 1932–1935*, Norderstedt, 2004

Ryback, Timothy, W., *Hitler's Private Library: The Books That Shaped his Life*, London, 2009

Ryback, Timothy W., *Hitlers Bücher: Seine Bibliothek—sein Denken*, Cologne, 2010

Sabrow, Martin, *Der Rathenau-Mord: Rekonstruktion einer Verschwörung gegen die Republik von Weimar*, Munich, 1994

Schäche, Wolfgang and Norbert Szymanski, *Das Reichssportfeld: Architektur im Spannungsfeld von Sport und Macht*, Berlin and Brandenburg, 2001

Schad, Martha, "'Das Auge war vor allen Dingen ungeheuer anziehend': Freundinnen und Verehrerinnen," in Leutheusser (ed.), *Hitler und die Frauen*, pp. 21–135

Schad, Martha, *Sie liebten den Führer: Wie Frauen Hitler verehrten*, Munich, 2009

Schäfer, Claus W., *André François-Poncet als Botschafter in Berlin 1931–1938*, Munich, 2004

Schäfer, Kerstin A., *Werner von Blomberg: Hitlers erster Feldmarschall. Eine Biographie*, Paderborn, 2006

Schauff, Frank, *Der Spanische Bürgerkrieg*, Göttingen, 2006

Scheck, Raffael, "Swiss Funding for the Early Nazi Movement," in *Journal of Modern History*, 71 (1999), pp. 793–813.

Scheel, Klaus, *Der Tag von Potsdam*, Berlin, 1993

Schenk, Dieter, *Hitlers Mann in Danzig: Albert Forster und die NS-Verbrechen in Danzig-Westpreussen*, Bonn, 2000

Schenk, Dieter, *Hans Frank: Hitlers Kronjurist und Generalgouverneur*, Frankfurt am Main, 2006

Schenk, Ernst Günther, *Patient Hitler: Eine medizinische Biographie*, Düsseldorf, 1989

Schieder, Wolfgang, *Faschistische Diktaturen: Studien zu Italien und Deutschland*, Göttingen, 2008

Schildt, Axel, *Militärdiktatur auf Massenbasis? Die Querfrontkonzeption der Reichswehrführung um General Schleicher am Ende der Weimarer Republik*, Frankfurt am Main and New York, 1981

Schildt, Gerhard, "Die Arbeitsgemeinschaft Nord-West: Untersuchungen zur Geschichte der NSDAP 1925/26," diss. Freiburg, 1964

Schlüter, André, *Moeller van den Bruck: Leben und Werk*, Cologne, Weimar and Vienna, 2010

Schmeer, Karlheinz, *Die Regie des öffentlichen Lebens im Dritten Reich*, Munich, 1956

Schmidt, Julia, *Kampf um das Deutschtum: Radikaler Nationalismus in Österreich und im Deutschen Reich 1890–1914*, Frankfurt am Main and New York, 2009

Schmidt, Matthias, *Albert Speer: Das Ende eines Mythos*, 2nd edition, Berlin, 2005

Schmidt, Rainer F., *Die Aussenpolitik des Dritten Reiches 1933–1939*, Stuttgart, 2002

Schmidt, Ulf, *Hitlers Arzt Karl Brandt: Medizin und Macht im Dritten Reich*, Berlin, 2009

Schmiechen-Ackermann, Detlef (ed.), *"Volksgemeinschaft": Mythos, wirkungsmächtige soziale Verheissung oder soziale Realität im "Dritten Reich"? Zwischenbilanz einer Kontroverse*, Paderborn, 2012

Schmied, Jürgen Peter, *Sebastian Haffner: Eine Biographie*, Munich, 2010

Schmölders, Claudia, *Hitlers Gesicht: Eine physiognomische Biographie*, Munich, 2000

Schneider, Michael, *Unterm Hakenkreuz: Arbeiter und Arbeiterbewegung 1933 bis 1939*, Bonn, 1999

Schneider, Thomas Martin, *Reichsbischof Ludwig Müller: Eine Untersuchung zu Leben, Werk und Persönlichkeit*, Göttingen, 1993

Schoenbaum, David, *Die braune Revolution: Eine Sozialgeschichte des Dritten Reiches*, Cologne, 1968

Schönberger, Angela, *Die Neue Reichskanzlei: Zum Zusammenhang von nationalsozialistischer Ideologie und Architektur*, Berlin, 1981

Scholder, Klaus, *Die Kirchen und das Dritte Reich*, Vol. 1: *Vorgeschichte und Zeit der Illusion 1918–1934*, Frankfurt am Main, Berlin and Vienna, 1977; Vol. 2: *Das Jahr der Ernüchterung 1934: Barmen und Rom*, Berlin, 1985

Scholtysek, Joachim, *Der Aufstieg der Quandts: Eine deutsche Unternehmerdynastie*, Munich, 2011

Schorske, Carl E., *Vienna: Geist und Gesellschaft im Fin de Siècle*, Munich, 1994

Schreckenberg, Heinz, *Hitler: Motive und Mehoden einer unwahrscheinlichen Karriere. Eine biographische Studie*, Frankfurt am Main, 2006

Schreiber, Gerhard, *Hitler: Interpretationen 1923–1983. Ergebnisse, Methoden und Probleme der Forschung*, Darmstadt, 1984

Schulz, Gerhard, *Von Brüning zu Hitler: Der Wandel des politischen Systems in Deutschland 1930–1933*, Berlin and New York, 1992

Schwarz, Birgit, *Geniewahn: Hitler und die Kunst*, Vienna, Cologne and Weimar, 2009

Schwarzschild, Leopold, *Chronik eines Untergangs: Deutschland 1924–1939*, ed. Andreas P. Wesemann, Vienna, 2005

Schwarzwäller, Wulf C., *Hitlers Geld: Vom armen Kunstmaler zum millionenschweren Führer*, Vienna, 1998

Schwilk, Heimo, *Ernst Jünger: Ein Jahrhundertleben*, Munich and Zurich, 2007

Seidler, Franz W., *Die Organisation Todt: Bauen für Staat und Wehrmacht 1938–1945*, Bonn, 1998

Sereny, Gitta, *Albert Speer: His Battle with the Truth*, new edition, London, 1996

Sieg, Ulrich, "Ein Prophet nationaler Religion: Paul de Lagarde und die völkische Bewegung," in Friedrich Wilhelm Graf (ed.), *Intellektuellen-Götter*, Munich, 2009, pp. 1–19

Siemens, Daniel, *Horst Wessel: Tod und Verklärung eines Nationalsozialisten*, Berlin, 2009

Sigmund, Anna Maria, *Des Führers bester Freund: Adolf Hitler, seine Nichte Geli Raubal und der "Ehrenarier" Emil Maurice—eine Dreiecksbeziehung*, Munich, 2003

Sigmund, Anna Maria, *Die Frauen der Nazis: Die drei Bestseller vollständig aktualisiert in einem Band*, Munich, 2005

Sigmund, Anna Maria, *Diktator, Dämon, Demagoge: Fragen und Antworten zu Adolf Hitler*, Munich, 2006

Sigmund, Anna Maria, "Als Hitler auf der Flucht war," in *Süddeutsche Zeitung*, 8/9 Nov. 2008

Smelser, Ronald, *Robert Ley: Hitlers Mann an der "Arbeitsfront,"* Potsdam, 1989

Smelser, Ronald and Rainer Zitelmann (eds), *Die braune Elite: 22 biographische Skizzen*, Darmstadt, 1989

Smelser, Ronald, Enrico Syring and Rainer Zitelmann (eds), *Die braune Elite II: 21 weitere biographische Skizzen*, Darmstadt, 1993

Smith, Bradley F., *Adolf Hitler: His Family, Childhood and Youth*, Stanford, 1967

Sösemann, Bernd, *Das Ende der Weimarer Republik in der Kritik demokratischer Publizisten*, Berlin, 1976

Solleder, Fridolin (ed.), *Vier Jahre Westfront: Geschichte des Regiment List R.I.R 16*, Munich, 1932

Sommer, Theo, *Deutschland und Japan zwischen den Mächten 1935–1940: Vom Antikominternpakt zum Dreimächtepakt*, Tübingen, 1962

Sontheimer, Kurt, *Antidemokratisches Denken in der Weimarer Republik: Die politischen Ideen des deutschen Nationalismus zwischen 1918 und 1933*, Munich, 1968

Sprengel, Peter, *Gerhart Hauptmann: Bürgerlichkeit und grosser Traum. Eine Biographie*, Munich, 2012

Stachura, Peter, *Gregor Strasser and the Rise of Nazism*, London, 1983

Stachura, Peter D., "Der kritische Wendepunkt? Die NSDAP und die Reichstagswahlen vom 20. 5. 1928," in *Vierteljahrshefte für Zeitgeschichte*, 26 (1978), pp. 66–99

Stegmann, Dirk, "Zwischen Repression und Manipulation: Konservative Machteliten und Arbeiter- und Angestelltenbewegung 1910–1918. Ein Beitrag zur Vorgeschichte der DAP/NSDAP," in *Archiv für Sozialgeschichte*, 12 (1972), pp. 351–432

Stegmann, Dirk, "Zum Verhältnis von Grossindustrie und Nationalsozialismus 1930–1933," in *Archiv für Sozialgeschichte*, 13 (1973), pp. 399–482

Steinert, Marlies, *Hitler*, Munich, 1994

Steinweis, Alan E., *Kristallnacht 1938: Ein deutscher Pogrom*, Stuttgart, 2011

Stern, Fritz, *Kulturpessimismus als politische Gefahr: Eine Analyse nationaler Ideologie*, new edition, Stuttgart, 2005

Stierlin, Helm, "Anziehung und Distanz: Hitler und die Frauen aus der Sicht des Psychotherapeuten," in Leutheusser (ed.), *Hitler und die Frauen*, pp. 253–98

Stöver, Bernd, *Volksgemeinschaft im Dritten Reich: Die Konsensbereitschaft der Deutschen aus der Sicht sozialistischer Exilberichte*, Düsseldorf, 1993

Stribrny, Wolfgang, "Der Versuch einer Kandidatur des Kronprinzen Wilhelm bei der Reichspräsidentenwahl 1932," in *Geschichte in der Gegenwart: Festschrift für Kurt Kluxen*, Paderborn, 1972, pp. 199–210

Süss, Dietmar and Winfried Süss (eds), *Das "Dritte Reich": Eine Einführung*, Munich, 2008

Tennstedt, Florian, "Wohltat und Interesse: Das Winterhilfswerk des Deutschen Volkes. Die Weimarer Vorgeschichte und ihre Instrumentalisierung durch das NS-Regime," in *Geschichte und Gesellschaft*, 13 (1987), pp. 157–80

Terveen, Fritz, "Der Filmbericht über Hitlers 50. Geburtstag: Ein Beispiel nationalsozialistischer Selbstdarstellung und Propaganda," in *Vierteljahrshefte für Zeitgeschichte*, 7 (1959), pp. 75–84

Thamer, Hans-Ulrich, *Verführung und Gewalt: Deutschland 1933–1945*, Berlin, 1986

Thamer, Hans-Ulrich, "Faszination und Manipulation: Die Nürnberger Reichsparteitage der NSDAP," in Uwe Schultz (ed.), *Das Fest: Eine Kulturgeschichte von der Antike bis zur Gegenwart*, Munich, 1988, pp. 352–68

Thamer, Hans-Ulrich and Simone Erpel, *Hitler und die Deutschen: Volksgemeinschaft und Verbrechen*, Dresden, 2010

Thies, Jochen, *Architekt der Weltherrschaft: Die "Endziele" Hitlers*, Düsseldorf, 1976

Thompson, Dorothy, *Kassandra spricht: Antifaschistische Publizistik 1932–1942*, Leipzig and Weimar, 1988

Thoss, Bruno, *Der Ludendorff-Kreis 1919–1923: München als Zentrum der europäischen Gegenrevolution*, Munich, 1978

Tobias, Fritz, "Ludendorff, Hindenburg, Hitler: Das Phantasieprodukt des Ludendorff-Briefes vom 30. Januar 1933," in Uwe Backes, Eckhard Jesse and Rainer Zitelmann, *Die Schatten der Vergangenheit: Impulse zur Historisierung des Nationalsozialismus*, Frankfurt am Main and Berlin, 1992, pp. 319–43

Toland, John, *Adolf Hitler: Vol. 1*, New York, 1976

Tomberg, Friedrich, *Das Christentum in Hitlers Weltanschauung*, Munich, 2012

Tooze, Adam, *The Wages of Destruction: The Making and Breaking of the Nazi Economy*, London, 2007

Treue, Wilhelm, "Hitlers Denkschrift zum Vierjahresplan 1936," in *Vierteljahrshefte für Zeitgeschichte*, 3 (1955), pp. 184–210

Trimborn, Jürgen, *Riefenstahl: Eine deutsche Karriere*, Berlin, 2002

Trimborn, Jürgen, *Arno Breker: Der Künstler und die Macht. Die Biographie*, Berlin, 2011

Turner, Henry A., *Die Grossunternehmer und der Aufstieg Hitlers*, Berlin, 1986

Turner, Henry A., *Thirty Days to Power: January 1933*, London, 1997

Tyrell, Albrecht, *Vom "Trommler" zum Führer: Der Wandel von Hitlers Selbstverständnis zwischen 1919 und 1924 und die Entwicklung der NSDAP*, Munich, 1975

Ueberschär, Gerd R. and Winfried Vogel, *Dienen und Verdienen: Hitlers Geschenke an seine Eliten*, Frankfurt am Main, 1999

Ullrich, Volker, *Die nervöse Grossmacht: Aufstieg und Untergang des deutschen Kaiserreichs 1871–1918*, Frankfurt am Main, 1997

Ullrich, Volker, *Die Revolution 1918/19*, Munich, 2009

Ullrich, Volker, "'Drückeberger': Die Judenzählung im Ersten Weltkrieg," in Julius Schoeps and Joachim Schlör (eds), *Antisemitismus: Vorurteile und Mythen*, Munich and Zurich, 1995, pp. 210–17

Ullrich, Volker, *Kriegsalltag: Hamburg im Ersten Weltkrieg*, Cologne, 1982

Ullrich, Volker, "Kriegsalltag: Zur inneren Revolutionierung der wilhelminischen Gesellschaft," in Wolfgang Michalka (ed.), *Der Erste Weltkrieg: Wirkung – Wahrnehmung—Analyse*, Munich and Zurich, 1994, pp. 603–21

Ullrich, Volker, "Anpassung um jeden Preis? Die Kapitulation der deutschen Gewerkschaften 1932/33," in Inge Marssolek and Till Schelz-Brandenburg (eds), *Soziale Demokratie und sozialistische Theorie: Festschrift für Hans-Josef Steinberg zum 60. Geburtstag*, Bremen, 1995, pp. 245–55

Urban, Markus, *Die Konsensfabrik: Funktion und Wahrnehmung der NS-Reichsparteitage 1933–1941*, Göttingen, 2007

Valentin, Veit, *Geschichte der Deutschen*, Berlin, 1947, new edition, Cologne, 1991

Verhey, Geoffrey, *Der "Geist von 1914" und die Erfindung der Volksgemeinschaft*, Hamburg, 2000

Voegelin, Eric, *Hitler und die Deutschen*, ed. Manfred Henningsen, Munich, 2006

Vogelsang, Thilo, *Reichswehr, Staat und NSDAP*, Stuttgart, 1962

Vogelsang, Thilo, "Neue Dokumente zur Geschichte der Reichswehr 1930–1933," in *Vierteljahrshefte für Zeitgeschichte*, 2 (1954), pp. 397–439

Vogelsang, Thilo, "Zur Politik Schleichers gegenüber der NSDAP 1932," in *Vierteljahrshefte für Zeitgeschichte*, 6 (1958), pp. 86–118

Vorländer, Herwart, *Die NSV: Darstellung und Dokumentation einer nationalsozialistischen Organisation*, Boppard am Rhein, 1988

Walter, Dirk, *Antisemitische Kriminalität und Gewalt: Judenfeindschaft in der Weimarer Republik*, Bonn, 1999

Walters, Guy, *Berlin Games: How Hitler Stole the Olympic Dream*, London, 2006

Watt, Donald Cameron, "Die bayerischen Bemühungen um Ausweisung Hitlers 1924," in *Vierteljahrshefte für Zeitgeschichte*, 6 (1958), pp. 270–80

Weber, Thomas, *Hitler's First War: Adolf Hitler, the Men of the List Regiment, and the First World War*, Oxford and New Yark, 2010

Wehler, Hans-Ulrich, *Deutsche Gesellschaftsgeschichte. Vol. 4: Vom Beginn des Ersten Weltkriegs bis zur Gründung der beiden deutschen Staaten 1914–1949*, Munich, 2003

Wehler, Hans-Ulrich, "Hitler als historische Figur," in idem, *Land ohne Unterschichten? Neue Essays zur deutschen Geschichte*, Munich, 2010, pp. 92–105

Weinberg, Gerhard L., *The Foreign Policy of Hitler's Germany: Diplomatic Revolution in Europe 1933–1936*, Chicago and London, 1970

Weinberg, Gerhard L., "The May Crisis 1938," in *Journal of Modern History*, 29 (1957), pp. 213–25

Weissbecker, Manfred and Kurt Pätzold, *Adolf Hitler: Eine politische Biographie*, Leipzig, 1995

Weissmann, Karl-Heinz, *Das Hakenkreuz: Symbol eines Jahrhunderts*, Schnellrode, 2006

Wendt, Bernd-Jürgen, *Grossdeutschland: Aussenpolitik und Kriegsvorbereitung des Hitler-Regimes*, Munich, 1987

Wernecke, Klaus (with the collaboration of Peter Heller), *Der vergessene Führer: Alfred Hugenberg. Pressemacht und Nationalsozialismus*, Hamburg, 1982

Wieland, Karin, *Dietrich & Riefenstahl: Der Traum von der neuen Frau*, Munich, 2011

Wilderotter, Hans, *Alltag der Macht: Berlin Wilhelmstrasse*, Berlin, 1998

Wildt, Michael, *Generation des Unbedingten: Das Führungskorps des Reichssicherheitshauptamtes*, Hamburg, 2002

Wildt, Michael, *Volksgemeinschaft als Selbstermächtigung: Gewalt gegen die Juden in der deutschen Provinz 1919 bis 1939*, Hamburg, 2007

Wildt, Michael, *Geschichte des Nationalsozialismus*, Göttingen, 2008

Wildt, Michael and Christoph Kreutzmüller (eds), *Berlin 1933–1945*, Munich, 2013

Willems, Susanne, *Der entsiedelte Jude: Albert Speers Wohnungsmarktpolitik für den Berliner Hauptstadtbau*, Berlin, 2000

Willing, Georg-Franz, *Die Hitler-Bewegung: Der Ursprung 1919–1922*, Hamburg and Berlin, 1962

Winkler, Heinrich August, *Der Weg in die Katastrophe: Arbeiter und Arbeiterbewegung in der Weimarer Republik 1930 bis 1933*, Berlin and Bonn, 1987

Winkler, Heinrich August, *Musste Weimar scheitern? Das Ende der ersten Republik und die Kontinuität der deutschen Geschichte*, Munich, 1991

Winkler, Heinrich August, *Weimar 1918–1933: Die Geschichte der ersten deutschen Demokratie*, Munich, 1993

Winkler, Heinrich August, *Der lange Weg nach Westen*, 2 vols, Munich, 2000

Winkler, Heinrich August, "Die abwendbare Katastrophe: Warum Hitler am 30. Januar 1933 Reichskanzler wurde," in idem, *Auf ewig in Hitlers Schatten? Anmerkungen zur deutschen Geschichte*, Munich, 2007, pp. 93–104

Winkler, Heinrich August, *Geschichte des Westens. Vol. 2: Die Zeit der Weltkriege 1914–1945*, Munich, 2011

Wirsching, Andreas, *Vom Weltkrieg zum Bürgerkrieg? Politischer Extremismus in Deutschland und Frankreich 1918–1933/39: Berlin und Paris im Vergleich*, Munich, 1999

Wirsching, Andreas, "'Man kann nur Boden germanisiseren': Eine neue Quelle zu Hitlers Rede vor den Spitzen der Reichswehr am 3. Februar 1933," in *Vierteljahrshefte für Zeitgeschichte*, 49 (2001), pp. 517–50

Wirsching, Andreas (ed.), *Das Jahr 1933: Die nationalsozialistische Machtergreifung und die deutsche Gesellschaft*, Göttingen, 2009

Woller, Hans, *Geschichte Italiens im 20. Jahrhundert*, Munich, 2010

Wollstein, Günter, "Eine Denkschrift des Staatssekretärs Bernhard von Bülow vom März 1933: Wilhelminische Konzeption der Aussenpolitik zu Beginn der nationalsozialistischen Herrschaft," in *Militärgeschichtliche Mitteilungen*, 23 (1973), pp. 77–94

Wright, Jonathan, *Gustav Stresemann 1878–1929: Weimars grösster Staatsmann*, Munich, 2006

Xammar, Eugeni, *Das Schlangenei: Berichte aus dem Deutschland der Inflationsjahre 1922–1924*, Berlin, 2007

Zdral, Wolfgang, *Die Hitlers: Die unbekannte Familie des Führers*, Frankfurt am Main and New York, 2005

Zehnpfennig, Barbara, *Hitlers "Mein Kampf": Eine Interpretation*, 2nd edition, Munich, 2002

Zelnhefer, Siegfried, *Die Reichsparteitage der NSDAP: Geschichte, Struktur und Bedeutung der grössten Propagandafeste im nationalsozialistischen Feierjahr*, Nuremberg, 2002

Zimmermann, Peter, "Die Parteitagsfilme der NSDAP und Leni Riefenstahl," in idem and Kai Hoffmann (eds), *Geschichte des dokumentarischen Films in Deutschland. Vol. 3: "Drittes Reich" 1933–1945*, Stuttgart, 2005

Zitelmann, Rainer, *Hitler: Selbstverständnis eines Revolutionärs*, 2nd revised and expanded edition, Stuttgart, 1989

Zitelmann, Rainer, *Adolf Hitler: Eine politische Biographie*, Göttingen and Zurich, 1989

Acknowledgements

I received a great amount of support during the extensive research that went into this book, and for that I owe many people my thanks. The first I should mention are the women and men at the archives who opened their doors and allowed me access to the treasures within: Torsten Zarwel at the Bundesarchiv in Berlin-Lichtenberg, Annegret Neupert at the Bundesarchiv in Koblenz, Dr. Klaus A. Lankheit at the Institut für Zeitgeschichte in Munich, Dr. Sylvia Krauss at the Bayerisches Hauptstaatsarchiv in Munich, Dr. Nino Nodia at the Bayerische Staatsbibliothek in Munich and Marlies Hertig at the Schweizerisches Bundesarchiv in Bern.

Mirjam Zimmer and Dr. Kerstin Wilhelms at *Die Zeit* newspaper were extraordinarily helpful in procuring literature for me. Karl-Otto Schütt repeatedly gave me access to books from the extensive holdings of the Bibliothek der Forschungsstelle für Zeitgeschichte in Hamburg.

Above all I would like to thank my friend Walter H. Pehle, the veteran history editor at the Fischer Verlag publishing house. He not only helped inspire the project but also thoroughly edited the manuscript and helped select the illustrations. His successor, Dr. Tanja Hommen, took over the coordination of the project as the book went to press. Dr. Peter Sillem, the publishing director of Fischer's non-fiction department, was consistently encouraging throughout the various stages of this work. The S. Fischer Foundation provided a generous stipend that allowed me to do my archival research.

My greatest thanks, however, go to my family: my wife Gudrun and my son Sebastian. With them I had many enlightening conversations about this unpleasant topic, and their critical questions and objections have greatly helped shape the text.

Volker Ullrich
Hamburg, May 2013

Index